MW00605879

MURDER OF JUSTICE

NEW JERSEY'S GREATEST SHAME

MURDER OF JUSTICE

NEW JERSEY'S GREATEST SHAME

LONG AWAITED
TRUTH
PROVES HAUPTMANN INNOCENT OF THE
LINDBERGH KIDNAPPING

WAYNE D. JONES

VANTAGE PRESS
New York

FIRST EDITION

Published by Vantage Press, Inc.
516 West 34th Street, New York, New York 10001

Manufactured in the United States of America
ISBN: 0-533-12023-3

Library of Congress Catalog Card No.: 97-90803

0 9 8 7 6 5 4 3 2 1

Bruno Richard Hauptmann
1899-1936

"My God, My God, where is justice in this world? I simply cannot believe that his state in order to cancel a case will break the life of an innocent man in such a way. This would be not only more than ordinary murder but - **MURDER OF JUSTICE!**"

Taken from a letter written by Richard Hauptmann from his prison cell to his mother in Germany shortly before his court appointed execution.

This Book is
Most Respectfully Dedicated
To Our Dear Friend
Anna Schoeffler Hauptmann,
Who Never Doubted Her Husband's
Complete Innocence,
And To My Own Dear Wife
Anna Mae,
Whose Support She Willingly Gave
At All Times
In Order to Make It Possible

****
Which keepeth truth forever. Psalm 146:6
****

T R U T H
Is a severe and jealous mistress.
She suffers no deviating to the right or to the left.
She demands unconditional faithfulness.

Author Unknown

"My faith in my husband is unfaltering. I know that he passed away like a Christian who believed in his God and Saviour. He has not passed out of life as a kidnapper or a murderer but as an honest man. I feel not ashamed but am proud of him. I know that his innocence will come to light. Therefore, I can rest assured and be at peace with my God at this time while I know that the murderers who have put him, an innocent man, to death, will never find peace as long as they have not condoned for this crime and repented before men and before God. They have taken away from me my faithful husband and a loving father from my child."

Anna Hauptmann
Trenton, New Jersey
April 3, 1936

"There has never been the slightest doubt in my mind but that Bruno Richard Hauptmann was erroneously convicted, and never a thought that he was in any manner, shape or form connected with the kidnapping of the Lindbergh baby. I am confident that had the baby kidnapped been the child of Joe Jones or Sam Smith of Hamilton Square, Ohio, and Hauptmann had been accused of the kidnapping and the evidence presented as was presented at his trial, he would have promptly been acquitted."

Lloyd Fisher
February 14, 1955
(Taken from a letter to the author)

CONTENTS

I - Foreword
III - Prologue
V - Introduction

BOOK I
THE CRIME

Chapter		Page
One	An Empty Crib!	1
Two	Hours of Anguish!	8
Three	Conspiracy!	24
Four	Police in Action!	34
Five	An Inside Job!	42
Six	Enter Doctor Condon!	48
Seven	"Jasfie" Meets John!	64
Eight	Confusion!	82
Nine	A Sleeping Suit and a Mysterious Woman!	93
Ten	Another Cemetery!	102
Eleven	Searching, Searching!	117
Twelve	A Stark Discovery!	135
Thirteen	A Great Controversy!	146
Fourteen	Violet Sharpe!	159
Fifteen	Aftermath of Sudden Death!	177
Sixteen	The Wood Detective!	190
Seventeen	A Theater in Greenwich Village!	205
Eighteen	1279 East 222nd Street!	215

BOOK TWO
THE TRIAL

Nineteen	Richard Hauptmann!	233
Twenty	"Justice" Grinds Away!	247
Twenty One	The Assembly of the Liars Club!	264
Twenty Two	Evil Plans Afoot!	286
Twenty Three	Twelve Honest Unsuspecting Jurors!	302
Twenty Four	Millard Whited - Five Star Liar!	316
Twenty Five	Your Turn, Amandus!	330
Twenty Six	An Epidemic of Lies!	349
Twenty Seven	What Lies We Mortals Tell!	367

Twenty Eight	Ay, Docktor!	397
Twenty Nine	Never Doubt --- An "Expert"!	408
Thirty	The Flip Side of the Handwriting Issue!	432
Thirty One	A Skeleton in Court!	443
Thirty Two	The Wood Man!	459
Thirty Three	What More Can Happen!	479
Thirty Four	Two Old Chisels!	486
Thirty Five	Hauptmann Needed Friends!	508
Thirty Six	Witnesses From Out of Nowhere!!!	530
Thirty Seven	The Rest of the Mess!	562
Thirty Eight	Who is Isidor Fisch?	577
Thirty Nine	A Fisch Turned Bad!	595
Forty	Isidor's Other Friends!	615
Forty One	Fingers Keep Pointing!	621
Forty Two	Bruckman Finds a Closet	633
Forty Three	Guess What? Cassidy Claimed the Closet!	650
Forty Four	The Star Attraction!	671
Forty Five	Verbal Carnage!	687
Forty Six	Court Without Ethics!	708
Forty Seven	The Defense is Heard!	716
Forty Eight	"Truth Sayers" and "Manic Depressives"!	729
Forty Nine	Doctor Hudsons Day in Court!	743
Fifty	Back to Wood Again!	754
Fifty One	Final Accusations!	769
Fifty Two	Reilly's Big Show!	780
Fifty Three	The Dependable Wilentz and Accommodating Judge!	800
Fifty Four	Trenchards Charge!	812
Fifty Five	The Sentence!	819

BOOK THREE
THE AFTERMATH

Fifty Six	Rumblings!	833
Fifty Seven	Hauptmann's Questions!	848
Fifty Eight	A New Investigation!	866
Fifty Nine	The Great Defender!	887
Sixty	Look I See a Star!	905
Sixty One	Richard's Faith!	914
Sixty Two	Anna's Faith!	925
Sixty Three	The Truth Slowly Surfaces!	935
Sixty Four	A Man Named Stover!	946

Sixty Five	In Search of Truth!	964
Sixty Six	Scaduto's Investigation!	983
Sixty Seven	Where Have You Been?	991
Sixty Eight	Doubts of the F.B.I.!	1003
Sixty Nine	Martin Stover, Hauptmann's Best Witness!	1016
Seventy	Unexpected Evidence!	1040
Seventy One	A Book is Found!	1054
Seventy Two	Convincing New Evidence and Letters of Proof!	1072
Seventy Three	Devious Deception! How Deep Can It Go?	1103
Seventy Four	Important Bits and Pieces!	1116
Seventy Five	The Elusive Fingerprints!	1131
	Epilogue	1146
	Chronology	1153
	Sources	1155
	Acknowledgements	1158
	Index	1161

FOREWORD

The evening of Friday, April 3rd, 1936 was a dismal one. Outside the high walls of the New Jersey State Prison at Trenton the early chill of the weather had turned cold. A large throng of anxious persons crowded near the main entrance. Their unrest had become quite evident. Many of them had waited hours for news from within,-an announcement all were expecting momentarily, but one which seemed would never come. Signs of unruliness were quite apparent as they pressed against ropes which restricted any attempt to move nearer the steps guarded by two rows of uniformed state police officers. Cat-calls were shrill, becoming more threatening with repeated demands of "Kill him", the volume reaching a near crescendo. The scene had taken on a ghostly appearance as the beams from giant searchlights played over the prison and the angry crowd. The explosions of hundreds of flash bulbs from press cameras gave forth the aspect of a thunderstorm with intermittent lightening flashes.

Within the walls, Bruno Richard Hauptmann, the man found guilty of kidnapping and murdering the 20 month old son of Charles and Anne Lindbergh, had been taken from a small cell and led through a door where, just a few feet away, he would face the state's legal instrument of discharging its sentence of death - the dreaded electric chair.

The man's life on earth would soon be over. His final breath would soon be drawn, within minutes this man would be deprived of ever seeing another daybreak.

Robert Elliott, the state's official executioner, expertly completed his task of securely strapping the prisoner into the chair. The leather straps were taut, all bonds secure. At exactly 8:44 p.m. Elliott placed his hands on a wheel and gave it a turn. The lights in the room dimmed as 2000 volts of lethal electricity were sent coursing through the man's body. The seated man was seen to jolt slightly forward, stiffly attempting to fight against the restraining entrapment. Tiny wisps of smoke were noticed as an odor of singed flesh permeated the room of death. The victim's body seemed to surrender itself to its ultimate fate. Two more successive electrical charges of 2000 volts each were administered during the next several minutes. Soon the body pulsations ceased. It appeared to be over.

Three doctors stepped forward and, in turn, each leaned over and placed his stethoscope to the bared chest of the now still person. Dr. Howard Wiesler, the prison physician, straightened and turned toward the ashen faces of the official witnesses who had been called to view the horrifying enactment of legalized death. The grim surroundings, the heat of the small room, and the trauma of the moment, coupled together with Dr. Wiesler's terse official statement: "This man is dead!", caused his voice to sound very hollow. The time was exactly 8:47 and one-half minute. An utterance made by a newsman, one of the witnesses, expressed it all: "God, it's terrible!"

Moments later Gabriel Heatter, well known radio newscaster, after broadcasting for hours reviewing the highlights of the famous kidnapping, was finally handed a note. Nearing exhaustion due to the marathon he had conducted, Heatter, quickly turned back to his microphone and gave, quite simply, the announcement his listeners had been anxiously waiting for; "BRUNO RICHARD HAUPTMANN IS DEAD! Good night!"

Before the dawn of the next morning most everyone in America had heard these words. Before the arrival of another sunset almost every person around the world would know it.

Colonel Mark O. Kimberling, warden of the prison, when asked by reporters if Hauptmann had said anything before he died, merely stated: "No, he said nothing after he left the cell. He said nothing!"

Minutes after learning of the execution, C. Lloyd Fisher, Hauptmann's attorney and friend to the very last, reaffirmed his unwavering faith in his client's innocence. His voice broken by the emotion of the hour, said: "This is the greatest tragedy in the history of New Jersey. Time will never wash it out!"

PROLOGUE

Richard Hauptmann died for a crime he did not commit. His explanation as to how he had acquired some of the Lindbergh ransom money was a very reasonable and logical one. His chief problem was quite simple- almost everyone who knew anything at all about the case simply refused to accept his explanation by exercising fair reasoning. It was popular to join the crowds and condemn him. And so he died! Accused of committing a crime of which he knew absolutely nothing other than, what he too, had read in the papers of that day.

Today we are far removed from the hysteria of the courtroom, the theatrics and the travesties that prevailed during the days of the Depression years of the 1930s years of anguish. The anti-German bigotry that existed then, promoted largely by those whose only desire was to see Hauptmann dead, has been replaced by a host of people all over the world who clamor to know the truth of just what actually happened in the "Crime of the Century". These are those who believe Hauptmann, the lonely Bronx carpenter, got a "bum deal" to say the very least.

In late 1987 a book titled *The Lindbergh Case* by Jim Fisher was published defending the actions of the authorities which led to the conviction of Bruno Richard Hauptmann. The publication was, to say the least, quite unfair since it failed to present the many new facts in the case that have been unearthed since the time of the trial. Mr. Fisher completely ignored the irregularities of the Flemington court room; the findings uncovered by Anthony Scaduto and related in his book, *Scapegoat*, (Putnam 1976) and those of Ludovic Kennedy in his fine book, *The Airman and the Carpenter* (Viking 1985).

Through the years Anna Hauptmann suffered as no other woman as she heard a multitude of accusers lash out their hatred toward her innocent husband. After 58 years her valiant effort to prove to the world that her beloved husband Richard was innocent suddenly ended. At 12:40 a.m. on Monday, October 10, 1994, a tired and weary Anna Hauptmann was taken in death to join her husband.

This book "MURDER OF JUSTICE", finally absolves him of all blame. It is THE FINAL WORD!

Wayne D. Jones
Phoenixville, PA

INTRODUCTION

On Saturday, May 21, 1927, a young man of 25 years piloting his Ryan single engine monoplane, lifted it from the runway of Roosevelt Field, Long Island, New York to land safely the following day at LeBourget Field, Paris, France. The trip had been made in the almost unbelievable time of 33 1/2 hours, 29.8 seconds. He had successfully made the trip alone. It was a feat never before accomplished. In addition to winning a $25,000 cash prize, he received instant fame. Over night he had become a world hero. His name was Charles Augustus Lindbergh.

Because of his courageous act, his appearance was demanded at cities throughout the world, and on December 14, of that same year, he made a goodwill trip to Mexico. While there he stayed at the home of United States Ambassador and Mrs. Dwight W. Morrow. During his visit he became acquainted with the couple's pretty 21 year old daughter, Anne Spencer Morrow. The attractive Anne proved to be more than a gracious host. Lindbergh was fascinated with the small, demure and somewhat shy young lady.

Her beautiful blue eyes and brown hair were additional charms "Lindy" could not fight. He surrendered to love, and following a whirl-wind courtship, proposed. They were married on Monday, May 27, 1929 at "Next Day Hill", the Morrow's estate at Englewood, New Jersey.

On Sunday, June 22, 1930, Anne's 24th birthday, the couple was blessed with the birth of a seven and three-quarter pound blue eyed blond baby boy. He was named Charles Augustus Lindbergh Jr.

Records show that officially he remained nameless for 17 days. Other records claim he lived only 618 days.

In order to escape the prying eyes of the inquisitive public, Charles and Anne hoped to find a location where they could build a home that would not only give them the seclusion they wanted, but provide safety for their infant son as well. A search from the air resulted in what they believed to be the ideal spot.

They agreed that the perfect location on which they could build their home, and thus avoid the stares of the curiosity seekers, would be near the crest of one of the hills that help form the eastern slope of the Sourland Mountain range. They decided the house would be erected on a site known as Sorrel Hill three miles directly north of Hopewell, New Jersey. Whether it was by design or not, their home would be built near a point where three of New Jersey's counties intersect. It would be located in Hunterdon County, a short distance from the Mercer County line to the south, and that of Somerset County to the east.

Hopewell, nestled snugly along the southeastern foothills of the Sourland Mountain, in what is known as the Amwell Valley-Hopewell Valley, was but a small village in the early 1930s. A rural hamlet that was the home of nearly 1500 hard working loyal American families. Many of its citizens were farmers living in immaculate small frame dwellings. Its exact location is East Amwell Township in Mercer County.

The small town was brought into existence when a man named Jonathan Stout came into the area in 1706 and encouraged others to also locate their homes in this choice section of the Amwell Valley. This many others did, but the residents failed to select the name of Hopewell for their little community until 1825. In 1891 it was incorporated as a borough. Prior to the Lindberghs coming into the area to make their residence there, the only item of interest its citizens could ever boast of was that at one time General George Washington had actually visited there. Although it was not much more than the proverbial "dot on the map", the villagers were provided easy accessibility to several other small communities surrounding Hopewell. Stoutsburg, Blawenburg, Skillman, Zion, Neshanic, Wertsville, and Ringoes could all be reached within minutes of travel time. To go south out of Hopewell, along a good highway, a drive of twenty minutes would take one to the state capital at Trenton, only 14 miles distant. By taking a southeasterly route along Princeton Avenue, through Mount Rose, would bring one into Princeton only eight miles away. New York City, 48 miles north-east, would require, at a moderate speed, one and one-half hours of travel time.

The Sourland mountain range, on which the Lindberghs had agreed to build their home, is located in the north-central part of the state, approximately six miles inland from the eastern bend of the Delaware River at Lambertville. Here begins a 12 mile range of vast mountain area that extends in a northeasterly path across the state. Known as the dreaded Sourland of "lost land" by the natives of the area, its southern slopes skirt Hopewell, a mere three miles north of the town. This mountain range was literally steeped in tradition. Over the years legends had been handed down by the ancestors of many of the residents who still live there. More than a few of these mountain people boasted of the area's reputation as being of the weirdest regions in the eastern section of the United States. Mysterious stories were told of the area regarding Hessian soldiers who, while serving under Lord Cornwalis during the American Revolution, roamed through the mountainous wilds, and after finding no way out of the thickly wooded area, married indian natives of these wilds, the legends continued, and to that day there were residents who claimed to be living descendants of those unions.

Other tales commonly told by the local townsfolk related to the "Jersey Devil", the phantom half-man half-beast, that for endless years had reportedly roamed through the Sourland mountain area of Central New Jersey, eventually meeting death at Three Brothers Rock high in the Sourlands. Other residents claim the Hopewell area had served as a perfect hideaway for escaping southern slaves during the Civil War.

It was here in the mysterious Sourland Mountains that Colonel Lindbergh and his wife had decided to build their new home. They reasoned that the small community of Hopewell, New Jersey, located directly south only three miles distant, would be easily accessible to them, chiefly over dirt roads, whenever they would be required to go to town for needed supplies.

In early March of 1931 the foundation for the home was begun. Ten months later it neared completion. Custom-built of rural fieldstone in a traditional French Manor style, the two and one-half story home had 20 rooms, a basement and a three car garage. Its 18 inch walls would provide comfort and warmth for this famous family of three. The provincial styled twin gabled edifice with its gray slate shingled roof and bright whitewashed walls, plus a multitude of shuttered windows with twelve individual panes in each presented a striking picture to the residents of nearby Hopewell. It appeared silhouetted against the vast woodlands that extended from the north, behind the home, and to the east and west on both sides of the clearing that had been made for the home on the southern side of the mountain.

Although the Lindbergh home could be clearly seen from the nearby village of Hopewell, it was actually the rear of the structure its residents saw. The Hopewell side of the home was constructed with a porch that measured 70 feet in length which faced a terrace overlooking an area of vast meadows, pastureland and swamps. The living room with its large French windows adjoined the porch overlooking the rural farmland to the south.

The front of the home faced the bleak Sourland Mountains and access to the main entrance could only be made by driving along a narrow dirt road for a distance of one-half mile. This road, destined to become known as "Lindbergh Lane", wound its way in an easterly direction for approximately one-half mile from the nearest traffic artery, the Stoutsburg-Wertsville Road. Entering this road would bring one to the imposing large walled-in parking area which served to enclose the main entrance to their home. The Lindbergh's nearest neighbors lived in a farmhouse at the other end of the lane. Virtually, the famous flyer and his wife had built themselves a home that was almost completely hidden. It was practically encircled by dense woods and underbrush. However, only detected, near the center of the 500 acres of land they had purchased, in a clearing amidst the thick forest of trees, the Lindbergh's "Mansion" appeared in stately fashion in all its glory.

The family would have very few close neighbors. The land surrounding the Lindbergh acreage had very few homes. The area, for the most part, had been abandoned as the kingdom of wildgame that inhabited and roamed the wooded terrain. In 1932 it still remained sparsely populated by members of the human race.

In turn, however, it was filled with many eerie tales. Superstitions and accounts of murders that were believed to have taken place somewhere within the vast area at some time in the past were prevalent. In spite of this, the Sourlands did provide an excellent stretch of mountainous territory that invited area hunters and trappers into its wilds seeking the mink, fox and deer that roamed through this 12 mile formidable mountain range in central New Jersey.

It had been Colonel Lindbergh's plan to build a landing field on his property, where he eventually could land his plane somewhere in close proximity to his home. However, by late February of 1932, he had merely started to clear out some of the timberland on the eastern side of the house. Until the proposed landing strip could be completed, the family would have to settle for the only means of available access to the home, traveling by automobile along Lindbergh Lane.

When leaving their home, at the end of the lane,

a turn north would take them over the top of the mountain toward Wertsville, Amwell and Zion, to a point known as Zion's Crossroads, often referred to as "the last outpost to the Sourland". Proceeding farther north would extend the trip over rough roadways to Montgomery and Neshanic, and down the north side of the mountain. To turn south at the end of their lane would take them over a dirt road down the mountain, a distance of three miles, to the outskirts of Hopewell. Here is where the Lindberghs would shop for their daily requirements. A general store, post office, barber shop and a few specialty stores were there to supply most of their customary needs. In addition to churches and a railroad station, the community also boasted of having its own police department.

Hopewell, New Jersey, in early 1932, had been and still was a rather remote little town, practically unknown, except for a small dot which located it as having its rightful place on the world's map. However, certain events were beginning to take form. Events which were to soon thrust it boldly into the center of attention of all the depression-weary citizens of the United States.

Hopewell, New Jersey was destined to leap overnight from its obscurity to world-wide prominence. It had its beginning when the Lindberghs decided to build and move into their new home a few miles away. It gained its fame following a horrible event that occurred on that fateful night of Tuesday, March 1, 1932.

THE LINDBERGH BABY HAD BEEN KIDNAPPED, AND HOPEWELL, NEW JERSEY WOULD NEVER BE THE SAME!

MURDER OF JUSTICE

NEW JERSEY'S GREATEST SHAME

BOOK ONE

THE CRIME!

CHAPTER ONE

An Empty Crib

Following another night of intermittent sleep, Anne Lindbergh awakened at dawn on Tuesday, March 1st to another day that promised to be one of more inclement weather. Although she realized that her little son's cold was somewhat better, she decided that since she also had the symptoms of catching a cold herself, it would be better if the family stayed another day at Hopewell. It was the normal custom for them to return to Englewood on a Monday. However, since they had already stayed over one extra day, Anne reasoned it would be safer to stay where they were, rather than risk taking little Charles out in such unfavorable weather. She concluded that the damp, cold air would pose too much of a threat to the health of both mother and son. As the morning hours passed, the weather remained especially dismal as occasional gusts of rain, directed by heavy winds, pelted the windows of the new home. By this time Anne Lindbergh was quite satisfied that her decision to stay at Hopewell another day and night had been a proper one.

Betty Gow, little Charles' nursemaid, as was her week-end custom, had remained at Englewood. However, Mrs. Lindbergh, realizing she needed some rest, decided she could use Betty's help. About 11:30 a.m. she telephoned and asked her to come and aid her in caring for her "fat lamb", the pet name she called her little son. Due to this phone call Betty had to make a change in her own plans.

Bessie Mowat Goway, a pretty, 27 year old Scotch lass, had shortened her last name to Gow and was affectionately called "Betty". She was quite attractive, having blue eyes, short bobbed brunette hair, and a slender figure.

It had been Betty's principal duty to look after the child's welfare full time, especially on the many occasions when Mrs. Lindbergh found it necessary to be away from home. At the time of her engagement as a nursemaid, on February 21, 1931, the child was but eight months old. She immediately captured the love of little Charles, and because of this she was adored by the entire family. Betty had come to the Lindberghs, highly recommended by former employers, most recently by a Mrs. Sullivan of Glenwood Road, Englewood, and the Whittier Hotel in Detroit. She had gained the complete trust of everyone.

Betty was not surprised to receive Mrs. Lindbergh's call summoning her to Hopewell since she was aware of little Charles' illness. Violet Sharpe, a maid at "Next Day Hill", the spacious 54 acre estate of Anne's mother, took the message and relayed it to her. However, Betty had anticipated a call of this kind when the Lindberghs failed to return to Englewood earlier that morning. Betty, however, had already made plans for that evening. Plans which necessitated a quick change. Putting through a hurried call to their friend, Henry "Red" Johnson to inform him that she could not keep her date with him, she was informed that Mr. Johnson was not in his room at the Englewood boarding house where he lived. Not able to reach him, she left a message that he should call her later that day at the Lindbergh home in Hopewell.

At approximately 1:20 p.m., Betty stepped from the sleek limousine driven by Henry Ellison, the Morrow's second chauffeur. They had arrived at Hopewell and were greeted at the door by Oliver Whateley, the Lindbergh butler. Hurrying inside to escape the cold licks of the fierce wind that whipped around the house, she was soon warmed by the friendliness of the heat coming from the living room fireplace. Its warmth soon removed the chill that seemed to have penetrated her very bones. It was cold, raw, and rainy outside the Lindbergh's Hopewell home, that afternoon of March 1, 1932.

Following a tasty lunch, prepared for her by Elsie Whateley, housemaid and wife of Oliver, the two women sat in the kitchen discussing the baby's health. Betty was relieved to learn that his cold had somewhat improved, and that he was sleeping soundly in his crib taking his customary afternoon nap.

Soon Mrs. Lindbergh entered the room, greeted Betty, and voiced her pleasure at having the nursemaid present to help with the baby. She told the two women that she had noticed the rain had subsided and, in spite of the otherwise horrid weather, she was going outside and take a short, but much needed, stroll around the house. Betty decided to go up to the nursery and look in on the baby. Finding him still sleeping, but realizing, he would soon awaken, she sat next to the crib and read for a short while.

Moments later she was distracted by the sound of something striking the panes of the southeast window. Going over to the window she peered out and saw the child's mother standing below throwing pebbles up against the glass. Anne motioned to her to bring the baby to the window for her to see.

The baby, having awakened, was lifted from his crib and carried to the window where Betty pointed down to his mother who smilingly waved to her "fat lamb". Taking his tiny wrist in her hand, Betty waved his little arm as he, in happy recognition, smiled back at his mother. The time was approximately 3:30. Upon returning from her walk, Anne went to the baby's nursery where she found Betty and Elsie busy playing with the child. The three women spent a short time together enjoying the youngster's gleeful mood. All agreed the child was feeling much better.

Feeling a need for the warmth of the living room fireplace, Anne left her two employees and went downstairs to the "sitting room" where she glanced out of the large French windows which overlooked the meadows on the southside of the house. She was aware that since her return from her walk the weather had grown even more miserable.

Around five o'clock little Charles joined his mother, and the two played together for another half hour. He spent most of the time dashing in and out of the kitchen and servants' quarters, gleefully playing with his pet wirehaired terrier, "Wahgoosh". The dog has been a gift to the family by the child's paternal grandmother, Mrs. Evangeline Lindbergh. The friendly little animal, although a member of both the Morrow and Lindbergh households for the past 18 months, had failed miserably in his desired and intended role as a watchdog.

Becoming aware of the time, Betty glanced at her watch and put an end to the child's frolicking. She hustled him upstairs to the nursery and seated him in his chair at the little maple table in the center of the room. Hurrying back to the kitchen, she quickly returned with a bowl of cereal she had prepared for her charge. Little Charles ate all of his supper, another indication of his improved health.

It was nearly 6:15 when Mrs. Lindbergh came to the nursery to help Betty prepare the baby for bed. Although his cold seemed much better, some trace of it was still evident. Because of this it was decided to give the youngster a physic. However, Charles apparently had an aversion for being fed his medication from a spoon, and as they attempted to place it between his lips, he suddenly turned away causing the spoon's contents to spill over the front of his sleeping suit. This necessitated an unexpected change in his bedtime attire.

As they undressed him, they agreed that for extra warmth, he should wear a flannel shirt next to his skin. This, they decided, would afford him added protection from any possible draft that might be in the room. Anne brought a flannel petticoat, one he had worn shortly after he was born, and asked Betty if she would fashion a suitable shirt for him. After acquiring scissors from the kitchen and the necessary needle and thread, a blue English Silco, from Elsie, she set about her task. The nursemaid proved to be a very adept seamstress. She took the scalloped edged petticoat given her and hastily made a little shirt ready to be placed on the child.

That completed, once again Anne selected dry clothes that the child would wear. Betty was busy rubbing little Charles' chest with Vicks VapoRub, a patented medicated ointment. In addition to two pair of diapers, covered by rubber pants, she then slipped the newly made flannel shirt over his head. On top of this they put a sleeveless woolen shirt, cut low in both front and back. Over all, completing his attire for the night, he wore a Dr. Denton's No.2 woolen sleeping suit. Next came the placement of a metal thumb guard over each of the little fellows thumbs. This would prevent him from thumb sucking while sleeping. Betty attached the guards by wrapping the tapes twice around his wrists, tying them in secure knots over his sleeping suit.

After giving him their goodnight kisses, Betty placed him beneath a sheet, a quilt and double blanket. In order to make it difficult for him to crawl out from beneath his covers, she fastened two large, two and one-half inch, safety pins securely to the mattress, one on each side of the child.

Checking all three windows, they were assured that the shutters were locked, with the exception of those on the southeast window that had somehow become warped and could not be completely fastened. The French window on the south side, which opened into the room, was left slightly ajar for ventilation. However, its shutters were secured.

It was shortly after 7:30 when Anne left the room

and went downstairs to the sitting room. Betty continued to attend to several details in the nursery. For a short time she sat beside the crib until she was certain the baby was sound asleep. At 8 o'clock she put out the light and went down to tell Mrs. Lindbergh that little Charles was sleeping peacefully, breathing very easily and apparently was comfortable settled for the night.

Leaving Mrs. Lindbergh, Betty joined Elsie Whateley in the kitchen which was located in the west wing of the house. Oliver was busy in the adjoining pantry. At 8:25 they heard the horn of Colonel Lindbergh's tan Franklin sedan as it approached the garage. His arrival at this hour had not been expected since Anne had informed the servants that her husband would not be arriving home until quite late due to a speaking engagement he was to make in New York City that evening.

Colonel Lindbergh entered his home from the garage and greeted the servants as he passed through the kitchen. At the same time he inquired about the health of his child. Receiving a favorable report from Betty immediately relieved his anxiety. After a few remarks about the inclement weather and the extremely high winds that had finally chased the rain away, he went to join his wife who was busy at her desk in the living room.

Anne, surprised at her husband's early arrival home, reminded him of his scheduled engagement to address 2,000 of the alumni of New York University, an appointment he had entirely forgotten. He attributed an afternoon appointment with his dentist as the possible reason for his memory lapse. After phoning his regrets to the NYU alumni committee the couple went upstairs for several minutes while Charles washed for dinner. A short time later, they returned to the first floor where Whateley served them a late evening meal in the dining room.

While the Lindberghs were enjoying their dinner, Betty Gow received her expected call from Red Johnson. He expressed his disappointment that their scheduled date for that evening had been broken. The two conversed for approximately five minutes. The time had now reached 8:35.

After finishing her dinner, Betty went to the servants sitting room where she turned on the radio and glanced through some magazines for about a half hour. Elsie and Wahgoosh joined her there and shortly after 9 o'clock they went upstairs to Mrs. Whateley's bedroom to look at a dress the housekeeper had recently purchased. During the remainder of that hour the two women discussed the news of the past few days.

Meanwhile, at 9 o'clock, having finished their dinner, the Lindberghs entered their living room to relax. They sat on a sofa enjoying the warmth of a roaring fire in the fireplace for approximately 15 minutes. As they sat side by side, sharing with each other the events of the day, at approximately 10 minutes past the hour of 9, they were startled by a strange noise. A noise loud enough to be clearly heard above the sounds of the snapping and crackling of the logs in the fireplace and the roar of the wind outdoors.

"What was that?" the Colonel questioned his wife. Although they were not able to detect the cause of the sound, or from where it had come, the two passed it off as possibly coming from the breaking of a tree limb outside, and that there was certainly no need for any alarm.

Shortly after hearing the unexplained noise, Charles and Anne went up to their bedroom where they continued their conversation for another 15 or 20 minutes. Following a bath, Lindbergh again dressed and returned downstairs to his library. Here, in the room located directly under his son's nursery, he decided to do some reading.

Anne, who was expecting her second child in August, and fearing that she might have caught her son's cold, also decided to take a bath and retire early. Before entering her bathroom, she rang for Elsie and asked if she would prepare a glass of hot lemonade that she could drink before retiring.

Elsie's friendly discussion with Betty had ended moments before when the baby's nursemaid realized it was almost 10 o'clock, her customary time to take the baby for his nightly visit to the bathroom. Meanwhile, in answer to Mrs. Lindbergh's request, Elsie entered the kitchen, and after asking her husband to heat a kettle of water on the stove, she began slicing a lemon in preparation for the hot drink.

The weather outside had turned colder; the bitter March wind was more intense, its "wailing and howling" could be clearly heard as it whipped around the corners of the well built home.

During all this time the occupants continued their normal movements about the house. None had reason to fear any danger.

However, lurking outside in the ominous blackness

of the night were fiends in the form of human flesh, silently watching every movement of the five adults inside. Fiends who could clearly peer through windows which were still without curtains or shades. Fiends who had been actively perpetrating and setting into motion the final and most dangerous phase of their diabolical plot to bring harm to the family of Colonel Lindbergh. Entering the nursery, Betty crossed the 15 feet to the large French window. Realizing a cool air was entering the room, she closed the window. The light from the hall furnished enough illumination to plug in the electric heater. Waiting a moment for the chill to disappear, she then crossed the room to the crib and instinctively sensed that something was amiss. She could not hear the child breathing. Alarmed, with one hand on the crib's side rail, she bent down and felt all over for him. Realizing the baby wasn't there, she entered his mother's room and inquired: "Do you have the baby, Mrs. Lindbergh?" Receiving a negative answer, the bewildered Anne suggested that Colonel Lindbergh might have him, informing her she would find him in his study.

The anxious and alarmed Betty lost no time as she hurried down the stairs to question the baby's father. Approaching the study through the livingroom door, she asked: "Colonel Lindbergh, do you have the baby? Please don't fool me." His answer was an immediate: "The baby? Isn't he in his crib?" Informing him that he was not, Betty followed him as he dashed up the stairs and into the nursery. After a hasty glance about, they entered Mrs. Lindbergh's room, and without saying a word, he returned with a Springfield rifle in his hand.

Each visibly concerned over the child's unexplainable disappearance, they hurried back into the nursery to the empty crib. Glancing about the room, the distraught father noticed an envelope resting on the radiator cover located under the southeast window. Seeing this, gave vent to his gravest suspicions. With a look of sincere concern on his face, he turned to his wife, and in a voice filled with alarm, said: "ANNE, THEY HAVE STOLEN OUR BABY!"

C H A P T E R   T W O

Hours of Anguish

The Lindbergh baby had been stolen! The new home both parents hoped would provide the protection they demanded had been violated by the intrusion of unwelcome persons. The villainous act had taken their baby from the warmth of his crib. Taken him away, to somewhere unknown, to face the ravages of a March night's bitter weather. From the initial discovery of their childs disappearance, it became apparent to the family that the kidnappers had made their departure from the home a successful one.

Had anyone been looking in the direction of the Lindbergh home shortly after the hour of 10 p.m. they would not have failed to notice, what would seem to be, a sudden transformation in the mansion's appearance. From its ghostlike white, silhouetted against the mountain background, into a maze of illumination as each light in the home was brought into use to aid in searching for their missing baby.

Within the home, each of the five occupants moved systematically from room to room seeking any trace of the child. But, they were unsuccessful. Their continued search proved to be futile. The Lindbergh baby had been stolen!

Lindbergh, realizing his need for outside assistance, asked Betty to summon Whateley and have him call the police. Finding the butler in the kitchen, she screamed with emotion, as she told him what had taken place. With Elsie at her side, she rushed back upstairs to the nursery, where the now distraught father issued implicit orders that no one should touch anything in the room. The three women continued their search of every closet in the home. Every conceivable hiding place was scrutinized, upstairs and downstairs, as well as the cellar and attic.

Whateley, finding the telephone usable, lost no time in contacting the Hopewell police. It was shortly before 10:30 when the operator on duty on the second floor of the small Hopewell post office placed the butler's call directly to the home of Officer Charles E. Williamson. Had the operator been listening as Whateley relayed the message to the policeman, she would have been the first civilian to hear the news which soon terrified citizens from coast to coast: "Colonel Lindbergh's son has been stolen. Will you please come at once?"

Williamson quickly put a call through to his superior, Chief Harry H. Wolfe, and several minutes later, after stopping to pick the chief up at his home, the two officers were speeding toward the Lindbergh residence. The two Hopewell officers, in addition to realizing the enormity of this crime, had difficulty comprehending the fact that soon they would be standing in the very presence of the world's most famous hero Colonel Charles A. Lindbergh.

At 10:45 p.m. the beam of the headlights of the approaching police car penetrated the intense blackness of the night as Officer Williamson maneuvered his car between the stone walled entrance of the Lindbergh home.

Parking near the front door, the Hopewell officers approached the brilliantly lighted home where tragedy had struck so suddenly. In the meantime Colonel Lindbergh had placed a telephone call to the New Jersey State Police at Trenton. After advising them of the kidnapping, he then called his good friend and legal advisor, Colonel Henry C. Breckinridge, requesting that he also come to Hopewell.

These calls being completed, while they waited for the police, Lindbergh armed with his rifle, in the company of Whateley, resumed their search of the property outside the home with flashlights. However, the rays of light revealed nothing more than dense underbrush and trees.

With rifle in hand, Lindbergh met the two Hopewell officers at the front door and immediately led them to the nursery. Following a cursory examination of the room, the Colonel pointed to an envelope on the southeast window sill. In spite of the fact that he believed it would contain information from his child's kidnappers, he ordered the Hopewell officers not to touch it until the arrival of the State Police. During this time, the three women had remained downstairs in the brightly lighted living room pacing about in bewilderment during their first of many hours of anguish.

While waiting for the arrival of the state police, the worried father decided to continue an inspection of the ground surrounding the home. Williamson and Wolfe accompanied him making a close examination of the area directly under the southeast nursery window, the one through which they believed the baby had been abducted. With the aid of a flashlight, a closer look revealed a shallow impression in the red yellow clay There was no doubt that it had been made by someone's foot, more than likely that of a man. Also quite discernible were two holes in the soft turf. Both agreed that these had been made by the legs of a ladder that had been placed there.

The men had been taking every precaution not to step off the narrow wooden planks on which they were walking. Evidently placed there by the builders, these planks served as a cat-walk for persons who had occasion to walk along the east side of the house. A step off the planks, which varied in width from six to twelve inches, could possibly destroy any existing evidence the soft earth might reveal. Anne Lindbergh had stood on these same planks earlier in the day as she tossed pebbles up to the window to attract Betty's attention.

The beam of Williamson's flashlight focused on an area in a southeasterly direction from the corner of the house. There, laying on the ground, approximately 60 feet away, were two sections of a ladder. Another 10 feet farther, brought within the beam of his light, lay a third section. Walking over to where the ladder sections were, they took a close look and were of one accord concerning the construction. They concluded that each section was crudely and carelessly put together, and evidently had been made by someone whose work displayed only a sparse knowledge of carpentry skill.

Lindbergh's call to the State Police had been received at the Trenton headquarters at 10:28 p.m. By 10:30, Trooper Joseph A. Wolf, of the Lambertville barracks, had received the relayed dispatch from his station as he was leisurely traveling along the roads of the area in his patrol car. Upon hearing the news, he immediately increased his speed and headed for the home high in the Sourlands. Colonel Lindbergh and the two Hopewell officers met him at the front door at exactly 10:55 p.m. Trooper Wolf was the third police officer to arrive at the crime scene.

After being escorted to the nursery, Wolf decided it would be wise to leave everything in the room untouched until the arrival of a commanding officer. Returning outdoors, the four men proceeded to make another inspection of the terrain around the home, once again concentrating on that portion under the window where it was determined entry into the nursery had been made. As they were showing Trooper wolf the footprint and impressions where the feet of the ladder had apparently been placed, their attention was drawn to the sounds and lights of approaching cars entering the main areaway.

Stepping from the first car at approximately 11:15 were State Police Detectives Lewis J. Bornmann and Nuncio DeGaetano, who were greeted at the front entrance by Colonel Lindbergh and Trooper Wolf. Closely following the detectives, were cars whose occupants were the first of a host of reporters representing most major eastern newspapers who, upon hearing the alarming news of the kidnapping, were ordered by their editors and publishers to rush to Hopewell and give the crime firstpage coverage. Highways leading to Hopewell from all directions were soon clogged with thousands of automobiles filled with reporters, cameramen, private detectives, amateur sleuths, and the morbid curious.

Desiring to make their own survey of the nursery, the two detectives were ushered there by Colonel Lindbergh who showed them a few clues that had already been noted by the two Hopewell police officers. Calling Bornmann to the southeast window, he pointed to the ladder laying where it remained undisturbed, but before going out to take a closer look at the ladder, they took special notice of the nursery condition.

There was the shocking appearance of the empty crib, its covers pinned near the top with two large safety pins. Near the crib was a folding pink and green wooden screen painted with a little red schoolhouse and farm animals. It had served as protection for the baby from any possible drafts which could come from the windows. Near the center of the room was a child's small table and two chairs. Below, and in front of the southeast window, they gave special attention to a small chest of drawers on which had been placed a small leather suitcase. A smudge, appearing to be yellow clay, could be seen on the lower left corner of the suitcase. The floor in front of the chest revealed another smudge of like appearance. Glancing toward the crib, located on the far side of the room, they noticed several other markings, apparently footprints of the same clay-like substance. It was evident that these had also been made by the intruder.

At 12:05 a.m., Trooper Frank A. Kelly, the State Police fingerprint expert, arrived on the scene. The investigation was beginning to move at a more intensive pace. Kelly had no sooner started his task of processing the nursery for any incriminating latent fingerprints, when shortly thereafter, Colonel H. Norman Schwarzkopf, Superintendent of the New Jersey State Police, entered the room, to be followed, only minutes later, by his assistant Major Charles H. Schoeffel.

After conferring with one another, all agreed that the crime committed just a few hours earlier was one of great magnitude, due largely to the world-wide prominence of the family whose child had been stolen. Because of this fact, it was further decided that the investigation would be conducted by on-the-scene directions from the state's top police officials.

By this time, Lindbergh's close friend and attorney, and former Deputy Secretary of the United States Navy, Colonel Henry C. Breckinridge, had joined the group up in the nursery. Other members of the New Jersey State Police detective division who had arrived just moments earlier were; Samuel J. Leon, Andrew Zapolski, and E.A. Haussling. Continuing to arrive, in what seemed to be droves, were more members of the press. These joined the many others who had been milling and roaming around the property, at the same time keeping themselves within close proximity of the house in the event a news release should be announced by the investigators.

Trooper Kelly's initial attention was centered on the envelope found on the windowsill. Colonel Lindbergh called down the stairs to Betty and asked her to bring a knife to the nursery. Gently lifting the envelope from the radiator cover, Kelly placed it on the fireplace mantle. Taking all the precaution necessary, Kelly donned a pair of gloves, took a small brush of very fine camel's hair bristles, and lightly dusted the envelope with a black powder. His exacting work brought negative results.

Major Schoeffel stepped forward, took the envelope from the trooper's hands, and proceeded to neatly slit the top of it with a fingernail file. Carefully removing the enclosed note it contained, he handed it back to the fingerprint expert for processing. Kelly proceeded to dust the note with the powder but the results were even more disappointing. Not the slightest segment of a fingerprint had been detected. There was nothing that could be developed for possible comparison at a later time.

Schoeffel again retrieved the note and read its penciled contents:

Dear Sir!
Have 50,000 $ redy 25 000 $ in
20 $ bills 15 000 $ in 10 $ bills and
10 000 $ in 5 $ bills. After 2-4 days
we will inform you were to deliver
the mony.
We warn you for making
anyding public or for notify the Police
the child is in gute care.
Indication for all letters are
singnature
ans(3holds. (SYMBOL)

The symbol chosen by the kidnappers, one that apparently was to serve as identification for all their future contacts, consisted of two interlocking circles, each about the size of a fifty-cent piece. The circles had been drawn with blue ink. The center oval, fashioned by the intersecting of the two circles, was approximately the size of a dime. It was colored to form a solid ball of red. The symbol had been pierced across the center by an instrument which made three small holes, each one spaced about an inch apart.

Momentarily abandoning his scrutiny of the ransom note, Trooper Kelly's attention was directed to other parts of the room which might reveal some clues that had not been noticed. The imprint of yellow clay on the suitcase top was examined, as well as those on the carpet between the window and crib. The results were indisputable. They had been made by the footsteps of a man. A closer inspection revealed that the marks bore traces of a yellowish-red pigmentation. Other officers informed Kelly that the color was identical to that of the soft clay-like soil outside, beneath the window.

While Kelly was occupied with the inspection of the nursery, Bornmann and DeGaetano were paying particular attention to the wood planks and the footprint impressions where they believed the base of the ladder had been placed. Aided by their flashlights they observed at close range a man's footprint and the two indentations they were certain had been made by a ladder. These two holes were located about 18 inches from the wall of the house and approximately two inches on the farside of the six inch walkway. The so-called temporary catwalk had been placed approximately two feet away from the house wall, extending along the entire east side of the home.

It had been determined earlier that the person whose footprint they could clearly see had either worn heavy stockings or had his feet wrapped in burlap. The imprint, they concluded, had been made by a man standing, two inches to the right, on the farside of the walkway, as he faced the home. It was evidently made as the ladder was placed against the wall, since it was near the two holes the ladder feet had made.

The investigators attention was attracted to the other visible footprint which they determined had been made by a woman who had apparently stepped off the walkway into the soft mud. This they found to the left of the two holes, between the planks and the wall of the house, facing, and quite near a step where a person could make entry onto the porch or open veranda that extended along the 70 foot south side of the Lindbergh home.

Walking in a southeasterly direction, Bornmann had his men direct their attention to the ladder laying near a bush approximately 60 feet away. First, special note was made of the two sections. Although at one time they had been somewhat securely connected, they were now semi-attached, due to a break in one of the boards. A split in the bottom upright section had caused the wood dowel pin, which was used to hold the two sections together, to become disengaged, causing the broken side to hang loose.

Playing their lights around the area revealed the ladder's third section laying another 10 feet away. The men observed that all the sections were approximately equal length. However, aside from that one fact, any speculation of the ladder having been constructed by an expert carpenter was immediately abandoned. It was a crudely built excuse for a ladder.

By this time the Lindbergh property had become a bee-hive of activity. Nearly a hundred more police officers had arrived, most of them neatly attired in uniforms which bore an official patch, identifying them as members of the New Jersey State Police. The addition of so many officers gave the home an appearance of an army barracks as they patrolled the grounds in their semi-military elite corps uniforms of horizon blue coats and flared deep blue riding breeches with broad yellow stripes. Their natty campaign hats and freshly polished gleaming black boots added even more toward a convincing impression that the troops had invaded and taken over the Sourlands.

Due to the influx of Jersey's official constabulary, and realizing that their duties had been, more or less officially completed, the ruddy faced Chief

Wolfe and his assistant Williamson soon ascertained that they had been relegated to the status of merely onlookers. Together, they decided the hour had come when they should vacate the premises. But, regardless of the length of time these two Hopewell police officers were in charge of the proceedings in the kidnapping investigation, it can never be denied that they hold the distinction of being the first to arrive on the scene in answer to Colonel Lindbergh's call for help.

Bornmann, deciding the ladder should be moved inside where it could be more closely examined in a better light, carried the connected sections into the foyer and hallway. As he placed them on the floor he called to Kelly to come and process them for possible fingerprints. Going off to retrieve the third section, he quickly returned with an additional find. Gently placing the ladder on the floor next to the other sections, he showed the group of officers a loose dowel pin and a 3/4 inch wood chisel. This he had found laying partially covered in mud, not far from the point where he had found the separated single ladder section. A close inspection of the ladder revealed that although it showed some evidence of skill in its construction, for the most part, it had been carelessly made. As they had surmised, it was found that all the sections were of equal length. Each measured exactly 6 feet, 10 inches. The side rails of each section had been crudely fashioned, each made to allow a narrower distance between its upright mate. By using the shorter, roughly made cross pieces, which served as rungs or steps, permitted all three sections to nest together, each inside the other for easier transportation. When it was raised to its full height, in order to prevent it from collapsing, wood dowel pins would be inserted into small holes that had been drilled into each section's upright side rails. The investigators concluded that the break in one side rail had occurred as the kidnapper descended the ladder with the added weight of the baby in his arms.

It was 1:30 a.m. when Trooper Kelly finished his work on the three ladder sections. His labor had proven fruitless. No trace of any semblance of a fingerprint was discovered. Likewise, nothing on the chisel could be noted. Bornmann, showing his disappointment, ordered his fingerprint man to return and complete his job in the nursery.

Outside the home, Officer DeGaetano had been kept busy with his examination of the footprint impressions in the ground below the window. The print, already conclusively agreed upon as being made by a male foot, was also imagined to have been that of the person who went up the ladder and into the nursery window.

To say the very least, DeGaetano's investigation of the footprint was UNDENIABLY VERY UNPROFESSIONAL! With flashlight in hand, this man, with nearly six years experience as an officer with the State Police, went through the process of attempting to determine the exact measurement of the questionable footprint by using nothing more than his flashlight. Rather than seeking an accurate measure, DeGaetano was willing to settle for an approximate "guess". The length of the footprint was "estimated to be from 12 to 12 and 1/8 inches"; the width "seemed to measure about 4 to 4 and 1/4 inches". But, DeGaetano's flashlight had not been used for illumination. Instead, as it was held horizontally by a fellow officer over the impression in the clay, it was employed a "as a unit of measure" that could give them nothing more than a poor estimate of the overall measurement of the imprint.

Explaining his "unscientific" method of crime detection as he testified on the witness stand in the Flemington courtroom nearly three years later, DeGaetano said: "I measured from the rear end of the flashlight and the print ended just about where the groove is on the other side of the switch." This "expert investigator" claimed he DID NOT, at the very least, place his flashlight into the depression; he simply held it over the depression. That, he said, "accounted for the length of the imprint". As for its width, he claimed he merely made a "guess", measuring it "with the palm of my hand". At best, the worth of this important clue would rest only in a conclusion drawn in the mind of a man who, very unprofessionally conducted a shoddy, amateurish and incompetent job. He simply had taken his five cell EverReady flashlight, one that measured 14 and 1/2 inches in length, and held it over the depression made by a foot. A professional investigator would have had a plaster cast made for future use in the courtroom, the use of which could prove the possible guilt or innocence of a person.

While this "masterful piece of investigation" was taking place outside, Trooper Kelly was conducting a far more professional one in the nursery. As he stood with his back to the southeast window, as he faced the crib, he noticed three blotches of yellow mud in three different locations. He first detected a smudge on the top of the suitcase at the upper righthand corner closest to the fireplace. Another could be clearly seen on the wood floor directly in front of the chest on which the suitcase rested. The third was a deposit of yellow clay on the carpet midway between the window and crib. Due to the size of this clearly discerned mark on the carpet, it was agreed that because of its size, determined by both its length and width, it had undoubtedly been made by a man.

Trooper Kelly continued his task of processing the nursery, holding high hopes of finding some incriminating latent fingerprints. But, in spite of his ability as a well trained professional identification officer, and after hours of tedious work, he had been unable to raise one single print. He seemed almost apologetic as he expressed his disappointment to his superior officers, Colonel Schwarzkopf and Major Schoeffel: "I'm sorry to report sirs, that no fingerprints were found anywhere in the nursery." Did you process everything, the crib, toys, table, windows, and doors?", he was asked. "Yes sir, everything sir. I missed nothing and found not one semblance of a fingerprint. The results were all negative," Kelly reiterated. "And as for the ladder, you say you couldn't find even a single print?" "That's right sir." Kelly responded in answer to Superintendent Schwarzkopf's further inquiry.

These facts were astounding! Too hard to grasp! Too hard to believe! And yet Kelly knew his work. He was a master of his profession. Surely there should have been the fingerprints of the child's mother, Betty Gow, the baby, the butler, the father! The medicated Vicks VapoRub, a greasy substance they had used to rub the baby's chest surely would have left unmistakable, easy-to-lift, clear latent fingerprints. But there were none, absolutely none! Had someone washed all traces of prints from the room? Even from the doors, the window frames and ledges? Preposterous, absurd, ridiculous! Nevertheless, someone had undoubtedly done just that!

Through the long night of darkness, each passing hour brought new fears to the worried parents. Fears that were intensified as Charles and Anne Lindbergh, after enduring the initial anguish of discovering the empty crib, and realizing their precious little son had been stolen, could only hope and pray that they would ever see their child again. With the passing of the black hours of night came new hours of early morning gray. And with them came new hope - and many more prayers.

With the arrival of daylight, the three sections of the ladder were carried to the location where it had been determined it had been placed against the house the previous night. When the sections were nested together, it was found the total weight to be exactly 40 pounds. Being very careful to hold the legs of the bottom section directly over the two holes in the soft earth, they gently placed the base of the uprights into the holes. The officers were not surprised - they fit perfectly. As they hoisted the other two sections into position, and after connecting them with the dowel pins, they could see that the kidnappers had not used the top section. To gain entry into the nursery, it had been necessary for them to use only the middle and bottom sections.

Deciding this, the officers agreed to use only these in their demonstration. By doing this, they discovered that the uprights of the top section of the two, lined up perfectly with two marks clearly seen on the whitewashed wall of the home. A close scrutiny of these marks revealed them to measure approximately 1 1/2 to 2 1/2 inches in length. Most certainly, these marks had been made by the ladder's top uprights at the very point where they had leaned against the wall. It was further determined that as the kidnapper ascended the ladder, his weight had caused it to move in a slight downward motion, causing the white paint to be scraped off the surface of the house, exposing the gray fieldstone underneath. Additional evidence of this was the discovery of small particles of wood from the ladder still clinging to the wall at those points where the uprights had rested. Even more conclusive evidence, proving that only two sections had been used, was presented by Trooper Kelly when he found traces of whitewash from the wall of the house on the inside of both uprights.

There was however, much cause for conjecture as the officers attempted to agree on the reason the kidnappers had placed the ladder where it would require such great difficulty to enter the room. They also reasoned that leaving the nursery with a child in his arms would complicate the task to an even greater degree. A person would have needed the dexterity of an acrobat. Nevertheless, they justified the action as being more or less unimportant, since the kidnapper's accomplices, no doubt had aided him in his entry and exit.

With the ladder placed where they were certain it had been during the enactment of the kidnapping, the state's investigators proceeded to note for the official police record, the location and dimensions of the ladder and its related window. They found that the top rung of the ladder's top section was exactly 30 inches below the windowsill and about one and one half feet to the right of it. While standing on the top rung, the culprit would have been allowed only a 3 inch toe-hold, and forced to lean against the wall of the house due to the absence of any side rails. In addition to these facts, it was evident that the kidnapper had either worn heavy stockings, or that he had wrapped his feet in burlap.

Analyzing what they already knew, the one great question of primary importance was why the kidnapper had set the ladder to the right of the window, its closest upright about one and one half feet away, instead of directly in front of the window? I believe the answer is a simple one. Had the kidnapper gone up the ladder with it placed directly in the window's center, upon reaching the top rung, he would have found himself leaning too close to the shutters, thus making it practically impossible to open them and then raise the window without falling. Furthermore, regardless of the foreseeable problem he would have with the shutters and window, there remained too great a possibility that Colonel Lindbergh might discover them putting the ladder in place or actually climbing it. The illumination from his desk light might have caused the attention of the child's father to be attracted by the movement of persons outside his study window. This risk was just too great, hence the reasons for placing the ladder where they did.

The sun's rays were warm as it rose on Wednesday, March 2nd. The bright clear day was one which promised the investigators every opportunity they needed to continue their search for the missing child. The inky blackness of the night had at last vanished, and with the early dawn, the Lindbergh mansion once again took on its ghostlike appearance as it stood in stately fashion amid the clearing of scrub cedars and second growth timber surrounding it. Its appearance was much as usual, with but one transformation. The atmosphere, in and around the home, had lost its tranquility, and in its place, had become a veritable hodgepodge of intense activity.

Around 8:00 a.m., Trooper Kelly turned his attention to taking the official photographs of the crime scene. These included those of the footprint impression and the marks where the base of the ladder had been placed, and of course, the ladder itself, showing both the two and three sections in position against the wall. Among others that were deemed to be necessary, those mentioned above were the chief photographs taken.

Although very little fault can be found in the police investigation up to this point, there was, however, ANOTHER INEXCUSABLE AND UNFORGIVABLE VIOLATION OF PROPER POLICE PROCEDURE HAD BEEN COMMITTED AT THIS JUNCTURE OF THE CASE! NO MOULAGE OR PLASTER CAST WAS MADE OF ANY OF THE IMPRINTS IN ORDER TO PRESERVE THEM FOR FUTURE USE IN A COURTROOM!

As news of the kidnapping of Lindbergh's baby from "the big white house up on the mountain" spread, it brought a virtual invasion of automobiles from all directions and many miles distant, speedily converging toward the small New Jersey town. From the very moment, at exactly 10:46 p.m. when the first announcement: "LINDBERGH BABY KIDNAPPED!" was flashed over the police teletype, the impact of those words penetrated the minds of the nation's depression-weary citizens. Something terrible had happened! It triggered and electrified the public into a very conscious realization that they just heard the disclosure of the most diabolical and heart-rending act that could ever be committed against mankind. A baby had been stolen. And that baby was the son of the world's hero, Charles A. Lindbergh. Although it seemed unbelievable, they had heard the news which soon would shock the world.

The greater majority of Hopewell's residents generally made it a practice to retire for the night no later than 10:00 p.m. The night of Tuesday, March 1st, 1932 was, most certainly, no different. But, hours before daybreak of the next morning, most of the residents of this quiet little town had come to realize that something they had never experienced before was actually happening. It was certainly something they were never to forget. They awakened to the sound of hustle-and-bustle in their streets. The little village was humming with a congested mass of humanity within its limits. And it kept growing as the daylight hours advanced.

In addition to those who came offering their aid in any way possible toward bringing the lost baby back to his mother's arms, were thousands of others with an assortment of talents. The largest number among them were the curiosity seekers, an overabundance of concessionaires, food vendors, newsboys, amateur detectives, spiritualists, telegraph men, many hysterical women, and a multitude of plain kooks and nuts who were all certain they knew where the baby was and could solve the crime successfully in a few short hours.

All of these, plus the authorized police personnel and the hundreds of members of the various news media and their respective camera crew, each one seeking to gain entrance into the half-mile muddy lane, located somewhere off the Stoutsburg-Wertsville Road. This lane would eventually take them to the Lindbergh residence. However, if they had been successful in finding the entrance to "Lindbergh Lane", they were prevented from entering because of a State Police barricade that had been set up at that point.

"COLONEL LINDBERGH'S BABY KIDNAPPED SOMETIME BETWEEN 7:30 AND 10:00!" As these words emblazoned themselves across the headlines of the nation's newspapers and were starkly reported by radio announcers, a country was literally transformed. Radio programs already in progress were terminated as the terse news of the progress of each hour was announced throughout the day, bringing the latest developments to the shocked citizenry. News of the war in the Far East was completely knocked off the front pages of newspapers. Type which had already been set to tell of the war's progress, was dumped for new and larger headlines, and in its place, appeared the latest news of the kidnapping. Nevertheless, glaring newspaper headlines were not needed to attract readers. Everyone was anxious to read everything about the kidnapping. Papers were at a premium since most news stands and newsboys experienced a complete sell-out of every issue. People could not wait to get their hands on the latest news of the case. Beneath the headlines appeared stories that virtually screamed with words which seemed to penetrate the innermost emotions of all who read them. The accounts told not only of the deep mystery of this inconceivable kidnapping, but the sincere concern, expressions of love, pathos and tears shed for the grieving parents. Words of anger were vented as the world's citizens spoke out, seeking revenge on the ones who had committed this most dastardly act. Everyone was offering their help to the Lindberghs during their hours of great need.

Ironically, the Lindbergh tragedy played an

important role in the lives of most Americans living in that year. It changed their life-style. It diverted their minds, at least temporarily during the course of the next several years, from the plague of worries that had been blighting the living habits of most American families since the dawn of the 1930s.

On October 29th, 1929, a day which would become known as "Black Tuesday", the Stock Market collapsed; and with it the financial structure of the country became prostrate. The bottom had dropped out! the result --- a disaster of national scope. It brought financial suffering to both the poor and the rich. During the succeeding years, in what was believed to be the greatest economic catastrophe to ever strike our country, the citizens of the United States found themselves trapped in the throes of a long and terrible Depression!

On that fateful "Black Tuesday" sixteen million shares of stock were offered for sale at whatever price could be obtained on the New York Stock Exchange. The crash fostered a loss of nearly 60 billion dollars in listed shares. Hysteria hit as a sudden torrential flood, not only on Wall Street, but in every nook and cranny of the country. Panic ruled! Nearly eighteen million employed citizens now found themselves without jobs. Bank accounts were wiped out and valuable properties lost. People from all walks of life were among the unemployed; they stood in breadlines seeking free handouts; they stood behind carts selling apples, hoping to earn a few spare dollars. People were willing to do anything that would possibly enable them to pay at least a portion of their many overdue bills.

Times during the '30s were tough ones indeed. Every person had his or her own financial problems; problems which, almost overnight had become constant day-long cause for distress. Adding to this, many had no idea where they would find their next meal, nor where they could acquire lodging for the night. Only temporary work was available, and this for just short periods and for low pay. Jobs of this type would be taken in order to earn even a small portion of the next month's rent or mortgage payments on a home they realized they were eventually going to lose. Vital problems! Vital questions? All of which seemed to have no answer.

From coast to coast, all were searching for the prosperity that was constantly reported as being "just around the corner". People walked as though in a daze, and then would bury their pride as they forced themselves to ask others, some of them much worse off, the heartrending question, "Brother can you spare a dime?" Desperately troubled people were legion during, what seemed to be, the endless, hopeless '30s. Every city, town village, and hamlet had been caught up in the evil and haunting clutches of the vicious depression that, before it was to end, would both destroy and claim many lives. And so it was at the time of the Lindbergh kidnapping. The citizens, worn and weary with their many troubles, seemed to go on an "emotional binge" as they put aside their own problems and centered their thoughts and prayers on the anguish and suffering of Charles and Anne Lindbergh.

CHAPTER THREE

Conspiracy!

THE LINDBERGH KIDNAPPING HAD BEEN COMMITTED BY A GROUP OF PERSONS! This was, and remained, the decision of the police from the very beginning of their investigation. They never held a doubt that the crime had been fashioned by anyone other than in the criminal minds of a conspiracy!

To begin with, they reasoned, how did the kidnappers know the Lindberghs would be spending that Tuesday night at Hopewell? Their past practice had been to return to Englewood on Monday mornings after a weekend in the Sourlands. This was their custom, one from which they had never deviated. And, so the police correctly reasoned: "Who could have been the informer?"

Although the authorities had much difficulty wrestling with the "Who could have known?" question, the fact surely was quite obvious that many persons did know, and had known, from the time Betty had been called to come to Hopewell. Surely, the Whateleys knew it; Violet Sharpe, who took the call in the Morrow home, knew it; Henry Ellison, the chauffeur, knew it; Mrs. Morrow, Anne's mother knew it; and there can be little doubt that many of the other 27 employees in the Morrow home had learned of it.

It is therefore to be assumed that, either deliberately or unintentionally, the "news": "The Lindberghs are staying in Hopewell again tonight." was passed along to the ears of those who were waiting to obtain this valuable information. Very few of the officers subscribed to this theory.

However, a majority of the investigators were willing to rationalize that the kidnappers had been lying in wait behind the surrounding trees. And then, at the proper time, whenever that could be, they would act, preferably, of course, when the Lindberghs would be spending a week night at Hopewell. But, this we should cast off as nothing more than ridiculous supposition.

Without the help of inside information, one would be expected to believe that the kidnappers would have guessed correctly which of the upstairs bedrooms was the child's nursery. Could they have taken another chance guess, and made another correct one? That, from the 22 windows on the second floor of the house, they had selected one of the three windows in the child's nursery, and the only one that could not be latched because of a warped shutter.

The element of "luck" is much too great a factor to consider. Instead we should accept the certainty that someone had "tipped off" the kidnappers informing them of the exact location of the nursery window.

Consideration was presented regarding the logic behind the time the kidnappers had chosen to steal the baby. It was generally accepted they had decided on mid-evening as the proper time, since during these hours the house would be filled with the normal sounds of the occupants as they went about performing their nightly activities. Hence, this would allow them to take better advantage of help from inside the home, heeding their warnings, rather than risk the danger of sounds being heard more distinctly after all the members of the household were in their beds.

Many of the police argued that had the kidnappers waited until after midnight; it would have, quite possibly, afforded them many more hours in which to make their getaway. But, this can only be an argument for conjecture. The fact remains that the abduction and removal of the youngster from the Lindbergh estate was successfully executed without detection. The accomplishment of the kidnappers, regardless of any quarrel against the way it was done, proves that in whatever decisions they had made --- they had been correct.

Obviously the perpetrators had planned to use all three sections of the ladder. Had they been able to do this, the height they had predetermined would be necessary, all problems of reaching the window's bottom ledge would have been eliminated. However, something unforeseen happened. Possibly due to the added stress, applied by the person's weight as he started to climb, caused one of the side rails and the top rung of the bottom section to split where the two had been joined with a dowel pin. If this be so, is it not feasible to reason that the noise Colonel Lindbergh heard while sitting with Anne in the living room was made by the sharp cracking sound of this break in the kidnapper's ladder? If a supposition of this kind is correct, then the time of the actual abduction can be established as "shortly after 9:00 p.m." since it was then that Lindbergh exclaimed to his wife: "What was that?" A further supposition would pose this question. Had the father immediately gone to investigate the cause of the sound, isn't it possible to assume that the Lindbergh kidnapping would never have taken its place in the annals of the world's history of crime?

Time, quite naturally, was of intense importance to the kidnappers. Realizing they must abandon their plan to use all three sections of the ladder, they continued their evil deed by using only two. Again we must emphasize the required gymnastic ability necessary for whoever climbed that rickety ladder and entered the nursery window.

To this day we are continually asked to believe the ridiculous theory that the kidnapper, acting alone with his feet wrapped in burlap, went up the ladder and, after reaching the top rung which afforded him only a three inch toe hold, found himself still 30 inches below the windowsill. Here the left upright of the ladder was nearly two feet below the window and almost two feet away from its right-hand casing. At this location he would have had nothing on which to secure himself, except to grasp for the right shutter. This would then necessitate his standing in an extreme upright position, leaning against the wall of the house, and at the same time, balancing himself fourteen feet above the ground. An accomplished acrobat might have been able to perform such a feat of agility, but hardly an inexperienced kidnapper in the darkness of a windy night.

Once he had maneuvered himself into some sort of workable position, he would then have had to reach across and open the two shutters. Once he had them open he would have been faced with the somewhat difficult task of raising the window, not directly above him, wide enough for him to enter. The window now open, he would reach over, grasp the sill and pull himself up and over and into the room. This he had accomplished without disturbing a musical beer stein sitting inside on the broad windowsill, and not moving a toy standing on the top of a suitcase directly inside and below the window. Now inside the nursery, without making a sound, he had made his way across the room to the crib where the baby lay sleeping.

From the evidence uncovered at the scene, based on the yellow clay found on the steps of the ladder, plus that identified as being the same yellow substance clearly seen on the suitcase, floor and carpet in the baby's room; we must conclude that this is a strong indication that someone certainly must have ascended the ladder and entered the nursery from the window. However, evidence cannot be found, and did not present itself, which would support the assumption that the kidnapper, with a child now in his arms, had left the room in the same manner as he had entered.

It must not be forgotten that the police never deviated from their dogmatic belief that the kidnapping had been the work of a conspiracy. That is, they never swerved from this --- until an arrest was made two-and-one-half years later. THIS WE SHOULD REMEMBER!

However, the facts, as we know them, definitely contradict even the initial theory of the authorities. First, however, we must examine the ludicrous claims they make. Finding himself in front of the crib, the kidnapper reaches down and, after taking the child in his arms, retreats across the room to the window. Here, he would have to be partially turned as he backed his way across the suitcase and windowsill, with articles on top, and lower himself out the window, at the same time feeling with his burlap encased feet for safe footage on the top rung of the ladder which afforded him only a three inch toe hold. And, all this was done with a 30 pound baby under one arm. Or possibly he had to shift the baby, forcing him to use both arms. A baby that did not cry. And while he manipulated himself into a position which would allow him the "unhindered advantage" to reach up and place a ransom note on the windowsill. And all this was accomplished during a heavy wind, that for some reason failed to disturb the note. But all was not over, he then had to lower the window, close both shutters, and make his way down the crude ladder. This clever abduction he had mastered by using only one hand.

But, the folly of this police theory continues. They would also have us accept their line of reasoning that upon reaching the ground in safety, the kidnapper instead of hurriedly making his exit from the Lindbergh property; had taken the ladder, weighing a total of 40 pounds and a baby weighing 30, had carried both to a spot 60 feet from the southeast corner of the house where he deposited two sections of the ladder. And then, at a spot 70 feet in the same direction from the house, had dropped the other section of the ladder. Or are we to believe that he placed the baby on the ground under the southeast window while he went off with the ladder sections to dispose of them? This is nothing more than a ridiculous supposition! It is pure nonsense! The kidnapping was not committed in that fashion! It could not have happened that way! The very facts prove it! To begin with, it is utterly absurd to believe that the kidnappers, who had just successfully stolen the world's most famous baby, the son of the world's hero Charles A. Lindbergh, would have bothered to remove the ladder from its position, leaning against the home. The child had been removed from the safety of his crib by fiends whose first thoughts would naturally be to place as many miles as possible between them and the house, and do it quickly - as quickly as possible without being detected. Good common sense would have us ask why would anyone be concerned as to where the ladder would be found? It would not have made one iota of difference if the ladder had been found still leaning against the wall or six and seven hundred feet from the house. The question of time most certainly would have been a major factor, especially so if a lone kidnapper had been involved. Surely, he would not have wasted the valuable minutes it would have taken to remove the ladder. The fact that it was moved gives further proof substantiating the involvement of more than one person. It goes far to prove that an accomplice, or accomplices, waiting at the foot of the ladder as the kidnapper entered the room, had taken the top section and carried it 70 feet away; then returned to remove the two sections, those used, and carry them 60 feet distant where they knew they would eventually be found.

This theory naturally brings two questions to mind. First, would be the possibility that the kidnapper had fallen as he attempted to maneuver his way down the ladder with the child in his arms? An examination of the clay-like earth, made soft from the day's rain, failed to show any evidence of a depression in the ground that could have been made by a fall from any height. Secondly, we have the problem as to how the kidnapper holding the baby could descend to the ground if the ladder had been removed as he was making his way across the darkened room to the crib? This too, is easily answered when we realize that the kidnapper never vacated the home by the way he entered. He simply went down the front stairs and out the front door, being led there by the person who had given him the inside help he needed; the person who had actually removed the baby from his crib. Someone the child knew, would trust, and therefore not utter a cry.

Returning now, to the question as to why Trooper Frank Kelly failed to find any latent fingerprints in the nursery? His ability as a fingerprint expert cannot be questioned. He certainly was qualified in every sense of the word. True, it is highly possible the kidnapper was wearing gloves. However, Kelly was not able to process, or raise, at least one latent print of anyone - from any point in the room. Unbelievable, you would say, but nevertheless true!

Surely, one would think Kelly would have found at least some semblance of a print from some section of the room. Those of the Lindbergh family and their employees most certainly would have left their fingerprints. Mrs. Lindbergh, Betty, Elsie and Oliver Whateley had handled, at least touched, the nursery furnishings on many occasions. We can be certain that little Charles had touched his toys, table, chairs, crib and other things in the room. And yet none of his prints were found. Slightly more than four hours earlier, Anne and Betty had rubbed Vicks VapoRub, an oily substance, on the little fellow's chest. The application of oil on one's fingers normally makes the job of developing latent fingerprints much easier; quite often the prints made by oily fingers can be detected with the naked eye before the area is dusted with powder. Then why, we ask, were none found?

The answer to that question is obvious beyond words. A very unreasonable and preposterous thought would be for someone to accept the ridiculous explanation that a lone kidnapper would have taken the time, either before or after he had removed the baby from his crib, to go about the room and wipe every item, including the doors and window frames, clean of all trace of prints anywhere. If we can believe such foolishness, then we should ask the question, did he use a dry cloth or a wet rag?

It is understandable why no fingerprints were found! There were absolutely none there to be developed and lifted! They had been permanently destroyed by the "good housekeeping" assistance of an accomplice working within the walls of the Lindbergh mansion. He, and he alone, would have been the only logical one to have rendered such valuable help to the kidnapper. He alone would know whether a dry or wet cloth had been used.

Returning to one of the most blatant examples of police neglect was their failure to have plaster casts made of the footprints, clearly evident, found on the ground beneath the nursery window. Officer DeGaetano offered nothing more than his guesswork as to the size of the impressions. This "efficient" detective admitted in court, when asked why he hadn't gone into the house and inquired of Elsie Whateley or Betty Gow if they had a measuring tape he could borrow, replied: "Well, I guess I didn't think of it." Instead of obtaining an exact measurement of the print, this seasoned officer, investigating a crime of major importance, had chosen a very incompetent method, one which possibly a child might have thought of doing. Combining the use of his flashlight and the palm of his hand, he had, and for the lack of a better word, "guessed" the size of the male footprint. It is also apparent that the thought had not entered his mind, nor for that matter the minds of the other officers, to measure the size of the Lindbergh butler's shoe against this most important clue, which obviously had been left behind by one of the kidnappers.

To be perfectly fair, however, we must admit that the police did question Whateley as to whether he had been outside the home, standing under the window? And then, they readily accepted his immediate answer that he had not been outside the residence at all that day. In unison, the officers accepted their initial "foregone conclusion" belief that the distinct impression found near the step entrance to the porch had "no doubt" been made by Mrs. Lindbergh the afternoon before as she stood on the wooden walk and waved to her baby. They assumed she had stepped off the plank, thus causing the footprint. But this is again an assumption and should have, at least, allowed for some skepticism on the part of the cops. But no, once again we have police "guesswork" playing a role in police professionalism. Although we are lead to agree that in this instance the police could have been correct; nothing conclusive was ever presented to prove it was Anne Lindbergh's footprint. Nevertheless there will always remain the doubt that it could have been that of an accomplice.

Are we to regard these failures on the part of police as mere oversights? Or should we consider something which raises its ugly head, something quite evident, a definite lack of police professionalism? A combination of these two lend themselves to a very poor initial investigation.

As for the chisel, we can only speculate that it had probably been brought there by the kidnappers with the intention of using it to pry open a locked window. However, fortunately for them, it was not needed and had evidently been discarded on that part of the property where the ladder sections were found.

With these facts assembled, as they were known to the police authorities on that night of March 1, 1932, it can be construed in no other way than to arrive with a final conclusion that the kidnapping had been successfully executed by a group of people. This is what the police deduced! And rightly so! They claimed there was not even a remote possibility that the kidnapper had acted alone!

Since we know of no one living today who actually witnessed the kidnapping, it is still possible to reconstruct the crime as we believe it could have happened. However, as close as our enactment might be, please bear in mind that our speculation is one of mere conjecture.

It can be definitely established that a kidnapper ascended the ladder based on the fact that particles of the yellow clay from the ground beneath was found on the ladder steps. His weight apparently caused a break where the two sections were joined. This break could possibly have made the cracking noise heard by the Colonel and his wife as they sat together in the living room shortly after the hour of nine. If this is true, then we can establish the kidnapping as taking place approximately between nine-five and nine-ten p.m. At any rate, the man continued his climb and entered the window. He definitely did not fall since there was no evidence supporting this possibility. An indentation in the soft earth, made by a fall, would have been proof of this claim, however,there was absolutely none.

After experiencing the great difficulty of getting himself off the ladder and into the nursery window, one of his two accomplices took the discarded and unused top section of the ladder and carried it to the location where it was found, 70 feet away. Its weight was slightly more than 13 pounds. Rather light and easy for anyone to carry, especially over a short distance. As he entered the nursery, the person at the base of the ladder, who had steadied the shaky affair, removed the two sections, folded them as one, transported them 60 feet distant and abandoned them there.

As this was taking place outside the home, the abductor was making his way stealthily across the room to the crib, leaving tell-tale proof, the yellow clay found on the suitcase and carpet, that he had entered by way of the ladder and window. Almost across the room, he was met by an accomplice who had already removed the youngster from the crib. Quickly following his inside helper, the two made their way down the front steps, into the foyer and out the front door. The child, still not completely awake, was then handed to one (possibly a woman) of the two accomplices on the outside. It had taken them only minutes to accomplish their fiendish act, and now, once outside, they lost no time as the three, one of them carrying the Lindbergh's precious little son, made their way into further darkness where a car awaited them not far away.

There are four lines of reasoning that I use in determining that the kidnapped child was taken out the front door. The decision to do so could have been made at the last minute due to the break in the ladder; making an exit with a baby in one's arms almost an impossibility without a fall occurring. Secondly, there were no visible marks on the carpet which indicated an exit had been made on any return trip to and through the window. My third point is made when we take into consideration the fact that the kidnapper left a ransom note on the windowsill. Keep in mind that there was a very high wind that evening and for him to have placed the note there and then proceeded to make his difficult and time consuming exit, there would have been the grave possibility that the note would have blown away. As to my fourth bit of reasoning, supporting the safety of such a bold venture as taking the child out the front door, I draw on a statement made by Colonel Lindbergh. When asked by the police if he believed that someone could have taken the child out the front door without his or Anne's knowledge, he readily admitted: "They could have." His answer was based on his knowledge that from the location where he and his wife had been sitting, facing the living room fireplace, it would have been impossible for either of them to see anyone come down the front staircase and leave by way of the front door. Both were completely out of their viewing range. And so, the risk taken of fleeing from the home by going out the main entrance was not too great.

True, the possibility remains that they could have taken the baby across the hall, down the back stairs, and out through the servants quarters entrance. But, this would have been a longer route, and time was of the essence. We must also take into consideration that Betty and Elsie were both in that end of the house and either or both might have detected strange movements and discovered the abduction as it was taking place.

And as the kidnappers were speeding away to parts

unknown, the lone confederate inside the Hopewell home was diligently making certain that all traces of fingerprints were successfully removed from the nursery.

As we briefly review the movements of the members of the Lindbergh household during the precise hours of that fateful evening, those between eight and ten; we have Charles and Anne either together or knowing where the other was from 8:20 until a few minutes after 10 when the kidnapping was discovered. Betty and Elsie were together from the time Betty left the baby at 8:00 p.m. until 10:00 when she went to look in on the baby and take him to the bathroom. Oliver Whateley, and we have his word for it, was alone in the servants sitting room contentedly reading The Saturday Evening Post.

During a period of one solid hour not one member of the Lindbergh household had seen the trusted butler Oliver Whateley!

CHAPTER FOUR

Police In Action

Hopewell, the quiet little New Jersey community, was soon to be transformed into a town of excitement and hub-bub. It literally changed overnight, with a large portion of the activity centered in and around Gebhart's General Store on Broad Street. Paul Gebhart, the owner, had been aroused from his sleep at 1:30 a.m. when the first contingent of reporters arrived on the scene. Their persistent pounding on the door, demanding him to open his store and allow them to use his telephone, had given him, not only early knowledge of the kidnapping, but in addition, the awareness that something big had taken place in his little community. This realization was fast becoming a reality as he soon found his stock of coffee, candy, cigarettes and pipe tobacco completely depleted. From the time of the first knock on his door, Gebhart's small store would never be the same.

Many of Hopewell's residents would soon be laying bets that before the pandemonium brought on by the kidnapping was over, the jolly, sandy haired proprietor, Paul Gebhart, would be able to retire a millionaire. Before nightfall on Wednesday, he had completely sold out of everything in his store. As the days wore on the demand for more provisions became even greater. Each day his "tenants" were largely those of the news media. Those whose employers were willing to pay hundreds of dollars for lodging and sleeping quarters in order that their reporters and camera crew could stay close to the story and report its latest developments. To meet the demand of their daily requirements, replacement of supplies were coming into Hopewell daily out of Trenton. Gebhart's General Store was vital in meeting the demands of the increasing host of visitors. And with it, the stout Mr.Paul Gebhart was becoming fatter and fatter in a financial way.

As the hours of Wednesday moved on, the State Police at the Lindbergh home were conducting their investigation at an intensive pace. Under the direction of Superintendent Schwarzkopf, their chain of command consisted of the following officers: Major Charles H. Schoeffel, serving as Deputy Superintendent, second in command of the Lindbergh investigating force; Captain John J. "Jack" Lamb, known for his work in the famous Hall-Mills murder at New Brunswick, New Jersey in 1922; Lieutenant Arthur T. (Buster) Keaten; Detective Corporal Samuel Leon; Detectives Lewis J. Bornmann and Nuncio DeGaetano; and Troopers Frank A. Kelly and Joseph Wolf.

Assisting these top officials of the State Police were Harry W. Walsh and Detective Robert Coar of the Jersey City Police Department; Lieutenant John J. Sweeney and Detective Hugh J. Strong of the Newark Police Department; and Captain Russell N. Snook, Chief of the Identification Bureau of the New Jersey State Police.

Captain Lamb quickly set up headquarters in the Lindbergh garage for the more than 100 state troopers and 16 detectives that had been assigned to the case. The so-called command post was soon furnished with a 20 line telephone switchboard with 20 troopers assigned to man them. Shortwave broadcasting and receiving equipment was installed; a police teletype machine was brought in, one capable of connecting the Lindbergh residence with every law enforcement unit in the state. Communication lines were extended in every direction for a distance of 30 miles. Many troopers, serving as security guards, were seen patrolling in all sections of the vast estate.

The Lindbergh property appeared to be in a state of siege. In addition to the police, the grounds were crowded with hundreds of reporters and cameramen, plus the many communication experts who were at work setting up the intricate system.

Realizing his property was being invaded by many unauthorized persons; it was Colonel Lindbergh who finally asked those who were not there in any official capacity, to please leave in order that the police could conduct their investigation without unnecessary interference. Reluctantly the members of the press complied, many taking up residence in a farmhouse near the end of Lindbergh Lane. Those who were unable to find lodging near the Lindbergh home retreated into Hopewell where, after agreeing to have their employers pay a rather exorbitant price, unheard of in 1932, were given a place to catch some sleep in a back room at Gebhart's "make-shift" hotel.

The primary objective of the police was to make

contact with all the residents living in the immediate vicinity of the Lindberghs. The occupants of every household within a 10 mile radius had been interviewed and questioned. The results proved to be useless. No one had seen anything of importance that would be of any aid to them in their continuing investigation. In addition, troopers conducted a systematic search into every abandoned building, culvert, viaduct, thicket and other probable places where a baby could be hidden, with negative results.

Investigators working nearer the house were paying special attention to the possible route the kidnappers had taken in their departure from the crime scene. A closer look at the ground in broad daylight permitted them to trace other signs of footprints. They agreed that a path, believed to have been taken could be clearly seen leading from the house to the location near the bushes where the ladder was found. From this point, they reasoned, although it was barely discernable, they pointed to an indication of someone's passage, evidenced by the broken underbrush leading to Featherbed Lane, a seldom used dirt road about a half mile south of the Lindbergh home. Here they found additional evidence that a car had been parked there, and had apparently made a turn on the narrow lane. They concluded that the appearance of the bushes on one side of road, having the bark scraped off them, substantiated their belief. It was also quite clear to them that there had been persons on foot who had entered a car at this point. THE OFFICERS, HOWEVER, SEEMED TO DISCOUNT THESE FACTS AS UNIMPORTANT TO THE CASE! The police had been aware of a man living in the Sourlands who had the reputation of knowing more about the mountain region than any living person. They decided it would be advantageous for them to seek his help. Oscar Bush, whose ancestry was part Indian, not only lived on the mountain, but had hunted and trapped throughout the entire range of mountainous area for many years. Their decision to contact him was a proper one. His aid would have been quite valuable had the police listened to his advice. But, when he was summoned to help them, many officers scoffed, claiming he was merely a woodsman, and could offer nothing very scientific that would assist them. Bush immediately confirmed the possible route the kidnappers had taken in making their getaway. He stressed his belief that the footprints were those of a man, in all probability those of a small person in his stocking feet, a man who would possibly wear a size eight shoe. He further explained that from the spot where the ladder was found, the sharp imprint of their feet was not discernable, but nevertheless, the beaten down grass could be distinguished from that around it on the path of exit he was certain they had taken. Bush strongly believed the kidnappers had entered the car after it had been turned. He ascertained that no one crossed the road to the other side since their imprints would have been clearly legible in the muddy road had they done this. The ruddy six-foot outdoorsman went so far as to tell the officers he felt certain the abductors escaped apprehension by traveling north over the mountain toward Zion and Neshanic.

With this kind of evidence at their disposal, why did the police relentlessly claim in the Flemington court room nearly three years later that they had only discovered two footprints outside the Lindbergh home? Why did they fail to mention the evidence they had uncovered which clearly pointed out that more than one person had left the premises by way of Featherbed Lane? As proof that the officers were aware of this evidence, we should examine some quotes taken from the official investigation report of Trooper Joseph Wolf, one of the first State Police officers to arrive on the scene. In part, Wolf's report reads: "The kidnappers consisted apparently of a party of at least two or more persons...Apparently two members of the party proceeded on foot to the east side of the Lindbergh residence and assembled a three-piece homemade extension ladder...Two sets of fresh footprints led off in a southeast direction...Kidnappers arrived in a car which was left parked some distance from the house either in Lindbergh's private lane or a rough road known as Featherbed Lane...I detailed several troopers SO THAT FOOTPRINTS WOULD NOT BE DESTROYED (emphasis supplied)." Why, we must ask again, did the police deny the existence of these footprints? Why were they not introduced in court? Again the answer seems quite apparent. Admitting this in court would have destroyed their case against a man they were "proving" had acted alone. It just would not have fit their purpose. However, the evidence was certainly important enough to Trooper Wolf, otherwise he would not have written in his report that he detailed several troopers to protect the footprints from destruction.

Further evidence should be noted here of another official report substantiating Wolf's report. A portion of Detective Nuncio DeGaetano's report reads: "We traced rubber boots or overshoes impressions from the ladder down an old road and appeared to stop alongside impressions from an auto." Were casts ever made of these? Were measurements of these ever taken? Ridiculous questions, since no one ever bothered to make any of those found below the nursery window. JUST ANOTHER EXAMPLE OF BUNGLED POLICE WORK!

Oscar Bush was very critical of the troopers for ignoring his advice to employ the use of a pack of bloodhounds. He wanted to get the hounds there so that they could acquire the scent of the baby by smelling his clothes, and then combine this along with any possible trail which might have been left by the fleeing kidnappers. But the lanky trapper claimed his advice seemed to fall on deaf ears, and when he pressed them for an answer to his prodding, the officers informed him they "did not own any dogs for that purpose." Bush, however, claimed he knew of an owner of a fine bloodhound who offered the animal for their use but was turned down in no uncertain fashion.

The big woodsman seemed to hold a vendetta against the investigators who, in his estimation, did not appear anxious to search the deep mountainside. He further stated that the police appeared afraid to enter the wilds of the Sourland Mountains "lost land" and examine the many abandoned shacks that would be found there. It is evident that the troopers resented the advice given them by this rugged mountaineer. By all means, they should have taken advantage of his suggestions, since he told them to use nothing but "clear logic and plain common sense." Most police officers are well aware that by using logic and common sense in their investigations many a criminal case, large or small, has been brought to a successful conclusion. And this was a large one. A real large one!

Of the hundreds of people questioned, mainly farmers who lived in the immediate area of the Lindbergh home, a glimmer of hope was realized when a man named Nelson Wyckoff reported that Ben Lupica, a friend of his, had mentioned to him that at about 6:00 p.m. on the night of the kidnapping he had seen a man with two sections of a ladder in a car near the entrance to Lindbergh Lane. Encouraged with this news, the police summoned Lupica to come to the Lindbergh home for questioning. Sebastian Benjamin Lupica was a 17 year old student who attended Princeton Preparatory School. The hopes of an early arrest ran high as the police listened to his story. He reported that as he was returning from school on the afternoon before, at approximately 6:00 p.m., he had stopped at his mailbox, which was located along the side of the road at the end of Lindbergh Lane. In no great hurry to get to his home, about a mile north of the Lindbergh home, and anxious to check his mail, he sat in his car along the roadside reading a letter. It was during this time that he heard the sound of a car approaching.

Glancing up from his letter, he had taken note that the car was a 1929 Dodge sedan, and was driven by a man wearing a black overcoat and a dark fedora hat. Lupica went on to say that the man had pulled the car over on the wrong side of the road and stopped. Pressing him for more details, the young man went on to say that the driver appeared to be between 35 and 40 years of age and that he had thin facial features.

The police were especially interested with the information he supplied them relative to the ladder he had noticed. Lupica claimed the ladder was in two sections, one laying on top of the other, and was resting from the front windshield, across the top of the seat, extending to the rear window. The car had stopped about 50 yards in front of him, and believing the driver wanted him to pass, Ben said he then drove off toward his home, once more making a hasty observance of the incident.

Quite interested in Lupica's information, the officers questioned him further. The color of the car, he related, was either black or dark blue. Yes, he had noticed the license plate and it was definitely that of New Jersey. However, he said he took no special note as to its registration number, but he was certain it bore a letter designation "L", which identified it as one issued for Mercer County cars.

Although Lupica's description of the driver was considered by the police to be rather sparse, they could not sway him in any respect from the story he told them. It definitely had given the troopers something on which to work.

The young preparatory student's story was somewhat substantiated by a woman who was convinced she had seen a car as it passed her farmhouse sometime between the hour of 5:00 and 6:00 p.m. Mrs. Henry Wendling, who resided along the Zion-Wertsville Road, gave the identical description of the car as had young Lupica. Mrs. Wendling claimed the car had attracted her attention, but that there was no reason to observe it in a more detailed way since it had been just another car passing her home. She was not able to give the police any information about the driver.

It seems more than strange that from the time (half past seven on the morning after the kidnapping) Nelson Wyckoff reported to the police that Ben Lupica had something which should be helpful to them, the authorities evidently were in no hurry to interview the youthful student for details. Ben was permitted to travel on to Princeton to attend classes that day before he was requested to go to the Lindbergh home and tell them what he had observed the night before. Nine and one-half hours after the child was discovered missing, the police seemed to be disinterested in interviewing a witness who could have given them valuable information that could have resulted in an early arrest. At 4:30 p.m., another nine hours had been allowed to pass before Lupica was finally interrogated by the police in the flier's Sourland Mountain home. Instead of hurriedly ushering the young man into the residence when they had first received word of information he had to relate to them, they had chosen instead to allow eighteen and one-half hours to go by before they would get down to the serious business of obtaining some valuable information. - Information which they could have learned nine hours earlier. - Information which could have given them, at least a vague description of one of the kidnappers before 8:00 that morning, providing they had been diligent in their investigation.

Judging by the lackadaisical effort the state police were making to question Ben Lupica, would cause one to wonder if they were at all anxious to solve the crime. A redundant thought, but nevertheless prompted by more facts involving young Lupica and his desire to help them. Lupica's first interview with the police interrogators was one of intense questioning. He willingly related his experience of the afternoon before, at the end of Lindbergh Lane. After telling them everything he could about the man and the car, he was excused, being told that if they needed him again, they would get in touch with him.

During this period of questioning, Lupica failed to identify the ladder sections found at the site of the kidnapping as being the same ones he had seen in the Dodge sedan. The reason for this is easily explained -- - the police simply failed to ask him! Would we be redundant to ask why? Either the police did not deem it important enough or "they just plain forgot about it!" At any rate Lupica never saw the ladder. However, he was asked to return at 7:00 p.m. and told that he would then see the ladder. When Ben returned at the appointed time, without a glimmer of doubt, he identified two of the sections as those he had seen on the afternoon before in the car at the end of Lindbergh Lane. Another two and one-half hours had gone by before this necessary identification was made. The Lupica affair is nothing more than another prime example of police impropriety in the Lindbergh case.

C H A P T E R   F I V E

An Inside Job

The reaction of the public to the news of the kidnapping was varied. During the first twenty-four hours after the first shocking announcement was made most people found themselves experiencing an attitude of skeptical disbelief. However, the truth was to soon saturate the minds of people throughout the world, as hour by hour radio newscasts blared forth with the latest developments. Others, who had possibly not yet heard of the tragedy, had it passed on to them by relatives, neighbors and friends. All were startled persons who kept the telephone lines busy throughout the night, attempting to find someone with whom they could share the news and express their sympathy for the Lindbergh family.

The events of what had occurred within the walls of that mountain home on Tuesday, March 1st were to remain a private matter for only a very short time. Recognizing that the privacy of their home had been invaded {their child had been stolen and could not be found}, little did they realize that the tragic occurrence would soon become property in the minds of the general public. A public, who for years to come, would violate the fundamental truths of what actually had taken place, and instead, substitute them with thousands of their own favorite garbled and distorted versions.

Within thirty minutes, following Whateley's call to Officer Williamson, the police of three states had been triggered into action the moment they were alerted of the crime. Immediately their most important assignment was to "find Lindy's baby!". All vehicles moving out of New Jersey into New York by way of any bridge or tunnel were stopped and searched. Cars, busses, and trucks were ordered to stop, their occupants asked to step outside, while the officers closely checked the interiors. Mothers wheeling baby coaches were delayed while the cops examined their babies; some mothers were taken to precinct station houses where they were kept for hours, attempting to prove, which they eventually did, that the questionable baby was really theirs and actually belonged to them. The Lindberghs, after a sleepless night, showed visible signs of the anguish and strain they were under. After spending approximately an hour alone with Anne, at a breakfast neither could eat, Charles went outside to join the searchers whose number had already reached several hundred. Cognizant of the fact that many of them, excluding the official police, included reporters and camera crews from various news services, lots of self appointed amateur detectives, and the usual morbidly curious persons who did nothing more than get in the way and hamper the investigation.

As the Colonel observed the apparent disorganized procedure that was being tolerated by the police, the disturbed father was slightly less than polite when he ordered all persons other than the police and those present on official business to immediately vacate the premises in order that the police could work without any hindrance. This command should have been given by the police since it had become quite apparent that the over abundance of needless persons, tramping aimlessly around the estate, could possibly be destroying some valuable evidence. However, any damage which might have been done, had already been accomplished by the unnecessary busybodies who, with great reluctance, withdrew from the property, some to find lodging in the few neighboring farmhouses.

"Slim" Lindbergh, the 30 year old aviator who nearly five years earlier had flown over the Atlantic Ocean alone, had momentarily "blown his cool" as he directed both Colonel Schwarzkopf and Major Schoeffel to bring some semblance of order out of the seeming chaos, disorder, hysteria and frenzy that he witnessed as he looked at the hundreds of people trampling over his property on that Wednesday, March 2nd.

This bareheaded airman, not having shaved and wearing an old pair of gray trousers, a tan leather flight jacket and shirt open at the neck, appeared to be very tired as he barked out his orders. The good looking six foot, four inch young man had temporarily lost his usual boyish compelling smile as he made it very clear to the police and other observers that he was taking charge of the investigation. And furthermore, if Schwarzkopf and his aides had any doubt of his sincerity, they agreed to condescend to his wishes, at least temporarily. Colonel Lindbergh was very angry and in no mood to deal with anyone who might want to trifle with him.

Anne, who did not venture a step outside, could be clearly seen moving about inside the home. Her cold had grown worse and she appeared tired and worn, caused largely by the anxiety of not knowing if her baby was safe. Despite her facial appearance, she was trimly dressed in a plain navy-blue sports frock trimmed with a white collar; a blue plaid scarf was neatly tied around her dark brown hair.

Mrs. Morrow, having been summoned from Englewood during the night, arrived at Hopewell early in the morning and had immediately taken charge of the necessary household duties. The grief stricken young mother, looking frail and tiny as she stood next to her tall husband, was outwardly displaying immense courage as she faced the days which lay ahead. Weary as she was, she refused the urging of her mother to lie down and rest.

Throughout the day, Lindbergh, with the encouragement of his good friend Henry Breckinridge, was assured by the police officials that everything that could possibly be accomplished during the early hours of the investigation was being done. Anne, in addition to the comforting presence of her mother, had the help of Mrs. Breckinridge, who, as the former Aida DeAcosta, was a member of one of the most socially prominent families in America. Mrs. Breckinridge, as well as her husband, was a close friend of both Anne and Charles.

As the hours continued to pass on, a complete description of little Charles was sent by wire to all the police and law enforcement agencies. And as the word of the kidnapping continued to spread, thousands of people jammed the roads leading into Hopewell. Cars were soon lined bumper to bumper on the Wertsville-Hopewell Road as hundreds of late arriving reporters, anxious to "be at the scene", were parking their cars near the gate and on foot were wending their way toward the home.

The influx of reporters had become too great. At one point, Colonel Lindbergh detected groups of reporters peering through the windows and doors watching the movements of those inside. He hurried outdoors, admonished them, and once again ordered them to please leave the property. He did, however, promise that if they would vacate and stay off his estate, he would reward them by personally informing them of any break in the case when it occurred.

Messages of condolence literally poured into the home of the grieving family. Messages came from all parts of the nation expressing love for the Lindberghs and hatred for the kidnappers. Telegrams, letters, and phone calls, plus the personal visits of family friends, numbered into the thousands. The mail alone, brought to the home by Edward Copner, the Hopewell mail carrier, was delivered by truck containing three large sacks addressed to the Lindberghs on the afternoon of March 2nd. This was only the first of his daily trips which would bring an increasing number of sacks with each delivery.

The great and the small, the rich and the poor, all blended their voices in chorus as they expressed their feelings of contempt toward those who had performed the dastardly kidnapping, a vicious crime soon to become not only known as "The Crime of the Century", but "The Crime of the Ages."

President Herbert Hoover immediately sent his personal message, as did Governor A. Harry Moore of New Jersey, who offered a reward of $25,000 for the capture of the kidnappers. New York's Governor Franklin D. Roosevelt sent word that the New York State Police and its entire law enforcement system awaited any command of the Lindbergh family. Dr. John Grier Hibben, President of nearby Princeton University, visited the Hopewell home and offered the assistance of the entire student body as a means of being used to possibly track down the kidnappers. Offers of help came from everywhere. Members of all religious faiths, Catholic, Jewish and Protestant, prayed for the safe return of the child. Messages of hope were largely sent by sincere persons, but as to be expected, there were the usual, and too numerous, caustic crank letters written by the many nitwits, crackpots, kooks and the maliciously insane who used the occasion as a field day to instill more anguish in the already troubled lives of the Lindberghs.

Regardless of the emotional chaos created by the crime, as genuine as it all was, the more important and valued reactions were those voiced by the experts in crime detection; those whose reputations were documented with records of successfully closed cases, and more importantly the worthy opinions of members of the law enforcement agencies already assigned to the case, as well as those of the victims themselves, the

Lindberghs.

From the very beginning of the investigation it became known that Colonel Lindbergh was convinced that the abduction had been committed by an underworld crime syndicate. His opinion never changed. As far as he was concerned, it had been the work of a conspiracy. In addition to this, when he was asked if it were possible for the child to have been taken down the main staircase and out the front door, had without any hesitation, answered: "It might have been possible." And then it was suggested that if there was disloyalty among the servants in his home, would it be reasonable to assume that they, being acquainted with the layout of the rooms, could have taken the baby down the servants staircase and then hand him to someone waiting in the garage, the yard, or at the rear entrance? When the Colonel was first asked this question, he strongly defended the integrity of his servants. His reaction to the possibility of any of them being guilty was too preposterous and impossible for him to consider had been his reaction. However, some time later, when the authorities asked him this same question, his answer was: "It would have been possible."

It should be taken into consideration that the baby had uttered no outcry as he was lifted from his crib; nor had the little dog, Wahgoosh, been heard to bark. These facts strongly indicate that the child, who was not accustomed to strangers, had not cried or made a fuss because he found himself in the arms of someone he knew, and although an outsider was also present, he felt perfectly safe. The terrier, not accepted as a good watchdog, possibly did not bark simply because the person holding the child was known to him as someone who belonged in the home.

The Hopewell police, from the very outset, were certain that three persons had committed the crime. This belief was based on the evidence of footprints which they determined led from Featherbed Lane to the Lindbergh home with each of the persons carrying a section of the ladder. Although this evidence could be counted as nothing more than conjecture, most of the police authorities agreed with them. All were in perfect accord that more than one person was involved.

Mrs. Dwight Morrow, Anne's mother, was outspoken in her belief that the crime was an "inside job". "How," she inquired, "would the kidnappers have known the Lindberghs were staying at their place at Hopewell on Tuesday night when Charlie and Anne had never done so before? It was their practice to spend the weeks with me at Englewood and the weekends here at Hopewell. Someone who knew about their change in plans due to the child's cold must have kidnapped the baby.", was her unshaken opinion.

Frank J. Loesch, President of the Chicago Crime Commission, said it was obviously the work of professionals. "It was a marvelously arranged affair. It showed marked familiarity with the Lindbergh premises and those who did it must have been waiting for a long time and must have benefitted from inside information. I mean casual or unwitting information gained from some member of the household."

The Jersey City police immediately theorized it to be an "inside job" assisted by an "outside gang." Colonel Breckinridge had no difficulty believing they were dealing with an organized gang. Colonel Schwarzkopf, Lamb, and Walsh were certain that there had been inside help. Schwarzkopf agreed that it could have been entirely possible for anyone to have left the house by any door between 8:00 and 10:00 p.m. without Colonel and Mrs. Lindbergh knowing it. The Superintendent of New Jersey's State Police, after being briefed by his chief investigators, decided they were all of one mind. Based on the evidence they had at hand, it definitely pointed them to their one and only conclusion --- the job was done by a gang who had worked with the help of at least one of the Lindbergh employees.

Shortly after the kidnapping, the *Associated Press* ran a story that it had learned "from an authoritative source" that a specific inquiry was being made into an alleged plot by five men to kidnap the Lindbergh baby. Herbert Garwood, a shrubbery salesman from Hopewell, reported that he had seen a man and a woman taking photographs of the Lindbergh home shortly before March 1st.

As the investigation moved on, bringing together the largest assemblage of professional and amateur sleuths, the one purpose confronting all of them was to apprehend the kidnappers and return little Charles A. Lindbergh, Jr. to the safety of his mother's arms.

Many and varied were the clues. Almost everyone agreed it could not have been accomplished without the help of someone inside the Lindbergh home. All agreed it had been a "treacherous" conspiracy. They offered no doubts, they were all in agreement --- more than one person had been involved in the crime.

CHAPTER SIX

Enter Dr. Condon!

The police lost no time in getting posters printed which bore two clear pictures of baby Lindy together with his complete description. Hundreds of thousands of these were printed and distributed throughout the country urging anyone with information as to his whereabouts to get in touch with either Colonel Schwarzkopf or the child's father.

Each of the household help was subjected to intensive questioning. This was also true of the 29 servants in the Morrow home at Englewood. During the interrogation of Betty Gow, she revealed to them the information regarding the phone call she had received from her friend Red Johnson at approximately 8:30 on the evening of the kidnapping. It was at the time of this call, Betty informed them, that her friend had been made aware of the child's presence at Hopewell. In spite of the close proximity of time between his call, made from a drug store many miles away in Englewood, and the hour the police accepted as the time the abduction took place, Red Johnson immediately became their prime suspect.

In response to continued questioning as to Johnson's whereabouts, Betty informed them that he might be located at the home of his brother in West Hartford, Connecticut. Contact was made with the police of that city where they were successful in quickly locating him and placing him under arrest.

Henry "Red" Johnson was a good looking, 26 year old Norwegian sailor with red hair. He had a special fondness for Betty Gow and milk, and because of this he was arrested, remained in custody for 18 days and subjected to intense questioning. However, he finally was released when the only shred of evidence that pointed to his possible guilt was an empty milk bottle they found on the floor of his car. They discovered that he was in America illegally, having jumped ship in 1931. For 18 days he explained to them: "I often buy a quart of milk and drink it while I'm driving." He exhibited a wide grin as he attested his innocence. Frustrated with their inability to pin anything on the sailor, they were successful in having him deported for his illegal entry into the United States.

The Lindbergh home was alive with activity due to the increased number of guests who were continually coming and going. The state troopers were in and out of the house at all hours. Mrs. Morrow had taken immediate charge of the 20 room house; she kept busy making beds, helping in the planning of the meals, as well as aiding in serving meals to the "chief" cops and her family. Each morning she would call her home in Englewood and have her own kitchen staff prepare an abundance of food which was then transported to Hopewell by auto. The troopers who were living and maintaining their command post in the garage had been furnished army cots on which they could lie. Whateley was kept busy serving them coffee and sandwiches. Their makeshift headquarters had many advantages provided by the Lindberghs.

The Lindbergh living room and library provided space for the regularly conducted conferences where the police planned their strategy. It was during these early sessions that more thought was advanced that the crime was the work of organized professionals, with mention made that Detroit's notorious Purple gang could have been responsible.

Although they were certain the infamous "Scarface" Al Capone was securely locked in the Cook County jail in Chicago, awaiting his transfer to Atlanta's federal penitentiary where he would begin serving an 11 year term for income tax evasion, many of the police agreed that he might have been the one to mastermind the diabolical crime.

From his prison cell Capone made it known that he had a compassionate heart in spite of all the gang killings which had been attributed to his mob of hoods. "It's the most outrageous thing I ever heard of. I know how Mrs.Capone and I would feel if our son were kidnapped, and I sympathize with the Lindberghs. If I were out of jail I could be of real assistance. I have friends all over the country who could aid in running this thing down." He informed Arthur Brisbane, the famous *Hearst* newspaper columnist, that he could return little Charles, Jr. to his parents in return for his freedom from prison. Brisbane wrote of Capone's offer in his syndicated column. Lindbergh was made aware of the proposal, considered it, and then dropped the idea after the police discouraged his acceptance of the gangster's proposed transaction. In spite of this, however, Lindbergh still considered dealing in some way with the underworld, but through a different source.

On Thursday, March 3rd, the baby's diet appeared on the front pages of the country's major newspapers. It read: Mrs. Anne Morrow Lindbergh asks that the

> baby's diet be adhered to, as follows:
> A half cup of orange juice on waking.
> One quart of milk during the day.
> Three tablespoons of cooked vegetables once day - preferably peas, carrots, spinach or potatoes.
> The yolk of one egg daily.
> One baked potato or rice once a day.
> Two tablespoons of stewed fruit daily.
> Half cup of prune juice after the afternoon nap.
> Fourteen drops of viosterol, a vitamin preparation, during the day.

Alarmed that there had been no further contact by the kidnappers, and nearly frantic because of the silence, the Lindberghs decided to issue a statement in the form of an appeal to those who were holding their son. Their unemotional plea was made at noon on Friday, March 4th. It was read over the radio from a plain typewritten sheet and was published in the newspapers. It stated:

> Mrs. Lindbergh and I desire to make a personal contact with the kidnappers of our child.
>
> Our only interest is in his immediate and safe return and we feel certain that the kidnappers will realize that this interest is strong enough to justify them in having complete confidence and trust in any promises that we make in connection with his return.
>
> We urge those who have the child to select any representative that they desire to meet a representative of ours who will be suitable to them at any time and at any place that they may designate.
>
> If this is accepted, we promise that we will keep whatever arrangements that may be made by their representative and ours strictly confidential and we further pledge ourselves that we will not try to injure in any way those connected with the return of the child.
>
> CHARLES A.LINDBERGH
> ANNE LINDBERGH

The Lindberghs greatest desire was manifested by their every effort to bring about the return of their child. This included their pledge that they would do absolutely nothing that would bring harm of any kind to the abductors. Because of this, New Jersey's Attorney General, William A. Stevens, decided it was about time to draw the line. Although he clearly understood the sincere concern of the parents, Stevens promptly issued a statement in which he explained that in spite of any desire the Lindberghs entertained about not wishing to prosecute the kidnappers, they had no authority in the matter, and that the state would most certainly bring the criminals to the bar of justice just as soon as they were apprehended.

Before many more days passed, it became apparent that the crime had already claimed the attention of three distinct investigating bodies. At the top were Colonel Lindbergh and his chief advisor, Colonel Breckinridge; second in command were Colonel Schwarzkopf and his staff of chief assistants; and thirdly, those with wild speculations and distorted stories - the news media which included a few of the reporters who had been among the first to arrive on the scene. They had come representing the *Hearst International News Service, The Associated Press, The United Press, The New York Daily News, and The New York American.* These reporters had been assigned solely to cover this one story until its completion --- the end of which seemed to be, at that moment, only a guess.

Breckinridge and Lindbergh, continuing to hold fast their belief that the underworld was responsible, decided to seek someone who would act as go-between.

Meanwhile, a post card had been intercepted in the Newark, New Jersey post office by Maurice Grady, a postal clerk as he was sorting the mail. The card was addressed to: CHAS. LINBERG HOPEWELL N.J. RUSH and printed on the message side of the card appeared:

BABY TAKEN GOOD CARE OF
LOOK FOR INSTRUCTIONS SATURDAY
IF POLICE GET TO CLOSE LOOK OUT

The card had been mailed from Auburn, New York and was postmarked with the date March 3, - 4:30 p.m.

The police, however, determined that the card was obviously a hoax since it failed to designate the signature the nursery note had said would appear on all future contacts. The police concluded that it had no doubt been sent by someone of the same mentality as those parents in whose automobile the police had mistakenly believed they had found the missing baby, and who later exhibited their child in typical side-show fashion by placing a sign in front of their home which read: SEE THE BABY THAT LOOKS LIKE THE LINDBERGH BABY - 15c.

Saturday, March 5th brought the anguished parents their first authentic communication from the abductors. The envelope bore a Brooklyn postmark with the date March 4, - 9 p.m. The message was written on both sides of a single sheet of paper.
It read:

> Dear Sir: We have warned you note to make anyding Public also notify the Police now you have to take the consequences. ths means we will holt the baby untill everyding is quiet. We can note make any appointment just now. We know very well what it means to us. It is rely necessary to get yours baby back as sun as possible. To settle those affair in a quick way will better for both seits. Dont by afraid about the baby two ladys keeping care of its day and night. She also will fed him according to the diet. (SYMBOL)
> Singtuere on
> all letters

And turning to the other side it continued:

> We are interested to send him back in gut health. ouer ransom was made aus for 500000 $ but now we have to take another person to it and probable have to keep the baby for a longer time as we expected So the amount will be 70,000 $ 20.000 in 50 $ bills 25.000 $ in 20 $ bills 15000 $ in 10 $ bills and 10.000 in 5 $ bills. dont mark any bills. or tacke them from one serial nonmer. We will inform you latter were to deliver hte mony. but we willn note to so until the Police is out of ths case and the Pappers are quiet.
> (THREE HOLES) The Kidnaping was preparet for yeahs. so we are preparet for everyding

The letter bore the identical two interlocking circles as the nursery note with the three holes piercing them. The envelope had been addressed in this fashion:

Mr. CoL Lindbergh
Hopewell N.J.

Lindbergh, heeding to the urging of Colonel Breckinridge and the advice of other friends, decided to appeal to someone who had connections with the underworld; a person who might already know who the kidnappers were. Breckinridge suggested the name of Morris "Mickey" Rosner who was summoned to come to Hopewell for a conference. Rosner, who was quickly approved, informed his interviewers that he would need the help of two men to serve as his assistants. His request for Salvatore "Salvy" Spitale and Irving Bitz, both of New York City, was granted. With tongue-in-cheek apprehension, the police, who recognized the trio as typical underworld characters, with great reluctance agreed to accept the men as intermediators.

There seemed to be no better way of informing the kidnappers of the selection of their go-between than to use the newspapers, with the following announcement making its appearance on the front pages of the major papers on Sunday, March 6th. It read:

> If the kidnappers of our child are unwilling to deal direct we fully authorize "Salvy" Spitale and Irving Bitz to act as our go between. We will also follow any other method suggested by the kidnappers that we can be sure will bring the return of our child.
>
> CHARLES A. LINDBERGH
> ANNE LINDBERGH

Just as soon as the message was set in type, the presses rolled, and the announcement was read, criticism mounted to a near crescendo as well-intentioned citizens from all sections of the country raised their voices in protest. Why, they asked, had the Lindberghs resorted to help from the underworld to find their son? Religious leaders voiced their disapproval since all three of the appointed contacts had police records of some sort. But Lindbergh, troubled and anxious for help, was willing to obtain the assistance of any person regardless of their status in life. After first asking for and receiving $2,500 expense money, Rosner prevailed upon Colonel Lindbergh to allow him to take the original ransom note and have copies made in order to share it with his "buddies" at their speakeasy headquarters on Forty-first Street. The request was granted, with only God knowing how many people had access to the note; thus opening a possibility of extortion threats being made by persons other than the kidnappers.

Colonel Schwarzkopf who had graduated from West Point in 1917, and served as a former floorwalker in Bamberger's department store in Newark, had absolutely no knowledge of police investigative work prior to his appointment in 1921 to serve as New Jersey's State Police Commissioner at the age of 26. He did, however, have the good sense to protest allowing copies of the note to be made. Nevertheless, the 37 year old man, who had served three months of active service as an artillery officer during World War I, once again acquiesced to Lindbergh's demands, but continued to fume over the direction the case was taking.

It must be said of Schwarzkopf, who had just started his third five year term as Commissioner, that soon after the investigation into the Lindbergh case began, the head of the State Police suffered much condemnation, due largely to the inability of his troopers to bring the criminals to justice. For two-and-one-half years, his department reported nothing but "little progress", and because of this they were subjected to "bashing" by the public. In his fine book *"KIDNAP"*, George Waller bears this out very clearly. He wrote:

"Schwarzkopf's critics suggested that the State police, though admirably suited to preserve everyday law and order, were incapable of coping with such a major case; that they were insufficiently trained in modern detection techniques; that more money had gone into uniforms than laboratory equipment; and that the temperament of the corps, thanks to Schwarzkopf's zealous tutelage, was hostile to the spirit of cooperation that must obtain if the kidnappers and murderers were to be brought to justice.

"The critics enlarged upon the charge of noncooperation. They recalled that within four days after the kidnapping representatives of the federal government had gone to the Lindbergh home and offered every assistance it was in their power to give. Since kidnapping was not a national offense, federal investigators were not completely free to act; but no law stood in the way of their providing advice and technical help. Apparently neither had been wanted.

Their suggestions had been received politely; no use had been made of their scientific equipment. Although federal agents had stayed close to the scene of the crime, they had been little more than unofficial observers, barely informed by the State police of developments in the case.

"Detective Sergeant James J. Finn of the New York City police had met similar indifference. True Lindbergh had telephoned Police Commissioner Edward P. Mulrooney in the early morning hours after the kidnapping and asked to borrow Finn for the case (in the tumultuous reception New York had given the Lone Eagle after his return from Paris, Finn had been one of his guards and Lindbergh had admired his efficiency) and, welcoming him to Hopewell, had told Finn to do everything he could, go as far as he liked. But neither these instructions nor the New York City postmarks on the ransom-note envelopes, indicating that the kidnapping was at least partly a New York police affair, had made the New Jersey detectives more communicative, and Finn had left with the observation that he could learn as much about the case by reading the newspapers."

So much, at this time, regarding the "lack of cooperation" given by the New Jersey State Police under the "very able" direction of Colonel Norman Schwarzkopf.

The kidnappers next contact with the Lindberghs was made by dispatching a note to Colonel Breckinridge at his office at 25 Broadway, New York City. It was mailed in a long 9 1/2 inch envelope, and was postmarked from New York, N.Y. Station D, at 1 p.m. March 7. Addressed to Mr. Co. Henry L. Breckenridge 25 Broadway N.Y., the note to the Colonel gave these terse instructions:

> Dear Sir.
> Please handel inclosed letter
> to Col. Lindbergh. It is in
> Mr. Lindberg interest not to
> notify the police.

Breckinridge immediately called one of his staff members, James Phelan, and told him to lose no time getting to Hopewell with this latest communication from those he believed were holding the baby.

Opening the envelope, Lindbergh's hopes sprung high as he at once recognized it as coming from the kidnappers when he saw the same identifying interlocking circles in red and blue, and identified further by the three holes. It, like the other, had been written on both sides of a single sheet, the same consistency as the others - a cheap type, such as that sold in 5c and 10c stores as a bond paper.

The Colonel read the contents with renewed interest: Dear Sir: Dit you receive ouer letter

> from March 4. We sent the mail in one off the letter pox near Burro Hall -- Brooklyn. We know Police interfere with your privatmail; how can we come to any arrangements this way. In the future we will send ouer letters to Mr. Breckenbridge at 25 Broadway. We believe Polise cupturet our letter and tit note forwardet to you. We will note accept any go-between from you seid. We will arrangh thiss latter. Thers is no worry about the Boy. he is very well and will be feed according to the diet. Best dank for Information about it. We are interested to send your Boy back in gud Health.
>
> singnature (SYMBOL)

The note continued on the other side:

> It is nessisery to make a word's affair out off it, or tao gett your Boy back as son as possible: Wy tit you ingnore ouesr letter which we left in the room; the baby would be back long ago. You would note get any raesult from Police, becauce this Kidnapping whas planet for a year allredy. but we was afraid the boy would not bee strong enough. and ransom was madeout for 50.000$ but now we have to but another lady to it and propperly have to hold the baby longer as we exspectet to it will be 70.000 $20000 in 50 $ bills 25000 in 25 $ bills 15000 in 10 $ bills 10000 in 5 $ bill. we warn you agin not to mark any bills or take them from one serial No. We will inform you latter how to deliver
>
> (THREE HOLES) the mony, but not befor the Police is out of this cace and the pappers are quiet. Please gett a short notice aboud this letter in the New-York American.

After examining and comparing both of the mailed letters, the authorities had no difficulty concurring that the writer of both had been one and the same. This conclusion was reached when they discovered that when they placed one on top of the other, the holes were in exactly the same position on both sheets and light could be clearly seen through them. It was further determined that a sharp punching instrument had been used to make these holes. The space measured from the left side and bottom of both letters were of equal distance. The police reasoned that the holes had been punched first, before the message was written, since the writer always was able to avoid writing over the holes. They also arrived at the conclusion that the same person had written both due to certain characteristics that were quite evident in both letters.

The publicity of the kidnapping had reached out to everyone. But its pathos tugged in a special way at the emotions of a 72 year old man living in the Bronx. Deeply troubled over the sorrowing mother who mourned the loss of her little son, he decided there was something he could do about it.

Sitting at his desk, he penned a letter "written in the Spencerian flourishes of my schoolhood days and with my favorite purple ink of my own manufacture", as he later described it, offering his help. Leaving his home in the dark of night, he took it to the nearest neighborhood mailbox. The time was three o'clock in the morning of Monday, March 7th. The letter had been addressed to *The Home News*, his favorite paper, published in the Bronx. The man was Dr. John Francis Condon, a boyhood chum of James O'Flaherty, owner and publisher of the paper, and also a close friend of both its editor, Harry Goodwin, and his assistant, Gregory F. Coleman.

The good doctor knew all the right people, and because of this he had no trouble having his contributions of poetry and patriotic articles printed. Although they were never refused, seldom if ever were they published over his own name. Instead, he chose to use pseudonyms such as L.O. Nestar (Lone Star), P.A. Triot (Patriot), L.O. Nehand (Lone Hand), J.U. Stice (Justice), among others he might choose in order to keep his identity a secret. However, in the instance of this 3 a.m. letter, it did run over Dr. Condon's correct name. Although it was received too late to appear in that day's edition, it did run on Tuesday, March 8th, exactly one week after the kidnapping. It read:

> "I offer all I can scrape together so a loving mother may again have her child and Col. Lindbergh may know that the American people are grateful for the honor bestowed upon them by his pluck and daring.
>
> "Let the kidnappers know that no testimony of mine, or information coming from me, will be used against them.
>
> "I offer $1,000 which I have saved from my

salary as additional to the suggested ransom of $50,000 which is said to have been demanded of Col. Lindbergh.

"I stand ready at my own expense to go anywhere, alone, to give the kidnapper the extra money and promise never to utter his name to any person.

"If this is not agreeable, then I ask the kidnappers to go to any Catholic priest and return the child unharmed, with the knowledge that any priest must hold inviolate any statement which may be made by the kidnappers."

The Home News, with a paid circulation of slightly more than 105,000 subscribers, was a daily newspaper read chiefly by residents of the Bronx. Following the appearance of Condon's letter on the paper's first page, an avalanche of inquisitive people reached him, most of them by telephone, at his home.

As Dr. Condon left his home and walked along the streets, he was stopped by many persons wanting to know why he was trying to, what they called, interfere in the case. He was a well known man in the neighborhood, and while most of the comments were peppered with mild to severe criticism, there were also among them those who commended and thanked him for his generous offer to help. However, his action displeased and caused apprehension among all the members of his family which included his wife, daughter Myra, and sons John and Lawrence. His closest friends were skeptical and thought him to be foolish. Others who barely knew him were openly critical, believing he was nothing more than a publicity seeking nut.

But, Condon was far from being any of those things. Born June 1, 1860, he lived in a two story home at 2974 Decatur Avenue, near 201st street, in the Bronx. He was a large man, weighing 250 pounds, who carried himself erect to every inch of his full six foot stature. Well respected by his neighbors, he was loved by the children in the area where he had spent his lifetime. A man with unmistakable features, he presented a striking figure with his apple cheeked square face, generous growth of gray white hair, and full mustache. He was the picture of a man enjoying perfect health, brimming with vitality and exuberance. He enjoyed boasting that he never had missed teaching a class in 48 years, and had lost only 19 hours of teaching in 50 years.

Dr. Condon was one of the best known educators in the Bronx and was very proud of his reputation. He had earned his Bachelor of Arts degree at the College of the City of New York, and Master of Arts at Fordham University. His honorary doctorate in Pedagogy was conferred on him by New York University. He had been the principal of the Bronx Public School No. 12 for 28 years, and had met his wife, Myra, while she was teaching at the old Public School 68 in Harlem. His daughter, Myra (Mrs. Ralph Hacker), was also a teacher. Both sons were lawyers.

Dr. Condon, despite his age, could not be referred to as a retired person. He was a man who loved the outdoors and for keeping himself physically fit, as well as helping young people properly develop their own bodies. He was particularly proud of the fact that he had never seen a doctor professionally, simply because he never had experienced a sick day in his life. After keeping himself active each day, his evening hours were also busy ones as he lectured on many nights as Professor in Education at Fordham University and at the Morris Evening High School. He was known to be a religious man who loved his family, his home, and his country. He was often called "the big man in the black derby hat" who always recited poems - a patriot who waved the American flag, and talked and bragged a lot. It was this boastful, prideful, conceited, sentimental gentleman who had decided to make his personal appeal to the kidnappers of the Lindbergh baby by means of placing a letter on the front page of the *Bronx Home News*.

In doing this, there remained only a remote possibility that Condon's letter would be read by the abductors. The readers of the Bronx newspaper were relatively few, and concentrated in a very small area, in comparison with the much greater number who read the major New York City papers each day. However, despite the odds, the seemingly impossible soon became a reality.

Wednesday, March 9th had been an exceptionally busy day for Doctor Condon. He had delivered four lectures at four different locations. Feeling somewhat tired as he entered his home shortly after 10:00 p.m., he went into his dining room and picked up his mail from beneath a bronze Tiffany clock where his wife had placed it. Hurriedly glancing at the envelopes, which numbered about 20, his eyes were directed to one printed boldly:

Mr. Dr. John Condon

2974 Decatur Ave New York and mailed from New

York, N.Y. Station T, March 9 at 12 - M.

Excitedly, his heart beating a bit faster, Dr. Condon nervously tore open the envelope. He withdrew a letter with explicit instructions for him. Hurriedly he read it, fully realizing that while the entire world was waiting impatiently for word from the kidnappers, he alone had actually been contacted by them. The message read:

> Dear Sir: If you are willing to act as go-between in Lindbergh cace pleace follow stricly instruction. Handel incloced letter personaly to Mr. Lindbergh. It will explain everything. Don't tell anyone about it. As soon we find out the Press or Police is notifyd everything are cansell and it will be a further delay.
>
> After you gett the Mony from Mr. Lindbergh put these 3 word's in the *New York American*
>
> mony is redy.
>
> After that we will give you further instruction. Don't be affrait we are not out fore your 1000 $ keep it. Only act strickly. Be at home every night between 6-12 by this time you will hear from us.

No signature appeared on the note to Dr. Condon. It was in a plain white envelope that apparently had been mailed at noon of that day. Inside, in addition to the letter to Condon, was a smaller envelope addressed to:

Mr. Col. Lindbergh
HopeweLL
N J.

Almost beside himself with the excitement of the last few minutes, Condon realized fast action must be taken. He must get to Hopewell with Lindbergh's letter just as soon as possible. Since he did not own or drive a car, Condon rushed from his house and boarded a trolley that took him to his favorite restaurant, one owned by his friend, Max Rosenhain at 2469 Grand Concourse. Here he hoped to find another friend, Alfred J. Reich, an ex-prize fighter, who had completely supported the doctor inserting his letter in *The Home News*. Condon was certain Reich would drive him to the Lindbergh home.

But Al was not to be found at the restaurant. Realizing that time was of the essence, and not being able to restrain himself from telling the news, Condon, bursting with the thrill of being involved in the case, and desperately in need of transportation, confided his secret to Rosenhain. The restaurant owner immediately called his friend, P. Milton Gaglio, a clothing salesman, who agreed to drive Condon to Hopewell in his car. It was decided that all three men would make the trip and they excitedly prepared for the journey. But, before they left, Condon had one more thing he had to do.

Entering a phone booth, he was soon connected with someone at the Lindbergh residence. After speaking, first with two male voices, he was assured by a third person that he was finally conversing with Colonel Lindbergh. Identifying himself as Professor Condon of Fordham University, he read the note that had been sent to him, which he believed was from the baby's kidnappers. He told Lindbergh of the separate enclosure, an envelope addressed to the Colonel, that he had not opened. Without hesitation, Condon was asked to open it and read its contents to him. Removing the letter, Condon read:

> Dear Sir, Mr.Condon may act as go-between.
> You may give him the 70000 $. make one packet. the size will bee about ...
> (Following this was a crude drawing of a box which showed the measurements of seven by six by fourteen inches.)
> We have notifyt your allready in what kind of bills. We warn you not to set any trapp in any way. If you or someone els will notify the
> Police ther will be a further delay affter we have the mony in hand we will tell you where to find your boy You may have a airplain redy it is about 150 mil. awy. But before
> telling you the adr. a delay of (SYMBOL)
> 8 houers will be between.

As Doctor Condon finished reading, Lindbergh inquired if that were all. As best he could, Condon explained the symbol, or signature, at the bottom. From his description, the Colonel recognized it as the same as those which appeared on the previous communications- the intersecting circles of blue and red with the three holes punched through and across the horizontal diameter.

Sensing the increased interest Lindbergh failed to hide, Condon inquired: "Is this letter I have important?"

"It is very important, Professor Condon." was the

answer, with extreme emphasis on the word very.

Although Lindbergh offered to come see Condon, he was told it would be far better if the doctor came to Hopewell with the important letter. And so, with Gaglio behind the wheel, Maxie and the doctor piled into the car. Traveling most of the way at a speed of close to 50 miles an hour, and after making several wrong turns, they at last found themselves at the entrance of Lindbergh Lane. As they drove toward the mansion, one of the men looked at his watch; the time was nearly 2:30 a.m.

Entering the home by way of the kitchen door, they were greeted by Colonel Breckinridge, who escorted Dr. Condon upstairs to a bedroom where Colonel Lindbergh had agreed to join them. After meeting the anxious father, and closely examining the letter, the two Colonels decided it to be genuine. Definitely another contact had been made. Gaglio and Rosenhain, before returning to their homes in the Bronx, were granted the privilege of shaking hands with the famous flying hero, both promising him they would not reveal to anyone the events that had recently taken place.

It had been decided that Condon should remain in the Lindbergh home for the remainder of the night. After meeting Mrs. Lindbergh and giving her reassurance that he would do everything possible to return her baby, the doctor was given the only bedroom available, the child's nursery. This was caused by the influx of people who had recently moved into the home, most of whom had been complete strangers until nine days earlier. Lindbergh, apologetic for having to ask Condon to sleep on the floor, brought his own army blankets and made a somewhat satisfactory bed of them.

As the lights were extinguished, Dr. Condon was stricken with a feeling of deep emotions. Realizing that he was alone in the darkness of the very nursery from where little Charles Lindbergh had been abducted, he silently crawled from between the blankets and grasped the rungs of the missing baby's crib. There in the quiet of the room, he slipped to his knees and whispered this prayer:

> "Oh Great Jehovah, assist me in the work which I am about to carry on in Thy honor and that of the most glorious Blessed Virgin Mary, Mother of the Son of God, whose anguish, too, was great, as her divine Son suffered crucifixion. Divine Mother assist me in my cause. By Thy grace and that it may redound to Thy credit and that of Thy

immortal Son, I swear that I shall dedicate my best efforts and, if necessary, the remaining days of my life, to helping these unfortunate parents. Let me do this one great thing as the crowning act of my life. Let me successfully accomplish my mission to the credit of Thy Holy Name and that of Thy Divine Son. Amen!"

CHAPTER SEVEN

"Jafsie" Meets John

Dr. Condon awakened at 8:00 that morning, having received less than five hours of sound sleep. Feeling refreshed however, and anxious to get started with the new day's events and his important role in them, he arose, dressed, and then spent some time inspecting the nursery. He reached into the crib and removed the two large safety pins that had been used a week earlier to pin the baby's blankets securely around his shoulders. He put them in a small canvas pouch he carried in his pocket. He then opened a window box beneath the French window and withdrew three of the child's wooden toys, a lion, a camel, and an elephant. He explained his actions later to Colonel Lindbergh, telling him that he had taken the items, on what he called "French leave", with the precise purpose that they could possibly be helpful in the return of his child. Lindbergh readily agreed that he should take them.

Following breakfast, a conference with Lindbergh and Breckinridge was held in an upstairs bedroom. Here, Condon was shown photographs of little Charles in order that he have the child's features indelibly fixed in his mind. He was further assured that the child was perfectly normal in every respect, and that both Colonel Lindbergh and his wife had complete faith in him to act as their intermediary. To assure him of this, the Colonel handed Condon a note dated March 10, 1932 which read:

> We hereby authorize Dr.John F.Condon to act as go-between for us.
>
> Charles A. Lindbergh
> Anne Lindbergh

Colonel Breckinridge had agreed to insert the "Money is ready" notice in the *New York American* that afternoon. However, realizing that the notice should be signed with a pseudonym when it appeared in the classified columns of the paper, Dr.Condon, who had proven to his own satisfaction that he had been quite a genius at selecting anonymous names for his earlier contributions in *The Home News*, suddenly exclaimed: "By putting my initials together, I get one: J.F.C. - Jafsie". Since it was one that had not been used previously, they decided it would be excellent.

Returning to the Bronx in Colonel Breckinridge's car, they arrived in front of the Condon home at two o'clock. It had already been decided that the doctor's home would be used as their headquarters for all of their New York operations, and that Breckinridge would "move in" as a temporary guest of the doctor for as long a time as the kidnapping negotiations deemed necessary.

As the two entered the house, they found two persons waiting for them. Al Reich, after learning from Rosenhain of Condon's trip to Hopewell, was anxiously waiting for him to return and give a first hand report, just as soon as possible, as to what had transpired with Colonel Lindbergh. The other person was Greg Coleman of *The Home News*, who assured Breckinridge and Condon that his knowledge of Condon's involvement as the intermediator in the kidnapping would be kept in strict confidence. After meeting Mrs. Condon and daughter Myra, Breckinridge hurried off to insert the ad in *The New York American*. At the same time, Condon took leave to keep a 4 o'clock appointment at Fordham University where he was scheduled to deliver a lecture.

In the Friday, March 11th issue of *The New York American* an ad appeared reading: MONEY IS READY. JAFSIE. It was the cause of much speculation among its hundreds of thousands of subscribers who had spotted the first of these mysterious classified advertisements - What did it mean? Who was Jafsie?

Upon his arrival home late that afternoon, Condon, while conversing with Colonel Breckinridge and Al Reich, was summoned by his wife to see her alone in the back parlor. She gave him some interesting information. "Someone called you on the telephone this noon. It was a man. He asked me to tell you that he would call again about seven this evening. He said you were to stay in and await his call." She went on to tell him that although he had not given his name, he had explicitly asked for Doctor Condon. Removing his watch from his pocket, Condon noted the time to be exactly six-fifteen.

Breckinridge agreed with Condon that the call had been unquestionably made by the kidnappers. Although the seconds seemed to tick by slowly, they actually did not have long to wait before the jangling of the phone brought Doctor Condon to his feet. Picking up the receiver, he inquired: "Who is it, please?" "Did you gottit my letter with the singnature?", came the caller's question in return. Condon concluded that the guttural voice had a pronounced German accent. Informing him that he had received the letter, the voice went on: "I saw your ad in *The New York American*. Inquiring where the voice was calling from, he was quickly told: "Westchester."

Again in the sharp guttural voice, came another question: "Doktor Condon, do you write sometimes pieces for the papers?" After assuring his caller that he did, on occasion, write articles for the newspapers, he heard the man speak with subdued intensity, as he apparently turned to someone standing nearby and relayed Condon's answer: "He say sometimes he writes pieces for the papers."

Then came a clear order from Condon's unknown caller: "Stay in every night this week. Stay at home from six to twelve. You will receive a note with instructions. Ect (act) accordingly or all will be off." As the doctor assured him that he would stay in and await the message, the old educator suddenly heard another voice coming from somewhere in the background: "Statti citto!" The voice was definitely not that of the caller. He recognized the expression as Italian, one that amounted to the equivalent of an English admonition meaning "Shut up!". Immediately the guttural voice of his caller uttered a hasty: "All right, you will hear from us." And with that the conversation ended.

There was no doubt that Condon had been talking with one of the kidnappers. All three men agreed to this. The telephone call made them certain that at least two, and possibly three, were involved.

Colonel Breckinridge volunteered to inform Lindbergh of the latest developments, and ask him to make arrangements for the preparation of the ransom money in the specified bills that were requested. Condon said he would take care of having the box constructed to the exact size given in the ransom note. Reich then departed after being asked to return by six o'clock the following evening.

On Saturday afternoon Condon located a cabinet-maker who told him he would have the required box ready in about four days. It was to cost him about three dollars.

That evening the living room at 2974 Decatur Avenue was a center of tension as five men sat in wait for additional instructions from the kidnappers. In addition to Condon, Breckinridge and Reich, the curious

Gaglio and Rosenhain were also on hand. As time passed, the men moved to an upstairs bedroom in order to hinder their voices from being heard outside. The hands on the clock revealed the time as nearing 8:30 when the loud ring of the front doorbell was heard, jolting them all to attention. Condon rushed down to answer it. Opening the door, he faced a man holding an envelope. From his cap and general appearance he was unmistakably a taxicab driver.

"Doctor Condon?", the man inquired. "I am Doctor Condon", came the quick reply. Handing Condon the envelope, he stepped inside at the doctor's invitation. Three inquisitive men had been waiting in the front parlor. The envelope was addressed to Mr. John Condon, 2974 Decatur Ave. He opened it and read:

> Mr.Condon
> We trust you, but we will note come in your Haus it is to danger. even you cane note know if Police or secret servise is watching you follow this instrunction. Take a car and drive to the last supway station from Jerome Ave line. 100 feet from the last station on the left seide is a empty frank-further stand with a big open Porch around, you will find a notise in senter of the porch underneath a stone. this notise will tell you were to find uns.
> (SAME IDENTIFYING SYMBOL HERE)
> Act accordingly
> after 3/4 houer be on the place. bring mony with you.

Identifying himself as Joseph Perrone, a cab driver, he informed them that he had been hailed by a man on Gun Hill Road at Knox Place. He told them the man was wearing either a brown overcoat or topcoat and a brown felt hat. He said he was asked if he knew where 2974 Decatur Avenue was, and when he informed him that he did, the man withdrew an envelope from his pocket along with a one dollar bill, and asked him to deliver the envelope to a Dr. Condon at that address.

Before Perrone was permitted to leave the residence, Gaglio noted his license badge number and went outside to check on the corresponding identification card posted within the cab.

Deciding it would not be advisable to waste any time reaching the designated spot referred to in the delivered note, Condon accepted the offer of Al Reich to drive him to the location. Within minutes Al's light Ford coupe was headed in the direction of Jerome Avenue with Doctor Condon on the seat next to him. Turning north on Jerome Avenue they continued to the point where the last subway station on the line was located. About one hundred feet farther they could see the frankfurter stand that was mentioned in the note.

Because the stand was on the opposite side of the street, Reich had to swing his car around before he stopped at the curb in front of the typical summer style refreshment stand with a large open porch. Due to it being a winter month it was abandoned.

Stepping from the car, Condon walked to the center of the porch where he found the large stone mentioned in the letter. Under it he found a small envelope addressed to Dr.Condon. Tearing it open, he read with the help of illumination from a street lamp, a note with the following instructions:

> cross the street and follow the fence from the cemetery.
> direction to 233 street
> I will meet you.

Realizing the meeting place to be approximately another half mile away, Reich told Condon to get back in the car since he had to turn and travel the distance, once again in a northerly direction. Glancing out the car windows they observed the deserted Van Cortlandt Park on their left and the eerie looking tomb stones of Woodlawn Cemetery to their right. As they came within 50 feet of the designated intersection of Jerome Avenue and 233rd Street they stopped along the curb. Just ahead of them was the impressive main entrance to the cemetery. Its nine foot iron gates had been set back from the intersection on a triangular plaza which had been built on an angle in order to have the entrance face both thoroughfares. Nine foot iron fencing ran along both sides enclosing the cemetery.

In spite of strong protests from Reich, who thought it was unwise for Condon to go alone, the doctor walked to the main gate. The heavy metal gates were locked. In each direction, the streets were deserted. There was not a sound. Taking the note from his pocket, he read it again, hoping his action would prove to the person, probably watching him, that he had kept his part of the bargain. As he waited, he was aware of only the cold stillness of the night. For nearly ten minutes he walked about the area and then decided to return to the warmth of Al's car. As the two conversed about the apparent failure of the meeting, Al gently nudged his friend and asked: "Do you suppose that could be ...?"

Walking south from 233rd Street, on the same side on which their car was parked, a man approached. After stepping from the car, Condon started walking in the same direction, but since the person had already passed by, not a word was said.

Once again Condon returned to the cemetery's entrance and continued to wait. The excitement and anticipation of the hour was proving to be more than he could endure. As he stood within ten feet of the gates, he turned slightly away, and as he did so, observed something moving. From behind the bars of one of the gates, he saw a person's arm waving a white handkerchief up and down. Due to the extreme importance of the events which followed, I deem it absolutely necessary that Doctor Condon tell the "truth" of what transpired during his meeting with a member of the kidnapping gang on that cold Saturday evening of March 12th, 1932. Therefore, the following dialogue has been set down here exactly as he related it in his book *Jafsie Tells All!*

"I see you," I said.

I walked over to the gate. In the shadows, three feet behind the gate, stood a man. He wore a dark overcoat and a soft felt hat, its brim pulled down. He held the handkerchief before his face.

He spoke, and I recognized at once the guttural voice that had talked to me over the telephone the night before.

"Did you gottit my note?" he asked.

"Yes, I got it."

I listened intently to every word he spoke. I studied his inflection, his accent, his pronunciation. I wanted all of those things to be indelibly impressed on my mind for that day in the future when I might again be face to face with him.

"Have you gottit the money with you?", he asked.

"No," I replied. "I could not bring the money until I saw the baby or ..."

Somewhere behind the bushes in that gloomy cemetery, there was the pistol-sharp snap of a broken twig. The man inside the gate wheeled abruptly. He plunged the handkerchief into a pocket, glared at me accusingly.

"A cop. He's with you? You sended him?"

"No, I wouldn't do that."

With the agility of an athlete, the man inside the cemetery gate seized the top of the fence,clambered up on it. His face, sallow in the light from the street-lamp, looked like an inverted, doughy triangle, its point lopped off. Even as he was jumping, his right hand plunged into the right pocket of the dark overcoat he was wearing.

With the grace and sureness of a cat, he landed on both feet, directly in front of me. His hand, as he turned to run, did not leave its place in that coat pocket.

"Now it is too dangerous," he said swiftly.

The cemetery guard whose approach threatened to destroy this, my first face-to-face contact with the kidnapper, rushed to the gate.

"Hey," he shouted at me. "What's the matter with that fellow?"

In a voice equally loud--loud enough, I hoped, to reach the ears of the running man--I responded:

"He's all right. He's with me."

I started, on the run, after the fleeing kidnapper. It must have been between nine o'clock and nine-thirty when he had first hailed me from inside the gate. His course took him, now, in a northerly direction, away from the cemetery. North of 233rd Street, both sides of Jerome Avenue form part of Van Cortlandt Park.

Running was no new sport to me. Years before, when I had been attending the College of the City of New York, I had won trophies in the five-mile, mile and half-mile races. Though that had been years before and though this fellow was half my age, I still felt confident that I could run him down.

"Hey," I shouted after him. "Come back here. Don't be so cowardly!"

He ran into a little clump of trees near a shack in Van Cortlandt Park before I got close enough to get a grip on his left arm, just above the elbow.

I bawled him out unmercifully. For that, too, I have been dubbed erratic. But my psychology, I feel, was not at fault in that moment. By giving him a dressing down, I expected to accomplish two things:

First, to surprise him enough so that he would forget his fear of danger and remain with me until I had talked to him.

Second, by that same element of surprise, to take from his mind any ideas he may have had about using on me the gun that he gripped in his right-hand coat pocket.

Maybe he didn't have a gun in that pocket. I didn't see the gun. I couldn't swear that he had one there. But I do know that the moment after the guard frightened him and his right hand was free, it dove into that pocket. And it stayed there every second of the time that he was with me.

I am not a coward. Nor am I a fool. I did want him to stay and I didn't want him to shoot me. So I bawled him out.

"You should be ashamed of yourself," I scolded. "Here you are, my guest. No one will hurt you. And you wanted to leave me, a poor unarmed schoolteacher, there at that cemetery gate and be drilled by a guard."

His left hand had grasped the lapels of his coat, drawn them together up over his chin so that the lower part of his face, inclined forward, was buried between them.

"It was too much risk," he said sullenly. "It would mean thirty years."

He pronounced "risk" as though it were spelled with a "z".

The fingers of my right hand were still clamped firmly in the left sleeve of his thin coat, above the elbow and, as I stood at his side, I forced his arm forward a little. Friends have told me that this would have been small protection had the kidnapper decided to shoot me, but I have been able to demonstrate convincingly in every instance, that it would have been simple enough for me at any time to have thrown him off balance before he could have pulled a gun out with his right hand and pointed it at me.

His words indicated that he was still uneasy and there remained nothing for me to do but quiet, as much as possible, that uneasiness. I led him to a bench near the shack--a park tool storage structure still used, often, as a dressing-room by tennis players. The bench faced 233rd Street.

"Sit down here," I commanded. "I'll have a look about. I'll make sure that we are entirely alone."

I walked around the shack. No one was in sight. I returned to the bench, told him reassuringly:

"We are alone. It is safe to talk."

Again I took his left arm between my fingers, forced it forward gently so that I could instantly throw him off balance.

"You shouldn't have run," I said. "You shouldn't be afraid. I am the one who should be afraid. And I am square with you. My word to a kidnapper is the same as my word to my own mother. You shouldn't have run as you did. Don't ever do that again."

I saw his eyes moving furtively from side to side as he sat there, motionless, beside me.

"The risk was too much. I would get thirty years if I am caught. And I am only go-between. I might even burn."

He must have felt the instinctive pressure of my fingers digging into his arm as he said "burn."

The horrible implication of his statement put an anxious note in my voice as I shot the question at him.

"What was that you said--about burning?"

"Vat if the baby is dead?" he asked dully. "Vould I burn if the baby is dead?"

I felt sick at heart. Was this then to be the end of my mission? So soon this awful ending? Was I to be the one who would carry back to Anne Morrow Lindbergh the tragic news that her infant son--the son I had sworn to return to her hungry arms--was dead?

Wearily, I asked the man at my side:

What is the use of this? What is the meaning? Why should we be here, carrying on negotiations, if the baby is dead?"

"The baby is not dead. The baby is better as it was. We give more for him to eat than we heard in the paper from Mrs. Lindbergh. Tell her not to worry. Tell the Colonel not to worry. The baby is all right."

The very matter-of-fact way in which he told me this, in the monotonous, expressionless voice he was to employ throughout our entire conversation, carried tremendous reassurance. There was no over-emphasis, no over-eagerness, no raising of the voice such as nine men out of ten, seeking to impart the quality of truth to an untruth, would erringly have demonstrated.

His statements, too, carried conviction.

"The baby is better as it was. WE GIVE MORE FOR HIM TO EAT THAN WE HEARD IN THE PAPER FROM MRS. LINDBERGH."

Lies! Cunningly conceived. Diabolical in their heartlessness. Yet serving well their sinister purpose: to establish the impression that the child was in good health and that it enjoyed excellent care.

Sitting there on the bench in Van Cortlandt Park beside this man who designated himself go-between for the kidnappers of the Lindbergh baby, I was not unaware of the possibility that he might, somehow, be an impostor.

"Tell me how I am to know that I am talking to the right person," I demanded.

"You gottit my letter with the sing-nature," he replied. "It is the same like the letter with the sing-nature which was left in the baby's grib."

Though I had never seen the original ransom note found in the Lindbergh home on the night of the kidnapping, I knew of the existence of such a note with its symbol signature of interlocking circles.

Eager, now, to have further proof that I was dealing with the right man, I took from my pocket the little canvas pouch in which were the two blanket pins, each nearly four inches in length, that I had removed from the Lindbergh child's crib on the night I had slept in the nursery at Hopewell. I removed the pins from the pouch, showed them to him.

"Have you ever seen these before?" I asked.

His shifting eyes halted, looked at the heavy safety pins. His chin moved slowly up and down between the lapels of his coat collar as he nodded his head.

"Yes," he replied. "Those pins fastened the blankets to the maddress in the baby's grib. Near the top. Near the pillow."

"That is right," I agreed and returned them to my pocket.

I was jubilant. There could be no doubt, now, that I was dealing with the proper person. But, in addition to that assurance, another thing became immediately obvious. In his eagerness to convince me that I was dealing with the right man, this fellow on the bench had entrapped himself beyond escape.

For, by identifying and giving the exact location of those two blanket pins, this man established positively one glaring fact:

He, in person, had been present in the Lindbergh nursery on the night of the kidnapping!

"Do you know Colonel Lindbergh personally?" he asked

"Yes," I answered, and put a question to him. "What is your name?"

"John."

"My name is John, too," I continued conversationally. He seemed to have shed much of his uneasiness, though his alert eyes continued to dart from side to side at intervals. Otherwise he was motionless enough. "Where are you from, John?" I pursued.

"Up farder than Boston," he replied.

"What do you do, John?"

"I am a sailor."

His guttural voice, the frequency with which his "t's" became "d's" and his "c's" became "g's", coupled with the Teutonic phraseology of his telephone conversation and letters, convinced me that he was a German. Our conversation was running smoothly: Question, reply; question, reply. Then came my next question:

"Bist du Deutch?"

That question--- "Are you German?" --- inserted casually and unexpectedly in the native language of a man, would have elicited instinctively a reply in the same language from nine out of ten, would have thrown them immediately off guard. But not this fellow! Crafty, cunning, cool, his mind as furtively alert as his eyes, he made no reply whatever.

I framed the question in English:

"Are you German?"

"No, I am Scandinavian," he answered promptly.

I was determined, despite his obvious wariness, to get inside his guard. In teaching thousands of pupils in the past fifty years, I have learned something of the art of inviting confidences. From a professor of education this may be treason, but it has been my experience that infinitely more can be done through an appeal to the emotions, rather than through an appeal to the intellect.

"You don't," I told him softly, "look like the kind of man who would be involved in a kidnapping. Is your mother alive, John?"

"Yes."

"What would she say if she knew you were mixed up in a thing like this?"

"She vouldn't like it. She vould cry," he answered.

He coughed once, sharply, into the lapels of his coat as he sat beside me. Through the thick, warm folds of my own great-coat, I could feel the sting of that bitterly cold night. His coat seemed much too thin for the biting weather.

"Your coat is too thin for this time of the year," I told him. "Take my coat. I have another at home."

"No," he said.

"Come with me, then, and I will get you something for your cough."

A shrug was his answer.

His taciturnity clothed his emotions like an impenetrable armor. Or was he possessed of emotions? I wondered. His cautious, shifting eyes, suggested that he felt little beyond fear for his own safety.

"You have nothing to be afraid of," I assured him. "We are alone. I have been square all my life and I am square with you now. You have nothing to fear from me." My next words were a crisp command.

"Take down that coat!"

He hesitated,then:

"Well ...."

"Well,nothing," I snapped. "Take down that coat!"

Reluctantly his right hand left the side coat pocket in which it was hidden. I let go of his left arm and he put down the collar of his coat. Immediately his right hand returned to his pocket and my right hand fastened once more about his left arm above the elbow, pushing the arm forward.

His mouth was small, his eyes deep-set above high cheek-bones. His complexion, sallow in the semi-darkness, was light. I guessed his age to be about thirty-five.

"Give me a chance," I pleaded. "I promised Colonel Lindbergh and Mrs. Lindbergh that I would help them get their baby back. That is what I am here for, nothing else. I am not here to harm or trap you. Where is the baby?"

His taciturnity vanished at once.

"Tell Colonel Lindbergh the baby is on a boad." He talked on and on. The "boad" he said, was six hours away and the child was in the care of two "womens." There were six members in the kidnap gang and one of them, he told me, took away their papers with the signature. I gathered from this that there existed a paper containing the master symbol or key symbol from which was carefully copied the symbol of the interlocking circles whenever they wished to write a note. Or he may have intended to convey the thought that the gang possessed a number of sheets of paper, blank except for the symbol, on which they could write further letters and that these had been stolen. Anyway he assured me:

"We can't send you anymore signals."

I asked him how he could tell the boat on which the baby was being kept. He said that the boat was marked with removable white cloths on its masts so that he could recognize it from the shore and signal to it.

"When the Colonel goes to get the baby," he said, "I will stand on the point two hours away (he meant two hours before, I suppose) and signal the boad it is all right to give the baby."

He was talking, now. Expressionlessly, in a low, guarded conversational tone, between thin lips that scarcely parted. But he was talking. And I wanted, as I studied him, to keep him talking. I plied him with questions about the kidnap gang.

Number One was the boss, he told me, a smart man who worked for the government and was, in private life, a very high official.

Number Two," he said, "knows you well. He says we can drust you."

"Then why doesn't Number Two come to see me?"

"He is afraid. He might be caught from you."

"What are you getting out of this, John?"

The leader, Number One, was to receive $20,000. John and two other "mens" and two nurses each were to receive $10,000, a total of $70,000 in all.

"But," I reminded him, "you made a bargain with Colonel Lindbergh to return his baby for fifty thousand dollars. You should stick to your word."

"Colonel Lindbergh talked to the police," he replied. Besides, he said, the negotiations were lasting longer than had been expected, one of the nurses was dissatisfied, one of the men in the gang was in trouble and, because this member had taken their signature with him, they were in danger while he lived. And, too, they needed a fund for lawyers should anything go wrong.

It may seem amazing to the reader that this man, hunted throughout an entire nation, should have sat with me on a park bench for more than an hour discussing in detail the "gang" that had abducted the Lindbergh baby. It seemed amazing to me, too, until I reasoned it out.

My genuinely sympathetic interest in his cough, his cold, elicited nothing but monosyllables and shrugs from him. But my curiosity about the kidnap gang was rewarded with minute explanations. His psychology was as sound as mine. He knew that I wanted the baby. He wanted the money. Therefore, he had to give me a convincing picture to take back to Colonel Lindbergh if he hoped to obtain the money.

I cannot truthfully say that I was entirely convinced by his story of a gang of four men and two women. Yet I realized that in this fantastic criminal case, his story might be true.

Fear and greed---the second sentence he had spoken to me that night had been: "Have you gottit the money with you?" --- had so far been the only emotions he had shown. If his story of a gang were true and if I could play on that emotion of greed, I might get further.

"It seems to me, John," I said, "that you are doing the most dangerous work in this case."

"I know it," he answered.

"You are getting only ten thousand dollars. I don't think you're getting what you ought to get."

"I know, I'm sorry I got mixed up ..."

I seized hopefully on that expression of regret.

"Look John," I argued. "Leave them. Come with me to my house. I will get you my one thousand dollars. Then I will take you to Jersey and see if I cannot get the money for you from Colonel Lindbergh. That way, you will be on the side of the law. There are lawyers in my family and if it can be done, I will do everything in my power to help you, if you will restore the baby to its mother."

He did not reply.

"On the other hand," I warned him, "if you double-cross me I will follow you to Australia, if necessary!"

My voice was vehement, almost angry.

I will give any man his due. And this man, uneducated though he was, had an instinctive mastery of psychology. For he parried my vehemence with a soft promise that stirred my own heart, ever full of the oath I had taken beside the Lindbergh baby's crib.

"We won't double-cross you," he promised. "You are the only one who will get the baby, who will put it back in its mudder's arms."

No word picture he could have drawn could have gone so deftly, so precisely to the very center of the single purpose to which I had dedicated my life, the avowed purpose which brought me, unafraid, to the cemetery rendezvous this night---the return of the child. Again, I was the pleader.

"Take me to the baby." I begged. "Take me there now. I promise you that I shall act as hostage until every cent of the money is paid."

He did not understand "hostage."

"I shall stay with the baby," I explained, "until the money is in your hands."

"No," he refused. "They vould schmack me oud. They voud drill me."

"Leave them," I repeated. "Don't you see? Sooner or later, you will be caught."

"Oh, no," he replied. "We have planned this case for a year already."

I began to despair of making any progress.

"Come, now, John. You can't expect us to pay the money without seeing the baby and knowing it is alive and the right baby." I tapped my coat pocket. "I have some of the baby's toys here with me. And I know some words the baby can speak. I will be able to tell whether it is the right baby. And I shall remain with the baby until every cent of the money is paid. But you must take me to the baby, let me see him."

He was obdurate.

"No, the leader vould drill the both of us. He vould be mad if he knows I said so much and stayed so long."

"Don't go yet. We have to make arrangements. I want to return that baby personally. But I would gladly give up that privilege if you wished to handle things without me, just so the baby is returned to its parents. You will only get in trouble if you do not get out of this affair. You don't have to return the baby to me. Transfer it to any priest, John. He will keep your name a secret. He will not report you to the police. He will see that it is returned safely to its parents."

My plea fell on deaf ears.

"I go now," said John. "I have stayed too long already. Number One will be mad. I should have gottit the money."

Again, greed! Again, fear! I began to believe that the man was incapable of any emotions.

"All right," I replied. "Get your men together in a decent way and have the work done on a cash-and-delivery basis. You are sure the baby is all right?"

"The baby is better as it was. It is happy and well. Number One told me I should tell you the baby is well. So you put an "ad" in *The Home News*, Sunday, like this, to show Number One that I gave you the message: 'Baby is alive and well.' And you put this in, too: 'Money is ready,' to show my friends I saw you and you will pay the money."

I nodded. My repeated efforts to stir some gentle emotion in this man had met with pitiable failure. And then something occurred to me. This man had been willing enough to give me details concerning his "gang." Perhaps he'd give me one more.

The newspapers, immediately after the kidnapping, had been full of rumors concerning an amiable lad whom they called "Red" Johnson. I prefer to refer to him by his proper name, Henry.

A Norwegian seaman, Henry Johnson had been a hand on the yacht of Thomas W. Lamont. He was a friend of

Betty Gow, nurse-maid of the Lindbergh baby.

Police held and grilled him, when after the kidnapping they had found an empty milk-bottle in a corner of his green Chrysler coupe. The police apparently found it difficult to believe the perfectly normal explanation that any adult could be fond of so mild a liquid as milk. And that had been Johnson's explanation.

My interest in Henry Johnson---another matter over which police later were to proclaim mystification---arose from two things.

Lamont's yacht had put in at City Island, where my real estate office is located and Johnson had become well acquainted with many of the Norwegian residents there. Further, he was a friend of Betty Gow, the charming young woman I had the pleasure of meeting at the Lindbergh home in Hopewell.

Everything I had learned from those on City Island who knew Johnson, had been unreservedly to that young man's credit. But now I was in position to inquire about him from someone who would definitely know whether or not he had any connection with the kidnapping. I put the question to him bluntly:

"John, what about Henry Johnson?"

"Red Johnson?"

"Yes."

For the first time, John's voice raised as he replied with almost fervent emphasis:

"Red Johnson is innozent! Betty Gow she is innozent too!"

These positive, heated statements were utterly out of character. Here was a man who, in nearly an hour and a quarter of talking had not previously exhibited a single trace of any decent emotion.

"Red Johnson is innozent. He must be free. The girl, too," he repeated.

For a moment I cherished the belief that this man was not a cold-blooded, greed-obsessed creature, eager for nothing but the spoils of a vicious crime. For a moment I felt a spark of admiration, of liking, for him. Kidnapper though he was, he had not sunk to such depths that he was willing to remain silent while another man suffered wrongly. How else explain his almost instinctive burst of altruism, his eager championing of the two innocent persons? That had to be the explanation.

But that wasn't the explanation. His next words were:

"Red Johnson had nutting to do wid it. It was worth my life to come here and now it seems you don't trust me. Don't you believe that we are the ones who gottit the baby, that we are the ones who should gottit the money?"

The irony of the situation was bitter as gall. I seek good in all men. And I tried hard---quite hard---to find some spark of goodness, some redeeming quality in even this man.

And I had found none.

"Now, I go," he told me. "I will send by ten o'clock Monday morning a token."

"A token?" I inquired.

"The sleeping suit from the baby," he promised.

The sleeping suit! He moved a bit on the bench and I released my grip on his arm. We stood up and my eyes studied every feature of his smooth-shaven face once more, though by now I knew every line of it as intimately as a well-remembered poem.

In the nursery, through a study of the smudged handprint on the window-frame, I had estimated his height as five feet ten or ten and one-half inches. I realized, now that five feet nine and one-half inches would be a closer estimate. The latter figure was the measurement I later gave to police who found his actual Bertillon measurement to be five feet, nine inches.

Now, standing beside him,I said:

"I will put the 'ad' in *The Home News* tomorrow."

I held out my hand---not entirely a gesture of friendship. I was still thinking of that smudged hand-print in the nursery---the hand-print, valueless for any practical purposes of finger-print comparison but exhibiting plainly definite signs of muscular over-development at the ball of the thumb.

His right hand came from the coat pocket, reached out, clasped mine.

The hard lump of muscle I had expected to find at the base of his thumb was there.

"I must go," he repeated. "Good-night."

He turned, walked, not hastily, north in the direction of the nearby woods. I started back toward the car and Al Reich.

I walked away from my first personal contact with the man who called himself John and did not know whether he was German or Scandinavian, whether the crime in which he had taken part was the work of a gang or of but one or two men. And I failed in my endeavor to persuade him to take me to the baby.

But I was supremely happy!

I had his assurance---and no reason to doubt it---that the child was alive and well and that negotiations would be continued until they had reached the happy termination for which, each night, I had prayed."

It is gratifying that we have Doctor Condon's personal account of his first meeting with one of the kidnappers. The story he related was a peculiar one, filled with many strange and unbelievable statements. As our story unfolds, these will be dealt with in their proper order. However, it is well that you remember, and take into honest consideration, one statement in particular --- "my eyes studied every feature of his smooth-shaven face once more, though by now I knew every line of it as intimately as a well-remembered poem."

Doctor John F. Condon was a peculiar man. A very peculiar man!

CHAPTER EIGHT

Confusion!

Upon his return home, an excited Dr. Condon reported to Colonel Breckinridge the results of his meeting with the intermediary. Feeling certain that they were well on the way to getting the child returned, the two men put together the ad: BABY ALIVE AND WELL. MONEY IS READY. CALL AND SEE US. JAFSIE. for insertion in the next day's edition of *The Home News*. Sunday's paper carried the ad without incident as the men waited patiently, fully expecting to hear something more that day. Not willing to wait another day, they inserted a new ad on Monday which read: MONEY IS READY. NO COPS. NO SECRET SERVICE. NO PRESS. I COME ALONE LIKE LAST TIME. JAFSIE.

Condon had been expecting the arrival of the baby's sleeping suit before 10:00 a.m. John's promise to send it brought nothing in the 10:30 mail delivery but a few letters of no importance. The doctor was fast drawing to the conclusion that the kidnapper's promises were worthless, when he was summoned to the telephone.

"Yes?" the professor inquired. "Doktor Condon?" came the answer in the form of another question. There was no doubt in Condon's mind that his caller was John, the same person he had talked with in Van Cortlandt Park the previous Saturday evening. He spoke in the same expressionless guttural voice.

"Yes, John. What is wrong? I have been waiting ...", came Condon's quick response, urging the man for an explanation. "There has been delay sending the slipping-suit. It will come. You will have it soon." His terse reply allowed Condon no time to frame another question; the caller had broken the connection.

A time of tense waiting was being experienced by the residents of the Condon home as Tuesday passed with no new occurrences. However, in Hopewell it was another story. Here, confusion seemed to be the order of the day as the state police investigators were kept busy chasing down leads, based primarily on false clues.

The Lindberghs were being deluged with offers from

"well meaning" persons who claimed they were in touch with the actual kidnappers. All were volunteering to act as negotiators.

This confusion served only as a hindrance to the investigators, who by this time were well aware that Colonel Lindbergh had taken the matter into his own hands and had apparently hired an intermediary of his own choice, the identity of whom they had no idea. This proved to be quite exasperating to many of the police.

During the morning of March 2nd, shortly after the news of the kidnapping had been broadcast, a friend of Colonel Lindbergh, Colonel M. Robert Guggenheim entered the kidnap drama with his "cast of confusion". Guggenheim had received a telephone call from the notorious Gaston Bullock Means, a former secret service agent, con-artist, swindler and ex-convict, who claimed he knew the head of the Lindbergh kidnap gang, and offered his help. Guggenheim seemed interested in the message and promised his cooperation. Means promised to call him again after he contacted with the gang and started negotiations. But, Guggenheim waited in vain.

In the meantime, Mrs. Evalyn Walsh McLean, fearless and warm-hearted, was unknowingly waiting for Means final hoax. Mrs. McLean, the wealthy estranged wife of Edward Beale McLean, millionaire publisher of *The Washington Post*, empathized with the grief of Anne Lindbergh and decided to lend her aid in helping to return the child to his mother.

Evalyn McLean, certain that gangsters were in back of the kidnapping, lost no time in reaching someone she thought could aid her. After obtaining the location of his residence and unlisted phone number; at 6:30 p.m. on Friday, March 4th, she placed a phone call to his home in Chevy Chase, Maryland. A call she was to regret making for the remainder of her life.

She called Gaston Bullock Means and played right into his hands. He had no reason now to go back to Guggenheim when he had the aid of none other than Evalyn Walsh McLean to take him right into the center of "the Lindbergh thing" as he chose to call it. Now he would be aiding the owner of the famous Hope Diamond, once owned by Marie Antoinette, as well as playing benefactor to the famous Lindberghs.

Means rushed to the McLean home at 2020 Massachusetts Avenue in nearby Washington, D.C. and found himself waiting at the front door at exactly 8:00 p.m. Great anticipation raced through his mind as he thought of what new adventures lay ahead for him.

Gaston Bullock Means was a 53 year old charmer. He was bald and had a dimpled, moon-shaped face. With the use of his glib tongue he captured everyone's confidence with his friendly innocence and open honesty. A large man, weighing 200 pounds, he carried his weight well, as he did his captivating smile.

In spite of Mrs.McLean's knowledge of his background as a former Department of Justice investigator who had gone bad and ended in jail for his deeds, she agreed to follow his instructions implicitly after convincing her that he had already been contacted by the kidnappers, and that negotiations were already underway for the safe return of the Lindbergh youngster. Mrs. McLean was easily convinced. Shortly thereafter, and during the many intervening days following, a group of trusting people were to be led astray by the pompous Mr. Means and his co-horts. A Catholic priest, Reverend Francis J. Hurney, pastor of Washington's Church of the Immaculate Conception was drawn into the case; as was Captain Emory S. Land of the U.S. Navy, a cousin of Colonel Lindbergh's mother, Mrs. Evangeline Lindbergh of Detroit. Both gave Mrs. McLean their whole-hearted support in her endeavor, as did many of her closest friends and trusted servants of many years of faithful employment.

Probably the most convincing statement that Means offered Mrs. McLean was his insistence that she inform the Lindberghs that the gang he was in contact with knew the police had given out an erroneous description of the sleeping suit the baby was wearing. Means said they had told him the suit worn by the child when he was taken was nothing like the one the police described in their bulletins. Taking the gangs word for it, Means claimed it to be a smart piece of business on the part of the police. He explained it was done to thwart impostors from securing a duplicate suit and make an attempt to pull a scam and eventually embezzle the ransom money. He told Mrs. McLean the brand of suit they said little Charles was wearing was one with little flaps on the back; but the suit he actually had on that night did not have a flap on the back.

Anxious to find out if this were true, and at the same time to check on the veracity of the wily Mr. Means, Mrs. McLean telephoned her friend, Captain Land, and asked if he would question Colonel Lindbergh about the truthfulness of Means statement. Captain Land's answer was one that cemented her confidence in Means claim that he was actually in touch with the kidnappers.

Lindbergh gave his cousin, "Jerry" Land, a very emphatic and affirmative reply: "He's absolutely right. We purposely gave out an erroneous description of the suit so that we could eliminate false tips." With that straightforward statement, who could ever blame Evalyn Walsh McLean for her jumping into the case with both feet and her bags of money.

In addition to the enticement of working with the infamous Gaston B. Means, the two Hopewell Colonels, Lindbergh and Breckinridge, suggested that she continue her negotiations with the known culprit, both believing he could be in contact with those holding the baby. And so, the wheels of a bizarre saga were now set in motion as the owner of the famous 44 1/2 carat blue diamond placed her implicit faith in the promise of a man who was to lead her and her friends on a futile chase for the child.

From the very beginning of their venture, Means claimed he had first hand information that the baby was safe in the care of a group. For the purpose of fostering a successful contact with them, Gaston's plan to reach the abductors seemed to thicken with all the elements of a fictional mystery drama brought into play.

To each of his aides, he assigned a code number. Mrs. McLean was to become known as No. 11, Father Hurney was No. 12, and Captain Land was to be known only as No. 14. The McLean butler, Anthony Garfoni, would be called No. 30, Miss Elizabeth Nelson, a nurse and trusted friend of Mrs. McLean, was No. 15. Harry Kohler, her chauffeur of 30 years would be No. 16, while Inga, Evalyn's maid was assigned No. 37. Means decided he did not need a number, but instead would be known only as "Hogan", while the Lindbergh child, he insisted, would be referred to only as "the book". During the weeks which followed Means led his group of numbered players into many sections of the country including trips to Juares, Mexico; El Paso, Texas; Aiken, South Carolina; and Concord, North Carolina.

Means' astounding story of his many contacts with the kidnap gang, headed by a man known either as "The Fox" or Number Nineteen, fascinated Evalyn McLean and her allies as they were led from pillar to post in search of "the book". However, after several "ghostly" experiences at "Far View", (her unoccupied country home at Bradley Hills, Maryland) where its caretaker, Number 22, made a practice of entertaining his own winter visitors, Means failure to obtain the baby, brought nothing but new discouragements with each passing day.

After giving Means one hundred thousand dollars to pass on to the kidnappers, the ever trusting Evalyn McLean soon found herself minus another $4,000 and no baby to show for it all. The gang of kidnappers, headed by the fictitious "Fox", to whom Means claimed he had paid the money, just did not exist. Mrs. McLean had been fleeced by the "honest" Gaston B. Means who made himself quite a bundle for a few weeks work. But Means' "success" was short lived. He had made fervent statements that he had not only been in communication with the kidnappers, but that he had also actually seen the baby on March 22nd in Aiken, South Carolina. Although he vehemently held to these "facts", proven to be pure unadulterated products of a criminal mind, Means was taken into police custody on Thursday, May 5th for the hoax he had perpetrated on Mrs. McLean. The charge, conspiracy to defraud, "larceny after trust".

For the part Means played in the Lindbergh kidnapping he received his just reward. Sentenced to a term of 15 years in the federal prison at Leavenworth, Kansas, he died there in 1938. His accomplice in the fraud, "The Fox", turned out to be a former lay lawyer, one Norman Whittaker, who received a two year sentence behind bars.

Ironically, Mrs. McLean received a visitor at her home in Washington shortly after the conviction of Means and Whittaker. He told her his conscience was bothering him because of his involvement in the Lindbergh kidnapping. He identified himself as merely another person named John, but told her he had been the man with the handkerchief that Lindbergh saw as he was sitting in the car outside St. Raymond's Cemetery when Condon paid the ransom money. He told Mrs. McLean that he had delivered dope to Violet Sharpe and Oliver Whateley and that the Lindbergh butler had put dope in the baby's milk the night of the kidnapping, which accounted for him not awakening as he was taken from the house. Evalyn reported this incident to J. Edgar Hoover of the FBI, but nothing ever came of it.

As to whatever became of the $104,000 that Mrs. McLean so willingly provided by her heartfelt effort to return the baby to his parents, one can only guess. Quite possibly Means stashed it away somewhere, hoping that when he completed his prison term he would retrieve it and live in the luxury of his ill-gained fortune. Nevertheless, to this day it has never been found.

There is however, one thing of which we are certain. Shortly after 11:00 o'clock on the night of

Monday, March 7th, 1932, the very trusting Mrs. McLean placed $104,000 of her money in the hands of Gaston B Means --- and never saw it again.

During the span of time the sordid McLean-Means "misadventure" was recording itself into the historical annals of the Lindbergh kidnapping, another chapter was being woven into the fabric of grim activities. The scene was Norfolk, Virginia.

It started about 10:30 on the evening of Tuesday, March 9th when John Hughes Curtis was about to enter his car outside the Norfolk Country Club where the well-known gentleman had attended a board meeting of the club. From somewhere out of the darkness of the night, he was approached by a man known to him as "Sam".

Sam, a big lumbering person who spoke only broken English, had been an acquaintance of Curtis for several years. He told the startled Curtis that he had come to Norfolk seeking someone who could possibly reach Colonel Lindbergh. He said it was imperative since he, not only knew the kidnappers of the baby, but had been asked to act as intermediary for them.

Curtis, shocked by the news, listened further, and after promising to keep what was told him in strict confidence, was finally convinced that Sam's story must bare some semblance of truth when it was explained that no money was to pass through him, but would instead be deposited in a Norfolk bank, to be paid to the abductors, only after the child was safely returned.

During the course of their conversation, Sam made one rather significant statement. Although at the time it meant nothing of importance to Curtis, it would later bear witness to the fact that the man honestly had definite knowledge of the current inner transactions taking place in the kidnapping investigation. "Don't you get surprised, Captain John, if you hear of some negotiations in the North." Sam stated, "We got one feller in our gang, he says we are too slow. He's trying to get in touch with Colonel Lindbergh through some other guy. But it don't mean nothin'. We got the baby!"

Curtis, now enthralled with Sam's story, but before agreeing to help, insisted that another prominent person be allowed to join him in the task. Sam readily consented. The conversation ended within 30 minutes, leaving an excited Mr. Curtis watching the mysterious Sam drive away in his 1930 five passenger Buick sedan. He made special note of the number on his New Jersey license plates.

John Hughes Curtis of 702 Redgate Avenue, Norfolk, was known as a social leader in and around the community. A distinguished looking man of 43 years, he presented an appearance that commanded attention. He was a large man, weighing 200 pounds. His erect muscular carriage measured a full six feet, 2 inches in height. Combining this with his ruddy complexion and iron gray hair made him a person easily recognizable to most people wherever he traveled.

Curtis was Commodore of the Norfolk Yacht Club and a former president of the Norfolk Country Club. His professional livelihood was that of boat builder, serving as head of one of the largest ship yards in the south. He and his wife, the former Constance Robeteau, had been happily married for 15 years. They were the parents of two children, John, Jr., 12, and Constance, 11. After suffering great financial losses during the early years of the Depression, Curtis was forced into bankruptcy in 1931. In every respect the Norfolk ship builder was known as a man of impeccable character.

Greatly troubled by his unexpected confrontation with Sam, Curtis arose the following morning after a sleepless night with his mind set on calling a man he only knew by reputation, The Very Reverend Harold Dobson-Peacock, Dean of Christ Episcopal Church in Norfolk. He arrived at this decision during the night when he became convinced he needed to seek the advice, confidence, and counseling of a man of God.

After receiving the excitable call from Curtis, Dean Dobson-Peacock insisted that the two meet in his rectory at once. Shortly after the noon hour Curtis stepped out from behind the wheel of his green sedan and hurried to the minister's front door. Upon hearing the details of the events which took place the night before, the two men agreed that Colonel Lindbergh must be contacted at once. "You have no choice. To refuse would be inhuman. It would cause you regret the rest of your life.", the Dean emphasized.

Following two unsuccessful attempts to reach Colonel Lindbergh by telephone, and after being told by Mickey Rosner, who by this time had assumed the role of the Colonel's personal secretary, that they should send him undeveloped pictures of the baby, Curtis and Dean Dobson-Peacock decided it would be advantageous for them to take a trip to Hopewell and personally talk with Lindbergh.

Although the minister had known Mrs. Morrow while serving as rector of the Episcopal cathedral in Mexico

City, it was at the suggestion of Constance Curtis that they should first contact a friend of theirs, Rear Admiral Guy Hamilton Burrage, USN retired, whom they knew to be a personal acquaintance of Colonel Lindbergh. She reasoned that if any one of them was to reach the father, Admiral Burrage would be the most successful.

Locating the admiral in his home at 731 Yarmouth Street, the two men explained in detail exactly what had taken place in their attempts to talk with Colonel Lindbergh. The distinguished looking gray-haired man, who appeared to be much younger than his 67 years, listened intently. It had been on Admiral Burrage's ship, The Memphis, where he had established a close friendship with Lindbergh following his historic flight to Paris in 1927. The Memphis had been designated not only for the return of the pilot to New York, where a mammoth welcome home awaited him, but as the means of transporting his airplane, The Spirit of St. Louis, as well. As the Burrage mentally digested the gravity of the tale his two visitors unfolded to him, he, with no hesitation, decisively told them: "I'd go to the ends of the earth, if necessary, to help Colonel Lindbergh get his baby back!"

Putting his words into action, Burrage put in a call to the Lindbergh home. However, after a conversation which lasted almost a half hour with a mere voice of someone who identified himself as being Colonel Lindbergh, the admiral became frustrated. Burrage was certain it had not been the grief stricken father with whom he had spoken.

Disappointed with their progress, the trio decided to journey to Hopewell, but only after a letter was first sent to the family. On Saturday, March 12th Burrage mailed his letter to Hopewell, addressed to the personal attention of Colonel Lindbergh. Thursday, March 17th arrived and still no answer. At this time Curtis was becoming quite dissatisfied and impatient. Although he was reluctant to do so, he talked of removing himself as an intermediary, a suggestion both Dobson-Peacock and Burrage vehemently disagreed.

Later that day, however, the interest of Curtis was renewed when he was again contacted by Sam, who reported that the "gang was getting restless." Sam related to him that they had hired a special nurse to care for the baby and that she was closely following the diet Mrs. Lindbergh had broadcast over the radio and had published in the newspapers. Sam said they had bought a new outfit for the baby, and (although Curtis thought it might have been a careless slip of the tongue) had mentioned something relative to the effect that, not only was the baby well and in good care, but that he was somewhere on a boat.

The following day more instructions came from Sam. He said the gang was asking Lindbergh to deposit a sum of $25,000 in a bank in the name of all three of the negotiators. The choice of any bank in Norfolk would be satisfactory with Sam's crowd, while Curtis insisted that no money would be paid over to them until the baby was safe in his father's or mother's arms.

By this time the three men held no doubt that they were definitely in contact with the actual kidnappers, but they were becoming more than frustrated with the apparent lack of interest of Lindbergh. However, as with the coming of dawn after the darkness of night, Burrage came with the good news that the Colonel had agreed to meet with them in his Hopewell home on Tuesday, March 22nd. And so, early on that very rainy morning the Norfolk trio, with Curtis at the wheel of his car, started their trip north with Hopewell, New Jersey their destination.

It was late that same afternoon when a weary Curtis, Dobson-Peacock, and Burrage entered the Lindbergh driveway and asked to see Colonel Lindbergh, who would be expecting them. They were ushered into the library where the colonel was waiting. After an exchange of greetings, the flier expressing his pleasure of once again meeting Admiral Burrage, the three men began explaining in detail the reason for their visit.

After listening attentively, Lindbergh expressed mixed interest in their story, explaining that he believed they were possibly being used as victims of deception. He further stated that he hesitated to tell them this since his good friend Guy Burrage was so certain they were not being victimized. However, since the $25,000 asked for by Sam was not to be paid out by a Norfolk bank until the baby had been identified and placed safely in his arms, he willingly gave them his blessings to continue their negotiations with Sam's group.

Although he appeared not to be in whole-hearted accord with what he was told, his interest seemed to be stimulated when it was explained by Curtis what had been related to him: "Sam says the man up here wants $50,000, maybe as much as $100,000. Sam is willing to deliver the baby to me for $25,000." the shipbuilder informed the aviator.

Upon hearing this, the attention of Lindbergh and his associates was renewed. Knowing perfectly well that no word of the Condon negotiations had leaked out to the press, it seemed to be very apparent that the group Curtis was dealing with was aware of the other payment being arranged through the negotiations of Doctor Condon. They had told Curtis to warn Lindbergh not to fall for this ruse.

Based on this additional information, the men from Norfolk were requested to continue with their negotiations in the south. Lindbergh was given further assurance of the veracity of the group when he was told that Dean Dobson-Peacock had been a friend of his father-in-law in Mexico City.

Remaining for a dinner snack, brought to them on a tray served by the butler, Oliver Whateley, they were joined by Mrs. Lindbergh, whose charm and grace were especially noted by the visitors. As they were enjoying the food and pleasantries, Mr. Curtis NOTICED A CERTAIN MYSTERIOUS MANNER ABOUT OLIVER WHATELEY, ONE THAT BOTHERED THE SHIP-BUILDER TO SUCH AN EXTENT THAT HE WAS TO SPEAK OF IT TO OTHERS AT A LATER DATE. Here, we again draw on the words of the person himself as he told of his first contact with the Lindbergh butler. Curtis said: "HIS MANNER WAS A DISTINCT SURPRISE, FOR IT COULD IN NO WAY BE DESCRIBED AS THAT OF A SERVANT. HE CAREFULLY AVOIDED MY GAZE AS HE SET BEFORE US THE BRUNSWICK STEW, BREAD, COFFEE AND PIE."

Curtis went on to say that Anne Lindbergh, having the trained eye of a perfect hostess, realized at once that THE TABLE SERVICE WAS INCOMPLETE. THE TRAINED BUTLER HAD FAILED TO SET THE KNIVES IN THEIR PROPER PLACE. He wondered if the butler had merely forgotten them, that it was just an oversight of the moment, or could it have been caused by the fast-moving events that had been taking place in the Lindbergh home since the fateful night of March 1st.

Whatever the reason, Curtis had more to say about the "unintentional mistake": "I ASKED MYSELF THEN, AS I HAVE DONE MANY TIMES SINCE, WHY DID OUR PRESENCE SO UPSET THIS SERVANT, PRESUMABLY TRAINED IN HOUSEHOLD DUTIES SINCE CHILDHOOD, THAT HE FORGOT SO ORDINARY A PIECE OF TABLE SERVICE AS A KNIFE?" Although unimportant as it appeared to be at the time, it was a most unusual blunder for a well-groomed English butler to make. However, his error was given greater emphasis when Mrs. Lindbergh, apologizing for the mistake, hastily retreated to a cupboard and brought the much needed missing knives to the table herself.

Upon returning to their homes in Norfolk on Thursday afternoon, the 24th, they were well aware that word of their mysterious trip to Hopewell had been leaked to the news media. The very reverend Dean was found to be in a talkative mood, proving to be very satisfactory with the press. But on the other hand, Curtis was displeased that the news had trickled out and was reluctant to talk. Nevertheless, a news story appeared, much of it quoting the loquacious minister who admitted that the three men had gone to Hopewell and talked with the father of the stolen baby. He told the over-zealous reporters, all anxious for their story, that: "I am sure we are in contact with the kidnappers and that soon there will be a happy ending to the case."

The gabby Dean Dobson-Peacock explained: "We believe that the kidnappers are acting in good faith. They want to deliver the baby and are willing to wait for their compensation until after it has been delivered. We have a good idea where the child is --- to say any more now could prejudice the case." Being prodded as to whether they had any real proof that they were in contact with the actual kidnappers, the good dean nearly exploded: "Proof? What more proof is needed than that the kidnappers have agreed to turn the baby over to us and demand no payment until Colonel Lindbergh has taken the child in his arms and said, 'This is my baby.'?"

The story appeared in the Norfolk evening newspapers. Repercussions followed the next day in morning editions of papers throughout the nation. Colonel Schwarzkopf literally "popped his cork" in a statement which quoted him as vigorously denying what the southern gentlemen claimed. It read in part, "The three citizens of Norfolk who visited Colonel Lindbergh gave him information which, on being investigated, was found to have no special significance." And what added more fuel to the fire, Lindbergh gave his complete approval of the Schwarzkopf statement.

Confusion and bewilderment prevailed. Which group had Mrs. Lindbergh's "fat lamb"? Who was holding Colonel Lindbergh's little "Buster"? Or amidst all the jumble, who had actually been accepted as the official go-between? "Jafsie" Condon? The Norfolk Trio? Certainly not Gaston B. Means!

And as the minutes of the hours of confusion ticked away --- a baby's life was being held in the balances.

CHAPTER NINE

A Sleeping Suit
and
A Mysterious Woman!

While the somewhat haphazard negotiations were being attempted in the south, things were continuing at a more rapid pace in the home of Jafsie Condon in the Bronx. During the morning of Wednesday, March 16th, following the delivery of the 10:30 mail, Condon entered his living room with a soft oblong package in his hand. He had just retrieved it from his mailbox. Although it was addressed to him, he decided not to remove the brown wrapping. Instead, he placed a telephone call to Colonel Breckinridge at his New York City office. Learning of the delivery, Breckinridge called Lindbergh at Hopewell, telling him of the apparent arrival of the child's sleeping suit, and making arrangements to meet him later that day at Condon's home. Colonel Breckinridge was in front of 2974 Decatur Avenue 45 minutes later. But their wait for Lindbergh to join them proved to be a long one.

Deciding to open the package, they found the contents to be a baby's sleeping suit and a note they were certain would contain further instructions from the kidnappers. But the hours of waiting for Colonel Lindbergh had taken their toll. The men were, by this time, pacing nervously, anticipating he would join them at any moment. But, midnight had passed and with the coming of 1:00 a.m. there was still no sign of the Colonel.

It was shortly before 1:30 when they heard a car stop in front of the Condon residence. A man jumped from the driver's seat, hurried to the veranda, and entered the front door as Condon held it open. Regardless of his disguise, consisting of a pair of amber colored large lensed glasses and a tourist cap that he had pulled down to almost completely cover his forehead, hiding his facial features so as not to reveal his identity, Condon and Breckinridge were confident the long-awaited Lindbergh had finally arrived.

In spite of the frosty air of the early morning hour, their visitor wore no overcoat. He explained that his tardiness had been caused by his efforts to escape the attention of reporters, whose curiosity would have been aroused when they saw him leave his home, and would in all probability, have followed him.

It was certainly no time or place for a suspicious press. The three men entered the Condon living room. Colonel Lindbergh took the package from the top of the piano and removed the sleeping suit. After carefully examining the gray woolen suit for several minutes, looking at both the front and back, checking its number of buttons and inspecting the fabric, he turned to face Breckinridge and Condon and stated: "This is my son's sleeping-suit. It is the one he wore the night he was taken." But, in spite of his certain identification, he was apparently troubled about its condition. "I wonder why they went to the trouble of having it cleaned?", he inquired. "This sleeping-suit has been cleaned before being sent here. I wonder why?", he repeated

Nevertheless, the Colonel was definitely satisfied that the suit he examined was the one which had been worn by his son. Soon after the kidnapping, a detailed description of the suit had been published in the newspapers. The information had been obtained from a saleslady at the store where the sleeping suit had been purchased, and was publicized as being: "A one-piece sleeping-suit of fine, white balbriggan. Stitched feet. Long sleeves. Close-fitting neck. Six buttons from crotch to neck and three across the back at the hips. Size Number 2."

Surely anyone who would read such a detailed description could obtain a suit of the same style, make, and size, and forward it to the father as a hoax. But Lindbergh had no fear of any deception by an imposter.

Had anyone attempted to defraud, by perpetrating a hoax to embezzle money from them, the family was protected from this happening by an honest mistake, made by the New York City department store saleslady who had inadvertently given out a wrong description of the suit. The correct information should have read: "It was of gray woolen material, twenty-four inches long. A straight line of four buttons allowed it to be buttoned up the back. Two other buttons on the back were a flap-over. It was size two. On the front, on the upper left-hand side, was a small pocket. On the back, inside the neck-band, was a small red label which bore the name of the manufacturer, Doctor Denton's." Because the suit received was not identical to the publicized description, Lindbergh was certain the persons who mailed the suit were the ones holding his son.

Turning his attention to the note in the sealed envelope addressed to him, he read the scrawled writing which contained further instructions:

> Dear Sir: Ouer man faills to collect the mony. There are no more confidential conference after the meeting from March 12. those arrangements to hazardous for us. We will note allow ouer man to confer in a way licke befor. circumstance will note allow us to make a tranfare licke you wish. It is imposibly for us. Wy chould we move the baby and face danger to take another person to the plase is entirerly out of question. It seems you are afraid if we are the rigth party and if the boy is allright. Well you have ouer singnature. it is always the same as the first one specialy them 3 hohls (and here appeared the identifying symbol)

And continuing on the reverse side:

> Now we will send you the sleepingsuit from the baby besides it means 3 $ extra exspenses becauce we have to pay another one. Pleace tell Mrss. Lindbergh note to worry the baby is well. we only have to give him more food as the tied says.
>
> You are willing to pay the 70000 note 50000 $ without seeing the baby first or note. let us know about that in the *New York-american.* We can't to it other ways. becauce we don't licke to give up our safty plase or to move the baby. If you are willing to accept this deal put those in the paper. I accept mony is redy
>
> ouer program is: after 8 houers we have the mony receivd we will notify you where to find the baby. If thers is any trapp, you will be responsible what will follows.
>
> (on the left appeared the 3 holes of the symbol punched from the first side)

As the men enjoyed a light lunch in the dining room, prepared for them by Condon's daughter Myra, they discussed future plans. They had been joined by Myra's husband, Ralph Hacker, and Al Reich, who were also of the opinion that the latest communication must have been sent by the same person who had met with Condon in Van Cortlandt Park on Saturday, March 12th.

The time was well past 4 a.m. as Lindbergh picked up the sleeping suit and note, donned his disguise, and drove away toward Hopewell where Anne was anxiously awaiting the news he was to share with her. Somehow his heart seemed a bit lighter as he dwelled on the spark of renewed hope that soon they would have their baby safely returned to them.

Dr. Condon had already placed another ad in the *Bronx Home News* which appeared on Thursday, March 17th. It read: "I accept. Money is ready. You know they won't let me deliver without getting the package. Let's make it some sort of C.O.D. transaction. Come. You know you can trust me. Jafsie." This, however, did not deter them from following the kidnappers explicit order to place an ad in *The New York American* and another in *The Home News*. The ads were placed by Colonel Breckinridge and ran the next two days, reading identically the same in both newspapers: I ACCEPT. MONEY IS READY. JOHN, YOUR PACKAGE IS DELIVERED AND IS O.K. DIRECT ME. JAFSIE.

While these developments were being formulated, the much needed $50,000 ransom money had been deposited in the Fordham branch of the Corn Exchange Bank. Armed guards from J. P. Morgan and Company had brought the money there following arrangements made between bank manager, Henry E. Schneider, and Doctor Condon. However, Elmer L. Irey, Chief of the Intelligence Unit, of the United States Internal Revenue Service was quite displeased with the manner in which the money had been prepared. It was Irey's contention that the major portion of the ransom bills should have been made up of United States gold certificates and that an exact description of all bills should be noted together with the serial numbers of each.

A meeting was arranged for Tuesday, March 15th in the Hopewell home with, in addition to Lindbergh and Breckinridge, two of Irey's most trusted men, Frank J. Wilson, his special agent whom he had placed in charge, and Arthur P. Madden, an agent from the Chicago bureau. At this meeting it was decided to have the money returned to the Morgan company where a new package containing the requested gold notes would be put together and made ready for payment.

On the following Tuesday, March 22nd, the money was returned, and under the direction of Stuart W. Cragin of J. P. Morgan and Company, with a staff of 20 assistants working eight hours, a new selection of bills was made ready for delivery when needed. The package was comprised of 1250 bills in the denomination of $20 each, totaling $25,000; 1500 bills in the denomination of $10 each, totaling $15,000; and 2000 bills in the denomination of $5 each, totaling $10,000. The package consisted of 4,750 bills worth a grand total of $50,000. A smaller package containing the extra $20,000 the kidnappers had demanded was made up of four hundred $50 gold notes.

The total number of bills packaged was 5,150 with each of their serial numbers all properly noted. The main package of bills, those to be placed at the proper time in the box being made for Doctor Condon, would hold the entire $50,000 comprised of $20 bills of either U.S. Gold Certificates or Federal Reserve Notes; $10 bills in Gold Certificates; and $5 bills in U.S. Notes, allowing them a total of $35,000 in gold certificates, all issued in the year 1928 with none of the serial numbers running in sequence.

Meanwhile, the placement of ads continued with no response to their latest attempts to re-contact the kidnappers. It proved to be discouraging, since advertisements had been running for three consecutive days in two papers. Finally Doctor Condon took it upon himself to draft a new ad to run in the Sunday edition of *The Home News*. It read: INFORM ME HOW I CAN GET IMPORTANT LETTER TO YOU. URGENT. JAFSIE.

On the afternoon of Saturday, March 19th, Condon attended the opening of a bazaar in a store at 194 East 200th Street, the proceeds from which were to go toward the erection of a chapel on Harts Island where prisoners were incarcerated. Through his generosity, Condon had contributed several violins from his collection of more than 50 as an aid to help in the raising of the necessary funds.

The store proved to be a rather busy place that Saturday afternoon. Although the doctor was interested primarily in offering help to anyone who might be a possible buyer of his violins, his attention was soon drawn to a woman who had entered the shop. Because of the importance of the events which followed, once again, in fairness, it becomes our duty to allow Jafsie Condon to tell it now exactly as he did in his book,: *Jafsie Tells All*:

"Late that afternoon, a short-middle-aged woman with the oval face and olive skin of an Italian, came into the bazaar. Plainly dressed in dark clothes, she looked about her a bit timidly, now at .the customers, now at the merchandise exhibited for sale, now at me.

"I sensed her discomfiture, went over to her.

"May I assist you, Madam?",I inquired.

Her eye fell upon the violins.

"I would like to see a violin," she said quickly. "How much are they;?"

"I gathered that she must know very little about violins.

"Different violins cost different prices," I explained. "There are several here." Two customers standing nearby, examining some hand-made towels, moved to one side and I took down a violin.

"The make, the quality and age of wood, all help to determine the value of an instrument," I continued, turning back to my little Italian customer. "The back of a good violin, like this one, is usually made of curly or rock maple, well-seasoned. The sides are of cherry, which gives it easy vibrations with the tone sent in by the bow. The top, well-seasoned spruce, catches the tone and relays the vibrations. I'll show you ...."

"I got the impression that she was neither listening to me nor watching me. I looked at her and found the impression correct. Her swift glance was darting from the doorway of the store to the two customers, who had moved away to another corner. Suddenly her dark eyes fastened upon me.

"She stepped close, began to speak rapidly, in a whisper: "Nothing can be done," she said, tumbling the words out clearly, "until the excitement is over. There is too much publicity. Meet me at the depot at Tuckahoe Wednesday at five in the afternoon. I will have a message for you!"

"As swiftly as she had come, as swiftly as she had spoken her amazing message, she was gone. Her skirts swished as she wheeled rapidly about. She walked to the door, opened it and stepped out into 200th Street, vanishing from my sight as she turned east.

"Like blows from the heavy hammer of Thor, her significant words impinged upon my consciousness. Other customers were staring at me as I stood there, anxiety written on my face. They stared at me even more curiously as I raced across the floor, pulled open the door and peered cautiously out in the direction the woman had taken.

"I saw her cross Webster Avenue, looking neither to right nor to left. Her steps took her in the direction of the uptown stairway of an extension of the Third Avenue elevated that travels north to the Williamsbridge section. I watched her climb the steps, vanish into the station.

"It would have been simple enough to have followed, to have overtaken her. Why didn't I? For the same reason that I did not attempt to follow the kidnapper after our meeting at Woodlawn Cemetery. For the same reason that I did not attempt to trace either of the two telephone calls from him received at my home.

"Throughout, Colonel Lindbergh, Colonel Breckinridge and myself instinctively refused to take any aggressive moves, to set any traps, to do anything, in short, that might give the kidnapper cause for alarm and destroy the precious contact we were maintaining with such difficulty.

"My very position as intermediary made any direct or independent action impracticable. I could best serve Colonel Lindbergh by obeying, without question, as a good soldier obeys orders. That those orders came from both Colonel Lindbergh and the man named John added difficulties to the mission for which I had volunteered.

"I can truthfully say, then, that it did not even occur to me to follow the mysterious woman caller that Saturday afternoon.

"Wondering about her got me nothing. I was convinced, at that moment, that she, too, was connected with the kidnapping. If the kidnapper's story of a "gang" were true, she might well be one of the two "womens" acting as nurse for the abducted child."

Here we have, in Condon's own words, exactly as he wrote it, the account of his meeting with this "mysterious woman" on Saturday, March 19th, 1932. A meeting of quite evident importance, that was to be completely, purposefully, and deliberately "forgotten" with the passing of time.

Later that evening Condon related his strange meeting with the "suddenly appearing, suddenly disappearing" woman; all agreeing that he should not fail to be at the Tuckahoe railroad station at five the following Wednesday. Although he kept the requested meeting, the mysterious woman did not appear.

An uneventful Sunday passed as the group waited impatiently for further developments. However, with the arrival of Monday morning's mail came their anxiously awaited answer. The envelope was addressed to Mr. Dr. John Condon, 2974 Decatur Ave., New York. It bore the post-mark March 19, 1932, 7:30 P.M., Station N. New York. As with their other mailed communications, it also had two one-cent stamps affixed. But there was one exception, the address had not only been printed, but part was written. Carefully opening the envelope, the message read like an ultimatum:

> Dear Sir: You and Mr. Lindbergh know ouer Program. If you don't accept den we will wait untill you agree with ouer Deal, we know you have to come to us any way But why shoul'd Mrs. and Mr. Lindbergh suffrer longer as necessary We will note communicate with you or Mr Lindbergh until you write so in the paper. We will tell you again; this kidnaping cace whas prepared for a yaer already so the Police would have any look to find us or the child You only puch everyding further out didyou send that little package to Mr. Lindbergh? it contains the sleepingsuit from the baby Baby is well. (THE IDENTIFYING SYMBOL APPEARED HERE)

And on the reverse side appeared this one sentence:

> Mr Lindbergh only wasting time with hiss search
>
> (AT THE BOTTOM WHERE IT HAD BEEN PUNCHED THROUGH FROM THE OTHER SIDE WERE THE THREE HOLES)

The conclusion drawn from this letter caused Condon and Breckinridge to assume that the kidnappers had evidently failed to see the latest advertisements that had been placed, asking for further instructions.

But, although the kidnap gang had failed to see the ads, the reading public had noticed them. Many members of the press had their curiosity aroused to the point where they were completely convinced that the appearance of the ads with their mysterious messages certainly had something to do with the Lindbergh kidnapping.

Reporters speculated that the ads in the "SPECIAL NOTICES" columns held the key to the mystery of the missing child; but answers to questions to newspaper editors and publishers pertaining to this, brought nothing but vehement denials. Some newspaper executives actually did not know the significance of the mystery ads. Only to close friends of Dr. Condon's at *The Home News*, who had been taken into his confidence, did the ads make sense; to all others the ads were merely topics of conjecture.

Fearing that a break-down in communications had taken place, Doctor Condon had the following ad placed in *The Home News* on Tuesday, March 22nd. THANKS. THAT LITTLE PACKAGE YOU SENT ME WAS IMMEDIATELY DELIVERED AND

ACCEPTED AS REAL ARTICLE. SEE MY POSITION. OVER FIFTY YEARS IN BUSINESS AND CAN I PAY WITHOUT SEEING GOODS? COMMON SENSE MAKES ME TRUST YOU. PLEASE UNDERSTAND MY POSITION. JAFSIE. The ad continued to run on Wednesday, Thursday, and Friday with no response from the kidnappers. However, it generated more and more speculation from the press, with many reporters already beginning to guess that Doctor Condon could be the mysterious Jafsie mentioned in the ads.

While Condon and Breckinridge were kept busy with plans for possible further negotiations, Lindbergh and his underworld mediators of Rosner, Spitale, and Bitz, were making absolutely no progress whatsoever. Confusion among the investigating authorities continued. More than a few of the police officials deeply resented their exclusion by Lindbergh, who insisted that he, and he alone, should be the one to set up a probable contact with the criminals who had stolen his baby and arrange for him to be safely returned.

The reports coming out of Hopewell, New Jersey were filled with speculation. Some were factual, but for the most part, they were loaded with sensationalism. Reporters were having a field day. News stories of the latest developments covered the front pages of every major newspaper in the world. Readers were hungering for something new, and while they waited for the latest truths, reporters fed them what they had. Rumors, rumors and more rumors! And the people were satisfied.

CHAPTER TEN

Another Cemetery!

It was difficult for Condon and Breckinridge to find any justification for the failure of the kidnappers to answer the ads they had placed. This was especially so because Lindbergh and Schwarzkopf were putting no credence whatsoever in the contacts the men in Norfolk claimed to have made. Things certainly seemed to have come to an impasse.

However, not to be thwarted, they placed another ad in the *Bronx Home News*. It ran on Saturday, March 26th reading: MONEY IS READY. FURNISH SIMPLE CODE FOR US TO USE IN PAPER. JAFSIE.

Another four days of waiting followed. Days filled with anxiety, frustration, and contemplation as each one rationalized that the interference on the part of the Norfolk group had caused this further breakdown in contact.

However, with the arrival of the mail on Wednesday, March 30th, the silence was broken when another letter addressed to Mr. Dr. John Condon, 2974 Decatur Ave. New York, was hurriedly opened. The envelope bore the post mark, MAR 29, 1932

9-A.M. New York, N.Y. STA. M.

A two-cent stamp was affixed on an angle in the upper right-hand corner. The message read: Dear Sir: It is

> note necessary to furnish any code. you and Mr. Lindbergh know ouer Program very well. We will keep the child on ouer save plase until we have the money in hand, but if the deal is note closed until the 8 of April we will ask for 30000 more.- also note 70000-100000. how can Mr Lindbergh follow so many false clues he know's we are the right paety ouesr singnature is still the same as on the ransom note. But if Mr. Lindbergh likes to fool around for another month. - we can help it. once he hase to come to us anyway but if he keep's on waiting we will double ouer amount. there is absolute no fear aboud the child, it is well (HERE APPEARS THE IDENTIFYING SYMBOL)

Things had been set in motion once again. A phone call by Breckinridge brought Colonel Lindbergh back to the Condon home for another midnight meeting. Using his same disguise, he had again escaped the curious news hawks who were watching for any questionable moves anyone might attempt to make.

Within the confines of the Condon living room, the three men discussed the advisability of paying the ransom money without first seeing the child. Although Condon strenuously objected to a move of this kind, he was over-ruled by Lindbergh and Breckinridge who believed that, considering the circumstances, it would be the proper thing to do. It was 3:30 in the morning of Thursday, March 31st when Lindbergh decided it was time to take his leave and begin his lengthy trip back to Hopewell.

Later that day, in *The Home News*, the following ad appeared:

I ACCEPT. MONEY IS READY. JAFSIE.

Condon's mail delivery of Friday, April 1st brought them another envelope. This one, also bearing a two-cent stamp, had been postmarked from Fordham Station, N.Y. 9:30 that same day. It was addressed to:

Mr. D. John Condon
2974 Decatur Ave.
New York, N.Y.

Within two hours both Lindbergh and Breckinridge were at Condon's home where the contents of the latest directive were shared:

> Dear Sir: have the money ready by saturday evening. we will inform you where and how to deliver it. have the money in one bundle we want you to put it in on a sertain place. Ther is no fear that somebody els will tacke it, we watch everything closely. Pleace lett us know if you are agree and ready for action by saturday evening.--if yes--put it in the paper
> Yes everything O.K.
> It is a very simble delivery but we find out very sun if there is any trapp.after 8 houers you gett the adr; from the boy, on the place you finde two ladies. the are innocence. (THE IDENTIFYING SYMBOL ON THE RIGHT)

Turning the paper over, they read on the other side:

> If it is to late to put it in the *New York American* for saturday evening put it in *New York*

Journal.

(AND ON THE LEFT WERE THE THREE HOLES
PUNCHED THROUGH FROM THE MAIN SIDE)

Feeling certain that the time of possibly negotiating the safe return of his child was fast approaching, Colonel Lindbergh quickly notified Colonel Schwarzkopf of the latest development. Learning this, the state police superintendent insisted that, since he had been cognizant of all the transactions between the parties thus far, he should be permitted to place a cordon of plain clothes police officers around the, yet to be decided, rendezvous where the money would be paid. But, once again Lindy won out with his argument that nothing should be done that would in any way hinder the safe return of his child. Finally Schwarzkopf condescended to the father's request that whoever would be the person chosen to meet with the kidnappers, he would not be followed.

Doctor Condon took care of inserting the requested advertisement, not only placing it in *The New York American*, but in *The New York Evening Journal*, and *The Home News* as well. It ran in the Saturday, April 2nd editions and read: YES. EVERYTHING O.K. JAFSIE.

Sensing the immediacy for his every action, Lindbergh notified the officials of J. P. Morgan & Co. that he would be picking up the prepared ransom money from their Fordam branch of the Corn Exchange bank that afternoon. But there was another slight hitch in the arrangements for the pick-up of the money. He was informed that the two packages were at the home of one of the firm's partners, Mr. Francis D. Bartow. They had been safely stashed away there by his butler, Thomas Tring. This change in plans necessitated another count be made. This was completed on Saturday morning, the count proving to be accurate, as Bartow, upon receiving instructions from Colonel Lindbergh, finally placed the packages in the hands of Al Reich who personally delivered it to the Condon home.

With Myra Hacker and Reich watching, Lindbergh, Breckinridge, and Condon placed the two packages of bills into the box that had been especially constructed to hold the currency. The larger package containing the $50,000 fit rather well, but as they attempted to force the additional package of $20,000 inside, they had difficulty closing the lid to completely shut. Lindbergh, in attempting to apply pressure by placing his right knee against the top, caused one side of the box to split. Noticing this, they decided not to lock the box, agreeing that to merely latch the hasp would make it possible for them to open the box with the least amount of difficulty, should the kidnappers wish to examine the contents.

The activity involving the placement of ads and the preparation of the ransom money had kept Lindbergh, Condon, and Breckinridge well occupied with thoughts of the much overdue meeting with the abductors. Everything they had been asked to do had been completed. Their meeting with destiny was drawing near ---now all they had to do was wait.

Meanwhile, at Hopewell, developments had come to a complete standstill. Aside from running down false leads, in addition to continuing their interviews with neighbors living in the area, the police were performing their role as "guardians of the manor". The negotiation attempts of Rosner, Spitale, and Bitz had proven to be fruitless and had virtually ground to a halt.

However, on Friday, April 1st, something of note took place. In spite of the fact that hundreds and hundreds of people had traversed the Lindbergh property, including the lane leading to the entrance of the home, since the early morning hours of March 2nd, a discovery was made on Friday, April 1st that was nothing less than remarkable. A DISCOVERY THAT SHOULD HAVE BEEN MADE MANY DAYS EARLIER! A DISCOVERY THAT SHOULD HAVE BEEN MADE NOT 31 DAYS LATER!

Thirty days had passed, with no noticeable results on the part of the police. During this time they had continued to make their presence known by a continual and repetitious search of the terrain. In addition to the uniformed police officers patrolling the ground, there were the myriad of members of the press, including reporters and cameramen, radio commentators, technicians, motion picture news photographers, and interested civilian spectators who continued to attempt a breakthrough of the police blockades.

During the span of this 31 days, aside from the Colonel, the residents of the Lindbergh home had become virtual prisoners of the property. As a means of escaping the monotony of their confinement, weather permitting, it had become the practice of Betty Gow and Elsie Whateley to take an afternoon stroll together down to the end of Lindbergh Lane, to the gate house, where they would converse for a few minutes with the troopers stationed there. On Friday, April 1st, the two ladies, walking leisurely on their return to the house, noticed a "shiny" object laying on the fifteen foot wide gravel pathway, located only 50 feet from the main entrance to the Lindbergh home. Both women took notice of it simultaneously. As Betty stooped to pick it up, she recognized it immediately as one of the missing thumbguards she had securely tied around the baby's wrists as she tucked him in his crib on the night of the kidnapping.

To believe that this thumbguard was laying in a spot, one we might call "center stage", where so many, many people walked for 30 days, in and around and over it, as it glistened in the sunlight of many of those days, and not be noticed, JUST CANNOT BE ACCEPTED AS EVEN A REMOTE POSSIBILITY!

Its discovery had given the police a new clue --- and with it a puzzle. The thumbguard was reported as being "still bright and shiny". Not anywhere on its surface was any trace of either mud or rust. It was still fastened to the knotted tape Betty had tied to it. With this find the authorities were plagued with an entanglement of new questions.

Why, they asked, had this been found in a completely different location from the direction which they were certain the kidnappers had taken in their retreat to their getaway car waiting for them on Featherbed Lane south of the home. The fresh sets of footprints had established this as factual. But, they reasoned, THE THUMBGUARD HAD BEEN FOUND IN SUCH A PROMINENT SPOT, NEAR THE ENTRANCE TO THE LINDBERGH HOME, AND IT WAS IN ALMOST NEW CONDITION IN SPITE OF THE WEATHER DURING THE PRECEDING 30 DAYS.

To say the police were baffled, would be to put it mildly. Had someone thrown it there recently? Their reasoning told them this question could only have an affirmative answer. This being so, then why? They were certain the thumbguard could not have been there for that length of time. If it had been, surely it would have been seen much before this date. Their most ridiculous theory had been the inconceivable thought that the kidnappers had returned to the scene and dropped it there purposely to further confound them.

Was the finding of the child's thumbguard important evidence? We doubt it. However, the way it was found, where it was found, and the time it was found goes far to intensify the conclusion that SOMEONE INSIDE THE LINDBERGH HOUSEHOLD SHOULD HAVE BEEN HELD RESPONSIBLE FOR DROPPING IT WHERE IT WAS VERY CONVENIENTLY FOUND 31 DAYS LATER BY BETTY GOW AND ELSIE WHATELEY! Additional proof that more than one person was involved.

Back in the Bronx, five men waited for additional words of instruction from the kidnappers. Saturday, April 2nd had turned into a trying one, brought on by the necessity of having to recount the ransom money plus the anxiety they felt as they waited for a message they fully expected that evening. Lindbergh, Breckinridge, Al Reich and Ralph Hacker, Condon's son-in-law, all showed evidence of emotional strain. Myra Hacker moved about the room, waiting for her assignment to go to the door in the event someone should step onto the porch. Mrs. Condon remained upstairs.

At approximately 7:45 the doorbell rang and Myra stepped hurriedly to the door and opened it. Her dad was close at her heels. Standing there was a rather short man of swarthy complexion. Due to his thin stature, he appeared to be rather young. Aside from a cap, identifying him as a taxi driver, he was dressed in normal streetwear. He was definitely not Joseph Perrone, the cab driver who had delivered the earlier note to Condon. Handing Myra an envelope, he immediately returned to his cab and drove away into the night. WHAT AN OVERSIGHT! Here we have an unknown man, delivering an important message pertaining to the return of the kidnapped child of Colonel Charles A. Lindbergh, and NOT ONE OF THE KEY PERSONS INVOLVED IN ORGANIZING PLANS FOR HIS RETURN HAD THE FORESIGHT OR GOOD JUDGEMENT TO INVITE THE CAB DRIVER INTO THE HOUSE IN ORDER TO OBTAIN HIS NAME AND FROM WHOM HE HAD RECEIVED THE ENVELOPE. Undoubtedly this man could have told them something. Joe Perrone had been of some help. Why did they fail to question this man? Some folks called them blundering idiots.

At any rate, they completely lost forever any help the man could have given them. He never identified himself in answer to requests that he make himself known and pass along whatever help he could give them.

The envelope was addressed to Mr. Dr. John Condon
2974 Decatur Ave
New York

and the note bearing the familiar symbol with the three holes, read: Dear Sir: take a car and follow tremont Ave to the east until you reach the number 3225 east tremont Ave. It is a nursery.
Bergen Greenhauses florist there is a table standing outsied right on the door, you find a letter undernead the table covert with a stone, read and follow instruction. (SYMBOL)

Turning it over they read further instructions:

> don"t speak to anyone on the way. If there is a ration alarm for policecar, we warn you, we have the same equipment. have the money in one bundle. We give you 3/4 of a houer to reach the place. (THREE HOLES)

Ten minutes later, with Lindbergh at the wheel of Al's Ford coupe and Condon sitting next to him holding the box with the ransom money on his lap, the two men hastened to their rendezvous with destiny. Reich had suggested they take his car, reasoning that John might grow suspicious if another automobile was used and thus cause unnecessary alarm to the kidnappers.

In addition to taking note that Lindbergh was an excellent driver, Condon also was made aware that the colonel was wearing a shoulder holster, making it quite evident that he was carrying a concealed revolver under his overcoat.

It took but a brief time for them to reach Williamsbridge Road and head south, soon crossing Pelham Parkway and entering Washington Square. As they proceeded south a short distance further, they then headed east on Tremont Avenue toward the designated trusting place. Arriving at the location of the greenhouse, which was across the street, they could not help but realize that at this point Tremont Avenue ran along the north side of St. Raymond's Cemetery. Could it be, they wondered, that the kidnappers had again selected a burial grounds as their meeting place?

Noticing that the greenhouse bearing the name, J. A.Bergen, was on the opposite side of the road, Lindbergh made a U-turn and parked in front of the establishment. The shop was closed. A table stood on the right side of the entrance. With the exception of their car, the area appeared to be deserted. Leaving the car, Condon was very aware that he was across from St. Raymond's Cemetery and its assortment of tombstones.

He walked to the entrance of the greenhouse, noticed that under the table was an envelope held secure by a stone. As he stooped to retrieve it, he noticed that it was addressed to his attention: Dr. John F. Condon, 2974 Decatur Ave.. Removing it from beneath the stone, he crossed the sidewalk to the car as Lindbergh shut off the motor. Taking the envelope from the doctor's hand, the flier opened it and withdrew the note as the two read its contents by means of the dashboard light. It read:

cross the street and walk to the next corner
and follow <u>Whittemore</u> Ave to the soud
take the money with you. come alone and walk
I will meet you (SYMBOL)

Lindbergh expressed a desire to accompany Condon in his meeting with the writer of the note, but Jafsie refused, pointing out that he had been directed to come alone. The colonel then attempted to hand over the box of ransom money, but Condon declined to take it, explaining that he did not believe he would need the box immediately, but would come back for it at the proper time.

At this point, we should study Condon's personal account of his second meeting with the kidnappers, exactly as he recorded it in his book: *Jafsie Tells All*.

"I turned, crossed the street. I walked east until I had reached the point where Whittemore Avenue cuts into Tremont. A man and a little girl of about twelve were standing there. 'Is this Whittemore Avenue?' I asked. 'I don't know,' the man replied. 'We're strangers here.'

They moved on. A corner lamp showed a street sign. It read: Whittemore Ave.

I looked to my right. Stretching to the south, lay the bleak, deserted, dirt-surfaced road that was Whittemore Avenue. On its eastern side was St. Raymond's Cemetery. There is a stone or concrete wall along that edge of the cemetery today. It was not there that night. Only bushes, interspersed with huge marble tombstones, monuments and crosses, behind which a dozen men could easily hide-- a perfect ambush.

I didn't like the looks of things. If I followed the kidnapper's instructions and turned south down Whittemore Avenue, I would walk down that road without knowing what lay behind those gaunt grave markers.

I decided, for the moment, that caution was the better part of valor. I deliberately disregarded the instructions contained in the note and followed Tremont Avenue east. This enabled me to look behind the tombstones and bushes that fronted Whittemore Avenue, the path I had been directed to take. I walked perhaps 100 yards east of Whittemore Avenue, peering intently into the eerie semi-darkness of the cemetery. I saw no one.

I returned to Whittemore Avenue, said in a loud, clear voice: 'There does not seem to be anybody here, Colonel.' Instantly from behind one of the monuments fronting Whittemore Avenue, the guttural voice of the kidnapper called:

'Hey, Doktor!'

'All right,' I replied.

'Over here!' directed the voice. And repeated: 'Over here!'

The corner of the cemetery at which its boundaries of Tremont Avenue and Whittemore Avenue meet, is elevated ground. As I heard the kidnapper issuing his directions, I looked into the cemetery, saw him moving between the tombstones, coming ever nearer to Whittemore Avenue at the same time moving south. As I started down Whittemore Avenue there were times when I saw nothing of him, followed his directions only by the sound of his movements.

My own path took me south on Whittemore, along a down-grade, away from the friendly stores and residences that line Tremont Avenue. It was a singularly desolate rendezvous and each down-grade step plunged me deeper in dreary darkness.

I am not ashamed to admit, frankly, that I felt uneasy as I trod that dirt road, away from the yellow glow of the street-lamp on Tremont Avenue. The only building nearby was a three-story frame structure to my right. It seemed deserted, and the kidnapper was leading me south; and away from it, to a spot, where we would have with us only the dead.

Cautiously, still wary of an ambush, I plodded along in the direct center of the dirt road, where no throttling hand, stretched out from the drear recesses of that cemetery could reach my throat.

I had gone perhaps 100 feet south when I noticed, to my left, a connecting road that entered St. Raymond's Cemetery. A wall formed its northern boundary. My eyes had grown accustomed to the gloom by this time and I heard and saw the man I was following reach the five foot wall. He stood there for a moment facing me, then jumped down. He crossed the road, mounted a low fence and came to a stop, stooping low, behind a hedge, directly opposite where I stood waiting in the center of Whittemore Avenue. 'Hello,' he greeted me. I walked over to the hedge. 'How are you?' I asked. 'What are you doing crouched down there? Stand up if you want to talk to me.'

He stood up. He wore no disguise, nothing over his face. He wore a fedora hat, its brim snapped down in front. His suit seemed to be of dark material. He did not--as he had in the early moments of our first meeting--hide his face between the lapels of his coat.

Perhaps, this time, he relied on the gloom and darkness of the spot where we were talking. No street intersection lamp, no light of any sort was nearby. Yet we stood face to face, not an inch more than three feet apart, and the night itself furnished sufficient light to permit me to see his features and, seeing them, know positively that he was the same "John" I had contacted twenty-one days before.

I could not, for example, distinguish this night the color of, say, his eyes, or his hair. But there was sufficient light to see and recognize his features. And, had his clothing been of light colored material, I would have been able to mark that lightness of color. It was dark, or medium dark.

His own answer to a question I put to him at once will, perhaps, serve best to establish the visibility that evening.

'Did you ever see me before?' I asked. 'Yes,' he answered. Don't you remember? Saturday night in the cemetery at Woodlawn vere we talked?' He paused, put a question to me eagerly: 'Have you gottit the money?' 'No, I didn't bring any money. It is up in the car.'

'Who is up there?'

'Colonel Lindbergh.'

'Is he armed?' I lied promptly. 'No, he is not. Where is the baby?'

'You could not get the baby for about six, eight hours.'

Still determined to exert every effort to see the baby before turning over a cent of ransom money, I pleaded with him, begged him to let me have a sight of the child.

'You must take me to the baby,' I concluded.

The thin thread of his patience snapped. Irritability, sullenness, anger were in his voice when he answered.

'I haf told you before,' he retorted, 'it is imbossible. It cannot be done.' He added a sentence. 'My father wouldn't let me.'

This was news to me, fantastic news.

'Is your father in it, too?' I asked incredulously.

'Yes. Give me the money.'

I shook my head. 'Not until you give me a receipt; a note showing where the baby is.'

My statement, I suppose, was just as fantastic. At least I know of no other kidnapping case where the intermediary demanded a written "receipt" before paying over the money.

'I haven't got it with me,' he replied.

'Then get it,' I said.

'All right,' he agreed. 'You will wait?'

Failing to persuade him to let me see the child, I had still another card that I wished to play.

'Listen,' I said, 'these are times of depression. You know
that. It is difficult, today, for any man to raise seventy thousand dollars. Colonel Lindbergh is not so rich. He has had a hard time raising fifty thousand and that is what you bargained with him for. Why don't you be decent to him? He can't raise the extra money, but I can go up to the auto right now and get the fifty thousand.'

There was a pause. I saw "John" shrug his shoulders.

'Since it is so hard it will be all right, I guess. I suppose if we can't get seventy, we take fifty.'

'That will be paid,' I promised. 'But tell me, where is the note?'

'In ten minutes,' he replied, ignoring my question concerning the whereabouts of the note, 'I come back again with the note and give you the note.'

He vanished amid the tombstones and I turned back toward Tremont Avenue, my hand delving in my pocket for a watch I had brought with me.

It was not an ordinary watch. Within its delicately designed, enamel case, are virtually three watches. Originally made for one of the royal heads of China, this chronometer watch, or repeater, stood me in good stead that night. Had I struck a match to consult it, that action might have aroused the suspicions of John.

I could not know where he was going to obtain--or write--his note, but I could at least determine how long it would take him to go there and return.

I pushed the lever on the side of the watch, listened as I walked. It chimed nine times for the hour. There was a pause. A second chime struck three times, to indicate the first quarter past nine. Another pause. It chimed once--9:16 o'clock.

Another thing was in my mind as I walked back to the parked auto--and Colonel Lindbergh.

This man had represented himself to be go-between for the Lindbergh kidnap gang. When, on my first meeting with him, I had asked to be taken to where the baby was, he had pleaded fear of the gang's leader.

I knew now, that he had lied. Perhaps he had accomplices, perhaps there was a gang. But he was no subservient go-between.

He was the leader.

For, without hesitation, he had agreed to a reduction of twenty thousand dollars in the amount of ransom demanded.

Colonel Lindbergh looked up at me eagerly as I put a foot on the running-board of the auto.

'Well?' he asked.

'I've met him. He wants the money.' Colonel Lindbergh's hand reached down swiftly for the box. 'Just the fifty thousand,' I told him.

I told him of my plea to the kidnapper, of the kidnapper's agreement to accept the smaller amount. He handed the box to me through the car window, kept one package on the seat beside him. 'Thanks, Doctor Condon. Saving me that amount helps a lot. Sure you'll be all right going back there alone?'

'Quite sure,' I answered. 'The kidnapper's alone. I could handle two like him.'

I retraced my steps slowly down dark Whittemore Avenue, passed the roadway where John had jumped from the stone wall, and stood waiting, ten feet from that roadway, at the hedge where we had been talking several minutes before. I waited for several minutes. Then deep in the cemetery, I heard and saw him coming toward me.

Again my fingers found the lever of the watch, pushed it. It chimed nine strokes of the hour, a series of three for the first quarter and a final series of fourteen for the minutes to announce the time of 9:29 o'clock.

The kidnapper had been gone thirteen minutes!

'Have you gottit it?' he asked, as he reached the hedge.

'Yes. Have you got the note?'

He had approached with his hands in the side pockets of his coat. The coat, unbuttoned, swung loosely at his sides. Ever wary, he was poised for instant flight, with nothing to impede his free movements.

I should like, at this time, to give the reader an exact and minute description of how the money transfer actually was made. It has never been published before. Invariably, our contemporary writers have said that I "tossed the money over the wall." As casually as that! It wasn't a wall, and I didn't "toss it" over.

Here is what really happened:

With the box balanced on my left hand, I reached out with my right hand toward John's left to receive the note. At the exact moment that his right hand reached out for the box, my fingers closed upon the note which he took from his coat pocket. I pocketed the note as he placed the box at his own feet, knelt down to inspect it, saying:

'Vait until I see if it is all right.'

'It is all right, as far as I know,' I assured him. 'I am only intermediary. There is fifty thousand dollars in 'fives', 'tens', and 'twenties', as you instructed in your note.'

I leaned over the hedge and watched John as he opened the box, pressed his left hand down on one of the bundles of bills and examined it.

'I guess it is all right,' he said. He put one of the bundles of bills in his left-hand coat pocket, rose holding the box. 'Don't open that note for six hours,' he admonished.

'I will not open it. You can trust me.'

'Thank you, Doktor,' he replied. 'We drust you. Everybody says your work has been perfect.'

We shook hands across the hedge and while I held his hand, I renewed my plea once more to be taken to the place where the baby was held. Again, I met with refusal.

'If you double-cross me...'

'The baby is all ride,' he answered quickly. 'You find him on the boad, Nelly, like the note says. Good-bye, Doktor.'

'Good-bye.'"

With great enthusiasm Condon returned to the car where Colonel Lindbergh was anxiously waiting. Telling him what had transpired, he made special emphasis of his promise to the kidnappers to wait for six hours before they would read the note. He explained he had promised this in order to allow them to make a clean get-away. Pocketing the note that Condon had given him, Lindbergh said he would honor their request, as he put the car in gear and headed back toward 2974 Decatur Avenue.

But Condon's curiosity as to the contents of the message in the note, proved to be too much for him to deal with. He wrestled with his conscience as long as he possibly could, finally giving in to a strong desire not to wait any longer. As they approached Westchester Square, realizing they were almost a mile distant from

St. Raymond's Cemetery, he urged Lindbergh to stop in front of a house he claimed he owned. He needed but little persuasion to convince Lindbergh that the proper time had come to open the envelope, read its contents, and have the satisfaction of knowing where they must travel to get the baby. As the two men sat on the small front porch, with the aid of illumination from the street light, they tore open the plain white envelope and read:

> the boy is on the Boad Nelly
> it is a small Boad 28 feet
> long, two person are on the
> Boad. the are innosent.
> you will find the Boad between
> Horseneck Beach and gay Head
> near Elizabeth Island.

It was written on a plain piece of paper and did not contain any identifying symbol or signature.

Both men agreed that the information in the note appeared to be authentic. Feeling confident that he would have his child back in his arms before many more hours passed, Lindbergh together with Condon could not restrain the jubilation they felt within themselves. As they entered the Condon home, they were greeted by Colonel Breckinridge, Al Reich, Myra and Mrs. Condon. They all rejoiced together over the apparent success of the trip. A private conference between the two colonels, one which lasted but ten minutes, brought forth the announcement by Lindbergh that they would be leaving immediately for Martha's Vineyard, Massachusetts, where they hoped they would quickly locate the Elizabeth Islands. Doctor Condon and Al Reich were invited to join them, and soon with Lindbergh at the wheel of his own car, the group headed toward the center of Manhattan, in New York City.

About midnight they entered the stately home of Colonel Lindbergh's late father-in-law, Senator Dwight W. Morrow, at 2 East 72nd Street, near Central Park. It was presently used as Mrs. Morrow's townhouse. Entering the enormous library, they were met by a group of men whose presence had been arranged beforehand by Colonel Breckinridge. Among them were two of the top men in the United States Internal Revenue Service - Special Agent Frank J. Wilson and his boss, Agent Elmer L. Irey. All were police officials of some degree, each holding an intense desire to see the case brought to a successful conclusion.

After a meeting-of-the-minds, one that lasted

nearly two hours, a phone call from Washington, D.C. assured them that arrangements had been made for the use of a plane by Colonel Lindbergh. The four men, now accompanied by Chief Irey, left the Morrow residence about 2:00 a.m. and headed toward the airport at Bridgeport, Connecticut. They arrived there an hour before daybreak, Sunday, April 3rd. As they awaited the arrival of the huge Sikorsky amphibian, it was decided that Al should drive the Lindbergh car to the Aviation Country Club, near Hempstead, Long Island, where the colonel decided he would land his plane later that day.

Lindbergh took little time making his personal inspection of the big airship. Soon Condon, Breckinridge, and Irey joined him as passengers, all exhibiting high spirits. The experienced flyer, an anxious, hopeful father at the controls, nosed his plane into the sky, high above the Connecticut shoreline and headed toward the northern end of Long Island Sound and Martha's Vineyard, where he would begin his search for the "Boad Nelly" and his little lost boy.

CHAPTER ELEVEN

Searching! Searching!

With the rising of the sun that Sunday, April 3rd, the four searchers were provided a bright clear day. With Lindbergh at the controls of the giant Sikorsky, they swooped low over every boat they spotted in the quiet waters of the bay. For hours they scanned the entire area of water along the Connecticut and Rhode Island shoreline --- but without success. The search was proving to be nerve wracking to all four as they closely scrutinized every boat they saw; swooping dangerously low, enabling them to read the names at close range --- with none bearing the name "Nelly".

From the sky they scoured every body of water; that around Buzzard's Bay and Gay Head, Vineyard Haven, Vineyard Sound, Cuttyhunk Island (where they landed for lunch), Horseneck and Woods Hole, without success. Late in the afternoon they returned to the mainland where they were met by Al at the flying field. The expressions on their faces told him they had failed.

In the mind of each man, they feared they had been betrayed. Driving home in silence, Lindbergh again at the wheel, heeded to the request of Condon and Reich allowing them to return to their homes by means of the subway. Stopping in front of the stairway leading to an elevated station on Third Avenue (somewhere in the Avenues of the Thirties), the two men boarded a train which would take them uptown to their homes in the Bronx.

As they departed company, a very distraught father turned to Condon and declared: "Doctor, we've been double-crossed." Reaching into his pocket, Colonel Lindbergh made an attempt to offer him a monetary gift for his services, a gesture Condon emphatically refused, bringing forth the father's parting words: "I'm sincerely grateful."

A downhearted father would soon be back at Hopewell bearing the discouraging news to his wife, Anne. In an attempt to keep her hopes high,. he insisted that, regardless of the thoroughness of their search, the boat Nelly had "just been overlooked", and another search would be made the following day.

Early Monday morning, in a Lockheed-Vega monoplane which had been flown from the Newark airport to the Teterboro airfield, located in Hasbrouck Heights, New Jersey, Colonel Lindbergh took off alone. Within an hour, he was once again combing the waters of Martha's Vineyard.

By mid-afternoon, after flying back and forth over the same areas he had covered the day before, he landed and inquired if there was anyone who could give him some information as to the whereabouts of a boat named Nelly. Receiving only negative replies, he went back into the sky, searching, searching, ever searching; his hopes diminishing. As time moved on, he became aware of the lengthening of shadows and his visibility growing poorer. Admitting another day of failure, he decided there was nothing more he could do but head back to the Teterboro airport. As he climbed out of the cockpit he noticed the time was nearing 7 p.m. Carrying the small blanket and suitcase he had hoped to use, he wearily walked to his car, ready to start his lonely journey back to Hopewell and his anxious wife. Knowing she was eagerly anticipating the good news of the safe return of her little "fat lamb", the colonel's heart was heavy, extremely heavy---since he was bringing her nothing more than added discouragement.

Revenue agent, Elmer Irey, had raised an interesting question of Doctor Condon, one he deemed to be of vital importance. He wondered if Cemetery John could possibly have left an impression of his feet in the earth at the location in the cemetery where the two men had met the previous Saturday. Condon claimed the possibility of this could exist, promising to look into the matter at his first opportunity on Monday.

However, before doing this, his first obligation to the Lindberghs was to place another ad in the newspapers as a further attempt to contact the kidnappers again and find out what had gone wrong. His last advertisement: YES. EVERYTHING O.K. JAFSIE. continued to run on both Monday and Tuesday and caused much unrest to Condon's already tired mind. However, he was able to place the new ad, to begin that day, in their Special Notice classification and run daily until further notice. It read:

WHAT IS WRONG? HAVE YOU CROSSED ME? PLEASE, BETTER DIRECTIONS. JAFSIE.

Following the completion of his transactions with the newspapers, Condon, in the company of his son-in-law, Ralph Hacker, made a return visit to St. Raymond's Cemetery, now in broad daylight. Condon had enlisted Hacker's help, not only to drive him to the cemetery, but to perform the task of making a plaster cast of any possible visual evidence of the kidnapper's presence there.

Their search for this was rewarded when Condon pointed to the exact spot where he was certain John had jumped from the wall. And sure enough, there it was, a rather deep, clear imprint of a man's foot, an impression at the base of the wall. Hacker proceeded to pour a pasty liquid over it, and within a few minutes, proudly displayed the results of his efforts. He had developed for future use, a clean plaster mold, one they enthusiastically believed to be a perfect moulage of one of the kidnapper's feet. One they could use by comparing it with a foot of any suspect they might arrest in the future.

Why Hacker was selected to develop this evidence instead of the Department of Justice agent who had accompanied them, has never been understood. However, Condon's son-in-law at the very least, did produce a cast, one that was never used. Although the three men continued to look for additional clues, some which might have directed them to the path that John had taken in his departure from the cemetery, their scrutiny proved to be in vain.

Reveling in the fact that they had produced something that should be of importance to the investigators, they returned to the Condon residence. They waited there for news of Colonel Lindbergh's second day of searching for the "boad Nelly" in the Massachusetts's waters, but were more than disturbed when he phoned to report that once again he had experienced failure.

Hoping against hope that the new advertisements would bring further instructions from the abductors, Condon's family and friends continued to spend countless hours waiting together at 2974 Decatur Avenue. Amid a host of police officers and newspeople who had assembled themselves at the Sourland mountain home at Hopewell, the Lindberghs spent hours of continued distress.

However, while there appeared to be a lull in the activities taking place in the Bronx, the tempo of happenings in Norfolk, Virginia were moving at a rapid pace. When the news media became aware of the involvement of John Hughes Curtis in the Lindbergh kidnapping, the shipbuilder and his family had not enjoyed a day of privacy since the story first appeared in the papers there, and used in the metropolitan dailies the next day.

Surprisingly, the gang had agreed to voluntarily reduce the ransom payment requested from the original amount of $50,000 to $25,000. Although Sam himself could not understand why the gang had cut the ransom demand in half, he said they had good reasons for doing it.

The Norfolk trio decided that another trip to Hopewell was in order, but due to the inability of Curtis to make the long tiresome journey, Dean Dobson-Peacock volunteered to go alone and report the latest developments, as they knew them, to Colonel Lindbergh. And so, with Lieutenant Richard at the controls of the plane, this time with the clergyman his lone passenger, they landed once again at the Philadelphia Naval air station and made the rest of the trip by automobile.

It was Captain Emory Land, a cousin of Colonel Lindbergh, who met Dean Peacock at the Hopewell residence. In spite of Peacock's insistence that the colonel was expecting him and that he carried an important message from the kidnappers, Land insisted that Lindbergh was much too busy to see him. Dean Peacock's patience began to grow thin, becoming quite indignant, questioning why the child's father could not spare him a few minutes, since he had made the lengthy trip from Norfolk. One of Schwarzkopf's assistants, overhearing the confrontation, left the room, soon to reappear with Colonel Lindbergh close at his heels.

"Have you been here long, Dean Peacock?" the Colonel inquired.

"Yes, about a half-hour; and I prefer to talk to you in private."

"Very well. I will ask my cousin and the other gentlemen to withdraw."

"I suppose you have seen by the papers that John Curtis has again been in communication with his contact."

"Yes, I know he has. Has he secured the desired information for me?"

"Only as to the amount of ransom. The gang has named $25,000 as the desired amount, and as you already know, it is simply to be deposited in the name of Admiral Burrage, John Hughes Curtis, and myself."

"This I will be glad to do when the identification

of my son is furnished me."

"But suppose, Colonel, that this man Sam is prepared to hand over the child when John Curtis next sees him. So that there will be no delay, will you not agree to receive the child, and pay the money when you have said 'This is my child,' without going through the form of a preliminary identification?"

"I prefer to handle the matter in the way I previously told you, Dean Peacock."

This attitude taken by Lindbergh, father of a child who had been mysteriously snatched from the confines of his home, and whose whereabouts were sought by citizens in every country of the world, never ceased to amaze the dean and his two Virginia cronies. They concluded, and rightly so, that it would have been much safer for the father to have run the risk of looking at a hundred children who proved not to be the missing baby, than to have little Charles held in captivity for one more unnecessary hour.

News of the continued attempts of Curtis, Burrage and Peacock to successfully bring the baby back into his mother's arms brought more coverage from the press. Excitement continued to spread as news articles told of the latest developments in the south. Another contact by Sam took Curtis to the New York City cafeteria for another midnight rendezvous. Here Sam instructed Curtis to follow him through the Holland Tunnel and then on to the Hudson-Manhattan station in Newark where they would meet the rest of the gang waiting for them there.

From the appearance of the man whom Sam referred to as "Boss", Curtis experienced a feeling that he had met the man somewhere before, possibly around his shipyard in Norfolk. The man was of medium height, wore his drab-colored hair straight back without a part, and had the swarthy complexion of a man of the sea. He appeared to be in his early forties. Although he was "Boss" to Sam, his companions called him "Dynamite" or "Din". Curtis, nevertheless, soon found out his proper name was George Olaf Larsen and that he was a Scandinavian.

The number two man was introduced only as "Nils". Judging from his appearance, Curtis guessed him to also be a Scandinavian. He had a florid complexion and blond hair; he appeared to be about thirty-two years of age. The third member of the group was a good looking man named John. He had the physique of a person who had engaged in athletics for the better part of his life. Curtis estimated his age to be in the mid-fifties. His accent gave a hint that he was either Norwegian or Dutch. The fourth man, the one who seemed to be of minor importance, looked to be about forty-five. They called him Eric and his speech caused Curtis to guess that he had come from the same homeland as John.

Curtis was informed that he must take a trip with them to Cape May, New Jersey, and because his car was the largest, they asked him to drive them there. It took but a short time for the shipbuilder to realize that John was the actual leader of the gang; and that he, together with Eric and Nils, had drawn Sam and Larsen into their plan to kidnap the Lindbergh child. The conversation among the six men as they journeyed to Cape May gave Curtis added information, but at the same time completely befuddled his mind as he drank it all in as absolute truth; each fact impressing him as entirely reasonable.

John did most of the talking, addressing much of his discourse to Curtis, who listened in utter amazement at the facts he was told: "Sam he says you want some proof we do this job. Well, suppose I tell you exactly how we do it. One night about one month before the kidnapping, I go to some party with a girl friend of mine, a German trained nurse, at a roadhouse outside Trenton. There I meet a member of the Lindbergh and Morrow household --- which one I don't say. For some time I think I do this job, and put the child with my girl friend, the nurse. I know I need inside help, so I get this person to help me. I promise plenty good money for the trouble..."

Finally arriving at Larsen's Cape May cottage, the group was led into the dining room by Larsen's wife, Hilda. Here Curtis continued to press John to continue with his story of the parts each of the five had played in successfully stealing the baby from his home.

In order for you to more easily follow the events as told by John, the following dialogue appears exactly as John Hughes Curtis related it to his attorney, C. Lloyd Fisher, at a later date: "Ya," John continued. "On this night, March 1, Nils, Eric, the German nurse, and myself, we drive in a green sedan to the lane leading up to Lindberghs'. We park some three hundred feet away. Sam follows us in his car. He parks still further away, on a high spot by the main road, so he can signal me with his lights if some other car comes into the lane.

"Nils and me we walk to the nursery window and put up the ladder which we have with us. It is in three parts so as to fit in the car. When we climb through the window, we have a blanket, a rag, and some chloroform, just enough. We do not leave by the way of the window, because the ladder it is so unsteady. We come down the stairs and out the front door."

John then reached into his inside coat pocket and brought out a homemade chart, drawn on a piece of ordinary paper that measured approximately twenty-four by thirty inches. It exhibited a rather crudely drawn layout of the interior of the Lindbergh's Hopewell home. It had been very accurately done, showing the location of the rooms both on the main floor as well as the upstairs, particularly where the baby's room would be found.

"You see this here," John went on, as he pointed to a small passageway near the front door, "That's a pantry, and it's a hallway between the kitchen and the front hall. We had this locked on the hall side, so if they got wise in the kitchen or servants' quarters they'd have to go all the way round through the dining room and living room to get to the front hall. You'll find that key on the hall side even now."

Armed with this new information, Curtis insisted that they leave for Hopewell at once and that Larsen accompany him in order to meet Colonel Lindbergh personally. It took much persuasion however, to convince Larsen that he should make the trip. Only after promising that no harm would come to him, based on Lindbergh's emphatic promise that immunity would be granted to any person responsible for the baby's safe return, did he reluctantly agree to make the trip.

As they approached the outskirts of Trenton, John Hughes Curtis entertained thoughts nothing short of complete success. The date was Monday, April 4th.

Entering the city, Curtis drove to the telephone office on State Street, from where he put in a call to Lindbergh's Hopewell home. Using the code word "Memphis" that the two men had agreed upon, he had no difficulty reaching the Colonel. Informing Lindbergh that he had one of the kidnappers with him, and being certain that the distraught father would be anxious to talk with him, Curtis was astonished to be told by the Colonel that he was "much too busy on an important errand and cannot meet you". This was more than a rejection; it was a definite refusal --- one that came on the heels of their long trip from Cape May to bring him first hand information about his baby. However, the best the man would agree to do was to offer the suggestion that they contact him again that evening about 8 o'clock.

With much doubt in his mind as to the advisability of doing this, Curtis consented. Looking at his watch he realized they would have a long wait of eleven hours, since the time then was just nine a.m.

It was about seven that evening when Curtis placed another call, this time from the women's waiting room in the Trenton railroad station. Receiving the call at Hopewell, he was told that Colonel Lindbergh was not there and had left no message. By this time Larsen was becoming very edgy, bordering on panic, telling Curtis that they had fooled around much too long and that he feared they were setting a trap for him.

Curtis won his plea that he wait another hour. He again called the Lindbergh residence but was politely told he would have to call back later. Upon hearing this news, Larsen blew his top and insisted that they return to Cape May at once.

The Norfolk boatbuilder, who had not enjoyed the pleasure of sleep since the previous Saturday night, found himself in a depressed mood. He had been, he believed, so close to success, and had failed. Failed not because of his lack of desire, but due to Lindbergh's apparent disinterest in speaking with Larsen personally.

On Wednesday, April 6th the world was informed that a ransom of $50,000 had been paid by Colonel Lindbergh, and that his child had not been returned. It was on this date, upon the order of W. C. Wood, Treasurer of the United States, that circulars containing the serial numbers of each one of the ransom bills be sent to banks throughout the world. Along with the list were instructions to every bank employee to be on the lookout for any of the listed bills. If any were located they were further instructed to wire or call the United States Treasury at once. The circular carried listings on fifty-seven pages of fine print, stating that they were precisely looking for twenty dollar bills which were either United States of America gold certificates or Federal Reserve notes. The ten dollar bills would be gold certificates, while the five dollar bills were United States notes.

Although the issuance of the circulars containing the serial numbers of the ransom bills was not for public consumption, it took only the curiosity of a teller in a Newark, New Jersey bank to inform a friend at the Newark News that he had seen the numbers, and before nightfall the story was in print on the front pages of most newspapers that picked up the latest developments of the case from the wire services. If Lindbergh and the authorities had wished the news of the ransom payment to have remained a closed secret between them, the damage, unfortunately, had already been done. They now feared the kidnappers would believe, through a misunderstanding, that they no longer could trust them in any possible further negotiations.

However, one week after the ransom payment, on Saturday, April 9th, in spite of any additional danger the disclosure might bring to his child, Colonel Lindbergh issued the following statement through Superintendent of State Police Schwarzkopf. It was broadcast over both the red and blue radio networks that evening:

Colonel Lindbergh has authorized the statement that a ransom of $50,000 was paid to the kidnappers---properly identified as such---upon their agreement to notify him as to the exact whereabouts of the baby. The baby was not found at the point designated.

Several days were permitted to elapse to give the kidnappers every opportunity to keep their agreement.

It was not intended to use the numbers on the specie in which the ransom was paid, but inasmuch as the kidnappers have failed to keep their agreement and have not communicated since the ransom was paid, it is felt that every remaining possible means must be utilized to accomplish the return of the baby, and to this end the cooperation of the Federal Government was requested in tracing the bills used.

Upon learning this news, Curtis was beside himself. How could Lindbergh have been so foolish to pay his $50,000 to someone who had presented no actual proof that he had the baby, especially so since the trio from Norfolk were certain they were dealing with the real kidnappers. Had the colonel forgotten that Curtis had warned him that one of the members of the gang he was dealing with was attempting to embezzle additional money from the child's family by arranging private negotiations of his own? It was on Tuesday, March 22nd, when they had met with the Colonel in his Hopewell residence, that he had been told this.

Realizing that Lindbergh had been fleeced out of $50,000, Curtis attempted to pin-point in his own mind, which of the five men he knew as the kidnappers, had probably been the one to whom Condon had passed the money in St. Raymond's Cemetery.

Quickly excluding Sam, Nils, Eric, and Larsen, he satisfied himself that it had, in all likelihood, been John since he seemed to fit Jafsie's description closer than the others.

Lindbergh, realizing that he had allowed $50,000 to slip needlessly through his fingers, and now experiencing utter failure in renewing contact with "Cemetery John", at last began to pay more attention to the progress his "friends" from Norfolk were making by centering his interest on the Curtis negotiations.

In the meantime, the police investigating units of both New Jersey and New York City were literally beside themselves in anger and frustration when they became aware that all this time Lindbergh had been negotiating with the kidnappers, embezzlers or just plain swindlers, and had been bilked out of $50,000 without their knowledge.

Curtis, now satisfied that he had gained more of Lindbergh's attention and confidence, exhibited more exuberance in the progress he appeared to be making. His hopes were again high as he, once again, headed through the Holland Tunnel for another secret meeting at the Newark railroad station. Four of the gang met him there in Sam's car in front of the building. Only John was missing. Inviting him into the car, they drove to John's home, in what was known as the Scandinavian section of the city.

Before long he found himself seated in a rather unkempt room that evidently was used for the combined purpose of sitting, eating, and sleeping. Beginning to admonish Curtis, assuming that he possibly had some responsibility for allowing the Condon payoff, John quickly interjected.

"Sure, I did the work with Condon." he explained. "That was the idea all along--to chisel this Lindbergh through Condon, and then turn the baby in through you. That's why we were willing to let the kid go cheap to you."

"Do you call $25,000 cheap?", Curtis answered sharply?

Assuring him that he did, Curtis saw John, Eric, and Nils reach into their pockets, each withdrawing $500 in five, ten and twenty dollar bills. Handing him a copy of the published list of ransom bills they had obtained, they challenged Curtis to check their $1500 against it for further proof. Comparing five of the bills taken from each man's pocket, Curtis was astounded to find that the serial number of each bill he checked tallied perfectly with corresponding numbers on the official list of ransom bills that had been turned over by Doctor Condon on Saturday, April 2nd.

This then, clinched it, Curtis concluded. It was no longer a possibility that he and his aides were dealing with the kidnappers. It was now factual. He had just seen actual proof that the men in whose very presence he now found himself, were the persons who, not only had abducted the baby, but knew where the child was being held captive at the present time.

Prepared to divulge this valuable information, Curtis made another visit to Hopewell on Monday, April 18th to personally inform the Colonel. Lindbergh admitted to the boatbuilder that every attempt of his, as well as those efforts put forth by the New Jersey State Police had run into a dead end. There seemed to be no new clues to follow. The endeavors of the underworld trio of Rosner, Spitale, and Bitz had failed to produce one solid lead, and now the negotiations of Condon had failed.

As early as Monday, April 11th, the front page of *The Bronx Home News* stated that the elderly resident of 2974 Decatur Avenue, the Bronx, was the mysterious "Jafsie" of the newspaper ads, and that it was he who had paid Lindbergh's $50,000 to an unknown person in St. Raymond's Cemetery, receiving nothing in return.

This announcement brought with it an avalanche of reporters converging on the Condon home in search of additional news, as well as obtaining the eccentric gentleman's own version of the role he was playing in the sensational Lindbergh case. Through it all, Condon was fast becoming a symbolic, almost instant hero. The name Jafsie captivated the imaginations of the public. Doctor Condon was thrilled at his overnight rise to notoriety. He gloated over his important, new-found, fame.

It was at this point in time that Lindbergh showed more interest in the claims of Curtis. He reasoned that the Norfolk men must certainly be doing business with the actual kidnap gang. With all the information he had been given, there seemed to be nothing remaining for him to do but place his implicit faith in their operations.

During the weeks that followed, Lindbergh gave Curtis and his associates every consideration, cooperating with all the demands made by the kidnappers. Sincere efforts were made by the group of men, comprised of Curtis, Edwin Bruce, Lieutenant Richard, and Colonel Lindbergh as they traveled by car, boat, and plane between Cape May, New Jersey, Norwalk, Connecticut, and Norfolk, Virginia, fulfilling their part of the bargain with the apparent kidnappers, to arrange for the transfer of the missing baby to his father.

But as the days passed on, with Curtis claiming they were reaching nearer to success; with the passing of each hour, their hopes would rise, only to fall again. Once more failure seemed imminent.

During the course of his negotiations, Curtis enlisted the aid of a few influential persons by taking them into his confidence. These men were more than willing to help in any way possible, even to expending themselves in the use of their financial resources, their possessions, and their facilities. His friend, Colonel Charles H. Consolvos, proprietor of the Monticello Hotel in Norfolk, allowed him the full use of his yacht, The Marcon, commandeered by its capable skipper, Captain Frank H. Lackmann. The entire facilities of the Navy's Hampton Roads Base were made available by order of Rear Admiral W.D. MacDougal, Commander of the Navy District. Captain Kenneth Whiting of the Naval Air Station informed Lieutenant Richard that he should be ready to pilot the Norfolk boatbuilder in the U. S. Navy Vought Corsair at any time he was needed. Ed Bruce, manufacturer from Elmyra, New York, volunteered his assistance at all times. The management of the Prince George hotel on 28th Street were cooperative by helping Curtis set up his New York City headquarters. And a wealthy friend, A.L. Foster of Atlantic City, loaned him his giant yacht, " The Cachelot".

In his quest to obtain more information from the abductors, Curtis had arrived at one main conclusion; that he was actually dealing with two groups within the one. He was certain that John, Eric, and Nils comprised one segment, while Sam and Larsen belonged to the other. He believed he was not wrong in assuming that it was John who had collected the money from Condon in St. Raymond's Cemetery. He spoke kindly of the Bronx educator, showing great respect for him, and referred to him in only the friendliest of terms. He further stated that Condon had proven himself O.K. in every way during his negotiations with him.

The intensity of the search increased in momentum as Consolvos' yacht, Marcon, was pressed into service. Lindbergh insisted that he accompany Curtis in his quest for another contact with the gang, and thus began days of close fellowship between the flyer, Curtis, Ed Bruce, and Lieutenant Richard. The four men spent many hours together searching the waters of the Atlantic Ocean in an area extending from as far north as New York City to Norfolk in the south.

Their search put forth an attempt to locate a two-masted Gloucester schooner, one they had been told, could be identified by her white cabin and dark green hull, and bearing the name --- "The Mary B. Moss". During the hours of darkness, Captain Whiting, in a giant seaplane equipped with searchlights, closely searched the water from the air.

Curtis had been told that it was on this boat, the lost baby would be found, and that they could easily identify "The Mary B. Moss" by two white towels flying from her forward mast. Their intense desire to locate the schooner, and their many thwarted attempts to contact those who held the child, had begun to take on all the elements of mystery and intrigue. In many respects, the "cloak and dagger" scenario surrounding the Curtis group, seemed to put the escapades of the Gaston B.Means-Evalyn Walsh McLean entourage to shame.

Means had his Father Hurney, plus the mysterious code numbers he had assigned to each of his assistants, plus "The Fox". Curtis had his Dean Dobson-Peacock, Admiral Burrage, plus Sam, John, Nils, Dynamite, Eric, Olga, and a newcomer known as "Inez". To say the least, the Curtis troop of actors certainly out-numbered those of the Means swindlers.

The latest acquisition to the gang turned out to be the group's radio operator, whose principal job was to send messages from land, by means of a portable radio, to the gang on their ship at sea. Curtis estimated her age to be about 25, noting that she was "neatly dressed and had a good form." He soon learned that she was married, her husband being a ship's captain who worked out of Hampton, Virginia.

On the evening of Tuesday, April 19th, Lindbergh, Ed Bruce, and Lieutenant Richard journeyed to Cape May Court House and registered at a small hotel there. The Colonel had decided to use the name "Axel" Swanson as an attempt to conceal his identity. Joining them there at midnight, Curtis reported that he had received definite information that Lindbergh's baby was being held on the two-masted schooner, "The Mary B. Moss", and that the gang had decided to take Lindbergh on board, provided the colonel would agree that there would be no activity by the Coast Guard in the area of their boat, and furthermore, that there would be absolutely no publication of the serial numbers of the new ransom bills, following the second payment for the return of his child. To all this Lindbergh readily agreed.

Reporting the Colonel's agreement to the gang, Curtis was picked up at the hotel by Hilda and Inez. Driving an old Ford sedan, equipped with a portable two-way radio in order to keep in touch with "The Mary B. Moss", he found Hilda to be very talkative, and more than willing to reveal some facts about themselves. Curtis held little doubt that the gang would have preferred this information to have remained untold.

Hilda, speaking with a decided German accent, said she was Olaf "Dynamite" Larsen's wife, and that she and Inez were sisters. She said she was a nurse by profession, and had three sons, ranging in age from seven to twelve years. She revealed to him that Sam's name was actually Morris Truesdale. She emphatically stated that she was not at all proud of her husband's involvement in the kidnapping, since it was not of her choosing. However, she did admit that she had been the one who had written all of the ransom notes.

Curtis was soon taken to the waiting Gloucester fishing schooner, easily recognized with its identifying two masts and temporary aft deck cabin painted white and dark green. On deck, Curtis, once again, found himself in the midst of the five men he still believed to be the kidnappers.

Although he saw no sign of the baby, Curtis had every reason to believe that little Charles was being held below deck in the care of a nurse. Dynamite informed the shipbuilder that they were headed toward the water around Block Island, and would be in the vicinity during the early morning hours of Thursday, the 21st.

The conference over, Curtis rushed back to report his latest findings to Colonel Lindbergh at Cape May Court House. The excited boatbuilder told him that the gang was very close to an exchange for his child, and that it could possibly be enacted the next morning. He further divulged some added facts he had learned as to how the kidnapping had been pulled off so successfully.

Regardless of Lindbergh's reluctance to believe it, Curtis insisted on relating the new information, that "one of his three servants was implicated, and without his aid they would not have known where the child's room was located."

The Norfolk gentleman went on to explain in more detail what he had learned from the gang, especially of the events which led up to the kidnapping. It was John who had told him that he had become acquainted with the servant after meeting him in a roadhouse located on the outskirts of Newark. Entering into a discussion with him about the position he held in the Lindbergh household, they came to a mutual agreement that the flyer's child could represent a lot of money if he could be snatched from his home and held for ransom. The servant obliged by drawing a rather rough, but nevertheless detailed sketch of the house, showing the location of the various rooms. Curtis claimed to have been shown this sketch.

The enthusiastic Curtis continued with John's discourse on the kidnapping events. He told Colonel Lindbergh that the perpetrators of the harrowing crime had first, very subtly questioned a doctor regarding the proper amount of chloroform that could be safely administered to a child of that age, thus rendering him unconscious and causing no outcry. Once they learned this, they were ready to strike.

A green Hudson sedan drove into Lindbergh Lane and parked on the driveway just several hundred feet from the home. In the car were John, Eric, and Hilda. Farther on, in another car, were the lookouts, Sam and Nils. The hour was nearing nine o'clock. The pre-arranged signal came from the servant inside the house.

At once, John and Eric carried the ladder to the southeast corner of the home and propped it against the wall near the nursery window. Inside, they immediately went to the crib and chloroformed the sleeping child. Meeting the servant in the doorway, and given his word that everything was clear, they hastened with boldness down the stairway and out the front door. Hurrying to the waiting car, the ladder sections having already been moved by Sam and Nils, they headed in undetected safety, back to Cape May.

Although Lindbergh refused to accept the fact that one of his servants had betrayed him, he did feel, from the contacts made by Curtis, that they were much nearer to finding his child than Condon had been. His eagerness increased as they relentlessly searched the waters near East Quarter Light, below the high clay cliffs of Block Island. It was at this point that it had been agreed the two ships would meet for a rendezvous of those on aboard and a final consummation of negotiations would be made. But they failed to site "The Mary B. Moss".

During the next three weeks, with Hilda acting as

the gang's liaison agent between them and Curtis, Lindbergh was kept apprised day-by-day of the movements of those reportedly holding his baby. " The Marcon", with her anxious passengers, patrolled the waters of the Atlantic, sailing from and into each designated spot where contact was promised to be made. The scenario, carried out during the remaining days of April and early May, was one experienced by emotion filled persons, realistically portraying themselves in a script that closely resembled that of a well-written mystery thriller.

Diligently, "The Marcon" continued to search the waters with Captain Kenneth Whiting at her helm. Her passengers now consisted of Lindbergh, Bruce, Richard, and the ever-present Curtis. The yacht gave no appearance of resembling a pleasure cruiser. Whiting and Richard each carried a Browning machine gun, in addition to their other rifles and pistols. Under his jacket, Lindbergh carried a pistol in a well-concealed shoulder holster. As the days dwindled on, the men grew restless, and finding much time on their hands, they turned to other interests. In reporting the activities on board ship, Curtis claimed there were occasions when the group was actually jovial.

The shipbuilder told how Lindbergh, in an attempt to relieve the strain and tension brought on by the constant wait, would instigate boyish pranks. The flyer, known since the barnstorming days of his youth for playing practical jokes on his friends, would generally select Richard and Bruce as the chief objects of his tricks. On one occasion, the distraught father tossed a full bucket of water on the sleeping and unsuspecting Lieutenant Richard. True, Lindbergh had always been known for his love of horse-play; and now, "Axel" as he was known by his present associates, seemed to enjoy his time at sea by either swimming or holding target practice with the weapons.

On days when calm waters prevailed and visibility was perfect, "The Marcon" searched back and forth with no success in her crew's attempt to contact "The Mary B. Moss". On gloomy days when the sea was too choppy to set sail, they remained anchored at their base. But their hopes plummeted as important time went by; time they believed to be wasted because of unnecessary waiting.

Curtis' offer to board the kidnapper's schooner and allow them to hold him captive until little Charles was returned, had been strongly rejected by Lindbergh.

The Colonel reasoned that the plan was senseless since Curtis was the only person able to communicate with the enemy's boat, and that it would be foolish to have him marooned far at sea on "The Mary B. Moss".

After several more meetings with Hilda at Cape May and New York, Curtis, now very discouraged at the lack of progress, received Lindbergh's approval to abandon the use of the Marcon and move their base of operations to a new location farther up the coast at Atlantic City. Here, Curtis said they could take advantage of A.L. Foster's offer to use his ninety-foot yacht, "The Cachelot".

However, before boarding her, Curtis placed a telephone call to Hilda at Freeport, Long Island, telling her that he was near Five Fathoms Banks in the waters off Cape May. From her he learned that the identification of "Dynamite's" boat was now to be distinguished by the flashing of her foremast lights instead of the designated two white towels flying from her mast.

On Monday, May 9th, at exactly 7:00 p.m., with Captain Edward Leighton Robb at the wheel of the ketch, and Captain Edward T. McLain on board, "The Cachelot" set sail for the waters that had now been specified as the final point of rendezvous with "The Mary B. Moss". Again Lindbergh, Curtis, Bruce, and Richard were on board. It was close to midnight when they reached their destination. Colonel Lindbergh, certain he would soon have his young son safe on board with him, had arranged a code with some friends on shore --- the flashing of signal lights, which would announce the good news.

But again new failures faced them. Flashing lights from "The Cachelot's" foremast brought no response from any ship lurking out in the darkness of the night. Additional trouble brought more distress to the crew. The sea had turned choppy due to increased wind; a storm at sea had been brewing. After almost five hours of searching, the yacht, with her downcast crew, returned to port at Cape May harbor.

Upon reaching land, Curtis immediately contacted Inez who was occupying a cottage along the shoreline. She informed him that in her last conversation with Dynamite on board "The Mary B. Moss", she had been told that the gang was still at sea with the child, and in spite of the inclement weather, they were waiting for the Curtis group to contact them. She hastened to tell him that all the members of the gang seemed to be in very bad moods, and that their surly manners had made it plain to her that their utmost desire was to get rid of the baby just as soon as possible.

Regardless of the need to make immediate contact, the intensity of the storm kept "The Cachelot" in port for the duration of that day. With the arrival of dawn on Wednesday, May 11th, the inclement weather still showed no signs of improvement, causing the Curtis ship to remain anchored at her dock.

During the idle hours of this day, forced upon them by their inability to sail once again, the men temporarily separated from one another. Curtis took advantage of this time to travel to Atlantic City, while Bruce and Richard journeyed to New York City. Lindbergh remained behind in Cape May, keeping busy helping the steward with small tasks aboard "The Cachelot". By doing this, the Colonel believed he could best keep away from the prying eyes of the press, who, eager for news, were still not aware of the maneuvering of the Curtis group.

The morning of Thursday, May 12th saw little change in the weather than the previous two days, although the intensity of the storm had somewhat subsided. The sea was giving every evidence of possibly allowing "The Cachelot" to set sail once again, permitting her to head for the waters off Five Fathoms Banks. The pelting of the incessant rain had turned into a steady cold drizzle.

The decision had been reached. It was now safe to renew their search. Curtis, however, had decided it would be advisable for him to remain on shore and contact Hilda again for any additional instructions she might have. And so, on board A.L. Foster's yacht, "The Cachelot", with Captain Edward Leighton Robb again at the wheel, they slowly sailed away from shore shortly after one o'clock in the afternoon. Colonel Lindbergh's hopes were never higher.

Charles Lindbergh firmly believed that it would be on this trip that he would finally make contact with the kidnappers. He was certain "The Cachelot" would finally meet "The Mary B. Moss" at sea.

Before they parted company, Curtis and Lindbergh had made arrangements to meet again late that evening -- - at approximately eleven. However, something was soon to happen which would prevent this meeting from taking place.

CHAPTER TWELVE

A Stark Discovery!

Throughout the morning and early afternoon of Thursday, May 12th, the inclement weather with its cold rain continued to saturate the entire area. A dismal drizzle had swept inland to envelope Hopewell and the Sourland Mountain home of the Lindberghs.

Traveling along a macadamed secondary highway, known as Mount Rose Road, taking them from Princeton to Hopewell, was a truck loaded with cut timbers that had just passed through the tiny village of Mount Rose with its few homes and general store. Within minutes the truck driver, 46 year old William J. Allen, and his assistant, Orville Wilson, would be making their delivery in Hopewell. The two men were both employees of Willard S. Titus, owner of a house moving concern in nearby Glenmore, New Jersey. Allen was a happily married man, father of four children, living in Trenton; Wilson resided in Woodsville.

Most of their trip from Princeton had been made through an increasing drizzle. The incessant and steady slap, slap of the windshield wipers played a tattoo on the nerves of the two men; both quite anxious for their final delivery of the day to be completed. Traveling conditions had become horrible.

At a point just over the crest of Mount Rose hill, a location which on a clear day would have afforded them visibility of the looming Sourland mountains ahead of them to the north, and a possible view of the Lindbergh home four miles in the distance, Bill Allen was becoming aware of his increasing discomfort. He had been experiencing a rather troublesome pain and decided he must stop and "answer nature's call". Telling Wilson of his intention, he pulled the truck to the side, jumped from the cab, walked across the road and stepped into the dense underbrush.

Making his way amidst the bushes and scrub oak, he was forced to lower his head in order to avoid some of the branches striking his face. He soon found what he thought to be a suitable place 90 feet from the highway.

As he glanced toward the ground, his eyes were directed to a startling sight, one that momentarily shocked his senses. On the ground, directly in front of him, was an object laying in a shallow scooped out hollow, partially covered by dirt and rotted leaves. In order to afford him closer scrutiny, he leaned over it and found what he first believed to be the skeleton of an animal was actually the badly decomposed body of a child.

Hurriedly making his way back to the location near the point where he had entered the woods, the excited Allen summoned his partner who was patiently waiting in the truck. With alarm in his voice, he shouted: "My God, there's a child --- a dead child over there!"

Orville Wilson lost no time joining Allen, and quickly followed him to his horrible discovery. Here, the two men made a closer inspection of the object on the ground in front of them. The body was lying face down in the shallow depression. What appeared to be a few fragments of clothing clung to the small corpse. It was evident that the combined elements of time, rain, and wind had taken their toll on the remains. There also seemed to be little doubt that scavengers had feasted on it, and now, although entirely veiled with vermin, Allen and Wilson knew they were viewing what at one time had been the body of a small human being.

Leaving the scene exactly as they found it, they scrambled back to the highway and their truck. "What are you going to do?", Wilson excitedly inquired. Climbing behind the wheel, Allen gasped his answer; "Get hold of Charlie Williamson and report it to him!" The mile and one-eighth remaining distance to Main Street, Hopewell was covered in mere minutes. The time was now shortly after 3:15 p.m.

Locating the Hopewell police officer in the local pool room, Allen asked him to come outside where he told him of his find. Realizing the possible importance of the discovery, he instructed Allen to follow him to the township police station and repeat his story to Chief Harry Wolfe. By this time it had begun to dawn on Bill Allen just whose body it might have been that he had stumbled upon.

Wolfe, without delay placed a call to the Lindbergh home and reached Sergeant Andrew Zapolsky of the New Jersey State Police. Realizing the importance of the call, Zapolsky, with Detective James Fitzgerald of the Jersey City Police department accompanying him, arranged to meet the two Hopewell officers at the gatehouse located at the end of Lindbergh Lane. From this point the four officers sped away to the spot, three and one-half miles away, where William Allen had been the first civilian to view the gruesome find, and where Sergeant Zapolsky would soon be the first police officer to see it. Soon this spot would herald the arrival of thousands of persons --- the morbid curious.

The first thing officer Zapolsky did was turn the body over on its back. According to Zapolsky, its face was white. Reaching into his pocket he extracted a picture of the missing Lindbergh baby and compared it with the face of the corpse before him. To his satisfaction HE WAS CERTAIN HE WAS LOOKING AT THE BODY OF LINDBERGH'S CHILD. Returning to Hopewell, he called his superior officer, Captain Jack Lamb, at the Lindbergh residence. Lamb was soon joined by four of his best men, Lieutenant Arthur Keaten of the New Jersey State Police; Inspector Harry W. Walsh and Detective Robert Coar, both of the Jersey City Police Department; and Sergeant Warren Moffat of the Newark Police Department. Meeting these officers in Hopewell, Zapolsky turned south on Princeton Avenue and led them out Mount Rose Road to the spot where, just an hour earlier, there lay an undiscovered corpse amidst the drops of falling rain that pierced the underbrush.

Upon his return to the scene, Sergeant Zapolsky informed his fellow officers that the face of the corpse had already turned a decided blue in color. Lamb, who now had taken complete charge, ordered the sergeant to go find Allen and Wilson; also telling Walsh, who was intently making a closer inspection of the body, to return to the Lindbergh mansion and obtain a piece of cloth from Betty Gow. Walsh completed his assignment and made a speedy return to the crime scene, where Lamb took the cloth and compared it with the badly stained clothing on the corpse. To his satisfaction, he found that it matched the finely scalloped embroidered edge of the shirt on the body. Convincing evidence, Lamb reasoned, that Allen's discovery was the famous kidnapped baby.

Taking a stick, Walsh attempted to raise the corpse about an inch off the ground, but in doing so, due to the badly decomposed condition of the body, he accidently pierced the skull, the puncture creating a hole about the circumference of an ordinary lead pencil. After having the official police pictures taken by Trooper Frank Kelly, Walsh held the body slightly elevated from the ground and cut the clothes from it. As the corpse was raised, he estimated the shallow grave in which it had been found to measure approximately eight to ten inches in depth; its length, the size of the child's torso, about two and one half to three feet.

The inspector, after collecting samples of the earth and underbrush surrounding the immediate area where the body had been found, took care in preserving some strands of loose blond hair, about five inches long, that lay nearby. After completing a thorough search within 20 yards in all directions from the place where the corpse lay, nothing of importance was found, with the exception of one other item --- an empty burlap bag. Taking the clothing remnants with him, Walsh returned to the Lindbergh home. Here they were surrendered to Colonel Schwarzkopf, who ordered the rain saturated clothes to be taken to the boiler room, where Walsh, with Captain Lamb's assistance, nailed them up to completely dry.

Betty Gow was again called into service, being asked to come and inspect the two small shirts that had been removed from the corpse. She readily identified them as the ones she had placed on the child as she prepared him for bed on the fateful night. Although they were now covered with dirt and were discolored by stain, upon close examination, she pointed out to the officers the similarity of the scalloped edge of the shirt with the piece of cloth from which she had cut the garment. In addition, she stated that the blue thread in the stitched border of the shirt was identical to the thread she had used that night. Now completely convinced that the skeleton found by William Allen was the body of the Lindbergh baby, Schwarzkopf entered the garage where the command post of the State Police had been operating, at this time, at a near stand-still. Having already notified the governor and the state house press corps in Trenton, he instructed a trooper to call Paul Gebhart's store in Hopewell and request the members of the press who were staying there to hurry to the Sourlands on the double. Schwarzkopf's terse statement was merely: "There will be an important announcement in Colonel Lindbergh's garage." Schwarzkopf had hoped to delay as long as possible the unpleasant task he had facing him. He realized that a further delay would only make it more difficult --- Anne Lindbergh must be told that her little son was dead. Finding her in the living room with her mother, the Colonel, gathering all the strength he could possibly muster, quietly informed her: "Mrs. Lindbergh, I have very bad news, your baby is dead." He told her briefly of the events leading to this fact, and then, quietly excused himself as Mrs. Morrow embraced her daughter. The two women were silently weeping together. Their grief was not only mutual, it was very, very great.

During this time, Captain Jack Lamb had called the Mercer County Coroner, Walter H. Swayze, and instructed him to come to the site where the body was found, perform his official required duties, and remove the corpse. Arriving on the scene, Swayze made a rather perfunctory survey of the skeletal remains, loaded it in a removal grip, and drove the hearse to the county morgue, his gray frame house, which also served as his funeral parlor, at 415 Greenwood Avenue in Trenton.

At 6:45 p.m., amidst a literal mob from the news media assembled in the Lindbergh garage, Schwarzkopf stood to his feet to address them. Speaking in a firm voice, in order that all could hear, he read: "We have to announce that apparently the body of the Lindbergh baby was found at 3:15 this date by William Allen - Negro, of Trenton...who was riding on a truck load of timber...Allen went into the woods...going under a bush he lowered his head, and as he raised his head, he saw a skeleton on the ground..."

*Note: This statement of Colonel Schwarzkopf has been condensed. The events which transpired were covered in the text. However, for the sake of emphasis, I have taken the liberty of underscoring the words apparently and skeleton.

As Schwarzkopf read his prepared, typewritten statement of seven paragraphs, containing 378 words, the overly anxious news hawks had already anticipated what the message would be.

Schwarzkopf's statement, as he read the first startling words, created a stir which caused many of the reporters to immediately bolt for the door. But, his sharp command: " No one will leave this garage until I have finished!" brought them reluctantly back to their seats. However, at the completion of his reading, the reporters in mass unorganized formation hurried out into the night to telephone their newspapers and radio stations with the terse words that would soon furnish their front pages and broadcasts with the shocking, heartbreaking news: "LINDBERGH BABY FOUND.DEAD!"

But the rush of reporters from the garage that evening, all hoping to be "first" on the street or on the air with the news break, proved to be fruitless, when they were all soon to learn they had been "scooped" by an *Associated Press* reporter named Francis Jamieson, whose daily "news beat" assignment was to cover the happenings as they occurred, or were issued, from the State House in Trenton.

As Jamieson was walking through the state house corridors during the late afternoon hours of May 12th, he wandered into the office of Governor A. Harry Moore, hoping the governor would have some late developments to report relative to additional news of political interest that he could send over the AP wires before he completed his work for the day. Just as Jamieson entered the room, the governor hung up the phone. Informing the youthful reporter of the news he had just received, Jamieson rushed back through the corridors to the nearest telephone. In minutes, the news went out over the AP wires, beating the other news sources by a considerable length of time, and winning for Francis Jamieson the coveted Pulitzer prize for journalism for the year 1932. Young Jamieson had truly been at the right place --- at the right time.

Colonel Schwarzkopf, after personally visiting the location where Allen's discovery had been made, became very apprehensive about the sudden turn of events. He was extremely anxious to have someone make a positive identification of the remains. Since Colonel Lindbergh was at sea searching for his son, and should the corpse now laying on a coroner's table in Trenton prove to be him, the father's search must end. For him to ask Anne to make the identification would have been too emotionally devastating for her. Betty Gow remained the only logical person to visit the morgue.

Dr. Charles H. Mitchell, County Physician from Mercer County, was summoned by Coroner Swayze to come to his mortuary and perform an autopsy on the child. But before this could be done, someone should attempt to identify the body. Shortly after 7:00 p.m., Swayze called Schwarzkopf at the Lindbergh home and insisted that someone come to his morgue for the purpose of making an identity. Yes, Schwarzkopf reasoned, he would insist that Miss Gow go to Trenton for that purpose.

And so, a few minutes before the hour of eight, Betty, accompanied by Detectives Robert Coar of the Jersey City Police Department and Samuel J. Leon of the New Jersey State Police, who had driven her in a state car to Trenton, was ushered into a room in which were several persons whom she did not recognize. However, it appeared they had all been waiting for her arrival.

Slowly she walked to the autopsy table and glanced down at the putrefying remains which lay before her. A few seconds passed. Covering her eyes with her hand, she turned her head and walked back to the door through which she had entered only a few minutes before. When she finally became composed enough to speak, she uttered the words they were all waiting to hear: "No, there has not been any mistake. Those are the remains of Charles A. Lindbergh, Jr.!"

A visibly shaken Betty Gow returned with the officers to the Hopewell residence. Colonel Schwarzkopf, after questioning her, issued the following prepared news bulletin to the waiting press:

"Betty Gow has positively identified the garments found on the body discovered today as being the garments in which the Lindbergh baby was clothed on the night of the kidnapping. The sleeping suit was not on the baby, but the two shirts on the body have been positively identified by Betty Gow. Mrs. Morrow and Mrs. Lindbergh were at the Hopewell home when it became known today that the baby found today was the Lindbergh baby. The body was found on the left side of the road going from Mount Rose to Hopewell. More than twenty additional troopers were immediately ordered to duty upon the discovery of the facts which have come to light today. Additional men are also being detailed."

In Trenton, Dr. Mitchell, assisted by Coroner Swayze, went about the grim task of performing the necessary autopsy on the body of the child. Upon its completion, the Mercy County physician issued this official written statement:

"The child died of a fractured skull caused by external violence."

The doctor could very well have added that it was a severe, extensive fracture. Evidence after examining the inner wall of the skull, revealed that at the point of the fracture, were the remains of a blood clot, proving that the youngster had been alive when the fracture occurred. Had he been already dead when he received the blow, causing the fracture, there would have been no blood clot. The doctor also estimated that death had occurred at least two months earlier, and that possibly he had been dead for a longer period.

Coroner Swayze, an undertaker by profession, issued and then signed the death certificate of Charles A. Lindbergh, Jr., certified by the Department of Health of the State of New Jersey. The contents of the certificate were based on information received by him from Dr. Charles H. Mitchell.

With the issuance of the statements of Colonel Schwarzkopf and Governor Moore, and the promptness of the news media in making the announcements public knowledge, it is quite possible that nearly everyone in the world had learned of the discovery in the New Jersey woods except the child's father.

Meanwhile Schwarzkopf had been successful in contacting Curtis at the President Hotel in Atlantic City, where he claimed to have been waiting for another pre-arranged meeting with Hilda. Upon learning the tragic news, Curtis appeared baffled at the sudden turn of events. Schwarzkopf brusquely informed him a state police car would be dispatched to Absecon, where an officer would furnish transportation for him back to Hopewell. Ironically, the Norfolk boatbuilder arrived there just a short time before Lindbergh; the treatment he was to receive would be decidedly cool, and he would soon realize he was in the midst of a hostile army of uniformed New Jersey police officers.

Another futile day of searching had been spent by those on board the Cachelot as she cruised through the waters around Five Fathoms Banks. Colonel Lindbergh, his eyes ever peeled for some sight of the elusive Mary B. Moss, never lost hope of rescuing his son. But as darkness descended, the disappointed and frustrated father, weary from fighting the elements of the weather, asked Captain Robb to head back to the now familiar shoreline of Cape May Harbor.

Ed Bruce and George Richard, who had remained in New York City, learned of the discovery of the body that afternoon and left immediately for Cape May, making several attempts to contact Lindbergh on board the Cachelot without success. As they waited for the Cachelot to dock, their uneasiness increased as they watched this brave father come ashore, walking toward them. Breaking the strained silence that had fallen between them, Lindbergh proceeded to tell them about his day of failure, expressing his hope for better luck the next day.

As he waited for some comment of their possible success, he sensed a reluctance on their part to relate the news they feared would be too great for him to bear. "What is wrong?" he stammered. Bruce, gathering all the inner strength he could, answered: "Colonel, I have a message for you. They have found the baby ---." His voice broke as he continued, "He is dead!"

Driving through the dark night on the long journey that would bring him to the home he had hoped would provide safety and security for his little son, he was once again left alone with his innermost thoughts. A constant rain pelted his windshield. There was never a night so dreary. He pondered the words he would use to console his dear Anne. Broken and crushed in spirit, he drove his car into the entranceway of his home. It was nearly 2:00 a.m. Friday, May 13th. There had never been a day so dreary.

The sky also seemed to be in mourning as the dismal rain continued to fall throughout the day. But, in spite of the bad weather, the funeral parlor at 415 Greenwood Avenue in Trenton had become the center of much activity. Outside, a large crowd of the morbid curious had gathered, hoping to catch a glimpse of some of the notables in the kidnapping. They were especially anxious to see the bereaved father. As the day moved on, people passed in and out of the morgue with very few of them being recognized. However, it was mid-afternoon when a car slowly edged its way to the curb in front of the main entrance. The lean figure of the famous flyer, bareheaded and looking worn and tired, emerged and quickly entered the door. Following close behind was Colonel Breckinridge, who upon learning of the new sadness which had entered his friends life, had placed himself at their disposal. Dr. John F. "Jafsie" Condon, who accompanied the two men, refused to enter the mortuary and view the remains.

The distressed father, looking much older than his 30 years, walked to the table where he expected to see the body of his son under the white sheet that covered him. "Please, take that off." he said, motioning toward the sheet. One of the coroner's staff members complied, stepping back to allow the Colonel to view what lay below. A look of combined horror, grief, and pain crossed the father's countenance. His sagging shoulders were seen to shudder. Staring down at what had once been his active little son, he stooped to more closely examine the decomposed form. He looked at the structure of the mouth, counting the teeth. He glanced over the entire form. With tears in his eyes, visible to the 20 people present, Colonel Lindbergh turned and slowly walked away. He had been in the morgue a total of only 90 seconds.

At the door of an adjoining room, Erwin E. Marshall, Mercer County prosecutor, shook hands with the father, and quietly asked: "Colonel Lindbergh, are you satisfied that it is the body of your baby?"

"I am perfectly satisfied that it is my child," the famous aviator answered.

Outside the morgue, Lindbergh and his associates entered the car driven by Colonel Schwarzkopf. The two other Colonels, Lindbergh and Breckinridge, sat in the rear as the crowd gawked inside for a better view. As they waited, the remains of the cute little blue eyed, curly blond haired baby boy were being wrapped in a shroud and placed in a small oak casket. At 4:30 p.m. a gray hearse was observed leaving the funeral home as it began its journey over the New Jersey hills headed for Rose Hill Cemetery in Linden, just south of Elizabeth, a trip of nearly 40 miles.

Upon their arrival there, they were met at the front of the crematory by M.L. Howard, the cemetery supervisor. Lindbergh walked alone, following the men who carefully carried the tiny coffin bearing his son, into the interior of the chapel. Because no religious service had been requested, the little coffin was taken to an elevator and removed on the floor below. Lindbergh, who had descended by way of the stairs, met them in front of the cremation chamber. He watched as the glass doors were opened and the small casket was guided in on rollers. Making certain the doors were closed and securely sealed, the flame from the fireclay was seen to burst into a roaring inferno that enveloped the entire chamber. A heart-broken father closely watched the searing white hot flames consume and reduce to a small deposit of ashes, what minutes before had been all that remained of his child.

Supervisor Howard, promising to provide a suitable urn for the child's ashes, assured him that one would be delivered to the Lindbergh family within a few days.

The time had reached 6:15. Nightfall was fast approaching as the three Colonels wended their way back toward Hopewell. Very little conversation had taken place between them as they silently dwelled on the events that had transpired over the past days. As they drove down the Hopewell-Mount Rose Road, one can only wonder if they noticed the hub-bub around the spot where the crushed little body had lain unnoticed until just a little more than 24 hours earlier.

In George Waller's excellent book, *Kidnap*, (The Dial Press, 1961), he describes so well the activity that had sprung up along that secondary highway. His graphic description is repeated here: "In the woods between Mount Rose and Hopewell, State troopers stood guard over the shallow hole that held the small body, and close by, on the rainswept road where William Allen had stopped his truck, cars drove bumper to bumper. Still more of the curious came on foot. At the spot Allen had entered the woods, now barricaded and guarded by troopers, the mounting traffic had converged into a tangle in which almost no movement was possible. Peddlers hurried up with peanuts and popcorn others hawked postcards of the Lindbergh house. An enterprising merchant from Trenton arrived with the materials to set up a refreshment stand, and soon the smell of hot dogs was in the air."

Just another act more kooks and clowns would follow before it all ends. The three ring show must go on!

The dismal rain continued to fall as Colonel Lindbergh paused momentarily at the front door of his home. He had returned to Anne --- and to John Hughes Curtis.

CHAPTER THIRTEEN

A Great Controversy

At this point in my narration of the events as they have already taken place, I feel it is essential to pause briefly and elaborate on a discussion of the corpse found by William Allen on May 12, 1932. This, I believe is especially important since so much controversy has arisen through the years, debating the claim that the remains found were not actually those of Charles Lindbergh, Jr., but instead, those of another child.

In my discourse I have attempted to be factual and fair, taking into consideration the events as they developed, including the identification of the remains, not only by the police, but more importantly that of Betty Gow, the nursemaid; and Colonel Lindbergh, the father.

I have related the time taken by both persons as they stood beside the broken body. Betty's identification was largely made by her comparison of the cloth from which she cut the little flannel nightshirt; and her comparison of the scalloped edge and the blue thread she used to sew the garment.

Quite enough, you might say. Well, I wonder, and what is more, I have good reason to do so. As for Lindbergh's absolute identification, we must remember that he had already been told that he was going to view the body of his son. And so, he went into the morgue with the preconceived knowledge that he would definitely be seeing his son, and no one else but his son. There would be no doubt about it.

In addition to Lindbergh's understanding that he was to view the remains of his son, we also acknowledge that he checked the number of teeth in the mouth and found that the corpse had the same number as were in the mouth of his youngster when he was kidnapped. However, it should be pointed out that it is not at all unusual for a great number of children at that age, or for that matter, children slightly younger or older, to have the same number of teeth in their mouths, eight upper and eight lower. All of which leads us to the conclusion that age cannot be definitely determined by a count of teeth, and therefore should be ruled out as a determining factor.

Colonel Lindbergh also said he noticed that the foot of the corpse had two overlapping toes, peculiar only to his son. But here again, I must point out that this in no way was a deformity of the foot by any stretch of the imagination. It could not even be termed a peculiarity, since the slightly "overlapping toes" are quite natural among young children to this day.

However, regardless of any arguments we might put forth today, it is not my aim to convince you one way or the other since I am by no means an authority on either teeth or toes. Nevertheless, I deem it quite important that we seek out the opinions of those persons, the professional doctors of that day; those who viewed the remains; and in addition, draw our own deductions on the conclusions rendered at that time --- and then, consider them to be invaluable and essential to the case at hand.

First let us take into consideration the statements made by the child's personal physician, Dr. Philip Van Ingen, who visited the morgue and made a thorough and complete examination of the skeletal remains. "If someone were to come in here and offer me ten million dollars I simply wouldn't be able to identify these remains." And that is the professional opinion of a man who had been very familiar with the baby's physical characteristics when he was alive. A man who now was expected to agree that the decomposed skeleton and little Charles Lindbergh were one and the same. Doctor Van Ingen very simply, could not do it. Not for ten million dollars.

Dr. Van Ingen, who had given the baby a routine examination on Thursday, February 18th, eleven days before the abduction, recorded that the child weighed between 27 and 30 pounds, and measured exactly 29 inches. This then, was the official record given to the state police for use on their official "Information Wanted" notices.

Once again, on May 13th, after making another detailed and minute examination of the body, Doctor Van Ingen gave additional emphasis to his former statement: "The condition of the body is such that positive identification by me is impossible." Dr. Van Ingen simply would not be moved from his firm opinion.

In order that you better understand what was the exact condition of the corpse, we can go to no one better than the Mercer County physician, Dr. Charles H. Mitchell, who performed the official autopsy. To begin with, Dr. Mitchell's findings stated that THE CORPSE MEASURED 33 1/2 INCHES IN LENGTH, A DIFFERENCE OF FOUR AND ONE-HALF INCHES. A CONSIDERABLE AND IMPRESSIVE VARIANCE WHEN WE TAKE INTO CONSIDERATION THAT A PERSON DOES NOT GROW IN DEATH. This fact remains true, even allowing for the probability of a very slight disparity, which could possibly be caused by the separation of dead tissue being severed from bone structure.

Here is a further look into some of the pertinent excerpts from Dr. Mitchell's report:

> "Sex undetermined, due to marked decomposition of body. General appearance --- badly decomposed. Left leg from knee down missing. Right forearm missing. Abdominal organs except liver missing. Eyes softened and decomposed. Thoracic organs except heart missing. Skin of head, face, portion of chest and right foot discolored and decomposed. Body shows evidence of prolonged exposure and unusual decomposition that would occur in the course of approximately two or three months' time, depending on climatic conditions that might produce such results. Special characteristics: Unusually high and prominent forehead and cranium, apparently greater in circumference than would be found in a child of this age. Height, thirty-three and a half inches."

It is a proven fact that it takes a 20 month-old child anywhere from one year and a half to two years to grow four and one half inches in height. We must then assume that the skeleton had been that of a child at the age of about three years. In this, Doctor Mitchell readily concurred, adding that the head of the corpse seemed unusually large for a mere child of 20 months. He further stated that there were certain features of the skeleton that led him to believe it was that of a female, due largely to the pelvic structure and other characteristics common in a female skeleton. The sex of the child could not definitely be determined because the area around the genitals was completely gone.

Taking these deductions into consideration, we must then conclude that the corpse was that of a three year old girl that had been found. As we look further into the facts surrounding the remains that continued to baffle and mystify the minds of many medical experts, we must sift out a few other findings from Dr. Mitchell's official report:

"The first toe of the right foot completely overlaps the large toe and the second toe of the right foot partially overlaps the right toe."

And once again, we must in all fairness consider the report of Dr. Van Ingen following his examination of the baby on February, 18th:

"The two things I specially noted when I examined him were that his skin was unusually dry all over his body, and the fact that both little toes were slightly turned in overlapping the next toe."

Now, in case you find these statements confusing, and you should, let us look ahead to the time of the Gaston B. Means trial in Washington, D.C. later that year, when Dr. Mitchell, now on the witness stand, testified of his findings relative to the condition of the corpse:

"The left leg from the knee down was missing and the left arm from the elbow down was missing. The right foot was missing. It had an unclosed fontanelle. In other words, to make it clear to you, it is what is commonly known as the soft spot on the top of a child's head after birth, which usually closes within the first year, but in this case the fontanelle was still open. I made the measurement of the fontanelle, which was larger than normally should be present. I would say that the youngster died within a short time after its disappearance. It is rather difficult to state accurately the time, but basing my conclusions upon the degree of decomposition, I would say that the child died within probably forty-eight hours, at least, following the disappearance from its home."

You have probably already noticed the grave discrepancy in Doctor Mitchell's testimony. The contradictory statements he made in his written and oral reports, topped by his confusing court testimony, leaves us in nothing less than a quandary. We are told he had a corpse with both feet missing; or in other words, a corpse with no feet, but did have queerly formed toes. Quite an oddity, to say the least.

In addition to the vast difference in the reports of the physicians, those medical professionals who should have been more than accurate in their analysis of every aspect of the condition of the corpse, apparently did not deem it important enough to have a pathological or toxicological examination made of the remains. Very bluntly we can state --- there were absolutely no tests of this nature ever made. And who prompted the decision to hurry and have the body quickly taken to a crematory the very next day and having it disposed of into a small pile of ashes?

To have held the remains a few days should have been of great aid to the police; pathologists and toxicologists could have conducted detailed tests which could have revealed much and bring them to a successful conclusion to the case. But then, Colonel Lindbergh, from the very opening of the case, had been making all the decisions.

Alan Hynd, one of the most prolific newsmen to personally cover the case, inquired of Dr. Mitchell why he had not focused official and public attention on these discrepancies. The doctor, "a blunt and earthy man" according to Hynd, gave him his immediate answer: "The reason Lindbergh made that identification was that he wanted to get the thing over with. How he could possibly have made an identification is beyond me. What he saw in the morgue was nothing but a blackened skeleton. Why, I didn't even know the sex of the remains. I'd have been crazy to tangle with Lindbergh. Why, with his power, he could have ruined me --- and don't think he wasn't just the boy to do it!"

Moving along in our study, we should take a look at another aspect that directly pertains to the skeleton as found. Since the "experts" seemed to be "convinced" and "content" that the body found was that of Lindbergh's "little eaglet", their extreme "scientific deduction" caused them to arrive at the conclusion that the body of the child had been in that location from March 1st to May 12th, a total of 72 days, --- "just waiting to be found". Their assumption is incorrect and can easily be proven so.

To begin with, it would have been impossible for a body to decay to that extent, in the prevailing, near freezing, temperatures that plagued the area during that period of time. During the entire month of March, the average temperature had been only 37 degrees Fahrenheit, only five degrees above freezing. The average for April had been only 49 degrees, while 55 degrees had been registered as the average for the first 12 days of May. The highest single day's reading during March had been

54 degrees on the 26th; the lowest daily average for that month had been 20 degrees; the April thermometer readings only once registered a high of 64 degrees, while still maintaining a low daily average which dipped to 37 degrees. Considering the first 12 days of May, we find the highest temperature reached was 62 degrees.

Now, taking all these figures into consideration, and realizing that a temperature of 32 degrees arrests decomposition, we find a shocking significance as we come to a very logical conclusion. The degree of temperature, proven to be most favorable to appreciable decomposition, must be 70 degrees or higher. We must also take into consideration that where Mr. Allen found the body was a spot that was a secluded, shaded one, where no bright sunlight could enter. Furthermore, it was a dark, windy location where temperatures would generally be several degrees lower than those in an open and exposed area.

Edward P. Mulrooney, Police Commissioner of New York City, when presented this same temperature evidence by Alan Hynd, and asked what he, the commissioner, thought of it, reported his response in this fashion. Hynd said: "He just smiled cynically and said, 'You figure it out.'"

Although Evalyn Walsh McLean, the Washington D.C. socialite had been bilked out of $104,000 by Gaston B. Means, it by no means deterred her from seeing justice done in the Lindbergh case. By this time she had hired a prominent private investigator, Lieutenant Robert W. Hicks, a Washington criminologist. His reputation for ferreting out true facts in criminal cases was excellent.

Upon his entrance into the case he became involved in substantiating the identity of the body that had been found. Here is that portion of his report to Mrs. McLean: "First of all, it would have been to the advantage of certain interests to have planted a body. The great police activity centering around the search for the Lindbergh child had seriously interfered with the enormous bootlegging industry, resulting in the seizure of many whiskey trucks plying between New York and Philadelphia. And the big bootleggers were just the men who would have stopped at nothing to remove an obstacle; and the planting of a body, so that the police activity would be curtailed, would have been a most logical thing for them to do.

"Colonel Lindbergh was told, when he went to a Trenton morgue to make an identification, that the body of a child believed to be his was there. Therefore the Colonel went into that morgue expecting to find the remains of his son. Is it not possible, in view of the mental suggestion and the hysteria surrounding the whole business, that he made a most understandable mistake? There are on record other cases wherein relatives and parents have made faulty identifications, and with considerably more to go on than Lindbergh had."

Lieutenant Hicks, in one of his reports pertaining to the condition of the corpse, reiterated that the temperature would have had to maintain a degree of near 70 for many, many days running in order that such a severe state of decomposition would be warranted.

In addition to Hicks' viewpoint regarding the temperature, he joined a multitude of others who disputed the belief that the child's body had been where it was found during the entire 72 days. For that matter, he, as well as others, honestly disputed that it was ever there, until, of course, that time when it was deliberately thrown there as a plant. "Thousands upon thousands of people had traversed the very spot where the body was found. Proof of this was the trampled underbrush under the spot where the skeleton was discovered.", his report went on to explain.

Furthermore, in addition to the Hicks' report relative to the variance in the child's measurements and other differences in physical characteristics, Mrs. McLean reports other evidence uncovered by her investigator which support the contentions that the corpse could not possibly have been that of baby Charles.

"Lieutenant Hicks obtained a sample of the hair that had been taken from the remains. He compared this with two samples of hair known to be that of the real Lindbergh baby. One of these two he obtained from Mrs. Dwight W. Morrow, the baby's maternal grandmother. The other he obtained in the plumbing of the Lindbergh home, in the elbow of a pipe leading from a washstand where the baby's hairbrush had been cleaned.

"The two known samples of the child's hair did not resemble that taken from the skeleton, even when allowance was made for the fact that the elements would have done certain things to the hair of a human being who had been buried for seventy-two days. The hair on the skeleton was darker in color, even when bleached to remove the discoloration caused by burial, and it was coarser.", Mrs. McLean stated.

But, in addition to Hicks' findings, and the

statements of the doctors, we must also look to the testimony of others to prove our point.

Ellis H. Parker, the celebrated chief of detectives of Burlington County, New Jersey, a man whose career spanned four decades, during which time he successfully solved thousands of crimes, including 226 murder cases of the 236 he actively worked on, was called to render his opinion of the Lindbergh case.

Parker, because of the great reputation in crime detection he had earned, had often been called on by investigators in large cities throughout the world to aid them in solving many difficult criminal cases. The "Old Fox of Mount Holly", as he was affectionately called, was a burly man of fine Quaker stock, who claimed he knew nearly everyone in Burlington County. He attributed his success in criminal work largely to the fact that, because he knew so many people, he had informants everywhere, who, in strict confidence, would turn vital information over to him, a trust he would never violate. This feeling was a mutual one, since Ellis, through the years, had learned to implicitly trust them and the information they would pass on to him.

Ellis Parker had worked for 44 years out of a small cubicle he called his office, located on the second floor of the Mount Holly courthouse. If his claim that he knew "nearly everyone in Burlington County" might have been slightly exaggerated, it is entirely possible that, on the other hand, if each of the citizens did not know Ellis personally, they most certainly did know him by sight. He was a well known personage in and around Mount Holly, and easily recognizable with his balding head of sparse white hair and ample white mustache that covered his upper lip, with a pipe usually clenched between his teeth. He looked every part the typical "home-spun" detective. He was a kindly man, whose only vice was "murdering the king's English", and had the habit, when asked, of "telling it like it is."

Although Parker had been ordered by Governor Moore to aid in the investigation, both Colonel Schwarzkopf and Captain Lamb had refused to comply with the governor's wishes. However, regardless of this, Parker entertained some of his own beliefs as to what had transpired in the Lindbergh case. It was largely because of this that the detective became so outspoken about the body that was found.

In an interview with Alan Hynd, Parker said:

"Lindbergh went into that morgue expectin' to make an identification because the State Police told him it was his kid. That whole identification was a state of mind." Parker, in addition to this statement, based entirely on the condition of the severely decomposed remains, stated further: "Several friends of mine, involved in the bootleggin' racket, told me that mobsters connected with the big bootleggin' interests in the big cities, dug up a corpse from some cemetery and planted it where it was found. They did this so that the whiskey and beer traffic could keep movin' unmolested between New York and Pennsylvania." Parker explained that he had learned this reliable information from racketeers who told him the "big boys" in the "booze business" were fearful of being put out of business, with many of them already facing prosecution, due to the police impeding the former easy flow of liquor traffic by the cops searching their trucks and cars for the missing baby.

Parker claimed he knew this to be factual, with signed papers to prove it. And strangely enough, from the time of William Allen's discovery, the liquor traffic continued as usual unmolested by police searches.

In one of my trips to Mount Holly, I learned of a man who could possibly corroborate this strong evidence which Ellis Parker had offered. His name was Frank Fitzpatrick. I was told he had been a reporter with the *Philadelphia Inquirer* during the time of the kidnapping, and in addition to this, had been a close friend of Ellis Parker, even working out of the detective's office.

Anxious to hear what Fitzpatrick could tell me, I found him at his home. After informing him of my mission, he invited me inside. I soon found him quite willing to talk about the famous case and his involvement in it. "Sure, I'll tell you whatever you want to know if I can." he fairly shouted. "They sure got the wrong man on that one. Why, as a matter of fact that body they found was definitely not the Lindbergh kid and I can prove it once I get my hands on some medical reports and photographs that have never been made public before. Ya' know, no one around here believes that was the baby. Everything old Ellis told 'em about the body was the truth and there's no doubt about it.", Fitzpatrick went on. "I spent many hours with Ellis Parker, I holed into his office by the hour, I went with him on some of the leads he ran down. Ellis

Parker could have solved that case and did, but they just didn't want him to. The guy they got was framed and I know he was." the reporter concluded his diatribe.

Yes, Frank Fitzpatrick was emphatic regarding his personal, first hand knowledge of the case, and in my questioning of other elderly citizens of the county seat, I found each of their knowledgeable viewpoints to be quite the same.

Through my years of investigating the Lindbergh case, I have visited Hopewell and Flemington innumerable times. During my many trips there, one thing which seemed to put doubt in the minds of those I spoke with, (measured only by the preponderance of times this question would be thrust back at me), was: "Why, if the baby was placed there on the night of March 1st, wasn't it found before May 12th?" They all emphatically were of the belief that the child had not been there for "all that length of time". The voices of the great majority could have spoken in unison with their statement. "Hundreds and hundreds of people had walked over and around that same spot for days after the kidnapping, hunting for the baby. The police, civilians, Boy Scouts who aided in the search, Princeton University students and lots of others were walking around there constantly ever since the baby's disappearance. So, if it had been there, why wasn't it found?"

Several of those questioned confirmed what Ellis Parker had been told, and had momentarily stumped him, during the course of his private investigation. Parker had learned that just a few feet away from the spot where the body lay, emergency telephone wires had been strung along the ground only a few days before. " Why," the detective asked, "was that body not noticed by the linemen as they passed so close to the scene?" Why didn't they stumble over the grave as Allen did? The only logical answer to this is the one Parker arrived at --- there was no body there which could have been found at that time --- it was placed there later!

In addition to the information I have placed at your disposal, we should delve more deeply into our study as to whether the corpse found was someone other than Lindbergh's baby. A report bearing the date May 27, 1932 from the E.R. Squibb and Sons Biological Laboratories reads: "It is established that the burlap bag found near the purported body of Charles A. Lindbergh, Jr., in addition to containing numerous fine, curly, light brown hair and locks of hair corresponding to that found on undershirt from body matted with leaves and pressed between leaves, the scientists found one phalange corresponding to foot of infant".

We also make note of a report made by Corporal Joseph A. Wolf of the New Jersey State Police on Saturday, April 9, 1932, in which he says: "Mr. Hervey Hill stated that he had on several occasions run his hunting dogs in that vicinity during the time the body was supposed to have been there but his dogs never gave any signs of finding anything as they usually do on finding dead animals at times."

Then, as late as Tuesday, March 13, 1934, we find another report of Corporal Wolf, in which he states that, a Dr. Robert Miller "noticed a man walking across the open field between his home and where the body was found ... he observed the man had a bag over his shoulder with something in it and when he stopped he placed same on the ground, when he continued he dragged the bag along the ground ... also stated that a Mr. Hervey Hill ... had been training hunting dogs in the vicinity where the body was found. This took place during the time the body was supposed to have been buried there but the dogs never uncovered anything to arouse his interest or suspicion."

There also exists an investigator's report, dated Thursday, January 2, 1936, to Governor Harold G. Hoffman of a detailed account given by George P. Pearson, a member of the board of directors of the bank in Hopewell. Mr. Pearson explained that about fifteen days prior to the discovery of the body, "right opposite to where the body was found, there was a bundle in the road and he nearly ran over it." He said after the body was discovered, "he was talking to Mr. J. B. Hill, who has a lumber yard there in Hopewell ... Mr. Hill told him that about twenty (20) days previous to the baby being found, that he went with two of his men up to the place where the body was found and that he had his dogs with him and that he dug out of a ravine some decayed matter such as leaves ... to put in the bottoms where he was planting some box bushes and he said, had that baby been there at the time they positively would have known it, because he went there later and saw it was in the same place and in Mr. Hill's judgement, the baby was placed in one of these places where they dug out."

Now, once more I urge your indulgence in allowing me to prove another point which goes far to disprove the "lone wolf" theory of the authorities, the "facts" they used to convict an innocent man. Again, we take into consideration the badly decomposed corpse and the belief that it had been where it was found the entire 72 days. Here now, is our honest question.

If the kidnapper, acting alone, had killed and buried the baby in that lonely wooded area off Mount Rose Road on the night of the kidnapping, how could he have known positively that no one had discovered the dead child in that length of time? We must remember that Doctor Condon met with the kidnapper for an hour and a quarter alone on a park bench in Van Cortlandt Park in the Bronx on the night of Saturday, March 12th,; and then again met with him on Saturday evening, April 2nd when he was paid $50,000 at St. Raymond's Cemetery for a child he did not return.

Had the baby's body been discovered prior to the March 12th date, Lindbergh would have been apprised of the finding, and a cordon of police could have been set around the park and "Cemetery John" would have been arrested. Had the body been discovered between the March 12th and April 2nd dates, the same thing could have occurred, with an arrest being made at the time the payment was made.

Our question then, answers itself - there was no body there to be found. And if we are ludicrous enough to even entertain the thought that the person who met with Condon had a look-out back near Hopewell, who each day would watch the happenings along the Mount Rose Road, and then make a daily report to the person in the Bronx that all is safe, then we just refuse to use plain good logic.

Instead, we have only the true facts before us. As Ellis Parker was told by his friends who were "in the know", a child's body, possibly that of a three year old girl, had been placed there in a fashion "suitable to the needs" of the bootleggers just several days before it was found by William Allen, who later received a reward of $5,000 for his efforts of "answering a call of nature" and finding a mess of bones and mutilated flesh, and that before it was all to end would play a prominent and important role in convicting an innocent man.

It is my honest belief that the authorities could formulate no definite belief as to just how the baby died and what caused his death. If we are to assume that they truly believed the remains were those of the Lindbergh baby, we are still left in a quandary as to what method of death was inflicted on the child, since the prosecuting attorney in the Flemington courtroom, simply failed to make up his own mind. In his opening remarks to the jury, he informed them that the child was killed when the ladder broke, throwing the kidnapper and the baby to the ground, the youngster's head striking the side of the house, inflicting instant death. And then in his closing charge to the jury, he insisted they believe that the kidnapper had used the chisel to crush the child's skull as he lay in his crib.

It apparently made little difference with the members of the jury as to what caused his death, how he died, when he died, and where he died. I, as an unbiased member of a lone jury of one, refuse to accept any of their lines of reasoning, because, studying the facts as they are already known to us, truly believe they are miles off base.

I am certain that Charles A. Lindbergh, Jr., barring an accidental death or natural death during the intervening years is alive today. And because this is true, and it is, then no murder was committed --- and I plan to prove to you, beyond any question of a doubt, that the wrong man died.

In conclusion, I present one more statement from an eminent authority, Doctor Alexander O. Gettler, who was head toxicologist of New York City and professor of chemistry at New York University in 1935 at the time of the trial. Dr. Gettler said: "The authorities do not know today how the Lindbergh baby died. The medical testimony in the case was terrible, and it was only mob psychology that convicted the man."

CHAPTER FOURTEEN

Violet Sharpe

Now that the kidnapped baby had been found dead, Colonel Schwarzkopf and his men were faced with an even greater task. They now had murderers to apprehend.

Topping the list of persons the police must first interrogate were those who had participated, without police sanction, in various endeavors to return the child to his parents. The three persons were Morris "Mickey" Rosner, Dr. John F. Condon and Commodore John Hughes Curtis.

Condon had been summoned to the Lindbergh home by Schwarzkopf late Thursday afternoon, arriving shortly after the body had been taken to Trenton, while Rosner appeared there that evening. Curtis took up residence there very early Friday morning. All three men were available for the necessary interrogation they were facing.

Each was questioned individually on Friday morning by Captain Jack Lamb of the State Police and Special Agent Frank Wilson of the Internal Revenue Service.

Rosner, who with his associates, Irving Bitz and "Salvy" Spitale, having by this time been removed from active participation in the case, told the officers that as early as March 12th he believed they had good leads as to who committed the crime. He told them he had every reason to believe that up to that time they were dealing with the kidnappers and that the baby was then alive and well. He further claimed the gang had shown them the identical symbol signature that was being used by the abductors. He said it was the result of other negotiations going on at the same time that caused a break-down in their role as mediators. Although he had nothing concrete to prove his statement, he claimed all three of them were convinced, by their own deductions, that the crime had been an "inside job". Spitale, an outspoken and straight-from-the-shoulder type guy, was quoted as saying: "Somebody inside the Lindbergh house, whether he knew it or not, was doing a lot of tipping off. No amateur could have done it without poolroom luck. If a real mob did it, the baby is alive and well and you can bet on that. Don't think they'd spare a thing in getting the best care for him."

Condon gave them a complete run-down of all of his escapades. He left nothing out, and in addition offered several of his own ideas as to how he believed the baby had met his death. At times he attempted to play the role of amateur detective; advancing his ideas that the child had been strangled, smothered, or struck with a chisel while asleep in his crib, and that he was carried dead through the window and down the ladder. He did, however, fail to include another of his theories, that chloroform may have been used.

The interrogation of Curtis proved to be one of much greater intensity. Sergeant Mullins and Trooper Holt of the State Police were assigned to take him back to Cape May in an attempt to locate Hilda and Inez. They were met at the Cape May Court House by Lieutenant Jones of the Morristown barracks. But, the trip proved to be a fruitless one; after spending the entire day running down every lead Curtis could furnish them, they arrived back at Hopewell about 9 that evening.

With Curtis remaining under guard, Troopers Williams and Agnew were assigned to spend, what seemed to be endless hours attempting to gain some logical statement from him. Grave doubts as to the integrity of his accounts with the kidnappers were beginning to mount.

Colonel Schwarzkopf's main objective for the present was to keep Curtis away from the grasp of the news media. In an attempt to do this, he assigned Sergeant Mullins to the task of driving him to Trenton, where the two would stay overnight at the Hildebrecht Hotel. On Saturday morning, in the company of Detective Cobb and Sergeant Hastings of the Newark Police Department, they searched for the house in which Curtis claimed he had made his initial contact with the gang. This too, proved to be unsuccessful.

A visit to the Newark rogues' gallery, looking for a face that he might recognize as one of the men or women he had been dealing with, also brought no results. The entire weekend was one of disappointment, as they continued their search, without a lead. After spending another night in the Trenton hotel, they returned to Hopewell on Monday, May 16th. It was then Curtis learned of their intention to place him under arrest for obstructing justice.

Continued pressure from the police as they

attempted to gain a confession, was taking its toll on Curtis. He insisted he be allowed to see Lindbergh. When the colonel finally arrived, and after listening to the man's plea for help, Lindbergh claimed he knew nothing about the pending arrest. Promising Curtis he would go at once and check on it, he departed. He never returned.

The attitude of most of the police had grown intensely worse. It was horrible. They constantly complained about the numerous articles which were appearing in the major newspapers about their failure, "during this length of time", to apprehend the abductors. They were surly about Lindbergh's insistence that he direct the investigation himself, while they were assigned to "this Godforsaken hole" as they referred to the Sourlands, and not permitted to operate from their own headquarters.

Because of the ill-temperament of the officers and the mounting evidence they believed they were uncovering against him, Curtis was finding himself subjected to an intense and relentless grilling throughout the long hours of the day and night. They continued to press him to sign a confession, admitting that his story was a hoax. They told him if he would do this, it would not become public knowledge, and they would then permit him to return home to his sick wife and two children.

Curtis, weary from weeks of lack of sleep and the constant harassment of the police, coupled with the tormenting fear of the embarrassment of the accusation, (false as he claimed it to be), and the possible impending imprisonment, submitted to the pressure. In doing this, he "foolishly" signed a prepared typewritten confession, which he later claimed "he never read."

Explaining why he surrendered to their demands to sign such an incriminating statement, Curtis said they worked on him from 10 o'clock that evening until 4:30 the next morning, when at that time, he agreed to sign it. Claiming it was entirely a lie, Curtis said later: "By that time I think I would have signed anything, just to get a little sleep."

Curtis was now kept under heavy guard. There were very few times when less than two troopers watched his every move. He observed the presence of Prosecutor Anthony M. Hauck,Jr. conferring with Lindbergh and Schwarzkopf, fear striking him, when he suddenly realized he could face possible arrest because of the "voluntary" confession they had forced him to sign.

Curtis later related the virtual "nightmare" he

suffered during the time of his confinement. Claiming the police made him the brunt of a barrage of false accusations which caused him to endure indignities beyond comprehension; he charged them with being belligerent far beyond reason: "The grilling that I went through was terrible. It was led by Agnew. Oaths were in order, it seems. At one time they would make out they believed the confession; at another time they would doubt it. They seemed to think I was still withholding information. It was a terrible ordeal. Just at dawn when I was reeling with nausea and fatigue, Agnew strode dramatically to the center of the room and threw down a copy of the *New York Daily News*. On the front page was a picture of myself, my wife, and my children, and the text of the supposed confession. 'Now!' he shouted, 'you're ruined for life!'" Curtis claimed he was put through this painful experience on Wednesday, May 18th.

As the intense grilling finally came to an end, Lamb ordered him to be taken to the cellar. Here, he was put in a room where he was left alone to suffer more mental torture. On the other side of the securely locked door a state trooper was stationed. Glancing about the dank basement laundry room, he observed, hanging nearby, the clothes they had removed from the corpse of the dead baby. His improvised cell was extremely damp; a sun lamp was kept turned on day and night, providing slight warmth. Exhausted, he fell to the cot that had been put there for his use.

Following a short rest, Curtis decided to examine more closely the child's clothing. He noted that they comprised a little shirt, and an article which appeared to be a cloth band with a length of colored thread that apparently had been used to sew the band. On the floor lay the matting and blankets from a crib, evidently brought there from the baby's nursery. In addition, he noticed a broken shovel, the kidnap ladder, and another ladder, a new one, which they evidently were building.

Believing that the days of the long gone Spanish Inquisition had returned and were presently being enforced in this damp New Jersey cellar, Curtis arrived at the conclusion that since he, thus far, had not been arrested, and was merely being "detained" by the authorities, there was a possibility they might later deny that he had ever been incarcerated.

It was because of this reasoning that prompted Curtis to make a sketch of the dark wash room. He went about jotting down the numbers taken from the oil burners, noting the numbers and sizes of the valves, and in general, making a complete description of the entire room. Folding it, he hid it in the lining of his coat, for future use, should the occasion present itself.

During the remainder of the day, Troopers Agnew and White brought more papers for him to sign; papers which, once again, he claimed not to have read, stating that he was completely worn in body and spirit. He said he had signed them with mixed emotions, reluctantly, and yet willingly; his only purpose in so doing, to speed the time of his release from imprisonment in order that he be allowed to return home to his family whom he dearly loved.

About five o'clock that afternoon, Trooper Kelly read him a warrant calling for his arrest. Taken to the library, in the presence of Colonel Lindbergh, Colonel Schwarzkopf, Colonel Breckinridge, Prosecutor Hauck, and before magistrate George Webster, he waived the official reading of the charges in the complaint. Bail was set at $10,000. Broken in spirit, Curtis registered a complaint as to the amount of bail. The state police superintendent informed him that the attorney general's office had wanted it to be set at $50,000, but that he, Schwarzkopf, had insisted it be the lower amount. Two troopers escorted him out into the open courtyard where a car awaited them. He was driven directly to a jail cell in Flemington.

The emotions and temperament of the public were hostile toward Curtis, and rightly so. Stories which had been appearing in all newspapers were filled with prejudice aimed at the Norfolk boatbuilder and his allies, who had knowingly mislead and deceived a sorrowing mother and father. Citizens everywhere could find no room for forgiveness of such an outrageous series of lies. Lies they believed had been deliberately fabricated in order to lead America's favorite son and his family on nothing more than a "wild goose chase", when the evidence at hand "proved" that the child had been dead during that entire period of time.

But the attitudes of Dean Dobson-Peacock and Admiral Burrage were ones of complete dismay. They first refused to accept the fact that they also had been duped by their friend Curtis. But the press badgered them for statements, and at times the men seemed to vent their feelings toward one another. Dobson-Peacock replied quite sharply when he was accused of using Curtis' ruse as a publicity stunt for himself, and that it was he whom Curtis was now accusing as the one who insisted on keeping the "publicity going" while Burrage and Curtis wanted to call a halt to the negotiations at the time the Condon payment became known by the public.

Regardless of the mild disagreements, charges, and counter-charges made by the dean, Admiral Burrage very calmly professed his complete innocence of any wrong-doing, refusing to make any other statement.

Of the three gentlemen from Virginia, Curtis was the only one to be arrested, charged with the crime of "having knowingly and willfully given false and untrue reports of the person or persons guilty of the crimes of kidnapping and murder, for the purpose of hindering the apprehension of those persons."

The only blame, which possibly could be placed at the feet of Peacock and Burrage, was in finding they had "placed too much faith in Curtis, by accepting his incredulous tale with too much enthusiasm."

With the discovery of the body identified as that of the Lindbergh baby, the intensity of the police investigation to apprehend his kidnappers, had now been increased with the order to now apprehend his killers. During the early morning hours of Friday, May 13th, the day following the gruesome discovery, the nations Chief Executive, President Herbert Clark Hoover issued the following statement:

> "I have directed the law-enforcement agencies and the several Secret Services of the Federal Government to make the kidnapping and murder of the Lindbergh baby a live and never-to-be-forgotten case, never to be relaxed until the criminals are implacably brought to justice. The Federal Government does not have police authority in such cases, but its agencies will be unceasingly alert to assist the New Jersey police in every possible way until this end has been accomplished."

In his directive, President Hoover had been all-inclusive in his demand that the agencies, under the command of the Attorney General of the United States, were to be the Division of Investigation (later to be known as the Federal Bureau of Investigation, the FBI) of the Department of Justice; the Secret Service of the United States Treasury; the United States Coast Guard (both the espionage and police arms); the Bureau of Internal Revenue; the Postal Inspection Service; the Intelligence Unit of the Bureau of Internal Revenue; the Bureau of Narcotics; the Bureau of Customs; and the

Bureau of Prohibition.

To prevent any confusion among so many investigative agencies, President Hoover's attorney general had ordered the various departments to be available to the New Jersey State Police, all to be coordinated, as found to be needed, under the direction of John Edgar Hoover, chief of the Justice Department's Division of Investigation. But, although fear of jeopardizing the safety of the baby had now been removed, the federal forces realized a reluctance on the part of the state police to allow them to share in the progress the state authorities had already made.

The New York City police also found it difficult to examine the existing clues, the physical evidence, and statements already gathered by Schwarzkopf's men. By this time, the State Police were making it very evident that if anyone was going to solve this baffling crime, it would definitely be the blue clad gendarmes from the state of New Jersey.

In spite of this, the Internal Revenue Bureau was one department of the federal government that took an active role early in the investigation. Frank Wilson, the bureau's chief, had the assistance of two very capable special agents, Arthur Madden and Pat O'Rourke. The special agents in the Justice Departments Division of Investigation were headed up by Thomas H. Sisk. In New York City, a detective division with 23 of the city's finest, was directed by Lieutenant James J. Finn, a friend of Colonel Lindbergh.

A giant task lay before them --- to apprehend the diabolical fiends who had stolen and killed an innocent little baby. The public's cry for blood could not be pacified.

The police had apparently done all they could do, in spite of the clues left behind by the criminals. The personal interviews with persons living a reasonable distance from the Lindbergh home had netted them nothing. Except for the information given them by Ben Lupica, the young Princeton student, no one had seen any strangers in the vicinity. The checking and re-checking of Condon's statements were filed for future use, if and when they were needed. The escapades of Curtis were completely discounted as being nothing more than those of "a psychopathic nut".

However, since the payment of the ransom by Condon, there appeared new clues, which, if followed properly, just might lead them directly to the kidnappers. As early as Monday, April 4th, one of the bills had been found in a deposit made in a branch bank of the East River Savings Bank, 96th Street and Amsterdam Avenue. A twenty-dollar note had turned up in the deposit of a David Marcus. When advised of this, Marcus, although unable to give the police any explanation as to where he had acquired the money, was quickly absolved of any suspicion in the kidnapping. Not many of the ransom bills turned up quite that soon, although a trickle of largely five and ten dollar notes, did appear in various locations. But, every attempt to trace the passers was unsuccessful.

From the outset of the investigation, the police had formed an undisputed opinion that the kidnapping could not have been pulled off with such perfection without the aid of someone on the inside. They reasoned further that the someone was, at least one member, of either the household help of the Lindberghs or the Morrows, or possibly both. This necessitated more than just a sketchy inquiry, but a close scrutiny of the lives, habits and actions of, not only Betty Gow and Oliver and Elsie Whateley in the Lindbergh employ, but the 29 other men and women who served in the Morrow household in Englewood.

Among those at Englewood was a young English girl who had faithfully served as one of the Morrow maids for the past two years. She was known to be a sober, industrious, willing, and loyal employee. She was a vivacious, jolly person who enjoyed having good times. She was endowed with bright twinkling dark eyes, brown hair, and a well-rounded figure. Her name was Violet Sharpe.

The 27 year old Violet had been hired by the Morrow's head butler, Septimus Banks, a man with whom she became enamored soon after her employment began. Banks evidently liked what he saw in her, since her credentials were rather sparse, telling him she had lived at the YMCA in New York City and had come to the United States from Tufts Clump, Bradfield, England. As for her previous employment, she said she had worked in Toronto, Canada for six months prior to her arrival in New York. Here she visited her sister Emily, employed as a maid in the home of Miss Elizabeth Chilton, who with Miss Elizabeth Morrow, Mrs. Lindbergh's sister, was co-owner of a school for children.

Aware that the Morrow home in Englewood was in need of a maid, Emily suggested that Violet seek employment there. This she did, and was quickly hired by the very dignified and reserved Mr. Septimus Banks at a salary of one hundred dollars a month. The "butler's butler" had evidently wilted at his first glimpse of the fun-loving Miss Violet Sharpe.

During the course of the methodical inquiry of the servants, it soon became Violet's turn to answer some questions. The police approached her for the first time on Thursday, March 10th, by having her accompany them to the Hopewell home in a State Police car, in order that she be interrogated there. Minutes after she left Englewood, a special group of detectives conducted, without her knowledge, a thorough search of her room in the servants quarters of the Morrow home.

In the course of their search, the detectives found nothing they deemed to be of any importance. Small items, for the most part, were found. Among them were the names and addresses of apparently a few of her friends, six business cards of a White Plains, New York cab service, called the Post Road Taxi Company, some books which included two which revealed her apparent love of mysteries and the macabre, "Murder on Broadway" and "The World's Best detective Stories", some letters from her parents who lived in a small village in Beenham, England, and a bankbook which listed her savings as $1,600, a substantial amount for a girl to have saved in such a comparatively short time. During that period she had managed to mail some of her earnings to her parents each month. Her ability to do this is understandable when we take into consideration that her living expenses were probably very low since she lived at the Morrows and had no rent to pay.

Among the other insignificant findings, the detectives located a hand written note, one Violet had penned to herself: "Banks promises to try and be straight for twelve months.", a note that baffled the police, since they had found nothing in their investigation of the Morrow butler which would mar his impeccable character. In their questioning of Banks they had learned of his occasional visits to speakeasies, the illegal drinking dens of those who enjoyed to take a "forbidden nip" during the years of prohibition. But this, the police reasoned, was hardly a vice that would prompt the young lady to phrase her note "try and be straight." Why, they asked themselves, didn't she just say that he promised to try to stop drinking?

At Hopewell, Violet Sharpe proved to be very belligerent and unresponsive to most of the questions the police asked her. She was evasive regarding her personal affairs, informing them that they were her business and "none of theirs". Nearing the end of an exhaustive and rather lengthy session, they begged her to be more cooperative and give them some answers as to her whereabouts on the afternoon and evening of Tuesday, March 1st. Explaining that it was for her own good that she answer, she reluctantly gave some response to what she termed their "nosey inquisitiveness".

Violet explained that Mrs. Lindbergh had telephoned from Hopewell at approximately eleven-thirty that morning, and that she had been the person who had received the call. Mrs. Lindbergh informed her she wished to speak with Betty, whom she summoned to the phone. Violet said the nursemaid told her the reason for the call was a request that she come to Hopewell that afternoon and aid in the caring of the baby.

She continued to tell the police that the remainder of the afternoon and early evening had been spent at Next Day Hill performing her normal duties as a housemaid. At about quarter to eight that evening she received a telephone call from a new male acquaintance she had made the previous Sunday, having met him while she was out for a walk with her sister on Lydecker Street. The call, she explained, was an invitation to see a movie with him, one she readily accepted, informing him that she would be ready when he called for her at eight-thirty.

According to the police, Violet Sharpe told the following details of the evenings events in a very precise manner. She said at exactly eight-thirty she met her friend at the pantry door and walked a distance with him down the back driveway to where his car was parked. Waiting in it were a young man and his young female companion, to whom she was properly introduced. She claimed their one and only stop had been at the Englewood Theater where they saw a movie, and then immediately, she emphasized, they had gone directly back to the Morrow mansion. She said it was a few minutes before eleven when she bid goodnight to her friend outside the servants' entrance.

The police continued to press her for more information, particularly about her date, but drew a blank. She claimed she had not seen him since that night, and furthermore she could not remember his name. Nor could she recall the names of the young couple who had shared the evening with her. She was asked the name of the movie they had seen, her response being "I can't remember." Who were the actors in the film?, the police inquired, with the results being the same: "I don't remember." Asked what the picture had been about, brought the same negative response: "I really don't remember." Violet Sharpe finally admitted that she could not remember one thing about the movie she firmly claimed she had seen the night of Tuesday, March 1st.

Violet, however, was quite responsive in answering their questions pertaining to where and when she first had become acquainted with the man, "whose name I can't remember." She again told her questioners, she had met him while she was out for a walk on Sunday, February 28th, two days before the kidnapping. Strangely enough, her memory seemed adequate to clearly recall the time and place of their first meeting --- and nothing more.

We must take into consideration the fact that Violet Sharpe had been officially questioned for the first time, nine days after the abduction, and 11 days after her first meeting with her mysterious date, and "could not remember anything". This certainly and naturally, by her own evasiveness and deceitfulness, caused her to be elevated to the top of the list as one of the prime suspects in the case. Can there be any question as to why the police slated her for another interrogation at a later date?

But the police were kept busy with other details of the case and were not able to return to the task of questioning Violet again until Wednesday, April 13th. This time they had planned to conduct a more intense line of interrogation by Inspector Walsh. It was to take place in the Morrow homestead, since the inspector believed Violet might be more inclined to answer his questions in an atmosphere she was accustomed to.

By this time, the girl's memory seemed to have improved. She said she was mistaken, and that the reason she could not remember the name of the movie was because they simply had not gone to the theater, but had instead gone to a roadhouse, known as the Peanut Grill in Orangeburg, New York, about a half hour drive from Englewood. She said she thought her friends name was Ernie, but then she "couldn't be sure." She still could not remember the names of the other couple.

Inspector Walsh expressed surprise, telling her he could not imagine a respectable girl such as she would frequent a roadhouse with three people who were practically strangers to her. Hearing this, she became highly indignant, insisting she had only coffee while the other three drank beer. She claimed she had two witnesses who would vouch for the time she had returned to the Morrow home that night. One was the night watchman, George Marshall, who opened the gate for her, and the other was Marguerite Junge, another of the Morrow domestic help, who Violet said entered the home shortly after her, and with whom she conversed with for awhile. She said it was soon after this that the telephone rang. Violet claimed she answered it and called Mrs. Morrow. This was the call which brought the news of the baby's kidnapping to those of the household of Next Day Hill.

Walsh continued to probe for more details about this so-called Ernie, and the other two people she told them she had spent the evening with, but the investigator was to learn little more. She told him she thought Ernie was tall and guessed his age to be about 23; he had blond hair and a fair complexion. He was dressed in a navy-blue suit, a dark gray overcoat and a gray hat "as well as I can remember", she went on to say.

When asked to describe the couple who rode in the back seat, she offered nothing much they could claim was helpful to them. The man was about the same age as Ernie, also fair haired, but somewhat shorter. He was wearing a gray overcoat and a soft gray hat. She told them the girl appeared to be in her early twenties, and was dressed in a navy-blue suit and black patent leather pumps. She said, on the top of her head was "perched" a tiny black tam-o-shanter hat. Violet remarked that she was a rather pretty girl, dark complexioned, of medium height and a good build. As for the car, she recollected it was dark green, but could not remember, if she had even noticed, whether it bore New Jersey or New York license plates.

Violet volunteered the information that none of them seemed to speak with any trace of an accent; all seeming, in her estimation, to be Americans. When asked if any mention had been made of the Lindbergh baby by any of them, she affirmed that there had been. "Yes, the girl asked me, 'How is Lindy's baby?', and all I told her was that he was a cute little fellow," was Violet's explanation.

Not at all satisfied with the answers this sometimes brash person had given him, Walsh decided she would have to be questioned again at another time. Several of her answers to important questions bothered him. Before he, in any way, could rationalize her actions, she would have to come up with far better reasons and, more importantly, honest answers.

Why, he asked himself, would this servant girl, an employee in the home of the distinguished Morrow family over a span of two years, and who, according to the other servants, was seriously considering marriage with the "very proper butler" Septimus Banks, suddenly take up with a perfect stranger, and in the eyes of many, become nothing more than an easy pick-up off the street? In doing this she had seriously risked the alienation of affections of Mr. Banks. Inspector Walsh was correct. Something was very much amiss in Violet Sharpe's story.

Another event for Walsh to ponder over, was the sudden action of Violet's sister Emily. On Wednesday, April 6th, she departed for her homeland, England, only four days after Dr. Condon had turned over the ransom money to Cemetery John. Emily had sailed without so much as hinting it to the authorities. To the very talented Walsh, this seemed to be more than just a coincidence. Yes, the inspector had many more questions for Miss Violet Sharpe.

But another obstacle was to stand in the way of arranging a repeat session with the evasive Violet, whose blatant lies had marked her as the investigator's chief target as the one person whose testimony would eventually help them break the case. Having been advised by the Morrow physician that she must enter Englewood Hospital for the removal of diseased tonsils and adenoids, Violet chose the date of Wednesday, May 11th as the proper time for the surgery to be performed. A few of the police voiced their opinion that she had chosen the date intentionally to avoid further interrogation.

Mrs. Morrow, upon learning of the disbelief the police held for her maid's answers, came to Violet's defense and informed them that she strongly believed their suspicion of her was unfounded. She went on to tell them that Violet, in every way, had proven to be a loyal servant whose reputation was excellent. She went so far as to make the point that, had Violet divulged any information about the routine of the Lindbergh's living habits, things which could have been used advantageously by the kidnappers, it had been done unwittingly. Mrs. Morrow was adamant in proclaiming her maid's innocence.

But Violet could not avoid the next session of questioning indefinitely. Having recuperated from her recent surgery, she now faced another session with the authorities in the Morrow home. Inspector Walsh requested that in addition to him, Colonel Schwarzkopf, and Lieutenant Keaten, that Colonel Lindbergh also be present for her interrogation. And so, on the evening of Monday, May 23rd, in the Morrow library, their third meeting with Miss Sharpe began.

From the very beginning it became very apparent that the Morrow maid was once again withholding information. Without a doubt, they all agreed that she could tell them some valuable facts if she chose to do so. As a matter of record, they were all convinced she was out-and-out lying.

Lieutenant Walsh, the ever alert inquisitor, was sharply critical of many of her answers. "Why" he asked, "did you tell us one story when we talked to you on March 10th and a completely different one on April 13th? Which one do you expect us to believe?" Stating that her true story was the second one she had told, and that the reason for her two versions was prompted by her being so nervous. She said that later she had thought more clearly about the things the foursome had done, and that her last version was absolutely the truth.

Walsh continued to probe for more "truths" from the evasive girl, questioning her about those she was with that night. When she claimed there was nothing more she knew about them, he inquired as to whether it was a habit of hers to be picked up by men she didn't know. And once again came her indignant retort: "Of course not!" Continuing his relentless line of questioning, he closed in with a question that he believed would break down one of the maid's strongest statements.

Violet evidently seemed convinced that the police had accepted her story that her friend Ernie telephoned her at the Morrow residence about 7:45 on the evening of March 1st. But Walsh had other knowledge of this important call. Again he had her reiterate the time as being about quarter to eight. As she reaffirmed this once more, Walsh broke in for the kill. "Isn't it a fact, Miss Sharpe, that Ernie telephoned you at one o'clock that afternoon? You talked with him just an hour and a half after you learned, at eleven-thirty that morning, that Mrs. Lindbergh's baby was going to remain in his Hopewell home that night, isn't that correct?" the clever inspector demanded, awaiting her reply, one he felt she might possibly still attempt to deny.

But, he did not have long to wait. Violet shifted slightly in her chair, looked down at her hands that remained clasped in her lap. She appeared defeated. She, at least for the moment, had lost her arrogance. She flushed as she raised her head, ever so slightly.

The four men stared at her, awaiting an answer. But, no audible reply was to be heard. Violet Sharpe could only nod her head in agreement. Violet Sharpe had blatantly lied to them about a very important issue in the Lindbergh case.

Having developed this successful break, through Violet's submission to finally admit to this truth, and the belief that it had been she who had informed Ernie of the Lindbergh's change in plans to remain at Hopewell that Tuesday night, the police intensified their search for the mysterious Ernie and his two unknown companions. With the coming of Thursday, June 9th they were no nearer locating them than they were the first time they had been told the man's name was Ernie. It was high time, Inspector Walsh decided, to pay Violet another visit. And this he did at eleven o'clock that morning.

Laura Hughes, Mrs. Morrow's secretary, had been assigned to take notes of Violet's story, as she once more was asked to go over it, relating all the facts, from beginning to end. Walsh was certain she had more to tell. Listening intently as Violet went through her account, by now a very familiar dissertation to him, the inspector noticed that she was extremely nervous and was obviously upset that her friend, Laura, was taking note of each word as she spoke. As she continued on, she appeared to be progressively unsure of herself. At those times when she appeared to be hesitant in giving an answer, Walsh took advantage of the delays, claiming that her failures to respond were only feeble attempts to hide her own guilt in the crime by her inclination not to answer.

Suddenly Walsh reached into his pocket and removed a photograph, asking her if this were a picture of Ernie. She stared at the police Rogues' gallery photo a moment and responded: "Yes, yes, that's the man." When the inspector inquired why she had failed to tell him who Ernie was before this, she vehemently denied, stating she had never known. And with this, Walsh snapped back: "Oh, yes you did. We found his business cards among your personal effects."

"I did not know who he was!", the terrified Violet screamed. Saying that he refused to argue with her about the veracity of her statement, Walsh continued to plod forward with his questions. "One more time, all I want to know is; is this or is it not the man you were with that night?", he continued on with his rapid-fire questioning. Emotionally upset, at a point of near hysteria, Violet screamed in a shrill piercing voice,

"Yes, it is! Yes, it is!" and then broke down with uncontrollable sobs.

The Morrow's personal physician was summoned and after his examination of Violet, he respectfully asked Inspector Walsh if he would defer his further questioning of the, by now semi- hysterical young lady, until another time. Informing her he would return the next day and take her to his office in the State Police Headquarters at Alpine, the interrogation came to an end.

Laura Hughes reported an interesting segment of information relative to what took place as the conference adjourned. Mrs. Morrow's trusted secretary claimed that as the distraught Violet was being led from the room, and passed the desk where Miss Hughes looked at the pathetic figure of the young maid with eyes of sympathy, much to her amazement, though appearing to be mentally and physically exhausted; --- the weary and worn Miss Sharpe was seen to smile and wink at her.

Nevertheless, the night of June 9th proved to be a nightmare to the greatly troubled Morrow maid. Her mind ceaselessly entertained the agonizing thoughts of having to face another session of questioning the following day. Her fear of this seemed to intensify, and as the hours passed on she became paranoid about her problem. She had informed her friends in the servants quarters with vehement declarations such as: "They'll never take me from this house again! They'll never question me again!"

Friday, June 10th, had been set aside by Inspector Walsh as his day of victory. This was the day he planned to question Violet in the State Police barracks at Alpine. After arranging for a doctor to be present to check the condition of her health, and to be available should she again become hysterical due to her extreme fear of being questioned, he proceeded with his plans to bring her to Alpine.

At ten o'clock that morning he telephoned the Morrow mansion. Finding neither Mrs. Morrow, nor the Lindberghs (who had temporarily moved back with Anne's mother in her Englewood home) there, he asked to speak with Arthur Springer, secretary to the late Dwight Morrow, who had continued on as Mrs. Morrow's personal secretary. The inspector informed Springer that he wished to question Miss Sharpe in his office at Alpine and that Lieutenant Keaten would soon be in Englewood to drive her there. He asked that Violet be informed of this and that she be ready to make the trip when Keaten arrived.

Using the house phone to notify Violet, who was in the servants hall, Springer passed on to her the instructions he had received, asking her to willingly comply with the inspector's request. Terrified at the news, Violet did not answer him. She slammed the receiver back in its cradle and ran to her lover, Septimus Banks, shouting hysterically: "Walsh wants to question me again, he wants to take me to Alpine, but I won't go! I won't go! I won't go!"

The butler attempted to calm her fears. He gripped her hand trying to comfort her and reassure her that there was absolutely nothing for her to be afraid of. But she slipped away and ran past him into the pantry. She grabbed a large measuring glass from a shelf and hurried up the stairs to her bedroom. She went over to her wardrobe closet and removed a tall six-inch tin can she had securely hidden. On a strip of yellow paper that had been glued around it were the heavily penciled words of warning. It read: Poison. Do not unpack.

She lost no time as she ripped off the warning strip. Her nervousness caused a fine trickle of the glittering powder to spill out on her clothes, the closet and floor. Hurrying to the bathroom and, without bothering to measure, she poured an ample supply of the sparkling crystals from the can into a glass, spilling much of it onto the washbasin's white surface. Turning one of the spigots, she filled the measuring glass with enough water to dissolve the crystals. She rushed back into her room, placing the can on a table. Raising the glass, loaded with lethal poison to her mouth, she drained its contents.

Violet, noticing that some of the undissolved crystals still clung to the bottom and side of the glass, was already aware that enough of them were now inside her. She quietly placed the glass on the table next to the can from which she had poured the fatal crystals and slowly descended the stairs to the pantry where Emily Kempairien, a chambermaid, was attending to some household duties, all the time unaware of the tragic event that had taken place upstairs.

Violet staggered in and made an attempt to speak, but her words were unintelligible and incoherent. She swayed to one side and fell at Emily Kempairien's feet. Horrified at the appearance of the person before her, the chambermaid shrieked for help. Banks came rushing into the pantry and attempted to revive his close friend and fiance, but everything he did proved unsuccessful. Anne's brother, Dwight Morrow, Jr. came and leaned over the still form. Realizing the gravity of the situation, he immediately ran to the house intercom and asked Springer to notify a doctor to come at once, and to inform the police of the shocking event.

Banks and the others present carried Violet back to her room where they laid her on the bed, tearfully awaiting the arrival of a doctor and Charles A. Peterson, Englewood's police chief.

Eventually the doctor arrived --- but much too late.

As a result of drinking a lethal dose of cyanide of potassium crystals, Violet Sharpe was dead! And in her passing she had taken with her many answers to questions the police sorely needed to successfully solve the mysterious Lindbergh kidnapping.

CHAPTER FIFTEEN

Aftermath of Sudden Death!

The tragic suicide of Violet Sharpe brought sudden reactions from, not only citizens of the United States, but from people around the world. Severe criticism by Great Britain was leveled at the New Jersey State Police through many newspaper accounts accusing the police officials of using "third degree brutality" and "merciless grilling methods" in their questioning of the "young English lass." A prime example was that of the *London Daily Herald* in a stinging account that accused the Jersey police of "venting their chagrin at their failure in the Lindbergh case on a poor English servant girl." Another instance of England's feelings was displayed by *The Telegraph*, whose vicious headline called it "A DISGRACE TO AMERICAN JUSTICE". But, there were many of the American papers that followed the same pattern with boldface headlines such as: "PUNISH COPS WHO DROVE MORROW MAID TO DEATH!" There were those who made unfair accusations claiming Violet Sharpe had been tortured. However, headlines, stories, and editorials, such as these, were all terribly unfair. They were nothing more than thoughtless allegations against the police, those authorities who, in spite of their occasional mistakes and irregularities, were doing all they could, regardless of obstacles being thrust in their way, by attempting, as best and as soon as they could, to successfully solve the "crime of the century."

To be frank, the police were growing extremely embarrassed and edgy at the accusations at nearly every turn, relative to their failure to come up with a solution of the case, one that was now almost four months old. The public was constantly making slurring and snide remarks at the inability of the authorities to solve the crime.

With Violet gone, and no longer available for future questioning, the police could do nothing more than review the facts they had learned from her previous interrogations. One outstanding thing, above everything else, was that of her unusual character and temperament;

two of the first things a detective makes note of in a person under surveillance as a suspect in a crime.

From their very first interview with the pretty English maid, she had proven to be very uncooperative. Her attitude had been puzzling to them, to say the least. She immediately had taken the defensive. She had been brash, smug, flippant, evasive, disrespectful, and defiant. During the course of their interrogations, as each session continued, although she had at no time been threatened or badgered, they had seen her attitude change from that of being lighthearted, to becoming sullen, fearful, morose, nervous, and hysterical.

It had been determined early that Miss Sharpe was withholding valuable information about some knowledge she had of the kidnapping. And, it was for that reason only that she had been subjected to four police inquisitions, with implicit orders that she be brought to the Alpine barracks on June 10th for her fifth session with them. Unfortunately, however, the meeting on this date was never held.

With all of the accusations being directed at the police, they refused to remain silent by issuing statements in answer to their accuser's unfair assertions. Colonel H. Norman Schwarzkopf gave the newspapers and radio the following statement for publication and broadcast:

> "VIOLET SHARPE HAS BEEN IN CONSTANT SUSPICION GIVING CONFLICTING STATEMENTS IN A HIGHLY NERVOUS CONDITION. THE SUICIDE OF VIOLET SHARPE STRONGLY TENDS TO CONFIRM THE SUSPICION OF THE INVESTIGATING AUTHORITIES CONCERNING HER GUILTY KNOWLEDGE OF THE CRIME AGAINST CHARLES A.LINDBERGH, JR."

Confirming Schwarzkopf's statement was one by Inspector Harry Walsh, who had personally conducted the interrogation sessions with Violet. Pertaining to the accusations made against him and his allies, he had this to say: "There is no basis for such criticism. She was always treated gently, never roughly. We pleaded with her to help us." Walsh went on to point out the things that confronted the police due to Violet's evasive answers and uncooperative spirit as:

> "1) VIOLET HAD TOLD THE POLICE CONFLICTING STORIES CONCERNING HER MOVEMENTS ON THE NIGHT OF MARCH 1.

2) VIOLET HAD PERSISTENTLY REFUSED TO REVEAL THE IDENTITY OF HER ESCORT ON THE NIGHT OF MARCH 1."

And the inspector went on to say:

"NO ONE CAN DENY THAT AFTER THE DISCOVERY OF THE LINDBERGH BABY'S BODY, VIOLET HAD CHANGED FROM A CHEERFUL, CONFIDENT YOUNG WOMAN TO A MOROSE SHADOW OF HERSELF.

"WHY?" the inspector asked, "IT SEEMED OBVIOUS THAT HER CONSCIENCE WAS TORTURING HER. UNTIL THE CHILD'S BODY WAS FOUND, SHE HAD TAKEN IT FOR GRANTED THAT THE KIDNAPPERS WOULD RETURN HIM TO HIS PARENTS, THAT SHE WOULD BE GIVEN HER SHARE OF THE RANSOM MONEY AND THAT NO ONE WOULD EVER BE THE WISER."

"THE BABY'S DEATH HAD SHAKEN HER; THEN SHE SAW THAT THE CASE AGAINST HER WAS GRADUALLY PUSHING HER INTO A CORNER FROM WHICH THERE WOULD BE NO ESCAPE.", and so, Inspector Walsh concluded:

"SHE HAD TAKEN THE ONLY WAY OUT --- TAKEN IT JUST BEFORE SHE WAS TO BE QUESTIONED AGAIN, WHEN HER GUILT WOULD HAVE BEEN EXPOSED --- THE GIRL'S SUICIDE WAS AN ADMISSION OF GUILT. AN INNOCENT GIRL WOULD NOT KILL HERSELF."

This frank conclusion of Inspector Walsh was not exclusively his. It was shared (during those years) by all of the police officials who were actively engaged with the gigantic task of solving the horrible crime. The citizens of that day were easily convinced of her involvement. However, it is interesting to note that an apparent naive attitude, coupled with extreme loyalty to one of her servants, prompted the elderly Mrs. Dwight Morrow, concerning the suicide of her maid, to tell reporters she was sure: "Violet had simply been frightened to death."

The charge of police brutality being employed in the questioning of Violet was investigated by the British Consulate; but the accusations were found to be of no significance. A statement issued by His Majesty's acting consul-general, Edward H. Gerald Shepherd in New York, claimed they were entirely satisfied that the charges were groundless and that Miss Sharpe had not been treated unjustly in any way. Finally, the New Jersey police were absolved of any wrong doing.

Nevertheless, Harry Walsh, a man confident of his convictions, made another incriminating statement of his feelings regarding Violet's guilt in the case:

"I AM CONVINCED THAT VIOLET SHARPE DECEIVED US, AND THAT SHE DID SO DELIBERATELY. I AM CONVINCED THAT SHE WAS THE INFORMANT ---- THE AGENT --- OF THE KIDNAPPERS. I BELIEVE SHE COMMITTED SUICIDE IN PANIC, FEARING HER GUILT HAD BEEN DISCOVERED, OR OVERBURDENED WITH HER GUILTY KNOWLEDGE AFTER NEWS OF THE BABY'S DEATH."

When, on June 9th, Violet identified the Rogues' gallery picture as that of the man with whom she had spent the evening of March 1st, the police at once put out an all-state alarm for the arrest of one, Ernest Brinkert. The card bearing that name stated Brinkert had a record of petty larceny with three previous arrests. And while the police drag-net for this Ernie was set in motion, the police had Doctor Condon come to the White Plains headquarters, hoping he could identify the picture on the card as the man to whom he had paid the ransom. But Condon, after studying the picture, could only shake his head and say: "It looks something like the man, but this picture is too light to tell. I can't be sure."

The authorities, however, did not have long to wait for the apprehension of Ernest Brinkert, and their right to question him. Ten hours after the issuance of the bulletin calling for his arrest, Brinkert turned himself in. The date was Friday afternoon, June 10th, just hours after Violet had taken her life.

The man immediately found himself under intense police interrogation, as he relentlessly and firmly held on to his alibi. He said the true account of his movements on that Tuesday night would be supported by his wife. The couple, he told them, had spent that evening at the home of his friend, Frank Page in Bridgeport, Connecticut, and that they had enjoyed the entire evening playing cards. He claimed he knew nothing at all about the Lindbergh case except the daily accounts he had been reading in the newspapers.

Brinkert was then removed to the New Rochelle Police Department where he underwent intensive questioning until four o'clock the next morning. Ernie claimed he could verify his whereabouts that night and that furthermore: "I never knew Violet Sharpe, I never knew Violet Sharpe, and for that matter, that goes for her sister, too!", he emphatically denied any involvement with them. Hoping to have been able by this time to tie Ernie Brinkert with Violet Sharpe, the police realized they had failed miserably. Disappointed, they transported him to their barracks at Alpine to be held there for another grilling the next day.

At six o'clock Saturday evening, after putting in a hard day of work on the case, as Inspector Walsh was leaving his office, he was approached by a man who identified himself as Ernest Miller. He told Walsh he was from Closter, New Jersey and that it was he the police were looking for, that he was the man Violet Sharpe had dated on the night of March 1st.

He gave his age as 22 years and volunteered the names of the couple who had accompanied him and the unfortunate Violet. Their names were Elmer Johnson, also of Closter; and Katherine Minners who lived in Palisades Park, New Jersey. The couple was promptly picked up, questioned, and corroborated the "new Ernie's" story, and just as promptly, were released as each one proved they had no involvement with the crime.

With this turn of events, the police now completely confident of the innocence of Ernie Brinkert, had the embarrassing responsibility of informing the press that Ernie had been released. The newspapers, already having printed their stories of Brinkert's arrest, were now forced to retract their earlier news and now relate this new development.

But, this unavoidable turn of events did not sit well with the public. Citizens everywhere were clamoring for an arrest, and now, with this apparent flub on the part of the authorities, the police were inundated with new attacks being leveled at them by an angry public. These unfair attacks, multiplied by the charges that they had used inhuman treatment in the questioning of Violet Sharpe, proved to be all the police could take without fighting back in their own defense.

Again it was Lieutenant Walsh who issued a statement regarding this latest disclosure to the representatives of the newspaper and radio, who were demanding an explanation:

"THIS IS A PECULIAR TURN OF EVENTS. IT IS NO FAULT OF OURS. I CAN'T UNDERSTAND WHY VIOLET SHARPE, IF SHE HAD NOTHING TO DO WITH THE KIDNAPPING, PREFERRED DEATH TO REVEALING MILLER'S NAME. I CANNOT UNDERSTAND IT AT ALL."

But this statement only brought on new attacks from the news media who were reporting the accusations of Violet's sister from England. Emily, upon receiving the news of Violet's suicide, spoke out in no uncertain terms, venting her feelings: "Ever since the baby disappeared, she was badgered and questioned by police until she didn't know what she was saying or doing. She was driven nearly mad. And it was all so cruel. Violet would never have done anything to the child or to anyone who wanted to find it."

Emily herself, however, was not to escape an interrogation session by the police, having brought suspicion on herself by leaving America for England as soon as the ransom was paid. Acting on the advice of Superintendent Schwarzkopf, Detective Inspector John Horwell of Scotland Yard, was assigned the task of interviewing Miss Sharpe, with the possibility of uncovering some enlightening news. Nevertheless, the only added information they were to learn from Emily was that of Violet's marital status. She was not a single woman as everyone understood her to be, but had been married two and one half years earlier in London to a man named George Payne.

Detective Inspector Horwell's report to Schwarzkopf completely cleared her of all suspicion. His report read: "I am satisfied that Emily Sharpe knows nothing about the Lindbergh case. She appears to be a girl of excellent character and has been in the best of situations." But, this was not so of her sister, Violet, as articles continued to appear in many newspapers, arguing the pros and cons of her guilt or innocence.

Violet's body had been removed to the Greenleaf morgue in Englewood, where a post-mortem was performed. Her body was then prepared for burial, a viewing being held on Tuesday, June 14th. During the late afternoon of Wednesday, she was lowered into a grave in Brookside Cemetery in Englewood with a small group of friends in attendance. The most grief stricken person was her loyal friend, Septimus Banks, who had visited the morgue each day, standing at the side of her coffin since the tragic suicide. Her grave was covered with red roses sent by His Majesty's acting consul-general, while other wreaths were sent from the Morrow family and their servants, including Betty Gow. These floral tributes would designate her burial site for many days; a grave not far from that of Anne Lindbergh's father, Dwight W. Morrow.

Ironically, the day of Violet's burial was also the day of sentencing for Gaston B. Means, the heartless fiend who had conned Evalyn Walsh McLean out of $104.000 with his home-made fantasy, that he, and he alone, would effect the return of the baby. Means' trial had opened on Wednesday, June 8th in federal court in the District of Columbia with Justice James M.Proctor presiding. Before a jury comprised of 11 men and one woman, United States attorney, Leo A. Rover, in spite of Means' strong denials of his innocence, presented convincing arguments of his guilt, and after a deliberation of only two hours, the jury returned its verdict of guilty on Monday, June 13th. Judge Proctor sentenced the embezzler on Wednesday to a term of 15 years imprisonment in the federal penitentiary at Leavenworth, Kansas. For the embezzlement of the $100,000 he received 10 years; the other five years were for the additional larceny of the $4,000.

The aftermath of the Sharpe suicide seemed to intensify the efforts of the police to solve the case just as soon as possible. The criticism for their failure to apprehend anyone after nearly four months, was understandable. The crime of the century had been committed, and they seemed to be no nearer a solution than they were during the earliest hours of their investigation. Dr. Condon was being driven from jail to jail by detectives Bob Coar and Sam Leon, as Jafsie continued to look at Rogues gallery pictures and observe men standing in police line-ups. But all to no avail.

But, the suspicion of Jafsie, and his probable involvement, did not subside. Throughout the summer months, he was subjected to intermittent inconveniences of having the police visit him at his home for additional questioning. On one occasion, the authorities, while conducting a search of his house, tore a piece of wallpaper from the wall of his study. Condon accused them of looking for the missing $50,000 ransom, saying they also had dug up the earth around the foundation of his summer shack on City Island, searching for it there. He became highly irritated, claiming they had tapped his phone line, and had tampered with his mail deliveries, delaying and checking them, before they arrived at his home.

Monday, June 27th marked the opening date of the trial of John Hughes Curtis in Flemington, New Jersey. W.L. Pender, a lawyer of Norfolk, Virginia, and friend of Curtis, had considered retaining Harry L. Stout, a veteran lawyer of the New Jersey bar, to represent the shipbuilder from Norfolk. However, C. Lloyd Fisher, a young Flemington attorney, was later selected to defend

Curtis.

It had originally been Stout's plan to have the manager of the telephone company at Trenton testify that he had seen Curtis with the man known as Larsen. Other persons whom Stout had told them would be valuable for the defense were the telephone operator at Cape May, who had received many of the calls from Hilda, as well as the taxi driver Curtis had hired to drive him to his meeting with Hilda. All these had agreed to testify on Curtis behalf.

In addition, Stout had planned to attack the State's case (based primarily on Curtis' confession), by issuing subpoenas to Betty Gow, Oliver Whateley, and possibly Colonel Lindbergh, whose testimony would attest to the fact that the Norfolk gentleman had not only been subjected to incarceration in the Lindbergh basement, but also the testimony of the servants would include their first-hand knowledge, of having witnessed on several occasions, him being a victim of police brutality.

But, this plan of the defense was not needed. Upon entering the Hunterdon County courtroom, their eyes were drawn to those at the prosecution's table. Sitting there were assistant Attorney General Joseph P. Lanigan and Prosecutor of Pleas Anthony M. Hauck, Jr., and between them, the man Fisher had trusted to help in the preparation of the case for the defendant, sat, with notes piled high in front of him, one Henry L. Stout who had taken his information to the adversary.

Realizing that the tips Stout had given them could no longer be used to advantage, they also decided not to call the witnesses they had deemed necessary. The state's case had taken a complete turn-about. The prosecution had decided to no longer present evidence that Curtis had played the role of a hoaxer, but instead were now willing to accept the fact that he had definitely been in touch with the kidnappers; and that the reason for his arrest was brought on by his refusal to reveal where they could be found. Their reasoning behind this could be clearly seen --- they agreed that Curtis was not guilty of a hoax, but instead had told them the truth.

In Hauck's opening remarks to the jury it was made crystal clear that he planned to scrap the Curtis confession. He said: "We will prove that John Hughes Curtis was actually in contact with the kidnappers, that he knew who they were and knew their whereabouts, and that he did not disclose their whereabouts to either

Colonel Lindbergh or to the authorities because there was no satisfactory arrangement with Colonel Lindbergh as to the amount of the ransom."

However, when on the witness stand, Colonel Lindbergh, when asked if he believed that Curtis was ever in touch with the actual kidnappers, shook his head and said: "I do not at this time believe that Mr.Curtis was in contact with the kidnappers. I do not believe that he ever knew who took the child or in whose possession he was."

In his cross-examination of the Colonel, when Fisher asked about the sum of $25,000 he had been asked to deposit in a Norfolk bank as a sign of his good faith, he was forced to admit that Curtis, whether his allegations were true or not, had not made one thin penny out of the entire negotiations. He also agreed that it had already been established that the Curtis contacts with the gang were definitely not a hoax.

In his charge to the jury, comprised of seven men and five women, Judge Adam O. Robbins, asked them to accept the testimony of what Curtis had told them, that he did know "THE GANG OF KIDNAPPERS, NUMBERING SEVEN OR EIGHT, WHICH INCLUDED A MEMBER OF THE LINDBERGH AND MORROW HOUSEHOLD." This was a complete reversal of what had been testified to earlier before a grand jury.

Curtis had been adamant in his testimony, particularly regarding his accusation that he had been confined under guard in the Lindbergh basement. Called to give testimony relative to this was Captain John J. Lamb of the New Jersey State Police. His questioning by Fisher follows:

Q. You swore a little at Curtis up there?

A. No, sir.

Q. Did not swear at all?

A. No, sir.

Q. Captain, as you sit in that stand, do you want to tell Court and jury that you did not swear at John Hughes Curtis while you were up at Hopewell?

A. I did not.

Q. Did you not use any foul language toward Curtis?

A. No, sir.

Q. You always treated him with the utmost courtesy?

A. Yes, sir.

Q. Captain, there is a cellar in the Lindbergh home?

A. Yes, I believe there is.

Q. Did you not give orders that John Hughes Curtis should be taken to the cellar?

A. No, sir.

Q. Do you say, Captain Lamb, that you did not give orders to the guard of John Hughes Curtis that he, John Hughes Curtis, should be taken to the cellar and put down there in the cellar?

A. No, sir.

On the face of this sworn testimony of the state police captain, one would certainly believe that the credibility of the police officer should not be questioned. The very oath he had taken when joining the force should certainly put the testimony of "this man in blue" as being above reproach.

However, the Lindbergh case had already become known as one of many questionable developments, as already evidenced in the Curtis trial. Contradictory evidence was heard in the same courtroom on that very day by another police officer. Inspector Harry Walsh was called to the stand. His testimony was:

Q. You visited him down in the cellar on one occasion, did you not?

A. Yes, sir.

Q. So that when Captain Lamb said he had never been put down there, he was mistaken?

A. I don't know.

Q. Curtis was down in the cellar of the Lindbergh house?

A. Yes, sir.

Q. You say that it was on the 18th that you saw him in the cellar?

A. Yes, sir.

Q. Was there a guard in the cellar with him?

A. There was a trooper down there; yes, sir.

Here we have the testimony of two police officers, each one giving a totally different account. The one, however gave testimony supporting what Curtis had told them, which went far to bear out the veracity of the man from Norfolk.

Judge Robbins in his charge, clearly stated: "In order to convict, you must find that John Hughes Curtis ... had contact with the kidnappers or knew their exact whereabouts."

And this, after deliberating four hours and five minutes, is exactly what the jury did. The state of New Jersey had now accepted those persons named by Curtis, and the yet to be identified member, one of the Lindbergh and Morrow household help, as being the "actual kidnappers' of Charles A. Lindbergh, Jr.

The results of this trial were almost unbelievable. John Curtis had been absolved as a "hoaxer and faker". Nor had he been convicted of "obstructing justice". He had, however, been found guilty of "honest truly" being in contact with the kidnappers, but had simply not been able, or had failed to disclose their whereabouts.

Curtis, found guilty as charged, was sentenced to one year in jail and a fine of one thousand dollars. His maximum sentence could have been a term of three years. Nevertheless, Fisher announced he was appealing the decision.

The verdict was glaring proof that, after hearing the testimony of all the state's witnesses, the judge and jury had believed the account as told by John Hughes Curtis to the point that he had actually been in contact with the kidnappers. All that now remained to be done, with the detailed description given to them by Curtis, was for the police to locate the five men and a woman, apprehend them, and bring them to justice. But, stranger things than this were to happen in the Lindbergh case. The police made no further effort to search for them. Even though there was little doubt that Olaf and Hilda were known to many people who resided in Cape May where the Larsens also lived. The authorities demonstrated no further interest in following up on the leads Curtis had given them. The court, judge and jury, believed him --- but the police simply would not. Free, after posting $10,000 bail until his appeal could be heard, Curtis returned to Flemington alone on Sunday evening, November 6th. Entering the courtroom the following morning, he evidenced a genuine feeling of warmth and friendship among the opposing attorneys as well as his own counsel. It was evident that an agreement had been reached between Curtis' lawyers and Hauck and Lanigan. Attorney Fisher asked the honorable Judge Robbins to show compassion on his client in re-sentencing him. The bench, hearing no objections from the prosecution, complied with the request as Judge Robbins stated: "This court has imposed a term of one year in jail and a fine of one thousand dollars upon this defendant. It is now within the province of this court to suspend operation of the jail sentence, which I hereby do."

A smiling Curtis paid his fine with a thousand-dollar bill, shook hands with Judge Robbins and all the attorneys, and drove back to his family in Norfolk, a free men at last. In issuing one last statement to the press who constantly badgered him, he said: "I firmly consider the action taken by the court as 'a vindication' of any wrong the authorities believe I might have done. I have paid the fine imposed in order to avoid any longer the 'uncertainties' of Jersey justice."

His close friends and associates believed in him implicitly. The Very Reverend Harold Dobson-Peacock, the publicity seeking dean, and Rear Admiral Guy Hamilton Burrage, USN retired, his "friends" through much of his search, had evidently deserted him since they failed to attend any of the trial sessions. His ill wife, mentally tortured by the accusations that had been hurled against her husband, had not been able to attend.

However, his 11 year old daughter, Constance, sat alone for two days in the courtroom listening to the world's hero, Charles A. Lindbergh, tell those in attendance that he believed her daddy had lied to him in all of their associations together. She appeared thin, pale, and withdrawn as she saw Harry Stout point to her father and shout: "There sits the most monumental liar God has ever permitted to tread this earth!" At this point she was seen to reach over and grasp her daddy's hand in childlike love and devotion.

While the chronicles of the Curtis phase of the Lindbergh case appeared to have closed, reflection should be made on the fallacy of the law in allowing an apparent injustice to be perpetrated on John Hughes Curtis. Here was a man whose only crime, a misdemeanor, had been his sincere and honest attempt to restore a stolen child to his father; unfortunately followed by his subsequent failure to do so.

Colonel Lindbergh had testified in court that, at no time, did Curtis gain anything for himself during the transactions. He further stated there had been only one time when a discussion of money was mentioned, that being when Curtis asked him to deposit $25,000 in a Norfolk bank, in trust, "as a means of showing good faith." Lindbergh also admitted that Curtis, during the negotiations, had telephoned him at Hopewell and informed him that he had a member of the gang with him who wished to meet with the Colonel. The Colonel confessed that he, on this occasion, had told Curtis "he was too busy to meet with the man." A decision he made that was unexplainable.

So, at this point, we have a case where one man is

found guilty for "honestly" negotiating with a gang of kidnappers that numbered seven or eight including a member of the Lindbergh household. For this he was fined $1,000; only to have Hauptmann charged and "proven", three years later, to have been the lone kidnapper.

On the other hand, we have the highly respected John Francis "Jafsie" Condon, the eminent doctor, who carried on negotiations with his own "gang" of kidnappers, carrying out the same type of enactments as John Hughes Curtis, and also accepted as factual.

But, in the case of Condon, we find he had also victimized Colonel Lindbergh, but in this case to the tune of paying $50,000 to a virtually unknown person, known only as "John", to have every dollar of it vanish into the thin air of St. Raymond's Cemetery in the Bronx. And for this Condon remained free, with nothing more than the honest doubts of Inspector Walsh and a few other skeptical officers to mar his otherwise spotless reputation; while Curtis, who had done much less, was made to suffer great indignities.

This gross irregularity on the actions of the police must always hang heavy in judgement of the integrity of the New Jersey authorities of that day.

CHAPTER SIXTEEN

The Wood Detective

The summer, fall, and winter months of 1932 were only the beginning of a long drought of developments in the famous kidnapping case. Nothing of major importance developed as the police continued their diligent search for ransom notes to appear. Aside from a few bills which trickled in here and there, these finds led them absolutely nowhere. Nor did their search for the man who might possibly fit the description of the person who had received the money from Doctor Condon net them any leads. The officials had been following a rather detailed sketch of the man; a drawing furnished them by the Department of Investigation, hoping it would aid the police in their pursuit of Cemetery John. But, this too had proved futile.

The Lindberghs sensed joy returning to their lives, on Tuesday, August 16th, with the birth of their second son, Jon Morrow. The healthy baby, weighing six pounds, eleven ounces, was born at Mrs. Morrow's town apartment at 4 East 66th Street, New York City. The attending physician was Dr. Everett Hawks, who had brought the ill-fated baby Charles into the world almost 26 months earlier. Assisting Dr. Hawks was Dr. Edward H. Dennen. Colonel Lindbergh made a public appeal to the press, asking that they allow his new son to grow up under the normal conditions most children enjoy. He told the news media that any undue publicity would be a disadvantage to the safety of the child, as had been the case in the life of his first son. His request received their collective promise, as they passed along their congratulations through him to Anne.

The various arms of the law, each operating without the assistance of the others, thrust forth their individual efforts to solve the case. Lieutenant James J. Finn of the New York City Police Department had erected a giant map of the city on the wall of his office. Using brightly colored map pins, he would diligently insert a pin at the location where every ransom bill was discovered. As the bills were spasmodically reported throughout the various sections of the city, and after checking on the validity of the find, Finn or one of his assistants would place another pin on the map.

Frank Wilson of the Treasury Department had previously issued an order to have 250,000 copies (57 pages) printed and circulated listing the serial numbers of each bill, but this proved to be of insufficient help. The lists were cumbersome, the type too small, the pages too bulky and awkward to wade through as each business transaction was made. Because of this very few bills were found. However, Lieutenant Finn devised a better plan. He ordered his detectives to make daily rounds of all banks. By taking this action, the bank tellers were alerted, becoming more diligent in checking for ransom money. Finn's men were aided in this venture by federal agents, and also Colonel Lindbergh, who offered a two-dollar reward to every person who found a ransom bill and turned it over to the officials. The task of finding the money was not an easy one. A large proportion of the bills passed in most transactions were of five and ten dollar denominations, many of them going unnoticed because of their lower value.

On Sunday, March 13th, during the early days of the investigation, Doctor Erastus Mead Hudson was ushered through the front door of the Lindbergh residence by Oliver Whateley. The eminent doctor had been invited to enter the investigation by James F. Minturn, a former justice of the New Jersey Supreme Court. Judge Minturn, aware of Dr. Hudson's scientific development of his silver-nitrate method of raising latent fingerprints (known as the "Hudson Process"), held great confidence that he would have success in developing prints where others had failed. His belief of this proved correct.

Dr. Hudson, in the presence of the Lindberghs, Mrs. Morrow, Colonels Schwarzkopf and Breckinridge, Frank Kelly and other state troopers, succeeded in raising clear prints of the baby's fingers and palms from various furnishings in the home that had been touched by the child. These prints, after being sprayed with silver nitrate were lifted from the high chair, books, toys and other things the baby had been accustomed to playing with. The prints were then permanently preserved by pouring shellac over the surface on which they appeared.

To this time, a set of either the fingerprints or toe prints of the baby was nonexistent due to his being born at the Englewood home of the Morrows, instead of a hospital, where the inking a newborn's toes was becoming a practice. The absence of any portion of the child's fingerprints, before Dr. Hudson's experiment, is undeniable.

Finishing his work, Dr. Hudson was completely satisfied that the authorities now possessed a set of the fingerprints of the missing child. The elated doctor announced that they have "FINGERPRINTS THAT STOOD OUT AS HARD AND SHARP IN CONTOUR AS THOUGH THEY HAD BEEN ENGRAVED IN STEEL." With great emphasis Dr. Hudson stated further: "WE NOW HAVE FINGERPRINTS TO IDENTIFY OR DISQUALIFY WITHOUT DISPUTE ANY 'LIVING LINDBERGH BABY' THAT MIGHT BE PRESENTED IN THE FUTURE."

Upon inquiry as to why Trooper Kelly had not been able to lift any prints from the furnishings in the nursery despite the greasy substance Mrs. Lindbergh and Betty had used when they rubbed the baby's chest, the doctor explained in these exact words: "NO PRINTS WERE FOUND, ALTHOUGH BETTY GOW, THE CHILD'S NURSE, AND MRS. LINDBERGH HAD OPENED AND CLOSED THE WINDOW THAT SAME NIGHT. MISS GOW HAD RUBBED THE CHILD'S CHEST WITH AN OINTMENT THE OLEAGINOUS BASE OF WHICH WOULD HAVE AUGMENTED THE SECRETION OF THE FINGER RIDGES IN LEAVING CLEAR PRINTS. OF COURSE THERE WOULD HAVE BEEN OLDER PRINTS AS WELL. THE REASON KELLY FAILED TO GET ALL THESE PRINTS WAS BECAUSE THEY MUST HAVE BEEN WASHED OFF. SOME ONE WITH A PAIL OF WATER AND CLOTH UNDOUBTEDLY BATHED THOSE SPOTS WHERE FINGERPRINTS MUST HAVE BEEN LEFT. THEY DID SO BETWEEN THE TIME BETTY GOW PUT THE BABY TO BED AND ABOUT FOUR HOURS LATER, WHEN KELLY BEGAN INVESTIGATING."

Doctor Hudson, a criminal investigator with a sharp mind, went on to explain his further feelings about the case: "IT IS LUDICROUS TO SUPPOSE THAT THE KIDNAPPER CLIMBED THE LADDER WITH THE PAIL AND RAG AND DESCENDED WITH THIS IN ONE HAND AND THE BABY IN THE OTHER. IT IS EQUALLY UNREASONABLE TO SUPPOSE THAT ONE ALIEN TO THE HOUSEHOLD, WEARING GLOVES, WOULD HAVE ANY INTEREST IN ELIMINATING THE NORMAL FINGERPRINTS TO BE FOUND IN THE NURSERY."

"BLUNTLY, THE ABSENCE OF FINGERPRINTS ON THE WINDOW PROVES CONCLUSIVELY THAT OTHERS WERE INVOLVED; THAT THE KIDNAPPER HAD AN ACCOMPLICE PROBABLY WITHIN THE LINDBERGH HOUSEHOLD.", Doctor Hudson concluded.

Betty Gow, in Trooper Kelly's estimation, had proven to be a very cooperative witness on the night of the kidnapping, by pointing to the exact spots on the window and crib where she had placed her hand, among other helpful things. But the trooper was unsuccessful in finding any trace of fingerprints. It is quite evident that Doctor Erastus Mead Hudson spoke factually from the wisdom of his profession.

Several days after Hudson's accomplishment of raising latent prints from articles the baby had handled, Kelly and his associate, Sergeant Louis Kubler, both fascinated with the expertise of the method the doctor had used, invited him to return to see what success he might have by processing the surface of the make-shift ladder. Hoping against hope that he would be more successful than they had been, he, once again using his silver nitrate process, sprayed, with the help of Kelly and Kubler, the entire 5,000 square inches of the ladder for the next three days.

Again quoting Doctor Hudson as he tells what he found: THE LADDER WAS LITERALLY COVERED WITH PRINTS. ALMOST EVERY SQUARE INCH OF ITS SURFACE WAS RIDGED WITH PALM-AND FINGERPRINTS, SOME FRAGMENTARY, A FEW OVERLAPPING, ANOTHER FEW BLURRED, BUT MANY COMPLETE AND CLEAR. CLOSER INSPECTION SHOWED FINGERPRINTS ON THE END OF THE RAILS AND EVEN UNDER THE RUNGS WHERE THEY HAD BEEN NAILED DOWN." Kelly and Kubler spent the next few days photographing the more than 500 prints and fragments that were visible.

Captain Russell A. Snook, Supervisor of the State Bureau of Identification at Trenton, after examining the photographs of the prints, stated that "thirty or forty perfect prints" could not be identified as belonging to those who were known to have handled the ladder.

When Doctor Hudson learned of this good news, he urged the state police to submit the prints for identification to the Department of Justice in Washington where the most complete file of fingerprints in the nation was maintained. But his suggestion went unheeded. Informed of this rebuff of his, Doctor Hudson related what he had been told, exhibiting contempt in his statement: "When there's any glory to be had," a New Jersey official told me scornfully, "the Jersey troopers will grab it."

"I offered to have them submitted through the many connections I maintain in Washington, so that the Department of Justice would not know who wanted them identified. I was turned down by the Jersey police."

Later, an official of the Department of Justice smiled and said, "Don't be naive! The Jersey police never gave any of us a chance to examine any of their evidence in the case. They don't seem to know about our files and laboratory facilities." Doctor Hudson lamented.

Colonel Schwarzkopf, from the night of the kidnapping, had been reluctant to share the evidence his troopers had gathered with members of the other investigative bodies. He had resolved that if anyone were to solve the crime it would be his nattily attired officers in blue. But as time went on, they were failing miserably in their attempt.

In New York City, Lieutenant Finn had his own plan for the apprehension of the gang. Finn was advised early in April by a Doctor Dudley D. Shoenfeld, a 39 year old New York psychiatrist, that he had come up with the "psychiatric certainty" that the police should be looking for a lone criminal rather than a gang. Now, in spite of the fact that in years to come this man would be regarded as a professional, he was no more than an amateur in 1932. However, he drew Finn's attention with his firm belief negating the gang theory of the multitudes.

It was soon after the discovery of the corpse that Shoenfeld contacted Finn and presented him with his theory. After listening to the many persuasive arguments the psychiatrist put forth, together with Dr.Condon's description of Cemetery John and the sketch made from it, Finn decided to place his complete faith in the Shoenfeld argument and issued the following description of the man they were looking for. It appeared in the newspapers during the month of June.

> Age, 30 to 35; 5 feet 9 inches; athletic build; speaks with Scandinavian or German accent; 150 to 160 pounds; rather light complexion; medium light hair; sharp almond eyes; high forehead, pointed chin; when last seen, wore soft brown hat, long black overcoat of light fabric, and black leather shoes.

Back in New Jersey, the outspoken Inspector Walsh, who had by this time been promoted to Police Chief of Jersey City, was highly agitated with the progress being made. In an article, written by him and published in the November 22, 1932 issue of *The Jersey Journal*, he had this to say: "ORDINARY POLICE METHODS WERE NOT FOLLOWED IN THE LINDBERGH CASE. NEITHER VIOLET SHARPE, NOR JAFSIE, NOR ANY ONE ELSE CONNECTED WITH THE CASE --- EXCEPT CURTIS AND HENRY JOHNSON --- WAS ARRESTED AND HELD PENDING INVESTIGATION." He went on to say that Doctor Condon should have been booked as a material witness, and that the arrest of the kidnappers should have been accomplished at St. Raymond's Cemetery when Jafsie paid the ransom.

The three sectioned ladder, the clue the police hoped would prove invaluable to them, had been the one item that held their continued and primary interest. From its hand-made appearance they hoped to possibly establish some information about the one who had constructed it, or even some knowledge as to the type person who had ascended and descended its steps.

One of the first things accomplished was the construction of a duplicate ladder. In it they were careful to use the same kinds of wood and follow the exact dimensions of the original ladder. After placing it in exactly the same position as the kidnap ladder, they had seven men, each of a different size, ascend it and climb into the nursery window. Each man carried a 27 pound bundle measuring 29 inches in length. By doing this they discovered that the ladder could not hold more than 180 pounds, and at that weight it would splinter in the same place. The result of this experiment brought them to the conclusion that the man they were looking for was one who weighed no more than 180 pounds and not less than 150.

The deductions the police made as a result of this experiment are certainly noteworthy. They reasoned that the baby's top weight to be 30 pounds, while the kidnapper's would be about 150 pounds or slightly more. They agreed that a man of this weight could successfully climb the ladder, enter the nursery, and remove the child; but in his descent, with the added weight of a 30 pound baby, the upright had cracked. The splintering of this wood could possibly have been the noise Lindbergh heard shortly after 9:00 p.m., prompting him to inquire of Anne: "What was that?" Later he described the noise as sounding like "the slats of an orange box falling off a chair." The sound at the time was passed off as one possibly caused by the cracking of a tree limb.

Their decision to construct a duplicate ladder was a good one; however, good as their line of reasoning was, it was far from perfect. By their experiment with the extra ladder, they realized that as the man was exiting himself from the nursery carrying his 30 pound bundle, the ladder wood again split at the exact location where the original had broken, with the retreating man and his package being thrust into the wall of the home. It was estimated that they would have been dashed against the wall with a pendulum force of at least 180 pounds, enough to cause them to fall from the ladder. But, had this been the case, where was the evidence in the soft ground that anyone had fallen? Furthermore, there was no indication that anything had either struck or brushed against the whitewashed stone wall.

From these facts, as the police found them, it should have been good judgment on their part to reason that in all probability the kidnapper had not gone back down the ladder with the 30 pound child, but instead had left the home by way of the front door.

However the kidnap ladder became the source of greater attention than just its initial examinations for fingerprints. It had been subjected to numerous studies by the police in their attempts to determine the types of wood that had been used in its construction.

Arthur Koehler, employed by the Forest Products Laboratory of the United States Department of Agriculture, in Madison, Wisconsin, was made aware of the Lindbergh kidnapping as he read of it in the newspapers the following morning. He was fascinated with the information given relative to the three-sectioned wood ladder that had been used. Known in his area of the country as a "Sherlock Holmes of wood", Koehler, his interest aroused, lost no time in writing to the Jersey authorities, offering his services in helping them trace the wood used in the ramshackle contraption. His reputation as a specialist in the identification of wood, had earned him the right to be referred to as a "wood" detective. Although Koehler had offered his services to Lindbergh in March, he heard nothing from the colonel until after the "presumed" body of the baby had been found. At this time Koehler was beckoned to come east and lend his aid. Early examinations of the ladder by the Bureau of Standards, and the analysis of some wood slivers by the Forest Service Laboratory had revealed absolutely nothing of significance that was helpful to the police. Because of this, the authorities anxiously awaited the arrival of Koehler at the State Police Headquarters in Trenton, where he, upon his arrival, was eagerly welcomed by Colonel Schwarzkopf and Captain Lamb.

Lamb drove Koehler to the State Police Training School at nearby Wilburtha, New Jersey, where the ladder had been stored after undergoing tests. From here, an investigation would soon begin that was to take Koehler into many eastern cities in his attempt to tie a criminal mind together with the construction of the crudely made kidnap ladder.

Starting with the tedious dissecting of the ladder, during which the wood expert separated each part, numbering them accordingly in order that they could be exactly reassembled again at a later date, it took him but a short time to determine that four kinds of wood had been used in its construction. He at once recognized that the two side rails of the bottom section had been made of second-growth Southern pine; while those of the middle section were Douglas fir; with both of these woods being used in the top section. The steps, were boards that had been turned on their edges and set into rather shallow recesses. These had been cut from ponderosa pine. The fourth wood the builder had used in the construction was in the dowel pins, those that held the sections securely in place when extended, preventing them from collapsing when fully extended.

Koehler studied the chisel marks, measuring each for its length, width, and thickness. Distances between nail holes were measured and every minute characteristic of the wood was carefully noted.

During his early examination of the ladder, one very outstanding difference was observed relative to the side rails. In the top section, the left-hand Southern pine side rail, the one Koehler had marked "Rail 16", he noticed contained four nail holes, evidence pointing to the possibility that the board had been used before. The holes were located in one end of the rail, with no sign of rust around them, which led Koehler to believe that the board had been previously used indoors, where it was protected from adverse weather conditions which would have caused rust to develop due to moisture and rain.

The four nail holes were square, not round as those in the other Douglas fir rails. From their appearance, they resembled those made by old-fashioned square nails, used in a by-gone era. Furthermore, he discovered, the holes were made by driving the nails at the same angle, and spaced the same distance apart. He said this could not be duplicated by anyone, if they made over ten thousand attempts, to precisely match the holes in "Rail 16" of the kidnap ladder.

The wood detective was then left with one tremendous challenge. Although the odds were probably one in ten billion that he would ever find the spot where this board had been nailed, he decided that as long as there remained a remote possibility, and in spite of the mathematical chances against such a find, he would, nevertheless, make such an attempt.

During the months that followed, Koehler lived up to the reputation he had earned, proving himself in every way to be a "wood detective" as he relentlessly traced the wood used in the ladder all over the country. He had great confidence that he would eventually find the planing mill that had dressed the wood for shipment. However, he realized that once he found the mill, his job would become even greater, since he then must locate, from among the hundreds and possibly thousands of lumber shipments, the customer that had purchased the finished lumber used in the ladder. Once finding this mill, obtaining a list of their customers holding the names of the firms which purchased the lumber from the planing mill would be a relatively easy task. However, once he obtained this list, locating the lumber yard that had sold the wood to the kidnappers would be his toughest job.

He decided it would be easier for him to begin his task by centering his attention on the wood used in two of the side rails. Koehler was certain, after tracing the grain, the two rails had at one time been a single board. Both were Carolina pine and, using the assumption that they had once been joined together, tracing them would undoubtedly afford him his greatest hope of success.

Upon close examination of these boards under a microscope, Koehler found certain distinguishable marks which had undeniably been made by the planing machine --- marks that would be peculiar to all those from other mills, but also a positive identifying characteristic of wood coming from some "as yet to be located" mill. Further observation revealed that the two knives used to trim the edges of the boards apparently had a very distinguishable imperfection, one that created a series of shallow grooves which marred the otherwise smooth surface at consistent intervals of eighty-six hundredths of an inch. Evidence of another defective knife in the edge trimmer was clearly seen under the microscope; the flat surface of the boards displayed another scar which appeared every ninety-three hundredths of an inch. These blemishes, Koehler reasoned, should certainly identify, without any doubt, the planing mill that had cut and shipped out the lumber.

Using the expertise he had acquired through the years of performing his role of "wood detective", Koehler discovered many other valuable points about the distinctiveness of the Carolina pine lumber used in the ladder. The dressing of the boards, he determined, had been done by a planing machine with six knives in the cutter, which had been used to trim the edges, while one with eight knives was used in the surface cutter. He figured that a fair estimate of the speed at which the lumber had been moving as it passed through the planer was approximately 230 feet a minute. Knowledge that this speed would be more than double that of most Eastern mills led him to believe that his task of locating the planing mill might be a rather easy one.

Therefore, letters were sent to every one of the 1,598 pine mills along the Atlantic Coast. Each firm was asked if they had a planer that would feed, especially one-by-four-inch Southern pine, as fast as 230 feet a minute. And if so, did it have six knives in the edge cutter heads? How about its face cutters, the letter inquired, are there eight knives in them? Does the first revolve at a faster speed than the second? Of the great number of letters dispatched, only 23 mills responded in the affirmative to all the questions. Encouraged by the answers, Koehler wrote again to each of the 23, urging them to send him samples of pine wood that came through the processing of their planers.

Among the responses was that of the M.G. and J.J. Dorn Company of McCormick, South Carolina. Complying with the request, a sample forwarded by this firm proved to be precisely what Arthur Koehler was looking for. There could be no doubt, for the evidence showed its surface had gone through a planer at approximately the same speed as the ladder lumber. The sample, however, lacked the markings which should have been there, the evidence of defective knives. But, Koehler reasoned, these blades could have possibly undergone systematic sharpening since the wood in the ladder had been planed, hence the changed appearance. He decided a trip to the mill in South Carolina was necessary.

Joseph J. Dorn, a South Carolina state senator and one of the owners of the company, upon learning of the vital importance of Koehler's visit, offered his full cooperation. Koehler had hoped to find a scrap of old one-by-four Southern pine that had been turned out by the firm many months earlier, one which might possibly reveal the blade imperfections he was looking for. But a thorough search of the yards brought him no results.

He did, however, discover that the Dorn planer that had dressed the ladder wood, had been operating at its excessive speed since September 1929. Why, thought

Koehler, couldn't he make an effort to trace each individual shipment of wood from that planer to its eventual destination where it could have been purchased by a customer at a retail outlet? Answering his own question, he decided to do just that.

Realizing he must now trace every shipment made by the Dorn Company since 1929 to the date of the kidnapping, a total of 30 months, he set out by acquiring the lists of customers who had purchased the one-by-four-inch Southern pine lumber from the company, especially those north of the Potomac River, and particularly in the New Jersey-New York area.

Completing his indexing of the list, he found there had been 46 carloads shipped out by them during that time span to 25 firms. These shipments had been for orders made up either wholly or partially of Southern pine. Considering that many of these customers had probably sold parts of their order to other firms, and they in turn had sent portions of their purchase to other lumber yards, Koehler decided he would begin his search within a 25 mile radius of Hopewell. By doing this, he found that 18 carloads had gone to the Johns Manville factory at Manville and a box factory in Trenton, two firms in New Jersey, both located within the area he had established.

Detective Lewis Bornmann was assigned by Superintendent Schwarzkopf to accompany Koehler until his search for the wood came to either a dead-end or proved successful. Unfortunately their visits to Manville and Trenton proved to be futile, being told at both factories that the purchase of this wood had been used for internal purposes and not sold to the public.

Not disheartened during the months that followed, the two men continued their quest of what seemed to be an endless tour, traveling to many neighboring states in their search for the Southern pine lumber which they hoped would match the wood used in the kidnap ladder. Going into cities and towns, both large and small, visiting firms in New York, Connecticut, Massachusetts, and Pennsylvania, as well as those in New Jersey, the officials of the many places they visited, anxious to help, would lengthen the list of those Koehler and Bornmann had hoped to see. Remembering at times, other places where, when, and to whom they had sold the elusive pine, these men would consult their account books, supply the names and addresses of additional purchasers, and send the two detectives off on, what sometimes turned out to be, a new search resembling a house-to-house check. However, among their list of new stops, they visited a lumberyard in Ozone Park, Long Island, where the owner remembered he had used some of the wood they inquired of in erecting new storage bins on their property some time earlier. With renewed interest, they followed the executive to the bins. Here he cut off a protruding board from one of them, handing it to Koehler for his examination. Looking at it closely, Koehler found the blemishes made by the defective cutter knife of the Dorn company could definitely be seen, but barely visible along one edge of the board. Believing their search had ended here, Koehler took note that the blemishes were not identical; they were a fraction farther apart and also closer to the center of the edge of the board.

This mathematical difference baffled Koehler until he rationalized that the wider spacing on the board pointed to only one clear fact --- the lumber yard board had passed through the planer at a faster speed because of a difference in the Dorn pulleys in McCormick. His good reasoning told him that this board had been dressed when a fast-speed pulley was used with the edge cutters placed in either a higher or lower position, therefore accounting for its difference with that of the ladder wood. Further thoughts brought him to the conclusion that, either before or after the special shipment to the Ozone Park firm was made, the defective knife had been used, and that either before or after, the middle-size pulley was on the planer, hence the reason the marks appeared as they did on the kidnap ladder.

Now, more certain that he was closing in on the shipment of lumber, he and Bornmann took another look at the list he carried with him. He found a shipment had been made 20 days after the Ozone Park delivery, to a firm in Youngstown, Pennsylvania. Finding the order was comprised of Southern pine one-by-fours, he learned they had been dressed an eighth of an inch narrower.

However, he discovered an order which offered hope. Nine days before the November, 1931 shipment to Ozone Park, an order calling for a portion of Southern pine lumber, the exact width and thickness as that of the ladder rails, had been filled and shipped out in a carload of lumber to Halligan and McClelland in New York City. In an interview with the management there, they learned the entire carload had been purchased by a lumber company located in the Bronx. The National Lumber and Millwork Company on White Plains Road in the

Williamsbridge section would be their next stop.

Greatly encouraged by this news, the two men held the hope that their long search had almost reached its end. Wednesday, November 29th proved to be their day for rejoicing. Approaching the entrance of the National Lumber and Millwork Company, they noticed it was more than just a lumber company, but also an established retailer that handled a wide variety of building supplies. Finding the foreman quite agreeable to help as he fingered his way through his office records, Koehler and Bornmann watched as he finally spotted the entry he was looking for. Its record showed that on Tuesday, December 1, 1931 the firm had received a shipment from the Dorn Company. But, it also informed them, the entire shipment had been sold out many months before their visit. Their initial encouragement was immediately reversed to discouragement. Wondering if the same procedure could have been possibly followed here as with the Ozone Park lumberyard, Koehler decided to put his question into audible words: "Is it possible for you to have used some of the wood from this shipment of Southern pine to construct storage bins?" Thinking a moment, the foreman agreed that there was a slight chance that this could have been done. Leading them out to the bins, he then proceeded to saw from a bin an irregular projecting piece from a one-by-four-inch Southern pine board. Handing it to Koehler, the wood expert studied it intently for just a minute under the revealing enlargement of his magnifying glass and shouted: "This is it!"

This was truly their day for rejoicing. The lost shipment had been found, the comparison was a perfect one. In every respect the wood clearly exhibited the proof Koehler needed. The wood the abductors of little Charles Lindbergh had used to make their ladder had been purchased from this lumberyard in the Bronx.

Excited beyond description, Koehler asked if he could see their customer-purchase list but learned that none existed since the firm sold on a cash basis only. "Yes," the foreman answered, "this had been our practice two years ago." Learning that no records were kept of sales made in 1931, Koehler, with Bornmann carrying the tell-take convincing piece of lumber, took their leave, discouraged once again with the knowledge that their lengthy search had evidently brought them face-to-face with another stone wall.

Realizing that their last remaining hope had been shattered in their search for the Southern pine, they decided to begin what could be another endless hunt, this time intensely searching for the discernable imperfections which were visible on the ladder rails made from Douglas fir.

With Koehler and Bornmann continuing to be kept busy traveling about the east coast, now on their renewed lumber hunt, other things of importance had been transpiring in the long and detailed history of the Lindbergh kidnapping.

On Friday, May 19th, 1933, Oliver Whateley, the Lindbergh's very sedate English butler-chauffeur, was taken suddenly ill. He had been living alone at Hopewell awaiting his wife Elsie's return from Europe where she had gone to visit relatives. The soft-spoken butler had been suffering increasingly alarming pains in the abdomen. Deciding he should not put off any longer a visit to a doctor, he motored to nearby Princeton where a doctor ordered him hospitalized at once. He was operated on that evening, for what was diagnosed as a leaking ulcer, but peritonitis soon set in, his condition becoming grave. Colonel Lindbergh visited his loyal servant shortly before he passed away early Tuesday morning, May 23rd. Whateley had lost his valiant attempt to remain alive until his faithful wife Elsie could be at his bedside.

The Whateleys had come to this country in 1930 from Birmingham, England, and after sporadic employment here, were hired through an employment agency for work in the Morrow home. But instead of the 45 year old "gentleman's gentleman" and his wife working in the Englewood home, Mrs. Morrow presented the Whateleys as a gift to her daughter and son-in-law shortly before they moved into their first home, a small farmhouse they had leased near Princeton. Here they would live until their new home at Hopewell was ready for occupancy. And then, for several months before establishing their permanent residence in the Sourlands, the three Lindberghs and their servants moved back to "Next Day Hill", the home of Anne's mother in Englewood.

Olly, as he preferred to be called, even using it as his official signature, and his middle-aged wife had proven to be everything desired as servants to the Lindberghs. It was at the time of his death that prompted the Lindbergh's decision to abandon ever living at Hopewell again. They rightly reasoned that things at Hopewell could never be the same. They fondly remembered Olly enjoying his swims in the river near Zion, a few miles from the Lindbergh home. Olly was recognized as a daily visitor on the streets of Hopewell, entering its few stores to purchase the needed items and the necessary food supplies to feed, not only the family, but the legion of state troopers camped in their temporary headquarters in the Lindbergh garage. Their faithful Olly would never return to Hopewell --- and neither would they.

With the passing of Oliver Whateley, much speculation arose regarding his ill health and sudden death. One belief as to the cause was that it had been brought on by a combination of worry, fear, and concern over his involvement in the kidnapping. Although there are strong arguments supporting this theory, Olly was no longer alive to defend himself of these accusations. Writing in *Plain Truth Magazine* in an article titled Jittery Jersey "Justice", Seymour Friedman asked this question: "Why did O. Whateley, Lindbergh butler, die unexpectedly just as he was about to confess his part in the alleged Lindbergh kidnapping? What Oliver Whateley did know, and did not tell, will in all probability, never be known. But, we do have the police with their original dogmatic belief, that the kidnapping had been the work of a conspiracy, and that someone in the employ of the Lindberghs and Morrows had undoubtedly been involved. However, we also have Oliver Whateley's word that he was "busy reading the *Saturday Evening Post*" during the time of the baby's kidnapping. Everyone's presence that night was accounted for, with the exception of this "gracious gentleman" who alone "proved" he was where he said he was during that fateful hour.

Whether from grief over the loss of her husband, or of natural causes, Elsie Whateley joined him in death on Monday, January 13, 1936.

C H A P T E R   S E V E N T E E N

A Theater In Greenwich Village!

The result of the national election held on Tuesday, November 8th, 1932 brought about a change in the administration in Washington. Franklin Delano Roosevelt and his promise of a "New Deal" resulted in a defeat of President Herbert Hoover by a resounding landslide. His inauguration, held on Saturday, March 4, 1933, not only gave the country a new president, but one who would soon enact legislation that would prove to be of tremendous help to the investigators working to solve the enigma of the Lindbergh case.

Rumor had always been a factor in enlarging the wild stories that were told of the "mysterious happenings up in the Sourlands". Among the unfounded tales was the claim made by the natives that the State Police feared to go into the "lost land" and patrol the many unfinished dirt roads and lanes that threaded their way through the wooded mountain area. Also there existed the highly illogical rumor that the Lindberghs were resented when they decided to build their home there. The reasoning behind this assumption was based merely on the incredible belief that there were persons who were operating illegal stills in the mountain where bootleg whiskey was being made. The bootleggers feared the added attention to the mountain, brought on by the aviator's fame, would result in the stills being "flushed out", and arrests being made.

It was true, however, that the "demon rum" as it was called, was manufactured by the mountaineers and sold for fifty cents a gallon. But with the repeal of Prohibition by the new president in 1933, the bootleggers suddenly found themselves out of business, ending an era of "individual prosperity" they had enjoyed during the years of the Depression.

The repeal of Prohibition offered nothing of significant value to the investigators in their desire to solve the case just as soon as possible; however, another act mandated by the new president did prove to be quite helpful as time went on.

Shortly after the stock market crash of 1929 it had become a practice of a great number of people to hoard their gold. This, coupled with the large numbers of depositors making runs on banks and withdrawing their life savings, soon threatened the financial condition of the country to such an extent that the industrialist wizards feared for its collapse. President Roosevelt then, based on the authority vested in him through his recently approved Emergency Banking Relief Act, requested the nation's citizens to exchange their gold by redepositing or exchanging it at their banks. But this proved to be of little value with only $633 million in gold coins and gold certificates being turned in. An estimated billion more dollars still remained in private coffers was the belief of the Federal Reserve Board. It was determined that it would be necessary for this additional $600 million in gold certificates and $400 million in gold bullion and coins to be turned in before the welfare and anticipated prosperity of the country could at last become a reality and encourage its citizens to sing "Happy Days Are Here Again."

As an added effort to impress those who were continuing to hoard their gold, and show them the utter uselessness of holding on to it for even a short time, and how it would seriously slow the progress of the country's financial recovery, the President's new Secretary of the Treasury, William H. Woodin, instead amplified a truth the citizens needed to know - how the deposits of their gold in the Federal Reserve Banks would render a sound security for the nation's currency and credit. However, even this admonition brought nothing more than a mild compliance.

Taking the proverbial bull by the horns, President Roosevelt on Wednesday, April 5th, 1933 issued an order compelling everyone who held any gold, either coins, certificates, or bullion, valued at more than one-hundred dollars, to deposit it in a Federal Reserve Bank, or any bank which was a member of the Federal Reserve System. Failure to do this within 26 days would make them subject to a ten thousand dollar fine or a ten year term in prison, or possibly both. The final day for compliance with this edict was Monday, May 1st.

In New York City, Lieutenant Finn, actively engaged in attempting to capture the kidnappers because of their possible carelessness in spending the ransom dollars, renewed his interest when he learned of the President's order. Realizing, with the deadline set by the president for the compulsory deposit or exchange of gold, and that nearly two-thirds of the ransom had been paid in gold certificates, what had been, up to this date, only a remote chance of finding an occasional ransom bill, now was changed with his assurance of locating many.

Finn's reasoning was sound. All tellers in banking institutions were now made aware of the president's orders, pledging anew that they would be more alert toward spotting the ransom bills when they were turned in. And if, Finn's logic directed his thoughts, John or any of his gang feared detection by attempting to exchange their ill-gotten money, and held on to it, defying the federal order, their wealth of gold certificates at a later date would be cause for even greater suspicion to be focused on them. Finn was pleased with his plan. He now had a trap set; one which was bound to lead them to a possible imminent arrest of one or more of the gang. Perhaps all of them.

But, once again, Finn's hopes were dashed asunder. The combined hope of the chiefs of staff of the three units intensively involved in the investigation were soon to be thwarted by the very trap Finn believed to be nearly invincible.

The increased activity at which the bills were being turned in presented an almost impossible task for the tellers. The few bills which were detected had not been discovered until hours after the tellers had completed the transaction with a customer, and sometimes not until the end of the day. Lieutenant Finn of the New York City Police, Special Agent Wilson of the Treasury Department, and Special Agent Sisk of the Department of Justice had certainly guessed wrong and had been disillusioned in their anticipation of immediate success.

A week before the deadline only a few bills were reported. New York's Chemical Bank acknowledged the appearance of 50 ten dollar notes, with 50 more turning up several days later at the city's Manufacturers Trust Company. The report of these proved rather encouraging to the investigators. However, these bills also escaped detection while the banks customers were still present and could be questioned.

With the arrival of May 1st the officers expectancy of success was at its highest. Their hopes were strong that thousands of Lindbergh ransom dollars would be turned in on this day. Once again they were proven wrong --- but not entirely so. Tuesday, May 2nd proved to be a banner day for them. On this date the

Federal Reserve Bank of New York reported that $2980 had been exchanged the day before by a customer making a single transaction, when he turned in two-hundred ninety six $10 bills, and one $20 bill, all serial numbers corresponding to the list of bills which had been passed to Cemetery John on Saturday, April 2nd, 1932. On the exchange slip used in the transaction was written the name and address: J.J. Faulkner, 537 West 149th Street, New York City. Unfortunately, the teller who had given his customer perfectly good money in exchange for the ransom bills could remember nothing at all about the mysterious J.J. Faulkner.

Disappointing as this news proved to be, the investigators were certain these gold notes would lead them to the man who had, until one day before, possessed this large amount of ransom money. Once he was located, an arrest of the entire gang was practically a certainty.

But the police were again wrong in their assumptions. Standing at the front door of 537 West 149th Street they were told that no one with the name of Faulkner lived there. Learning this, the police searched for the names of previous residents at that address and found that a person named J. Faulkner had lived there 12 years earlier. However, the J. Faulkner turned out to be a Jane Faulkner who had married a German immigrant named Carl Oswin Geissler on May 21, 1921.

Now, believing to be hot on the trail of the former Jane Faulkner, they traced her to 120 North Chatsworth Avenue, Larchmont, New York, where she and her husband had moved. But Geissler, a partner in the ownership of a flower shop on Madison Avenue, had an impeccable reputation and was above suspicion. Again the hopes of Finn, Wilson and Sisk plummeted.

It seemed that the anonymous J.J. Faulkner had selected an address at random, one that by coincidence had been occupied by a person with that same name years ago. Another oddity in the selection of the 149th Street address was noted when the police discovered that a car stolen from Lakehurst, New Jersey, a few days before the kidnapping, had been found abandoned across the street from the home of the unknown Faulkner, shortly after the crime was committed.

Although it seemed the search would end there, Finn, feeling he was close to something important, continued to probe for additional information about J.J. Faulkner. He learned that another person resided at the

Larchmont address, one Alvin Weigner who had married a sister of Mary Faulkner. He then obtained a photostatic copy of a passport issued to Geissler, a copy of his marriage license, a picture of him, and the bank deposit slip. Wilson had them forwarded to the government handwriting expert, Mr. Saunder in Washington, D.C., who confirmed a day later that the handwriting on all of the documents had been written by the same person. The lead Finn was following seemed to be getting hotter every minute. Regardless of the fine character Mr. Geissler was known to have, serious doubts as to his innocence in the crime began to increase.

But the trail grew cold once again when it seemed impossible to tie-in the two Geisslers or Weigner with any concrete evidence as to their involvement in the case. Nevertheless, another piece of information they uncovered caused the three detectives to turn their attention toward the Geissler's two children from his previous marriage; Carl D., who was in business with his father, and Phyllis Ann, who was married to a Henry Clay Liepold.

The web of mystery continued to spin around the children of Jane Faulkner Geissler. A check issued by the young Mr. Geissler, made payable to one Herman Halpern of 25 Almeda Street, Mount Vernon, was uncovered. This caused increased interest when it was discovered that Halpern was a brother to a Max Halpern who conducted a business where, at an earlier date, one of the Lindbergh ransom bills had been traced to his store. Furthermore, it was learned that Phyllis Liepold had departed for Canada under an assumed name. These coincidences brought about serious probing into the lives of the Faulkners, Geisslers, and Liepolds, but again the investigation led the police up another dead-end street, or better still, a blind alley.

This, however, seemed to be their plight for just a short time. A proverbial bolt-out-of-the-blue struck home when they discovered a toll call had been placed from Liepold's White Plains home at 11:08 a.m., April 7, 1933. Its message related to what might have been a conspiracy. The cryptic cablegram caused their adrenalin to flow at a faster rate. It read WILLIE KRIPPENDORF 33 BAVARIAN RING MUNICH GERMANY ADVISE YOU STRONGLY TAKING CHEAPEST STEAMER RATE POSSIBLE EVEN THIRD CLASS REGARDS HENRY C LIEPOLD.

The police arrived at a reasonable theory. Realizing by this time that the authorities were in hot pursuit, and knowing they were attempting to find

Phyllis in Canada, Liepold had taken this means of informing Krippendorf to show no display of wealth which could possibly tip their hand. The cablegram could very well have been instructions for him to leave any ransom money he had with him in Germany. Now armed with this new name, Finn determined to search the records of the Immigration Bureau at Ellis Island and find what they might reveal about Willie Krippendorf.

Finn completed his findings with the following report: "Willie Krippendorf first entered this country on the steamer Ventan on December 26, 1923, and left again in 1932. He is thirty-three years of age, born in Germany, weighs 155 pounds, is five feet eleven inches in height, has gray eyes and blond hair." In accordance with the cablegram, this same Krippendorf again arrived in this country, in company with his wife, Teresa, on the steamer Deutschland of the Hamburg-American Line, on May 5, 1933. Upon his arrival here he stated that he was going to live with a Leo Rodel at 353-355 Tom Hunter Road, Fort Lee, New Jersey. Further investigation revealed that Krippendorf and Leo Rodel were closely associated with Ralph Hacker, 9 Crescent Avenue, Palisade Park, New Jersey. The same Hacker, who was none other than, the son-in-law of Doctor John Francis Condon; the famous "Jafsie" of the Lindbergh case.

This latest information practically caused Finn to "blow a gasket", as his excitement was brought on by the realization that the trail of the ransom money was leading them straight back to Condon.

Lieutenant Finn was another police officer who, as had Inspector Walsh, distrusted the old man in many of the things he claimed to have done. As for Hacker, he had been on top of many of the movements made by his father-in-law during the negotiations with the kidnappers. It had also been Ralph Hacker who had drawn the precise plans for the construction of the wooden box in which the ransom money was placed for delivery. And it had been Hacker, not an identification expert, who had made the plaster cast of the footprint of the extortioner in St. Raymond's Cemetery. This all appeared to be more than just a set of coincidences.

Lieutenant Finn, was more vociferous than Inspector Walsh in his denunciation of Doctor Condon. He did not trust the man. To prove this we must read what Finn had to say about the pompous Bronx educator: "Jafsie Condon would talk---and how he would talk! Then he would shut up like one of his own City Island clams. He was always doing strange things---like hunting for

Red Johnson along the water front and then defending him as violently as if Red had been his own son. And why did he go around with a bodyguard?

"One time we'd see him, he'd be himself, the old master. The next time, he'd be rigged up like an Englishman's idea of a tough in a Bowery dive. Then he'd turn up as a half-witted tottering old party, pretending to be almost totally deaf.

"All in the interest of the great amateur sport of crime detection!

"It was funny, in a way, because Jafsie's physical proportions did not lend themselves to a successful disguise. He stood six feet or more and weighed 250 pounds. Besides, he had a generous growth of mustache, unmistakable features, and eyes you don't forget. It wasn't funny though, to have your chief witness going around and saying things that tended to discredit him with the public. Then there was the way he came into the case. Some of the boys could never see why he chose a small paper like the *Bronx Home News* as a medium of communication with the criminals, or why, having done so, he got such an immediate answer. And why was he, an obscure ex-schoolteacher, so readily accepted by the kidnappers as the ransom intermediary?

"He was shaky, too, on some of the details of his story. He never did tell where he got the wood out of which the ransom box was made. He professed not to remember the carpenter who made it, and when he did remember, the man had disappeared. He said that his son-in-law, Hacker, made the plans for the box; later referred to them as 'my plans'. He claimed to have the plans in his house; but nobody ever saw them.

"The feeling grew in many high quarters that the old schoolmaster knew a lot more about the kidnapping than he was letting on. But nobody could do anything about it. He was protected by Colonel Lindbergh's confidence in him. And the Colonel was the boss."

But, in spite of all the suspicion, nothing surfaced that pointed to the direct involvement of Leo Rodel and Willie Krippendorf with Ralph Hacker and any connection with the kidnapping. In spite of the suspicion of Condon, he was able to "weather the storm" very well.

However, once again, proving that truth is definitely stranger than fiction; Henry Clay Liepold, not able to endure the concentrated investigation of him as a suspect, committed suicide in October. According to Finn, Wilson, and Sisk, his suicidal death was an outward admission of his guilt. The increased attention, brought on by the exchange of the $2,980 on May 1, 1933, had come to a near standstill.

Monday, May 8th, 1933 saw Gaston B. Means back in the courtroom of the Supreme Court in the District of Columbia. Means' accomplice, "The Fox", who had remained a fugitive for more than a year, had been arrested in Brooklyn and identified as Norman T. Whitaker.

Brought from his prison cell to testify in this second trial involving his fleecing of Mrs. McLean out of $104,000, Means glibly answered the questions put to him by his attorney, J. William Tomlinson. On the witness stand the embezzler continued to relate another more unbelievable "cock-and-bull" story in another attempt to escape justice. After deliberating two hours and twenty minutes, the jury found Means and Whitaker, himself a former convict, guilty of conspiracy to defraud Mrs. McLean of $35,000. A sentence of two years in prison for both was imposed on Friday, May 12th, one year to the day after the finding of the corpse.

As they were led from the courtroom, Means gave the spectators one of his most gracious smiles in spite of the fact that he was now facing an additional two years in Leavenworth. In 1936, hoping that he would gain a temporary leave from prison, Means confessed that he had kidnapped the child. The fake confession of an already mentally disturbed man.

Gaston B. Means, who had come from a highly respected family in Concord, North Carolina. His grandfather had once served as governor of that state, His father had at one time served as mayor of Concord, and his uncle had been the chief of police. Means, a man who had received his education at the University of North Carolina and had been a former investigator with the Department of Justice; an author of some repute; a man whose wife fondly called "Bud", died in disgrace in the Federal prison in 1938, marking the end of the life of a person who would always be referred to as "the world's greatest swindler" or "the world's greatest embezzler".

The police continued to run down every report they received, many from fanatics, whose "leads" would eventually take them on dead end searches that were, not only time consuming, but absolutely worthless. Their trail to the kidnappers apprehension had grown absolutely cold. Their only vestige of hope lay in possibly tracing the few ransom bills which would turn up occasionally in various locations. But running these down had led them nowhere.

Monday, November 27th, 1933 turned out to be a red letter day of sorts when, during the mid-morning hours, Lieutenant Finn received a telephone call from William M. Cody of the Seventh Avenue Branch of the Corn Exchange Bank, located at Seventh Avenue and 14th Street. Mr. Cody told Finn that while he was counting the receipts in a deposit of the Loews Sheridan Square Theater in Greenwich Village he had found a five dollar bill that, after checking it against his list, was definitely one of the Lindbergh ransom notes. The money, he said, had been brought to the bank by the theater manager, Mr. J.H. Simons.

Finn's immediate visit to the bank confirmed that Cody had spoken the truth. A $5 gold note bearing serial number B35435796A had been a part of the receipts made up from ticket sales to customers of the theater the night before. The Lieutenant lost no time traveling to the theater at 12th Street and Seventh Avenue to talk with the manager. He was a man with high hopes as he explained the latest developments to his two assistants, Agent Manning and Corporal Horn, who accompanied him.

Mrs. Cecile M. Barr, the cashier, an employee of the theater for nearly 25 years, was very enlightening in her interview with Finn. She claimed she well remembered the customer who had given her the five dollar bill.

She told Finn she was sitting in her ticket booth occupied with her regular job of counting the receipts of the night. She said the time was about nine-thirty, and that she was certain of this because the final show had just begun. As she was concentrating on counting the bills and coins in her cashier's tray, her attention was distracted by a five-dollar bill that had been thrown on the counter in front of her. This customer was almost her last of the evening. His bill, she explained, had been folded three times, the creases forming a small eight sectioned, easily discernable pattern on its surface. She said she had to open it and flatten it in order to make it fit the paper money compartment of her receipt tray.

Finn asked her to be more explicit. "Well, it was first folded lengthwise in half," as she took another bill to demonstrate, "then again in half to a size one-half its length, and then a third time that reduced its size to what became almost a small square." Finn inquired if the bill in its folded form revealed the denomination? To this she asserted: "Not until I opened it up." Continuing with her explanation of the events of the night before, Sunday, November 26th, Mrs. Barr stated that the man said nothing, and did nothing but stare at her. When she inquired as to what he wanted, he looked up at the sign in her booth on which was posted the three ticket prices available, 35, 40 and 60 cents. She said she continued to stare back at him while he made his decision. She claimed he seemed "almost surly" as he decided on a forty-cent ticket. Mrs. Barr said she then proceeded to have his ticket extracted from the automatic machine, his change clicked out from the coin machine, as she counted out his four dollars change in paper money and sixty cents in silver. He disappeared as he walked into the darkened recesses of the theater to view Walter Winchell's film "Broadway Through A Keyhole", starring Paul Kelly and Constance Cummings.

The exuberant lieutenant asked the friendly and very cooperative Mrs. Barr if she could describe her customer in detail. Again Cecile Barr had no trouble. The following description she gave is taken from Lieutenant Finn's official report dated November 28, 1933. "Apparently an American; about 30-35 years of age; slender build; 5 feet 8 inches or 5 feet 9 inches; about 155-160 pounds; light complexion; thin face; light-brown hair; smooth shaven; high cheekbones; wearing a dark soft hat with the front pulled down and no overcoat---dark suit. This man was alone."

But in spite of this latest turn of events, even though Mrs. Barr's description tallied nearest to that given by Jafsie and Joseph Perrone, and the certainty with which she stated: "I will never forget that man's face, and I am quite certain that, despite the severe cold night, he wore no overcoat.", the "almost contemptuous man" had literally disappeared, not only into the theater, but also deep into the night.

The year 1933 ended, 22 months had passed by, and the police still appeared to be no nearer a solution of the case than they were a few hours after the kidnapping. The crime of the century had reached an impasse. The public clamored for an arrest to be made! The authorities could not comply! This created, as it had from the beginning, a very embarrassing situation; one that was growing more acute with each passing day the case remained unsolved!

CHAPTER EIGHTEEN

1279 East 222nd Street

As the year 1934 dawned, the police files contained no new clues that could possibly raise even their slightest hope of solving the baffling kidnap-murder. With the exception of reports of occasional ransom bills found during the latter months of 1933, the authorities could only wonder when and where more bills were going to appear. To this date it seemed there was to be no sun appearing for them on the horizon. Every incriminating bill recovered was a challenge to their ability to tie it to the person who passed it. So far they had been unsuccessful in accomplishing this. Their morale badly needed a lift. On February 14th, 1934, two men entered the Bronx lumberyard of Cross, Austin and Ireland Lumber Company, at 149th Street and the East River. They were looking for a piece of plywood to be cut to a specified size. Miss Alice Murphy, the company's cashier, told them the cost would be forty cents. As one of the men offered to pay her with a ten dollar bill, she hesitated to accept it because she had noticed it was a gold note, one which should have been turned in the previous May.

While calling to the yard foreman, William Reilly, to have the wood cut, the men changed their minds, deciding to pay her the forty cents in change. Informing the men it would take but a few minutes to have the plywood cut, they decided not to wait and hurried away, telling her they would return for it later. By now, their strange actions had aroused her suspicions and, watching them leave, she followed them to where she could see their car and proceeded to jot down the license number on the sales slip. Back in her office, she joined the two men who had been there inspecting the company's books. Their names were Arthur Koehler and Lewis Bornmann.

As Miss Murphy related the incident to the police, she said that one of the men was a "wiry sort", with flat cheeks, a pointed chin and sharp blue eyes. He had spoken with a decidedly German accent, she stated. It seemed that Koehler and Bornmann had never been, during their nearly two year search, any closer to the possible kidnappers than they were on that Valentine's Day.

President Roosevelt, on Friday, May 18th, affixed his signature to a bill that was to add much strength to the already existing punishment for the crime of kidnapping. The law in its new form now defined it a federal offense to send a kidnap or ransom note across a state line, and called for the death penalty to be enacted against persons who transported their kidnapped victims across a state line, and failed to return them unharmed.

The progress of the police during the hot summer months had stagnated. Current news of the case had virtually disappeared from the newspapers simply because there was nothing new to report.

However, on a late afternoon near the end of August, a bit of activity took place while Jafsie was riding on a bus in the Bronx. The bus traveling in a southerly direction on the Williamsbridge Road was approaching the intersection of Pelham Parkway, a broad four-lane highway, with traffic moving in two lanes from both the east and west. The two lanes were separated by a grass-grown island-type strip. Since the night Condon had paid Lindbergh's $50,000, he had kept himself busy traveling, at his own expense, up and down the eastern seaboard searching for a man who might closely resemble "Cemetery John". Condon delighted in the notoriety and publicity he had received on these expeditions, never ceasing to let it be known that he was the famous Jafsie of the Lindbergh case. As the bus neared the wide thoroughfare, Condon peered through the window and was startled at what he saw. Here is how he described it in his book, *Jafsie Tells All*.

"We were within a few feet of the Parkway, about to cross it, when I saw a man in the garb of a workman walking in a northeasterly direction toward a nearby woods. It was broad daylight and in that wild instant that I saw him, and jumped eagerly to my feet, shouting at the driver to stop the bus, I had recognized the man.

"He was John, of Woodlawn and St. Raymond Cemeteries.

"As I fought my way toward the front of the slow-moving bus,; I continued to shout: 'Stop this bus! Stop this bus!'

"The bus-driver's face, a familiar one, turned for a startled second in my direction. 'I can't stop her, Doc. There's cross-traffic.'

"A glance out showed me that we were already crossing busy Pelham Parkway, and I realized the bus could not possibly be brought to a stop until it reached the southwest corner on the other side of the Parkway.

"I tried to look out, but could see nothing of John, who had been walking in the direction opposite that in which we were traveling. In those exasperating few moments I felt as though we would never reach the south side of the parkway.

"But we did finally, and the driver pulled open the bus door. I stepped out hurriedly, turned about and looked across Pelham Parkway. Several pedestrians were walking north on the other side of the thoroughfare, but at that distance I could not tell whether or not John was among them.

"Crossing the thoroughfare, with its speeding traffic, ate up another precious moment or two. When I had reached the other side, I could see nothing of the man I was seeking. Whether he had disappeared in the nearby woods, whether he had entered an automobile and driven away, I could not tell. He was gone---and I didn't know which way to go to look for him.

"I did what I considered the best possible thing under the circumstances.

"I sought out the nearest telephone and called the New York Office, Federal Bureau of Investigation of the Department of Justice, on Lexington Avenue. I reported in full the incident, and their records, today, should disclose the report I made to them."

But, this incident of Jafsie's, although noteworthy at the time, did nothing more for the police than to give them the opportunity to view, once again, the pompous Doctor Condon basking in the lime-light engendered by the importance of the Lindbergh case.

However, with the arrival of September more of the ransom bills were turning up in deposits of various banks. On Thursday, September 6th The National Bank of Yorkville discovered a ten dollar gold certificate, number A57232100A, in a deposit made by a Salvatore Levatino, proprietor of a vegetable store at 152 East Third Avenue near Eighty-ninth Street. Levatino said the customer who handed him the bill had made a purchase of only six-cents and, although an argument ensued as to the needless size of the bill offered in payment, he reluctantly gave in and handed the man his change of $9.94.

Two days later, Saturday, September 8th, another bank reported finding a Lindbergh ransom bill among its deposits. This time it was The Chase National Bank located on East Fordham Road in the Bronx that spotted bill number A35272048A in a deposit made by Jacobsen Brothers Exquisite Shoe Store, 266 East Fordham Road. The bill was a twenty-dollar gold note that had been accepted by clerk Albert Shirkes in payment for a pair of women's black suede shoes, size 7 1/2. The price had been $5.50 and the transaction had been made the day before. Shirkes' description of his customer closely matched those of other witnesses who had dealt with the man.

Two more ten-dollar gold certificates were reported, and checked out as Lindbergh money, during the early hours of Monday, September 17th. Each had been deposited at the Irving Trust Company in the accounts of two vegetable markets located on Second Avenue in Yorkville, but neither proprietor could describe the person who had passed the bills. The discouragement of the police was at a new low. However, had they known it, fate was about to play into their hands a set of circumstances that would allow them to "solve" the case that had stymied them for more than two and one-half years. A mystery that had baffled them for exactly 933 days.

It was just a few minutes before the hour of ten o'clock, Saturday morning September 15th, that a dark blue Dodge sedan drove up to an Ethyl gas pump of the Warner-Quinlan service station on the corner of 127th Street and Lexington Avenue, located near the eastern fringe of what is called upper Manhattan.

The driver stopped, turned off the car's motor, and waited while the station's two attendants, Walter Lyle and John Lyons, came out to take care of the needs of their lone customer. Lyle, the manager, removed the hose from its clamped position at the side of the pump and unscrewed the car's gas cap. "Fill her up, sir?" he inquired. Lyons was busy filling the car's radiator with water.

"No, just five gallons of Ethyl." the man behind the wheel replied.

Lyons was now busy cleaning the windshield as Lyle inserted the nozzle of the hose in the gas tank. The driver opened his door and stepped out. Lyle determined his customer to be German because of his accent. The man was clean-cut in appearance, although he was dressed in the attire of a mechanic.

While the manager filled the tank with the five gallons requested, he studied the face of the man. He had a pointed chin and high cheekbones. He believed the man to be a new customer, or possibly he had just not served him before.

Withdrawing the hose spout, he replaced it firmly in its original position. Tightening the gas tank cap, he said: "That's ninety-eight cents."

Reaching into his inside coat pocket, the man withdrew an envelope and removed a ten-dollar gold certificate. He handed it to Lyle.

Having been told by the police to be wary of any money that appeared to be even slightly irregular, Lyle studied the bill for a few moments. His partner, Lyons, also seemed to be dubious about the currency. After all, it was a ten-dollar gold note; one of those the men had been warned about as being questionable legal tender. Their customer, noticing the apparent doubts they held about his money, gave them a slight smile and said: "They're all right. Any bank will take them."

Still studying the bill on both sides, Lyle said: "You don't see many of them any more."

"No," his customer agreed, "I have only about a hundred left."

Taking the bill into his station, Lyle quickly returned and handed the man his change, two pennies and nine one-dollar bills. Once again behind the wheel of the Dodge, the customer drove away as Walter Lyle carefully observed the exact numerals of the car's license plate. Taking the gold note he had received, he wrote in pencil on the end margin of its back --- 4U 13-41, making mental note that it was a New York plate issued for the year 1934.

Approximately two hours later, only minutes before the noon hour, John Lyons entered The Corn Exchange Bank at 125th Street and Park Avenue. He had brought with him that mornings receipts of the Warner-Quinlan station. Miran John Ozmec, the teller on duty, willingly exchanged the ten-dollar gold certificate for two five-dollar United States notes. The marked bill, bearing the license number, was counted and placed with the other money in the station's deposit, where it would remain unnoticed amid the other bills --- but not for long.

Shortly after one o'clock, the afternoon of Tuesday, September 18th, William R. Strong, head teller of The Corn Exchange Bank, picked up a stack of recently deposited bills from his associate teller, Miran Ozmec. It now remained the head tellers job to check through this assortment of bills, and as he proceeded to do so, he was surprised to find among them, two ten-dollar gold certificates. Strong, ever alert to the task of checking these against the list of ransom note serial numbers, picked up the list and scanned it closely. Although one was not among them, the other certainly was. Number A73976634A had very definitely been a part of the ransom payment.

Just as soon as a phone call could be put through to him, at his New York office, Special Agent Thomas H. Sisk was notified of the find. Immediately summoning his aide, Special Agent William F. Seery, they, together with Lieutenant Finn and Detective Corporal William F. Horn, were, within minutes, speeding toward the bank.

Seery himself was experiencing mixed emotions about the call. He had been running down, without success, most of the reports of ransom bills being found for the past year and a half. Finn too, had been kept busy responding to reports of them in his immediate neighborhood. As recently as Wednesday, September 5th he had gone to The National Bank of Yorkville and found that a deposit there had contained a ten dollar gold note. The deposit had been made by a grocery store on Third Avenue. After questioning the owner, Finn had become encouraged. The man told him he clearly remembered his customer because he had paid him with a ten-dollar bill for a purchase that totaled only six cents. During the week that followed, this same man had passed a dozen Lindbergh ransom gold certificates in both Yorkville and the Bronx. The pins being placed by the lieutenant on his large wall map had begun to form a pattern.

Arriving at the bank the three detectives examined the bill, confirming that it certainly was one of those to ransom the child. It looked like all the other ten-dollar notes that had been found and were unable to trace. Turning it over once again, Corporal Horn's attention was drawn to some pencil markings on the margin. On closer inspection the three men believed the figures could possibly be someone's license number; and if this were so, why had it been placed there?

Taking a blind guess, the trio surmised it had probably been done by someone working at a gas station. Asking teller Ozmec if he remembered who had deposited the bill proved worthless, although the teller thought if he could look at the deposit slips again, he might remember. But when the slips were placed in front of him they proved to be of no help.

At Finn's suggestion, they removed the deposit

slips of those made by gas stations, and this proved helpful since there were only three. But again Ozmec could not be sure which one had made the deposit which contained bill number A73976634A.

Deciding their best move would be to check out the nearest station, slightly more than a block away, the three men soon were talking to the pleasant mannered manager of the Warner-Quinlan service station, Walter Lyle. It had been the suspicions of this honest young man that pointed the detectives to question him.

"Yes", Lyle answered their question, "I put that number there myself. It's an auto-license number." After questioning him further about his customer's appearance and the conversation that had passed between them, the detectives were convinced they would at last learn the identity of this latest bill passer. The description Lyle and his assistant, Lyons, had given them again tallied with those of others who had dealt with "this mysterious man."

Lieutenant Finn was jubilant, again he could barely restrain himself. The three detectives were certain they now possessed the license number of the car that would undoubtedly lead them to one of the kidnappers of Charles A. Lindbergh, Jr. The gold certificate Finn held in his hand would, in all probability, help them to solve the case.

The trio of detectives returned to the bank from where Finn phoned his friend, Gus Reich, at the New York Motor Vehicle Bureau. "I've got a number, Gus, that I want you to look up" Finn requested. Very slowly and distinctly, he read off the number that had been placed on the margin of the bill --- 4U 13-41.

"All right, Lieutenant," Reich said. "I'll have it right away."

The silence seemed deafening as Finn waited nervously for the answer. The other two officers pressed close to the phone. A click was heard at the other end of the line. Reich lost no time in obtaining the information and he didn't waste a word in repeating it:

"Name, Richard Hauptmann ... 1279 East Two-Hundred and Twenty-second Street."

At last they had a suspect with a name!

Finn jotted it down as fast as this long-awaited information reached his ears. After being told the man's age was 34, and still anxious to learn more, the lieutenant urged him to continue to read any further information, brief though it may be, from the registration card of this man, Hauptmann. Leaving the phone again, Reich was away only a few seconds when he returned with only sparse information about the man, who had now become, at last, a suspect with a name.

" 'Description: five feet nine and a half ... hundred and eighty pounds ... blue eyes ... light brown hair ... German ... carpenter.' Sorry, that's all I have on him, Lieutenant" the voice at the motor vehicle bureau concluded.

After thanking his friend Reich, Finn turned from the phone, his spirits elated. At long last he had a name to work with. Never had he been more positive, more certain of success, as he reported the progress he had made to his superior, Inspector John A. Lyons. Seery and Horn were also busy contacting their respective headquarters with the good news.

Inspector Finn, having been placed in charge of arranging for the arrest, had already decided that the suspect should be apprehended away from his home. A calling of a meeting of the minds included Seery and Horn, Federal Agent Thomas H. Sisk, and Lieutenant Arthur T. Keaten of the New Jersey State Police. Soon to join them were four additional detectives, Sergeant John Wallace of the New Jersey State Police, Chester Cronin and William Wallace of the New York department, and Trooper Dennis Duerr of New Jersey.

The men decided their first move would be to locate the Hauptmann residence on 222nd Street, set up a surveillance, and then agree on the proper procedure they should follow to capture the man. All acknowledged the place of apprehension should be at a location where no possible harm could come to anyone; they wanted to avoid the possibility of a shoot-out with the suspect, where even an innocent by-stander could be injured or killed.

As the officers proceeded north in three unmarked cars, their objective was to locate the suspect's home, observe it from a considerable distance, and then make their plans accordingly. Near the extreme northern end of the Bronx, not far from the Westchester line, they found 222nd Street. Turning east, they began scanning every house. The street extended from its western entrance at Woodlawn Cemetery and its adjoining Van Cortlandt Park, at Bronx Boulevard, to its eastern terminus, near Pelham Bay Park on the east.

The homes which lined the street were mostly small, built of wood and stucco with shingled roofs. Small well-kept lawns, many edged with flowers gave evidence that the owners took pride in their properties. Patches of trees offered some shade. Vacant lots awaited better times when buyers would erect more homes there. It was a neighborhood resembling that of a small town community, similar to those found not too far distant from the outskirts of the nation's average major cities. In these homes lived families who, although plagued by the many problems brought on by the ravages of the Depression, were nevertheless, honest God-fearing people. But Finn reflected, as he continued to look at each doorplate, this was not altogether true, since in one of these houses there lived a kidnapper and murderer.

The three detectives in the lead car, Finn, Sisk, and Seery, all realized at the same time they were passing in front of number 1279. It was a single two and one-half story stucco home. It had been built far enough away from the thoroughfare to allow for a four foot sloping bank, and a three and one-half foot stone wall at its base, which extended along the ample sidewalk at the front. A hedge and an abundance of flowers adorned the lawn, and a large vine grew against the front wall, reaching to the four first floor windows. Needham Avenue, a mere lane, but wide enough for an automobile to enter, ran along the east side of the home, separating it from a vacant lot. At the rear of the property, across Needham Avenue, was a single-car garage. Behind the home a row of large trees, towering above it, were clearly seen from 222nd Street.

Following a late afternoon meeting held in a little German restaurant not far from the Hauptmann home, the detectives decided to stake-out the residence throughout the night. Three vantage points were chosen where they could effectively watch for any activity that might take place. One of the cars was stationed on Boston Road at 222nd Street. In it were detectives Sisk, Keaten, and Cronin. Car number two with its occupants, Finn, Seery, and Horn, parked at 221st Street. The third car with Detective Sergeant John Wallace, William Wallace, and Dennis Duerr, pulled up at the corner of 222nd Street, near a small lane, at a position diagonally across from the Hauptmann home. From this location they could more closely observe any household activities.

The long night passed with no sign of activity in the house, except seeing the lights being turned on in two of the rooms. No one was seen leaving or entering the house. As the morning sun rose in the sky the anticipation of the nine watchers grew more tense. Nine o'clock would soon arrive and still no sign of life had been observed around the home. But at 8:55, the front door opened and down the steps strode the man they had been waiting to see. From his physical appearance, they all agreed later, he certainly answered the description of Cemetery John. The detectives watched as he turned east on 222nd Street, entered Needham Avenue alongside his home, and walked to his garage, about 50 feet across the lane. After unlocking its padlocked double doors, the man they now knew to be Richard Hauptmann, entered and backed the car out. He stopped, alighted and returned to relock the doors. Watching him intently, they saw him slowly drive out Needham Avenue and turn east on 222nd Street.

And as he did this, nine officers in three black unmarked Ford police cars quickly followed in pursuit, unknown to the driver of the Blue Dodge sedan who was now traveling away from Needham Avenue, heading east toward Boston Road.

Hauptmann appeared to be in no hurry as he made a right turn onto Boston Road and headed in the direction of Manhattan. He picked up speed as he continued south. The three cars remained at a reasonable distance behind, so as not to attract Hauptmann's attention that he was being followed. Hauptmann was keeping his speed between 40 and 45 miles an hour, The other cars were keeping their safe distance when the officers realized they had already crossed Gun Hill Road, and that Hauptmann was reducing his speed in order to make a right turn on Pelham Parkway.

Traveling west on the Parkway, through Bronx Park, and continuing on Fordham Road (its new name east of the Park), he then made a left turn onto Washington Avenue which had him heading south once again. By this time the detectives had at least gained respect for Richard Hauptmann's ability as a driver. He had shown them his skill by threading his way through traffic and maneuvering his Dodge past several dozen traffic lights without being forced to stop for a red signal. Two more turns, an unexpected right at 189th Street had him moving once again in a western direction, when he suddenly turned left on Park Avenue and was moving south again. The officers could see the man showed no hesitation, and knew the route well to where he was going, by driving with such assurance.

Now headed south again, the officers in the car not too far behind Hauptmann, decided it was about time to act. They knew Park Avenue was a unique stretch of road. To the left, the tracks of the New York Central railroad ran parallel with it. An iron grilled fence prevented any southbound motorists from making any left turns. The four cars continued on Park Avenue past 180th Street and 179th. As they crossed 178th Street and were nearing East Tremont Avenue, Hauptmann, realizing he was about to be blocked in by a municipal sprinkling truck, attempted to pass it on the right. But, while endeavoring to do this, he was forced to stop. Detective William Wallace gave the Ford sedan he was driving a sudden burst of speed, passing Hauptmann's car, and at the same time, edging him toward the curb. As the two cars were abreast, Trooper Duerr, seated alongside the driver, shouted to him to pull to the curb and stop, as car one drove in front, trapping the Hauptmann vehicle.

In what seemed to be one quick movement, car number two pulled in behind, Trooper Duerr leaped from his front seat, and John Wallace jumped from the back shouting directions to the driver of the trapped Dodge. Wallace rushed around to the right side of Hauptmann's car, opened the front door, and slid into the seat beside him. Both Duerr and Wallace held drawn pistols. Wallace pressed his weapon into Hauptmann's ribs, ordering him to pull his car a little closer to the curb. The bewildered driver complied to the curt command.

Holding the prisoner's right wrist, Wallace pulled him from behind the wheel to the sidewalk as they heard Hauptmann's voice for the first time. "What is this? What is this all about?", he asked. Without answering, Officer Wallace took a pair of handcuffs from his person and snapped one cuff on Hauptmann's wrist and the other on his own, securing their captive to him. Their prisoner was visibly frightened.

The distance from Hauptmann's home to the point of his arrest had been 4.7 miles. The time was now 9:25 a.m. Finding himself surrounded by the nine arresting officers who had effectively captured him, a confused Hauptmann watched as Lieutenant Keaten searched his person, removing a wallet from his left rear trouser pocket. In it were twenty-nine dollars; four ones, a five dollar bill and a twenty dollar gold note, which, after checking it against their list, was found to be one of the Lindbergh ransom bills.

Returning to the temporary privacy of Hauptmann's car, they thrust other questions at him, insisting on honest answers. "Where did you get this gold certificate?", "How long have you had it?", "Do you have any more?", they asked in rapid fire order.

Hauptmann's answers, although not evasive, were not satisfactory. He claimed he had been collecting gold notes for the past two years because he feared inflation, having seen paper money become valueless in Germany. Believing the same thing could happen in the United States, he had collected nearly three hundred dollars worth, but then he realized his fears were groundless and had started to spend it. He said the bill they found in his wallet was the last one he had. "Why then," they asked, "did you tell the man in the gas station last Saturday that you still had about a hundred left?"

Hauptmann's response to this was more evasive. He explained that he really hadn't told the officers the exact truth; to be quite honest he actually did have about a hundred left back at his home in a tin box. Keaten, Sisk, and Finn then affixed their signatures to the face of the incriminating twenty-dollar gold note, bearing serial number A35517877A, the one they had extracted from Hauptmann's wallet.

Having already notified Inspector John Lyons of the capture of Hauptmann, the men arranged to meet him at the corner of White Plains Avenue and Gun Hill Road. The men had agreed that the commanding officer of their New York unit should share in the honor of having had a part in the arrest of the kidnapper. They proceeded to the specified location, but had to wait 35 minutes there for the inspector to join them. Upon his arrival, the convoy started to wend its way back to the Hauptmann home at 1279 East 222nd Street.

The entourage, now comprised of five cars, included Hauptmann in the lead car seated between Officer John Wallace, to whom he was securely handcuffed, and Lieutenant Finn. Hauptmann's blue Dodge, driven by one of the other officers, brought up the rear, until the convoy was met by Inspector Lyons, who followed them adding yet another car to what already resembled a small parade.

It was close to eleven o'clock when the cars entered Needham Avenue, next to Hauptmann's home and drove to the rear of the property. The men, anxious to find what the home would reveal, scrambled from their cars and entered by way of the front door. Once inside, they hurried up the steps to the second floor apartment where the Hauptmann's lived. The accused man had told the men of his wife and baby, but as they entered they found the apartment empty of occupants.

The police continued their inquisition in the back bedroom as they pressed the prisoner for more information regarding the gold certificates Hauptmann claimed he owned. Bringing them a small tin box with a combination lock, he proceeded to open it for them. Inside were six twenty-dollar gold coins. "There is the hundred or so." Hauptmann said, pointing to the contents.

"Where are the gold certificates, like the one we found in your wallet?" Finn hammered on. The much confused Hauptmann explained that he had no gold certificates of this kind, that he had been referring to the gold coins he had hoarded.

Suddenly one of the police officers gave Hauptmann a violent push, a shove that caused him to fall heavily back on his bed. "Where are the gold notes you told the gas station man you had?", they probed further. "How did you get hold of so many?", the investigators threw their questions at a faster pace. "Isn't it true that you extorted them from Charles Lindbergh? Isn't it true that you kidnapped his baby? Isn't it true that the bills you have were part of the ransom payment? You are the kidnapper!." In rapid-like fire their questions and accusations at last made him aware as to the reason for his apprehension. They had not picked him up for the crime of gold hoarding. They were arresting him for a far more serious offense --- that of kidnapping the world's most famous baby.

"What are you saying?" Hauptmann protested. "I know nothing about any kidnapping! I know nothing about ransom money!"

As the interrogation was taking place in the bedroom by Lyons, Sisk, Keaten, and Finn, other officers were literally tearing the five-room apartment to pieces searching for additional evidence they could bring against Hauptmann. Drawers of cabinets were pulled out and emptied of their contents, the floor becoming the main depository. The baby's nursery was ransacked, with clothes and toys strewn about as the searchers exhibited no concern for their value. The officers appeared to be obsessed with an intent desire to find more incriminating evidence in order to confirm their suspicions that their prisoner was deeply involved in the crime. The baby's rocking chair, high chair, and playpen, all constructed by his daddy, revealed nothing of use to the investigators, but they were nevertheless promiscuously thrown about with utter disdain. Mattresses were pierced and torn open, stuffed toy animals received the same treatment, and the contents of shelves were removed and not replaced. The apartment resembled a scene of an aftermath of a battle.

A woman entered the apartment and stood momentarily terrified at what she saw. She glanced about at the shambles that had been made of her once neat living quarters by a group of strange men. Men who seemed intent on taking her possessions and those of the two dearest people to her heart and tossing them asunder with a viciousness such as she had never seen.

The woman was Anna Hauptmann, wife of Richard, who just a short time earlier, after having breakfast with him, had carried her little son Manfred to a window from where he could wave good-bye to his daddy as he departed for work. After bathing and dressing her little "Bubi", the name they affectionately called him, she took him out into the backyard to play. The day was a beautiful one and while mother and baby were enjoying the warmth of the autumn sun, she reasoned little Manfred might enjoy a ride in his coach. Taking her young son in her arms, she walked toward the back door where she was greeted by Louisa Schussler who, with her husband Victor and young daughter Viola, shared the first floor rear apartment beneath the Hauptmanns.

After an exchange of pleasantries, Mrs. Schussler inquired if Mr. Hauptmann was still at home. "No" Anna replied, "He went to work as usual."

"But, I hear voices and movement upstairs in your apartment. Surely someone is up there.", Anna's friend and neighbor emphatically continued.

Asking Mrs. Schussler if she would look after Manfred while she went up to investigate, she turned and at the same time was accosted by a stern faced man who gruffly demanded of her: "What is your name?"

Although somewhat hesitant, thinking it was really none of his business, she nevertheless answered: "I am Mrs. Hauptmann."

Showing her his detectives's badge, he told her to follow him. "Come upstairs" was his curt order, "the police want to ask you some questions."

And the scene she viewed was one of nearly complete destruction. As she entered their bedroom she saw her dear Richard sitting on the bed, his arms secured by handcuffs.

Crying, she ran to his side: "Richard, what is this?" Placing her arms about him, she held him close.

"Richard", she pleaded, "did you do anything wrong?"

"No, Annie." he answered her quietly.

"Oh, yeah!" one of the cops jibed. "You'll find out pretty soon."

"Take that woman outside." Lyons commanded, as the now distraught wife was pulled away and led down to the front room. She had started to weep. What was taking place? Why were they treating her Richard with such contempt? The woman was visibly shaken by the unexpected happenings of the last few minutes.

Once Anna Hauptmann was removed from the bedroom, the officers continued their sharp questioning of her husband. Special Agent Seery showed him a pair of women's black suede shoes. "Didn't you buy these shoes with a twenty-dollar gold certificate about a week and a half ago?"

"Yes." Hauptmann conceded that he had. "I bought them for my wife."

"How about these two bills, Hauptmann? Did you pay Mrs. Rauch with these gold notes?" they countered with their rapid-fire questions.

The two ten-dollar bills they put before their prisoner were those they had retrieved from Mrs. Pauline Rauch, the Hauptmann's elderly landlady, who lived with her son Max, in the first floor front section of the home.

Hauptmann agreed that he had definitely paid Mrs. Rauch with the bills as part of his September rent. Pressed now for an explanation as to where he had acquired the bills, he told them he had probably been handed them by other merchants or possibly even bankers. He again admitted his purchase of gasoline with another ten-dollar gold note the previous Saturday.

As the search of the Hauptmann quarters continued, more items were found which appeared to the investigators to be more than incriminating. Seventeen memorandum and account books were located in which they saw notations had been made in both German and English. These, Hauptmann explained, contained records of transactions made by him and a close friend who had been buying, trading, and selling furs together for approximately two years. Some held a record of their dealings as partners in the stock market for the same time period. Also retrieved from among Richard Hauptmann's possessions was an expensive pair of German field glasses, causing the police to jump to an immediate conclusion that their prisoner had used them to spy, from a great distance, on the activities which had taken place, in and around the Lindbergh home, as he made his plans for the kidnapping.

In order to get to the attic, reached by means of entering a small linen closet, removing the shelves, and using the cleats which had held them in place, the investigators had to climb through a small trap-door opening in the ceiling. Here in the unfinished attic they found one hundred Hudson sealskin pelts and very little else of anything worth noting. Hauptmann explained that the pelts belonged to a friend and that he was merely keeping them for him.

The wild bedlam of the hour had literally turned into one of household destruction as their unsystematic hunt continued. Although their search had turned up letters, pictures, maps, and other items usually owned by an average family, their relentless quest to find the incriminating missing box, which had held the ransom money, eluded them.

During the interrogation Special Agent Sisk had become aware of Hauptmann's demeanor while sitting on the bed. Sisk noticed the accused man's attempt to peer out of the window. Walking to the window, the officer glanced out and saw the small frame garage across the lane, some 50 feet away.

Taking advantage of this as a possible clue which could lead them to something of value, Sisk, hoping to catch Hauptmann off guard, suddenly thrust forth his question as he pointed in the direction of the garage: "Is that where you hid the money?"

"No," came Hauptmann's quick response, "I have no money."

Informing Inspector Lyons and Lieutenant Keaten of his suspicions, the heads of the three investigating forces moved their personal search to the garage. It took them little time to break the lock which held the double doors secure. Inside the small interior, which measured 11 by 15 feet, they noticed an assortment of items. The contents were comparable to those most families would store in a garage because of the limited space a small apartment would afford. In addition to Hauptmann's carpentry tools and work bench, they found various pieces of lumber of different lengths, an assortment of tin cans and household items, including several trunks, a folding cot, a wash boiler, a baby carriage, folding chairs, several mens shirts still in their original laundry wrappings, a bassinet, and countless other items of no importance to the investigators. All of these items were found stashed neatly against the walls. However, once the police had finished their initial search, all the contents were tossed outside in disarray at the front of the garage.

They discovered that the garage floor had been constructed of heavy two and a half inch thick planks, eight inches wide. The flooring showed evidence of wear and soiling from oil drippings of automobiles. As they moved about the interior, continuing to search for additional evidence, Sisk noticed that two of these middle planks tilted loosely as he walked across them. Taking a crowbar, he pried the loose boards completely away from the rest of the flooring. Beneath them the soil gave evidence of having recently been dug up and smoothly recovered. Taking a spade, the overzealous agent started to dig with increased intensity, motivated with a hope that he was to soon find the ransom box and missing money that Hauptmann had hidden under the garage floor.

After digging a hole nearly a foot deep, his spade struck a solid object that sounded much like metal. Carefully digging the dirt from around it, the men were disappointed to find that "the sunken treasure" they hoped to find was nothing more than a heavy metal jar. After prolonged tugging the jar was finally forced loose. Wiping away the coating of mud and dirt that encased it, the officers pried off the stubborn lid. Peering in, they found it to be absolutely empty except for a few inches of water that sloshed away at the bottom when the jar was shaken.

Collectively, the police realized that the past hour and a half had failed to be beneficial to them. Since the questioning of Hauptmann in his home, and the search of his premises had both proven to be unfruitful, they agreed it would be more advantageous to move him to the Greenwich Street police station in Manhattan where a more intensified interrogation could be conducted. Their decision was to take him to the headquarters of the Second Precinct at 156 Greenwich Street, located in the lower West Side, close to the elevated tracks, where on the second floor they could interrogate their prisoner safe from the prying eyes of the press. Although, safe from the news media, Hauptmann was not to be kept safe from the "third degree" he would soon be forced to endure.

It was about twelve-thirty when the prisoner was taken from his home. Inside, Anna watched through a front window as he was led, shackled by handcuffs, to a police car waiting at the curb. This was to be the last time she would ever see her dear husband leave his home. As the car sped away, Richard Hauptmann glanced back. It was the last time he would ever see his home. Behind its walls were those he held dearest to him. His wife, whom he affectionately called "Anny", now shedding tears of sorrow for her departing husband, and his little "Bubi", whom she held tight in her arms.

Enroute to the police station they made a stop at the Central Savings Bank at Broadway and 73rd Street. Here they checked a safe deposit vault that Hauptmann said he maintained. However, it contained nothing but a few documents that proved to be absolutely worthless to the investigators. Just another disappointment for his captors.

From here the cars moved on to the place of incarceration, called by many, "the old bastille", where the police were certain they would be able to wring a confession from Hauptmann's lips.

Meanwhile, back on 222nd Street, Anna Hauptmann was pleading with the police to tell her where they had taken her Richard. Ignoring her pleas, they continued to concentrate on their search of Hauptmann's personal possessions, while at the same time, they proceeded to destroy the physical appearance of the apartment over the unheeded protests of Mrs. Rauch, the Hauptmann's distraught landlady.

During the next two hours, Anna was successful in learning that Richard had been arrested and taken to the Greenwich Street police station. She did not have to beg the police to take her to him. This had already been their plan. While they had taken a great deal of time in questioning Anna, they learned nothing that would implicate her involvement with her husband in the crime. They decided she was nothing more than a devoted German housewife who loved her husband dearly and trusted him implicitly.

The time had now reached 2:30 as she arranged with Louisa Schussler to look after her little "Bubi".

As they led Richard's "Anny" from her home, she pleadingly inquired: "Where are you taking me?"

The terse answer she received left little doubt in her mind: "The same place where your husband is!"

END OF BOOK ONE

Charles and Anne Lindbergh (Courtesy of UPI/Corbis-Bettmann)

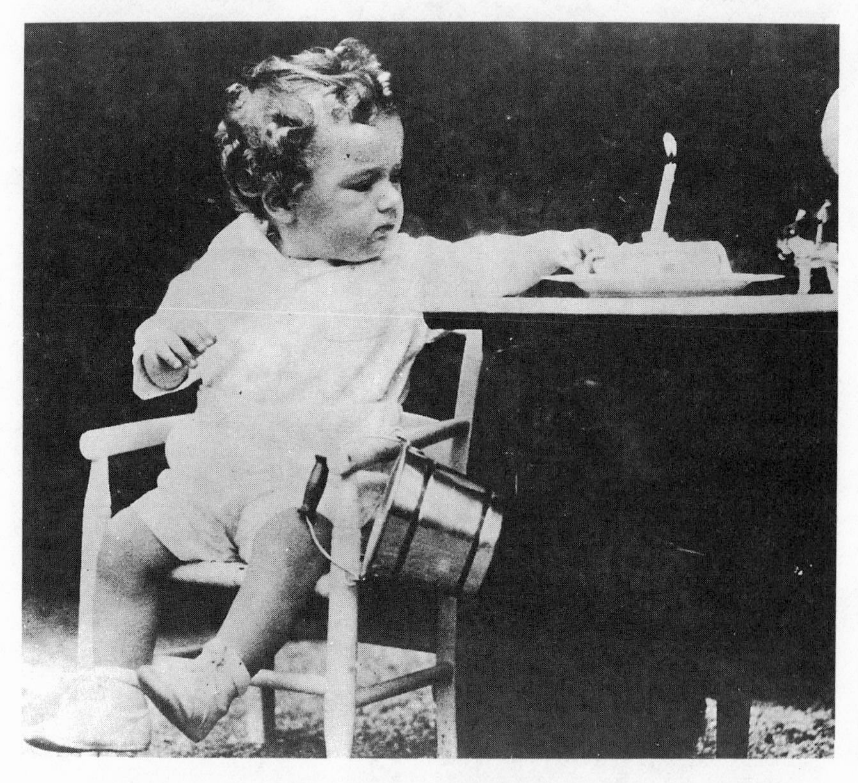

Charles A. Lindbergh, Jr. The kidnapped baby on his first birthday. (Author's collection)

Betty Gow, the child's nursemaid, and Oliver Whateley, the Lindbergh's butler. (AP/Wide World Photos)

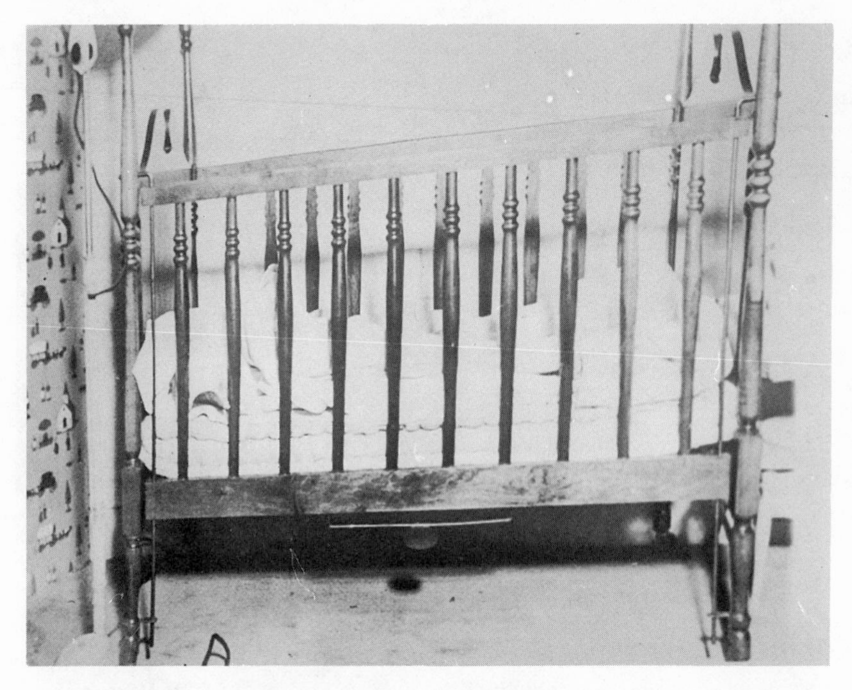

The empty crib—from where the baby was taken. (AP/Wide World Photos)

The southeast nursery window from where it was believed the baby was taken. (Courtesy of UPI/Corbis-Bettmann)

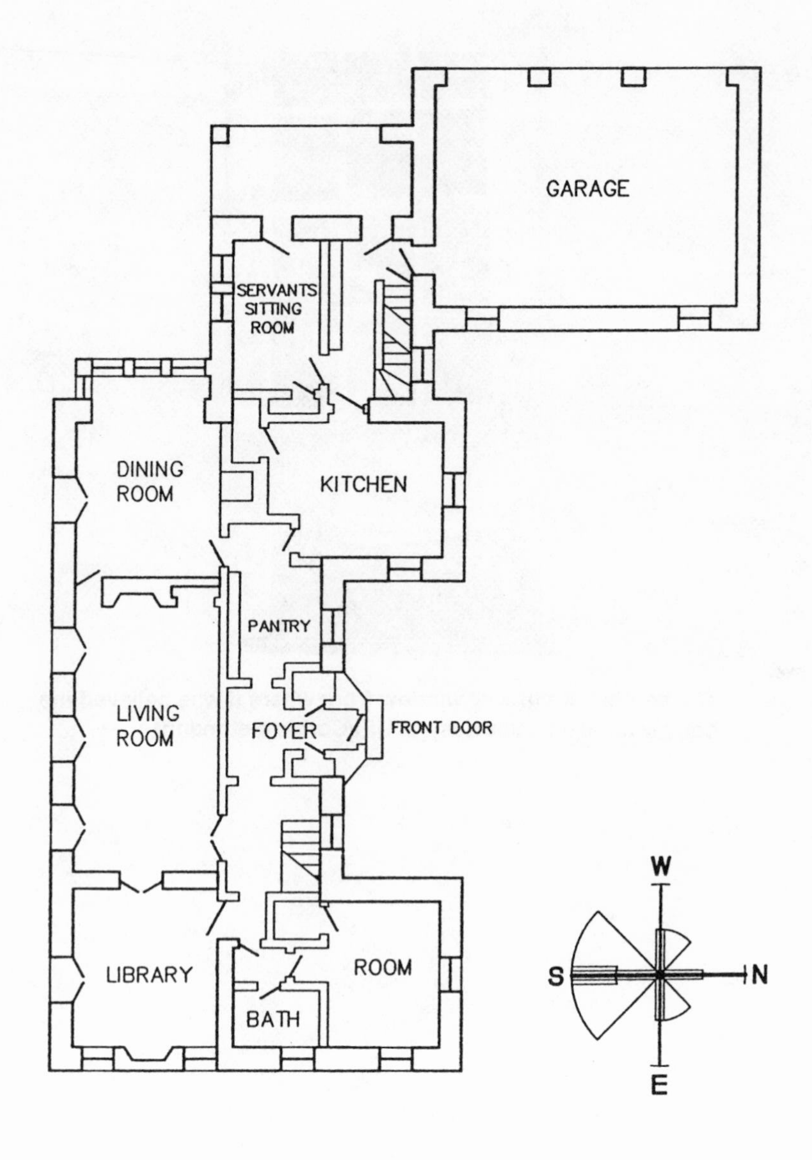

Floor plans of the Lindbergh Hopewell, New Jersey, home: Helmut Vickus.

HOME

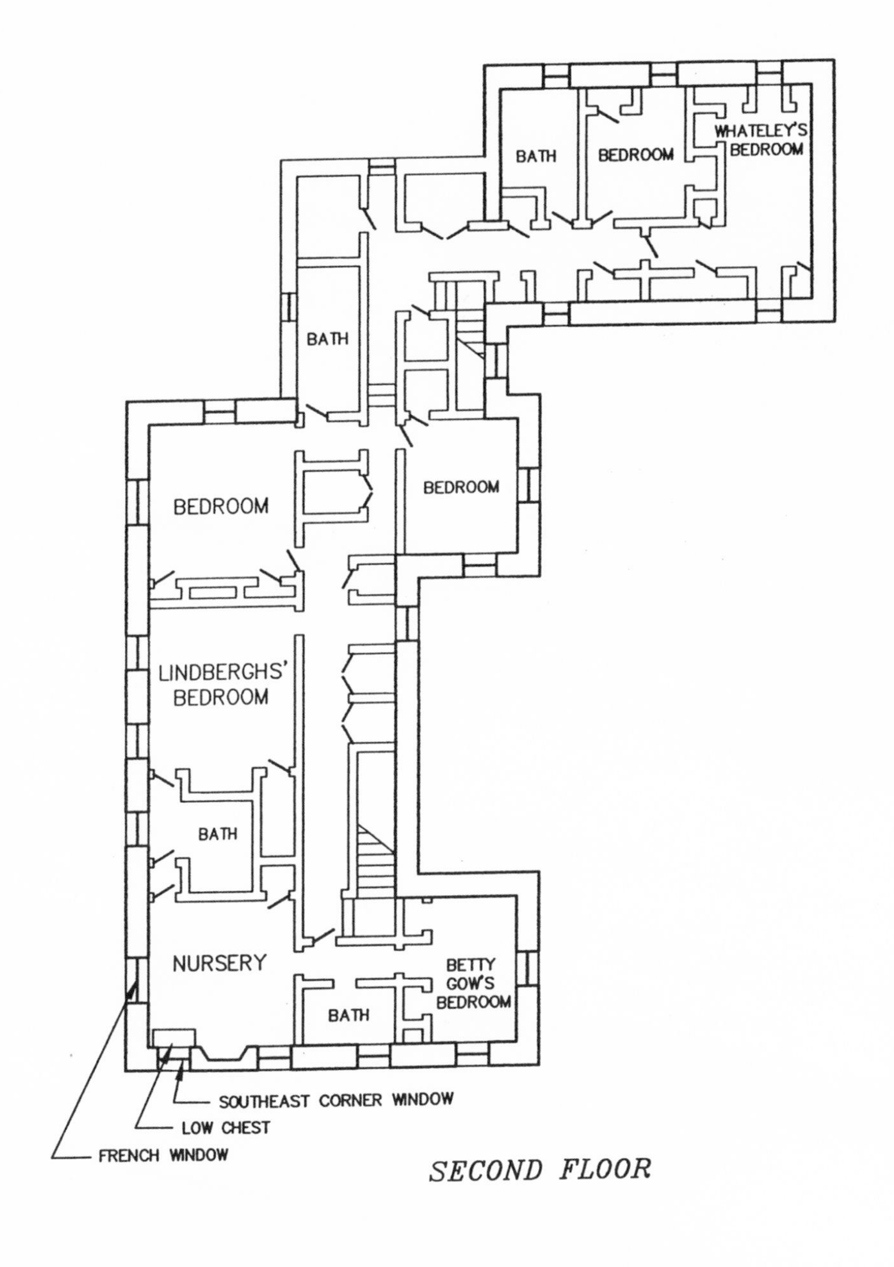

SECOND FLOOR

Dear Sir!

Have 50.000 $ redy 25 000 $ in 20 $ bills 15000 $ in 10 $ bills and 10000 $ in 5 $ bills. After 2-4 days we will inform you were to deliver the mony.

We warn you for making anyding public or for notify

the child is in gut care.

Indication for all letters are singnature and 3 holds.

The note the kidnapper left on the nursery windowsill. (UPI/Corbis-Bettmann)

WANTED

INFORMATION AS TO THE WHEREABOUTS OF

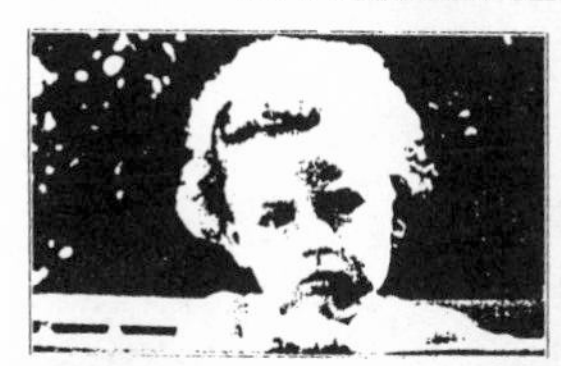

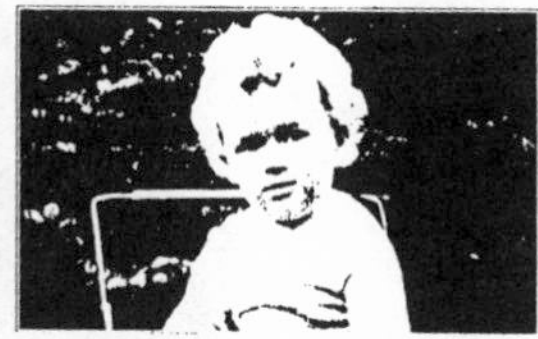

CHAS. A. LINDBERGH, JR.

OF HOPEWELL, N. J.

SON OF COL. CHAS. A. LINDBERGH

World-Famous Aviator

This child was kidnaped from his home in Hopewell, N. J., between 8 and 10 p. m. on Tuesday, March 1, 1932.

DESCRIPTION:

Age, 20 months	Hair, blond, curly
Weight, 27 to 30 lbs.	Eyes, dark blue
Height, 29 inches	Complexion, light

Deep dimple in center of chin
Dressed in one-piece coverall night suit

ADDRESS ALL COMMUNICATIONS TO
COL. H. N. SCHWARZKOPF, TRENTON, N. J., or
COL. CHAS. A. LINDBERGH, HOPEWELL, N. J.

ALL COMMUNICATIONS WILL BE TREATED IN CONFIDENCE

March 11, 1932

COL. H. NORMAN SCHWARZKOPF
Supt. New Jersey State Police, Trenton, N. J.

The wanted notice issued shortly after the kidnapping. (AP/Wide World Photos)

Aerial picture of Lindbergh Estate taken just hours after kidnapping. (UPI/Corbis-Bettman)

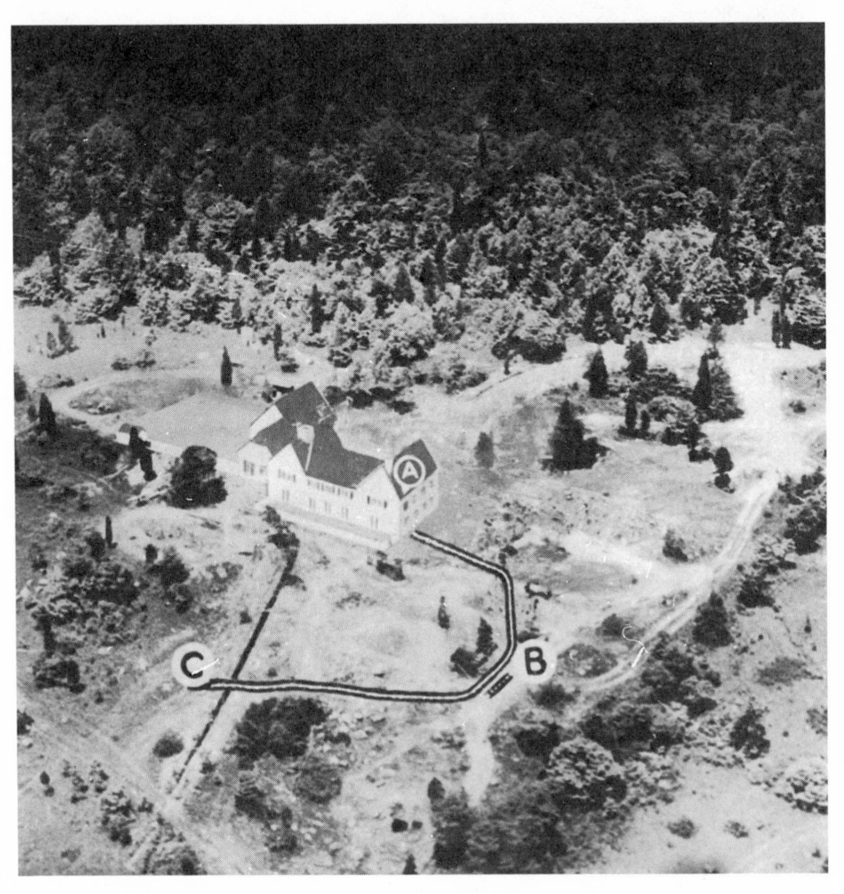

Aerial picture of home used by police showing what they believed was the route of departure taken by the kidnappers (read early police reports). (AP/Wide World Photos)

Violet Sharpe—maid in the Morrow home in Englewood, New Jersey, who took her own life in fear of questioning by police. (AP/Wide World Photos)

Dr. John F. Condon—the mysterious "Jafsie." (AP/Wide World Photos)

Joseph Perrone—who delivered the letter to Jafsie. (UPI/Corbis-Bettmann)

Woodlawn Cemetery entrance gate—where Condon first met "Cemetery John." (UPI/Corbis-Bettmann)

St. Raymond's Cemetery—where the $50,000 ransom was paid. (UPI/Corbis-Bettmann)

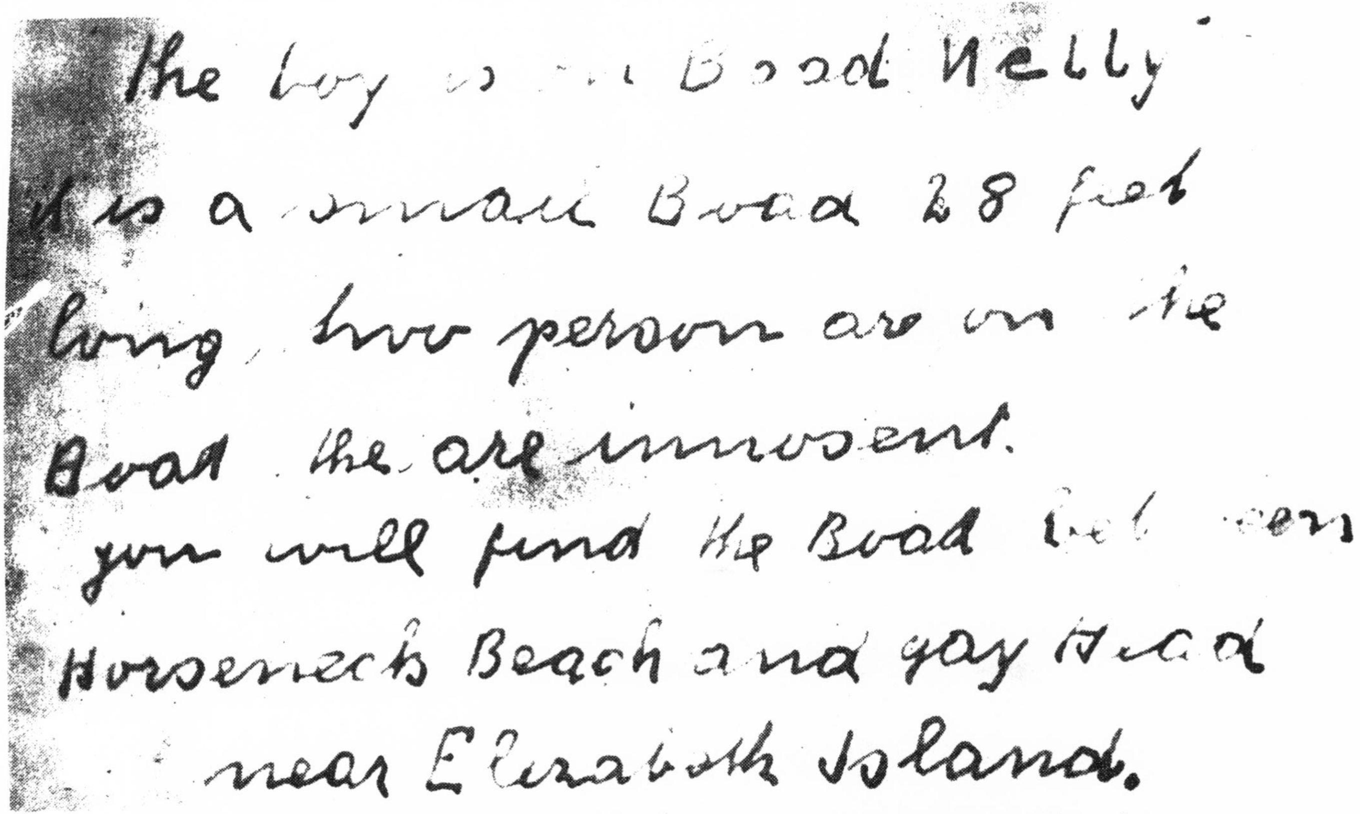

the boy is on Boad Nelly
it is a small Boad 28 feet
long. two person are on the
Boad. the are innosent.
you will find the Boad between
Horseneck Beach and gay Head
near Elizabeth Island.

Note received by Condon in exchange for $50,000 ransom. (AP/Wide World Photos)

Corpse shown exactly as it was found by William Allen. (Author's collection, New Jersey State Police)

William Allen—points to exact spot where he discovered the human remains identified as those of the kidnapped child. (UPI/Corbis-Bettmann)

B O O K T W O

THE TRIAL!

C H A P T E R N I N E T E E N

Richard Hauptmann

On Sunday, November 26, 1899 in the little town of Kamenz, Saxony, Germany, approximately 75 miles south of Berlin, Bruno Richard Hauptmann was born. His parents, Herman and Paulina Hauptmann, had three other sons, Herman, Max, and Fritz, and a daughter, Emma.

His father worked as a stone-mason in the little town of nearly ten thousand people, while his mother looked after the needs of her five children at 64 Bautzenerstrasse. Here, in a two story brick home, is where the Hauptmann family lived, in rather close quarters, on the first floor. The second floor they rented to another family.

Richard's years as a little boy were largely spent exploring the woods and fields near his home. It was during these days that his love of nature was first recognized, due to his interest in the birds, animals, and flowers of the area.

The youngest Hauptmann began his schooling at the age of six, and after his teacher helped him overcome an embarrassing speech impediment, he seemed to enjoy life among his schoolmates, learning many new and interesting things about the world around him.

Paulina Hauptmann was a devout Christian woman who believed in reading stories from the Bible to her children. At a time when she believed Richard had reached an age of true understanding, she encouraged him to make his decision to receive Christ as his saviour. Every Sunday the five children and their mother attended church services together. However, their father disassociated himself from any form of religious service, rather instead to seek out the local beer halls.

Richard's early years of learning were those spent primarily under the teaching and influence of his mother. His father, unfortunately, was spending more time away from home, drinking more heavily, and arriving home at late hours each night. Nevertheless, the children and their mother enjoyed these early years just being together. Richard would always remember the annual Christmas celebrations, when they would deliver food baskets to those families less fortunate than they, and the carol singing each night in the town square. He would likewise never forget the annual Kamenz Forest Festival, held each August, when a thousand children, dressed in white and carrying wreaths made of flowers and oak leaves, would march in procession through the town's streets.

As he grew older, Richard was fascinated with the German soldiers when they arrived in town, many of them taking up lodging in the local homes. The young boys would march along at their side in parade fashion. They would watch them clean and load their rifles, and at times were permitted the exciting task of helping the military men polish their boots.

Before long Paulina Hauptmann experienced the trauma of seeing her children taking leave of their home. Her sons, Herman and Max were the first to depart for service in the army. Emma, still in her teens, decided it would be best to seek her fortune in the United States, while Fritz abandoned his home soon after to study the tailoring trade, which left Richard the only one remaining at home to help his mother.

Richard attended grade school for eight years and, after completion, then entered a trade school. Here, for two years, he learned much about the profession of carpentry and machinery. At the age of 14 he served as a carpenter's helper for a salary of three or four marks a week and maintenance. As his skill improved, he worked as a first class carpenter in Kamenz until, at the age of 17, he was called into the military service of his country during World War I.

The war was a horrible experience for everyone who had loved ones away at the front, but it proved to be an especially tragic one for Paulina Hauptmann. Two of her sons, Max and Herman were killed; Fritz had been reported missing in action; and Richard, serving as a machine gunner with the 12th Machine Gun Company on the Western Front, was slightly wounded. After returning to duty he was gassed and sent back to a field hospital where he remained until the war ended. In addition to the heartache Paulina Hauptmann had been brought to suffer, she lost her husband in death, a man she dearly loved, during the summer of 1918. Richard, having served honorably for the defeated German army, and after receiving his discharge papers, returned home to his widowed mother and ill brother Fritz shortly before

Christmas of 1918.

Arriving back in his poverty stricken community, and the small house he called home, he was greeted by his mother who gave thanks to God for His faithfulness in returning Richard to her. He soon realized that his desperate search for a job in this war-torn country, one that would allow him to support them proved to be unsuccessful. By the time March rolled around the young man, now 19, became desperate, realizing that both food and money were needed in order for them to survive. In spite of the knowledge of the wrong he would be doing, he decided to resort to stealing. This, he rationalized, was what some other returning servicemen had done. They too had come back to their war-ravaged homeland, now experiencing a period of reconstruction, and had turned to crime. And so on the night of Friday, March 14th, 1919 Richard, in the company of Fritz Petzold, a young man with whom he had served in the same regiment, robbed a home in Rackelwitz, a small village nearby, by removing 2000 marks in securities, and two hundred more in cash, and a gold watch and chain from a living room desk. Their first venture into a life of crime had proven to be successful. The next night, on Saturday, March 15th, the two went to the nearby town of Bernbruch and burglarized a home there. With the use of a ladder they entered the second floor of the dwelling of the burgomaster, Herr Schierach. For their trouble, which seemed to them to be rather easy, they were able to steal three hundred marks and a silver watch. They split the money evenly, Richard keeping the watch for himself.

Deciding to continue their crime spree, five days later, in broad daylight at ten o'clock in the morning, on Thursday, March 20th they saw two women wheeling perambulators on the road between Wiesa and Nebelschutz. Their plan was to rob them of the contents of the carriages, but when they accosted the pair, one of the women rejected their order to stop. Petzold foolishly drew a pistol and threatened to shoot as they emptied the carts which netted them nine loaves of bread, eight ration cards and three marks. That same night they brazenly entered the home of Edward Scheumann, a leather merchant, who lived just two doors away from the Hauptmann home. The desk in this home netted them another 200 marks and another watch. They were gaining confidence in their ability as thieves, once again getting away without detection.

But, their boldness in robbing the two frightened

women of their foodstuffs and ration cards, and leaving them screaming and empty handed, was to be their undoing. A good description of the two young men resulted in their arrest on Wednesday, March 26th, 1919. On Tuesday, June 3rd they were found guilty of all four crimes, three counts of burglary and one of highway robbery. Both men were sentenced to a term of five years and one week in Beutthen prison at Bautzen. On Friday, March 23rd, 1923 Richard was paroled.

A much shamed man returned once again to his mother in Kamenz. Welcoming him with open arms, she told him of her love and begged him to never again do anything that would bring dishonor to his family and promise that he would never again resort to criminal practices. Richard Hauptmann, who loved his mother dearly, sincerely meant to keep his promise to her.

However, since he had already served time in prison for crimes he readily admitted, he was now known as a branded criminal. Every crime committed in the area caused him to be considered a suspect. In June, bales of leather belting strips were stolen from a machine shop, a sawmill, and a pottery shop. Richard was immediately arrested, although he vehemently denied any knowledge of the thefts. Unable to prove his claimed innocence, or find anyone who would accept his professed innocence, he was again thrown in the local jail awaiting trial.

Realizing that if he were found guilty, innocent though he was, he would have to serve the final year of his former sentence, plus the penalty for this new crime, he decided to try to escape. In this hope, fate proved to be with him. He remained in jail only two days. Since he was allowed the privilege of going outside to exercise in the jail yard, he took advantage of an open gate with no guard nearby. He nonchalantly walked through it unmolested into the fields and nearby woods never to return.

But, his escape from jail only served to increase his record as a criminal. He was now listed as a fugitive from justice. Anxious to flee his homeland, rather than face a possible rearrest for a crime of which he insisted he was innocent, Hauptmann decided to seek a new start in America. However, the odds of his accomplishing this were against him. He had neither money nor passport. Undaunted by this, after accepting what food and money his mother could spare, and receiving her blessings by promising he would live the life of a Christian in the new land and never do anything that would bring discredit to his name, he set off for Hamburg.

In late June of 1923, young Richard Hauptmann went on board the SS George Washington and stowed away by hiding in the hold of the giant steamship bound for New York City. It was here that he hoped to start a new life for himself.

Suffering from the elements of cramped and confined quarters and trying to exist on the small amount of food and water he had brought with him, he became ill and was discovered by a crewman several days before the ship was due to dock. Questioned by the United States immigration officials on Ellis Island, he explained it had been his intention to enter America in this manner since he had run out of money. He gave his name as John Perlmeyer, and apparently his questioners took this for granted, since they ceased their brief interrogation, neither photographing or fingerprinting him. He was merely turned over to the ships captain who took him back to Hamburg on the ships return trip.

His failure to gain entrance into the United States was not a serious disappointment to him. In August he made another attempt, but this time he was discovered shortly after he sneaked on board. Since the ship had not yet left the pier, and realizing he would be turned over to the German police, he jumped overboard and was able to make his way safely to shore and escape apprehension.

However, in November, Hauptmann's third attempt to enter America proved successful. This time he had boarded the ship at Bremerhaven, once again on board the George Washington. He stowed away in a coal bunker, among the engines, with only two loaves of bread and two bottles of water, where he was able to remain undetected for 10 days. Although he was filthy from his stay in the bowels of the ship, he was able to make his way to a washroom. As the ship docked at Hoboken, New Jersey, he bravely walked unmolested down the gangplank to the land which was to be his new home. Realizing he was free at last, and although he was aware that he had entered America illegally, he gave God his thanks for the safety of his passage.

After crossing the Hudson River, from Hoboken to Manhattan on a ferry boat, he attempted to find the only person he was acquainted with in New York, a friend he had met on board ship during his first attempt to enter America. He remembered his name as Albert Diebig, but after going to the 86th Street address that had been given him, he was told that he had moved to an unknown location. Discouraged and tired, Hauptmann had walked from 23rd Street to 96th Street and Amsterdam Avenue. Here he encountered a man named Fred Aldinger who, after realizing Richard was from his homeland Germany, and recognizing his inability to speak English, befriended him and took him to his home nearby.

It was only a few days before Hauptmann's 24th birthday that he found himself quite comfortable in the home of his new friends, Fred Aldinger and his mother Lena, a German washerwoman who also had not learned to speak English. Richard was content indeed, as he mailed his mother a post-card telling her of the success he had entering a new land of opportunity.

The door of opportunity opened further for Richard when, a week later, he found employment as a dishwasher in a restaurant down near what was known as the South Ferry, in Greenwich Village. His salary was $15 a week. However, after working there for a month and a half, he abandoned this job to accept one that paid slightly more ($16) with a firm called Washburn and Wild. But his time here was short, because he left to hold various other positions, each paying him a better salary working as a dyer in a dyeing business and a machinist in Brooklyn. His salary had increased to $26 a week.

Each time Richard changed jobs he improved the status of his position. Finally he landed a job as carpenter, the trade he had been schooled in, which paid him a dollar an hour for his services. His work was chiefly that of repairs, his average weekly salary being $44 since the firm he worked for at Sixth Avenue and 40th Street had him employed on a full time schedule.

During this time Richard's ability to speak and write the English language was improving due to the help given him by Fred Aldinger, his mother Lena, and the various German bosses for whom he worked. Richard soon found an apartment of his own on 156th Street, but remained there only a short time. His next move to more comfortable living quarters took him to another apartment, this one located on 88th Street between Park and Lexington Avenues in a German colony known as Yorkville. Although he remained here only a few months, it was during this time that his friend Albert Diebig located him and renewed their previous brief acquaintance. The two decided to share an apartment at 154th Street between Parkway and Amsterdam Avenue, but once again after a short time, a change of residency was made with the two men moving to another apartment on

97th Street in New York's East Side.

While Hauptmann's changes in living quarters had been many, his employment as a carpenter had continued uninterrupted. On October 24th, 1924 he began working in Lakewood, New Jersey at a job he had acquired by answering a newspaper advertisement. This position paid him approximately $50 a week. This enabled him to bank $38 weekly in an account he had opened in the downtown Manhattan branch of the Bank of the United States. The job was an excellent one, but it lasted only two months.

Christmas day arrived and Hauptmann found himself unemployed. However, this afforded him the opportunity of completing the bungalow he and his helper, Diebig, had constructed in Lakewood.

His period of unemployment proved to be only for a short time since he soon acquired more work where his skill of carpentry was needed. He was paid union wages of one dollar an hour and was provided 44 hours of work each week at a construction job near Bronx Park. In addition, he began working for a man named Heinzelmann on East 9th Street between First and Second Avenues, which allowed him to continue banking a large amount of his earnings.

All the while Richard Hauptmann was working at various jobs and struggling to improve his grasp of the English language, something had taken place that was to play an important part in his future.

On Tuesday, January 1, 1924, a young lady of 25 years, walked down the gangplank of a ship that had safely carried her to the soil of New York City. Her entrance into the United States, unlike that of Richard Hauptmann, was legal. Her name was Anna Schoeffler. She had left her father and mother, Frederick and Katherine, back in the village of Markgroningen, the province of Wurttemberg, Germany. Her father, a saddlemaker, had found it difficult to earn anything more than a meager living in post-war Germany. Anna attempted to help by working as a maid in Zurich, Switzerland. But her wages were quite small and added little to aid the family's finances, so she decided to journey to America and seek better employment in the new world.

Once on the shore of her new homeland, she was greeted by her cousin, Marie Freiermuth, who resided in the Borough of Queens and with whom she remained for ten days. Her niece, Wally Freiermuth, had already mastered the English language quite well and the companionship of her relative proved to be beneficial to Anna as she observed and quickly learned and followed the customs and language of the new country she had chosen as her home of future years.

Anna Schoeffler was also quite fortunate to gain almost immediate employment. On Thursday, January 10th she started working for a Mrs. Rosetta Rosenbaum at 316 West 79th Street. Her duties were those of general housework.

Lena Aldinger, who did the wash for the wealthy Rosenbaum family, soon became friendly with the attractive Anna as she stopped each week at the Rosenbaum home on Riverside Drive. Lena, in attempting to play "match-maker", continued to rave to her about Richard Hauptmann, hoping that the two would meet. She told Anna that she considered Hauptmann as another son of hers. Finally, approximately three months after her arrival in America, and after much persuasion, she met Richard in the Aldinger home.

Anna was much impressed with the man's fine character, his handsome appearance, his kindness, and genuine concern for her. Their first meeting was a pleasant one during which they sat listening to the radio and singing German songs with another guest who was there. Anna told them it was exactly as they did in her home in Germany. When it was time for her to leave for her home Richard walked with her to the subway station.

During the months which followed the two saw much of each other. A memorable time was spent at Coney Island, New York's famous fun park, where they rode the amusements, a thrill Anna would never forget. However, their dates consisted primarily of walks along Riverside Drive as they enjoyed watching the boats passing by on the Hudson River, the frolicking of the squirrels in the park, feeding the pigeons as the two sat talking on a park bench until darkness set in. Both spoke often of the days of their youth back in Germany. It was during these times that Hauptmann came to the realization that he had "found my dear wife, an upright Christian woman to whom truth is sacred." He recognized in Anna Schoeffler that he had found a woman who held the same Christian morals as those of his mother Paulina.

He asked Anna to be his wife, but only after he had told her of his imprisonment for crimes he committed in Germany as a youth and of his illegal entry into the United States. Admiring him further for his honesty in telling her, Anna had no difficulty understanding this. She too had experienced the hard times her family had been subjected to in Markgroningen after the war, when there was no work, no food, and no money. Agreeing that this should be put behind them and not impair their future happiness together, on Saturday, October 10th, 1925, in the home of Marie Freiermuth, they were united in marriage.

Their marriage was a happy one. Together they enjoyed the simple things of life, more walks in the park, sitting on benches feeding the birds, and talking to the little children playing in the area. Richard and Anna both loved children and held fond hopes of becoming parents in the future. Financially they had no problems since both were working and bringing in enough money to bank a good portion.

Two or three weeks before his marriage Richard was earning $66 a week and had purchased a second hand car, a Chevrolet, which cost him somewhere between $200 and $300. Anna, while working for Mrs.Rosenbaum since shortly after her entrance into America, had earned $50 a month during her first year and $55 each month of her second year. She had opened a savings account in the Central Savings Bank at 173rd Street and Broadway. She terminated her employment with Mrs Rosenbaum in October, shortly before her wedding. Between the two they had been able to save $1600 prior to their wedding, and in addition to this Richard had saved another $1000 without Anna's knowledge of it. He had planned to use it as a surprise toward the purchase of a house his future wife had expressed as her wish that they could someday own.

During the first two weeks of their life together they lived in one room at 154th Street near Broadway, between 4th and Amsterdam, then another move took them to an apartment on 122nd Street at Park Avenue. But their residence here was also one of short duration. Shortly before Christmas of 1926, they moved to Needham Avenue in the Bronx.

Soon after their move here, Anna and Richard purchased a lunch room at 223rd Street and Lexington Avenue for $900, but after operating it for only a month, they sold it to Hauptmann's friend, Albert Diebig, making a profit of $400. Anna had obtained employment as a waitress in a bakery operated by a Mrs. Ella Achenbach on 191st Street near Third Avenue, and for her duties there she was paid $16 a week plus tips.

In June of 1928, after obtaining a four month leave of absence, Anna sailed for Germany as a third class passenger on the boat "York". While there she visited her ill and aging parents in Markgroningen, as well as Richard's mother in Kamenz. Accompanying Anna on her trip to Europe was Mrs. Achenbach's nine year old daughter, Pauline "Mutzi", who visited her grandmother in Siegen in the Province of Westphalia. They returned home on the liner Bremen and Anna immediately resumed working for Mrs. Achenbach on October 26th, remaining there until December. Early in 1929 she continued working for the new owner, a Mr. Wiletz who, after purchasing the business from the Achenbachs, required her experience as a waitress and counter-girl for a short time.

In June of 1929 Anna began working for Christian and Katy Fredericksen in their bakery-lunchroom at 3815 Dyre Avenue in the Bronx. For her duties as the experienced counter girl and waitress she proved to be, she received $18 a week and tips. Her salary, however, was soon increased to $20. Although the hours of work were somewhat longer, she never complained since the pay was larger, she was able to eat her meals there, and on many occasions was allowed to take food home with her at the end of the day. Her work schedule called for her to begin each morning at seven and remain there until five in the afternoon. The only exception to this routine occurred regularly every Tuesday when she was required to stay on the job until eight p.m. due to Mrs. Fredericksen's absence from the shop on that evening. Occasionally she would stay until 9 or 9:30 p.m. Monday was Anna's day off.

As she continued to work at this popular and well patronized Danish owned bakery, Anna's raises in pay soon found her taking home, with tips included, amounts as high as $33 a week. This, combined with the salary Richard was earning, permitted them to live quite comfortably. Her husband, soon after their marriage, had acquired employment with a man named Herman Olson, who required his steady services as a carpenter for the next three or four years. Whenever work became slack, he seemed to always find work with someone else. On Saturday afternoons and Sundays during 1928 and 1929 he worked for his two friends, a Mr. Haberland and a Mr. Tolksdorf building two houses in the Bronx. For this he was paid approximately one thousand dollars.

The money the Hauptmann's were jointly earning allowed them, after setting aside their living expenses, the luxury of enjoying weekends without feeling they were squandering their earnings. They especially enjoyed the time spent with their friends on Hunter Island, a small strip of land located east of their

Bronx home, which extended into the southern shore of the Pelham Bay section of Long Island Sound. It was on this island that the German families would congregate regularly for relaxation and fun.

The plain living Hauptmanns, since the time they first started to frequent Hunter Island in 1928, had met many persons there, many of whom had become their closest friends. Among these were Hans Kloppenburg, Karl and Gerta Henkel, Henry Lemke, Otto and Louise Wollenberg, Isidor Fisch, and others. During the spring and summer months they would enjoy boating in Hauptmann's canoe, bathing, fishing, playing soccer and volleyball. Other things in which all would partake were the times spent sitting together and singing songs of their native Germany accompanied by Richard on the mandolin and Hans Kloppenburg on the guitar. Winter evenings were even more enjoyable as they gathered around a huge bonfire, some sitting in the openings of their tents and lean-tos they had erected. The fellowship was warm and innocent. Sincere friendships were made and shared together on Hunter Island.

During the latter part of 1929, whenever steady employment as a carpenter would become slack, sometimes for a period of months, Richard and Tolksdorf became interested in Wall Street and what was taking place in the Stock Market there. Because of this he began frequenting the firm of Steiner-Rouse and Company on 86th Street, between Third and Lexington Avenues, where he would watch the changes of the Stock Exchange on the board in their office. He had opened an account with Charleton Mott and Company and was soon using some of his savings to buy stocks. Although Anna had at first expressed some disapproval of this, Richard's spasmodic work as a carpenter, and his seemingly sincere promise that his increased interest in the Stock Market would help compensate them for their loss of income, she finally condescended to his wishes.

By the end of 1929, including a mortgage of $3,750, the Hauptmanns were worth, in cash and bank accounts, approximately $9,000. Thrifty as they were, they had not put all of their money in a bank. Instead Richard kept most of his earnings at home, to be used as ready cash when needed. In March of 1931 he bought a brand new 1930 Dodge four-door sedan for $725 and paid for it in cash, taking it from the slightly more than $4,000 he had in a trunk in their apartment. In the bank they had about $600.

Financially, in spite of the Depression, Richard

and Anna Hauptmann were by no means destitute. On July 5th, 1931 they, accompanied by their good friend, Hans Kloppenburg, left on a three month tour of the United States, that included a two week stop in Los Angeles, California, where they visited Richard's sister Emma Gloeckner and her husband Charles. This was a happy reunion for the brother and sister since they had not seen each other since their years they spent together in Germany as youngsters. They made the trip in Hauptmann's Dodge, their supplies neatly contained in a large box the two men had built and mounted on the rear of the car. Their expenses of the trip, a total of only $370 were equally shared. The price of gasoline was only 18 cents a gallon.

Upon the completion of the trip, Anna resumed her work for the Fredericksens and Richard continued working at carpentry jobs for various employers. Agreeing that the apartment they had been sharing with Hans and Henry Lempke on Needham Avenue had grown too small for them, they moved to one they could now share alone on the second floor of a house at 1279 East 222nd Street, only a few blocks away. They moved into their new quarters on Thursday, October 15th, 1931. Their new landlords were Max Rauch and his mother Pauline who lived on the first floor. Their rent was $45 a month.

By the time the year 1932 arrived, Richard's success in the stock market, and together saving their money, allowed Anna to make plans for another trip to visit her mother Katherine in Germany. Mrs. Schoeffler would soon be celebrating her seventieth birthday and Anna was exuberant that she could journey once more to her home in Markgroningen and share the day with her mother. She also planned to visit Richard's mother, and while there, to go to the police authorities and inquire of the possibility of Richard returning to Germany without fear of arrest. On Sunday, July 3rd, her hopes high, she sailed for her homeland, traveling third class on the North German Lloyd. She had a most enjoyable visit with her parents and mother-in-law. Her only disappointment was learning that Richard would be required to wait at least two years longer before he could return to Germany without fear of apprehension and imprisonment. Anna returned to her Richard on Monday, October 10th.

During Anna's lengthy absence, Richard wrote long letters to her, and in one of them, he enclosed a picture of himself. He loved to please his dear wife in many ways, and in this instance he had gone into a photographer's shop on East Eighty-sixth Street and had his picture taken in order to send it to her. The colored picture was an excellent one, his handsome facial features accentuated. Richard had sent her the picture, "So I can be with you over there." The photographer evidently thought so much of the picture he placed it in his show window for all to see.

Upon Anna's return, Richard told her that he had entered into a partnership in the fur business with his new friend, Isidor Fisch. He related to her the fascination he held as Fisch described his many tales of adventure. He said the partnership involved their joint investment in the fur business and the stock market; Fisch taking care of buying and selling furs, himself being responsible for the investment in stocks.

Sometime near the middle of February, Richard met a customer in Fredericksen's Bakery, and when he learned of Hauptmann's inability to find regular work in the carpentry trade, he suggested that he apply at The Reliance Property Management Agency on 6th Avenue. This Hauptmann did, and was informed by a Mr. E.V.C. Pescia that in all probability there would be an opening very soon for a skilled carpenter at the Majestic Apartments which were nearing completion. Richard made a practice of reporting each morning to Pescia, and on Saturday, February 27th, the employment manager told him to post the customary fee of $10 since he was slated to begin work on the morning of Tuesday, March 1st at a pay rate of $100 a month. The elated Hauptmann, after returning home and sharpening the tools he would be using, went on Monday morning to the Majestic Apartments, located at 72nd Street and Central Park West, and left his tools in the basement carpenter's shop, where he would report for work the next day.

Success seemed to smile on the young married couple since Anna had resumed work at Fredericksen's Bakery, and Richard continued to pick up odd jobs requiring his carpentry skills. Richard also continued to realize profits from investments in stocks and furs. And now with the promise of steady work in downtown Manhattan, things were flourishing for them financially.

In December 1932, after realizing earnings of more than $7,000, and saving most of it, since she entered the United States, Anna terminated her work with the Fredericksens. Early the following year she discovered she was pregnant and on Friday, November 3rd, 1933, blond and blue-eyed Manfred Richard Hauptmann was born in Misericordia Hospital on 86th Street, New York City.

Happiness would fall short in describing the contentment of this family. Richard Hauptmann truly loved his little, innocent and faithful, German "hausfrau", whom he affectionately called his "Anny". She was hardworking and thrifty and had complete trust in her handsome husband. Their love of children increased even more after the birth of their own son, little "Bubi", the affectionate nickname they chose to give him.

With the coming of 1934 new hopes were anticipated by the Hauptmann family. A strong desire to see his aging mother, who would soon reach the age of 70, prompted Richard to write to her during the summer. His letter carried to her the good news that his family of three would visit her during the Christmas season. They reasoned that little "Bubi" would by then be in his second year and would be certainly capable of enduring the boat trip to meet his grandparents. Their plans never looked brighter. But, soon after the dawn of Wednesday, September 19th, these plans were dashed and torn asunder, never to become a reality for Richard, Anna, and little Manfred Hauptmann.

CHAPTER TWENTY

"Justice" Grinds Away!

The police quickly hustled their captive up the steps to a second floor room of 156 Centre Street, Greenwich Village, New York's 2nd Precinct Police Station. This lower West Side, out-of-the-way, Manhattan station was one the officers seldom used. They brought Hauptmann here to keep him away from the prying eyes of reporters who, had they taken him elsewhere, would no doubt have noticed the increased police activity, and published a premature announcement in their papers of an arrest being made in the Lindbergh kidnapping. The police were not ready for the public to have any knowledge of what had taken place that day.

The handcuffed prisoner was ushered to a wooden armchair near the center of the room and told to sit there. The arresting authorities, some in uniform, others in plain clothes, gathered around him. The rumbling of an elevated train on the tracks nearby could be clearly heard. As soon as Hauptmann had been seated the barrage of questions began. After receiving answers to their customary initial inquiries; what was his name?, his age?, his place of employment?, how long he had lived in the Bronx?, among other necessary facts needed to complete their official police record, they suddenly turned on him with intense severity.

"What were you doing on the night of March 1st, 1932?" He couldn't remember.

"Weren't you at the Lindbergh home in Hopewell, New Jersey?"

No, he had never heard of Hopewell until he read about it after the kidnapping, was his answer.

Had he ever been in New Jersey?, was their next question. He answered in the affirmative, telling them he had worked in the state when he constructed a few houses there.

The intensity of the questioning moved on at a more rapid pace. "Isn't it true that you helped build the Lindbergh home?"

"No!" he said emphatically. "I told you I was

never in Hopewell!"

"You knew the Lindbergh servants, Betty Gow and Oliver and Elsie Whateley, and no doubt you knew Violet Sharpe in the Morrow home, didn't you?" came their firm declarations.

"No, I don't know any of them. I told you I have never been in or near the Lindbergh home." Hauptmann answered their accusations.

His interrogators continued their unrelentless verbal attack on the prisoner, who had already begun to realize the magnitude of his arrest. Surely, he thought, they can't be serious about his being involved in the Lindbergh kidnapping. Wouldn't his complete lack of knowledge about the crime be enough to prove his innocence to them? This whole thing could not be real. Why, he wondered, had he been singled out as the kidnapper.

"You took that baby from his crib on Tuesday, March 1st and killed him." Their serious accusations continued. "You might as well confess and get it over with." The tormenting charges they were accusing him of were piercing the innermost resources of his now fearful and troubled mind. What are these men saying? He reasoned they surely knew he could not have done this terrible crime --- he loved little children.

The emphasis the men were making on where he was on Tuesday, March 1st, and realizing that Anna had been working at Fredericksen's bakery during that time, caused him to interrupt their questioning. "Yes, if it was a Tuesday night that the child was taken, I can tell you where I was." he shouted, hoping they would understand.

Hauptmann went on to explain that he had worked that day as a carpenter on the construction of the Majestic Apartments at 72nd Street and Central Park. After finishing work at five o'clock, he returned home by subway, and took his car from the garage and drove to Fredericksen's Lunchroom and Bakery, arriving there at about a quarter to seven. He told them he always ate his supper there on Tuesday evening because his wife worked late on that day, sometimes not finishing until 9 p.m. They would then drive home together and go immediately to bed since they both arose early the following day. He was certain, he emphasized, that he had picked his wife up on March 1st because it was a Tuesday, and because Mrs. Fredericksen took off every Tuesday, it was mandatory that Anna would have been working and he would have been there to take her home.

Hearing this, his captors decided to pressure him about other dates relating to the case. Let's see what he has to tell us about Saturday, April 2nd, 1932. He certainly won't be able to explain his way out of this one, they reasoned.

"Okay, Bruno.", they proceeded. "Do you know where St. Raymond's Cemetery is?"

"Yes." came Hauptmann's quick reply.

"Yes, and you were in it on the night of Saturday, April 2nd, 1932 when you were handed $50,000 in Lindbergh ransom money by Doctor Condon" they charged, then countered with another question: "What have you done with the rest of it, the $45,000?" Hearing this, he vehemently denied having any knowledge of the money and of knowing a Doctor named Condon.

Although he was thoroughly confused by their line of questioning, Richard apparently was thinking clearly as he reflected back to this date his inquisitors had inquired about. They had mentioned that April 2nd, 1932 had been a Saturday, and if this were so, then he would have been at home, since the first Saturday night of each month was reserved for him and his friends to get together in the Hauptmann apartment for an evening of music.

"April 2nd was the first Saturday of the month and I was at home." he countered. "Hans Kloppenburg would bring his guitar and I would join him on the mandolin and we would all sing German and American songs together." Hauptmann went on to explain. "I know I was at home since it was our custom and we never missed our meeting on the first Saturday. Hans would come about seven and we would sing until almost midnight." He emphatically denied their accusations that he had been in St. Raymond's Cemetery at 9 p.m. on that date. Although he told them he had a knowledge of where St. Raymond's Cemetery was located, he denied he had ever been in it.

In their attempt to place him in Greenwich Village on Sunday night, November 26th, 1933, Hauptmann had an ironclad alibi, but nevertheless, one they refused to accept.

"O.K. Bruno!" they continued with their attempts to break him down and wring a confession from him.

"We know you passed a Lindbergh ransom bill at the Loews Sheridan Square Theater in Greenwich Village on Sunday night November 26th, 1933. The cashier has already identified you. She says you threw a five dollar ransom bill folded in a small square at her in payment for your ticket." their accusations came on without stopping.

"I've never been to Greenwich Village in my life." Richard earnestly protested. "Furthermore," he continued, "that night was my birthday and Anny gave me a birthday party and had a few of our friends over to celebrate. I can prove it." he pleaded.

"No, I don't fold my money that way. I carry it in my wallet the way you found my money when you arrested me." Hauptmann continued to protest and deny their fast repeated accusations.

Before long Hauptmann completely realized the enormity of the reason he had been arrested. But surely they could not be serious in believing that he had kidnapped the little Lindbergh baby. But then, why were they so intent on having him confess? He could tell them nothing about it. But their accusations continued. And now they had brought Anny in and were attempting to force her to tell what she knew. But, just as he, she could tell them nothing. And Hans Kloppenburg, his good friend, what were they trying to do to him in the next room? Oh merciful God, he thought, please help me. I could not hurt anyone. Richard's tormented brain continued to bring this line of reasoning to his senses.

Hours had passed since they first brought him in, and now the unrelentless barrage of questions were beginning to take their toll on the weary prisoner. New teams of detectives with fresh vigor were called on to pursue the inquisition. Richard, near exhaustion from the monotonous hostility and badgering, and the knowledge that they had now dragged Anna into it, had been brought near the breaking point. However, through it all, he maintained a strong affirmation of his innocence, giving them his honest answers without hesitation, as well as he could remember the facts and events that had taken place several years earlier. Basically his story never changed. He knew absolutely nothing about the kidnapping and could prove it if they would only listen to reason.

In another room Anna Hauptmann was undergoing this same line of questioning. She confirmed the movements her husband had told them he made on the dates in question. She was certain he had called for her at Fredericksen's Bakery on the night of Tuesday, March 1st, 1932. She was more than certain because she knew, that since it was a Tuesday, Mrs. Fredericksen had taken off as she always did on Tuesdays, which made Anna's working there a necessity. "Yes" Anna said, "I am sure of it."

As for Richard's presence in their apartment on Sunday, November 26th, 1933, she became indignant that the police could even suggest a doubt that he wasn't there.

"Why, that was Richard's birthday, and I had a party for him. Of course he was at home. Hans Kloppenburg was there with us, and so was my niece, Maria Mueller and Mr.Fisch who gave him a gift, a black fountain pen, and I can prove it. It was his birthday and we had a celebration for him." She answered their strong accusations which clearly demonstrated their refusal to believe her.

By this time Anna Hauptmann had also come to realize the seriousness involved in her husband's arrest. When the police informed her that the money they had taken from Richard's wallet had been part of the Lindbergh ransom payment, they had inquired: "Didn't he tell you his money is from the Lindbergh kidnapping?" "What do you mean?" she hurled her accusing question at them.

"We know your husband, Bruno Richard Hauptmann, kidnapped and killed the Lindbergh baby. Had been paid $50,000 for his trouble and now he is going to burn for it." came their rapid response.

"No! No! It is not the truth. My Richard could never do such a terrible thing." Anna shouted her denials against their horrible accusations of her husband's guilt. She loved him and knew he was innocent.

As the police continued questioning her about any possible knowledge she might have of her husband's involvement in the kidnapping, they were kept constantly alert of any slip-up she might make as to a part she may have possibly played in the crime. However, she was adamant regarding her mate's innocence, and, without realizing it, had supported everything Richard had told them in an adjoining room. She had informed her questioners that Richard had been with her on Tuesday, March 1; Saturday, March 12; Saturday, April 2, 1932; and Sunday, November 26, 1933. Of this, she said she had no doubt; that she could prove it, as could many others.

The host of detectives, led by Inspector John Lyons, involved in the questioning of the Hauptmanns and Hans Kloppenburg, who also had been picked up and brought in as a possible accomplice, were Inspector Finn, Sisk, Keaten, Francis Fay, in charge of the New

York office of the Division of Investigation, and Colonel Schwarzkopf of the New Jersey State Police.

The authorities had received an answer to their cabled report to Germany informing them of Hauptmann's arrests over there. However, although this information gave the police knowledge of Hauptmann's former criminal record and his illegal entrance into the United States in 1923, it did nothing to aid them in their attempt to place him in the Lindbergh home on the night of the kidnapping. Thus far his friends, Hans Kloppenburg, Maria Mueller, and the Fredericksens, had all confirmed the validity of his activities, exactly as he had related them to the police. Realizing they would need much more evidence, the police, with renewed intensity, set out to find the missing pieces.

For ten hours Hauptmann had been subjected to the intense staccato-like questioning of the police authorities, and although he appeared to be very tired, near exhaustion, and on the verge of sleep, he continued to plead with them, claiming his complete innocence. Constantly blinking his eyes, shying away from the glare of the spotlight they played on him, he attempted to pull himself away from the constant jabs in the ribs he was forced to endure. Intense jabs that caused him to grimace and squirm in the chair in which he had been sitting since he was brought in. His captors showed no desire to give him any rest. They must break this man was their only intent.

It was near midnight when Inspector Lyons decided it was time to turn to another means that would surely prove Hauptmann's guilt. Certainly his handwriting would match that of the ransom notes, so they would have him write.

In May of 1932, Albert S. Osborn, the internationally known handwriting expert, assembled a paragraph in which he laced a good percentage of the letters, words, and syllables as they appeared in the actual ransom notes to the Lindberghs. It was his belief that when the guilty author of the ransom notes was arrested, this sample typewritten paragraph, although appearing to be innocent enough, could be very incriminating after the sample paragraph was written by the suspect. Osborn claimed it would leave no doubt as to the suspect's guilt or innocence after he or she had written the statement. At midnight Inspector Lyons decided it was time to test Osborn's innocent appearing dictational trap on Hauptmann.

Osborn had instructed the police not to tell

anyone taking the test that it was being done in order to check their natural handwriting with the ransom notes. However, in this instance they decided to warn Hauptmann of their purpose for having him submit to the request writings. Osborn's reason for withholding this information from a suspect was his belief that, had the suspect known this beforehand, he would make every attempt to disguise his handwriting. A disguised writing would make it extremely difficult to clearly determine that he or she had actually been the writer of the notes.

Inspector Lyons approached Hauptmann with the prepared paragraph in his hand and told the prisoner the purpose of the test. He explained that the statement would be dictated to him and that he should take his time and spell the words in his normal way. He emphasized that by doing this Richard could clear himself quite easily. Hauptmann readily accepted the opportunity and challenge it offered.

"I will be glad to write because it will get me out of this thing," the weary prisoner answered.

Sergeant Thomas Ritchie of the New Jersey State Police was selected to dictate Osborn's prepared paragraphs. Handing Hauptmann a pen and paper he began reading very slowly as the nearly exhausted man sitting at a desk in front of him began to write.

Over and over and over again Ritchie dictated, by this time, the familiar paragraph. And over and over and over again Hauptmann wrote the requested words. Finally, Hauptmann blinking his eyes with great frequency, sagged in his chair; but in spite of this, he never lost his composure. However, weariness was fast taking over his numbed body.

The dictation that had begun as request writings, intermingled by new questions, had turned into demand writings, intermingled later again by these two paragraphs Osborn had prepared:

> "Cross the street and walk to the next corner follow Whittemore Ave. to the Sound. Take the money with you. Come alone and walk. I will meet you. The boy is on the boat Nelly. It is a small boat 28 feet long. Two persons are on the boat. They are innocent. You will find the boat between Horseneck Beach and Gayhall near Elizabeth Island."

The second paragraph was slightly longer:

"We were not near Smith Hall where the robbery took place, between 6 and 12 by our time. During all the time I was out of the house, but later came home. Did you not write letters to New York sending back anything that was stolen from Mr. Conway? Police keep those letters and papers, they will be good for something later maybe. One of the letters said Dear Sir, thank you for the bills and for your money. We will send back the bills later perhaps. Where shall we send them, the address we lost? Be at home every night so you will hear from us. You can not tell when that will be."

The onslaught of questions continued without interruption. Although fresh teams of detectives took their turns interrogating their prisoner, Hauptmann was forced to sit in the same chair, the victim of not only the verbal abuse of the police, but of their constant jabs into his sides and midriff. As early dawn approached, deciding that the past six or seven hours of "penmanship school" had accomplished their purpose, the host of police officers felt certain that their prisoner, Bruno Richard Hauptmann, was, without any doubt, the writer of the ransom notes. Now all they had to do, they reasoned, was to get an official confirmation of this from the author of the dozen or more sentences they had forced their prisoner to write, one Albert S. Osborn, recognized as the master of all handwriting experts.

Basking in what they believed was success, the police, all untrained in the analysis of handwriting specimens, pointed out to one another the various reasons they felt certain Hauptmann had penned all of the ransom notes. Hadn't both writings clearly exhibited the transposition of g's and h's as in the word night, appearing as nihgt; the hyphenation of the two words "New York"; the spelling of the word boat as "boad". Oh yes, they rejoiced together, revelling in their belief that because of the way their prisoner had written the demand writing, and what they believed was convincing and convicting evidence, they had, after two-and-one-half years were now successfully bringing the killer of tiny Charles A. Lindbergh, Jr. to justice.

During the long hours of the night, in another room, Hans Kloppenburg, was forced to write the same paragraphs dictated by another officer. They reasoned that if Hauptmann had not been the penman of the ransom letters, then quite possibly his German friend Kloppenburg had been the writer. However, after a few hours they determined that Kloppenburg was not involved. For the present they would not hold him for any possible guilt as a conspirator with Hauptmann in the crime. This also proved to be their feelings about Anna Hauptmann. Following a few hours of questioning they returned her to her home in the Bronx. They had arrived at the conclusion that she knew nothing at all about the kidnapping. The authorities seemed perfectly content with the one major arrest they had made.

Entering the door of her second floor apartment at 1279 East 222nd Street, a partial cry escaped Anna Hauptmann's lips as she glanced in horror at the mass of destruction in front of her. Her home resembled a battlefield. All their possessions had been removed from drawers, shelves, and closets and thrown about with utter abandon. Furniture had been destroyed, mattresses were torn apart, pictures had been removed from walls, stuffed toy animals had been ripped apart and the stuffing pulled out. The customary neat and orderly home of Richard and Anna Hauptmann had been destroyed. The disorder of the normally quiet, comfortable, and peaceful appearance was now one of chaos. Police were moving about with disregard to Anna's cry, as tears flowed freely from her eyes: "Why?" she pleaded. "Why has this happened to us?"

Realizing she could not stay any longer in her apartment, she hurried to the home of her niece, Maria Mueller, who lived at 2701 Marion Avenue, not too far distant. Maria had taken Manfred with her when the police took Anna to the Greenwich Street Police Station. When Anna arrived at the home of her niece, she was in a very distraught emotional condition. Being told that her little son was already sound asleep, she yielded to the offer of her niece to spend the night with her. The thought of going back to her apartment was a devastating one, and since the police had granted her permission to stay at the Muellers overnight, she took advantage of the opportunity. However, they had informed her that she must return to her home early the next morning.

Sleep for Anna Hauptmann that night was an impossibility. The angry questions and accusations the police had thrust at her, claiming her dear husband was involved in the terrible Lindbergh kidnapping, kept her far from spending even a time of rest as they came back to haunt and trouble her. What had they meant when they angrily shouted at her: "Didn't you know it was

Lindbergh ransom money your husband was spending?" "Oh, my God, my God, what are they saying?" she wailed. These and other frightful thoughts continued to plague her throughout the night, sapping her strength.

Arising early, and after feeding "Bubi" his breakfast, she left him in Maria's care and hurried back to her home. As the police began arriving, they found Anna pacing about, inspecting the wreckage they had wrought to her cozy little apartment. The floor was littered with debris, consisting of things which had once been an assortment of perfectly usable household items; at least they had been before they fell prey to the carnage of the police.

The small German housewife was demoralized and mentally confused as she looked at the pillage which had been brought at the hands of some of the very police officers who were now ordering her to accompany them out to Richard's garage. Once there, she watched in unbelief as she saw the men viciously destroy the entire contents of the garage. Her husband's workbench was torn apart, the floorboards were pried up, the contents of everything within the small confined quarters were tossed outside, and at the same time the roof was being ripped off. Nothing resembling a garage was left standing.

During the course of a more systematic and intensified search, Detective James Petrosino's attention was drawn to the south wall where a board had been nailed across two uprights, directly above the location where Hauptmann's workbench had been anchored. He removed the board and discovered a shallow compartment with a narrow shelf on which rested two bundles wrapped in newspapers. Gingerly he lifted them and went about unwrapping the paper to examine the contents. Much to his surprise, he found that each package contained a thick packet of money which, upon quick scrutiny, proved to be more Lindbergh ransom bills, all of them ten dollar gold notes. The money was wrapped in a copy of the June 25, 1934 issue of *The New York Daily News* and one of *The New York Daily Mirror*, dated September 6, 1934.

Detective Petrosino's discovery immediately brought the other searchers to his side, all hearing his shout: "Look! Look at what I've found!" Excitedly Sergeant John Wallace of the New Jersey State Police, Special Agent Leon Turrou of the Division of Investigation, Washington, D.C., and Detectives Edward Murphy and Frank Dunn of the New York City Police were literally whooping it up, celebrating this latest incriminating find. Their tumult of shouts acclaiming victory, confused the unbelieving ears of Anna Hauptmann. What could this all mean she questioned herself? She heard their voices, "Now we have him!" They were filled with hate for her husband, causing her to grow faint; her heart began beating at a faster pace, and she was experiencing a strong feeling of nausea approaching. She could not believe this was actually happening to her. Surely she must be experiencing a terrible dream of some sort. "Now, we've got Bruno!" the shouts continued. "He's going to burn for this!" they went on with their mad ravings.

The men, occupied for several minutes with their individual inspection of the discovery, suddenly turned on the visibly shaken Anna. "What do you know about this?" they demanded of her. "Where did it come from and who put it there?" they continued to bark out their accusing questions at her. And while they were leveling their attention toward the trembling little housewife, Detective Murphy noticed another board, wider than the one they had just removed, nailed across two uprights beneath where the bed of the workbench had been nailed. Ripping the board loose, he found a one-gallon shellac can resting on the base of the recess that helped form the right window. Lifting the can, he anxiously pried off the lid, and reached in, pulling two tightly stuffed cloths that had been wedged in at the top. Under this, the detective removed several more bundles wrapped exactly as those they found several minutes earlier. The police had hit another jack-pot. The contents revealed, what appeared to be, more Lindbergh ransom money.

Anna Hauptmann seemed in a trance as she watched the men extract the money. Again they turned on her, the object of their impassioned accusations, as they continued to spit out their mind-penetrating questions at her. "What do you know about this, Mrs. Hauptmann? Who put it here? I guess you're going to tell us you don't know anything about this?", came their rapid-fire statements which betrayed their doubts of her innocence.

Shaking her head again and again, she pleaded with them to believe that she knew nothing about where the money came from. But her protestations fell upon deaf ears as the officers continued to dismantle and wreck the garage her husband had built just a year ago. "Please stop," she cried, "Why are you doing this to us? Why? Why?"

But in spite of the poor woman's denials, the officers literally pounced upon the money they had found. Money that had been so carefully stashed away. Money they were certain, every bill of it, would prove to be Lindbergh ransom cash.

And in this they were correct. Close inspection found them to be gold notes in denominations of tens and twenties. The first two bundles contained all $10 bills; 100 in the one package totaling $1,000, and 83 in the other totaling $830. The sum total of both packages amounted to $1,830. The shellac can held ten bundles, each containing $1,000 (50 - $20 bills in each) for a sum total of $10,000; and another two packages, one holding $990, the other an additional $940. The grand total of cash they uncovered was $13,760, comprised of 493 bills in $20 and 390 bills in $10 denominations.

The police, certain they would find more, continued with their plundering. Their efforts did not remain unrewarded. Officer Maurice W. Tobin, of the New York City Police Department, while probing about, removed another short board from off the garage wall. It had been nailed as a connecting board between two uprights, its inner surface flush against the south wall. Upon examining the short 2 by 4 inch plank, they found it contained six holes that had been drilled into it as a hiding place for more Lindbergh money. Five of the holes were round, each one filled with tightly rolled $10 gold notes, that fit snugly into each hole. As the officers removed the contents of each hole it was carefully counted and added to the previously confiscated notes. Hole one contained $190; hole two $200; hole three $150; hole four $200; hole five $100. Eighty-four more $10 gold notes gave them $840 more to be added to the already counted $13,760. The grand total found in the Hauptmann garage now totaled $14,600. Although the search continued as the garage was demolished they found nothing more in any form of currency.

Hole number six, larger than the other five, gave the police another piece of valuable evidence to be used against their prisoner who was still being quizzed at the Greenwich Street Police Station. From it they extracted a three-inch pearl handled Lilliput German automatic pistol. The compartment in the wood had been gouged out with a chisel, allowing the small calibred hand-gun to fit compactly inside.

Other items taken from Hauptmann's garage were his tool box, (complete with tools) and a few other personal possessions including letters and legal papers. The only other possible piece of evidence they could find was a workman's wooden plane bearing the trademark Sargent. It measured about 18 inches in length and bore the serial number "3418" and the initials "V.B.M." and "H".

Now armed with the indisputable proof that Hauptmann had $14,600 of Lindbergh ransom money securely hidden in his garage, plus the twenty dollar gold note they found in his wallet at the time of his arrest, the officers were overjoyed at the prospect of facing their prisoner with this new and damning evidence --- A total of 966 pieces of currency, each one pointing directly to the guilt of Bruno Richard Hauptmann. And, in addition to these, there was the bill he used on September 15th to purchase gasoline at the Warner-Quinlan station, as well as the one they surmised he had taken to pay for his ticket at the Loews Sheridan Square Theater in Greenwich Village on the night of November 26th, 1933, plus those they believed he had previously spent in various stores.

Although they had not officially checked the serial numbers of the garage bills against the official list of the Lindbergh ransom bills, they were certain there would be a perfect match. With this evidence against the man they already determined was guilty, they hurried back to the Greenwich station to share the good news with their fellow officers who were still busy grilling Hauptmann.

It was nearly two o'clock in the afternoon. Hauptmann had not been permitted a moments sleep since his arrival there twenty-four hours earlier. However, relays of refreshed detectives soon grew weary of hearing the prisoner continually evade the issue of their continued line of questioning. They were certain he would break at any moment and make a complete confession as a result of the severe torment of their accusations. But such had not been the case.

Now, with the news of the discovery of so much additional ransom money in his possession, they lashed out at him with renewed vigor.

"C'mon Bruno, you might as well tell us everything about it." they prodded him. "Where'd you get all this money?" came their demanding questions as they showed him the bundles of cash still wrapped in newspapers. "It's Lindbergh ransom money, Bruno, and you know it. All you have to do is tell us where you got it and we'll let you sleep awhile," was their promise.

After being told that it had been found in his garage, Hauptmann explained that he had originally lied to them about the money because he knew the bills were gold notes and that it was illegal to own so many. He realized that if he were caught with so much of it he could be prosecuted for hording it.

"Bruno, how stupid do you think we are to believe that cock and bull story? You knew it was ransom money. You took it from the old man in St. Raymond's Cemetery in payment for the Lindbergh kid, the one you killed." They hammered away, never ceasing long enough for his protests and denials to be heard above the charges they aimed at him.

Realizing he had unknowingly set a trap for himself by his original denial of the truth about the garage money, Hauptmann decided, since it had been found, the time had now arrived when he must tell everything he knew about it.

"It is not my money. It belongs to a friend of mine, Isidor Fisch, who went to Germany. I didn't even know it was money when he left it with me." Hauptmann told them. "And that is the truth, please believe me, I don't know how it can be Lindbergh money. It belonged to Mr. Fisch. I already told you I never have been in St. Raymond's Cemetery and I don't know any Dr. Condon. Why don't you believe me?" He pleaded over and over again for their understanding, professing his absolute innocence as to any knowledge of it prior to it being left with him by his friend, Isidor Fisch.

"O.K. Bruno, suppose you tell us how you got it, and then maybe we'll believe you!" his tormentors goaded him for his complete explanation.

"Mr. Fisch was a friend of mine, in fact we're in business together." he began. "We had formed a partnership and shared everything fifty-fifty. He was in the fur business, buying and selling them for both of us, while I bought stocks for the two of us since Isidor didn't have a brokerage account. We did rather well, although Isidor did make some poor investments on his own, and I loaned him several thousand dollars, some of it as late as just before Christmas last year, right before he left for Germany." For a man under great duress, he nevertheless continued to expound his explanation in a calm manner.

"Well, go on. Let's hear the rest of it.", came the impatient prodding of the police. "We want to hear more of this fish story of yours!"

"Mr. Fisch was a Jew and was concerned about his

parents safety in Germany and had gone over to Leipzig to see them with hopes that he could convince them to come to America and live in safety from the threats of Adolph Hitler. Before he left in December last year, he gave me two suitcases with his personal effects in them and 400 Hudson sealskin pelts. He asked me to take care of them for him until his return two months later."

"The Saturday night before he sailed for Germany we had a little farewell party for him in our apartment. On that night he brought me a wrapped shoe box and asked me to store this for him until he came back. He said it was more personal papers and that I should keep it in a safe place. I put it up on the top shelf in our broom closet and forgot all about it." Hauptmann continued without faltering, believing the men would certainly accept this true account of how he came into possession of the money. But, he was wrong.

"Oh yeah! Surely Bruno, you don't expect us to believe that. How come Fisch never got his money back if it belonged to him?", they chided him with their taunts of unbelief. "Go on, let's hear the rest of this amazing story of yours," they urged him to continue. "Mr. Fisch died in Germany last March. His brother, Pinkus, wrote to me and told me about it a few months ago. I was waiting for his brother to come to America and settle Isidor's affairs. I had explained to him however, that what he had left with me seemed to be of no real value. Just some papers and books and furs. You see, Isidor owed me $7,500. I had loaned him money on several occasions and now I didn't have much hope of getting it back, because Isidor was dead and had no money," the prisoner continued his discourse.

"C'mon Bruno, let's get to the money in your garage. How are you going to explain that away? If it belonged to Fisch, why did he leave it with you?" they urged him on for his explanation of these important questions.

"I tell you it's the truth. The shoe box I put in my broom closet last December and forgot all about it. It was nothing so important that I should make a point of remembering it.", the prisoner hurried on, anxious to tell the rest of the story. "Anyway, about three or four weeks ago, on a Sunday in the middle of August, I went to the broom closet to get a broom, I was transplanting a rubber plant for my wife, and the handle punctured the box. It was watersoaked. We had a leaking pipe in the closet and the water had soaked into the box and it broke open and then I saw all the money. I reached up to take it down and it was so wet, the water ran down my arm. As soon as I saw the box I remembered that Isidor had left it with me to keep for him." Hauptmann paused and studied their reaction to his true explanation.

"Bruno Hauptmann, you can't expect us to swallow that story, do you?" the interrogators laughingly chided him. "Tell us, if this money belonged to Fisch, why were you spending it all this time? Don't expect us to swallow this "dead fish" story of yours. We know you've had that money since you got it from Condon in April of 1932 and you might as well confess it now!" came their angry demands.

Distressed that his truthful explanation had not been accepted, and nearly broken in spirit, he continued: "When I saw it was money, I lifted it down and put it in a pail and took it down to the garage. The box was so water soaked it was falling apart. When I got it in the garage I squeezed the water out of the bills, they were all stuck together, and flattened them out so they would dry. Then I took the money and put it in a basket and after I put it in I covered it, and then put it on a shelf up near the ceiling and nailed a couple of strips of wood in front of it so that no one would see it. After several days, when it had dried, I took some of it and started to spend it. I only spent about a dozen bills. I thought it wouldn't hurt since Mr. Fisch owed me $7,500," was the prisoner's impassioned account.

When asked why he had wrapped the dried bills in newspapers, hidden them where the police had found them, and then lied to them when questioned about his possession of having any more money, Hauptmann was quick to explain his reason: "After several days, and I was able to separate the bills and count them, I found out there was nearly $15,000. I could see they were all gold notes and were illegal and that if I was caught with them I would be in trouble with the government for having so many. That is why I spent only a few and why I didn't admit having any more money when you asked me. I didn't have any idea it was Lindbergh ransom money. I don't know how Isidor could have had any of that money. I just can't believe it is Lindbergh money," he droned on in an attempt to have his captors understand the truth.

But the truth the police wanted was far from what Hauptmann had told them. His words fell on ears that had already been stopped by their closed minds. No reasonable explanation any prisoner could have given them at this time would have been acceptable. After two-and-one-half years of failure, they now had their man. And now all that remained for them to do was build their "air-tight" case against him and proceed with the prosecution.

By mid-afternoon word had been leaked to the press and public that a major arrest had been made in the Lindbergh case. Hundreds of people converged on the police station, all demanding their "pound of flesh" in payment for the diabolical act that had been committed against their idol Charles A. Lindbergh.

Reporters with their companion photographers rushed to the already clogged Greenwich Street. A mob of unruly citizens moved closer to the door of the building which held the as yet unnamed "criminal". Extra police were called to quell the disturbance on the street, with orders to keep everyone moving, a momentous task, since the mob's enraged hatred for the "already guilty nameless person" was fast reaching a crescendo.

As late afternoon arrived, the number of people surrounding the station house increased. However, their unruliness had subsided, with only occasional shouts being heard. As they moved uneasily about, a police car slowly drove near the curb and stopped. Two police officers stepped from the front seat as the rear door opened and a large man emerged and walked with the detectives along the crowded sidewalk to the steps of the police station. The crowd showed no difficulty recognizing this third man. They could not be mistaken. He was tall, walked erect taking great strides. His gray hair and ample mustache made him appear quite dignified. They could not be wrong. It could be no one else. As one, although in chorus, they shouted over and over: "It's Jafsie! It's Jafsie!" to be followed by a host of exclamations: "Jafsie will see that he burns!" "Give it to him good, Jafsie!"

Cheers for Doctor Condon and jeers for no matter who the prisoner was filled the air. And Jafsie Condon basked in it. He loved his fame, acclaim and notoriety of it all.

As the three men entered the front door another bizarre chapter in the Lindbergh case was about to begin.

CHAPTER TWENTY ONE

The Assembly of the Liar's Club!

Dr. John F. Condon was escorted up the stairway and down halls now jammed with reporters representing newspapers that, upon hearing of the arrest, had once again assigned their most capable persons to cover the case first hand. Bedlam seemed to reign as police officers raced up and down, to and fro, many displaying their officious demeanor. With the arrest of a suspect, interest in the Lindbergh kidnapping had sprung wide open again, renewing memories of March 1932. Striding amidst the enthusiastic members of the news media, Jafsie was deluged with requests to grant them interviews when he completed his business there, but, following orders from the police officials, he refused them all.

As he entered the large police line-up room the elderly intermediary found himself in the midst of a great number of police officers. Glancing toward one side of the room he noticed thirteen men standing in line on a stage. He reasoned they were there to afford a clear view of prisoners for identification purposes. At the direction of Inspector John Lyons he was asked to look at each of the men, study them closely, question them if necessary, and then determine if any of them could be the mysterious John whom he had dealt with in Van Cortlandt Park and St.Raymond's Cemetery over two-and-one-half years earlier.

Of the thirteen men in the line-up, all were attired in civilian clothes. However, twelve of them were police officers. Now, the objectivity of any fair line-up should always include only participants endowed with the same general characteristics as those of the suspect as he had been originally described by the eyewitness. If he had been depicted as being short and stocky, then at least most of the men used should be of like appearance; if tall and thin, the others standing with him should, for the most part, be of similar stature. This would also apply to the color of hair, facial features, color and type of clothing. To conduct a line-up in a contrary fashion would be prejudicial and could unfairly influence the persons attempting to make a fair identification. This unfairness could be carried out further if the suspect had a decided foreign accent while none of the others spoke with anything less than a clear distinctive American-English. It was also customary that the prisoner be granted the privilege of selecting the numbered position in front of which he would stand in the line-up. But of course, this privilege had not been extended to Richard Hauptmann.

Regardless of the propriety of proper police procedure, one that dogmatically insisted on fairness to suspects in criminal cases, it was found noticeably lacking in Hauptmann's case. The police were so certain they had apprehended the proper person involved in the kidnapping they could not have cared less how unfairly the cards of additional evidence would be brought in and stacked against him. In order to get him properly identified none of the other twelve men in the line-up even closely resembled Hauptmann. All of the police who cooperated were of short stature and could be easily described as being stocky; none of them spoke with an accent but Hauptmann.

Condon went immediately to the business at hand. The police anxiously awaited what they anticipated would be his foregone decision, his naming Bruno Richard Hauptmann as the man he had met on three occasions during the ransom negotiations. But, what should have been a rather easy and painless task for the Bronx educator, developed into somewhat a difficult one. After speaking briefly to each man, he signaled to four of them to take a step forward. To these, Hauptmann being the only one who spoke with an accent, he urged each to tell the truth as they answered his questions.

After learning each man's name, his first question was: "Have you ever seen me before?" Each answered with a definite "No!" He next asked for a pencil and paper. This was done with Inspector Lyons approval since he had granted Condon the privilege of conducting the interrogation in any way he desired. On the paper he wrote: "He would smack me out. I stayed already too long. Your work is perfect." and then handed it to the men, instructing them to, in turn, each read aloud from the paper. Each took his turn reading the quotations as they were written. But, unlike three of them who spoke perfect English to the satisfaction of Dr. Condon and the police, Hauptmann was the only one who spoke with a dialect, and therefore the only one who could possibly have been Cemetery John. His German sounding rendition held a distinctiveness all its own as he read: "He vould schmack me oud. I stayed already too long. Your vork is perfect."

Learning of Hauptmann's German extraction, Dr. Condon decided to use another method that would possibly reach the innermost being of the prisoner and bring forth a confession, something the police had been unable to do. He motioned Richard to a corner of the room and in German said: "Konnen Sie Deutsch sprechen?" (Can you speak German?) In a grateful and much relieved voice the weary German carpenter immediately answered: "Ja Ich kann. Sprechen Sie zu mir auch Deutsch." (Yes, I can. Speak to me in German.)

Confident that by using this new approach, Condon was sure he could break through the denials of Hauptmann. The certainty of this is based on the fact that it could work only if the man were guilty. An innocent man would certainly not be trapped by any devised means. But it was apparent at this point that Condon was not at all positive of Hauptmann's guilt. Leaning closer to the prisoner, he whispered to him: "Wahrheit ist besser, Richard." (The truth is better, Richard.) To this there was no reply.

Next the doctor thought it appropriate to recite a poem:

"Willst du immer weiter schweifen
("Will you always seek still farther
Sieh das gute liegt so nah
See the good that lies so near
Lerne nur das Gluck ergreifen
Learn at once to grasp your fortune
Denn das Gluck ist immer da."
Then happiness is always there.")

Again there was no outward reaction by the prisoner to Condon's brief recitation. At this point Jafsie walked away declaring: "I am through."

Although silence had permeated the room during the identity session, it immediately burst into a noisy center of activity as the police pressed Condon for an identity of Hauptmann as the recipient of the ransom money. The place took on a carnival atmosphere as reporters and photographers, who now were allowed to enter, hurried to Jafsie's side to better hear every word of his anticipated accusation.

But in this they were disappointed. Anxious to learn the results, one police officer could barely wait for the results of Condon's private and personal interview with their prisoner: "Which of the four men was John? Was it Hauptmann?", he pushed Jafsie for a reply, fully expecting him to name their prisoner. But instead, showing some irritation at the demands of the multitude of voices, he gave them a very unexpected answer: "I am holding my identification in abeyance for the present." He announced this much to their disapproval.

"C'mon Condon. Either you can pick the man out or you can't" came an angry protest from one of the other policemen. "Tell us which one is John."

"I shall not declare an identification at this time." The doctor retorted, indignant that he should be treated in this manner.

Inspector Lyons, himself annoyed at the evasiveness of Condon in not giving them a definite identification, followed through with a pointed question pertaining to Richard Hauptmann.

"Would you say he is the man?", he inquired.

"He resembles the man. I can see a resemblance, but I cannot swear to it." was the best answer Condon would give.

At this point in my narrative I wish to emphasize that it has been my endeavor to relate each and every event that occurred in the famous Lindbergh kidnapping case. I have attempted to tell the facts of each event exactly as they happened. In doing this I have been more than fair in pointing out the few times the authorities displayed excellence in their police work. In other instances I have signified their failures. Regardless of this, however, I believe I have leaned over backward to support the work of the police throughout the early years of the case. But, now with the arrest of Richard Hauptmann, more than just a few of these same officers "turned their backs to the facts" by displaying utter disregard to the truth, and tainted their careers by framing an innocent man. The remainder of this book continues as an honest factual report, telling in detail all of the deliberate things which were unfairly perpetrated against a man who was given no opportunity to prove his innocence, but instead, thru the forces of an evil criminal justice system, made no way for him to escape. The events which follow relate a series of inhuman events Richard and Anna Hauptmann were forced to endure. Contrary to a person being innocent until proven guilty, Hauptmann was "guilty" from the very first moments of his arrest.

We continue our story at the Greenwich Street Police Station and the identity line-up session with the eminent Doctor John F."Jafsie" Condon.

One of the officers present on that afternoon of Thursday, September 20th, 1934 was Special Agent Leon G. Turrou of the Federal Bureau of Investigation. In order to present some valuable information in defense of Hauptmann I have extracted the following from Mr. Turrou's book *Where My Shadow Falls*, published in 1949 by Doubleday and Company. It had been Special Agent Turrou who had driven Dr. Condon to the police station that afternoon. Here is exactly the way Turrou reported it in his book.

"While I was driving Dr. Condon to the Greenwich Street Station where Hauptmann was being held I told him we had a suspect I wanted him to identify.

"Who? The kidnapper?" he asked.

"I don't know, Doctor. It may be." At that stage I wasn't sure myself. I was convinced that Hauptmann had a very close connection with the crime, but I could not hazard a guess as to whether the man whose footprints were found beside the broken ladder and the man whom Dr. Condon had met on three occasions and to whom he had given the ransom money were the same.

"Don't worry, son," Dr.Condon said. "If he's the fellow I met I'll know him. If I live a million years I'll know him." Then he quizzically tilted his head toward me and whispered, "Now look here, describe this suspect you've got."

That surprised me. "I'm sorry, doctor--I can't tell you that. The whole point to this is that you pick him out by yourself."

He protested. "Why? Just tell me why. That's nothing but a fool notion."

When we got to the station Hauptmann was in the line-up with a dozen detectives. It wasn't much of a deception. The detectives were shaved, bright-eyed six-footers. Hauptmann looked like a midget who had wandered through a Turkish bath for two sleepless days and nights.

"Doctor, have you ever seen any of these men before?" Inspector Lyons of the New York City Police asked.

J. Edgar Hoover, Colonel Schwarzkopf of the New

Jersey State Police, and the whole Lindbergh squad were on hand to watch the proceedings, but the doctor was Inspector Lyons' show.

The old man scratched his head and squinted at the group. Suddenly he straightened up and barked "Tenshun!" in his best 1917 doughboy manner. The big policemen did as they were told. Hauptmann remained slumped and defeated. Then Dr. Condon began putting them through a series of complicated drill maneuvers, marching them around, right flanking, left flanking in a voice sharp and military. Those few moments in that little police station should by rights have belonged to the stage.

The tragi-comic picture of Hauptmann stumbling along in a file of tough bruising cops was more than Inspector Lyons could bear.

"Stop, Dr. Condon!" he shouted. "Enough"

The drilling came to a halt. The doctor turned furiously. "Now if you're going to start interfering I'll wash my hands of the whole mess!"

Inspector Lyons laid a huge hand on the doctor's shoulder. "We're tired," he said softly. "We want to go home and sleep. We deserve it. Now, do you know any of these men or don't you?"

"For the love of God!" Dr. Condon snapped. "I can't identify an innocent man."

"Doctor, we're not asking you to. Please now, are any of these men here familiar to you?"

"Go ahead, Doctor," I urged, but in a small and humble voice.

He turned then and walked directly to Hauptmann.

"Do you know me?" he asked in German.

Hauptmann shook his head wearily.

"Well, do you think we've ever met?"

"No," Hauptmann said.

For several minutes the doctor queried, permitting himself to comment freely on extraneous matters. Finally Inspector Lyons nerves snapped.

"All right, all right! Stop stalling! Do you or don't you know this man?"

Dr.Condon spun on his heels and stalked from the room. I followed him.

"I won't identify him for those insolent morons! he told me.

"No," he said. "He is <u>not</u> the man. But he looks like his brother!"

Special Agent Turrou had been given the assignment to watch Doctor Condon and "not permit him to talk to strangers." Here is what Turrou wrote in one of his official reports:

"Dr. Condon impressed the Agent that he has no desire, for some reason, to identify Hauptmann. ...Several times he asked me that he be permitted to talk to Hauptmann for half an hour, following which he would render a definite opinion as to whether Hauptmann is the man known to him as John. ...He remarked on one occasion that <u>Hauptmann is not the man</u> because he appears to be <u>much heavier</u>, <u>has different eyes</u>, <u>different hair</u>, <u>etc</u>. ...

Here we have provided a detailed report of Special Agent Leon G. Turrou of the Federal Bureau of Investigation in which he clearly states that when he asked Condon several times if Hauptmann was the man he met on three occasions, heard him distinctly answer: "NO, HE IS NOT THE MAN!" "HE APPEARS MUCH HEAVIER! "HE HAS DIFFERENT EYES!" "HE HAS DIFFERENT HAIR, ETC." Condon absolutely refuses to identify Hauptmann.

Are we expected to believe that this man who had spent so much time with "Cemetery John", and had bragged to Federal Agent Turrou that "If I live a million years I'll know him.", the man who was now arrested for committing the most heinous of crimes, kidnapping and murder, was not to be identified simply because Condon had been irritated by the police. The very thought is ridiculous! Condon refused to identify Hauptmann for one reason and one reason only! And we have only to look once more at the answer he gave when Inspector Lyons urged him to make a positive identification: "FOR THE LOVE OF GOD! I CAN'T IDENTIFY AN INNOCENT MAN!" At that very time Condon knew beyond a doubt that the prisoner before him was not the John of the cemeteries. His very words prove this! However, the police were not, and would not remain, satisfied with his answer.

Things moved at a faster pace following the "identification" of Hauptmann. Allowing their prisoner a short period of rest, while still sitting in a chair, the taunts, accusations and questions continued on until late that night. About midnight he was taken to the office of Bronx District Attorney Samuel J. Foley. Here he was confronted with the appearance of Joseph Anthony Perrone, the taxi driver who had delivered the note to Condon at his home on March 12th. Perrone had no trouble identifying Hauptmann as the man who had handed him the note for delivery. Next came Mrs. Cecile M. Barr, the theater cashier, who also added her confirmation that the prisoner was indeed the very person who had tossed the bill at her on Nov. 26th, 1933.

Now armed with the admissions of Perrone and Barr that Hauptmann was the right man, Condon was again brought back to face the prisoner. After spending the best part of the next evening in the District Attorney's office, where the police implored him to make a definite identity of Hauptmann, the intermediary staunchly refused their requests that he add his identification to that of the others. After hours of statements being read to him by the police, which should surely have refreshed his memory, and after his examination of hundreds of full-face, profile and three-quarter profile pictures they showed him of their prisoner, Doctor Condon remained adamant in his refusal to condemn Hauptmann as his "Cemetery John".

Regardless of Condon's rejection in naming Hauptmann as the man to whom he paid the ransom, the police authorities were convinced they had the right person. Anxious to get a confirmation on the two test paragraphs they had him write, they contacted Albert S. Osborn at his home in Montclair, New Jersey and implored him to read the request writings and compare them against those of Hauptmann's natural hand. Finding the 70 year old handwriting expert ill and not able to accommodate them, he suggested they contact his son, Albert D., at his New York City office in the Woolworth Building. Special Agent Turrou and Sergeant Ritchie hurried there and delivered the manuscripts to him asking for his quick decision. The two officers turned over a copy of the two paragraphs Hauptmann had written as dictated to him. In addition to these, there were nine pages of dictated words and statements, plus other papers containing the Bronx carpenter's natural writing, found by them in his home. In writing the seven samples for the police, Hauptmann had used three different pens as they ordered him to write sometimes using an upright hand, and at other times a slanting one.

We must keep in mind that the dictated request writings were not actually "requested" ones in the true sense of the word, but instead were "demanded" writings, since the police ordered Hauptmann to write the words exactly as they were dictated to him, even to the point of having him mis-spell certain ones. Words which Hauptmann had always spelled correctly in correspondence with persons years prior to his arrest had been dictated to him incorrectly in order to give them the "evidence" they needed to use against the unfortunate man. They had him write the word note as "not", money as "mony", good as "gute", our as "ouer". These are but a few examples of the deliberate way they had him mis-spell specific words.

After leaving the papers with young Osborn, the men returned to the police station where Hauptmann was still the victim of police harassment. About four a.m. the handwriting "expert" phoned and informed Colonel Schwarzkopf that he was having difficulties in reaching a final determination of the writings. Osborn stated that at first he "thought they were the same, and that there were some striking similarities, but after examining them for a while HE FOUND A LOT OF DISSIMILARITIES ... AND HE IS CONVINCED HE DID NOT WRITE THE RANSOM NOTES.

Upon hearing this unexpected news, the greatly disappointed police officers promised to send him more specimens of Hauptmann's writings, and at once ordered their prisoner to write more dictated statements from news publications, interjecting words from the ransom notes, hoping these would prove conclusively that one man had written all the documents.

By the time the new writings were delivered by Ritchie and Turrou, the two handwriting "experts", father and son, were both at their office and took up the examination together. The two men poured over all of the specimen handwriting that had been furnished them of Hauptmann, comparing them with the printed and written ransom notes. For two hours they made their study and were ready to give the police a report when the phone rang. Answering, the senior Osborn reported to Lieutenant Finn that he HAD FOUND NOTHING TO ALTER HIS SON'S PREVIOUSLY DECLARED OPINION! Finn could not believe what he had heard. A denial of the similarity of the two writings would greatly hurt their chances of a conviction. Finn was quick to inform Osborn of the new evidence they now held against their prisoner: "We found over $14,000 in the man's garage. WILL YOU BE GOOD ENOUGH TO RECONSIDER YOUR VERDICT? It will be of great help to us."

Finding themselves in a bind, realizing there had been times in the past when they, both of them known as "experts", had been wrong in other court cases, and now that the police had all this additional evidence, maybe they, the "experts" should hop on the bandwagon after all and claim the writings were made by the same person. It took less than an hour for the senior Osborn to call Schwarzkopf and inform him that the two "experts" were now certain that Hauptmann was the writer of all of the ransom notes. (IMPORTANT NOTE: It should be made a matter of record that in 1971 one of these same Osborns testified in the trial of Clifford Irving in which he was accused of a forgery of Howard Hughes writings. Osborn Jr. gave his clear statement from the witness stand that there could not be "the slightest question" that the handwriting was that of Howard Hughes, and that it was "impossible on a practical matter, based on our years of experience ... that anyone other than Hughes could have written the letters." IN 1971 OSBORN WAS WRONG! The writing was proven to be a forgery of Irvings. OSBORN WAS WRONG! AND HE WAS WRONG 37 YEARS EARLIER WHEN HE WAS WILLING TO CHANGE HIS ORIGINAL FINDINGS, AT THE SUGGESTIONS AND COERCION OF THE POLICE, TO TESTIFY AGAINST RICHARD HAUPTMANN! So much for the so-called "experts" who are willing to sell their testimony for a mess of pottage!)

The interrogation of Hauptmann continued throughout the weekend, and on Tuesday, September 24th he was taken before Magistrate Richard McKinery and held without bail for an appearance before the Bronx County Grand Jury, the county in which the extortion of $50,000 had taken place. Hauptmann was brought there without an attorney to represent him.

The authorities, at this point, realized that none of the evidence they had against Hauptmann, including his identity by the eye-witnesses, could place the accused man in the state of New Jersey on the night of the kidnapping. Realizing their need of this evidence, they went searching for someone who would verify that Richard had been there. Originally, they were of the opinion that this would be hard to do since no one living near the Lindbergh home had ever reported to the police that they had seen anything unusual around Hopewell, New Jersey that night.

Detective Arthur Johnson had been given the assignment of tracing the early life of Hauptmann and his friend Isidor Fisch. While visiting Germany he confirmed Richard's prior arrests and his illegal flight from his homeland; and that Hauptmann's correct name was actually Bruno Richard Hauptmann, not merely Richard, the name he had used since he entered America in 1924. He also learned that Fisch, who had sailed for Germany with his friend, Henry Uhlig, on Wednesday, December 6th, 1933, had died three months later on Wednesday, March 29th, 1934 at 2:00 p.m. in St. George Hospital in Leipzig. The cause of death was termed tuberculosis of the lungs. At his bedside had been his brother Pincus and sister Henna. Johnson's trip to Hauptmann's homeland had turned up little of value, except to confirm the status of Fisch's wealth --- he was a pauper.

The authorities discounted the possibility of it being Fisch with whom Condon had conducted the ransom negotiations. They saw little likelihood of this since Fisch was described as being decidedly underweight, of short stature, and having a pale complexion. Furthermore, the police claimed they had uncovered nothing conclusive which would prove that Hauptmann and Fisch were anything more than friends. As for Hauptmann's claim that they had a close partnership in furs and stocks, this, for the convenience of the police, was played down as unimportant and probably not true at all. On the other hand they easily established that Fisch, who came from Germany, and Uhlig, who sailed from England, had entered America together in 1925. Both were 20 years old, and soon after their arrival in America, they met and became fast friends, sharing an apartment together in New York City while Uhlig sought employment. From the information turned up by Detective Johnson, it appeared to the investigators that these two were closer friends than Hauptmann professed himself to be with Isidor Fisch.

Richard Hauptmann's troubles were just beginning. While the police were busy weaving a net of guilt around him, he was frustrated with the stark realization that the only person who could give credibility to his true explanation as to how he had obtained the Lindbergh ransom money was now dead. Had Isidor Fisch been alive, he would undoubtedly explain it all to the police and clear him of these charges. But would he? Hauptmann was starting to realize the seriousness of the situation he found himself in, one he could not explain, since the police refused to believe his true account. One that already was being referred to as "Hauptmann's fish story". "But", he rationalized to himself, "I have told them the truth! Surely they will believe me sooner or later! I know nothing more!" His mind raced on as he thought of the police and their apparent intent on pinning this thing on him regardless of the cost. He was extremely frightened. Would no one believe him?

At 11:00 a.m. on Wednesday, September 26th, before a Grand Jury of 23 jurists in the new Bronx County Court House at 161st Street and Walton Avenue, a building that helped form the intersection known as the Grand Concourse, Hauptmann was brought in to publicly face his accusers. A large crowd, numbering in the thousands, had gathered outside lining the sidewalks, anxious to catch a glimpse of, not only the accused man, but especially to see Colonel Lindbergh, who arrived exactly at 11 o'clock with his friend Colonel Schwarzkopf. Extra police called to duty formed a solid line of protection around the door of the court house where the participants would enter. Movement by automobile was diverted away from the large building onto side streets that were seldom used. Another scene had become carnival-like in atmosphere and appearance.

At the advice of friends, Anna Hauptmann had retained the services of a lawyer to defend her husband. James Mark Fawcett, a Brooklyn attorney, had been selected to represent the thoroughly confused prisoner. The prosecution was handled by Bronx District Attorney Samuel J. Foley and Attorney General David T. Wilentz of New Jersey.

Following the presentation of convincing evidence to the jury, Hauptmann was indicted for extortion of $50,000. Justice Ernest E.L. Hammer set bail at $100,000 and Hauptmann, handcuffed to Sheriff John J. Handy, was taken to the Bronx County Jail. A despondent man heard the door of cell number 19 clang shut in front of him. Hauptmann's troubles were growing with each passing hour. Despite the testimony given by the officers who had arrested and interrogated Hauptmann, giving the jurors knowledge of the money found in Hauptmann's possession, and his inability to give a satisfactory explanation as to how he had obtained it, the statement made by Colonel Lindbergh, when asked if he could identify the prisoner's voice, certainly could not be considered harmful to Hauptmann. Lindbergh's inability was strongly reflected in his answer: "IT WOULD BE VERY DIFFICULT FOR ME TO SIT HERE AND SAY THAT I COULD PICK A MAN BY THAT VOICE." His answer appeared to be an honest one, one that would certainly be expected from someone asked to identify hearing a mere two words "Hey, Doctor" after the passage of two-and-one-half years time.

But it was quite obvious that Lindbergh's explanation was in no way a satisfactory one to the police and Sam Foley. All had expected the Colonel to identify their prisoner immediately. The following morning Lindbergh was summoned to come again to the office of the district attorney. Lindbergh appeared this time in a semi-disguise, wearing a cap and dark glasses. He took a chair in the center of the large office amid a group of detectives already assembled there. His seat had been pre-arranged in order that Hauptmann would not detect his presence.

At exactly 9:50 a.m. the prisoner was brought in and ordered to take a seat in a chair already placed in their center. After a short period of questioning from Foley and some of the other officers, he was directed to sit in various positions, to walk back and forth before the witnesses, at the same time answering more questions. This was done to allow Colonel Lindbergh the advantage of observing him from many directions, hear his voice and its inflections, and study his walk, his posture and other characteristics. After ten minutes Hauptmann was taken from the room. During the entire time the accused man had been in the room the Colonel had not spoken one word.

Reporters had crowded around the outside of Foley's office door and pressed the District Attorney for the reason Lindbergh had been present. The agreeable Foley gave them this answer: "Colonel Lindbergh was here this morning in my office by arrangement, and at his own request he was confronted with the prisoner. He was in the room with Hauptmann for about ten minutes, and the prisoner was unaware of the colonel's presence. The purpose of the meeting and its outcome will not be disclosed by anyone concerned."

When asked if Lindbergh had identified Hauptmann, Foley refused to make any further comment about the meeting. However, Charles F. Brodie, the district attorney's chief clerk, did tell the members of the press that Colonel Lindbergh "didn't say anything after the confrontation."

Here we have a distraught father, one who should have been anxious to tell the world that the police had finally captured the kidnapper and murderer of his tiny son, refusing to make such an announcement. There could be only one reason for his failure to do this --- Lindbergh was not certain that they had the right man.

When the Colonel had first described the man he had seen on Saturday, April 2nd, 1932, the one believed to be an accomplice, Lindbergh told the police they should look for a man not over 30 years old, of dark complexion, five foot seven in height, and weighing about 150 pounds. And in addition, he informed them: "He had a pronounced stoop and walked with an unusual gait," one which he described as: "a rolling gait, somewhat like a sailor's walk, and somewhat awkward." It was after he gave this description to the authorities that he expressed to United States Agent Larimer his opinion that: "the crime had been committed by hardened, experienced criminals." Based on these former statements given by Colonel Lindbergh, we have every reason to believe that he was definitely uncertain of Hauptmann being the right man.

It was evident to the authorities that, although they had enough evidence to try Hauptmann for extortion, they were lacking the vital evidence that would prove conclusively that he was at the Lindbergh home in New Jersey on the night of the kidnapping. In this effort the police lost no time assembling the needed material and persons who would so testify at the extradition hearing scheduled to be held two weeks later.

From the time of Hauptmann's arrest on September 19th, the police had taken possession of his home. In addition to this they had confiscated and impounded everything in it. It had been agreed that only the authorities should have free access to the premises. Because of this Mrs. Hauptmann and her little son, Manfred, were forced to find other living quarters. Her niece, Maria Mueller and her husband Hans, lovingly provided this much needed accommodation.

Anna Hauptmann learned of her need for a "new home" when she arrived back at their apartment on Thursday, September 20th, and was told by the Rauchs that they had agreed to temporarily change the Hauptmann's lease over to Detective Lewis J. Bornmann of the New Jersey State Police, who had been given orders to keep Anna Hauptmann permanently away from the investigation. The state had rented the apartment for whatever time the police deemed necessary.

While this action spared Mrs. Hauptmann the grief of watching the police destroy her property, it proved to be a fatal mistake made by the trusting and unsuspecting German housewife. As for Max and Pauline Rauch, they were appalled and horrified at the barbarianism of the police as they maliciously hacked away with hatchets and saws, destroying its physical appearance, all done with an intense desire to uncover more evidence against their prisoner, whose name they now had learned, from the authorities in Germany, was actually Bruno Richard Hauptmann.

Statements given the press, issued from District Attorney Sam Foley's office, when turned into print by the nation's many newspapers and the spoken word over the radio, became quite clear that Hauptmann was not only being tried by the media, but was also being convicted by them as the kidnapper and murderer of

Lindy's baby. The wheels of destruction were already turning -- wheels which would ultimately crush Hauptmann.

Back at 1279 East 222nd Street, the newly established police "command post", a dozen detectives were endeavoring to "build" an ironclad case against the unfortunate prisoner, whose only claim of innocence had been the truth --- that he had received a package, not knowing it was money, from his friend Fisch; that he had worked the entire day of Tuesday, March 1st, 1932; and that he had brought his wife home from her job at Fredericksen's Bakery later that evening.

Constant searches of the Hauptmann apartment revealed nothing additional other than the usual things any married couple would possess. But Lieutenant Bornmann and his assistants, now having complete reign of the apartment, were busy seeing that something "began to happen". Something that would be advantageous in their conviction of the Bronx carpenter.

On Monday, October 8th, in order to be granted extradition, allowing them to move the prisoner for trial in New Jersey, a hearing was held before a jury of twenty men and three women in the Hunterdon County Court house at Flemington, New Jersey. The authorities were ready to proceed - the "necessary witnesses" had been "found" and were now coached well enough to be placed on exhibition. And there was a parade of them, as Attorney General David T. Wilentz presented his case to the jury. Judge Thomas Whitaker Trenchard presided, as the jury of 26 rendered its verdict which ordered Hauptmann to be extradited for trial by jury in the state of New Jersey.

The jury decided this in spite of testimony given in Hauptmann's behalf. Both Christian and Katy Fredericksen stated that: "If it was a Tuesday night that the child had been kidnapped" they were reasonably sure that Richard had called for Anna at their bakery. Although Hauptmann had expected to produce documented evidence, in addition to verbal affirmation that he had worked all that day at the Majestic Apartments, nothing was presented to back up his claim. "Utterly unbelievable" was the jury's answer to his Isidor Fisch story as an explanation for his possession of the money. Attorney James Fawcett, skilled in law though he was, could not combat the overwhelming evidence brought against his client.

Albert S. Osborn, who had gained fame as an "expert" in the "art and science" of handwriting analysis, testified that Hauptmann had written all of the ransom notes, including the nursery note found on the window sill. Another great plus for the prosecution! But in spite of this, they had yet to prove that Hauptmann had been seen in New Jersey. Proving this, however, seemed to be an easy matter for them. In order to do this they simply had to call on a man who lived near the Lindberghs at the time of the kidnapping. It was easier for them to pull Mr. Whited from his home in Lambertville than a magician to pull a rabbit from a hat.

Millard Whited, identified himself as a 37 year old "logger" who bought and sold timber. He said he had seen Hauptmann on two occasions in the vicinity of Lindbergh's Hopewell home. However, several other witnesses followed him to the stand and testified that Whited was not known as a very trustworthy person. According to William Geltz, a cousin of Whited's, when asked: "What is Millard Whited's reputation in Hopewell?" answered: "Not much!"

"Good or bad?" came the following question, with an immediate and decisive response: "Bad!"

A Hopewell farmer, William Diehl, informed the court that Millard Whited's reputation was: "bad, yes, sir!", and George J. Lentz, another neighbor who knew Whited well, when asked about the man's credibility, shouted for all to clearly hear: "Bad!"

Two days before the extradition hearing began, Whited had been taken to the Bronx County Court House at 3:00 p.m., and in the presence of Captain J.J. Lamb, Sergeant W. P. Kelly, Detective James Cashman, Detective William Gilmartin, and Trooper Wolf, all members of either the New Jersey State Police and New York City Police, had voluntarily made the following statement in answer to their questions.

Q. You have been given an opportunity to look over eleven men in the Bronx County Jail in the Bergen Building this date, were you not? A. Yes.

Q. Did you ever see any person that was in that line-up before this time? A. Yes just one.

Q. And where was this man standing in this line-up? A. The second man from the right as I faced them.

Q. Under what circumstances did you see this man before? A. On the road from Wertsville to Hopewell, New Jersey.

Q. When was that? A. I will say between the 18th day and the last day of February, 1932.

Q. Describe the place on this road and the time of the day? A. I will describe it the best I can, there is an old buttonwood tree at the corner of the Wertsville - Hopewell road which we call Buttonwood Corner, between there and a place known as the old William Dougherty farm, as near as I could tell, ten minutes to twelve to twenty minutes after twelve, on the first occasion that I saw him he was stepping out of the bushes on the left hand side of the road going toward Wertsville, he had a grey slouch hat, a light suit of clothes and he had a coat hanging on his arm, I don't know just what kind of a coat it was on account of this road being a narrow road, I only noticed him because he was a stranger in this section, he walked with his hat pulled down over his eyes and a frown on his face. I passed him with my window down and got a good look at him, I also looked at him through my mirror, he stood on the road looking in both directions, due to the condition of this road I was traveling about fifteen miles an hour and this gave me a good opportunity to look him over. The next time I saw him was between 4:00 P.M. and 5:00 P.M. about four days after the first time I saw him, he was at the cross road closer to the Lindbergh land than the Buttonwood Crossroad, this is the cross road that leads to Zion, he stood there on the left hand side of the road, he looked at me as though he was figuring which way to go, I was traveling in my truck and trailer and due to the condition of the road I was making about ten miles an hour, I had a good opportunity to look him over, and saw that he was the man that I had seen several days before at the Buttonwood corner, he wore the same clothes at this time that he had on when I saw him four days before. I am positive that this is the man who I talked to the Detective about in March, 1932.

The preceding statement appears exactly as it was given to the police. It was signed by Millard Whited with the following witnesses affixing their signatures: Typed by Sgt. W. P. Kelly, NJSP; Act. Lt. James J. Finn, NYCP; W. F. Seery, Sp. Agt. U.S. Dept. of Justice; Det.James Cashman, NYPD #127; Det. William Gilmartin NYPD; and J.J. Lamb, Capt., NJSP.

One of the first things the police did with the arrival of dawn on the morning of March 2nd was to systematically begin questioning all the residents living within a ten mile radius of the Lindbergh mansion. This was done with the intention of possibly finding someone who could tell them something that might be helpful in either recovering the baby or give them some information that might lead them to the apprehension of the kidnappers. This intensified search brought them results which were absolutely negative, not one resident reported seeing anything unusual in the vicinity of the home.

If no one had seen anything out of the ordinary, then we should ask: "Where did this guy come from?" Here we have a man, whose very friends testified they would not believe him, come to the center of the stage and vividly recollect all "he had seen" more than two-and-one-half- years earlier; and then reports under oath that the things he told were true. And what is more surprising, the police expected all who heard and read his statements to believe him. And they did!

For us to be content by accepting Millard Whited's "unusual recollections", as the jury did, would be derelict. Is it possible that Whited had either forgotten to mention these incidents to the police, or considered them of no importance at the time of the police survey of homes? This certainly could not have been the case. Whited's "grave discrepancy" was certainly worthy of further investigation. Why did the police fail to report this man's "important" testimony at the time of the kidnapping? Had he been overlooked? This was highly unlikely since the search for information was, to say the least, very complete and thorough.

Evidence in hand, but deliberately ignored by the investigators at the time of the Hauptmann trials, prove that MILLARD WHITED DELIBERATELY LIED IN ORDER TO CONVICT AN INNOCENT MAN AND WAS PAID TO DO IT!

In my possession is a copy of the police report made at Hopewell, New Jersey on April 26th, 1932. This statement was given voluntarily by our "excellent witness", Mr. Whited before Detective Robert Coar of the Jersey City Police and S.J. Leon of the New Jersey State Police. The questions and answers follow:

Q. Can you tell us where you were from 7:00 A.M. March 1st, 1932 till 12:00 midnight the same date? A. Yes. I got up about 6:30 A.M. and load my truck and took a load of popular (poplar) to Burlington, New Jersey. From Burlington I came back to the Chevrolet agency on Princeton Ave. Trenton, New Jersey and stayed here until about 6:15 or 6:20 P.M. then I came home arriving home about 7:30 P.M. and stayed home the rest of the night. I went to bed about 8:30 P.M. The next I knew the dogs started barking and woke me up, this was about 3:30 A.M. I then got up and went out to the barn as I thought that something was the matter with the horses. From the barn I went back into the house and started a fire. While I was starting the fire a State Trooper and four men in plain clothes came into the house. One of these men questioned me as to how many children I had and if I saw any suspicious cars or persons around the last day or two. I told them that I did not see anyone. They asked me a few more questions about my neighbors and then they said Good Night and left.

That was Whited's recollection of what had taken place as he related it to the police during the early morning hours of March 2nd. However, later in his statement, he was asked more pointed questions about things he might have observed prior to the kidnapping. Here again are his exact answers:

Q. Did you ever cut any timber in back of the Lindbergh home? A. Yes we cut timber in back of the Lindbergh home a year ago last summer.

Q. HAVE YOU NOTICED ANY PERSONS WALKING THROUGH THE WOODS IN THE VICINITY OF THE LINDBERGH HOME BEFORE MARCH 1ST, 1932 THAT ACTED IN A SUSPICIOUS MANNER A. NO I HAVE NOT.

Q. Have you ever heard any one holding a conversation about the Lindbergh family or their baby? A. No I never did.

Q. Has anybody ever asked you where the Lindbergh property was located? A. Last summer when Mr. Lindbergh's home was just started the school teacher at Bryam (Byram), New Jersey, who lives in Frenchtown, asked me where the Lindbergh home was being built and I told her. This is the only person that ever asked me this question.

Q. Have you ever been in the Lindbergh home while it was being built or since it's been built? A. No.

Q. Do you know where the Lindbergh baby is or who it's kidnappers are? A. No.

Q. IS THERE ANY INFORMATION THAT YOU CAN GIVE US THAT WOULD ASSIST US IN THIS INVESTIGATION OR HELP THE POLICE TO RECOVER THE CHILD? A. NO.

The above statement was signed by Millard Whited with Robert Coar and Samuel Leon, the witnesses.

Can we now even think of accepting the testimony of this "person" as he gave it at the extradition hearing? Regardless of the police knowing of Whited's earlier statements, they still dragged him into court to deliberately lie in order to "prove" that Hauptmann had been seen near the Lindbergh home in February, 1932 prior to the kidnapping. The police needed a witness badly, and believe-you-me they found him in one Millard Whited. His statement was not even worth the price of the paper the court stenographer typed it on. But, oh no, the police considered him a "valuable witness".

Where had this man Whited been? This person who had the audacity to be so easily used by the police in the deliberate frame-up of an innocent man. They evidently believed in a new system, one of their own concoction, that a man was no longer to be considered innocent until proven guilty, but that he must be considered guilty, without any doubt, and to discard any proof to the contrary.

This is the way things were in the state of New Jersey during the frenzy of the 1930's when the writings in the news media had already enraged the nation's citizens. The public were now "screaming" for a quick trial and conviction of Hauptmann, the "fiend" whom they were convinced had killed the infant child. On Tuesday, October 9th, the extradition warrant was quickly drawn up and taken by the police to Governor A. Harry Moore of New Jersey, who signed it and directed that it be presented to New York's Governor Herbert Lehman, who affixed his signature to it on Thursday, October 11th. This being completed, Attorney Fawcett exercised his permissible legal recourse by contesting the warrant at habeas corpus proceedings in the Bronx County Supreme Court with Justice Ernest E.L. Hammer presiding. At the hearing held on Monday, October 15th, Hauptmann testified in his own behalf and seemed to be much at ease under both direct and cross examination. This, however, was the first time he faced the eyes of hate shown toward him by such a contemptuous crowd of hostile onlookers.

Fawcett's attempt to keep Hauptmann from being transferred to New Jersey proved to be a lost cause when, on the following day, Justice Hammer ruled against Hauptmann and dismissed the writ. Richard's lawyer, using his final legal maneuver, appealed to keep his client out of Jersey, but was again turned down three days later by the Appellate Court which confirmed the decision of the lower Court. It was now inevitable that the Bronx carpenter be turned over to the state of New Jersey to stand trial for the murder of Charles A. Lindbergh, Jr.

Shortly after eight o'clock on the evening of Friday, October 19th, one month from the date of his arrest, Bruno Richard Hauptmann was securely handcuffed to Captain John Lamb and Lieutenant Arthur Keaten of the

New Jersey State Police and escorted to a rear seat of one of the four cars making the trip down to the jail in Flemington, New Jersey. It was nearly 10:30 when the caravan rolled into the Hunterdon County seat.

At this hour, the rural little town with its population of 3,000, would normally have closed its shops and businesses, a great number of its residents having retired for the night. However, earlier in the day, word had leaked that Hauptmann, the killer, would soon be brought to town that night. What seemed to be at least a third of the town's citizens were seen milling about the jail located next to the courthouse. Hundreds of reporters and cameramen were already there awaiting the approach of the motorcade as it drew near the point where Hauptmann would be taken from the car to his jail cell. A dozen uniformed State troopers were stationed near the front door of the prison.

Although the town was ablaze with lights usually extinguished at this hour, many folks, anxious to get a better glimpse of the prisoner, had brought flares which added to the grotesque atmosphere. The explosion of hundreds of flash bulbs gave the night scene a carnival appearance, one which under normal circumstances would have been just another one of restful quiet.

Motorcycle policemen, with rifles at their side, had by this time joined the entourage. The cars eased their way slowly to the curb. The door of the fourth car opened and out stepped three men. Handcuffed in the middle was Bruno Richard Hauptmann, probably the most closely guarded prisoner in the history of the United States. He was remanded to the custody of Sheriff John Curtiss, who promptly led him to cell number 1, where he would remain a closely watched prisoner for many days to come.

Facing the many hours he would spend alone before his trial, Hauptmann spent them reading his Bible and a book which told the life story of his boyhood hero, Baron Manfred Albrecht VonRichthofen, Germany's air ace "The Red Baron", who, in his scarlet colored plane, had shot down 80 enemy planes during World War 1. As he passed his time away by reading, he had no idea of the great trouble he would soon be called to face.

From his Capitol office in Trenton, Governor A. Harry Moore issued the following official statement:

"The New Jersey State Police, working with other agencies, have arrested a suspect after two and a half years of tireless effort.

They have been diligent in their search and have

traced down every lead.

New Jersey will be diligent in its prosecution of the man charged with the commission of the crime.

There is an old maxim in law that a man is innocent until he is proven guilty.

NEW JERSEY WILL SEE THAT BRUNO HAUPTMANN GETS A FAIR TRIAL."

What a pity that Richard Hauptmann's loyal wife, his mother, his relatives, and his friends, who never doubted his innocence, and now those of us who have since learned the truth, find this final statement of the governor to be nothing more than shallow, hollow, empty, meaningless words, all to be encased in a batch of lies, cleverly and connivingly woven together, by evil New Jersey culprits and their associates!

CHAPTER TWENTY TWO

Evil Plans Afoot!

With Hauptmann securely tucked away in the Flemington jail, plans were fast being made by the prosecution to "prove beyond any doubt" that Hauptmann was the kidnapper and murderer of little Lindy. In order to do this successfully, they were faced with checking out things their prisoner had told them. Things, if proven to be true, would go far to help him prove his innocence. Some of the answers had a ring of truth to them, and this bothered the officials.

Richard had told them that he worked the entire day of Tuesday, March 1st. Realizing that if this were true, it would have been next to impossible for him to have been over in Hopewell, New Jersey to accomplish the kidnapping. One of the first things they must do was to break down his alibi and "prove" that he did not work as he said he did.

Attorney James Fawcett, during the six weeks he represented Hauptmann, had been busy obtaining evidence to back-up the claims which would prove his client's innocence. Fawcett interviewed and was given confirmation by the Fredericksens, Hans Kloppenburg, Maria Mueller, among others, all friends and acquaintances of Hauptmann, that he had been exactly where he said he had been on the various dates in question. He next went about the task of checking Richard's alibi relative to his work record. His client had said he was "certain" that he had worked at the Majestic Apartments on March 1st. Fawcett had only to prove this by contacting someone in charge at the apartment building and have him confirm this.

His attempt to locate the supervisor of the construction at the Majestic Apartments, Joseph M. Furcht, proved unsuccessful. Furcht, he learned, had been employed there since September 1931 and had left his job almost two years earlier. None of the present employees could offer any information as to his present whereabouts.

Undaunted, Fawcett moved on to the office of E.V.

Pescia who ran an employment agency on Sixth Avenue. The attorney had been told that the workers at the apartment in 1932 had obtained their jobs through this agency. Hoping that Mr. Pescia could render him some helpful information, Fawcett was not disappointed.

"Sure, I remember Hauptmann.",

Pescia answered the question put to him without hesitation.

> "He came to me near the end of February and asked if I could get work for him. He paid me the ten-dollar fee I required and when I got Furcht's call, I assigned him to work at the Majestic."

Pescia was dogmatic in his statement.

> "You see, Furcht is supervisor of construction there, and I got a call from him the day before and I promised him I'd have the help there that he needed."

Although he was confident the information he gave Fawcett was accurate, Pescia continued:

> "Let me check my records and I'll tell you exactly when he started."

Opening a record book to a designated page, the agent went on:

> "Sure, here it is! Richard Hauptmann started work at the Majestic Apartments on Saturday, February 27th. Now, if Hauptmann had not started work on that day I would have been called by Mr. Furcht first thing in the morning because he was in need of a carpenter very bad. Yep, you can be sure Hauptmann worked the following Monday, Tuesday, Wednesday, and for that matter the rest of the month. If he hadn't I'd have been told about it. I never heard any more from Mr. Furcht, so I know he was working when he says he was."

The employment agent left no doubt in Fawcett's

mind that his client's statement had been a truthful one when he told the police he had worked at the Majestic Apartments during the entire day of March 1st. He not only had Pescia's word of this, he personally had seen a printed record of it. Fawcett was elated. This, he reasoned, would be a major factor in proving Hauptmann's innocence.

Jim Fawcett had become quite concerned over his clients lack of alertness, and because of this he suspicioned that Richard was not receiving proper treatment at the hands of the police. The attorney was very upset that the accused man had been badgered and harrassed constantly from the time of his arrest. Lack of sleep, their constant questioning him and subjecting him to such mental torture with their false accusations had caused him to lose weight. Hauptmann's weakened condition had become very apparent to all who had seen him the first time he was brought in to the Greenwich Street Police Station.

Troubled by all this, Fawcett had his suspicions and planned to find the reason for Hauptmann's poor change in appearance. So great had become his concern that he decided to inquire of Richard as to what was causing his change in demeanor and loss of weight. But he first approached Anna and inquired if she had detected any change in her husband's appearance. "Oh, yes!" she answered.

> "When I saw Richard in the Bronx after the police had him for two days, I was shocked." she went on. "I saw him sitting in a room with a detective at his side. I noticed that his eyes were swollen and black and blue. I walked over to him and said: 'Richard, what have they done to you?' I touched his face where his eyes were puffy and again asked: 'Richard, what happened?' And then he looked at me and said 'Nothing!' But I couldn't believe it, he seemed to be so badly hurt."

A short time later she and Richard were left alone for a few minutes, and it was then that her husband was able to tell her what had happened to him:

> "Anny, they punched me and kicked me. They turned the lights out so I couldn't see who was hitting me. They had me strapped in a

chair and they kicked me in my chest and stomach."

His small wife was aghast at the things he told her.

> "The police gave me such a terrible licking I fell downward to the floor. They showed me a hammer, then they put the lights out again, and started to beat me on the back of my head, on my shoulders and arms. They kicked my legs and all the time they kept on yelling, 'Where is the money? and where is the baby? We'll knock your brains out if you don't tell us!'"

Although he had no doubt whatsoever that Hauptmann had told the truth about his beatings, Fawcett decided to obtain evidence that would legally support his accusations, by having a doctor examine him.

On Tuesday, September harassed, Dr. Thurston H. Dexter subjected Hauptmann to a physical examination. Present, in addition to Hauptmann's lawyer, Mr. Fawcett, was Louis L. Lefkowitz, assistant medical examiner. When the examination was completed, the official report read in part as follows:

> "SCAB AND ABRASION BETWEEN LEFT EYE AND MOLAR REGION, AND UNDER THE LID A FAINT YELLOW DISCOLORATION ... ON RIGHT SHOULDER A TENDER LUMP, AN INCH AND A HALF, AND A LUMP ON THE SPINE OF THE LEFT SCAPULA AND ABOVE IT ... ALL OF LOWER SHOULDER BLADE SHOWS A SWOLLEN WELT WITH DISCOLORATION AND ABRASIONS ... A LARGE MARK AND DISCOLORATION, YELLOW AND BLUE, EXTENDING INTO THE AXILLARY REGION ... IN THE LOWER LEFT QUADRANT OF THE ABDOMEN, CLOSE TO THE GROIN, AN AREA OF THREE BY FIVE INCHES OF FAINT GREENISH-YELLOW DISCOLORATION ... IN THE UPPER CHEST REGION, INVOLVING PRINCIPALLY THE STERNUM, A LARGE IRREGULAR REGION DISCOLORED YELLOW AND FAINT BLUE, SUPERFICIALLY ABRADED ... RIGHT THIGH MUCH SWOLLEN, VERY TENDER, AND MARKEDLY DISCOLORED."

It is already quite evident that Richard had told

Anna the truth. However, if there should still be some doubt, here is Doctor Dexter's summation:

> "I CONCLUDE FROM THIS EXAMINATION THAT HE HAS BEEN SUBJECTED RECENTLY TO A SEVERE BEATING, ALL OR MOSTLY WITH BLUNT INSTRUMENTS. THE INJURIES RESULTING FROM THIS ARE GENERAL AND INCLUDE THE HEAD, BACK, ABDOMEN, AND THIGHS."

This report clearly speaks for itself as we keep in mind that the examination was made just a week after Richard Hauptmann's arrest. But it was quite obvious that the police planned to "rough up" their prisoner, and in anticipation of this, in order to cover their indiscretion and protect themselves from any possible charges that they had subjected him to physical abuse, they had Hauptmann undergo a physical examination of their own on the second day of his incarceration. To this time the police had done nothing but plod him to answer their questions by frequent "pokes" in the ribs. But they had other plans, and to carry them through successfully, they needed the help of a doctor to thoroughly examine the prisoner before they "went to work on him."

On Friday, September 21st they called on Dr. John H. Garlock, New York City Police Surgeon, to come to the station at 9:30 a.m. and give their prisoner a cursory examination to "prove to the world", just in case anyone should be interested in asking whether Hauptmann had or had not any marks on his body, which would indicate that he might have been beaten. Assisting Dr. Garlock was a Dr. Loughlin. After giving Richard their customary routine physical scrutiny, this was Dr. Garlock's report:

> "Complete physical examination failed to reveal any evidence to suggest recent injury of any sort aside from the fact that this man was pale and suffered from loss of sleep, nothing was found. The heart was negative. All the joints of his body were normal. The head was normal, and there was no break in the skin. The patient's gait was normal. An entry to this effect was made in the police blotter."

With this report now in the record, the police were now covered and all set to do whatever they wished with their prisoner. Who, they reasoned, would ever believe Hauptmann's claims that he was beaten? They now had the protection they needed when Richard Hauptmann, broken in spirit and crying for their mercy, begged them to: "Stop, stop, I didn't do it! I already told you everything I know! I don't know anything more!" and then told Anna: "I was handcuffed in a chair and they said, we'll knock your brains out." With this report of the police surgeon in our possession - we are safe - we are the arresting police - "the good guys!"

James Fawcett had been quite willing to defend the Bronx carpenter. He had agreed to do this even though he had little hope of receiving much money in return for his services. Fawcett had established an enviable reputation among his fellow barristers as one of Brooklyn's cleverest attorneys. He was acquired by Anna Hauptmann to defend her husband and to present the best possible defense for Richard. Consequently, Fawcett had put in many hours gathering valuable information for his client who had already been "declared guilty" by the newspapers and radio. Their daily declarations contained statements issued from District Attorney Foley's office, as well as those of other officials, who were "convinced" that Hauptmann was guilty, and furthermore, apparently did not care in the least what methods were employed as a cover-up for them to "prove it".

Attorney James M. Fawcett had sensed, that soon his opportunity to defend Hauptmann and be of help to his wife, had to be done with very few funds. At the time of Hauptmann's transfer to Flemington's jail, Fawcett named Harry Whitney, a business representative of the Hauptmanns, as an aide to him. Shortly after Richard's arrest, Anna had turned over, in Whitney's name, two mortgages of $3,750 each on property in Brooklyn and Queens. However, the name on the document was Weisensee, rather than Whitney. This represented the sum total of money available to defend Richard Hauptmann.

During this time, Fawcett refused to speak to the press and referred all their inquiries to Whitney. His terse comment was always the same: "Any statements on this case will have to come from Mr. Whitney. You'll have to see Mr. Whitney." But, Mr. Whitney's statements did little to satisfy the hungry news hounds since he merely emphasized Mrs. Hauptmann's devotion to her husband and her belief in his complete innocence. The legal moves of defense counsel were being kept from the news media. Rumors of dissention were rampant however, while the reporters waited for Fawcett to choose the New Jersey attorneys who would serve as associate counsel of record for the state in the county of Hunterdon.

But, something entirely unprecedented occurred on Friday, November 2nd. Something that wrote finis to Fawcett's term as chief defense attorney for Richard Hauptmann. It occurred in this fashion. Mrs. Hauptmann, together with Harry Whitney, had arranged to meet with Fawcett in his Brooklyn office and then go to Flemington. The purpose of the trip was to find suitable New Jersey lawyers to assist Fawcett in his presentation of the case for the defense. But, they never reached their destination. As Anna and Whitney were approaching the entrance to the building in which Fawcett's office was located, they were halted by a man who addressed Mrs. Hauptmann with these words: "Fawcett will take your husband to the electric chair. You had better get another lawyer at once; if you don't he will go to the electric chair." Startled by these curt statements, Anna Hauptmann, believing the man to be a friend who was offering his honest help, inquired as to whom he would recommend, and without hesitation, the man answered: "Ed Reilly."

Although Anna Hauptmann knew nothing about Reilly, she consulted with Whitney, and realizing their need for the best lawyer possible to represent Richard, they made a hasty decision and decided to rely on the man's apparent earnest wish to help them. This decision was to prove itself, over and over, a bad mistake.

They learned that the stranger's name was Jack Clements, a representative of *The New York Mirror*, one of the many newspapers of the *Hearst* chain, owned by millionaire publisher William Randolph Hearst.

The irony of this poor decision was self-evident, since it was a known fact that this newspaper, as well as the other Hearst publications, had proven themselves to be violently anti-Hauptmann from the time of the carpenter's arrest.

Nevertheless, without giving a thought to the negative slant of the articles, commentaries, and editorials, the paper had taken relative to her husband, the consent of Mrs. Hauptmann was all that Clements needed. Within minutes, after putting in a call to Reilly, the trio were on an elevator enroute to "Big" Ed Reilly's law office.

After spending a short period of time listening as Reilly explained to them that he had been retained by the newspaper chain to represent her husband at absolutely no cost to her; and that the change of lawyers, of course, would only be done with her approval; and that he, Reilly, was a "famous criminal lawyer who had lost very few cases", Anna, realizing her lack of funds and desiring to procure the best attorney possible, consented, with no remorse, to allow him to defend her husband.

It took only a short time for the flamboyant Reilly to give the news media the latest development in the case with the announcement that: "Edward J. Reilly, a Brooklyn lawyer has been retained to serve as chief counsel for Hauptmann." Reilly told them he was succeeding James M. Fawcett, "who will retire from the case."

Apparently the news came as a shock to Fawcett as he clearly stated his complete surprise: "It is news to me. Of course, if Mrs. Hauptmann wishes me to withdraw and wants to engage Mr. Reilly, she has a perfect right to act." Confirmation of the Reilly announcement was made by both Whitney and Mrs. Hauptmann. It left little doubt that Fawcett had been discharged from the case. Neither Fawcett or Reilly would discuss the change in chief defense lawyers. The press could only surmise, and therefore wrote their reports of the change accordingly.

Relieved that she had made the proper decision, Anna was asked to sign a brief contract in which she agreed not to talk to any representative of the press other than those employed by *The Mirror*. It was also agreed that Miss Jean Adams, a writer for the Hearst paper, be assigned as Mrs. Hauptmann's constant companion until the end of the trial. This was done in order to gain exclusive news whenever the prisoner's wife had a story to tell.

The transfer of attorneys was made without either the consent or knowledge of Richard Hauptmann, although when he was told, he readily agreed since his concern for additional money to pay for his defense had been solved.

The pretentious Mr. Reilly, from the moment he was hired, began his "peacock strut" in and around Flemington. "Death House Reilly" or "The Bull of Brooklyn" were two names he had acquired during his more than 25 years as a successful lawyer, and he wore both titles well. At an age of 52 years, he had earned his reputation as a defense attorney for many murderers and had successfully won acquittals for them. This afforded him the right to proudly boast of his legal victories in more than two thousand cases. And this he did without difficulty, his braggadocio always finding ready listeners.

Enhanced and blown-up with the importance of his appointment as Hauptmann's chief lawyer, "Big Ed" at once found the closest printing house and ordered several thousand business letterheads, which when printed across the top of the page and centered in capitol letters, read:

THE LINDBERGH-HAUPTMANN TRIAL
FLEMINGTON, N. J.

and slightly below this near the right-hand margin appeared:

OFFICE OF
EDWARD JAY REILLY
CHIEF DEFENSE COUNSEL

But this was not enough for the bombastic, pompous lawyer, who was so thrilled with himself and his position as the "center attraction" in what was destined to become the world's most important criminal case, to be forever referred to as "The Trial of the Century". Mr. Reilly conjured another way to go one step further. Since he had already banked Hearst's retainer fee of $7,500, he decided it would be entirely proper for him to spend some additional money by "jazzing up" his correspondence paper which he thought to be too conservative, especially for an important man such as him. The case was a big one, and so "Big Ed", who would soon acquire the new nick-name of "Big Head Reilly", ordered a sketch of the three sectioned kidnap ladder to be printed in crimson red along the left-hand margin of his writing paper. Looking at the finished job, a broad smile broke across his face as he remarked: "Boy, that's more like it!". Certainly Edward J. Reilly could never be referred to as a humble man.

Reilly decided his initial item of business was to pay a visit to his client who was still closely guarded in cell one in the Hunterdon County jail. After greeting him and listening to Hauptmann's explanation as to how he obtained the ransom money plus a few other particulars which Reilly evidently deemed to be unimportant at that moment, he departed with these words of encouragement: "Don't worry, there is no jury in the world who can convict you." He went away singing to himself. The entire time he spent with Richard Hauptmann at the time of their first meeting had not lasted more than five minutes.

Next on the Reilly agenda was the important task of meeting with the press and issuing a formal statement. Two days after his appointment to defend the accused man, he called a press conference, and as the newsreel cameras recorded his brilliant oratorical mannerisms, and with reporters taking notes on steno pads, Reilly rose to the occasion as he uttered these words: "We must remember that a man must be considered innocent until he has been proven guilty. That, of course, we recognize as a principle of American jurisprudence and that a mere accusation of guilt is not proof of guilt. In my examination of the case, brief though it necessarily was, I am convinced beyond a doubt of the innocence of my client."

Reilly's selection of associate lawyers from the state of New Jersey appeared to be "cut and dried" since he immediately chose Flemington's own C.Lloyd Fisher, Frederick A. Pope of Somerville, and Egbert Rosecrans of Blairstown. In this same Flemington courtroom in which Hauptmann would be tried, Fisher had defended John Hughes Curtis in 1932 for his role as a "hoaxer" of Colonel Lindbergh in his attempt to gain his son's return.

The defense efforts to learn the specific accusations against their client proved to be difficult. At best they could only obtain a broad charge. It was Hauptmann's legal privilege and right, under all judicial decisions, to be informed as to exactly what each charge was in order that his attorneys properly defend him to the best of their ability. However, the team of defense barristers claimed the prosecution's charges were much too vague. Specifically, the defense was anxious to learn from the prosecution staff, the answer to these questions. Does the State contend that Bruno Richard Hauptmann alone committed the crime against the Lindberghs, or did he have associates, and where and when did the actual murder of Charles A. Lindbergh, Jr., occur? Another major question the defense attorneys believed they were entitled to be given an answer was, by what method the State contends the baby met his death?

Reilly and Fisher brought the matter in a formal demand before the Court. Attorney General David T.

Wilentz, assisted by Anthony M. Hauck, Jr. the prosecutor of record from Hunterdon County, represented the State in their argument before Justice Thomas W. Trenchard, who ruled that the prosecution must advise the defense as to what lethal instrument had been used to kill the Lindbergh infant. However, the justice added the stipulation that this be done only when the identity could be made with a degree of certainty.

Wilentz and Hauck accepted Trenchard's decision as a victory for them. His order seemed to place more emphasis on the manner of death rather than by what means the child had been killed. In order to satisfy the demand of the defense attorneys, they had only to turn to the medical examiner's official verdict, the phraseology being broad enough to cover many variations, the interpretation to be determined merely by the mind of the person reading the report. It read: "Death was caused by a fracture of the skull, due to external violence." This could mean death might have come as a result of anything from an accidental fall to extreme violence caused by the impact of an automobile, a truck, a locomotive, a baseball bat or even a baseball itself, to name but a few. On the other hand it could also conveniently cover a lethally inflicted blow from a hammer, hatchet, knife, gun butt, or a bullet fired from a gun.

Justice Trenchard's term was due to expire on January 20th, 1935, and facing the prospect that the Hauptmann trial would already be in progress at that time, the newly elected governor, Harold G. Hoffman reassured Trenchard that he planned to reappoint him to another term on the bench. This was done in order that there would be no fear of an interruption or a possible mistrial which would create grounds for the trial to be started anew.

The trial was slated to begin in January, and with the passing of each day during the month of December, the press were fed statements issued by representatives from both sides. Reilly and Fisher claimed they would bring 50 witnesses to the stand who would prove that Richard Hauptmann was not in New Jersey at any time on or about March 1st, 1932. A report from Anthony Hauck made it clear that: "The prosecution will bring a hundred witnesses who will link Bruno Hauptmann unmistakably to the crime."

Battle lines were being drawn. Rumors grew with intensity. Speculation was overwhelmingly against the possibility of the accused Bronx carpenter being acquitted. The area became electrified with pre-trial predictions that Hauptmann would die for the heinous crime he had committed. The gathering crowd had already pronounced him guilty.

The little town of Flemington was in no way prepared for the onslaught of people who were moving enmasse over its boundaries. The residents, most of them at least, had grown accustomed to the normalcy of the depression life of the thirties. However, with the Hauptmann trial about to begin in the center of their town, regardless of their unpreparedness for the thousands of visitors cascading on them, they seemed to enjoy the circus-like atmosphere as well as the notoriety and fame it was bringing them. People from all walks of life were coming from near and far to view the big event. They wanted to catch a glimpse of the many notables coming to enjoy the trial, while others wanted to see the "main actors" in the trial. Flemington's population was growing by the thousands.

Tickets were printed for admission to each day of the approaching trial, to be sold on a first come, first served basis. Miniature three sectioned ladders and tiny airplanes had been constructed to be sold by hawkers and vendors on street corners outside the courthouse. The appearance of the small town which served as the County Seat was being transformed from a quiet little hamlet into one of intensive activity. Its citizens soon found themselves busy making preparations for an onslaught of visitors that proved to be greater than the wildest imagination of any of its native residents.

Flemington, New Jersey had its origin as a settlement of Dutch immigrants during the seventeenth century. In 1624, a boatload of 30 families sponsored by the Dutch East India Company, under the direction of Captain Cornelis Jacobsen May, put ashore on land later to be named New Jersey. The town did not officially receive the name chosen until sometime in the 1750s when Samuel Fleming, a local innkeeper was chosen as the person whose name the town would bear. Located in Hunterdon County, approximately 10 miles north of Hopewell, it is situated in what one would term north-central Jersey, about 60 miles west of New York City. The State Capitol at Trenton lies 20 miles to the south.

In 1828 an impressive two and one half story courthouse was built of native Jersey stone. Four massive Doric columns on the main entrance porch, reached by seven steps from Main Street's sidewalk extended across the front, gave the white stucco building a handsome appearance. A moderate size Colonial cupola adorned its roof. Behind the courthouse, a small building, very modern for that day, served as the county jail. It was here that Hauptmann had been incarcerated in cell number one.

The residents of the town, numbering nearly 2800, were mostly God-fearing folk who took pride in their clean well-kept law abiding community, however, occasionally the town's one policeman had to escort a citizen to his home after he had spent too many hours imbibing at the local pub.

The townfolk believed in the practice of going to bed at an early hour in order to arise early to take care of their immaculate white-walled, green shuttered homes. Many of these were festooned with various styles of vintage ornamental woodwork and generous flower gardens in their front yards. The community of Flemington was neat, orderly, and quiet -- that is, until the thousands of visitors came to town.

Among the notable people who arrived early for the trial, were those whose tickets had been reserved for them. These included many stars of the stage and screen, United States senators, members of Congress, well known concert singers, social celebrities, and any number of those who rarely missed an important sports event or major murder trial.

The town would shortly be entertaining a combined assortment of Hollywood, Broadway, and Washington, D.C. big shots, something the community had never experienced before, and never would again. Quite naturally, as the news of the upcoming trial spread, an assemblage of star-struck and morbid curious were likewise being drawn to it.

It was estimated that no less than three hundred reporters swarmed into Flemington, with newsmen and newswomen from every major publishing network in the country. The *United Press* and the *Associated Press* had their ace reporters there, as did the overseas papers such as the *London Daily Mail* and the *London Daily Express*. Other foreign representatives from Paris and various major cities throughout the world were present. The names of the news media who had been assigned to cover the trial read like an all-star cast of the fourth estate. There was Damon Runyon, Alexander Woollcott, Arthur B. Reeve, Fannie Hurst, Edna Ferber, Heywood Broun, Walter Winchell, James Kilgallen, Ford Madox Ford, Kathleen Norris, Adela Rogers St.John, Dorothy

Kilgallen, Earl Rogers, Arthur Brisbane, many of them reporters, while others were famous novelists, most of them intent on attending every session of the trial with the desire of writing a best selling novel, based on the famous trial, one everyone now titled "The Trial of the Century".

Covering the daily events for the radio audience who would be intently listening for the latest news at the end of each day's court session were Boake Carter and Gabriel Heatter, both well known news personalities of that era.

With the influx of so many people into the town, a two-fold problem presented itself. Those who planned to stay until the trials end, largely those of the news media, found it quite difficult to find lodging. Representatives of the major news organizations had obtained reservations for rooms when it was first announced that the trial would open on Wednesday, January 2nd. The other problem was fostered on those who owned hostelry suitable for housing persons in search of rooms for just a day or two. More than a few citizens placed signs in the windows of their homes offering spare rooms for rent. And all of these were immediately claimed with exorbitant charges being paid by those willing to meet the highest dollar demanded.

The Hauptmann trial had at least made it possible for the little town to temporarily escape from the pangs of the depression in which it had found itself enmeshed since the stock market crash of 1929.

The majority of those who planned to remain for the duration of the trial found lodging in the Union Hotel, directly across from the courthouse. Its 50 rooms were quickly filled. Many folks who were total strangers when they came to Flemington, doubled up, to become fast friends before the trial's end. The four-story brick hotel with its long second floor porch was soon to become famous, and remain so, as a tourist attraction in the years to come. Its third floor served as quarters for the broadcasters, Carter and Heatter, with the other six rooms on that floor, set aside for the members of the jury. The bar on the main floor soon became known as "Nellie's Tap Room", due to a black and white mongrel dog that strayed in to become attached as a pet to one of the reporters. She soon became the pet of almost everyone who frequented the bar, which had become the dog's favorite lodging place. She answered to the name of "Nellie", hence the reason for the bar's "distinguished" identity. The Union Hotel was soon to earn its individual fame as the nerve-center of everything that happened in Flemington when the legal sessions came to a close each day in the century-old Hunterdon County courthouse.

As the Christmas holiday season ended and with the New Year's Day festivities ahead of them, many persons decided to dispense with the midnight revelry and journey into Flemington to await the opening of the trial the following day. Visitors came from most every state as far away as California, Colorado, Florida, Utah, Arkansas, Iowa, as well as from the neighboring states of New York, Pennsylvania, Delaware and Maryland.

Ladies from the social circles of New York City and Philadelphia arrived in chauffeur driven limousines and stepped to the curbside near the courthouse to inquire where they should go to obtain passes to the trial. Of the fur coats they wore to protect them from the chill of the January air, mink seemed to predominate. Sports and movie fans were not to be disappointed, as many of the celebrities were identified as they looked for places to park their cars. Among those recognized were Jack Dempsey, Jack Benny, Robert Ripley of "Believe-it-or-Not" fame, Ginger Rogers, Lynn Fontanne, Lowell Thomas, Moss Hart, Clifton Webb, and Elsa Maxwell, plus many others. The citizens of Flemington, New Jersey were enjoying a "field day". Their little town had suddenly become the center of the world.

As the crowds approached the steps of the courthouse, their appearance resembled that of a throng of enthusiastic fans about to enter the doors of an arena where a major fight or ball game was about to start. As Flemington's natives looked upon the scene in amazement at the great number of people who had come to their community, they gazed aghast at the changed appearance of their courthouse. Forty telegraph wires hovered above their heads, thousands of feet of wire had been strung from a pole outside, their thickness forming a black mass against the sky. The heavy strands of black cable had been inserted into the ancient attic of the courthouse to serve the 40 wireless operators who would soon be dispatching important messages, directly from the courthouse, to points in the distant world. From their vantage point high in the balcony, thousands of words from scribbled messages would soon be sent around the world many times a day directly from the courtroom floor as the reporters enjoyed an overall view of the scene as it was to be enacted before them.

The great "circus" in the hippodrome was about to begin. Most of the participants had received their subpoenas, many of them already on hand to take their seat in the witness chair and swear that the testimony they were about to give would be "the truth, the whole truth, and nothing but the truth, so help me God!"

CHAPTER TWENTY THREE

Twelve Honest Unsuspecting Jurors!

Wednesday, January 2, 1935 provided clear weather for the thousands of people who left their homes early that morning bound for Flemington. Their purpose in this was to arrive there before the courthouse doors opened and thus gain entrance to the court room. Most folks, however, had already obtained either passes or tickets that would admit them, although that would only be true if the small court room would accommodate them.

All roads leading into the tiny town were virtually clogged with incoming cars, taxis, buses, and trucks. Many people in nearby areas chose to walk the distance. Those who had not found lodging within the town itself had been forced to find temporary living quarters in the neighboring communities of Clinton, Stockton, and Califon. The Hildebrecht and Stacey Trent Hotels in Trenton accommodated many, as did a country club on the outskirts of Flemington that had been leased by a New York newspaper in order to provide quarters for its employees assigned to cover the trial. Before 10:00 a.m., the hour the trial was scheduled to begin, most of the 250 spectator seats were occupied. Outside, thousands of disappointed people hoping to be admitted, were kept away from the entrance doors. The snappily dressed contingent of State Police officers, in their attractive winter coats of horizon-blue and flared riding breeches sporting broad yellow stripes, saw to it that there was no disorder. Members of the press, having presented their passes and moving to the front of the courtroom, had already taken their seats located behind a pine board table. This table allowed them a rather restricted 18 inch space for each one of the 150 reporters, comprising all of the major media networks, to perform his or her duties while covering the trial. Inside a rail enclosure at the front of the room were the chairs where the prosecution and defense attorneys would sit. Although most of them were already seated, a few were to be seen milling about conversing with other courtroom officials.

At exactly 9:45, a stir among the spectators was noted. Bruno Richard Hauptmann had entered the room accompanied by Lieutenant Allen C. Smith of the New Jersey State Police and Deputy Sheriff Hovey Low. Each had one of the prisoner's wrists firmly in his grasp as they led him to a chair reserved for him in the center of the room where he was immediately seated directly in front of the attorney's enclosure rail. Directly in front of Hauptmann was the table where his own lawyers were sitting. To his right was another table where the prosecution attorneys were located.

Reilly, Fisher, Rosecrans, and Pope were observed conversing with their client in what appeared to be a light conversational manner. Hauptmann, knowing he was innocent and looking forward to a fair trial, after being promised by his attorneys that he could never be convicted of the crime, was seen to smile along with the four men as they awaited the call to order which was only minutes away.

Those representing the state prosecutors were Attorney General David T. Wilentz; Judge George K. Large, chief assistant to Wilentz who had prepared the case; Anthony M. Hauck, Jr., prosecutor of record for Hunterdon County; and assistants to the Attorney General, Joseph Lanigan, Robert Peacock, Richard Stockton, and Harry Walsh.

Four chairs to Hauptmann's right sat Colonel Lindbergh. His countenance displayed signs of the nearly three years of turmoil he had passed through since the night of his son's disappearance. On the Colonel's left sat his friend Colonel Breckinridge and Colonel Schwarzkopf, Superintendent of the Jersey State Police. Approximately 15 feet away from the prisoner sat Anne Lindbergh and her mother, Mrs. Morrow. Anna Hauptmann was sitting one seat away from her husband, a police officer between them.

As the courthouse bell ceased its bonging, announcing the hour of ten o'clock, a door at the front of the courtroom opened and as everyone in the room rose to their feet, the black robed Justice Thomas Whitaker Trenchard walked in and took his seat on the judges' bench. Elmer Hann, the court crier intoned the ancient announcement of the English law courts of the old country homeland: "Oyez! Oyez! Oyez! All manner of persons having business in this Court ... on this second day of January in the year of Our Lord One Thousand Nine Hundred and Thirty-five, let them draw nigh, give their attention, and they shall be heard!"

As the final words of his cry echoed through the yellow high-vaulted steel metal walls and ceiling of the century-old courtroom, excited spectators once again lowered themselves into their seats, including those who had perched themselves on the sills at the base of the ten tall recessed windows. The cramped quarters of the tiny courtroom provided anything but comfort for most of the observers. The court of Oyer and Terminer of Hunterdon County, New Jersey had been formally declared open by the white-haired court crier and the session was ready to begin.

Clerk of Court, C. Lloyd Fell and Sheriff John H. Curtiss, who served as Hauptmann's chief custodian, took their official designated seats at the front of the room. Tension seemed to mount among the onlookers - the trial of the century was about to begin, and they were there to enjoy it.

Sheriff Curtiss poled the seventy prospective jurors seated in the rear, all answering to their name as it was called. Each initially agreed that Bruno Richard Hauptmann was certainly entitled to a fair trial, and if they were selected they would see that he received one. However, of this number, only twelve of them would serve. It was emphasized before the trial that: "No Hunterdon County jury can be stampeded into railroading an innocent man to the electric chair." The motive behind the statement was to avoid any accusation that the jury exercised prejudice because of the prominence of the family on which the crime had been perpetrated.

Rapping his gavel for order, the room quieted, and Justice Trenchard was heard to ask the first necessary question: "Is the State ready to proceed with the case of the State against Bruno Richard Hauptmann for murder?"

"The State moves the indictment of Bruno Richard Hauptmann for murder.", so answered Anthony M. Hauck, Jr.

"Is the defense ready?", Justice Trenchard inquired.

"Yes, your Honor.", came Lloyd Fisher's immediate response.

And the trial was underway.

The first juror called was a machinist of High Bridge named Charles Walton, Sr. Married and the father of four children, Mr. Walton was a slim gray-haired man of 55 years of age. Since he was the first selected, he would act as the jury foreman.

Of the seventy prospective jurors from which Mr. Walton was chosen, it is well that we first have an insight on how the 70 were selected. Harold G. Hoffman, who served as governor during the year of the trial, relates the following:

> "Cicero wrote, 'Let us remember that justice must be observed even to the lowest.' Our understanding of American justice has been built upon this concept; we have always held that members of the jury, especially those in whose hands may lie the life of a human being, must be free from prejudice and from a preconceived idea of the guilt or innocence of the person on trial.
>
> "The state of New Jersey overlooked no bets in the selection of the jury in the Hauptmann case. Perhaps these precautions were wise, but shall place the facts before the public so that it may be determined in individual minds whether or not it was possible for the German carpenter, under the circumstances, to receive what we so often refer to as a fair trial. "Lloyd Fisher, a defense attorney, was worried over the impression that would be created in Hunterdon County by the appearance of Edward J. Reilly of Brooklyn as the chief defense counsel. He suggested to Mrs. Hauptmann that an effort be made to add to the counsel staff former Judge George Large, highly regarded in Hunterdon County. Fisher found that Judge Large was interested, and when Mrs. Hauptmann said she had no money to retain the judge, Fisher felt that under the circumstances, with Reilly being paid from funds that came from an outside source, Justice Trenchard might assign Large to the defense. A few days later there came news that Judge Large had been retained by the state. Large, ostensibly, had been secured to help draw the jury. For this he received from the State of New Jersey $8,043.
>
> "Ten special investigators were paid $100 each to check the persons from whom the jury was to be drawn. Local people were used for this purpose. I have before me their findings, as compiled by Detective Sergeant John Wallace of the state police for the information of the prosecution. Some of the people were drawn; some were not. I am obliged to withhold their names, lest a lot of good Hunterdon County folk be

embarrassed. Every person on the jury list was carefully labeled 'Republican' or 'Democratic.' 'Here is some of the illuminating information:

* Advised she wants to see Hauptmann get all that is coming to him. Should be a good juror.
* Very good type. Had remarked that Hauptmann should get the chair.
* Good type of juror. Father-in-law of Sergeant -- -- -- of state police.
* Very poor head. Had remarked that she couldn't send Hauptmann to the chair if found guilty.
* Good type of juror. Belongs to KKK and they are against Fisher in that township.
* Good type---easily led---should make fair juror
* Would make good juror. Not friendly to Fisher.
* Learned he may be led $$$$ Poor type juror.
* Would go along with state.
* Can be reached $$$$$
* Her reputation is questionable. Gossiper.
* Believe she could send Hauptmann to the chair without any hesitation.
* Carpenter, approachable $$$ Poor type juror.
* She would be weak and hesitate about sending a person to the chair; also learned she had said Hauptmann resembles a person she knows and she couldn't convict him.
* Would favor the state, provided several good Lambertville jurors were on the panel to influence him.
* States state has weak case against Hauptmann. Poor juror type. OUT.
* He is acquainted with Millard Whited and would doubt very much the veracity of this man's statements or testimony.
* May be handicapped by his age, but would go along with the state.

Even the constables selected to guard the jury were checked and double- checked."

Prior to Walton's acceptance as the first member of the Hauptmann jury, he had as all the others that followed him, been asked a series of questions relating to his viewpoint and knowledge of the case. Lloyd Fisher was the defense attorney chosen to examine him. These are the questions he asked and Mr. Walton's answers:

"Mr. Walton, have you formed any opinion as to the guilt or innocence of the defendant in this case?"

"Not exactly, no."

"Have you read the Winchell column in the *Daily Mirror?*"

"No, I haven't."

"Or heard his broadcast?"

"Well, occasionally."

"And from what you have heard in his broadcast, you have formed an opinion?"

"No, not necessarily." Walton's answer was followed by a brief pause as he considered it again, and then responded with another "No."

"Do you feel, Mr. Walton, if you were permitted to sit on this jury that you would be guided by the evidence and render a fair verdict in accordance with the evidence as presented to you?"

"Yes, I would, sir."

"And do you understand that rule of law that the defendant is innocent until he is proved guilty beyond a reasonable doubt?"

"Yes, sir."

"And would you be willing to give him the benefit of that reasonable doubt?"

"Yes, sir, I would."

Lloyd Fisher, having completed his line of questioning, indicated he was perfectly satisfied with Mr. Walton as a juror. It was now Anthony Hauck's turn to interrogate the prospective juror. His questioning proceeded as follows:

"Mr. Walton, have you any conscientious or religious scruples against capital punishment?"

"No."

"I understood you to answer Mr. Fisher, as to whether or not you had formed an opinion, that you said, 'not exactly.'"

"Well," Walton explained with an accompanying gesture, "well, not to any extent, not more than anyone else would that read the paper."

"In other words, even though you might have been affected in some small manner, you could be guided by the evidence and by law as charged to you by the Court solely?"

"Yes." Walton nodding his affirmation to the

question.

Hauck, turning to Fisher, announced that he was also satisfied with the first selection. Mr. Walton was then directed to step into the jury box located on the right side of the attorney's enclosure rail.

Although it had been the belief of both the prosecution and defense attorneys that the selection of a jury of twelve persons would take several days, it developed that the processing of the seventy talesmen and the seating of the 12 found to be agreeable to both sides, had taken considerably less time than had been expected.

A few weeks before the trial was scheduled to begin, *The Law Journal*, an official publication of the legal profession, had pronounced great confidence in an editorial by stating: "Due to an aroused and inflamed public sentiment by reason of the prominence of the victim and the atrocity of the crime, and the unprecedented publicity which every step and phase of the investigation has been given by the newspapers, it will be difficult to secure a jury for the trial of Hauptmann in New Jersey, the members of which shall possess the fair, impartial, and unbiased minds deemed essential to the proper administration of the criminal law."

But, in spite of these and other predictions, the selection of the jury members progressed rapidly, and at the end of the first days session, nine more jurors had met the requirements of all the attorneys and had taken their seats, as had Charles Walton, in the jury box. They were:

Juror No. 2. Mrs. Rosie Pill, a 55 year old widow from Califon. She had two grown sons.

Juror No. 3. Mrs. Verna Snyder, a 36 year old housewife who lived with her husband in Readington.

Juror No. 4. Charles F. Snyder, a 40 year old farmer of Clinton Township. Father of two sons.
(Not related to Mrs. Verna Snyder.)

Juror No. 5. Mrs. Ethel Stockton, a 32 year old housewife of Pattenburg. Worked as a stenographer in the office of a former district attorney. She was the mother of a seven year old son. Insisted she was not related in any way to Mr. Richard Stockton of the State's counsel.

Juror No. 6. Elmer Smith, a 42 year old

insurance salesman of Lambertville. Father of a three year old son.

Juror No. 7. Robert Cravatt, a 28 year old unmarried Civilian Concentration Camp supervisor at High Bridge.

Juror No. 8. Philip Hockenbury, a 58 year old railroad laborer. Lived at Annandale with his wife and two grown children.

Juror No. 9. George Vorhees, a 54 year old farmer of Clinton Township. Married and the father two grown children.

Juror No. 10. Mrs. May F. Brelsford, a 38 year old housewife and stepmother of two children. She lived in Flemington.

Following the selection of Mrs. Brelsford, Judge Trenchard, noting the lateness of the hour, adjourned court until ten o'clock the following morning, announcing that the completion of the jury would be determined at that time.

The first day of the Hauptmann trial had drawn to a close. Justice Trenchard's final announcement informed the jury that they would find rooms reserved for them during the length of the trial on the third floor of the Union Hotel across the street. Sheriff's deputies escorted them to their quarters where they would enjoy their evening meal in the dining room and shortly thereafter retire for the night. They were to be sequestered for the duration of the trial.

When court reconvened the following morning it took but a short time to complete the selection of the final two jurors.
They were:

Juror No. 11. Liscom C. Case, a 60 year old retired carpenter of Franklin. A widower who suffered from a serious heart condition.

Juror No. 12. Howard V. Biggs, a 55 year old unemployed bookkeeper of Clinton Township. Married and the father of two sons.

Clerk of Court Lloyd Fell announced that the selection of the jury had been completed and immediately Judge Trenchard instructed Attorney General Wilentz to begin. A slight stir was noted among the crowded and cramped spectators, but was soon reduced to a quiet hush as the young prosecuting attorney rose and began his opening address for the State. Glancing at each of those as he mentioned them, he said: "May it please your Honor, Mr. Foreman, men and women of the jury." And with these words the trial was underway.

David T. Wilentz, a 39 year old Jewish lawyer, had been appointed attorney general for the state by Governor A. Harry Moore because of his success as a young political aspirant by convincing a large majority of traditional Republican voters in Middlesex County to switch their allegiance to that of the Democrats. He was a graduate of New York University Law School. After serving a hitch in the military as a lieutenant in France during the war, he was admitted to the New Jersey Bar in 1919, soon establishing a reputation as a very competent attorney.

Wilentz was a man of slightly dark complexion, short in stature, impeccable in attire. He presented himself as a person of importance as he was observed moving about the courthouse; dapper was he in his Chesterfield coat with velvet collar, one which permitted his white silk scarf to be exposed for contrast. He appeared to be a man of "real class" as he was seen "strutting his stuff" outside the building among the thousands of onlookers. An off-white felt hat adorned his head, a fedora that covered his slicked-down immaculately combed black hair, topped-off his "slick" appearance which resembled that of a movie star who enjoyed cavorting in front of his fans.

Regardless of his appearance, which seemed out of place in the rural Hunterdon County courtroom, attorney Wilentz brought with him an excellent record as a trial lawyer. He also brought his caustic tongue which would soon be publicly exhibited. However, regardless of his fine record as a successful lawyer, and his intense desire to prove that Hauptmann, and Hauptmann alone, had been responsible for the kidnap-murder of little Lindy, this trial would be the first murder case he had ever tried.

In his opening address to the jury, Wilentz explained that Hauptmann was being tried for first-degree murder because baby Lindbergh had been killed during the course of a burglary, and this he would prove. Furthermore, he stated, he would prove that the child's murder had taken place in Hunterdon County and not in Mercer County where the corpse was found. Quite naturally the prosecutor went on making other bold statements as to what else he would prove. Initially, in his opening remarks, we should accept his description of the child as being factual, otherwise Anne Lindbergh would have refuted this. Wilentz made this quite clear by stating: "The child was a happy, normal, jovial, delightful little tot at that age, -- blue eyed, curly headed, blond haired. He had been playing around that entire day with the family."

Before we make our move to disqualify their "proof" with evidence either known at the time of the trial and not permitted to be presented, or evidence which was later discovered and would have voided the claims of the State's staff, we should take a closer look at what the Attorney General said in his opening: "The State will prove to you jurors that the man who killed and murdered that child sits in this very courtroom -- the gentleman in the custody of the Sheriff's guards right in the rear of the distinguished members of the Bar who make up the defense counsel.

"This crime had been planned for some time. This defendant Hauptmann had conceived this plan and had undertaken it, had plotted it, prepared it, and we will show you that by the fact that he was in and about the vicinity of this Lindbergh home on many occasions before as well as at the time of the crime.

"He came there with his ladder, placed it against that house. He broke into and entered at night the Lindbergh home with the intent to commit battery upon that child and with the intent to steal the child and its clothing. And he did. Not only with the intent, but he actually committed a battery upon the child and did steal it and did steal its clothing. I will refer to its clothing and its stealing a little while later.

"Then as he went out that window and down that ladder of his, the ladder broke. He had more weight going down than he had when he was coming up. And down he went with this child. In the commission of that burglary, that child was instantaneously killed when it received that first blow. It received a horrible fracture, the dimensions of which when you hear about it will convince you that death was instantaneous.

"Getting down there he took the ladder and about 70 feet away the load was too heavy. In one hand he had the ladder and in the other he had this bundle, this dead package to him. The ladder was of no particular use to him. He abandoned that. Then he proceeded on his way until he had gotten about a half mile, the child was dead. Knowing it was dead, he wasn't a bit concerned about it and there, three thousand or more feet away and still on the Lindbergh estate, he yanked and ripped the sleeping garment of that child off its body. Though it was cold and raw, he yanked and ripped that sleeping garment off that child, because he didn't need the child, as we will show you, he needed the sleeping garment.

"Then, of course, at the very first convenient spot, some few miles away, he scooped up a hastily improvised and shallow grave and put this child in face downward and on he went on his way to complete the rest of his plans in this horrible criminal endeavor."

Had Wilentz been able to do all he had promised, no fault could be found. He stated that he would prove that Hauptmann was "in and about the vicinity of this Lindbergh home on many occasions before as well as at the time of the crime." With this statement, he had certainly set up for himself a big order to fill in light of the fact that the police had never found a person who had seen anyone, strangers or otherwise, around the Lindbergh home either before, during, or after the kidnapping. After questioning all the residents within a ten mile radius of the home, the police had come up empty handed when it came to finding any witness who had seen anything strange or any stranger. Ben Lupica, the Princeton student, had been their only hope and he had proved to be of no real help to them.

The attorney general knew very well they had no one to testify that Hauptmann had been seen there, and this presented a real problem for the state. In order to convict Hauptmann they must find witnesses, even if they had to "dig them up" two and a half years later --- and this they did. Millard Whited and Amandus Hochmuth were two liars and perjurers they could count on.

It will soon become very clear how Wilentz went about using the testimony of these two persons, plus others, with their seared consciences, the blatant liars who were willing to sell their souls for a "mess of pottage", that the prosecution used to "dupe" the jury. A jury, surrounded by a hostile atmosphere that permeated a courtroom filled with spectators who were willing to accept anyone's testimony that was "tossed into the arena" in order that they, the police and prosecutor's, could get "their pound of flesh" from their already determined guilty prisoner. Wilentz was caught up in the "excitement and notoriety" of the case and was swept away with it in order that he gain a conviction.

However, before going on with the truth about Whited and Hochmuth, we should examine further some of the statements made by the attorney general in his opening remarks. His claim, of which he spoke with assurance, stating the child had been killed when the kidnapper, with the extra weight of the youngster under his arm, had caused the ladder to break, thus plunging them to the ground, was nothing more than a "guess", "pure speculation" or "conjecture".

The evidence of this happening was just not there. His claim that the baby had been "instantaneously killed when it received that first blow" does not hold water. It does not make one shred of sense. After an examination of the ground by the police, of either the soft earth at the base of the ladder, or in the immediate vicinity at the bottom of the ladder, there was not one bit of ground which gave evidence that anything had fallen there.

Wilentz, using his persuasive eloquence, rambled on as he led the jury to believe that Hauptmann had disposed of the dead baby after he had first "yanked and ripped the sleeping garment off its body". He rationalized this bit of "senseless reasoning" simply because the kidnapper, "no longer needed the child" but "did need his sleeping garment". Here, we can blast his "reasoning" asunder by merely posing the question as to why he would have disposed of the "body in the first convenient spot" where it should have been found. If the kidnapper had realized he had killed the child, why then didn't he dispose of the baby many miles from the Lindbergh home instead of just a short distance away where he should have known it would surely have been found? Wilentz said the kidnapper realized "he no longer needed the child". Rubbish! The child had been taken for ransom. They needed a live baby to return in exchange for the money. Knowing the baby was dead, to keep the sleeping garment would have been, not only dangerous, but senseless. There is no evidence to substantiate any of the happenings as David Wilentz presented them to the jury; but, on the other hand, there is much to prove that the kidnappers made a clean get-away and had many hours to accomplish the task of taking a very live Lindbergh baby back to their point of operations.

It must be reasoned, that if as the attorney general insisted, it had been tossed where it had been found 72 days later, several sincere questions must be dealt with. As we stated before, hundreds, and possibly thousands, of people had walked over and back across that ground off Mount Rose Road where the corpse was found. No one had seen or reported seeing any semblance of a corpse simply because there was nothing there to report. This fact alone explains the boldness of the kidnappers who allowed one of their gang to meet with Condon for over an hour in Woodlawn Cemetery and Van Courtlandt Park on the night of Saturday, March 12th, and in St. Raymond's Cemetery on the night of Saturday, April 2nd, 1932. Cemetery John and his associates had no fear or reluctance in keeping their date with Condon, simply because they knew no corpse had been found due to the fact that there was none anywhere to be found. Had a body been found at some time during the negotiation period (March 1 thru April 2), the investigators would have been notified and a cordon of police would have encircled the meeting place and an early arrest made.

One other question arises at this point. Assuming that we accept the line of reasoning Wilentz had the jury believe, in that Bruno Richard Hauptmann, acting alone as he claimed he was, "at the very first convenient spot, some few miles away, he scooped up a hastily improvised and shallow grave and put this child face downward and on he went on his way to complete the rest of his plans in this horrible criminal endeavor", how then, could Hauptmann, working alone, have been certain that the body had not been found sometime between the nights of March 1st and April 2nd? Surely he would have been a fool to have taken the chance that it had not been found and had "gambled" on his safety from arrest on the two nights Wilentz claimed he met with Condon. Had the body been discovered and reported, as it certainly could have been during that period of time, it is an absolute false assumption that the police would have failed to surround Condon's arranged meeting, captured his Cemetery John, and arrested him for murder.

Things did not transpire in this way simply because there was no body laying there, or anywhere, to be discovered. It is ridiculous and illogical to assume that "Cemetery John", working alone, made a daily trip from his home in New York City to Mount Rose Road in order to "check-up" on the possibility that the body had been discovered. To do this would have been a ludicrous act on the part of the kidnapper, one which would almost certainly have been brought to the attention of someone who would question why a person was "scouting the area in such a suspicious manner. Time alone, would not have allowed for such a daily performance, especially over the clogged highways in and around Hopewell during the early days of the kidnapping. There is absolutely no doubt whatsoever that Cemetery John, Richard Hauptmann, or whosoever, working alone, would have thrown caution to the wind and been brave and foolish enough to have risked arrest had they tossed the body where it would have been found so easily by someone of the great number of persons searching for the stolen child. Once again, no body had been found there for the main reason that there was no body there to be found --- the kidnappers knew this and had the security of knowing this!

Moving back once again to the statements of Wilentz that he would prove that Bruno Richard Hauptmann "was in and about the vicinity of this Lindbergh home on many occasions before as well as at the time of the crime", let us first make a study of Mr. Millard Whited - the State's liar number one who was used to "prove" that Hauptmann was seen in New Jersey near the Lindbergh home.

Whited was without a doubt one of the State's valued witnesses. Originally, when he was visited during the early morning hours of March 2nd, 1932, he had been awakened by the sound of the barking of his dogs. As he answered the knock at his door he was greeted by four New Jersey State police officers, Trooper Joseph Wolf, Lieutenant Arthur Keaten, Detective William Horn, Sergeant Haussling, and Colonel Lindbergh. Entering his home, they inquired if he had been aware of any suspicious persons or cars in the vicinity of his house during the last few days. He informed them that "I DID NOT SEE ANYONE." They asked a few other questions pertaining to his neighbors, the number of children he had, and other general inquiries, then bid him goodnight and departed.

We already have examined Whited's official report given to the police when questioned by Sergeant Samuel J. Leon of the State Police and Detective Robert Coar of Newark on Tuesday, April 26, 1932. At this time Whited answered without hesitation when asked if he had seen anyone acting in a suspicious manner in the vicinity of the Lindbergh home before March 1st, 1932, and if there was anything he could tell them that would help them recover the Lindbergh baby, his answer had been a decided "NO".

CHAPTER TWENTY FOUR

Millard Whited - Five Star Liar

And now, with the trial at hand, we must ask from where did this man come, this man who boldly testified at the trial nearly three years later that he had seen Hauptmann on several occasions? In order to properly do this we must study his testimony as he gave it in court at Flemington. After identifying himself and stating that he was 37 years of age and had lived in New Jersey all his life, he went on to say that he had resided within a mile of the Lindbergh estate at the time of the kidnapping. However, he stated he now lived in Lambertville and that he was in the timber and farming business. He claimed to know every person who lived in his vicinity. The following are selected, pertinent questions asked by the attorneys regarding any knowledge he might have pertaining to the case. His answers to the questioning of Mr. Wilentz were as follows;

Q. In February, 1932, did you see any strangers in that vicinity? A. I did.

Q. Tell me particularly did you see the defendant, Bruno Richard Hauptmann? A. I did.

Q. When did you see him? A. As near as I could, to the best knowledge, around the 18th of February, 1932.

Q. Did you see him again after the 18th of February? A. I did.

Q. When to your best recollection? A. Between the 25th and 27th of February.

Q. Was this the February before the Lindbergh crime? A. It were.

Q. Now tell us the first time you saw the defendant Hauptmann, where it was and what circumstances. A. I was coming home from dinner with my car and he came out nearly on my ground or, I would say, within two or three feet, one way or the other---I could show you the very spot if I were there---and he stepped out to the side of the road when I came face to him, with the car, and I saw him when I was coming to him, and when I passed, through my window, I looked at him and wondered why and where he came from.

Q. Through the window of what? A. Out of my car window; that is, the window was down, but out of the left hand side of the car.

Q. Now, the second time you saw him, where was he and where were you? A. He was on the cross road that leads to Zion and I was coming up the road with the truck and trailer, and I saw him on the cross roads standing.

Q. How far away from him were you when you saw him that time? A. Not quite as far as from here to the railing.

Q. To the rail? A. Yes.

Q. Indicating the distance between--- A. Between the rut of the road---

Q. Will you give us your judgment about how many feet you think that is? A. Not over six.

Q. Not over six feet. So that you were within six feet of him the second time. A. Yes, sir.

Q. How far away or how close were you the first time you saw him? A. Perhaps about eight feet.

Q. About eight feet. Did you see his face on both occasions? A. I did.

Q. Now, in the early morning of March 2nd, 1932 being the early hours of the morning after the Lindbergh child had been taken did you report to troopers or investigators that you had seen a stranger? A. I did.

Q. Now, is there any doubt in your mind at all with reference to the man you saw on those two occasions in February, 1932? A. No, sir.

Q. You say that was this defendant? A. I do.

Q. Since that time you saw him in the Bronx, did you not? A. I did.

Q. You testified in the extradition proceedings in the Bronx at that time? A. I did.

Q. Some time around the 25th or between the 25th and 27th or whenever it was you say you saw him the second time, in February, 1932, tell us what he wore, if you remember? A. A gray suit and a gray felt hat.

Q. How did he wear the hat? A. Just tipped a trifle forward.

Q. When you say a trifle, did it go over his forehead? A. Just about like that (illustrating). A. Did you see his eyes? A. I could.

Q. Did you see them? A. I did.

Q. Did you see his eyes the first time you saw him? A. I did.

Q. Did he have an overcoat on? A. He had a coat of some description hanging on his arm.

Q. Carrying it on his arm? A. On his arm.

Q. When you saw him was he in the roadway or near the bushes, or what? A. Just stepped out of the edge of the bushes.

Q. Stepped out of the edge of the bushes? A. Just stepped out of the edge of the bushes.

Q. The bushes on whose property? A. On to---practically on to mine and on what is known as the William Henry Wacker's Estate later.

Q. How close to any part of Colonel Lindbergh's Estate? A. The first time I would say it was a mile and a quarter.

Q. The second time? A. Not over a half a mile from the Estate.

Q. Now, some time in September, 1934, when the defendant was arrested, where were you living? A. In Lambertville.

And now the Cross-Examination by Mr. Fisher:

Q. You can recognize a picture if you see it, can't you? A. What is that?

Q. You could recognize a picture if you had seen one? A. To a certain extent.

Q. Well, if you saw a picture of yourself, for instance, you would recognize that, wouldn't you? A. Not some of them.

Q. Down at your home in Lambertville when you first got in the case, did you get any money to have your picture taken? (The Court ruled the witness did not have to answer the question.)

Q. Now, how far do you say now it was from the Lindbergh gate the second time you saw the man whom you identify as Mr. Hauptmann? How far away from the gate? A. The first time?

Q. Yes---the second time. A. The second time, about a half a mile.

Q. Do your remember testifying in the Bronx that it was three-quarters of a mile? A. No.

Q. Well, if you testified in the Bronx that it was three-quarters of a mile, were you mistaken at that time? A. To the best of my knowledge I didn't testify to that, that it was three-quarters. (Checking Whited's testimony as given in the Bronx revealed that he had answered the question in this fashion: "Not over three-quarters of a mile.)

Q. Not over three-quarters of a mile. Now, were you mistaken on that occasion or are you mistaken now?

A. I didn't check it or have ever checked it. It could be checked with a speedometer if somebody took time to do it.

Q. What day is it that you say you saw Mr. Hauptmann up there the first time? A. I said around the 18th.

Q. Well, will you fix the date definitely for me? A. No, I wouldn't know.

Q. But you will say now that it was as late as the 17th? A. It might have been as late as the 17th.

Q. Then how far the other way might it be, the 21st? A. The first time?

Q. Yes, the first time. A. That I couldn't say because I had too much on my mind to remember dates and I kept no record.

Q. Do you remember testifying in the Bronx--- A. Yes--and I wish to rectify that because I got the two men mixed in my knowledge.

Q. Yes, and you gave another name over there that you told the story to first? A. I did because the name---

Q. Well, --- A. I wish to rectify that by the two men's faces that is here. I would like to rectify that mistake.

Q. Yes. Well, I will give you plenty of chance to rectify it, sir. You told over there under oath that you gave the information to Captain Wallace, didn't you? A. No I didn't go to that actual questions.

Q. Didn't you? A. No.

Q. I will ask you did you testify in the Bronx in reference to this visit of the police and Colonel Lindbergh, at from three to four o'clock in the morning: "Naturally, what was in my mind was that they came there thinking I was a thief." Did you so testify? A. I think I did.

Q. And that is what you thought, wasn't it, when you came in there? A. To a certain extent.

Q. Now, when were you called on to identify the prisoner, Hauptmann, the first time? A. The 6th of October.

Q. The 6th of October? A. Yes.

Q. Do you know what day he was arrested? A. I don't.

Q. Do you know that he was arrested on the 19th day of September? A. That I couldn't say.

Q. But you say that the first time you were called was the 6th of October? A. Right.

Q. During all that period of time you lived in Lambertville, didn't you? A. I did.

Q. From the 19th of September till the 6th of October? A. From when?

Q. From the 19th of September to the 6th of October, 1934? A. I lived there before that.

Q. But, you lived there during that period? A. Yes.

Q. Didn't you? A. Yes, sir.

Q. How far is Lambertville from your home in the Sourland Mountains? A. About twelve miles.

Q. You made no effort to hide yourself in Lambertville, did you? A. No.

Q. You were available there every day and every night, weren't you? A. I was.

Q. You had given this statement to the State Police the night of the kidnapping, hadn't you? A. Only just that I saw a stranger.

Q. Were you called on from the 19th of September to the 6th of October to identify anybody? A. I was called on, the first was a newspaper, on the 1st of October.

Q. Were you called on--- A. With a picture out of a newspaper, by the State Police.

Q. Were you called on by the State of New Jersey to identify this man Hauptmann until the 6th day of October, 1934? A. Just explain just what you mean by that.

Q. I mean, were you taken to see the prisoner Hauptmann? A. I---

Q. Prior to October 6th, 1934? A. The 6th was the first.

Q. That is the first time you were taken? A. That is right.

Q. In the interim you had seen some pictures of Hauptmann, hadn't you? A. I saw two.

Q. Who brought those to you? A. Mr. Wolfe, Trooper Wolfe.

Q. He brought you first a picture out of a newspaper, didn't he? A. Right.

Q. And did you look at that? A. I did.

Q. And then he came back with a regular photograph? A. Right.

Q. Photographer's picture? A. Yes.

Q. And you took a look at that, didn't you? A. Yes.

Q. So that you had two perfectly good looks at a likeness of Hauptmann, didn't you, prior to going to New

York City? A. My estimation as to that question, when those papers were brought to me, my answer was that I wouldn't identify no one by a paper or by a picture.

Q. But you took a look at the pictures, didn't you? A. A glance look.

Q. Yes, just a glance? A. Yes.

Q. Now, when the officer, the police officer came over to your home in Lambertville with a picture, and said, "Here is a picture, look at it," you simply glanced at it, is that right? A. That is right.

Q. And knowing that you only glanced at the first one, he brought back another one so you could take another glance? A. Right.

Q. I suppose. A. Right.

Q. Yes, he came back with a second picture when you refused to do more than glance at the first one? A. Yes.

Q. Yes. A. Because I was in Pennsylvania when he delivered that one to me, working.

Q. Well, you saw it, didn't you? A. I saw it, yes.

Q. You took this glance at it? A. Yes.

Q. And the officer was satisfied and went on home? A. That is all he could be, couldn't he?

Q. Yes. Now he came back with another picture? A. No.

Q. Didn't he come twice? A. Twice. I said he was there that night and requested a better picture.

Q. The next day he brought you a better picture. If you remember now, what did you do with that picture, glance at it? A. I glanced at it, because I was getting in the truck. I just glanced at it.

Q. You took another glance at that one? A. Yes.

Q. So that you must consider that you had two glances of two separate pictures, is that right? A. Right.

Q. Before you went to New York? A. Right. Just those two glance pictures.

Q. All right. Now what about in New York, did you see any newspapers? A. No, sir.

Q. You say you didn't see any newspapers? A. I saw them laying around, but not---

Q. Well, did you see any pictures of Mr. Hauptmann in the newspapers? A. No, sir.

Q. What? A. No, sir.

Q. Did you know that his picture was on the front page of the newspapers at that time? A. Might have been in the front; might have been in the back. I didn't pick it out to read it.

Q. Did you know it? Did you know it? A. No.

Q. You didn't pay any attention to it? A. I didn't pay any attention to the paper, because I didn't have none in my hands.

Q. You didn't know a thing about that, did you? A. I answered that question, I didn't have no papers in my hands.

Q. In the Bronx did you testify as follows: Q. Did you know his picture was on the front page of the newspapers almost every day for the last three weeks? A. Why would that interest me?

Q. Did you know that? A. Why would that interest me? I have not saw it.

Q. Who told you it was on the front page of the newspapers for the last three weeks? A. Just hearing other people talk.

Q. How much money were you paid for testifying in the Bronx? A. None.

Q. No expense money paid? A. Expense, yes.

Q. How much expense money? A. I was took over there and my dinner.

Q. Yes. Nothing for your day's work? A. No.

Q. No newspaper money from no newspapers over there? A. No.

Q. Were you told by anyone that you would be compensated for the time you are losing in this case? A. No, sir.

Q. You are simply here in answer to a subpoena? A. That is right.

Q. Did you get your subpoena fee? A. No.

Q. You haven't even had that? A. No.

Q. So you are here without any fee whatever of any kind, or any promise of any kind. A. I supposed that you always got paid for your subpoena when you answered to your subpoena.

Q. I see. Well you haven't been paid yet and you have been here quite a few days.

Q. Now, tell me about the car you were riding in at the time you first saw the man you identify as Hauptmann. What kind of a car was it? A. 1931 Chevrolet sedan with a wheel on each side.

Q. Anybody riding with you? A. Wine color. Nobody but myself.

Q. Where had you been working that day? A. I answered that question. I didn't know whether I was working or not.

Q. You didn't know whether you were working or

not? A. No.

Q. You are sure of that now? A. I am sure of that.

Q. I see. Well, what were you doing, driving along there, just at that time? A. A man has a right to go home at any time, I would think.

Q. I am asking you what you were doing there just at that time. A. I answered that. I was going home for my dinner.

Q. For your dinner. But you don't know whether you were working or not? A. I don't.

Q. And if you were working you don't know where? A. That is just it.

Q. Is that right? What kind of weather was it?

A. That I just can't recall, too. It was March weather.

Q. March weather? A. Or, I mean, February weather.

Q. Oh. A. I beg your pardon. I misspoke myself.

Q. Yes. Did you have your windows down in your car, any of your windows? A. One window, one window down.

Q. Which window? A. On the driver's side.

Q. Did you have an overcoat on? A. Who?

Q. You. A. It is very seldom I ever wear an overcoat when I am out.

Q. Well, was it a chilly day or a warm day? A. That is something I couldn't answer.

Q. Don't you know whether it was hot or cold? A. That is going back pretty well, to ask a man whether it is hot or cold at a certain day or not.

Q. That's right. I think it is going back quite a ways. Was it snowing? A. It wasn't snowing, no.

Q. Was it raining? A. I couldn't say whether it was raining or not, but I don't think it was raining.

Q. Was the condition of the road muddy or was it dry? A. It happened to be right where I was there was a little bit of stone throwed up.

Q. Stony? A. On top of the road. Just a few fresh stone the county had spread there.

Q. Well, just a little in the other direction or a little before you got to that point, was the road muddy or perfectly dry? A. It was naturally dry, but slippery, up there; it is always slippery up there.

Q. Well, was it cold enough that the ground was frozen? A. At the night the ground would freeze. During the day it would thaw.

Q. But you say the man you saw stepped out of the woods didn't have an overcoat---or rather, he had an overcoat, but he was carrying it over his arm; is that right? A. That is right.

Q. How far was he from your car on that first occasion? A. I said about eight feet.

Q. A man was in your house with lights for fifteen minutes and you can't even attempt to describe him. A. The man sat there and didn't say anything and I didn't pay no attention to him. I was paying attention to the one who was talking to me.

Q. How long was the man on the road under your observation in point of time? A. About two minutes.

Q. And you were traveling in an automobile at the rate of 15 or 20 miles an hour in one direction. A. That is right.

Q. And he was walking at you diagonally. A. I didn't say he was walking.

Q. Did you say he stepped out of the woods? A. I said he stepped out of the woods.

Q. From the side of your automobile? A. Not from the side; ahead of me, before I got to him.

Q. Ahead of you? A. Yes.

Q. And you kept moving? A. Certainly.

Q. And he was in your view for two minutes? A. That is right.

Q. Part of which time was while you were looking at him through a mirror in the front of your car; is that correct? A. I don't know how a man would look through the windshield.

Q. Didn't you do that? A. He would have to look through the windshield.

Q. Well, how about when you passed the man? A. Then I looked through my mirror.

Q. All right. That is what I am talking about. A. No. You said when I was facing him.

Q. All right. A. I beg your pardon.

Q. I mean when you passed him, after you had gone by him. A. Yes.

Q. You looked up in the mirror? A. That is right.

Q. And you saw him then through the mirror or something? A. That is right.

Q. Is that correct? So that part of your two minutes of observation was through a mirror as you were going away from the object which you were viewing; is that correct? A. Not two minutes, no.

Q. Well, you said you saw him altogether two

minutes? A. Yes.

Q. And part of that time was looking in a mirror as you are going this way and the man stands back here, is that correct? A. I passed the man.

Q. That is right, and then you continued to observe him in the mirror? A. Yes.

Q. Of your car? A. Yes.

Q. Where was the mirror, inside your car? A. Inside.

Q. Yes, and that is the look you had at him? A. The first time, yes.

Q. Yes. Well now, the second time how long did you have him under your observation that time? A. I was not traveling over ten miles an hour, I imagine, I was going upgrade in second speed.

Q. Yes. How long did you have him in view? A. For about four minutes.

Q. The road curves there, doesn't it? A. No, not exactly; after you pass you can see quite a little piece up the road.

Q. But how far can you see up the road? A. 500 yards.

Q. 500 yards. All right. Now, how near the turn is the intersecting road where you say you saw this man? A. How near the turn?

Q. Yes. How near were you coming in view, how far away were you when you first viewed him in the direction in which you were traveling? A. I was coming straight down.

Q. How far? A. I was just coming over a hill, starting down over it.

Q. Yes, and there is the intersecting road to Blawenburg, is that right? A. No to Skillman.

Q. Now, when you first turned the corner, when you got your first vision in the direction in which you were traveling--- A. I didn't turn no corner there, I was coming direct straight.

Q. Well, is the road straight for endless miles on down there? A. Did you ever see one straight for endless miles? I said I was coming straight up the main road.

Q. All right. How far was it that you had a vision from the main road where you say you saw the man? A. I told you about 500 feet each way.

Q. Each way? A. Yes.

Q. Feet? A. About 500 feet as you---

Q. That is a thousand feet then altogether? A. Yes.

Q. And you were traveling at what rate of speed? A. About ten miles.

Q. So that all you could possibly have seen, looking at this man out ahead was for a distance of 500 feet ahead of you, is that correct? A. Yes, that is right.

Q. And you say that it took you four minutes to travel 500 feet? A. Yes, about that.

Q. I see. At ten miles an hour how many feet a second are you traveling, do you know? A. I was never educated enough to figure that out.

Q. Never figured that out, but you still think it took four minutes to travel 500 feet? A. I said about four minutes.

Q. It might have been longer? A. I might have been longer or shorter. I had a truck and trailer, understand, not a pleasure car.

Q. Were there any mirrors in that car so you could see in back of you? A. Yes.

Q. Did you again look up and watch in the back? A. I did

Q. And did he stand still for the entire time you were watching him? A. As far as I could see.

Q. Like a statue? A. No.

Q. Perfectly still? A. He was looking up and down the highway.

Q. But not moving up and down? A. No.

Q. That is right. And did you speak to him as you went by? A. I didn't.

Q. Did he speak to you? A. No.

Q. What time of day? A. About---from four to five o'clock in the afternoon.

Q. Did you mention to any person in the world until you talked to the policeman in your home, the early morning of March the 2nd, the fact that you had met this strange man two separate times in the hills? A. No, sir.

Q. Never mentioned it to a soul? A. No, sir.

Q. Two brothers living with you at the time? A. Yes.

Q. Father living with you at the time? A. Yes.

Q. Wife living with you at the time? A. I hope so.

Q. How many children? A. I have five; four at that time.

Q. Four living with you at that time. And on neither occasion did you mention to any of these people that you had met this man. A. No. For the reason I thought that was my business and not theirs.

Q. Now, did you see the man stepping out of--- whose land? A. Off of my property.

Q. Off of your property? A. Yes.

Q. Well, I understood you to say this morning that it was at the line of your property and somebody else's. A. It is, right on the line; it is practically right on the line of the two properties.

Q. So that you can't tell definitely whether it was your property or the next neighbor's property? A. I can tell definitely. If I go up there I can show you definitely, yes.

Q. Now, did you sign any statement that early morning? A. I didn't.

Q. Have you signed any statement yet about this man that you say you saw along the--- A. Yes.

Q. When did you sign that? A. That I couldn't answer that question, simply because it has been too long for me to bring that back.

Q. Well--- A. But it was during--- I think it was the latter part of March or perhaps the middle of April.

Q. You signed a statement about seeing this man? A. I signed a statement of all I knew.

Q. Well, did you include in the statement the fact that you saw this man along the road on two occasions? A. I won't say whether I did or not.

Q. Did you ever see Ollie Whateley in his lifetime? A. I don't think I did.

Q. And do you know whether or not he looked like the defendant Hauptmann? A. Who.

Q. Whether or not in his life time he looked like the defendant Hauptmann from pictures that you have seen of him published since? A. Who was this man Whateley that you are mentioning?

Q. That is one of your neighbors up in the hills.

Q. Did you ever see a picture of Ollie Whateley, the butler, or the employee of Colonel Lindbergh? A. I can't say that I did.

Re-direct Examination by Mr. Wilentz:

Q. Mr. Whited, I think I asked you before; you said you couldn't read very much didn't you? A. That's right.

Q. You can't write very much either, can you? A. No, sir.

Q. Did you go to school at all? A. I went until I was eleven years old.

Q. I see. And from that time on, I take it--- A.

I have worked.

Q. You have worked. Did you say you had five children now? A. I have.

Q. Mr. Whited, your father is still living? A. Yes.

Q. Mother? A. Yes.

Q. This Blawenburg, is that the place where that robbery--- A. Blawenburg.

Q. Do you know of your own knowledge whether or not a man admitted and was convicted of that robbery? A. He was.

Q. Now, Whited, you didn't know Colonel Lindbergh, did you? A. No, sir.

Q. And you didn't know the Attorney General, did you? A. No, sir.

Q. And you didn't know Prosecutor Anthony Hauck, did you? A. No, sir.

Q. And you didn't know the police very well, did you, the troopers? A. No.

Q. On the very morning after this kidnapping and this crime, you did give a statement verbally, that is, you spoke to the police officers and told them the story you are telling now. A. Yes, sir.

Mr. Fisher: I suggest that is leading, and object to it on that ground.

The Court: Well, I think I will allow it to stand.

Q. You didn't have a camera with you, did you? A. No, sir.

Q. And you didn't take a picture of anybody on the road that day?

Mr. Fisher: It is objected to for the same reason. Let the witness tell what he did.

The Court: I think the questions are perhaps objectionable in being leading.

Q. Were you awake that day when you were riding down in your car on both those occasions? A. Yes, sir.

Q. Were your eyes open? A. Yes, sir.

Q. Your eye sight was fair at that time, was it? A. Yes, sir.

Q. Were you able to see as you came along that highway those things and objects that were within your view? A. Yes.

Q. Within the roadway? A. Yes.

Q. Did you see Hauptmann, the defendant in this case on those occasions that you have testified to? A. I did.

Q. Are you in any way at all interested in this

case except as a resident of this county? A. No, sir.

That ended the "very honest testimony" of Millard Whited as he told it in court. A man who originally said he saw nothing in the neighborhood of the Lindbergh home both before and after the kidnapping. In our next chapter we tell you the truth about the perjury of Millard Whited, the five-star liar.

CHAPTER TWENTY FIVE

Your Turn, Amandus!

Without the unmitigated lies of Millard Whited it is extremely doubtful if the prosecution could have fostered the extradition of Hauptmann over to the New Jersey authorities to be tried for the murder of little Charles Augustus Lindbergh, Jr. It had been largely Whited's testimony that convinced Justice Hammer that he should order the prisoner to be remanded to the custody of the Jersey State Police and taken to Flemington for trial.

At this point we should literally bi-sect the real Millard Whited and learn the actual truth as to what prompted the man to appear on the scene and allow his services to be used by the police in the prosecution of Hauptmann.

To begin with, the authorities knew they had to find someone who would be willing, for a price, to say they had seen Hauptmann near the Lindbergh home on or about the time of the kidnapping. After studying the list of nearby residents they had interviewed, starting with the date of March 2nd, 1932, they found the name of Whited who, because of his reputation, seemed the most likely candidate to fill their purpose. Without a doubt, Whited's reputation was deplorable. He was not only extremely poor, he owed money to many, many people in the neighborhood, with apparently no intention of paying them back. He was known as a man who told lies as easily as most folks tell the truth. It was this man who was approached by the police and first shown a picture of Hauptmann. Colonel Schwarzkopf had taken a giant risk with this move. However, realizing that he needed someone to place Hauptmann in New Jersey, and after studying the list of possible potential witnesses who would attest to this fact, he had chosen Whited as the most likely to fill his needs.

And so, it was on Saturday, October 6th, 1934, that Whited was taken to the Bronx County Jail, in a State Police car by Captain Jack Lamb of the New Jersey State Police. Here Whited picked Hauptmann, from a line-up of uniformed police officers, as the man he had seen near the Lindbergh home on two previous occasions prior to March 1st, 1932.

Lamb had assured his superior, Schwarzkopf, that "Whited is a thoroughly honest man and reliable witness", which in turn prompted the State Police Superintendent to respond, "his identification will greatly strengthen our case against Hauptmann." Schwarzkopf was no fool. He realized that without the aid of Whited they barely had a case at all. The State's "actors" were playing their roles well.

Schwarzkopf went a few steps further, to out-lie Whited, by stating that on the night of the kidnapping Millard had told the police that he had recently seen a man coming out of the bushes near the Lindbergh estate and had given them at that time a description of a man that matched Hauptmann. Schwarzkopf claimed they had no reason to doubt Whited since "he is a poor man who is absolutely upright and honest." And in support of this claim, he told of a statement made by Whited's wife: "My husband is a truthful man," and one by his father: "He has never been known to tell a lie." Much was being done to "prove" the honesty of their witness to the general public. However, in contrast to this we have the statement of Detective William Horn who had interviewed Whited about eight hours after the kidnapping. Horn reported that he very well remembered speaking with Millard Whited that morning and that he was quite certain that Whited "AT NO TIME MENTIONED SEEING A SUSPICIOUS PERSON IN THE VICINITY OF THE LINDBERGH HOME BEFORE THE NIGHT OF THE CRIME."

Yet, two and one half years later, this same Whited claimed he had told the authorities that he had seen a man who resembled Hauptmann when he was questioned on the morning of Wednesday, March 2nd, 1932. His statements, so widely conflicting, as presented in a criminal case of such magnitude, were nothing more than a "batch of lies". Lies, this man had been instructed to state in court as factual. They present for us one of the most raw and repulsive pieces of blatant "evidence" ever brought into a courtroom anywhere.

Governor Harold G. Hoffman, while there still remained hope of saving Hauptmann from his appointment with the electric chair, had Whited brought into his office in the New Jersey State House at Trenton on Saturday, February 22nd, 1936. Here in the presence of Anthony M. Hauck, Jr., prosecutor of Hunterdon County;

C. Lloyd Fisher, one of Hauptmann's defense counsel; and Andrew K. Dutch, the governor's confidential investigator, Mr. Whited stated the following, as taken from a stenographic transcript of the meeting. After admitting that he had been paid "about $150" and that he had "hollered" for thirty-five dollars a day before he agreed to go to the Bronx, the following is an important excerpt of the questioning as it was taken down:

> Fisher: Now, Millard, in the trial you testified. You were asked if you got any money or not, and you said all you got was being taken to New York for dinner?
> Whited: I know it.
> Fisher: Did you lie about that?
> Whited: I absolutely thought that was my business what I got out of it.

Governor Hoffman's own account of his investigation relative to the veracity of Millard Whited was set down as follows:

"It was brought out during the questioning that Whited had been told he would be entitled to share in the reward. Asked how much he thought he was entitled to, he said. 'As much as the rest were---about one third.'

"Whited tried to explain the change in his testimony from the answers he had given two years before by saying the state police had told him to "keep secret" the knowledge that he had really seen a suspicious person near the Lindbergh home before the crime. It seems to me utterly fantastic that the State Police would never place in their files, if this were so, Whited's true statement, and that they would make part of their records a statement that they knew to be false.

"Once Whited had identified Hauptmann in the Bronx, the State Police took no chances on Whited again changing his story. For weeks troopers were assigned to watch him day and night, and even to ride with him into the woods when he went to haul timber.

"It would take pages to set out all the discrepancies in the testimony and the statements of Whited. All that searchers for the truth in the case will have to do to obtain an estimate of his value as an important witness for the state is to take a day's jaunt into the Sourland Mountains and ascertain the opinion of his neighbors as to his integrity and veracity."

Governor Hoffman had no trouble in summing up his conviction that Whited was a liar by stating that: "It is beyond belief that the state police would have made Whited's false statement a part of their official records while eliminating from the files all mention of the important prior disclosures he claims to have made."

During my own search for the truth in my many visits to the Hopewell area I have yet to find one person who could say a kind word when we inquired about Whited's honesty. Every person who remembered him claimed they never believed anything the man said. In one of my trips into the Sourland Mountain area of New Jersey I was accompanied by Sydney L.Smith of West Chester, Pennsylvania who lived in Hopewell at the time of the kidnapping. Mr. Smith, told me he not only knew, but remembered Whited well for the reputation he had earned as being nothing more than a liar. This then, was the reputation of one of state's star witnesses, one the jury was led to believe, one who LIED IN ORDER TO CONVINCE THE JURY TO ARRIVE AT THEIR VERDICT OF GUILTY!

The emphasis of this chapter has much to do with the testimony of a person who perjured himself by testifying of something he knew to be absolutely untrue. However, much should be said about the importance of eyewitness testimony given in court by those who have "honestly believed or honestly thought" they had seen a "certain person" perform a "certain act". Many are they who have spent considerable time in prison, and on occasion, some even sentenced to their death, because of testimony given in court by persons who were sincerely convinced they had witnessed someone perform an act of criminal nature. There are innumerable cases in the records of criminal jurisprudence where the testimony of an honest eyewitness has later been proven to be false; not because the witness was dishonest, but because their testimony was "sincerely wrong".

Anthony Scaduto in his great book *Scapegoat* published in 1976 (G.P. Putnam's Sons, New York) had much to say about the danger of trusting in eyewitness testimony.

As we move along in our discourse on the innocence of Richard Hauptmann, it would be wise to remember the fallacy of placing too much emphasis on eyewitness identification. This should be extremely so as we relate to you the testimony of one more liar who was used to "prove" that Hauptmann was near the Lindbergh home at the time of the kidnapping.

Another "star" witness for the state seemed to appear from out of nowhere. His name was Amandus Hochmuth, an 87 year old former Prussian army veteran, who said he lived at the corner of Mercer County Highway and the road that "goes up to the Lindbergh place." The gray haired octogenarian with his bushy-gray mustache and matching beard trimmed in a VanDyke style, seemed rather feeble as he slowly ambled his way to the front of the Flemington court room. Appearing noticeably stooped, his hands trembled as he reached out for the arms of the witness chair. However, once comfortably seated, he could be judged as "quite anxious" and very ready to "spill his batch of lies" along-side those of Millard Whited.

Attorney General Wilentz began the direct questioning:

Q. On the 1st day of March, 1932, where were you residing? A. I was standing on the porch---"

Q. Where were you living then? A. The corner of what they call the Mercer County Highway and the road that goes up to Mr. Lindbergh's place.

Q. In other words, that is at the main highway intersection with the lane that runs up to the Lindbergh place? A. Exactly.

Q. And is that where you were living? A. Yes.

Q. And were you outside that day? A. Yes, sir.

Q. Did you see a car coming along? A. Yes.

Q. Tell us about your experience that morning.

A. Well, I saw a car coming around the corner, pretty good speed, and I expected it to turn over on the ditch. And as the car was about 25---I should judge 25 feet away from me, the man in there looked out of the window like this. (Hochmuth attempted to imitate the man's facial expression).

Q. Out of the window of the car you mean? A. Yes, and he glared at me as if he saw a ghost.

Q. What time of the day was that? A. It was in the forenoon.

Q. And the man that you saw looking out of that automobile glaring at you in the manner that you say, is he in this room? A. Yes.

Q. Where is he? A. Alongside of the trooper there.

Q. Alongside of the trooper? A. Yes.

As Hochmuth's hoarse and husky voice was heard uttering his affirmative response; his shaking bony, knotted and gnarled right index finger pointed simultaneously toward Hauptmann, the old man's face, in contrast to the gray of his beard appeared to turn extremely white. At that precise moment the lights in the courtroom went out. This, together with the heavy fog of the weather outside, cast the room into semi-darkness for a period of 20 minutes. The apparent nervousness of the witness, plus a very noticeable senile tremor, gave one cause to doubt the man's mental faculties. However, the questioning continued in the gray-dark atmosphere of the unlighted courtroom.

Q. Well, at any rate, would you mind stepping down, please, and showing us?

Reilly: I object to that until he first points out the man from where he sits.

Wilentz: He did that.

Reilly: No, he did not. He said a man sitting next to the trooper.

Q. Which side of the trooper? A. The man sitting between the trooper and the other man with the white shirt on.

Q. The other man with what on? A. The man with the white shirt.

Wilentz: Now may the gentleman come down without objection?

The Court: I think so.

Amandus Hochmuth, with Attorney General Wilentz helping him, stepped down from the witness chair with what could be termed a noticeable generalized tremor to his walk as he shuffled to Hauptmann's side and placed his right hand on the prisoner's shoulder.

Wilentz: May we have on the record, "Indicating Bruno Richard Hauptmann?"

Q. You were telling us a minute ago about a car coming around the corner. Did it come around your corner? A. It couldn't have come any other way but from Hopewell.

Q. Along what road did it come, sir? A. It can't come any other way.

Q. I know, but you will have to tell us what road it did come, not how it cannot come. A. I can't state exactly.

Q. I mean on what highway was it as it turned that corner? A. Mercer County Highway.

Q. Mercer County Highway, and coming from the direction of---what town was the nearest town? A. Hopewell.

Q. Hopewell. And did it make the turn, as you said, into the lane? A. Yes.

Q. And when it made the turn into the lane, did it proceed or did it stop? A. It stopped as it got in the ditch.

Q. Did it get into the ditch? A. Not yet but it stopped there, and he pulled the ladder over to him.

Q. You say that he stopped as he got into the ditch in making the turn? A. Into the ditch.

Q. How long did it---did the car stop at all for any period of time? A. Well, I should say about quarter of a minute, or something like that.

Q. A quarter of a minute? A. Yes.

Q. Yes, sir. All right sir. Now, you said just now something about a ladder: Was there a ladder in the car? A. I saw something, some of the ladder in it.

Q. Something?---Now where do you spend your---I will withdraw that. I think you said you live in this county about ten years. A. Yes, sir; lived in Skillman first, and my son-in-law lived there.

Q. You lived in Skillman with your son-in-law first? A. Yes.

Q. I see. And you spend some time in New York, do you, too? A. Yes.

Q. With your daughter? A. My elder daughter, yes.

Q. And who lives here at this corner that you talk of, this house here, in Hopewell? A. My daughter.

Q. Your daughter? A. And my son-in-law.

Q. Your son-in-law and daughter. A. Yes.

Thank you sir. That is all.

Q. Oh. You remember the color of the car? Yes, I omitted that. A. Yes. A dirty green.

Q. A dirty green. A. (Hochmuth nods affirmatively).

The time had now arrived for Reilly to shoot his questions at Hochmuth. He began immediately with a blistering attack on the veracity of the feeble 87 year old witness.

Q. When did you first tell this story to anybody? A. Never spoke to anybody about it.

Q. Before you took the witness stand you never told a soul about what you were going to testify to today, is that correct? A. That is correct.

Q. You give me your word on your oath that that is correct? A. Certainly I do.

Q. Did you stand at that door, the left hand door of this court room yesterday? A. Yes.

Q. At noon recess, at a quarter of two, with a State Trooper? A. Yes.

Q. Alongside of him? A. I guess so.
Q. Don't you know? A. Yes, I think it was.
Q. And didn't the State Trooper bring you to the left door and point Bruno Richard Hauptmann out to you as he sat in his seat? A. No, sir.
Q. And weren't you then taken back up the stairs to the Grand Jury room? A. No.
Q. What did they bring you to that door for yesterday at a quarter of two? A. I don't think---
Q. Look at me, please. What did they bring you to that door for? A. Oh, I went to the toilet.
Q. The toilet in that room is to the rear of the room; you know that, don't you? A. Yes.
Q. The toilet is nowhere near this door, here, is it? A. I don't see what you are aiming at.
Q. I am aiming at this: Do you remember yesterday at a quarter of two being brought down the staircase of this room in here, the library, by a State Trooper? A. Yes.
Q. Do you remember being brought to this doorway here, and facing out into the courtroom: do you remember that? A. Yes.
Q. Do you remember the State Trooper pointing Hauptmann out to you yesterday? A. No, sir.
Q. What did they bring you to the door for? For what purpose? A. I don't know.
Q. You don't know? A. I don't remember---I went out---the officer took me out to the toilet once.
Q. Well, of course, the toilet is not in that doorway. A. I know that.
Q. Your health is rather poor, isn't it? A. My health?
Q. Yes. A. It don't seem like it.
Q. Well, I notice that you are shaky. A. I have had a good deal of rheumatism.
Q. Did you ever have a stroke? A. No.
Q. Just rheumatism. You say you are shaking from rheumatism, and that you are eighty-seven years of age? A. Yes.
Q. Are you near-sighted or far-sighted? A. My eyes are all right.
Q. I didn't ask you that, mister. You are wearing glasses.
Wilentz: He has answered it. He asked if he was near or far-sighted.
The Court: He says his eyes are all right.
Q. Why do you wear the glasses, to see better? A. At a distance, yes. For reading, I read without

glasses.

Q. When did you come to live at this particular corner you are telling us about? A. Oh, that is about five years.

Q. Five years. I want to know what month? A. What month?

Q. Of that year, you came to live there. Had you been living there for a year or two before that? A. I had been in New York in the summer time, celebrated my birthday there, the 25th of July, and then I left and came out here.

Q. When did you come out here? A. To stay?

Q. August, September, October or when? A. July.

Q. July? A. After my birthday.

Q. And you stayed on continuously, is that correct? A. True, yes.

Q. Now what day of the week was this you say you saw the dirty green car? A. That was on the 1st of March.

Q. What day of the week? A. Well, I think it was Tuesday.

Q. And--- A. I am not quite---

Q. And what time did you get up that morning? A. Oh, I am up at six o'clock.

Q. And what time do you say you saw the dirty green car? A. Well, it was pretty late, towards noon.

Q. Noon on March the 1st? A. Yes.

Q. Is that so? A. It was a clear day.

Q. A clear day. Was it a cold day? A. Well, yes.

Q. How long had you been out of this front gate or at the road? A. Beg pardon?

Q. How long had you been out at this spot that you say you saw this green car? A. Why, I had just come out.

Q. How far was it away from your house? A. Well, I should judge it is about---what do you mean, the car?

Q. No, you. The spot that you were standing. A. How far was I from where?

Q. Your house. A. Oh, I was right on the porch.

Q. You were on the porch? A. Yes.

Q. And you are sure you were on the porch? A. Yes.

Q. Correct. Now how far does the house set back from the road? A. About, I should judge, about five feet.

Q. Five feet? A. The house stands back.

Q. The house stands back from the road? A. Yes.

Q. Now, this is some highway, isn't it? A. Yes.

Q. What is the name of the highway? A. Well, it is a road up to Lindy's. I call it Lindy's Road.

Q. Is it a dirt road? A. No, it is not a dirt road.

Q. Is it a State macadam road? A. No, a stone road.

Q. A stone road? A. Yes.

Q. And is there a fence between the house and the road? A. There is a hedge.

Q. A hedge? A. Yes.

Q. And, is the porch right up against the hedge or doesn't the house set back? A. The house is back from the ---

Q. The house sets back from the hedge? A. Yes.

Q. You know that? A. Yes, sir.

Q. How many feet twenty, or twenty-five feet back from the hedge, doesn't it? A. I would say five feet.

Q. Isn't there any lawn between the house and the hedge? A. That is about five feet wide.

Q. Did you ever measure it? A. No.

Q. There is a lawn between your porch and the hedge, is that correct? A. Yes, there is quite a---

Q. And, you say there is only five feet between the porch--- A. It isn't as wide as this is (referring to space between judge's bench and jury box.)

Q. It isn't as wide as this? A. No.

Q. How big is the porch? A. Oh, the porch is about three feet square.

Q. Three feet square? Room for any chairs? A. Well, if you want to.

Q. Just what portion of the porch were you on? A. Facing the road going up to Lindbergh's.

Q. Had you come out the front door of the house? A. The back door. This is the back porch.

Q. This is the back porch. This is the kitchen porch, is it? A. Yes.

Q. And you had come out there and you were just standing there, is that right? A. Yes.

Q. You did not expect anything to go past there, did you? A. No.

Q. Your mind was not on the road at all? A. No.

Q. You were not interested in anything, is that correct? A. Yes.

Q. This is some day in 1932, right? A. Yes.

Q. And all of a sudden a car passes very fast? A. Coming this way.

Q. I don't care which way it was coming, it was going fast? A. Yes, pretty good speed.

Q. Pretty good speed. Forty or fifty miles an hour? A. Yes.

Q. Faster than that? A. No, I don't think so.

Q. Forty or fifty miles an hour? A. About forty miles an hour.

Q. And there was a turn in the road there? A. You see, I have seen many a one going into that ditch, and I expected to see him going over, but the car stopped.

Q. The car slowed down? A. It stopped.

Q. Stopped. It came to a dead stop? A. Yes.

Q. And then started up again? A. Yes.

Q. Is that right? A. Yes.

Q. And the man that you saw, was he driving? A. Yes.

Q. And there were windows in the car? A. Yes.

Q. Was it a cold day? A. Well, I can't exactly state.

Q. What month was it? A. March. You know the weather we have in March.

Q. How many cars had you seen go in the ditch before that? A. I saw seven go in in one week.

Q. Seven. A. Yes, before it was fixed. It is fixed now.

Q. This dirty green car did not drop over? A. No.

Q. It didn't go in the ditch? A. It went slanting.

Q. It did not go in the ditch? A. No.

Q. It did not ask you for any assistance, did it? A. No.

Q. It slowed up, started up again, and drove off; is that correct? A. Yes.

Q. How was the man dressed, if you can remember? A. Well, I think he had a dark shirt on.

Q. You think he had a dark shirt on? A. You see all I took in was the face and these glaring eyes.

Q. Give me this again. What was it? A. All I took in was his red face and glaring eyes.

Q. I see. He had a red face? A. Yes

Q. Like mine? A. A little more red.

Q. A little more red than mine? A. Oh, yes.

Q. And he had very piercing eyes, did he? A. Yes.

Q. Well, you as a bank man know that you have seen many people in your bank with piercing eyes, right?

A. Yes.

Q. And you have seen many people with red faces, is that right? A. Yes.

Q. Of course you told nobody about this? A. No.

Q. Not even your son-in-law? A. No.

Q. Your daughter? A. No.

Q. Nobody, correct? A. Correct.

Q. So that we have your solemn word before this jury that before you took this stand---am I right? A. Correct.

Q. Nobody in the world knew what you were going to say, is that so? A. Exactly.

Q. That's all---pardon me, it isn't all. Were you taken into the jail some time ago by a State trooper? A. Yes.

Q. When? A. Oh, it is several days ago.

Q. You saw the defendant, Hauptmann, there, didn't you? A. I saw a figure in there, but I couldn't see him.

Q. Didn't they have you in there thirty minutes? A. Maybe so.

Q. What? A. Yes.

Q. There was nobody there but the defendant, was there? A. That's it and two troopers.

Q. And they were in uniform? A. Yes.

Q. You knew they were troopers, because they wore---A. No, one wasn't in uniform.

Q. What did he have on, trooper's pants, didn't he? A. I cannot exactly---

Q. You cannot remember only a few days ago that he had on his trooper's pants? A. A few days ago, it is longer than that.

Q. A month ago? A. Yes.

Q. You can't remember whether he had on his trooper's pants? A. I think he did.

Q. You remember that he had his cartridge belt on? A. No, I didn't look.

Q. And do you remember that he was in his shirt sleeves? A. Oh, yes.

Q. Yes. And he wore a gray shirt, didn't he? (Witness nods affirmatively.)

Q. The second trooper. A. Which one do you mean, the one outside?

Q. No, in the jail. A. In the cage?

Q. When they took you to see the defendant. A. In the cage?

Q. Yes. A. Yes, he was in his shirt sleeves.

Q. Yes. A. And I think---

Q. Trooper's pants? A. Trooper's pants.
Q. With a nice--- A. Yes.
Q. ---Yellow stripe, is that right? A. Yes.
Cross examination by Attorney General Wilentz:
Q. You spoke to me this morning, didn't you, Mr. Hochmuth? A. Yes, sir.
Q. Just a few minutes before you got on the stand. A. Yes.
Q. So that you, as I understand it, you said you spoke to me this morning? A. Yes.
Q. And, did you speak to any officers about this case recently? A. No.
Q. Well, I mean--- A. Not---
Reilly: Now, I object, that is his answer.
Wilentz: Well, now, certainly it is his answer.
A. You know, you can't prevent from speaking to anybody in the case.
Q. What do you mean by that, sir? A. Why, if one will speak to you and the other speak to you, one say, "How do you do," and, "How do you feel?" and this way, so you can't help it.
Q. Did any of the officers speak to you about the case? A. Well, well, I tell you, after I seen him---I said "That is him."
Q. And by "him" who do you refer to? A. Hauptmann.
At this point Hochmuth was turned over to Reilly for a period of re-cross examination.
Q. Who gave you the name Hauptmann? A. I saw the name in the paper.
Q. Yes. Now, have you ever been in any institution? A. What do you mean?
Q. Hospital? A. Hospital. I was employed in a hospital once.
Q. Where? A. Poughkeepsie.
Q. Whereabouts in Poughkeepsie? A. Hudson River State Hospital.
Q. The what? A. Hudson River State Hospital.
Q. When were you employed there? A. I was employed as a kitchen boy.
Q. How long ago? A. Oh, I think that was in '73, '74---1874.
Q. Ever been back there since? A. What?
Q. Have you ever been back there since? A. Yes; my wife is buried there, and three children.
Q. Have you ever been back to that institution since? A. I went there one summer. My son took me up,

showed me the change that had been made since I was there.

Q. Did you ever stay there? Did you ever stay there? A. No.

Q. Were you ever in any other institution as an employee or as an inmate? A. No.

Q. Or any hospital? A. No.

Q. Sure about it? A. Yes.

Q. So that you got the name Hauptmann from the newspapers? A. Yes.

Q. How long ago? A. When it came in the papers.

Q. Why, that's months ago. A. Yes.

Q. And you saw his photograph in the paper, didn't you? A. Yes.

Q. Day after day and day after day; is that right? A. No, when the first papers came out, I saw that face.

Q. You saw the photograph? A. I saw---

Q. Now, just answer my questions.

Q. Am I correct in saying that you saw Hauptmann's picture in the newspaper? Is that correct? A. When the first paper came out.

Q. Yes. A. After his arrest.

Q. How long ago was that? A. Oh, I don't remember.

Q. You don't remember that day do you? A. That is when he was arrested.

Q. You don't remember that date, do you? A. No.

Q. Now, can you remember the second time you saw his picture, what date? A. Oh, in every newspaper.

Q. Can you remember the date that you were in the jail? A. That must have been---

Q. Not what it must have been---can you? A. No, not exactly.

Q. That was within the last couple of months you were in the jail? A. Huh?

Q. You were in the jail in the last couple of months? A. Yes, I think it was.

Q. You think it was? A. About a month ago or something like that.

Q. What day of the week were you in the jail? A. I think it was on a Sunday.

Q. You are not sure? A. No.

Q. You are not sure about the date? A. No.

Q. And that only happened a month ago, is that right? A. It is not quite a month ago, I don't think.

Q. Is that right? A. Yes.

As Hochmuth completed his testimony, a five minute recess was called by the Court. What a perfect time for you to learn the true facts about Amandus Hochmuth and the amazing lies he was capable of telling, under oath, at the age of 87.

Hochmuth's testimony had been used effectively by the prosecution to add more nails to the coffin of Bruno Richard Hauptmann simply because the jury was not aware of facts it should have known. Information which unfortunately did not come to light until months after the trial had ended.

Bearing in mind, once again, that at the time of the kidnapping every person living within a radius of 10 miles of the Lindbergh estate had been questioned about the possibility of them having seen a strange occurrence in their neighborhood. The results had proven to be negative with the exception of the Princeton student, Benjamin Lupica, who reported seeing a person in a car with a ladder near the entrance to Lindbergh Lane.

Knowing this to be factual, it then poses the question, where then did this Amandus Hochmuth with his "Johnny-come-lately" story come from? Under routine questioning by the police during those early days of the investigation he had been stout in his denials that he had seen any suspicious stranger in the vicinity of the Lindbergh home, and yet three years later, he, under oath,identified Richard Hauptmann as the driver of the dirty green car he swore he had seen before the kidnapping.

Great credit must be given the late New Jersey governor, Harold G. Hoffman, who conducted his own investigation after the completion of the trial and compiled many true facts about, not only the perjury of the witnesses used against Hauptmann, but of the distorted and manufactured evidence brought against the accused German carpenter.

To begin with, the 87 year old Hochmuth must have suffered a sudden deterioration of his eyesight shortly after he had "observed" Hauptmann on that day of March 1st, 1932. In a report issued by the Division of Old Age Security, Department of Public Welfare, New York City, over the signature of Edward Carey, investigator, dated June 29,1932, just four months later, pertaining to Hochmuth's general health, we read: "Health is very poor, APPLICANT PARTLY BLIND." And then, thirty-six days later, on August 4, 1932, over the signature of another investigator, Joseph A. McGovern, of the Old Age Security Department, we read this further interesting notation pertaining to the eyesight of the state's "excellent" witness: "FRAIL. FAILING EYESIGHT DUE TO CATARACTS."

Governor Hoffman's comments on the deplorable testimony of Hochmuth has been taken from his excellent book, *The Crime-The Case-The Challenge* which was serialized in *Liberty Magazine* in 1938. It read as follows:

"The first record we have of Mr. Hochmuth's interest in the case is found in a report to Trooper W.O. Sawyer of the New Jersey State Police. It is dated November 28, 1934---two months after Hauptmann's arrest, and after pictures of him had been published in every paper in the country. Frank Storey, a neighbor, related to Trooper Sawyer a story told by the eighty-seven-year-old Hochmuth, who claimed he 'saw a car containing a man with a ladder pass his home on the morning that the Lindbergh baby was kidnapped.' Sawyer proceeded to Hochmuth's home. Hochmuth repeated the story to him, and after being shown a picture of Hauptmann remarked: 'He looks like the man.'

"Hochmuth's interesting story, as reported by Sawyer, is as follows: 'On the morning that the Lindbergh baby was kidnapped a car turned the corner of his home coming from the direction of Hopewell and made too wide a turn and went into a ditch on the right side of the road. The car contained a ladder and before the man attempted to drive out of the ditch he straightened the ladder as it had fallen against the window. The car was a greenish sedan.... The driver wore what appeared to be a dark blue sailor cap with a shiny peak. Hochmuth stated that his reason for not divulging this previously was that he did not want any publicity and that he thought if he identified the man with the ladder it would be the cause of the man going to the electric chair and he did not want to do that.'

"On December 20, 1934, Sawyer reports that he took Hochmuth to the State Police Training School, where 'he identified the Hauptmann car as the car he had seen.' In a statement given to Captain Lamb on the same day Hochmuth said: 'I am almost positive that it is the same car.'

"In the same statement Hochmuth said: 'The car was going so fast it slid into the ditch.' He told Troopers Sawyer and Genz that the car slid into the ditch. On the witness stand he said (page 448, volume 1, Official Trial Transcript, State of New Jersey vs. Bruno Richard Hauptmann) that the car stopped as it got into the ditch, and again, as a witness (ibid on page 460), that the car did not go into the ditch.

"Troopers Sawyer and Genz reported that they took the old man to the Flemington jail and that Hochmuth identified Hauptmann as the man he saw on the morning of the kidnapping. To Captain Lamb he said: 'The man I saw today looks exactly like the man I saw in the car that morning, but his face was little more ruddy and might have been a little heavier.' On the witness stand (ibid on page 461) Hochmuth admitted that he 'SAW A FIGURE IN THERE BUT COULDN'T SEE HIM.' He admitted that he was there about thirty minutes.

"On the witness stand Hochmuth said he had lived in Hunterdon County for about the past ten years, and visited New York occasionally.

"I have in my possession a certificate signed by Ruth Hill, Third Deputy Commissioner in charge of the Division of Old Age Security, Department of Welfare, New York City. It is dated June 17, 1935, and I quote it herewith:

'The individual record #14106, of the Division of Old Age Security, regarding Amandus Hochmuth, contains the following two excerpts under health: June 29, 1932, over the signature of Edward Carey, investigator. "HEALTH IS VERY POOR, APPLICANT PARTLY BLIND, SUFFERING FROM A COMPLICATION OF DISEASES.' August 4, 1932, Joseph McGovern, investigator, noted this information supposedly received from Mr. Hochmuth: 'FRAIL...FAILING EYESIGHT DUE TO CATARACTS.'

"Here was Hochmuth, living in New Jersey, drawing aid upon the representation that he was a resident of New York City (he gave the addresses 595 East 134th street, and 370 Willis Avenue, Bronx) of undoubtedly defective eyesight, going upon the stand and swearing away the life of a man whom he had seen for a fleeting second, supposedly on the morning of the Lindbergh crime.

"Hochmuth, in my office on December 15, 1937, could not identify an eighteen-inch silver loving cup, filled with flowers, on top of a cabinet located within ten feet of the chair in which he sat. On that day, when I examined Hochmuth in connection with the reward, in the presence of Leon Hoage, a crime analyst, the old man gave the following fantastic story, never told before, in an effort to convince me that he had really seen Hauptmann and was entitled to a share of the reward; I am quoting from the stenographic record: 'WELL, WHEN THE BABY WAS KILLED, THAT WAS ON MARCH 1, I

SAW HAUPTMANN, AND BEFORE THAT I SAW A FELLOW HANGING ON THE BRIDGE THERE---THIS IS THE FIRST TIME I HAVE MENTIONED IT. HE WAS HANGING ON THE BRIDGE, AND WE HAVE A GOOD MANY GERMANS COMING TO THE NEIGHBORHOOD, AND I SAID, 'ARE YOU LOOKING FOR A JOB?' AND I DIDN'T GET A SATISFACTORY ANSWER, BUT I SAW HE WAS A GERMAN AND I SPOKE GERMAN TO HIM AND WE HAD QUITE A TALK. I SAID, 'I AM FROM HAMBURG,' AND HE SAID **HE CAME FROM SAXONY.** I said, **'WHAT IS YOUR NAME ?'** and he said, **'HAUPTMANN.'**

"Get the picture, readers, of Hauptmann, planning a crime that would shock the world, prowling around Hopewell telling people his name and origin! Hochmuth repeated this fabulous story in the presence of over twenty newspaper reporters on the day that the reward announcement was made; but little was said about it in the public press. NOTHING MUST BE DONE TO DISCREDIT A WITNESS IN THE HAUPTMANN CASE!

"And Justice Trenchard, in his charge to the jury, referring to Hochmuth, asked, among other things, 'Do you think there is any reason, upon the whole, to doubt the truth of the old man's testimony?'

"The jury evidently believed him. Remembering that he was one of the important witnesses who placed Hauptmann at the scene of the crime; that he was drawing relief in New York City while a resident of New Jersey; that there were wide discrepancies between his statements and the testimony he gave on the stand; that for over two years after the crime he kept it "secret" that he had seen a man in the car with the kidnap ladder; **DO YOU BELIEVE HIM ?**"

Knowing the facts, as we now do, how could any person put any credence in the testimony of this unscrupulous man? What a horrible reality that Hochmuth was prompted and allowed to testify of things he knew to be untrue in a court of law where a man's life hovered in the balances. This same man who told Trooper Sawyer: "He did not want any publicity and that he thought if he identified the man with the ladder it would be the cause of the man going to the electric chair and he did not want to do that." This same man that Attorney General Wilentz was so concerned would not "mislead" the jury. This same man that, as he pointed to Richard Hauptmann as the man he had seen near noon on Tuesday, March 1st, 1932, near the Lindbergh home, saw, as did all other spectators, the lights of the courtroom flicker out, throwing the room into 20 minutes of semi-darkness. This same man whose rheumatic limbs enabled him to slowly walk alongside the defendant and dramatically place a gnarled hand on the shoulder of Bruno Richard Hauptmann. This man's silent action might as well have been a verbal one, shouting its intensity: "Right here. Here is the man!"

Here we have Amandus Hochmuth, the man who failed to identify a vase of flowers in the office of Governor Hoffman. The man whose first guess had been "a woman wearing a hat", and again missed on his second guess by claiming it to be "a bowl of fruit sitting on a piece of furniture." A man of veracity, the very honest Amandus Hochmuth.

Is it any wonder that, as Hochmuth placed his hand on Richard Hauptmann's shoulder, the condemned man slowly shaking his head again and again, leaned toward his wife and spoke to her in their native language: "Der Alte ist verruckt!"

CHAPTER TWENTY SIX

An Epidemic of Lies!

Hochmuth and Whited were not the only liars that were paraded in to testify against Hauptmann. Let's now consider the testimony of the cab driver who delivered the note to the Condon home on the night of Saturday, March 12, 1932. Perrone, a small bespectacled man with carefully combed black hair, identified himself as a taxicab driver who had driven for Rosenblatt Brothers in the Bronx for sixteen years. On the stand, in answer to the questions thrust at him by the attorney general, he had this to say:

Q. In your capacity as a taxi driver did you have occasion to visit the home of Dr. John F. Condon? A. Yes, sir.

Q. At what address? A. 2974 Decatur Avenue.

Q. What date was it, if you remember? A. March 12th, 1932.

Q. What was the occasion of your visit to the home of Dr. John F. Condon? A. I had a man give me an envelope addressed to Dr. Condon.

Q. Who is the man that gave you that envelope? A. Bruno Richard Hauptmann.

Q. Is he in this room? A. Yes, sir.

Q. Come down and point him out, please. Perrone stepped down and made his way to where Hauptmann sat. Placing his hand on Hauptmann's shoulder, he announced: "That is the man." At this point Hauptmann was heard by those nearest him to calmly say to Perrone: "You're a liar." Reilly, who had clearly heard it, insisted that Richard's response to his accuser be placed in the record, but Justice Trenchard claimed he had not heard it, nor had the court stenographer, and therefore ruled that the record stand as it was for the present.

Wilentz: All right. Just go back.

Indicating the defendant, Bruno Richard Hauptmann.

Reilly: I move that the record be amended to take the answer of the defendant to the witness.

The Court: The record is presumed to be correct. I have no reason to doubt that it is correct.

Reilly: I am prepared to show proof right now, by five or six people here, that the defendant made an answer to the accusation of the witness, and I believe it belongs in the record. I am sorry the stenographer didn't hear it. We all heard it.

Wilentz: I did not hear any answer.

Reilly: We all heard it---the press heard it.

The Court: The press may be called as witnesses at the proper time, Mr. Reilly. If there is any such thing as that, you will have the opportunity at the proper time to show what was said; but let the record stand as it is for the moment.

And so, the response of Richard Hauptmann to his accuser, "You're a liar." was disallowed, the greater number of spectators never being made aware of the words of denial spoken by the accused man in answer to the direct and fatal accusation of a man who was, as Whited, proven to be a habitual liar.

The remainder of Perrone's testimony, as he rendered it to both attorneys, had to do with his "absolute knowledge" of Hauptmann's guilt, based simply on his "certainty" that it was the accused man who had given him the envelope to deliver to Condon's home on that given night. On several occasions the witness, who seemed to have a reluctance to speak above a whisper, had to be admonished to answer in order that he be heard by the jury.

Q. By Wilentz: Just exactly what happened when you received that note and just prior to that? A. I happened to be on a hack stand at Mosholu Parkway and Jerome Avenue, March 12th.

Q. Is that in the Bronx? A. Yes, sir.

Q. While on the hack stand, tell us what happened? A. While on the hack stand, I had a young man ask me to drive him to 3440 Knox Place. After discharging this fare, I drove east on Gun Hill Road and when I got---

Q. Take your hand down. You drove to Gun Hill Road. A. Yes, sir.

Q. What happened then? A. I arrived at Knox Place in Gun Hill Road and a man came running to me with his hand raised motioning me to stop. I stopped my cab and this man tried to open the front right side of my door and I motioned to this man to wait a minute, that I would lower the window which I did. This man kept looking around first before he ever said a word to me. When he did he asked me if I knew where Decatur Avenue was. I told him I did, that I was familiar with the neighborhood. With that he put his hand in his overcoat pocket and brought out an envelope, looking at the envelope he said, "Do you know where 2974 is?" I said, "Yes, I am familiar with the neighborhood." This man, looking around again put his hand into the very same pocket and gave me a dollar bill to deliver the envelope.

Q. Did he ask you to deliver it? A. No, sir; he did not.

Q. Just gave you the envelope and a dollar? A. Yes, sir. And when he did that he walked to the rear of my cab and put his hand in his pocket; now, I don't know which it was, and taking down my license plate number.

Reilly: I object to that as calling for a conclusion.

Q. Well, he was writing something? A. He was writing something.

Q. And when he was writing, right immediately prior to his writing, were his eyes focused or directed at any thing, as you saw it? A. Yes, sir.

Q. What was it? A. Right at the license plate number.

Reilly: Well, that is a conclusion. I object to it. The man might have been looking at the back of the car.

The Court: Well, he says looking at the license plate. I suppose that is competent testimony, for what it is worth.

Reilly: Yes.

Q. How did it happen that you observed that when you are seated in front and he is in back? A. Well, the way he acted, I had my eyes on him---

Reilly: I object to the way he acted.

Perrone: (continuing) from the moment he gave me the note and started speaking to me, and he---

Q. Did you look around? A. Yes. And he had to go like that (illustrating) to me before I left.

Q. From the back? A. From the back.

Q. When you say he went like that, you are

motioning with your hand, your right hand? A. Yes, sir.

Q. And waving your hand away from you? A. Yes.

Q. Is that the manner in which he waved that night? A. That is right.

Q. And where was he when he was waving his hand that way? A. In the rear of my taxicab, at the rear of my taxicab.

Q. And you saw him while he was doing it? A. Yes.

Q. Was the wave directed to you? A. Yes, sir.

Q. And as the result of that wave, did you comply with it and proceed then? A. I did, yes, sir.

Q. Where did you go then? A. I drove south on Jerome Avenue---

Q. Still in the Bronx? A. Still in the Bronx.

Q. Yes. A. When I passed the hack stand I showed this letter with the dollar; I waved it to another driver on the hack stand that I had just previously left.

Q. What was his name? A. James O'Brien.

Q. Did you then proceed? A. Why, he asked me where I was going with the letter.

Q. Yes. A. I told him to---

Reilly: I object.

Perrone (continuing) I said---

Q. Well, whatever you told him, you told him something and then what did you do? A. I delivered the envelope.

Perrone went on to tell more facts about his delivery of the note; that he had been paid fifty cents above the normal taxi fare, and that the time was between 7:45 and 8:30 when the man approached him. He said his visibility was good at this "point and place" because there was "an arc light there right underneath the street light." Asked if he knew where both Woodlawn and St.Raymond's cemeteries were, he assured attorney Wilentz that he did. He went on to say that Woodlawn Cemetery was "about two miles" from where he received the note; and that St. Raymond's Cemetery was "about five or six miles" away. He also said that since Hauptmann's arrest he had seen his home in the Bronx and that it was "about three miles" from the spot. Once again, Perrone claimed he was making a "positive identification" when asked:

Q. And that man that you are talking about, when you talk about the man that stopped you, the man that waved his hand and the man that did this and that, you are referring to one man, are you not? A. That is right.

Q. Who is the man you are referring to? A. Bruno Richard Hauptmann.

Q. The defendant in this case. A. Yes, sir.

During Reilly's cross examination the cab driver continued to speak inaudibly at times and gave the appearance of being confused with the line of questioning. The evasiveness of his answers should have caused much doubt as to his honesty and integrity.

Q. Who did you come down here with today? A. Today? I came down here with a State trooper today.

Q. Keep your voice up. State troopers? A. Yes.

Q. Did they come to New York and get you? A. No, sir.

Q. Where were you? A. I was sleeping in the barracks in West Trenton.

Q. How long have you been sleeping in the barracks? A. Well, I arrived here yesterday morning by train and I slept there last night.

Q. Do you know of Van Cortlandt Park? A. Yes.

Q. It is a large area in the City of New York, is it not? A. Yes.

Q. You have been driving in the Bronx how many years? A. Oh, I have been driving in the Bronx about six or seven years.

Q. Now on this particular day it had already been published in the newspapers, had it not, in the *Bronx News* and other papers, Dr.Condon's connection with this case? A. Not that I knew of at the time.

Q. That came out March 7th, 8th or 9th, didn't it? A. I don't know anything about it.

Q. Don't you read the papers? A. Not the Home News at that time.

Q. Had you read about the Lindbergh case? A. After it happened, yes.

Q. Now what day of the week was this you say this happened, the incident of the envelope and the dollar? A. March 12th, 1932.

Q. What day of the week? A. Saturday evening.

Q. Sure about that? A. Positive.

Q. Now what time did you have your car out that day? A. I got out of the garage about 4:30 that day.

Q. Describe the passenger just before you received the letter? A. A young man.

Q. Driven from where to where? A. Mosholu Parkway and Jerome Avenue.

Q. Young man? A. Yes, sir.

Q. What was the fare for that young man? A. Fifteen cents.

Q. As you were returning back to your cab stand, you say this incident happened. A. That is right.

Q. You were coming down this parkway. A. Gun Hill Road.

Q. Gun Hill Road. Where does that run? A. Well, that runs all the way over to the Boston Post Road.

Q. Isn't that in the middle of a parkway or near a parkway, Gun Hill Road? A. Well, it is right opposite Van Cortlandt Park.

Q. Now, at what portion of that Gun Hill road do you say a man waved at you? A. Knox Place in Gun Hill Road.

Q. All right. Was there anybody with you? A. No, sir.

Q. What time at night? A. Between the hour of 7:45 and 8:30.

Q. Well, that is three-quarters of an hour, isn't it? A. That is; yes, sir.

Q. And what day was that, that this man waved to you? A. March 12th.

Q. On Saturday night, you say? A. Yes, sir.

Q. Between half past seven--- A. 7:45 and 8:30.

Q. 7:45 and half past eight? A. That is right.

Q. Now, of course, Van Cortlandt Park on a Saturday night in March at 7:45 is dark, isn't it? A. It was at that time.

Q. Yes. A. Yes.

Q. And all that area is dark except wherever there is a park light? A. That is right.

Q. There are no traffic lights in there? A. No.

Q. No reds, greens, stops or anything else? A. No, sir.

Q. So that when you are coming through you can come through on the loop, can't you? A. That is right.

Q. Were you coming through on the loop at a pretty fast rate? A. Yes, I was. I wouldn't say too fast.

Q. Well, you were coming back to your stand? A. I was going back to my stand, yes.

Q. And looking for more work? A. That is right.

Q. And what did the man do? Suddenly jump out of the bushes? A. No, he did not.

Q. What? A. He came running from Knox Place, with his hand raised.

Q. Well, where he came from on Knox Place, could he see a car coming towards him? A. I don't know.

Q. He didn't know you were coming along, did he? A. I don't know how he ever came running to me.

Q. You were just coming along? A. That is right.

Q. And he was running towards you? A. That is right.

Q. No expectation on your part of seeing anybody there at all to you? A. I was surprised to get a hail that way.

Q. You got a hail and stopped? A. That is right.

Q. And of course you stopped under the great big arc light; is that correct? A. Yes, sir.

Q. Yes. Brighter than this, wasn't it? A. Well, it was an arc light. You know what a street light is.

Q. Now, where in Gun Hill road is there any kind of a light like this? A. On the southwest corner, Knox Place.

Q. It is on a pole, isn't it? A. Yes, sir.

Q.. An ordinary park light? A. Street light.

Q. In a park? A. Yes, sir.

Q. In the Van Cortlandt Park section? A. That is right.

Q. Right? A. It is opposite the park, the street light.

Q. Yes. It is opposite the park, bordering on the park?

Q. Now, how was the man dressed? A. He had on a brown double breasted overcoat and a brown soft hat.

Q. Peaked hat, fedora hat? A. Felt hat.

Q. Felt hat? A. Felt hat.

Q. Pulled it down or pulled it back? A. Pulled it back.

Q. Pulled it back? A. Turned up in the front.

Q. Oh, yes, turned up in front. A. Turned up in front, that is right.

Q. It wasn't down like the way men wear them at all? A. No, no,sir.

Q. But he had folded his back? A. He didn't fold it, but that is the custom of that hat that he wore. Well---

Q. Now, just a moment. A. I---

Q. Was it a hat such as I hold in my hand? A. Can I see the hat, Mr. Reilly?

Q. I don't mean about the make, I mean was it a soft hat like that, a Fedora hat? (Exhibiting hat to witness.) A. It was turned up a little more than that.

Q. It wasn't a derby? A. No.

Q. And it wasn't a cap? A. No.

Q. It was a soft hat? A. Soft hat.

Q. And it had a front on it like this? A. No, it was turned up more.

Q. Well, it didn't have it up like that, did it? (indicating by bending brim of hat against the crown.) A. Well, I can explain it to you, if you give me the hat back again. It was turned up with a seam like that, all the way around (witness indicates by bending the brim back a little.)

Q. A bevel edge, is that what you mean, a beveled edge? A. Yes, something like that.

Q. A beveled edge hat, right? A. That is it.

Q. Did he have glasses on? A. Who?

Q. The man? A. No, he did not.

Q. Did you have yours on? A. Yes, sir.

Q. Are you near-sighted? A. Well, evenings, I am, yes.

Q. Evenings you are near-sighted, is that right? A. Yes.

Q. This was in the evening? A. Yes.

Q. Now, the man reached in his pocket---if I am wrong, stop me---which pocket did he reach in and get this note? A. The right hand pocket.

Q. Did he have any rings on his hands? A. I don't know.

Q. You did not notice? A. I didn't notice.

Q. Did you notice his hands? A. No, sir, I did not.

Q. Well, he had hands, did he not? A. He must have.

Q. What do you mean he must have, were you not looking at him? A. Yes, he had hands.

Q. He gave you his right hand? A. That is right.

Q. Now will you tell us---if I may have this blotter for a second---will you show me how he handed you this note from your pocket? A. I don't quite remember how he handed it to me, but he handed it to me.

Wilentz: Please repeat the answer.

A. I don't know how he handed it to me, the exact way he gave me the envelope, but I know he handed me the envelope.

Q. Where did he get the dollar bill from, the other pocket? A. The same pocket he had the envelope in.

Q. He reached in twice and changed the envelope from the one hand to the other, reached in again after asking you some questions about this address and produced a dollar bill, is that correct? A. He gave me the envelope first, and then just before he walked to the rear of my cab, he gave me the dollar.

Q. Well, did he not give you the dollar and the envelope at the same time? A. No, he did not.

Q. Did you tell him how much it would cost him? A. He asked me how much it would cost to get there.

Q. What did you say? A. I told him about fifty cents.

Q. You did not tell us that before, did you? A. I may have forgot it.

Q. Anything else you have forgotten? A. (No answer.)

Q. Is there? A. Well not that I can remember.

Q. When you said "It will cost you fifty cents," did he say anything about the balance of the dollar? A. No, he did not.

Q. Didn't he say "Here is half a dollar for a tip."? A. No.

Q. Did you ask what the balance was for? A. I did not.

Q. You took it for granted that was what it was for? A. He walked right to the rear of my cab.

Q. But you saw his hands, were they large hands? A. I didn't take notice of his hands.

Q. But you saw his hands? A. I only saw the right hand he gave me.

Q. Right hand. Bare like mine? A. I wouldn't say it was bare or covered. I didn't take notice to it.

Q. You weren't looking at anything but the dollar bill? A. That's it.

Q. And that was in his hand? A. And the envelope.

Q. And the envelope. How many times have you gone over this story? A. What story?

Q. The story you are telling on the stand here now? A. How many times?

Q. Have you told this story over and over again,

15---20 times? A. About that.

Q. Who suggested to you that you should answer "I don't remember whether his hand was covered or not"? A. Nobody ever said anything to me.

Q. You won't say his hand was not covered and you won't say it was covered, will you? A. I didn't take notice at the time.

Q. You know, don't you, that if his hand wasn't covered, that the imprint of his fingermarks were on the envelope he gave you, right? A. I don't know.

Q. You don't know anything about that? Nobody ever told you anything about that or to be careful about that, did they? A. No, sir, nobody said anything to me.

Q. It is a fact that as soon as you rang Dr. Condon's doorbell he came and answered the door? A. That's right.

Q. Do you know Dr. Condon? A. No, sir.

Q. Had you ever seen any pictures of him? A. No, sir.

Q. Did you ask him to identify himself before you gave him the note? A. No, sir.

Q. You asked for Dr. Condon and handed it to this man, is that right? A. That's right.

Q. When were you next questioned about that? A. About a month and a half later.

Q. Where? A. Jersey State Police.

Q. At the Jersey State Police? A. Yes, sir.

Q. During the month and a half did you tell anybody? A. No, sir.

Q. About this note? A. No, sir.

Q. Did you give Dr.Condon your name and address? A. Yes, sir.

Q. He asked for it? A. Well, Dr. Condon---

Q. Did he ask for it, that is what I asked. A. He didn't.

Q. Were you driving taxicabs during that month and a half after this note? A. Right along, yes, sir.

Q. Can you tell me anybody you had in your cab on the 13th of March? A. No, sir.

Q. Can you describe anybody you had in your cab on St. Patrick's Day? A. No, sir.

Q. The 17th of March? A. No, sir.

Q. Can you give me a description of anybody that ever rode with you during the month of March, 1932, except this description that you have of the defendant? A. No, sir.

Q. Nobody? A. No, sir.

Q. Can you give me a description of anybody that rode with you in February? A. No, sir.

Q. What time did you get to Dr. Condon's home? A. Well, between the hour of 7:45 and 8:30.

Q. How many times have you seen Dr. Condon since? A. Twice.

Q. Where? A. At his home, at the Bronx Grand Jury room.

Q. When did you see him at his home? A. March 12th, 1932.

Q. After that? A. Why, in May; in May---16th or 17th at the Bronx Grand Jury.

Q. Not between--- A. No, sir.

Q. May 16th or 17th, what year? A. 193---1932.

Q. 1932? A. Yes.

Q. Who sent for you to come to the Bronx Grand Jury? A. Why, I don't know the detective's name.

Q. You didn't appear before any Grand Jury? A. Yes, I did.

Q. In March---in May, 1932? A. No. May, in May, 16th or 17th, 1932.

Q. 1932? A. Yes, sir.

Q. Have you seen Dr. Condon since? A. No, sir.

Q. Sure about that? A. Positive.

At this point the witness was turned over to the Attorney General for re-direct questioning, with Wilentz attempting to clarify some of the statements Perrone had made:

Q. Counsel asked you whether or not you had the fare that you had prior to Mr. Hauptmann---whether you read the second fare and the third fare, and he has inquired as to other dates. Now, on the day that the defendant hailed you, was there anybody else that gave you a note to deliver, or was that the only note you received that day? A. That is the only note that I received that day.

Q. Nobody else gave you any note that day to deliver? A. No, sir.

Q. Have you ever gotten any note from anybody else to deliver to Dr. John F.Condon, Decatur Avenue? A. No, sir.

Q. Now, shortly after you delivered that note, that is to say, within a few days, I suppose you read in the papers about Dr. Condon, did you not? A. No, sir, I did not.

Q. Well, when did you finally read about it? A. April 10th or 11th.

Q. Somewhere in April? A. April 10th or 11th.

Q. So that is to say within a month? A. Within a month.

Q. Now, the question about your meeting Inspector Lyons and other police officials, have you met these officials since your experience which you related about today with reference to Hauptmann or did you know them before? A. After.

Q. So that on account of and since the time that you took the note from Hauptmann you have become acquainted with and met the various officials in the various states that are working on the Lindbergh case. A. That is right.

Q. You have met all these people on account of and since the case. A. That is right.

Q. Whenever the police wanted you and summoned you, you came. A. Yes, sir.

Q. Prior to the arrest of Bruno Richard Hauptmann, had you been called upon by the police to come to various places for questioning for the purpose of providing such information as you had in the Lindbergh case. A. Yes, sir.

Q. Since that time you have again been called, have you not? A. Yes, sir.

Q. To various places? A. Yes, sir.

Q. And it is in pursuance of those calls from the various governmental agencies, whether it is State, National, New York or New Jersey that you are here today, isn't that the fact? A. Yes, sir.

The testimony of Joseph Anthony Perrone, in spite of Reilly's attempt to dissuade the jury, was obviously believed as factual in every sense of the word. However, the cab driver simply stretched his "truth" almost beyond comprehension. It was unfortunate that the truth, which should have been known about Perrone at that time, was not properly exploited by Reilly. Had this been done, any jury would have most certainly disregarded the words spoken by Perrone from his seat in the witness chair at Flemington.

The claims of Perrone might, at the very least, almost be acceptable until we examine the truth surrounding the actual advance knowledge of the cab driver regarding the accused Hauptmann. It should also be understood that Perrone had become, well acquainted with Hauptmann's appearance through the many, many photographs of him that had been published, from the time of his arrest until the time of his trial, in a great number of newspapers and magazines. However, in spite of this, Perrone's testimony seems to be non-conclusive in every aspect. For us to believe that he "well remembered" a night nearly three years earlier and could well remember just "which pocket an unknown man reached into with his hand" is incomprehensible. It is pure hogwash. And yet the jury believed him.

For the facts regarding Joseph Anthony Perrone's "certainty" of Richard Hauptmann being the man who gave him the envelope let's examine the record together. Information gathered from Governor Harold G. Hoffman's *The Crime-The Case-The Challenge* "What Was Wrong With The Lindbergh Case?", (a series of articles published in *Liberty Magazine* in 1938), we learn so much about Perrone's uncertainty of Hauptmann, it makes us nauseous. The Governor's report of his investigation follows:

"I have before me the signed statement in which he says that he was taken to the New York Police Headquarters on September 19, 1934, and was told that six men were to be brought in and he was to see if he could identify the man who gave him the note. 'Six men were brought into the room,' Perrone states. 'They were in the room for about three minutes and then walked out again. Inspector Lyons then asked me if I saw the man that gave me the note. I said there was a man in the group that looks very much like the man who gave me the note. They were brought in the room again. Hauptmann was in the middle of the group....I put my hand on Bruno Hauptmann.'

"Now let's look at the police record of the identification of Hauptmann by Perrone, as it actually took place at the Greenwich Street police station:

"A line-up is arranged in the room consisting of Patrolman John McNamara, Bruno Richard Hauptmann, Detective Thomas Coake.

Inspector John A. Lyons resumes questioning:

Q. On March 12, 1932, at about 8:30 P.M., you were driving a taxicab in the vicinity of Mosholu Parkway and Gun Hill Road. Did anybody accost you at that time? Do you see him in this room?

A. Yes, that's the man. (Perrone walks over to Hauptmann and puts his hand on his shoulder.)

"What a travesty of justice! A man held for murder and kidnap of the Lindbergh child, a German carpenter in ordinary clothes, stuck between two police officers, while a nearsighted taxi driver is called upon to identify him! And the taxi driver had said there were six in the lineup, which would have been bad enough.

"But the police had reason to be wary of Perrone's identification. On twelve or fourteen different occasions he had either identified or had picked out as "closely resembling" the note-giver various photographs in police rogues' galleries. Once he had said that he saw Dr. Condon at City Island, talking to a man whom he thought was the man who had given him the note. He had the police check a man named Hognell whom he met at an American Legion affair, and who he said must be the double of John. He sent the police after a man who he said had hired his cab and who went into an address on 203rd Street.

"At another time Perrone said he saw a man coming out of 412 West End Avenue, a perfect resemblance of John. He said, again, that a man named "Chetel" ran as he (Perrone) looked at him, and went into a movie. At another time he said the man who gave him the note had some facial characteristics of Colonel Schwarzkopf. He then saw "John" and a woman come out of the Hotel Albert, and reported it to the police. He identified one Otto Steiner, under arrest for stealing harness at Princeton, as the man who gave him the note. He reported once that he had seen another man resembling "John", but that this man was now wearing a monocle.

"I have examined all these reports, and have photostatic copies of them to exhibit to doubters. I also have copies of some of the pictures of persons identified by Perrone as bearing a great resemblance to the man who gave him the note. They look no more like Hauptmann than I look like Haile Selassie."

Perrone, on at least a dozen different occasions, had given the police a decidedly different description of the man who hailed his cab at Knox Place and Gun Hill Road. And, then in April of 1932, when he was asked by the police if he could identify the man, he said he had "only a fleeting glimpse" of him. He certainly proved to be of no help to the authorities whatsoever, when he was shown hundreds of rogues' gallery photographs in an attempt to have him pick out the man. When asked if he could tell them of any physical characteristics the man had which might prove to be helpful, Perrone said: "No, I didn't pay any attention to anything", followed by the question: "Is there anything about this man that fixes itself in your mind?", his immediate answer was again a decisive "No".

The answers Joe gave at this time were no doubt honest ones, since it was next to impossible for him to clearly see at the location where he had stopped his cab. At this point the dark street was afforded light from the beam of a nearby overhead arclight, which not only illuminated objects, but cast some in the shadows.

When in April of 1932 the police asked the Bronx cab driver: "Would you know him if you saw him?" and his reply had been "No, sir.", we can only imagine the amount of persuasion the police had to use on "poor honest Joe" to convince him to go into a Flemington court and "lie through his teeth" in order to play such a major role in convicting an innocent man.

Perrone's short honest answer of "No, sir" given to the police in 1932 was, at the direction of someone, turned and twisted into another "batch of lies" that developed into quite an elaborate story by the time he took his seat in the witness chair in January of 1935. One clue as to who it was that had coerced Perrone into aiding the prosecution is found in a memo from the New York Police Department. Special Agent Thomas H. Sisk of the Federal Bureau of Investigation reported seeing a typewritten New York Police Department memorandum dated October 20,1934, that told of Perrone being given a "pep-talk" by the NY police prior to the Hauptmann trial in which the cab driver was told: "NOW WE'RE COUNTING ON YOU, JOE."

Sisk also reported a conversation he had with Inspector John Lyons, in which the inspector told him that it was he who had persuaded Perrone he should testify so convincingly. As with other witnesses, Perrone had been coerced into giving "valuable" evidence that would help the prosecution. Here is Lyons word-for-word account, as told to Agent Sisk, of the things he told Perrone: "Now, Joe, we've got the right man at last. There isn't a man in this room who isn't convinced he is the man who kidnapped the Lindbergh baby. He answers the description of the man that gave you the note perfectly and there is no doubt about him being the man. Now we're depending on you, Joe. Take a good look at him when we bring him in, but don't say anything until I ask you if he is the man." This is what should be termed "coercive coaching" in a criminal case where a man's life was at stake.

And this persuasive diatribe was conducted in the presence of none other than the great distinguished head of the New Jersey State Police, Colonel H. Norman Schwarzkopf, who practically worshipped the ground Colonel Lindbergh walked on; Schwarzkopf who earlier had stated that Perrone "is a totally unreliable witness." Lieutenant James Finn had referred to Perrone as "a screwball."

And so, at the trial, Joe whatever he was, obediently following orders, informs a jury how keen a mind he has; that he "clearly remembers" those "specific things" that happened regarding his delivery of a note to a man's home on Saturday, March 12th, 1932. Claiming he never forgot the man's appearance, and from which coat pocket he had removed the note, among many other obscure things that to most persons would have gone unnoticed.

Inspector Lyons was always "more than willing" to allow himself to be used in any way to bring a conviction of Hauptmann. At the time Perrone walked to the prisoner's side and placed his hand on his shoulder, Lyons asked Richard to repeat the words Perrone had testified were asked him by the note bearer on the night of March 12th. And at the direction of Lyons, Hauptmann willingly obliged. Liar Perrone, without hesitation stated: "I recognize the voice and manner of speech. It was exactly as he spoke to me that night." The State, possibly fearful that the jury would have some difficulty believing Perrone's conglomeration of lies, made certain they had a back-up ready to take the stand and swear before God that certain events "very definitely" had taken place. James J. O'Brien was called as a witness, identifying himself as a taxi driver who worked in the Bronx and knew Joe Perrone. Here is his brief testimony in response to the Attorney General's questions:

Q. And did you know Mr. Joseph Perrone, the young man who was just on the stand? A. I do.

Q. Some time in March, 1932, did you see him? A. Yes, sir.

Q. And what was the address and name on the paper?

> Mr. Pope: I object to the question, sir; whatever took place between the taxicab driver and this gentleman was not in the presence of the man who gave the taxicab driver the envelope, and if that happened to have been the defendant in this case, of course, it was not in the presence of the defendant, and anything that was said or done at that time between two strangers is not evidence against this defendant.
>
> The Court: Well, the question does not seem to relate to any conversation.

Mr. Pope: No, but---

The Court: But it is part of a transaction and if the Attorney General desires to put it in, he may do it.

Mr. Pope: But, it relates to a physical fact.

The Court: Yes, it relates to a physical fact.

A. He held a letter in his hand showing me that, Dr. John F. Condon, 2974 Decatur Avenue, Bronx.

Q. And where were you at the time? A. At a hack stand.

Q. And where was he? A. In his cab.

Q. Did he leave his cab? A. No, sir.

Q. What were the circumstances under which this incident occurred? A. He was driving down Jerome Avenue and I was on a hack stand at Mosholu and Jerome Avenue. He saw me standing there and he called me over to this cab. He said that was a---

Reilly: I object.

Wilentz: Never mind what he said.

Q. But, at any rate, as a result of that you happened to walk over? A. I walked over to his cab.

Here the questioning ended with no attempt being made to cross-examine the "back-up liar" O'Brien.

This testimony could very well be the most ludicrous bit of testimony offered during the entire trial. It was presented purely to bolster the tale of Joe Perrone, the man who had previously testified that he had "waved" the letter to O'Brien as he passed the hack stand. Perrone in his testimony had attempted to relate what he had told his fellow cab driver when he was asked his destination with the note, however, an objection by Reilly had prevented his answer from going into the record. Reilly's objection to the question and his failure to cross-examine O'Brien could have been serious mistakes on the part of the Hauptmann defense.

So we now have the quite supportive evidence of Mr. James O'Brien who says "yes", he well remembers his pal Joe showing him the letter and, what is more, he also well remembers that the envelope was addressed to Dr. John F. Condon, 2974 Decatur Avenue, Bronx. Of course, we now have the envelope being referred to as a letter. And to top all this, we have Mr. Perrone admitting he could not identify, or even tell anything at all about any of his customers before being accosted by the mysterious man who asked him to deliver a note. But, of course, he could relate everything the police wanted to know about this mystery man. But "obliging Joe" was not able to give any specific information about any of his passengers on days, either preceding or following, the Gun Hill Road, Mosholu, Jerome Avenue, Knox Place incident of March 12th, 1932. Joe Perrone and Jim O'Brien worked well together playing a little more than bit roles in the scenario that was being enacted to place Richard Hauptmann in New Jersey's electric chair.

C H A P T E R   T W E N T Y   S E V E N

What Lies We Mortals Tell!

The "incriminating" testimony of Whited, Hochmuth, and Perrone, as damaging as each had been, proved to be nothing more than "minor sideshows" to the "headlined acts" of the "main event" scheduled to be performed in the Flemington, New Jersey "circus" conducted in January and February of the year 1935.

John Francis Condon, the garrulous, pompous 74 year old "Jafsie", cast all other witnesses into the background with his rambling account of the "big role" he played in the Lindbergh case.

Realizing his self-imposed importance in the successful conclusion of the crime, Condon did all he could to thrust the spotlight on himself. Rather than test your patience of having you digest all of the lengthy and tiring testimony given by this man, you will find the dialogue of only those important questions and answers which directly led to Condon naming Richard Hauptmann as the recipient of the $50,000 ransom payment. Remembering that Condon had been reluctant from the very first time he met Hauptmann to identify him as the person he talked with on two occasions in cemeteries, he, as had the other "false witnesses" came through in fine fashion for the prosecuting attorney.

Condon informed the Court that he had every authority to be referred to as a doctor since he held "the title, the degree, and the diploma" with a Bachelor of Arts degree from the College of the City of New York that he had earned in 1882. He said he also held a Master of Arts degree from Fordham University and a Doctor of Pedagogy from New York University. He informed his listeners that he had taught in schools and universities since 1884, and after a career that ended with his retirement in June of 1930 at the age of 70, he had continued to teach and lecture several days a week, which time he counted as a total of 51 years.

Most of the police who had worked with Condon during the years of the Lindbergh kidnapping investigation, would have been only too glad to award him another degree, sanctioning it with a loud "Amen". The degree would be that of "Master of Arts in Prevarication", since the doctor was nothing more than an "out-and-out liar."

For quite a few months Condon had told so many different stories about his work on the case; had identified or failed to identify suspects; plus had given irrational statements and actions, that the authorities were afraid that his value to them as a witness, at the most, would be very questionable. Nevertheless, before the Flemington trial got underway, Doctor Condon had put his act together by bringing enough credence into his "tall tales" that the jury could not help but believe such a man of "honor and integrity".

In part, here is what the doctor of letters had to say precisely about his meeting in St. Raymond's Cemetery on the night of April 2nd, 1932 as he was questioned by Attorney General Wilentz:

Q. Now, Doctor, did you go down Whittemore Avenue that night? A. I did.

Q. Did you meet a man there? A. I did.

Q. Did you have with you some time or other that night, you and Colonel Lindbergh, a box of money? A. The Colonel had the box of money with an extra package besides.

Q. All right, sir. Did you give some money in a box that night? A. I did.

Q. And who did you give that money to? A. John.

Q. Who is John?

The aging doctor appeared to enjoy the prominence and importance his testimony would have on the spectators as they eagerly awaited his reply. Frowning, he stared down at Hauptmann. The shrill ring of his voice penetrated the "quiet pause of expectancy" as he very carefully pronounced and separated each syllable of the name:

A. John is Bru-no Rich-ard Haupt-mann.

Condon's immediate reply had caused the accused man to glare back and shake his head ever so slightly. Lindbergh was seen to lean forward, appearing pleased with the identity, his eyes never turning away from Condon.

With the announcement, the hush which permeated the courtroom was broken by a ripple of comments and exclamations from the spectators. Justice Trenchard called for order. Up in the balcony a spontaneous burst of revived activity took place as the excited members of the press sent new headlines and stories to their papers for publication that evening --- headlines reading: JAFSIE IDENTIFIES HAUPTMANN.

Again, during the proceedings, Condon was called upon to register his affirmation that Hauptmann was the kidnapper, therefore assuring the jury of his "honesty" in making a definite identification:

Q. Now did he shake hands with you that night? A. He reached his hand over the hedge: "Your work was perfect. Good night." I said, "Good night, John. Remember, don't try to double cross me."

Q. And the man that you handed that money to was John, you say? A. Is John.

Q. That is the man you are talking about in this conversation? A. That is the man I am talking about on that night.

Q. And John is who?

Although he should have well rehearsed his part, having acted it out once earlier in the day, his apparent attempt to announce the name in an ever more dramatic fashion, the proud doctor, in spite of his "title, degree, and diploma", went on to miserably flub his lines as he blurted out: "John is Bruno Rudolph--- or Bruno Richard Hauptmann."

Regardless of this one flaw in his testimony, Condon held up well as he withstood the intense questioning of Reilly during cross-examination. At 4:31 p.m. Justice Trenchard called for adjournment until ten o'clock the following morning, Thursday, January 10th, the seventh day of the trial.

Much controversial testimony was heard regarding the envelope Condon had received on the night of Wednesday, March 9th, 1932. The question as to whether Doctor Condon had opened the letter bearing the symbol signature before he took it to Hopewell to Colonel Lindbergh, or whether he had delivered it still in its sealed envelope to the Colonel was made a matter of great importance, and was discussed at great length. It is very possible the jury was never brought to completely realize the significance of these questions, and quite probably never had it made clear to them as to just what Condon's answer to the question actually was.

The significance of Condon's claim that in late August of 1934 he had sighted Hauptmann from a bus on which he was riding, and his reason for doing nothing about it was because he "thought it was none of my business" is too ridiculous to be believed.

Reilly's questioning of Condon leading to his

testimony of this incident follows:

Q. Now, Doctor, do you recall being in Childs' Restaurant, New York, Broadway, in the neighborhood of 67th Street, during the month of December, 1934? A. I was there at Childs' Restaurant, visited it frequently, but the exact moment I don't know.

Q. Well, which Childs' Restaurant? A. Well, I will tell you---

Q. Let's see if we can get that? A. There is a kind of an opening in a northeasterly direction---

Q. What street? A. Well, St. Nicholas Street, I think, is about 66th Street or near that, and then it was one block south, or near it, 65th, 64th or 63rd, about that. I can point it out.

Q. Did you meet there a man named Marcus Griffith, or Griffin? A. Marcus Griffuth?

Q. Yes, of the *New York Inquirer*? A. Not to my knowledge.

Q. Did you talk to a man in Childs' Restaurant the last time you were there in December, 1934? A. Yes, sir.

Q. About this case? A. I couldn't tell you, but if you specify I will remember.

Q. Did you tell Marcus Griffuth of the *New York Inquirer* in Childs' Restaurant during the month of December, 1934, that the child's body was brought back to the spot where it was found buried and you knew that to be a fact? A. I don't remember having said so.

Q. Is your memory poor? A. It is not. It is a question of my belief that I am thinking of.

Q. You won't say you didn't say it? A. I won't say I didn't---I don't know.

Q. Now, after the defendant was arrested and you saw him in Centre Street Police Headquarters---is that correct? A. Police headquarters I think---yes, yes.

Q. Did you ask a question in the Bronx for some pictures of the defendant so you could study them? A. Not to my recollection.

Q. Will you say now that you did not, after the arrest of this defendant, ask Detective Callahan of The Bronx for some pictures of this defendant so you could study them? A. I did not.

Q. Did Detective Callahan of The Bronx give you some pictures of this defendant? A. I don't know---I don't know him.

Q. Did anybody give you any pictures in The Bronx of this defendant? A. Not that I remember.

Q. And did you say to Detective Callahan--- A.

I don't know; I don't remember---

Q. Wait a minute, please. A. I see.

Q. Did you say to him when he gave you the pictures, "Don't tell anyone you gave me these pictures?" Yes or no. A. No.

Q. Now, I want the exact date, if you can recall, when you say you saw Hauptmann in The Bronx and you were riding in a bus. A. The exact date of the month I do not know, but it was in the latter part of August, 1934.

Q. And what bus were you riding in? A Riding from the New Rochelle section down, that is in a southerly direction toward New York.

Q. And you didn't think it of enough importance to write that date down, did you? A. Not the date.

Q. Give me the number of the bus. A. I didn't take that. The number of the bus I was in.

Q. Yes. A. No, sir; I didn't take it.

Q. Did you take the chauffeur's number? A. I did not.

Q. Did you call out to the chauffeur, "Get that man?" A. "Get that man?" No, it was none of my business.

Q. None of your business? A. No, sir.

Q. To get the man? A. For me; no, sir.

Q. Do you want this jury to believe that it was none of your business---I will reframe the question. A. Yes.

Q. If it offends the General. It is your sworn testimony then, is it, that you saw the man in August, 1934? A. Yes, sir.

Q. On the street in The Bronx, the man to whom you had handed the $50,000 ransom, the man you believed had double-crossed you, and you made no outcry? A. I didn't say that. I didn't say that I didn't make any outcry.

Q. Did you make an outcry? A. I did.

Q. In the bus? A. In the bus.

Q. Give me the name of a person that heard you. A. I don't know anybody. I was alone.

Q. Did you take anybody's name? A. I didn't know anybody.

Q. Did you make any effort to have the bus driver run the man down? A. He couldn't---

Q. Did you ask him to? A. Yes, sir.

Q. To run him down? A. No, I didn't on account of the traffic. You see, he couldn't run him down; there might have been fifty people killed.

Q. That is what you think about it? A. That was

my thought then.

Q. Did you ask anyone in the bus to give their name and address? A. I did not.

Q. In what direction did this man go that you saw in August? A. Northeasterly direction, that is---

Q. Where did he disappear? A. He disappeared in the woods north of Pelham Parkway.

Q. And where did you ride in that bus before you got off? A. Rode to the crossroad of Pelham Parkway and Williamsbridge Road. Williamsbridge Road runs, well, almost in a northerly and southerly direction; Pelham Parkway goes to the west, towards City Island.

Now here is the "remarkable" Doctor Condon, who claimed he had been so vitally interested in seeing to it that his "friend", Cemetery John would be apprehended ever since he made the payment of $50,000 to him in St. Raymond's Cemetery and his failure to return the baby, now actually "turning his back" to a wonderful opportunity to bring about the possible arrest of the man. Regardless of how one looks at the facts, it fails to make any common sense at all, since Condon's actions, by his own strong verbal admission, proved to be contradictory to those of his often voiced claims.

One other glaring omission regarding the actions of the "highly respected doctor" was the failure of at least one, if not all of the persons in the Condon home on the night of Saturday, April 2nd, 1932 to obtain the name and any other necessary information that would identify the messenger who brought the letter to the doctor. This had been deemed important enough, and rightly so, to have obtained the name of Joseph Perrone who had delivered the first note on March 12th. Why then, did each of the men present --- Lindbergh, Condon, Breckinridge, Reich, and Gaglio fail to question the man who brought the note to the door? Condon, by all means, should have pursued the matter, since it was he who had personally taken the note from the man. Gaglio, who was standing directly behind should have prompted Condon to do so.

The neglect to learn the messenger's name, was without a doubt, one of the major mistakes committed by novice "investigators" in the Lindbergh case. Through the years, more than a few professional authorities have been highly critical of the manner in which the investigation was conducted. Many referred to it as outright stupidity on the part of the police for allowing the direction of the investigation to fall into the hands of non-professional civilians. But then, it must be also remembered that it was Colonel Lindbergh who was calling most of the shots.

John F. Condon was indeed a multi-faceted person. He was many things to many persons, an enigma who proved to be a contemptuous mystery-man to the police, who came under the suspicion and severe criticism by the authorities. He had originally presented himself as the ultimate example of a man of moral, spiritual, and patriotic character. However, as the police came to know Condon in a more intimate way through their dealings with him in their investigation of the Lindbergh case, they found him to be a man capable of expounding untruths, innuendos, and outright lies, while at the same time attesting to the things he told them as gospel truths.

Lies, lies, lies, and more lies were issued from the lips of this man, who for many months, told tales which caused the police to become suspicious of him as having played a role in the enactment of the actual crime.

To properly bi-sect Condon's many "tall tales" we must begin with three initial questions. Just why and how did he get involved in the case? Why did he select *The Bronx Home News* as the means of possibly making contact with the kidnappers? And, why was he so certain that Arthur "Red" Johnson, Betty Gow's boyfriend was innocent?

Governor Hoffman, in his series of *Liberty Magazine* articles, refers to Condon as the confusing confused "ace" witness of the State of New Jersey against Hauptmann. The governor's research of the case was thorough to say the very least; the facts he uncovered were not only astounding, but the real truths when parlayed against the "rotten deliberate lies" that were used against Hauptmann are absolutely revolting. Since there is no better way to inform you of these, the following is Governor Hoffman's first hand report of his findings exactly as he told it in his *Liberty* articles:

"The first question that may be asked is, Why did Doctor Condon enter the Lindbergh case? We shall let him answer it. To District Attorney Breslin of the Bronx, on May 14, 1932, he gave the reasons: "I heard many people, most of whom had decided foreign accents, stating that such an outrage could not occur in any other country of the world ... my American spirit was aroused ... the distress of the Lindbergh family." To the Bronx Grand Jury on May 20 he gave practically the same reason: "talk in various restaurants." *In Jafsie Tells All* the reason was derogatory talk on the night of the crime in Bickford's Restaurant, where he threatened to fight some men who were "reviling" the United States and the Department of Justice. On the witness stand in Flemington, Doctor Condon said that he inserted the ad in the *Bronx Home News* because the other papers "all led toward one poor miserable fellow that I thought was innocent. His name was Arthur Johnson."

"In his *Liberty* articles Doctor Condon said that he selected the *Bronx Home News* for his advertisement because the Bronx was an easy exit from Hopewell; to Inspector Harry Walsh of the Jersey City Police he said that he "didn't think to use the large dailies."

"The Doctor was asked the question, after he had already admitted that he did not even know "Red" Johnson, 'Did you learn that he (Red) phoned Betty Gow at half past eight on the night of the kidnapping?' 'I knew that, snapped back the witness, on the night of the kidnapping.' Later Jafsie tried to correct this blunder; blamed his misunderstanding of the question on Reilly's "English."

Before we continue with Governor Hoffman's report of Condon, it is wise to dwell for a moment on the ridiculous "confusion" that occurred as to who it was that received the telephone call from the eccentric Condon in the Lindbergh home around midnight on Wednesday, March 9th. A close friend and advisor of Colonel Lindbergh, Robert H. Thayer (who incidentally was never called as a witness) was very certain that he was the person who spoke to Condon. When asked, appearing a bit confused, Lindbergh "did not think he talked directly with Doctor Condon." The Colonel either could not recollect it, or was deliberately evasive as to who it was that took the call. But Thayer was positive it was he who had talked to Condon. Thayer's statement as given to Lieutenant Keaten on May 16, 1932 reads as follows:

"At about 12 o'clock on the night of March 10 I was answering the telephone, and a voice on the telephone stated that he was Doctor John Condon of the Bronx and that he had received a letter addressed to Colonel Lindbergh. He said that he did not know if there was anything to it, that it might be just a crank; but that he had put an advertisement in the *Bronx Home News* offering a $1,000 reward to any one who returned the baby safely, and possibly this was in answer to the advertisement.

"We had just been discussing the question of the difficulty of the kidnappers communicating with Colonel Lindbergh and Colonel Breckinridge, due to the great publicity in the case and the activity of the press, and we had been discussing the possibility of the kidnappers sending letters to Colonel Lindbergh through a third party. For that reason my curiosity was particularly aroused, and I asked Doctor Condon how the letter to him was signed. <u>He stated that it was signed with the sign of the Mafia. I then asked him to open and read the letter addressed to Colonel Lindbergh.</u>

"I took this letter down on pencil and paper as he read it to me, and it was apparent to me from the first few words that this letter was from the same people that had left the ransom note. This was confirmed when I asked him to give me a vague idea of the signature. I also took down on pencil and paper the letter addressed to him from the same people. I then told him to get into a car as quickly as he could and come down to Hopewell, bringing the letter with him. I gave the copies of the letters that I had made to Colonel Lindbergh and I have not seen them since."

Governor Hoffman's remarks on the contradictory statements of Thayer and Condon are best expressed in this belief he held: "The letter to Condon, as a matter of fact, <u>bore no symbol or signature</u>; so how he could have told Thayer or any one else that the letter bore the sign of the Mafia or any other sign, prior to getting instructions to open up the sealed letter addressed to Lindbergh, will always remain a mystery. (At Flemington, Condon, on the stand, was skating on thin ice under cross-examination about the symbols, but was saved through an interruption by Attorney General Wilentz.)"

Governor Hoffman bears down hard on this issue, one of Condon's very apparent initial lies: "The matter of opening the sealed letter addressed to Colonel Lindbergh has brought forth many contradictory statements. Thayer, as I have pointed out, said that Doctor Condon told him that his letter bore the "sign of the Mafia" <u>before</u> the Doctor was asked to open the sealed letter. In his *Liberty* articles Condon says he first saw the symbol when Lindbergh told him to open the sealed letter. In his testimony (page 714) he says he told Lindbergh he had a letter with the symbol upon it. He later testified that he showed the symbol (page 725) to Gaglio and Rosenhain <u>before</u> he made the telephone call to Hopewell.

Under oath, questioned by Reilly, he said (page 721) that he did not phone to Colonel Lindbergh until he saw the symbol. Then he testified (page 724) that the letter addressed to the Colonel was still sealed when he delivered it at Hopewell. The following day, at Flemington, under patient redirect questioning by Wilentz, Condon retracted both of these latter statements, making it clear to the jury then that the letter received by him bore no symbol and that he did not see the symbol until, at Rosenhain's, he had been directed by the voice at Hopewell to open the letter addressed to Lindbergh; and that, therefore, the letter had been opened when he handed it to the Colonel.

"To Inspector Walsh and Lieutenant Keaten, on May 13, 1932, Condon gave a signed statement that he had received at his home "two telephone calls (from the kidnappers) ... and in both places there were a number of people talking; they were directing John in the same room." He told the same thing to Detective Leon, to Lieutenant James J.Finn (as reported in Finn's *Liberty* articles), to Department of Justice investigators, to the Bronx Grand Jury. In most of these statements he recalled that he distinctly heard one voice say, "Statti citto!" the equivalent of "Shut up!"

"Special Agent J.E. Seykora, on March 8, 1934, reports that Condon said that at about 3 P.M., March 12, 1932, he received a telephone call from an unknown man who stated that he was calling from Westchester Square. The report says: "Doctor Condon stated that this man spoke with an Italian accent and stated that Doctor Condon was selected as a go-between and instructed him to remain home that evening."

Hauptmann, you will recall, was being tried as a "lone wolf" at Flemington. Nothing is mentioned by Condon, anywhere in his testimony, about hearing other voices---about "Statti citto!" To those who may feel the defense should have brought out this fact it must be pointed out that these statements of Condon were not given to the jury and the public until long after the trial, and the defense could have had no knowledge of them.

Nor was it brought out that Doctor Condon, on July 25, 1934, had furnished the Department of Justice with a pencil sketch of the "kidnapper's left hand," <u>showing fleshy development at the base of the thumb</u>. On this sketch, as reported by Special Agent Sisk, "Doctor Condon had placed an arrow pointing at the fingertips ... 'just as disease, such as pulmonary inroad, would cause.'" Hauptmann had a normal mechanic's hand.

Nor was anything said about the suspected "lookout" observed by Doctor Condon and Al Reich walking south on Jerome Avenue the night of Condon's Woodlawn Cemetery conference with "John". "Doctor Condon describes this man," says Agent Seykora, "as apparently being a Calabrese Italian, short and swarthy, wearing a cap."

In *Liberty*, in the official records of District Attorney Breslin, Lieutenant Keaten, and Detective Leon, and in the trial testimony, Condon said he inserted the "Money is ready" ad in the *New York American*. To Inspector Harry Walsh, on June 2, 1932, he denied it.

On the stand Doctor Condon testified that he saw "John" inside the Woodlawn Cemetery gates, waving a handkerchief. He approached him within about three feet, and John asked, "Did you got the money?" In about a "minute or so" there was a rustle in the leaves, according to Condon, and "John," saying, "There is a cop," climbed up the vertical bars of a nine-foot fence and ran away. To the Bronx Grand Jury, on May 20, 1932, Condon said, "We had been talking there for maybe twenty-five minutes when an officer appeared in back of him, the officer being a cemetery guard in uniform. ..." In *Liberty* the Doctor writes that he talked with "John" three minutes before the guard came.

In *Jafsie Tells All*, Condon reports "John" as saying the people "down South" had nothing to do with the kidnapping. On May 14, 1932, Condon told Assistant District Attorney Breslin that "John" said, "I will go back and tell them what you say. He told me that the baby is not in Norfolk, Virginia, nor in the North." Detective Sam Leon of the New Jersey State Police reports Condon as saying, "John told me to tell Colonel Lindbergh not to pay any attention to the other gang, meaning Curtis, as they were not the right parties." Remember, please, as you read this amazing information, that Condon's alleged conference with "John" was held on March 12, 1932, and it was not until March 19 that Curtis first made his appearance in the case, or that the Norfolk angle was mentioned.

"On May 18, 1932, a conference was held by Colonel Schwarzkopf, Major Schoeffel, and Lieutenant Keaten of the State Police with Mr. Nathan and other representatives of the Department of Justice and the Treasury Department, Assistant Attorney General Lanigan, the prosecutors of Mercer and Hunterdon Counties, and Inspector Walsh of Jersey City. This is from the record:

"Mr. NATHAN: Are you convinced that Condon is on the level?

"INSPECTOR WALSH: No."

"Walsh went on to inform the government officials that discrepancies in statements given by the Doctor were being investigated.

"One of the statements made by Colonel Schwarzkopf at the conference is very interesting. He said that at St. Raymond's Cemetery, after Condon passed over the box containing the money, "John" shook hands with the Doctor and said, "Your work has been perfect in this arrangements." The Doctor then said that John must tell him where they could get the baby. At that time, according to Schwarzkopf, "John said, 'I will have to talk to my partners,' and he went off to two men standing in the background some distance off. ..."

Department of Justice officials conferred at Englewood with Colonel Lindbergh over a year after the crime, and in his report of this conference, United States Agent Hugh Larimer says: "Colonel Lindbergh made that remark that were Doctor Condon a younger man he would be immediately suspicious of him, but that in spite of Condon's age there were several little things which raised a doubt as to Condon's sincerity." Among the "several little things" cited were the prompt reply to Condon's advertisement in the *Bronx Home News*, Condon's recital of the way he---a 72 year-old man---overtook "John" at Woodlawn Cemetery when he jumped the fence and ran, and the fantastic story about Condon and "John" covering each other with revolvers during the conference on the bench. The report continues: "The Colonel was suspicious of Al Reich who claimed that he observed John jump the fence and run. ... Lindbergh was not impressed with the arrangement whereby Condon and Al Reich were to make the contact and deliver the money."

"Inspector Harry Walsh, now Police Chief of Jersey City, wrote in the *Jersey Journal*, November 22, 1932, that "ordinary police methods were not followed in the Lindbergh case. Neither Violet Sharpe, nor Jafsie, nor any one else connected with the case - except Curtis and Henry Johnson - was arrested and held pending investigation." Walsh, in his article, says that Doctor Condon should have been booked as a material witness, and the arrest of the kidnappers should have been accomplished at St. Raymond's Cemetery when Jafsie paid the ransom.

"On September 21, 1934, the day after he had been

assigned to watch Doctor Condon and "not permit him to talk to strangers," L.C. Turrou, special agent of the Department of Justice, wrote, in a report:

"Dr.Condon impressed the Agent that he has no desire, for some reason, to identify Hauptmann ... Several times he asked me that he be permitted to talk to Hauptmann privately for half an hour, following which he would render a definite opinion as to whether Hauptmann is the man known to him as John ... He remarked on one occasion that HAUPTMANN IS NOT THE MAN because he appears to be MUCH HEAVIER, HAS DIFFERENT EYES, DIFFERENT HAIR, ETC. ..."

Shortly before he was taken to the District Attorney of Bronx County he intimated to the writer that he was not going to identify Hauptmann and "would tell the true story later on."

There is before me a copy of a report by Special Agent J.J. Manning, dated September 29, 1933, entitled "Dr. John F. Condon, 2974 Decatur Avenue, Bronx, New York, apparently untruthful in his statements concerning identity of persons alleged by him to have made box in which was contained the ransom. ..."

"Condon, according to the report, said that the box had been made by an old friend whose name he could not recall. Later he pointed out a vacant store to Agent Manning and said, 'The man who made the box used to have his business in there.' He then recalled the name of the man as "old man Peretty." Subsequent investigation showed that the store had been formerly occupied by a cabinetmaker named Frank Peremi, Jr. Peremi denied that either he or his father, who had died in 1931, made the box. He did state, however, that Doctor Condon and Al Reich, approximately ten days prior to the payment of the ransom money, had brought plans and inquired as to the price for making such a box. Informed that it would be three dollars and fifty cents, Condon remarked that it was too much money for such a job.

Later, Department of Justice investigation revealed that a cabinetmaker named A. Samuelsohn had made the box. Doctor Condon was taken by Agents O'Leary and Seery to Samuelsohn's shop at 3037 Webster Avenue. Samuelsohn immediately recognized Jafsie and said, "I remember you. I did a little job for you a couple of years ago." He then produced records showing that on March 25, 1932, he had made the box for Condon. Samuelsohn charged $3.

At Flemington, on the stand, Doctor Condon when

asked who made the box, answered, "I couldn't tell you."

Now let's take up the matter of identification. It would take pages to give all the descriptions of "John" given by the good Doctor to various police officials. As to some characteristics there is at least a degree of consistency. The age of the man estimated by Jafsie ranges from thirty to thirty-five, and he invariably mentions that "John" had a "pointed chin", although he also claimed, continually, that the mysterious man kept his coat collar turned up over his face. Whenever a police official or juror was smart enough to ask the Doctor how he could see the chin and other facial characteristics so well, Jafsie would say that he asked "John" "not to be afraid" to turn the coat down, "which he did".

Good-natured criminal,this "John". Sitting there with Doctor Condon at a time when he knew the baby was dead and that he could be arrested any moment for kidnap and murder, he was kind enough to respond to every request made by Condon that would enable the latter to help bring about his arrest and conviction. He obligingly turned down his collar; he let the Doctor feel his muscles so he could judge his weight. He let Condon shake his hand upon several occasions so that the go-between (had Condon, Lindbergh, or the police officials been smart enough---and they apparently weren't) might have gotten his fingerprints.

And "John", the baby kidnapper and murderer, was a kindhearted person, too! When, at St. Raymond's Cemetery, Doctor Condon told "John" that "these are times of depression ..... Colonel Lindbergh is not so rich ... why don't you be decent to him ... he can't raise the extra money." the murderer immediately replied (as quoted by Condon in *Jafsie Tells All*), "Since it is so hard it will be all right, I guess. I suppose if we can't get seventy, we take fifty."

Kindhearted -oh, yes - a very sentimental fellow, this "John" who had brutally murdered a baby and thrown its little body in the woods. Before the Bronx Grand Jury, on May 20, 1932, Doctor Condon testified as follows: "I said, ... what is your name? He said, 'Call me John.' Well, John, did you ever think of your own mother? 'Yes,' and a tear came into his eye, which I saw on that night on the northerly side of the large gate of the cemetery." "John's" heart must have been almost breaking. And what vision the venerable Doctor had on that dark night when he even spied that telltale tear!

He was rather consistent about the weight of the man. His estimates ran from 150 pounds to 165 pounds. Hauptmann's weight in 1932 was 175 pounds, as shown upon his application for an automobile driver's license, issued before the crime. His weight in 1934 was 180 pounds. Hauptmann lost thirty pounds between his arrest and the time he went on the witness stand---which fitted in very nicely with the estimate given by Doctor Condon at that time.

Then too, although the Doctor continually said that "John" wore a hat which he kept pulled down over his face, he referred always to the forehead as being "high" or "prominent". Probably John also took off his hat to accommodate the Doctor, for he was able to describe the hair very nicely. It was "dirty blond" or "medium light".

The eyes (to Walsh and Avon) were "blue-grey", (to Keaten and Moffat) they were "almond-shaped) and quite a distance from the nose ... never opened wide ... rather semi-closed ... not big eyes"; (to Breslin) they were "wide, almond eyes"; (to the Bronx Grand Jury) they were "separated a little from the nose such as Chinese or Japanese"; in *Liberty* they were "deep-set".

Doctor Condon appears to have remembered more as time went by. In July of 1934, to Agent Sandberg of the Department of Justice, he mentions for the first time that "John's" ears are "unusually large; protruding somewhat".

As reported by Condon, "John's" complexion, at times, was "medium", "rather light", and "sallow". His height, according to various statements by Condon, ranged from five feet eight to five feet ten. Lieutenant Finn reports Condon as saying at one time that "John" wore gloves; at another, that he didn't. His eyebrows, as reported to Sandberg, were "medium heavy and in a straight line across forehead, almost joining each other".

Once in a while "John" was "Scandinavian or German". On June 2, 1932, when asked, "What makes you think John is a Scandinavian?" Condon replied, "He told me---and his accent." Again he said, "I figure he is not a German."

Now "John's" cough deserves special mention. In the statement just referred to, given to Inspector Walsh, Jafsie says, "The skin was smooth and it gave me the impression that disease had started its inroads into his body. He had a hacking cough." To Detective Avon, Condon said that "John coughed continually." At numerous other times Jafsie said that John "coughed continuously."

At Flemington, under oath, Doctor Condon, the state's number one witness, said "John" only coughed once.

To Inspector Walsh, Condon said that "John" told him he was not married. To Lieutenant Finn, Condon reported that "John" had told him he was married.

On May 14, 1932, Condon told Assistant District Attorney Breslin that "John" had a "hatchet face". (Incidentally, in this same statement, taken stenographically, he said that "Colonel Lindbergh did not want any interference from the police; he laid down the law; he said that if he was interfered with in this case, being that it meant so much to him, they would hear from him personally." On this same day, significantly, Condon told Breslin, "I would not like to be indicted in New Jersey by the Grand Jury, for they would choke you for a cherry in New Jersey.")

So it appears Jafsie had no use for the police authorities, and the police, in return, were suspicious of him.

But he was permitted to go merrily on his way. It was Condon, alone, who conceived the idea of putting the ad in the *Bronx Home News*; Condon alone, who received the notes delivered by the taxi drivers; Condon, alone, who went to St. Raymond's Cemetery and, out of sight of Colonel Lindbergh, delivered the $50,000 to the mysterious "John".

There is much more to be said about Jafsie, who advertised that he would offer all he could "scrape together"---$1,000 which he had saved from his salary, "all of my life's savings---for the safe return of the Lindbergh child. There is much more to be said of this same Jafsie, who, in his story in *Liberty* March 14, 1936, said that "since I entered the case I have spent more than twelve thousand dollars of my own money on trips and investigations."

There are glaring discrepancies in the stories told by Condon to the police and, under oath, to the Bronx Grand Jury before and after the arrest of Hauptmann. Why didn't he identify Hauptmann in the Greenwich Street police line-up---a man whose face, he said, he could remember "as intimately as a well remembered poem"? Why did he change his story so many times even upon the witness stand? Why, long after his supposed identification of Hauptmann, was he still looking for the "John" to whom he paid the Lindbergh ransom money? What part did his testimony play in sending Hauptmann to the electric chair? What part of his story would have been believed by the jury if the police had not withheld from them the records now being made available to the public?

If Doctor Condon did not do, or did not say, the things I have mentioned and will mention, then the reports of the Flemington trial and the Bronx Grand Jury, the statements of Colonel Lindbergh, the records of the Department of Justice, the New Jersey State Police, and the New York City Police are in error. I am quoting from these records, and I challenge any one to disprove my statements.

Jafsie was given pretty much of a free hand in a case that involved human life and the interests of society. He played, it has always seemed to me, a puzzling game with himself---a sort of psychopathic solitaire in which he was permitted to make all the cards and deal them as he pleased.

The things that Doctor Condon had done and said that fitted into the scheme of the prosecution were paraded at Flemington. His unexplainable actions---the things he wrote and said that did not fit in---are still being carefully protected from public scrutiny.

"On February 17, 1936, Colonel H. Norman Schwarzkopf wrote to J. Edgar Hoover of the Federal Bureau of Investigation, requesting transcripts of the statements taken from Doctor Condon during the course of the Lindbergh investigation. In reply to this belated request---made over a year after Hauptmann had been convicted, largely on Doctor Condon's testimony---Assistant Director Harold Nathan, of the Bureau, advised that "Doctor Condon was interviewed by agents of the Bureau on more than one hundred occasions and that, consequently, the information obtained as a result of these interviews is distributed throughout the ninety volumes of files maintained by the Bureau in this case."

A request for permission to examine these files was denied by Director Hoover, who held that under a regular department ruling an examination of the files could not be made by any person "not having a current official interest therein." A similar request made to Police Commissioner Valentine of New York brought forth a like refusal.

But when C. Lloyd Fisher, later a Prosecutor of Hunterdon County, and who certainly had an <u>official</u> <u>current</u> <u>interest</u> in the case, and who desires to bring to the bar of justice <u>all</u> persons who were involved in the Lindbergh case, subsequently asked permission to view the records, he, too, was refused access.

Why this secrecy? One side of this case has been given the fullest public airing. If the police officials are sure that complete justice has been served, they should likewise be willing to prove to the world that they and their witnesses, including Jafsie, were right.

It is represented today by the Department of Justice and by the New York Police that all important statements have already been turned over to the New Jersey authorities. If that is so, they have been removed from the files. Here and there I have been able to find a copy of a statement taken by the Bureau of Investigation agents; but there is much of the record missing. The publication of these records in their entirety would be, I am sure, illuminating to the lovers of justice in America.

There is enough in the available record to arouse the suspicions of those who want, and are entitled to, the complete truth in this case.

I have shown, from authentic records, that there were numerous discrepancies among the statements of Doctor Condon and changes in his testimony; that even Department of Justice records denounce some of his statements as "apparently untruthful"; that he was suspected by Colonel Lindbergh, by Department of Justice agents, and Inspector Harry Walsh of the Jersey City Police, one of the smartest police officers who worked upon the Lindbergh investigation, of knowing more than he told about the crime and subsequent happenings.

It has been brought out previously that Jafsie gave different reasons for his use of the *Bronx Home News* to offer himself as a go-between, without authority, for the Lindberghs; that he changed his testimony on the stand and in various statements given to the police, as to his knowledge that the sealed letter to the Colonel bore the telltale kidnap symbols; that he had said, prior to the trial, that men with Italian accents had been heard giving instructions to "John"; that he reported "John" as mentioning "the people down South" and "Norfolk, Virginia" long before Curtis and the Norfolk angle were even brought into the case.

I have shown, from the stenographic transcript of the meeting with Department of Justice officials, that Colonel Schwarzkopf had reported Condon as saying that "John" went off to two men in the background on the night the ransom money was paid over the hedge in St. Raymond's Cemetery; that Schwarzkopf had maintained that the suicide of Violet Sharpe had tended to "confirm the suspicions of the investigating authorities concerning her guilty knowledge of the crime.

Now, let's take up, in greater detail, Doctor Condon's visit to the Lindbergh home, where he spent the night in the nursery. There is his own story in *Jafsie Tells All*. On the night of March 9---or was it March 10? Condon's version differs from the official record---the good Doctor accompanied by Rosenhain and Gaglio, had hurried to the Lindbergh residence. He had shown Colonel Lindbergh the letter, bearing the symbols, that he had received from the kidnapper. He had been immediately designated as the go-between for the Lindberghs, and invited to stay overnight.

Gaglio and Rosenhain were sent back to the Bronx. The only available room in the house, according to Condon, was the nursery, where Colonel Lindbergh, with army blankets, made a bed for him. He awoke at 8 A.M., and then began to find important clues that had been overlooked by a score of investigators and police for nine days. His hand strayed to the pillow of the crib, and "touched something, amid the bedclothing, that was metallic." The something turned out to be two large safety pins. The good Doctor had an idea. "Removing them," he said, "I placed them in ... my pocket, and began an inspection of the room."

Walking to the east window, he found the "eloquent' imprint of the kidnapper's hand (how this must have chagrined Kelly, the fingerprint expert of the State Police, who testified that he didn't find a single fingerprint in the nursery!) right where the man had supported himself against the sash frame with his left hand while holding the child with his right." Right away he estimated the intruder's height to be five feet ten or ten and one half inches. He found footprints, too!

Then he took three toys---wood-carved miniatures of a lion, a camel, and an elephant--out of the window box, and he was seated on the floor apparently playing with them when Colonel Lindbergh came in. After breakfast, Lindbergh, Breckinridge, and Condon agreed that it would be necessary to use a pseudonym in conducting the negotiations. Condon suggested several. Significantly, two of them were "L.O. Nestar (Lone Star)" and "L.O. Nehand (Lone Hand)". Condon, in the Lindbergh case, was to be a Lone Star and a Lone Hand, but it was decided that his sudden happy choice was the best. "By putting my initials together," he said, "I get one: J.F.C.---Jafsie." "Fine, said Colonel Lindbergh. "Use that one. It will mask your name from every one but the man who wrote to you."

So Condon became Jafsie; but why? Condon's first note to the *Bronx Home News* was signed "Condon." The ransom letter to Lindbergh said that "Condon may act as go-between." Then, without the knowledge of the letter writer, they concocted the name "Jafsie." How would the kidnapper know any more than anybody else that Jafsie was Doctor Condon?

The police and the prosecution repeatedly tried to create the impression that no one but the writer of the original nursery note could have obtained the "symbol signature" and that, therefore, the writers of the subsequent notes were the actual kidnappers. I have shown that Rosner made a copy of the symbol from the note; that he showed it to Spitale and to Bitz; and that photographic copies were shown to members of the State Police. Condon, by his own admission, made a copy of the symbol, and <u>showed it to every one he met</u>. His exact words are: "I sketched it on a piece of paper and carried it with me. I showed it to every one I met, asked about it. And finally, late that evening, I found some one who recognized it. A Sicilian friend of mine explained the symbol. It was, he said, the symbol of a secret organization in Italy and was known as the <u>Trigamba</u>, or Three Legs.

Bear in mind, please, that Condon is writing about <u>late that evening</u> of the day after his visit to Hopewell. Robert H. Thayer says that, before Condon was told to open the enclosed envelope addressed to Colonel Lindbergh, the Doctor had stated that "it was signed with the sign of the Mafia."

"On March 6, 1934, (I am now quoting from a report of Agent J.E. Seykora of the Federal Bureau of Investigation) Doctor Condon said, in contradiction to his other statements, that "John" spoke with a Scandinavian or German accent; that he had received on March 12, 1932, a telephone call from an unknown man who stated that he was calling from Westchester Square, Bronx, New York City, and that "this man spoke with an <u>Italian accent</u>." The report continues: "Doctor Condon further stated that during this telephone conversation he heard other Italian voices apparently speaking to others in the room, telling them "Stat Zit' (phonetic), which he stated was an Italian expression meaning 'Shut up.'" Doctor Condon was later to tell also of seeing a man "apparently a Calabrese Italian," near Woodlawn Cemetery. A State Police report says that it "is an Italian characteristic to do business in a cemetery."

Let us go through the few available records to get Doctor Condon's stories of the safety pins, which he held to be highly important.

Here is the Woodlawn Cemetery story, as he tells it in *Jafsie Tells All* (*Liberty*, February 1, 1936): "Eager now to have further proof that I was dealing with the right man, I took from my pocket the little canvas pouch in which were the two blanket pins.... "Have you ever seen these before?" I asked. ...'Yes,' he replied. 'Those pins fastened the blankets to the maddress in the baby's grib. Near the top. Near the pillow.' "That is right," I agreed, and returned them to my pocket. I was jubilant. There could be no doubt, now, that I was dealing with the proper person....For, by identifying and giving the exact location of those two blanket pins, this man established positively one glaring <u>fact</u>: He, in person, had been present in the Lindbergh nursery on the night of the kidnapping!"

On a <u>phonograph</u> <u>record</u> for the Federal Department of Justice by Doctor Condon, recording his version of the meeting with the kidnapper near Woodlawn Cemetery, the Doctor, although he now attaches such importance to the safety pins, <u>does</u> <u>not</u> <u>even</u> <u>mention</u> <u>them.</u>

In his statement to Inspector Walsh on May 13, 1932, giving, supposedly, an accurate account of his activities (the body of the baby had been found the day before), Doctor Condon <u>makes</u> <u>no</u> <u>reference</u> <u>to</u> <u>safety</u> <u>pins</u>.

In a report, Meeting the Kidnapper at Woodlawn Cemetery, written by Doctor Condon in longhand, <u>he</u> <u>does</u> <u>not</u> <u>even</u> <u>mention</u> <u>safety</u> <u>pins</u>.

He did not mention safety pins in a statement given to the New Jersey State Police at Alpine, New Jersey, on June 2, 1932. Neither did he in the statement given to Assistant District Attorney Breslin on May 14, 1932, or in subsequent statements given to Detective Leon and Agents Manning, Sisk, Sandberg and Seykora of the Department of Justice.

Yet on May 20, 1932, <u>before</u> <u>the</u> <u>Bronx</u> <u>Grand</u> <u>Jury</u>, Jafsie, under oath, said: "I am here to tell the truth. I spoke to Colonel Lindbergh and asked him if I might take the two safety pins for this reason; the crib was long and wide enough to pin the over blanket of the child with large safety pins to the under sheets.... A child kicks a great deal and those two safety pins were placed up there. Would you like to see one? I have it here. I kept it with me. That is part of the oath. I know how bizarre it is. I don't mind it. I had an object in view. I put it in there if I haven't lost it. You will pardon me. I was in such earnest that I determined to have at least something. I didn't show that to the kidnappers, as stated. I mentioned it many places to attract attention."

Under oath again at Flemington, Jafsie told an entirely different story from any he had told before. The record:

> MR. REILLY (referring to Woodlawn Cemetery): Now, then what else was said there?
>
> DR. CONDON: In order to find out whether he ("John") was the proper party or not, I said, "How am I to know that I am talking to the right man? Tell me." I trust if this hurts anybody's feelings--
>
> MR. REILLY: No, what did he say?
>
> DR. CONDON: I trust that I may be excused. "The baby was held in the crib by safety pins."
>
> MR. REILLY: Who said that: John?
>
> DR. CONDON: John
>
> MR. REILLY: Yes, sir. And what---did you have the pins with you?
>
> DR. CONDON: I had the pins with me because I took them out of the baby's crib on the night that I slept there.
>
> MR. REILLY: I see.
>
> DR. CONDON; They had been, as nearly as I could judge, to the right and left of where the baby's neck was.
>
> MR. REILLY: Did you take them out with the consent and knowledge of Colonel Lindbergh?
>
> DR. CONDON: I took them out first and asked him afterwards--- what they call French leave.

So much for the safety pins---putting Doctor Condon in the position of giving a mass of weird, contradictory statements! How about the height of the fence over which "John" jumped at Woodlawn Cemetery, as estimated by Jafsie, who prided himself on his ability to judge weights, distances, ages, etc.? He told Assistant District Attorney Breslin that "John", at the approach of the cemetery, "caught hold of the cemetery gate, which was about twelve or fifteen feet high, and got over it in two seconds and alighted on the ground.

He ... started to run;. He got about twenty yards away and I said, 'Don't run away, you are my guest.'"

On the stand at Flemington, the amazing Doctor Condon said the fence climbed by "John" was less than nine feet high, but "John" climbed it in "Turner fashion." (Jafsie had never mentioned the "Turner" business before, but it may have helped to convince the jury that the climber was Hauptmann, who might have been a German Turnverein athlete.) At Flemington Condon testified that what he called to "John" was: "Hey, come back here. Don"t be cowardly. Here I am a poor schoolteacher and you are leaving me here to be drilled."

The cemetery guard who frightened "John", as testified by Condon, was a man named Riehl.

Now (in the event that you are one of those busybodies who dare to question the administration of justice in New Jersey) you might ask why Riehl, who would it seems, be an important witness, was not placed on the stand at Flemington. So let's go to the New Jersey State Police records, where we find a signed statement by Robert Riehl, guard at Woodlawn Cemetery, given to Sergeant Zapolsky on July 19, 1932. Riehl, then fifty-four years of age, recalled very well, it seems, the happenings at the Van Cortlandt gate on the night of March 12. He says: "I observed a man sitting on top of the stone column of the gate, talking to the other fellow who was outside of the gate. The man sitting on the column seen me. I was then about seventy-five feet away from him. He hollered to the other man who was on the outside of the gate, 'There's the cop coming.' The other man did not answer at all. The fellow on top of the column then jumped down and I thought he had broke his leg. When he got up he ran across 233rd Street into the park and disappeared. I went near the gate and questioned the other man who was outside as to what the young fellow was doing on top of the column, and his reply was, 'I don't know, I have no idea, and if you wait a minute I'll go over and ask him.'"

When asked by Zapolsky to describe the man, Riehl replied, "I could not describe his face or give you the color of his hair, as it was too dark to see it, but to the best of my judgment he was about five feet six or seven inches in height; weight about 130 or 135 pounds, and from his action while running I would judge him to be about twenty-three or twenty-four years old; dressed with dark pants, white shirt, no coat on, and wearing a cap. When this man hollered I did not notice foreign accent in speech."

Riehl, unfortunately, was not as keen as Condon. He could not distinguish a middleweight from a heavyweight, or see a tear in a man's eye on a dark night, or the color of hair through a cap or hat pulled down, so he would not have made a good witness for the state. He would have been a bad witness if he had testified, in line with his signed statement, that the man outside the gate did not resemble Doctor Condon, and was apparently between fifty and fifty-five, and about five feet six inches in height, and had no mustache. Had Riehl testified, and had his conscience not have permitted him, as in the case of so many others, to change stories between 1932 and 1935, the jury at Flemington might have been convinced that "it was two other fellows" at Woodlawn, not Hauptmann and Condon. No, Riehl's testimony just wouldn't fit.

Then there's the time consumed in that conference between Condon and "John" on the bench in Van Cortlandt Park. It was reduced from one hour and forty minutes, in earlier statements, to one hour and ten or fifteen minutes, when the good Doctor was upon the witness stand. Even an hour and ten minutes, for the conversation reported, might have taxed the credulity of the jury. But that's not important, perhaps.

And while we are on the subject of credulity of the jury, it might be well to consider another strain put upon it. Mrs. Ella Achenbach was placed upon the stand by the state to prove that on March 3 or 4---she wasn't quite sure---Mr. and Mrs. Hauptmann visited her home, and Hauptmann was limping so badly that he had to support himself by a rail or wall on the stoop. This, of course, was to show that Hauptmann had injured himself when the kidnap ladder broke. Yet the jury was asked to believe that less than ten days afterward Hauptmann had climbed vertical bars in two seconds and had jumped from the top of a fence nine feet high, landed on his feet like an athlete, and quickly run away.

The jury was not asked to believe, however, that Joseph Perrone, the taxi driver, had taken a passenger to City Island a few days after the Bronx County Grand Jury session, and that there, as he reported to Detective Claude Patterson of the New Jersey State Police, he had observed Doctor Condon <u>talking to a man who he thought was the man who gave him the note</u> to be delivered to the Doctor arranging the Woodlawn Cemetery meeting. Such information as this was kept carefully locked in the breasts, and in the files, of the State Police until my investigation, long after Hauptmann had been condemned to die, brought it to light.

Let's proceed to the circumstances surrounding the delivery to Condon of the sleeping suit, which formed the basis of the payment of the $50,000 for the return of the then dead Lindbergh baby. First we will review Doctor Condon's testimony, under oath, at Flemington. My parenthetical references are to the page numbers in the official record:

"Doctor Condon states (page 630) that "John" said, "I will send you the sleeping suit."

"Doctor Condon states that the following Wednesday, with two letters (page 633), the sleeping suit arrived.

"Doctor Condon, in answer to the question, "Who was present when you opened it?" (page 634) said, "Colonel Lindbergh and Colonel Breckinridge." When asked, "Anybody else?" he answered, "Those are all that I remember."

"Doctor Condon (page 636) said, "I immediately upon getting that suit brought Colonel Lindbergh into my parlor and, spreading the suit on the piano, I asked him to direct me and see if I was making any mistake."

"Doctor Condon (page 757), on cross-examination, said that he actually received the package containing the sleeping suit in the morning mail, at about half past ten. He said it was put on top of the mail box; that he couldn't recollect if he found it there, but "I know I got it" (page 758). He then said (page 759) that he opened it himself and "sent for Colonel Lindbergh to see if it was his son's sleeping suit."

"Doctor Condon, after recess of the court, and under direct examination by Attorney General Wilentz, said (page 814) that Colonel Breckinridge was the only one he remembered being present when the sleeping suit was opened. He then admitted that his daughter, Mrs. Hacker, was there.

Mrs. Hacker testified (page 849) that only she, her father, and Colonel Breckinridge were present when the sleeping suit arrived.

"To the Bronx Grand Jury, on May 14, 1932, Doctor Condon said, "The sleeping suit was rolled up in a package and I opened it out and I sent word to Colonel Lindbergh and to Colonel Breckinridge, as I had promised." He further said that, although he received the suit in the morning, Colonel Lindbergh did not come to his home until evening, when he took supper with Condon, after which he showed him the suit and the letters. He added, "Colonel Breckinridge was there, too."

There are many other conflicting statements to add to this confusion, but I must proceed to an important statement, and I am quoting verbatim from the stenographic record. Colonel H. Norman Schwarzkopf, head of the New Jersey State Police, told Assistant Director Nathan of the Federal Bureau of Identification, and other police officials, on May 18, 1932: "The family ... asked for positive identification, and they sent back to Doctor Condon the sleeping suit ... which was the same kind that the baby had worn the same night the baby had been taken away; however, this suit had one button off and it had apparently been washed and <u>was not accepted as conclusive</u>. It was accepted as being the same kind of a suit, but as being the suit, <u>there was nothing to positively identify it</u>."

This being so, may I ask, <u>why in the name of common sense was Colonel Lindbergh's $50,000 paid to an extortioner or extortioners at St. Raymond's Cemetery on the night of April 2</u>?

It cannot be said that the authorities did not know that the money was going to be paid. Doctor Condon, before the Bronx Grand Jury, had reluctantly divulged his "secret"---that there had been a meeting of the Secret Service (as he called it), the Jersey Police, and a representative of the New York Police at the "Morrow Home around Sixty-ninth or Seventieth Streets," when plans were laid for the payment of the ransom.

Doctor Condon's rambling, inconsistent statements had set forth much to raise a doubt that "John" had ever been in the nursery. He had not described the nursery, he had not been called upon to present one iota of real evidence that the child was in his possession, and his statement that the note "had been left in the baby's <u>grib</u>" should have been the final warning that Condon was dealing with an imposter. For had not Colonel Lindbergh, Betty Gow, and every one else at the Lindbergh home on that fateful night given information that the note was left on the <u>windowsill</u> and <u>not</u> in the <u>grib</u>?

Here is a question for the authorities to answer. There were good fingerprints of the baby in existence---I have copies of them---in spite of denials of the police that satisfactory fingerprints of the baby existed. Why was not Doctor Condon directed to hand

"John" a ten-cent ink pad and told to mail fingerprints as proof that the baby was in his hands or in the hands of his confederates? Even a photograph of the child, taken with a dollar camera, would have been better evidence of possession than a sleeping suit that was "the same kind as that worn by the child."

But Condon, on this flimsy bit of identification, was permitted to go alone to make the delivery of the ransom money; the police, knowing that the money was to be paid, made no effort to apprehend the kidnapper or extortioner.

There had been much to arouse the suspicions of the police as far as Doctor Condon was concerned. He had told conflicting stories about many things that I have been unable to mention in detail but which I am prepared to supply. There were a dozen different versions and descriptions of the second taxi driver---the one who delivered the note on the night of the ransom payment.

There had been the "coincidence" of the appearance of Condon's *Bronx Home News* letter offering himself as a go-between on the same day that the third ransom note, addressed to Breckinridge, had rejected Spitale and Bitz as go-betweens; there had been wide discrepancies in the phone calls reported by Condon from the kidnappers.

On March 19, 1932, according to his story *Jafsie Tells All*, Doctor Condon was approached at a bazaar at 194 East 200th Street, where he was selling old violins, by "a short middle-aged woman with the oval face and olive skin of an Italian." This woman stepped close to the Doctor and whispered, "Nothing can be done until the excitement is over. There is too much publicity. Meet me at the depot at Tuckahoe Wednesday at five in the afternoon. I will have a message for you!" The Doctor says that he went to Tuckahoe driven by one of his daughters-in-law, but "the woman never appeared."

"With variations, he told this story to a number of different police officers; but---to the Bronx Grand Jury on May 20, he made this sweeping denial:

Question: Now, Doctor, it has been mentioned in the public press at one time during your negotiations with the alleged kidnappers that you visited Tuckahoe to get a supposed communication or make an appointment with some unknown woman. Are those reports correct?

Answer: They are absolutely false. I saw no one at Tuckahoe, except my relatives. I never went to Tuckahoe to see anybody about anything.

There are a dozen different stories, too, about

seeing "John" long after the ransom payment, when Condon was riding in a bus. He saw the man to whom he had paid the ransom at the corner of Williamsbridge Road and Pelham Parkway. This, he testified, was in August, 1934, nearly three months "before I saw him in the New York police station." But I have in my possession a photostatic copy of a statement given to Corporal William Horn, dated July 12, 1933, in which Doctor Condon says that he saw "John" from a Throggs Neck bus on White Plains Avenue.

In this statement he says he got off the bus at the next corner, but "lost sight of the man." At Flemington, when asked, "Did you call to the chauffeur, 'Get that man'?" Dr.Condon replied, "No. It was none of my business." And this from the man who had repeatedly asserted that he had told "John" he would "follow him to Australia" if "John" had "double-crossed" him!

Most people do not know, as shown in the records, that Condon told stories of needle salesmen and scissors-grinders suspected of being members of the kidnap gang. They do not know that on one occasion he told that "John" had "fair and regular gold teeth." They do not know of the conflicting stories told by the Doctor about the mysterious woman driven to his Decatur Avenue home, during the period of the negotiations, by taxi driver Maurice Silken. They cannot be expected to know because these have not been made public, the conflicting stories of the payment of the ransom money at St. Raymond's Cemetery.

They do not know of Condon's mysterious doings at his summer camp in Becket, Massachusetts, which even drew the attention of the Department of Justice.

The police have every reason to smart, as do the prosecuting authorities, over several "let-downs" that the good Jafsie has given them. Among them are his refusal to believe that Hauptmann wrote his telephone number on the board in the closet, his insistence that more than one person was involved in the crime, and his criticism of the police line-up method of identification;. In *Jafsie Tells All* he declares that Hauptmann was lined up with "twelve or more broad-shouldered, florid-faced, bull-necked chaps who could not by any stretch of the imagination have been confused with the man I had described, over and over, as 'John'".

To show that the police were not without suspicion of Jafsie, may I quote from Lindbergh case memoranda in the official files of the New Jersey State Police these phrases: "He maintains junk shop." "Has private room in house---lots of vanity." "Makes own ink---has great imagination." "loves publicity," "travels all the time with Al Reich," "got upset in boat on presumed investigation." "Does he handle tools?---what size shoe does he wear?" "Where was Al Reich on night of March 1?" "Why did Condon wait to see if Col. L. was nervous Apr. 2?" "Does he read detective stories?" "Get his fingerprints if possible." "How did he act when body found?" Lamb phoned him---what did he say, and how?" "He had blanket pins---get details." "What is financial status?" "He changes subject---avoids direct answers." "Goes into long digressions off the point discussed." "Get a hypnotist to hypnotize him---can't harm him." "Have him psychoanalyzed." "He loves show---parades---speeches, etc." "Chase up police rumors about him." "Condon promised to keep faith with kidnappers." "Dick Oliver says no cab came to Dr's on Apr. 2." "Try out lie detector on Doctor---use party plan."

There were hundreds of such notations in Colonel Schwarzkopf's files. But Jafsie was painted, at the trial, as a patriot and public benefactor.

In spite of the good Doctor's refusal to participate in the reward (the declination came through second and third parties) the evidence is clear that he attempted to commercialize on his participation in the Lindbergh case. He advertised himself under the management of Lester Lockwood as available for appearances in vaudeville or motion-picture theaters. He exhibited himself in store windows with replicas of the kidnap ladder, Hauptmann's tools, and other real or fancied exhibits of "evidence."

He told, at Lynn, Massachusetts, a fantastic story of having been offered $250,000 to change his testimony and throw the blame for the Lindbergh crime on Isidor Fisch. He told (and I have affidavits to support these statements) a story of protecting the name of a woman in the case. "Supposing," he said to Arthur Sullivan, a reporter for the *News*, of New York, "there were a family in which most of the members were bad but one of them was very good, and suppose the good one came to you and went down on her knees, asking your protection. Wouldn't you do everything to shield her name?" "The Doctor, Sullivan adds, said that he would "carry her name a secret until I die."

Condon, long after Hauptmann was arrested and after he is supposed to have identified him, was at the Raisford Prison Camp, in Florida, interviewing Samuel Garelick, a Bayonne youth imprisoned for kidnapping, and still making an apparent effort to find "John" to whom he paid Colonel Lindbergh's money.

Rambling, inconsistent, volatile, garrulous Jafsie---from material in hand, I could write volumes about him. But I must go on---to other phases of my story.

His age, it may be pleaded, offers an excuse for his digressions from the path of accuracy and consistency. But the point as I see it, is that, largely upon his incoherent testimony, a human life was taken and a case that was a wanton challenge to society has been marked, in the police records, as "closed".

And with that we conclude this amazing evidence brought together by the governor of the state of New Jersey, Harold G. Hoffman; one person who believed it his business to make a thorough and complete study and investigation of the crime. Harold G. Hoffman, a man willing to sacrifice his political future in an honest attempt to reveal the real truth about the Lindbergh kidnapping.

When we come to understand this truth, emblazoned by the unfortunate fact that, because the public, the authorities, and the jury in their effort to see justice done, at any cost, were willing to be gullible enough to believe the "stack of lies" told by this man, one who painted himself as a "patriotic saint", cannot help but make us very, very nauseous.

C H A P T E R   T W E N T Y   E I G H T

Ay Docktor!

Many other irregularities were to raise their ugly heads as the Hauptmann trial proceeded; irregularities that added to the mass confusion that already existed, largely due to the outright lies and "poor memories" of the witnesses. Because of this we must first study more discrepancies in the testimony of the "eminent doctor of many letters" as he released his "batch of lies" regarding the voice he and Colonel Lindbergh claimed they heard on the night of Saturday, April 2nd, 1932 as they waited for "John" to appear at St. Raymond's Cemetery.

First we have the discrepancy of what the Colonel claims he heard in variance to what Condon said he heard. Surely the acute hearing of Lindbergh, which enabled him to "identify" the voice he remembered hearing two-and-one-half years earlier, should certainly have been of great help to him in demonstrating his ability to remember exactly what the words of that person had been, when he called to the Doctor as he waited for Condon to return to the car. At Flemington he testified he had heard the words, "Hey, Doctor."

Governor Hoffman raised an interesting question when he said it was hard for him to understand why "the kidnapper and murderer" would have dared to shout to Condon. The doctor was standing just outside the cemetery, with "John" close-by on the inside, and yet the "supposed abductor" was nervy enough to call out so loudly that persons within a few hundred feet of him could have heard his call, causing their attention to be drawn to the unusual activity in the cemetery at that time of night.

Regardless of this, however, we must go along with their story that "John" did shout and the following miss-mash of statements is what Lindbergh and Condon claim they heard.

On May 20, 1932 in a signed statement to Inspector Harry Walsh, Colonel Lindbergh said: "A voice from the cemetery called, "Ay, Doctor."

But, thirty months later, on September, 26, 1934, to the Bronx Grand Jury in answer to this question by District Attorney Sam Foley: "Did you receive any impression as to whether or not the voice you heard was a voice of a foreigner or a man of foreign extraction?", Lindbergh answered: "It undoubtedly was. It was a very distinct foreign accent. The voice simply called to Doctor Condon, saying, '<u>Hey</u>, <u>doc</u>,' but there was a very distinct accent."

How Colonel Lindbergh could detect a "very distinct accent" when he merely heard two words, each one a single syllable, is quite difficult to understand and very hard to accept as factual. During the passing of time since the kidnapping, I have heard those same words repeated by several persons who came from foreign countries and, other than the volume and pitch of their voice, it was virtually impossible to detect or determine, by hearing just two words, from which country they came. Even to accept the stressful condition Lindbergh was under at the time, I cannot be persuaded to agree, after the passing of two and one half years of time, with this most preposterous statement that he was certain, beyond any doubt, that the voice was the same.

In support of my contention, we have only to select another statement made by Lindbergh when he appeared before this same Bronx Grand Jury and was asked: "Do you think you would recognize that man's voice if you heard it again?" And in answer to this the Colonel replied: "<u>I can't say positively</u> I remember the voice very clearly. I would recognize the voice to be identical with the one I heard. It would be very difficult for me to sit here and <u>say that I could pick a man by that voice</u>."

Now here we have the kidnapped child's father testifying under three different occasions and giving three different versions of "exactly" what he supposedly heard "John" call to Doctor Condon.

Was it "<u>Hey</u>, <u>Doctor</u>"? Was it "<u>Ay</u>, <u>Doctor</u>"? Or was it "<u>Hey</u>, <u>Doc</u>"? You could use your best speculation and take a good guess, after, of course, you decide on which foreign accent you care to choose.

We should now examine exactly what Doctor Condon claims he heard. To Inspector Harry Walsh, in a statement taken at Hopewell on May 13, 1932, Condon said: "I started to walk away, but some one from the cemetery yelled, '<u>Hey</u>, <u>Doc</u>, <u>here I am</u>!'"

But, on May 20, 1932, just seven days later, as he testified before the Bronx Grand Jury, he said: "I turned to go back ... and some one yelled out, '<u>Hey</u>, <u>Doc</u>.'"

A month later, on June 21, 1932, the record tells us that while at Alpine, New Jersey, he told Inspector Walsh: "I was called by the man ... he said "<u>Doc</u>." Yet, five days later, on June 26, 1932, he claimed, in testimony given to Detective Leon, also at Alpine, that: "<u>The</u> <u>man</u> <u>called</u> '<u>Doc</u>, <u>Doc</u>.'"

None of the officers seemed to care enough about these discrepancies to question Condon, and pin him down with a conclusion as to what exactly "John's" words had been. But the variances do not end here.

Doctor Condon, while being questioned on March 23, 1934, stated: "I walked a short distance, when I heard some one call, '<u>Doc</u>'". This last bit of testimony was given six months before the arrest of Richard Hauptmann, the German Bronx carpenter, who would soon be tried as the lone kidnapper of the Lindbergh baby.

How conveniently Condon's story was now being bent, formed and shaped to fit the "German beast" Bruno Hauptmann (a name he never used from the time he entered America), but had now been tacked on him by the police and the press in an effort to make their prisoner appear and sound more brutal. The establishment conveniently used every means to change the original "conspiracy" theory into a solid conviction that "Hauptmann had acted alone." The following examples clearly show the intent and purpose of Condon to agreeably go along with this, persuaded, of course, by the urging of the police and prosecution.

In his book *Jafsie Tells All*, (page 149), he relates the call to him by "John" and leaves no doubt in anyone's mind that he was dealing with no one other than a German. He wrote: "Instantly, from behind one of the monuments fronting Whittemore Avenue, the <u>guttural</u> <u>voice</u> of the kidnapper called: '<u>Hey</u>, <u>Docktor</u>! <u>Over</u> <u>here</u>! <u>Over</u> <u>here</u>!'"

But, on the stand at Flemington, realizing that he no longer needed to describe the voice as guttural since his role was now to personally identify Hauptmann, his description of what took place was: "<u>Some</u> <u>one</u> <u>said</u> <u>in</u> <u>a</u> <u>very</u> <u>loud</u>, <u>clear</u> <u>tone</u>, '<u>Hey</u>, <u>Doctor</u>, <u>over</u> <u>here</u>.'"

How was it possible for two men to tell so many different versions of what had taken place in a crime of such magnitude, one in which a man's very life depended on the honesty and integrity of witnesses who had been sworn to relate the truth? The jury, however, certainly cannot be held responsible since only one of these "concocted stories" had been told at Flemington. After all, what else could any jury do but believe what it was told by two such well respected God fearing citizens, whose integrity could not be doubted. What the Flemington jury heard was: "Hey, Doctor, over here." Had they heard the assemblage of "Ay, Doctor,"..."Hey, Doc," ... "Doc, Doc," ... "Hey, Doc, here I am," ... "Hey, Doctor," ... "Hey, Docktor (guttural), ...and "Hey, Doctor, over here, over here." it is very doubtful the members of the jury would have placed much faith in the testimony of both men. Or would they? After all, these two men were gallant heros, while Hauptmann was nothing more than a brutal beast according to the picture being painted of him.

Before we take a look at some of the other liars who were involved in the Lindbergh case, it is only proper that we examine the absolute absurdity of Condon's "ridiculous reasoning" as to why he did not make a positive identification of Hauptmann being "Cemetery John" when he first confronted the prisoner in the Greenwich Street Police Station. Here, as he was brought face to face with Hauptmann, he demonstrated his first sign of doubt as to Hauptmann's guilt, when asked by Inspector Lyons: "Would you say he is the man?" and had given this answer: "He resembles the man. I can see a resemblance, but I cannot swear to it".

Later, after studying Hauptmann in the Bronx office of District Attorney Samuel J. Foley, and examining many pictures of him in profile, three-quarter profile, and full-face poses, and in spite of the constant prodding of the police, urging him to make a definite announcement that they had the right man, Condon still refused to identify Hauptmann as "John".

Next, in the jail in Flemington, after talking to Hauptmann in his cell for more than an hour, the doctor was heard to say that he could "never testify against this man." Standing outside the cell at the time, and within hearing distance, was Anthony M. Hauck, Jr., of Hunterdon County, one of the prosecuting attorneys, who denied later that he had heard such a statement. Nevertheless, we have the condemned man's word for the exclamation being uttered by the doctor; and in light of the fact that someone of authority, most certainly, would have been standing close to the cell; and since so many untruths had already been issued by so many people for the good of the state's case, we should give Hauptmann the benefit of any doubt, and believe that his hearing had been perfect.

In support of Hauptmann's report of Condon's visit to his cell, we have a statement made by the condemned man's spiritual advisor, Reverend D.G. Werner, as he told of a conversation he had with Hauptmann pertaining to the visit. The following is a portion of the prisoner's conversation with Reverend Werner: "I was glad when Dr.Condon was called to the stand," he told me. "I thought to myself, 'Now that old man will clear me!' I had reason for thinking so."

"Some weeks before my trial started, he came to see me in the jail at Flemington. We talked for a long, long time. Over an hour, I think it must have been. When he got up to leave, the Doctor said: '<u>I never can (or I never will</u>') <u>testify against this man</u>!""

"This disclosure startled me. I gazed at Hauptmann in astonishment. His eyes were fixed intently on mine. I opened my mouth to ask a question, but he stopped me with a gesture and continued:

"Pastor, I myself heard him say those words. I am so careful in repeating it to you that I give you both versions. I am not sure if he said 'I never can' or 'I never will.' Mr. Hauck was standing right there, and I am sure he must have heard it, too."

"Now, remembering this, how could I believe that Dr. Condon would stand up in the courtroom--as he did--and point his finger at me and shout, 'John is Bruno Richard Hauptmann!'"

"Yes, pastor, Mr. Hauck did hear Dr. Condon. I know he did. He was there, outside the bars of my cell, and when the Doctor jumped to his feet, very excited, shouting that he never would (or could) identify me, Mr. Hauck tried to calm him down. He told him, in soothing tones, 'It will be all right, Doctor; it will be all right.' This is true, pastor, and I am giving you every word just as I heard it that day."

We can well understand why Hauptmann, after sitting in the open courtroom and hearing Condon accuse him of being the mysterious "John", would insist that the Bronx educator would pay him another visit in the Flemington jail. "I want to see Dr. Condon. I want him to come here, in this jail, and talk to me!", he pleaded. Richard became extremely anxious to learn what had persuaded Condon to change his mind. Pastor Werner, also dismayed at Condon's reversal of opinion, questioned Hauptmann again and again, in a soul-searching way, for his own opinion as to why Condon had identified him, when originally, he had been so determined that he would not, or could not, testify against him. Reverend Werner received this explanation to his question:

"This is the question I would like to ask Dr. Condon. I would like to put it to him in person. Why, did he change his mind after saying he would not identify me? Who talked to him and what was said? I would like to ask the Doctor if he would dare to face me here and deny that he made that statement in my presence."

Reverend Werner went on to tell what took place prior to Condon's amazing Flemington cell declaration that he "never could" or "never would" testify against Hauptmann. Here is exactly the way Hauptmann related it to the minister, first telling him that the aged educator sat down beside him and asked: "Richard, are you the man I talked to in the cemetery?" To which Hauptmann responded: "I never saw you until that day in the Bronx courthouse."

Then, not content with this denial, Jafsie kept repeating the question---Hauptmann---did not know how many times---receiving the same answer each time: "I do not know you. I saw you only once before, and that was in the Bronx."

It was at this point that Condon shouted his surprising declaration that he would not testify against the accused man.

Condon's answers to questions in his cross-examination by defense attorney Reilly regarding his failure to make an identification of Hauptmann before the trial were certainly void of good reasons, nor were they valid poor excuses, but rather ones that bordered on the ridiculous. The questioning follows:

Q. Did you see any newspaper men while you were there? A. Plenty.

Q. Did you tell them at that time that Hauptmann was not the John? A. No, sir.

Q. How many newspaper men did you see? A. Oh, I couldn't count them, they were flocking in there in such droves that I couldn't count them.

Q. How many interviews did you give? A. I couldn't state that they were interviews, but I had conversations with anybody that came to my room or to my table.

Q. They asked you about this case didn't they? A. They did.

Q. Yes. You never once told any newspaper man that this defendant was John, did you? A. What defendant?

Q. This defendant here. A. Oh. I never did. I never told or mentioned his name to them or in public, never,--note the words Colonel--of affirmation or denial. I make a distinction between "identification" and declaration of identification."

Q. In other words, I am to understand that you split hairs in words? A. No hairs at all. A man's life is at stake and I want to be honest about it.

Q. There was nothing preventing you from telling the press, was there, that this was the right man? A. Yes, there was; yes, there was.

Q. If you wanted to be honest about it, why did you not blazon forth that fact to the world when they asked you? A. Because I didn't wish to do it and perhaps interfere with this case itself.

Q. If you were honest and telling the truth, do you not know that nothing could interfere with the truth, no matter how many times you said it was the man? A. It didn't. It didn't. It didn't interfere because I didn't say.

Q. In Greenwich Street, New York police station, you said it was not the man, did you not? A. No, sir. Get all the people that were there, I did not.

Q. You never said it was the man? A. I never said it was or was not.

Q. Because you know you are not sure? A. Because I made the distinction between declaration and identification. The identification meant what I knew mentally, the declaration meant what I said to others. There isn't a man who breathes who ever heard me say that that was the man but one.

Q. You were brought there for the purpose of identifying Hauptmann, were you not? A. I was, yes, sir.

Q. And you didn't identify him, did you? A. No, sir. Beg pardon, there is the word "identification" again. I take exception to your language. It would make a mistake and when you begin to divide the identification and declaration and denial, you would make it appear as though I were dishonest and I am not. I won't--is that too severe, Judge?

The Court: No.

Q. Come on, I can take it. A. That is good. I want you to know, Counselor, that the identification is purely a mental process after the senses have known, after the senses have distinguished, and unless that is taken that way to answer quickly, fast, I don't know but what it might be a kind of trap that you were getting me. The <u>declaration</u> is where I tell it to others. <u>Identification</u> is what I know myself.

Q. And that is what you think is the common definition of identification, is it? A. No, I don't think that way at all.

Q. Now you are talking down here to a lot of plain people. Do you understand that? A. I do perfectly.

Q. Yes, plain people, and identification means only one thing, the picking out of a person. A. Yes.

Q. Did you ever announce the identification of this defendant? A. I did.

Q. In any court of law before today? A. I did not.

Q. And nobody had any muzzle on you, did they? A. Nobody. But, if you will allow me--

Q. Please answer my question. A. Yes.

Q. And how many times in the past two years--- A. What?

Q. have you been asked concerning "John?" A. I don't---

Q. How many times in the past two years have you been asked by anybody about "John?" A. I didn't count how many times, but---

Q. Numerous, weren't they, thousands? A. Right; right; curiosity seekers.

Q. You wouldn't call Inspector Sullivan of the Police Department of New York a curiosity seeker, would you? A. I didn't tell him pro nor con.

Q. No. A. Or con.

Q. You wouldn't call a judge that sat in the extradition proceedings up in the Bronx a curiosity seeker, would you? A. What do you mean?

Q. Judge Hadding, is that the name? A. I don't know anything about that.

The Reporter: Hammer.

Q. Judge Hammer. Do you know Judge Hammer of the Bronx? A. Very well, but I wasn't before him.

Q. Well, the State didn't call you, did they? A. (No answer.)

Q. Neither New York nor Jersey called you, did they? A. You will have to specify when.

Q. When Bruno Richard Hauptmann was on trial for extradition only two or three months ago, in October, in The Bronx, and you with the secret locked in your heart---you were not called, were you? A. Only by the Jury---under---under---

Q. I am talking about that proceeding---were you

called? A. No.

Q. And that proceeding was after you saw Bruno Richard Hauptmann in Greenwich Street and Centre Street? A. To the best of my recollection, yes.

From the Flemington testimony of Doctor Condon, we find him bending to the probing questions of Attorney Reilly, and then finally admitting that he had not been called to testify against Hauptmann in the Bronx courtroom. The only reason Jafsie had not been called is extremely apparent. Condon simply had not, up to that time, been able to identify the prisoner as "Cemetery John", the man he had met with on the nights of Saturday, March 12 and April 2, 1932.

In support of his inability to identify Hauptmann prior to the Bronx extradition hearing, we have Condon taking a trip to Florida for the sole purpose of visiting the Raisford Prison Camp. Here he interviewed a man named Samuel Garelick, a prisoner whom the authorities there believed was the "John" that Condon was still searching for. This trip was made, along with others, quite some time after the professor had seen Hauptmann in the Bronx. Condon, in his confused state, was having a difficult time deciding just who was going to be his "guilty John."

Another interesting point should be made regarding the doctor's court testimony; that was his reluctance to mention Hauptmann by name as he answered the many questions. At all times he referred to the accused man only as "John". Surely, by this time, Condon knew quite well he had been called for the primary and important purpose of linking Hauptmann to the crime. And yet, he was hesitant to a fault to speak the name of Hauptmann, until he was afforded the opportunity to answer the direct question which allowed him to blast forth boldly with the theatrics of an accomplished actor, and announce: "John is Bruno Richard Hauptmann."

Condon's inability to vocally mention the name Hauptmann throughout the trial demonstrates the great probability that his conscience was giving him pangs of guilt. Guilt which was brought on because he was certain he had been called on to identify a man whom he knew, within his innermost thoughts, was an innocent victim.

Anthony Scaduto in his book *Scapegoat* gives rise to some interesting questions about the amazing Doctor Condon: "For example in recreating the trip he made with Al Reich to Woodlawn Cemetery, where he met John for the first time, Condon testified,'I got out of the car with the letter that I had picked up at the frankfurter stand and went over to the middle of that space, like a little piazza or area in front of the gates. I took the letter out. One man walked down 233rd Street in the direction of the automobile, between me and the automobile. Mr. Reich was in the automobile and I saw this man come down there, but I didn't pay any attention or any account to him.'

"Almost immediately, he said, he saw a handkerchief being waved inside the gate. The man waving it turned out to be John.

"But who was the first man? I wondered. Condon was convinced he was dealing with a gang, including the Italian who had said "statto citti" and the Italian woman who asked him to meet her at the Tuckahoe station. I thought: If he was so convinced a gang was involved, wouldn't he have believed this man he first saw at the cemetery was a lookout? Wouldn't he be very curious about this man? He most certainly would have been. Then why did he skim over it so lightly in his testimony and in his book?

"Again, I wondered once more why there was no mention of the Italian man Condon had heard over the telephone and the Italian woman who had approached him at the charity bazaar. But now my suspicions went even further. Obviously, the defense didn't know about these two incidents which established that more than one man had been involved in the extortion plot. Just as obvious, the prosecution had suppressed this evidence because it would have made a mockery of the claim that Hauptmann had acted alone. And if that evidence was kept from the defense and public, how much other evidence helpful to Hauptmann had been similarly concealed.

"Another question: During Condon's long recital of his experiences with John, he again slid quickly past an incident which could be vitally important. After the ransom had been paid, Condon told federal agents, John had climbed a low railing in the cemetery and leaped to the other side, landing on a freshly dug grave. Perhaps he had left his footprint, Condon suggested. Condon returned to the cemetery accompanied by his son-in-law, Ralph Hacker, and federal agent Thomas Sisk. They found a print where Condon said it might be. A plaster of paris cast of that footprint was made. But it was never introduced into evidence. Had it matched Hauptmann's shoe, I was certain, the prosecutor would have put it into evidence because he held back no evidence in his files that could have convicted Hauptmann. His failure to use the plaster cast against the prisoner must have meant that it didn't match Hauptmann's shoes. Was this also deliberately suppressed?"

Yes, it was these, and a multitude of other things that caused "Tony" Scaduto to seethe when he realized the unfairness of the trial; the manipulation of Condon's testimony in order to "prove" to the jury that Hauptmann had acted alone.

As I add my own thoughts to the plaster cast of the footprint on the freshly dug grave, it brings forth a question. Why, with a federal agent present, did he allow Hacker, Condon's son-in-law, to make the moulage? Here we have a government agent, assigned to perform a very important official police duty in an attempt to obtain concrete evidence in the nation's most famous kidnapping case, allowing a rank amateur, Hacker, to perform the task.

We can be certain that the print found in St. Raymond's Cemetery had not been that of Hauptmann. And we can be just as certain that the footprint found below the nursery window at Hopewell was not his. Had either one, or both, even slightly resembled his, we can be more than certain the authorities would have broadcast this evidence to the highest rafters of the Flemington courtroom.

As we uncover the "truth" of the other "undeniable evidence" against Hauptmann, as the state referred to it, we cannot help but notice a stench of something "undeniably rotten" permeating these pages.

CHAPTER TWENTY NINE

Never Doubt --- "An Expert"

Albert S. Osborn, a resident of Montclair, New Jersey, who maintained a business office at 233 Broadway in New York City, identified himself in pompous fashion as "an examiner of questioned documents, disputed handwriting and typewriting, ink, paper and so forth." To put it bluntly, he was the first of a battery of eight "big guns" the state used to pepper Hauptmann with their accusations that he, and he alone, and there could be no doubt about it, had written every one of the fourteen ransom letters. These were the handwriting "experts" who confused the jury so badly that they were left with no alternative other than their belief that "because they said so", and they were the experts, Hauptmann undoubtedly had written every thing that was written or even printed.

Osborn and his cohorts, with their unfair and biased testimony, in a very significant way, helped destroy any likelihood of an acquittal for Richard Hauptmann. But don't take our word for it. Examine the true evidence for yourself.

The great Albert S.Osborn presented himself as having the greatest set of credentials. His braggadocio "trumpeted" his possession of great expertise in his chosen profession. He claimed he had testified in courts on the subject of handwriting for a period of time "upwards of thirty years," and that he had appeared as a witness in courts in 39 states of the USA, various parts of Canada, Newfoundland, and Puerto Rico. He stated that he had evidence in cases submitted to him from London, England and New Zealand, and that he was the author of two books on the subject of handwriting; the one titled *Questioned Documents*, the other *The Problem of Proof*.

But, in spite of all this man's fame as an "expert" and an author, we must register our firm denial, from beginning to end, that his testimony against Hauptmann was not conclusive in any way. You will learn that Osborn and his seven "sanctimonious buddies" were no more certain as to who wrote those "documents", as they had come to be called, than Snow White and her Seven Dwarfs. You will find that the handwriting evidence used against Hauptmann was false from the very word go. Bruno Richard Hauptmann, based on overwhelmingly conclusive evidence, never wrote those ransom notes. We can only take a good guess as to who did write them, but they most certainly were written by someone other than Hauptmann. The handwriting testimony of the "experts", which lasted for hours, proved to be boring to the jury and the spectators as well. Osborn and his seven associates, with their giant charts exhibited behind them, went about, with great flourish, pointing out the "great number of similarities" in the writings which "to them were quite apparent" in all of the fourteen notes.

Throughout Osborn's lengthy discourse, the elderly "wizard" of writing, displayed by means of "courtroom theatrics", his method of tracing the course of the various downstrokes, the upswings, the thickness of letters and numerals, their pressures and other persuasions of his "magical" influence, all of which caused the honest, but bewildered, members of the jury to render at the end of the trial, what each one believed to be "an honest verdict."

It is not necessary to repeat the "tiring" dissertation of these eight handwriting experts. Anyone interested in reading what each man testified, can surely find it in the official trial transcript. It was tiring double-talk, presented in glowing terms by men whose "integrity and facts demonstrated" were not to be denied. The testimony was largely dull, monotonous, and repetitious. It nearly lulled most of the gallery of spectators, as well as those of the jury, into a state of semi-sleep. But, regardless of the well sounding assertions and declarations of "truth" in their testimony, we, who stand in Hauptmann's corner, aware of his innocence, deem it our solemn obligation to his wife Anna, to tell you the pure and unadulterated facts that should have been presented at the Flemington trial, but were not for obvious reasons.

Ludovic Kennedy, one of Great Britain's foremost journalists and broadcasters, is not just another man who is convinced of Hauptmann's innocence. In 1985 he published his monumental work on the Lindbergh case after making an exhaustive study of the crime. Kennedy leaves no doubt about the complete innocence of the unfortunate Richard Hauptmann.

Because the noted British author accomplished such a remarkable piece of reporting the many facets of the case, I have borrowed the following from his book, *The Airman and the Carpenter*. He relates so well the facts that must be known the world over; about the unfairness of the handwriting evidence used in the court proceedings.

Kennedy's report begins as he relates the happenings that took place in the 2nd Precinct Police station in Greenwich Village late on the night of Hauptmann's arrest: "It was now getting on for midnight, and Schwarzkopf was keen for one of the Osborns to give an opinion on Hauptmann's handwriting. So he telephoned the father, Albert S., aged seventy, at his home in Montclair, New Jersey; he said he was in bed and not feeling too good but if the matter was urgent, why not get in touch with his son? The son, Albert D., agreed to go to his office in the Woolworth Building, where presently Sergeant Ritchie and Agent Turrou delivered to him the copies of the two statements that Hauptmann had written as well as other samples of his writing found by police in his apartment. There were nine other specimens of his writing located in his apartment. There were nine sheets of dictated writing in all; two of the first statement and seven of the second. Sisk, who glanced at them before they went, said it was obvious that Hauptmann had tried to disguise his writing. In fact the police officers supervising the writing had asked Hauptmann to write the seven versions with three different pens, some with an upright hand and some slanting; so there were even greater discrepancies between the various copies of the dictated writings than there were between the dictated writings and the ransom notes.

"Schwarzkopf and the others had little doubt that Osborn would declare that Hauptmann was the writer of the ransom notes. But for Osborn, apart from the lateness of the hour, this was a routine assignment (the news of Hauptmann's arrest had not broken in the papers) and he wanted to take his time. After Ritchie and Turrou had handed over the samples, he asked them to wait. They waited fifteen minutes. Unconvinced that Hauptmann had written the ransom notes, Osborn asked if he could be given some printed specimens by him, particularly the name and address of Dr. Condon as it had appeared on the envelopes of the ransom notes. Turrou and Ritchie hastened back to Greenwich Street with this information, Hauptmann was set to work writing out Condon's name and address, and Turrou, this time with Zapolsky, retraced his steps to Osborn. Asked if he had yet formed an opinion, all Osborn would say was that the samples were 'interesting', and that he would telephone Schwarzkopf with an opinion when he had one.

"Convinced that Hauptmann was guilty, yet frustrated by Osborn's reluctance to confirm it, the police now resorted to their own methods of obtaining proof. We want you to write some more, they said. Hauptmann, by now exhausted, said he couldn't, he hadn't slept for twenty-four hours, and Kloppenburg who was also writing for them heard them say, 'You'd better write, it's bad for you if you don't,' and they hit Hauptmann in the ribs once or twice to keep him awake. 'You write,' they said to him, 'you write.'

"This time Hauptmann was told to spell certain words as they had been spelled in the ransom notes. 'I was told to write exactly as it was dictated to me,' he said, 'and this included writing words spelled as I was told to spell them.' Kloppenburg said the same. 'I had to copy it the way it was spelt.' Many of the words mis-spelt in the ransom notes seem to have been done so haphazardly, without any recognizable pattern and, some think, deliberately. Among those Hauptmann was instructed to copy were 'bee' ('be'), 'The' ('They'), 'note' ('not'), 'mony' ('money'), and 'hte' ('the'), which last appeared only once in the ransom notes but <u>three times</u> in Hauptmann's dictated writings, according to evidence of handwriting expert John F.Tyrrell, (Testimony Page Trial 1168.) Hauptmann was a good speller, and one has only to look at the reproduction of his letter to Mrs. Begg (page 133) to see that he knew perfectly well how to spell 'money' (which he was dealing in every day at Steiner, Rouse) and 'not' and 'the'. 'Be' also is one of the first English words a foreigner learns, and when the notes were written Hauptmann had been in the States for ten years. Other words he was told to mis-spell were 'singnature' ('signature'), 'were' ('where'), 'ouer' ('our'), 'haus' ('house'), 'gut' ('good'), 'letter' ('later') and 'Sond' ('Sound') all of which had been mis-spelt in the ransom notes.

"In addition to the mis-spelt words in the dictation of the composite statements, Hauptmann was also told <u>to copy</u> both the two composite statements <u>and</u> the photostats of the actual ransom notes. There are a number of sources for this, the main ones being the *New York Times* of September 22 which reported, "The New York

Police disclosed that they had caused Hauptmann to copy the notes',that of Osborn Senior when he wrote of Hauptmann 'copying the prepared matter and other matter', (Albert S. Osborn. *Question Document Problems*), and of Agent Turrou who spoke of Hauptmann 'having to work constantly at adding curlicues to 'y's or crossing 't's in different ways'. He was also told to write a passage without dotting his 'i's (he almost always dotted his 'i's) because 'i's were not dotted in the ransom notes; to write many capital 'N's as '-'s (as on the ransom notes); and to write with the left hand (it was thought that the first five lines of the nursery note had been written with the left hand). 'If I had known at the time,' Hauptmann wrote later, 'to what use the writing was to be put, I would never have undertaken the dictation.

"At around 4 a.m. the telephone rang. Schwarzkopf took it and when he heard it was Osborn, raised his hand for silence. According to Sisk, who was there, Schwarzkopf 'listened to what Mr. Osborn had to say for several minutes and then inquired as to whether further specimens would help out any, after which he remarked, 'We'll send them over.' He then hung up the receiver and advised those present, 'It doesn't look so good. He says that when he first looked at the specimens he thought they were the same, and that there were some striking similarities, but after examining them for a while he found a lot of dissimilarities...and he is convinced he did not write the ransom notes.' 'His father is coming to examine them in the morning first thing. I told him we would give them more specimens to work with, but he doesn't think that would change his opinion.'

"Other police officers than those present might have paused to consider whether they might be barking up the wrong tree, and that anyway at this late hour enough was enough. But Osborn's verdict seems to have goaded Schwarzkopf and the others into even greater activity. More 'specimens' were demanded of Hauptmann, not just the two statements again but, said Turrou, other matter such as the *Wall Street Journal* and the *Congressional Record* into which Turrou admitted 'interjecting a word or two from the ransom notes now and then'. Bornmann, who must have been getting almost as sleepy as Hauptmann, said, 'Why don't you tell the truth, Richard, and get it over with? Why don't you get it off your mind?' "For what remained of that night, he was allowed to doze in his chair; but the questioning went on."

We must keep in mind that at that hour the search of the Hauptmann home and garage had not been completed. Officers from the New York City Police, the New Jersey State Police, and the Federal government continued their task the following morning, and at about 10 o'clock they agreed that they had found nothing incriminating in their search of the prisoner's home. Their attention was now centered on the demolition of the Hauptmann garage. It was here they "struck pay dirt" as they uncovered $13,760 of Lindbergh ransom money , with another $840 found soon after. However, with their initial find of $13,760, they were now certain they had the "absolute proof" of Hauptmann's guilt. Word of their important discovery was passed along rapidly, reaching the bastille where Hauptmann was being held. And with the news came a more intensified series of questions which they felt sure would "break their prisoner" into a certain admission of guilt. Ludovic Kennedy continues with his report of the events which followed:

"This news was speedily conveyed to Greenwich Street where two things happened. First Lieutenant Finn telephoned the Woolworth Building where the Osborns, father and son, had been studying Hauptmann's request and acknowledged writings for the past two hours without finding anything to alter the son's previously declared opinion. Now Finn told them that the suspect whose writing they had been examining was under arrest, and that nearly $14,000 of the ransom money had been found hidden in his garage. Would they be good enough to reconsider their verdict?

"This news put the Osborns in something of a fix. It was true that certain characteristics in both the ransom notes and Hauptmann's various writings -- uncrossed 't's, 'x's formed like back to back 'e's, 'g's shaped like 'y's -- indicated the writers of both as having German as their first language. It was also true that there were many mis---spellings common to both the ransom notes and the request writings. But when they compared the writings found in Hauptmann's house (a surer guide, they knew, than anything coming out of a police station) with the ransom notes, and saw how different were the formation of words and letters, the angle at which they were written, the shading, the spacing between words and lines, they knew that the writer of the one was certainly not the writer of the other.

"And yet, supposing they were wrong! They had

both been wrong before, and had seen plaintiffs or defendants for whom they had testified lose their cases in court. (In thirty-seven years' time the son was to make the biggest mistake of his career in testifying along with another four "experts", that writings said to be that of Howard Hughes but forged by Clifford Irving was genuine.) If the police were as certain as they seemed to be that the man they had arrested had written the ransom notes, who were they to contradict them? Less than an hour after Finn's call, Osborn Senior rang Schwarzkopf to say that the author of the specimens was also the author of the ransom notes. When this news was passed on to the other police officers in Greenwich Street, they burst out laughing. 'Those handwriting experts!' they said. 'Oh, boy!'"

Anthony Scaduto, in his book *Scapegoat* delved deeply into the value of the testimony of the prosecution's "so-called handwriting experts" as it was offered in the Hauptmann trial. I quote from his excellent treatise on the case:

"Wilentz led Osborn through a lecture on the art and science of identifying disputed writings, as one journalist of the day put it. Art and science? Nonsense. American courts have held repeatedly that the testimony of so-called handwriting experts represents the lowest degree of evidence, and with good reason. The analysis of questioned documents is neither science nor art. It is a very subjective process in which the examiner looks for "similarities" between two sets of writings and, depending on whether or not he finds enough similarities, renders his <u>opinion</u>. Legal scholars to this day question the value of such opinions, primarily because each side in a legal dispute always manages to find enough experts to support its particular contention.

"The value of handwriting analysis is questionable, moreover, because so many "experts" have so often been proved dead wrong. For example, a short time before the trial one of the handwriting experts who testified against Hauptmann had helped convict an innocent man by swearing the defendant had forged a number of checks. Again, Albert S. Osborn's son, who also testified against Hauptmann, still headed the family firm in 1971 when it reported there wasn't 'the slightest question' that Clifford Irving's forgery of the handwriting of Howard Hughes had actually been written by Hughes; further, the Osborns said, it was 'impossible as a practical matter, based on our years of experience ... that anyone other than' Hughes could have written the letters written by Irving. Further evidence from the Hughes-Irving fiasco shows how "scientific" this field is, even with improvement in techniques in the forty years since the Hauptmann trial. Alfred Kanfer, another handwriting authority, was asked to compare Irving's forgeries with authentic handwriting by Hughes. After studying the materials, Kanfer said they'd been written by Hughes and asserted: 'The chances that another person could copy this handwriting even in a similar way are less than one in a million.' Finally, another piece of evidence attesting to the extreme fallibility of handwriting experts emerged in 1970, during one of Hughes's many court battles. In this one, the former commander of the FBI forgery school gave it as his expert opinion that a document purportedly signed by Hughes was a forgery. Later events in court proved that Hughes had indeed signed it.

"But to return to the transcript of the Hauptmann trial: Bulletin boards are wheeled into the courtroom. On them are dozens of photograph blowups of letters, words, sentences. Osborn the elder steps down from the witness chair and over to the photos, takes pointer in hand, and begins his lecture. He is questioned only occasionally by Wilentz.

"He explains to the jury: 'The thirty pieces of script before us include fourteen ransom notes and sixteen specimens of Hauptmann's known writings. Among his known writings are some of the pages he wrote as police dictated to him at Greenwich Street in the days after his arrest. We will break down all these writings into three categories: the disputed ransom notes; the 'conceded writings,' such as Hauptmann's automobile license applications; and the 'request writings,' done at the dictation of police.

'Have you made a careful comparison and examination of the so-called ransom notes with the conceded writings and the request writings of Bruno Richard Hauptmann?' Wilentz asks.

'I have.'

'Based on your examination and comparison, what is the opinion you have reached?'

'My opinion is that the ransom notes were all written by the writer of the various papers signed 'Richard Hauptmann.''

'Explain the reasons.'

"In the first of several lengthy, rambling lectures, Osborn said he'd found all the writings were connected with each other in a large number of ways, a number of which were outside the question of handwriting. By that he meant, he said, a discernible pattern in the use of words and the peculiar spelling connecting them; the fact that the second note referred to ideas expressed in the first note, such as the amount of the ransom, and each note that followed made reference to something previously written; the crude symbol with the three circles and three holes found on all notes, so that when all the notes were placed one upon the other, the three holes matched so perfectly that by holding them to the light 'you can see right through the holes.' Here the reporters scribbled more quickly to record his implication that the kidnapper had punched holes through a pad of paper at one time, tearing off a sheet whenever he wanted to write another note.

"Through almost all the eighth day of the trial and into the morning of the ninth, Osborn went over individual letters in the ransom script and in Hauptmann's writings to show that peculiarities in the ransom notes were the same as peculiarities in Hauptmann's writings. The witness dissected individual words to demonstrate that they appeared in all sets of writings. He summed it all up by saying the evidence proving Hauptmann had written the ransom notes was 'irresistible, unanswerable, and overwhelming.'

"Reilly took the witness for cross-examination. Handing Osborn two of the ransom notes, he said: 'I ask you whether there is, in your opinion, a visible difference between them?'

'Oh, there is a <u>little</u> variation,' Osborn replied, 'but in my opinion they are substantially the same.'

"Another note was handed him, one sent to Dr. Condon. 'Isn't the phrasing of the letters, the general outline, a little clearer than the preceding notes?'

'I would say that it is clearer than the nursery note and perhaps a little more freely written than some of the others, but it is essentially the same.'

'Well, is this disguised, in your opinion?'

'I think they are all disguised, all the ransom notes. That is, they are all disguised to a certain extent. That is, they are not natural, free writing.'

"<u>Disguised</u>. I turned back now to the earlier part of Osborn's speech, where he had originally brought up the theory of disguised writings. He had said: 'In my opinion the ransom letters are all written in a disguised hand, somewhat disguised.' Then he explained that it is customary, when taking a handwriting sample from a suspect, to have him write the same material three times. And then he went on:

'The writing is taken away and another sheet is supplied and the same matter dictated. Now, if they differ from each other it is not the habitual genuine honest writing of the writer. And that is exactly what we find in this request writing. In one instance we find it on the same sheet of paper. In my opinion these ransom notes are disguised writings, part of the request writings are disguised writings, and the writer didn't have but one disguise. So that when the request writings were asked for, part of them are written in the style of the ransom notes and part ... are like the writings of the automobile registrations' and a promissory note Hauptmann had signed.

"Wait a minute ... wait just a minute, I thought. From everything I'd read Hauptmann had been forced to write 'from dictation' for many hours. 'From nine that evening until early the next morning,' one handwriting authority in the employ of the prosecution later wrote, 'he covered page after page with writing.' Scores of pages, no doubt, perhaps a hundred or more, in those hours; on the ten pages of that dictation I was able to find reproduced in several books, police officers present had written the precise time of dictation, and they ranged from nine in the evening of September 19 to ten the next morning. It seemed plain that only a small portion of the pages he had written had been introduced into evidence and were used to demonstrate similarities between those writings and the ransom notes. Would it be unfair to suggest that prosecution witnesses had been very selective? That only those samples with the greatest similarities would do for their demonstration?

"Disguise? Or had it been weariness? The elder Osborn had said it was customary to have a subject write three times under dictation. One reason not to have a man write dozens of times would be the distortion in the handwriting that repetition naturally brings. There was also something else, I remembered from my readings in the Clifford Irving forgery. One of the Osborns who had wrongly attributed Irving's writings to Howard Hughes, while attempting to explain to interviewers how they'd made the error, had stressed two important procedures that an analyst must follow. One is to obtain samples of the subject's writings that have been written at roughly the same time as the questioned documents, because the style and character of handwriting changes;

that, of course, was not done in the Hauptmann case if only because his arrest came more than two years after the ransom notes had been written. Second, the analyst must make certain the samples have not been done deliberately for a specimen. 'Writing is a semiconscious act and it's as difficult to do naturally if you have been asked for a specimen as it is to walk into a room naturally if you are being filmed,' a member of the Osborn firm explained. The Hauptmann samples, then, were doubly unnatural: they were written under dictation as handwriting samples to be submitted to an expert, and they were written after Hauptmann had been told he was a suspect in the Lindbergh murder.

"The train of thought leaps back further as the mind filters and digests, as it recognizes nuances. Osborn had said the ransom letters were written in a disguised hand. 'Part of the request writings' were similarly disguised, he said; Hauptmann 'didn't have but one disguise.' The logic is defective: building a positive identification by placing disguise upon disguise with no glue to bind them is like building a house by placing brick upon brick and omitting the mortar. For if Hauptmann was the criminal genius Wilentz etched for us and had actually written the ransom letters in a disguised hand, would he then attempt to disguise the words he was writing for police? Hardly. He would write as naturally as possible so that the dictated writings wouldn't accidentally resemble the disguised writings in the ransom letters. To repeat the disguised writing would defeat the very reason for disguise. It would be absolute lunacy.

"Osborn and the other six witnesses agreed that Hauptmann wrote every one of the ransom notes. And as I read through their testimony I was struck by an odd omission. Osborn had said at the very beginning that the ransom note which had been left in the nursery was written by the same man who had written all the other notes. But he had made the statement, 'That first letter was written with more deliberation than any of the other letters, written somewhat more slowly and with more deliberation....' He quickly added that he was certain it had been written by the same man. Yet his statement quite explicitly pointed to differences. When I looked through all the handwriting testimony for a discussion of the first ransom note, I realized that every one of the prosecution's experts had ignored the letter found in the nursery. They made general statements that it had been written by the man who wrote all the later notes, but they offered no specifics. In all their charts breaking down the notes into sentences, words, and individual letters, only a single word, 'is,' was taken from the first ransom letter. They ignored thirty-nine other words and nine numerals. Was it because they could not say Hauptmann had written them? I found it all rather strange. My thoughts returned again to Mickey Rosner, the bootlegger and Lindbergh's "secretary," and the assertion that he had displayed the first ransom letter all over Manhattan, permitting it to be copied and recopied until many con men and thieves had an exact reproduction of it. Could that event, if it indeed occurred, be an explanation for something else Osborn said? 'The first two lines of the second letter are written with great deliberation,' said Osborn, 'and very distinctly like the writing in the first letter. The rest of the second letter is written somewhat more freely.'"

Tony Scaduto, an excellent police reporter and investigative journalist, had used little more than common logic in his study of the sworn testimony of the handwriting "wizard" Albert S. Osborn, as well as those of his associates, to arrive at the opinion that their deductions "should have been absolutely worthless." He wondered if it were possible that one person, the actual kidnapper, had written the first letter, and then had been scared off when he realized the baby had been killed? Scaduto then turned his thoughts to a second man, an extortionist, who possibly obtained a copy of the first letter and, after starting to write the second letter in the same style as the first, grew careless and continued to write the remainder of it "somewhat more freely." Is it possible this is what happened? Tony's mind raced on with more questions. A phrase in the testimony of Osborn's son, Albert D., leaped out at him. Once again I borrow from Scaduto's book to more clearly show his line of reasoning:

"He, too, swore Hauptmann wrote all the ransom letters. But when asked for specific reasons, he fell back primarily on the fact that certain words which had been misspelled in the ransom notes had also been misspelled by Hauptmann when the test paragraph was dictated to him again and again. Osborn was asked whether any of the words had been deliberately misspelled by the police as they dictated. He replied he didn't know 'of my own knowledge,' but insisted that could not have happened because he had the utmost confidence in the police and especially the federal agents. 'Of my own knowledge': how many witnesses have I heard or read about who avoided a direct perjury charge by denying personal knowledge of an event they have heard, secondhand, did take place? Men accustomed to testifying under oath and wise in the ways of legal deception repeatedly use that expression or variations of it---'to the best of my recollection' is another example---and though I could not know whether Osborn was deliberately fudging, those phrases have always been a warning signal for me. (Hauptmann, of course, swore when he took the stand in his own defense that all the misspellings had been dictated by police. I could no more take that as truth than I could take Condon's stories, for the defendant more than anyone else can be expected to lie. I would have to find other evidence to prove or disprove my suspicions.)"

Scaduto becomes more decisive as he continues to tell of many other erroneous statements of "findings and discoveries" that the Osborns claimed to be absolutely factual. These claims should never be doubted by anyone since "the infallible father and son" said they were "truthful statements that went far to prove Hauptmann's guilt in the crime. Tony's findings give us a completely different aspect, one we cannot deny, as he provides us with more reasonable and very believable arguments for Hauptmann's complete vindication. He writes;

"When Albert S. Osborn and his son, Albert D. Osborn, testified at Hauptmann's trial as the foremost experts on questioned documents the prosecution could find, they unequivocally declared Hauptmann had written all the ransom notes; there could be no question about it, they said, and there was no other possibility.

"But there are, in the documents at hand, several questions which make their conclusions less than perfect.

"To start, the elder Osborn in all his published work over more than thirty years had always maintained that any handwriting expert worthy of carrying the title would not attempt to arrive at an opinion until he had studied a large sampling of the suspect's undisputed writing and compared those writings with the originals of the writings in question, in this case of the ransom notes.

"Yet the elder Osborn, testifying at Hauptmann's extradition hearing three weeks after his arrest, said that he had worked from photographs, the handwriting experts have always said, tend to distort and should be avoided at all times. More revealing still is a letter from the elder Osborn to State Police Superintendent Schwarzkopf, dated September 21, 1934, the day after Hauptmann had completed his dozen hours of writing in the police station. In it, Osborn says he had 'examined a large number of writings' by Hauptmann and concludes that Hauptmann was the writer of the ransom notes. But in this brief report, as Osborn called it, he lays particular stress on Hauptmann's 'automobile registration cards' and mentions no other documents in the 'large number' of writings he examined. Lieutenant Finn has written that the morning Hauptmann was arrested, on September 19, Hauptmann's auto registration applications were sent to Osborn for his study. Handwriting authorities have repeatedly said that a proper analysis of questioned documents requires days and sometimes weeks of study. Osborn himself, in a letter to Bronx Assistant District Attorney Breslin dated October 5, 1934, asked for all the material in the 'Hauptmann matter' so that 'I will not have to rush my preparation' for the extradition proceedings, more than a full week away. It appears quite likely Osborn identified Hauptmann's handwriting on the basis of the very incomplete writings on the automobile registration forms.

"Did Osborn commit himself so early that he could not easily declare he'd been in error, assuming he later reached that conclusion? That he was uncertain of his ground more than two weeks after Hauptmann's arrest is illustrated by a letter he wrote to District Attorney Foley on October 5. In it, Osborn asked, 'Do you have any of the handwriting of Mrs. Hauptmann? If she is examined again, I think it would be a good plan to have her do some writing, especially of figures.'

"This rather strange request makes it appear Osborn is suggesting that although he would be willing to swear Hauptmann had written the ransom letters, he was having difficulty with the numerals in those letters. Could Osborn have possibly believed Hauptmann had written the words and Mrs. Hauptmann was called in to write the numerals? Or is he in doubt about Hauptmann's hand in writing any part of the notes? In either case, he does not appear to be as certain in this private letter to Foley as he was at the trial. And that letter takes on added significance when one reads through the trial transcript and realizes that not a single one of the handwriting experts testifying for the prosecution mentioned any of the numerals in any of the notes. Not one of their enormous number of photographs illustrated any of the numerals that were liberally sprinkled through all the ransom notes.

"Every one of the prosecution's experts conveniently ignored the first ransom letter, the one left in the nursery, when comparing Hauptmann's writings with the letters sent to Lindbergh. In all their charts they took from the first ransom note only a single word, 'is,' and declared it looked similar to Hauptmann's writing of that word. They ignored thirty-nine other words and nine numerals because, it seems clear, they could not say Hauptmann had written them. Which brings us back again to Mickey Rosner and the ransom note he displayed all over Manhattan, raising the possibility that if Hauptmann were guilty that if Hauptmann were guilty of anything it was at the very most of being an extortionist.

"But even that seems unlikely, not only because of all the evidence which shows rather conclusively that he had nothing to do with the Lindbergh case until finding the money Fisch left in his care, but also because of compelling evidence that handwriting experts were less than scientific in their methods of analysis.

"The truth is that those experts based their identification of Hauptmann as author of the ransom notes almost exclusively on the writing that he produced in the police station after his arrest. The point is worth emphasizing: Hauptmann was called the writer of all the ransom notes almost entirely as a result of comparing those notes with the specimen paragraphs he wrote at the dictation of police, and <u>not by comparison with his natural handwriting</u>.

"Like all writers who had come before me, I had originally accepted the assertion of the elder Osborn and the other experts that they had examined 'a large number of writings' by Hauptmann before arriving at their opinions. Those witnesses and all contemporary writers said Hauptmann was proved to have been the author of the ransom letters after the experts had made a careful study of the "conceded writings"---that is, Hauptmann's writing during the normal course of his life and in the police station. It hadn't occurred to me earlier that in lumping all Hauptmann's writings into a category called "conceded," the prosecution and its experts could have falsified even this "scientific" evidence. But now, after having read police and FBI documents relating to Hauptmann's notebooks,I realized I may have accepted too much on faith. I returned to the trial transcript to learn precisely which of Hauptmann's writings from the years <u>before</u> his arrest had been analyzed by the experts.

"There was one promissory note, with Hauptmann's signature only. One insurance application, with his signature only. Nine automobile registration applications, each of them containing his signature and several other words such as address and descriptive characteristics, his height, weight, color of hair and eyes.

"That was all. Eleven examples of Hauptmann's natural writing before his arrest. Eleven signatures. Perhaps one dozen other words, not counting repetitions of "blond" under a question about his hair coloring and "Bronx" in the space for his address. And some of those words were not written in script, but were printed in block letters.

"According to all contemporary newspaper and magazine stories, however, police had seized in Hauptmann's home between fifteen and nineteen notebooks in his handwriting. In a relatively few official documents in my possession there are discussions of at least eight such books---ledgers, address books, memo books---with hundreds of words written in them. I've counted the words in police and FBI reproductions of several of Hauptmann's notebooks. There are, in Hauptmann's hand, 235 separate words, omitting repetitions. Police also retrieved from Hauptmann's home copies in his own hand of the letters he had written to Pinkus Fisch, five pages of script with another couple of hundred words. Thus there were available to the handwriting experts many scores of pages of Hauptmann's natural writing, filled with hundreds upon hundreds of words in both English and German.

"And yet the handwriting analysts ignored all of that material. They condemned Hauptmann almost entirely on the "evidence" of the police station writings.

"It is difficult to understand why the expert witnesses did not consult the enormous body of writing by Hauptmann which was available. There are two possibilities. Either the police withheld from the experts all of Hauptmann's natural writings because they realized from a visual examination that those writings wouldn't support their contention that Hauptmann was the author of the ransom notes. Or the expert witnesses saw those writings and pushed them aside because they couldn't be made to fit the only conclusion acceptable to the prosecution, which was paying their fees: that Hauptmann was guilty.

"In either event, the handwriting evidence against Hauptmann was as twisted and dishonest as every other piece of evidence and testimony presented by the prosecution.

"It must again be stressed that Albert D. Osborn, in discussing with reporters many years later why his firm committed such a dreadful error when it authenticated Clifford Irving's forgery of Howard Hughes's signature, described the two basic techniques of handwriting analysis which his firm had embarrassingly ignored in that case.

"To be absolutely accurate, Osborn said, a handwriting expert must obtain samples written at about the same time as the questioned documents so as not to be deceived by changes in style and character of writing that usually occur as time goes by. That condition was not met in Hauptmann's case. In Hauptmann's writings for the period 1931 to 1933 that were consulted by the expert witnesses there were three auto registration applications, one promissory note, and one insurance application---documents containing only seven or eight individual words. The amount of writing involved was much too sparse to permit anyone, no matter how expert he claimed to be, to render a valid opinion.

"Osborn's second prerequisite for an accurate opinion is that the analyst must be certain the samples he's studying are in the subject's "natural" handwriting. How natural could Hauptmann's writings in the police station have been? From all the evidence available, Hauptmann and his wife were up late the night before his arrest, seeing a friend off on a trip to Germany; there had been a bon voyage party and the Hauptmanns didn't get home until past midnight. They were awake by their usual time, 6:30 the next morning. Arrested several hours later, seeing his home torn apart and his wife in a state of shocked bewilderment, being hammered by police with questions about the gold notes and then being told he was a suspect in a horrible child murder, Hauptmann must have been under enormous stress and in great fear. And then, for at least thirteen hours that night and through the next morning, he was made to write at least sixteen specimen letters (that number were introduced at his trial) and probably three or four times more than that. Furthermore, police had told Hauptmann that the writing they demanded would be used to prove or disprove his guilt, even after the

Osborns had warned investigators not to inform any suspect about the reason for wanting his handwriting specimen.

"And finally,in his memoirs of the case published in *Liberty*, Lieutenant Finn wrote that the specimen paragraph 'was handed to Hauptmann' in the police station. Handed, Finn said, not dictated, and Finn was there.

"Under those circumstances would any person's handwriting be natural? Most decidedly not. Given the intense mental stress that Hauptmann must have felt as he wrote those specimens, even if he had not been beaten as he had charged, his writings would have certainly been as unnatural as the handwriting of someone whose mind was fogged by alcohol or drugs; his writings would have been so far from natural as to have been useless for honest comparison. Yet Hauptmann's writings were used for comparison, they were used to convince the jury and the world of his guilt.

"If Hauptmann had been made to write several dozen pages of the specimen paragraph, as I believe was done, and only sixteen were introduced at his trial, that selectivity was a deliberate attempt by police or the handwriting experts to suppress any of those writings which didn't appear to match the handwriting in the ransom notes. Even after such selectivity the experts were forced into some strange contortions to make their opinions more believable. The experts, especially the two Osborns, swore Hauptmann had written 'in a disguised hand' when he produced the police station specimens. They didn't seem to be troubled much by the patent absurdity of their logic: that a man who wrote several ransom notes in disguise would later use the same disguise in writing specimens for the police. Most naturally, they did not consider the more logical possibility: the "disguise" they saw was the result of Hauptmann's stress and fatigue.

"The handwriting evidence fails on every count. The standards required for accuracy, cited by the Osborns and other experts before the Lindbergh kidnapping and over the subsequent forty years, were violated in Hauptmann's case. The handwriting analysts not only drew their opinions from a stacked deck by relying almost exclusively on the specimen writings for comparison, but each expert also ignored the fact that the ransom notes are written in a system of penmanship completely different from the one Hauptmann had always used in all his writings. The ransom notes are written in the vertical round hand system. Hauptmann wrote in the Palmer-Zaner system, according to Samuel Small, a scholar of penmanship. Small conferred with Governor Hoffman after the trial, begging him not to permit Hauptmann to be executed. Spreading out magnifications of all the writings before the governor, Small declared:

"The shadings are different---the downstrokes and the upstrokes. Every letter has different characteristics---they are started in different places. The smartest criminal in the world, with all the writing in the ransom notes, couldn't do that, couldn't disguise his writing in that way.

"It isn't a question if Hauptmann wrote those letters. It is a question whether he could write them. I tell you that if you went to the prison and said to Hauptmann, 'I will let you free if you can write a single sentence the way it is written in the ransom letters,' Hauptmann would have to stay in prison the rest of his life. Any expert who has studied types and methods of writing will tell you that.

"The vital point is that the elder Osborn, in his own published writings, had himself maintained that no person could ever disguise his handwriting from one system to another. Although Osborn did state at the extradition hearing that the ransom notes had been written in a style 'very similar to our old round hand in English,' neither he nor any of the other men who testified about Hauptmann's handwriting at Flemington ever pointed out that the defendant's basic penmanship style differed from the penmanship of the person who wrote the ransom note.

"The elder Osborn went to some absurd lengths to defend his original judgment, that Hauptmann wrote all the notes. At the extradition hearings he said that one of the important similarities between Hauptmann's writing and the ransom letters is that in both cases 'there is hardly an i dotted.' Hauptmann's lawyer asked:

'There are thousands and thousands of people who don't dot their i's when writing, isn't that so?'

'I would say,' Osborn replied, 'that there are thousands and thousands of people that occasionally omit it but to omit it entirely, for instance, is an individual characteristic in my opinion.'

"Pressed on whether there weren't 'hundreds of thousands of people' who do not use the dots, Osborn replied, 'Well, I think they are very, very scarce.'

"That of course, just isn't so; any manuscript

collector could point to dozens of specimens in his collection in which the i is un-dotted. Further, although Hauptmann did not dot his i's in the request writings dictated by police, he did occasionally do so in his automobile registration applications---a further hint that perhaps police did tell him precisely how to write those specimens.

"That both Osborns were heavily involved in working with police, as amateur detectives, to prove Hauptmann's guilt and were thus ignoring the objectivity expected of scientists, can be seen in several letters found in the files.

"On October 2, 1934, the younger Osborn wrote to District Attorney Foley and enclosed photographs of the writing on the door and closet panel in Hauptmann's apartment 'which I made last Friday.' Osborn continues: 'If this writing on the jamb did not mean anything, why did someone smear it over, as was clearly done?' Yet that writing, which Osborn-as-detective considers so vital to the prosecution's case against Hauptmann, is demonstrably a fraud. In that same letter, Osborn makes another suggestion in his role as a sleuth: 'In the photograph of the figures on the door there seems to be part of a fingerprint. Perhaps this is Inspector Bruckmann's. I understand he discovered this, but it might be interesting, at least, for one of your fingerprint men to compare it with Hauptmann's.'

"And in the same letter in which the elder Osborn implied he was having trouble tying Hauptmann into the "figures" in the ransom notes and asking the district attorney to get samples of Mrs. Hauptmann's writing of numerals, he also came up with a brilliant idea for detectives to investigate. 'I have suggested to Lieutenant Finn,' he wrote, 'that if it hasn't been done, it would be a good plan to check up the gas and electric bills of the Hauptmann household, which would show when they were both absent and might give some useful information,'

"There are other examples, in police and district attorney files, which show rather strongly that the Osborns, rather than being independent scientists, behaved like members of the prosecution team gathering evidence against Hauptmann.

"What was it that some legal scholar once said about "scientists" such as handwriting experts? 'Skilled witnesses come with such a bias on their mind to support the cause in which they are embarked that hardly any weight should be given to their evidence.' Or to quote again a famed trial lawyer: 'It has become a matter of common observation that not only can the honest opinions of different experts be obtained upon opposite sides of the same question, but also that dishonest opinions may be obtained upon different sides of the same question.'

"While exploring the evidence of the handwriting experts, I considered gathering photographs of all the ransom notes and Hauptmann's conceded writings that I could find, and submitting them to one or more authorities on questioned documents for a fresh analysis. But the first man I called, a man who was recommended by my friend in the New York City police department who had secured so many of the documents from which I'd been working, told me I'd be wasting my time. 'Anyone in this business of questioned documents' he said, 'has cut his teeth on the Lindbergh case. Even someone who disagrees with the Osborns opinion---and that's all it was, an opinion---will not say so publicly. The accepted verdict is that Hauptmann did it and to swim against the current might mean a man's losing his standing in the field. His very career could be jeopardized if he disagreed with the findings of history.'

"'Do you disagree?' I asked.

'I will not give you an opinion and I will not permit my name to be used in your book. I'm sorry. But I will say this---if I were free to give an opinion it would run counter to old man Osborn's testimony. That's all I will say about it."

Theo Bernsen, a European writer who has been conducting his own investigation of the Hauptmann evidence, did have photographs of many of the writings examined in London. During a trip to New York Bernsen discussed his findings.

"Through a friend," he said, "I made contact with language experts for the German embassy in London. The man I went to is in charge of translating English to German and German to English, getting the proper language and syntax and grammar, all that sort of thing. He is an authority on German writing, a recognized authority.

"I showed him certain parts of the ransom letters. Enough to get his opinion but not enough to make him aware this was the Lindbergh case; I insisted it was historical, had nothing to do with current affairs in any way.

"He said the letters---he didn't know they were

kidnap letters---but he said they were not written by a German who had been taught English. They were written by a man who knew English, was brought up in English, and was trying to write the way a German would. The language structure is so peculiar that even the most illiterate German wouldn't make those mistakes, he said. All of it was written by a man who thinks in English and is trying to write Germanic. The grammatical errors show it clearly, the attempt to make a Germanic construction by a man thinking in English.

"He particularly stressed the word 'boad,' the word that Osborn and the others claimed was German. But in German it is written with a t---boot---and it's not possible a German just learning English would make that mistake. It was someone who knew English and who believed, from pronunciation he'd heard, that that's the way Germans spelled it.

"Although it isn't possible at this date to get a fresh comparison of Hauptmann's handwriting with the ransom notes, because the originals have been locked away by New Jersey state police officials, my research has developed enough evidence; to make it possible to state that there is absolutely no proof he wrote any of the ransom notes. I can't claim, from the materials available to me, that there is evidence proving Hauptmann didn't write those notes, but simply that the state did not actually prove what it claimed to have proved. Most important of all, from the legal point of view, is that the state's contention that Hauptmann was the kidnapper because it was proved he wrote the first ransom note (and so was proved to have taken the child from the nursery) is a lie. The experts used only one word from the nursery note. They used only seven of eight words from Hauptmann's natural writings. Their conclusions proved nothing except to reaffirm the accusation that some handwriting experts will swear to anything their employers demand.

"All the evidence, including the elder Osborn's difficulty with the numerals in the ransom notes, the fervor with which both Osborns became detectives aiding the prosecution in its search for evidence, and, most of all, the peculiar omission from the experts' exhibits of the notebooks written in Hauptmann's hand, leads to only one conclusion: the testimony of the prosecution's handwriting analysts was deliberately and grossly distorted to help police and prosecutor rush Richard Hauptmann into the electric chair. Those experts were not impartial scientists, as they claimed. They were detectives, they were avengers, they were a part of the mob; their vaunted clinical detachment collapsed in the face of the intense need of the police to convict Hauptmann and thus expiate their guilt over not being able to solve the case for more than two years, the need of the public and the press to avenge this foul deed against the heroic Lindy, and the need of Lindbergh himself for ... I'll leave that to the psychiatric theorists. What is undeniably plain is that, when considered with all the other documentation showing Hauptmann was the victim of an enormity of contrived evidence, the handwriting experts in this case appear to have been as lacking in ethics as Colonel Schwarzkopf, who encouraged perjured testimony, and as all the police and FBI men and eyewitnesses who fabricated evidence and who lied repeatedly."

It is my earnest desire that Anthony Scaduto will be publicly commended for his excellent report on the fallacy of the prosecution's handwriting testimony used against Richard Hauptmann. He clearly pointed out the many "weaknesses" of the eight "experts" who blatantly stepped to the witnesses stand and "hood-winked" almost everyone, most importantly the judge and jury, with their "legal sounding jargon" that Hauptmann was the author of everything ever written in the Lindbergh case. Scaduto, with his reams of evidence, certainly leaves no doubt in anyone's mind today that Hauptmann was unjustly accused by the prejudicial testimony of these "wizards of the written word."

The handwriting testimony, linked with all the other falsified, manufactured and perjured testimony, that was thrown into the "Roman carnival" atmosphere of the Hunterdon County Courtroom, makes it extremely visible for us to see, even with impaired vision, that Hauptmann was caught in such a mesh of the prosecution's lies that he didn't have a chance to prove his innocence.

The efforts of the state's handwriting genius's "sold the jury" with the belief that the accused man had been unable to correctly spell simple words such as 'boat', 'note', and other uncomplicated one syllable words, and yet, at the same time, had them believe that he was capable of being able to correctly spell words such as 'according', 'immediately', 'arrangements', and many other difficult words. It is utterly ridiculous, but nevertheless the jury swallowed this "hook, line, and sinker."

It is absolutely asinine to think that a jury of

twelve persons with their sound minds could even entertain the thought that Hauptmann had written the "words", while his wife, Anna, had penned the "numerals" used in the notes. At the very outset of his study of the notes, chief handwriting "wizard" Osborn, Sr. implied that this might possibly have been done. If such a tactic had been used, and the jury believed such a ridiculous insinuation, Anna Hauptmann could very well have been implicated as an accessory to the crime, and been found guilty along with her husband. It was just the grace of God that prevented such a thing from happening, since the jury seemed anxious to accept anything these "brilliant handwriting men" fed them.

The violation of truth in the "well plotted" case perpetrated against Richard Hauptmann at Flemington, New Jersey in 1935 is almost too difficult to relate. It wrenches our innermost being. Today, the sad fact remains, as a miserable commentary, that the twelve members of the jury were "cheated" by clever "double-talk and gobble-dy-gook" of knowing the "hanky-panky" used in the presentation of the deceptive handwriting evidence. However, the truth about this terrible miscarriage of justice must be told --- and we are telling it!

CHAPTER THIRTY

The Flip-Side of The Handwriting Issue!

Although the handwriting evidence, as it was presented, had shattered Richard Hauptmann's claims of innocence, and in spite of the "excellent reputations" of the eight so-called experts and the glib words they "spat out" over a four day period in that little courtroom in Flemington, I firmly believe, without a shadow of a doubt, that had the facts, as we know them now, been properly presented without prejudice, the jury could never have convicted the man on the basis of his handwriting.

In spite of the claims of the two Osborns, Elbridge W. Stein, John F. Tyrell, Herbert J.Walter, Harry M. Cassidy, William T. Souder, and Clark Sellers who said that their findings and conclusions were "irresistible, unanswerable and overwhelming"; looking at the evidence now known, the jury would have had to concede that the evidence largely proved that Hauptmann could not possibly have written the notes, while the evidence as presented was weak and nothing more than mere supposition. The truth of the handwriting testimony had been cleverly hidden behind the mass of enlarged charts and confusing double talk of the "eight geniuses". One of the most glaring portions of "unfair and untrue" statements, was one left to slide by unnoticed, made by the chief prosecuting attorney, David T. Wilentz. In order to properly present this, we must first examine the testimony of John W. Trendley, the lone handwriting expert to testify in Hauptmann's defense. Here we pick up that portion of his testimony, beginning on page 3243 of the official court transcript, as he was being questioned by Mr. Reilly:

Q. Now I call your attention particularly to the word "singnature" do you find that? A. I do.

Q On Mr. Osborn's chart? A. I think I do. Let me see that. (Witness examined ransom note.) I find it on Exhibit S-109.

Q. Is that the only place you find it? A. That

is all.

Q. In its entirety on the ransom notes? A. That is all.

Q. And would you say that this S-109 is a photographic reproduction of the word "singnature" on the ransom note? A. I would.

Q. Now in your examination of the request writings did you find that Hauptmann wrote the word "singnature" as spelled here, did you? A. I did.

Q. Now, do you find anything in the Osborn column of Hauptmann request writing, comparative writing, where he has the word "singnature" as written by Hauptmann photographed? A. I never have.

Q. Now let us take---Have you in your folder there the chart of any other expert who compares "singnature" of the nursery note with anything Hauptmann ever wrote, in its entirety? A. No, I haven't in this one. I don't think there was, I don't remember.

Q. Well, if there is the Attorney General very likely will ask you on cross-examination. Now, I call attention to this exhibit, the nursery note, and ask you whether or not the "S" beginning "singnature" is not more or less missing? A. It is not legible.

Q. It is not legible? A. No.

Q. In fact, there is a certain portion of the downward stroke of the "s" that didn't respond to the pen,---am I correct? A. Yes, you are right.

Q. Do you think it would be safe for any expert to pass an opinion upon an "s" that was not fully made, such as this "s"? A. No, I wouldn't.

Q. Now, I ask you to look at the "g," s-i-n-g (showing exhibit S-18 to the witness). Is there any difference from that "g" and some of the other g's in the ransom note? A. In the one in "making" there is a vast difference.

Q. And that is the "g" at the end of the seventh line? A. That is it.

Q. The "g" in the word "making" extends to the right like a right angle? A. It does.

Q. The "g" in "singnature" is a more or less straight up and down double loop oval; correct? A. Correct.

Q. Did that demonstrate to you that it was a disguised writing? A. It sure would be, because there are so many different directions of lines, formation of letters.

Q. Is it not a fact in this ransom note left in the crib that one part is straight up and down and the rest, another part, rather, is to the left, another part to the right there is a continual variance in the writing and printing? A. All throughout.

Q. All throughout. Now I ask you to pay attention to the "a" in "singnature." A. That is distorted like an "o" laying over on its left side.

Q. It is a distorted "a," isn't it? A. It is.

Q. It looks like an "o" that somebody bent and pressed down? A. Laying over on the left side.

Q. Now I ask you to look at Hauptmann's writing and I am going to point to a's. I now point to Exhibit S-109, the "a" in "hands," is it anything like the "a" in "singnature"? A. It is not.

Q. And the "a" in "and"? A. It is not.

Q. And the "a" in "at"? A. It is not.

Q. And the "a" in "sa"? A. It is not.

Q. And the "a" in "year"? A. It is not.

Q. And the "a" in year," Exhibit 108? A. It is not.

Q. And the "a" in "was"? A. It is not.

Q. Or the "a" in "was"? A. It is not.

Q. Or the "a" in "Avenue"? A. That is a capital.

Q. A capital. Now I ask you to look at the latter part of "singnature," t-u-r-e is there anything in the Hauptmann writing as shown by Mr. Osborn's charts, any sample t-u-r-e from any of the Hauptmann request writing? A. (After examining charts) There is not.

Q. We now have eleven lines of the note found only one i-s on Osborn's chart? A. And another one, in the nursery, and we find in the eleven lines, do we, "singnature," two of them. I's and "singnature."

Q. But on his chart as to "singnature," you do not find any comparative word spelled the same way or anything like it in the Hauptmann request writings? A. None whatsoever.

Q. Now we come to the last line of the nursery note a-n-d, and I ask you to look at that "d." Does it appear from that "d" that the pen skipped in part of the stroke and no ink was registered? A. It does, that looks like a-n-s-l.

Q. A-n-s-l? In fact, is there not a loop to the left on the first stroke of what we read as "and" reading the intention of the note. A. Of the last letter, do you mean?

Q. Yes. A. Yes.

Q. Now, is there anything on Mr. Osborn's chart

that corresponds to that "and'? A. I find one "and," two ands, they do not correspond. A. You are not pointing to and's on Exhibit 112. Does this "and" correspond to the "and" on the ransom note? A. It does not.

Q. The ransom note "and" differentiates from the "and" on S-112 in what manner? Please tell the jury. A. In the letter "a," this is the oval, these a's, the length is about one and a half times the width, or one and a quarter. The slant is different. The "d" is different. Instead of---We have a-n-d with a little upstroke and a heavy downstroke, and we have the same in the "and" on the fifth line. The "d" downstrokes all show that curve of an oval writer.

Q. And the "and" in the nursery note stands up more, doesn't it? A. I think it slants to the left---yes, left, and one part of the "d" looks like a letter "s," the loop part of the "d," the shoulder.

Q. You don't find that "and" on Mr. Osborn's chart? A. No.

Q. You don't find the figure "3"? A. No figures whatever.

Q. Now, the last word "holds," h-o---something, do you find that collection of pen-strokes---the last word in the note on Mr. Osborn's chart? A. I know that is not on there. "Holds" is not on the chart.

Q. Now calling your attention to this particular word "holds," does it not appear that after the word was written an added loop was put over the third letter? A. (Examines note with glass.) No, I think it was written in its entirety.

Q. With a lighter stroke? A. Yes.

Q. You don't find it on Osborn's charts? A. No, sir.

Q. So taking the whole ransom note from top to bottom, we find that Mr. Osborn, testifying for over forty years all over the country, with samples of the defendant's handwriting before him, and with this note, the first note found in the nursery, as a comparative test upon which he makes his observations and opinion to this jury, picks out the word i-s "is," and compares it with i-s's of Hauptmann's is that correct? A. It is.

Q. Picks out the word "singnature" and compares it with nothing on the chart from Hauptmann's writing. A. That is correct.

Q. In your opinion would that be sufficient to send a man to the electric chair?

Mr. Lanigan: That is objected to.

The Court: The objection is sustained.
Mr. Lanigan: I ask the Court to instruct the jury to disregard counsel's remark.
The Court: I didn't hear the remark.
Mr. Reilly: It wasn't a remark it was just a question.

If it were true, as Justice Trenchard stated, that he did not hear the question asked by Reilly, then how in the name of good common sense could Trenchard sustain an objection to a question that, he, himself, the Court, had not heard in the first place? The whole thing was ridiculous! But, again Reilly failed to pursue the issue any further.

The prosecution, in turn, attempted in every way possible to intimidate Trendley in cross-examination by inferring that he lacked the proper qualifications to be accepted as a "first class" handwriting expert. Trendley, on the other hand, accused state's assistant district attorney, Joseph Lanigan of not allowing him to examine the questioned writing as we shall see from the following questioning:

Q. Now, Mr. Trendley, when you testify as a witness, you frequently prepare charts and enlarged photographs to illustrate your testimony, do you not? A. Sometimes we do.

Q. Sometimes. How often do you do that? A. Well, if it is a big case like this---

Q. Cases of major importance? A. Yes, cases of major importance.

Q. Cases as big as this? A. Yes, certainly.

Q. Yet, in a case like this you prepared no charts, did you? A. How could we when you wouldn't surrender nothing.

Q. Who? A. You. You didn't even want to let me look at the original.

Q. When was that? A. When I was down at Trenton for two days and got two hours on them.

Q. Have you since requested them? A. I had a time getting these copies from you.

Q. When did you get them? A. About ten days ago, I think; I don't remember. I was tired waiting for them.

The lack of cooperation and blatant unfairness of not allowing the defense handwriting expert ample time to prepare his enlarged photographs and charts is quite apparent. It closely resembled the tactics used by the state police during the early months of the investigation when they refused the original ransom notes to be released to the other investigating authorities, namely the New York City police and the Federal Bureau of Investigation.

Returning to my earlier mention of "one of the most glaring portions of not only unfair, by defiantly untrue, statements" made by Attorney General David T. Wilentz, was my reference to his summation for the state (found on pages 4453 and 4454 of the official trial transcript, State of New Jersey vs. Hauptmann, Volume 5) where we take up his referral to his questioning of Hauptmann pertaining particularly to the spelling of the word signature. His unfair summation pertaining to his interrogation of Hauptmann went along as follows: "Q. How do you spell 'signature'? A. S-i-g-n-a-t-u-r-e. That was in this court. You remember it. Q. Did they tell you to spell it s-i-n-g---? A. They did. Q. So when they were dictating the spelling that was not your own free will in spelling? A. It was not.

"Now, he swears we told him to spell 'signature' that way. You can take the request writings. Here is one of them. You go through every one of those misspelled writings and there isn't the word 'signature' on one of them to show that we ever asked him to spell it, right or wrong. What do you think of that?

"And here he is in this court room. He knew the importance of that 'signature'. There isn't the word 'signature' in any one of these exhibits, the request writings, that we asked him to write. Why, there isn't, as I said before, in fourteen pages of request writings the word 'signature'. It doesn't appear any place. We never asked him to write it, and you have it here before you, his request writings. Look through them and see. And still he swears on the stand in this court room that we told him to spell 'signature' in the request writings with an 'n.'

"What a fake! What a fraud! What a joke! Defense! Wasting the taxpayer's money here. Sure, if there is any wasting, that is where it is, with that kind of a phony defense. Perjury is a joke in this case. They seem to take it so lightly. They would swear to anything---anything to save Hauptmann."

And the ranting and raving of the prosecuting attorney continued as he presented his summation. But in the midst of it all he had made statements that were absolutely in error; those pertaining to his claim that Hauptmann had at no time been asked to spell the word 'signature' in the request writings, or the 'demand writings' as I choose to call them. In the cross-examination of John Trendley by Joseph Lanigan the word 'singnature' was on one of the prepared charts of request writing and had been compared with the word 'singnature' of the ransom notes and had been determined that there was absolutely no similarity whatsoever. Mr. Wilentz had not done his homework well. He was entirely ignorant of the fact that during his assistant's cross-examination of Trendley much discussion had been made of the word 'signature' or 'singnature.' (Pages 3243-3247 official trial transcript). Attorney General Wilentz had been absent from the courtroom at the time this segment of questioning was pursued, hence his lack of knowledge of the dialogue pertaining to the mutual agreement that it did not resemble that of Hauptmann's writing. **BUT IT DID MUCH MORE**! **IT PROVED HAUPTMANN CORRECT IN HIS STATEMENT THAT HE HAD BEEN ASKED TO WRITE THE WORD 'SIGNATURE' INCORRECTLY AS 'SIGNATURE' IN THE NEW YORK POLICE STATION**! **ONCE AGAIN HAUPTMANN HAD TOLD THE TRUTH**!

Again we must ask why Reilly didn't pounce upon this unfair accusation of the attorney general's? Why did he allow this outrageous lie to stand in the record as factual? As for Attorney Wilentz and his caustic accusations leveled at Hauptmann as a fake, a fraud, a joke, a phony defense wasting the taxpayer's money, and perjury being a joke in this case, claiming that anything would be said in order to save Hauptmann, let us simply bi-sect this statement of the "brilliant" attorney general: "We had him at his arrest with the twenty dollar bill."

Of course they had him. After two and one half years they finally came up with "an innocent victim", one who had a perfectly honest answer and a legitimate reason as to where, when, and how he had come into the possession of the money. Of course they had him. And, in this little century old courthouse in Flemington, nearly three years after the crime was committed, who is accusing who of perjury?

In 1977, Joe Sharkey, a police reporter on the staff of the *Philadelphia Evening Bulletin*, visited me. He had learned of my involvement in the Lindbergh case, and was anxious to learn of the evidence I had obtained which would prove that Hauptmann had paid with his life as a scapegoat in the famous case. Joe arrived in Phoenixville and enthusiastically recorded my story on audio tape. He spent many weeks developing a series of four articles for his paper, one which told of his findings during a visit he made to a handwriting expert who had not been permitted to testify in the trial by none other than Hauptmann's chief defense counsel, Edward Jay Reilly himself.

Sharkey had visited the handwriting expert at her home in Clearwater, Florida. Her name was Hilda Zaeglein Braunlich and the *Bulletin* reporter found her quite willing to tell her story of what had taken place at Flemington in 1935. Sharkey's account of this, as it appeared in the Monday, October 3, 1977 issue of the *Philadelphia Evening Bulletin*, follows:

"Mrs. Braunlich, now 80 and living quietly here, said she was threatened and prevented from testifying as scheduled by Hauptmann's chief defense lawyer, Edward J. Reilly.

" 'I told Reilly I could prove Hauptmann innocent in five minutes in front of that jury,' Mrs. Braunlich said during a recent interview.

'Only photographic copies of the ransom notes were used as evidence in the trial. The well-guarded originals, when examined with a magnifying glass, showed obvious overwritings, some in a different hue of ink, Mrs. Braunlich said.

'Not only that, she said, a close examination of the notes indicated to her that Hauptmann did not write them, as the prosecution successfully convinced the jury with its own battery of eight handwriting experts.

"Instead of welcoming her findings, which she related to the defense lawyer the night before she was to testify, Reilly 'flew into a rage and told me to leave town within the hour,' she said.

"Afraid, confused and concerned about her status as an alien, she fled Flemington, N.J. Soon after the trial she went to Switzerland and then to her native Bavaria, she said. She returned to the United States in the late 1930's.

"Mrs. Braunlich said Reilly flatly ordered her to leave town, telling her, 'Do not talk to any reporters,' after she informed him she was prepared to prove the ransom note originals had been tampered with to the extent that they were virtual forgeries.

"A young, widowed immigrant who had made her living in New York City as a portrait painter, Mrs. Braunlich, had entered the Hauptmann case reluctantly. A physician acquaintance, impressed by her expertise, sought out a friend on the defense team and Mrs. Braunlich was then persuaded to enter the case as an expert in European script.

"In her native Bavaria, she had been for two years an assistant to Alois Runge, handwriting authority who founded the International Organization for Scientific Graphology.

"In all, the defense invited eight handwriting experts to Flemington. Newspaper files and other documents from the trial confirm that Mrs. Braunlich was one of them.

"Only one of the defense experts, the late John Trendley, testified in Hauptmann's behalf. Trendley later claimed Reilly prevented him from fully discussing the apparent tamperings. Trendley testified, trial transcripts indicate, that the ransom note writing was not Hauptmann's---but his opinion was outweighed by the battery of prosecution experts who testified otherwise.

"She and several of the defense experts, including Trendley, demanded to see the originals of the 14 ransom notes before they testified, Mrs. Braunlich said.

" 'The prosecution made it very difficult for us to get to see the originals of the notes,' she said as she sat in the parlor of her two-story home and combed through piles of documents.

" 'When the request was finally approved, she said, policemen stood behind each of the four defense analysts who examined the originals using a powerful magnifying glass.

" 'What I saw, I was shocked,' said Mrs. Braunlich. (She was widowed a second time in 1970 and uses the name of her second husband. She asked that her current surname not be published.)

"I saw evidence of a crime which one could not detect with the naked eye and which never showed up in photos or facsimiles,' she said. 'Clear out and large, the ransom notes showed forged strokes.'

"She and another defense expert, now dead, hoped to project the original notes onto a screen and indicate to the jury where the forged strokes could be seen, she said. But Reilly, she said, was an obstacle.

" 'He was very friendly, we knew, with the prosecution officials,' she said. 'He dined with them at the hotel. Could we trust him?'

"Hauptmann himself blamed Reilly for his plight, in a death cell letter written to his mother just before he was executed: 'I am 100 percent certain (Reilly) worked with the prosecution.' The letter was suppressed by prison officials and surfaced just last March.

"Mrs. Braunlich also was prepared to testify that the writing on the notes appeared to be that of Isidor

Fisch, she said. The mysterious Fisch was the man from whom Hauptmann claimed he innocently received the $14,000 in marked ransom money which was found in the Hauptmann home in the Bronx. A total of $50,000 was paid in ransom money.

"The 14 Lindbergh ransom notes, together with 16 samples of Hauptmann's known writing (most of which had been dictated to him by police after his arrest), were the bedrock of the circumstantial evidence which sent the German carpenter to his execution in 1936.

"Not only was a different color ink used to change key strokes in some of the writing, the overall script clearly was not Hauptmann's, Mrs. Braunlich says she was prepared to swear.

'The pressure points and shaping strokes in the notes did not match Hauptmann's known writing, she said, although superficially the samples shared an 'undeveloped grouping' of handwriting common to thousands of unschooled European immigrants, Fisch and Hauptmann among them.

'And you want a projector and the original ransom notes?' Reilly asked incredulously after she had explained her analysis to him the night before she was to testify, according to her account.

" 'Of course. In five minutes the jury will be convinced,' she replied. 'I'll show how the ransom notes have been made over to look like Hauptmann's script.'

"Reilly demanded to know if she had shown her analysis to anyone else, especially any of the 700 reporters who had descended upon Flemington to cover the sensational "crime of the century," as the kidnap case was called. She had not, she said.

"Ordered to leave, she fled Flemington in disguise, she said, and sailed to Switzerland to stay with relatives.

"Mrs. Braunlich said she took only $60 in advance expenses for her stay in Flemington. 'I could not be a further burden on poor Mrs. Hauptmann,' she said.

"Why did she not speak out during or immediately after the trial?

'I was afraid. I was a stranger in America. They threatened me with being deported,' said Mrs. Braunlich, who only began speaking out in the past year about her role in the case.

"She became a U.S. citizen in 1954, about a decade after moving to this pleasant Florida Gulf Coast resort where she lives, surrounded by her dog-eared notes and her paintings.

"During the trial, the elder Osborn---reacting to claims that handwriting analysis was a subjective art at best---called his trade a science 'as exact as the science of astronomy.'

"Mrs. Braunlich does not believe this. Besides training, it requires talent, perception and deduction, she said. But, she stressed, there can be no doubt among serious handwriting authorities examining originals when something has clearly been overwritten and tampered with.

"The original ransom notes are thought to be sealed in a cache of trial evidence now being combed through by New Jersey state police at their West Trenton headquarters. A. spokesman, Lt. Gordon Hector, would say only, 'I wouldn't be surprised,' when asked if the originals of the notes were among that evidence.

"The younger Osborn, meanwhile, still headed the family firm in 1971 when it reported that there was not "the slightest question" that writer Clifford Irving's purported letters from Howard Hughes' biography, were genuine samples of the billionaire's handwriting.

"Irving later served a prison term for his role in the forgery and hoax. Irving, himself, had written the letters."

And so, we now have Joe Sharkey's report of Hilda Zaeglein Braunlich and John Trendley confirming the fact that, contrary to the "sworn testimony" that Hauptmann had been the author, he could not possibly have been the writer of the ransom notes. This certainly puts a stamp of approval concerning Samuel Small's firm statement of belief that "IT WOULD HAVE BEEN **IMPOSSIBLE** FOR HAUPTMANN TO HAVE WRITTEN THEM!

Tony Scaduto is also well aware of Mrs. Zaeglein Braunlich's willingness to testify for Hauptmann and of her being prevented from doing so by Edward J. Reilly, the pompous lawyer who had been hired to defend an innocent man, but did a better job of convicting him. Scaduto clearly relates this in the excellent television documentary, *In Search of the Lindbergh Baby*.

The word INNOCENT has not, by far, reached its intensity. There is much, much more to tell. And the facts grow more sickening. Read on!

CHAPTER THIRTY ONE

A Skeleton In Court!

At the conclusion of the eleventh day of the trial, all the monotonous testimony and "the words of unquestionable wisdom" of the state's eight handwriting experts had been absorbed by the jury as "just so many facts". "Facts" that already were deeply rooted in each of their minds so that there now remained no doubt as to Hauptmann's undeniable guilt.

Before we take under consideration more of the prosecution's ridiculous charges, trumped up for the sole purpose of framing Hauptmann, it is well to take a more serious study of the remains of "a child" that the authorities contended had been placed where it was found by no one other than Bruno Richard Hauptmann.

Thursday, January 17th brought revived interest back into the courtroom when, shortly after 10:00 a.m., William J. Allen was called to the witness stand. Mr. Allen related how he had quite by accident found a human remains, later identified as those of Charles A. Lindbergh, Jr. In response to Attorney Robert Peacock's direct questioning, Mr. Allen answered: "Well, when I ducked my head and went under the bush, I seen something, a <u>skeleton</u>. It looked like an animal when I first seen it. Naturally, I was going in the woods anyhow, so I went right straight to it and I walked there and I looked down on it and I said 'Gee, that looks like a human being.'"

Here we have Mr. Allen who found the decomposed remains using the identical word, "<u>skeleton</u>" as Governor A. Harry Moore and Colonel Schwarzkopf also later used when each one issued their initial announcements to the press of exactly what Allen had found.

Viewing pictures of the body in its original resting place, "in the woods about 30 yards off the highway", it cannot be denied that it was nothing more than a "<u>skeleton</u>", one that Dr. Philip Van Ingen claimed he could not identify as the remains of Charles A. Lindbergh, Jr. if he were given ten million dollars.

Orville Wilson, who accompanied Allen into the

woods to see what his partner had found on that dismal afternoon of May 12th, 1932, corroborated the testimony of Allen.

Sergeant Andrew Zapolsky of the New Jersey State Police told of his being summoned from the Lindbergh estate, and accompanied by Detective James Fitzgerald of the Jersey City Police Department and Officers Williamson and Wolf of the Hopewell police, and making a hasty trip to the scene of the gruesome find.

Zapolsky related how he had found the child lying on its face in a shallow grave with some leaves covering parts of the body. He said he was the one who had turned the body completely over on its back and that when he did this, together with the help of Fitzgerald, he was able to compare the facial features and its apparent likeness to a picture he held of the child, as well as a comparison he made from mental notes he had made of a description of the baby which had been given to him by his superior officers. In answer to Mr. Peacock's question: "Comparing the picture with the body, who was that child?", the police sergeant responded: "Colonel Lindbergh's child."

The witness stated further under cross-examination by Attorney Fisher that the body was covered "somewhat with leaves" and that "where the clothing was on it was intact, and the face, that was in the ground, was preserved; when we turned it over it was white, and then when we returned from Hopewell it turned blue, we found it was blue."

And Fisher went on to ask: "And you say that the body was in such condition that you could recognize it from the photograph of a living child, is that correct?" to have Zapolsky respond: "Yes, the features were there."

The witness also testified that although he had turned the corpse from its face down position over on to its back, someone had taken it upon himself to again move the body to the position Allen had originally found it in order that pictures be taken. He stated that when he returned to the scene with Lieutenant Keaten and Inspector Walsh the skeleton was once again on its face.

The testimony of Inspector Harry W. Walsh of the Jersey City Police Department had much to do with the flannel shirt he had cut from the body of the child. He said that as he was lifting the body about an inch off the ground, which he had done with the use of a stick, and in so doing the stick had accidentally penetrated the skull, making a little hole in it about the diameter of an ordinary lead pencil. The direct testimony regarding this incident as given to the questioning of Attorney Wilentz follows:

Q. What clothing did you cut besides the shirt that I just exhibited to you, being Exhibit S-13? A. Another similar sleeveless shirt.

Q. I show you State's Exhibit S-14 and ask you whether that is the sleeveless shirt that you refer to? A. It is.

Q. And having cut these garments from the body---did you cut them from the body of the child? A. Yes, sir.

Q. How did you cut them, Inspector? A. With a knife, while I held the body elevated from the ground.

Q. How did you hold it, with the hands? A. With a stick.

Q. And then I take it that you removed from the child's body these articles of clothing which you just testified you cut? A. Yes, sir.

Q. And you took those pieces of clothing where? A. Back to the Lindbergh estate or home.

Q. What did you do with it? A. May the 12th was a stormy day and the clothes were saturated with rain and Captain Lamb nailed them up in the boiler room to thoroughly dry them.

Q. Then I suppose you surrendered them to Colonel and Mrs. Lindbergh and the family? A. No, sir, I surrendered them to Colonel Schwarzkopf.

Q. Oh, I see. At the home you mean? A. Yes, sir.

Q. Tell us, please, in addition to that, while you were at the scene, referring to the place where the body was found, did you take a look at the ground there? A. Yes, sir.

Q. Will you tell us whether or not there was any place there that indicated some sort of an excavation of one kind or another? A. There was a depression in the ground, possibly about, I'd say roughly eight inches deep, ten inches deep.

Q. And about the length? A. Well, about the length of the torso of the child.

Q. And had the child been removed from that excavation or depression? A. When I arrived there it was laying on its back paralleling that depression

Q. Paralleling. About how close to it? A. Six inches.

Q. And did you examine that excavation or depression in the ground there? A. Yes, sir.

Q. And what, if anything, did you find there? A. I'd been informed---

Q. What did you find there? A. A quantity of blond hair about five inches in length laying in semi-circle form at the end of the depression formed by the head of the body.

Q. And what did you do with that hair? A. I removed it with the clothing to the Lindbergh estate.

Q. And surrendered it to Colonel Schwarzkopf? A. Colonel Schwarzkopf.

The cross-examination by defense attorney Fisher developed these facts:

Q. Inspector, about how long was the depression in the ground in feet and inches? A. Well, I am giving you a rough guess now; I would say about two and a half to three feet.

Q. Two and a half to three feet. That is longwise? A. Yes, sir.

Q. And from eight to ten inches deep? A. About.

Q. And how did it seem to have been made? I mean by that, did it look as though it was dug out by hand or were there signs of instruments being used? A. I don't know. It gave me the impression that the child had been laying in it. I couldn't tell you whether it was dug out or whether it was caused by nature or whether or how it was made; I know that it was there, however.

Q. In other words, there is a possibility that the child might have been left on the surface and gradually nature worked the body down to where you saw it? A. That is altogether possible.

Q. Now did you report this matter of making a hole in the baby's head with a stick to the County Physician, Dr. Mitchell, who made the examination of the baby's body? A. I didn't have any occasion to make a report to the County Physician. No, sir, I didn't.

Q. Did you report it to Mr. Swayze, the Coroner? A. No, sir.

Q. Did you report it to any of the examining physicians at all? A. No, sir.

Q. When did you make mention to anybody of the fact that you had made a hole in the child's head with a stick? A. I reported it to Colonel Schwarzkopf immediately.

Q. The same day? A. Yes, sir.

Q. The very same day? A. Yes, sir.

Q. Did the hole you made go right through the bone structure of the baby's head? A. It slightly penetrated the skull; I don't know what it went through.

Q. To penetrate the skull, it would have to go through some bone structure, would it not? A. It may have been just the flesh; I don't know.

Q. You think the brain is immediately adjacent to the flesh and might be penetrated without anything else being touched? A. From the condition of the body I doubt if there was a brain in it.

Q. The body was in pretty bad shape, was it not, Inspector? A. It was badly decomposed.

Q. How long was it, Inspector, from the date of the kidnapping till the day the body was found? A. The kidnapping occurred on March 1st and the baby's body was found on May 12th.

Q. That would be 72 or 73 days, about? A. About.

Q. Why was it necessary for you to use a stick to raise the body, Inspector? A. Because the entire body was veiled with vermin.

Q. You couldn't have used gloves? A. I didn't have them.

Q. How far is Hopewell from the scene? A. By the speedometer on the car I was in that day, four and a half miles.

Q. From Hopewell village? A. Main Street, one mile and one-eighth.

Q. By Main Street you mean from Wearts' garage, where you make the turn? A. I guess that is where the garage is, Gebhardt's Hotel is there.

Q. From Gebhardt's Hotel to the scene is one mile and a tenth? A. One mile and an eighth.

Q. Did you make a survey of the scene, Inspector? A. Immediately surrounding the body, yes.

Q. Did you find anything at all there? A. I found a sack.

Q. What kind---burlap? A. Burlap bag.

Q. For what area did your examination extend? I mean, now, taking the body as a center, 20 yards in all directions? A. About.

Q. Twenty yards. And you found nothing at all except a burlap bag? A. That is all.

The questioning continued regarding the identification of a piece of flannel cloth:

Q. Now what material is that, Inspector, if you know? A. A piece of flannel, as I understand it.

Q. Flannel? A. Yes, sir.

Q. Referring now to S-30. And what is there that is peculiar to you that identified that? A. Scalloped embroidered edge.

Q. I see. And do you say also, referring now to Exhibit S-13, that that is a piece of flannel? A. Yes, sir.

Q. And it has a similar edge, scalloped edge, is that it? A. Identical.

Q. Identical. And because of that you say that that convinced you that the garments were the same? A. Yes, sir. That and the information that I had.

Q. Yes. Now, is that hand stitching? A. I don't know.

Q. Or is it machine stitching? A. I don't know.

Q. Did you ever see such stitching as that before in any garment of any kind, Inspector? A. I am not interested in sewing. I didn't.

Q. Did you ever see it? A. No, sir.

Q. You are not interested in sewing, are you, Inspector? A. No, sir.

Q. And you don't know much about it, do you? A. No, I don't.

Q. No. And for that reason you are not qualified to state whether that is a common stitching in flannel or not, are you? A. I can tell you now that it identically matches the scalloped edge on this piece of cloth that you are holding in your other hand.

Q. That is right. But whether both of them are very common, the flannel sleeping garment or the flannel shirt, you don't know that, do you? A. I couldn't tell you that.

Q. No. It is quite possible, isn't it, Inspector, that such garments as that may be on sale in a thousand department stores in America? A. That is altogether possible.

Q. That is altogether possible. A. It is altogether possible.

The testimony of Walter H. Swayze, coroner of Mercer County, related to his initial examination of the child's body after it had been removed to the County Morgue in Trenton. During cross examination by Reilly he was asked these pertinent questions:

Q. Are you a physician? A. No

Q. What is your business? A. I am an undertaker.

Q. So when you made out the (death) certificate,

it was based upon information furnished to you by someone else in so far as affecting the principal cause of death? A. Correct.

Q. Is that right? A. Right.

Doctor Charles H. Mitchell, Mercer County Physician, said he had practiced medicine within the state of New Jersey for nearly 35 years and that he had been the County physician for almost ten and a half years. He told how he had examined the corpse and was able to state that there was no question as to the cause of death: "The child died of a fractured skull." During Reilly's questioning Mitchell told of his examination of the remains as he performed the autopsy in the morgue.

"We examined very carefully by opening the mouth, putting the finger down the throat, also opening the chest, looking at the various organs that were left---very few of them left---examined the teeth, examined the tongue, tried to make as careful an examination under the conditions that we had to work on as it was possible to do. The odor itself almost made it impossible for a man to work over this child."

In answer to Reilly's question as to how long it took him to determine the cause of death, the physician went on: "Well, I first made a general examination of the external portion of the body, made different measurements of the length of the body, examined the teeth, examined the condition of the muscles, which were in a badly decomposed state; then after that I made an effort to open up the scalp, to dissect it, but in dissecting, in cutting, it was in such a decomposed state, it brushed back. Then I found this marked fracture on the left side, extending upward to the frontal posterior occipital bone, the bone in the back of the head. There was no laceration of the scalp over that point. There was no reason why there would be any external bleeding, because there was no opening in the scalp. But in taking it off the top of the skull, which I endeavored first to do, but the bones finally separated and fell off, and I found the various sutures, I found this evidence, the evidence of it on the inside as well as externally, and for an area, I would say, two inches in diameter around this centralized point where this fracture radiated from was an area of decomposed blood clot.

"The brain substance itself was just past doing anything with, it was in the form, I would say of almost, well, probably a thick soup. We poured it out onto a table and made a very thorough examination of the entire contents of that brain, put our hands through it with gloves of course, and hunted very carefully for anything that might have been in that brain substance, and we also examined carefully the inner structures of the skull after we got the brain out.

"The only thing I found was that in a hole on the opposite side of the head about an inch posterior, I think, it was about an inch posterior to the right ear, an opening into the skull about close to a half an inch in diameter, an irregular rounded hole.

"Now, do you want me to describe the loss of these various organs, Mr. Reilly? I can tell you them, I think I have them right in my mind---the left foot was gone from the knee down; the both hands were gone."

"No." Reilly assured him, "I am only talking about organs from which you could determine a cause of death."

After further questioning pertaining to the thickness of a child's skull in comparison to that of an adult, the length of time it would take for rigor mortis to set in, and how long it would take for a child to die of exposure under average temperature conditions, Reilly pressed on with questions about the hole found in the skull, suggesting the possibility that it might have been made by the entrance of a bullet. Soon his probing questions centered on the doctor's actual performance of the autopsy and the surgical instruments he had used:

Q. What instruments did you bring with you from your office to perform the autopsy? A. We didn't bring any from the office. We have a set of them, furnished by the County, down there.

Q. What instruments have you there? A. Oh, we have scalpels, forceps, costotomes, probes, scissors, saws---the usual routine set-up that we have for post mortem work.

Q. Now as you had this little body in front of you from which some of the hair had fallen off the back of the head---am I correct? A. You are right sir.

Q. And you said you put your finger down the child's throat? A. Yes, sir.

Q. What organs are down the throat? A. Trachea, and the larynx, pharynx, tonsils.

Q. Well, they were missing, weren't they? A. No, they were not missing. The larynx and trachea were still there.

Q. What do you call the thor--- A. Thoracic cavity, you are referring to?

Q. Thoracic organs. A. Why, the lung and heart-

--the lungs, rather and heart. The lungs in this case were absent, they were not there.

Q. Well, now, I just want to know what you did with the skull. Was the skull connected with the rest of the vertebrae to the body? A. Yes, sir.

Q. That had not been disconnected? A. Had not been separated in any way.

Q. Had not been disconnected in any way? A. Not at all.

Q. Nor separated? A. It had not.

Q. The face had turned a brown color, had it not? A. Rather a dark color when I saw it, sir.

Q. The eyes were missing? A. No, they were there, but they had softened up considerably.

Q. Now I want you to tell me, please, just what you did to the skull. A. Well, the face--- I presume you include in the skull the face as a part of it?

Q. Yes. A. I first counted the teeth. I don't know whether that was just first or not, but that is one of the things.

Q. Were there any bruises on the face? A. There was no evidence of bruises. There was an evidence of this discoloration due to decomposition. The facial muscles were very much still in what I would consider a natural formation, although discolored; the eyes were softened, that is, when opening the lid, the eyes had a different appearance than the normal eye. I don't know how I could describe it to make the jury understand it, but we call it a softened condition of the eye. The lips were swollen and slightly averted, the teeth were showing, were quite prominent due to this elevation of the lips.

Q. Which is natural in death? A. Well, in this case I think it was due to the fact that there was some distinction of the parts, probably due to decomposition as well.

Q. There was no doubt in your mind but what you were examining the Lindbergh baby, was there? A. At that time I didn't know. I didn't know at that time whether it was the Lindbergh baby or whose baby. Of course we had our own ideas.

Q. I mean you hadn't been told when you came over there? A. We were told that it was suspected to be the Lindbergh baby. I didn't know at that time.

Q. Had Colonel Lindbergh identified it? A. Not at that time.

Q. Had Betty Gow identified it? A. No, but I called the State Police and requested that Betty Gow come down and see the child to aid us in identification.

Q. Did she come down while you were there? A. She came, but I didn't go in the morgue while she was there.

Q. You knew it was a case of very importance? A. We gave that case the same consideration that we give every case. We don't consider it important, we consider the individual, one we consider about as good as another when we come to do our work.

Q. You didn't consider this case important enough---wait for a question, please. You didn't consider this case important enough to call in some other doctor of standing of either Pennsylvania, New Jersey or New York to join in the certification of the cause of the death? A. No, I didn't think I needed them.

Q. An hour and a half after you looked at the body you determined the cause of death? A. I certainly did.

Q. Where was this blood clot? Point it out on your own head, please. A. About an inch and a half posterior---this is inside the skull, not outside.

Q. You laid the skull open? A. We laid the skull open by endeavoring first to saw off the top of the skull, but then it began to come apart of its own.

Q. The skull was so pliable in a child of that age--- A. That it broke off.

Q. ---that you could practically open it like an orange, could you? A. At that time?

Q. Yes, certainly at that time. A. Yes, sir; decomposition had set in. Do you want me to answer this other question or do you want me to wander off into this new thing?

Q. No, we won't wander off at all. We will go back into whether or not the skull of this unfortunate child at this time wasn't so pliable because of its youth and exposure to the elements to practically open it like an orange. A. Yes, you could; it fell apart.

Q. Yes. A. Absolutely.

Q. And you don't want to convey to the jury that you had to use a saw, the same as you would do on my skull or on yours? A. We started to, but we found the bones were beginning to separate so we decided---

Q. And you decided that was a good autopsy,---to use a saw on a child? A. I certainly considered I did a good job.

Q. In your opinion, you did a good job? A. I am well satisfied with it.

Q. Yes, and well satisfied with yourself? A. Not at all.

Q. Now, I want to know whether or not you photographed the blood clot? A. We did not. My memory still holds to me, just as I saw it on that occasion.

Q. Didn't you think that at some time it might be possible, in view of the fact that it was afterwards determined, before this child had been sent for cremation, you knew it was the Lindbergh child, didn't you? A. That was taken---

Q. Yes. A. That was taken away, I did, yes.

Q. Yes. Didn't you think it important enough to preserve the evidence by picture, of what you found, didn't you? A. I felt my memory was just as good as the picture of that.

Q. There had been nobody arrested, had there? A. For this crime?

Q. At that time. A. At that time?

Q. Yes. A. Not to my knowledge.

Q. And did you take into consideration the fact that possibly before a suspect would be arrested you might die? A. I didn't give that a thought.

Q. Did you consider the fact that if you did die before an arrest was made no one could testify to the autopsy from a medical viewpoint? A. I don't know the law, to tell you the truth. I don't know how you work it. You fellows have got it around some way before you get through with it. (Laughter.)

Q. Just a moment, Doctor. You want it to appear now that you are ignorant of the law? A. I am ignorant of that part of the law. I really don't know what would happen if I did die.

Q. You have been performing autopsies for the Government---and by the Government I mean the State of New Jersey and a certain County---for many years? A. Yes, sir.

Q. And you have been testifying in court? A. Many times.

Q. On homicide cases and on other cases? A. You are right.

Q. And you say from the number of times and the years that you have testified, that you do not now know the law applicable to this preservation of a physician's testimony, a physician in your official capacity? A. All I know is I file a report. The report is accepted, I presume, as authentic. I give that to the prosecutor of my County, if it occurs there, or, in this case, to the State, and that is what I consider the evidence that

I am going to abide by when I testify. Now, if I should die---I don't want to appear ignorant of the law, but I am ignorant of that fact, ---I don't know what would happen.

Q. Did any official, Colonel Schwarzkopf, or any official connected with this case, suggest that night that it might be advisable to not only have your findings but the findings of another physician? A. I don't recollect the Colonel speaking to me about that. At least, I am quite sure he didn't.

Q. And you say there is no photograph in existence except your recollection and your memory of this blood clot? A. Absolutely. To my knowledge there isn't.

Q. Now, what is the medical term for this blood clot? A. That is what it is: coagulated blood.

Q. What is a thrombosis? A. That is a clot in a vessel.

Q. Yes. And a person or a child suffering from a clot in a vessel of the body can die, can they not, when the clot reaches the brain? A. You are right, sir.

Q. And you never saw this child, as you have testified, in life? A. Never in my life; no, sir.

Q. And don't know what it was suffering from? A. Haven't the slightest idea.

Q. If it was suffering from anything. A. I don't know, sir.

Q. So you came to your conclusion that because there was a clot on the brain and there were evidences of a cracked skull that the child died of a fractured skull? A. Based my conclusions on those facts.

Q. On that, is that right? A. On those facts, yes.

Q. Yes. Doctor, is it true that blood decomposes more rapidly than any other portion of the body or changes its chemistry? A. It is one of the softest tissues we have and, of course, the density of the tissue is in proportion to the decomposition. The softer it is the more quickly it decomposes. A blood clot I can safely say would decompose quite rapidly.

Dr. Mitchell admitted that he had only an idea or slight suspicion that he had examined the Lindbergh baby. He said it was only after Betty Gow's identification that he felt certain it was the Colonel's child. However, he did this despite the badly decomposed body which lay before him, and the statement of a qualified doctor, the baby's personal physician,

Dr. Philip Van Ingen who knew the child well, and had stated the body was definitely unrecognizable.

With this fact being widely known, isn't it strange, you might ask, why the Hauptmann attorneys made no attempt to challenge the prosecution's claim that the skeletal remains found by William Allen were not those of Lindbergh's son. By doing this they could have put a battery of doctors on the stand contesting the find. Several days of contradictory testimony would have then been entered into the court's record. However, this was not done and it is easy to understand why when the stupidity, or deliberate oversight of Reilly is seen.

It had become very apparent early in the trial that Edward J. Reilly was not too interested in defending his client in a proper legal manner. The Brooklyn lawyer had been hired by William Randolph Hearst, whose chief purpose in doing this was to obtain exclusive news reports of the trial for his chain of newspapers. His newspapers were to get first-hand accounts from, not only the bombastic "Bull of Brooklyn", but from the human interest accounts given, either personally to, or observed by, the constant female companion he had assigned to stay with Mrs. Hauptmann at all times.

Discussions about the trial had many folks speaking of the apparent dislike Reilly held toward his client; as well as his utter disregard to prepare and present a sound defense for Hauptmann, whom he certainly recognized, for the most part, had little more than circumstantial evidence against him that needed to be explained away with reasonable arguments.

This fact was never more apparent than during the testimony given by Mrs. Elmira Dormer, who identified herself as a custodian of St. Michael's Orphanage in Hopewell where she resided. Mrs. Dormer stated that of the 306 children, ranging in ages from two weeks old to sixteen years, cared for in the orphanage, none had been reported missing during the latter part of February or early March, 1932. Nor had there been any missing through the month of May. The orphanage, she explained, was located on the opposite side of the highway from the spot where the corpse was found on May 12th. She said the orphanage school was situated about "ten good sized blocks" from where William Allen had made his discovery. Attorney General Wilentz inquired:

Q. Are these books the books of attendance of your school? A. Yes, sir.

Q. As of those months? A. Yes, sir.

Q. If there is any dispute about the attendance I will offer them. If there isn't, I won't.

Mr. Reilly: There is no dispute.

Mr. Wilentz: There is no claim that the child came from the orphanage.

Mr. Pope: No.

Mr. Wilentz: Am I to understand that there is no claim that this child came from the orphanage?

Mr. Fisher: I thought your proposition was if we didn't dispute the attendance you would not offer the books.

Mr. Wilentz: If there is any claim about it, I will offer them

MR. REILLY: I WILL SAY NOW THAT THERE HAS NEVER BEEN ANY CLAIM BUT THAT THIS WAS COLONEL LINDBERGH'S CHILD THAT WAS FOUND THERE. However, I am glad you brought the lady here because I want to ask her a couple of questions about the terrain. May I have the pointer, please?

And "Death House Reilly" went on to question her about the landscape and a police dog named "Dannie"; all questions of virtual unimportance.

But the damage had been done. Lloyd Fisher, hearing Reilly's admission that he was not contesting the remains as being any other than Lindbergh's child, stood to his feet and in a strained voice, shouted at the chief defense lawyer: "YOU ARE CONCEDING HAUPTMANN TO THE ELECTRIC CHAIR!" His countenance expressed a combination of disgust and contempt for the Brooklyn barrister, and with an inaudible utterance escaping his lips he rushed out of the courtroom.

Scaduto in his book *Scapegoat* described the occurrence this way: "Fisher, rising to answer, but too late, appeared as if struck in the face with a club; Reilly had just destroyed the slimmest chance to save Hauptmann's life. Even if he protested and tried to correct the record, the jury had heard the concession. Fisher shot up straight now and shouted at Reilly, 'You are conceding Hauptmann to the electric chair!' Then, with an inaudible word that was a short sharp hiss of contempt, he rushed from the courtroom. Hauptmann started to rise, as if to flee with the lawyer he most trusted, but thought better of it as his guards stirred. He sat heavily and whispered, 'You are killing me.' Anna Hauptmann sat, the wrench of recognition twisting at the edges of her mouth, understanding that a crisis had been reached---and lost"

This tragic admission by Reilly was inexcusable even if it had been an accidental one, which was definitely not the case. Lloyd Fisher had made it quite clear to Reilly that it would have been a fatal mistake to concede, in any way, that the child found was Lindbergh's. Realizing the importance of this, Fisher had pointed out to Reilly that the weakest link in the case, built on almost nothing more than circumstantial evidence, would be to agree to the identification of the skeleton. "Whatever you do, Ed, don't concede that the skeleton was the Lindbergh child's. We can put doctors and scientists on the stand for a week to prove that it wasn't." Big Ed readily agreed to this, admitting it was certainly sound logic.

But, setting aside the unacceptable and very vague possibility of it being "an accidental admission or omission", I arrived at the conclusion many years ago that Reilly deliberately made his startling announcement with complete knowledge as to exactly what he was doing. He, as I have already pointed out and will continue to do, was doing everything he could to "prosecute his own client." He, on many occasions, had shown his contempt for Hauptmann.

Although it was another known fact that Reilly, on many days of the trial, had appeared to be "far from sober" as he entered the courtroom, was certainly not "in a drunken stupor" when he made his blundering admission. "Big Ed" was seen by a host of people spending his evenings, usually with a woman on his arm, at the bar of the Union Hotel. Alan Hynd, in the numerous articles he had written covering the Hauptmann trial, had a unique way of describing the bulbous Brooklyn barrister and his nightly escapades: "Big Ed Reilly spent his nights drinking. He arrived in court each morning thoroughly bushed, afraid to lean over, and reluctant to open his eyes for fear of bleeding to death. He was never fully awake until after lunch, when he drank eight to ten orange blossoms out of a coffee cup in the hotel across the street."

Writing about Reilly's intentional "goof-up" which denied the defense the opportunity of placing even the slightest doubt in the jury's minds that the skeleton could have been that of anyone other than Lindbergh's son, Hynd reported: "While the little men with the hammers were at work on the inside of Big Ed's temples, the question of the identification of the body came up.

Lloyd Fisher, Reilly's associate counsel, was supposed to arise at that point and begin introducing evidence to dispute the state's claim that the body of the Lindbergh child had really been found. Reilly was on his feet first. 'We concede,' he said, 'that the corpse that was found was that of the Lindbergh baby.' The state's lawyers could hardly believe their ears, Fisher left the courtroom to give his temperature a chance to drop."

Reilly, pompous buffoon of a lawyer that he was, had played the "fool's part" to perfection as he generously handed the prosecution staff a valuable piece of evidence they didn't have to put forth even the smallest argument to prove. Whatever fairness the innocent Richard Hauptmann felt would be granted him at Flemington was being crushed each day inside a courtroom filled with liars, manufactured evidence, and a very inept lawyer.

C H A P T E R   T H I R T Y   T W O

The "Wood" Men!

Probably the most outrageous piece of framed evidence, if we can select one above another, used to convict Richard Hauptmann was the testimony of Arthur Koehler, the wood "expert" of Madison, Wisconsin, supported by the "fabricated" evidence fostered on the jury by Detective Lewis J. Bornmann of the New Jersey State Police. Their combined testimony, no doubt, proved to be most damning to the innocence of Hauptmann.

The evidence of Koehler had to do primarily with the wood used in the ladder. He had traced at least a part of it from the M.G. and J.J. Dorn Company of McCormick, South Carolina to the National Lumber and Millwork Company, in the Bronx. He testified that Hauptmann had not only worked there, but had undoubtedly, purchased the lumber from there. He "proved" that one rail of the ladder had come from the Hauptmann attic at 1279 East 222nd Street, the Bronx. The one incriminating rail, later to be identified as "Rail 16", was a pine upright which completed one of the ladder's sections.

Koehler demonstrated that the eight foot rail contained four nail holes made by the old fashioned square cut nails as the board had been nailed into the joist in a staggered pattern. He "proved", to the evident satisfaction of the jury, that this "Rail 16" had been removed from the attic flooring, leaving a conspicuous eight foot space, with tell-tale sawdust remaining as more incriminating evidence that it had once been a part of the attic floor.

Koehler was quite convincing as he "proved beyond any possibility of anyone's doubt" demonstrating with pictures, official photographs, drawings, tracing, knots, texture, rings and grain, in addition to other "factual points" that "Rail 16" had at one time been taken from Hauptmann's attic and used in the construction of the kidnap ladder. He pointed out that when the tongue and groove eight foot plank had been placed over the uncovered joist, the four nail holes coincided exactly with the holes in the joist, and that by merely holding the same size cut nails above the holes in the board, with the slight pressure of one's thumb, they would drop into the holes in the joist. The "wood genius" stated that for this to happen by sheer coincidence it was figured mathematically as 1 in 10,000,000,000,000,000. And this figure would not take into consideration the allowance for the inclined or sloping of even one nail hole, which would increase the chance of any accidental resemblance.

It would be unfair of me to bore you with more of the obnoxious irritating testimony of this man Koehler, who enjoyed the title of "wood detective". The jury obviously believed every word he said, since his testimony, on the surface, was very convincing, especially to those who knew nothing, or very little, about wood in any shape or form. The clue as to how and why at least one police official decided it would be profitable for them to make use of an attic board in convicting Hauptmann can be clearly seen, especially when we take a look at what actually took place after the arrest of the Bronx carpenter.

But first, we should remember something that Koehler, shortly after his entrance into the case, had told Colonel Schwarzkopf regarding the appearance of "Rail 16". He had explained that since the four nail holes showed no trace of rust, it was very evident that the board had been used in a place that had been sheltered from the weather. "Whenever you get a suspect", he emphasized, "look around his premises for a place indoors where there are empty cut-nail holes, and possibly some boards to match with the ladder rail." And with the utterance of that statement the door was opened wide for the terrible deception that was to take place within the Hauptmann home in 1934.

When Richard Hauptmann was arrested on September 19th of that year we must bear in mind that Mrs. Hauptmann did not live in her home one more day until after the trial ended in mid-February of 1935. The home had been rented by the New Jersey State Police, with Detective Bornmann its chief resident. Remembering then, that it was Bornmann who had been assigned to accompany Koehler in his nationwide search to locate the lumberyard from where the ladder wood had its origin, and that the two men had been together as traveling companions from June of 1932 until the autumn of 1934, we can use our reasonable assumption that since Bornmann and Koehler had spent so many months together, it is therefore, not difficult to imagine that the wood expert had also divulged his theory to his partner: "Whenever you get a suspect, look around his premises for a place indoors, where there are empty cut-nail holes, and possibly some boards to match with the ladder rail."; or for that matter, that Schwarzkopf had also shared with Bornmann the theory he had been told by Koehler.

Only minutes after Hauptmann's arrest, the police started dismantling his living quarters. They lost no time in checking into, tearing into, and searching everything within the apartment, including the attic and garage. Due to their efforts they confiscated many things belonging to the Hauptmanns, mainly the $14,600 of Lindbergh ransom money that had been stashed away in the garage adjacent to the home. The garage was demolished to the very ground it had been erected on.

During the time intervening between the date the arrest was made and Wednesday, September 26th, the police had made repeated searches of the Hauptmann attic. During those eight days, no less that thirty-seven police officers, representing the New York City Police, the New Jersey State Police, the Federal Bureau of Investigation, and the Jersey City Police, had gone up there, and not one of them had disclosed any information regarding the missing attic board.

Tony Scaduto's feelings on the possibility of such a dereliction of duty by those thirty-seven men, and possibly many others who had searched the attic, were well stated in his book *SCAPEGOAT* when he reasoned that they "must have been as blind as the witness Hochmuth."

Now armed with the knowledge bestowed on him by the "wisdom" of Koehler, the seed of an idea had been planted in the mind of Lewis Bornmann. This seed, watered with an over zealous and fervent desire to prove beyond any doubt the involvement of Hauptmann, captivated his mind with his "own distorted certainty" of Hauptmann being the only person capable of carrying out every facet of the crime. Detective Bornmann lost no time in setting the wheels in motion to prove this, and at the same time establishing himself a hero of sorts.

Now it is expedient that we study the actual court testimony of "super-cop" Bornmann as he answered some questions put to him under direct questioning by Mr. Robert Peacock of the prosecution staff: (Pages 2151-2156)

Q. Mr. Bornmann, do you know where the defendant Hauptmann lives in New York or did live? A. Yes, sir.

Q. Where was it? A. 1279 East 222nd Street,

Bronx.

Q. On September 26th, 1934, were you at his home? A. Yes, sir, I was.

Q. And for what purpose? A. For the purpose of searching for evidence.

Q. Did you make a search for evidence? A. Yes, sir.

Q. Did you make a search of the attic of the defendant's home at that time? A. I did.

Q. How did you get in? A. Why--

Q. Pardon me. Were you going to say something? How did you gain entrance to the attic? A. Entrance is gained by going to the small linen closet leading off the hall. It is necessary to climb through this linen closet to the attic.

Q. What was the size of the closet? A. It is 28 inches deep, 22 1/2 inches wide, and has a small door 15 1/2 inches wide with a lock.

Q. And where was the closet located in the house? A. It is located between two bedrooms, rear bedroom and what is known as the nursery bedroom.

Q. And how did you get from the closet up into the attic? A. It was necessary to remove the shelves and climb up.

Q. And where were the shelves located in the closet? A. As you open the door there are three shelves spaced apart.

Q. And how wide were those shelves? A. They are made of 1 x 12, what is known as shelving, 22 and a half inches wide,--

Q. Who was with you? A. Long.

Q. ---this day? A. On the 26th, I was accompanied by Police Carpenter Cramer, Enkler and Detective Tobin of the Bronx.

Q. Now, did the three of you remove those shelves to get into the attic? A. Yes, sir, we did.

Q. Now, when you got into the attic what did you find? A. We first made a search for money, we didn't find any money and during this search I found that all the floor boards were not of the same length, that is the one in the south west corner, a portion of it had been removed.

Mr. Reilly: I move to strike that out as calling for a conclusion, there was one board, he can describe the boards that were there, but the conclusion one had been removed, was missing, I say is objectionable, he can't testify to that.

The Court: Well, Mr. Reilly, he may have

seen evidence that it had been removed. I do not know about that.

Mr. Reilly: And may he say what he saw, Judge?

The Court: Yes, he may say what he saw, that is the best way, I think.

Q. Now, Mr. Bornmann, referring to Exhibit S-215, will you show to the jury where that board was missing that you---

Mr. Reilly: Now. I object to that word "missing." Let him tell us what he saw.

Q. I withdraw that question. Referring to Exhibit S-215, show the jury the condition that you found the attic. A. Well, this is the south west corner, this is the south side, and this is the west side (indicating) and the end board, approximately 8 foot of it had been removed---

Mr. Reilly: Now, I object to that as calling for a conclusion; he can say there was no board there.

Q. Well, there was no board there, was there? A. There was no board, and upon examining it further, I found that there were nail holes still in the beams, and between the 7th and 8th beam here there was a small quantity of saw dust.

Q. Now, where was that saw dust? A. That was between the 7th and 8th beam, right down in here, laying on the plaster.

Q. Referring to the end of the piece of rail that still was on the floor, is that what you mean? A. Yes.

Q. In between the two beams at the end of this rail? A. In between this 7th and 8th beam; it was also on this adjoining board there, a small indentation made by a saw where, when this board had been sawed off, the saw went into it.

Mr. Reilly: I object to that, where the board had been sawed off.

The Court: Well, there seems to be some little justification for that sort of an inference, doesn't there, Mr.Reilly?

Mr. Reilly: There might be an inference, Judge, but it is not such an inference that a guilty conclusion can be drawn from it. This board might have been well nailed down with that saw cut in it, and I take it that we are only concerned in---

Mr. Wilentz: Well, he doesn't say anything to the contrary. Mr. Reilly's statement may be so, that it may have been nailed down with the saw mark in it, but the fact remains that there is a saw mark.

Mr. Reilly: Yes.

Mr. Wilentz: That is all the witness has testified to.

Mr. Reilly: Yes, the fact there is a saw mark, yes, sir.

Mr. Wilentz: That is all that he is testifying to.

The discussion regarding the location of the saw mark followed, with the direct questioning continuing as to what was done with the board:

Q. And what did you do with that board? A. I had Police Carpenter Cramer remove the cut nails from it.

Q. And what--- A. And I then took the board down to the second floor and locked it in a bedroom.

Q. Did you have the key to that closet? A. It was in the custody of a policeman, a uniformed man on duty.

Q. Then what further was done with that board? A. I made a report to Captain Lamb as to---

Mr. Reilly: I object.

Q. Well, you made a report with reference to what you had done that day? A. Yes, sir.

Q. Now were you at the same building on October 9th with Mr. Koehler? A. Yes, sir. In compliance with instructions from Captain Lamb I took Mr.Koehler---

And the witness went on to tell of his "marvelous find", the tell-tale attic board and how he and the "scientific wood expert" Koehler matched the board with the holes, the holes with the board, and the nails with the holes and the board until the jury and spectators were lost in the maze of wood. To claim, however, that Koehler and Bornmann failed to prove their point to the satisfaction of the jury would be trite. Hauptmann was convicted largely because of the testimony and evidence presented by these two men. But as we all know, there is always two sides to a coin, just as there are two sides to the facts of "Rail 16" and the attic board. Let us now look at the truth. We will start with the cross examination of Bornmann by Mr. Frederick A. Pope:

Q. When was the first time you were up in the

attic, Officer? A. September 26th.

Q. And how many times were you up there after that before Mr. Koehler came? A. Once more I believe.

Q. And during that interval how many local policemen were up there? A. To my knowledge there has never been a local policeman in that attic.

Q. How many troopers were up there? A. Myself only and Sergeant Schultz, the photographer.

Q. How many Department of Justice Agents up there? A. None to my knowledge.

Q. None to your knowledge? A. No, sir.

Q. They all had access to the house, did they not? A. They did to a certain extent but the New York Police Department took it over, they acted as custodians of it.

Q. After the arrest of Hauptmann, the State Police took possession of his apartment, did they not? A. No, sir.

Q. You rented it for a couple of months, did you not, you yourself? A. After Hauptmann had moved out, yes,sir.

Q. Well, that was after his arrest, he didn't move out before his arrest, did he? A. After he had vacated the premises, I rented it.

Q. Well, you rented it for a couple of months, didn't you? A. That is correct.

Q. And locked it up? A. Yes, sir.

Q. And refused admission to the defense or their representatives?

Mr. Wilentz: I object to that, if your Honor please. In the first place he doesn't know anything about that. However, I withdraw the objection.

The Court: He either did or he didn't.

Mr. Wilentz: I withdraw the objection.

Q. You are the tenant, aren't you? A. I am what?

Q. The tenant, the one that rented it? A. Yes, sir.

Q. And paid for it, and you locked it up? A. I rented it anyhow.

Q. You rented it, and you have refused to permit the defense to enter the premises, haven't you? A. I have never had any request from the defense for permission to enter.

This testimony is ridiculous. As you will learn, the defense made many requests to inspect the house and were refused.

Bornmann gave another recital of the size of the linen closet which led to the attic and was then asked to be more precise. The questioning follows:

Q. Now, was there a trap door leading from that closet to the attic? A. Well, as you went to the top there was the covering over the closet.

Q. Well, was it a trap door? You know what a trap door is. A. Well, you wouldn't call it a trap door. It wasn't on hinges; it was just loose.

Q. Just a loose trap door? A. Yes.

Q. Set in a frame? A. It was part of the flooring that had been cut out to allow access to the attic.

Q. Now, that was the only method of access to the attic, wasn't it? A. Yes, sir, it was.

Q. And it was apparently constructed that way when the building was built? A. That is correct.

Q. There was no other entrance to the attic except the one that you have just described? A. No, sir.

Q. Were you in this closet before the Hauptmanns moved out? A. I had to go into it, to go to the attic.

Q. Well, were the Hauptmanns living there at the time you were in the attic? A. Their furniture was still there.

Q. Was Mrs. Hauptmann there? A. No, sir, she was not. She came in a couple of times while I was there.

Q. And she had not been there for several days, had she? A. Not living there, no, sir.

Q. Well, the property was infested with police, wasn't it? A. Well, there were a few policemen around there.

Q. Yes. How many do you call a few? A. Detective Tobin, myself, two police carpenters and two police guards, I believe.

Q. About 7 or 8? A. I call it 6.

Q. Now, how many times were the police carpenters up in the attic before Mr. Koehler arrived on the scene A. They were there with me, that was all.

Q. How many times? A. Once.

Q. Just once? A. Yes.

Q. To your knowledge? A. Yes.

Q. And when was that, what date, if you know? A. September 26th, 1934, about 10:30 a.m.

Q. Now, so far as you know that was the first

time that any policeman went up to the attic? A. As far as I know, yes.

Q. And then after that you don't know how many policemen were there, do you? A. I don't know how many were there.

Q. Yes. A. No, sir. There were none there to my knowledge.

Q. None to your knowledge, no. When did Mr. Taylor arrive at the scene after September the 26th? A. First took him over there on October the 9th.

Q. That was about 14 or 15 days later? A. Approximately

Q. And at that time this other piece of board had been removed from the flooring, hadn't it? A. It had been removed from the attic and was still in the house, in the bedroom of the second floor, under lock and key.

Q. That is, the board was under lock and key? A. Yes, sir.

Q. In your possession? A. Yes, sir.

Q. The key was in your possession? A. No, sir, the key was in the possession of the Police Department.

Q. Of the New York Police Department? A. New York Police Department.

Bornmann's testimony, a great example of the truth being bent out of proportion, is clearly exhibited when he stated, for the record, that he had gone up into the Hauptmann attic for the <u>first time</u> on September 26th about 10:30 a.m., and that "as far as he knew this was the <u>first time any policeman went into the Hauptmann attic</u>.

Bornmann lied. If it were so, as he testified, then the many police who worked in and around the Hauptmann home from the date of his arrest, September 19th, until September 26th had been derelict in their work. Police reports prove that many officers, at least 37, had been up in the attic on many occasions. And with Bornmann the tenant of the home, it is impossible to believe that he had never ventured into the attic himself before that date.

J. Edgar Hoover and his FBI agents, shortly after the arrest of Hauptmann, had learned of this "matching wood testimony" the prosecution staff were planning to use against their prisoner as a "catch-all" in convicting their Bronx prisoner. Hoover and his men became quite dubious of "Bornmann's great discovery", and stated openly that they believed "the wood had been fabricated by the joint efforts of the New Jersey State

Police and the New Jersey prosecutor's office in cooperation with Arthur Koehler." Hoover was expecting to be subpoenaed by the defense for someone in his department to come to the Flemington trial and testify as to their beliefs --- but Hauptmann's lawyers failed to do this. Reilly failed again!

Governor Harold Hoffman's remarks about this amazing late discovery were related in one of his writings:

"This important evidence is something that should have struck any experienced investigator 'smack in the eye'; yet, if it was there, New York City Police, F.B.I. investigators, and the New Jersey sleuths passed it by until Bornmann arrived on the scene, September 26, and accompanied by two carpenters from the New York City Police Department, discovered the important evidence that had been waiting, for a week, for him to find.

"Corporal William Horn, in a report of his activities for September 19, says that he searched the Hauptmann residence with representatives of the New York City Police Department and the U.S. Department of Justice, under the supervision of Lieutenant Keaten of the New Jersey State Police and Inspector John Lyons of the New York City Department. The partially missing floor board is not mentioned in this report.

"On September 20 Corporal Samuel Leon reported that, with Lieutenant Frank McCarthy of the New York City Police and Agent Wright of the Department of Justice, he searched the Hauptmann garage, and he adds: 'We then searched the kitchen, bedroom, nursery, parlor, and attic, and cellar, but were unable to find anything connected with the Lindbergh case.'

"On September 22, in compliance with the orders of Lieutenant Keaten, Sergeant A. Zapolsky of the New Jersey State Police went to the Hauptmann home, accompanied by Sergeant P. Kelly and Sergeant Wallace of his department, and four New York City detectives. 'We were assigned,' writes Zapolsky, 'to search the attic.' He adds: 'In the attic we picked up a mason's bag containing two trowels, two pieces of pipe, one ruler, one plane blade, and one empty fiber suitcase.' There is no mention of the partially missing floor board.

"Can it be possible that all these sharp-eyed Sherlocks--several Department of Justice investigators, a half dozen or more New York City detectives and policemen, and eight New Jersey State Police officers--had gone repeatedly to the Hauptmann attic to search it, and had passed over what subsequently turned out to be the most important piece of evidence in sending Hauptmann to the electric chair?

"But read this report signed by Detective Bornmann, and setting out his activity of September 26, the day the evidence is supposed to have been found: 'This date detailed by Captain Lamb to continue search on the above-captioned home. Meeting Detective Tobin, two police carpenters, and Superintendent Wilson on the premises at 9 A.M., we immediately proceeded to make a thorough search of the attic. Nothing of value was found, with the exception of several small pieces of wood and shavings and several cut nails that may possibly have a bearing on the case.'

"It is true that there are several supplemental reports citing the 'great find', but I am at a loss to understand why Bornmann, in what apparently was his first written report of that day's activities, maintained that 'nothing of value was found.'

"Bornmann, you will recall, is the State Police officer who, according to his testimony, pulled up the remaining half of this floor board, filled with nails, and with a tongue inserted in the groove of the adjacent floor board, with his bare hands. He certainly played an important part in sending Hauptmann to his doom. Bornmann didn't apply for any of the New Jersey reward money.

"The wood angle represents another phase of the case upon which whole volumes might be written.

"Hundreds of pages of testimony were devoted to the wood angle, undoubtedly confusing the jury. Some of the claims made were absurd, but they were undoubtedly swallowed by the expert-awed jury.

"I have in my possession a photograph of the ladder made the day after the commission of the crime. It is a clear photograph, in which the knots and grains are distinctly shown and rail 16 can be easily identified; but in neither the original nor in a copy magnified ten times can the alleged nail holes be found."

Anthony Scaduto in *Scapegoat* delves further into the attic-ladder wood testimony of Bornmann, proving beyond anyone's doubt that the State Police detective, not only perjured himself, but had his own manufactured evidence brought into court to frame the hapless Richard Hauptmann. Mr. Scaduto tells it well:

"I call as my next witness Lewis J. Bornmann."

"Detective Bornmann, please!"

"Bornmann rises from the prosecution table and steps to the witness chair. He has not been outside, in the corridor or in an anteroom, nor kept segregated from the proceedings so that his recollections, his mind, would be uninfluenced by the testimony of witnesses who proceeded him. He has sat day after day at the long table of the prosecution, with Lindbergh and Wilentz and a half dozen prosecution lawyers.

"Bornmann. The cop who took over Hauptmann's apartment hours after his arrest, who cheerfully agreed with Mrs. Hauptmann that she should move in with relatives and then confiscated the apartment. The man who still lived there, keeping out defense lawyers and investigators who sought entrance; mistrustful, they wanted to see where Bornmann had located certain evidence they heard he had found, how he had come across it, what the apartment now looked like. But Bornmann turned them back, an officer of the law protecting the law's castle, repelling the outsiders. For after all Bornmann had exercised a peculiar brand of annexation and he wasn't going to permit the dispossessed to interfere with the sovereign states of New York and New Jersey.

"Wilentz asked: 'And did you again search that apartment?'

"Yes, I did, Bornmann said. It was on September 26 (seven days after Hauptmann's arrest) that I conducted another search of said premises with other police officers. Said search took us to the attic. We gained access to the attic by entering a small linen closet, pushing up a trap door in the ceiling, climbing up the closet shelves, and pulling ourselves through.

"When you got into the attic what did you find?

"Well, first we searched for money and during the search I noticed that a length of one of the attic floorboards had been sawed off one end of this long floorboard. I knew it had been cut off because there were nail holes still in the beams and between the seventh and eighth beam there was a small pile of sawdust lying there. Also, on the floorboard adjoining the end of the piece that had been sawed away, you could see a small saw cut where the saw bit into the adjoining board.

"So, he continued, I called for Arthur Koehler, a wood expert for the U.S. Forest Service. Koehler had been helping us trace wood in the kidnap ladder for two years. And he came as soon as he could get away and on October 9 we returned to the attic of said premises.

"What did you do when you arrived there?

"Well, we brought with us one of the side rails in the ladder, one of the uprights. It's marked Rail 16, that's what we marked it when we tagged each piece of it for lab analysis. Rail 16. There are four nail holes in Rail 16. Up in the attic, we put Rail 16 down on the beam that also had four nail holes. Then we pushed nails into the holes in Rail 16 and they went right in with just a little finger pressure and they went right in and right down into the holes in the attic beam. They fit perfectly, no doubt about it.

"The prosecutor paused, turned to the jury with a smile, let it sink in. An earlier witness, the owner of the house, had testified that when the Hauptmanns moved into the apartment in October 1931, the attic floor had been intact. A couple of the jury members nodded. It was plain now. Hauptmann had run short of wood and had removed a length from his attic to finish the kidnap ladder.

"Now, Detective Bornmann, I show you a board. Did you take this board from Hauptmann's attic?

"Yes, sir, I did. That's the board that had a piece cut from it.

"Who removed that from the attic floor?

"I did.

"Was it the same color that it is now?

"Oh, yes sir, it is.

"And what was the color of Rail 16?

"The same color as the attic board.

"Your witness, the prosecutor said. He sat down, quite pleased. The kidnap ladder had now been rammed home---right into Hauptmann's attic.

"Frederick Pope, a local lawyer, one of the assistants to Reilly and Fisher, rose to challenge for the defense.

"He asked: 'Before you put Rail 16 into place there was nothing between the attic board and the end of the building, was there?'

"No sir, Bornmann replied. There was about eight feet missing from the floor, the board that was cut out was about eight feet long.

"Now, even after you put Rail 16 into place it didn't reach from the end of the floorboard to the end of the building, did it?

"No sir, there was a space about an inch and a quarter between the board on the floor and the beginning of the ladder rail. When we put the ladder rail into place with the nails, there was this gap of more than an inch.

"Yes, the defense attorney said, but I'm talking about the other end also. The missing length even after laying Rail 16 down is about thirty-six inches, isn't it?

"Well, Bornmann said, about eight foot of it had been taken out and Rail 16 is about six foot, eight and a half inches.

"The implication was clear to the spectators and the jury. Hauptmann, a skilled union carpenter, had removed a board from his attic that was between fifteen and thirty-six inches too long and had to later cut a foot or more from it. Or, perhaps---another inference that could be drawn---was it that Bornmann had been so sloppy in manufacturing his evidence he had cut off and threw away a length of attic floor a couple of feet longer than the board he was going to claim had come from Hauptmann's attic?

"But it wasn't made sufficiently clear to the jury. The cross-examination had been too brief. Nowhere in it does the lawyer shout: 'Do you expect this jury to believe this ladder upright, Rail 16, came from that attic? Let us see what you expect this jury to believe. Wasn't there a lumberyard two blocks from the defendant's home? Didn't you find enough wood in his garage and in the basement to make this upright? Is it your expert police opinion that Hauptmann climbed into his attic in search of a length of wood to complete his ladder? He knows he needs precisely six feet, eight and a half inches. He is a carpenter, he measures his work, he knows the length he needs. In his attic, he begins to saw. Without measuring. Is it your expert opinion he sawed off a piece about eighteen inches too long? That he took it down through the trap door into his house and then down into his garage and sawed off the eighteen inches? And then, finding it was still too long, he cut off another inch and a half from the opposite end? Or is it more logical to believe there was an inch-and-a-half gap between the ends of those two boards in the attic because that was the only way to get the nail holes to match up? Did you, Detective Bornmann, drive nail holes in the beam so they'd match the holes in the rail?'

"But the questions were not asked. The information received by the jury was that the board had come from the attic. More than a foot off one end, an inch and a fraction off the other. Nuances never highlighted by questions to force the jurors to think.

Nuances suggesting manufactured evidence.

"Coils of suspicion uncoiled in my mind. Eyewitnesses, suspect. Handwriting analysts, suspect. A board from the attic, suspect. A commander of police willing to suborn perjury . . . suspect. Was it all like this? Layer upon layer of perjury, a meandering river of lies that swallowed Hauptmann and carried him over the abyss?"

Scaduto is just as convincing in his bonafide accusations of the "expert" testimony of the "wood man" Arthur Koehler:

"And now the really vital evidence from Koehler was about to come. Koehler, wood detective, on the Flemington stage for his second day of glory, was asked by the prosecutor: 'After you removed from the ladder this section of wood, Rail 16, what did you find?'

"Detective Bornmann and I took it to Hauptmann's attic, Koehler said, and I found that the nail holes in the rail corresponded exactly with the grain in the piece of wood still in the attic.

"Then you say there is a relationship between Rail 16 and the board found in Hauptmann's attic?

"Yes, there certainly is, the witness responded. Those two pieces at one time were one piece. They were cut in two in the attic. I know that because there are a number of similarities between the two that make me believe they had been one.

"Is one of the similarities the nail holes?

"Yes, exactly, Koehler said. I took nails from the board still in place in the attic, because they would naturally be the same as the nails which had once been in Rail 16, and I lined up Rail 16 over the beam on the attic floor with the nail holes in it. I pushed down on the nails and each of them went through Rail 16 and into the holes in the beams. They fit perfectly into those holes.

"Tell us, what is your opinion as a wood expert?

"In my opinion, he said, that rail had at one time been nailed down on that beam in the attic. The nail holes in the rail and in the beam are irregularly spaced, both in distance between holes and in direction, and even in the slant at which they were originally hammered into place. It would not have been possible that there could be another board somewhere, spaced exactly as those nail holes are spaced. The same distance apart, the same direction separating them, the same slant to the nails. No other board anywhere could have fit into that attic.

"Wilentz turned to the jury and smiled; I have driven this ladder directly into Hauptmann's home, his eyes and mouth seemed to be saying. Upstairs, in the upper gallery of the courtroom, the din of teletype machines again emphasized the prosecutor's point: guilty, guilty, guilty. Wilentz returned to the witness.

"'What other reason do you have,' he asked, 'for giving as your opinion that Rail 16 and the board from Hauptmann's attic were at one time the same piece of lumber?'

"Because, the witness explained, speaking directly to the jury, when the rail was laid down in the attic and the nails inserted and fit perfectly, the rail was perfectly parallel to the adjoining board. If it had been an accident that these nails fit perfectly, it would not be expected that the board would necessarily be parallel to the other boards in the attic floor. That it was parallel proves even more conclusively that it had once lain in the attic, as part of the floor.

"And now Wilentz glided into his spectacular dramatic scene: Koehler had said earlier he was certain the ladder rail and the attic board had once been a single piece. Will the witness please explain to us further why he stated that?

"Well, when I was up in the attic with Bornmann I had peered down at the board still nailed into place and saw that a piece had been roughly cut away from it, Koehler said. I could see that a saw cut had been made at the end of the attic board, the end of what remained of the original long piece of board. Looking closer, I discovered on the adjoining floorboard a small cut of a saw directly in line with the board that had been cut out. Furthermore, there was a little pile of sawdust on the plaster of the ceiling below the board, directly under the end which had been cut. And furthermore, the piece of board left behind, still nailed down after the builder of the kidnap ladder had taken away the length he required, projected over the beam into which it had been nailed. Now, a carpenter wouldn't let the end of a board overlap and hang free that way. He would have placed the edge across the joists and finished it off perfectly. That indicates the board was not in its original condition.

"Not only that, he went on, but by matching the grain from the upright rail in the ladder with the board remaining in the attic, I find that it matches up practically perfectly, considering there is a gap between the two. The gap, of an inch and a quarter, can easily be explained, Koehler said. After the board had been removed from the attic it had been trimmed slightly at that end, doubtless because the ladder-builder decided it was too long for his purpose.

"'Will you show us on these photos,' Wilentz said, 'the grain and how you matched the grain?'

"Koehler, handling several enlargements of the two pieces of wood, explained why he was certain the grain of the ladder rail corresponded precisely with the grain of the floorboard. Every year, he told the jury, a tree produces a layer of wood under the bark. Those are known as the annual rings and by measuring them we can determine the rate of growth and the age of the tree. There are the same number of annual rings in the floorboard as there are in the ladder rail.

"Does that indicate the two boards are of the same age?'

"It indicates that it took the same number of years to produce that much growth, the witness said. Further evidence the two boards were once a single piece, Koehler said, is that the variation in the width of the rings is the same. There are three narrow rings in the floorboard and then the next two are thicker and the next two are narrower again. And as you can see---pointing to the photo of the ladder rail---the pattern here is precisely the same. But there is one apparent inconsistency, he went on, again touching each photo with his pointer. In this part of the floorboard the rings are wider and more distorted than they are in the end of the ladder rail which had once been attached to this board. The reason for that---a knot.

"Just a minute now, Wilentz said. Can you show us on this next photo?

"Another enlargement was introduced and mounted on the bulletin board. Koehler stood before it, his pointer down at his side, waiting for the next question.

"Can you show us the knot you are talking about?

"Yes, this is the knot right here, at this end of the attic floor board.

"Proceed from there, please, Wilentz said.

"The witness: You see, knots distort the grain in wood. And the closer you get to a knot the more the grain is distorted. Here, in this corner of the floorboard from the attic, you see the grain is greatly distorted. But you will notice that on this edge of the ladder rail that was sawed from the floorboard, the annual rings are wider. That shows there was some factor influencing their growth right there. And that factor, in my opinion, is the influence of the knot in the floorboard extended over into the end of the rail of the ladder. The reason the grain is not so greatly distorted in the rail is because it was farther away from the knot.

"And on and on Koehler went. The 'inconsistency' in the grain is due to a knot. Since there is an inch-and-a-quarter piece missing between the two lengths of board, we must 'imagine' the manner in which the grain traveled along the missing piece and was changed somewhat by the knot before it got to the ladder rail. No inconsistency if one is able to 'imagine' as I have done the natural course of the grain over that missing piece.

"Wilentz said: 'I notice that the ladder rail is not as wide as the attic board. Will you explain that?' He was quite skillful, this Wilentz, for a man who had never tried a criminal case. By asking the question now, with great candor, he deflated a defense attack. 'Why is the rail narrower than the attic floorboard?' he asked again.

"'In examining the ladder rail,' Koehler said, 'I noticed that both edges were planed with a hand plane.' And the witness went on quickly, not giving any juror a chance to wonder why a carpenter who was so slovenly about his work he didn't plane or sand the other uprights in the ladder would have planed this particular board on both edges: 'The plane,' Koehler rushed on, 'was not in very good condition and left ridges.'

"Wilentz stepped to a table on which were spread out several of Hauptmann's tools and his metal toolbox. He lifted an old wooden-bodied plane and carried it to Koehler. 'Can you tell us whether or not this plane was used in planing the ladder rail?'

"'It was.' Koehler said.

"'Is there any question in your mind about it?'

"'Not the least.'

"'Why do you say that? Will you explain it?'

"'Because on the ladder rail there are a number of ridges of different sizes and when I plane a piece of wood with that plane it makes similar ridges of the same size and same spacing apart as are found on the ladder rail.'

"'Would any other plane, in your opinion, make those ridges and those marks?' Wilentz asked.

"'No, that would be out of the question.'

"Wilentz asked Koehler to demonstrate for the jury

why he felt so certain Hauptmann's plane and only Hauptmann's plane could have left the marks found on the ladder rail. The witness planed a piece of wood, using Judge Trenchard's bench to work. He then placed a sheet of paper over the newly planed area and rubbed lightly with a pencil---'A very simple method I learned as a youngster,' Koehler said. The impression of the plane marks that came up in the pencil rubbing was precisely the same as the impression of marks left in a piece of the ladder, Koehler swore. Hauptmann's plane had been used to trim wood in the ladder. And the teletype machines chattered in the attic above.

"The prosecutor moved on to the chisel found under the nursery window and once more I read of Koehler's dramatic discovery: there was no three-quarter-inch chisel in Hauptmann's toolbox. And now Wilentz moved to link the chisel even more closely to Hauptmann. He asked Koehler to carry the ladder to the edge of the jury box and show the jurors the places in the wood where a chisel had gouged. Koehler did so, pointing to chisel marks in several places. Then, using the chisel found under the nursery window, the chisel which the state had just proved must have been Hauptmann's because his toolbox lacked a chisel of that size, Koehler gouged into another sample piece of wood. Once more he rubbed his pencil over a sheet of paper to get an impression of the marks. Once more the impressions matched.

'Hauptmann's chisel' had been used on the ladder. Actually, what Koehler had proved was that a three-quarter-inch chisel had gouged into the wood of the ladder, <u>any</u> chisel of that size and not necessarily the one found outside Lindbergh's home. But the subtlety was undoubtedly lost on the jury, for it escaped reporters, most of whom wrote that the wood detective had proved Hauptmann's own chisel had been used to build the ladder.

"It didn't much matter, of course, in the long run. Hauptmann was so demonstrably guilty, according to the script, that a distortion here or an exaggeration there made little real difference. Yet Koehler's testimony was highly significant, for if he was willing to go along with the charade and distortion of the meaningless chisel evidence, if he was willing to tailor his later writings to fit the prosecution's carefully woven garment, if he could justify in his own mind a minor falsification in this instance and a bit of glossy misrepresentation in that instance---then all his testimony could be a lie. I would have to prove it, not through intellectual analysis alone but with hard facts. Somewhere, perhaps in police files, would be the cold documentary evidence I needed to demolish the state's case against Hauptmann.

"Koehler, whose offense is the most reprehensible since he claimed to be a man of science, was given over to Frederick Pope, associate defense counsel, for cross-examination. Pope questioned him for a couple of hours. It was futile. Koehler could not be budged. The best Pope could do was get him to admit everything he had sworn to had been his 'opinion'---as if any juror distinguished between the <u>opinion</u> of an expert witness and the <u>facts</u> shown in a document or in a scientific analysis. Pathologists, for example, may be called to tell a jury certain medical facts which are not matters of opinion, perhaps that the victim died of a bullet wound in the heart. Doctors can hardly disagree on such facts. But in the area of mere opinion the experts differ so widely among themselves that little credit can be given to expert opinion as such. Lawyers know or should know the difference between fact and opinion, judges know it, seasoned observers do also, but few jurors are sophisticated enough to sort it all out."

After reading *Scapegoat* in 1976 I telephoned Scaduto at his home in Connecticut congratulating him on his excellent work. I then informed him of the things I had learned in my search for the truth which began shortly after Hauptmann's execution. Hearing this, Tony exclaimed "Where have you been?" which brought forth my own question: "Where have you been?"

I know that had we known of each other's research, Tony's book would have had a different ending. *Scapegoat*, in my estimation, and in the opinion of many, many others, remains a classic source of study for those who want to learn the truth about the Lindbergh case.

The book you are now reading is a compilation of the facts Tony uncovered, plus the amazing revelations that I uncovered during my 57 years of probing for the truth. Read on, the half must yet be told!

CHAPTER THIRTY THREE

What More Can Happen?

Before moving on to expose the other unfair irregularities that were permitted to be brought into the courtroom as factual evidence, deliberately overlooked and unquestioned by the judge and jury, and especially to remain uncontested by Hauptmann's chief defense attorney, I believe much more emphasis should be made on the framed evidence used against the accused man by Lewis Bornmann and his co-hort Arthur Koehler.

To begin with, it is just good common sense to question why it took Bornmann so many days to "find" the missing attic board. Hauptmann had been arrested on September 19th and the State Police detective claimed he noticed the questionable "missing board" on the 26th. Police reports exist which emphasize that no less, and possibly many more, than 37 pairs of eyes had searched every inch of the Hauptmann home and garage at 1279 East 222nd Street - and this included the attic. The garage had been torn to the ground, and in the process $14,600 of ransom money had been found. Why then had this man believed that the attic had been so neglected that seven days later he decided to take "one lone look" up there and see what he could ferret out that the other officers had missed?

How is it possible, that during the eight days the police had occupied the Hauptmann home, every one of had failed to notice the missing attic board? That is, they all missed it except, due to the "eagle-eyed" inspection of the "amazing" Detective Bornmann on the eighth day, it was "conveniently found."

Hauptmann's landlord, Max Rauch, testified in the Flemington trial that the attic flooring had been complete when the home was built in 1926. He stated further that it was still complete before the Hauptmanns moved in on the 15th of October, 1931, he knew this because he had gone into the attic around the 5th of that month and could attest that the floor was complete.

In direct examination by Mr. Peacock, in answer to his question: "Now, do you remember when Hauptmann was arrested, September, 1934?", Mr. Rauch responded: "Yes."

Q. How soon after that did you go into the attic? A. I didn't go up there two weeks after.

Q. I show you a picture of your attic and I ask---will you come down here---is this the board, referring to this section between the end of this board and that end that was missing when you went into the attic after Hauptmann was arrested? A. Yes, sir. This is on the southerly side as I walk up to my right side.

Q. At the time you went into it in October, 1934, was that board there? A. It was complete.

Q. It was complete? A. Yes.

Testimony willingly offered, confirming Hauptmann's statement that he had never removed a board from his attic, and yet the defense made no effort to follow Max Rausch's conflicting statement that could have done much to damage the claims of the prosecution that Hauptmann had done that very thing.

And then we have the statement of Gustave Miller, the plumber who had been called by Mrs. Rausch to check out and repair a pipe that was leaking water in a kitchen closet in the Hauptmann apartment. Mr. Miller said he had to go up into the Hauptmann attic to trace the origin of the leak and that if an 8 foot board of the flooring had been missing he would most certainly have noticed it. Miller said it was in August of 1934 that he repaired the cause of the leak, a fact which surely confirms Hauptmann's true statement of finding the water-soaked shoe box that very month.

Every piece of evidence brought against Richard Hauptmann seemed to be tainted with a very questionable validity. Had this all-important ladder testimony been so all-fired important, why then was it not used in the extradition hearing on October 19th? Surely they would have used this evidence, had it existed at that time, since they had nothing more than the testimony of a confirmed liar, Millard Whited, who claimed he saw Hauptmann near the Lindbergh estate prior to the kidnapping.

The known facts point a strong finger of accusation in the direction of Bornmann that he was the manufacturer of "very crooked" evidence. Had Reilly been a competent defense lawyer he would have taken this "batch of lies" spread by Bornmann and Koehler, reversed the questioning in such a way that the testimony of both men would have been clearly seen by the jury as nothing but untruths. But this simply did not happen. The twelve men and women, although they certainly did not completely understand the technical twists given by the "wood detectives", they had no trouble swallowing the distortions and lies - hook, line and sinker - and with nothing more on their conscience than their inability to understand, they were able to render their "just" verdict of guilty.

Tony Scaduto continues with his thoughts about these two men and their skulduggery in *Scapegoat*:

"The first line of Bornmann's report reminded me to turn to other documents I'd skimmed through, concerning fingerprints on the ladder, which I'd intended to explore in greater depth later. Bornmann had written: 'This date detailed by Captain Lamb to continue the search....' Captain Lamb? A rather interesting gentleman, this Captain Lamb.

"Back during the first week of the kidnapping, long before Hauptmann had been arrested, New Jersey state police told newspaper reporters that not a single fingerprint had been found on the kidnap ladder. Upon reading those stories about the peculiar lack of prints, Dr. Erastus Hudson, a respected New York physician and criminologist, volunteered his services to the police. Hudson had been experimenting with the relatively new silver nitrate process, far superior to older fingerprint "dusting" technology. He persuaded State Police Superintendent Schwarzkopf to permit him to demonstrate the process, and was able to raise over five hundred prints from the ladder. Most of them were the prints of policemen and reporters, for by then the ladder had been handled by a great many people. But at least twenty could not be identified as the prints of anyone known to have touched the ladder. These unidentified prints were photographed by Dr.Hudson, for use in the event a suspect was later arrested. Police confiscated the photographs and negatives. FBI Director J. Edgar Hoover later told Governor Hoffman those photographs were never sent to Washington for comparison against the prints of thousands of known criminals.

"Hauptmann's fingerprints no doubt were not found on the ladder; had they been, Wilentz would have used that evidence in court. After his arrest, state police repeatedly fingerprinted Hauptmann, forcing him to let them ink his fingertips and even his palms and the edges of his hands. Hauptmann protested that he had been printed many times in several days since his arrest, but the New Jersey troopers insisted none of his earlier prints had been clear enough.

"After those prints had been taken from Hauptmann, two New Jersey police officers consulted Dr. Hudson. They asked: Is it possible to counterfeit fingerprints? And how do we go about it? Those officers seemed quite disappointed, Hudson later said, when he told them that although counterfeiting was possible, 'I would be able to detect the difference between real and counterfeit fingerprints.'

"One of those officers was Trooper Kelly, the fingerprint man for the state police. The other was the superior investigating officer on the case, the man coordinating the work of all New Jersey police and detectives, Captain John Lamb.

"That name, of the man who was seriously asking whether it was possible to counterfeit fingerprints---Hauptmann's, no doubt---seemed familiar. Someone, had mentioned Captain Lamb in connection with the other famous New Jersey criminal case of this century, the Hall-Mills murder. The Rev. Edward Wheeler Hall and Mrs. Eleanor Mills, his choir singer and his mistress, had been found murdered in a lover's lane in New Brunswick, New Jersey, in September 1922. Both had been shot several times and Mrs. Mills's vocal cords had been slashed. Strewn around the bodies were fragments of letters from Mrs. Mills to Rev. Hall---'I want to look up into your dear face for hours as you hold my body close'---and the murders became, most naturally, a newspaper sensation. But after a rather casual investigation by police and a purple-prosed one by reporters, the case was closed. Four years later, as a result of a campaign by the *New York Daily Mirror*, during a circulation war against an upstart paper, the *Daily News*, the investigation was reopened. One of the leading investigators on the case was then Sergeant John Lamb. It was Lamb who persuaded the sluttish, middle-aged Mrs. Jane Gibson (known as the Pig Woman) to belatedly come forward and swear she had witnessed the murder while she was out on her mule, Jenny, looking for the thieves who'd been raiding her corn bin. The Pig Woman testified that the killers were the Reverend's wife, Frances, two of her brothers, and her cousin. As she testified, Mrs. Gibson's elderly mother sat in the front row of the court muttering, 'She's a liar, she's a liar, she's a liar.' The jury reached the same opinion, especially after other witnesses testified that she was home in bed when the murders occurred, and the four defendants were acquitted. Sergeant Lamb's reaction was never recorded.

"All in all, the circumstances surrounding Bornmann's claimed discovery in the attic of a missing piece of floorboard, and Captain Lamb's propensity for contriving testimony against murder suspects makes it highly probable the attic evidence was contrived---as fingerprints would have been had Dr. Hudson not discouraged Captain Lamb. What I believe most probably occurred in the attic is that either Lamb or Bornmann, remembering the comment of the wood expert, Arthur Koehler, that Rail 16 had once lain indoors and that a search of any suspect's home should be made for a place where the rail had previously been used, decided to fake the evidence once it was clear all prior searches were fruitless. Bornmann then went into the attic. He laid Rail 16 down across one of the floorboards so that the nail holes in the rail would lie above one of the joists. Measuring only roughly, he cut off a length of lumber that would approximately correspond to the length of the ladder rail, but he cut it at least eight inches too long, forced to do so, perhaps, because of the sixteen-inch spacing between joists. He threw that length of lumber away. He then placed Rail 16 over the joist nearest the remaining piece of floorboard, took four of the square-cut nails which he had found in Hauptmann's attic, and slid them into the nail holes in the ladder rail. He then hammered them home, so that they would create holes in the joists precisely corresponding to the angle and spacing of the holes in the rail. When he removed the nails, he had his evidence to directly link Hauptmann to the ladder.

"There can be no other explanation. As has been pointed out, a carpenter who works in a lumberyard which is only two blocks from his house, a man who is supposed to be a criminal genius, does not take wood from his own attic should he be lacking a piece. If Hauptmann had made that ladder, he no doubt would have made it in his garage, where he had a workbench and tools, and where he could work in secret. It would have been easier for him to walk two blocks to the lumberyard and buy a piece of lumber of the proper length and width, than to climb into the attic and cut a piece that he later had to plane down on both edges to bring to the proper width.

"There is circumstantial evidence which tends to further support the conclusion that Bornmann created the attic scenario. For one thing, through all the days in which Hauptmann was questioned by police and the Bronx district attorney's staff---questioning that continued after the date Bornmann claims to have found the attic proof of the prisoner's guilt---no investigator ever questioned Hauptmann about it. He was repeatedly interrogated about the ransom money, about the board with Condon's telephone number which had been found in his closet, about his tools and his purchases of lumber, and dozens of other questions connected with the ladder. But not once was he asked to explain the missing board in the attic. From a close examination of transcripts of those sessions in which Hauptmann was questioned and from the memoirs of FBI Agent Turrou, it becomes rather clear that the investigators were absolutely convinced of the prisoner's guilt and were throwing bits of 'evidence' at him in an attempt to break him down and get a confession; for some, especially federal agents, the greatest interest was to wear him down so that he would confess and tell them where he'd hidden the remainder of Colonel Lindbergh's money. But it is peculiar that the most dramatic piece of evidence police later claimed to have found, the attic floorboard, was never used to destroy Hauptmann's obstinate disavowal of guilt.

"Similarly, it is difficult to believe that if the attic evidence existed at the time of Hauptmann's extradition hearing in mid-October, District Attorney Foley and Attorney General Wilentz would not have produced it in the Bronx court. Hauptmann was suing to overturn the extradition order signed by New York Governor Lehman. The prosecutors had to show that Hauptmann had been in the area of Hopewell on the day of the kidnapping. The only proof they had was the eyewitness, Millard Whited, who testified he had seen Hauptmann near the Lindbergh estate on two occasions, the last of which was a couple of days <u>before</u> the kidnapping. And Hauptmann's attorney put on the stand three men from Hopewell who had known Whited for many years; each of them said his reputation in the area was dreadful, he was a liar and a cheat. Albert S. Osborn had testified that Hauptmann wrote all the ransom notes, but that was not evidence Hauptmann had been in the Lindbergh nursery and personally left the note there; even if he had written it, someone else could have performed the actual abduction. Had the attic evidence been discovered on September 26, it seems logical to conclude that the prosecution would have presented it at the extradition hearing even if Arthur Koehler had not yet made the very thorough study he later swore he did make. With so relatively weak a case against Hauptmann in the Bronx, the prosecution would probably have introduced the attic evidence had it truly been discovered almost three full weeks before the Bronx hearing.

"Bornmann, who lived in the Hauptmann apartment from the day after the arrest until the trial, must have manufactured the attic evidence long after September 26 and then back-dated his reports so that it would appear he had simply decided to make another search of the attic on that date. He could not pretend to have found the evidence before September 26, because his report and the reports of other investigators said that up to that date nothing of interest had been found. And he could not have filed a report a week or a month after that date, because the delay would have been more suspect. So he filed his fake report with a date and time immediately following his last authentic report of his fruitless search of the attic.

"The evidence discovered by Bornmann is probably the most demonstrably false of all the evidence against Hauptmann. And it is Bornmann's evidence upon which the credibility of Koehler's testimony hinges. Without that ladder rail, none of Koehler's testimony can be considered even circumstantial evidence connecting Hauptmann with the kidnap ladder; without that ladder rail, in fact, Koehler's testimony is absolutely valueless."

Tony Scaduto's work on the case as an investigative reporter was a masterful one. Sadly, however, his discoveries were uncovered 40 years after the trial; uncovered from among musty files of records that many of the police authorities and prosecutors had hoped would never be looked at again. Scaduto in his search and review of these records, no doubt, agonized and retched on many occasions as he was brought to realize, not only, the innocence of Richard Hauptmann but the beastly tactics that had been used to frame him for the horrible crime. Man's inhumanity to man in its most brutal form he had seen exhibited. We, then, can clearly understand why he asked himself the soul-searching question: " Where does all this lead us?" And his clear answer: "Down that inevitable path I had seen traced in my mind so early---Hauptmann was the victim of manipulated evidence and had been sacrificed on the altar of retribution: cleanse this stain on society and destroy the stainer as a warning to other men of evil."

CHAPTER THIRTY FOUR

Two Old Chisels

The testimony of the wood evidence as presented in the Hauptmann trial must be recognized as possibly the most deliberate of frame-ups ever perpetrated in a criminal case. Nevertheless, as foul as it proved to be in sending an innocent man to his death, the truth of the deception could not be kept under cover forever. Shortly after Hauptmann's conviction the testimony of Bornmann and Koehler was scrutinized extensively by two government wood specialists. They examined the attic, the disputed board, Rail 16, and all other physical evidence used by the "wood experts". The findings of the two men, Roy Knabenshue and Arch W. Loney, after conducting an objective investigation, revealed things which were quite contrary to those of the dishonest "experts".

One must seriously question why and how a jury, in spite of the so-called expert evidence presented by Koehler, could count his testimony as worthy of being given any consideration at all. Had not his testimony been largely that of tracing the grain of one board over an empty space which measured one inch and a quarter, at the same time following an imaginary grain (since it could not actually exist over an imaginary space) and tell the bewildered jury that the two boards had at one time been one board, that is, until Hauptmann took it to be used in his kidnap ladder? Of course that is what he said, and the jury believed him without a doubt. But then, why shouldn't they? The accused man was already guilty, they all knew it, including Lindbergh, so how could they even as much as question this testimony? This was the trial of the century and they were all members of a jury that had been called to see "justice" done. And they were going to do this no matter what the cost, even to taking the life of an innocent man.

Again we borrow from Tony Scaduto's *SCAPEGOAT* since he tells so very well the findings of Knabenshue and Loney:

"But after the trial two other wood specialists

working for the federal government, Arch Loney and Roy Knabenshue, came forward and said that when they read of Koehler's testimony and studied photographs of the boards, they immediately contacted the defense and offered to testify that by no stretch of anyone's imagination could they have come from the same lumber stock. But chief defense counsel Reilly told the two men they were not needed.

"One of the things these two wood specialists cited, according to newspaper reports, was a knot in the wood of Rail 16 on which Koehler leaned heavily. Koehler had testified that this knot created a distinctive pattern that could be traced over to the attic board despite the missing piece. However, Loney and Knabenshue maintained, Koehler had minimized the significance of the difference in quality of the knots in each board, and that difference alone would make it unlikely the boards had once been connected. The knots in each board produced clearly defined rings around them. But the rings in Rail 16 were in no way as distinct or similar to the rings that could be seen in the attic board. They were flatter and fuzzier. Had the boards once been connected, the two men said, the knots and their rings would surely have looked more alike. That they were dissimilar made it likely they had not been part of the same length of lumber. This lack of similarity, it must be pointed out, was not a defect of the photographs the two wood specialists studied; Koehler mentioned it in his testimony as he handled the two boards, but he passed hurriedly over it.

"Koehler had used other photographs to back up his conclusion, and Loney and Knabenshue separately pointed to them as even greater evidence Koehler was distorting the truth. One of the photographs showed the butt ends of the ladder rail and the attic board. One was placed on top of the other to demonstrate that the annual rings of the tree from which the boards had been cut were precisely the same on each edge, indicating they once had been connected. The photographs seem to show the same curvature, the same arc in the annual rings, and their evidence can be convincing. But then Koehler carried his demonstration an unnecessary step further, and damned his own evidence.

"What Koehler did was to take the portion of the photograph showing the butt end of the ladder rail and cut off the left side of it. He then superimposed the remaining side of the butt upon the photograph of the floorboard's butt end. This demonstrated, he said, that the rings which could be seen in one board matched perfectly the rings seen in the other---'the grain in the end of the ladder rail matched that in the end of the floorboard,' as he put it in his testimony.

"In truth, the photographs demonstrate most clearly that Koehler was forcing his "scientific" evidence to fit his need to prove Hauptmann guilty. As one can see upon examining the pictures, Koehler had to lift the ladder rail, the right-hand section in his reconstuction, perhaps as much as a quarter inch in order to get the rings to match. There is no possible way that a board, cut in half across its width, can have its grains matched up unless the surfaces of each piece are flush.

"However, there was testimony that the ladder rail had been planed across one surface so that it was about one sixteenth of an inch thinner than the attic floorboard. Is it possible that planing had removed enough wood so that Koehler was justified in lifting the ladder rail section of board in his photograph to take into account the missing wood? A close examination of the pictures shows that is not possible. The right-hand board, the ladder rail, juts out far above the attic floorboard, much too far to be accounted for by the planing of the other surface. A precise measurement, even in the reduced-sized photographs, makes it clear that for Koehler's speculation to be accurate, then the upper surface of the board from the attic floor must also have had some of its surface removed. And that never occurred.

"Still, the annual growth rings do appear to match rather precisely. If my conclusion was correct, that the two boards had never been one piece of lumber, is it possible that two pieces of wood cut from different trees at different times---even years apart---could produce growth rings that would match almost precisely?

"I remembered that there had been an article in my town's local newspaper, the *Ridgefield Press*, about a rare botanical event, the growth to maturity of an American chestnut tree. Once quite common, the chestnuts were decimated soon after the turn of the century by a fungus bark disease that usually kills the trees off before they attain more than fifteen or twenty feet in height. But a forty foot chestnut was found growing in the town and the paper ran a long article on it. The reporter interviewed J. Mortimer Woodcock, who had run a nursery in the town for several decades and who was also 'a former U.S. forester.'

"I called Mr. Woodcock. He remembered Koehler's testimony very well, he said. He had graduated from Syracuse University's School of Forestry in 1927 and had of course been interested in the wood expert's detective work in the Lindbergh case. I asked: Do you remember what you thought about his testimony at the time?

"'Certainly,' he said. 'You can't match up grains of wood and say this board came from the same tree as that board. You can tell what type of tree it was. You can tell how good the growth was in one year compared to another year, by the annual rings in the board. But matching up the grain the way he says he did is not possible.'

"I went over to see Mr. Woodcock, bringing with me copies of Arthur Koehler's photographs. He studied them for a time.

"'You see,' he said,'each tree grows according to the weather. If you had a stand of this pine down in Carolina, growing in the same area, each tree would reflect the climate...'

"'So you might have a number of trees in the same area with precisely the same growth, the same configuration of annual rings?' I asked.

"'I would say so. But then again there could be variations because of soil variations. Still, if you cut a number of pine trees from the same area of the same woods it would be very difficult to ever identify one board as coming from a certain tree or to say that two pieces are from the same tree. It is always going to be possible to have one board and then find another board from a different tree that has the same size rings as the first, the same grain, the same good growing seasons and bad growing seasons. Especially if both trees that the boards came from were growing in the same area under the same climatic conditions.'

"I had brought with me a couple of pieces of common pine which I had cut from one length of lumber, to help demonstrate what Koehler had done with his photographs of the board edges. Woodcock began examining them. He held the edges toward me.

"'You can see the rings here are both running the same size,' he said. 'If you trimmed this piece off another board that had the same size rings, the same growth, I wouldn't know that they'd come from two different boards or from the same board. And I don't think anyone could swear to that for certain.'

"We discussed Koehler's photograph, in which he superimposed a part of the ladder rail on the attic floorboard in order to show that the grains matched. I explained my deduction, that by lifting one board in order to make its grains match with the second, Koehler actually proved they had come from different stocks of lumber.

" 'It certainly would be logical that by raising this piece higher than the other,' Woodcock said, 'he's forcing grains to match where they really don't. The only time that could happen is if one piece had been planed across the surface...but that can't be in this case because the top surface of one board is lifted up above the surface of the other. If these pieces were supposed to be attached and there wasn't a really large gap between them, then it can't work the way Koehler claimed it did.'

"Let's go back to the surface grain that Koehler said he could trace from one board to the other. You said it would be difficult for anybody to say that one piece of wood was cut from the same long board that another piece came from."

'Very difficult,' Woodcock said.

"Another way of putting it is that grains of wood are nowhere near as distinctive as, let's say, your fingerprints. In theory, no two people have the same sets of fingerprints. Is that true of wood grains?'

"'Absolutely not. You can identify varieties of wood easily enough and you can tell from the rings a great deal about the growth of the tree. But to come down and identify individual trees and individual boards of lumber and match them, that's not possible. A lot of trees have the same growth and a lot of lumber is going to be easy to match up. There isn't enough variety among growths, especially from the same forest, to be able to say that this board came from the same tree as that board and from no other tree, or that this board was once attached to that board. It's just not possible.'

"As I was leaving, Woodcock stopped me at the front door. 'You know,' he said, 'if Koehler did that to make the end grains match, well...he was highly respected, he was the leading authority in the field. How he could have done it is beyond knowing.'

"I drove home and returned to the reports that involved Arthur Koehler. And what I found in those documents helps impeach Koehler's testimony even further, for they make it plain that Koehler, like so many others, was distorting the truth in order to create a more perfect case against the defendant.

"Koehler had testified that Hauptmann's plane and only that one plane could have left the distinctive marks in the ladder's wood that he had found there. At his trial, several carpenters testified in Hauptmann's behalf that almost any plane would leave the marks Koehler claimed were so distinctive, if the tool was held in a distorted position no carpenter would use. I consulted several carpenters in town, and tried it myself, and in every case it was demonstrated that by holding the plane at an unnatural angle to the surface of wood being worked on, any gouge you're trying to make will show up. Koehler's experimental gouges with Hauptmann's plane in court appear to be the result of his need to reproduce for the prosecution the patterns he claimed to have found in the ladder's wood.

"Koehler's demonstration of those gouges was based on the premise that after making the kidnap ladder some time in late 1931 or early 1932, until his arrest in September 1934, Hauptmann neither used nor sharpened that plane blade. But it is clear from police reports that Hauptmann did use that plane on several occasions after the kidnapping. And since he was a skilled carpenter, with an emery wheel in his garage, it is likely he had sharpened the blade at least once. Had he sharpened it, this part of Koehler's testimony would collapse. It isn't possible at this time to learn whether it had been sharpened during that thirty-month period. But even if the blade had never been laid against the emery wheel in that period, the nicks that existed in it before the kidnapping would have assumed a completely different character during its quite frequent use up to the day of his arrest.

"For Hauptmann used that plane during his work at the Majestic apartments. (And he had told police several times during their days of questioning, before he ever learned of the existence of Arthur Koehler, that when he was hired to work at the Majestic he sharpened all the tools in his toolbox the day before reporting for work.) In October 1932, Hauptmann made a door for another tenant in the building in which he lived. That tenant, Victor Schussler, told police without possibly knowing the significance of his remark that he frequently went into Hauptmann's garage 'to borrow a chisel and a plane and other tools.' Hauptmann built a wardrobe closet and a crib for his son after the child's birth in November 1933. He also said, and it was confirmed by police, that even after quitting work to concentrate on his stock market speculations, he occasionally did carpentry for customers of the lumberyard near his home who had projects they couldn't handle themselves and who asked the yard foreman to recommend a good carpenter. In all of these carpentry projects, and possibly many more that I have not learned about, Richard Hauptmann must have used his plane. And it is inconceivable that he did not sharpen it at least once.

"Koehler, you'll remember, also testified at the trial that Hauptmann's toolbox was lacking a three-quarter-inch chisel. Conclusion: Hauptmann had dropped his chisel under the nursery window, where it was found by police.

"During the questioning by police on September 20, a full day after his arrest, Hauptmann was asked whether he owned any chisels and he replied that he had a mixed but full set of National Tool and Stanley chisels ranging in size from one-quarter inch to two inches. Koehler knew the chisel found on the Lindbergh property was a Bucks brothers brand, manufactured before 1900. Yet he blithely reported a chisel missing out of Hauptmann's set of more modern chisels. If he were the absolutely disinterested man of science he claimed to be, Koehler would have questioned that curious discrepancy and would, perhaps, have wondered about the other evidence---for certainly it is difficult to conceive that a carpenter who had lost his chisel early in 1932 would by late 1934 have failed to replace it, even though he had worked for at least a couple of weeks at a professional construction job.

"I have found further evidence that once again either the police or the prosecution committed an illegal act against Richard Hauptmann in order to convict him. A New York City police department document dated September 29, 1934, is an inventory of the tools found in Hauptmann's toolbox. In that list of several dozen hand-tools is the line: "1---cold chisel 3/4"---National Tool make."

"Hauptmann did have a three-quarter-inch chisel on September 29. Some time between that date and Koehler's theatrics at Flemington, police or prosecutor removed it.

"There is additional evidence that Hauptmann had a <u>second</u> three-quarter-inch chisel which was hidden from the jury. At around this time in my investigation I was told that all the evidence in the Hauptmann case which was once in the possession of Attorney General Wilentz was stored in a small basement room at New Jersey State

Police Headquarters in Trenton. I called the Superintendent of Police, Major George Quinn and, after giving him my background as a newspaper reporter and free-lance writer, I asked permission to examine the Hauptmann material.

" 'I'd just like to see the ladder and the wood and other exhibits used in the trial,' I said, 'and maybe take fresh photos for my book.'

"'That can be arranged,' Quinn said. 'Unfortunately, there is no one currently on the force who was connected with the case, no one who is still on top of it. I'll assign someone to help you go through the material, but it's going to be difficult.

"'You know,' he added, 'the file is still marked open because there's a feeling that others were involved.'

"I wanted to say, <u>you people convicted him as a lone killer</u>, but I held it back and instead said, 'Yes, from what I've been reading it seems pretty certain this man Fisch was Hauptmann's accomplice. And there's also the question of the ransom money.'

"'That's correct,' he said, 'A large part of it has never been recovered. For a lot of reasons, the case is still open. No one is actively working on it, of course, but it is still open in the event something develops or some new information comes in.'

"I drove down to Trenton a few days later. Major Quinn was not in that day, but he had assigned Major William Baum, the chief of the Criminal Identification Bureau, to assist me in my search. And Major Baum disappointed me. Because all the documents on the case were haphazardly piled in a small room, he said, it would not be possible for me to go through them. Any documents filed in an orderly manner, in several file cabinets, could not be seen 'because I don't know what happened to the keys, it's been so many years since anyone's been in that room that it's all a mess.' He quickly added, cutting off my obvious suggestion: 'And I don't want to take responsibility for breaking the locks on the files.' The upshot was that Baum would assign one of his aides to accompany me and to take photographs of the ladder and the wood from the attic. I didn't care about the photographs, that had been simply a ruse to get into the files. 'But Major Quinn said I could look through some of the documents,' I said. 'When we were talking the other day we discussed the fact that Hauptmann must have had accomplices and I said I'd like to see the files because I wanted to make an intelligent guess in my book as to who those accomplices were. He agreed about that.'

"'I don't care what he said then,' Baum replied, but very politely. 'We've decided it would be too much trouble giving you access to everything, considering the condition of that storage room.'

"He took me across a courtyard to an old building he said had been the first barracks erected on the grounds. We went down into a basement, along a dingy corridor to the end, then stopped at what appeared to be a prison cell. On the heavily padlocked steel bars securing the cell was a small hand-lettered sign that read: "Lindbergh Case File." Beyond the steel bars I could see four locked file cabinets on top of which were dozens of cartons of investigative reports, and several score of other cartons similarly filled with material. Resting on top of a stack of cartons that lined one wall were the original kidnap ladder, the attic floorboard, and other lengths of wood. Much as I hated it, Major Baum had underestimated the 'trouble' which would have been created were I given free access to all the files; it would take me at least six months simply to sort everything.

"A trooper was called to assist me. 'Mr. Scaduto wants to take photos of the ladder and perhaps the handwriting exhibits,' the Major said, pointing to a dozen or so large display cards with photographs of the handwriting that had been used by Osborn and others to explain their opinions to the jury. 'Just those things, nothing else,' the major added. He left us.

"I took my pictures. When I was done I took a chance and began to rummage through Hauptmann's tool box, rusting on top of one of the cabinets. I'm looking for chisels, I said, evidence that Hauptmann made this ladder. There were several chisels in the toolbox. I measured them with a tape measure I had brought along. None of them was a three-quarter-incher. A few moments later the trooper, his curiosity apparently overwhelming the orders he'd been given to restrict my researches to the ladder and the fingerprint exhibits, pulled from a tall metal locker filled with boxes a rolled-up manila envelope. 'This could be it,' he said. There was some writing on the outside of the envelope. It said: "Two old chisels found in Hauptmann's garage."

"We opened the envelope and discovered two chisels inside. I measured their cutting edges. Both were three-quarter-inch chisels. One of them was a Bucks Brothers brand similar to the one found under the nursery window. But this one was almost new, definitely not the chisel which had been found and was introduced at the trial, because it wasn't old enough and it didn't have a tag attached with an exhibit number as it would have had were it the one placed into evidence. The other chisel was much older, a Stanley. One surface of the wooden handle had been whittled flat: a carpenter's technique for preventing a round-handled tool from rolling off a shelf.

"It was possible the Stanley was the chisel police had taken from Hauptmann's toolbox so that the prosecution could claim it was missing, but since the notation on the envelope said the chisels had been "found in Hauptmann's garage" it is more likely I had located two additional three-quarter-inch chisels. Either way, the evidence was strong: on the day Hauptmann was arrested police had confiscated two or three of his three-quarter-inch chisels so that Arthur Koehler could add one more piece of damning but false evidence to his testimony "proving" Hauptmann had built the ladder and had killed the child.

"(I also found a small box filled with photographs of "Latent fingerprints---Hauptmann case." There were possibly two hundred photos. Most of them appeared to be of prints found on the ladder; some were prints which had been lifted from smoother surfaces, perhaps in the nursery. Prints the police denied they had ever found.)

"Koehler's scientific objectivity and his impartiality are open to question in still another incident connected with his work in "tacking Hauptmann to justice," as the newspapers put it in those days. Apparently to demonstrate to his readers that Hauptmann was guilty beyond all doubt, Koehler had written in the *Saturday Evening Post* that a man later identified as Hauptmann had come into a Bronx lumberyard with a companion on a day that Koehler and Bornmann were poring over the records in an attempt to find the customer who had bought common pine of the size and type used in the ladder. The men acted very suspiciously, offering a gold note in payment and then fleeing without taking their purchase, after they glimpsed the badge on Koehler's vest as he sat in an open office behind the counter. The foreman of the yard, Koehler said, later identified one of the men as Hauptmann. This event, in late 1933, was absolute proof that Hauptmann possessed gold notes long before he claimed he had found the horde in Fisch's shoe box and that he had guilty knowledge those bills were from the Lindbergh ransom payment.

Otherwise, why would he have run away?

"The foreman was never called to testify, a curious omission because it was so vital that Wilentz prove Hauptmann's possession of ransom money before August or September, 1934. The reason he did not become a prosecution witness can be found in the transcript of this foreman, William F. Reilly, by Bronx Assistant District Attorney Breslin and Captain Lamb.

"Can you relate to us this transaction with reference to a gold certificate?" Breslin asked.

Reilly said, "I couldn't say it was a gold bill. I never seen the ten-dollar bill."

"Do you think you can identify Hauptmann as the man in the lumberyard that day?"

"Yes, I think I can identify him," Reilly said.

"What did the other man, his companion, look like?"

"He was a little guy, short, skinny, and dark. He might be of Italian descent, but <u>he speaks perfect English</u>. <u>In fact, they both did</u> [emphasis supplied].'

"Later, after failing to identify Hauptmann, foreman Reilly said: 'He looks something like the man, but not exactly the same. There's just a resemblance to the man. But the man didn't have the accent this Hauptmann has.'

"And yet, long after the trial, the impartial scientist Koehler said it was Hauptmann who had fled the lumberyard that day, distorting truth so that he could further establish Hauptmann's guilt in the minds of his readers."

On Wednesday, November 29th, 1933 the two "wood detectives", Bornmann and Koehler, still attempting to trace the ladder wood, made a return visit to the office of the National Lumber and Millwork Company at 3541 White Plains Road in the Bronx. It was at this time their search proved successful when they found some of the lumber they had been searching for, several planks of 1 by 4 yellow pine, that had been planed by the M.G. and J.J. Dorn Company of McCormick, South Carolina.

But their finding evidently proved to be of no significant importance. Reporting their find would not be necessary to mention to the Federal Bureau of Investigation. It was customary for the Jersey authorities to snub the FBI whenever inquiries were made by the Federal authorities. The usual answer, when asked as to what progress was being made, was nothing. In a later chapter you will read a series of letters I own, which clearly reveal the difficulty FBI Director

John Edgar Hoover had in obtaining important information from Colonel Schwarzkopf.

Although at the time the discovery of the wood proved worthless, it certainly became invaluable to the authorities after the arrest of Hauptmann and they came to realize that their prisoner lived just a short distance from the National Lumber and Millwork Company, and it was also here that he purchased his lumber and sometimes did work for some of the firms customers. A beautiful scenario was taking shape. The man in whose garage they had found $14,600 of Lindbergh ransom money, had also purchased lumber from the very lumber yard which had "no doubt" sold him lumber they had received earlier from the planing mill down in South Carolina. It was all fitting together very beautifully for them. All they had to do now was "prove" it by concocting some timely frame-up.

When we analyze the whole picture objectively, the pieces fail to fit together well. In fact, we find many missing elements and "manufactured guesses". One thing it failed to prove was that the buyer of the lumber lived in the Bronx. The one who built that ladder could have been any one of the hundreds of other people who had purchased the yellow pine boards to construct the ladder. And to go a step further, the lumber could have been purchased from any one of the many other lumber companies that had done business with the South Carolina firm. Even from one located in Phoenixville, Pennsylvania, my home town, if such a thing were possible.

Again we call on our investigative reporter friend, Tony Scaduto, who uncovered so much valuable evidence that had aided us in proving the innocence of Richard Hauptmann. In his book *SCAPEGOAT*, he writes:

"Because the ladder was connected to a crime in New Jersey, Koehler felt it sensible to begin his search for the ultimate purchaser of that wood among Dorn customers north of the Potomac. He copied from the Dorn ledgers the date and destination of each shipment to the north. The completed list showed that forty-six carloads had been sent north to twenty-five firms. And it was obvious where he would have to start: eighteen of the carloads had gone to two firms in New Jersey that were within a twenty-five mile radius of the Lindbergh home. These were a box factory in Trenton and the Johns Manville plant at Manville.

"Koehler took the next train north to Trenton. He told Chief Schwarzkopf of his findings and Detective

Lewis Bornmann was assigned to accompany Koehler on his search. At the Johns Manville plant, Koehler and Bornmann were told that all the wood from the Dorn mill had long been used up in making crates for Manville products. None was sold to the public. High fences around the plant had protected the lumber from theft. The wood, when used, had been cut into lengths too short to have later been used in making the ladder. At the box factory in Trenton the story was the same.

"So with relief, Koehler later said, 'I crossed off shipment after shipment, to leave but twenty-eight.'

"Koehler's assumption that none of the lumber in those eighteen carloads could have been stolen because of 'high fences' ignored a common event, employee theft. Even back in those more innocent times workers would not have been above stealing a few lengths of lumber from the boss. The ladder, built as it was of three distinct types of wood and one piece showing prior use, made it likely the kidnapper had picked up the lumber wherever he could find it and had not bought from a lumberyard the precise quantity he required. (Which creates another thought: Hauptmann building a ladder, would have known as a carpenter precisely how much lumber he needed and would have bought from a lumberyard a consistent type of lumber.) For Koehler to arbitrarily cross those shipments from his list was naive. There is no evidence---in fact it would be highly unlikely---that the shipments to both plants were cut into shorter lengths as soon as they were received; no doubt the lumber was cut as needed and the original lengths were on hand for quite some time. Koehler must have eliminated those firms only because there was no possibility of tracing the wood they'd been shipped, only because the wood had been so thoroughly dispersed it was impossible to trace.

"And as long as I found myself indulging in that favorite pastime of skeptics, poking holes in someone's story, I decided to take it from the beginning, point by point.

"Koehler, a wood expert, said the ladder showed evidence its maker was a dreadful carpenter. The construction of the ladder was amateurish. The carpenter's tools were unsharpened. His chisel bit much too deeply. But Hauptmann was a skilled union carpenter, and had been for at least six years before the kidnapping. He had helped build some of those tacky houses that dot the Bronx. He had built for his newborn son several pieces of well-constructed and finely detailed furniture, a rocking chair, high chair, and playpen. On the last job he held, at the Majestic apartments, around the time of the kidnapping, he was employed as a finisher, the carpenter responsible for putting into place door and window trim, kitchen cabinets, moldings, all the small details of carpentry that require skill and patience and in which the slightest carelessness would glare like a full moon on a cloudless night. No, Koehler's assertion that the builder of the kidnap ladder was a poor carpenter doesn't fit what we know of Hauptmann. The record seems to be speaking of two different men.

"And the chisel? At one point during his examination Wilentz asked Koehler to step to Hauptmann's toolbox and see whether it held a three-quarter-inch chisel. High drama for the jury's benefit: Koehler rummaged around and then grandly announced the chisel was missing. That could only mean Hauptmann had dropped it while descending the kidnap ladder. Koehler later went to great lengths to stress that the chisel found under the nursery window matched the 'right-angle lines' left in the kidnap ladder by a chisel. What did that mean exactly? I consulted the trial transcript, Koehler under cross-examination. Well, he said, it meant the mortise cuts in the ladder had been made by a three-quarter-inch chisel, and a three-quarter-inch had been found under the nursery window. That's all. Of perhaps several million chisels of that size in use at that time, Koehler was trying to imply both chisels were one chisel---when he possessed no such evidence.

"Why was everyone stretching so hard to fill in every single gap in the Hauptmann case in an attempt to convince us all that he was indeed the guilty one? So many people, during the trial and for many years after, from John Condon to George Waller (Author of *Kidnap, The Dial Press*, 1961) distorted the evidence, attributed to Hauptmann a personality he didn't seem to own, tried to make us believe the case against this man was super-perfect. No murder case is ever perfect, obviously, for only the victim might tell us the truth (perhaps) and the victim cannot be present. Even seeing on our television sets Jack Ruby kill Lee Harvey Oswald could not bring into the courtroom a case so brilliant in its perfection, in its wholeness and completeness, that it would absolutely satisfy. For what would we learn of motive? Had Ruby testified about his motive we could never be certain he was being truthful. We would never have been certain he had acted alone and not as the agent of some dark conspiracy. And by attempting to bring such perfection to the case against Hauptmann, all writers and all witnesses automatically damn their own stories and damn the truth. Michelangelo may have been correct when he said that trifles make perfection. But only in art. If, in a criminal trial, every trifle is absolutely perfect and all trifles add up to a perfect whole, then we must assume the trifles have been deliberately shaped to attain the perfection of art. But a courtroom is not an artist's canvas or a sculptor's block of marble. To create, in a trial, an artistic masterpiece so perfect there can be no question the result is truth, means truth has been shaped and distorted to fit the artist's concept.

"To return to Koehler, then, still testifying. He had searched high and low for the wood from the Dorn mill, in lumberyards, in chicken coops and garages where some of the wood ended up, climbing fences with Bornmann like a couple of weird burglars with badges. Always disappointed. Until one day he arrived at a lumberyard in Ozone Park, Queens. The dealer told him all the lumber from the Dorn shipment had been sold months before. The familiar tale, to Koehler's ears, he was much too late. But, said the dealer, now that I think about it, I'm pretty sure we used some of that pine here in the yard, to build storage bins. He led Koehler and Bornmann to the bins and sawed off a length of protruding board. Koehler walked into the sunlight with the strip of pine and studied it under his magnifying glass.

"Along one edge of the board were the familiar scars of the defective cutter knife. But there was a slight difference. The blemishes on this board were a trifle farther apart and nearer the center of the board edge than were the scars of the ladder rail. Koehler thought about it for a while, as Bornmann drove them back into the city. The only possible explanation for the wider spacing of the blemishes was that this piece of wood had been fed through the planing machine at a slightly faster speed than the wood in the ladder rails. The pulleys, of course, Koehler surmised. This board had gone through the planer either just before or just after the Dorn mill hands changed the pulley on the machine. Perhaps then the shipment he sought, the shipment from which the kidnapper had bought his common pine, had gone to a firm on his list either immediately before or immediately after the shipment to the Ozone Park lumberyard.

"He consulted his list. The subsequent shipment had been made to a lumberyard in Youngstown, Pennsylvania, but Koehler had made a note next to that yard's name which indicated the wood it had received had been trimmed an eighth of an inch narrower than the ladder board. Clearly, he saw, 'I could rule it out!'

"Now, Koehler said, he was certain the shipment he had sought for so many months had gone to the customer on the list prior to the lumberyard they'd just left. That was the National Lumber and Millwork Company, in the Bronx, which had received a Dorn shipment nine days before the Ozone Park firm.

"Bornmann drove directly to the Bronx yard. The date was November 29, 1933. Once more the sleuths were disappointed. All the pine from the Dorn shipment, they were told, had been sold long before. Koehler later wrote: 'But then occurred another lucky break. It might be, the yard foreman thought aloud, that he had made his molding bins out of that Dorn mill one-by-four-inch stuff. He looked just once, then got a saw. A piece projected; he cut if off and handed it to me. One look was enough! The marks on the edge were the same!'

"It seemed strange. Two lumberyards somehow managed to have a piece of the Dorn pine and each yard employed such sloppy carpenters that a piece of wood projected from the bins constructed of them. Was every carpenter as careless as the man who'd made the ladder? Does every lumberyard contain bins with projecting pieces so that employees might scrape and tear skin, overalls, lumber? Even stranger is Koehler's assertion that he and Bornmann had searched in upstate New York, Connecticut, and Massachusetts for almost a month and only after many disappointments found the wood he was seeking in the Bronx. If it were true, then Detective Bornmann wasn't a very smart cop. He knew the extortionist almost certainly lived in the Bronx. All the evidence pointed to it and all police authorities were certain of it. Why on earth didn't Bornmann start with the Bronx lumberyard? Why give the kidnapper more months to dispose of his ransom money? And, since the criminal was known to be a German, according to all accounts, why give him more time to perhaps flee to Europe?

"Koehler never explains. He wrote and testified that he was now positive he'd traced the lumber to the yard that sold it to the kidnapper. That detective work was a vital point for the prosecution because Hauptmann always purchased his lumber at that yard. He was well known there, had in fact been employed by the yard, sent out to work for customers who needed a carpenter. The implication was stunning: Hauptmann had bought the lumber used to make two of the ladder uprights.

"Koehler testified and wrote that he now had come up against a solid wall hampering further search---the lumberyard dealt in cash. It had stopped giving credit long before the Dorn shipment was received and therefore no names of customers were available. That is the reason, we must all infer from Koehler, he was unable to personally arrest Hauptmann by sleuthing in wood.

"However ... and however and however. Another contemporary writer, Sidney Whipple of the *United Press*, who reported on the search for the kidnapper as a police reporter, published a complete cops-and-robbers account of the case immediately after Hauptmann's conviction, and alter edited and annotated the trial transcript published by *Doubleday* in 1937, provided some enlightening information in just a few sentences in his books. Whipple had written:

The known customers of National Millwork & Lumber were then thoroughly investigated and one by one eliminated from the case.... And at this point [a reporter] made the logical suggestion to the authorities that every one of the automobile license applications from within a certain well-defined zone of the Bronx be examined for comparison with the ransom notes. Such a search was conducted. Of the thousands of such documents on file, all but 480 were eliminated, and there remained only forty-eight possible suspects by the end of 1933. All of them were closely shadowed by Lieutenant Finn's men.

"Known customers of the lumberyard. Licenses issued to drivers living in a certain area of the Bronx. Hauptmann's name must have appeared on both lists since he was a steady customer and occasional employee of the lumberyard and since, at his trial, the handwriting experts claimed the writing on his license applications was the same as the writing in the ransom notes. Why was he "eliminated" from both lists and cleared of all suspicion? Had his name appeared on either list---and it must have---he certainly would have been kept under surveillance as forty-eight men had been. Most especially since all the minute details of the description Condon swore to at the trial fit Hauptmann. The mind leaps with questions, the questions stumble over each other like kittens playing with string and getting tangled in it. Is it possible Hauptmann didn't fit the description of John in 1933 and that Condon revised his description a year later to fit the man who'd been arrested? Was this further support for my instinctive feeling that Condon had lied? Is it possible Hauptmann's handwriting was ruled out in 1933 as unlike the writing in the ransom notes, then was made to match by mental gymnastics in 1935? Could it be possible Hauptmann was eliminated because he was not passing ransom money in 1933? Had not begun to pass it until August 1934, as he claimed, because that's when he discovered the gold notes in Fisch's shoe box? Doesn't it seem more likely now that Hauptmann was telling the truth and the witnesses against him lied?

"Including, perhaps, Arthur Koehler, the wood expert now in the witness chair. In fact, another major discrepancy in Koehler's story now became clear to me. In one section of an article he wrote for the *Saturday Evening Post*, he said National Millwork and Lumber could not provide names of its customers because they sold only for cash. But later in that same article he said that after Hauptmann was arrested police found in that lumberyard a sales slip showing the prisoner had bought nine dollars' worth of lumber late in 1931, little more than three months before the kidnapping. That purchase most certainly would have placed Hauptmann in the list of customers Whipple says were thoroughly investigated. Why wasn't Hauptmann arrested in 1932, when Condon's memory of the extortionist would have been much fresher? Why, most of all, did Koehler contradict himself? Police most certainly found the sales slip, for it was introduced as evidence against Hauptmann at the trial. Koehler's claim that the lack of such a sales slip made it impossible for him to trace Hauptmann in 1933 forces us into the man's mental processes, the workings of his mind. He could have been gratifying his own ego, a sleuth who failed only because of forces beyond the control of science. Koehler took such pride in his role as detective that he published a learned article in the *Journal of Criminal Law* describing his achievements and suggesting that the techniques he had employed in the Hauptmann case could be useful to other detectives and to prosecutors. If Koehler was motivated by vanity, by a delight in valuing himself and his creations above all other things, then all he contributed to the case against Hauptmann becomes as small as all vanities. If ... that's an enormous qualifier, that word, I thought. I can't prove ego and vanity ruled Koehler and twisted his reasoning; I'm only thinking that was possible.

And, thinking that, I must examine Koehler's story with a sharply critical mind.

"Back I went to something he'd written in his detailed report of his detective work in tracing the Dorn shipments. I could rule it out! he had exclaimed. The shipment to a lumberyard in Youngstown, Pennsylvania, could be eliminated because the wood involved was an eighth of an inch narrower than the ladder board. If so, it was strange that Koehler included this yard in his list in the first place. For Koehler had written, in his article for the professional journal: 'Two of the North Carolina pine rails were cut from one board which was fourteen feet long originally. It could be determined that it had been dressed to three and three-quarters inches in width, which made it unnecessary to pay any attention to similar stock dressed to three and five-eighths inches in width. In fact, that eighth of an inch difference in widths narrowed down the tracing of lumber from sixty-three to forty-five carloads.' Certainly, if Koehler was eliminating wood that had been dressed a mere eighth-inch too wide, an even greater logic would have demanded he eliminate lumber trimmed narrower than the ladder boards. Koehler testified he had eliminated all shipments of board that had not been dressed to the precise measurement he sought. Why had he listed the Youngstown shipment, only to dismiss it later? I didn't know and since Koehler died many years ago, I'd never find out. But I knew what I suspected---Koehler ignored the Youngstown shipment because he was in New York, 300 miles away; he lied about it later because he didn't want to be left open to the criticism that lumber with the same scarring he'd been searching for might have been found hundreds of miles from Hauptmann's home.

"The circuits of the mind make further connections. Those two pieces of pine in which Koehler claimed to have found telltale mill scars enabling him to trace them to the Bronx lumberyard clearly were not planed or sanded by the man who built the ladder. Had they been, the marks of the Dorn mill's planer would not have been visible. Would Hauptmann, a skilled carpenter, have neglected to sand smooth the lumber in his ladder? Doesn't a total amateur carpenter like me sand every piece of wood I work with? Most certainly, if only to avoid splinters. When I built the bookcases that fill two complete walls around me, didn't I sand each board, even the edges that were to go flush against the wall? And I am not a meticulous man, as Hauptmann is said to have been. I am known for being careless and sloppy, yet I sanded. And I am sure a professional would have planed and then sanded his lumber before putting the pieces together as a ladder.

"As I read on, I found that Koehler was again stretching to bring his case the perfection of detail that damns it all in my mind. He claimed that after tracing the Dorn pine to the Bronx lumberyard and reaching the end of the road in his investigation, he set out to similarly trace the Douglas fir that had also been used in the ladder. One day in December 1933, he and Detective Bornmann sat in the rear office of a lumberyard at 149th Street and the East River, also the Bronx. The sleuths were copying from a ledger names of customers who had bought Douglas fir of the size found in the ladder.

"As they worked, two men entered and bought a forty-cent piece of plywood. One of the men offered a ten-dollar gold certificate in payment. The clerk asked the customer whether he had a smaller bill, a five perhaps. Retrieving the ten, the customer handed her a five-dollar bill. She accepted it and went into the rear, where Koehler was sitting, to get change. The men must have glanced over the low partition that separated him from the front of the shop and noticed his Forest Service badge, ordinarily concealed under his jacket but now possibly exposed, Koehler later wrote, because when the clerk returned with the change the men acted extraordinarily suspicious. One of them said: 'Never mind, I have the change.' As he threw forty cents on the counter the other man took from the clerk the five one-dollar bills she had brought out front. Muttering something about going to a nearby restaurant to eat, promising to return later, the two men left without the plywood they just bought. So suspicious were their actions, the foreman of the yard went into the street and took down the license plate number of the small green car they drove away.

"After Hauptmann was arrested, the clerk and foreman saw his picture in the newspapers and recognized him as one of those two customers who had behaved so strangely. Hauptmann and his associate fled the lumberyard because the gold certificate was undoubtedly, a ransom bill, police told newspaper reporters. Surely this was further evidence of Hauptmann's guilt. Koehler agreed. That little incident was important to everyone who condemned Hauptmann because it punctured a facet of Hauptmann's alibi, that he didn't know the gold notes he'd been passing were Lindbergh money. That story told by the murderer had to be proved a lie; showing his guilty behavior proved it was a lie. And now I understood the motive behind another anecdote police had related to the press, which had made banner headlines---BRUNO TRIES SUICIDE! I had ignored the story before, that Hauptmann while in jail in the Bronx had stolen a pewter spoon and sharpened it into a blade with which he could slit his wrists or throat---because it seemed an aberration of a tale. Now it became all of a piece. Hauptmann had plotted suicide because he was guilty. But even writers absolutely certain Hauptmann was guilty commented after his execution that the suicide tale was no more than a bit of dramatics by police, nothing more than coming up with a harmless little story to satisfy reporters' demands for more color.

"That the authorities were stacking the deck against Hauptmann long before his trial I had no doubt. Consider the police story about the two men who acted so suspicious that the foreman of the lumberyard took their license number. Yet neither the foreman nor the clerk was ever called to testify at the trial. No doubt even police realized they were mistaken, no doubt the physical evidence didn't support their eyewitness testimony. Had the license number been Hauptmann's number; had the bill given in payment been folded in that unusual way all the ransom bills were folded; had it matched a serial number on the Lindbergh list---had even one of these facts been true, prosecutor Wilentz most certainly would have called the lumberyard employees to testify in order to prove Hauptmann's guilty behavior months before he claimed he found the ransom money. Yet police, prosecutor, and Koehler-as-detective, knowing they were distorting the truth, publicly stated that the link had been connected. (Further evidence of the falsity of the story: police said it had happened around noon, but Hauptmann's stock market accounts show he made several trades that day in his broker's office about ten miles away.) The police and Koehler, trying so hard to create that artistic masterpiece, the perfect case.

"Another thought lights the mind. These men, all of them, were making so great an effort to convince us of Hauptmann's guilt because they were trying to convince themselves, hoping to relieve their own doubts."

Before Tony Scaduto was to complete his investigation aimed at proving the innocence of Richard

Hauptmann, he discovered many more truths which proved the honesty and innocence of Hauptmann, but nevertheless were turned inside out into "sickening lies" in order that his captors could, with their seared consciences, lead their prisoner directly to a seat they had already reserved for him in the Trenton electric chair.

CHAPTER THIRTY FIVE

Hauptmann Needed Friends!

Every door was being bolted closed, every avenue of escape was made impassable for Richard Hauptmann as he desperately tried to have his truthful explanation, and those of his witnesses, accepted. At the very least, it should have been accepted as possible truths until hearing the evidence against him presented, evaluated, and then given fair consideration. This law is mandatory and never to be refused in a "fair" trial. But, of the charges brought against Richard Hauptmann, such was not to be the case. To begin with, the prisoner's own lawyer disliked him. Hired to defend the accused man by the owner of the powerful Hearst newspaper chain, who, like the lawyer, believed in the man's guilt and stood by watching from the sidelines as his "hired attorney" refused to permit some excellent witnesses to take the stand, instead sending them back to their homes without an opportunity to even approach the witness chair and speak in Hauptmann's defense.

And then we have the many other blunders and failures of the "Bull of Brooklyn", Edward J. Reilly, too many to enumerate at this time, but which will be dealt with later.

It soon became quite obvious that Hauptmann was not being represented properly. C. Lloyd Fisher, second in command of the defense counsel, recognized this from the very start of the trial. But unfortunately his hands were tied by the conceit and arrogance of the chief of staff, "Death House Reilly".

Before we delve into the other "unfair tactics" which closed the door on any hopes Hauptmann might have had to prove even the remotest possibility of his innocence, we should completely understand that it was his incompetent lawyer, hired to defend him by the Hearst enterprise, that deliberately locked the door himself.

The unfairness used in forbidding the testimony of anyone who wanted to refute the wood evidence presented by the wood master, Koehler, is enough to make one gag.

After the trial, Roy Knabenshue, an authority on wood employed by the government's interior department, and Arch W. Loney, a wood specialist, also employed by the federal government, came to Lloyd Fisher and reported that their testimony would have greatly differed with the "opinions" of Koehler. Loney stated he had reported his belief prior to the trial but had been turned down as a witness.

He reported he had contacted Governor Hoffman by means of a statement sent to him by a mutual friend, George H. Maines, in which he said: "rail 16 came from the heart of a tree, while the attic board from which it was supposed to have been torn came from the top, or 'sap' of the tree, the floor board was fine grain, while 'rail 16' was coarse grain." This information was passed on to the prosecuting attorneys who, quite naturally wanted no part of any such information. Colonel Schwarzkopf sent Loney the following answer: "In conference with the Attorney General, we have decided to restrict our evidence along this line to the findings of this man, Arthur Koehler, Agricultural Experiment worker over a two year period." The door was not only locked but bolted as well. Very well bolted!

Hauptmann was trapped all because of the "phony" evidence brought in by one man, Lewis Bornmann, and his ridiculous statement which was held together by nothing more than "silly putty" but, nevertheless, believed by a "trusting jury" who not only swallowed his every word as factual, but also the words which were spoken by his "undoubtable" accomplice in the matter of "intricate wood", the one-and-only expert Arthur Koehler.

In spite of the official police records which state that between September 19th, 1934, the date of Hauptmann's arrest, and the 26th of that month, there were no less than 37 police officers who made nine trips up into the Hauptmann attic. And yet, none of them ever noticed the missing attic floor board. But to this very day, Bornmann still insists that no one had been in the attic until he himself had gone there on two occasions, one in the morning and again in the afternoon of the 26th when he finally made his "amazing great discovery of the century".

In one of his final interviews made public in Ludovic Kennedy's filmed documentary *Who Killed The Lindbergh Baby?*, (produced in 1985) Bornmann explained his find in this manner: "Naturally one of the first things I noticed was ah, it was a partially floored, was tongue and grooved lumber. But on the end board approximately 8 foot had been removed, why I started to get very curious and I thought to myself this, this looks pretty good. I immediately got, called for the carpenter to come up and saw off another piece of the board from the remaining, it was originally about 20 feet there, and I thought it well I got best get back to West Trenton and let Koehler look at it, eh, for it looks pretty good to me."

What a script Bornmann wrote for himself back in 1934; one he dare not ever change. What was it that prompted him to think to himself "this looks pretty good - this looks pretty good to me?" The evidence is clearly seen - it was Bornmann's evil decision to plant some evidence which would gain him the fame he needed, thus granting him the right to say in the years to come, that he played an important role in the solving of the famous Lindbergh case. But, in so doing, he wrote for himself a major role in helping to frame an innocent man and, at the same time, write finis to the life of Bruno Richard Hauptmann. What a dastardly deed! Such an act, in the eyes of all mankind - unpardonable!

But the prosecution was by no means through with Hauptmann. They had many more persons willing to sell their souls in order to "prove" their case against the prisoner, who by this time was visibly showing signs of concern. Knowing he was innocent of any wrong doing, Hauptmann did not fail to see the ineffective way Reilly was defending him. Both Richard and Anna Hauptmann had begun to question many of their lawyer's actions. Had they known what lay ahead for them, their concern would have turned to sincere advanced worry.

More of the state's "big guns" loaded with their convicting "ammunition" had yet to be heard - and heard they would be - and believed they would be! After all, the case against Hauptmann could not fail in any way or by any means at this point in time.

One major problem Hauptmann faced was the inability of the jury to believe he had been at work at his place of employment in Manhattan during the daytime hours of Tuesday, March 1st, 1932. During the early police interrogation sessions with their prisoner, he had insisted he had reported to work at the Majestic Apartments located on the corner of 72nd Street and Central Park West, and from the earliest indications this appeared to be true.

Hauptmann had explained to the police how he had been looking for steady work, when one morning near the end of February of 1932 a customer at Fredericksen's

Bakery, where Anna worked, had told him that an employment agency, the Reliance Property Management Company on 6th Avenue, was looking for skilled carpenters. Hauptmann lost no time in going there and was encouraged by a man named E.V.C. Pescia, who told him there was a strong likelihood that he could obtain steady employment at the nearly completed Majestic Apartments. With this hope of at last finding work, Richard made it a practice to check back with the agency daily in either the morning or afternoon.

On Saturday, February 27th, Richard, while making his daily contact with the agency, was told to pay the required ten-dollar fee, and then, along with Gustav Kassens, another applicant, to report for work at the Majestic Apartments. After arriving there, he and Kassens were instructed by a Mr. Joseph M. Furcht, the construction supervisor, to report, ready to work, on Tuesday, March 1st at 8:00 a.m. During the remainder of Saturday afternoon he and his good friend Hans Kloppenburg spent their time on Hunter Island. Here they played soccer with Emil Muller, Ludwig Kubisch, and other friends. The men returned to the island on Sunday and it was then they were told by Hauptmann that he was starting work at a new job on Tuesday and would be paid $100 a month.

On Monday he spent the greater portion of the morning sharpening his tools in order to have them ready for his new job the next day. Following this, he drove down to the Majestic Apartments and left his tool box in the basement's carpenter's shop.

Supporting Hauptmann's claim that he started work on that fateful day of Tuesday, March 1st, was the statement made by the Majestic Apartment's construction supervisor, Mr. Furcht, who said when the police checked with him: "On 1 March, 1932, at 8 a.m., Bruno Richard Hauptmann and Gus Kassens reported for work at the Majestic Apartments and worked throughout that entire day until five o'clock...Hauptmann was a skilled carpenter who much against my wishes I was forced to put on maintenance work which is ordinary work instead of skilled carpenter work."

But, even with this evidence which supported Hauptmann's honest claim that he had started work on March 1st, his attorney, (at that time James M. Fawcett), found himself in a dilemma because the "forces of evil" had already begun their pernicious work.

Fawcett was certain that when he presented his defense of Hauptmann at the Extradition Hearing, the

Writ of Habeas Corpus Proceedings in the Bronx County Court on Monday, October 15, he would have no trouble proving that Hauptmann had started work on Tuesday, March 1, 1932. After all, he would have the sworn testimony of this very fact as given by both Pescia and Furcht. But that was where he was very, very wrong. Neither man put in their appearance. Instead, scheduled to appear was one Edward F. Morton, who had been a timekeeper at the Majestic Apartments at the time Hauptmann was hired. Surely his time sheets would prove Hauptmann's claims correct. However, when Mr. Morton was called as the first witness, he failed to appear. Later attorney Fawcett again called for this important witness to take the stand, and still there was no response. Morton was very simply - not present --- absent from the very courtroom to which he had been subpoenaed to appear. Because of this flagrant failure, without just cause, Morton could be found guilty of contempt of court. The absence of Morton, Furcht, and Pescia meant only one thing to James M. Fawcett. It was now impossible for him to prove where his client was on March 1st, 1932.

Ludovic Kennedy explains very clearly in his book *The Airman and the Carpenter* why no one appeared at the trial who could have supported Hauptmann's contention that he had worked on the controversial date of March 1st. The evidence had quite conveniently disappeared. Mr. Kennedy did a splendid job of pulling out all the stops and letting the chips fall where they may. He writes: "What seems to have happened is this. Soon after Fawcett had discovered that Hauptmann's name was on the time sheets and payroll records for the first half of March 1932, the District Attorney's office had discovered the same thing. Both these records, so highly damaging to the prosecution's case, together with the payroll records for <u>the last half of February 1932 which must also have included Hauptmann's name</u> - were then hastily removed. The payroll records were put under lock and key in the Office of the Assistant District Attorney, Mr. Breslin, where they remained until October 29 when Breslin handed them to Detective Cashman of the New York City Police. The time sheets, according to David Wilentz, came into the possession of the police even earlier. It is inconceivable that Mr. Wilentz, who was working in close co-operation with Foley and his staff, did not know the contents of both the time sheets and the payroll records, and know that if ever they saw the light of day, they would virtually clear Hauptmann.

"Mr. Morton therefore did not appear because the time sheets on which he was relying for his evidence had been removed; and in his place the Reliance Property Management Company sent along their assistant treasurer, Howard Knapp, not with the records for the first half of March which was what mattered, but with the altered and quite irrelevant payroll records for the second half. He claimed that these showed that Hauptmann had not started work at the Majestic until March 21, and in support of this Wilentz produced a check for $36.67 dated March 31, 1932, paid to Hauptmann by the Reliance Property Management for eleven days' work between March 21 and March 31, and with Hauptmann's signature of endorsement on the back. It would seem therefore that unless the checks were faked as the time sheets were, Hauptmann was away sick between March 16 and 21 and had only been paid for eleven days' work.

"That the Reliance Company and Mr. Knapp had gone along with the prosecuting authorities is clear from other evidence of Mr. Knapp. Asked by Mr. Fawcett where the records were for the first half of March, he gave a reply that put him in the same league as Whited and Schwarzkopf. 'Our records,' he said, 'do not indicate that any such records exist at this time,' then added lamely, 'or at that time either.' As this company employed over a hundred people it was, on any reading, a ridiculous reply. Then Fawcett turned to Wilentz and asked if he had got the payroll records for the first half of March and Wilentz, who must also have known they were in Breslin's office, replied truthfully that he hadn't.

"Frustrated at having been deprived of the evidence that might have set his client on the road to freedom, Fawcett sat out the rest of the hearing with barely concealed disappointment. When Whited spoke about seeing Hauptmann come out of the bushes, a voice in the courtroom was heard muttering that anyone could see he was lying. (Whited said he was driving a truck, so even if a stranger had been there, he could have had no more than a fleeting glimpse of him.) Old Osborn gave evidence about the handwriting, and was lucky to survive a skillful and damaging cross-examination. Hauptmann electrified the court by shouting 'No!' to Wilentz's accusation that he had kidnapped and murdered the Lindbergh baby. His testimony until then, said the *New York Times*, had been given quietly, in a sing-song fashion, 'but the voice that said "No!" was emphatic and booming'. The team of Bornmann and Koehler, although claiming to possess by far the most powerful evidence for Hauptmann being in New Jersey on March 1, still thought it wiser not to disclose it.

"Having seen the time sheets that showed Hauptmann was working at the Majestic Apartments on March 1, Fawcett was determined not to let the matter drop. As soon as Justice Hammer had declared that in his view Hauptmann had failed to establish that he was not in New Jersey at the time, Fawcett asked for a stay of extradition until he had filed notice of appeal; and the court granted him forty-eight hours.

"In the event it was not he who found the vital evidence he needed, but Tom Cassidy of the *Daily News*. It will be recalled that the superintendent who had taken Hauptmann on at the Majestic on February 27, 1932 was called Joseph Furcht, but that when questioned at Greenwich Street after his arrest, Hauptmann could not remember his name, nor that of E.V.C. Pescia of the Reliance Employment Agency who had sent him there. However Mr. Knapp in his testimony had mentioned Furcht as the official responsible for the payroll records during the first half of 1932, and Cassidy, sniffing another good lead, immediately set about locating him.

"Furcht worked for the Department of Public Welfare on Eighth Avenue and two days later, having just finished his lunch in the cafeteria, he saw Tom Cassidy bearing down on him.

In a signed affidavit Joseph Furcht states:

Cassidy asked me if I was the Superintendent of the Majestic Apartments around March 1st 1932, and I said 'Yes'. He then asked me if I had any records and I said'No"...Cassidy then told me that there were no records showing the employment agency which sent Hauptmann. I told him what the agency was and suggested that we go to the agency and get their records. We left the office about 2 p.m. and went to the E.V.C. Pescia Employment Agency, 779 Sixth Avenue, and there interviewed Mr. Pescia. Pescia then presented the records to us ... which clearly brought out the fact that Bruno Richard Hauptmann worked for me on March 1st 1932...

At eight o'clock on the morning of that day Bruno Richard Hauptmann and Gus Kassens reported for work ... and worked throughout that entire day until 5 p.m.; subsequent thereto they worked there the 2nd, 3rd, and 4th days of March 1932 from eight o'clock in the morning until 5 p.m. in the afternoon.

"With this information Cassidy took Furcht to the offices of the *Daily News* where he was interviewed by someone on the staff, and a photographer was despatched to Pescia's office to take a picture of the records. Next day Furcht informed Fawcett of his findings and also signed an affidavit before a notary public. At the end of the affidavit he wrote - and this is significant: '<u>Annexed hereto, and made a part of this affidavit, is a photostatic copy of the record of E.V.C. Pescia</u>.'

"Another photostat copy found its way to the Bronx District Attorney's Office where Foley and Wilentz, now deeply worried, saw the whole case against Hauptmann beginning to slide from under them. In a statement Foley said he had never heard of Furcht and Pescia before, showing how poorly his staff had done their homework. He was forced to admit that Hauptmann had worked at the Majestic Apartments on March 1 but added - in order to create time for Hauptmann to have reached Hopewell without rushing it - that he believed he quit work at 1 p.m. He gave no evidence to support this, and it was Hauptmann's first full day at work.

"Wilentz, equally disturbed, issued a statement saying he wasn't disturbed and, to lift his morale, brazenly declared that even if the statements of Furcht and Pescia had been before Justice Hammer, they would not have affected the outcome of the proceedings (he could have been right - in the prevailing climate of hysteria anything was possible). Indeed, so rattled was he that on returning to Trenton he issued a further statement in which he too admitted that Hauptmann had been employed at the Majestic Apartments on March 1 'but did not put in a full day's work'. He added, 'The police know that because they have the timecard record of the Majestic Apartments.' They certainly had, and no defense lawyer or nosey journalist who might upset the apple-cart was going to be allowed a peep at them. He went rambling on about records being a lot more definite than statements based on memory. Yet, Pescia's statement was not based on memory but records, and the timesheet records in the hands of the police would have confirmed it. Later still, when reports that the police had been tampering with the payroll records were appearing in the press, Wilentz issued another statement that he was convinced this was untrue. 'The police at no time had possession of the payroll,' he claimed, but evidence shows the police receipt for the payroll.

"Next day, October 19, was the deadline for

Fawcett's appeal, and in the Bronx Appeal Court he sought leave to bring Furcht and Pescia with Pescia's records before Justice Hammer for a presentation of fresh evidence. He added that he had subpoenaed the Reliance Company for their records before March 15 1932, 'but had been informed they had disappeared' (which must have given Wilentz and Foley a quiet laugh). The five judges of the Appeal Court turned down the proposal. The new evidence was in conflict with evidence already heard, they said, and issues of fact should await the trial of the action: the writ of habeas corpus would be dismissed.

"Often in criminal proceedings when it is discovered that new evidence is likely to challenge the prosecution's case, certain things are found to happen: embarrassing documents disappear; new witnesses are discovered to counter the defense witnesses; and existing witnesses for the defense are persuaded (by various methods) to go back on their earlier statements.

"In this case all three of these things happened. All copies of Pescia's records (and maybe the originals as well) mysteriously 'disappeared'; they have not been seen from that day to this. Gus Kassens, the carpenter whom Furcht had engaged at the same time as Hauptmann, was run to earth and persuaded to sign an affidavit that Hauptmann 'had not started work until several weeks after March 1st' - though why any credence should have been placed on the memory of a man who had only met Hauptmann briefly two and a half years before, is hard to tell. (When Wilentz read it, did he remember what he had said about records being more reliable than memories?)

"And then there was Joseph Furcht who, until now, had seemed so confident about the hours that Hauptmann had worked, who had told Fawcett (who had told Hauptmann) that he would take the stand for him at Flemington - he too was broken. What caused him to change his mind - threats or bribes or a call to duty - we shall never know, but on October 23, in the Office of the District Attorney, he went back on almost everything he said.

"'I wish to state that I do not know whether or not Bruno Richard Hauptmann worked on March 1st, 1932 at the Majestic Apartments ... I have heard an affidavit given by Gustav Kassens that Hauptmann did not work on March 1st but at a later date ... I believe Mr. Kassens as I know that he was always honest when he worked for me ... If I knew at the time that I made the statement to the *Daily News* people what I know now, I never would have made that statement, but I would have stated that he did not work on March 1st at the Majestic Apartments.'

"It was a pathetic climb-down and when he read it through Furcht must have thought so himself, for right at the end he wrote: 'If the payroll from March 1st to March 15th 1932 does not contain the name of Bruno Richard Hauptmann for that period, and if the payroll is signed by me, then Hauptmann did not work on March 1st 1932.'

"He knew well enough that Hauptmann's name did appear in the payroll record for March 1 to 15, and that he had signed it himself. By lobbing the ball back into the prosecution's court, by challenging them to go and check the record for themselves, he had salvaged a little of his self-respect.

"On conclusion of the habeas corpus proceedings on the evening of October 19, Hauptmann was put into a New Jersey Police car between Captain Lamb and Lieutenant Keaten, and with an escort of New York and New Jersey Police cars and a posse of motor-cycle outriders with sirens screaming, set out for Flemington."

It is quite natural for the thought to have crossed your mind that possibly Hauptmann did not work at the Majestic Apartments on March 1st, and that since it cannot be proven that he did, there must always remain a doubt. And this would be true, had not our favorite investigative reporter, Anthony Scaduto, uncovered the facts about the "missing" work records.

The ever probing Scaduto reports in his book *Scapegoat*: that during his investigation (and the gathering of information for the book) in 1974 he was granted permission by the Bronx District Attorney, Mario Merola, to search the files of the Hauptmann extradition proceedings. "If the files are still around, you're welcome to see them, spend whatever time you need to copy them. I'll put a Xerox machine at your disposal. But let me check first to see whether they're here.", Scaduto reported Merola's instant agreement.

The files were most certainly there, and within a few days Scaduto had a desk outside the office of his friend, the chief assistant, Seymour (Sy) Rotker. On this desk were "four very large folding envelopes tied with purple ribbon which didn't appear to have been loosened in many years." Hand-printed across the face of one of these envelopes was: "Hauptmann---Reports, Letters, Etc. Important." Excitement and great expectations joined together as Tony Scaduto started to untie the bow and extract the six-inch thickness of Hauptmann documents.

Selecting envelopes at random, Scaduto soon found one addressed to Edward D. Breslin, the assistant Bronx district attorney. It was a letter relating to handwriting specimens which drew his immediate attention since it was dated earlier than a year before Hauptmann had ever been heard of in connection with the kidnapping. The letter proved to be of interest to Scaduto. His finding proves to be quite informative: "I found a letter from the district attorney of upstate Albany County, enclosing reports from Albert H. Hamilton, 'Chemical and Microscopical Investigators, Auburn, N.Y.' The first item from Hamilton was a letter dated August 29, 1933, more than a year before Hauptmann was arrested. In it, Hamilton requested specimens of the handwriting in the ransom notes so that he could compare them with the writings of suspects. There was and still is a state prison at Auburn and I suspected Hamilton was one of dozens of investigators across the country who had been hired since the kidnapping to find the kidnapper by comparing the ransom writing with the writings of men and women in prison.

"Attached to that letter was a report, dated some months later, but still long before Hauptmann had been arrested. In it Albert H. Hamilton said he had compared the handwriting characteristics of the person who wrote the Lindbergh ransom notes with specimens taken from a man named "Manning Strawl" --- Hamilton himself put quotation marks around the name --- and after careful study he concluded that:

> The person who wrote the request writings and then signed the name "Manning Strawl" to same was the person who wrote all the "kidnap" letters and envelopes.
>
> This finding can not be modified by any other standard.

"The document was signed Albert H. Hamilton.

"Now I know how Schliemann must have felt when he discovered the ruins of Troy, or Sutter when he came up with gold in the Sacramento hills, I thought. This brief document made a mockery of Osborn and all the handwriting experts whose services had been purchased by the State of New Jersey. Albert Hamilton, whoever on earth he may have been, was obviously respected enough by New York law enforcement officials to have been employed in the search for the man who wrote the ransom notes. He was, no doubt, a recognized handwriting expert. And in August 1933, long before anyone even suspected the existence of Bruno Richard Hauptmann, this expert had examined some suspect's handwriting and opined that that man had written the ransom letters.

"Putting aside "Manning Strawl" for the moment---the important thing was that Hauptmann had been convicted at least in part on the testimony of seven handwriting authorities who swore he had written every ransom note, yet here was another authority who swore that some other man had written those letters. And Hamilton didn't know a man named Hauptmann lived; he had no interest in helping convict or acquit Hauptmann.

"I returned to the covering letter from the Albany district attorney to the Bronx district attorney and realized it was dated December 22, 1934, three months _after_ Hauptmann's arrest and a few weeks before his trial. Plainly, this report was kept secret by the prosecution. In reading through the records in the Hauptmann case I had come to suspect that some evidence had been suppressed so that there would be no flaw in the prosecution script. But here, in my hands, was the first tangible proof to support that suspicion. And I knew it was likely that within these files I would find many other documents that had been kept hidden from Hauptmann's lawyers back then and from the public for forty years.

"I resisted the temptation to dance on my desk, and also fought down the urge to continue riffling through the files at random. Hauptmann's alibi, I decided, was my main goal for now; I'd have plenty of time later for the other aspects of the case, for Merola and Rotker had both said I could use the records as long as necessary.

"That alibi demolished by Wilentz's witnesses still disturbed me enormously. It seemed peculiar that Hauptmann had originally claimed to have been working on the day of the kidnapping, then changed his starting date on the construction job to March 15, even though the prosecution claimed to prove he did not begin work until March 21. I thought that perhaps in the transcript of Hauptmann's extradition hearing, the first opportunity the prisoner had to test the state's evidence against him, I could find some evidence to support my feeling that the payroll records had been altered to damage Hauptmann's alibi. I began reading the transcript of that hearing, held in Bronx supreme court on October 15, 1934. Hauptmann's lawyer was James Fawcett of Brooklyn. The state was represented by District Attorney Samuel Foley and by Mr. Wilentz, the New Jersey Attorney General, appearing in a New York court apparently to chalk up some experience in this skirmish before the big trial in Flemington.

"Hauptmann's lawyer called to the stand Howard Knapp, assistant treasurer of Reliance Property Management, the agents of the Majestic Apartments, on which Hauptmann had worked. Knapp brought with him the payroll records for March and April, 1932---but he did not have the records for the first half of March, the critical period from March 1 to March 15.

"'Where are the records for the first half of March 1932?' Fawcett asked.

"'Our records do not indicate that any such records exist at this time---or at that time, either,' Knapp quickly corrected.

"'Any records at all respecting the first half of March 1932?'

"'Chronologically speaking, this is the first payroll that we have.'

"'You have no payroll records before that date?'

"'Nothing before that on the Majestic Apartments.'

"Hauptmann's lawyer pressed Knapp on the point and practically called him a liar as the witness continued to insist, 'To my belief there is no payroll record in existence.' Yet Knapp admitted his company had been in charge of employment at the Majestic since long before March 1, 1932, and employed more than one hundred men and women on any given day. How can you expect us to believe, Fawcett obviously was stating in his questions, that the payroll records for this particular date do not exist?

"I certainly couldn't believe it. I felt strongly that Knapp had been lying: the slip of the tongue in which he said no 'such records exist at <u>this</u> time' made me feel certain they had existed at least until Hauptmann said he'd been working on that day. And I wasn't imagining a slip of the tongue, because in the transcript the stenographer used both a comma and hyphens to mark a distinct pause between that phrase and Knapp's attempt to cover his lie by adding, 'or at that time, either.'

"The folder in which I had found the 240-page transcript contained a file envelope marked: "Hauptmann-

--Notes taken during extradition." If the payroll record was not produced in court, it could only mean those records would have supported Hauptmann's alibi and been harmful to the prosecutor. So I began searching through the folder with notes of the extradition, looking for a copy of the payroll record or any evidence that it had once existed.

"I was certain I wouldn't find it. It didn't make sense that a prosecutor would deny the existence of an employment record and then leave it in the files---unless he was so arrogant he felt certain his files would never be examined by an outsider.

"The small sheet of yellow legal paper on which someone had hand-written a receipt almost escaped my notice. That receipt read:

> Received from Asst. D.A.Breslin, the following records:
> Employment card record of Richard Hauptmann,
> Carbon copy of payroll Feb. 29, 1932,
> Carbon copy of payroll March 15, 1932 ...

"The payroll record had existed, for here was some kind of receipt for the semimonthly records which would cover the dates surrounding the kidnapping. I said to myself, they did suppress it and lie about it---Foley and Wilentz and Knapp and everybody else involved, they had to know those records existed and they had to know they were dooming Hauptmann by suppressing them.

"I looked around me, at the secretaries in an adjoining room and the assistant prosecutors and policemen strolling around the offices. Should I slip this evidence into my pocket and walk out with it? Or should I ask someone to Xerox it? The first would be illegal, stealing city property. The second could be disastrous, for if anyone in that office learned I was discovering material which could prove Hauptmann had been wrongfully convicted the files might be sealed on me. I couldn't be certain Merola would cooperate in what could eventually become a condemnation of an earlier DA and I wasn't about to test him. Besides, the receipt proving the payroll records had existed and had been in the hands of the district attorney was unsigned. It was either a rough copy of a formal receipt or, more likely, the prosecutor's note to his secretary to type out an official receipt. Somewhere, the original receipt must exist, or at least a carbon copy of it.

"I rummaged quickly through the papers in this

file folder but could find no receipt. Still, I did find other material of even greater significance. One of these was an affidavit made three days after the extradition hearing by a man named Joseph M. Furcht. He swore that he had been hired as supervisor of construction at the Majestic in September 1931. Shortly after he came on the job, he said, the contractors who were working to complete the building suddenly quit and Furcht was put in charge of construction. His first need was for carpenters to fill the jobs vacated by the contracting firm, so he called upon E.V. Pescia, an employment agent on Sixth Avenue, to supply him with the necessary skilled carpenters.

"'On or about the twenty-fifth of February, 1932, it became necessary for me to hire two skilled carpenters,' Furcht's affidavit continued. 'I thereupon again called Mr. Pescia's office and he sent me Gus Kessenes and Bruno Richard Hauptmann ... I hired Gus Kessenes on February 26 and Bruno Richard Hauptmann on February 27, 1932, both of whom were directed by me to report to work on March 1, 1932 at eight o'clock in the morning.

" 'On March 1, 1932, at 8 A.M. Bruno Richard Hauptmann and Gus Kessenes reported for work at the Majestic Apartments and worked through that entire day until five o'clock; subsequent thereto they worked there the second, third, and fourth days of March from 8 to 5 P.M. The work of Bruno Richard Hauptmann was such that he was constantly at the premises of the Majestic Apartments from eight to five during that period.' Furcht ended by stating that he remembered Hauptmann and Kessenes because he was in such 'great need of two carpenters' at that time and he clearly remembered Hauptmann because Hauptmann was 'a skilled carpenter who, much against my wishes, I was forced to put on maintenance work, which is ordinary work instead of skilled carpenter work.'

"There it was---Hauptmann, according to the construction superintendent, had begun work on March first as he had originally told police when he was arrested. There was no doubt any longer in my mind that the Majestic employment records had been doctored because it would not have been possible for Hauptmann to have worked until five, taken the subway home, put the kidnap ladder in his car, and drive out to Hopewell in the time span involved. Even if it were possible, police and prosecutor clearly recognized this as a grave defect in their case, but instead of considering the possibility Hauptmann was telling the truth, they bent the evidence to fit the guilty verdict they had already reached.

"Furcht's affidavit was sworn to three days after the extradition hearing. In the transcript of that hearing I read that Hauptmann's lawyer, Fawcett, had asked several witnesses connected with the Majestic whether they knew where to find Furcht, the superintendent, and each said they had no idea where he was because he had quit the Majestic years before. Plainly, Furcht had read about the hearing in the papers and had come forward. But why, I wondered, didn't his testimony force a reopening of the extradition hearing? What happened to Furcht's testimony?

"I found a telephone and again called Lenny Katz at the *Post*. Please pull out the clips on a Joseph Furcht, I asked, in connection with the Lindbergh case---especially clips from October 1934, during Hauptmann's extradition hearing in the Bronx. Lenny said he'd call me back in a little while. I continued going through the file of material concerning the extradition. And I promptly came across a second page of Furcht's affidavit, separated from the first for some reason. His statement continued: 'At the time that Bruno Richard Hauptmann and Gus Kessenes were employed under me, during that period, I signed their payroll sheets.

"'On October 17, 1934 [that is, two days after the extradition hearings] I personally went to the offices of the employment agent, Mr. Pescia, and again examined the records in connection with my request for two carpenters which I made to him in February 1932. His records clearly brought out the fact that Bruno Richard Hauptmann worked for me on March 1. 1932. Annexed hereto is a photostatic copy of the record of E.V. Pescia.'

"The photostatic copy was missing, probably turned over to the Jersey prosecutor along with the Majestic payroll records. Although I still did not have in my hands the actual document, I was certain it once existed because Furcht would not have attached to his affidavit a document that would have shown him to be mistaken or lying. Yes, all those documents proving Hauptmann had worked on the day of the kidnapping most certainly did exist at one time.

"Following this second page of Furcht's affidavit was an affidavit from Pescia, the employment agent, who confirmed that his records showed Hauptmann had come to him for a job in the closing days of February, paid a ten-dollar fee, and was sent to Furcht on Saturday, February 27. Pescia's records also showed that Hauptmann was scheduled to begin working on the following Tuesday, March 1, and that Furcht had so informed Pescia. 'If Bruno Richard Hauptmann had not started work on that day I would have been notified by Mr. Furcht, for he was quite in need of a carpenter,' Pescia added.

"Lenny Katz called and read me a clipping from the *New York Times* about the 'new evidence' provided by Furcht and Pescia. Reporters assigned to the Hauptmann case asked Wilentz and Bronx District Attorney Foley to comment on this evidence and in their comments lies further proof that the payroll records which 'didn't exist' were indeed in the hands of the prosecutors. Foley said, according to the *Times*, that 'he believed the employment records showed that Hauptmann had quit work at the Majestic at 1 P.M. on the day of the kidnapping.' Wilentz told reporters: 'The police know definitely that Hauptmann did not work those hours, nor did he put in a full day of work on March first ...'

"Both Wilentz and Foley admitted in those statements that they knew of some records reflecting Hauptmann's employment on March first. In effect, both admitted the prosecution had not been truthful at the extradition hearing and that it had suppressed the records. Both men, sworn to uphold the majesty of the law, to protect the innocent as a priority over convicting the guilty, not only condoned the lies of Mr. Knapp at the hearing but indulged in further verbal contortions to buttress the official position, that Hauptmann was the killer of the Lindbergh child. Sure, they said, Hauptmann worked on March first, but he quit early so that he could get out to Hopewell. No reporter, not even chief defense attorney Edward Reilly, asked why Hauptmann would call attention to himself by leaving work early on his very first day on the job simply to get out to Hopewell in time to kidnap a baby while the baby's parents and their servants were still awake. Hauptmann did no such thing, I was positive. And I began to understand now that when he wrote his script and got his witnesses to swear Hauptmann did not begin working until March 21, David Wilentz knew it was all a lie, every bit of it.

"Lenny read me another newspaper clipping, an article about a second affidavit signed by Furcht in which he 'retracted' his first, the alibi for Hauptmann. The story said that after Furcht's original affidavit was made public, Wilentz immediately began to inquire about this disturbing news. And so it was that a few days later Furcht was summoned to the office of District Attorney Foley where, in the presence of prosecutor Anthony M. Hauck and several police officers, Furcht made his second sworn statement. In it he said:

"'I am not positive at this time whether or not Hauptmann worked at the Majestic Apartments on March 1,1932. ...At this time I wish to state that I do not know whether or not Hauptmann worked on March 1,1932, at the Majestic Apartments, as the only information I have is the record of the employment agency. ...

"'The system that we used for keeping a record of the time that the men worked was as follows: There was a bimonthly time book which was kept by me and also by Edward Morton. This book showed the names of the men working, and next to the names the date, and in the evening either Morton or I would mark whether the men worked that day. If I were to refer to this book <u>as of March 1, 1932, it would be possible for me to determine whether or not the particular workman worked a full day</u>....I do not know whether or not those records are still available, but they were when I left in December 1932.'

"According to the receipt I had just found in the district attorney's files, those records were available. And it becomes plain, once more, that prosecutors of two states were distorting their evidence to fit their preconceived certainty that Hauptmann was guilty. For what clearly happened is that Furcht was called into Foley's office and was questioned about the affidavit he had given to Hauptmann's attorney.

"During that questioning he was no doubt made to concede that his first affidavit had been based on memory and on the employment agency's files. Then, told the only real evidence to support his statement would be the actual employment records---'and they are missing'---he was forced to say he was 'not positive' whether Hauptmann had worked on the day of the kidnapping. That is the only logical explanation for this "retraction" that was not quite a retraction.

"I found further evidence within the next documents in the folder that someone had tampered with Hauptmann's time sheets in order to prove he had not begun to work until March 21. Those documents were photostatic copies of sheets from that portion of the Majestic's time book which the prosecution did produce in court. The time sheets demonstrate that several prosecution witnesses had lied about Hauptmann's employment.

"Hauptmann is said to have begun work on March 21. Several witnesses connected with the Majestic or with Reliance Property Management testified at the extradition hearings or at the later trial that the construction workers were paid at the end of the month for the two-week period ending the last Saturday of the month. In this case, that would have been March 26; one witness, in fact, specifically said he had prepared the payroll checks based on the work the men had performed up to March 26. Hauptmann therefore should have been paid for working six full days his first week on the job.

"But he was paid for eleven days. According to all the witnesses against him, Richard Hauptmann was paid for eleven days when, the state claimed, he had only worked six days.

"I examined the time sheets more closely now---and there was no notation next to Hauptmann's name, as there was next to the names of several others, that Hauptmann had put in any overtime. Plainly, the extra five days' pay could not be attributed to time and a half.

"There was further internal evidence of tampering within the time sheets themselves. It appeared quite likely that whichever police officers altered these time sheets went even further. Those time sheets are divided into columns. The left-hand, widest column lists the names of the employees, seventeen of them including Hauptmann on the sheet in question. To the right are the columns for the dates. When a man was marked present and working on any specific date, a check mark was used, according to several witnesses. A man who was absent on any date would have a zero entered in the column for that date.

"Along the line following Hauptmann's name there are, for the sixteenth through the twentieth---dates during which Hauptmann had not yet been employed, according to the prosecution---zeros entered in the column for each date, indicating Hauptmann did not work on those days. But the zeros are more than zeros. They are heavy blobs of ink, circles with no center holes. Of all the zeros on these pages only those circles proving Hauptmann had not yet begun work are solid black dots. All the others are neat and round, proper doughnut-shaped zeros. Leading me to the inescapable conclusion that those blobs of ink were affixed to the page after Hauptmann's arrest in order to cover up the original check marks that would have shown he was working. That's the only possible explanation, I felt, for the suddenly sloppy penmanship. Taken together with the fact that he'd been paid for eleven days when it was claimed he had worked only six, this evidence, I was certain, proved the time sheets had been altered.

"But there was more. Two other men had begun working on the twenty-first. While the column next to Hauptmann's name for the five days before the twenty-first contained these questionable zeros, the columns for those dates next to the other two names had lines drawn through them. Only in Hauptmann's case were "zeros" used to indicate he had not yet been employed. Why? Because a simple line would not have erased the check marks of employment; only a round blob of ink could do that.

"Also, something else became clear. I remembered that the time-keeper who testified at the trial, Edward Morton, had sworn Hauptmann was not hired on March first and had been told to return in two weeks 'because we only hire on the first and fifteenth.' Yet Hauptmann, it was said, was hired on the twenty-first. And in the time sheets two other carpenters, Angus Morrison and William Bowie, are listed as having been hired on the sixth. Clearly, another lie to convince jury and public of Hauptmann's guilt.

"Further, the documents I was now studying shed some fresh light on when Hauptmann resigned his job. It was a vital question. Condon had turned the ransom money over to Cemetery John the evening of April second. Hauptmann swore he had worked that day, a Saturday, and then quit, effective immediately. His payroll checks showed he did work for two days in April. The prosecution insisted, and "proved" through the time sheets, that Hauptmann had worked on the first, been absent on the second, then worked the following Monday, the fourth. That "proof" permitted Wilentz to say that Hauptmann, so busy preparing to collect the ransom money and so confident he would get it, did not come to work that Saturday. Once again, however, the "zero" alongside Hauptmann's name for April second is a solid ball of black ink and not one of the perfect circles that appears throughout the time sheets. Also, there is additional evidence that someone tampered with that date of resignation. The last column of each time sheet is headed "Remarks." On Hauptmann's line there is the notation "Out 4/4." That is, it shows he quit April fourth, not on the second as he claimed. But the second

"4" bears no resemblance to the first. It quite clearly was written over another number.

"Similarly, the last element of Hauptmann's explanation of why he had resigned in early April had obviously been doctored. Hauptmann said he quit when he realized that instead of being paid one hundred dollars a month, which he thought was to be his salary, he was receiving only eighty. Prosecution witnesses said he was lying; he was being paid one hundred dollars. There is, in the time sheet, a column devoted to each man's rate of pay. Every single one of the figures---whether "70" or "90" or "100"---is written very clearly beside each man's name. Except for Hauptmann. There is a small stroke for the numeral "1" and then another of those very strange ink blots that seemed to drop out of the time keeper's pen only when that pen was being used on Hauptmann's line in the ledger. Not only that, but Furcht in his affidavit had said he was forced to assign Hauptmann to "ordinary work, not skilled carpenter work." All the skilled carpenters on the time sheets are recorded as being paid one hundred dollars. Hauptmann, on "ordinary work," must have been paid less.

"All these coincidences of leaky pens and the unbelievable discrepancy between the number of days Hauptmann worked and the number of days for which he was paid were simply too much. Hauptmann, beyond question, had been victimized by police who altered the time sheets to fit their belief in his guilt, by witnesses who went along with the alteration, and, most of all, by David Wilentz, who had conceded to the press that Hauptmann had indeed been employed at the Majestic on March first and then later presented "evidence" to prove he had not begun work until three weeks later.

"Was Hauptmann also victimized by his defense attorney, Ed Reilly? I wondered now why Reilly did not point out to the jury all of the discrepancies and alterations I had found, why he did not question Morton, the timekeeper who testified at the trial, more thoroughly and more harshly? Did Reilly feel so certain his noted powers of oratory would seduce the jury into a verdict of acquittal that he neglected to defend his client properly?"

The diligent intensity of Anthony Scaduto's investigation and the invaluable evidence he uncovered pointing to the malfeasance and misfeasance of public officials and police officers can be clearly seen. It is largely due to his intense desire to see true justice proclaimed much too late, but nevertheless proclaimed, but unfortunately after the damnable miscarriage of "what we thought was justice", had claimed the life of an innocent man.

The terrible shame of it all is that it involves more than a few guilty persons who had taken solemn oaths to defend and protect the innocent, and yet allowed themselves, with malice aforethought, to violate and corrupt the very sacred trust invested in them by showing no shame as they stooped to a new low in American jurisprudence.

With this pointed evidence already proving to you how Richard Hauptmann was soundly framed; and with more to come, you will clearly see that the poor innocent Bronx carpenter had no chance whatsoever of escaping a future date in the electric chair.

C H A P T E R   T H I R T Y   S I X

Witnesses from out of Nowhere!!!

The State had by no means finished presenting its case against Hauptmann. If the parade of witnesses had been brought to the stand to tell of truthful events or actual happenings the verdict would be understandably a just one. However, from information gathered since the trial it is obvious that the prosecution was in dire need of finding "honest" witnesses. The remainder of persons who pointed their fingers at Hauptmann as the lone culprit have certainly raised many doubts as to their veracity. Hallucinating, might be a good word to describe their stretching and bending the truth in order to obtain a conviction for the benefit of "justice". However, regardless of who they were, or what they said, if the words flowing from their mouths were against Bruno Richard Hauptmann they were believed, regardless of any testimony refuting their claims, as espousing "nothing but the truth, so help us God!"

Appearing from out of what seemed to be "nowhere" came 26 year old, Miss Hildegarde Olga Alexander. She identified herself as a salesperson and clothing model, who resided at 730 East 236th Street, the Bronx. The young lady testified that she had been a resident of the Bronx her entire life and that she had known Doctor Condon, just casually, since the year 1923. Her testimony given from the Flemington witness chair is overwhelmingly "absurdly ludicrous", one that taxes the wildest stretch of our imaginations. Or possibly we should term it what it really was, --- simply "unbelievable"! That would be true with the exception of the jury, who collectively believed her.

We pick up her answers to the direct line of questioning by Attorney General Wilentz:

Q. Did you see Dr. Condon in the month of March, 1932? A. I did.

Q. Was it before it was publicly known that he was negotiating in the Lindbergh case or after? A. After.

Q. Was it before or after it was chronicled that

the money had been paid, the ransom money? A. Before.

Q. Sometime between those dates you mean? A. Yes.

Q. Where did you see him? A. I saw him in front of the telegraph office in the waiting room of the Fordham Station of the New York Central.

Q. In front of the telegraph office? A. Inside.

Q. Inside. Has the New York Central a Fordham station there? A. Yes.

Q. Were you in that station that day? A. In the platform of the station, yes.

Q. About what time of the day or night was it? A. I should judge about 6:15 or 6:30 in the evening.

Q. Dark, I suppose, I mean night time? A. Yes.

By the Court:

Q. Can you fix the day, Madam? A. Not definitely, not the date.

Q. But was it in March? A. It was in March. It was either on a Monday or Tuesday evening.

Q. 1932. A. Yes.

Mr. Wilentz continues:

Q. Now, who else was in that station besides you and Dr. Condon? A. I saw a man looking at Dr. Condon.

Q. How far away from Dr. Condon was this man? A. About from where I am sitting to where you are sitting, probably just a little further.

Q. May we stipulate it is about from 10 to 15 feet? A. Yes.

Q. Was there anybody else in that station besides Dr. Condon and this man and yourself? A. There may have been but I didn't notice anyone particularly.

Q. Well, were there many people there? A. I wouldn't say that. There are never very many people there.

Q. On this occasion particularly? A. No.

Q. You noticed Dr. Condon and you say you noticed another man? A. Yes.

Q. What were you doing in the station? A. I went into the station to telephone my mother, to tell her I wouldn't be home for dinner.

Q. And will you tell me again what you saw Dr. Condon do in the room. A. Dr. Condon was in front of the telegraph office and he seemed to be having an argument.

Mr. Reilly: I object.

Q. Well, he was talking to somebody there? A. He was.

Q. Yes. At the telegraph station: is that it? A.

Yes.

Q. And what was the other man doing that you observed? A. Watching him.

Q. Now, the man to whom you refer and whom you saw in that station that night, did you see him again, madam? A. Yes, I did.

Q. When approximately? A. Approximately two or three evenings later.

Q. Where? A. He was walking at Fordham Road and Webster Avenue, there is a comfort station there and he was turning the bend.

Q. Were you walking in that vicinity? A. I was.

Q. Who was the man you saw in that station watching Dr. Condon on this night in March and whom you saw a few nights afterwards walking down Fordham Road? A. I say the man was Bruno Richard Hauptmann.

Q. Now when Mr. Hauptmann was arrested in the Bronx, did you see his picture in the paper? A. I did.

Q. And when you saw his picture in the paper did you report the incident to anyone? A. First to my mother.

Q. And then to whom? A. Then I discussed it one evening when I was coming uptown with some friends and it was reported to the foreman of the Bronx Grand Jury and the following day I was called upon to report it to the foreman of the Grand Jury.

Q. Did you also come to Flemington to the jail to see the defendant Hauptmann? A. I did.

Q. Now, when you saw Dr. Condon in the railroad station that night and you also saw this man, on that very night did you say anything about it to anyone? A. Well, I was talking to my mother over the telephone, I was recounting the incident to her---

Q. You spoke to your mother about it? A. Right.

Q. Now, at that time did you know who the man was? A. No.

Q. Did you attach any particular significance at the time? A. Well, I thought that he may have been---

Mr. Reilly: I object to what she thought.

Mr. Wilentz: All right, I will withdraw it. That is all, Miss Alexander. Mr. Reilly may inquire.

Cross examination by Mr. Reilly:

Q. What time of the day was it that you finished your work this particular day? A. Five-thirty, I always finish at five-thirty.

Q. And where did you live then? A. At the same address.

Q. Where is it? A. 730 East 236th Street.

Q. And how do you go home from Park Avenue in the neighborhood of where you work to that address on 236th Street? A. Yes, I walked over to the Third Avenue "L". I take the local up to 42nd Street and then I change for the express.

Q. The "L"? A. Yes, the Third Avenue "L".

Q. You don't take the subway? A. No, I don't.

Q. And then change at 149th Street? A. No, I don't.

Q. And how long does it take you to get home? A. Usually about a half hour, thirty-five minutes, it all depends.

Q. Now, how far away from your home was this railroad station? A. How many stations, do you mean?

Q. The railroad station you say you saw Dr. Condon at? A. Well, part of my--well, on the Central, the next station is the Botanical Gardens, the one after that is Williamsbridge, and the one after that---

Q. Could you go on the Central? A. No, I occasionally use it, but not very often.

Q. Did you use the Central that night? A. No, I did not.

Q. You went up on the "L" and got off where? A. Fordham Road and 190th Street.

Q. Fordham Road and 190th Street? A. Yes.

Q. Where, in connection with Fordham Road and 190th Street is the railroad station? A. You walk down from the Third Avenue "L" and then you walk probably a few steps west and there is a platform right there, there is a connection, I mean, you can enter the New York Central train.

Q. What station of the New York Central do you say it is? A. Fordham Road, 190th street.

Q. But you were getting off at 233rd Street? A. No, I wasn't. I got off at Fordham Road and 190th Street.

Q. Why? A. Because I attended evening school.

Q. Where? A. Fordham Road; Theodore Roosevelt Evening High School, at the time.

Q. What time does that evening school start? A. It starts at 7:30.

Q. How far is the high school from your home? A. By stations or by time?

Q. Time. A. I should judge about 20 minutes or 15 minutes by train.

Q. You would have time to go from your place of business, leaving at 5:30, go up and get your dinner and come back to the high school, would you not? A. Yes, I would.

Q. Did you? A. No, I didn't. I had dinner in Fordham that night.

Q. Where? A. At a Chinese restaurant.

Q. With whom? A. I had no escort.

Q. You had no escort, did you? A. I was by myself.

Q. Where is this Chinese restaurant? A. On Fordham Road and Webster Avenue, 190th and Webster.

Q. How near is that to the elevated railroad station that you say you came down on? A. It is on the west side of Webster Avenue.

Q. You know, do you not, that there are telephone booths in every elevated station in New York City? A. Yes.

Q. There are telephone booths in every subway station in New York City? A. Yes.

Q. And there is a telephone in your Chinese restaurant? A. Yes.

Q. So you walked down the stairs of the elevated station and over to the New York Central Railroad Station? A. I just had to turn a few steps.

Q. For the purpose of telephoning your mother, is that correct? A. That is right.

Q. And on the railroad station you found Dr. Condon, right? A. Inside the platform of the waiting room.

Q. Now I want you to describe for this jury that railroad station at 190th Street and Fordham Road of the New York Central. A. Well, I would say this was the main entrance coming in (indicating).

Q. Yes. Now where is the ticket booth? A. The ticket booth is in the center.

Q. And what time were you there that night? A. About 6:15 or 6:30.

Q. Yes. And where was the ticket agent at 6:30 that night? A. He may have been in the booth. I didn't take particular notice.

Q. Don't you know that the station closes at five o'clock? A. I have never known it to close at five o'clock. I have always been in there.

Q. Did you ever try to buy a ticket at that station, going north on the New York Central? A. No, I did not.

Q. After six o'clock? A. No.

Q. Now it is nothing more or less than a local station on the New York Central for local trains, am I correct. A. That is correct.

Q. How near is it to Mott Haven Station? One station further north or one south? A. Well, Mott Haven is going north.

Q. And how near is it to Spuyten Duyvil? A. Spuyten Duyvil is not in that direction at all.

Q. What road is this on? A. What road is it on?

Q. The New York Central; where do the trains run that pass this particular station you are talking about? A. Park Avenue---

Q. If Spuyten Duyvil is not on the station, not on that road. A. Well, the trains run east of White Plains Avenue, west of White Plains Avenue, east of Webster.

Q. Where does this particular road start, this railroad? A. At 42nd Street.

Q. All right. It is not the spur up around 133rd Street bridge that runs into Boston, is it? A. Not that I know of.

Q. Do you know the Boston and Maine Road that starts at 133rd Street, of the New York Central? A. No, I don't.

Q. And how long have you lived in the Bronx? A. All my life.

Q. All your life and you don't know that there is a road that begins in the Bronx and runs to Boston of the New York Central? A. No, I don't.

Q. All right. Now, do you know anything about the Putnam Division? A. I do not.

Q. Of the New York Central. You don't? A. No, I don't.

Q. Do you know that there is a Putnam Division of the New York Central that runs through the Bronx and runs through---maybe this will refresh your recollection Pocantico Hills, the home of the people up there--- A. I do not.

Q. Now, you have told us that sometimes you take the New York Central home; is that right? A. That is right.

Q. And when you do you go to 42nd Street and Park Avenue: correct? A. That is right.

Q. Now, what line do you take? A. I go to the lower level and I buy a ticket and I find out what track the train leaves on, and I go on that track and get into the train and get off at either Fordham or 233rd Street; I never pay any attention to whether the train goes further or not, or whether it goes--

Q. Well now, is there a station of the New York

Central at 233rd Street? A. There is; it is called Woodlawn.

Q. Called Woodlawn? A. That is right.

Q. Then that is on the White Plains Division, is it? A. That is on the New York Central.

Q. Is it the White Plains or is it the Yonkers Division? A. It is on the White Plains Division.

Q. Yes. Now, you say you get a ticket and you walk to a gate and you pay no attention to where the train goes: is that it? A. Well, I know where it is going, because I ask.

Q. Well, don't you have to look at the indicator alongside of the station entrance, the train entrance? A. That is right.

Q. Now, have you ever taken a train and changed before you got to Fordham? A. No.

Q. Did you ever change at Highbridge? A. No.

Q. Is Highbridge above or below your station? A. I don't know where Highbridge is; I imagine it is below.

Q. Yes. Now isn't it a fact, young lady, that anyone desiring to go in the way you have indicated must change at Highbridge for the Putnam Division and the White Plains side? A. Not that I know of.

Q. Don't you know that at five o'clock at night and six o'clock at night there are no local stops? A. There are so.

Q. Between the Grand Central on that line and possibly Mount Vernon? A. Well, there are local stops.

Q. How many times have you ridden on the New York Central to your house? A. Often enough to know what train leaves there.

Q. How many times? A. I can't approximate the number of times.

Q. What is the fare? A. The fare to Fordham varies.

Q. What varies on the New York Central, what fare? A. The fare from 42nd Street to Fordham.

Q. Is how much? A. I think it is thirty-five cents.

Q. Don't you know? A. I can't remember definitely.

Q. What is the fare to 233rd Street? A. I believe it is 44 cents.

Q. Don't you know? A. Or 49; not definitely either.

Q. When was the last time you rode? A. Possibly several years ago. I don't know. I am not in a position to state that definitely.

Q. Several years ago you rode on the New York Central to your station, is that right? A. That is right.

Q. Several years ago means what, five years? A. Maybe two years.

Q. Maybe two years? A. Maybe three years.

Q. It made no impression, did it? A. No.

Q. How long do you know Dr. Condon? A. Since 1923.

Q. Where did you meet him? A. In a theater.

Q. Who introduced you? A. The manager of the theater.

Q. Where was the theater? A. At 195th Street and Webster Avenue.

Q. And under what were the conditions that you were introduced to him? A. Well, I worked at the theater at the time, while I was going to high school.

Q. What were you doing in the theater? A. I was cashier in the theater.

Q. And Dr. Condon was a frequent visitor? A. He was a patron.

Q. What? A. A patron of the theater.

Q. And why should the manager of the theater introduce you, his cashier, to Dr. Condon? A. Because the manager conversed with Dr. Condon very, very often. There were never crowds that came into the theater during the afternoons and the manager knew I was going to high school at the time, mornings while I worked in the afternoons and he also knew that Dr. Condon was connected with either the Board of Education or was a principal, and he thought it was nice to let Dr. Condon know that I was going to school while I was working.

Q. Was Dr. Condon a principal then? A. I don't know.

Q. Was he ever connected with the Board of Education? A. I don't know that either.

Q. How many times after that did you see Dr. Condon? A. Just during the time that I worked in the theater.

Q. How many years ago was that? A. 1923.

Q. You left the theater in 1923? A. 1924.

Q. '24, and from 1924 down to 1932, you tell us you had never seen Dr. Condon once, is that right? A. That is right.

Q. What was Dr. Condon doing when you first saw him in this railroad station? A. He was standing in front of the telegraph office, walking back---

Q. Where is the telegraph office? A. Inside of

the platform, the waiting room.

Q. This is a local station, is it not? A. That is right.

Q. What telegraph operator was ever on duty there in March? A. I don't know.

Q. Did you see one? A. Yes, there was a telegraph operator---because Dr. Condon was talking to someone.

Q. Talking to a telegraph operator in this station? A. Talking to someone.

Q. Which is it now? A. A telegraph operator, most likely.

Q. Did you see the man telegraphing? A. No, I did not.

Q. You came to the conclusion that he was a telegraph operator? A. That is right.

Q. And Dr. Condon had his back to you, did he not? A. He was directly in profile to me.

Q. But you were not in front of him? A. No, I was not in front of him.

Q. You did not hear what he said? A. No, I didn't hear what he said.

Q. You came to the conclusion he was talking? A. He was very much excited, I came to that conclusion.

Q. You came to the conclusion he was excited? A. He was excited.

Q. Did you make your telephone call to your mother? A. I did.

Q. From that station? A. I did.

Q. And of course you went into the booth. A. I did.

Q. When you came out you went out? A. That is right.

Q. And went upstairs and went on the street? A. No, I didn't go upstairs. It is on a level with the street.

Q. Then you were on the upper station, you were not on the platform? A. I was on the level. The waiting room is on a level with the street.

Q. Did you get off the train and walk through the station out into the street? A. I walked downstairs from the Third Avenue elevated station.

Q. I am talking about the station. A. Yes.

Q. Is that on the level with the street? A. Yes.

Q. You can walk into the station--- A. Yes.

Q. Through the station to the platform where the train is, is that right? A. You walk downstairs.

Q. Yes, for the train? A. For the train.

Q. Yes. A. That is right.

Q. Yes. So you don't walk off the street for the train, do you?

Mr. Wilentz: She didn't say she did.

A. You walk from the street right into the waiting room where the information room is and the Western Union office is.

Q. And that is back now in 1932? A. That is right.

Q. And where was this booth? A. The telephone booth?

Q. Yes. Then--- A. There are booths on both sides.

Q. Both sides of what? A. Of the waiting room, the ticket office.

Q. Well, now, your object in going there was to phone? A. That is right.

Q. And you came right in and you glanced around and went to your phone, didn't you? A. May I demonstrate how I came in?

Q. Do you want to come down here and show how you came in? A. I will say this is one way of coming in--- there are several---I don't know how many there are, and I came in from an entrance that showed Dr. Condon to me directly in profile, and there were phone booths directly where I entered.

Q. And you went to the phone booth? A. I didn't use the phone booths where I entered. I walked directly to the opposite side where Dr. Condon was standing.

Q. But you used a phone booth? A. And I used the phone booths there.

Q. That didn't take more than two minutes, to phone? A. Several minutes. I had a conversation with my mother at the time.

Q. Then you came out, right? A. That is right.

Q. And you went on about your business? A. That is right.

Q. When did you next see Dr. Condon, or have you seen him since? A. No, I have only seen him in the papers, that is all.

Q. Have you had any conversation with him over the phone or any way? A. No, I have not.

Q. Has anybody come to you from his house? A. No.

Q. Has anybody come to you from anybody's house? A. No.

Q. Has anybody come to you from any place at all?

A. No.

Q. You haven't talked to a soul about the testimony you were going to give here this morning, have you? A. Oh, yes, I have discussed it.

Q. Who? A. Discussed it first with my mother.

Q. Outside of your mother. A. And members of my family.

Q. Outside of your mother. A. My employer.

Q. Yes. This is all recently? A. Yes, a few months back.

Q. And who brought you down here today, young lady? A. District Attorney Breslin.

Q. Who? A. Mr. Breslin, of The Bronx.

Q. Do you know him? A. I don't know him personally, no.

Q. When did he come to the house for you yesterday? A. Yes, he came to me last night.

Q. Before that when have you seen Breslin? A. About two weeks previously, on a Friday when he called for me to drive me out to Flemington.

Q. Were you in The Bronx courtroom at the extradition hearing of this case? A. In the courtroom, no.

Q. Were you around the building? A. In September I was around the building, yes, or in October, I don't know when it was.

Q. In October. Did they bring you there? A. They brought me.

Q. And how long were you there? A. Possibly an hour or so; I don't recall.

Q. And you didn't testify, did you? A. I did.

Q. In court? A. No.

Q. That is what I am talking about. A. No, I did not.

Q. You didn't testify before the Judge? A. No.

Q. This is the first time you have testified? A. Yes.

Mr.Reilly: That is all.

Re-Direct Examination by Mr. Wilentz:

Q. In addition to coming here with Mr. Breslin, you came here with your mother this morning? A. That is right.

Q. When you were in the Bronx Court House you came there as the result of the invitation of the foreman of the Grand Jury, did you not? A. That is right.

Q. And when you got there you spoke to District

Attorney Foley and told him your story? A. That is right.

Q. You asked at that time, as you have asked since, to try to keep away from any publicity, haven't you? A. Absolutely.

Mr. Wilentz: Thank you, miss, very much, and we are sorry to trouble you.

The Witness: Thank you.

(Witness leaves stand.)

Miss Hildegarde Olga Alexander had played her role to perfection as Attorney General Wilentz led her to "brilliantly explain" how she had "remarkably remembered" a mere incident. An incident which had occurred (if it had actually occurred at all) nearly three years before she volunteered to give her "incriminating testimony" which was used against Richard Hauptmann's hapless and hopeless defense to prove his innocence.

Miss Alexander's testimony actually proved nothing; except to add another person who was willing to point their fingers at Hauptmann as the lone culprit in the Lindbergh kidnapping. Alexander said she saw a man she positively identified as Bruno Richard Hauptmann staring at Doctor Condon in a train station. Furthermore she claimed she only had a profile view of Condon, a man she knew just casually and had not seen since 1923, nine years before this occurrence took place. Criminal investigators will tell you that it is a known and accepted fact that hundreds of mistaken identities have been made in cases where someone has been asked to point out a person, and have either failed to do so or named the wrong person, simply because they were not acquainted with the person's profile appearance. This fact results from most of us being, quite naturally, more familiar with the full-face appearance of the people around us. This is true even in the case of close friends, simply because this is the way we look at, see, and come to know most everyone.

Based on this fact, the evidence presented by Hildegarde Olga Alexander amounts to "nothing more than an empty nothing" since we have no more assurance that the man she identified as being Richard Hauptmann was actually him, than we have that the person she identified as Condon was really him. She had not seen Condon since 1923, and even then did not know him well. As for Hauptmann, he was a man she "believed" she had seen three years earlier, making her judgement of this only from a newspaper photograph published of the arrested man.

And so, without any more being said of Miss Alexander's identification of Hauptmann, we will write it off as a preposterous illustration as to the depths some folks will sink to gain a fleeting flash from the "instant but dying spotlight" of unearned fame in the Lindbergh case. In spite of her asking to be "kept away from any publicity", Miss Alexander's hallucination has etched her name in the "rotten clay" of The Crime of The Century.

Taking her place by the side of Alexander comes the already mentioned Mrs. Cecile M. Barr, the cashier of Loew's Sheridan Square Theater, located at 12th Street and 7th Avenue, Greenwich Village, New York. It was Cecile Barr who testified she had been given a folded $5 Lindbergh ransom bill on the night of Sunday, November 26, 1933, by no one other than Bruno Richard Hauptmann, as he paid for a ticket to enter the movie house. She claimed he had the bill folded in a curious way, first lengthwise, and then twice over, making a small compact one. In her description of him, she had told Lieutenant James Finn that her customer was apparently an American, had been somewhat surly with her, and that he was wearing a hat but no overcoat. Had the man been Hauptmann, she would most certainly have easily detected his German accent from the short conversation she had with him.

Now we have no problem with Mrs. Barr's statement that she had a customer around nine-thirty on the night of Sunday, November 26th, 1933, and that her customer had definitely passed her a Lindbergh ransom $5 bill. This much is a matter of record. However we vehemently dispute her contention that her customer was Mr. Hauptmann.

On this specified night Richard Hauptmann was fifteen miles away in his home in the Bronx where he and his friends were spending an enjoyable evening celebrating Richard's 34th birthday. Present at the party, in addition to Anna Hauptmann, was Maria Mueller, Katie Fredericksen, Paul Vetterle, and Isidor Fisch. There can be no denial of this. It is factual. However, in spite of this, the jury refused to believe the very apparent and quite obvious lifestyle of the average citizen, and believe instead that Hauptmann had left his wife and three week old son and had ventured 15 miles away from his home to see a movie alone without wearing an overcoat on a cold night near the end of

November. To this we say baloney sliced thin. If you still want to believe such foolishness, it is your privilege. However, we must question your reasoning for not looking at the situation fairly.

Before we move on to another "gem" of a witness, it is well that we make note of a statement made by a young New York City psychiatrist, Dr. Dudley D. Shoenfeld. The doctor had predicted, since the ransom bills turning up during the remaining months of 1933 and 1934 were folded in like fashion as the one given to Cecile Barr, the kidnapper, when arrested, was certain to have a bill in his wallet folded the same. Isn't it odd that on September 19, 1934 when Hauptmann was arrested, although he had a ransom bill in his wallet, it was not folded in this manner. Neither were any of the other ransom bills, attributed to being spent by Hauptmann, folded in this way. Dr. Shoenfeld's empty prediction had fallen to the ground as a deflated balloon.

The State's case against Hauptmann was progressing along at a rapid rate. The female witnesses, Alexander and Barr, had certainly had their fair say; and now it is proper to learn what another of the male gender, one Charles B. Rossiter, had to say about Richard Hauptmann.

Rossiter,after he had been properly seated in the witness chair, told his listeners that he had lived in Maplewood, New Jersey in 1932 and that he was a salesman who covered the entire state of New Jersey for Perfect Foods, Incorporated of Lansdale, Pennsylvania. He said during the month of February, 1932, he had seen the defendant, Bruno Richard Hauptmann, on Route 31, near the Princeton Airport. He claimed it was the Saturday evening before the kidnapping. The hour, he said, was around 8:00 p.m.

The food salesman said he was on his way to Philadelphia to stay with his wife's people there when he saw Hauptmann standing at the rear of a car parked about 100 to 150 yards north of the Princeton Airport.

Attorney General Wilentz's direct questioning continued in this fashion:

Q. You say he was in the rear of it? A. He was standing at the rear of it.

Q. What did you do as you drove along? A. As I drove up I pulled to the rear of the car.

Q. Why? A. For the simple reason that I could be to the rear of it and not pull up around the front of it.

Q. Well why did you stop? That is what I mean.

A. For the simple reason to see if I could render any assistance, thinking it was a motorist in distress.

Q. Was it a section that is not thickly populated? A. Yes. There is only one house there, to my knowledge.

Q. How far away from this point? A. Well directly across from where his car was.

Q. I see. And did you get out of your car then? A. I did.

Q. And what did you do? A. I walked to the rear of his car.

Q. Did you speak to him? A. I did.

Q. What did you say to him? A. I wouldn't say verbatim what I said to him---

Q. Substantially--- A. To the effect of whether I could help him any.

Q. What did he say? A. He said he was all right; he didn't need any help.

Q. Did you then proceed on your way? A. No, I stood there and looked the man over pretty well.

Q. Why?--- Never mind that 'why.' At any rate, you stayed there for a while? A. I did.

Q. What sort of hat was he wearing? A. A slouch hat.

Q. And then you proceeded on your way? A. After looking him over, yes.

Q. Did you then proceed on your way? A. No, not right away, no.

Q. Well, within how soon? A. Well, a period of anywheres from five to eight minutes, I would say.

Q. Then where did you go? A. To Philadelphia.

Q. And you stayed there that night? A. That is right.

Q. That was Saturday night? A. That is right.

Q. When did you return to work? A. I returned to my home the next afternoon, which was Sunday.

Q. The next afternoon? A. That is right.

Q. Now, when was the next time that you saw this man or a picture of him? A. The next time I saw a picture of him was the day after his arrest, September 20th.

Q. And when you saw that picture did you call it to the attention of the authorities? A. I did not, at once.

Q. What did you do? A. I felt at the time when I saw his picture---

Mr. Reilly: I object to how he felt.

Q. Never mind how you felt. When did you call it

to their attention? A. On the 22nd of September.

Q. And as a result of that did you go over to see him in The Bronx? A. I did.

Q. Did you see him there? A. Yes.

Q. Now, you have been subpoenaed by the state, have you not, to this trial? A. That is right.

Q. And in that connection and capacity you have been the guest of the State at its headquarters in the Hildebrecht Hotel in Trenton, have you not? A. That is right.

Q. Awaiting your call to be a witness, isn't that so? A. That is right.

Q. And you are here today in answer to a subpoena? A. That is right.

Q. I understood you to say on occasions you returned to your wife---you are married, are you? A. Yes.

Q. Are you employed at this time? A. I am.

Q. Have you any interest in this case in behalf of either the complaining witness in this case, Colonel Lindbergh, or the State, or the State Police, or anybody else? A. No, only interested in justice.

Q. I recall that you stated you lived in the State of New Jersey for how long? A. All but three years of my life.

Q. Are you employed now anywhere? A. Yes.

Q. Where? A. American Automobile Association.

Mr. Wilentz: Take the witness.

Cross-Examination by Mr. Reilly:

Q. Now, will you turn around and face me, please? A. Sure thing.

Q. Did you ever make a mistake in identity in your life? A. Did I ever make a mistake in identity?

Q. That is the question. A. Yes.

Q. How many times? A. Why, possibly two or three times.

Q. And those mistakes of identity, were they occasions where you thought you saw some person you knew and attracted the attention of that person, that you stopped, and then it turned out that you were in error? A. That is right.

Q. Such as touching on the shoulder? A. That is right.

Q. Or addressing him by name? A. That is right.

Q. And there were certain characteristics about the person that you looked at that you associated with some person that you knew and that you found out you were in error? A. That is right.

Q. Correct. Now, the man on the road you had never seen before, had you? A. No, sir.

Q. And this was a well traveled highway, one of the main highways, isn't it? A. Yes.

Q. Super-highway, is that what they call it? A. Oh, no.

Q. Well, it is one of the main arteries between what cities? A. Why, it runs between Somerville and Princeton. It is not one of the main highways.

Q. It is a busy road? A. Well, I would say it is fairly busy, not too busy.

Q. Were you ever a private detective? A. No.

Q. Did you ever study law? A. No.

Q. Ever been a witness in any case before? A. Once.

Q. Have you ever been convicted of any crime? A. Not that I know of.

Q. Now, on this particular evening, you say it was a Saturday evening? A. That is right.

Q. I suppose you wrote that down in a diary, didn't you? A. No, sir.

Q. You are now depending upon your recollection in 1935 of something that happened in 1932, is that correct? A. (No answer.)

Q. Yes or No. A. I am basing it on the fact that I know what I am talking about.

Q. You are relying on your recollection of something that happened in 1932, testifying in 1935, is that correct? A. That is right, yes.

Q. And you made no memorandum in writing, did you? A. No memorandum.

Q. And you pride yourself on your memory, is that it? A. Well, I wouldn't exactly say that, but I can remember faces.

Q. And remember dates? A. Well, not all dates, some dates.

Q. This particular Saturday night, was there anything about that Saturday night that you remember, a wedding anniversary or something like that? A. Nothing particularly that Saturday evening, no.

Q. Just a Saturday evening? A. Just a Saturday evening.

Q. And where had you started from? A. 26 Berkley Street, Maplewood.

Q. To ride to Philadelphia? A. That is right.

Q. Were you driving with anybody? A. No, I was driving by myself.

Q. What time did you leave this Maplewood

address? A. Well, I would say it was around 7 o'clock, 7 p.m.

Q. Dark? A. Yes.

Q. Dark all along the road? A. Yes.

Q. Where had you been that afternoon? A. Well, now, of course, that is an easy question for me to answer for the simple reason I always had---

Mr.Wilentz: Answer the question, please.

A. I was in my warehouse, which I was manager of at that time, checking stock.

Q. Is that your usual Saturday afternoon job? A. That is right.

Q. And Saturday morning where had you been? A. Working on my ledgers.

Q. When had you come in from the road? A. I didn't come in from the road. I was---

Q. Where were you on Friday? A. On Friday, I had no definite procedure to follow, and at that time I wouldn't say that I was at any particular place, other than you might say running in all directions.

Q. Do you recall any direction you ran in? A. Well, offhand I couldn't say definitely, no.

Q. Can you recall anybody you met on Friday? A. Can I recall anyone I met?

Q. On Friday. A. Yes, my wife.

Q. You meet her every day, don't you? A. That is right.

Q. Let's have somebody else besides the members of your family. A. My neighbors.

Q. Anybody in business on Friday? A. Well, not at present, for the simple reason I don't remember just where I was on that particular day.

Q. Do you recall any strangers you met on Friday? A. Any strangers? Possibly I met a lot but I haven't met them since.

Q. Can you recall any of them now? A. I wouldn't say I could, because I haven't seen them since.

Q. The day before, Thursday, where were you? A. Well, one of many places; I couldn't say offhand where I was.

Q. Did you meet any strangers on Thursday? A. No doubt I did.

Q. Can you describe any of the strangers you met on Thursday? A. Describe any of the strangers?

Q. Yes. A. No, I wouldn't attempt that.

Q. Now where did you spend the 22nd of February, 1932, Washington's Birthday? A. 22nd of February---at my home to my best recollection.

Q. Did you meet anybody there that day? A. That day?

Q. Outside of the members of your family? A. Not that I remember now.

Q. February the 12th. A. February 12th?

Q. Was Lincoln's Birthday. You recall that, do you? A. Oh, yes.

Q. Did you work on that day? A. Home, to my best recollection..

Q. Did you meet any strangers that day? A. Not that I remember.

Q. Where were you on the Sunday after this Saturday night? A. The Sunday after this Saturday night?

Q. Yes. A. At the home of my wife's people in the Frankford section of Philadelphia until late that afternoon.

Q. And you started back with your wife? A. No, by myself.

Q. Covering this same route? A. Same Route.

Q. How many automobiles did you see on the road between Philadelphia and your home that was standing either in front of you or at the side of the road? A. How many did I see standing in front of me or to the side?

Q. Yes. On Sunday. A. Well, possibly a lot in the cities.

Q. On the road? A. Not any to my knowledge.

Q. Do you recall any automobile on Sunday---did you come back in the afternoon or evening? A. Afternoon.

Q. Daylight? A. Well---

Q. Dusk? A. Towards dusk, yes.

Q. Towards dusk? Did you see any automobile there that you can recall where anyone was changing a tire? A. No.

Q. You say no, or that you don't remember, which? A. That was not to my knowledge, I didn't take any notice.

Q. You didn't take any notice of? A. No.

Q. There might have been some but you don't recall? A. I say I didn't see any.

Q. You say you didn't see any. Now, you can remember definitely that on Sunday---what date in February was this visit to Philadelphia? A. What date?

Q. Yes. A. Well, I would say, I am not saying positively, but I believe it was the 27th of February.

Q. You think it was? A. Well, I would say, I believe so.

Q. You believe so? A. Yes.

Q. And would that be Sunday, the 28th? A. No, that would be---

Q. Sunday, the 27th? A. The 27th yes.

Q. Saturday was the 26th? A. That is what I believe, yes; I haven't checked the dates.

Q. You haven't checked the dates? A. No.

Q. Could it have been the 19th? A. No.

Q. It couldn't have been February 19th? A. Pardon me. May I ask what you are driving at?

Q. On Saturday. A. The Saturday that I saw Hauptmann?

Q. Yes. A. Well, the date to my best knowledge, of course, in close relation to the kidnapping, and to my mind I am aware of that date, I would say it was around the 26th.

Q. But you are not positive of that? A. Why, I wouldn't be positive of that date, no.

Q. It could have been the week before? A. Oh, no; it couldn't.

Q. You have absolutely got that date set in your mind: is that it? A. Oh, yes; that evening.

Q. That evening. Well, now, was there anybody else around the road? A. Anyone else around what road?

Q. Yes, around the road where you say you met Hauptmann. A. No.

Q. And was the car standing out in the center of the road or towards the side? A. Two wheels were off the highway.

Q. Two wheels were off the highway,---was he jacking up a tire? A. No, sir.

Q. Did you see any blow-out? A. No, I didn't look for any.

Q. Did you see the rear light out? A. The rear light was on.

Q. The rear light was on. This man didn't signal you to stop? A. No.

Q. He didn't indicate that he wanted any assistance? A. No.

Q. Was he near any house? A. Yes, directly opposite a house.

Q. What is the number of the house? A. I didn't go to the house to look for a number.

Q. What kind of a house was it? A. Well, it is a very, very large house, I would say that to the best of my knowledge it is a three-story house.

Q. People in it? A. Well, now, I don't know about that.

Q. Was it lighted up? A. That I didn't look to see at that time.

Q. What light was there on the road? A. What light?

Q. Yes. A. Well now, let's see. There was a light, I believe the beacon light was operating at that time at the airport.

Q. The beacon light at the airport? A. Yes, sir.

Q. Are you interested in aviation? A. Me? No, sir, I have never been up in my life.

Q. The beacon light of the field is how high? It is only a tower, is it not? A. Yes, sir, I guess it is.

Q. It is a revolving light? A. Yes, sir.

Q. It shows white and shows red? A. To the best of my knowledge, I never looked at it to pay much attention to it.

Q. Were you there? A. Yes, but I didn't look up at the beacon light.

Q. Is it a stationary light or swinging light? A. I believe it is a swinging light.

Q. Don't you know whether it is or not? A. I have passed there on several occasions and I have noticed it takes a wide swing around there.

Q. Does it take a swing? A. Yes.

Q. Always white? A. I wouldn't say the color because I never paid any attention.

Q. But you have passed there many times? A. That is right.

Q. This is a beacon that stands out at this field, correct? A. That is right.

Q. And a person driving within say a half a mile of the field either way is attracted by this light, is he not? A. That is right.

Q. While it doesn't play on the road, it sweeps the heavens, doesn't it? A. That is right.

Q. It is a signal to the aviators in the heavens, is that correct? A. That is right.

Q. It doesn't light up the road? A. Oh, no.

Q. Now, what other light was there? A. No other lights except mine.

Q. Your headlights? A. That is right.

Q. How close did you come to the car in front of you? A. Well, within ten to fifteen feet.

Q. And you got out of your car? A. That is right.

Q. You walked up to this man, is that correct? A. That is right.

Q. How was he dressed? A. Well, at that time he had on an overcoat, I would say, I did say was black, and a light suit which I described as being gray.

Q. What kind of a shirt? A. What kind of a shirt? Couldn't see, because he had the collar pulled up covering the shirt.

Q. He had his collar up around his neck? A. No, he didn't have his collar up, but it was pulled so close that you couldn't distinguish the color of the shirt.

Q. A fedora hat? A. A slouch hat, if that is what you call a fedora.

Q. Pulled down over his eyes? A. No, he didn't---

Q. Pushed back off his forehead? A. No.

Q. Even--- A. Even, I would say, right across the top of his forehead.

Q. You came up to this man and what did you say? A. I asked him if I help him---Those are not words verbatim; they were words along that line.

Q. And he said no, he didn't need any help? A. That is right.

Q. And then did you get in your car and drive away? A. Not immediately, no.

Q. Stand there looking at the beacon light? A. No, sir.

Q. Standing there looking at the man, I suppose? A. That is right.

Q. No further conversation? A. No further conversation.

Q. From either one of you? A. No.

Q. When did you drive away? A. When did I drive away?

Q. How many minutes after this? A. Five to eight minutes.

Q. Are you related to anybody in the State Police? A. In the State Police?

Q. Yes. A. Not to my knowledge.

Q. Or any other police? A. Not to my knowledge.

Q. That is what I am talking about---your knowledge---Is there any member of your family connected with any police force or detective force? A. No.

Q. Do you know any of the State Police? A. A few of them.

Q. How many? A. Well now, it would be hard for me offhand to number them.

Q. Well, about how many? A. Well, a conservative

estimate, at least ten.

Q. They are all under Colonel Schwarzkopf of the State---of the New Jersey State Police? A. I am speaking collectively of the men that I have come in contact with, whether they were State Police or New York police or Department of Justice, I wouldn't distinguish because unless I actually was told I wouldn't know.

Q. Well, how many State Police do you think you know? A. Just a minute. I will figure them for you. I can name five, at least.

Q. State policemen? A. Yes.

Q. Will you name them, please? A. Well, there is Wallace.

Q. How long have you known Mr. Wallace? A. How long?

Q. Yes. A. Oh, at least since September 22nd, that is, known him to see.

Mr. Wilentz: Give us the date, please.

The Witness: You mean the length of time?

Mr. Wilentz: That is what you wanted, isn't it?

Mr. Reilly: Yes.

The Witness: How long do I know him?

Q. Yes. A. Since September 22nd.

Q. Last year? A. 1934, yes.

Q. Did you know any State Police before that date? A. No.

Q. Did you know any police in your local town? A. In the local town? Know them to speak to, yes.

Q. Did you know any New York police before September, 1934? A. No, I didn't.

Q. Now, what is your business? A. District Manager, Cumberland County, American Automobile Association.

Q. How long has that been your business? A. Oh approximately three months.

Q. Before that what were you doing? A. With the Universal Producing Company in New York City.

Q. What do they do? A. Why they book amateur theatricals.

Q. Have you been an actor? A. Actor? No.

Q. Never took part in any amateur dramatics of any kind? A. Not that I can recall.

Q. Ever written any articles for any newspaper or magazine? A. No.

Q. How long were you connected with this organization that furnishes amateur--- A. Theatricals.

Q. ---actors---is that what it is? A. No, no.

Q. Just what do they do? A. They put on shows for civic organizations with their own talent, that is, the community's home talent.

Q. They go around to a community and they--- A. Book shows.

Q. They gather local talent, is that it, put on a show and divide the profits, if there are any. Is that it? A. With the organization, that is right.

Q. And how long have you been doing that? A. About two weeks.

Q. Well, now, before that what did you do? A. I was with Perfect Foods, Incorporated, Lansdale, Pennsylvania.

Q. Perfect Foods? A. Incorporated, Lansdale, Pennsylvania.

Q. Did you live there? A. Did I live there? Yes. For about a year.

Q. And how long were you employed by them? A. Close on to six years.

Q. Before that what did you do? A. Before that I was with the Jacob Horning Brewing Company in Philadelphia.

Q. And lived in Philadelphia? A. Yes.

Q. For how long? A. About three years; about three years.

Q. I suppose before that you were at school, is that right? A. No.

Q. What was your occupation before that? A. Before that? With the Ward Baking Company in Philadelphia.

Q. In New York or Philadelphia? A. Philadelphia.

Q. Now, when did you first see a picture of Mr. Hauptmann? A. The afternoon of September 20th.

Q. In the daily papers? A. That is right.

Q. And how many days did it take you to make up your mind that you had seen that person before? A. A day and a half.

Q. And during the day and a half you saw other pictures of him in the newspapers? A. That is right.

Q. Every edition---? A. That is right.

Q. ---you bought had his picture in? A. That is right.

Q. And then you---what did you do, go some place? A. Did I go some place?

Q. Communicate with the State Police? A. That is right.

Q. How did you do that, call them on the

telephone? A. That is right.

Q. Where? A. At the training school in Trenton.

Q. And who did you ask for? A. Colonel Schwarzkopf.

Q. Did the newspapers say that Colonel Schwarzkopf could be found at the training station or school in Trenton? A. No.

Q. You just picked up the receiver and asked for Colonel Schwarzkopf or for the training school? A. Colonel Schwarzkopf.

Q. He invited you to come over and see him, is that correct? A. No.

Q. Did he come to see you? A. He didn't.

Q. Sent one of his men? A. That is right.

Q. Did he have some pictures of Hauptmann? A. Not then.

Q. Later on did he have some pictures of Hauptmann? A. Later on that day.

Q. Yes. How many pictures did he bring you? A. Three.

Q. And did you see any more pictures of Hauptmann in the press or from the State Troopers before you went to the Bronx? A. Yes, on a Sunday I saw some pictures.

Q. I would like to know if you can tell me how many pictures of Hauptmann you saw between the day you saw this picture for the first time in the paper and your visit to the Bronx. A. Collectively, you mean, all of them?

Q. Yes. A. Well, I wouldn't number them, they were plenty.

Q. Fifty? A. Oh, no, not that many, I didn't buy that many newspapers.

Q. Twenty-five? A. Oh, I would say offhand about ten or twelve.

Q. Ten or twelve, some newspapers and some pictures brought by the State Police? A. That is right. They weren't brought.

Q. You saw them anyhow? A. Yes.

Q. The State Police had them? A. That is right.

Q. Whether they came to you or you went to them is of no consequence, you saw the pictures, didn't you? A. That is right.

Q. So that you had a view of at least ten or fifteen pictures. A. That is right.

Q. Covering a period of how many days before you saw the defendant in the Bronx? A. Three days.

Q. Three days. And of course when you went to the Bronx, you saw the man that you saw in the pictures?

A. That is right.

Mr. Reilly: That is all.

Mr. Wilentz: That is all.

Mr. Reilly: Just a moment, please.

Q. I have been asked by my brothers of the defense to ask you to give us a better description if you will of this house on the side of the road. A. A better description?

Q. Yes, if you can. A. Well, as far as I can remember, I never took any special note of that house and never went back to the point to distinguish the house or place that house in my mind.

Q. Have you ever passed along that road since? A. Have I passed along that road since? Yes.

Q. Have you ever seen the house? A. Not to take any particular note of it.

Q. You say there was a house there that night? A. That is right.

Q. Will you describe the airport? Is it an open space? A. An open space?

Q. Has it gates? A. It is all open, no gates there.

Q. All right. Is it all an open field? A. Yes.

Q. How do you get into the airport, can you walk off the road into the airport? A. Why, yes, you can drive in from the road into the airport.

Q. There is a driveway? A. Oh, yes.

Q. A person walking along could walk right over the road in on the airport grounds, is that correct? A. I would say so. I have never been in there, but that is---

Q. Have you ever seen any fence? A. No, I never noticed any fence.

Q. Now is this road you were traveling on macadam? A. At that time, yes, sir.

Q. At that time? A. Well, it is a combination of stone. I suppose you would call it tar or something along that line.

Q. Now in relation to this driveway in the airport, which you now have firmly fixed in your mind, have you? A. The driveway in the airport?

Q. Yes. A. Well, now, I am not---

Q. Can you recall now in your mind a driveway leading into the airport as you have testified to? A. I wouldn't try to place the driveway into that airport, no.

Q. Well, would you try and place this particular car you say you saw in relation to some monument, driveway or something else in connection with the airport? A. Place it in relation to something?

Q. Yes. A. At that spot.

Q. Yes. A. The only thing I could place it in relation to is the fact that it is you might say directly opposite that house.

Q. Directly opposite the house? A. That is right.

Q. And how near to the driveway of the airport do you say this house is? A. How near to the driveway?

Q. Or was at that time, in 1933, yes. A. I would say that is at least 200 yards.

Q. 600 feet? A. Close to that, yes. That is my---

Q. As you drive toward Philadelphia, is the house before you get to the entrance of the airport or beyond? A. It is north of the airport.

Q. Beyond---you are driving toward Philadelphia, correct? A. Towards Princeton, towards Princeton.

Q. You have not yet arrived at the road that leads into the airport? A. No.

Q. It is the house before you get to the driveway or beyond? A. Before you get---

Q. Before? A. That is right.

Q. Now, in relation to this man's car, was it in front of the house? A. Not in front of the house, no.

Q. How near to the house? A. Directly across from the house, on the opposite side of the house, that is, on the side going towards Princeton.

Q. Was the car facing Princeton? A. That is right.

Q. Describe the car. A. The car at that time that I noticed it, I didn't distinguish the make of the car; the car that I saw had on the rear of it a three-pronged tire holder, and it had a license plate on the left rear fender with, of course, a stop light on top of it, and any more than that I didn't go into any more detail as far as taking any mental notes of the car.

Q. You are in the automobile business now? A. That is right.

Q. You don't know the make of the car? A. No, sir, it wasn't distinguishable on the back.

Q. You didn't take the license number? A. No, sir, I did not.

Q. Was there a tire on the rear? A. There was.

Q. On a three-prong holder? A. That is right.

Q. What kind of a rear light was there? A. What kind of a rear light?

Q. Did it have any name indicating the make? A. No, it didn't.

Q. Did it have one or two rear lights? A. One.

Q. Did it have one or two rear tires? A. One.

Q. What color were the wheels? A. What color were the wheels?

Q. Yes. A. Very dark; I couldn't determine the color.

Q. What color was the body? A. A very dark color.

Q. What type of car was it? A. Well, that I wouldn't--

Q. Sedan---landaulet, limousine, or roadster? A. It was a sedan.

Q. A sedan? A. Yes.

Q. Did you come around the front of it? A. Did I go around the front of it? No.

Q. Only at the back of it? A. Just to the rear.

Q. Was there anybody in the car? A. I didn't look for that.

And that completed the testimony of Charles B. Rossiter, just another witness whose statements should have been torn to shreds by the defense attorneys.

Mr. Rossiter had only observed what he chose to observe --- and nothing more. My reasoning says that "good old Charlie" probably saw no motorist stranded "by the side of any road" on that Saturday evening in February, 1932. His story just does not fit well. There were many questions that should have been asked of Mr. Rossiter. Important questions that were not probed and developed by "Death House Reilly", whose job it had been to defend Richard Hauptmann --- not prosecute him.

Had it not been for Attorney Lloyd Fisher, Rossiter would have been dismissed from the stand without even being asked to describe the car "the man by the side of the road" had been driving. And when, during the final minutes of his testimony, he literally "blew it", Reilly was not equipped to go "in for the kill" and prove the man to be nothing more than a prevaricator of the worst kind --- in court they are commonly known as perjurers --- a criminal offense.

As proof of this I offer the following facts. Rossiter, who said he had spent the entire time (five to eight minutes) at the rear of the man's car could give only a casual appearance of the car. He said he "didn't go into any more detail as far as taking any mental notes of the car." But he was very specific when it came to stating that the automobile had a "three-pronged tire holder on the rear".

Rossiter failed to note the make of the car (which he stated was "indistinguishable") and although he said he was there for a length of time, he failed to notice whether the car contained any passengers, its license number and other features. It is hard to believe that the motorist "to whom he offered help" would have said nothing to a silent person who just stared at him "from the rear of his car" for the period of time Rossiter claims neither man spoke. A ridiculous dialogue to say the very least.

The truth which should have been made known by Hauptmann's attorneys was never made public because of the inept way Richard was defended. Had the jury known the truth it would never have believed one word said by Charles B. Rossiter.

The evidence proves that Rossiter had certainly not seen the Hauptmann car that evening. Richard was driving a 1931 blue Dodge Sedan. When Rossiter was asked if there was a tire on the rear? He answered: "There was." "On a three-pronged holder?" he was asked. And again he said: "That is right."

Hauptmann's car never had a three-prong tire holder on the rear. Instead it carried a large wooden trunk that had been constructed and mounted on the back by Richard. This had been done in 1931 in preparation for the trip he, Anna, and his friend Hans Kloppenburg, were planning to take to California during that summer. The trunk was still securely mounted on the rear of the car when Richard was arrested in September, 1934. As for where the spare tire was located, it had always been carried in a fender well, positioned for this purpose, in the left front fender. Also on the back of the car, above the top of the frame which held the license plate was the appropriate, and easily recognized, size logo which clearly spelled out the name Dodge.

And so, Mr. Rossiter had not only falsified the truth, but his powers of "observation" had failed him when he needed them most.

Had the defense lawyers been apprised of some interesting facts in Rossiter's background, they could have certainly used it to some advantage in discrediting his testimony. It seems that Charles was never "too sure of himself" when he was called in to take a look at the prisoner, then being held in the Greenwich Street Police Station. He first had stated, two days after Hauptmann's arrest, that "this man looks very much like the man I saw in front of the airport." When he was shown some glossy photographs of Hauptmann, he still remained uncertain in his identification. Detective Lewis Bornmann's police report states that regardless of this, Rossiter claims the man in the newspaper picture: "does bear a striking resemblance."

But, when Charles B. Rossiter was ushered into the New York City jail to personally observe the unfortunate Bronx carpenter, he lost no time in making judgement - Hauptmann was definitely the man he had seen "by the side of the road" on Saturday night, February 27th, 1932. There could be no doubt about it now. He went on to describe the man as being identical to Hauptmann. Wasn't this some "terrific accomplishment"? Especially for a man who had just seen the prisoner in the flesh.

In addition to the information regarding "little-known" facts about Charles B. Rossiter, it should be also noted here that this "Man of Integrity" had some "skeletons in his closet" which, if had they been made known at the proper time, would have caused one of the State's Star Witnesses, more than a little embarrassment. Let the record show that Rossiter had been fired from several of the jobs he held. The reason --- stealing company funds as recently as shortly before his involvement in the Lindbergh case brought him the "tarnished fame" he deserved by helping the police frame Richard Hauptmann.

Governor Harold G. Hoffman's "last-minute" involvement in the case uncovered many disturbing facts relative to how the frame-up of Richard Hauptmann was accomplished. Unfortunately his help came much too late to be of any aid to the already doomed man. Hoffman's report in his book *The Crime-The Case-The Challenge What Was Wrong With The Lindbergh Case?* clearly shows to what depths mankind will sink in order to exploit "man's inhumanity to man." This is quite apparent in his following report on the Rossiter matter:

"Now comes Charles B. Rossiter, another of the state's identification witnesses. It was a great trio of witnesses who gave the important testimony that convinced the jury that Hauptmann had been prowling around in New Jersey--Whited, Hochmuth, and Rossiter.

"Rossiter is another fellow who never came into the case until after Hauptmann had been arrested. On September 22, 1934, he called Sergeant A.G. Varrelman at the Mount Ephraim barracks of the State Police, and told a story reported by Varrelman as follows:

"'The Saturday evening before the kidnapping he

left his home in Maplewood ... proceeded along his regular route (he was then a pretzel salesman), route 29 in Somerville, then to Princeton. Between Princeton and Bellemead he noticed a large dark-colored sedan with New York plates, the color which he believes might have been green, parked on the right side of the road, headed toward Princeton and opposite the Princeton Flying Field. The car appeared to be in the ditch, so he stopped and asked the man who was standing in the rear of the car if he could be of any assistance, and was told no, the car was all right, so he got into his car and proceeded on. ... Last evening he saw several pictures in the paper of Bruno Hauptmann, recently arrested, and he stated that this man looks very much like the man he spoke to in front of the Princeton Airport.

"Rossiter was rushed to the State Police School, where he gave a signed statement to Detectives DeGaetano and Bornmann. He says that he pulled up to within fifteen feet, got out, walked to the man standing in the rear of the car and asked if he could help. 'He seemed very much irritated,' stated Rossiter, and very abruptly answered, 'No, I don't need any help,' or words to that effect. 'Whereupon I got into my car and drove away.' He described the man as having 'a sallow complexion, very prominent nose, five feet six inches in height, very stocky build, and weighed about 170 to 180 pounds'--one of the hundreds of varying descriptions given of men supposed to have been Hauptmann.

"In this signed statement he said that 'I noticed New York registration and spare tire mounted on a three-prong tire carrier.' He was shown several photographs of Hauptmann and said, 'None of these pictures look like the man I had seen'; but he went on to say that in a group of four, published in a New York newspaper, he had seen one that "bears a striking resemblance.'

"The Hauptmann car never had a three-prong tire carrier on the rear. There was a trunk on the rear, and it was one of the type of cars where the spare tire is carried in a well in the front left fender.

"Colonel Schwarzkopf's men made a check of Rossiter to ascertain his reputation, and although that investigation showed that his character and reputation were questionable, Rossiter was brazenly used as a state witness, and an important one. Detective De Gaetano found out some interesting things about Rossiter. I have a photostatic copy of that report before me. Here are some excerpts: 'Visible signs of financial distress

... fired for some unknown reason ... failed to turn in collections ... said some one had entered his house when he and his wife were away and stole the $400 collections ... a trial was given him but after two months he returned to his old practices, which again caused his dismissal ... Mr. ----- (an employer) brands him as being a good composer and wonderful liar ... Mr. ----- (another employer) says: ... This company received a telegram from New Rochelle, New York, signed by Charles B. Rossiter, stating that he was held up and robbed and requested more money ... received $60 worth of merchandise he has failed to account for.!'

"Voluntarily, a number of other employers of Rossiter have written to me stating that Rossiter had been dismissed for irregularity in financial transactions. When he was used as a witness, in the face of knowledge that he had an unenviable reputation, he told a story, under oath, differing widely from the initial statements he had given the State Police. But such witnesses as Whited, Hochmuth, and Rossiter, none of whom had been heard from prior to Hauptmann's arrest, evidently convinced the jury that Hauptmann, in different cars, answering different descriptions, had been seen in the vicinity of the Lindbergh home. The jurors might have been impressed by the consistency with which the defendant had followed his habit of running cars into ditches."

Hasn't it already been made clear that Hauptmann did not have even the slightest hope of escaping the electric chair? If you still are not convinced --- read on, you will be!

CHAPTER THIRTY SEVEN

The Rest of the Mess!

Just as a fighter, losing his battle, has been pummeled incessantly by heavy torturous blows and is reeling hopelessly on the ropes, so was Richard Hauptmann. Failing to realize that his point of no return had passed, he also could not visualize there was nothing remaining but the hopelessness of a vain, but valiant, attempt to prove his innocence. Nevertheless, he kept swinging away, with the assistance of a very inadequate attorney, to prove to the world that he was innocent of the crime which had been laid at his doorstep.

Hauptmann had been certain he would never be convicted. How could they ever prove that he was guilty of such a dastardly crime? One of which he knew absolutely nothing. As for the money found in his possession, he had explained to them, over and over again, how it had been left with him by his friend, Isidor Fisch. It had only been a wrapped package left with him to take care of until Fisch returned from Germany. He had not known the package contained money. He could not believe that his partner, Fisch, could have been involved in the famous kidnapping. And because of his naive belief and faith in his friend he failed to realize the seriousness of his own arrest and possible conviction. He constantly assured his Anny that he would soon be returning home to her. They could never, he assured her, prove his involvement in something of which he knew absolutely nothing.

Bruno Richard Hauptmann, a peaceful man, a loving husband and father, had placed his absolute faith in his innocence, which was to soon be proven, and that in the end justice would undoubtedly prevail. Soon, he believed. he would return to his sweet wife, Anna, and his dear little son, Manfred, where the three of them could take up a tranquil life together in their home at 1279 East 222nd Street in the Bronx.

But the authorities were making every assurance that this was not to happen. Richard's hopes and dreams of contentment with his family were being thwarted at every turn. Utterly impeded by "clever" moves of the prosecution staff, aided by the astute judge who was hearing the case, not to mention the "cunning" and ridiculous permissible cross-examination of the attorney general who was basking in the limelight of publicity.

To begin with, the prosecutors were immediately aware of the fact that the initial and chief thrust of their case was the fact that they had arrested a man in possession of $14,600 of Lindbergh ransom money. There was absolutely no doubt about this. Literally Hauptmann had been caught with the goods. Although he gave a perfectly reasonable and honest explanation as to how he had come into possession of it, the authorities after spending a fruitless two-and-one-half years of searching for the kidnapper, had "at last" been handed their long-awaited break, and they were in no mood to listen to any form of an explanation, reasonable or not, as to how their prisoner had come to possess it. Fortified with this basic fact, they were now ready to go into court. That is, just as soon as they were able to manufacture enough other evidence and gather together enough witnesses willing to perjure themselves, by offering testimony "for a price" which placed Hauptmann in New Jersey, principally by means of their "fake" eyewitness accounts of having seen him there.

However, there was a problem which troubled the prosecution staff. Now that they had arrested Hauptmann, and charged him as being the only person involved in the kidnapping, they were faced with the task of explaining that since they had caught him with just a part of the ransom money ($14,600), they would have to "prove" that "in some way and at some time" since April 2, 1932, he had been in possession of every "penny", or at least every dollar, of the original $50,000 of Colonel Lindbergh's money.

Well, now, with the aid of an agent who had served with the United States Treasury Department for twelve years, eight years in the Intelligence Unit of the department, the information they needed could quite easily be furnished. Mr. William E. Frank was another person they found who had been willing to offer his services for the convenience of the prosecution.

One large factor in the successful prosecution of Hauptmann had been the state's ability to render to the gullible jury the belief that the accused man had not worked a day after the payment of the ransom on Saturday, April 2nd, 1932. But, just because the twelve jurors were willing to accept this as fact, the truth proves otherwise.

Actually Richard had resigned from his job at the Majestic Apartments at the completion of work on that Saturday. He had placed his tools in his tool box and returned to his home where that night, with his wife present, he and his good friend Hans Kloppenburg had their regular first Saturday of the month get-together playing their guitar and mandolin. The following Monday Hauptmann had returned to the Majestic Apartments hoping to collect his wages for the two days he had worked in April, an amount totaling $6.67. However, he was informed that he must wait until April 15th because payments were made only twice a month. Hauptmann's reason for resigning had been prompted by the employment agency's failure to pay him the $100 weekly salary he had been promised, but instead the agency had paid him only $80.

The prosecution, coupled with the jury's inability to clearly follow the complicated explanation Hauptmann gave of his finances, had successfully blanketed the truth and left everyone with the misconception that the man had never worked another day after his resignation. This was done in order to have them believe that since April 2nd, he had received the $50,000 ransom and therefore had no immediate need for additional money.

But, this was simply not the case. During the summer months of 1932 he did free-lance construction work for the National Lumber and Millwork Company of the Bronx; often he aided his friend, Hans, building display stands and cabinets for neighborhood merchants. By doing this he was able to earn the going contract rate for carpenters. He was now afforded the opportunity to spend many hours at the brokerage firm of Steiner, Rouse and Company where he played the stock market. Here he suffered only a minor loss of $5,216.03, an amount he could well afford when we look at the total of the Hauptmann's finances during the years immediately before the kidnapping.

Through the willing assistance of Mr. Frank, the state "proved" that Hauptmann had suffered heavy losses in his dealings in the stock market and that by the end of 1931, due to the fact that by then he was a man in great financial distress, he perpetrated the kidnapping of the Lindbergh baby and gain for himself a $50,000 ransom.

But such was far from the case. Frank's "proof" topples like a house of cards when the true facts are recognized as we study the FBI accounting reports of the Bronx carpenter's bank and brokerage transactions.

Basically we must understand that the Hauptmanns were a thrifty couple. During the early years of the Depression existing records show that they had a total of $4,000 cash salted away in a trunk they kept in their apartment. However, most of this money was later removed for the purpose of investing in a second mortgage. Incidentally, and yet of primary interest, should be the knowledge that the cash turned in for the purchase of this mortgage was accepted at the Bank of Manhattan at the end of 1932 and not one bill was identified as being gold certificate ransom money. This fact was attested to by the bank manager, a Mr. McCron.

In addition, the happy couple had collected and saved more than $1,000 in gold coins and gold certificates as a precautionary measure against possible inflation. They also had in a bank account of somewhere between $12,000 and $15,000, a sum which, in addition to a mortgage of $3750 Richard and Anna had taken out in 1927, certainly earned them a rather nice interest.

Although Richard's employment as a carpenter during the years of '32 and '33 was not as steady as he hoped it would be, he was far from being characterized as unemployed. And he certainly was not suffering heavy losses at the stock market. Hauptmann, in January 1934, was listed in the following fashion with the New York Retail Credit Company as a capable and honest freelance carpenter:

> Richard Hauptmann ... has a small jobbing business of his own. He works for small property owners in the Bronx and has been receiving a fair amount of work in spite of generally slack conditions in the building trade. He is a hard-working and industrious type of individual and he is able to get along on his income at the present time; although in the past good years, he has earned more than he is now. They (the Hauptmanns) lead a normal home life and have the name among their neighbors of meeting their local bills when due.

Anna's steady employment at Fredericksen's Bakery was earning her $30 weekly. The rent the couple paid amounted to only $10.50 each week, while their weekly household expenses did not exceed $30. Looking at the total income of the Hauptmanns during those questionable years certainly goes far to prove that they were not virtually paupers.

Hauptmann, from the time of his arrest, had told them to bring him the "big book" in which he recorded all his financial dealings. If they would do this he would prove to them that his partnership with Isidor Fisch did exist and was not merely his "fish" story. Please, he begged them, let me see it and it will explain everything. But in this, as in other requests of his, the "very cooperative" police refused.

Because the testimony of the state's financial wizard, William Frank, was so repetitious and tiresome, he practically lulled everyone in the courtroom to sleep as he went back and forth over the so-called transactions of Bruno Richard Hauptmann. But Mr. Frank had a job to do and he performed it well. Surely it was over the heads of the spectators. It was something which possibly the judge and jury did not completely understand, but nevertheless that did not matter as long as the twelve members of the jury were at least impressed with his eloquence and "proof" that Hauptmann had spent every dollar, or at least nearly all, of the Lindbergh ransom money. And this Mr. Frank did by cleverly manipulating and maneuvering the dollars the accused man had in his possession and spent from the year of his marriage in 1925. The bottom line totals always served his purpose as he "proved" again and again that the balances were the result of (not Hauptmann's) his own "clever explanations" of the debits, credits and "end results" which proved Hauptmann had spent just what he, Frank, said he did. The results of his testimony were damning for the accused man.

Tony Scaduto's investigative skill as a reporter once again is brought to the forefront. It was largely due to Scaduto's intuitiveness that much has been uncovered to prove Richard Hauptmann's innocence. His discovery of the 'big book' Hauptmann so desperately wanted proves, to an even greater degree, that everything the accused man said was factual. Had Tony not found the "big book", the one the authorities continually denied ever existed, along with letters from Pinkus Fisch, Isidor's brother in Germany, the proof of Richard's innocence would have certainly been much more difficult to prove. However, with the factual evidence of its existence, along with the statements of the FBI, together with all the other facts of deception set before you in this volume, the finger of Richard Hauptmann firmly points to all those persons who sent him, an innocent man, to such a cruel and needless death. The shame of many is great. The blood of Hauptmann has been on their consciences for many, many years. It can never be wiped away.

So as not to confuse you, nor bore you, as did the testimony of Mr. Frank in the Flemington courtroom in 1935, I am again using Tony Scaduto's excellent account of his discovery of the "big book" and what it revealed. The following is taken from his book *Scapegoat*:

"Thus far I had found evidence that about a dozen men and women, among them police officers, had lied, and that police and prosecution hid from the defense evidence that would have supported Hauptmann. And now I turned to what was perhaps the most crucial of the suppressed evidence.

"The 'Fisch story,' police and prosecutor called it, thereby dismissing Hauptmann's alibi in advance and destroying his main chance---to prove Isidor Fisch had been his business partner in the stock market and in the fur trading and had given Hauptmann large sums of money to invest. On this part of his alibi hung Hauptmann's primary defense, that Fisch had also given him the gold notes found in his garage. Wilentz, at the trial, said that of course there was a man named Fisch, we concede that, Mr. Hauptmann didn't simply pull his name out of the air. But what proof is there that Fisch was anything more than just a poor German immigrant, sickly and dying? None, none whatsoever. When Hauptmann asked for his ledger book, for letters from Fisch's brother, the prosecution said they did not exist or, alternately, that it was too much trouble to search for such evidence.

"That ledger, the 'big book' Hauptmann begged for when he was testifying, did exist. And so did the letters from Pinkus Fisch which show that Isidor told his brother that back in America there was a man named Hauptmann and he, Isidor, and Hauptmann were speculating as partners and growing wealthy together.

"Among the files are dozens of official FBI and police reports about Hauptmann's finances, his memo books, his letters, and his dealings with Isidor Fisch. There are also a handful of reports on an investigation into Fisch's life in America. Reading through those reports, one thing becomes clear: Isidor Fisch was a confidence man who borrowed money from friends to invest in firms that did not exist and who seems to have cheated Hauptmann out of more than $7,000 by counterfeiting receipts to show he had bought furs which actually didn't exist.

"But before exploring Fisch's character and his business partnership with Hauptmann, I was led by certain documents into an examination of David Wilentz's evidence that supposedly explained why Hauptmann had committed so brutal a crime.

"In trying to prove motive for the kidnapping, the state demonstrated through its expert witnesses that Hauptmann had lost heavily in the stock market by the end of 1931, was almost without funds, and kidnapped the Lindbergh child a few months later in order to extort $50,000.

"But that 'proof' collapses upon an examination of several memorandum books found in Hauptmann's desk the day he was arrested and of FBI accounting reports on Hauptmann's bank and brokerage transactions.

"In one of those memo books Hauptmann kept a meticulous record of his and his wife's income and savings from January 1, 1926, three months after he and Anna were married, to January 1, 1930. In each of those four years the Hauptmanns' joint income ranged between $3,000 and $4,000. At the end of that period, on New Year's Day, 1930, they had accumulated savings of $7,666.

"The accounting demonstrates that the Hauptmanns were both hardworking and exceedingly frugal. Hauptmann worked through 1931 and part of 1932 and his wife worked into 1933. If their earnings and savings pattern continued, as he claimed it did when he testified that he had saved a great deal of money from his salary, then by the date of the kidnapping it is likely the Hauptmanns were worth about ten thousand dollars. Anna Hauptmann, in fact, had told one friend that they'd saved that amount or a little more.

"There is no evidence and it had never been suggested in the newspapers or at the trial that Mrs. Hauptmann was the kind of woman to flaunt her wealth or boast about her savings. On the contrary, she was usually very circumspect about her personal life. Several of Anna's friends, questioned by police about her personal life or her finances, replied: 'I don't know, she never told me.'

"There is, however, one exception, and it bolsters the other evidence indicating Hauptmann had saved a large sum of money up to a year before the kidnapping.

"In a report by FBI agent John Seykora, dated a

few weeks after Hauptmann's arrest, he summarizes an interview with Mrs. Otto Wollenberg, who came from the same town in Germany where Anna Hauptmann was born and who had grown friendly with her over a few years before Hauptmann was arrested. During the interview Mrs. Wollenberg said, in the FBI man's words:

" 'That before the Hauptmanns' California trip, early in the spring of 1931, Mrs. Hauptmann told Mrs. Wollenberg that they had saved about ten or twelve thousand dollars since they were married; that both of them worked all the time and that she hardly had time to sleep'

"There is additional evidence that Hauptmann's memo books faithfully and accurately recorded the amount of savings he and his wife were accumulating. An FBI report on Hauptmann's bank accounts notes that he had savings of $5,700 at the end of January 1928. Hauptmann's memorandum lists savings of $5,780 on January 1, 1928---only an $80 disparity. It is likely, from the evidence contained in FBI documents, that Hauptmann was worth more than $10,000 by the spring of 1931, less than a year before the kidnapping.

"But it is true, as Wilentz said in explaining to the jury why Hauptmann had kidnapped the Lindbergh child, that he had begun to use his savings for stock market speculation. He opened a trading account with a brokerage house on November 1, 1929, by withdrawing $2,800 from his bank account and adding $200 in cash. According to the FBI accounting report, Hauptmann was required to deposit another $1,500 in cash in June 1930, because he had 'suffered large losses.'

"However, the accountant's characterization of Hauptmann's loses as 'large' and Wilentz's statements to the jury that the defendant kidnapped young Lindbergh because he had gone broke in the stock market are patent falsehoods. The FBI report states that this stock market account 'was inactive during 1931' and continued to be inactive up to the time of the kidnapping. And at the conclusion of the report on this account, in the final summary of Hauptmann's losses, the accountant reported: 'Losses--$363.65.'

"Hauptmann's total stock market losses from 1929 through the early part of 1932 were less than $400.

"Plainly, if he had a net worth of perhaps $10,000 at the end of 1931 and suffered stock market losses of under $400, Hauptmann had not been so completely impoverished by his speculations that can serve as a motive for kidnapping. Another part of Wilentz's script collapses.

"This FBI document, sixty-five pages of single-spaced type, is unfortunately only a synopsis of Hauptmann's finances. Its main goal was to demonstrate the amount of cash flowing into Hauptmann's various accounts in an obvious attempt to prove he had been spending well above his means and could only have done so because he had received $50,000 in Lindbergh money. A federal accountant who testified at the trial, William Frank, had sworn his figures showed Hauptmann had possession of more than $49.000 that could not be accounted for through his income and savings before 1932. The writers of the day threw kudos at the federal agents who had proved 'to within a few dollars,' as they put it, that Hauptmann had had his hands on every bit of the Lindbergh money.

" 'How could they say they proved I had fifty thousand dollars ransom money,' Hauptmann asked Governor Hoffman during that visit to his death house cell, 'when the police came to me after the trial and said they would help me stay out of the chair if I told them where the other thirty thousand is to be found?'

"This FBI document makes plain why the New Jersey state police were still trying to find $30,000 in ransom money after Wilentz had proved Hauptmann dumped every cent of it into his stock market binge. The truth is that in all Hauptmann's market trading, even in the transactions which took place before the kidnapping, he suffered a total loss of only $5,216.03. Not $49,000 or $35,000, but a rather modest $5,200 in almost five years of activity---little more than $1,000 a year.

"To sum up this point because it must be stressed, this FBI document shows that Richard Hauptmann suffered a loss of less than $400 before the kidnapping, which is hardly motive for purse-snatching when a man has thousands in the bank. And it shows that Hauptmann, rather than losing in market speculations all the Lindbergh money, with the exception of the gold notes found in his garage, actually suffered a loss of only $5,216.03.

"One other thing must be noted. When he testified at Hauptmann's trial the federal accountant, Frank, swore that 'my figures are accurate' and that he wasn't simply counting the same few thousand dollars that Hauptmann withdrew from his bank to buy stocks on margin, then withdrew from his brokerage house when his equity built up and returned to his bank account, and then back again, many dozens of times. No, Frank swore,

Hauptmann was playing around with enormous sums of money, cash money. The FBI report, however, shows that in his accounting, Frank was bending the truth somewhat. Hauptmann had certainly bought nearly $400,000 worth of stocks. He had made deposits of more than $21,000 into his brokerage accounts. But an examination of the document proves conclusively that Hauptmann was moving money from bank to brokerage house and back again, and was churning his stock account on margin; at no time did the amount of equity in his accounts exceed $11,000 or $12,000, and when it did come anywhere near that figure it appears from the records to have been, as Hauptmann said, because Isidor Fisch had become his investment partner and was funneling money in.

"And then something else suddenly leaps out of these pages and condemns the prosecution again for its distortions. A great deal was made by Wilentz at the trial of the date Hauptmann and Fisch first were introduced. Hauptmann had said it was March or April, 1932, and, the police and prosecution said, he was lying, he did not meet Fisch until July or August of that year. He lied because he had to fabricate an earlier date of introduction to Fisch to explain how he came to possess the enormous sums which he deposited in cash in his bank and brokerage accounts.

"What enormous sums? Reilly never asked that question and even Hauptmann accepted Wilentz's argument. Hauptmann was at a disadvantage because his own ledger was suppressed, and the records of his bank and stock accounts which were subpoenaed by the prosecution remained in Wilentz's hands at all times. Reilly and Hauptmann had little time to study those records in preparing for direct examination of the defendant.

"Had there been time, it would have become obvious Hauptmann had not lied, but the prosecution had distorted. Here in this FBI report there is a boringly complete list of every cent in cash that Hauptmann deposited to his bank and stock accounts after the day the ransom money was paid. Through the months in question, April to August, 1932, Hauptmann was putting into a bank account small sums that never exceeded $200 and were most often less than $100. The only money deposited in his single brokerage account at the time was $600 on April 8 and $22.75 on April 11. Hardly enormous sums.

"Hauptmann and his defense counsel had fallen victim to a hoary courtroom trick---make a statement supposedly based on accounting records, but don't permit your opponent time to examine those records so he will be forced to accept that statement as truth.

"That the police and prosecution knew Hauptmann and Fisch were business partners---in spite of Wilentz's implication that it was a fishy story---can be found in the final pages of this lengthy FBI report. There, the FBI agent lists the names of all potential witnesses to Hauptmann's transactions, including customer's men, bank clerks and treasurers, and investigating police officers. One of those listings includes the names of Inspector Lyons of the New York City police department, FBI agent Sisk, and Captain Lamb of the New Jersey state police. They would be needed at the trial, the report states:

'To testify as to finding record book or journal in the home of Richard Hauptmann and the questioning of Richard Hauptmann relative thereto and the general questioning of Hauptmann as to stock market trading and other transactions.'

"But the official fiction was that 'the record book or journal' did not exist and that 'other transactions'---meaning fur trading with Isidor Fisch---were part of the defendant's manufactured alibi. So Wilentz said, again and again.

"From page 31 of the FBI report:

'During a search of the premises occupied by Hauptmann, Inspector John A. Lyons of the New York City Police Force and Special Agent T.H. Sisk found, in a desk in the front room of the house, a record book or journal which was exhibited to Hauptmann and identified by him as his property. The book contains a number of entries which appear on pages 4 to 9, 50, 51, 72 to 77, 100 to 107, all of which entries Hauptmann admitted were in his handwriting. The book was later examined by Special Agent W.C. Dickson who has reported that it is evident that the book is a personal record of Hauptmann's interest in numerous transactions....'

"The first pages cited are Hauptmann's record of stock transactions between May 4, 1932, and August 8, 1932, listing the name and quantity of a particular stock, price paid, and price realized when sold. The FBI report does not duplicate Hauptmann's lists, simply summarizes them, and so it is not possible to analyze them. But there is some interesting information to be gleaned from the later pages.

"'The entries on pages 50 and 51 constitute a record of stock market transactions similar to the record on pages 4 to 9' the report says. It goes on to state that pages 4 to 9 had lines drawn through them, as if Hauptmann was starting a fresh accounting of his stock portfolio. Page 50 lists one new stock purchase, made on June 6, 1933. It is the only transaction noted on that page. And significantly, the FBI agent wrote in his report, there is a notation at the bottom of the page which indicates that on July 10, Fisch gave Hauptmann a little over $2,000 to buy into a partnership on a '20 percent basis.'

"While that notation is not fully explained, the FBI analyst makes it plain he believes that sometime in the early summer of 1933 Hauptmann and Fisch became partners in stock market speculations. That belief is strengthened by the next series of entries in the book, on two fresh pages. Those entries are headed '17,500---Richard Account' on one page and '17,000---Isidor Account' on the adjoining page. The FBI report says the headings and the entries that follow are probably 'accounts in a partnership's books.'

"What appears to have happened is this: In June or July, 1933, Hauptmann 'canceled' his own stock market accounts in his ledger and, on a fresh page, placed the stocks he already owned into a partnership account with Fisch. The FBI analyst suggests this is what occurred. And it conforms to Hauptmann's explanation to police, when he was questioned about this ledger, that he had begun trading in stocks for his partnership account with Fisch while Fisch was trading in furs.

"During that questioning by police in the first days after his arrest, and in his testimony at the trial, Hauptmann conceded that he had deposited large sums of money into his brokerage account in the spring and summer of 1933. Most of that money, he said, had come from Isidor Fisch. The prosecutor labeled this alibi the 'Fisch story.' And yet, based on Hauptmann's ledger, it seems to have been the truth.

"There is another transaction in the ledger that indicates Hauptmann and Fisch had become partners in speculation as early as May 8, 1933, a date which is important because it lends greater support to Hauptmann's explanation. The brokerage account in which Hauptmann did most of his trading was not opened until August 1932. But according to an officer of Hauptmann's brokerage house, whose affidavit is reprinted in full in this FBI analysis, Hauptmann did not begin speculating heavily until May 1933 (and not in 1932, as Wilentz claimed at the trial). The largest deposits Hauptmann made to this trading account were between April 28 and August 10, 1933. They came to a little less than $12,000. After September 1933, Hauptmann's account became inactive. And on October 21, 1933, on still another page of this ledger, Hauptmann calculated the balance in the partnership account as if he 'desired to make a determination of his position' on that date, the FBI agent comments.

"Isidor Fisch bought his ticket for Germany the following month. It appears likely the stock trading activity slackened in September and Hauptmann calculated his position in October because Fisch was preparing to leave the country. The evidence in Hauptmann's ledger, confirmed at least in part by the records of the stock brokerage house, indicates Hauptmann's major stock market trading began after the date he and Fisch had entered into a partnership of some kind, and that trading activity greatly diminished very shortly before Fisch returned to Germany.

"This section of the ledger alone, had it been shown to the jury and released to the newspapers, would have raised some serious questions about the prosecution's case against Hauptmann. That it was hidden---suppressed---can only be attributed to a deliberate decision by one or more officials to deny Hauptmann a fair trial.

"But an important question comes to mind: Did Hauptmann's ledger and memo books reflect an accurate accounting of his savings and of a partnership with Fisch, or were the documents carefully planned to create an alibi should he be arrested as the extortionist?

"All the evidence laid out in this accounting report indicates the books are exceptionally accurate in every area where the FBI was able to check entries against documented sources, such as bank and brokerage house statements. Hauptmann's notation in a memo book that he had over $7,000 in savings on a certain date, for instance, is confirmed by his bank statements; a notation that he had a certain amount in equity in his stock account on a given date is confirmed by statements from the brokerage house. In each case, when the FBI was able to check Hauptmann's figures against original sources, his figures were accurate.

"Furthermore, two pages in his ledger are devoted to an accounting of funds that Hauptmann and Fisch either deposited to the stock account or withdrew for personal expenses. The account was begun by Hauptmann on November 1, 1933. It ends July 28, 1934, three months after Hauptmann was meticulously accounting for every penny he withdrew from their partnership account for the day Fisch's brother would arrive to settle the estate. By checking these items in Hauptmann's ledger against bank and stock market transactions analyzed by the FBI, it is clear that Hauptmann's records are accurate and it becomes likely that this ledger was not composed as a future alibi.

"The FBI summary of Hauptmann's ledger continues with an analysis that makes more obvious the reason this book had to be suppressed. The report states:

'Pages 74 to 77 are given over to a record of the <u>purchases</u> <u>and</u> <u>sales</u> <u>of</u> <u>furs</u> and it is indicated ... that the transactions are for the <u>account</u> <u>of</u> <u>Isidor</u> <u>Fisch</u> <u>and</u> <u>Richard</u> <u>Hauptmann</u>' [emphasis supplied]. Hauptmann set up his ledger, the FBI report goes on, so that when it was opened to the pages concerning fur speculations he could promptly determine their financial position. The left-hand page showed the purchase of a specific lot of furs. When that lot was sold, Hauptmann followed the line across to the right-hand page and noted the details of the sale. The FBI agent wrote:

'Because of the relative importance [!] of these transactions and of the fact that they are comparatively few in number, the record as it appears in the book is shown hereunder .... ' It doesn't have to be said, but I intend to stress it---the transactions were so important to Hauptmann's defense that the book was suppressed.

"Precisely how this partnership worked, who contributed what funds and to which account, furs or stocks, is not clear from the ledger. Even the notation by Hauptmann indicating he had $17,500 to his credit and Fisch had $17,000 is deceptive. It is possible that was their investment on paper, for the stock account was margined as high as 80 percent and the furs that were purchased did not have to be paid for, in many cases, for ninety days; the ledger indicates most of the furs were sold at a profit within ninety days, in some cases within three days.

"Yet Hauptmann, when arrested and asked to explain why he had been "stealing" money from his late partner, Fisch, maintained he had simply been taking what was his because Fisch owed him $7,500. How Hauptmann arrived at that figure is impossible to determine at this point, because the original documents in the case are locked away at state police headquarters in Trenton and no writer is permitted to examine them. We know Hauptmann withdrew $2,000 from his brokerage account to finance Fisch's trip to Germany. The other $5,500 he said he was owed is hidden in this ledger book.

"But there is a clue. The accounting of fur purchases and sales shows that between May 8 and November 10, 1933, when trading seems to have ended at almost precisely the time stock market trading fell off, the partners had bought almost $51,000 worth of various skins, from Hudson seal to Russian caracul. (Again, it must be made clear that, as in the stock market account, the total sum cited is not moneys actually invested in cash, but the result of repeated buying and selling.) The profits on sales made by the partners came to $6,637. But there is something rather curious here. The ledger shows that on August 8, 1933, they bought 2,000 Hudson seal pelts at a total cost of $1,100. On November 3, their last recorded purchase, they bought almost 3,300 pelts ranging from silver fox to mink, at a total cost of $21,900. Only 1,600 of the Hudson seals were sold, at a profit of a dollar a pelt. The 400 sealskins and the 3,300 assorted pelts were not sold when Fisch went to Germany. According to Hauptmann's ledger, $24,100 worth of furs were owned by the partnership and should have been in storage somewhere.

"Hauptmann searched for those skins, but could never find them. And he slowly came to the conclusion that Fisch had cheated him."

Mr. Scaduto was not only an excellent investigative reporter, but a fine writer as well. I am deeply grateful to him for allowing me to borrow from his book, *Scapegoat*, in which he so clearly explains the contents of Hauptmann's "big book". I cannot emphasize my feelings enough, than to state them in this fashion: Had there been someone, at the time of the arrest, trial and conviction, willing to put forth the same intense desire as did Anthony Scaduto, forty years later, and help Richard Hauptmann's attorneys uncover the truth, the innocent Bronx carpenter would have never died in the electric chair. Instead he would have been exonerated. But alas, the entire world seemed to be against this hapless man.

CHAPTER THIRTY EIGHT

Who Is Isidor Fisch?

Shortly after Richard Hauptmann's arrest (and he told the police officers how he had come to possess the money), his explanation became known as "Hauptmann's fish story." The authorities refused to believe him, and so dubbed his true answers as a "fantasy", a falsehood, a lie, and what was to become "Hauptmann's unbelievable alibi." But such was far from the truth.

It was looked upon as his alibi simply because they did not want to believe him. His perfectly reasonable explanation as to how he had "fallen heir" to the $14,600 of Lindbergh ransom money was looked upon as a joke and consequently scoffed at as being ridiculous. But regardless of the public's acceptance or denial of his explanation, it definitely did not change the truth of what had taken place in the life of Richard Hauptmann, and the possibility of truth in his statement, of his account, at the very, least being a perfectly reasonable occurrence, of just how he had discovered the money in mid-August of 1934.

But, for the most part, the citizenry would not settle for any explanation, no matter how reasonable it might have been. Now that Bruno Richard Hauptmann was in the clutches of the police, they wanted revenge! They wanted blood! They demanded blood! And they would settle for nothing less. No stupid "fish story" of any kind would be accepted. But, to demand an unjust verdict by closing their eyes and mind to the truth is not only absurd, it is unjust. Unjust to the pointing of accusing fingers at everyone who consciously refused to at least look into Hauptmann's story with open minds. And in doing this they completely failed to learn the truth of Isidor Fisch and his alliance with the kidnappers of the Lindbergh baby and the absolute innocence of Bruno Richard Hauptmann for a crime of which he knew absolutely nothing more than what he had read in the newspapers and heard over the radio.

But Fisch was dead - and Hauptmann was very much alive. We must move in for the kill and now "fry the kraut" just as soon as possible at any cost. Just how in God's dear name could they do this? Well, they did! And now the truth must be told!

Hauptmann never deviated from his explanation that he had received this package, not knowing it contained money, from Isidor Fisch. He never once changed his story, from shortly after his arrest until he drew his last breath of life. And because of his insistent claim that he knew nothing else about it, the "possible" truth of this claim should have been investigated with vigor. But Fisch was dead, how could he help them? Nevertheless there were many persons, very much alive, who could have given the investigators new leads; that is, if they had been interested in searching out the truth of Hauptmann's story.

Members of the underworld of that day, when asked for their belief of Hauptmann's possible guilt, invariably came up with the same answer: "He has to be innocent, why the poor fellow doesn't even have an alibi." How true their answer proved to be. Two-and-one-half years after the kidnapping and the accused man had nothing better to tell his captors than such a cock-and-bull story as one that on the surface sounded utterly ridiculous. Ridiculous - only because it happened to be the truth - and the only story Hauptmann had to tell.

"Richard Hauptmann was far from being a fool. He was an honest God fearing man who loved his wife and son, an innocent man who said to Governor Harold G. Hoffman on October 16, 1935, nearly six months before his death: "They think when I die, the case will die. They think it will be like a book I close. But the book it will never close." How true his statement was. To this very date the book has never closed.

Because we have known of Richard Hauptmann's innocence and have, through the years, tried in the best way possible, to make you aware of the many unknown true facts in this famous criminal case, is the reason this book had to be written. I have literally lived with the Lindbergh case since I first became aware of Hauptmann's innocence shortly after his execution in 1936. Initially, the police failed by their unwillingness to uncover facts about Isidor Fisch. Facts which when learned would have put an entirely new light on the claims of innocence by Hauptmann. Through the passing of time, much has come to light about Hauptmann's dead partner. A partner who left him to hold the bag and be the fall-guy for the big part he actually played in the kidnapping. His so-called "friend" who allowed him to be a "scapegoat", to stand alone and suffer the agony of false accusations which eventually took him to the chair.

Much speculation has been advanced as to the part, if any, Fisch played in the kidnapping. Among Hauptmann's friends, those who knew Isidor, the great majority of them claimed they "did not trust him" and believed him to be "not all he said he was. Hauptmann, however, spoke highly of the man. It was because of his apparent "blind trust" that he was drawn into the case as an innocent person. Under a corresponding set of circumstances many of us could be falsely accused of something of which we knew absolutely nothing. Exercising blind faith in an evil person can easily permit a set of circumstances to arise which, even after close scrutiny, point to an innocent person's "apparent" guilt.

It is for this reason that we had to believe Hauptmann's claim of innocence and, in so doing, look objectively into the background of the man from whom he said he had received the box of ransom money. This, then, is what we found. Because Isidor Fisch was so deeply involved, more must be told of this vicious little man. Facts never before revealed about this mysterious man. Once again we turn to what Tony Scaduto learned about him and tells so well in *Scapegoat*:

"Isidor Fisch, it appears from the documents available, was most certainly dishonest. He also seemed to have been persuasive enough to make one group of friends believe he was starving so that he could cadge money from them and from an immigrant society to which he belonged. At the same time he was getting another group of friends (Hauptmann and his acquaintances) to believe he was a wealthy fur speculator and investor in small expanding businesses so that he could borrow money from them by claiming he was temporarily short of liquid capital but didn't want to miss out on a sure winner. None of the money Fisch borrowed was ever repaid.

"It is possible, from the FBI and police files, to put together a portrait of Isidor Fisch. Born in Leipzig in 1905, he came to America around 1922 and got a job as a furrier. He was making about fifty dollars a week, at first, and by the late twenties was earning about a hundred a week. He went to night school, learning to read, write, and speak almost perfect English and winning a certificate of merit. He lived frugally, sending large sums of money to his parents in

Germany, 'of whom he was very fond,' one friend told police. But he apparently had saved enough to enable him to buy a piece of land in Freeport, Long Island, in 1928. At the same time, however, he gave most of his friends in a fraternal lodge in which he was sergeant-at-arms the impression that he was always on the edge of destitution.

"In 1931, Fisch invested $15,000 in a pie-baking corporation. The details of that investment cast a little further light on Fisch and the kind of men he was associating with. In tracing Fisch's background, police interviewed Lamber D. Brush, who was the brother-in-law of New York City's coroner but who was estranged from his family because, it appears, he was continually involved in questionable businesses.

"Brush conceded that police information was accurate; he had once been a partner with Isidor Fisch in a pie company. That partnership came about, he said, when the pie-baking company he had begun in October 1930 had grown short of capital and was near collapse by the following January. At that time he was visited by an old business acquaintance, Charley Schleser, who suggested they form a corporation and seek an infusion of new capital. Charley said he would find a couple of investors among his contacts but, as finder's fee, he wanted a share in the new corporation even though he couldn't personally invest anything. Brush agreed to the proposition although he was fully aware of Charley's rather tainted business credentials. Brush had met Charley around 1918, when Schleser was running a delicatessen in upstate New York and Brush was general manager of a meat-packing firm in Brooklyn. Charley had had business reverses and had fallen behind in paying his bills to the firm Brush worked for, so Brush bought him out and assumed the debts. Apparently, Brush had been involved in manipulating the books in Brooklyn so that the debts in upstate New York would appear diminished, and eventually he was fired.

"Brush says he saw Charley occasionally up to 1925, then lost contact with him until he appeared with his offer to help the pie business. But, Brush said, he'd heard a few things about Charley. Charley had gone to prison for a couple of years for swindling a woman out of thousands of dollars. Most recently, Charley was involved in a crooked real estate business with a man named Joe DeGrasie, a <u>real</u> hoodlum---implying Mafia connections. As the FBI agent relates Brush's account:

'Brush said that he considered Charley as a

trickster very capable of successfully putting over a shady deal and undoubtedly closely identified with the criminal element.... During the time when the pie company was in operation, on several occasions undoubted gangsters had visited Charley and gave every evidence of being intimate with him. As a matter of fact, Brush says it was Schleser's boast that he could get gang assistance at any time should he need it.'

"DeGrasie was only one member of that criminal element that visited Charles at the pie company, Brush said. And DeGrasie loved to boast about how great a team he and Charley had been in their real estate swindles. They had a legitimate real estate office on Beekman Place, near City Hall, DeGrasie told him. And DeGrasie said 'that the plan of operation during their real estate days was for him to dig up the suckers and turn them over to Schleser, who was the office man who would put through the deals by which several people were victimized.'

"Brush told police that DeGrasie left New York in March 1931, shortly after the pie company was incorporated, because he had swindled someone out of about five thousand dollars. DeGrasie had fled to Germany; his wife was German. Investigators seemed to grow rather excited about that information and they asked Brush to describe DeGrasie. Well, Brush said, he was about thirty-five years old at this time, 1934, short and stocky with black hair and quite clearly of Italian descent and, 'There was something wrong with one leg, causing him to limp slightly at times.'

"That description, one police report dryly noted, 'seems to match the possible lookout seen in the cemeteries.'

"But DeGrasie had left a year before the kidnapping and FBI agents were assigned to check with immigration officials on whether he had returned. That particular trail ends, for us, because there are no further reports concerning DeGrasie's movements after March 1931 in the files to which I had access.

"It was DeGrasie and Schleser who brought Isidor Fisch into the Knickerbocker Pie Company. Whether Fisch was one of their 'suckers' or whether he was associated with them in other ventures cannot be determined from the small number of documents available to me. But that Fisch himself became a swindler---of Hauptmann and others---soon becomes apparent.

"Schleser told police that when Isidor Fisch came to him and offered to invest in the new enterprise,

Fisch said he was prepared to put about $800 into the corporation. Charley said that wasn't nearly enough, and about two weeks later Fisch returned with $1,500. He said it was all his savings, but Schleser felt certain it was borrowed money.

"Actually, Fisch had borrowed the money from Mrs. Augusta Hile, the mother of Karl Henkel. Fisch roomed with Karl and Gerta Henkel and it was Gerta who testified she introduced Fisch to Hauptmann in the summer of 1932.

"Schleser also told police that when Fisch first came into the pie firm as a stockholder in the corporation, 'he was in a run-down condition and no doubt already the victim of tuberculosis.' Fisch said he had become ill because of his years in the fur business, dressing fur pelts in chilled rooms until his lungs were affected. He wanted to get out of furs, he said, and into some other form of occupation, which is why he was going into the pie business.

"But Fisch also told Brush, the man who operated the original pie company until it was incorporated as Knickerbocker in January 1931, that he was still working as a furrier and making eighty to a hundred dollars a week. Brush said Fisch finally lost that job months later when the pie business interfered with his fur trade. And when the pie business folded around August 1931, because of a dispute between Schleser and Brush, Fisch's entire investment was lost.

"A couple of months later, according to Mrs. Hile, Fisch borrowed another $1,850 from her 'to put in the pie business so we can expand,' he said. To the day he sailed for Germany, Fisch told one group of friends that the 'pie business was doing fine.'

"After meeting Hauptmann in the summer of 1932, Fisch began hanging around with him at the brokerage office on East Eighty-sixth Street where Hauptmann watched the tape almost every day. Several customer's men told police they'd been introduced to Fisch by Hauptmann. Gerta Henkel, with whom Fisch roomed during 1932, told police shortly after Hauptmann's arrest: 'Isidor got on my nerves, he always get me nervous, pacing up and down the floor and looking out of the window to see if Hauptmann come or not. He was always there until about half-past nine in the morning. He would go away with Hauptmann;, but sometimes Hauptmann didn't come and he go away alone. I said, Where you go, working or what?' He said he go down to the stock market.

"By the beginning of 1933, which is several months before Hauptmann's ledger indicates they had become partners, he was telling friends that he and Isidor were going into business together. Hans Mueller, who was married to Anna Hauptmann's niece, told police that some months after Mrs. Hauptmann returned from a trip to Germany, in October 1932, Richard was talking about going into business with Fisch. Each of them would invest $17,500 in a partnership, Hauptmann to speculate in stocks with part of the capital and Fisch to buy and sell fur pelts, 'everything on a fifty-fifty basis.' In the statement to the FBI by Mr.and Mrs. Wollenberg, they said they had gone to the Hauptmanns' apartment some time in the early morning hours of January 1, 1933, to wish them a happy new year, and they met Fisch for the first time. 'Hauptmann seemed to show considerable respect toward Fisch,' Wollenberg was quoted in the FBI report. Wollenberg said he'd been drinking and at one point, forgetting his manners, he pointed toward Fisch and asked Hauptmann, 'Who is that little shrimp there?' And Hauptmann replied, 'That guy is worth thirty thousand dollars. He is my partner in furs and in the stock market. We have an agreement that we go half-and-half on everything.' Mrs. Louisa Schussler, who lived downstairs from the Hauptmanns, said she began to get friendly with Anna when the latter was growing large with her pregnancy, in the summer of 1933, and would come and visit and ask questions about giving birth and raising a child. At one point, Louisa told police, Mrs. Hauptmann began talking about Fisch. 'She said she thought Fisch is a nice man, he speaks nice English and she likes to talk with him, and Fisch and Richard are going in business together.'

"While cultivating the Hauptmanns as friends and business associates, Fisch was warning Mrs. Hile not to tell anyone he had borrowed money from her because 'he didn't think it was anybody's business but ours.' She agreed---and Fisch promptly borrowed another $1,000 from her 'to buy furs with Richard.'

"In June 1933, a month after the deadline for converting gold certificates into other paper money, a month after Wendel had said Fisch tricked him out of the gold notes, Fisch rented a safe-deposit box at the North River Savings Bank branch on West Thirty-fourth Street, in the fur district. When that box was opened by court order in August 1934, after Fisch's family had hired an attorney to seek out any assets in his estate, it was empty. In September, when Hauptmann was arrested, police verified that the box had indeed been empty and they wondered---in several reports---whether Fisch had been Hauptmann's "accomplice" in the kidnap and extortion and whether he had hidden his shoe box of gold notes in that bank until just before sailing for Germany. In August 1933, a few months after renting the box, Fisch started a trading account with a brokerage house on Broad Street, far removed from the East Eighty-sixth Street brokerage office he frequented with Hauptmann, and he began to trade in a relatively small way, in hundred-share lots never worth more than $1,000. Hauptmann evidently did not know about Fisch's solo market trading.

"By the autumn, shortly before buying his ticket for Germany with money borrowed from Hauptmann, Fisch was boasting that he was a wealthy man. Hans Mueller remembered that the only time he ever saw Fisch in Hauptmann's house was after Fisch had definitely decided to return to Germany before Christmas. Muller told police:

"Richard was at his desk and Isidor came in and they spoke about the fur business. They were talking that when Isidor came back from Germany they can start to buy fur from the trappers and I said to Isidor, 'That cost a lot of money.' He said, 'Oh, we make the money. We almost missed ten thousand today. If I would have bought the right furs and have money for it we could have sold it right away and make ten thousand dollars on it.' And at that point I was sent out of the room because Richard, he want to talk business with Isidor Fisch."

"Fisch boasted to a number of other friends of the Hauptmanns' that he was 'getting rich in furs' and that he 'had already a big bundle of money from fur profits.' At the conclusion of his going-away party, a few days before sailing for Germany in early December 1933, Fisch was driven to the subway station by Mrs. Katie Fredericksen, whose husband owned the bakery in which Mrs. Hauptmann had worked until her pregnancy. And Fisch practically propositioned her, she said, apparently trying to demonstrate that he had a great deal of money. 'I don't know if it was a joke,' she told the Bronx district attorney, 'but Fisch said, do you want to go downtown and raise the roof some place?' Mrs. Fredericksen said she couldn't possibly do that, she wanted to go straight home. 'And Fisch took some bills from his pocket and held them up and said we be spending that for a good time.' She replied that he'd go broke before getting to Germany if he carried on like that. Then they arrived at the Pelham station and Fisch got out without any further conversation.

"Yet at the same time he was causing members of the Hauptmann circle to believe he was wealthy, Fisch was presenting another face to another group of friends. The members of his lodge, the Chrzanower Young Men's Association, interviewed by FBI agent P.M. Breed during a meeting several days after Hauptmann's arrest, all swore that Fisch was always broke and nearly destitute, so broke that he was unable to seek medical aid for his pulmonary condition and on two occasions was unable to pay one-dollar assessments by the lodge. At the same time, most lodge members said he appeared to live at a near-poverty level because he was sending large sums of money to his parents. One member of the group told agent Breed 'that Fisch did a lot of overtime work as a furrier and had a small machine in his room. On this he frequently used to work until one or two o'clock in the morning stitching furs, explaining that he needed the extra money to send to his family in Europe. He also stated that he used the money secured from overtime work to pay his passage to Europe.'

"Another lodge brother said he had met Fisch on the street shortly before he sailed for Germany. Although it was very cold Fisch was wearing only a raincoat,and the friend remonstrated with him. Fisch said he had no money, 'that he was having hard work paying his room and board expenses which amounted to thirteen dollars a week.' The friend gave Fisch an old sweater to keep warm.

"Charley Schleser, the man with mob connections who brought Fisch into the Knickerbocker pie firm, although himself a confidence man, seems to have been conned by Fisch. He said that he saw Fisch occasionally after their business closed down and 'things had gone from bad to worse with Fisch.... He practically lived from hand to hand, earning a few dollars here and a few dollars there in the repairing of furs on small individual orders, his health getting worse by the minute.' Charley offered to take Fisch in, he could come and live with Charley and his wife until things improved, but because of his 'sensitiveness' over his financial condition Fisch refused. Eventually he took a thirteen-dollar-a-week furnished room in the building in which the Henkels lived. But, Charley told police, Fisch had been evicted from that room some time in the spring of 1933 and 'thereafter Fisch slept wherever he might find it possible to do so, including the benches in the Grand Central depot.' Charley was certain of that, because Fisch had told him so. However, police learned Fisch had moved out of the room, voluntarily, to take a large place on East Eighty-sixth Street, in the German community of Yorkville, near the brokerage office where he would frequently watch the tape with Hauptmann.

"Schleser said he gave Fisch money during this period, a few dollars at a time, to help him out. Still, Fisch was getting much worse. Several weeks before Fisch sailed for Europe, Charley met him outside the Pennsylvania Hotel in the fur district 'and because of Fisch's weakened condition took Fisch to a restaurant in order that they might sit down, Fisch having seemed to be about to faint while they were standing on the sidewalk. Fisch was very much depressed at the time, as he had been on recent earlier meetings, and renewed previous threats to commit suicide, stating that he felt there was nothing else left for him to do.' Schleser and another friend who had been helping Fisch with small sums of money during this period argued with him and suggested he return to Germany. Fisch said he would very much like to do so, but he couldn't afford the boat passage. Schleser and the other friend gave Fisch thirty-five dollars 'and with a few dollars raised here and there Fisch departed for Europe.'

"Up in the Bronx, meanwhile, Fisch was playing the rich speculator, borrowing money from Hauptmann and Mrs. Hile and several others, according to police reports, and leaving Hauptmann with the understanding that he had in storage more than $24,000 worth of furs on which they could expect a large profit when he returned from Germany, probably in March or April.

"At least one of Hauptmann's friends did not trust Fisch, however. Hans Mueller, married to Anna's niece, told the Bronx district attorney:

"Fisch didn't have no place of business, Richard told me. I asked him if they go partnership together don't they want to have office or storage house, or if they shouldn't go to a notary public if he is going to invest so much money in Fisch's fur business. They speak about thirty-five thousand dollars, each party seventeen five, and I said, 'If you want to invest so much money, Richard, you got to go to notary and have agreement and go to bank and have bank account so you know how much money you got and how much money you pay out.' And then he tell me later they wanted to get everything down on paper before Isidor went to Germany but they never did, they never make the agreement.

"I ask him one time, I said, 'Richard, if you go in storage business and you buy so much furs, don't you have to have storage house or loft? He said, 'No, that is not done in business like this, the furs is bought in lots and stored in storage house; and we get paper for it and we don't have our own place for that.'

"Fisch sailed on December 6, 1933, with a friend, Henry Uhlig, who had known Fisch as a child and who remained close to him when both emigrated to New York. Over the next months Fisch sent a couple of postcards to Hauptmann---which during Hauptmann's trial David Wilentz said was 'all the letters we could find'---and then there was silence. At the end of April 1934, Hauptmann received a registered letter from Pinkus Fisch, Isidor's brother. It said, in part:

'I am writing you in great sorrow the sad news of my brother's death. My brother, Mr. Isidor Fisch, died at the Leipzig Hospital on March twenty-ninth at 2 P.M.

Now that we are back again to normal functions, I have taken time to let you know about it, although I have not been able to write sooner....I feel it is my duty to let you know about it in America as my brother has often talked about you and your business connections with him, which I imagine were not only business but of a more friendly nature. I am saying that because of conversations between me and my brother about you.

[Isidor] has told me about several enterprises in which you were also active, and still are. He advised me that you and my brother used to speculate with stocks and silver fox furs. He also told me of a will which is supposed to be in the safe of a New York bank. That safe is supposed to contain all papers in regards to his business and private matters.

In his last few hours he mentioned your name and I supposed he wanted to say something to us about you, or something for us to tell you, but he did not have the strength, and so I beg you please in the name of my relatives and dead brother, let me know what your connections were with my brother in business and also in private matters. Please do not misunderstand me to write such a letter shortly after my brother's death but evidently you were his close friend and I presume that you are willing to help us in getting the estate of my brother, for which he has worked so hard, so it will not get into someone else's hands. He advised us that the stocks and merchandise would amount to quite a bit of money. He also mentioned that again on his deathbed and the same confidence my brother had in you is still good with me in memory of my brother.... I would be pleased to have a complete list of all the goods belonging to my brother, to your knowledge, knowing that you will do this as a last favor to my brother. If you believe that the news of my brother's death should be kept from some persons, in regards to creditors, I will leave that entirely up to you.'

"The emphasis in this letter has of course been supplied, for police and prosecutors knew of the letter and others to follow. They knew that Pinkus Fisch had been told by Isidor about his business arrangements with Hauptmann, but all officials denied the letters' existence, doubtless because to have produced them at the trial would have raised questions slashing at the fabric of Wilentz's case. To reemphasize it: Pinkus Fisch said that Isidor told him he and Hauptmann speculated in stocks and furs, and talked about it often. Pinkus Fisch suggested that Isidor had attempted to say something to be told to Hauptmann---and the defense could easily have drawn the inference that it was a warning about the Lindbergh ransom money in Fisch's shoe box. Pinkus said he'd been told by his brother that the stocks and furs were quite valuable. Pinkus suggested others should be kept in the dark about Fisch's death so that, presumably, they would be denied any claim against the estate. All these statements in the first letter from Pinkus were so completely the reverse of what Wilentz "proved" that the letter had to be kept from the jury and the public.

"Hauptmann replied to Pinkus on May fourth. His letter was introduced at the trial; Wilentz was able to attack it as lies and fantasy, since it appeared to exist in a vacuum, without connection to the letters from Pinkus or the material in Hauptmann's ledger books. In his letter, Hauptmann first expressed his grief "that I will never see Isidor again" and then went on to detail their business arrangements:

'In the spring of 1933 I bought stocks for Isidor, which I knew would bring a profit and they did. We used to talk about his business and I loaned him money several times, when he wanted to buy furs. In the summer of 1933 he gave me two thousand dollars for stock market speculation, with an agreement that he would get

20 percent of all winnings and also share 20 percent in money lost. This was my unlucky year and I have lost heavy. Isidor knew what it means to play the stock market, it is always a gamble. After this experience we decided to go into business and build up a future as he figured that we would make 20 to 25 percent on the capital invested in the business....

On November the first, 1933, we started the business with a capital of $35,000 which was supplied by both of us, each one putting up half the money. We figured out the value of my stocks which on November the first, 1933, amount to $12,000. Isidor's supply in furs is $21,900. I gave him $5,500 cash out of my private bank and my interest in the business would be $17,500.

On November the thirteenth, 1933, Isidor asked me to take $2,000 out of the business as he needed money for traveling expenses to Germany, otherwise, he would have to sell furs to get the money, and we decided that it would be unwise to sell them as they will bring more money later on, and on November the fourteenth I took $2,000 out of my business and gave it to him....

Our business standing is as follows: My interest in full is $17,500. Isidor was not in a position to pay the full amount as he had other expenses.... Amount of stocks---$10,000---Isidor one half, Richard one half. Amount of furs---$21,900, Isidor one half, Richard one half plus $7,500 on Isidor's half....

Isidor also told me he was interested in a bakery business in which he invested $10,000. For the past few days I have been running around trying to locate this bakery, but all I could learn was that the bakery went bankrupt about two years ago. I can hardly believe it because Isidor had told me, just before he left on the boat, that everything was all right. I think there is something wrong. I personally believe that this bakery is operated under a different name to cut the income tax, but I think that there are papers in his bank box which should explain everything.

Now, dear Mr.Fisch, I beg you to write to me in the near future giving me information on the most important things. Would it be possible for you to copy the bills, and also send the address of the warehouse where the furs are stored, and also the address of the bank. I don't know what warehouse he used in storing the furs, everything is in his name. I would like to have everything locked, also his bank box. After his visit to Germany we intended to write the business in both names, but as it stands now I am unable to get into the warehouse or the bank....Our business was built up in trusting each other. I have kept books on all items bought and sold but I don't know where it is stored....

"In his letter, Hauptmann appears to be somewhat anxious about his inability to trace his late partner's assets. But the letter also appears to be self-serving. The most serious question about it, one which Wilentz stressed in his cross-examination, is Hauptmann's statement about the amount he and Fisch had invested in their partnership. 'We figured out the value of my stocks which on November the first, 1933, amount to twelve thousand dollars....I gave Isidor $5,500 out of my private bank....' But Hauptmann's own ledger and the FBI accounting summaries make it plain that he didn't withdraw $5,500 from his bank or brokerage accounts during that period. And there has never been any evidence that Hauptmann had cash hidden in a 'private bank'---that is, money hidden in his trunk as he claimed at his trial. Although I've discovered that most of what Hauptmann told police when he was in custody and later swore to at his trial was indeed the truth, in this instance I must assume, perhaps unfairly, that he did not have money hidden away. Making that assumption, one must ask how he built up his assets from $12,000 he may have had before the kidnapping to the claimed $17,500 he invested in the partnership, while losing about $5,000 in the market.

"It isn't possible, with the small number of documents available, to understand Hauptmann's figures or to attempt to answer the question with certainty. But some inferences can be drawn from the material at hand.

"To start, the evidence clearly demonstrates that Hauptmann did not possess Lindbergh ransom bills until after Fisch had died. Condon stated positively that Hauptmann was not the man who received the ransom money; none of the Lindbergh bills were ever deposited in Hauptmann's brokerage or bank accounts, nor did any turn up when Hauptmann traveled out of the city, where he most logically would have disposed of such dangerous currency; police laboratory reports show conclusively that the ransom bills found in Hauptmann's garage differed from those passed during the two years before Hauptmann says he found Fisch's shoe box. In sum, it isn't likely that the $5,500 he claims to have given Fisch was part of the Lindbergh money.

"If Hauptmann did not have $5,500, the only

logical explanation for his statement in the letter to Fisch's brother is that he lied.

"But why did he lie? And why settle on $5,500 and not some other sum, such as $10,000?

"There are clues in his ledger. By the time he wrote that letter to Pinkus Fisch, Hauptmann had learned that he'd been fleeced by his business partner and friend. And from the transactions listed in the ledger and from statements he made to friends, it is plain that Hauptmann believed he had made many thousands of dollars in profits from Isidor's fur trades. In fact, Hauptmann's ledger indicates that he and Fisch had made profits of almost $7,000 speculating in furs and, based on past experience of a 25 percent profit on investment, should have realized gains of another $4,000 or $5,000 on the furs Isidor claimed to have bought and were supposedly stored in warehouses when he left for Germany.

"The figures in the ledger bring a little sense to Hauptmann's claim that he 'gave Isidor $5,500....' Hauptmann believed that Fisch had made a total profit of about $11,000. Hauptmann's share should have been $5,500. No doubt knowing that Pinkus, as executor of his brother's estate, would not admit that Isidor had been a swindler and would not recognize a claim based on unrealized profits, Hauptmann apparently decided to claim he had actually given Isidor the money in cash.

"Such a claim on Fisch's estate would not have been too unethical for Hauptmann, or for many men, under the circumstances. Hauptmann was buying stocks for their partnership through his own stock market account, using his own funds; the ledger clearly indicates stock purchases for the partnership. During the span of the joint venture, the stock trading account suffered thousands of dollars in losses. Hauptmann, as the partner who had put up his stocks, absorbed those losses. He must certainly have felt that to balance his loss, he should have been compensated by the 'profits' from Isidor's fur trading. When he could not find those furs that had not been sold, Hauptmann in effect established a claim on Isidor's estate for the amount he believed he would have received had Isidor been honest.

"That Hauptmann knew, before writing the first letter to Pinkus, that Isidor had been a swindler is obvious from the documents at hand. After Isidor's death Hauptmann began to discuss his partners finances with their friends. He learned Isidor was not a wealthy man, as he had claimed, but that he owed money to several people, including Mrs. Hile. Most distressing, for Hauptmann, is that Henry Uhlig, Isidor's childhood friend, who sailed with him to Germany and who was at his bedside when he died, told Hauptmann in this period that Fisch had cheated him. In an interview in the district attorney's office in October 1934, another friend of Fisch, Max Falek, said that he and Uhlig were at Hauptmann's house discussing their fruitless search for Fisch's furs and other assets. Hauptmann showed them a fur price book and Uhlig, who was also a furrier, looked through it and said, 'Isidor claimed he paid more for the furs than they really cost. He was cheating you.' Falek told the district attorney: 'I never knew Fisch to be that kind of fellow. I trust him with everything I did.'

"These events, and the transactions recorded in Hauptmann's ledger, make it possible to understand why he falsely claimed that he had given Fisch $5,500 in cash.

"Pinkus Fisch responded to Hauptmann's letter on June third, once more confirming in a few sentences that Isidor had said he and Hauptmann were business partners. 'He spoke very well of you,' Pinkus wrote, 'saying that you were his best friend and adviser with whom he talked over his private and business matters....'

"In this second letter, Pinkus asked a number of questions about the partnership and wrote that he'd given Henry Uhlig a letter which he hoped, would have the force of power of attorney so that Uhlig would be able to get information from banks in which Isidor had safe deposit boxes. After Uhlig conducted a search and compiled information on Isidor's assets, then Pinkus would come to America to settle the estate. And he supplied Hauptmann with a list of furriers and warehouses in which, he said, Isidor's $21,000 worth of furs were no doubt stored.

"By his next letter Hauptmann seems to have been growing frantic. He has, he said, investigated at the warehouse and furriers Pinkus named, but either the firms do not exist, or the warehouses never heard of Isidor Fisch and never had any of his furs in storage. 'We attempted to locate the firms you mentioned in your letter, but we could not find them,' Hauptmann complained.

"Richard was unable to locate those firms because Isidor had manufactured them. It is impossible at this date to know whether Richard understood the extent of the fraud Isidor had perpetrated upon him---although it is clear he suspected---but, after his arrest, police investigated those firms and learned that Fisch had been a confidence man. The safe-deposit box, which had been opened by court order a month before Hauptmann's arrest, was found to be empty. The largest furrier that Fisch claimed to have been doing business with, Klar & Miller Brothers, on West Twenty-eighth Street, was investigated by Detective Max Leef of the 32nd Squad. In a report dated October 5, 1934, Detective Leef says his inquiries in the fur district disclosed that the firm never existed; further, the telephone number for the firm listed on a bill left with Hauptmann by Isidor Fisch belonged to another furrier at a different address, and that furrier had never done business with Fisch.

"The strongest evidence that Fisch was a swindler is found in a report by Detective Leef dated October 7. In it he says that he had interviewed a Louise Helfert, 'a lady friend of Isidor Fisch,' who admitted that for the last year or so she had been making out for Fisch 'bills in the thousands of dollars on the letterhead of Klar & Miller, doing it because Fisch did not have a typewriter.' Detective Leef notes: 'Klar & Miller Brothers is the nonexistent fur company.'

"With Fisch proving to be a thief, police told the newspapers that he was believed to have been Hauptmann's 'accomplice' in the kidnapping and extortion. But by the time David Wilentz came into Bronx Supreme Court to fight Hauptmann's attempt to overturn the order extraditing him to New Jersey, all discussion of Fisch as a thief and a probable extortionist was forgotten. All information on the partnership between Richard and Isidor was suppressed so that the state could label Hauptmann's defense 'the Fisch story.'

"The evidence in these dozen or so police and FBI reports appears to confirm rather conclusively that Isidor and Richard had indeed established some kind of stock market and fur-trading venture, that Fisch was a rather unprincipled rogue with criminal connections, that he swindled Hauptmann and others, and that Hauptmann was owed several thousand dollars by Fisch, as he had claimed from the moment the ransom money was found in his garage.

"None of this evidence was ever presented to the jury at Flemington, or to the public."

Had Tony Scaduto not found and disclosed for us the contents of the Hauptmann ledger and Fisch letters, we would have been as naive and trusting as the twelve jurors. We too, could have, and no doubt would have, doubted their very existence. However, fortunately Scaduto did uncover them to aid us in formulating a clearer understanding of just what kind of "honest little man" Isidor Fisch was.

But, read on, there is much more to be told about this "mysterious Mr. Fisch" who allowed his friend Hauptmann's name to be listed in the annals of aberrant behavior as the world's worst criminal, receiving the endorsement of this title by David T. Wilentz, Attorney General of the state of New Jersey.

CHAPTER THIRTY NINE

A Fisch Turned Bad!

It had been established, without any dispute whatsoever, that a man named Isidor Fisch had once been a business partner of Richard Hauptmann. But since Mr. Fisch was deceased, they reasoned there could be no purpose in connecting him with the crime. Their decision was not only unreasonable but very unprofessional. They had arrived at an agreement that to name Fisch, even though there was evidence that he was a member of the gang, would serve no purpose to the police. And so, the authorities decided to seek the necessary "proof" that would saddle Hauptmann with the charge of being the lone culprit. But, what a pity this was! What a shame this was! Had they put some credibility and understanding in Hauptmann's honest explanation as to how he came to acquire the ransom money, their investigation could not have led them anywhere but to the very doorstep of Isidor Fisch and his connection with the actual kidnappers.

There is then, much more to learn about Isidor Fisch; and had the authorities delved into his so-called "mysterious life", it is altogether possible that Bruno Richard Hauptmann would never have stepped foot into the town of Flemington, New Jersey, except to offer the probable testimony he might have been called to give against his former partner. To begin with, it has been established that the first formal meeting of Hauptmann with Fisch occurred in the home of his friends, the Henkels, sometime during the summer months of 1932. Karl Henkel, a painter, lived with his wife, Gerta, in an apartment they rented from a Mrs. Selma Kohl at 149 East 127th Street in Manhattan. Fisch was another of Mrs. Kohl's tenants, as was Hauptmann's friend, Hans Kloppenburg. Although this was accepted as the initial meeting of Hauptmann and Fisch, Hauptmann somehow was under the impression that he had already known Fisch from an informal meeting that had occurred a few months earlier on Hunter Island. Another mutual friend was Henry Uhlig, a fur trader, with whom both Karl, before he was married, and Fisch had shared rooms together.

At any rate, this proved to be the beginning of a rather close friendship of Hauptmann with Fisch. A friendship that, from all appearances, had been one of great trust, at least on the part of Hauptmann, until he received the letter from Pinkus Fisch informing him of his brother's death, and requesting Hauptmann to investigate Isidor's assets in America.

This letter prompted Hauptmann to write to Pinkus inquiring of him the address of Isidor's bank where he held an account, and to also send him the location of the warehouse where Isidor stored the furs he valued at $20,000. News of Fisch's death brought Erich Schaefer, another friend of the dead man, to write to Pinkus inquiring as to how he, Schaefer, could regain the $2,500 he had loaned his brother, Isidor. This letter, written on May 2, 1933, should most certainly have caused Pinkus Fisch to have entertained some serious doubts about the integrity of his brother, for in it he had expressed himself with no uncertainty: "You must always think of him as he was, upright and honest, loyal and true to his ideals ..."

Several months after the demise of the Knickerbocker Pie Company, Fisch had written a letter, dated November 1, 1932, to this same Mr. Schaefer in which he stated: Allow me at the present time to use the capital further until such time that I can develop my plans further, about which I think every day.... Please do not lose your trust in me and I will prove to you I am an honest man."

Fisch had declared himself to be "an honest man." Fisch was now a dead man. Why should Hauptmann's captors try to pin the crime on a dead Fisch when they had in their hands a "live fish", one they could now "reel in and hang out" for the approval of all who had been screaming for the past two-and-one-half years for a successful conclusion of the famous kidnapping case?

They now had their man and the only thing left for them to do was to PROVE HIM GUILTY! And this they could best do by eliminating any mention of Isidor Fisch as being, even remotely, a partner in the crime.

The worst oversight, no doubt a deliberate one, on the part of the investigators was their failure to probe further into the life of Isidor Fisch. Their determination to accept the fact that since Fisch was dead and there was no need for them to learn any more about him, resulted in a decision which proved to be most devastating to Bruno Richard Hauptmann as well as one which was very advantageous to those who planned to prosecute him as the lone kidnapper and murderer.

Although hindsight generally proves itself better than foresight, had the police probed deeper into the life of Isidor Fisch, from the time they had first heard his name mentioned by Richard Hauptmann, they would have learned many additional facts about him. And in doing this their findings would have tied him directly to activities pointing to his participation in the Lindbergh kidnapping, and thus would have led them to the correct conclusion to the "baffling" case with the complete vindication of Richard Hauptmann.

Among those whom Fisch called his friends, very few of them placed much faith in the man. He appeared to be an enigma of sorts. To some he was known as a rather wealthy person, while to others he was looked upon as poor, bordering on extreme poverty. Truthfully, he was actually a "con man", who at every turn, by playing on their sympathy, bilked as many of his acquaintances as possible out of their hard-earned dollars in order to give himself what he claimed was "a much needed financial lift".

Of all the persons known to have been found by Fisch to be a "soft touch" for money, Karl Henkel appears to be the only one who was repaid the small amount the fur dealer had borrowed. In addition to the $7,500 he owed Hauptmann, we find a list of his other friends to whom he was indebted. There were William and Mary Schaefer, the parents of Eric Schaefer, a sum of $2500 in his now defunct Knickerbocker Pie Company at 61 Downing Street in New York City; Mrs. Hermann Kirsten, Gerta Henkel's mother, $4000; Mrs. Augusta Hile, mother of Karl Henkel, $4100; Max Falek $800; Henry Uhlig $400; Ottilia Hoerber $250; a Mrs. Kuntz $500; plus quite a few undisclosed sums to other friends, including Gerta Henkel"s sister, Erica, and Anna Stotz.

However, it had not been common knowledge among his friends that Fisch was using more than a few of them to obtain money. By not being aware of this, he was accepted as a "man of means" who always had money because of his lucrative business successes. To those who helped him financially with large amounts, he was cleverly selling himself as a smart businessman, one who sought their money for joint investments in his various projects such as the Knickerbocker Pie Company, the Long Sign Company, a daytime motion picture company, or for cash he needed to obtain from them as he served as their investment broker on the Stock Market.

But to others who knew him only as a penniless pauper, he borrowed smaller amounts to help him pay his room rent or to pay his doctor. To these friends he was looked upon as a person to be pitied, one who desperately needed their help for his very existence. These kind friends rarely expected a repayment and rarely received one.

But there is much more that we learned about Isidor Fisch than his indebtedness to his friends and the large sums of money he never intended to pay back. Fisch was truly a sinister man of mystery.

The son of Jewish parents, Salomon and Blime Fisch, Isidor was born in Leipzig, Germany on July 26, 1905. He attended school until he was seventeen. After finishing school he joined the firm of R. Schwarze and Company where he learned the fur business as an apprentice. He spent three years with the company and struck up a close friendship with a fellow employee, Henry Uhlig.

The two men learned the fur trade from their boss, Hermann Kirsten, who, while instructing them, instilled within them a desire to someday journey to America where greater opportunities would be afforded them. Kirsten was the first to leave and soon after his arrival in New York City with his wife and two daughters, Erica and Gerta, wrote to his former employees advising them to embark for the United States as soon as possible, where they could earn more money than they could in their homeland. Uhlig decided to take this advice and left immediately on the first available steamship. Upon his arrival he stayed with the Kirstens in a room of his own.

But Fisch was not happy about being left alone in Germany. He wrote to his good friend Uhlig bemoaning the fact that he did not have the money to come to the United States. Since Henry had already obtained employment, he sent his friend the necessary funds; and soon thereafter, on December 2, 1925, Isidor left his father, Salomon, his brother, Pinkus, and sister Hannah, in Leipzig, to join his friends in New York.

Despite the fact that Isidor registered complaints that neither of his friends had obtained any form of employment for him, as had been promised him by Kirsten, the new immigrant soon found work for himself as a cutter in the fur trade. His earnings, which ranged from a starting salary of $50.00 a week, soon increased to $100.00 enabling him to regularly send some money home to his parents.

Kirsten, had by this time abandoned his initial profession of fur trading for the far more lucrative business of prohibition bootlegging. Uhlig and Fisch, who were now sharing an apartment, continued with their work as cutters in the fur business in midtown Manhattan's west side. A new friend of Uhligs, a German lady, named Augusta Hile, had inquired if her son, Karl Henkel, could move in with the two men when he arrived from Germany, and they had readily agreed. It was through this arrangement, that Karl Henkel would soon meet his future wife, Hermann Kirsten's daughter, Gerta.

Soon Fisch moved to another location, an apartment owned by a Mrs. Selma Kohl at 149 East 127th Street, where he and Hans Kloppenburg had rooms, as did the recently married Henkels.

With these facts which permanently establish Isidor Fisch as a resident of the United States, it is necessary that we trace his tainted career from the time he became a naturalized citizen in the Bronx County Courthouse, New York, on August 26, 1931 and other factual events that took place during his lifetime until he returned to his homeland in December 1933 - where he would die on March 29th the following year.

Fisch was a small, rather frail man. A passport application records his height as being five feet, six inches. His friends, however, believed him to be much shorter. His weight was recorded as 148 pounds. His hair and eyes were brown. In addition to being short of stature, he had been blessed with a pair of oversized ears, set far enough away from his head which caused more than a few people to comment on his resemblance to the popular Eddie Cantor, the well known comedian of that day. In addition to his personal appearance, he was known to have a very bad cough, one with which he had persevered since the year 1931. Here we should remember the testimony of Doctor Condon when he related that his "Cemetery John" had a sharp cough which to him gave indication that the man was suffering "from the inroads of pulmonary disease." This leads us to wonder if the man who met with Condon for an hour and a quarter in Van Cortlandt Park on March 12, 1932 had been none other than Isidor Fisch?

That Fisch had been suffering from tuberculosis since 1931 is attributed to the findings of a report to Police Department, City of New York, given by Doctor August Spiegel, 842 Park Place, Brooklyn, New York, regarding information pertaining to Isidor Fisch. The interview was obtained on September 24, 1934. It reads as follows:

1. Interviewed Dr. August Spiegel at about 4:30 P.M. this date, at his office, and received the following information:-- he first treated Isidor Fisch on July 13, 1931, for T.B. He again treated him on July 20th, 25th and 31st, 1931. He did not again see the above mentioned person until November 4th, 1933, when he again called at the Doctor's office for treatment and was found to be suffering from T.B. of the right lung, high fever and in a very nervous condition. He was at that time asked if he could afford to go to a hospital and he answered "Yes" but refused; he asked if it were possible for him to visit his relatives and people in Germany and was advised against traveling.

2. The address given by Fisch in 1931 was 542 East 157th Street, at which time he was engaged in the fur business. In 1933 he gave an address of 149 East 127th Street. Dr.Spiegel did not recall how Fisch first came to his office for treatment, but did recall that he always came alone and paid $5.00 per visit. The doctor does not recall whether any of these payments were made in gold certificates or not. He also stated that Fisch never appeared to be in any other than ordinary circumstances and does not recall ever having seen Bruno Hauptmann until his picture appeared in the newspaper.

3. Dr. Spiegel further stated that he wanted to let the police know of the condition which he found Fisch, because of the articles he read in the newspapers to the effect that Isidor Fisch died from some poison and that his body was going to be exhumed.

4. Dr. Spiegel was of the opinion that Fisch, being of a very erratic and nervous type, would commit a crime of that sort quicker than Bruno Hauptmann whom he claims he had never seen other than the photographs that appear in our daily newspapers. Respectfully submitted, and this document was signed by: Detective F.J. Ruggiero, #-250 of the New Jersey State Police and Detective Charles Frank, #-530 of the Main Office Staff of the New York City Police.

In addition to the facts as we have related them to you, particularly to those pertaining to his practice of deception among his friends, and that of posing as a "man of means" to some while appearing as a "pauper" to others, thus keeping his true financial status a complete mystery, we now delve into some very interesting truths of other friends, better to be called fiends, and their involvement together in matters which directly connect them with the kidnapping of little Charles Lindbergh.

Among the earliest friends Isidor made upon his arrival in America, very few of them came to know his later acquaintances. With the exception of Henry Uhlig, Karl and Gerta Henkel, Hermann Kirsten and Augusta Hile, most of them never met the friends he made during the early 1930's, namely Hauptmann and Kloppenburg.

Hauptmann at first claimed he had only known Fisch by sight during the early summer of 1932, having seen him initially on Hunter Island. But, he said, he had formally met him several weeks later when they were introduced during one of Richard's frequent visits to the apartment of Karl and Gerta Henkel. Karl told him that Mr. Fisch was a tenant in the home of Mrs. Selma Kohl, the same lady who had earlier rented rooms to him, Henry Uhlig, and Hans Kloppenburg.

However, Richard was later convinced from statements offered by his friends that he and Fisch had known each other months before. This fact was later proven to be true since Hauptmann clearly remembered engaging in a partnership with his new friend, this small Jewish man, as early as May of 1932 when Fisch first proposed they enter a fifty-fifty alliance, Fisch trading in furs for them, while Hauptmann traded on the stock market. Their mutual agreement merger began in the middle of May, 1932 when Hauptmann turned over $600 to Fisch as his initial investment in furs. Nevertheless, it was not until August when Isidor gave Richard his first payment for stocks he was to invest for him.

And with this meeting a "friendship" was engendered between Hauptmann and Fisch which, through a series of bizarre circumstances, was to ultimately reserve a seat for Richard in the electric chair at Trenton four years later.

The findings in our study of the lurid career of Isidor Fisch prove beyond any doubt that he was a deceptive, shrewd individual who, until years later, had successfully kept hidden many unknown facts about his life, which, while he lived, were not to be collectively known until after his death. And when all these facts were put together, a web of intrigue had been spun into and around his life --- unfortunately not to be known until death overtook him.

These then are the things which you must know in order to properly evaluate the kind of person he was, the life he led, and his undeniable involvement in the Lindbergh case.

Fisch first decided to go to Germany shortly before May 12, 1932 since this date is clearly seen as it was stamped on his application for passage on the steamship Leviathan set to sail on July 19th. However, due to the person he had planned to embark with losing his job, a lack of the necessary funds prevented them from making the trip. Incidentally, the date they applied for his passport happened to be the very day on which the corpse was found near Hopewell, New Jersey.

However Fisch and his friend, Henry Uhlig, did take the trip more than a year and one-half later and the following is a record of the interesting events that took place during the months before he boarded the U.S. Manhattan on Wednesday, December 6, 1933, embarking from the port of New York bound for Germany.

The earliest recollections his friends had of Fisch were that he never seemed to have any money. He paid his landlady, Mrs. Kohl, a mere $3.50 weekly for a room in the attic, the cheapest she had to offer, and for which he quite often would keep her waiting for the payment.

Although he was recognized among many of his German friends as a sickly pauper, others acknowledged that they knew him as a furrier who dabbled in other interests that necessitated small investments of his own, and in addition possessing the ability to encourage his confidants to invest large sums of money in worthless enterprises, some of them even nonexistent. To others he was known as a rather wealthy young man, one who always had money for a good time. When the announcement of his death reached his friends in America, it was at that time that they recognized him as being nothing more than a clever con-man who had bilked many of them out of thousands of dollars. Of this group, Hauptmann had been the hardest to convince of this fact. For some reason or other Richard's faith in his friend Fisch never seemed to waver. That is, until he was finally brought to the bold realization that he had been tragically betrayed --- but by then it was much too late to rectify his mistaken trust in his little friend --- the police now had him in their clutches.

In retrospect the friends of Fisch said they were always a bit skeptical of him. He had always boasted to be doing well in his fur trading, and yet there was no substantial evidence to back up his claims. Hauptmann on the other hand had continued to make good investments on the stock market. Because of this it is hard to understand just how Richard had not become wary of his partner's claims of wealth.

Nevertheless, Hauptmann had remained very naive about Fisch and his tall tales. Certainly this would not have been so, had he been aware of the losses other friends were suffering at the wily, unscrupulous hands of Isidor Fisch, a man he trusted.

Surely if Eric Schaefer, Mrs. Kirsten, Mrs. Hile, Karl Henkel, Max Falek, or any of the others, had mentioned to Richard their losses to Fisch, this book would not have had to be written. But such was not to be the case; not one of those who had lost money to Fisch ever told Hauptmann of their trouble with the man. It had been Fisch's practice to emphasize with those from whom he borrowed money the importance of not letting anyone else know of the transaction because, as he stated: "It's nobody's business but ours."

Henry Uhlig seemed to have the correct evaluation of Isidor's business dealings with those he was about to hoodwink out of their money: "He incited his acquaintances against each other, so that they did not speak to each other about their private affairs, and so it was possible for him to borrow money from each..."

Hans Kloppenburg called Fisch "a sneaky, foxy sort of guy; you never knew where you were with him. When they were at Richard's place and wanted to talk business, they went into the bedroom and shut the door." In my last interview with him, Hans claimed he "never trusted the man. There was something funny about him. I could never trust him, but Richard always did, you know."

Anna Hauptmann said Isidor was a man she tried hard to like, but never felt at ease around him. "He was a mystery man. One moment at Hunter Island you'd be talking with him, the next moment he'd disappeared." One thing Fisch demanded of Hauptmann was that he keep all information pertaining to his partnership with him from the ears of Henry Uhlig. This was a mystery Richard never understood since Fisch and Uhlig were such great friends dating back to their boyhood days in Germany.

From the very beginning of their partnership they seemed to have prospered. Although Fisch talked of large profits coming in from his sale of furs, Richard could do nothing more than accept his words as factual. Although Isidor claimed to have made more than $6,000 profit in furs during 1933, it could not be proven. It might very well have come from one of his other fly-by-night scams.

On the other hand, Hauptmann had been doing very well on his end of the partnership. His stock market investments prospered. In February of 1933 he purchased shares of Curtis Wright stock for $850 and sold them in May for $1456; and in April of that year, he bought Pennsylvania Railroad shares for $1887 and sold them four days later for $2045. Dominion stock acquired for $1612 on April 25 we're sold for another profit on May 17 for $1978. Hauptmann was doing quite well with his stock dealings at the brokerage firm of Steiner, Rouse and Company, where he had opened an account on March 27, 1933 in his wife's maiden name, Anna Schoeffler. He, however, had maintained full control over the account.

Of the two partners, Richard was the one who kept the records and was by far the more businesslike. However, there was still much to be desired as to the legality of the jointure. The details of the partnership had not been officially set down before a notary public; they did not have a proper partnership bank account. Fisch apparently had no official place of business and had not disclosed where he kept his furs. To say the least, the partnership was formed in a very unprofessional way.

The lack of a proper businesslike headquarters certainly afforded Fisch every opportunity he needed to cheat his naive and trusting partner. Hauptmann never came to accept the fact that Fisch had been a real life Dr. Jekyll and Mr. Hyde whose chief aim was that of successfully living a "life of lies" among those he had befriended and had gained their trust in him.

Isidor had no misgivings about cheating members of his own family. During June of 1933 his brother Pinkus shipped a crate of cat skins from Germany for Isidor to sell. Their total value had been established at $84.00; but when Isidor sold them to fur dealers, Fishbein and Klar, he failed to send any portion of the profits back to his brother. He was truly a person who suffered no misgivings for his criminal acts. But, as you will see, he was a congenital liar, one who deliberately would allow whatever ill to befall his friends, whatever the cost --- even death.

From the very first days they became partners, Hauptmann had been under the impression that Fisch owned furs valued at $20,000. In order to successfully accomplish this fraud, Isidor had invented from out of the machinations of a "warped mind" the fake name of a bogus firm which he referred to as Klar and Millar. Through the unsuspecting help of his friend, Louisa Helfert, he had her type a list of purely non-existent furs, which he naturally did not own. But, nevertheless, in order to complete his perfect fraud, he had Louisa type alongside each, their estimated value, and again from his twisted mind, a figure ranging from between two and three times their actual worth --- if he had owned them. In order to successfully accomplish this "brilliant swindle" of his, Fisch had stationary printed with the fake letterhead of Klar and Millar brazenly appearing across the top. It is of no little wonder that the trusting Hauptmann was convinced that, although Fisch still owed another $5,000 into the partnership, there was no doubt that it would be paid just as soon as some of the furs, valued at $20,000, would be sold.

During the period of the Hauptmann-Fisch partnership, Isidor was known to have done much traveling. To those who knew him as a rather wealthy man, this act was above suspicion. To those who looked upon him as penniless, he simply disappeared for awhile with no knowledge by anyone of where he went. He was, most certainly, the "mystery man" in the German community of the Bronx.

Now, before we present facts which definitely tie Isidor Fisch together with other persons we know to have been participants in the Lindbergh kidnapping and the subsequent part he played, we should first prove to you that Fisch had, without any doubt, possession of at least part of the ransom money, in addition to the $14,600 he had left in a wrapped box with the unsuspecting Hauptmann in December of 1933, months before the police ever attributed any bills as having been passed by Richard Hauptmann.

During Hauptmann's trial most members of the press, as evidenced clearly through the tenor of their reports on the case, had been adversaries to the Bronx carpenter. However, there were a few journalists who appeared to be sympathetic to the situation Hauptmann found himself in and had come to the conclusion that the man might "just be as innocent as he said he was." One of these reporters was Patrick McGrady of the *Associated Press*. McGrady and his wife, Grace, had shown themselves to be friendly to Anna Hauptmann, going so far as to assist her in searching for facts which might be encouraging, and at the same time helpful, to the distraught wife of the accused man.

I was initially informed of the McGradys by Anna Hauptmann who suggested that I contact them for some important information they had collected during the trial and incarceration of her husband. I lost no time reaching Mrs. McGrady by telephone at her home in Lilliwaup, Washington, but learned that her husband had passed away some time earlier. I found Mrs. McGrady quite willing to talk with me about her more than 300 pages of data she had collected on the case, including some personal experiences of her own, and how everything when put together very clearly proved to her that Hauptmann had been framed. She inquired if I had read Anthony Scaduto's *Scapegoat*. Assuring her that I had, she reminded me that much of what she knew about the case had been used by Tony in his book. Thanking her for her cooperation and after completing my call, I hurried to once again peruse my copy of the book. Sure enough, much of what I had previously learned from my own investigation, as well as those things uncovered by Harold G. Hoffman, the late governor of New Jersey, had already been exploited by Tony in his fine discourse on the case.

Because of the magnitude of these facts and the excellent way Mr. Scaduto presented them to his readers, I must once again draw on his kindness in allowing me to set them down here exactly as he told them in *Scapegoat*.

"Another document given to me by Grace McGrady strongly supports that conclusion (that Fisch possessed and spent gold notes from the ransom). In a deposition taken by the private detective, a man named Arthur H. Trost swore that he had known Isidor Fisch since the summer of 1931, about eight or nine months before the kidnapping. Trost said he met Fisch frequently in a billiard parlor at Eighty-sixth Street and Third Avenue, in the Yorkville section of Manhattan. Between the summer of 1931 and through January 1932, he saw Fisch in the billiard parlor two or three times a week. In February, the month before Lindbergh's son was kidnapped, Fisch stopped going to the billiard parlor. Trost did not see him there again until the following summer. His deposition concludes with that last meeting:

> 'My occupation is painter and I have been acquainted since March or April, 1931, with a man who is also a painter and who I knew only by the name of Fritz.... In June or July, 1932, I met Fritz at a restaurant at 1603 Second Avenue at which time he asked

> me if I wished to buy some 'hot money' for fifty cents on the dollar from a friend of his. I told him that I would go with him to see the people who had it for sale and he then took me to the same billiard parlor and when we arrived there he started to introduce me to Isidor Fisch. I then told Fritz that I was already acquainted with Isidor Fisch and needed no introduction to him. I also told Fritz that Fisch was already indebted to me for borrowed money and that I could not believe any of Fisch's stories. I was led to believe by Fritz that this 'hot money' was in the possession of Fisch and that Fisch had it for sale.'

But this was not the only instance regarding the passing of Lindbergh ransom money by Isidor Fisch. There were others. However, none was more directly connected to him, nor more convincing, than that testimony given by George Steinweg who ran a steamship and tourist business at 226 East 86th Street, New York. Because of its tremendous significance and its damning evidence against Fisch, I have used a good portion of the official court transcript here, beginning with his direct questioning by defense attorney Reilly:

Q. Did you on some day prior to December the 6th, 1933, sell the transportation of Isidor Fisch to Isidor Fisch? A. Yes, I did.

Q. To Germany? A. To Isidor Fisch and his friend Mr. Uhlig.

Q. When? A. On August 18th, 1933.

Q. August 18th, 1933? A. 1933, was the first visit of Mr. Fisch.

Q. Yes, the first visit. Well, did he buy his ticket then? A. No, he only made reservation for himself and his friend.

Q. Made reservations for what ship? A. The Manhattan, steamer Manhattan.

Q. Sailing when? A. Sailing December 6th, 1933.

Q. So that in August, 1933, he made a reservation for December, 1933? A. Yes, sir.

Q. And sailing on the U.S.S. --- A. SS. Manhattan, yes, sir.

Q. United States lines? A. Yes, sir.

Q. And it stops at Bremerhaven? A. No, Hamburg.

Q. At Hamburg? A. Yes, sir.

Q. When did he come in and buy his ticket? A.

The final payment was made on November 14th, 1933.

Q. And did he come in alone? A. The second time, yes.

Q. That was the final payment? A. Final payment.

Q. How much did he pay for his ticket and for Uhlig's ticket? A. For the both tickets he paid the tickets $410.

Q. And how much did he transfer into German currency? A. Not German currency, he bought German registered mark checks, American Express checks.

Q. For how much? A. 1500 marks for himself and 500 for Uhlig.

Q. And how much was that in American money? A. Approximately $650.

Q. So he spent with you over a thousand dollars? A. Over a thousand dollars.

Q. Now, did he exhibit to you any money in addition to the thousand dollars that he spent with you? A. He had quite some money in his wallet he took out.

Q. Did you see his wallet? A. Yes.

Q. Describe to the jury the condition of the wallet in so far as money was concerned, after he was finished paying you over a thousand dollars. A. He had quite considerable more money in his wallet, because I asked him to buy more checks; but Mr. Fisch said that his friends would send some more money afterward if he needed it.

Q. Friends would send him some more money over to Germany if he needed it? A. If he needed it.

Q. Now, you had records showing the transaction, didn't you? A. Yes, sir.

Q. And where are those records now? A. I have the steamship record with me, but the travel check records were taken away from me by the officials.

Q. By the State Police of New Jersey? A. No, from New York.

Q. How long ago? A. Right after the arrest of Mr. Hauptmann.

Q. And you do know, do you, that Isidor Fisch and his friend, Henry Uhlig, sailed December the 6th, 1933? A. Yes, sir, Room C-31.

Q. Room C-31 on the U. S. Manhattan. A. U.S. Manhattan.

Q. Did Fisch ever return as far as you know? A. I heard from Mr. Uhlig when he returned. He called me up and told me that Mr. Fisch had died.

Mr. Wilentz: All right. Just a minute.

Q. All right. Now, in Fisch's visits to you did

you notice whether or not he had a cough? A. Yes, sir.

Q. Did you know he was suffering from consumption? A. Yes, sir---from consumption? I couldn't say, but he had a very bad cold and told me he had consumption himself.

Mr. Wilentz: I move that what he told him be stricken out.

The Court: Yes, that will have to go out.

Q. All right, tell us, please, without telling what he said, what you observed about his general condition of health? A. When he was in my office the first time on August 18, 1933, during our conversation he had a very bad coughing spell, and we got to talk about---

Q. No, not what he said, how long did the cough---- A. I asked him what's the matter.

Mr. Wilentz: No.

Q. How long did the coughing spell last? A. For quite some time, I had to wait till he was all done.

Q. Now the second time he came in, did he cough? A. He had, he still had the cough.

Q. About how tall a man was Fisch? A. About my height, five feet five or four, or five foot four or four and a half.

Q. What did he weigh? A. About 140, 145 pounds, approximately.

Q. I show you Defendant's Exhibit 39 and ask you if you recognize that as a picture of Fisch? A. No, it looks different. It looks a little different.

Q. Look at Defendant's Exhibits 5 for Identification. Is that the way he looked when he bought the ticket? A. It looks still a little---it is about that.

Mr. Wilentz: It looks still a little what?

The Witness: It looked to me a little sharper pointed chin he had.

Q. He had a little sharper pointed chin when he left you? A. Than it looks to me, yes, sir.

Q. But that's his picture, isn't it? A. It looks like him.

Q. Is there any doubt about it? A. Yes, there is.

Q. There is doubt about it? You say the man--- A. He had a sharper, sharper look.

Q. When you saw him you mean he had a thinner look? A. Yes.

Q. More wasted? A. His ears was standing off very wide.

Q. And how about his face? A. Very thin and pale.

Q. And his chin was much sharper? A. Pointed, more hollow in the cheeks.

Q. More hollow in the cheeks. But you think--- A. It looks like him.

Q. It looks like him. When he was healthier: is that what you mean? A. That may be it. (Examines photograph again.) Yes, he looked more haggard.

Q. He looked more haggard than that? A. Yes.

Mr. Reilly: All right; I think that's all.

Cross Examination by Mr. Wilentz:

Q. On November 14th, 1933, you sold to Mr. Fisch about four hundred and some dollars' worth of traveler checks, did you not? A. Four hundred---to Mr. Fisch?

Q. Yes. A. Four hundred and sixty some odd; four hundred and sixty, and a hundred and sixty for Mr. Uhlig. He took him along too.

Q. Four hundred and sixty? A. Dollars worth.

Q. To Fisch? A. For Fisch, and a hundred and sixty dollars---

Q. For Uhlig? A. ---he took along for Mr. Uhlig. Mr. Uhlig was not there then.

Q. Altogether six hundred dollars' worth? A. Over six hundred; about six hundred and thirty dollars.

Q. And on November the 14th, 1933, don't you know that Hauptmann gave him $2,000 for that very purpose? A. I don't know.

Q. The very same day? A. Well, I don't know. How should I know that?

Q. You didn't know Fisch when he was healthy, did you? A. No.

Q. The only time you saw him was when he looked emaciated. A. In August.

Q. Face drawn. A. Face drawn.

Q. Cheeks pointed. A. Very sick looking.

Q. Skinny and thin. A. Yes.

Q. Now when you say 140 pounds you are guessing about that, aren't you? A. Well, I have to guess that every day dozens of times with passengers when we make out the papers.

Q. Five feet four and a half? A. Five feet five, about.

Q. Very thin? A. Well, he was broad shouldered but thin, no flesh.

Q. Very thin, no flesh. A. No flesh.

Q. In fact, would you be surprised to know that he weighed 120 pounds at that time? A. Well then his clothes must have covered it.

Q. Well of course his clothes covered whatever weight he had, but would you be surprised to know that he weighed only 120 pounds at that time? No.

Q. It is possible. A. It didn't appear to me like that.

Q. You may be mistaken about that. A. Certainly. I guessed the weight.

Q. You may be ten pounds out of the way or twenty pounds? A. Yes.

Q. You weren't here, were you, when Mr. Hauptmann testified that he gave him $2,000 on November the 14th, 1933, to make this trip? A. No, sir.

Q. So you don't know where the money came from? A. No.

And with the conclusion of this cross examination, Mr. Steinweg was excused. And as Steinweg stepped down from the witness stand, so ended Reilly's golden opportunity to prove to the jury that Fisch had actually been in possession of the ransom gold notes months before Hauptmann had claimed to have found the shoe box filled with them. With the failure of Reilly to pursue this line of questioning, either because of his stupidity, incompetence, or a combination of both, he abandoned the heart of Hauptmann's only defense, that of proving beyond a doubt that Isidor Fisch had been spending Lindbergh ransom money.

A deposition, one of many in Grace McGrady's possession, is the report of a private detective who had been hired by Lloyd Fisher, now Hauptmann's sole defense attorney, in an effort to gather new evidence for his client's appeal for a new trial. The detective's interview with George Steinweg, reads as follows:

'On November 14 at 11 A.M., Fisch again came to the agency and bought $600 worth of marks and two tourist-class return tickets for $210 each. Fisch paid for the German money and the tickets with gold certificates of ten-and twenty-dollar denominations. Steinweg told me that Fisch paid for his tickets in Lindbergh ransom notes. The agent Steinweg remembered the transaction perfectly well for several reasons. First, he had been rather surprised to see so much money come out of the pocket of a fur cutter who had never looked as though he was very prosperous. Secondly, he remembered the gold certificates and saved most of them because they were nice and crisp and he wanted to give some of them to his wife on her birthday. But before this happened a friend of his, a Mr. Gartner, who also went to Germany, asked him for some of these bills and he paid by check for the amount. But when this man went to the Federal Reserve Bank to pass some of the bills he was arrested on the suspicion that he was J.J. Faulkner, and he had to write his own and Faulkner's name a good many times to convince the police that he was not this man nor the kidnapper of the Lindbergh baby....

The police claim that on November 14, 1933, Hauptmann gave Fisch $2,000 which Fisch then used to buy tickets and marks. But Fisch paid for all this at 11 A. M. but Hauptmann did not take out the money which he gave to Fisch until a few minutes before 3 P. M. that day. Therefore, Fisch must have paid with his own money and not with that that he received from Hauptmann....'

Now, we read of this same account in a book titled *The Lindbergh Crime* written by Sidney Whipple, a reporter for the *United Press* and published in 1935, shortly after Hauptmann's conviction, and months before his execution. Mr. Whipple wrote:

'George Steinweg, the steamship agent, remembered the transaction perfectly for many reasons. First, he had been rather surprised at seeing so much cash come out of the pocket of a fur cutter who had never appeared to be over-prosperous. Second, he remembered the gold certificates. Third, it appeared to him that Fisch was financing his friend Uhlig's trip abroad. When Steinweg therefore read in the newspapers that Fisch's name had been brought into the case, he went to the police and divulged what he knew about the transaction. And after that, going back to the flutter of gold notes over his agency counter he went to his own bankers and asked if they had a record of a deposit in such certificates, on or about November 14, 1933.

The bank officials also remembered the matter very well. They had discovered, upon checking over the certificates, that they were a part of the Lindbergh ransom money. But at that time they had no means of tracing them back to the depositor, and although the federal government was notified, the trail was lost.'

We now have Steinweg, after seeing the name Fisch in the newspapers, his conscience being stricken to rightly divulge to the police what he knew of the little fur cutter's possession of Lindbergh gold notes - and in addition to this the bank officials remembering the incident very well, we should properly ask if any more was needed for Reilly to present this line of questioning to the proper witnesses. But Reilly had failed miserably.

George Steinweg was, quite apparently, an honest man. A man who realized the predicament Hauptmann found himself in and wanted to help him by offering what true knowledge he had of the transactions preceding the sailing of Isidor and Henry on the liner Manhattan.

Again Tony Scaduto comes to aid us in proving the innocence of Richard Hauptmann. The police had refused to accept even a remote possibility that Isidor Fisch had anything whatsoever to do with the kidnap-murder of young Charles Lindbergh, Jr. They went on to deny there was any evidence that Fisch had ever been in the state of New Jersey. During a visit to the home of Anna Hauptmann in 1975, while doing research for his book *Scapegoat*, he asked Richard's widow if she knew whether Fisch had ever traveled over to New Jersey. Her immediate and direct answer appears exactly as he recorded it:

"But Isidor Fisch did have friends in New Jersey. He would tell us about visiting friends in New Jersey, I know that for sure. But I don't know where these people lived. We tried to find out if maybe they had something to do with the kidnapping, but we found out nothing.

"There are a lot of things I remember about Fisch, that I didn't have time to tell you before. I read in your reports that some of the gold notes were passed at burlesque houses. Isidor liked to go to burlesque, he always went to those shows because he liked them so much. He told us that.

"He also told us a lot of times that he loved to go to the court house, he would sit and watch the trials. And he told me, 'Most of the time they convict the innocent.' (Mrs. Hauptmann repeated it in German, to get Fisch's words precisely, and then translated it more accurately): "He said, 'The people who get convicted are the ones who are not guilty.'

"Isidor was a strange man, I told you that already. He was a loner and everybody thought he was very peculiar. We would go to Hunter's Island and Isidor would always wander away by himself, vanish for a half hour at a time. And people would say, 'Where's Isidor?'"

At this point Scaduto was about to learn from Anna Hauptmann some important, and very new, information pertaining to the attempt of George Steinweg to back up Richard's story that Fisch, very definitely, was spending Lindbergh ransom money.

Scaduto was asking Mrs. Hauptmann for

clarification of something Richard had written in a letter, when she broke in with:

"Oh, excuse me. I remember something about Isidor that I have to tell you. Mr. Steinweg, the man with the travel agency that sold the boat ticket to Fisch, he said to me one day, 'Find out what time Richard gave Fisch the money. This is important. I won't tell you now what it's about, but find out.' When I went to see Richard the next day I asked him about it. Richard said that Isidor met him at the broker's office. He said, 'I'll get a check for you from the broker,' and Fisch said, 'No, I want cash.' Fisch suggested Richard get the check and they cash it in Richard's bank. They rushed to the bank to make it in time, it was just before closing time late in the afternoon. Richard said he remembered they had to rush to get to the bank in time.

"When I told this to Steinweg he said Fisch had bought the ticket in the morning, before Richard gave him money. Fisch had a lot of money, Mr. Steinweg told me. He said he thought Fisch was wearing a money belt, filled with money, but of that he wasn't certain. He was certain Fisch bought his ticket and changed money into deutschemarks in the morning, a lot of money, before Richard gave him the two thousand. And Steinweg told me Fisch bought the tickets with gold notes."

Time magazine, in its issue of December 31, 1934, contained this statement: "Isidor Fisch, Hauptmann's partner in random business ventures, used ransom money to pay for his passage back to Germany where Fisch died of tuberculosis in 1933." But, the prosecution, in order to eliminate all evidence that would implicate Fisch, refused to make known this important fact. They knew very well that Fisch had paid for his passage with gold notes in the morning, many hours before Richard had cashed his check for $2,000 at his own bank, at Isidor's insistence, and handed the cash to his partner just before the bank's time of closing. This fact alone, controversial as it might have been, could have been used to present more evidence to Hauptmann's innocence, but Reilly was either too stupid or neglectful to argue such an important argument. Or had he been deliberately told to overlook it? You may draw your own conclusions.

CHAPTER FORTY

Isidor's Other Friends!

As time moved on more interesting facts were being discovered pertaining to the deceased Isidor Fisch by investigators who had been hired by James Fawcett, Hauptmann's initial lawyer. While city and state detectives seemed to be content to allow the dead Fisch to rest in peace, other investigators were turning up evidence of which even Isidor's most intimate friends were not aware. Evidence which pointed more directly to the double-life the man had lived.

To begin with, we must bring another of Mrs. Grace McGrady's depositions, into focus. It was one given by a detective, hired by C. Lloyd Fisher in his effort to gather new evidence on which he could base his plea for his client's appeal for a new trial. The deposition proves to be quite interesting as we read it. It was one offered by a husband and wife, Gustave and Sophie Mancke, who conducted an ice cream parlor and lunchroom on Main Street, New Rochelle, a suburb of New York, only a few miles north of their home in the Bronx.

Mrs. Mancke stated in her deposition that "During an eight- week period in January and February, 1932, and up to the Sunday before the kidnapping, Isidor Fisch ate at our lunchroom on several occasions. Each time, Fisch was accompanied by Violet Sharpe, and by Oliver Whateley, Lindbergh's butler." The deposition taken from her husband, corroborated the statement made by Sophie, but was more specific. It read:

"During these eight weeks and I believe usually on Sundays at about 9 P.M. or later, a man and a woman who I identify positively from photographs as Ollie Whateley and Violet Sharpe came to my place four or five times to eat. On three or four occasions they were accompanied by a short thin dark man who looked like Eddie Cantor only with much larger ears. He coughed badly and I slapped him on the back, saying, 'You resemble Eddie Cantor.' His friend said, 'No, his name is Fisch.' I said, 'Why not herring?' They laughed and went out.

This man who coughed always spoke to me in German. I positively identify this man as Isidor Fisch. The man who I identify as Whateley ... limped slightly and had blond hair thinning at the temples.

The woman who I identify as Violet Sharpe always ordered tea and sandwiches. She was hard to please and was always disagreeable. The whispering of these people attracted my attention and the attention of my wife. The man Fisch never came to my place alone. He was there with Violet Sharpe and Whateley three or four times. None of these people who I have mentioned above ever came back to my ice cream parlor after March 1, 1932."

Now are we expected to discredit the testimony of these two people who voluntarily offered such incriminating evidence, and then at the same time believe that it had been Hauptmann who had purchased a ticket at a movie house, miles away from his home on the night of Sunday, November 26, 1933, which just happened to be his birthday? I think not. The statements of all three should be accepted as truthful, especially so as we learn more of the involvement of Isidor Fisch with Sharpe and Whateley.

Theon Wright, the late author, who as a young reporter had covered the Hauptmann trial and believed that the true story of the Lindbergh kidnapping had never been told, in his book *In Search of the Lindbergh Baby* published by Tower Publications, Inc. in 1981, reported that he, together with a fellow writer, Joe Dunninger, had pursued a report of a meeting that had taken place on Sunday, March 6, 1932. They had learned that Colonel Schwarzkopf, Colonel Breckinridge and Mickey Rosner had been joined by a spiritualist minister on that date in Princeton, New Jersey for the purpose of obtaining some psychic or spiritual help in their endeavor to solve the crime.

Their information had been factual for they uncovered the record of these three men on that date meeting with a Reverend Peter Birrittella, a spiritualist who served a church called "Temple of Divine Power" located at 164 East 127th Street, New York City. They learned that also present was a Mary Cerrita, an associate pastor who later married Birrittella, who conducted her own church at 141st Street and Willis Avenue in the Bronx. The meeting, held in a hotel in Princeton, had been arranged by the two colonels because they had learned that through "divine powers possessed" by Birrittella, he had placed Mary under a hypnotic trance; and while under his spell she had revealed some, however sparse, information about the Lindbergh case. Hence, the investigators were more than anxious to learn what the spiritualists had to report, even though their faith in such a demonstration was small.

Although Mary had been unable to make any direct "contact with the spirit world", she did predict some information that turned out to be, somehow or other, remarkably true. While in her hypnotic state she made a sudden declaration: "I see initials. They are like a light. They are J.F.C."

It must be emphasized that Mary Cerrita made this announcement on Sunday, March 6th, five days after the baby's abduction, and that it was not until March 9th that Doctor Condon made his contact with Colonel Lindbergh and the decision was made that he should become the intermediary and use his initials J.F.C. as a pseudonym. This fact has been documented and the dates correct, so we have this spiritualist telling the Lindbergh investigators of Condon's entry into the case three days before the good doctor knew about it himself. Are we foolish enough to label this a mere coincidence? Especially when there is more to be told of what Mary said while hypnotized.

Before Mary came out of her trance, she continued with more information: "You are wasting your time here, Mr. Breckenbridge. You should go to your office. There is an important letter for you there." This was also a documented statement made by Mary Cerrita on that Sunday in March.

The following morning Colonel Breckinridge entered his office and found his first letter from the kidnappers. It was difficult for him to believe that his name had been spelled "Breckenbridge", exactly as Mary had pronounced it during her seance. Her amazing revelation caused much speculation that she must have seen or had first hand knowledge of the actual letter. However, this conclusion must be regarded as highly unlikely by an impartial investigator.

The police evidently placed some credence in the information Mary Cerrita had divulged to them on Sunday, March 6th. Shortly after the suicide of Violet Sharpe they again contacted her for a statement regarding her belief. They were no doubt disappointed with her answer. She merely shrugged her shoulders and replied: "If a person isn't guilty, they don't commit suicide."

Colonel Schwarzkopf apparently believed this. Inspector Harry Walsh was certain of this.

But, getting back to Isidor Fisch it should be pointed out that his residence at 149 East 127th Street was only three doors away and on the same side of the street as the Warner-Quinlan service station where Hauptmann used a $10 Lindbergh ransom gold note to purchase gasoline of Saturday, September 15, 1934. Diagonally across the street, also in the same block, was the "Temple of Divine Power" the Reverend Birrittella"s church at 164 East 127th Street.

Richard Hauptmann visited the home of Karl Henkel on many occasions where two of his best friends, Fisch and Kloppenburg, lived. Because of this, it is hard to accept the fact that the September 15th date was the first time Richard had purchased gas at the Warner-Quinlan station, although it is possible. Nevertheless, we must think it quite possible that he had bought gas there before, and that Walter Lyle, the attendant, and Hauptmann had seen each other prior to that fateful Saturday.

Peter Birrittella and Mary Cerrita were interviewed by Wright and Dunninger on Sunday December 30, 1934 prior to the opening of Hauptmann's trial in Flemington on the following Tuesday. During this meeting they learned some interesting facts which, quite naturally, were never considered of any value to the prosecution staff, but could have proved to be very helpful for Hauptmann's defense.

During the interview the men were informed by the two spiritualists of the closeness of their church "Temple of Divine Power", to the apartment house where Fisch and Kloppenburg lived. This information fostered their next question: "Were any of the persons involved in the Lindbergh case members of your church?" Birrittella seemed not at all hesitant to respond, stating: Well, they were not really members, but we knew them as frequent visitors. The man who signed himself as Faulkner on the deposit slip for the money he turned in that proved to be Lindbergh's money was known to us as Falconi. And then there was Jafsie Condon, Isidor Fisch, and also Violet Sharpe, the maid in the Morrow's home who committed suicide. Dr. Condon was very interested in spiritualism. Our little church held a fascination to lots of people. We even had Chinese in our services sometimes. They all wanted information from Mary who was our medium."

Armed with this information, Wright and Dunninger

next went to the apartment of Hans Kloppenburg in the Bronx where he had moved. Fortunately, they found Karl Henkel visiting him. They both admitted they were well aware of the little church across the street from where they lived, but neither had ever attended the services. Inquiring if any of their friends were members of the "Temple of Divine Power", Henkel was the first to reply: "Isidor Fisch was." And then he went on to elaborate: "Fisch was a strange sort of fellow. He lived in the house where I lived. He attended the church and said it was interesting." When Henkel was asked if Hauptmann was a member of the church, without hesitation he responded: "No, he was not. He was not interested in such things."

The investigation of Theon Wright and Joe Dunninger proved to be even more fruitful when they went to see a man known as Professor Victor who was quite cognizant of those who attended the church run by the Reverend Birrittella. Among those he mentioned were a maid and a butler from over in New Jersey, "the ones mixed up in the Lindbergh case," namely Violet Sharpe, who had committed suicide, and Oliver Whateley, the Lindbergh butler. Instinctively, the men had expected the butler Victor would mention could be none other than Septimus Banks, the chief butler in the Morrow home, with whom Violet was believed to have been romantically inclined. However, they learned that she had been making occasional visits to Birrittella's church with Whateley, lending more evidence that the two were seen together publicly prior to the kidnapping.

Intensified investigation of Isidor Fisch revealed that he also was a member of a lodge called the Chrzanower Young Men's Association located in the Bronx. Here he was known, according to a report given to FBI agent P.M. Breed, as a member who was "always broke and nearly destitute, so broke that he was unable to seek medical aid for his pulmonary condition and on two occasions was unable to pay one-dollar assessments by the lodge." Most of the lodge members said that he appeared to live at a near-poverty level because he was sending large sums of money to his parents. According to Anthony Scaduto in *Scapegoat*: "One member of the group told agent Breed 'that Fisch did a lot of overtime work as a furrier and had a small machine in his room. On this he frequently used to work until one or two o'clock in the morning stitching furs, explaining that he needed the extra money to send to his family in Europe. He also stated that he used the money secured from overtime work to pay his passage to Europe.'"

Throughout his adult life Isidor Fisch seemed to have been a past-master at deceit as he wove himself into the lives of his friends at the Chrzanower Young Men's Association and those of the Reverend Peter Birrittella's church. This appeared to be true with the possible exception of Hans Mueller who never quite learned to trust the man. On the other side of the picture were those close friends, the Henkels, Mrs. Hile, Louise Wollenberg, Hans Kloppenburg, Charlie Schleser, Paul Vetterle, Henry Uhlig, the Fredericksens and a few other acquaintances whom he had fascinated, and then captivated, with his "claims of wealth." And then, of course, there were the Hauptmanns.

But regardless of how he had been accepted by his "friends", today there remains a very distinct truth about the man. Isidor Fisch had definitely been in possession of Lindbergh ransom money. And this we will prove.

To begin with it was a well known fact among the underworld figures in and around the Bronx in late 1932 and early 1933 that a man called Fisch, who frequented the speakeasies there, was selling some "hot bills", which he explained to his potential buyers as being nothing more than counterfeit money. However, the word counterfeit was far from the truth, since they were gold notes, many of them later identified by their serial numbers as Lindbergh ransom bills of ten and twenty dollar denominations.

During the months of concentrated investigation of Fisch, much more evidence was uncovered that pointed to Hauptmann's partner having possession of a goodly portion of Lindbergh ransom bills. Among this evidence was a statement given by Henry Uhlig who had learned from a detective that Fisch had "actually been seen" exchanging money in a pool hall at 86th Street and Third Avenue; a man named Oscar J. Bruchman informed his lawyer, who took the story to the *New York Times*, that Fisch had solicited his help in disposing of some "hot money". And then we have the claim of a convict named Stephe Spitz, who in 1936 came forth and produced $1,000 of Lindbergh ransom bills, explaining that he had purchased them in New York City at forty cents on the dollar.

Yes, there can be no doubt that Fisch had access to some of the $50,000 Lindbergh had paid out with the hope of reclaiming his stolen little son. But how and where did he get it?

CHAPTER FORTY ONE

Fingers Keep Pointing!

It is understandable why Attorney General David T. Wilentz, after already parading before the court such a large assemblage of "gifted liars", each one more than willing to point their fingers of guilt toward the innocent Richard Hauptmann, proceeded to bring on others whose testimony succeeded in "tightening any loose bolts and screws" as he cleverly locked up the minds of the jurors, especially of those who might still have a slight doubt of the man's guilt.

Now, getting back to the trial, we, in fairness, allow each of them their brief time "on stage" before we permit you to read of those who came to the defense of Hauptmann, but who, however, were very tragically not believed in any sense of the word.

One of the witnesses who was used quite effectively by the prosecution happened to be a friend and neighbor of the Hauptmann's, a Mrs. Ella Achenbach who resided at 1253 East 222nd Street, the Bronx, five city lots and a private house distant from the Hauptmann home.

The witness said she had known Mrs. Hauptmann since 1927 when she had employed her as a waitress in her restaurant. She had come to know Richard when he would occasionally call for his wife after she had finished her work. Mrs. Achenbach claimed she clearly remembered the date of the kidnapping as being March 1st, 1932. As the attorney general prodded this "keen memory" of hers while he had her on the witness stand, an unexpected outburst took place from the courtroom floor, one which Wilentz intimated, in his snide manner, had been staged. The questioning of Mrs. Achenbach went along in this fashion:

Q. Did you see Mr. Bruno Richard Hauptmann some time in March, 1932, after the Lindbergh kidnapping? A. Yes, they came home from a trip.

Q. About how long after the kidnapping, March 1st, 1932, was it that you saw him the first time? A.

It was the following day after the kidnapping or two days after the kidnapping.

Q. One or two days? A. Yes, sir.

Q. Where did you see him? A. Anna Hauptmann came to my front porch and told me they just came home from the trip ... She halted abruptly as Anna Hauptmann rose from her chair and shouted:

"Mrs. Achenbach, you are lying!"

Confusion dominated the courtroom as counsel for both the state and the defendant jumped to their feet attempting to gain the attention of Justice Trenchard. Hauptmann appeared bewildered as he heard his usually demure and reserved wife publicly come to his defense. However, he remained quietly seated as he stared at the witness in astonishment.

Attorney General Wilentz could be heard pleading with the Court: "If your Honor please, we object to these demonstrations, whether they are staged or otherwise.", with Fisher's immediate retaliation: "I ask that those remarks be stricken" as Justice Trenchard responsive inquiry: "One moment. who said that?"

Wilentz was more than eager to furnish his quick answer: "Mrs. Hauptmann."

For you to completely understand the magnitude of this hasty exchange of words, and the difficulty both Anna and Richard Hauptmann must have realized themselves to be in as a result of this untrue statement of Ella Achenbach (which I will prove later was completely false), I have included the dialogue that took place between the Court and the attorneys which immediately followed Mrs. Hauptmann's sudden outburst:

The Court: This is the second time this thing has happened.

Mr. Fisher: I think the statement made is sufficient. What I resent, and I don't think it was intended, was the general remark, "whether they were staged or not."

The Court: Oh, well---

Mr.Wilentz: I insist upon that remark, so far as I am concerned, if your Honor please, very respectfully, I insist that it remain in the record, that is just what I meant, whether counsel resents it or not. This is the third time, if your Honor please, not the second, with a witness on the stand before and the delightful defendant addressed him from there yesterday and again today Mrs. Hauptmann. Now if your Honor please, is the

Court conducting it or Mr. and Mrs. Hauptmann? I know the Court is, and so, if your Honor please, I stand by the statement made by me for the State.

Mr. Fisher: The statement just made by counsel is far more unfair than the last statement.

The Court: One moment. I do not think that I will strike any of the statements of the Attorney General from the record. Of course, my anxiety is to conduct this trial in an orderly and fair fashion and I have assumed all the time that that is joined in by counsel.

Mr. Reilly: It certainly is.

The Court: Yes. Now, what has counsel to suggest to the Court in the way of dealing with this problem?

Mr.Wilentz: So far as the State is concerned, if your Honor please, I suggest that we may be permitted to bring witnesses here without being called names while they are testifying.

The Court: Of course, of course, but I am talking now about the outburst, these outbursts.

Mr. Wilentz: I have no suggestion, and I do not know as one can be made except that your Honor has already done to inform the parties offending. I have no desire to exclude any of the parties that are now in the room.

Mr. Reilly: Of course the Court will appreciate that both the defendant and his wife are under high tension, and as I said before, I have no desire to interfere with the judicial calm which has heretofore prevailed, and many times my patience has been attacked and I have sat under the benign influence of your Honor. I think the admonition which your Honor has administered is sufficient.

Mr. Wilentz: I agree sir. I think a judicial admonition to the defendant and his wife would be sufficient. I agree, sir.

The Court: Well, this woman who made this outburst a moment ago I understand is Mrs. ---

Mr. Reilly: The defendant's wife, yes.

The Court: Well, madam, don't you see the impropriety of your interrupting this trial in an outburst of this kind?

Mrs. Hauptmann: I am sorry, your Honor, but I couldn't help it ---

(She appeared to be almost at the point of tears.)

Mr. Wilentz: No. I am sorry if I am offending the Court, but may I state that I object to the lady making any addresses in the courtroom.

The Court: I am asking her whether or not she does not see the impropriety of that thing. Now you see that it was wrong for you to make that outburst, don't you, Mrs. Hauptmann?

Mrs. Hauptmann: Yes, I see it---

The Court: You see that it was wrong, do you not?

Mrs. Hauptmann: Yes, sir, your Honor.

The Court: Now will you promise me and these gentlemen here and the jury that you won't offend in that respect again?

Mrs. Hauptmann: Well, I will try to do, but sometimes I just can't help it.

The Court: But I am asking now whether or not you will promise to keep quiet?

Mrs. Hauptmann: I will.

The Court: Yes. And I think we have in effect that kind of a promise out of the defendant, haven't we?

Mr. Reilly: Yes, sir. In fact he wanted to address the Court yesterday, but I wouldn't permit it, because I didn't want anything interrupted, but he wanted to apologize to your Honor for his outburst.

The Court: Well, we will have to proceed.

Mr. Wilentz: I appreciate counsel's last remark, but I would appreciate it, too, if he joined with me in having it out of the record that the defendant wanted to apologize. I think telling that to the Court in chambers or at side Bar is sufficient. I don't want it to be a part of the record in a matter of argument.

Mr. Reilly: Your Honor invited my reply as to whether I could certify that he would not do it again.

Mr. Wilentz: I think the reply was proper.

The Court: This is rather an embarrassing situation. However, we will have to proceed.

Following the reading by the court stenographer of the question that had provoked the controversy, the questioning continued by Wilentz:

Q. She came to the porch that day? A. She came to the porch.

Q. Did Mr. Hauptmann come? A. She was there about...

Mr. Fisher: That is not responsive. He asked if Mr. Hauptmann came.

Mr.Wilentz: Just let her finish.

A. We were talking about 10 or 15 minutes, about her trip.

Q. Did he come? that is what I want to know. A.

After that Mr. Hauptmann came up also.

Q. All right. When he came there, there were Mr.and Mrs. Hauptmann and yourself on the sun porch: is that right? A. The three of us, yes.

Q. And in addition to what your were talking about, did you observe him; did you look at him? Did you see him? Was he all right? A. He was all right while he was sitting there.

Q. Then what? Did you observe anything about him? What did you see about him? A. Before they went home, she said, "Oh, another thing happened to Richard; he hurt his leg."

Q. Was he there? A. Of course he was there. She said he sprained his ankle pretty bad.

Q. What did he do? A. While she was talking about his injury he bent down and gave his leg a massage-like stroke.

Q. With his hand, you mean? A. With his hand.

Q. Now, let me ask you; did you observe when he got up whether or not this leg condition showed in any way? A. Not when he got up, but when he went down the steps I did.

Q. How did he walk when he went down the steps? A. When he went down my front steps he kind of supported himself on the side of the stoop.

Q. I see. Did he walk with a limp? A. As they were both walking toward their house, he was walking with a limp on the left leg.

During Reilly's cross examination Mrs. Achenbach related that, during the summer of 1928, Mrs. Hauptmann had taken her nine year old daughter along with her to Germany. While there, she testified, Anna had visited her parents, and that during this time her youngster had spent the time with Mrs. Achenbach's parents in Siegen in the province of Westphalia. She said that when they had booked passage for the trip on the steamship York she had purchased a half ticket for her daughter, and in addition had also provided fifty dollars expense money for train fare and whatever else for which it might be needed.

Mrs. Achenbach further testified that since her daughter had celebrated her tenth birthday in Germany, the price of her return trip ticket demanded that full fare be paid. Mrs. Hauptmann, she said, had paid the increased cost and had been reimbursed by her husband in an amount of either $32 or $34, she could not remember which. She claimed she had been repaid either of those amounts on the date Anna received her first pay following her return from Germany.

It is important that we take another look at the testimony of Mrs. Achenbach since it clearly reveals several conspicuous discrepancies. Returning to the date she claimed the Hauptmanns had visited her on the porch of her home, she had sworn under oath that the date had been either March 2nd, or 3rd, 1932. She said she had been informed by her neighbors that the Hauptmanns had just returned from a trip. It was this statement, relative to a trip, that prompted the outburst from Anna Hauptmann. And rightly so. At no time during the police interrogation had it even been as much as hinted that the Hauptmanns had been away on a trip around the March 1st date. And it was derelict of the defense in failing to have Hauptmann and/or his wife to prove this. Had Reilly pursued this statement of Achenbach's he, very easily, could have proved it to be erroneous, which in turn would have served the purpose of exploiting the deception of Achenbach who no doubt was alluding to the trip the Hauptmanns had taken during the summer of 1931. One enjoyed quite a few months before the very convenient, tie-in date of March 1st, 1932, which Achenbach eluded to. However, Achenbach's statement was allowed to stand, without a contradiction, for the record, and so it remained, not as a mere mistake, but instead as a manufactured, deliberate lie which was permitted to be used as another nail in the coffin of Bruno Richard Hauptmann. Because of this, there remains no wonder as to why Anna Hauptmann could not restrain herself and cried out in desperation to defend her innocent husband: "Mrs. Achenbach, you are lying!"

In addition to this, Ella Achenbach was very emphatic about her observance of Richard Hauptmann's <u>very convenient limp</u>, one the prosecution staff intended to tie-in with his <u>doubtless guilt</u>. The inference had been that Hauptmann was, without any possible doubt, Jafsie Condon's "Cemetery John" who had jumped, as he testified, "with the agility of an athlete; the man inside the cemetery gate seized the top of the fence, clambered up on it. Even as he was jumping with the grace and sureness of a cat, he landed on both feet, directly in front of me." Condon had written in his book *Jafsie Tells All* about his meeting with the kidnapper at Woodlawn Cemetery. But, the date of this meeting was Saturday, March 12th. Their plan to claim that Hauptmann had received an injury to his leg as he leaped over the fence should have gone awry at this point had Reilly been on his toes. Surely, in order to prove this as the date of Hauptmann's visit to the Achenbach porch would have had to have taken place on either the 13th or 14th of March and not on the 2nd or 3rd as Mrs. Achenbach contended.

However, in spite of their best laid plans to prove that Hauptmann had received an injury to his leg in a leap from the Woodlawn Cemetery gate on the night of March 12th, as the trial progressed, the prosecution certainly must have realized the error they had made in dates. If challenged on this they would have been forced to use the argument that Richard had been injured in a fall from the ladder outside the child's nursery window on the night of March 1st.

But, as fate would have it, no damage was done to their witnesses' testimony since no challenge came from Hauptmann's defense attorneys. Nevertheless, it would have been rather interesting, as well as embarrassing, to have heard Wilentz explain Hauptmann's fall on March 1st with absolutely no evidence whatsoever on the ground below that window that showed signs of anyone's having fallen there.

But regardless of this gross exaggeration of absolutely unproven "facts" the false words of Ella Achenbach were allowed to stand in the record, among the long list of liars who were willing to sit in the seat of the scornful and nudge Richard Hauptmann a little nearer to his seat in the electric chair.

Ella Achenbach, "a friend" of Anna Hauptmann, proved herself willing to be either coerced or bought into selling her soul to help convict an innocent man.

Another piece of rather convincing testimony, used rather effectively against Hauptmann, was that of Thomas H. Sisk, special agent in the Division of Investigation, U.S. Department of Justice. Basically his discourse had to do with the part he played in the arrest of Hauptmann, the search of his apartment and the discovery of the money found in the Hauptmann garage the following day.

In answer to questions asked by the Attorney General, he told of the happenings as he first entered the Hauptmann garage after breaking the lock on the door. His assistants had been Lieutenant Arthur Keaten of the New Jersey State Police and Inspector John Lyons of the New York City Police. When asked what they had found as they entered, Sisk replied:

We found that the two middle planks on the floor

of the garage were loose, and we took a crow bar and we pried them up.

Q. Yes? A. And underneath them was some freshly disturbed dirt, as though someone had been digging.

Q. Yes? A. So we got a shovel or a spade and we dug down and we found a crock.

Q. Crockery? A. I don't know what it was made out of. It was all covered with mud and I had it---

Q. Was it crockery? A. Yes, I imagine that is what it was, either crockery or some sort of heavy metal.

Q. Had it been buried there? A. It was about a foot underground.

Q. When you say a foot underground was it covered with dirt? A. It was covered with dirt and it had a lid on it and at the bottom was about a quarter---or, about two or three inches of water.

Q. Water? A. Yes, sir.

Q. Still in there, water? A. Yes, sir.

Q. All right now. Did you remove it? A. Yes, sir; we did.

Q. Did you find any money in there? A. No, sir.

Q. All right. A. We questioned Hauptmann as to that jug. He denied knowing anything about it, but the next day when we questioned him, he admitted that he had that money in there three weeks before he was arrested.

Q. In the jug? A. In that jug.

Q. All right, sir. What did you do that day?

Richard Hauptmann: Mister! Mister! You stop lying! You are telling a story!

The defendant could be clearly heard as he cried out, making a desperate attempt to refute the untrue statement made by Sisk. Due to this outburst, Hauptmann received a stern rebuke from Justice Trenchard:

"One moment. Let me suggest to the defendant that he keep quiet. If he has any observations to make, let him make them quietly through counsel."

The reports of tests made on the money, conducted in the police laboratory, confirmed Hauptmann's claim that the bills he found on the shelf of his broom closet had been water soaked, which he said had been caused by a leak in a water pipe in the closet. Because of this the prosecution had been faced with the task of concocting their own explanation as to why the bills they found showed evidence of having been in water.

Surely the testimony of Sisk as he told of finding the jug with two or three inches of water in the bottom would be all that was necessary to explain the condition of the bills to the satisfaction of the judge and jurors. The prosecution staff could now feel secure with this "logical" explanation devised by their own warped imaginations. The police scientists and technicians had found the bills to have at one time been subjected to water, and here then was the reason: "they had been in a crock containing water, two or three inches of it." Hauptmann said this was "pure nonsense" ---and it was. But who was there to believe anything the accused man had to say?

Once again the point had been made and the damage done. Hauptmann upon hearing the words of Sisk had suddenly, not being able to restrain himself, stood from his seat, causing his guards also to rise and force him back into his chair. Justice Trenchard's gavel was heard pounding on his bench.

It is my belief that at this moment, one which proved to be not only a very emotional one for the accused man, the stark realization for Hauptmann had arrived when he could not help but conclude that his accusers were successfully weaving a "web of lies" around things he knew to be truths. Truths which, if believed, would prove to all the honesty and sincerity behind them. To this very moment, I believe Hauptmann had reasoned that his prosecutors would have great difficulty proving his guilt. He was entirely innocent. He knew it. His wife knew it. How would it ever be possible for anyone to prove him guilty of a crime of which he knew absolutely nothing?

But now, with the testimony of Sisk, he was suddenly becoming aware of the dilemma he now was finding himself in. When he had been taken into custody the previous September, it had been quite some time before he came to realize why he was being charged with the horrendous crime. He had great difficulty believing that his friend, Isidor Fisch, could have even remotely been connected with the Lindbergh kidnapping and had left the ransom money with him. The entire matter seemed preposterous. The bold enormity of his arrest seemed to be a giant nightmare, one from which he would soon awaken. But with so many accusing fingers of persons pointing at him, with their tongues speaking lies against him, his belief that he would be acquitted, without any doubt, had begun to crumble. Richard Hauptmann was by this time a troubled man --- and rightly so.

The prosecution made much ado about the testimony of Henry Eichin, a licensed New York State land surveyor who held the position of surveyor for New York City. Mr. Eichen, with the aid of an enlarged map of the Bronx, pointed out the locations of Woodlawn Cemetery, St. Raymond's Cemetery, Dr. Condon's home and the Hauptmann home, and the relative distances between them. Eichin stated that the distance between Hauptmann's residence on East 222nd Street and the main gate of Woodlawn Cemetery, located at East 233rd Street and Jerome Avenue, was three and two-tenths miles; and the distance between Hauptmann's home and the main gate of St. Raymond's Cemetery at the corner of East Tremont Avenue and Whittemore Avenue was estimated to be about four and three-tenths miles. He also testified to the close proximity of Van Cortlandt Park, as well as the home of Dr. Condon, City Island and Hunter Island. The inference made was, quite naturally, the convenience of Hauptmann's home to the locations the kidnapper had chosen for his meeting with Condon. It was an outrage the defense attorneys saw no reason to place an emphasis on the convenience of the home of Isidor Fisch to any one or all of the meeting spots. But, then again, they apparently saw no importance in Hauptmann's true account as to where and how he had obtained the ransom money. Hauptmann needed help and needed it desperately.

Detective John Wallace of the New Jersey State Police told of the events pertaining to Hauptmann's arrest, his interrogation and principally about his personal account of the search of the prisoner's garage. He identified a wooden carpenter's plane, a "Sargent" model about 18 inches long bearing Serial No. 3418, with initials "V.B.M." as well as an "H". This he said was found in the garage. He claimed the other initials on the plane, J.W. to be his, along with the date and time, September 20th, 1934, 11:50 a.m., which he said he had placed there.

In addition to the plane, he identified the newspapers in which the money, also found in the garage, had been wrapped. He further identified the one-gallon shellac can and the twelve packages of gold certificates in ten and twenty-dollar denominations that were found wrapped in newspapers dated June 25th and September 6th, 1934. The papers were copies of the *New York Daily News* and the *New York Daily Mirror*. Sergeant Wallace stated he had placed his initials on everything he found.

Under cross-examination by Lloyd Fisher the

witness agreed that Hauptmann had been subjected to incessant questioning from shortly after his arrest until at least 2:10 a.m. the following day. This was verified by notes taken from Hauptmann and signed by Corporal Horn and Lieutenant Finn. Wallace stated that, regardless of Finn's testimony to the time being 2:10 p.m., September 19th, Finn was mistaken since he personally knew the time to have been 2:10 a.m. September 20th. Wallace also said that Hauptmann had told the police of his finding the money in his broom closet as early as 3:00 or 3:15 o'clock on the afternoon of his arrest.

I deem it very important to make a point here, relative to the two newspapers in which Hauptmann had readily admitted wrapping the money. It is quite evident that the prosecution wanted the jury to assume, as each of them apparently did, that he, the lone kidnapper, had been in possession of the bills from the time he had received the ransom money from Doctor Condon on Saturday, April 2nd, 1932; and, although no bills had ever been traced to Hauptmann's possession, he had kept them for a period of two-and-one-half-years and then suddenly in late August of 1934 had started to spend them.

We should, in fairness to Richard Hauptmann, assume that if he were the lone kidnapper, he would have taken the money to his home, examined it, and then wrapped it in newspapers and proceeded to hide it. Certainly this would have been the logical thing to have done. And in doing this the newspapers used would have been copies bearing the dates of April or some of the earlier months in the year 1932. The defense failed to even hint at this possible deduction which would have again aided their client to some extent.

I find it much more logical to believe Richard Hauptmann's true explanation as to how he found the box filled with money on the top shelf of his broom closet, and how he had dried it, hid it, and then started to spend some of it. We should again remember that not one bill had been traced as being passed from the hands of Hauptmann before September 6, 1934. The earlier bill which turned up in the National City Bank on August 30th of that year went through without the passer being identified. We can, however, reasonably assume that it had been passed by Hauptmann since it appeared shortly after the date he said he had discovered the money. But, again we must point out, it had not been traced to Hauptmann.

If we use just plain reasoning and sound logic it seems to me it would be much easier to put more faith in Hauptmann's explanation. Are we to believe that two and one half years after the crime Hauptmann decided to wrap the money? Yes we are, simply because that is exactly what he did. Proof of this is testified to by the dates of the papers in which the bills were wrapped when they were found by the police. But the authorities who prosecuted the poor man would not have us to believe such foolish tommy-rot. Instead they would have us believe, even to this day, their highly illogical theory they threw at him. It is my personal belief that Richard found the money, exactly as he said he did on Sunday afternoon, August 12th, 1934 (this date is estimated from my own deductions). Then after drying them in his garage, as he claims he did, he started to spend some of the bills rather promiscuously and bravely, without the slightest knowledge of their lurid background and the danger he was creating for himself. Certainly his claim of finding the bills is much more logical than the belief the prosecution had us swallow, that Hauptmann had committed the terrible crime, and failing to pass one bill in two-and-one-half-years, he on a Sunday afternoon in August, 1934, had suddenly decided to "trust his luck" and start spending them hither and yon. I certainly hope I am not asking too much of you by urging you to join me in believing Hauptmann's very reasonable explanation. An explanation that is extremely at odds with the highly illogical actions the prosecution would have us believe. The one the jury "swallowed" as the truth.

One final word about the newspapers in which the money was found. I believe the dates of these two New York newspapers "scream out the truth" of what Hauptmann professed, which if pursued would have gone far to prove the innocence of the Bronx carpenter. However, it was a truth the authorities were to push aside as nothing more than foolish fantasy, a product of Hauptmann's criminal mind. What a shame! What a terrible shame!

C H A P T E R   F O R T Y   T W O

Bruckman Finds A Closet!

David T. Wilentz and his staff of prosecuting attorneys were taking no chance whatsoever of allowing Hauptmann to slip through the web of guilt they had woven around him. The "police experts" continued to take their respective turns in the witness chair offering their "expert opinions" on "certain facts" they could "vouch" for - things they were "absolutely sure of" - things they would never admit there could be even a possible doubt as being "anything but positive factual truth." The pendulum of guilt was steadily hovering over the head of Hauptmann. With so many "positive facts" being presented, could there remain anyone who would still have the audacity to believe this man who had the accusations of so many "experts" mouthing off such a battery of "so-called truths" that "proved" him to be guilty even before the trial had reached the jury?

And yet somewhere in the background there remained a small group of citizens who had not been enveloped and captivated with the "Lindbergh frenzy" of being assured the kidnapper had at last been caught. Thank God there were those who still remained unconvinced of the man's guilt.

Stanley R. Keith of Montclair, New Jersey, employed by the Taylor Wharton Iron and Steel Company as a metallurgist, identified the metal tabs he said he had affixed to the three sections of the kidnap ladder in order to identify the nails. Keith said he had received the nails from Captain Lamb and had returned them to him. He further testified that he had not seen the nails removed from the ladder sections, but he had seen an assistant of Arthur Koehler replace them. He said he had received the nails while he was in Lamb's office in the State Police Training School at Wilburtha, and he had then taken them to his laboratory at his home in Montclair where he retained them for examination. He told the court he had the nails in his possession from October 19th, 1932, until January 15th, 1933, when, on that date, he had personally returned them to Captain Lamb at the Training School. He claimed he had witnessed the nails being replaced. His presence had been needed "in order to see that they were properly assembled so that I could properly identify them as such.", he testified.

I personally find it difficult to understand why it was necessary for Mr. Keith to testify relative to "his seeing" the replacement of the nails. Since he did not witness the original withdrawal of the nails, how then could he honestly testify that the nails he had seen placed in the ladder by Arthur Koehler's assistant had been put back in the exact holes from which they had been removed, especially so since he had not seen the original nails withdrawn? Or for that matter that they were the exact original nails which had been withdrawn by Lamb or whoever? This portion of the testimony was not only ludicrous but proved to be absolutely nothing of any value; that is, with the possible exception, however, of allowing the prosecution to further confound the jury with more "highly important technicalities" of the trial, which many layman accepted as being "additional valuable testimony from professionals" pertaining to the issue at hand. Without their realizing it, this testimony served its purpose, since it acted as aid toward further mixing up the already muddled and confused minds of the lay listeners. After all, this testimony had come from the minds and mouths of "experts" - should not they be speaking nothing but the truth? Of course, these were the authorities, they spoke out with confidence, they could not lie. Only Hauptmann the accused was capable of lying. And soon the jury would literally be told that Hauptmann was actually incapable of telling the truth.

James Paul Petrosino, a member of the New York City Police Department, testified that he, in the company of Sergeant John Wallace of the New Jersey State Police and Leon Turrou of the Department of Justice, had searched the Hauptmann garage and about 11:30 a.m. had found two packages containing Lindbergh ransom money. In one was 100 ten dollar U.S. gold certificates and in the other 83 ten dollar U.S. gold certificates, totaling $1,830. He said they had taken the money to the Hauptmann home where he and Turrou initialed each bill. In the afternoon at approximately 12:40 Detective Edward Murphy of the New York City Police had found a one-gallon tin can in which were stuffed twelve packages of U.S. gold certificates covered by two rags. He said the total value of the money the Erco shellac can contained was $11,930. This, he said, had been discovered in Mrs. Hauptmann's presence.

In addition to the money located, Officer Petrosino said Sergeant Wallace had found a carpenters plane bearing the name Sargent. Although Petrosino said he had searched the work bench, he failed to remember that there were four or five planes of different sizes also found there. Nor did he recall seeing any screw drivers or files. This very adept policeman, who could not remember any tools on Hauptmann's bench with the exception of a lone plane, also had incorrectly identified the date of the major discovery by stating that it had taken place on September 19th, when it had actually been found on Thursday, September 20th, 1934. Again Reilly's defense attorneys had glossed over a slight, but nonetheless important, inaccuracy.

James M. Cashman, a detective of the New York City Police Department, told the court that at approximately nine o'clock the night of Wednesday, September 19th, 1934, he had removed from the Hauptmann garage a chest of tools he found on the floor under the work bench. With him at the time was Sergeant E.A. Haussling of the New Jersey State Police. He testified that the tools were given to a Detective Cronin who put them in Hauptmann's car along with his clothing. The detective then delivered them to the Greenwich Street police station that same night. The chest of tools was brought into court and identified as the same, although he said he had not seen them since they had been turned over to Mr. Brody in the Bronx District Attorney's office several months earlier.

Charles F.W. Enkler, a carpenter employed by the New York City Police Department, told the court of his being sent to the Hauptmann home on September 25th, 1934, in the company of Anselm Cramer, also a carpenter with the New York City Police; a Mr. Wilson, Superintendent of Buildings; Detective Maurice W. Tobin and Inspector Henry Bruckman of the New York City Police; and Trooper Lewis J. Bornmann of the New Jersey State Police.

Enkler's testimony had to do primarily with the search of Hauptmann's garage and of Cramer's finding a piece of board which "to all outward appearances" was part of the garage wall and which also served as a brace. The board had five small holes drilled in it, and in each hole they found ransom bills. Anselm Cramer's testimony verified Enkler's account of the discovery.

Detective Tobin identified the board and the money they extracted. He stated that a total of eight hundred and forty dollars of Lindbergh ransom money had been wedged into the holes after it had been tightly rolled. He explained that hole one had contained $190; hole two $200; hole three $150; hole four $200; with the remaining $100 in hole five. He said that each bill found in the board had been a gold certificate.

But Tobin had much more to tell his audience. Relating to the search he and Inspector Bruckman made of the Hauptmann apartment he went on to tell of their finding some very incriminating evidence. Evidence which the jury had no reason to disbelieve. Evidence which attorney Wilentz pushed to the hilt in his effort to convict the unfortunate Hauptmann.

We pick up the testimony of Detective Tobin as he gave it under the direct examination of Attorney General Wilentz:

Q. Now, were you with Inspector Bruckman at anytime when there was a search of the house? A. I was.

Q. And do you remember when Inspector Bruckman tore down a piece of lumber from the inside of a closet? A. I do.

Q. I want you to take a look at this and see if this is the board that Inspector Bruckman of the New York Police discovered and took out of the Hauptmann home? A. It is.

Q. What day was it that Inspector Bruckman took this board? A. That was on September 25th.

Q. What closet was it? A. In a clothes closet in the nursery room.

Q. In the nursery room? A. Baby's room.

Q. The room that the Hauptmann family had for their child? A. That is right.

Q. Now, will you describe to us the kind of closet it was? Was it a large closet, a roomy closet or was it a narrow one, was it difficult to get in or was it easy to get in? A. It was an ordinary closet, I should judge---

Mr. Wilentz: Have we a picture here?---I should judge approximately four foot long and about a foot wide and I should judge about ten foot high.

Q. About ten feet high and the entrance space about four feet? A. Four foot.

Q. And the depth about one foot? A. About one

foot.

Q. Is that what you mean? A. (No answer.)

Q. If you can tell from this picture, officer, tell me---Will you take a look at it and tell us whether that correctly shows that closet with the door torn off it? A. It does.

Q. That is the closet? A. It is.

Q. And shows correctly that closet, particularly the size of it, I mean, the width and the depth and the height? A. That is about right.

Q. The door being taken off? A. That is right.

(The closet picture was offered and accepted into evidence as Exhibit S-203.)

Q. Now, as you look at Exhibit S-203, you are looking into the closet aren't you? A. I am.

Q. Now this board which I have here in my hand, and which I will ask them to mark for the time being for identification---

(The board was then assigned S-204 for identification.)

---204 for identification; as you look at the closet, in the room looking at the closet, just as you are looking at it at this picture could you see this board S-204 for identification? A. You could not.

Q. Was it on the outside as part of the closet? A. It was not.

Q. Was it on the inside? A. It was on the inside.

Q. What part of the inside part of the closet did this make, S-204? A. It was on the inside on the lefthand side of the closet, facing against the part of the outside.

Q. So that in order to get to this, would you have to get inside the closet, in order to see the outer part of the board, S-204? A. You would.

Q. All right. Did Inspector Bruckman squeeze in there? A. He did.

Q. And then this came out, is that it? A. That is right.

Q. This was taken out? A. Yes.

Q. Did it have "2974 Decatur Avenue" written on it when Inspector Bruckman brought it out? A. It did.

Q. And did it have this telephone number on---no withdraw that. Did it have this Sedgwick or something like that, 3-7154 on it? A. It did.

Q. And then of course it was taken by the department into its possession. A. It was.

The board was subsequently offered in evidence and

the questioning of Detective Tobin continued with cross-examination by Mr. Pope.

Q. As I understand your testimony, sir, this was a part of the trim on the inside of the door frame. A. It is.

Q. And as you stand in the closet and look out, on which side of the door was the board? A. It wasn't on the door.

Q. I mean on the door frame. A. It was on the inside.

Q. You have told us that. As you stand inside the closet and look out into the room, on which side of the door casing was this piece of board that is marked S-204 for identification? A. That would be on the right hand side.

Q. On your right hand side as you were looking out? A. Yes.

Q. Now, I want to call your attention to the markings that were referred to by the Attorney General. There are some figures there; can you see them? A. Yes; yes.

Q. Were they there when you took this board out? A. They were.

Q. Did you see them? A. I did.

Q. Did you see them before the board was taken out? A. I seen them before the board was taken out.

Q. And did you take it loose yourself? A. No, I did not.

Q. And were they in that condition when the board was taken out? A. They were slightly smudged, as you see there.

Q. Well, it appears as though this has been smeared, that is what I mean. A. Well, that is just what I mean; smudge is what I mean for smeared.

Q. And it was exactly like that when it was taken out? A. Yes; yes, I will say so.

Q. I call your attention to the figure 7---I don't want to touch it, but you see the figure 7 here? A. Yes.

Q. In what appears to be 7154? A. I do.

Q. Has that figure 7 been touched up and made more legible? A. I don't think so.

Q. Then I call your attention to the "4." I ask you if that has been touched up and made more legible with a lead pencil? A. I don't think so.

Q. Who was the first person that discovered this piece of wood in the door? A. Inspector Bruckman.

Q. Bruckman? A. Bruckman.

Q. B-r-u-c-k-m-a-n ? A. That is right.

Q. And were you there with him? A. I was.

Q. At the time? A. I was.

Q. And you were searching the house, too? A. I was.

Q. Now what time of the day was it, about? A. Around the noon hour. I should judge it was around eleven or twelve o'clock on the 25th of September.

Q. Now, no one noticed any figures on this piece of wood until Inspector Bruckman squeezed into the closet as you say and the came out and reported to you what he had discovered? A. Not that I know of.

Q. Well, you were there, weren't you? A. I was.

Q. And you know that no one did discover any figures there until after the inspector had squeezed into the closet as you say and then came out? A. That is right.

Q. And when he came out, he announced to the rest of you what he saw? A. I was alongside of the inspector when he found it.

Q. You were in the closet too? A. I was right in the room as Inspector Bruckman leaned into this closet or got into it and he discovered these numbers on the board.

Q. And when he discovered them, then he announced to the rest of you what he saw. A. That is right.

Q. And that directed your attention to it? A. That is right.

Q. And then you took a look? A. I did.

Q. I see. You are under Inspector Bruckman are you? A. I am.

Q. And is he present here today? A. He is.

Q. Now, so far as you know were these numerals, contained on this board, submitted to the handwriting experts? A. That I couldn't say.

Q. How many other closets were there in the Hauptmann house that were examined by you men? A. I believe there were two more besides this one here that we speak of now.

Q. Did Inspector Bruckman squeeze into both of those closets? A.. He did not.

Q. The only one he did squeeze into was the one the figures came out of? A. That is all I know of.

The direct examination of Henry D. Bruckman by the Attorney General proceeded as follows:

Q. Inspector, what is your rank in the Police

Department of the City of New York? A. I am Inspector commanding the 18th Division, Bronx, that is the Detective Division in the Bronx.

Q. What are the ranks, will you tell me so that we will know just the position of your various officers, the detectives, the patrolmen, Inspector? A. Well, the detectives, of course, that is a designation, it is not a rank. The ranks in the Police Department starting with patrolmen are, patrolman, sergeant, lieutenant, captain, deputy inspector, inspector, deputy chief inspector, assistant chief inspector and chief inspector.

Q. So that there is patrolman, sergeant, lieutenant, captain---what is next? A. Deputy inspector.

Q. Deputy inspector. A. And inspector.

Q. And inspector. Is that your rank? A. Yes, sir.

Q. How long have you been connected with the New York City Police Department? A. 29 years.

Q. Were you an inspector September, 1934? A. I was.

Q. And in that capacity were you in charge of the detectives in that section? A. I was.

Q. And particularly in charge of the detectives who worked up at the, in the Hauptmann case there? A. I was.

Q. Did you also participate personally in the investigation up there? A. I did.

Q. I am referring now in the house. A. I did.

Q. I show you exhibit S-204 and ask you if you won't tell me where this board came from, who got it, and the circumstances relating to it? A. As to the circumstances, as a result of the investigation, the interviewing of various witnesses, I had a conversation with the Assistant Chief Inspector. As a result of the conversation with the Assistant Chief Inspector I communicated with the Superintendent of Buildings, Mr. Wilson. That was on the 24th day of September. As a result of that conversation I appeared at Hauptmann's home on the morning of September the 25th. I had a conversation with the carpenters in the presence of the detectives who were assigned to conduct the search. I wanted to give them the benefit of such knowledge as I gained during the course of the investigation, and I went there for the purpose of directing their attention along certain investigational lines. When I got to the room in which this closet is located I found they were clearing the room. It had not been fully cleared. The shelf was still in this closet and a clothes rack and a pole was in the closet.

Q. Is that shown in Exhibit S-203, the clothes rack and the pole (showing exhibit to witness)? A. Yes.

Q. All right. A. I instructed the carpenters to remove the shelf and this pole.

Q. Yes. A. And I entered the closet, and I said to those who were collectively present---

Mr. Pope: Never mind what you said.

Q. Never mind what you said. What did you find, sir? A. I entered the closet---and I backed up into the closet and, as I was in there, I observed what appeared to be a smudge and I put my glasses on and I looked at it and I addressed a remark to Detective Bornmann.

Q. Now, is the smudge that you say you observed on that board the apparent---I think Mr. Pope referred to it as a smear of something, a smudge. Well, we will call it a smudge. Does it still have the smudge there that you referred to? A. Yes, sir.

Q. Now, was there any other smudge on there except that, which called it to your attention? A. No, sir.

Q. Was it the smudge, the smudgy appearance of it, that directed your attention to it? A. I observed that first.

Q. All right. Then you say you put your glasses on? A. I did.

Q. And then on close inspection what did you find? A. I observed the numbers.

Q. What were the numbers? Can you tell them now by looking at it? A. Yes, sir. "2974 Decatur" and 3-7154,---the first letter appears to me to be S, the second letter is not---I can't determine that; the next is DG, and I concluded it was "Sedgwick."

Q. 2974 Decatur Avenue, is that address familiar to you? A. Yes, sir.

Q. Whose address is it? A. Dr. Condon's address.

Q. And you found this you say in the closet of the Hauptmann home? A. Yes, sir.

Q. Did you check up at that time to find out what the other numbers with Sedgwick or what ever it is, 3-7154? A. I know what they were.

Q. What were they? A. Dr. Condon's telephone number.

Q. Was that Dr. Condon's telephone number in

1934? A. No, sir.

Q. That was Dr. Condon's telephone number when? A. In 1932.

Q. But you found the board there in 1934, did you? A. I did.

Q. All right, sir. When this board was found, I take it, Inspector, that eventually Mr. Bruno Hauptmann who was in custody was told about it, was he not? A. Yes, sir.

Q. Were you present? A. I was.

Q. Who else was present, sir? A. District Attorney Foley.

Q. Tell me, please, what if anything was said to Mr. Hauptmann or what he said with particular reference limiting it to this board? A. He was asked whether he recognized the board as coming from his house and he said yes; he was asked whose handwriting it was in; he said he recognized the 2974 as his handwriting. Then Mr. Foley asked him whether he didn't write it all and he said he thought he did. Mr. Foley asked him how he happened to write it. He said, "Well, I was a little bit interested, the papers were full of the Lindbergh case and I was a little bit interested and I must have had a newspaper and probably was putting paper on the shelf in the closet and I copied down this number.

Q. Now, were you in the court room in The Bronx during the extradition proceedings of the State of New Jersey against Bruno Richard Hauptmann in an effort to bring him to the State? A. I was.

Q. You remember when he was on the stand? A. I recall him being on the stand, yes, sir.

Q. If you don't recollect his testimony Inspector you tell me. Do you remember what his answer was when he was asked under oath whether or not that was his handwriting? A. I don't recall.

Q. You don't recall? A. No.

Cross examination by Mr. Reilly:

Q. Were you in charge of the Bronx when the ransom money was paid? A. I was.

Q. Before that you were in charge of Chinatown, weren't you? A. No, sir.

Q. The lower part of New York? A. No, sir.

Q. Were you ever a captain there? A. No, sir.

Q. When did you come into the Bronx as an inspector? A. I came back in April of 1930.

Q. April, 1930? A. Yes, sir.

Q. And all these detectives in The Bronx are working under you: is that correct? A. Those that are assigned to The Bronx; yes, sir.

Q. How many of them are here: four or five? A. No, I don't think there are that many. I think at the present time that there is just one: Detective Tobin.

Q. So that you knew before you went into this closet Dr. Condon's address. didn't you? A. Frankly I must admit that I did not know it. It had slipped my mind.

Q. Didn't you know that the ransom money was passed over the hedge? Did you know that? A. The ransom money?

Q. Ransom money was passed over a hedge. A. I have read about it; yes, sir.

Q. And you had never met Dr. Condon in all the time you had been in The Bronx? A. Oh, yes.

Q. And you never asked him where he lived? A. I know the house in general. I know Dr. Condon's house, but frankly I didn't remember the number.

Q. Well, you have a pretty good memory, haven't you? A. Yes, sir; I have.

Q. And you knew he had a telephone in 1932? A. I didn't have any personal knowledge that he had a telephone.

Q. Didn't you know your men were communicating with him and investigating him? A. No. I think that is a mistake, counsel.

Q. You don't know that? A. I know my men were not investigating him.

Q. You know the men from the main office were investigating him? A. I wouldn't have any knowledge of that, counsel.

Q. In other words, you want this jury over here in Jersey to believe that a matter in The Bronx in which you were interested, the Headquarters downtown, the chief, the Commissioner and others would not know anything about it: is that it? You want the jury to believe what you say, don't you? A. I suppose the jury will judge my testimony the same as anyone else's. I am not interested in the final outcome of the case. I am simply here to tell the story as I remember it and as I know it.

Q. Now you are not concerned in the final outcome of this case, you say? A. Not---

Q. Is that right? A. Not as a police officer, no.

Q. Well now, as a police officer, if the crime of extortion was committed in this case, it was committed in your territory, wasn't it? A. Yes, sir.

Q. Yes. And as a police officer you are interested in the crime of extortion for which this defendant has been indicted in the Bronx? Aren't you? A. Yes, I am interested in all crimes committed in my--

Q. I am talking about this case. A. Yes, sir. I am interested in the crime of extortion, as it occurred within my jurisdiction, it is my responsibility.

Q. And in your district and through your efforts this man was indicted in the Bronx, wasn't he? A. Well, I may have contributed, but I wouldn't say it was entirely due to my efforts.

Q. You did contribute? A. Yes.

Q. You testified before the Grand Jury? A. Yes, sir.

Q. Yes. In an indictment that now lies against him? A. Yes, sir.

Q. And under which indictment he was there when he was extradited here? A. That is correct.

Q. So you are concerned in the extortion case in New York? A. Not in the outcome. I am concerned in so far as my responsibility is concerned.

Q. You don't go into a case and arrest somebody and then sit down and say "I don't care if he is turned loose or convicted" do you? Now was there an electric light in the closet? A. This closet did not have an electric light.

Q. Was there any light in the closet, any artificial light? A. No, excepting that it was on the 25th day of September; I know I left there at 11:15 a.m.; there is a reasonably large window in this room and I would say the light was fairly good.

Q. In the closet? A. In the closet; yes, sir.

Q. In the corner of the closet in which this board was found. A. No, that isn't a corner, there is a trim on the inside of a door and---

Q. Inside of a door? A. On the---yes, it is the inside of a jamb of a door; it is a trim. I think that is what you call it.

Q. Does it swing with the door? A. Oh, no; it is stationary.

Q. Stationary? A. Yes.

Q. Well now, here is a doorway, will you show us where the trim was? A. Well, if you come inside of this door here, I would say the trim was right here. (Witness steps inside door in the courtroom and points to board.)

Q. In the closet? A. Right here.

Q. In the closet? A. That is right.

Q. All right. The inside trim of the door of the closet, which trim you would face if you had your back up against the wall of the closet? A. That is correct.

Mr. Wilentz: Immediately adjoining the door?

Mr. Reilly: Yes.

Q. And there was no artificial light in that closet? A. No, sir.

Q. Had any other detectives been in there before you that you know of? A. In the closet?

Q. Yes. A. Not to my knowledge.

Q. Had you been in any other closet? A. I think that I did, with other closets in a measure, something similar to what I did here.

Q. And you were the person that discovered these numbers, the first person, is that correct? A. Yes, sir.

Q. So far as you know? A. Yes, sir.

Q. And did your men search the house, were they ordered to search the house? A. They were.

Q. They are fine detectives, are they not? A. Well---

Q. By that I mean men of vast experience in the police department and length of time. A. They are not all trained, some are in the process of training and some are trained.

Q. Were there any trained ones there? A. Well, I would say reasonably well trained, yes.

Q. Yes. They were searching for evidence, weren't they? A. Yes.

Q. They only had one floor of an apartment to go through, is that correct? A. No, that is not correct.

Q. Well, how much more did they have, in the house? A. Well, they had the floor of the apartment; they had an attic or a hanging ceiling, I would call it; they had a cellar; they had a garage.

Q. I am talking about the house now, Inspector? A. Well---

Q. Stick to the house. A. Of course it would all be part of the same search.

Q. Yes. How many rooms in this apartment that they had to search for evidence? A. Four rooms and bath.

Q. And how much of an attic, over one room or over two? A. It is a hanging ceiling. It is over the entire house.

Q. Is it a Queen Ann shape front, peak roof? A. Yes, but it is a hanging ceiling, it is not an attic.

Q. And the cellar is equally shared by the people

who live downstairs? A. Yes, sir.

With those words the testimony of Inspector Bruckman came to an end. The judge and jury had been informed of how the writing, identified as being Hauptmann's, had been found by the alertness of a New York police officer. This, of course, should not be made light of in any respect, since it was a very damning piece of evidence used against the accused man --- and rightly so.

However, as important as it proved to be in bringing about Hauptmann's conviction, it should be understood that at that time the real truth, and the utter subterfuge behind it all, was not known by those who would soon be called on to render a verdict. The actual truth of the board and its markings had been learned from the "loose tongued mouth" of a member of the press, a person whose act was despicable and vile, to say the very least. But more about this fact later as we move on with more of the court testimony about this "sensational" find from inside a closet.

The next witness called was the confidential stenographer of the Bronx District Attorney Samuel J. Foley. Attorney General Wilentz inquired if he had taken down the questions the District Attorney had asked Bruno Richard Hauptmann, and his subsequent answers, on September 25th, 1934. Assuring Wilentz that he had, we now proceed with the questioning of Mr. Benjamin Arac from that point:

By Mr. Wilentz:

Q. Will you please proceed. A. Statement taken on September 25th, 1934, in the office of the District Attorney at 11:55 a.m.

Q. Will you tell us the first question. A. Hauptmann, I want to ask you some questions about this board. You know it is from your closet in your own house, don't you? A. It must be. At that point I marked a tag, marked it Exhibit 1, and put it around the board.

Q. Is the tag that you talk about marked around the board, which is now this exhibit referred to---I mean is this the board you were referring to, Exhibit S-204? A. Yes, that is right.

Q. The answer you say was, it must be. The questions are by District Attorney Foley? A. That is correct.

Q. All right. A. Q. It is the same kind of wood, your handwriting is on it. A. Yes, all over it.

Q. What did you write on that board? Read it to the stenographer. A. I can't read it anymore.

Q. Who rubbed it out? Can you read the address on it? A. 2974, I can't make out the first. I remember the number---. I read the number down below 37154.

Q. What else can you read on that board that you wrote yourself? A. I can't read, that's a t u and , another one I can't make out.

Q. That is Dr. Condon's address, isn't it? A. I don't know.

Q. Why did you write it on the board? A. I must have read it in the paper about the story. I was a little bit interest, and keep a little bit record of it and maybe I was just on the closet and was reading the paper and put down the address.

Q. How did you come to put the telephone number on there? A. I can't give you any explanation about the telephone number.

Q. Your only explanation for writing Dr. Condon's address on this board and telephone number is that you were probably reading the paper in the closet and you marked it down, is that correct? A. It is possible that a shelf of two shelfs in the closet and after a while I put new papers always on the closet and we just got the paper where this case was in and I followed the story of course and I put the address on there.

Q. Your answers to my questions here are made of your own free will, is that correct? A. Yes.

Wilentz was taking every advantage of Hauptmann's weak attempt to explain, and account for, the appearance of the "mysterious" writing which had been found on the jamb on the inside of the closet in his son, Manfred's, room. The writing had looked like his, and as bewildered as he was, his only explanation had been that he was a carpenter, and carpenters are known to write figures on wood. Nevertheless, in spite of his inability to give the police any logical reason for their being there, he continued to admit that he believed it was his writing.

The questioning of Benjamin Arac continued as he read more from the notes he made of the interrogation of Hauptmann in Sam Foley's office on September 25th, 1934.

Q. And the answers you make you make of your own free will without any compulsion or promise whatever? A. Yes.

Q. Is there anything more you want to say about it or add to it? A. No. About them two numbers, I am sure it was 500 or 1,000 dollar bills.

Q. When you say those two numbers, you don't refer to anything on this board, when you talk of the two numbers you don't mean anything on this board, but other numbers written on the door? A. On the door.

Q. But not on this piece? A. I can't remember where I put it.

Q. And you say that they refer to bills of high denomination? A. Yes.

"Q. Is there anything else you wanted to add? A. No.

"Q. Do you remember the day that you wrote this memorandum on the board? A. No.

"Q. You remember that you did write it? A. I must write it, the figures; that's my writing.

"Q. The writing is yours too, isn't it? A. I hardly can read it.

"Q. From what you see of it, it is your writing, isn't it? It is your figures and your writing? A. I really can't remember when I put it on.

"Q. Regardless of when you put it on, it is your figures and your writing, isn't it? A. The writing I can't make out so very clearly; I don't know.

"Q Do you know who rubbed it out or tried to rub it out? A. No.

"Q. Do you remember the date that you marked Dr. Condon's telephone number on the board in your house? A. Absolutely not.

"Q. You can't fix the time? A. No, sir, impossible.

"Q. Do you remember the time that you marked the numbers of the bills? A. No.

"Q. Did you mark first the telephone or the bills? A. I can't remember that. Question---"

Q. Just a minute. A. "Did you get---"

Q. Just a minute. I think that is all on that point. I want to see. I would like to have you refer to any other questioning about this particular exhibit that we have now and direct your attention specifically to September the 26th, 1934. A. There is some.

Q. Which is the next day. A. There are one or two---

Q. Please refer to that and tell me if by inspecting your notes you can tell me whether they referred to this piece of wood again? A. Yes.

Q. Please give me those questions and answers.

A. "Hauptmann, yesterday I showed you a piece of wood from your house with Condon's address and phone number on it; is that correct? A. Yes.

Q. You admitted that you wrote that on the board? A. Yes.

That is all on that statement about that board.

The prosecution had done everything they could to hog-tie, nail down, and lock up the apparent guilt of Hauptmann by his utter inability to offer them a logical explanation for the closet board with Condon's address and phone number on it. Most of the courtroom spectators, with Justice Trenchard's permission, of course, would have applauded the verbal maneuvers the attorney general had put into play as he clearly exhibited to them that by Hauptmann's own admission of having written them, he had all but sealed his own death warrant.

Although Hauptmann had explained that the numbers on the inside of the door were possibly those of large bills of $500 or $1,000 denomination that Isidor Fisch had given him to be used for the purchase of stocks, he said he could not verify this as true. However, after the federal agents checked the serial numbers, it proved that Hauptmann had been honest, inasmuch as the numbers checked out to be of bills of five-hundred and one-thousand-dollar denominations, as Hauptmann said he thought they might be. The inference, however, had naturally been that the numbers were those of some ransom bills, which Wilentz very well knew them not to be. But, the wily attorney let this slide by without any comment, and let the jury assume they were. And Riley, once again was willing to allow an important point to pass by without as much as a challenging comment.

What a shame so much time had been taken to "prove" something Hauptmann "confessed to doing", while in reality something of which he knew nothing about. In our next chapter we will exploit one of the most revolting perpetrations ever fostered on an innocent human being.

CHAPTER FORTY THREE

Guess What? Cassidy Claimed The Closet!

At this point it is hard to understand how you can still entertain even a semblance of a doubt that Bruno Richard Hauptmann could be anything but innocent of the crime of kidnapping and murder.

Although there is much more to tell, I am certain that most of you have already seen how that one lone element of circumstance, the finding of $14,600 of Lindbergh ransom money in his possession, of which he had a perfectly reasonable and believable explanation, had been taken and used in chorus with the cleverly assembled mass of manufactured evidence and despicable perjured testimony of many persons to nail their prisoner to the crime as its sole perpetrator.

But, how could these things be? How could they be possible, we are forced to inquire? It certainly must have taken the cooperation of a great number of "players" to have been crafty enough to have pulled such a giant ruse, one which was to be believed whole-heartedly by a trusting jury. But this was not necessarily so since the fact remains that only a few key "players" were positioned and moved in the proper way, as in a game of chess, each used to gain their objective by "check-mating" Hauptmann into a sentence of death in the Trenton State Prison.

It would have been dangerous for them to have used more. All they had done was to line up the few who were necessary for the success of their plot and who, of course, were willing to sell their souls deep in a performance of acts labeled "filthy treacherous deception". Acts much too diabolical for words to adequately express. These are those who were <u>just plain liars</u> in every possible description and sense of the word.

As despicable as the performance of some of the police authorities, as well as others, were in their willingness to condescend to tactics of such a low degree, it must be understood that most of the officers who had anything at all to do with the case were above reproach. They conducted themselves as men and women of honor who had only one objective in mind, that being their responsibility of doing their part in seeing the crime successfully solved in an honorable and truthful manner. No one would ever have dared to approach them with the proposition that they be willing to put the honor of the pledge they had taken and the badge of pride many of them wore to dishonor the police department they served in order to put Hauptmann in the electric chair. Thank God there were only a few who were "right ready" to have their integrity trampled in the mud, grime and filth of the ground under the feet of the very people they had pledged themselves to serve in any way other than an honorable fashion.

But to those who stooped to the very lowest in order to see Bruno Richard Hauptmann "fry", as they put it, we can only refer to them as contemptible "tiny people" who have earned for themselves the right to wear the title of "police wretches" at the top of the list easily identifiable as <u>police corruption at its very worst</u>!

"I pledge that while I am Police Commissioner, the Police Department will strive toward ... the ultimate end that every law-abiding citizen ... and this includes every member of every minority group, and every policeman as well ... , may be free to enjoy the liberty which such a climate will make possible." This promise was made by one of New York City's finest police commissioners, Vincent L. Broderick, at the time he was sworn into office. What he had promised to do was to see that all those who enforce the law, from him, the commissioner, to all under him including those who patrol beats, were not, under any circumstances, permitted to "wink at the law" simply because they are on the side of the law and are called on daily to see that laws are obeyed. To his credit, this is exactly what Commissioner Broderick succeeded in doing.

And yet, in 1934, '35 and '36 this was blatantly ignored in the investigation following the arrest, trial and conviction of Hauptmann in the Lindbergh case. This must be clearly recognized and conceded to by the convincing evidence I have presented to you in the chapters of this volume. But, there is much more I must relate before you can render your final verdict.

You will remember that immediately after the crime, Trooper Frank Kelly had been unable to raise even a portion of a fingerprint from anywhere in the child's nursery. This in spite of the fact that both Anne

Lindbergh and Betty Gow had raised and lowered the windows, touched the broad windowsills, as well as other items in the room, all done with their greased fingers which still undoubtedly carried the oil from the Vicks ointment which they had applied to the little boy's chest. And then after Kelly's inability to raise prints from the kidnap ladder, several days later, Doctor Erastus Meade Hudson offered his services and ability of lifting latent fingerprints by using a new silver-nitrate method he had developed. His offer was accepted and he was successful in raising more than 500 prints from the ladder. In addition to these, he discovered and developed a clear set of prints from the child's toys, table, high chair, and other objects all believed to be those that little Charles had left behind him on things he had touched during the previous week-end.

At the time of the arrest of Hauptmann he was subjected to almost constant fingerprinting of his inked fingers. In addition to the customary plain and rolled prints being taken, he was forced to have the police take inked impressions of his fingertips, his palms, as well as from the sides or edges of his hands, which was a very unusual procedure. This practice was done on many occasions on the days following his arrest, the police using the excuse for this that none of the previous prints they had taken were clear enough for comparison.

It was during this time that Dr. Hudson was approached by two New Jersey police officers, Captain John Lamb and Trooper Kelly. They questioned the doctor as to how one would go about counterfeiting fingerprints and whether it would be possible? Hudson told them that counterfeiting of prints was indeed possible but, "I would be able to detect the difference between real and counterfeit fingerprints." Lamb appeared to be disappointed when learned it would be impossible to do. There is little doubt that Lamb had it in his mind to further frame Hauptmann by means of falsified fingerprints. This over zealous Captain Lamb was desperate to play the role of "super cop."

Members of the FBI, under the able direction of John Edgar Hoover, voiced their own opinion of Captain Lamb. Keaten and Lamb were both regarded by Special Agent Thomas Sisk as nothing more than "third-raters", regarding Lamb in particular as being "None too bright", while a newspaper reporter likened his red face to that of "an angry tomato."

The following is Sisk's evaluation of them to his

superior, J. Edgar Hoover:

"...this agent had a conversation with them on one occasion during which they spent considerable time criticizing Scotland Yard. After exhausting this subject, they launched upon a tirade against the Northwest Mounted Police, then the New York Police, the Department of Labor Investigators, Post Office Inspectors and the Treasury Department ...

"On several occasions Lieutenant Keaten and Captain Lamb have openly bragged about the fact that their men have orders not to give the New York police officers or the Division [FBI] agents any information whatsoever. It is a practice of Captain Lamb to frequently criticize the New York Police, particularly Lieutenant Finn, who is characterized by Lamb as a 'nitwit', Captain Oliver as 'a sugar man' and Commissioner O'Ryan as 'an old broken-down General', that 'Roosevelt and his gang' were dangerous Communists, and that when the Republicans were elected, 'Hoover goes out and Schwarzkopf goes in.'"

The cooperation between the three investigating bodies from the opening of the case had been reprehensible. The New Jersey authorities, feeling certain they could solve the crime without the aid of either the Department of Justice or the New York Police Department, were a tragic example of shameful teamwork. Later in this treatise you will read a series of letters which passed back and forth between Colonel Schwarzkopf of the New Jersey State Police and J. Edgar Hoover, Director of the FBI. These letters explicitly demonstrate, as nothing else can, how appalling the deficiency in cooperation had become. The dispatches clearly point to Schwarzkopf as the offender by his downright refusal to lend his aid to the Federal Government. The attitude of the New Jersey State Police superintendent toward the FBI had no doubt been perverted, at least in part, by the constant reference of Lamb and Keaten of the Federal agents as "those educated investigators". But, regardless of his feelings toward Hoover and his men, there was still no reason for his failure to cooperate in such a case of this magnitude, or for that matter any case of any size, which would have caused Hoover to state: "It's hard to believe, but we still haven't received from them the fingerprints of Hauptmann for our files --- we never had them" ...

Director Hoover had his own opinion as to the way the investigation in New Jersey had progressed. In addition to the lack of cooperation he had been receiving from the Jersey authorities, and the doubts he held of Lindbergh's amazing ability, more than two-and-one-half years later, to identify Hauptmann's voice as the voice of the same man he heard from a considerable distance, call out only two words, 'Hey Doctor' to Dr. Condon while 'Cemetery John' was inside St. Raymond's Cemetery on the night of Saturday, April 2, 1932, Hoover had many other bothersome doubts.

Director Hoover's perplexity must have been great as two men, in whose integrity he had great faith, expressed to him their feelings relative to the voice identification of Lindbergh. Assistant Attorney General Lanigan and his own Special Agent Tamm stated their unbelief, with Tamm saying he thought it "remarkable" that such a claim had been accepted without any doubt whatsoever. Hoover, in a memo to Tamm, dated October 9, 1934, claimed he too, was "highly skeptical of it."

It should be noted here that the FBI withdrew itself from its involvement in the case on October 10, 1934, three weeks after the arrest of Hauptmann. Hoover was deeply concerned with his suspicion that the state troopers in Jersey were formulating a case against their prisoner. There were too many loose ends and unanswered questions which completely dissatisfied Director Hoover. To begin with he had grave doubts about the validity of the board which was removed from the Hauptmann attic and the prosecution's presenting it as being fashioned and used by Hauptmann in the construction of rail 16 of the kidnap ladder. Another factor in the case that Hoover had trouble accepting was that of the thousands of dollars they attributed as having been spent by Hauptmann as he played the stock market at Steiner, Rouse and Company, making substantial deposits of his own in various banking institutions, in addition to the money he admitted keeping in his home in a tin box, not one bill ever turned up that was claimed to have been passed by Hauptmann until dates following his discovery of the box of bills his "friend" Fisch had left in his care.

Hoover's skepticism about the wood taken from the Hauptmann attic had certainly been warranted because of his personal suspicions that Bornmann and Koehler had "played hanky-panky" by faking this evidence used against an unsuspecting and trusting Richard Hauptmann. This support, however, was of no help to the prisoner during his trial since it was not officially known until Hauptmann's execution.

Dated May 26, 1936, in a memo from Federal Agent Rosen to Special Agent Tamm, we read:

"The identification of the wood in the ladder, resulting in the opinion that the wood in the attic of Hauptmann's residence was identical with that of the ladder, was developed subsequent to the withdrawal of this Bureau from the active part in the investigation, and occurred after the New Jersey Police had rented the Hauptmann residence.

You will also recall that at one stage of the trial of Hauptmann it was indicated that efforts would be made by the defense counsel to subpoena records of this department relative to Arthur Koehler, with the thought in mind that the defense could establish and check that Arthur Koehler's story concerning the wood identification could be proved as having been fabricated by the joint efforts of the New Jersey State Police and the New Jersey Prosecutor's Office in co-operation with Arthur Koehler. However, this request was not received by the Bureau from the defense attorneys."

Of course it had not been received. Largely due to the poor defense Hauptmann was given by his very incompetent lawyer, "Death House Reilly." Years later when asked about this failure of the FBI to come to the aid of Hauptmann with testimony which could have helped Hauptmann, Hoover very tersely stated: "We simply were not subpoenaed."

Before the FBI departed from its participation in the case, Hoover had been aware that the New Jersey authorities were lacking evidence with which they could extradite and prosecute Hauptmann for kidnapping in their state. He realized they were faced with a dilemma. Director Hoover had been informed by his special agent Sisk that: "The New Jersey authorities do not have one single reliable witness who can place Hauptmann in the vicinity of Hopewell prior to or on the date of the crime."

With the press badgering Schwarzkopf for daily statements, the colonel had a difficult time satisfying their thousands of anxious readers with any concrete statements pertaining to Hauptmann's removal over to Jersey to stand trial. Schwarzkopf's delay was caused simply by his inability to find any eye-witnesses who would claim they had seen their prisoner near Hopewell.

Requesting Governor Moore for his cooperation by granting the necessary extradition papers which would allow them to take Hauptmann over to New Jersey, the good governor in turn kept asking for the evidence he needed which would permit him to sign the papers. Not being able to find anyone, the state authorities realizing they were in a bind, very simply set out to find someone, even if they must stoop to the vile act of "inventing" him. And by doing this they came up with one of their chief liars --- Millard Whited.

From the time of Hauptmann's incarceration hundreds of false rumors and stories had been printed in nearly every major newspaper. News accounts were invented by reporters in order to give them a story for the next edition of their papers. For instance there appeared a story that Hauptmann had attempted to commit suicide; one that related to its readers how Hauptmann had confessed to his cellmate that he was guilty of killing the child. All were ridiculous, but nevertheless harmful, since at no time had Hauptmann attempted to take his life, and at no time was he ever in a cell with another person. However, as untrue as these accounts were, many people believed them and passed them on as factual.

During the great activity generated by the interest in the solution of the Lindbergh kidnapping some newspaper reporters were granted special privileges by the police in order to help them gain first hand, on the spot, news coverage. A few of these "news hounds", the over zealous, went so far as to plant some phony items near the various crime scenes with the intentions of their being found by the police, thus giving them an "inside" story complete with pictures taken by a photographer from their paper who, "quite conveniently", just happened to be standing nearby.

One such occurrence had taken place at the time the corpse, believed to be that of Lindbergh's child, was discovered near Hopewell. In another report by Agent Sisk to Director Hoover two of these practices had been discovered and labeled as being bogus: "According to the newspapers some diapers were found near the body, but the State Police had conclusive proof that these were planted by a newspaper reporter. Also an old broken shovel was found there, but the State Police had a confession from a man who planted it and he admitted having received $5 from a New York reporter for making the plant."

Of all the reporters assigned to cover the arrest

of Hauptmann, Tom Cassidy of *The New York Daily News* seemed to be one of the most privileged when it came to obtaining police permission to enter otherwise restricted areas to others. It was a practice of some newspapers to put some police officers on a "special unofficial payroll" in return for favors rendered their star reporters. Such could possibly have been the case of Tom Cassidy. However, regardless of any prior arrangement, Cassidy certainly took advantage of the permissiveness the police gave him by allowing him "free access" to the Hauptmann home during the time Bornmann rented it for the State Police.

One other piece of evidence which proved to be a mystery, not only to FBI Director Hoover, but to others as well including old "Jafsie" Condon himself, was the board taken from inside the closet in Hauptmann's home on which had been penciled Condon's address and telephone number. Several people questioned why Hauptmann would have done such an incriminating thing. Since the Hauptmanns did not have a phone in their apartment, and could have used a public phone just a few blocks away, it seemed senseless to have put Condon's number where it was found, especially so when the Condon number was listed in the public directories. In addition to this the apparent serial number of a bill also listed on the back of the closet door was not one of the ransom bills.

When Hauptmann was confronted in District Attorney Sam Foley's office in the Bronx, he was asked to give a reason for the writing found on the board. Assuming it to be his, since they told him it had come from a closet in his apartment, (without mentioning which closet), Hauptmann gave them the only reasonable answer he could. Thinking Foley referred to the larger kitchen closet, where one could stand upright, he explained that he, as do other carpenters, often make notes on wood.

In his attempt to give Foley the only honest answer he could, Hauptmann had offered a very logical reason for their finding, what even he believed to have been put there by him. At this point in time, Richard Hauptmann was interested in only one thing, to be perfectly honest with his interrogator in order that he be permitted to return to his dear wife whom he knew was anxiously waiting for him. As for his entertaining even a remote thought that the writing had been put there by someone in an attempt to frame him was beyond belief at this time, so naturally he assumed what they found was of his own doing.

His answer to Foley's direct question pertaining to whether it was Dr. Condon's address and telephone number they found there, brought this response: "I don't know." And when asked why he had written it on the board, Hauptmann gave a very weak explanation: "I must have read it in the paper about the story. I was a little bit interest, and keep a little bit record of it and maybe I was just on the closet and was reading the paper and put down the address." And then, with a belief that Foley was talking about a larger kitchen closet, no doubt the one in which he placed their old newspapers before permanently discarding them, he explained: "It is possible that a shelf or two shelfs in the closet and after a while I put new papers always on the closet and we just got the paper where this case was in and I followed the story of course and I put the address on there."

Then followed Foley's question as to whether Richard remembered the day he had written it, to which he received a negative answer. And then his clinching questions with their convincing answers in which Hauptmann responded that it was his writing.

Q. You remember that you did write it? A. I must write it, the figures, that's my writing.

Q. The writing is yours too, isn't it? A. I hardly can read it.

Q. From what you see of it, it is your writing, isn't it? It is your figures and your writing? A. I really can't remember when I put it on.

Q. Regardless of when you put it on, it is your figures and your writing, isn't it? A. The writing I can't make out so very clearly. I don't know.

Unknowingly Hauptmann had doomed his own soul. The condemned man, never suspecting that a frame-up had been put in progress had agreed to something which had completely baffled him. Who else but me, he wondered, could have written it? Although he was to admit later that the only explanation he could give them had sounded ridiculous even to him, they were demanding an answer and this was the only "logical" one he could think of giving them. The very weakness of his answer had given them the "strength" they needed, with such conclusive evidence that Hauptmann knew Condon at the time of the ransom negotiations, for Foley to prove his case of extortion against Hauptmann before the Bronx Grand Jury the previous September.

Of all the things ever written, printed, spoken, or photographed which were brought forth to accuse Hauptmann and thus pave a broad path which eventually led him to the electric chair, nothing was more dastardly and vile than the accusations based on the penciled writings found inside his closet which the police claimed he had put there. For many months the truth as to who actually wrote them inside the small closet remained a mystery. Although the police, and most people who had learned of it, seemed to be thoroughly satisfied that "that terrible fiend Hauptmann" was the culprit, there were still some who would not believe he had done it. And how right they were! From beginning to end, the entire thing was a flagrant hoax. Diabolical in itself, the act stood far and above as the most beastly thing a person, declared to be in his right mind, could ever perpetrate and execute on a fellow human being.

It was unfortunate that this deception had not been known earlier. Had attorney Fawcett been aware of the "closet frame-up" it would have been impossible for the Grand Jury to have brought in a true bill of indictment against Hauptmann. This false evidence could have been exploited, showing what means the prosecution staff had resorted to in its efforts to extradite the unfortunate Bronx carpenter over to New Jersey for trial.

In fairness, however, it should be stated that it is my belief that the prosecutors, at least most of them, could not have been aware of this diabolical act. Had they been, it is difficult to think that they would have used it to the extent that they did. Nevertheless, the fact remains that they did use it, either knowingly or unknowingly, and it was effectively used to eventually place Hauptmann in the electric chair.

Hauptmann, although he remained in a complete quandary as to how and/or why he had written the references to Condon within the confines of his closet, had reluctantly accepted the statements of the police as factual since they had told him they had been found there, which generated his feeble explanation: "I must have read it in the paper about the story. I was a little bit interest, and keep a little bit record of it and maybe I was just on the closet and was reading the paper and put down the address. I can't give you any explanation about the telephone number." Of course he couldn't explain it. How could he? Hauptmann was not responsible for placing anything there. Had the truth of that writing been known at that time many aspects of the entire trial might have been changed. The verdict could have been reversed and Hauptmann just might have walked away a free man. However, this conjecture is based merely in light of this one segment of "framed evidence". We must not lose sight of the fact that much more additional "manufactured evidence" had been used against this innocent man.

Every segment of deception, plus the blatant lies used to convict Hauptmann, were heinous in every devilish way one would choose to describe them. However, if any one act can be singled out as being at the top of the list, the winner would have to be the "Condon closet writing". This selection is judged not solely on the vicious act of falsely and purposely planting the evidence which had served its purpose of pointing just one more accusing finger against the very innocent prisoner, but because of the manner in which, and by whom, it was done. The perpetrator was a newspaperman with "a sick mind", a member of the fourth estate who, when the truth was learned, proved to be a disgrace to everyone within the elite profession he had chosen to follow.

The hoax was played out in this fashion. Tom Cassidy, a reporter working on the case for his paper, *The New York Daily News*, was one of the privileged journalists permitted to enter the Hauptmann home at will in order that he obtain first hand developments of the case. It was "a crime in itself" that Cassidy allowed his zeal for information to "run wild" as he literally planted his "own manufactured evidence" which helped to convict an innocent person.

Because of an intense desire deep within himself to beat the competitive reporters of other newspapers assigned to the case, Cassidy decided to get a "scoop" of his own making and beat them all with a "red-hot" exclusive. And this is what he did.

At some point in time between the arrest of Hauptmann on the 19th of September and the morning of the 24th, Tom Cassidy, taking advantage of the liberty afforded him, slithered into the closet of little Manfred's room and scribbled on the inside the condemning name, address and phone number of Condon.

Whether Cassidy's evil mind had directed him to perform this dastardly deception as being nothing more than "a practical joke" to be laughed at later, or whether he hoped it would help the efforts of the police to tighten the bonds on their prisoner, it is certainly inexcusable since it served its purpose either way one looks at it. And to make matters worse, if that is possible, Cassidy bragged about his "foul trick".

Having accomplished his mission Cassidy successfully passed the report among the Bronx police that some writing had been found inside a closet of the Hauptmann home which was believed would help them convict the man. But Inspector Henry Bruckman apparently did not have to hear the "rumor" Cassidy had started. It appeared that the inspector already knew where he would find this "additional evidence" which would make him stand out as a "brilliant genius" in the profession of scientific criminology. And so Bruckman, accompanied by three police carpenters, made haste to the home at 1279 East 222nd Street being overly anxious to enter the dark closet and make his "amazing find".

Bruckman was certainly aware that during the preceding five days every part of the Hauptmann apartment had been thoroughly examined. However, in spite of this, the inspector dismissed all thoughts of what might be said pertaining to "his discovery" being overlooked by the other officers. Having received the news from Cassidy he was intent on claiming the credit for "the find" that would belong to him and him alone - and the sooner he could do this, the better. Ludovic Kennedy in his excellent treatise on the case in his book *The Airman and the Carpenter* does a fine job of explaining how the event transpired.

"Cassidy got word to the Bronx Police, and next morning they sent along their Inspector Bruckman, described by the FBI as 'evidently German, large, loud-spoken, easily excited and very brusque'. While accounts of searches of the apartment by officers like Bornmann, Wallace, Finn and Sisk were concise and direct ('Searched front room this a.m. Found two ledger books and photograph album, etc.'), Bruckman, in view of the tip-off, found it necessary to preface his report with a windy, half-apologetic preamble. 'As a result of a conference with Chief Inspector Sullivan ... we felt there might be some possibilities in connection with a further search of the premises ... the Assistant Chief Inspector authorized me to bring three police carpenters ... to do such work in connection with the search as was deemed advisable.'

"Why ask to bring police carpenters unless you know what you are bringing them for? Bruckman knew exactly why he was bringing them and what he was seeking, as this recorded telephone conversation between

Agents Sisk and Wright shows.

Sisk: 'Well, Mr. Wright, do you remember telling me that Bruckman walked straight to that number as though he knew right where it was?'

Wright: 'Well, he found it pretty quickly.'

Sisk: 'He walked right up to it, I mean, as though he knew it was there and then made it known that he had found something...'

Wright: '... he seemed to walk right into the room and hit directly for the closet where the number was found.'

"Bruckman turned to those around him and said piously that this was a good example of the thoroughness of search; but he enjoined everyone to the strictest secrecy. In fact, said Wright, 'he even went so far as to tell me that if it became known he would hold me responsible.' What the explanation of this is, is hard to say; but it would seem likely that Cassidy had promised Bruckman a scoop for the Bronx Police in return for Bruckman giving Cassidy a scoop for his paper. Bruckman had the carpenters dismantle the door and jamb, then took them along to the District Attorney's Office where Foley announced that he would interrupt the Grand Jury proceedings to hear this fresh evidence.

"Bruckman related what had happened, and stated categorically that the numbers on the jamb were serial numbers of the ransom bills. (Had Cassidy told him they were?) Why hadn't he bothered to check? Then it was Hauptmann's turn. It was unfortunate that his lawyer, Mr. Fawcett, was not present, as he would have counselled silence. But having, he thought, nothing to fear, he saw no reason to refuse to answer questions that might clear him. As with the handwriting tests, he had no idea what he was up against.

"Having been shown the jamb and the board with the writing, he was asked if the writing was his. If Hauptmann had been the kidnapper of the Lindbergh baby, if he had written the ransom notes and received the $50,000 from Dr. Condon in St. Raymond's Cemetery, he would either strenuously have denied that the writing was his or else kept silent. But who else but himself, he asked, would be scribbling things in pencil on the back of one of his bedroom closet doors? (The idea of a plant was as far beyond his own imagination as those of most other people.) Peering closely at the writing and saying he was unable to make it out (a great piece of acting, thought Foley), he was asked if it wasn't Condon's address and telephone number. 'I don't know,' he said. 'Why did you write it on the board?' Foley asked, and Hauptmann, knocking another nail into his coffin, replied, 'I must have read it in the paper about the story. I was a little bit interest, and keep a little record of it, and maybe I was just in the closet and was reading the paper and put down the address.' As he admitted later, it sounded a silly explanation even to him, but what other could there possibly be? Foley asked if he remembered what day he had written on the board, and he said No. 'You remember that you <u>did</u> <u>write</u> <u>it</u>? asked Foley, and Hauptmann, giving himself the <u>coup</u> <u>de</u> <u>grace</u>, said: 'I must write it, the figures, that's my writing.'

"For Foley, for the Grand Jury, for the three law enforcement agencies, indeed for the American people, here were the first glimmerings of the confession they had been waiting for during the past week, evidence that Hauptmann was the receiver of the ransom money and was at last admitting to it. Foley told the Grand Jury that this was 'conclusive evidence' that Hauptmann knew Condon at the time of the ransom negotiations (Condon changed his telephone number soon after), and that the extortion case against him was now complete.

"When Fawcett heard what had happened, he told the press, 'I have told the defendant not to talk any further to anybody. He talked enough before I got into the case. He disobeyed that advice this morning before I got a chance to talk to him. When I saw him late this afternoon, I advised him again not to talk to the District Attorney.'

"Bruckman returned to the Hauptmann apartment where, said Agent Wright, 'he invited every reporter and two news photographers into the house, spelled his name out for them, and explained the occurrences in detail.' History does not record whether Cassidy and his photographer were there, but the story duly appeared in the next edition of the paper."

Hauptmann had been hit extremely hard by the semantics of that day; an agreement made between the police and press, whose ruthlessness was a common practice, one which always resulted in the police granting certain reporters special favors and exclusive tips, which in turn would develop into a sensational story being written and published with the officer receiving ample plaudits for his part in the case. This practice worked in mutual ways with some newspapers going so far as to have certain cops listed on their payrolls, for which they would receive recompense for any "inside information" granted their ace reporters. But, then, this is the way things were done during the years of the depression.

Richard Hauptmann was hit extremely hard as he was caught in the middle of such a situation; first with the discovery of the "planted" incriminating closet evidence, to be followed the next day with the "fake attic antics" of Bornmann and the eight foot plank which he and Arthur Koehler "proved" had been removed and used by Hauptmann to become rail 16 of the kidnap ladder. Oh, what clever maneuvering on the part of some "honest" cops and a despicable dishonest newspaperman.

The aberrant and deviant manipulations of persons of this ilk could only be capped by the ridiculous actions of the man who was stupid enough to brag to his fellow journalists about the deceptive act he had performed against Hauptmann.

Tony Scaduto, while doing research for his book, *SCAPEGOAT*, interviewed a man in Mt. Holly who was well aware of Cassidy's evil trick. The man was Frank Fitzpatrick, a retired newsman, who worked out of Mt. Holly for *The Philadelphia Inquirer* during the days of the Lindbergh case, as did Tom Cassidy for the *New York Daily News*. While covering the case together the two men became friendly competitors. In his book Scaduto gives this account of Fitzpatrick's comments about Cassidy. The following dialogue with Scaduto is picked up with Fitzpatrick saying:

"Hauptmann was framed, I know he was."

"How do you know it?"

"The things they claimed they found in his house. For example, that board in his closet with Condon's phone number written on it. You know how it got there?" I shook my head.

"It was put there by this guy Cassidy, Tom Cassidy, he used to work out here for the *New York Daily News* and he went into the Bronx to help cover the Hauptmann arrest. And after they took Hauptmann away and his wife moved out, the police confiscated his apartment. And one day Cassidy is up in the apartment with a photographer and he needs a fresh story for his first edition. So he goes into Hauptmann's closet and writes that stuff on the closet board and then has his photographer take pictures of it. Then he calls the inspector or whoever was in charge and he says, 'Look what I found.' Front-page pictures and story in the

News that night."

"Can you prove this?"

"Cassidy was bragging about it all over Mt. Holly. Ask anybody in town who goes back that far and they'll tell you how Cassidy was bragging about it. He even showed us how he wrote it and when he showed us it looked the same as the writing on the board they brought into the trial to nail Hauptmann."

"Why didn't Reilly put Cassidy on the stand?"

"I don't know. Probably because he knew Cassidy would deny it and maybe because Reilly always worked with reporters and got a lot of publicity from them, so he wasn't about to get them mad at him."

"And the inspector swore that he found the board?"

"Sure. They all lied about the evidence. I mean, Hauptmann never admitted he wrote those numbers. He was confused because he was trying to tell the truth and he just didn't recollect putting those numbers on the board. Because he didn't put them there, Cassidy did. And that's how the whole trial went."

Seeking additional information about the Cassidy matter, Scaduto was told another retired newspaperman known as "Hoppy", a Russell Hopstatter, who could no doubt be of help to him. Without difficulty the author found "Hoppy" at the Elks Club in Mt. Holly and had merely started to question him when he received more confirmation on Cassidy's involvement. This is the way Scaduto reported it when he inquired:

"I've heard a story about the board in Hauptmann's closet ..." I started to ask, and Hop broke in: "Cassidy, *The Daily News reporter*. Sure, he wrote that phone number, whatever it was, he admitted that to me and to Ellis, he told everybody about it. He was sure Hauptmann was guilty so it didn't matter very much, that's how he felt about it."

It seemed to be common knowledge among the news media, due to the boasting tongue of Tom Cassidy who knew all about it, that the writing found in the Hauptmann closet was fabricated evidence made possible by the "distorted mind" of the braggart himself. Among those who verified the story was a reporter named Russell M. Stoddard of New Jersey's *Camden Courier-Post*, who was quoted as saying: "He told a bunch of us he did it to get a new lead for the story the next day." Joe Sharkey, a reporter working for *Philadelphia's Sunday Bulletin*, confirmed this in an interview with me while working on a story for his paper in 1977. Other persons who had heard of Cassidy's deception during the trial claimed it was common knowledge on the streets of Flemington, as well as in "Nellie's Taproom" in the Union Hotel across from the courthouse. There can be little wonder why this prompted Anthony Scaduto to ask Frank Fitzpatrick: "Why didn't Reilly put Cassidy on the stand?"

During an interview I had with Frank Fitzpatrick in his home in Mt. Holly, I was quite curious to hear at first hand the man's reaction to the mention of Tom Cassidy's name: "The guy pulled a lousy thing on Hauptmann. He framed him. It was awful. Why he was never prosecuted for it, I'll never know. I think they just wanted to throw the book at Hauptmann and didn't care how they got the evidence. Hauptmann got a lousy deal in that whole trial. His own lawyer didn't help him either." I had not had long to wait. From the moment he started to speak I was receiving my answer. Anyone hearing the emotion of his voice would never have doubted Fitzpatrick's knowledge of Cassidy's prank, nor his sincerity as he expressed his opinion of what the prosecutors had done to the innocent Richard Hauptmann.

From the very beginning the efforts put forth by the police in seeing that Hauptmann would be unquestionably charged, regardless of how they obtained a conviction, with the crime of kidnapping and murdering the Lindbergh baby should not come as a surprise. No sooner had the man been arrested than we find Captain Jack Lamb approaching Dr. Erastus Meade Hudson inquiring if it were possible to counterfeit fingerprints, and if so how would they go about it. And when told by Hudson that it could be done but that it would be easily detectable, Lamb seemed to be quite disappointed. Trooper Kelly, who had accompanied him, again reiterated his own knowledge that this could not be successfully done.

How stupid it had been for Lamb to have even broached the subject. Had he so soon forgotten that he had asked this same question of the doctor in 1926 when he first inquired if fake prints could be developed and detected. It had been Lamb's intent to convict Mrs. Frances Noel Hall and two of her brothers, William and Henry, for the murder of her husband and his mistress which had taken place during the early morning hours of Thursday, September 14, 1922.

The Reverend Edward Wheeler Hall and Mrs. Eleanor Mills, a choir singer in his church, whose bodies were found under a crab apple tree on De Russeys Lane in New Brunswick, New Jersey, was a crime that drew world wide attention. However, after several years it was recorded in police annals as an unsolved mystery. Nevertheless, four years later, our Jack Lamb, then a sergeant, reopened the investigation. He had at last found a witness who claimed she had seen the actual murders going so far as to name the assailants.

Jane Gibson, during the passing of four years was the previously unheard of witness who, during the trial in 1926, came forth to become infamously known as the Pig Woman of the Hall-Mills murder case. During the Pig Woman's testimony her own aged mother kept remarking in a loud voice which could be heard throughout the courtroom: "She's a liar, a liar, a liar! That's what she is, and what she's always been." Words clearly reminiscent of those we had heard may times during the Hauptmann trial.

In 1926 Sergeant Lamb dug up from somewhere this previously unknown witness, the Pig Woman, and dragged her into court on a literal death bed, and placed it in the center of the courtroom from where she testified to a batch of lies, which later were accepted as being no more than hallucinations she claimed she had seen.

Lamb now had his star witness willing to testify for the prosecution in this famous case. A case from which he hoped to eventually evolve as the "hero cop" who had, after four years of diligent detective work, successfully solved this most mysterious of cases.

Now the "brilliant" state police sergeant was ready "for the kill"; he was now ready to make the arrest. And how he did do it!!! A few minutes before midnight Sergeant Lamb, together with five officers drove into the circular driveway of Mrs. Hall's home. Mrs. Hall, widow of Reverend Edward Wheeler Hall, was a dignified middle-aged woman whose hair had already turned gray. As the wife of the rector of the fashionable Church of St. John the Evangelist she was well respected as a resident of her community.

At the time of her mother's death Mrs. Hall and her two older brothers had reportedly inherited a sum of nearly two million dollars that had been equally divided between them. The death of an aunt had added more wealth to their coffers leaving them all financially secure. At the front of the Hall's large two-story red brick mansion Lamb's car came to a stop. The time had arrived for the sergeant to go into his act, being sure to use all the embellishments and theatrics which were his style. By doing this he would exploit the power and authority of the police that the big man possessed, especially that of a person wearing the uniform of the New Jersey State Police.

Lamb had a style of doing things which was distinctively all his own. Although he had obtained two separate warrants for Mrs. Hall's arrest at ten o'clock that morning, he had waited until more than thirteen hours had passed to apprehend her. Lamb certainly had a great flare for the dramatics, especially when it came to his own enhancement.

Stepping from his car, Sergeant Lamb and his men approached the front door and rang the bell. A young servant girl responded and was curtly ordered to: "Tell Mrs. Hall that I want to see her." At the same time Mrs. Hall's brother had descended the stairs: "Hello, Willie. I came here to see Mrs. Hall right away," the officious voice of the sergeant informed him. "I have important business of an official character to transact with her." Willie, being only partially awake, called up the stairs, "Frances, they want you."

A few minutes later Frances Hall came down to greet her visitors. "Good evening gentlemen. Your visit is a rather late one. I suppose you want to question me again.", she inquired.

The officious Lamb wasted no time in friendly levity or diplomacy. He immediately came right to the purpose of his visit. "I have a warrant calling for your arrest. I have been instructed to take you to Somerville at once.", he stated. She asked if she might see the warrant, the curt trooper handed it to her as she started to read: "Frances Hall stands charged that on or about the fourteenth day of September, 1922, at the Township of Franklin, county aforesaid, she did willfully and feloniously and of malice aforethought, kill and murder Edward Wheeler Hall against the peace of the state." She merely glanced at the second warrant which was a duplicate with the exception of the name Eleanor Mills being substituted for that of her husband.

After being granted permission to notify her lawyer, the unfortunate woman was driven to Somerville the County Seat where she was officially charged with the murders at 3:00 a.m. and escorted to a detention cell on the second floor of the county jail. In making his arrest of this dignified lady, Lamb had employed all the theatrics he possibly could in order to make his hoped for "conclusion" of the Hall-Mills case as sensational as possible. He was certain he and his associates, armed with the "additional incriminating evidence" he had gathered together during the past four years, chiefly the testimony of the Pig Woman, would have no trouble proving to a jury that at last he had found the murderers. But, how wrong he was.

At the conclusion of the lengthy trial the jury had no difficulty clearing all three defendants. Most folks found the decision "most gratifying" since much of the testimony against the accused had been nothing more than circumstantial, linked together with charges which were termed to be nothing more than "lies, lies, lies" by the accuser's own mother, and the inclusion of a "mysterious fingerprint", which had also come into the picture four years later, to be identified as being that of Willie Stevens, Mrs. Hall's brother, on one of the Rev. Hall's calling cards, a card which the chief defense counsel, Robert H. McCarter, in a voice hardened by the audacity of the prosecutors to bring such a "rigged" piece of evidence, stated to the jury: "I charge with all the solemnity that is involved in it that that card is a fraud." Must we remind you that Sergeant Lamb had been informed that fingerprints could not be faked? We can find no reason to disbelieve the sincerity expressed in the answer of a member of the jury panel, when asked the reason they had reached a verdict for acquittal: "I would remain here for thirty years rather than vote a verdict of guilty on such evidence."

The investigator who convinced Mrs. Gibson's relatives to testify for the defense and who was directly responsible for ruining Lamb's attempt to convict the defendants on patently perjured testimony was the chief of detectives of Burlington County, Ellis Parker. An old friend of Mrs. Hall's family, Parker felt strongly that 'this here's a frame-up,' and he conducted his own investigation. (Years later, when the Lindbergh child was kidnapped, Colonel Schwarzkopf and his chief investigator on the case, Captain Lamb, refused to permit Parker to join the investigation even though the governor at the time, A. Harry Moore, had ordered Ellis to participate.)

"All in all, the circumstances surrounding Bornmann's claimed discovery in the attic of a missing piece of floorboard, and Captain Lamb's propensity for contriving testimony against murder suspects make it highly probable the attic evidence was contrived---as fingerprints would have been had Dr. Hudson not discouraged Captain Lamb."

What a pity that the Hauptmann jury had not been aware of all of the deception presented to them. Had they been cognizant of all the irregularities, their deliberations and ultimate verdict would have been quite different.

In 1927 Mrs. Hall and her brothers brought lawsuits in court for undisclosed sums rumored to be somewhere between $50,000 and $150,000. A similar suit, won by the three defendants, against William Randolph Hearst's *New York Evening Journal* which had boldly printed hundreds of thousands of words about the case on their front pages, buried the brief story of their settlement back on page 20.

The grief and frustration of having been forced to endure the experience of falling into the hands of the New Jersey police authorities is very clearly stated by Mrs. Frances Hall when she was asked if she intended to go to Europe after her trial? With a laugh, she said: "It is impossible for me to make any plans at the present time. I used to be a good American and I still am a good American, but I am getting skeptical. I have just reached the conclusion that New Jersey is not a fit place for decent people to live in. I don't know whether I shall continue to live here or not." Mrs. Hall was vindicated in 1926.

C H A P T E R   F O R T Y   F O U R

The "Star" Attraction!

The State had thrown all its heavy punches at Hauptmann; and although the prosecutors believed he should be reeling on the ropes, they could not wait until they had him seated in the witness chair to end the battle with a knockout.

Seated in the courtroom, Hauptmann, the accused, had been on the receiving end of every unfair accusation they could muster. He had heard this without being able to answer his accusers. And now he thought his time had come to explain the unfair charges and discrepancies that had been lodged against him. He was certain that with a reasonable explanation, a true account of what had taken place, he would undoubtedly be vindicated. However, this was not to be the case.

As unfair as their charges had been, we must realize that the jury, the judge and the multitude of citizens across the country and around the world did not know anything about the dishonest plot that was being enacted against the innocent Richard Hauptmann.

From shortly after the time of Hauptmann's arrest, we must also not lose sight of this one fact. He had not deviated from his original explanation - that he accidentally, or through a trick of fate, had come into possession of the $14,600 ransom money by simply being willing and agreeing to keep a wrapped package, not knowing and not inquiring what was in it, for his "good friend" Isidor Fisch. He then, sometime later, had accidentally discovered the package which, by then, gave evidence of being a box of water-soaked money. Realizing his "friend" had died, owing him $7,500, he felt no compunction in taking what he knew to be his and spending it. This act, and this act alone, led to his downfall.

Hauptmann had told the truth and from the time he drew his last breath his story never changed. What an unfortunate occurrence to take place in the lifetime of such a good man. A man who knew no more about the Lindbergh case than what he had read in the newspapers and heard on the radio. A man who, together with his wife and the mass of honest citizens of the world, wanted to see the crime solved in an orderly fashion by the honest hard-working police investigators who were actively working on the case since the night of March 1st, 1932; never expecting it to be "solved" by methods conjured up by those whose dereliction of duty was to eventually bring only shame and degradation on the annals of criminal investigation in the State of New Jersey.

The prosecutors, it appeared, had been "successful" in throwing everything at Richard. The two Osborns and their six handwriting cohorts, Hochmuth, Whited, Alexander, Condon, Lindbergh, Perrone, Achenbach, Barr, Rossiter, Bornmann, Koehler, to name only a few. However, New York police carpenters, Charles F.W. Enkler and Anselm Cramer, must be included because of the "important evidence" they willingly gave, supporting Bornmann's "missing floorboard" in the Hauptmann attic.

The two carpenters told the court, after "properly" identifying the nails, the holes and the spaces on the disputed board, they had arrived at the conclusion that, although a space of at least one half inch was missing between the remaining nailed-down board of the floor and the plank, and in spite of a knot in its grain where a cut was made, it had been used as "rail 16" of the kidnap ladder. However, in spite of the confirming testimony of the two men, which very "cleverly" fell into place "in detail" with that of Bornmann and Koehler, and regardless of the fact that neither carpenter had seen the nails removed from the holes, or closely examined or studied the holes, the spaces and the board, it went far to further impress the jury. Under cross-examination by attorney Frederick Pope, carpenter Cramer admitted they had not been told that the missing plank was to be used as evidence against Hauptmann until 15 days after Bornmann "claimed" he discovered his "amazing find". It was during a picture taking session in the Hauptmann attic, on October 10th, that they were first made aware of "the importance" the board was to play. More evidence that it was quite apparent that even the police, working in concert as they should have been, were keeping very "important secrets" from one another.

And so, at 12:20 p.m. on Thursday, January 24, day 17 of the trial, the "clever" prosecutors appeared to have played all their cards at the proper time. They were now poised and ready to verbally "tear Hauptmann to pieces." Attorney General Wilentz rose and announced: "The State rests."

Following a break for lunch at the Union Hotel, the jury returned to their seats in the jury box. The "main ring" of the Flemington circus had been made ready for the "star attraction", Bruno Richard Hauptmann, who would entertain the crowd by vainly making an attempt to squeeze his way out of the "web of crooked lies" that had been so maliciously woven about him by his captors. The crowds in the Coliseum at Rome had been no better entertained. However, the shouts for the victim's blood had been silenced by the stilled hush of a courtroom.

The crowd did not have long to wait; soon Richard Hauptmann would take the stand and the cry for the kill would be on. But first Egbert Rosecrans of the defense counsel addressed the Court making an impassioned plea in a motion asking for a verdict of acquittal for his client. Rosecrans might as well have asked the judge to release the prisoner forthwith. As far as the jury was concerned, I am sure they as a group could very easily have pronounced the verdict of guilt then and there. However they were enjoying the carnival atmosphere of the Flemington trial and were anxious to learn what was to be the next act with its "star attraction." The Rosecrans appeal for acquittal seemed ridiculous in light of all the evidence presented against Hauptmann. Following the tall lean attorney's attempt to persuade the Court that an acquittal should be reached, Justice Trenchard turned to Wilentz and inquired: "Does the Attorney General care to be heard?"

And this he certainly did with an intense attack against every argument put forth by Rosecrans in which he gave his strong closing appeal to the Court: "If your Honor please, let me just say in conclusion that is our view, very respectfully submitted to your Honor that there is not only sufficient evidence but overwhelming evidence, if your Honor please, which requires this defendant to answer."

By this time the jury and spectators were beside themselves wishing they could shout: "Let's get on with the show!" as Justice Trenchard finally announced: "The motion for direction of acquittal will be denied." His decision could not have been otherwise. This was "The Trial of the Century". They had their defendant; the time had arrived for them to prove his guilt. Nevertheless, the real crime was in trying Hauptmann with such manufactured evidence and the lies of witnesses who were willing to give perjured testimony in order to distort the truth. The trial would soon turn into a human debacle.

It had been expected that Chief Defense Attorney Reilly would be the one to make the opening statement for the defense; however, the choice of Lloyd Fisher for that task had been a wise one. Unlike Reilly, who on several occasions had shown a dislike for his own client, Fisher was compassionate, exhibiting an honest belief in Hauptmann's innocence, and was sincere in all his endeavors to prove it. Additionally, the good looking attorney was from Hunterdon County, with many local connections, which certainly would prove helpful to the Hauptmann cause. Reilly, on the other hand, had been boisterous, flamboyant and rowdy, always endeavoring to impress his "audience" wherever he went that he was the "big city all-knowing lawyer from New York."

Fisher made an excellent presentation, reiterating every facet of the charges made by each prosecution witness. He promised to prove to the jury that, although he was well aware of the gravity of the charges brought against his client and the magnitude of the trial, he was certain he would prove Richard Hauptmann's innocence when they were told the true circumstances.

He told them the testimony of the defense witnesses would confirm that Hauptmann could not have been in the Hopewell home of the Lindberghs on the night of Tuesday, March 1st, 1932; that he was not the man in St. Raymond"s Cemetery to whom Doctor Condon had paid $50,000 on Saturday, April 2nd of that year; and that he was not the man whom Cecile Barr claimed had passed her a ransom bill at the theater in Greenwich Village on the night of Sunday, November 26th, 1933. Fisher said he would show that Hauptmann's finances had been blown so far out of proportion by the prosecution that the true facts would prove that any money he and Anna Hauptmann obtained had been earned honestly. The attorney stated the evidence of the "so-called" kidnap ladder being traced to Hauptmann's Bronx home should not even be considered since the one brought into the courtroom in no way resembled the ladder found on the Lindbergh grounds the night of the kidnapping.

One thing Fisher urged the jury to remember was the shortage of funds the defense lawyers had to work with. He explained that unlike the prosecution who had been able to afford a large number of witnesses to come to Flemington to testify, the Hauptmanns had utilized every dollar they could scrape together to pay the necessary travel expenses of their few witnesses. Fisher stated: "Again may I say we will be terribly handicapped by a total lack of funds. We are in no such position as is the State in this case with the combined resources of the United States, the State of New Jersey and the State of New York at their fingers' tips." Hauptmann, on the other hand, had no more than a $3750 mortgage with which his lawyers could present his case.

Nevertheless, Fisher continued to make clear the encumbered circumstances the defense counsel was working with: "We are here battling along with our back to the wall, so far as financing goes, and we will prove that on this witness stand, and we will do the very best we can. We will give you everything we have got, everything we can get in this courtroom, by way of testimony. We will hide nothing and produce everything and, when you have heard all the testimony, we trust that if you are not already satisfied that the State of New Jersey has utterly failed to make out a case against Bruno Richard Hauptmann, we are quite sure you will be convinced, after you have heard such testimony related as we will present."

Unfortunately these words of Lloyd Fisher apparently fell on the deaf ears of those seated within the jury box. At this point, we feel certain, had it been possible to have taken an early poll, that most of the eight men and four women had already made up their minds and, if called upon for their verdict, would have pronounced the innocent Hauptmann guilty as charged.

Regardless of the odds against them, plus the errors and omissions made by the "Bull of Brooklyn", Edward J. Reilly, the defense put up a valiant effort to prove Hauptmann's innocence. The final 'unfair' verdict was rendered, without a doubt, due to the ineptness of Justice Trenchard as he clearly exhibited his bias, particularly during his charge to the jury, by improperly explaining both sides of the evidence which had been presented for their fair and impartial consideration. This, together with the unfair tactics used by Wilentz as he continually badgered and verbally abused Hauptmann, capped by the host of prosecution witnesses whose fabricated stories and perjured testimony convinced the jury that there was absolutely no way possible for the prisoner to be considered innocent in any sense of the word.

However, as unfair and dishonest as the case was as presented against Hauptmann, I must state that I do not fault the jury for the verdict they rendered, nor for the sentence they imposed. Not one of the members of the jury could have been aware of the vile false cunningly calculated accusations that were deliberately manufactured in the minds of evil men and "pounded" into the personal character of Richard Hauptmann, an innocent man. This was much more than character assassination - it was character murder.

However, I, as you, would have voted exactly as did the 12 good members of that jury in Flemington in 1935. They knew nothing different and, in ignorance of the true facts, although much of the "fake" testimony on the surface was highly questionable, they rendered a just verdict based on the evidence they were swayed to believe was true.

The time had arrived for Richard Hauptmann to be called to defend himself against a terrible accusation - the kidnapping and murder of the young son of Charles and Anne Lindbergh. How would he do it? Simply by telling the truth about all he consciously knew about the horrible crime.

It is needless to go into Hauptmann's detailed testimony. You have already been made aware of the facts as he gave them to the police shortly after his arrest. Hauptmann never changed his story. However, I would advise you not to forget that when he was first arrested he denied that he had any more than a hundred of the illegal gold notes. This he claimed he had done because he feared being charged with hoarding so much of the money President Franklin D. Roosevelt had declared to be illegal tender after May 1, 1933. To be caught with more than one hundred dollars of these bills, a person would be subject to a fine and imprisonment. Hauptmann was aware of this and, in order to avoid a further search for more in his home, he told the police that was all he had. Richard unquestionably had no idea the money he had found in his broom closet was Lindbergh ransom money. After being told that it was, he had difficulty accepting the fact that his "good friend" Isidor Fisch could have been implicated in the crime. To Richard it seemed inconceivable that Fisch could have had any knowledge of the crime, let alone have been a participant in it.

Remembering this, I would like to make it clear that Attorney Wilentz took great advantage of the fact that Hauptmann lied about how much of the "illegal" money he had. The questions asked of Hauptmann in the Flemington courtroom pertaining to the bills were questions the attorney general knew very well had been asked of Hauptmann in District Attorney Sam Foley's office in the Bronx shortly after the arrest had been made. However, Hauptmann readily admitted his possession of the larger number of bills after the police found the $14,600 in his garage and he learned it was Lindbergh ransom money. From this point, Hauptmann, realizing the seriousness of the charge being brought against him, explained how he had come into possession of the money. Regardless of this, Wilentz took advantage of the accused man's initial denial, made in the Bronx district attorney's office, and presented the denial to the Flemington jury as a "blatant lie" told, and never retracted, by Hauptmann. This simply was not true - Hauptmann's story never wavered once he learned it was Lindbergh money and that he was being held for a far more serious crime than the mere possession of illegal gold notes. This maneuver resulted in just another unfair major charge made effective by the "clever deception" of Attorney General David T. Wilentz.

Regardless, however, of whatever could be termed the merits of the case, and the various pros and cons of those who would argue for or against the man's innocence or guilt, it is imperative that I show you the testimony exactly as it was given in the Flemington courtroom by Hauptmann. In addition, I will make clear the unfair tactics used by Wilentz in his questioning of Richard; the abusive language used against him by the attorney general; the failure of Justice Trenchard to put a stop to the verbal attacks by Wilentz; why Hauptmann hesitated on many occasions before answering him; and finally you will read the very reasonable testimony of witnesses who came to the accused man's defense - witnesses whose truthful words were utterly cast aside by the judge and jury as simply unbelievable.

Hauptmann rising from his seat, made his way to the witness chair in a few strides. He appeared anxious to testify. Unlike the many descriptions given of him by the press, Richard Hauptmann was a good looking man. He was immaculately dressed in a double-breasted gray suit, which was somewhat creased, evidently the result of daily wear during the first 17 days of the trial. A blue shirt and a blue polka-dot tie complemented his apparel. A guard followed the prisoner and took a standing position behind the witness chair. Hauptmann was immediately sworn in and was asked to be seated. Crossing his legs, he leaned forward slightly, his eyes never turning from his interrogator, Mr. Reilly.

Because it is imperative that you read and clearly understand the testimony, pertaining to the vital issues of the case exactly as it was given by Hauptmann at Flemington, the following dialogue reveals the extremely unfair tactics used by Wilentz, on many occasions, in his questioning of Hauptmann. I have also used those sections of testimony applicable to the accused man's defense as given by his loyal wife Anna, as well as other defense witnesses who attempted to testify to the truth as they knew it. Truthful testimony which was deliberately shunted off by those who could have prevented it. Testimony which was to be eventually utterly discarded as nothing more than mere rubbish by those who hoped it would be forgotten forever by having it burned in a caldron of their hate toward an unfortunate Bronx carpenter who was completely innocent.

Bruno Richard Hauptmann whose very innocence continually convinced him they could never prove him guilty of something of which he knew nothing more than he had already told them. Bruno Richard Hauptmann, a God fearing man, who ardently trusted the fairness of our system of justice so fervently that he kept assuring his trusting wife that he would soon be cleared of this horrible crime and they could return to their home together.

But then, Bruno Richard Hauptmann had not been aware of the satanic devices which had been forged to be used against him. And although he had already heard the many lies spoken against him, he being innocent, was firmly of the belief that he could clear himself by convincing the jury that he was telling the truth. But the combined naiveness (apparent gullibility) of the jury, who refused to accept Hauptmann's very logical and reasonable explanation as to how he had come into possession of the ransom money, and their pre-conceived opinion that Hauptmann could not be anything else but guilty after listening to such a batch of lies (of which they could never have imagined were nothing more than vicious untruths based on vile manufactured evidence) which had been permitted to be brought into a court of justice by dishonest prosecutors.

Although Hauptmann was aware of the seriousness of the charges brought against him, his faith in his ability to prove his innocence never wavered. As he sat in the witness chair he appeared anxious to at last tell the public his side of the story. It is here that we take up with some of the direct questioning of him by Attorney Reilly:

Q. Do you remember when Fisch went to Europe? A. I do.

Q. When was that? A. December. '33.

Q. He never returned, did he? A. No.

Q. Now, before Fisch went to Europe, did he call at your house? A. He called several times at the house.

Q. When was the last time he was at your house before he sailed for Europe? A. The night before he sailed.

Q. Who was at your house, as you recall it now? A. Mrs. Fredericksen, my wife and I.

Q. Anyone else? A. No.

Q. Did anybody come in during the evening, any of your friends, that you remember? A. Can't remember.

Q. Did Fisch have anything with him, any bundles, or anything with him the night before he sailed? A. No, sir.

Q. Well, before he sailed did he leave anything with you for you to take care of while he was in Europe? A. Well, he left two suitcases.

Q. What else? A. Four hundred skins, Hudson seal.

Q. What else? A. And a little box.

Q. Now the 400 skins, or what kind of skins were they? A. Hudson seal.

Q. Hudson seal. And they were skins that were purchased in your partnership between Fisch and yourself. A. Yes.

Q. And did you have those skins in your possession when you were arrested? A. Yes.

Q. And are they now as far as you know in the possession of the New York City police? A. I guess they are.

Q. Now this little box that you described, what kind of a box was it, paper, cardboard or wood? A. Well, I find it later out it was a shoe box.

Q. What was it made of? A. Well, cardon.

Q. Carton, cardboard? A. Yes.

Q. Now, will you describe to the jury under what circumstances it was that he left this shoe box with you, what he said and what you said. A. Well, of Mr. Fisch request it was he was throwing a party when he left for Chermany, it was at his request in our house; we invited a couple of friends and about nine o'clock or a short while before nine o'clock, Fisch came out and got a little bundle under his arm. I answered the doorbell, my wife was in the baby's room. He came out and we went in the kitchen and he said, "I leave it, I leave it something, if you don't mind, keep care of it and put it in a tight place." I didn't ask what is in it, he only said that is paper in it. I thought maybe they are---

Mr. Wilentz: Just a minute.

---A. they are bills.

Mr. Wilentz: Just a minute. Now, I object to what he thought.

The Court: Never mind.

Mr. Wilentz: I object to what you thought.

Q. Tell us what you did, not what you thought. A. I put it in the broom closet.

Q. And where was the broom closet? A. The broom closet was in the kitchen.

Q. In what part of the broom closet did you put it? A. Please?

Q. In what part of the broom closet? A. On the upper shelf.

Q. And how long did that shoe box remain there before you disturbed it? A. The middle of August, '34.

Q. '34? A. Yes.

Q. And what caused you to disturb it? A. I was looking for---it was Sunday, it was nasty weather outside---was looking for a broom. I took the broom. The broom is on the left side in the closet. And when I took the broom I must hit the box with the broom handle, and I looked up, and that way I saw that it is money. I damaged the box.

Q. And you saw money? A. Yes.

Q. In the box? A. Yes.

Q. Well, now, had there been any moisture or wet or anything in that closet? A. All soaking wet.

Q. Were there some pipes that ran through the broom closet? A. Yes.

Q. What kind of pipes? Were they water pipes or gas pipes? A. No, no water or gas pipes. That is, I guess that is ventilation pipe, I guess, for toilets.

Q. Radiator pipes, is that what you mean? A. No.

Q. For the heating system? A. No, not for heating system.

Q. Ventilation? A. That is for ventilation.

Q. Did you take the box down, the paper box down then, and you disturbed it? A. I put it in the boiler and took it down to the garage.

Q. What money did you see in that box? A. Only gold certificates.

Q. About how much? A. I didn't count it from the beginning.

Q. Is that the money that you afterwards started to spend? A. That is the money.

Q. Is that the money that was found in your garage? A. It is.

Q. And was Fisch dead at that time? A. Yes.

Q. How many satchels did he leave with you when he went to Europe? A. Two.

Q. What did you do with those satchels after his death? A. After his death, I opened the big satchel and searched it for bills. I couldn't find anything in there and I closed it again and left it in the garage. That means the big satchel.

Q. While Fisch was in Germany, did he write to you? A. Yes.

Q. I am pointing now to State's Exhibit 1, which shows the estate of Colonel Lindbergh as of March 1st, 1932. Hauptmann, were you ever in Hopewell in your life? A. I never was.

Q. On the night of March 1st, 1932, did you enter the nursery of Colonel Lindbergh---? A. I did not.

Q. ---and take from that nursery Charles Lindbergh, Jr.? A. I did not.

Q. On the night of March 1st, 1932, did you leave on the window seat of Colonel Lindbergh's nursery a note? A. Well, I wasn't there at all.

Q. You never saw baby Lindbergh in your life, did you? A. I never saw it.

Q. Now, I want you to look at State's Exhibit 18 and the envelope in which it was contained, Exhibit 17. Did you ever see that note before? A. Why, I saw it in Bronx courtroom.

Q. That was the first time you saw it? A. It was.

Q. You never saw it except in the courtroom? A. No.

Q. Did you write it? A. I did not.

Q. Did you leave it in the Lindbergh nursery? A. I did not.

Q. March 1st, 1932, you referred to here yesterday in a general way. Will you again tell the jury where you were from the time you got out of bed on the morning of March 1st, 1932, until you went to bed that night, your movements that entire day? A. Well, I wake up about six o'clock, took my wife down to the bakery.

Q. About what time did you take your wife to the

bakery? A. Between half past six and a quarter to seven.

Q. How did you take her down? A. In automobile; in car.

Q. And again I ask you how many miles would you say it was from your home to the bakery? A. A good mile.

Q. She had to be there about seven o'clock, didn't she? A. Yes.

Q. How long did you remain at the bakery that morning? A. I didn't enter the bakery at all.

Q. Well, after Anna entered the bakery, where did you go? A. I went right home, put the car in the garage, and went to White Plains Avenue subway station.

Q. Well, you testified yesterday you were nine or ten minutes' walk from there. A. Six or nine minutes.

Q. And you took the subway, as you described yesterday, the White Plains, to some intersection? A. White Plains to 177th Street, and there I changed for Broadway subway.

Q. And where did you ride to? A. To 72nd Street, Broadway.

Q. And then where did you go? A. I went to the Majestic Hotel.

Q. And when you arrived there did you see anybody? A. Well, I went to the carpenter shop. Of course, my tools was down there already. I took the tools down the day before and was going to start to work. The foreman said, I got to see the superintendent first.

Q. Now, do you recall the name of the foreman? A. I can't.

Q. All right. Continue now your movements. A. Well, I showed him the letter from the agency. He said, "I'm sorry, it is filled up." So I left the tools right in the Majestic and took the letter and went down to the employment agency where I get the job trying to get them ten dollars aback what I paid for it. I couldn't get it them ten dollars and he said, "Come around next day, maybe something else coming in." And after that I went to another agencies and I went over to Radio City which was under construction, trying to get a job over there, but I couldn't. And I went home around five o'clock, maybe a little bit later or earlier, I don't know.

Q. Now when you arrived home, who was there if anybody? A. There was nobody at home when I arrived.

Q. What time did you go back and call for Anna? A. I was there around seven o'clock.

Q. When you arrived at the bakery, who was there? A. My wife alone, my wife was alone there, but there were customers in there always.

Q. People come in and go out and buy things, is that right? A. Yes.

Q. Did the Fredericksens at that time have a police dog? A. Yes, they did.

Q. Did you do anything with that dog during the evening while waiting for Anna to finish her duties? A. Oh, yes; I usually let the dog out for a walk.

Q. Did you take the dog out that night? A. I did.

Mr. Wilentz: Just a minute, your Honor please. I didn't want to object to the leading suggestion about the dog, but as long as the question was asked, specifically that night, the answer was, "I usually took him out." I think the next one is very leading and offensively leading, "Did you take him out that night?"

The Court: Yes, that is leading.

Mr. Reilly: I don't see how I could otherwise direct his attention to that night.

The Court: You might try.

Mr. Wilentz: He did specifically before and he refused to say anything but he usually took the dog out.

The Court: For the moment I have excluded this question.

Q. Well, tell us what you did there that night? A. When I came down I usually got my supper first. I took the police dog out and took it out on the street, sometimes for a quarter hour, sometimes for a half hour.

Q. On this particular night---that is what we are interested in, did you--- A. I did.

Q. ---take it out that night? A. I did, yes.

Q. Do you remember where you walked the dog? A. I went to the corner of the Boston Road, Boston Post Road, went a little farder up, came back again to the gasoline station; it is just the corner.

Q. Did you meet anybody? A. As far I can't remember. I met a gentleman, I guess he was put gas, gassing in the gasoline station, and he was talking about the---the dog, und he was asking me where I get him. I told he doesn't belong to me. I don't know whether he was asking about interest from the owner, that is what I can't remember.

Q. Do you remember meeting a man that talked to you about that dog? A. I do.

Q. On March 1st? A. Yes.

Q. At about what time of the night? A. I would say it would be between eight and half past eight.

Q. What did you do? Did you bring the dog back to the restaurant? A. Oh, yes.

Q. What time did you and your wife leave there? A. Came before nine o'clock; it was after nine o'clock. I can't remember exact the time.

Q. Well, it would be fair to say it was in the neighborhood of nine o'clock, is that right? A. Yes, that is about right.

Q. Did you drive your wife home? A. Yes.

Q. And after arriving at the house, did you again leave your house?

Mr. Wilentz: Just a minute. Now if your Honor please, I don't want to be objecting but I don't think counsel ought to be testifying.

The Court: Well---

Mr. Reilly: All through the examination of his witnesses, if the Court please, we never thought of interrupting the gentleman's continuity of thought; we allowed him to testify fully and freely. I don't want to do it, but I want to simply direct this witness's thought in the channel of March 1st, that night.

The Court: Well, suppose you ask him what he did.

Mr. Reilly: All right.

By Mr. Reilly:

Q. What did you do? A. I went home. We went home, took the car---

Q. Did you stay there? A. Took the car in the garage, went right away to bed.

Q. So that on March the 1st, 1932, I ask you again, were you in Hopewell, New Jersey? A. I was not.

Q. And on March the 2nd, 1932, do you remember what time it was that you got up? A. The same time again, six o'clock, a little bit later.

Q. And did you and your wife go any place? A. I took the wife down to the bakery. After that I took the car down home in the garage again and went down to Sixth Avenue. I entering the subway station one, 225th Street, I read the paper and is the first time I read about the Lindbergh case.

Q. Then you read for the first time of the Lindbergh kidnapping, is that what you say? A. Yes.

Q. I now refer you to State's Exhibits S-21 and 20. Were you---Withdrawn. Did you mail a letter in this envelope addressed to Mr. Colonel Lindbergh, Hopewell, New Jersey, on March the 4th, 1932? A. No, sir.

Q. Did you write that envelope? A. I did not.

Q. Now, I show you the letter which was contained in that envelope, S-20. A. I did not write any letter like that.

Q. You did not write that letter? A. Did not write it.

Q. When was the first time you saw that letter, if you ever saw it before? A. Well, I saw some of them letters in Bronx courtroom.

Q. You didn't put any marks on any in The Bronx? A. No.

Q. You saw some letters like this? A. Yes.

Q. You may have seen this in The Bronx and you may not have seen it, is that correct? A. Yes.

Q. When do you say for the first time you knew or learned that Colonel Lindbergh lived at Hopewell? A. Well, I---I heard it in the paper.

Q. The morning after the kidnapping; is that it? A. Yes.

Mr. Wilentz: That is what I object to, if your Honor please.

Mr. Reilly: He has testified already he read it.

Mr. Wilentz: He hasn't testified to that. The witness was waiting to determine his answer as to the time, if he was going to answer it at all.

The Court: I think the question was leading, but it has been answered.

Mr. Wilentz: I understood counsel answered it. Counsel suggested the day after the kidnapping.

By Mr. Reilly:

Q. When did you read in the paper of the Lindbergh kidnapping? A. March 2nd.

Q. Did it say in the paper that the baby was taken from Hopewell, New Jersey? A. It did.

Q. You didn't know Colonel Lindbergh, did you? A. I did not.

Q. You had never been in Hopewell, had you? A. No, sir.

Q. Now, when for the first time did you read that he lived in Hopewell, New Jersey, or did you know he lived in Hopewell, New Jersey? A. When I read from the kidnapping.

Now the only fair perspective which should be

taken at this point is that Richard Hauptmann is, or, to say the least, should be still presumed innocent until he is proven guilty. This should be so regardless of the massive evidence that had already been presented which pointed to his guilt. It is mandatory that a person have their so-called "day in court" to allow the judge and jurors to hear their plea of innocence. Now, from the time Hauptmann took the stand, he categorically and vehemently denied any knowledge of the crime until he read about it in the newspapers the next day. We must be emphatic once again by stating that Hauptmann never deviated from the explanations he gave the police. He remained firm in the denial of his guilt in every facet of the kidnapping. Under similar circumstances we would have done the same had we been innocent of a crime of which we knew absolutely nothing.

Bearing all this in mind, in our next chapter you will unquestionably see the unfair tactics used by David Wilentz in his cross-examination of Hauptmann. This is coupled with the permissiveness of Justice Trenchard in allowing such unjust badgering, taunting, jeering questioning, as was publicly demonstrated by the Attorney General in this so-called "fair" trial. A trial already acknowledged as "The Trial of the Century", but nevertheless, one which instead, as it slowly drew to its close, was speedily earning the title, "The Disgrace of the Century". However, to those who are unequivocally convinced of Richard Hauptmann's innocence --- <u>this is precisely what we have labeled it</u>!

CHAPTER FORTY FIVE

Verbal Carnage!

The moment David Wilentz had been waiting for had finally arrived. He had grown overly anxious to get to this German who had the audacity to still persist in declaring his innocence when such overwhelming "evidence" of guilt had been piled up around the man. He was "straining at the leash" to tear the man apart with his talented "tongue of verbal abuse". With the help of "lying compatriots" and their "framed evidence" he had nothing more to do than shout his accusations at the prisoner on the chair in front of him and he would win his case hands down. This case was gaining great political merit for him; he realized its successful conclusion would open a wide path for him to be elected the state's next governor.

But before this was to ever become a reality, he must get on with the business before him, the cross-examination of the man he despised.

Again, we deal here only with those charges which, if true, would definitely incriminate the man. Therefore, the questions and responses used here are those of only vital points covered during the cross-examination of Hauptmann by the attorney general as he attempted to "trap" Hauptmann into something he could call a "confession". His attempt to do this ended in complete failure.

The following abbreviated portion of the questioning by Wilentz pertains to Hauptmann's friendship with Isidor Fisch:

Q. So you are a carpenter? A. I am.

Q. When was the last time you did carpenter work? A. Last time?

Q. Yes. A. About four or six weeks before I get arrested.

Q. But you didn't do any work regularly as a carpenter since April, 1932, did you? A. That is correct.

Q. You have been a stock market trader, haven't

you? That has been your business? A. Trading in stock market, trading in furs, and through some mortgages coming in.

Q. Well, you were a partner in the fur business, but you didn't buy and sell furs? A. No.

Q. But your business really was trading in the stock market? A. Yes.

Q. That is what you really did? A. Yes.

Q. That is where you spent your days, isn't that a fact? A. Yes.

Q. And every dollar of money that went into those brokerage accounts that you have talked about today, every dollar that went in there you took yourself and gave to the brokers, didn't you? You delivered it to the brokers, didn't you? A. Yes, I delivered to the broker.

Q. Every dollar that you said that Fisch gave you or anybody else gave you, so far as delivering it to the broker, you are the one that gave it to him, aren't you? A. Yes, sir.

Q. And the only man that knows about any moneys between you and Fisch, so far as the stocks are concerned, is the man that is dead, Fisch: isn't that right? A. I don't know; I guess, he said to me he is keeping book.

Q. He is the only man, though? A. As far as I know, yes.

Q. Yes. And he is dead? A. Unfortunate.

Q. He was your best friend, wasn't he? A. Well, I don't say best friend, but---

Q. You don't say so? A. He was very good friend.

Q. Did he help you kidnap this Lindbergh child and murder it? A. I never saw---

Q. You never saw? A. ---Mr. Lindbergh's child.

Q. But Fisch didn't help you, did he?

Mr. Fisher: Objected to, your Honor. He has a right to finish his answer.

Mr. Wilentz: Yes, I suppose he has. I thought he had finished it.

Mr. Fisher: You knew he hadn't.

The Court: Mr. Fisher, you need not shout in that fashion. Make your objections in a quiet and orderly fashion and we will deal with them in a quiet and orderly fashion.

Now then what is the question?

Mr. Wilentz: The objection was that I hadn't permitted the witness to finish his answer.

Mr. Fisher: That is right.
Mr. Wilentz: That was the objection.
Mr. Fisher: That is correct.
Mr. Wilentz: He said he never saw the Lindbergh child, I think.

Here, I call to your attention that Justice Trenchard was swift to admonish attorney Fisher for his first rather shrill accusation "You knew he hadn't." when he responded to Wilentz's claim that it was his impression that Hauptmann had already completed his answer. This was done in spite of the fact that it was very apparent that Hauptmann had not completed his answer. I advise you to note as we read along, the restraint Trenchard used by not "blowing the whistle" on Wilentz as he flew into his continued verbal tirades, haranguing the witness with vile accusations.

Continuing on with Hauptmann's answers to the prosecutor's questions regarding his discovery of the shoe box filled with ransom money:

Q. Now, when Fisch gave you this box, this shoe box, he told you to keep it in a dry place, didn't he? A. Yes.

Q. Don't forget that now. He told you to keep it in a dry place? A. Yes.

Q. And a safe place. A. Yes.

Q. How much money was in that box? How much? A. (No answer.)

Q. You counted it many times. How much was in that box? A. I find it out later it was close to fifteen thousand.

Q. How much was in the box when you counted it? You counted it many times. A. I didn't count it in the box.

Q. How much money was in that box, gold, how much? A. I counted the money when the money was dry and it was close to fifteen thousand.

Q. How much money was in that box, not close, not far away, strange money, money you found when you were excited; how much was in there? A. All the money that was in my possession in gold certificates.

Q. How much? A. That's what I said, close to fifteen thousand.

Q. Fourteen six hundred, fourteen seven hundred, fourteen nine hundred, how much? A. Close to fifteen thousand.

Q. Why don't you know the amount? A. Because I

took a few out of there and I really don't know.

Q. Before you took the few out how much was in there? A. I didn't count it.

Q. You didn't count the gold you found? A. I did count it.

Q. You did count it? A. After I---

Q. How much was in there? Don't get away from it. A. Close to $15,000.

Q. You don't know how much? A. Not exactly.

Q. Was it $14,900? A. Can be.

Q. Was it $14,800? A. Can be.

Q. Was it $14,700? A. Can be.

Q. I don't want to know "can be," I want to know how much it was? A. I told you.

Q. You don't know? A. Not exactly.

Q. Not within a hundred or within two hundred or within three hundred or within four hundred, do you know? A. I said close to $15,000.

Q. How close? A. Say $14,800.

Q. $14,800? A. Yes.

Q. That is a guess? A. Pretty close.

Q. It is a guess, you don't know the exact amount? A. Not exactly.

Q. When you found that money and you took it into the garage to dry it, you didn't count it then, did you? A. When I bundled it.

Q. You just answer the question. You know what I am asking you. When you took that money from that shoe box down into that garage and you took those gold certificates and put them in a basket one after another, fives, tens and twenties, whatever they were, you didn't count it, did you? A. No.

Q. You left it lay in a basket all night and you didn't count it? A. That is right.

Q. You left it lay another night and you didn't count it? A. That is right.

Q. The reason you didn't count it was because you knew, didn't you? A. I didn't know anything. I didn't---

Q. Thousands of dollars lying around of strange money, you find it and you don't even count it, is that right? A. It was hard to count it.

Q. Hard to count it? A. Because it was all wet.

Q. For two weeks you left that money in the basket without counting it, didn't you? A. I counted always when I took the dry one out.

Q. After it dried, two weeks later, you counted the money, didn't you? A. Now listen, the first money,

I took out---

Q. Not took out, I want to know when you counted it. We will come to your taking it out. A. Always when I took the dry ones out, I counted the dry ones.

Q. You take a few out and count the dry ones? A. Yes.

Q. It took two weeks for you to count the money? A. Yes.

Q. It took two weeks for the money to dry? A. I suppose so.

Q. For two weeks you left gold lying in the basket and did know how much was there? A. That is right.

Q. The trunk was a safe place, was it not? A. It was.

Q. The trunk was a dry place, wasn't it? A. Yes.

Q. When you had money and you really wanted a safe place, you put it in the trunk, didn't you? A. Yes.

Q. Everything that you thought was dear to you in this world by way of physical assets, the thing you loved the most, money, you kept in that trunk because it was safe and dry, isn't that it?

Mr. Pope: We object to the form of that question.

Mr. Wilentz: Well, I think this is cross-examination, if your Honor please.

The Witness: That is not the way I lose most money.

Mr. Pope: He is characterizing---well, it is done.

Q. But you kept all the money you had in that trunk because you thought that was the best place for you to keep it? A. Yes.

Q. Better than the bank? A. No, no; not better as a bank.

Q. Better than the vault? A. No.

Q. Did you have a vault? A. Not this time.

Q. Not at that time? A. No.

Q. But you had a bank account? A. Yes.

Q. Now Fisch, he was your best friend, wasn't he? A. Not my best friend.

Q. Now you say he wasn't your best friend? A. I can't say the best friend, he was---

Q. Will you say that you didn't tell people he was your best friend? A. He was my best friend, what I say, in business.

Q. Didn't you tell people that he was your very best and closest friend? A. I got friends dey are just as good, I would say.

Q. Yes. A. Just as dear to me as Mr. Fisch.

Q. All the friends you got have known you only since you are in this country, isn't that right? A. Yes.

Q. Nobody that you know in this country today, none of them outside of your sister, did you know in Germany, did you? A. Oh, yes.

Q. Who? A. Mr. Heim.

Q. Mr. Heim? A. Yes.

Q. Who is he? A. He lives right in New Jersey.

Q. But not Fisch, not Kloppenburg? A. No.

Q. None of those people? A. No.

Q. Didn't you write letters saying that Fisch was your best and closest and dearest friend? A. Closest?

Q. Well, best friend, I think that is the expression we used before? A. Probably he write a letter.

Q. Probably he write a letter? A. Yes.

Q. But it wasn't true, is that it? A. It is true.

Q. It is true, so you wrote a letter he was your best friend and you think he was, one of your best friends? A. One of my best friends.

Q. All right. And he told you to keep this money in the box? A. Not money.

Q. Not the money, the box in a safe place? A. Yes.

Q. He was very sick, you knew that? A. Well, he was sick, but I really---

Q. You thought he would come back? A. That is true.

Q. But you knew he was suffering from tuberculosis, or something like that, you knew that, didn't you? A. I---now, listen. I was asking a couple of time about his sickness; he always said, "Never mind, I am all right."

Q. All right. A. So I think he is O.K.

Q. Well, did you know it? Did you know it? A. I know he was a little bit sick, but I never took it so serious.

Q. Well, he was sick, anyway? A. Yes.

Q. You didn't expect him to die though? A. No, sir.

Q. And here was your sick friend going home, and he asked you to keep this box in a dry place? A. Yes.

Q. You knew from the day you moved into that house that that closet was a wet place, didn't you? You had complained about it all the time, isn't that the fact? A. Complained a couple of times, yes.

Q. From the day you moved into that house you knew it was a wet closet, didn't you? A. Oh, I wouldn't say from the first day.

Q. Well, from the six months or so? A. Yes.

Q. You had complained about it? A. Yes.

Q. But even though you knew that was a wet place, it was a wet closet, even though Fisch told you to keep it in a dry place--- A. Yes.

Q. He told you there were papers in it, you put it in the closet? A. Because I couldn't go in the front room and I couldn't go in the middle room either when Fisch gave me this package. A. You mean that night? A. That night.

Q. Who was going to stop you? Weren't you the master of the house? A. Yes, but I got somebody in the front room; my wife was in the baby's room; and so I put it in this closet, and I forgot all about it.

Q. You didn't want to show it to your wife and you didn't want to show it to your baby, is that it? A. Oh, no.

Q. Well, why couldn't you take it right there, that very night---why didn't you take it there? A. I didn't like to disturb the baby.

Q. You didn't like to disturb the baby? A. Yes.

Q. Well, you didn't have a baby then, did you? A. Yes.

Q. You did? A. Yes.

Q. You didn't want to disturb the baby and you didn't want to disturb your wife? A. That is right.

Q. Is that right? A. Yes.

Q. And you forgot all about it afterwards? A. Yes.

Q. Well, finally, you found it? A. Yes.

Q. You made a mistake, you put it in a wet place; Fisch asked you to put it in a dry place, you put it in a wet place, but you finally found it? A. I found it, that is right.

Q. You found the money? A. Yes.

Q. And you found it because a broom hit it, isn't that right? A. Yes.

Q. There is no mistake about that, is there? A. No mistake.

Q. A broom hit the box and you saw money? A. Yes.

Q. When was that? When was that? What date, what month? You don't know, do you? A. It was the middle of August.

Q. 1933? A. 1933. It was on a Sunday---

Q. Middle of August? A. Yes.

Q. Was your wife home? A. My wife, she was home, yes.

Q. Yes. A. She was home.

Q. And you went to the closet? A. I went to the closet.

Q. And you took the broom? A. Yes.

Q. You were going to take it out, were you? A. I took it out to clean something.

Q. You went to the closet to take a broom out, isn't that it? A. Yes.

Q. And you were going out with it, isn't that right? A. That is right.

Q. And when you did that, walking out of the closet with the broom, you hit that box? A. No, walking that way I couldn't, I couldn't hit the box.

Q. Well, how did it happen then? That is what I want to know. A. Probably the broom was mixed up or there was another broom and stuff laying in the closet.

Q. What shelf on the closet was it? A. The upper shelf.

Q. Upper shelf, top shelf? A. Top shelf.

Q. I want you to take a look at this picture of the kitchen and tell me whether that is a correct picture of the kitchen and the closet, that part of it shown by the photograph? A. Yes, that's right.

Q. That shows your closet and shows your kitchen, does it? A. Yes.

Mr. Wilentz: All right, I offer it in evidence.

Wilentz also kept hammering away incessantly at Hauptmann about the "discovery" of the door panel in his kitchen closet with Tom Cassidy's fiendish plant. As best he could, Hauptmann attempted to explain the mysterious writing, but was thwarted at every turn by the cleverness of the attorney general who took every advantage of the witness's failure to give an immediate answer to some of his questions.

Q. Now, Mr. Hauptmann, what you mean then is this, that you have got a habit of writing down telephone numbers and addresses of things that are interesting; isn't that right? A. Yes.

Q. From the paper. A. From the paper or---

Q. Or from anything else? A. From books.

Q. Yes. And you must have read this in the paper, and you were near the closet, so you wrote it down; that is what you mean, isn't it? A. There is a possibility, but I can't remember---you took this piece of wood from the closet, you said you took this piece of wood from the closet, and it is impossible to stay inside in the closet and to write or read.

Q. That is--- A. That is, I guess that is what you said, or Mr. Pope meant, and so I said it is impossible that I would ever put this on this board.

Q. Well, you know you wrote some of it; you know that, don't you? You remember that. A. But I am positively sure I wouldn't write anything in the inside of a closet.

Q. You know that part of it, part of the numbers are your handwriting; you know that, don't you? A. It looks like it.

Q. Yes. Well, you know it is; you have said so many times, in the Bronx. A. I don't say it is.

Q. Well, didn't you say in the Bronx many times that you wrote the numbers on? A. I said it looks like.

Q. You told Mr. Foley that it was, and you told me in court that it was, in the Bronx, didn't you? A. (No answer.)

Q. And didn't you say at that time that the reason you wrote it in there was just like you said a minute ago, that you had a habit of writing those things. A. Yes, I said so, but that doesn't ---

Q-- And that is why---sir? A. That doesn't include this board. I wouldn't make any notice on the inside of a closet where you have no chance to stand to write or read, it is impossible.

Q. In the closet, no chance to stand to write or read in the closet, that is why you put it in the closet, you didn't think anybody could find it, isn't that why you put it there? A. No, I make notice sometimes when a person is born that means his birthday, I want it in a place where I can see it.

Q. That is why--- A. No, that is why I always put it in the kitchen.

Q. Now let me get back to your question and answer and don't get me off the track again. Did you tell Mr. Foley that that was your handwriting? We will start all over again. A. Yes, all over again. I don't know, sir, that I did.

Q. You think you did? A. I think I did not.

Q. Did you say to Mr. Foley when he asked you why did you write it on the board, do you remember that question, and you said to him substantially what you have just told us here, "I must have read it in the paper about the story. I was a little bit interest and keep a little bit record of it and maybe I was just on the closet and was reading the paper and put down the address." Did you say that? A. I say I don't know if it is exactly what I said to him.

Q. It sounds all right? A. I said something to him, I know.

Q. Something like that? A. Something like it, yes.

Q. Substantially that? A. What does "substantially" mean?

Q. It means practically that, that is what it means, the same thing. A. I said to him something about my habit of writing numbers.

Q. You had a habit of writing numbers? A. No, not numbers---for instance, I am interested in a book and for instance there is a person, when this person was born or that person, and that was why I was interested to remember this in history, I am much interested in history and so I couldn't forget. I always put it on the place. It was usually the place underneath the mirror in the kitchen.

Q. In other words, you were interested in historical events and dates? A. Yes, sir.

Q. And you had the habit of marking down in the kitchen on the wood, is that what you mean? A. Yes.

Q. Were you interested in historical events relating to aviation? A. No.

Q. You were interested in that? A. No.

Q. Do you know who was the greatest aviator for Germany during the World War? A. Yes, I know.

Q. What was his name? A. Richtofen.

Q. What was his first name? A. Manfred.

Q. Manfred Richtofen? A. Manfred Richtofen, yes. Besides I was just reading the book in the jail and that brings my memory back.

Q. You are reading a book about the greatest aviator in the German Army in the jail? A. About four weeks ago I read it in the jail here.

Q. Tell me what his name is again? A. Manfred Richtofen.

Q. Manfred Richtofen? A. Yes.

Q. Now, we will get back to this board again and

the telephone number or the words written on that board. So that you say now that when Mr. Foley asked you why did you write on the board you said something to him that you had a habit of writing dates and other things about historical events. A. I told him something, yes, about that.

Q. Well, Mr. Foley wasn't satisfied with that, was he, he asked the next question, "How did you come to put the telephone number on there?" And your answer was, was it not, "I can't give you any explanation about the telephone number." Do you remember that? A. No, I can't.

Q. You can't remember that? A. I can't remember all, in dem days---

Q. I want to know whether you can remember that question and answer and whether or not you gave that to Mr. Foley. A. I can't remember.

Q. You were then talking to the District Attorney of Bronx County, you were incarcerated, you were kept in custody and you were charged, you knew you were being charged with murder by the State of New Jersey. A. No, I didn't know that.

Q. You didn't know that? A. No.

Q. You knew you were arrested in the Lindbergh case. A. Yes.

Q. Yes, sir. You knew the Lindbergh child had been dead, you knew that, didn't you? A. Yes.

Q. You knew somebody had gotten $50,000 or so they said, from Dr. Condon, you knew that? A. That is what I read in the paper.

Q. And you were asked about Dr. Condon's telephone number and home address in your closet on a board which was right before you, you remember that. A. Yes.

Q. And today you don't remember what you said to Mr. Foley about that. A. I said I can't remember all them single questions, because there was so many questions at this time.

Q. You have answered the questions then, haven't you? A. (No answer.)

Q. You have finished that answer, haven't you? A. I have finished this answer.

Q. You wanted to tell Mr. Foley the truth, didn't you? A. Yes.

Q. Mr. Foley treated you well, didn't he? A. Very well.

Q. He is a very delightful man, isn't he? A. Yes.

Q. A very fine man? A. Yes.

Q. Yes. And you were sitting in there in his office and he was asking you about it, wasn't he? A. Yes.

Q. And you were answering him? A. Yes.

Q. And there was a stenographer there, isn't that right? A. Well, there were quite a few people in the room.

Q. Yes, but there was a man writing, wasn't there? A. I can't remember seeing anyone writing.

Q. Did you tell the District Attorney at that time the truth when he was talking to you about this board, S-204? A. Well---

Q. You don't know whether you told him the truth? Why don't you answer the question, Mr. Defendant? A. For the first time he brought this piece of wood and he said that's from my closet. Well, anybody can show me a piece of wood like that; you find it in every house. I didn't even think of it, what I said.

Q. Oh, you didn't even think of it. Did you tell District Attorney Foley the truth when he spoke to you about this board S-204? You might just as well answer it because I am going to stay here until you do. A. The truth? Well, I told him---

Q. Did you tell him the truth? A. I told him the truth, yes.

Q. You told him the truth? A. Yes.

Q. Did you tell the truth about this board in the Supreme Court in New York? A. I---

Q. Why do you hesitate? A. I am not.

Q. Well, then, why don't you answer? Either you did or you didn't. A. You have to give me a chance.

Q. I will give you all day, but you ought to know whether you told the truth in court. A. No, I have to trans--- I am thinking in German and I have to translate it in American language, and it needs quite a bit of time; so excuse me.

Q. Yes, sir. But just the simple question of whether you told the truth in The Bronx courthouse about this board--- A. When I told Mr. Foley---

Q. No, please. I am going to ask you the question again. When you were examined in the Bronx County courthouse specifically about 204, did you tell the truth there? A. I was.

Q. Please, will you--- A. I was not willing---

Q. Pardon me. Will you please answer the question? Can't you answer it Yes or No, you either told the truth or you didn't? Then you can give the explanation.

Mr. Pope: We think that the witness is trying to answer it and that he should be given an opportunity to do so.

The Court: Yes, he ought to be given an opportunity and I think he is being given an opportunity. The question was as to whether or not he told the truth there. He may answer that and then he may add to anything he desires to add to it by way of explanation. That I think the witness is entitled to.

Proceed, Mr. Attorney General.

Q. Did you tell the truth in the Bronx Courthouse, Yes or no? And then if you want to explain it you may explain it as far as I am concerned. A. Well, I guess I explain it first.

Q. Will you please do us the kindness of abiding by the rules of the court and answer first Yes or No did you tell the truth about this board when you were being examined in the Bronx County Court House under oath about this board. A. Then I say No.

Q. You didn't tell the truth there? A. No.

Q. All right. Now, just stay there for one minute.

Mr. Pope: Wait a minute, now.

A. You want to give me a chance to explain?

Q. Yes, sir.

The Court: He may have it.

A. When I saw Mr. Foley the first time speak about this particular board here I never said Yes and I never said No, because I never could make out and I never could remember ever putting it out, and when it came up in the court room I only said Yes, mitout thinking of it.

Q. You simply said Yes, what? A. When he asked me if I put it out.

Q. You simply said Yes, in the court room without thinking about it? A. Yes, without thinking about it.

Q. You mean that you just paid no attention, you have no interest in the case? A. No, interest--- Of course I got to have interest in it, but really is to get over it, first place, I didn't know what to say, so I said Yes. Just as well I could say No.

Q. When was that, before Foley or in the court? A. In the court room.

Q. Go on tell us. You want to explain. Go on and explain. A. I guess I am finished with the explanation.

Q. You are finished with the explanation? A. Yes.

Q. What do you mean by explanation? Do you mean that you said No, it didn't make any difference to you or rather you mean you said Yes, and that wasn't the truth? That is the first thing you mean, isn't it? A. Yes.

Q. That is in the court house when you said Yes you wrote that on the board, you really meant No? A. This came---

Q. Is that what you mean? Is that what you mean, Mr. Hauptmann? A. Will you---

Q. In the court house you say you didn't tell the truth because when you said Yes that you wrote this, you didn't mean it? A. I didn't mean it, that is right.

Q. That is right. So you did say in the court Yes you wrote it, in the Bronx County court, but that was not the truth? A. This was not the true.

Q. Not the truth? A. After I was thinking of it, this board, special from the place where they took them, and it is impossible I ever put it on.

Q. Now, you were examined by District Attorney Foley on September the 25th, 1934, you remember that, about a week after you were arrested. A. That is about.

Q. And after you were examined by District Attorney Foley, the hearing in the Bronx, October 17th, 22 days after you made the statement to Mr. Foley, you came into the Bronx County Court House to oppose the efforts of the State of New Jersey to bring you here on trial, so you had some time to think about the board, didn't you? A. I really---I never was thinking about it.

Q. You had a lawyer in court, didn't you, in the Bronx County Court? A. I did, yes.

Q. Yes, sir, and you were represented by a lawyer when this hearing was on? A. Yes.

Q. You were in the courtroom where they were taking your pictures every day, weren't they? A. Yes.

Q. You knew how important it was? A. Well, I don't know exactly how important it was.

Q. You don't know how important it was? A. No.

Q. Your wife was in there saying to you, "Richard, please tell the truth," every day, wasn't she? A. Yes, she was.

Q. And with all of that, with a charge of murder against you by the State of New Jersey and your wife pleading with you to tell the truth, you walked in before a Supreme Court Justice in New York State and you lied, and when you lied you knew you lied, didn't you? A. No, that is not lying, I give this answer mitout thinking anything, I could just as well say no or yes.

Q. Well, it wasn't one question and one answer, Mr. Defendant, was it? A. My physical condition wasn't so well at this time.

Q. At that time? A. No.

Q. October 17th? A. No.

Q. It was just as good as it is now? A. No, sir.

Q. It wasn't? A. No.

Q. Let's see. Did you say anything to the Judge at the time about your physical condition, that you couldn't answer or didn't want to answer? A. I can't remember to make any complaints.

Q. Did you say anything in court at the time that you would like to have the hearing postponed? A. I don't think I did.

Q. Your physical condition was good enough to deny that you were in the State of New Jersey on March 1st, wasn't it? A. That is one thing I am positively sure of.

Q. Sure. Your physical condition was good enough to deny that you murdered the Lindbergh child, wasn't it? A. I never saw the Lindbergh child.

Q. You jumped out of your chair when I asked you about that, didn't you, in the Bronx courthouse? A. In the Bronx courthouse I jumping out of my chair?

Q. Yes. A. I said No.

Q. Your physical condition was good enough for that? A. That is one thing that is so absurd that you can sleep when you are up against that.

Q. That is one thing you are sure of? A. Yes.

Q. You were never in that Lindbergh house, were you? A. No, sir.

Q. Certainly not? A. Certainly not.

Q. You never went in there and took that child out of that room, did you? A. No.

Q. You never took that chisel into that bedroom, did you? A. I never was.

Q. You never took that ladder up there, did you? A. I even didn't build that ladder.

Q. You didn't even take that ladder out of your attic, did you? A. No, sir.

Q. You didn't collect the $50,000 either? A. No.

Q. You got part of it, didn't you? Who got the rest of it? A. The---

Q. Who got the rest of it? A. I don't know anything about it.

Q. You don't know anything about it but you wrote Condon's name and address on this board, and that is what we are back to now. A. No, positively not.

Q. Positively not? A. Positively not.

Q. Let me read you some of your answers then: "How did you come to put the telephone number on there?" And your answer was, "I can't give you any explanation about the telephone number." Then your next question--- I read that to you a minute ago. "Your only explanation for writing Dr. Condon's address on this board and telephone number is that you were probably reading the paper in the closet and you marked it down, is that correct?" And wasn't your answer as follows: "It is possible that a shelf or two shelves in the closet and after a while I put the new papers always on the closet and we just got the paper where this case was in, and I followed the story of course, and I put the address on there." Did you say that to Foley? A. Yes.

Q. All right. A. I say that.

Q. You said that to Foley. It is possible you were reading a paper and you were in the closet and you were interested in the case, so you marked it down on the closet? A. But it is impossible to mark it down in the closet.

Q. And then the next question: "That's why you marked it on the door?" You had something on the door, too, didn't you? Some numbers of some bills, some big bills? A. On the panel.

Q. On the panel? A. Door panel.

Q. You had on the door panel, that same door, some numbers of big bills, didn't you? A. Yes.

Q. What were the size of those bills, $5,000 and $1,000, weren't they? A. It was a thousand, I guess.

Q. Thousand dollar bills? A. Thousand dollar bills.

Q. How many thousand dollar bills did you have? A. I can't remember now. When I put it on, it was summer time '32.

Q. Yes, sure, summer time '32; after April the 2nd, 1932? A. No; summer time '33; I wish to correct.

Q. Oh, I see. A. I got $2,000 I should put in the stock market, I brought it to the bank, and I kept it home for a few days.

Q. Two one thousand dollar bills? A. Yes.

Q. Tell me, where do you get those one thousand dollar bills? A. That is Mr. Fisch brought it in my house, to put it in the margin.

Q. Oh, Mr. Fisch brought it? A. Yes, sir.

Q. We are going to come to Mr. Fisch in a little while. A. Yes.

Q. Now let's get back to the board again. A. Yes.

Q. The next question---oh, I just asked you about that; that is, the next question was why you marked it on the door and you said, "That is the only explanation I can give."

Q. And then you were asked by Mr. Foley, "Your answers to my questions are made of your own free will: is that correct?" And you answered, "Yes." Isn't that right? That is, you made the answer to question Mr. Foley asked you if you made the answers of your own free will, and you said Yes, isn't that right? A. Yes; I guess I said to everybody, everything yes at this time.

Q. Now, do you remember being asked this, "Is there anything more you want to say about it or add to it," you were asked that, and your answer was this: "No. About them two numbers, I am sure it was five hundred or thousand dollar bills." Do you remember saying that? A. I guess I did say so.

Q. You didn't even know whether it was a $500 or a $1000 bill, isn't that right, it was one or the other? A. Yes, one or another.

Q. You mean to tell me that you sat in The Bronx courtroom, talking to Foley about $500 bills and $1000 bills, and didn't know whether it was five hundreds you had or thousands? A. That is true, I don't know if it was a five--

Q. You didn't know? A. ---hundred dollar bill or a thousand dollar bill.

Q. A man that had, the greatest amount of money you ever had in Europe was a hundred dollars, and you couldn't remember in 1932 whether the bills laying around the house were thousand dollar bills or five hundreds? A. This time, '33, I get quite a lot of money to put in the market, put in force, so I really, I couldn't remember if it was 500 or 1000.

Q. And that is what you told Mr. Foley? A. Yes.

Q. All right. As you remember, then, you were asked, "When you say those two numbers you don't refer to anything on this board, when you talk about the two numbers you don't mean anything written on this board, but other numbers written on the door," and your answer was, "Yes, on the door." That is true, isn't it? That is, you told Foley that you didn't mean anything on that board, you meant the numbers on the sash or the door? A. On the door pillar?

Q. Yes. On the panel of the door. A. Panel of the door.

Q. And then you were asked, "Is there anything else that you would like to add," and you answered "No," isn't that correct? A. Well, I can't---that is what I say; I can't remember.

Q. All right then, weren't you asked then, "Do you remember the day that you wrote this memorandum on the board," the memorandum referring to the memorandum on Exhibit S-204, you were asked that question, weren't you: "Do you remember the day that you wrote it?" and your answer was "No." You remember that, don't you? A. That is what I said, I can't remember them questions and answers.

Q. Then you were asked again, "You remember that you did write it?" And your answer was, "I must write it, the figures, that is my writing." Do you remember saying that to Mr. Foley? A. I guess I said it must be, it looks like my writing.

Q. Do you remember saying that to Mr. Foley? A. No, I can't.

Q. "I must write it, the figures, that is my writing"? A. I guess I said it looks like my writing.

Q. You guess you said it looks like your writing? A. I guess; I can't exactly remember, but I said---

Q. You say you didn't say that, "I must write it, the figures, that is my writing"? A. That is what I said, I can't remember that what I said.

Q. Well, at any rate, you had talked to Foley, all these questions, September, 1934, you knew when you were coming into the courthouse to answer the complaint of the State of New Jersey, you knew you were going to be asked about it, again, didn't you? A. Well, I didn't know if I was going to ask again about it.

Q. What did you think they were going to ask you about, your hunting trip up in Maine? A. No. I really don't know.

Q. You didn't know? A. I know there is a lot of things to put on the particular board.

Q. This is funny to you, isn't it? You are having a lot of--- A. No, absolutely not.

Q. You are having a lot of fun with me, aren't you? A. No.

Q. Well, you are doing very well, you are smiling at me every five minutes? A. No.

Q. You think you are a big shot, don't you? A.

No. Should I cry?

Q. No, certainly you shouldn't. You think you are bigger than everybody, don't you? A. No, but I know I am innocent.

Q. Yes. You are the man that has the will power, that is what you know, isn't it? A. No.

Q. You wouldn't tell if they murdered you, would you? A. No.

Q. No. Will power is everything with you, isn't it? A. No, it is--- I feel innocent and I am innocent and that keeps me the power to stand up.

Q. Lying when you swear to God that you will tell the truth. Telling lies doesn't mean anything. A. Stop that!

Q. Didn't you swear to untruths in the Bronx Court House? A. Stop that!

Q. Didn't you swear to untruths in the court house? Didn't you lie under oath time and time again? Didn't you? A. I did not!

Q. You did not? A. No.

Q. All right, sir. When you were arrested with this Lindbergh ransom money and you had a twenty dollar bill, Lindbergh ransom money, did they ask you where you got it? Did they ask you? A. They did.

Q. Did you lie to them or did you tell them the truth? Did you lie to them or did you tell them the truth? A. I said not the truth.

Q. You lied, didn't you? A. I did, yes.

Q. Yes. Lies, lies, lies, about Lindbergh ransom money, isn't that right? A. Well, you lied to me, too.

Q. Yes, where and when? A. Right in this court room here.

Q. We will let the jury decide about that. In this court room. Did I ever ask you a question outside of this court room? Did I ever come into that jail to ask you a thing? A. No.

Q. I asked you if you wanted a cigar or cigarettes when I brought you here from the Bronx, didn't I? A. I don't remember.

Q. I asked you if you would like to stay in the corridor or if you would like to go up to the cell, I asked you that, didn't I? Isn't that right? A. I can't remember those things.

Q. You can't remember that. Now let's get back to the Lindbergh ransom money. You were arrested by the police? A. Yes.

Q. You see you are not smiling any more, are you? A. Smiling?

Q. It has gotten a little more serious, hasn't it? A. I guess it isn't any place to smile here.

Q. "I am a carpenter." A. I am.

Q. That was funny, wasn't it? A. No, sir, there is nothing funny about it.

Q. There is nothing funny about it? You had a good laugh, didn't you? Did you plan that in the jail there, did somebody tell you to give that answer when I asked you about the ladder, to stand in front of the jury and say "I am a carpenter"? A. No, sir.

Q. You thought that out yourself? A. No, I didn't think a thing about it.

Q. Let me ask you something: You have got a peculiar notion about will power, haven't you?

> Mr. Pope: Well, I think this has gone just about far enough.
>
> The Court: What do you mean by that, Mr. Pope?
>
> Mr. Pope: Well, I mean this patent abuse of the witness. It seems to me it is about time we protested against it. It has been going on for quite a while.
>
> The Court: Whenever you have any occasion to protest, you make your protest to the Court while the thing is going on, and the Court will deal with it; it always has and will continue to do so. We will now take a recess for five minutes.

By this time it becomes quite obvious that Wilentz was using the "closet board plant" of Tom Cassidy to its greatest advantage by presenting the "find" as absolute and insoluble proof that Hauptmann was guilty, and there could be no doubt about it. Taking this evidence and confusing the jury, as well as Hauptmann, the attorney general played it for all it was worth. By presenting statements made by Richard when he was first confronted with the board, plus those made by him in the Bronx court room, together with the fact that the accused man had great difficulty in giving immediate answers because of the great difficulty he had on many occasions by first having to mentally absorb the questions in German, his native tongue, before he could render a suitable answer in English. This, coupled together with the verbal harassment which was directed at him by the caustic and scathing tongue of the prosecuting attorney and a judge who saw no reason to put a stop to it, could do nothing else but make Hauptmann appear to be very,

very guilty before the eyes of all mankind.

More than a five minute recess was needed. At this point Hauptmann surely must have realized his need for help was very great. However, depressing as things appeared to be, he was certain this help would come when some honest people willing to tell the truth, regardless of the cost, would be heard and judged for their reasonable testimony regarding his definite and very persuasive innocence.

The reasonable understanding and belief of a judge and jury should have been all that was needed. But, unfortunately for Bruno Richard Hauptmann, their belief in the truth was sadly and tragically missing.

CHAPTER FORTY SIX

Court Without Ethics!

Regardless of the answers or any reasonable explanation Hauptmann attempted to give regarding the things he did, the attorneys for the prosecution refused to accept any of it as even being remotely possible. Instead they hammered away at him without restraint. Hindered with a need to initially think out the question in his native tongue before giving his answer in English, Hauptmann gave the impression that he was, not only hesitant and uncertain in his response, but was also blatantly lying about almost everything he attempted to tell.

To understand the prisoner's difficulty and dilemma in giving spontaneous answers, one would have to also be of foreign parentage and have only a limited command of the English language as was the case with Hauptmann.

In addition to this it is easily seen that at no time and in no way did they ever entertain the thought of accepting Hauptmann's reasonable explanation as to why he, upon finding the money in Fisch's shoe box, did not take it to his bank. His reasoning was certainly a sane one. Had he done so, realizing most of it was in gold notes, he would have subjected himself to many questions of which he would be unable to answer; chiefly as to how he had come into possession of so much illegal currency, the end result would have undoubtedly revealed his illegal entry into the United States. And so, his decision to keep it in his garage was the only logical one he had.

Having been told that his partner, Isidor Fisch, had passed away earlier that year owing him a sum of $7,500, of which he had no hope of reclaiming, he proceeded to remove no more than 12 to 15 of the bills, estimated at their greatest value to be $300, and after drying them, went about putting them in circulation by purchasing necessities such as groceries, shoes and gasoline. But this perfectly acceptable logic was much too much for the prosecution to swallow as being even remotely the truth. To them it all added up to more fantasies in Hauptmann's famous "fish story".

But, in spite of the despicable cross examination by Wilentz, Hauptmann did very well in defending his actions on the questionable dates. As a matter of fact, as we study the trial testimony, at one point where Hauptmann was explaining what he did with the money when he discovered it on the top shelf of the broom closet, it seems quite evident by the remarks made by the attorney general, that he himself became lost in the possibility that Hauptmann had actually found the money as he testified, and that he, David Wilentz himself, probably believed, for that moment at least, and had accepted the perfectly logical explanation that Hauptmann had given. As I was watching some of the file film of this part of the courtroom cross-examination with Dick Cass, I was startled as Dick yelled: "See that, Wilentz actually believes Hauptmann? He gives himself away, but nobody caught it! Play that part back again.", he asked. And we did, over and over again. I had to admit that I also think that Wilentz momentarily, while lost in the heat of the moment, gave his unwitting sanction to Richard's explanation. The attorney's voice inflection gives him away.

The utter disregard Wilentz demonstrated by his failure to even remotely accept any of Hauptmann's statements is also clearly seen. Hauptmann said he lived about a mile distant from Woodlawn Cemetery, and was well aware of its location, but he had never been in the cemetery and very seldom had passed by it. As for his knowledge of St. Raymond's Cemetery he claimed to have read about it in the newspapers regarding its connection with the Lindbergh case, but it was his belief he had only driven by it possibly one time. These statements were looked upon by the prosecution as being highly unthinkable, incredible and absurd.

But then, Hauptmann's claims were certainly reasonable. We must remember that the Borough of the Bronx is rather extensive in size, and although Hauptmann lived in close proximity to one of the cemeteries, the location of his work took him in a completely different direction from it. I am sure that there are many points of interest, in small towns where you have lived for many years, and although you have known of them, you never went out of your way to see them.

Why then was such a big deal made about Hauptmann and their refusal to believe his perfectly logical explanation? Simply because they realized their need to use every possible means in order to connect him with both cemeteries, thus pulling together even the weakest facets of their case in order to convict their innocent victim.

Wilentz was relentless during most of his interrogation. By taking every advantage offered him by Hauptmann's inability to supply his answers immediately, or his handicap of not completely understanding the questions, the attorney general was successful in making it appear that Hauptmann was lying about every phase of the case. His sharp attacking accusations at many points added more to put the witness in what appeared to be a defenseless situation. But such was not the case. At many times Hauptmann was utterly struggling to give his answer, but he was not permitted to do so because of the rapid-fire questions of Wilentz.

In District Attorney Foley's office in the Bronx, Hauptmann had explained all he knew about the handwriting on the board taken from the inside of the bedroom closet of his home, the board with reference to Dr. Condon, which had been conveniently placed there through the "courtesy" of newsman, Tom Cassidy. However, when Richard finally learned from where it had been taken, he denied ever writing it. However, he did admit the writing resembled his.

But in spite of his constant and emphatic denials of having written it, Wilentz was persistent with his accusations of Hauptmann's guilt. Had Cassidy not provided such a controversial damning bit of evidence the cross-examination by Wilentz would have been greatly condensed.

And so it went, on and on, as Wilentz almost agonized in his attempts to draw an admission from Hauptmann of his involvement in something that in itself could be termed not only absurd and ridiculous, but preposterous as well. Our own good sense would lead us to ask the question: "Why in heaven's name would Hauptmann, had he been even remotely guilty of taking part in the kidnapping, have been stupid enough to write the name of the man he was negotiating with for the ransom money on the inside of a bedroom closet?" Of course he didn't write it! He didn't write it because Tom Cassidy did. But when he was first shown the wood panel, while undergoing a third-degree questioning session, he, not even being told where it came from, admitted it looked somewhat like his handwriting. However, when he was finally told it came from the inside of his child's bedroom closet, he vehemently denied writing it there or anywhere, furthermore denying that the writing could be his.

The questioning you have read is but a portion of the cross-examination of Hauptmann by Attorney General Wilentz regarding the board taken from the closet. It starts on Page 2659 of the complete trial testimony and continues until Hauptmann was finally excused from the stand with Wilentz still pounding away with his questions about the wood as we reach Page 2907.

Had the real truth of the "accepted faked evidence" been known by everyone, instead of just a few, regardless of how incriminating it appeared to be, Wilentz could have been accused of making "much ado about nothing" at the expense of a great deal of time and dollars. Nevertheless, regardless of the cost, Wilentz had gained a very apparent victory by branding Hauptmann, in the eyes of the members of the jury, who would soon judge him, to be nothing less than a calculating and devious cold-blooded killer. A biased majority of the world's citizens had already decided he was this, due largely by mass reaction and the "landswell of emotions" brought on by much unfair pre-trial publicity which the public had been feeding on daily.

One more point I would like to make clearly demonstrates how the attorney general, after further confusing the defendant, and continuing with a series of questions pertaining to the precise words Hauptmann used in a letter to Pincus Fisch when he informed him of Isidor's indebtedness of $5,500 to him. The questioning went this way:

Q. Didn't you write to Fisch's family, after Fisch died, after he died, didn't you write them, "I gave him $5,500 out of my private bank account"? A. Yes, to make it clearly I wrote him this way---

Q. You wrote him that, didn't you? A. Yes.

Q. Wait a minute, now. My God, don't you tell anybody the truth?

Mr. Fisher: That is objected to, your Honor.

The Court: Yes, that is objectionable. I sustain the objection.

The sudden outburst by Wilentz as he, in one stinging question, attacked the veracity of Hauptmann's previously given testimony was entirely uncalled for. Justice Trenchard realized the unfairness of the accusation by immediately sustaining Fisher's prompt objection.

It seems, however, that statements made by persons, at least in the Flemington courtroom, varied a great deal and would be determined by Wilentz alone as to who it was that he chose to decide was lying --- and who he declared to be telling the gospel truth.

This fact is made clear by his objections to the answers Hauptmann gave during the re-direct questions asked by his own attorney, big Ed Reilly. The discussion related to the Knickerbocker Pie Company in which Fisch had told Hauptmann he had invested some money. Reilly inquired of his client:

Q. Now, when Fisch and you first decided to go into business, did Fisch tell you that he was interested in the Knickerbocker Pie Baking Company? A. He said he is one of the founders.

Q. Did he say the business was still being carried on? A. He said the business is very fair and he said his investment is $10,000.

Q. And you replied on that, didn't you? A. Yes, I did.

Q. Did you find out after he died that the pie baking company folded up, went out of business two years before he told you that? A. I find it out after I start.

Q. Yes, that two years before he told you the pie baking company was making money, it folded up into bankruptcy, is that right? A. That is right.

Q. So he lied to you there, didn't he? A. Yes.

> Mr. Wilentz: I move that be stricken out. First I object to the question and the answer.
>
> Mr. Reilly: Well, you have been asking this man whether he lied or not.
>
> Mr. Wilentz: Whether Fisch lied to him, your Honor please, is a conclusion on his part and is objectionable, I submit.
>
> Mr. Reilly: He relied on his business honor and probity.
>
> Mr. Wilentz: But I object to this witness characterizing the statement of somebody else.
>
> The Court: Now the further question is whether or not Fisch lied to him.
>
> Mr. Wilentz: Yes, and that I object

to because that is his characterization and his conclusion.

The Court: Well, I am inclined to think that I will have to sustain the objection.

Q. Fisch didn't tell you the truth, did he?

Mr. Wilentz: I object to that as calling for a conclusion.

The Court: Well, you see you have got the facts in the case, Mr. Reilly. Now, what is the use of having the witness characterize it?

Mr. Reilly: All right, we will leave it to the jury as to whether he misstated it or didn't tell the truth or what was.

Here we see Reilly virtually "giving up" in this battle with the attorney general who was determined to prevent Hauptmann from stating his true knowledge about his partner. Although Fisch had definitely lied to Hauptmann, as well as to others, about his nonexistent Knickerbocker Pie Company, the man accused of the terrible act of kidnapping and murder had now been stopped from telling about one of the many fabrications of his deceased partner. This had been cleverly manipulated, maneuvered and played to the hilt, through the permissiveness of Justice Thomas W. Trenchard, by David T. Wilentz, the very man who had earlier inquired of Hauptmann: "don't you tell anybody the truth." Just another example of the "smart tactics" the attorney general used in his determination to place an innocent man in the electric chair at any cost.

Anna Hauptmann followed her husband to the stand and told of the events as they happened following the arrest of Richard and the interrogation she had undergone after she had been taken to the police station. She reiterated the complete faith she had in his innocence. She further explained why, when she had been initially asked if she remembered the night of the Lindbergh kidnapping in March, 1932, and where she and Richard were at the time, she had been unable to do so because she could not remember that far back. However, when she was told the night had been a Tuesday, she could now be certain that she had been working at Fredericksen's Bakery that evening and that Richard had called for her and they had driven home together. She was absolutely positive of this since it was necessary that she work late every Tuesday and Friday because it was customary for Mrs. Fredericksen to take those nights away from the bakery.

In answering questions about the dates of Saturday, April 2nd, 1932 (the night of the ransom payment), she affirmed that her husband had been at home with their friend, Hans Kloppenburg, playing their musical instruments; Sunday, November 26th, 1933, (Richard's birthday) she assured them that he was at home attending a party given in his honor. In addition to Richard and herself, others present were her niece, Mrs. Mueller, Paul Vetterle and Isidor Fisch she so testified.

Wilentz attempted several times to besmirch Richard's faithfulness to his wife by implying that her husband had become rather fond or even infatuated with Gerta Henkel. When asked the pointed question: "Now, Mrs. Hauptmann, from anything you saw or anything you heard in connection with Mrs. Henkel and your husband have you ever entertained the slightest suspicion concerning your husband's infidelity toward you?", her immediate answer had been: "Mrs. Henkel was not only a friend of my husband, she was my friend too." And when asked: "Did you ever entertain any thoughts or opinions that your husband was untrue to you?", she shot back: "Never." And when the suggestion of his unfaithfulness to Anna was suggested, Hauptmann angrily responded: "Do you know what you are talking about? You are talking about my wife and me." The implication of any unfaithfulness on the part of either of the Hauptmanns was quite unfair since it was very evident that both Richard and Anna were deeply in love, and they had remained true to each other, ever since their marriage in 1925.

A large part of the attorney general's interrogation of Anna Hauptmann were questions pertaining to her inability to see the wrapped shoe box on the top shelf of the broom closet. Her explanations seemed rather futile when confronted with a glossy photograph of the closet which clearly exhibited her apron, something she used daily, hanging on a hook located above the shelf. After examining the picture Anna seemed confused, as she offered no better reason than that she had not noticed the shoe box on the shelf because it was too high to see the articles placed there and that it was not easy for her to reach to that height. In a later chapter you will learn why Anna had more than a good reason why she had been unable to explain why she could not see the box on the top shelf. It was due to another diabolical scheme by those who were intent on framing Hauptmann. A fiendish act which tends to make us sick to the very pit of our stomach.

CHAPTER FORTY SEVEN

The Defense Is Heard!

With such an accumulation of "convincing evidence" as the prosecution presented against Hauptmann, it seemed difficult to expect his attorneys to bring any form of factual rebuttal in his favor. However, such was not the case. The defense witnesses proved to be quite positive in their statements, and had their testimony been accepted in light of the truth instead of the pre biased judgement of those who had been fed so many unmitigated lies, it is hard to believe that a jury could bring in any verdict other than an acquittal.

Elvert Carlstrom, the first witness for the defense, testified that he ate at Fredericksen's Bakery on Dyre Avenue in the Bronx regularly on weekdays mornings and evenings. He said he knew Mr. and Mrs. Fredericksen and also Mrs. Hauptmann. He further stated that he knew Anna Hauptmann was a waitress there and that she had waited on him on many occasions during the approximate two and a half months time he had frequented the restaurant. The youthful looking, 27 year old, witness was quite sure he had seen Mrs. Hauptmann's husband in the restaurant on the evening of Tuesday, March 1st, 1932.

Carlstrom said he was certain of the date because it was his birthday and he had journeyed from his home in Dunellen, New Jersey, to the Bronx and had stopped for a bite to eat at the Bronx bakery-restaurant before meeting a lady friend named Esther who lived two doors from the restaurant. He testified further that he had arrived at Fredericksen's at approximately 8:30 and had left there about 20 minutes later. He said Mr. Hauptmann was seated near the front of the restaurant reading a newspaper; that Mrs. Hauptmann had waited on him; that he saw neither Mr. or Mrs. Fredericksen; and that both Mr. and Mrs. Hauptmann were there when he left.

Elvert could not be shaken in his testimony, and although Wilentz succeeded in confusing him at times, he remained fervent in his statement that it was definitely

Hauptmann he had seen in Fredericksen's on the night of the kidnapping. He did admit he was not aware that the man he saw there that night was the husband of Anna, his waitress, until he read about it in the newspapers shortly after he learned of Hauptmann's arrest. Although he admitted when he recognized Hauptmann's picture in the paper as the man he had seen in Fredericksen's that night, he did not go to the police with his knowledge because he was not anxious to get involved. However, he said he had told some friends.

I am sure if Carlstrom had gone immediately to the police with his story they would have done everything "lawful" to discourage him from affirmatively testifying for their prisoner.

The next witness, Louis Kiss who resided in New York City, testified that he well remembered Hauptmann being present in Fredericksen's Bakery on the evening of Tuesday, March 1st. He said he came to defend Hauptmann when he read the published testimony given in court by the defendant regarding an incident that transpired on the evening of Tuesday, March 1st, 1932 in Fredericksen's Bakery regarding a police dog. Under the direct questioning by Reilly, Richard had given his testimony which Mr. Kiss had read.

It was this testimony of Hauptmann that had alerted Kiss to the fact that he had been in Fredericksen's restaurant on the evening of Tuesday, March 1st, 1932 and had witnessed the incident of Hauptmann telling his wife about the man "wanting to take away the dog". This is exactly the way Kiss told it in court:

Q. Well, the dog came in. Did anyone come with the dog? A. Yes, a man.

Q. What happened concerning that man? A. That lady who served me the coffee came from the back and that man about two or three feet in front of me met that lady, and that man saying to him in German, "Somebody want to take away the dog." That is the way how I remember the whole thing, because he saying that in German. Then I looked up at the man and I drink my coffee and I walked off. I forgot the whole thing.

Q. What did the man say in German to the lady? A. "Je mann hat voll das dog---das hunt vechnamen."

Q. Now, will you give us your translation of that as you understood it in English? A. "Je mann" is "somebody." "Hat voll" is "wanted." "Das hunt," "the dog."

Q. Somebody wanted to take the dog away? A. Yes. "Vechnamen," "take away."

Q. Now, did you get a good look at the man? A. Yes.

Q. The restaurant was well lighted? A. Yes.

Q. And it is a fact that that was said in German, as you testified, and that that impressed it on your mind. A. That is what I looked up from my coffee.

Q. When did you first see after that the picture of the man that said that in German? A. The first day when Mr. Hauptmann was arrested.

Q. Now, do you see the man in the court room? A. Yes, sir.

Q. That you saw come in with the dog and speak those words in German? A. Yes, sir.

Q. Where is he? A. (Arising and pointing.) Right there.

Q. Now, point out. (The defendant arose.) Is that the defendant you are speaking of? A. Yes.

Another good witness had spoken in support of Hauptmann's claim that he had been in Fredericksen's bakery on the night of the kidnapping. However, as convincingly sincere as the words of Mr. Kiss proved to be, they certainly fell dead at the feet of a jury whose members by this time had been stricken with a severe case of unbelieving ears.

During his testimony, Kiss had emphasized he was more than certain that the date he had seen Hauptmann in the bakery was March 1st, because "exactly a week earlier", shortly after midnight February 22nd, his seven year old son, Louis, had been rushed to Belleview Hospital with severe kidney trouble. Wilentz made much of the fact that since Kiss insisted the date had been Washington's Birthday (Monday, February 22nd) when his son had entered the hospital, "exactly a week earlier" would prove Kiss incorrect. The attorney general claimed that Kiss was mistaken and had been in Fredericksen's bakery on Monday, February 29th, and not Tuesday, March 1st, as he testified. Records of Belleview Hospital revealed that the Kiss child had been admitted at 1:20 a.m., the early morning of the 22nd.

But this in no way could have aided Wilentz in his argument. If the date had been a Monday, Kiss could not possibly have claimed to have seen Hauptmann there because Anna did not work on Monday evenings. Wilentz's argument that the night Kiss claimed to have seen Hauptmann in the bakery was Monday, February 29th, gave

Reilly an excellent opportunity to state that it could not have been a Monday since Hauptmann would have had no reason to have gone there. But the inept Reilly once again muffed an excellent chance to combat the claims of the prosecution. Quite a hullabaloo over the difference of one day.

Regardless of all attempts of Mr. Wilentz to discredit him, Louis Kiss proved to be an impressive witness. Adela Rogers St. Johns, daughter of Earl Rogers, the brilliant flamboyant trial lawyer, covered each day's events of the trial for her newspaper, *The New York Evening Journal*. Miss St. Johns was of the opinion that there was merit in the testimony of Mr. Kiss. She wrote: "If I had happened to be on the jury, I would have listened very carefully to Mr. Kiss because I had a conviction he was telling the truth."

Mr. August Van Henke of New York City was the next person called to the witness stand by the defense. He stated that he had lived in the Bronx in 1932 and that sometime during the middle of February his dog, a German Shepherd, had run away. He related that on the evening of Tuesday, March 1st, as he was driving home from New Rochelle on the Boston Post Road, he had stopped at a gasoline station in the Bronx. Mr. Van Henke's gave this account of an incident that took place there.

Mr. Reilly's interrogation follows:

Q. Do you know what street it is on? A. I believe one street runs in here from Dickerts Park, there is an end of the street, I believe it is what they call Ryer Street. I haven't looked at the name. Ryder Avenue, or whatever is the name. The Boston Post Road runs into it.

Q. It begins, you say at the Boston Post Road some place? A. Yes.

Q. Now, as you approached the gas station, you told us about,---did you see anybody and did you see anything that attracted your attention? A. Soon I get on the gas station with the car, I see a dog there on that street what runs west. I get out of the car, left the car on the station and I went out the car, followed the dog, went after that dog. As soon as I pass the station, the gas station, a man stepped up to me and asked me, he says, "Is that your dog?" He says, "It looks like my dog," or you know what he said, "No," I said, "if that is your dog," I says, "it is my dog. If you claim it, I will have you arrested." So he said---

Q. Did the man say who the dog belonged to? A. Yes.

Q. Who? A. He says it belongs to the baker, he points down to the street.

Q. And do you see that man in the court room? A. Yes, I believe that man, that is the man, yes (pointing in the direction of the defendant,) next to the man with the glasses.

Mr. Wilentz: Now just a minute. There is no necessity for the defendant to stand up to identify himself.

Q. Well, we won't have any doubt about it. Is that the man? A. That is the man.

Q. The defendant? A. Yes.

Q. Now I want you to tell the jury, you didn't know this man did you? A. Never seen him before.

Q. Never seen him before. You had lost a police dog? A. Yah.

Q. The dog looked like the dog you had? A. Yes, sir.

Q. And the conversation concerned your dog, didn't it? A. Yes, sir.

Q. Now, slowly and distinctly tell this jury what you said and what the defendant said to you? A. Now, soon I drove in the station. I see the dog there, end of the station, about fifty, sixty feet from the Boston Post Road. I went out my car, I jumped out the car and went after that dog. Soon I get end of station, the gas station. A man stepped up to me and I ask him, I says, "Is that your dog?" Of course he came up to me. He says, "No. It belongs to the bakery." So I said, I says, "If that is--- if that was my dog and you got him in your possession I will have you arrested."

Q. Did you think it was your dog? A. After I look him right, I call him, you know, I call him by name---

Q. What was your dog's name? A. My name was Rex.

Q. Was the general description of the dog--- A. As nearly---

Q. ---the same as yours? A. Nearly the same only this dog got some little black spots in the back of his, no know, neck, and he didn't listen to my call.

Q. Didn't listen to your call? A. No.

Q. But at first you thought it was your dog. A. Yes.

Q. And you are sure you were talking to this defendant. A. I was talking to this man right there.

Q. When he told you it belonged to the baker, what did you say? A. I said, "If it would be my dog I would have you arrested. I don't care who you belonged." And he said, "No." He said this way: "That dog belongs to the baker and I am not the baker," you know in German. We talked German right away, soon I found out, I call the dog in German and he call him in some---what he call him, some kind of a name, Rupier, or some kind of name, funny name.

Q. It wasn't Rex? A. It wasn't Rex. So he listened to the dog and then I got a little conversation with him.

Q. And what else did you say to the man? A. Oh, I told him---

Q. About the dog. A. I told him, I says, "If it would be my dog I would have him locked up."

Q. What else did you say to him? A. Well, I told him, I give him my name, where I was living.

Q. What did he say to you? A. He said "All right; the baker---" He calls him a different name, you know, what the baker's name was, and he told me his name is Hauptmann.

Q. He told you right there in that spot? A. That he did.

Q. That his name was Hauptmann, did he? A. Yes; and I should come along to the bakery to make sure that that dog belonged to the baker, I see--- I know it is not my dog.

Q. And you got into your car? A. I went to the car and took five gallons gas and I went to New York.

Q. And, as a matter of fact, you did find your dog, did you not, some days later? A. Yes, in March the 4th.

Q. Now, why do you place this and how can you place this date as March the 1st, 1932? A. Well, I believe that was the day when everybody knows that Lindbergh's baby was kidnapped.

Q. Did you hear of that any time during that night? A. I came home, you know, it was about nine o'clock; so I went, got my dinner, and then I went outside again. You know, there was a lot of noise on the street, you know people was talking and they said, "You know, Lindbergh's baby is kidnapped."

Q. What time of the night would you say that you heard that Lindbergh's baby had been kidnapped? A. That was around between ten, eleven, eleven o'clock; something like it.

Q. Now, you don't know me, do you? A. No.

Q. Mr. Pope; Mr. Rosecrans--- A. No.

Q. Mr. Fisher? A. No.

Q. And you do not know the defendant outside of

this identification: is that right? A. That night.

Q. And you are not related to them? A. No.

Q. Tell the jury how you became a witness in this case. A. After Hauptmann was arrested and I hear about it, that they got the fellow what kidnapped Lindbergh's baby, first I didn't pay no attention to it and then I thought myself---

Mr. Wilentz: Just a minute. I object to what you thought yourself. What did you do?

Q. After you thought a while, what did you do? A. I wrote to Mr. Fawcett, I believe was his name.

Q. You wrote to his first lawyer? A. A letter

Q. That was shortly after his arrest? A. After his arrest.

Q. Did you tell Fawcett in your letter what you told on this witness stand? A. I told him I know something abut the man that was arrested there. I gave---

Mr. Wilentz: Just a minute. You have answered the question.

Q. All right, you wrote a letter. That letter contained practically the same information that you have given from this witness stand, is that right? A. Yes.

Q. You have no interest in this case, have you, except to come here in the cause of justice? A. That is all.

Q. You know nobody connected with the case? A. I know nobody.

Q. You are absolutely sure that on March 1st, 1932, at what time was it? A. In the night time?

Q. Yes, what time do you say you were at the gas station? A. I couldn't say, a couple of minutes before eight or a couple of minutes after eight.

Q. In the neighborhood of eight o'clock in the Bronx at a gas station--- A. Gas station.

Q. ---you saw this defendant? A. Yes, sir.

Q. And talked with him? A. Yes, sir.

Q. And he gave you his name as Hauptmann? A. Yes.

Van Henke had been positive and sincere in everything he told as he related his chance meeting with Hauptmann in the Bronx at a time close to the hour the kidnapping was taking place over in Jersey. Although the attorney general made every effort to besmirch the man's testimony through character assassination with charges and insinuations that had absolutely nothing at all to do with the case, Van Henke was a strong witness for Hauptmann's cause. However, as indisputable and convincing as his statements were, and weighing them against all the "trumped up" fictitious charges Hauptmann had to face, it would have taken nothing less than an actual bonafide filmed "on the spot" version of the "police dog" episode to have convinced the jury of his innocence. My friends, the prosecution's deck had been deviously stacked against the innocent Richard Hauptmann.

Another witness for the defense whose testimony could not be shaken was Lou Harding of Trenton. He said he had reported to the police early Wednesday morning, March 2nd, that he had seen a car the day before with two men in the front seat and a ladder in the back. As a result of Mr. Reilly's questioning the spectators were informed of the details as the interrogation continued:

Q. Along the road; and do you remember the name of the road? A. Washington Road.

Q. Washington Road. Do you remember March the 1st, 1932? A. Yes, sir.

Q. Were you working? A. Social Service at Princeton.

Q. Were you working in Princeton? A. Yes, sir.

Q. Were you working on that road? A. Yes, sir.

Q. At about what time in the afternoon did you see an automobile? A. It was between two and three-thirty.

Q. On the afternoon of March the 1st, 1932? A. March the 1st, 1932.

Q. And where were you when you saw this automobile? A. I was right alongside the road, right on the road when I saw the automobile.

Q. Now I want you to tell the jury just what you saw, the conversation you had, if the Attorney General doesn't object; if he does, we won't have the conversation with the people in the automobile. A. Well, March the---March the 1st, 1932, it was two people come along in a car.

Q. Men or women? A. Men. And was asking me to direct them to Lindbergh's estate and I told them and directed them to the best of my knowledge, but I directed them out toward Rocky Hill and turn to the left and then they would find the way to the Lindbergh estate.

Q. And how long were you talking to those two men? A. I was talking to them at least about five minutes, four or five minutes.

Q. Was either one of those two men this defendant? A. No, sir, it was not.

Q. Now did you look in the car? A. Yes, sir, I certainly did.

Q. And what did you see in the car? A. What I seen in the car, was a ladder in the car.

Q. A ladder in the car? A. Yes, sir, and a pasteboard box.

Q. And a pasteboard box. What kind of a pasteboard box? A. Well, it was a brown pasteboard box about three-foot long I guess, I imagine about that long or maybe a little bit longer.

Q. Now will you describe the car, please? A. Yes, sir. It was kind of a dark blue suburban car.

Q. What kind of a license did it have on it? A. New Jersey license plates on it.

Q. And now you said a suburban car---will you describe that more fully and in more detail to this jury? A. Yes, sir, I will. A suburban car, what I mean, is a suburban car, it has got three or four seats into the car, see? And them seats was out. It was no seats in there at all, but the ladder was down in the bottom of this car and the box was on top of it.

Q. And were the two men sitting on the front seat of the car? A. In the front seat of the car.

Q. And it was daylight? A. Daylight.

Q. And you had a good look at them? A. I certainly did.

Q. And the car drove away in the direction--- A. Of Princeton.

Q. Of Princeton. Now, in the early morning of March the 2nd, 1932, were you taken in hand by the State Police? A. Yes, sir, not by the State Police, by the township police, Princeton.

Q. By the township police. And eventually did you get to Colonel Lindbergh's estate? A. Yes, they took me up to his estate.

Q. What date? A. March the 2nd.

Q. And did you see the Colonel there? A. Yes, sir, I shook hands with him.

Q. And did you see the same ladder that you had seen in that car anywheres around that estate? A. Well, yes, sir, the same ladder.

Q. Where was it? A. The ladder was right up by the window. As I went into the side door, the ladder then was up on the outside by the window, see? And I was in, I just can't say, just exactly what room I was in, but it was in the room where he had the round globes at.

Luther Harding had been another good witness for the defense with his very certain declaration that neither of the two men he had seen in the car on March 1st had been Richard Hauptmann. In addition to this he was strong in his affirmation that the ladder in the car had been the same as the one he had seen the following day at the Lindbergh home. His cross examination by Wilentz was intense. However, he never wavered or was confused in his answers. The attorney general did all he could to generate Harding to slip up in some way and give an evasive answer. But his efforts proved fruitless. His constant questions pertaining to the ladder bordered on the absurd. Over and over he repeatedly asked if the witness was sure it was a ladder he had seen?; what kind of a plain ladder?; was it a stepladder?; you only saw something that looked like a ladder?; was it a wide ladder?; describe the ladder?; was it a black ladder?; was it a white ladder?; was it a green ladder?; how tall was it?; how long was it?;

After Wilentz had exhausted all these repetitious questions about the ladder, during which time the witness said he had observed both of the car's occupants, as well as its interior, because he had talked to them at close range while standing alongside the passenger's side of the car with his foot on the running board for a period of four or five minutes in broad daylight. Harding never wavered in his positive statements about the ladder, although he could not testify to its width and length, he had nevertheless seen its steps, and said it was "just a plain unpainted one that you pull in and out because I seen it".

Wilentz seemed proud of the fact that Harding's evidence should be questioned simply because the witness had previously been arrested on two occasions for assault and battery; something entirely irrelevant to the case at hand. With all points taken into consideration, Lou Harding's testimony was quite favorable to Hauptmann.

In its February 3, 1935, report of the trial and Harding's stint on the witness stand, *The New York Times* offered this editorial comment: "Although negative, Harding's testimony fits in with the defense attempt to convince the jury that someone other than Hauptmann committed the crime, that the authorities, especially the State Police, neglected opportunities to follow up clues such as Harding's, and that they are now trying to cover up their failure to investigate the case properly by 'railroading' the accused man."

John M. Trendley, who identified himself as an imitator of handwriting, came from East St. Louis to testify for the defense. He said he had examined disputed documents since the year 1895 in 387 or 388 criminal court cases and went on to name many of the most famous. He testified of the peculiarities in the ransom notes and the request writings and said he had examined the charts of Mr. Osborn and the other eight handwriting experts and had reached an opinion. And when asked this question by attorney Reilly:

Q. And as a result of your study and examination of the ransom notes and the Hauptmann request writings, are you in a position to render an opinion as to whether or not Hauptmann, this defendant, wrote the ransom notes? A. In my opinion he did not.

The prosecutors, as they had done with previous defense witnesses, did all they could to malign the credibility of Trendley. But, in spite of their attempts, his opinion did not waver. He was as certain as Samuel Small and Theo Bernsen that Hauptmann could not have written the ransom letters.

Peter H. Sommer was the next person to take the stand for the defense. He testified that between 12 and 12:30, the night of March 1st (He meant the early hour of March 2nd) he had observed two men as he was riding in a trolley car enroute from Fairview, New Jersey, to the 42nd Street ferry at Weehawken. One he described as being about five foot nine, the other one shorter, possibly five foot four. When he boarded the ferryboat bound for the New York side of the river he noticed that one of the men, the taller one, was also on board.

Immediately after arriving there, Sommer said he got on the 42nd Street Crosstown trolley; the time was probably 12:40 a.m. While entering the car he observed two men, one of them he said he recognized as being the taller man he had seen previously on both the New Jersey trolley and the ferry. He said he watched this man in the company of a different shorter man assist a woman, whom they met at the ferry house, onto the car. The woman was carrying a baby. After helping the woman board the trolley, Sommer said he watched the two men walk to a car parked nearby. He testified he closely observed the woman during his ride to the Seventh Avenue subway from where he took a train bound for his home in Brooklyn.

He identified the woman as appearing to be "very nervous". The child was wrapped in a blanket; and when she lifted the baby, the blanket would slip and he was able to see that he (or she) was a blond child about two years old.

Sommer said he was certain the night was March 1st, 1932, and that when he learned of the kidnapping about 10:45 the next morning, March 2nd, he reported the incident to a Detective Mulaney of the 81st Precinct at Ralph and Quincy Street, Brooklyn, New York. He said he was accompanied there by two young men, Joseph Dutt and Carl Jugg. When asked: "Did you communicate again with the police after you spoke to this detective in New York, or was that the only incident?" His answer was: "That was the only incident." Followed by this question: "Did anybody from the New York police come to see you?", Sommer answered: "No, sir. When I reported there they told me they had hundreds of clues."

At the time this report was made by Sommer, Wednesday, March 2nd, the investigation was less than 12 hours old. Why was there no follow-up to this "red-hot" tip?

And why in Flemington did the Attorney General try to intimidate Mr. Sommer by referring to him as a "professional witness" as he testified to some things he had observed on the late night of the kidnapping? He did everything permissible, even overstepping legal bounds, to discredit the man's testimony.

When Sommer was shown a picture of Violet Sharpe (Defendant's Exhibit 7) and asked by Reilly if he could recognize the woman that was seated in the trolley car holding the baby? Sommer's answer had been: "I would say that resembles the woman very strongly." And when shown a photograph of Isidor Fisch (Exhibit D-5) and Reilly inquired: "I show you a picture and ask you whether or not that resembles the man, or is that the man, one of the men that you saw on the trolley car? Sommer replied: "No, but I saw this man on the ferryboat." He further stated that he had made his observations at close range, having been seated "across the way from him.", for a period of between eight and ten minutes.

When asked if there was anyone, other than Detective Mulaney, to whom he had reported the actions he had witnessed on the trolley and ferry ride, he said he had on the following Friday (March 4th) written to the State Police at Trenton, New Jersey. And when asked these questions by Reilly the answers seem very hard to understand:

"Did you ever get an answer?" A. "I did not."
"Nobody came to investigate?" A. "No, sir.

Especially so, since the time involved was at the outset of the investigation. At a time when we would certainly assume all leads, of any kind, would have been run down. What a pity for the sake of Richard Hauptmann that this was not done.

CHAPTER FORTY EIGHT

"Truth-Sayers" and "Manic Depressives"

One of the best witnesses the defense had in their corner was Sebastian Benjamin Lupica. The young Princeton Preparatory student had reported, as early as 7:30 a.m., Wednesday, March 2nd, 1932, that he had observed a man driving a dark colored car at the end of Lindbergh Lane on the afternoon before the kidnapping at about 5:30 p.m. In the car he had seen a ladder.

Why, you should ask, since Lupica told the authorities of this incident early the following morning, and, who certainly should have been aware of its vital importance, did they not deem his report relevant enough to take the time to question the student about it until 4:30 that afternoon? The search for the world's most famous baby and his abductors had begun less than eight hours before, and these "brilliant" investigators just did not bother themselves to interrogate such an important witness. Evidently they were awe-struck with the realization that they were standing in the very presence of the great aviator --- and forgot all else. Certainly they were not all that stupid to pass up those valuable hours, those during the early part of an investigation, to merely "look into this a little later". And yet, that is exactly what they did.

At any rate Ben Lupica was a good witness in court. He did not change his testimony one iota from that which he finally had given the police nearly three years earlier. He described the car as being a black or dark blue 1929 Dodge sedan. The driver had been its sole occupant; the ladder was the same one he later had seen in the Lindbergh home when he was there on the evening of March 2nd.

Wilentz appeared distressed with Lupica's straightforward answers and did everything possible to discredit his testimony. But in spite of this, Lupica was definite when he said there was no trunk on the rear of the car because it held a spare tire there; he was also certain it bore a New Jersey license plate with the letter designation "L", which identified it as one from Mercer County. Adding to this, a further defeat for Wilentz, he stated it was absolutely not a New York plate.

As for his identification of Hauptmann as the driver of the car, the attorney general was somewhat successful by persuading the Princeton student to admit that the driver "bore some resemblance" to the accused prisoner. However, when asked if he could identify Bruno Richard Hauptmann as the man he saw, Lupica, without any hesitation, answered: "No."

Ben Lupica's testimony had been positive and did not deviate from the truth he had told the authorities in 1932. The jury, hearing this, should have seriously considered a verdict of acquittal for Hauptmann. However, the odds by this time had been tremendously stacked against the innocent Bronx carpenter and a verdict in his favor would have been unheard of, uncalled for, and much less accepted.

Hauptmann's friend, Hans Kloppenburg, was the next witness for the defense and although Wilentz did everything he could to shake the man's testimony, he failed in every attempt. Although there were many dates asked of him which he could not be positive, he was absolutely certain that Hauptmann had been home on Saturday night, April 2nd, 1932, because: "I came up to his house about seven o'clock, maybe little bit before, maybe half past six, I don't know exactly. Then we played some music, played cards, had some coffee and cake and between eleven and twelve o'clock he drove me up to the White Plains Avenue."

Q. And he was in the house then the entire evening up to the time--- A. Yes.

Q. ---he drove you to the subway station, is that correct? A. Yes, he was.

Q. Was Mrs. Hauptmann there? A. Mrs. Hauptmann was there too, sure.

Kloppenburg was positive about his testimony since the date happened to be the first Saturday of the month, a time the two men had set aside for their regular monthly meeting to sing and play their guitar and mandolin together in the Hauptmann apartment.

He was just as certain about the events which transpired in Hauptmann's home the night of Saturday, December 2nd, 1933 when the farewell party for Isidor Fisch was held. Kloppenburg said he was already at the Hauptmann's when Fisch arrived: "Yes, I saw him when he came in."

Q. And where did you see him? A. I saw him when he came in the door, on top of the stairway is a door when he came in there.

Q. That leads to what room? A. Goes in the hall.

Q. Did you see him in conversation with Mr. Hauptmann? A. Yes, he was talking right away to Mr. Hauptmann.

Q. Did you notice whether or not he had any packages or bundles with him? A. Yes, he carried a package in his arm.

Q. In his arm? A. Yes.

Q. Now, will you describe that package to the jury and its size, width, if you can? A. It was about, I would say five to six inches high, and seven, eight wide and the length was about 14 inches.

Q. And how did he carry it? A. He carried that under his arm like that (indicating with left arm).

Q. Now, when was the last time you saw Fisch with that package in Hauptmann's house? A. The last time both went together through the hall in the kitchen.

Q. I see. Am I correct then in saying, without leading you, that you saw Fisch as you testified at the entrance of a room at the head of the stairs upon his arrival, is that correct? A. Yes.

Q. And that he had under his arm the package that you described, is that correct? A. Yes, that is correct.

Q. And that you saw him in conversation with Hauptmann, is that correct? A. Yes.

Q. And that you saw Hauptmann and Fisch then go to some other part of the house, is that correct? A. In the kitchen.

Q. In the kitchen? A. In the kitchen, that is right.

Q. Now, when Fisch came back and joined the group, did he come back and join the room gathering then? A. Yes, he came later.

Q. Did he have the package with him? A. No, sir.

Hans Kloppenburg was a good witness. His answers were forthright and without hesitation and indecision. He testified that in addition to him and the Hauptmanns, among those also present were Victor Schussler, Otto and Louise Wollenberg, Maria Muller, Mrs. Hauptmann's niece, plus a young German couple from Elizabeth, New Jersey, whose name he believed was Hein. He was not certain, however, if Mrs. Hauptmann's brother, Ernest Schoeffler, had been there or not.

During my personal investigation into the case I had the pleasure of visiting with Mr. Kloppenburg at his home in Jackson, New Jersey on three occasions. It was during these times that we were able to discuss in detail his friendship with Hauptmann and his personal knowledge of the crime as well as his belief in Hauptmann's guilt or innocence.

Hans was consistently adamant in his firm belief in his friend's innocence. He told me of the pleasant times they had with their many friends at Hunter Island; of the enjoyable vacation he had with Richard and Anna during the summer of 1931 when they took their three month trip to California together; of how honest a man Richard was; the kindness and love he showered on his wife Anna; how he enjoyed playing with children and animals; how extremely happy he was with the birth of his little son Manfred. "Richard was a good man. He would not hurt anyone. He did not kill that baby.", he expressed himself with emphasis.

When I questioned him about Fisch and the shoe box he said: "That was another thing Wilentz did. He said when it was my turn to be questioned in court if I used the word shoe box when I described the size of the package Isidor handed to Richard, he would have me arrested. That's why I gave the approximate measurements. He said I couldn't say the word shoe box. I could never understand why.

"And then there's another thing. Wilentz said I lied when I said I saw Isidor hand Richard the package. But I honestly did see him come in and hand him the package. I was right there. If I lied then why didn't I lie all the way? Why didn't I say that I saw Richard put the package on the top shelf of his broom closet? But I couldn't say that, I didn't see where he put it, I only saw him hand it to Richard and then they went down the hall with it into the kitchen. If I was going to lie for my friend, why didn't I lie and say I saw him put it on the shelf? But I couldn't do that!"

Among other things that had been deeply embedded in Hans Kloppenburg's memories of the case was the nightmare of those first hours following Hauptmann's arrest when he had been ushered down to the Greenwich Street Police Station and forced to write, for what seemed to be endless hours, under the threat of also being arrested as an accomplice in the crime. "They made me copy sentences and words over and over nearly all night and then threatened to arrest me.", Kloppenburg told me.

Attorney General Wilentz and the consenting police officers went to almost unbelievable lengths to prove Hauptmann guilty with threats to Hauptmann's good friend Kloppenburg: "He had his men take me into a small room and then they started to tell me what it would be like for me to sit in the electric chair, and that I better start to tell them the truth or I would find out. They even had it in the papers the day before I testified that they were going to arrest another man. I know it was me they meant, but even though they scared me, I just had to tell the truth about what I knew about the package Isidor gave to Richard." Hans Kloppenburg appeared relieved to have experienced another friendly visit from someone who also believed in Hauptmann's complete innocence. A person who had already become emotionally involved and now could agonize with him over such extreme diabolical injustices as he had personally experienced.

Paul Vetterle, another friend of the Hauptmanns, testified that he had attended Richard's birthday party held on Sunday evening, November 26th, 1933. He said he had arrived at the Hauptmann home at approximately three or three-thirty o'clock in the afternoon and had remained there until at least ten o'clock. Also in attendance were Mrs. Mueller, her baby, and Isidor Fisch. He said they spent the evening listening to the radio and talking about Germany. They all left together with Hauptmann driving them to the 225th Street elevated station. Vetterle's statements substantiated those of Richard and Anna Hauptmann and should have melted Cecile Barr's "identity" of Hauptmann to nothing more than another false accusation.

The trial continued with Colonel Schwarzkopf taking his turn in the witness chair. He stated that after Officer Kelly reported to him of his failure to find any fingerprints in the nursery the night of the kidnapping, he had ordered him to conduct a re-examination of the room and that this re-examination had also proven to be futile. He went on to say that he was aware of Dr. Erastus Mead Hudson's search for prints by using his own method about the 12th or 13th of March and of his success in raising nearly 500 latent prints from off the ladder. He also admitted that he had no knowledge of any of the prints being identified as those being made by the fingers of Bruno Richard Hauptmann.

Schwarzkopf's interrogation by Attorney Lloyd Fisher revealed that he had not been overly cooperative toward Dr. Hudson.

Q. Now you discovered by Hudson's process that you could get prints where Kelly couldn't find any? A. Yes, sir.

Q. Now did you submit to him the ransom notes and ask him to fingerprint those? A. (No answer.)

Q. Did you submit to Dr. Hudson the original ransom notes and say, Here Doctor, you have had great luck with the ladder, here are the ransom notes; see what you can do with those? A. We did submit the ransom notes to his process.

Q. Did Hudson ever see the ransom notes? A. No.

Q. Colonel, a man came down from New York and he taught your men and worked with your men and where your men could find no prints, he developed, we will say, dozens--- A. That's so.

And here Wilentz, apparently not particularly happy with the way Fisher was questioning his Superintendent of the State Police, interrupted by shouting: "Just a minute. Just a minute," and then followed with this statement: "The question has been answered on several occasions that Colonel Hudson (the attorney general must have truly been upset as he gave the good doctor another title) on March 12th or 14th, with a new process, that had been developed since March 1st, made the experiment for fingerprints on the ladder and that he found fingerprints. Now that question has been answered many times."

And of course Justice Trenchard did not fail to rule in this manner: "I think that is so, Mr. Fisher, the record speaks for itself."

Attorney Fisher pressed on with these questions:

Q. But after that had happened the original ransom notes never were submitted to Dr. Hudson for his examination, were they? A. No, sir.

Q. No. A. It was not necessary.

Q. You say it was not necessary? A. No, sir, it was not. He had shown us his process, and under his process we processed the notes.

Q. You say that it wasn't necessary to let the man who introduced this thing to you see the notes; that's your answer, is it? A. Yes, sir.

Q. Very good. Did you process the original ransom note with the Hudson method? A. With one of the Hudson methods, yes, sir.

Q. Well, now, as a matter of fact, Colonel, Hudson showed your men down in the basement of the Lindbergh home how to process wood for fingerprints, didn't he? A. Yes, sir.

Q. And at that time he didn't do a thing about paper, did he? A. No, sir.

Q. No. A. We inquired about it, though.

Q. And you say that you used his method on the letters. A. He had two other methods, that he also showed us, and we processed the paper with those.

Q. Now, Colonel, did you call any fingerprint experts outside your department in this investigation? A. No, sir.

Q. What about Federal fingerprint men? Were there any? A. I don't believe---no, there were not.

Q. Or New York State fingerprint men? A. No.

Q. That is men from New York City Police Department? A. No, there were not.

Q. Or Newark City Police Department? A. No.

Q. Nor Jersey City? A. No.

Q. So that the only fingerprint men that ever had a chance to examine and inspect the ransom notes for fingerprints were the men from your own particular department? A. Yes, sir.

Q. Is that correct? A. Yes, sir.

Q. And it didn't occur to you that anybody else should be called in? A. We used our men on it.

Q. That's right? A. Yes, sir.

And so it went, continuing with Schwarzkopf explaining how they had a duplicate ladder constructed and, when a man weighing 180 pounds ascended it, a break occurred at the same spot, the junction of the two sections, where it had in the original ladder. He also stated that he did not know how many times the original ladder had been taken apart and reassembled.

Louise and Otto Wollenberg testified that they were, in addition to the others named by Kloppenburg, in the Hauptmann home on the evening of the farewell party for Isidor Fisch on Saturday, December 2nd, 1933, and that they had remained there all that night. But, where Hans Kloppenburg's memory had failed him, Otto said Mrs. Hauptmann's brother, Ernest Schoeffler, had also been present.

Victor Schussler, who, with his wife and small child, occupied the rear rooms on the bottom floor beneath the Hauptmann's apartment, said he had attended the Fisch farewell party and also verified the names of the others who had been present. Hilda and Otto Heyne of 635 Livingston Street, Elizabeth, New Jersey, testified that they had arrived unexpectedly at the Hauptmann home at about 4:00 on the afternoon of December 2nd, 1933. They had been asked to remain for

Fisch's party, which they did, departing for home at approximately ten that evening.

George Steinweg, who had operated a steamship and tourist business at 226 East 86th Street, New York City, for twenty-five years, testified that he had been acquainted with both Isidor Fisch and Henry Uhlig. He said the two men, on August 18th, 1933, had visited his steamship agency and made reservations for their passage to Germany on the U.S.S. Manhattan which was sailing on Wednesday, December 6th of that year, its destination Hamburg.

Fisch, he explained, returned alone to the agency on November 14th and made his final payment of $410 for both tickets. At this time Fisch purchased German registered mark checks, American Express checks, 1500 marks for himself and 500 for his friend Uhlig, which had totaled approximately $650. In all, Isidor Fisch had given Steinweg over one thousand dollars.

"Big Ed" Reilly missed a wonderful opportunity to aid Hauptmann by his failure to ask Steinweg the hour Fisch had paid for his tickets. The purchase had been made in the early morning and it was not until late in the afternoon, just before the bank closed, that Richard and Fisch had gone to the bank to withdraw the $2,000 Hauptmann had loaned his partner. It had already been established by George Steinweg that the $2,000 Fisch used for the passage had been in gold notes. Once again the evidence points to the unquestionable fact that Isidor Fisch was not the pauper some folks knew him to be, but was rich in his possession of Lindbergh ransom gold notes.

Once again commenting on the Steinweg incident as it was mentioned in the book, *The Lindbergh Crime* by Sidney B. Whipple, which was published in 1935; Tony Scaduto in his book, *Scapegoat*, states it very clearly: "Except for the lack of reference to Gartner, the man who was sold some of the gold notes and was suspected of being the kidnapper when he tried to cash them, Whipple's account of the incident is remarkably similar to that in the investigator's deposition. Yet the investigator didn't interview Steinweg until September 1935, more than six months after Whipple's book was published. There can be little doubt that Whipple got his story, including the fact that bank officials had notified the Treasury Department about finding Lindbergh ransom bills in the steamship agency's deposit, from the police <u>before</u> Hauptmann went on trial; later the authorities denied the story because it would have marred their portrait of Hauptmann as the lone kidnapper and murderer and would have helped Hauptmann's defense.

"Most important, there can be no doubt at all that Steinweg was telling the truth: Isidor Fisch gave him more than $800 in ransom money a year before Hauptmann passed <u>his</u> first gold certificate. If his story were not true, Whipple would never have been given the vital detail that the ransom money had been discovered by bank officials. Isidor Fisch had most definitely possessed and spent gold notes from the ransom before the going-away party at which Hauptmann said he was given the shoe box."

With Reilly's awareness that this information existed, and had he not been so remiss in presenting it to the jury, he could have added valid strength to Hauptmann's claim that Fisch was indeed in possession of the Lindbergh ransom bills before he brought the package to Hauptmann for safe keeping on December 2nd, 1933. "Death House" Reilly had failed once again.

There can be little doubt that Reilly was unwilling to settle for the few witnesses that honestly testified they had seen Hauptmann in the Bronx on March 1st, 1932. It seems he believed in "padding" the list with a number of "weirdos" and "manic-depressives" who had either been in prisons or mental hospitals over the years and were either out-and-out liars or those whose imaginations were stretched to a point where they no longer knew what the real truths were. Or for that matter, could not have cared less. Some apparently were just willing to play their "bit part" in the trial of the century in order to, years later, say they had a role in the Lindbergh kidnapping.

It was a mystery to Reilly's associates, Fisher, Rosecrans and Pope, where the chief defense attorney had been able to find such characters as these who were willing to testify to just about anything he had instructed them to. And not only were they a disturbance to the other defense attorneys, they were causing Hauptmann much grief. There came a point in the trial when he asked Lloyd Fisher: "Where are they getting these witnesses from? They're hurting me! Tell Mr. Reilly he's got to find out if they are honest, good people before they are witnesses for me!"

The reason Richard had asked Fisher to relate his request to Reilly was very evident to the other staff lawyers. Reilly very seldom spent any time at all with the accused man, and when he did, it was for no more than five minutes. He had adopted an apparent dislike toward his client and did not care in the least who knew it. Rosecrans and Pope seldom saw the prisoner, while Fisher, who believed in his innocence and had developed a fondness for him, came to see him in his cell almost daily.

Returning to the remaining witnesses in the trial, the defense called Lieutenant E. Paul Sjostrom who identified himself as the Assistant Supervisor of the State Bureau of Identification, Department of the New Jersey State Police. He said he was assistant to Captain Russell A. Snook. Attorney Fisher's questions pertained largely to the failure of the police to obtain fingerprints from any article in the child's nursery as well as from the kidnap ladder, while a Doctor Hudson, several days later had been successful in developing several hundred from the surface of the ladder.

As Fisher continued his questioning of Sjostrom, he inquired of nine specific photographs which had been taken of some certain sections of the ladder. "And to your knowledge, that's all that was taken?", he asked the lieutenant: "Yes, sir."

Q. And you don't know which side of the ladder, or rungs, or anything about where these pictures are located? A. No, sir.

Q. You couldn't tell me, for instance, whether that is a picture of a side rail or a rung (showing photograph)? A. No, sir.

Q. Or of the front or back? A. No, sir.

Q. Or the inside or the out? A. No, sir.

Q. Just nine pictures of something on that section? A. Yes.

Another "brilliant" example of the professionalism of the New Jersey State Police. Quite some time was spent with Fisher probing the witness for a clear answer as to why Trooper Kelly did not develop any latent prints suitable for photographing; why nothing of importance was found on the sixty-eight photographs taken of the ladder on which "there were approximately about 125 finger marks shown", and then concluded with this very interesting, and quite informative, line of questioning:

Q. Now, Lieutenant, you ran down the fingerprints that you found on that ladder, didn't you, eliminated one by one, searched out the identity of the people whose prints you found? A. Some.

Q. Well, as far as possible didn't you? A. As far as possible.

Q. Yes. How many prints did you identify on there

out of the hundred and some that were found? A. "About eight.

Q. NOW, DID YOU IDENTIFY ON THE LADDER AT ANY TIME DOWN TO THE PRESENT DAY THE FINGERPRINT OF THIS DEFENDANT, RICHARD HAUPTMANN? A. NO, SIR.

Mr. Fisher: Take the witness, Mr. Attorney General.

Cross-Examination by Mr. Wilentz:

Q. If this defendant, Mr. Hauptmann, wore gloves when he was handling that ladder, would his fingerprints show? A. No, sir.

Q. Is it not a fact, Lieutenant, that your experience shows to you that men who are experienced in crimes use gloves? A. Yes, sir.

Mr. Wilentz: That is all.

Re-direct Examination by Mr. Fisher:

Q. Your experience is, Lieutenant, that mothers in putting children to bed and nurses in putting children to bed don't wear gloves, do they? A. That is not my experience, I don't know.

Mr. Fisher: That is all.

Re-Cross Examination by Mr. Wilentz:

Q. You have never been a nurse, have you? A. No.

By Mr. Fisher:

Q. Nor a mother neither, I take it? A. No, sir.

Q. In closing windows in nursery rooms the parent or the nurse doesn't ordinarily wear gloves, does she? A. No.

Q. In your experience--- A. Not that I know of.

Mr. Fisher: That is all.

As vital as these questions were, they bordered on mere banter, with Lloyd Fisher clearly winning the "round". The important question was not whether the kidnapper had worn gloves, but who was it that had wiped the entire nursery clean of every trace of fingerprints, including those of the baby, the mother and the nursemaid?

Sergeant Louis Kubler, a member of New Jersey State Police Identification Bureau, Troop B., was the next witness. He said he worked under the command of Captain Snook and Lieutenant Sjostrom and that he had been at the Lindbergh home when Dr. Hudson of New York came to demonstrate his silver nitrate process of bringing out latent fingerprints. Kubler's testimony was almost identical to that of Sjostrom since all his answers were in the negative as to whether he could tell from what section, or what part of any section, any given print had been found; nor could he tell whether it was found on a rail or a rung; and that he could not tell whether it was found on the left rail or the right rail. And when asked: "No way of knowing where the print was found on this section of the ladder?" Again his answer was the same: "No, sir." Kubler, as his superior, had been of little help. His answers to questions pertinent to knowledge of his chosen profession proved to be somewhat inadequate.

Trooper Frank A. Kelly was re-called to the stand but did nothing more than reiterate his inability to raise any latent fingerprints from the nursery during the early morning hours of the day after the kidnapping.

Appearing next as a defense witness was Oscar John Bruckmann, a taxi driver who lived on Manhattan Avenue, New York City. His time on the stand was short-lived. Reilly had him relate that he had worked for Isidor Fisch in 1930 at The Knickerbocker Pie Baking Company at 59 Downing Street, New York City. Bruckmann said he knew Fisch, having worked for him for about a year, and that he saw him again around the month of May of 1933 at the corner of 60th Street and Broadway from where he was stationed with his taxi for an independent cab company. He claimed it was about seven o'clock at night when Fisch came up to him.

Bruckmann, in an attempt to answer to Reilly's question: "And did Fisch talk to you?", received this reply: "He did, he wanted to know how I---" (the possible completion could have been "was doing?") but this utterance brought an immediate charge from Wilentz: "Just a minute. I object to what Mr. Fisch said to this gentleman in May, 1933." Reilly was quick with his follow-up remark to the bench: "I think it is competent. It is offered for the purpose of showing the sudden affluence of Fisch and his wealth and his display of certain gold-back bills that he had in May, 1933."

But in spite of the strong arguments put forth by Reilly insisting that the testimony of Bruckmann be permitted to be entered into the court record, and after numerous objections by the attorney general who protested that the evidence the witness intended to give was neither material or competent, the defense attorney made this impassioned plea: "I say it is material and it is competent to show---and we have charged here in the defense repeatedly---that this money was in the possession of Fisch and the box that he gave to Hauptmann, Hauptmann has testified he left with him, and it contained money which afterwards people have demonstrated here contained notes that had been registered as part of the Lindbergh money.

"Now it is unfortunate that Mr. Fisch is dead, but still it is part of our case, we contend, to show that Fisch was going around New York after the ransom money had been paid by Dr. Condon, exhibiting gold bills to different people and trying to exchange them with different people, and that he left part of them with Mr. Hauptmann."

The Court, however, sustained the objection. Nevertheless, Reilly continued with his effort to have Bruckmann tell what had taken place when he was approached by Fisch: "Well, did Fisch exhibit anything to you at any time during that night in his conversation?"

Mr. Wilentz: Just answer Yes or No, please.

A. Yes, he did?

Q. What did he exhibit?

Mr. Wilentz: That I object to, if your Honor please.

The Court: One moment.

Justice Trenchard then granted a request by Wilentz for a side Bar conference, one which stretched the Court's one moment into a lengthy 13 minutes, immediately followed by a recess.

Upon the resumption of Bruckmann's testimony, the only factual remarks the witness was permitted to make were these. That he had driven Fisch "down to Sixth Avenue" and he had "pulled a roll of bills out of his pocket and gave me a five-dollar bill." He said he could not swear they had been gold notes he had seen; and although the fare had not been five dollars, Fisch had given him a five-dollar bill for the ride.

Gustave Miller, a Master licensed plumber, testified that he had been called by Mrs. Rauch to repair a pipe which was leaking in a closet of an apartment in her home which she rented to Mr. and Mrs. Richard Hauptmann. Miller testified that he had gone there sometime in early August, 1934, had located the pipe (water still on the pipe, shelf and floor since the rain continued) and had then gone up into the attic to examine the cause of the trouble. He was quite certain that there was no attic flooring missing at that time since he was up there about two o'clock in the afternoon during broad daylight.

HERE WE HAVE THE HONEST TESTIMONY OF A MAN, WHO

CERTAINLY HAD NO REASON TO LIE, STATE THAT NO BOARD WAS MISSING FROM THE HAUPTMANN ATTIC (the date presumed to be Monday, August 13, 1934, the day after Hauptmann claimed he found the money left by Fisch) WHEN HE, THE PLUMBER, WENT INTO THE ATTIC TO FIND A LEAKING PIPE REPORTED TO HIM BY MRS. RAUCH! --- THIS TESTIMONY CONFIRMS THAT GIVEN BY MAX RAUCH, WHO EARLIER STATED, ALSO UNDER OATH, THAT HE HAD ENTERED THE HAUPTMANN ATTIC IN OCTOBER, 1934, AND THE ATTIC BOARD WAS COMPLETE!

Now, we must ask this one important question to each of you readers. By using every sense of fairness and by using just plain common sense, do you think it was possible for Lieutenant Lewis J. Bornmann, an honorable member of the New Jersey State Police, to locate a "missing board" (in his second report dated September 26th, 1934) a board which had not been previously reported as missing by no less than 37 other detectives and police officers (representing the New Jersey State Police, the Federal Bureau of Investigation, and the New York City Police Department) who had thoroughly combed that same attic on nine different occasions???? Had Mr. Bornmann performed this feat with the assistance of a Harry Houdini??, a Thurston???, a Blackstone????, or a David Copperfield????? --- No! No! No! No! Even with the combined deception, created by mystical illusion, as performed by these great masters in the art of wizardry, this "baffling feat" could not have been accomplished with the finesse and success that "magician" Bornmann exhibited for all to see in that Flemington courtroom, simply because in his "super presentation" ---- Mr. Bornmann had acted alone!

However, we should be aware of the fact that it is quite easy to be disillusioned, and thus give all the credit to "magicman Bornmann". We must remember that he did not perform this "act" alone. Working close by his side, in perfect chorus, was his "very able" assistant, Mr. Arthur Koehler, "master in the art of wood", who helped him "dramatize" this great "illusion" that was to penetrate deeply into the impressive minds of both the judge and jury ---- and the great Attorney General David T. Wilentz.

CHAPTER FORTY NINE

Doctor Hudson's Day In Court!

One of the most professional of all the witnesses to appear at the trial and to be heard relative to his findings in the Lindbergh case was Doctor Erastus Mead Hudson, of New York City. It had been the hope of the prosecutors that Dr. Hudson's testimony would be helpful to them in proving their case against Hauptmann; but unfortunately for those who were desirous of "railroading" the innocent Bronx carpenter into the electric chair, such was not to be the case.

It had been expected that Dr. Hudson, without a doubt, would be testifying for the prosecution with important fingerprint evidence against Hauptmann. However, because of his findings, due to a completely honest and unbiased investigation he conducted, it turned out that the results were indeed more beneficial to Hauptmann's defense. Hence, Doctor Hudson had been summoned to appear as a defense witness, much to the chagrin of the pompous Attorney General Wilentz.

Because of this, it appeared evident that Wilentz made no attempt to hide his disdain toward the witness. At times his treatment of Dr. Hudson was quite rude. He belittled the doctor's ability, making light of his silver nitrate method of developing latent fingerprints suitable for having photographs made, with his continuous aspersions that Hudson's method was not recognized in official police circles as being anything more than amateur.

However, the facts were made clear that Dr. Hudson had graduated from a medical institute, The College of Physicians and Surgeons in New York in 1917; served as a medical officer in the United States Navy where he supervised the taking of all fingerprints; had worked with fingerprints while in Liverpool with the men of Scotland Yard, and had done a great deal of work in fingerprinting with Frederick Kuhn of the New York City Police Department, and with Mr. J.H. Koehler of the Navy Department in Washington D.C. where they visited the eminent Dr. DeForest who conducted the largest laboratory on fingerprints in the United States where he studied further the chemistry of detecting latent fingerprints. With this realm of work and study behind him, which had begun in 1920, Doctor Hudson could hardly be alluded to as a novice. And yet the attorney put no value or credence to the doctor's ability, to say nothing of his faith in the Doctor's integrity.

During his time in the witness chair, in addition to telling of the proven success of his silver nitrate method on other occasions, Doctor Hudson clarified several important points. He said that, on March 13th, 14th and 15th, 1932, in the company of two New Jersey State Police Offices, Trooper Kelly and Sergeant Kubler, he had demonstrated his system on the Lindbergh kidnap ladder and had visually brought out more than five hundred fingerprints and fingerprint fragments, all suitable for filming, from the surface of the crudely built three-sectioned ladder. A particular point he stressed was that from out of the more than five hundred prints, not one of them had been Hauptmann's. He went so far as to say that if Hauptmann had been the maker of the ladder some of his prints would have unquestionably been found on it. There can be no doubt about this, he stated. This fact, he went on to say, is based on the proven certainty that fingerprints left on wood are known by fingerprint experts to remain there for a span of six months. These can be successfully revealed, had they been touched, by using the silver nitrate process at any time during that period. Sometimes satisfactory prints have been developed, under certain conditions, even years later, Dr. Hudson said.

One of the most annoying factors of Hudson's testimony to the chief prosecutor was the doctor's persistence that at the time he had closely examined the ladder sections, he had taken particular notice of the section known as "Rail 16" because it had a knot in it which had caused the wood to split. Two nails had been used on each side as a reinforcement, but only one nail was used on the face. He explicitly remembered it, he said, since it was the only rail that had one nail hole made by a square nail. Dr. Hudson stated: "I saw only one nail hole made by a square nail in the entire ladder." And it was due to this fact that he clearly remembered "Rail 16" from all the others. Then why do you insist it had only one nail hole, when this picture "taken in March, 1932" distinctly shows the presence of four nail holes? Wilentz wanted to know. Couldn't you be wrong, doctor? the attorney general persisted. No, not at all!, Doctor Hudson was certain.

Just how certain had Doctor Hudson been? Well, Doctor Hudson was very, very certain. Let's examine his answers to the badgering questions of Wilentz:

Q. All right. If this rail had been examined by persons other than the State Police of New Jersey in March, April and May, 1932, and reports were filed during those months, showing these four nail holes, would that induce you to believe that possibly you were mistaken? A. No, sir; that wouldn't.

Q. If the United States Government reports showed in 1932, that there were four nail holes, these very four nail holes, would that lead you to change your mind? A. No, sir; it would not.

Q. Doctor, assuming that this particular rail that we have been speaking about is the rail that you saw in March, at which time you say it contained only one nail hole? A. Yes.

Q. Have you explained the appearance of four cut nail holes in the rail as it is now? Can you tell how they got in there, Doctor?* A. No, sir, I have no idea.

Q. But they were not there when you saw it, were they? A. No, sir.

(*Officer Lewis Bornmann was probably the only person able to give the correct answer to that question.)

David T. Wilentz did all he could to make a mockery of Doctor Hudson's knowledge as a fingerprint expert, "This is sort of a hobby with you, isn't it?", he asked at one point. Throughout the time he spent cross examining the doctor, he attempted to belittle him by inferring that he may not be all he claimed to be in the medical field, by asking: "Now of course, you appreciate, Doctor, with your intelligence---you are a member of the medical profession, aren't you?", and this after the doctor had properly stated his qualifications and had offered the information as soon as he took his seat in the witness chair that he had been practicing medicine since the year 1917.

Wilentz showed no respect for Doctor Hudson, treating him as a hostile witness simply because it had turned out that the evidence the eminent doctor had uncovered was not in agreement with the "network of lies" he and his cohorts had been weaving to pin Hauptmann as the lone kidnapper. Oh, what the attorney general would have given to have heard Hudson say one of the prints on the ladder was Hauptmann's. But, unfortunately for the prosecution, Doctor Hudson was an honest man. He could not be manipulated. He had no alternative other than to speak out in defense of the accused man, who at this point in the trial desperately needed someone in his corner. However, regardless of the evidence presented by Doctor Hudson, the jury evidently paid no heed, showing that they favored the angry theatrics of, by this time, the frustrated Wilentz.

What follows is Doctor Hudson's account of the part he played in the Lindbergh case:

"On April 3, 1936, the State of New Jersey closed its books on the most publicized trial in the history of the world, when Bruno Richard Hauptmann shuffled to the electric chair.

"Yet the case never has been really closed, and many prominent authorities connected with it, as well as part of the reading public, are of the opinion that the bottom of it has not been sounded.

"Hauptmann was put to death for the kidnapping and murder of the twenty-months-old son of Colonel and Mrs. Charles A. Lindbergh purely on circumstantial evidence, much of it scientifically deducted. From the day of his arrest until his last mortal breath the prisoner denied inculpating evidence.

"Hauptmann's prosecutor, Attorney General David T. Wilentz, had told the jury that Hauptmann alone committed the crime, and the indictment on which he was tried included no recognition of possible accomplices.

"Four important phases of the case stand out in my memory as the points that led to his conviction: the defense admission of identification of the body as that of the Lindbergh baby; Hauptmann's admitted possession of almost $15,000 of the $50,000 ransom paid out by Colonel Lindbergh; the identification, through comparison of handwritings, of Hauptmann as author of the ransom notes; and Hauptmann's alleged construction of the rickety three-section ladder which the state contended had been used. Many jurists feel that, lacking all other evidence, sufficient proof of Hauptmann's guilt rested in these four points to secure a conviction.

"The case gave an excellent idea of what could have been done in the way of scientific investigation. It also brought to light certain frailties of our advanced methods of criminal investigation which should be corrected. The power of a jury of laymen to pass on the highly technical evidence of experts, to my way of thinking, is only one of the absurdities exposed. Unfair both to the defendant and to the ends of justice was the state's refusal to submit to other investigators and experts for pre-trial examination highly important material exhibits in the case, some of which even today might throw new light on the kidnapping.

"A few days after the child disappeared from the nursery, my old friend, the late James F. Minturn, formerly a justice of the New Jersey Supreme Court, induced me to enter the case to determine whether the kidnappers had left fingerprints. On the afternoon of March 13 Oliver Whateley, the Lindbergh butler, who has since died, greeted us at the front door and escorted us to the dining room, where Colonel and Mrs. Lindbergh, her mother Mrs. Dwight Morrow, and Lindbergh's friend and attorney Colonel Henry Breckinridge were finishing dinner. Mrs. Lindbergh looked drawn and weary, but she managed to smile and express the hope that I would find everything I needed, before she left the room. Colonel Lindbergh, though his eyes were clear and his color good, showed indications of being tired. We were told that he had had little sleep during the preceding two weeks.

"The Lindberghs could not conceal certain little glances of impatience and suspicion. They had been plagued by all sorts of cranks, well meaning nitwits, publicity seekers, etc. But while the futility of the investigation had told on their nerves, their patience, and their belief in human nature, it had no effect on their courtesy toward those sincerely sympathetic and in some measure helpful.

"Colonel Lindbergh looked on curiously as I opened my old medical bag, into which I had packed brushes, atomizers, and bottles. We covered the dining room table with old newspapers and laid the instruments on them. Colonel H. Norman Schwarzkopf, who headed the state police throughout the entire Lindbergh case, watched suspiciously. He complied gingerly when I asked him to lay his hand gently on a small piece of wood; he touched the board with his fingertips and withdrew his hand as quickly as if it had been a hot stove. I sprayed the wood with silver nitrate and handed it to him. He looked at it curiously for a moment, and offered it back with a tart remark; "Doctor, if you see anything there, your eyes are better than mine."

"Please take it over to the window and let the

sunlight at it for a minute," I asked. Plainly skeptical, he complied. He as well as the Lindberghs had been having a trying time of it. I felt that this little demonstration was necessary to gain their confidence.

"Colonel Schwarzkopf stood near the window through which the evening sun's rays slanted. As the golden beams played on the surface of the wood, he was joined by Colonel Lindbergh and later by Colonel Breckinridge. Gradually small dark spots took form where Schwarzkopf had placed his fingers. Another minute, and his fingerprints stood out, as hard and sharp in contour as though they had been engraved on steel.

"The trio looked at me, their eyes wide with astonishment. State troopers came to observe the results. Mrs. Lindbergh and her mother were called in. They expressed wonderment and pleasure.

"Newspapers have since referred to the silver-nitrate method of fingerprint detection as the "Hudson process." In truth this method was used many years ago in France by the famous Dr. Aubert; but I was first to use it in the United States, and in my own right I may lay claim to an original method of application and solution which, even today, police find some difficulty in duplicating. When I discovered the process twenty years ago, I did not know that any one else had ever used it.

"Trooper Frank Kelly of the state police suggested that we examine some toys in the Lindbergh nursery. He had managed to obtain, through ordinary methods, a baby's print from one of the tiny chairs. His problem was to preserve it. When I poured shellac over it, I could see Kelly shudder, turn away, and bury his eyes in his hands. But a moment later the print came out beneath the shellac, clearer than it had appeared before. **It should now last as long as the longest memory of the Lindbergh case.** Later, however, Kelly told me that for many months, whenever he heard the word shellac, cold chills played chopsticks on his spine.

"From the baby's books and toys we were able to produce and preserve enough palm- and fingerprints, under application of a new French chemical, **to identify or disqualify without dispute any "living Lindbergh baby" that might be presented in the future.**

"A point of great importance rested in the absence of any fingerprints on the nursery window and its remarkably broad sill. Kelly had powdered it a few hours after the kidnapping. No prints were found, although Betty Gow, the child's nurse, and Mrs. Lindbergh had opened and closed the window that same night. Miss Gow had rubbed the child's chest with an ointment the oleaginous base of which would have augmented the secretion of the finger ridges in leaving clear prints. Of course there would have been older prints as well. **The reason Kelly failed to get all those prints was because they must have been washed off. Some one with a pail of water and cloth undoubtedly bathed those spots where fingerprints must have been left. They did so between the time Betty Gow put the baby to bed and about four hours later, when Kelly began investigating.**

"It is ludicrous to suppose that the kidnapper climbed the ladder with the pail and rag and descended with this in one hand and the baby in the other. It is equally unreasonable to suppose that any one alien to the household, wearing gloves, as the prosecution contended the kidnapper did, would have any interest in eliminating the normal fingerprints to be found in the nursery.

"Bluntly, the absence of fingerprints on the window proves conclusively that others than Hauptmann were involved; probably within the Lindbergh household. Major Schoeffel of the state police called my attention to this fact when he told me, "Doctor, I cannot understand and Kelly cannot understand why the fingerprints of Betty Gow were not on that window." Miss Gow even showed Kelly where her hand was placed on the window. No reflection whatever is meant to be cast upon Miss Gow, least of all that she may have been an accomplice.

"Hauptmann's counsel, during the trial, made a grievous error in attempting to belittle the fingerprint work of Sergeant Kelly and Sergeant Louis Kubler, Kelly's associate, both of whom, considering their equipment and experience, did an excellent job.

"A few days after I entered the case, Kelly and Kubler agreed to my suggestion that we try to obtain fingerprints from the ladder which the state contends was used in the kidnapping and which at that time had been lying neglected in a rear hallway on the ground floor. Kelly's previous efforts with powder had failed. We moved the ladder into the laundry in the basement, and set to work on it. For three days, Kelly, Kubler, and I sprayed every inch of the structure without testing to see whether or not our labor bore fruit. Convinced of the value of the work myself, I hesitated to test for prints before the job was complete, because I feared that others might become disheartened with a fruitless test.

"We took the ladder out of the basement into the cold brilliant rays of the sun at last. The postman asked us if that was the famous ladder, and remarked, "Why, you fellows have covered it with a lot of shingle stain."

"He entered the house, and when he emerged the ladder was literally covered with prints. Almost every square inch of its surface was ridged with palm- and fingerprints, some fragmentary, a few overlapping, another few blurred, but many complete and clear. Closer inspection showed fingerprints on the ends of the rails and even under the rungs where they had been nailed down.

"Kelly and Kubler went over the 5,000 square inches of surface for days, photographing more than 500 prints and fragments, which, Kelly said, appeared clear and very well defined. Each picture covered six square inches of the ladder's surface, with at least two digital impressions possible to the square inch. More than a thousand pictures would have to be taken to cover the entire surface.

"When we took the ladder back into our improvised laboratory in the basement, Kubler summoned his superiors and Colonel Lindbergh. The aviator appraised the work minutely, going over most of it with a lens.

"He turned to me with an expression of satisfaction and said, "Doctor, you ought to write a book on this."

"Here the ladder prints and I parted company. Kelly told me the pictures "came out damn well." Captain Russell Snook of the state police said that **<u>"thirty or forty perfect prints"</u>** could not be identified as belonging to those who were known to have handled the ladder.

"I urged the state police to submit the prints for identification to the Department of Justice in Washington, which has the most complete file of fingerprints in the country. A New Jersey official told me scornfully. **<u>"When there's any glory to be had, the New Jersey troopers will grab it."</u>** I offered to have them submitted through the many connections I maintain in Washington, so that the Department of Justice would not know who wanted them identified. I was turned down by the Jersey police.

"Later, an official of the Department of Justice

smiled and said, **"Don't be naive! The Jersey police never gave any of us a chance to examine any of the their evidence in the case. They don't seem to know about our files and laboratory facilities."**

"Early in May, 1932, I wrote Colonel Schwarzkopf that I was quite sure an iodine-gas process, unknown to police, would develop fingerprints on the ransom notes. I never received a reply from him.

"When the news of Hauptmann's arrest came out, I called a state police officer at the Trenton barracks. He told me in high elation that **"We got our man."**

"Were his prints on the ladder? I asked.

The reply was, **"No."**

"Then you'll have to look further," I said.

"Good God, don't tell us that, doctor! he said, nonplused.

"When the press and police were at the height of their attack on Hauptmann, unheard, untried, and unconvicted as yet, I felt that, in fairness to the defendant, Colonel Schwarzkopf should make public that fingerprints had been found on the ladder and that none of them were Hauptmann's. He had repeatedly denied that prints had been found on the ladder.

"I wrote him to the effect that if he did not make this public I would see fit to do so, at the same time stating the opinion that **if Hauptmann had made the ladder from six to eight months prior to the kidnapping his prints should be on it.**

"When I entered the case, I told Colonel Schwarzkopf that I preferred to keep my name out of the papers and that I wanted his hard-working troopers to get any credit that might accrue from my work. Now I was in the embarrassing position of seeking some measure of justice for Hauptmann in the public prints, with Colonel Schwarzkopf repeatedly denying that any fingerprints whatsoever had been found on the ladder.

"Over Kelly's objections and unknown to myself, the state police washed all fingerprints off the ladder, once it was learned that Hauptmann's were not among them.

"Captain Snook advised me that Attorney General Wilentz would like to see me, that I might be used as a state's witness. I replied that, to my way of thinking, the fingerprint matter was one for the defense, and reiterated my request that the authorities clarify the fingerprint situation and save me the embarrassment of doing so. I was told no such announcement could be expected. So I called my friend MacGregor Bond of the

New York World Telegram and released the story the day before Hauptmann went on trial.

"I won a feeble victory over common police unfairness---by no means confined to the Hauptmann case---in with-holding evidence for pretrial investigation by defense.

"My investigation in behalf of the New Jersey police and later for Hauptmann's counsel and Governor Hoffman, all conducted without fee, drew heavily upon my long and varied experience in criminology.

"When I entered the Lindbergh case my background included a Bachelor of Science degree from Harvard, chemistry and mathematics as majors; summers of study in Harvard engineering camps; five years of study at and degree of Doctor of Medicine from the College of Physicians and Surgeons, New York; four years as a surgeon in the medical corps in the United States navy; twenty years in medical practice; and twenty years of study and application of American and foreign methods of criminal investigation and research into my own theories in several fields of the chemistry, forensic medicine, biology, botany, mathematics, and other sciences indispensable to complete criminal investigation.

"My criticism of the state police and the prosecution of the Hauptmann case is based not so much on what they did as on what they left undone. This despite the fact that the federal, state, and New York City police spent almost $300,000 plus the time of detectives and agents running down clues, and despite the fact that a much larger amount was invested in procuring evidence against Hauptmann. Experts calculate that, in all, more than $650,000 was spent in the conviction of the German carpenter. New Jersey drove a notoriously bad bargain. The defense, of course had access to no such expensive opinion or exhaustive investigation.

"The peculiar characteristics of Hauptmann's handwriting that identified him, in the minds of the state experts and apparently of the jury, as the author of the ransom notes are no affair of mine. It did interest me to learn, however, that defense experts were given little opportunity to examine these writings and that Department of Justice and New York authorities had no chance whatever to inspect them. Eventually a psychiatrist, to whom they were loaned for a short time, surreptitiously photographed them and gave copies to the New York police.

"In this connection, it is also of interest to

recall a point that did the Hauptmann defense no good.

"I was amazed to hear the famous handwriting expert, Albert S. Osborn, testify at length on the rarity of the hyphenated "New-York." Much of my mail from Germany hyphenates "New York." Many of my German acquaintances tell me they were taught in school to hyphenate "New York."

"Even today I cannot but wonder whether other opinions so glibly and profoundly asserted by experts before the Hunterdon County jury were in truth more accurate."

And so, there you have it. A truthful account told by a man with all the qualifications necessary to perform a task that he had been called to do --- to find hidden fingerprints and make them visible and suitable for photographing --- and he located over 500 of them.

And then, to read that this eminent and certified authority of the fingerprint science had been subjected to such harsh and rude ridicule, in addition to being treated as a belligerent witness in open court by an attorney, who himself knew very little to absolutely nothing about the profession, was quite difficult for me, a student of criminal identification, to take.

Yes, Doctor Hudson could have told much more, but he was too fine a gentleman to have gone farther. However, in a later chapter, you will read a series of letters exchanged between the New Jersey State Police and the FBI, which will enable you to see how shallow the cooperative teamwork was between the two agencies in their quest to solve the Crime of the Century.

CHAPTER FIFTY

Back to Wood Again!

The tempo of the trial was fast approaching its final week. Several more witnesses testified to the veracity of Millard Whited, the man who originally said he had seen no strangers in the vicinity of the Lindbergh home either on or preceding the night of Tuesday, March 1st, 1932, but who, following the arrest of the Bronx carpenter in September of 1934, came forth out of nowhere and, under oath, identified Hauptmann as a man he had seen in the area on two occasions several days before the crime.

William Whithead, a fifty-four year old resident of Hopewell, said Whited's reputation for honesty was: "No good."; while 45 year old George E.J. Lenz, who lived on Featherbed Lane, near the Lindbergh home, said he had known Whited about 20 years and that his reputation for truthfulness was: "not good" and that he "didn't pay his bills." William Diehl, another Hopewell resident, said he had always known Whited, having lived in the same neighborhood as he, and when asked what he would say about his reputation, answered: "Taint any good."

The defense could have brought many others to the stand who had known Whited and their endorsement of him would have been the same. Whited was known as a proverbial liar. Sydney L. Smith of West Chester, Pennsylvania, a friend of mine who was born and raised in Hopewell, knew Millard Whited very well and claimed the man "didn't know how to tell the truth."

It is shameful that the jury readily believed the testimony of Whited as factual, and at the same time could utterly disregard the statements of Whithead, Lenz, and Diehl who knew him to be a fabricator of lies, one whose testimony as a witness was purchased with the promise that he would be given a share when the distribution of the reward money was made. Whited later received $1000 for his trouble.

Mrs. Augusta Hile, the next witness, testified that Isidor Fisch was indebted to her for loans she had made to him which totaled $4,350. She said he died without ever paying any of it back.

Karl Henkel, whose wife, Gerta, the attorney general had implied as possibly having an affair with Richard, was a mutual friend of the Hauptmann's, Isidor Fisch, and Henry Uhlig was another witness. He testified that he and his wife were part of a group of friends that met together quite often at Hunter Island for fun and recreation. When he was asked: "Have you ever had the slightest thought in your mind that there was anything irregular or improper between Hauptmann and your wife?", his answer was a definite: "No."

Q. Did you ever see anything improper between your wife and Hauptmann? A. No.

Q. Did you ever have any feeling that there was anything improper between them? A. Never.

Q. When you visited Hauptmann's home, how did he treat his wife and child? A. Nice.

Wilentz, however, would not let up with his continuous insinuations by implying that he knew better, that there was "something going on" between his wife and Richard Hauptmann. "You were perfectly satisfied that Mrs. Henkel served coffee to Mr. Hauptmann two or three times a week when you weren't there?", he asked. Karl Henkel's immediate answer to this was: "I trust my wife."

Later, when Reilly asked Henkel: "You believe your wife, don't you?", his answer was: "Yes."; only to have the honorable David T. Wilentz blast away with his usual: "Just a minute now; just a minute now. I move that be stricken out." To which Justice Trenchard responded: "I sustain that objection and strike out the answer, if he has answered." Yes, the witness had already answered in the affirmative that he did trust his wife, only to have his honest answer stricken from the record by the Honorable Thomas W. Trenchard.

Oh, justice, sweet justice! Where were you in that Hunterdon County court room of Flemington, New Jersey in 1935?

Henry Uhlig was next to testify. He said he lived at 520 East 157th Street in the Bronx and that he had been Isidor's best friend, having enjoyed their boyhood together in Leipzig, Germany, and both coming to America in 1925, Fisch arriving a month later than he.

Uhlig became quite indignant when Reilly inquired: "He paid your passage to Europe?", by responding immediately: "That is a lie. He did not pay my fare. He paid my fare with the money he took from me to invest in his phoney bakery." And in the following series of questions also asked by Reilly, he told of Fisch's ill health and the length of time he had suffered with it:

Q. Now, will you describe, please, to this jury Fisch's physical condition when he left here, his appearance. A. Fisch was very sick and he was coughing. He also had a little blue bottle with him to expectorate into and I took good care of him on the boat, because he was also weak and went to bed early and didn't take part in anything.

Q. How long had he had that cough? A. He had that cough since 1929.

Q. Can you describe the cough? A. To me it sounded like a consumptive cough.

Q. He had it for how long? A. Since 1929.

Q. So that he had that cough in April, 1932, didn't he? A. Yes, he did.

Uhlig said their ship docked in Hamburg on Friday, December 15th, 1933. Fisch, now a very sick man, was taken to the home of his parents, where Uhlig visited his good friend at least twice a week until he entered the hospital in Leipzig. He testified further that he had not known Hauptmann until the fall of 1932, having first been introduced to him in the home of Karl Henkel on 127th Street, Manhattan.

One more resident of the Bronx came to the aid of Hauptmann. Walter Manley was another person who said he had seen Richard in Fredericksen's Bakery on the evening the kidnapping had taken place. He testified he had been there at about quarter after seven buying some Danish pastry and bread. He said Mrs. Hauptmann had waited on him and that her husband had been sitting in the front drinking coffee.

Manley went on to say that he had known the Fredericksens since 1928 or '29 having done some painting in the restaurant on two occasions. He said he also knew Anna Hauptmann, but had never met Richard. He testified that, although he was ill and confined to bed, had come to Flemington to tell what he knew to be the truth, he had seen the accused man in the Bronx restaurant on March 1st, 1932.

For some reason Wilentz' cross examination of this witness was mild compared to the stinging interrogation he subjected most of the others to, especially those who claimed they had seen Richard in New York on the night in question. This can be readily seen by the tranquility of his final questions:

Q. What time did you leave? A. I was there about

four minutes---four, five minutes---three, four, five minutes.

Q. Was Mr. Hauptmann drinking coffee then? A.Yes, sir.

Q. Just one cup? A. I couldn't tell how many cups; he was drinking coffee while I was there three or four minutes.

Q. Did it look like a lot of coffee he was drinking from quarter after seven until half past eight? A. Well, I don't know.

Q. You saw him drinking a cup of coffee? A. "Yes, sir.

Q. Nothing else? A. That is all.

Q. He had a cup of coffee in front of him? A. Yes.

Q. And he was drinking it? A. Yes.

Q. You are a very sick man, aren't you? A. I certainly is.

Mr. Wilentz: All right, sir, that is all.

Those questions cannot help but make us wonder just how well Mr. Wilentz was on that twenty-seventh day of the trial, Thursday, February 7th, 1935.

And so, we must add the name of Manley to the list bearing those of Carlstrom, Van Henke, Kiss, Fredericksen and Anna Hauptmann as having seen Richard miles away from Hopewell, New Jersey, on the night of the Lindbergh baby's kidnapping, which alerts us to once again ask the question: "How in the name of everything holy were they able to find Hauptmann guilty?" That is, of course, without concocting a massive frame-up!

Stanley Seal of Flemington, an expert on the use of planes, identified himself as a pattern maker who was accustomed to working with tools on wood. He testified that he was familiar with planes and plane bits and the markings plane bits leave on wood. He said a difference in the markings left from nicks in the plane bit could be seen on the wood's surface because of the angle or position in which the plane itself had been held while it was passed over the wood. He demonstrated this by first holding the plane parallel with the edge of the board, as near as possible, and planing it straight which revealed a wide mark. He then drew the plane across on an angle exposing a mark with a difference in width of about five-eighths or three-quarters of an inch between the ridges. He explained that as one turns the plane on an angle, the width between the plane markings gets narrower and would therefore change the appearance of any markings made by nicks on the blade.

A very impressive witness for the defense was Charles J. DeBisschop of Waterbury, Connecticut. He came with the finest of credentials, having worked with wood and lumber of all kinds since the year 1898 when he started working in lumbering at Wolcott, Connecticut. His experience was vast, having been employed as a contractor, a boat builder, and a house wrecker. He was familiar with, not only cutting down trees, but taking them to the mill and sawing them as well. He said he had worked with all kinds of wood including oak, chestnut, pine, spruce, hemlock, beech, dead chestnut, black birch, cherry, North Carolina pine, and what could be called an imitation of North Carolina pine, known as southern pine.

In 1913 he was in complete charge of the A.D. Bridge & Sons lumber mill in West Worthington, Massachusetts where about 150,000 feet of lumber would be produced weekly. Later, he said, he had gone into the contracting business for himself at the Scoville Manufacturing Company for Turner Construction Company of New York and handled all their lumber for the large ammunition factories where he had charge of all the lumber, all the brick, all the glass; "all the material, every pound in those large ammunition (factories) went through my hands.", he said. When asked how much lumber he handled in the course of a week or a year?, his honest answer had been: "Why, I couldn't tell that. Sometimes we had fifteen carloads a day and sometimes we didn't have but two."

Yes, according to the credentials he provided, Mr. DeBisschop could not be termed anything less than an expert in lumber.

However, after hearing the witness expound the years of experience he had in working with many kinds of wood, Wilentz who earlier had challenged DeBisschop's qualifications as an expert, was asked by judge Trenchard: "Well, now, Mr. Attorney General, do you think that he is qualified?", with Wilentz replying: "Not as an expert, if your Honor please."

The Court: Not as an expert?

Mr. Wilentz: No, sir.

The Court agreed that "for some purposes" he may be accepted as "a practical lumber man, since his test might be of value. And of course, its value and weight is a question for the determination of the jury. You may proceed with your examination, Mr. Pope."

DeBisschop was on the witness stand for a good

portion of two days and did not hedge at any point in his testimony as he explained and demonstrated in detail why "rail 16" of the kidnap ladder and the board still nailed as part of the flooring in the Hauptmann attic could never have been one piece of wood. The complete testimony he gave was very, very convincing. He presented himself as a man who knew exactly what he was talking about. During the cross-examination, Wilentz, as usual did his best to confuse DeBisschop, but without success. As he was led through the task of answering questions pertaining to the type of wood, the kind of nails, the planing marks and many other questions the attorney general hoped would "derail" him and reveal DeBisschop as nothing more than a "student of lumber" the man proved himself time after time to be far more professional than had Arthur Koehler who, without any hard-fast proof, had claimed the two pieces of lumber at one time, prior to March 1st, 1932 had been one piece.

It was largely due to Mr. DeBisschop's reading the account of Koehler's testimony in the newspapers, and then weighing it with his own knowledge of wood; he came to the conclusion that the testimony Koehler had given was not only ridiculous but preposterous as well. With a sense of fairness to help the accused man who had such unfair evidence presented against him, DeBisschop decided to do something about it. He immediately offered to give his testimony, based on his many years of experience in wood, as an aid to the defense and made the trip to Flemington at his own expense.

Shortly after DeBisschop had been seated in the witness chair Wilentz must have come to the realization that he had a strong adversary to overcome. The knowledge exhibited by the witness was overwhelming, so much so that at times it could have caused some doubts to be raised in his own mind as to the veracity of Koehler's testimony in which he, up to this time, placed great faith. From the very start of the interrogation of DeBisschop, Wilentz had done everything possible to discredit him as a qualified witness. He inquired: "Have you ever tried matching grains in two different pieces of lumber to see if they were the same?" To which DeBisschop casually answered: "I've been doing that for the last thirty years." The knockout punch Wilentz had attempted to throw had failed.

It would be tiring reading for you if I were to present the entire text of DeBisschop's answers to the many complex questions he was asked pertaining to the disputed attic board and the now famous "Rail 16".

Nevertheless, in deference to my ability to prove Richard Hauptmann's complete innocence, it is imperative that I show enough of the extremely convincing testimony of Charles DeBisschop which, in every sense of fairness, should have been enough to convince even the most biased jury.

We, therefore, begin with that part of the questioning where Frederick Pope, an assistant defense attorney, questions DeBisschop about the ladder rail:

Q. Now, have you made a study of the ladder rail, the ladder rail Number 16, and the piece of wood marked State's Exhibit S-226? A. I have.

Q. And how many times did you study them? A. Three times.

Q. Then where did you see them? Here in Flemington? A. In Flemington, yes; the court house.

Q. And have you also studied the photographs of the ladder rail and the board said to have been taken from the attic, which is S-226? A. Yes.

Q. And still another photograph, these photographs at the bottom of State's Exhibit S-231? A. Yes.

Q. Turn it over. A. (Ladder and board, Exhibit S-226, placed end to end on rail before the jury by the witness.)

Q. I ask you if from your study of these two pieces of board you believe that they are all a part of the same board, that they were sawed apart and that there is missing between the end of the ladder rail and the end of the board in the attic a small piece about an inch and three-quarters in length? A. I would say they are an entirely different board, owing to this knot here, which would show pitch and a darker color, far past the inch and three-eighths; probably that is a little more than that. Also, if you will notice, these here are not the same knot---

Q. Now, pardon me, 'These here' doesn't mean anything on the record. Will you call them rings, or whatever they are? A. These rings are not the same kind of a knot ring as those there. These project out. If it was the same piece of lumber, with an inch and an eighth put in there, this heart here, the pitch in this, would project down a good deal further than this does now. This knot here would project the opposite way, this way. Neither one has done that. This heart in here--- Now, if you notice any of the other hearts in here, you will notice how far they go--- a big circle heart in here. If you had a ---this is a big heart in here. I don't happen to see a big heart in here. But this big heart in here would project back a dark color in here; whereas this pine, North Carolina pine, has been exposed, as I understand it, to the weather; it would naturally be of a harder surface, soft--- when you laid your hand over this it would be a kind of a wooly thing; where this in here, by being under cover, should be harder; the pitch in it would be harder. Instead of that, the pitch in here is softer, the wood.

Q. Now, then, put it this way; no, let the ladder be. Now I am turning the board, the so-called attic board, S-226, over on the other side, and I ask you if there is any matching there? A. No.

Q. And if not, why? A. Well, you got the heart there. You have got a good deal the same type, but your heart is all set. It is too far that way.

Q. The heart is on which, on the attic board? A. Yes, it is here. See?

Q. Yes. A. And here is the heart here. No matter what you done, no matter where you put it, according to Mr.--- it should be over that way, an inch and three-eighths, and they certainly do not match. There is the heart, and here is the heart, running this way; also showing the year's growth in here; the grain is of a different type than that, considerable. That knot--- This should be all knotted. If you will notice, these grains are running, inclined to run, that way (indicating). You will notice they are all running that way and they should be--- you see the grains in the knot in here should be of a wavy side, like this. See what I mean? And yet these grains are clear, and they are running that way.

Q. So that in your opinion it doesn't make any difference which end of this board you turn up and try to match it against that end, it is impossible to do it? A. It can't match;, not so far as the face surface of either side---

Q. Now, taking the general appearance of this board marked State's Exhibit S-226 and comparing it on both sides with the general appearance of the ladder rail, is there in your judgement any similarity between the two boards which would lead you to believe that they were both at one time a part of the same board? A. No, sir, it is tree nature to have this pitch, if it runs in the top, that pitch comes from a bruise and it wouldn't certainly be a bruise so high, it would be a bruise down lower. Mr. Koehler has told me this is the top. That pitch would have to come---naturally you would have more pitch in the bottom. When your pitch on North Carolina pine increases on the height, it is because that tree has been bruised considerably when it was young and that board don't show any stains of pine like that whatsoever.

Q. Now, take the---comparing the general characteristics of the grain formation in State's Exhibit S-226 with the general characteristics of the grain formation in the ladder rail, is there any similarity? A. No. The knots in here, you look at those knots, see, knots in all trees go the same. These knots in here have got a good deal more curls all over, and are rougher as they go in here.

Q. The knots, I suppose, are limbs on a tree? A. Limbs on a tree. This originally was in here. You notice there is a knot in there, you see how much smoother they go with that curly thing like these in here, these knots in here look more curly; they are not in there, see how curly they are? A tree, the development of your upper part of your tree all depends upon the nature and the way and the lower bottom of your tree has been taken care of when it was young. If this tree had been bruised a lot in the bottom it would have gnarly spots, and it would increase as it grows to the top. This pitch, it is practically a disease, that pitch in there, injured.

Q. This streak of pitch, long streak of pitch--- A. You see---

Q. ---in the center of the board, S-226, you think represents an injury? A. Yes, sir; when it was younger. But here is--- This knot in here, you can see, you match in here. This is the way they are supposed to be matched, isn't it? Is that the way they are supposed to be matched? Which is the top? Which is the top here?

Mr. Wilentz: Just a minute. He wants to know---

Are you asking Mr. Koehler which is the top?

The Witness: Yes.

Mr. Wilentz: Well, I am afraid---

The Court: The witness ought not to ask questions. He ought to answer questions.

Mr. Wilentz: Is there any question now pending?

By Mr. Pope:

Q. Well, do they match either way? A. No.

Q. No matter which way you turn the board over. A. No.

Q. If you turn it as it is now or turn it over? A. No.

Q. What I wanted to ask you was is there sufficient similarity between the attic floor board, S-226, and the ladder rail--- A. No, sir.

Q. ---to enable anyone to say they are both a part of the same board? A. No, sir. If they were the same board there would be---one, two, three, four, five, six, seven---seven knots in that board there. Here you have got---

Q. In how many feet? A. They are the same length, aren't they?

Mr. Wilentz: You see, your Honor---

The Court: I have told the witness that he must not ask questions. He must confine himself to answering questions.

Mr. Wilentz: I have no objection to Mr. Koehler answering his questions, but I think it is irregular.

Mr. Pope: We don't need it.

The Witness: One, two, three. In this same length there is three knots and in this top limb there is seven.

Mr. Pope: That is an additional reason why you believe it is not a part of the same board?

Mr. Wilentz: I object to that. Oh, all right.

Q. Now, I want to call your attention to the photograph marked S-233. At the left of this photograph we are told that that is an enlarged photograph of the ladder rail, and at the right of this photograph we are told that there is a photograph of the attic floor, and there is the square in the notch showing an inch and three-eighths difference between the two. You see those blue lines on here, the blue pencil lines? A. Yes.

Q. Those pencil lines were put there by Mr. Koehler and he told the jury that in his opinion that was the way grain on that board originally ran before the inch and three-quarters notch was sawed out and they were separated. What have you to say about that? A. This heart, if it was sawed out, this heart would go back and project in here (indicating on the exhibit) where it hasn't. Here is your grain here. All the way through here is your grain. There is no similarity of a heart up above here whatsoever.

Q. I now call your attention to State Exhibit 231 and here we have a cut-off portion of the photograph of the ladder rail No. 16, butting up against the end of the board from the attic floor. Do you think that those rings are continuous and that they were a part of the same board? A. Whoever set this up here, it is on an angle, and by putting it on an angle, they compare fairly good. They don't compare in fact, but fairly good, but put up that way it should be---it is on an angle. This piece here is away up at the top there. It is put on there to make it match. This piece in here on this here is supposed to be the identical pieces, only it is reversed around. Now in this piece here, this end here, if you watch the circle, the trees, the years, every one of them is perfect. If you will watch them on this picture here there is a "V" on all them.

Q. Now I want you to show that "V" to the jury. A. You notice all that "V" in there going up. See them "V's"? See those "V's." There is one, two, three, four, five and then it jumps down to here, six. That was all "V's" in them. They are not in this. This is supposed to be---

Q. Now show it to these gentlemen back here. A. There is the "V's" in them, in them marks here. There is none in these whatsoever. That is the same picture as that. You see the "V's" in there everybody?

Mr. Wilentz: No. We don't want him to be asking questions.

The testimony rendered by Charles DeBisschop was indeed professional. It was apparent at times that Wilentz was unable to cope with his positive answers by failing to exploit his usual customary self-confidence. The knowledge DeBisschop possessed of wood seemed to have perplexed the attorney general.

In essence, Wilentz realized that DeBisschop had refuted Koehler at every turn. And this could present the prosecution staff a very serious problem. Ludovic Kennedy in his book *The Airman and the Carpenter* sums it up very nicely:

"He gave several powerful reasons why Rail 16 and the attic board were not related; the knots were different ('the lower rail has three knots and the top one seven which is contrary to anything there ever was'); the 'V's were different; the saw cuts were different; the nail holes in Rail 16 were smaller than those in the board; and while the end grains appeared to match, they didn't when laid end to end. The reason for the gap between Rail 16 and the attic board, he suggested, was because the grains **didn't** match and also that the holes in Rail 16 could fit over the joists. Holding up Koehler's drawing of Rail 16 and the attic board with the gap between he said, 'whoever has drawed those lines has drawn them to correspond and make it look as though they were meeting...look at the width there...they are tightening together ... **they had to do it to make them look the same'.** He even challenged the prosecution's claim that their so-called attic board had come from the attic. 'There are no marks on its under side to show it has lain on joists for the last few years, and no marks to show that it has been removed by hammer and chisel.' In his view it had never been part of the attic flooring."

However, despite this testimony which was definitely favorable to Hauptmann, any loss of confidence Wilentz might have suffered was gained back through the permissiveness of Justice Trenchard by not censuring him for his unfair summation to the jury, this in addition to the judge's own unfair and biased charge to the same.

Reilly had another "giant" in the field of wood skills to take the stand and speak in Hauptmann's defense. Ewald Mielk, who had his own plant at Lindenhurst, New York, gave ample proof of his experience in carpentry and millwright work since 1892 until 1910 with a firm in New York where he had become familiar with North Carolina pine, sometimes called southern pine.

Mielk was quite convincing with his knowledge and explanation as to what he determined caused nicks to develop in the blade of a carpenter's plane. The questioning by attorney Pope went smoothly until the witness was asked whether he was able to express an opinion as to whether or not the attic board and Rail 16 had ever been the same piece. At that time Wilentz again "popped his cork" shouting that Mielk was "not qualified to tell whether these two pieces were a part of the same board."

Apparently Wilentz was continuing to "run scared", having not fully recovered from the "heavy" testimony of DeBisschop, who had strongly affirmed that the two pieces had never been one, and now to realize he must face another confident witness who was about to say the same, was more than he had bargained for.

Again I draw on the fine writing of Ludovic Kennedy who dramatized the performance of Attorney

General Wilentz in his book *The Airman and the Carpenter*. Said Kennedy: "Then came Ewald Mielk who gave additional reasons: the rings in the attic board were darker and had more life, there was a marked difference in the size and spacing of the knots, and the board was thinner than Rail 16. As Wilentz saw his evidence being demolished brick by brick, and no doubt cursing the day he ever decided to introduce it, he became increasingly jumpy, popping up and down like a jack-in-the-box to object to almost every question put or answer given - an exercise in which the judge mostly sustained him. But Mielk stuck to his guns: rail 16 and the so-called attic board were not and never had been part of the same flooring."

Ludovic Kennedy stated it well, however, he could have gone one step further. By actual count taken from the official trial transcript, Wilentz objected no less than 52 times during the short period Mielk was on the stand. His constant "objections" were so tiresome, even to a reader, it must have been frustrating to listen to in open court. Wilentz put forth every effort to belittle the evidence given by Mr. Mielk, as he had with DeBisschop, but in doing so in both instances, he came out the loser. But the record still stands, unfortunately for Bruno Richard Hauptmann, the judge and jury failed to put any credibility in the testimony of these qualified wood experts, rather choosing to "place their chips" on the more "questionable and inconceivable", wholly unbelievable words of Koehler.

Koehler had testified previously that the two pieces were once one board regardless of the fact that a space of nearly an inch and one half existed between the ends of the two. And then this man, by tracing some "imaginary and non-existent" graining, had declared them, due to his "successful tracing of the imaginary grains, to have been at one time a solid piece of lumber. In order to "prove this to the jury", he had justified his visual evidence by raising Rail 16 a fraction of an inch and making the claim that one surface of Rail 16 had been planed off. But regardless of the possibility of this having been done, it would not have jutted out so far above the floorboard to be noticeably seen. This very unnatural "imaginary jointure" gives more evidence to the fabrication of the wood evidence, directed and allowed, to be brought into court by Arthur Koehler.

Taking the complex answer of Koehler which was hard to follow, it seems to be just plain good sense to take the simple and more truthful statement of Ewald Mielk, when he was asked: "If any board, any board were cut into parts, say two parts or three parts, you have stated that if there was anything missing in that operation, one piece of board cut off from the other, you would be unable to identify them as being the same board if they later came to you, you would be unable to do so? **A: "I DON'T THINK ANYBODY WOULD."**

One instance, taken from many like it, I use as an example of the unfairness in that Flemington courtroom during Mielk's testimony is shown in the following dialogue:

Mr. Pope: Q. I ask you this question: Look at these boards and in view of the fact that you have stated that there is more life in the one board, known as the attic board, than there is in the board known as the ladder rail, that there is a difference in the kind, the size and the spacing of the knots and that there is a difference in the grain colors, can you, as a practical wood man, tell this jury whether they ever were, in fact, a part of the same board? A. They are not.

> Mr. Wilentz: If you Honor please, I object to the question and I move that the answer be stricken out for; the same reasons heretofore advanced.
>
> The Court: Strike out the answer.

Mr. Pope: Q. I ask from your practical experience as a carpenter, a millwright, and one who has handled millions of feet of southern pine lumber, if, by looking at these two boards which I have shown you, the State's Exhibit, one known as the attic floor board and the other the ladder rail, bearing in mind the fact that the one board shows more life than the other board, that the one board shows larger knots and more of them in the same relative space, and that one board shows a different color in grain than the other board, I now ask you if as a practical mill man and from your years of experience you are able to tell this jury whether the two boards were ever one and the same board. Now just please answer yes or no. A. No.

> Mr. Wilentz: Just a minute.
>
> Mr. Hauck: He said no.
>
> Mr. Wilentz: He said he can't tell. All right.
>
> The Witness: There is a wrong impression there, on the question.
>
> Mr. Wilentz: Just a minute, please.

You wait until you are asked a question.

Mr. Pope: That's just what I thought. Now if your Honor please, we have some rights in this courtroom, besides the Attorney General. If the witness has given us a wrong impression, may we not correct that impression?

The Court: Certainly you may; certainly you may.

Mr. Pope: Now may I ask the witness this question?

The Court: Yes.

Mr. Pope: Will you tell us what you meant by your answer No?

Mr. Wilentz: I object to that, if your Honor, please.

The Court: I sustain the objection. You may ask him if he intended to stand what he did state.

Mr. Pope: Did you intend to state that you could not tell or that you could not tell that they were not a part of the same board? A. That they were not part of the same board.

Mr. Wilentz: That I move be stricken if your Honor please.

The Court: It will be stricken out.

Mr. Pope: Q. I now ask you were they any part of the same board?

Mr. Wilentz: Just a minute now. If your Honor please, Mr. Pope speaks of rights.

This "underhanded" courtroom scenario continued on throughout the remaining days of the trial, naturally to be interspersed with Wilentz's monotonous, needless, and what seemed to be, his endless objections.

Today, though we gaze upon the scene in hindsight, we find ourselves asking the question: "Were there not at least a few fair minded persons in that courtroom who, in spite of all the evidence presented against him, in honest sympathy, felt that "Hauptmann was most certainly getting a very raw deal!"

CHAPTER FIFTY ONE

Final Accusations!

At 12:10 p.m. Friday, February 8th, 1935, following a recess which had lasted only eight minutes, defense attorney Reilly made this unexpected announcement: "The Defense Rests." Then followed the testimony of the rebuttal witnesses who had been called to refute statements given by previous witnesses. However, none gave any convincing evidence worth noting. One exception would be that of George G. Wilton who identified himself as a photographer with the New Jersey State Police. He said he had taken the photographs of the portion of the ladder, known as Rail 16, on March 8th, 1932 and that at that time the rail had four nail holes in it. Stating that he had been a photographer for over eleven years, his testimony was naturally given to contradict and discredit that of Doctor Hudson, who had testified that when he examined the rail on March 12th it contained only the one nail hole. He said he had not only taken the picture, but had enlarged it as well. He said no one had witnessed his taking it, nobody had signed the plate, nobody had signed the proofs, and nobody had been with him in the darkroom when the enlargement was made. As a matter of additional fact, no one had seen any of the procedures involved with the presentation of the enlarged photograph in court that day.

Which prompted attorney Reilly to state: It is only your word?, to which Wilton answered: Yes.

Q. And you are a State Trooper? A. Yes.

Q. You were told before you came here that you were going to testify as to when you took those pictures in 1932? A. No, sir.

Q. You didn't know what you were called for? A. No. I have got a lot of pictures.

Q. You didn't know you were going to be examined? You say you didn't know before you took the witness stand what you were going to be asked about these pictures? A. No, sir.

Q. Not a thing? A. No, sir.

Q. Why did you take this report in your pocket concerning these two pictures? A. I have carried that report ---

Q. How long have you carried it? A. Since I have been in the courtroom.

Q. How many other pictures did you take for this trial? A. No other pictures.

It seems obvious that Trooper Wilton had received instructions from his superiors to have the questionable photograph in his possession for presentation when needed at the trial. As a matter of fact, he denied under oath knowing anything about the possibility of his being questioned about the picture before he was called to testify. Which prompts us to ask, why then did he have the controversial picture conveniently in his pocket?

Here we are asked to either take the word of Trooper Wilton or believe the testimony of Doctor Erastus Mead Hudson, who said that on March 12th, 1932, there had only been one hole in the ladder rail. Basing our decision on the facts we have learned throughout our study of the case, we choose to believe Doctor Hudson.

A succession of rebuttal witnesses followed, including Joseph O. Levenson, Erna and Henry Jung, three people who were called for the express purpose of presenting evidence that could prove Isidor Fisch was with them on the night of March 1st, 1932. Each of them testified that Fisch had been in the home of the Jung's that evening; however, they gave nothing more to prove this than each confirming the statements of the others that they had all been together.

They admitted having known Fisch for only a short time, Levenson saying he had met him on only one occasion. However, all claimed it had been March 1st since they well remembered that night but failed to have any recollection of where they had been on February 29th or March 2nd, nor could they state what the weather conditions had been on those dates. They said they had seen pictures of Fisch in the newspapers during the trial and had been taken to Flemington by detective Leef from the Bronx. Levenson said he had not known Leef "until about three weeks ago" when the previously unknown detective came to his real estate office and told him he should get in touch with Attorney General Wilentz pertaining to his being acquainted with Fisch.

So that you may better understand the type of witness these people presented, I relate here a portion of Levenson's answers to the questions Reilly thrust at him during his cross-examination:

Q. Did you ever see his picture? A. In the paper.

Q. When? A. Sunday I saw it in the *Telegram*. I don't remember what day, but I saw it in the *Telegram*.

Q. You have got a poor memory? A. I don't know.

Q. When did you see Fisch's picture in the paper? A. About two or three weeks ago.

Q. How did you come to be a witness in this case? A. I was called to be a witness.

Q. Who told you to be a witness? A. Detective Leef came up to my office.

Q. Who? A. Leef.

Q. Came to your office? A. Yes.

Q. When? A. That was over a week ago.

Q. That was over a week ago. Did you know Leef before he came there? A. No, sir.

Q. Did you ever see him before? A. No, sir.

Q. Did you know Isidor Fisch has been dead a couple of years? A. I heard he was dead.

Q. Do you know any of his relatives? A. No.

Q. You were not in court any time during the trial? A. No, sir, except yesterday.

Q. Before that you weren't here? A. No, sir.

Q. Did you have any communication with this family that you say you called on? A. No, sir.

Q. Since that night of March? A. No.

Q. Nobody knew what you knew, you hadn't written to the Attorney General, you hadn't written to him, had you? A. To the Attorney General, no, sir.

Q. Anybody else? A. No, sir.

Q. Did you write to anybody? A. Pertaining to this case?

Q. Yes. A. No, sir.

Q. How did anybody in the world know you were in Schwartz's home---I mean Jung's home? A. How did they know? Detective Leef has known.

Q. You didn't tell anybody? A. I don't know how he found out.

Q. A strange man out of the clouds dropped into your home and said, Come down to Flemington, and testify, is that it?

> Mr. Wilentz: Just a minute. He didn't come out of the clouds.
>
> The Court: I think you had better reframe that question.
>
> Q. He was a stranger, wasn't he? A. Yes, sir. Q. Right? A. Yes.

Q. You didn't know him? A. No, sir.

Q. He dropped into your office? A. Yes, sir.

Q. And he tells you about something that happened in Jung's house in 1932, right? A. He asked me about it, if that was so.

Q. Yes, but you hadn't told him. A. No, sir, after he asked me I answered the question.

Q. And you hadn't seen Jung? A. No, sir.

Q. And you hadn't talked it over with Jung? A. No, sir.

Q. And you hadn't been in the police station? A. No, sir.

Q. And you had no contact with the police? A. No, sir.

Q. And at the time you saw Isidor Fisch's picture you didn't tell anybody you had seen him in Jung's house? A. No, sir.

Q. You were just sitting in your office and the door opened and a strange detective came in? A. I wasn't there the first time he came.

Q. Well, whenever you were there, he did come in and saw you and you were sitting in your office? A. That is right.

Q. And the same man came in? A. That is right.

Q. And told you something about somebody whom you knew nothing about. A. That is right.

Q. And you expect us to believe that? A. That isn't---

Re-Direct Examination by Mr. Peacock:

Q. What you told us was the truth, wasn't it? A. Yes, sir.

Q. And he was there that night? A. Yes, sir.

Q. You have never been convicted of crime, have you? A. No, sir.

Mr. Peacock: That is all.

The testimony of the others had not been one snippet more convincing than had Levenson as to where Fisch had been on March 1st, 1932. However, we wonder why all the stir was made as to the location of Fisch on that night; it was Hauptmann they were trying, and had already come to the conclusion that it was he who had climbed the ladder and gone through the child's nursery window. Reilly touched on this thought during the Levenson testimony by stating: "We haven't produced any Mr.Jung in here at all, nor has anybody said that Isidor Fisch was in Hopewell March 1st, so far as I know, in this case."

Henna Fisch, a sister of Isidor, along with her brother Pincus and the nurse who had attended Isidor in the hospital, had been brought to the trial with all expenses paid by the State from Leipzig, Germany. Henna testified (through an interpreter} that her brother had lived at her home in Leipzig from the time of his arrival until he entered the hospital on the 27th of March, 1934, where he died two days later. She said he had in his possession only about 1500 German marks ($500 in United States currency) in travelling money. She also said she judged he was in poor physical condition because "he looked very badly" after landing in Hamburg and completing the six hour trip by fast train to Leipzig. Pincus Fisch was not called to testify.

Detective Lewis J. Bornmann was re-called to identify the eight nails which he had taken from the board he had removed from the attic flooring. He said he was certain they were the nails because they had been in his possession ever since he had pried the board loose. He stated he had done this with his bare hands, the nails remaining in the board were then drilled through with a hammer from the under side after it was removed. Then, he said, they were extracted with a pair of pliers "taking all precaution to keep them straight." With confidence he stated they were "Square nails; yes, sir; cut nails."

Naturally, in order to refute the testimony presented by the defense, the State recalled Arthur Koehler, "their wood wizard" who would "prove" even more conclusively that it was possible, minus the connecting piece of lumber, to "prove" that the two boards had once been "fitly joined together." Koehler's testimony, however, primarily had to do with distinguishable marks left on wood by a carpenter's plane. In rebuttal the witness answered Mr. Pope's questions with little assurance:

Q. The nick ridges on the rungs are solid bodies, aren't they? A. Yes.

Q. And they can readily be measured in their

three dimensions, can't they? A. It would be exceedingly difficult and practically impossible to measure the fine ridges made by the fine nicks on account of the variability of the wood itself.

Q. The fine nicks or the fine ridges made by the fine nicks are solid bodies, aren't they? A. Yes.

Q. Every solid body may be measured in its three dimensions, may it not? A. It may.

Q. Yes. You made no attempt to measure these bodies in any of their dimensions, did you? A. Except the distance apart.

Q. And did you make an accurate measurement of the distance apart? A. I compared them with others.

Q. And the distance apart varies with the angle to which the plane is held while being passed over the wood, doesn't it? A. Certainly.

Q. Yes. So that you never made any attempt to ascertain any one of the three dimensions of these solid bodies, did you? A. No; I didn't think it was necessary.

Q. Whether you thought it was necessary or not, you didn't do it, did you?

Mr. Wilentz: He has already answered the question that he didn't.

A. I made an observation as to their relative size, but not an accurate measurement.

Mr. Wilentz: Like what before, may I ask?

Q. Like testing out, undertaking to identify the markings of a plane bit upon a piece of wood. A. I have identified numerous markings on---

Q. Did you ever attempt before in your life to identify the markings of a plane bit upon a piece of wood?

Mr. Wilentz: He has already answered numerous times.

The Court: He has answered the question. He may answer it again, if he wishes to.

A. Yes.

Q. When? A. Oh, at various times.

Q. And for what purpose? A. To compare the marks on wood with those made by a plane.

Q. Was that done at various times during the pendency of this investigation? A. Even previous to that.

Q. And did you ever testify in court before in your life as to the plane markings on a piece of wood?

A. No.

Q. No. This is the first time you ever undertook to do that, isn't it? A. Yes.

Q. And even this time you didn't attempt to get any measurements?

Mr. Wilentz: He has already answered that.

A. I got relative measurements.

Q. Now isn't it a fact, Mr. Koehler, that in the absence of measurements of the three dimensions that the probability of the markings being alike or made by two different planes varies only with the number of planes in the world in that condition? A. No, it varies with the number of markings made by the plane, if there is only marking---

Q. I say the probabilities, the probabilities in the absence of accurate measurements, the probabilities of the markings being made by different planes from the one you examined varies only according to the number of planes in the world?

Mr. Wilentz: Well, he has answered that it doesn't.

Mr. Pope: No, he hasn't

Mr. Wilentz: That it varies according to the nicks in the plane, not the number of planes.

Mr. Pope: The nicks have nothing to do with the markings.

Mr. Wilentz: He says it has. Maybe you are right, but the witness says it has.

The Court: That I understood to be his testimony. If you have any doubt about it, you may put another question.

And so it continued on and on, with the monotonous and repetitious questions and answers that we are almost certain would have put some of the spectators to sleep.

Koehler attempted to defend his testimony of allegations that the markings made by Hauptmann's plane in the construction of the kidnap ladder sometime prior to March of 1932, were absolutely identical to those made by his plane as demonstrated in the courtroom three years later.

If we are to accept this as factual, then we must ponder one serious question. Here we have Hauptmann, a carpenter working on many construction jobs, large and small, during that span of time, never bothering to once sharpen his plane or change the blade. Are we expected to believe this? Wilentz and Koehler, with Bornmann thrown in for good measure, would say we should. Quite frankly we do not --- and never shall.

Ernest Miller of Closter, New Jersey, testified that he was the young man who had dated Violet Sharpe on the night of March 1st, 1932. He said he had picked her up at the Morrow Estate in Englewood at eight o'clock that evening and they had gone to the Peanut Grill, a speakeasy in Orangeburg, New York, just across the state line north of Englewood. He stated another couple accompanied them, Elmer Johnson, also of Closter, and Catherine Minners of Palisades Park, New Jersey. After spending two or three hours dancing, eating and drinking, he returned Violet to her home at "about half past ten to quarter to eleven."

Miller claimed he had met Violet as she was walking along the road near the Morrow estate about a week before March 1st. She was walking alone and she waved her hand, "She asked me for a ride.", Miller continued. "You didn't know her? There was no introduction?" "She waved her hand, I stopped." explained Miller.

Reilly continued with his questioning:

Q. All I want to know from you is what time in the evening did you see the strange girl on the road that you didn't know that hailed you and got into your car? A. I don't remember the exact date or time.

Q. And the very first time---it was dark, wasn't it, when you met her the first time? A. Very first time?

Q. Yes. A. I do not remember. I think it was in the afternoon. I am not sure.

Q. Do you pick up so many girls on the road around Englewood--- A. I am not in the habit of it.

Q. Wait a moment. Do you pick up so many girls in the afternoon on the roads around Englewood that you don't remember what time it was or what day it was? A. I am not in the habit of picking up girls.

Q. This girl you did take in your car? A. Yes, I did.

Q. That's what we call picking up, isn't it? A. Not exactly.

Q. What do you call it? A. If the girl takes me for somebody else, I don't call that picking up.

Q. Well, you found that out as soon as she got in the car, that you weren't the man she thought you were? A. No, I didn't know what was on her mind.

Ernest Miller stated further that he did not understand why Violet would not give the police his name, instead of leading them to believe she had been in the company of Ernest Brinkert, operator of The Post Road Taxi Company located in White Plains, New York, who was also known as a petty thief.

Catherine Minners testified that although she had been in Miller's car when they had called for Violet at the Morrow home and had returned her there later that evening, she was unable to give any description whatsoever of the Morrow's stately mansion. Neither was she able to tell her interrogator anything specific of the days immediately before or after the March 1st date, nor of the weather conditions as well. But she was very precise about the events of the "very questionable evening".

Elmer Johnson followed Miss Minners to the stand but could add nothing additional to that already offered by those who made up the foursome at the Peanut Grill. He also failed to remember anything about occurrences on the days before and after the kidnapping. However, he too, was certain the night they had been with Violet Sharpe was Tuesday, March 1st, 1932.

George Marshall, the 61 year old night watchman who had served in that capacity in the house for the past four and one-half years at the Morrow estate, said he well remembered the night in question. He claimed he had seen Violet come home around eleven o'clock and that it was close to that time when they learned of the kidnapping at Hopewell. This prompted Reilly to ask: "Then there was lots of confusion in the house after that?", with the watchman's surprising answer: "Not right away."

Q. Within a few minutes? A. Mrs. Morrow answered the phone after I told her about it.

Q. After she answered the phone there was great excitement? A. Well, no. Mrs. Morrow took quite a little while. I came down, rang up my clock. I had to ring up at 11 o'clock.

Q. Was there or was there not excitement in the Morrow home after Mrs. Morrow received word of the kidnapping? That is easy enough to answer. A. No, there was no great excitement.

Q. No great excitement? A. No. They had all gone to bed, the biggest part of them.

Q. And none of them got up? A. I wouldn't say

that. There wasn't very many home that night.

It seems rather strange that George Marshall was not certain if Mrs. Morrow's daughter, Elisabeth, was there that night. Miss Morrow, along with the Lindberghs, was a permanent member of the Morrow household. Yet, when the night watchman was asked: "Was Miss Elisabeth there that night?", his answer had been: "Well, I wouldn't swear that she was."

Mrs. Dwight Morrow was the final witness and confirmed that Miss Sharpe had definitely been in the Morrow home that evening. She said her maid had served dinner, that she had not seen her after quarter to eight, but she had seen her again shortly after eleven. Mrs. Morrow said her daughter was at home with her that evening.

Following her short time on the stand, Attorney General Wilentz made his announcement: The State rests. This was followed by defense attorney Reilly who made the same announcement since he had no rebuttal witnesses to be heard. At 2:39 p.m. Saturday, February 9th, court was adjourned until Monday morning, February 11th, at ten o'clock.

Attorney Anthony Hauck was chosen to give the summation for the State. He opened by congratulating the jury members for their patience in listening to over a million and a half words of testimony and watching some 380 exhibits. After reviewing the events of the case, he reiterated the state's contention that Bruno Richard Hauptmann was alone guilty of the kidnapping and murder of the Lindbergh baby. He said the testimony of state's witnesses Perrone, Condon, Hochmuth, Achenbach, Alexander, Rossiter, Lindbergh and Lupica (apparently forgetting the Princeton student had been a defense witness) was conclusive proof of his guilt.

However, as incensed as Hauck was in his declaration of Hauptmann as the lone participant in the case, nearing the close of his summation he stated: "Now you can disregard the personal identity, disregard the handwriting experts, disregard Whited, disregard the ladder, disregard Lupica, disregard all those things, but I want you to remember this: that the man who got the $50,000 handed to him was the man who had buried in his very garage approximately $15,000 of this very money."

Strangely enough, to this very day, almost everyone who still believes in his guilt, even some of those who claim themselves to be students of the case, hold firm to this very argument: "What do you mean he was innocent?", they ask. "Of course he was guilty, didn't they catch the guy with all that money on him? How can you say he was innocent?

To this we must reply: "Thank God" we were never swayed by the hatred of the public's many preconceived opinions. Those, who as one, were led and swayed by their narrow prejudices to cry out "Kill the Kraut!", at any cost!

I trust this book will "kill" all beliefs of Hauptmann's guilt. By far, not all of the evidence proving his innocence has been presented. I have much more to tell. However, to those who are still not convinced, I ask you to consider the statement attorney Hauck used in his summation. Then, based on the new facts you have already learned since you started reading this book, ask yourself this question: "If Hauptmann were alive today and, taking all the evidence the police used against him, then he could present you with ABSOLUTE, UNDENIABLE, UNQUESTIONABLE AND INDISPUTABLE PROOF AS TO HOW HE CAME INTO POSSESSION OF THAT RANSOM MONEY, would you then believe him? We unequivocally believe you would; because this book cries out the true answer for him. --- That is why it had to be written!

CHAPTER FIFTY TWO

Reilly's Big Show!

Because of Lloyd Fisher's strong belief in his innocence, Richard had requested that he be the attorney selected to make the summation for the defense. However, his wish was not to be granted. Reilly's huge ego would not allow this: "Why, I have been summing up cases for juries before Fisher was born.", he told Anna Hauptmann. He went on to explain that: "Even if this jury was made up of country people, which everyone recognizes it to be, country juries and city juries are all brothers and sisters under the skin because it is nothing more than a question of appealing to the human heart and the human heart doesn't change." Anna and Richard could only hope he was right.

Fisher also had hoped to make the summation for Richard. He was convinced of his client's absolute innocence and was certain he could do a better job than Reilly. Furthermore, since he was a resident of Flemington, it was his feeling that the jury might be more sympathetic to his plea. But again Reilly would have none of this: "I'm running the show here and I'm doing the talking.", his already flushed face nearing the color of crimson. And so it had been settled; Reilly would do the summation without further ado.

Anthony Hauck had closed his summation for the state with these words: "Remember, we are not required to have a picture of this man coming down the ladder with the Lindbergh baby; but we have shown you conclusively, overwhelmingly, beyond a reasonable doubt, that Bruno Richard Hauptmann is guilty of the murder of Charles A. Lindbergh, Jr.".

Now, all that remained for the defense to do was to erase from the minds of the jurors all of the false testimony they had been fed by the prosecution witnesses during the preceding days. Quite a task to be sure, however, not an impossible one since the entire case against Hauptmann had been built on "packs of lies and innuendos" and around nothing more than the fact that the defendant had been caught with almost $15,000 of the Lindbergh ransom in his possession. However, regardless of this fact, he had a perfectly reasonable and honest explanation as to how he had obtained it; but this was the tremendous obstacle he had to overcome.

It was a barrier so great Reilly would have difficulty explaining it to the twelve citizens who were sitting before him, those who would soon deliberate together on the ultimate fate of Richard Hauptmann and find him guilty "beyond a reasonable doubt." We believe their collective minds were already fixed, and because of this, it is doubtful if any lawyer, facing the same set of circumstances that transpired in that Flemington courtroom, could have won an acquittal for Hauptmann.

Although this was the first day Reilly had failed to wear a fresh white carnation in his lapel, he still maintained his appearance as a Beau Brummell of fashion. Dressed in his usual dark morning coat, striped trousers and spats he made a harsh contrast to the attire of the rural country folk he still hoped to convince of his client's innocence. However, in spite of this, he did have, what might be termed "his best day in court" by delivering a compassionate and emphatic summation, one possibly fostered by a "rather tardy" thought that "just maybe" Hauptmann might be innocent after all.

As the flamboyant attorney rose to address the jury, he removed a small Bible from his pocket and, holding it high above his head, he said to the jury: "I wish to give you a text from St. Matthew, 'Judge not, lest ye be judged,' and I ask of you in the consideration of this case that you bring into your hearts and into your consciences the feeling that you are weighing that which you cannot give back if you take it away---life."

As inept as Reilly had proven to be, he seemed to redeem himself as he proceeded with his summation. He began by pointing out the many facts that would have been essential for Hauptmann to have known before the kidnapping. "How in God's name did Hauptmann in the Bronx know anything about the Lindbergh home?", he asked the jury; claiming "it would have been impossible, for a man living in Bronx County, at least 75 to 100 miles away from Hopewell---to know anything about Colonel Lindbergh"s home."

"Colonel Lindbergh was stabbed in the back by the disloyalty of those who worked for him, and despite the fact that he courageously believes that there was no disloyalty in the servants' quarters, I say now that no one could get into that house unless the information was supplied by those who worked for Colonel Lindbergh. And this is no fairy tale. I am talking now from the record; I am talking from the evidence in this case." Reilly thundered on.

He drew a graphic picture of the impossibility of Hauptmann's entering the nursery window: "They would have you believe that Hauptmann went up two sections of that ladder. That brings him 30 inches below this window sill.

"And they'd have you believe that he had gloves on,---30 inches below this window sill. Now he has to inch up. There is no need of any chisel, no need of any chisel. He reaches up and he finds that the shutters are just closed together. He opens the shutters;, one back and the other back. Now how long do you suppose two loose shutters would stay back with a gale howling? They would be banging, banging, banging, back and forth. But nevertheless, with those shutters banging back and forth and a gale blowing, this man has to take himself by his two hands, and I don't see how he could get above the second section of the ladder, because he would have to hold on to the side of it, and he would have to hold on to the wall as he went up, to steady himself; but finally he is on the top rung now, and he is reaching three feet through the air, gripping the bottom of the window sill, of a house he had never been in, of a house where he doesn't know who is inside the room---and any fool would know that a Colonel of the United States Army would have a gun somewheres around and put a bullet through your heart; but nevertheless he pulls himself up until he gets in such a position that he can shove this window up. That makes him at least five feet away from the top rung of the ladder. Now he has got to shove the window up, get a purchase underneath as the witness did here, and raise up this window; and here is a window with a shelf, and a beer stein on it for decorative purposes, and I don't care where it was, he didn't know it was there, if anybody ever went in that window, and a strange man is able to swing himself in the window without knocking the beer stein down, and a room that is absolutely dark, mind you, in which there are toys, furniture, table and chairs, and he has never been in the room before, and across the room is a crib that he never saw in his life---this man is able to navigate that room without bumping into the table or falling over a chair, gets over to the crib, where there is a sick child, a fretful child, a child that has just been given a physic, just had its chest rubbed---why that child would sense immediately the presence in that room of a stranger!

"And the moment anyone put their hand on that child, that child's cry ringing out would have brought the mother from the room across the hall.

"Now, I will leave it to you mothers if I am not right. The person that picked that child out of that crib, I give you my solemn word, the inference I draw, knew that child and that child knew that person. Nobody---it is humanly impossible to pick up a child 20 months old, unless that child had been doped---of course instead of a physic, if that child had been given paregoric or something, then the child wouldn't cry.

"But who gave the medicine? Not Hauptmann. Who gave the physic? Not Hauptmann. And this little child is picked up and they would have you believe that Hauptmann, this man who never saw the child and never knew the child and the child didn't know him, with a dog downstairs---now you have got a strange man in the house and all the doors open, goes back with a 25 or 30 pound child in his arms, swings himself out the window in the darkness and is able to find the top rung of that ladder, three feet below the window shelf, that rickety old ladder, and then as he finds himself on the window seat and his feet touching the top of the ladder, is able to turn with a child in his arms and feel his way down the side wall and still hold on to the child and find the ladder, so that he can come down the ladder to the part where the dowel pin joins it together, and then they say the dowel pin broke---but unfortunately what they say is not evidence, because this is resting in mud, this is resting in mud."

Reilly had accurately described the impossibility of any one person entering that home by himself without the aid of someone inside. And then he describes, had the kidnapper acted alone, what he would have been forced to do: "Now a man with a baby that he has just stolen from the most popular American of the day---what did he do with the baby? Did he put it down some place and direct his attention to carrying an old wooden ladder? Because that's what somebody must have done, if you believe the State. The baby must have been put down, and the man picks up one section of the ladder and puts it here, and goes back, and gets two sections, joins them together, and puts them down here, all the time running the risk of detection and arrest, or maybe being shot. Now would a man that kidnapped the

Lindbergh baby pay any attention to the ladder?

"Folding it up nicely and putting it under a bush, and putting another piece here, and then picking up the baby."

Reilly's address to the jury hit hard every instance where the police had bungled their job. These included their failure to have plaster casts made of the footprints found at the Lindbergh home; their inability to develop any latent prints in the nursery; the stupidity in failing to have every mailbox in New York watched since they were aware the ransom letters were being mailed from the New York-Brooklyn area. "The writer of these letters could have been arrested or the mailer of these letters could have been arrested within 48 hours if somebody hadn't stumbled and bungled---just another Battle of Jutland---stumbling, bungling and blocking the path.

"Now when this second letter came to the Colonel, certainly when a letter came to Colonel Breckinridge, New York, N.Y., Station D, the New York police were assisting the New Jersey police. The police agencies of this country were aroused Federal, State, Internal Revenue, everybody; private detectives by the score.

"Don't you suppose, after the New York police saw that letters were being mailed in New York City that one word from Colonel Schwarzkopf, or somebody else, 'Cover the letter boxes,' would have had some result? But no! Bungling, bungling all the time."

Reilly attacked the police for allowing Condon the complete liberty of making all the arrangements with the kidnappers. He questioned why Condon was "always alone" during every meeting with the kidnappers. "Why, that graveyard of St. Raymond's should have been surrounded by police. That man, as he reached over and grabbed, wanted to grab fifty thousand dollars, should have been pounced on immediately.

"But it was Condon, the ad putter, Condon who received the letter within 24 hours, that must have advised the Colonel, 'I have got everything under control; don't worry, I will get it; we don't need the police.'

"And who saw Condon hand the $50,000 over the railing, or over a bush? Nobody---nobody in God's world but Condon.

"And if a man was there to receive it and he comes back and he has got another note---Condon alone,---always Condon,---gave him the money, Condon alone.

"Sitting on the bench, the golf bench in the park:

Condon alone.

"Woodlawn Cemetery: Condon alone."

Reilly made an impassioned plea, pointing out to the jury that the State had presented nothing but "guesswork", lacking direct evidence, when it came to proving how Lindbergh's child met his death, as well as when it occurred.

"Now, they must prove the cause of death by direct evidence." So they called in the Coroner's Physician.

"You saw him---a big, swaggering, blustering individual, who says he is a doctor.

"Are you connected with any hospital?"

"No."

"Now, you and I know from our experience that every respectable, high-standing professional man is always connected with some hospital if he is a physician, or if he is a lawyer, is connected with some Bar Association. He is either consulting surgeon or is administrating medical man, or he is diagnostician, or he is something. It is his standing in the profession.

"He doesn't belong to anything.

"And the poor little baby's body was so badly decomposed that all the important organs were missing, and the detective unfortunately, in lifting up the body---and even the Doctor had to admit that the baby's skull, of that tender age, and exposed to the elements as it was, would be more or less in the same condition that you might have a decaying orange or grapefruit: it would be easy to lay it aside, open it up.

"Now, we have---and he did it, no doubt, with the best of intentions, this detective picking up the body with a sharp stick, and as a result of his picking up the head with a sharp stick, he with sufficient force punctured a hole in this little child's skull.

"Now, I say that the pressure is sufficient---and I think it is borne out by the evidence, and it is a fair inference for you to draw---the pressure of that stick on the little baby's skull, which hadn't formed into bone yet,---was just more or less like muscular tissue,---if it was sufficient to force into that, it would be sufficient to almost crack it open.

"And the cracks he found in the skull are no indication that the baby in life received a blow. Then he tries to say in medical terms, 'Oh, yes, it was a blow, because I found a clot of blood on the inside of the brain, which I believe,'---he believes,---I would not take his word in an accident case, much less a case of death, a case of life and death like this,---'I believe,' he says, 'that that clot of blood inside shows me,' he is a professional man---'that that clot was formed before death.'

"'Well, Doctor,' I said,---and you would say the same thing,---'did you have anybody come in and look at you perform the autopsy?'

"'No.'

"'You gave your report. Did you write it down?' 'No,'---but he filled out a form which is on file. No inquest, no Coroner's jury called, no inquest, no care and attention that you would expect to be given to the child of Colonel Lindbergh.

"Now, where is there any security in a report of that kind of a medical man? 'Supposing, Doctor, you had died before anybody was arrested: What would happen to your evidence?' 'Well, I don't know.'

"Now, supposing the State of New Jersey at some time did get the real kidnapper, the real culprit---not Hauptmann, who is innocent---and Dr. Mitchell was dead. How would they prove anything? They couldn't--no photographs, no backing up by any other physician, no record that you could bring into court, except the filing of a form, Coroner's physician form No. 8, 'Baby came to its death by blow, external.' But even that, he can't say, nor is there any doctor living---and I challenge them to bring one in here,---is there a doctor living that can tell from the examination of that baby's body at that time, under those circumstances, when it died?

"And remember, you are limited to March 1st, between ten o'clock at night and midnight. There isn't a doctor living that can tell when that poor unfortunate baby died, or what it came to its death from. The mere fact that he found the skull might indicate a million things, but Mr. Wilentz in his opening said this: 'I will show you that when the ladder broke the baby was smashed up against the wall and then fell, I think on the catwalk.'

"Now where is there any evidence of that? That's Mr. Wilentz's assumption, his guess, his inference, and he would like to have you believe it. Now you can't believe it when you take Dr. Mitchell's report. You can't hang a man on circumstantial evidence unless all of the innocent constructions covering the act are wiped away and only the guilty construction remains. Now you can't guess that this baby received its death blow, as Mr. Wilentz said, because he wasn't there. He knows nothing about it; he is the Prosecutor; he may believe it, he may think it fits in fine with this indictment, but that's not the fact and that's not the evidence. The pressure of that stick by that police officer, careless and clumsy, more bungling---that little child should have been treated with the greatest reverence in the world; it was very easy to allow the little baby's body to stay there until some trained mortician came with a little basket, and who knew how to gather up the child, and then you wouldn't have this careless bungling of a great big copper with a stick, unfortunately puncturing the head and the skull of this child, and of course there was force enough for that undoubtedly to cause the little skull to crack, and that was the condition Dr. Mitchell found it in.

"Well, as I say they had the Colonel going from here, going there, and going everywhere. He came back, saw his baby for the last time, the baby's body was sent and was cremated."

As for the suicide of Violet Sharpe, Reilly belittled the inference that she had taken her life because she had a fear of losing her job. "A girl who can always get a position as a waitress, doesn't commit suicide because she fears she might lose her job. Life is too sweet. But the net is closing in. Sharpe has said something; Sharpe has given a clue. The clue was investigated. I think it was Walsh of New Jersey had investigated Sharpe. It was the New Jersey Police that was doing the investigating. Suddenly detectives come back and they say, 'Bring Violet down here again.' 'But you have just questioned her.' 'Never mind, we have got something we are going to ask her about now, bring her down.' And a poison which is never permitted in any home, cyanide of potassium, I think it was, the most deadly, effective and quick-acting poison in the world this girl drained when she knows Inspector Walsh and the police have checked up and found something. She didn't do it because she feared she would lose her job. She did it because the woman from Yonkers, Mrs. Bonesteel, told the truth. She was at the ferry with a blanket and she was at 42nd Street with a child and that child was the Colonel's child, and while I have the greatest respect and always will have for the distinguished Mrs. Morrow, who appeared here at the last hearing of the court, I will say this: that I believe that she is honestly mistaken and I will tell you the inference I draw, and if my inference does not amount to anything, please reject it. In great houses like the Morrows, where there are any number of servants and the mistress of the house is living practically in exclusive privacy as she was after the death of the late Senator and where there was nobody there but Miss Elisabeth on March 1st, it is a fair assumption to believe that the mistress of the house is served her dinner by the butler and the waitress serves the other members of the household who happen to be at the table.

And I have a right to assume from my knowledge of the world and the inference I draw, and I give this to you for your belief, that when Mrs. Morrow finished her dinner that evening she retired to her private quarters, very likely to read and to rest.

"People of her station in life do not associate with their servants. If Mrs. Morrow required a glass of water or a glass of milk that evening, or any attention, and if she pressed the bell or pulled the rope, the butler would respond; and he was on duty that night.

"There were five other maids. Any personal attendance Mrs. Morrow required that evening undoubtedly was given to her by her personal maid and not a waitress; so I don't think that Mrs. Morrow remembers correctly that she saw Violet Sharpe at 11 o'clock or 12 o'clock March 1st, because it doesn't fit in with Violet Sharpe's suicide.

"Whateley, who controlled the dog, his wife goes to Europe, he is suddenly stricken,---he is dead.

"The sinister hand of fate played strange tricks in Hopewell and in Englewood, concerning this unfortunate baby.

"The man that was there with the dog, the man that had charge of the ground floor, he is stricken while his wife is off to Europe,---dead in two days.

"Sharpe,---'bring her downstairs; I want to ask her something.'---Dead!

"And then you say---and you say that they had nothing to do with this kidnapping of this child, when Whateley was in control of that house that night, as butler, and controlled the dog, and Sharpe; that Mrs. Bonesteel---she is no convict, she is a respectable, decent woman,---do you suppose she comes down and she perjures herself? I don't believe it.

"She saw that girl before that night; she was introduced by another maid; it was the end of the Alpine Ferry; the Alpine Ferry was the nearest Ferry from Jersey, from Englewood to New York. The girl was there over an hour, she has a blanket on her arm; a car pulls up, she waves, she runs out, and then they bring this parade in here of witnesses who say they were with her, they were with her on March 1st."

"Then add to that her suicide; because in her guilty heart and conscience she knew what she did. But stricken with fear and stricken with her conscience, she didn't know how much the police had found out; and when they asked her the first time and she got away with it, she couldn't leave the Morrow estate without being subject very likely to arrest; but when they came back and said, 'Bring her down again, we have got something this time we want to ask her,' then the realization came to her, 'They have got me, but they will never take me.' Death was the quickest and the easiest way out of it. And this explanation that she did that because she was afraid that somebody would know she was in a speakeasy is ridiculous. I am asking for an application of common horse sense; David Harum sense, please. This girl never killed herself because she feared the loss of her job, any more than Whateley was suddenly stricken with appendicitis or something. He was stricken with something that they dare not bring in and didn't bring in the record of his death; but he was dead and he died while his wife was in Europe, and he died---I don't know how he died or why he died. But he is the man that had the dog and muzzled the dog and kept the dog quiet the night that this unfortunate child was taken out of that house, down those stairs, and not down any ladder."

Reilly took great issue with the State's charge that Hauptmann was responsible for spending $35,000, the amount in excess of that found in his garage. Hauptmann, they charged, had at one time been in possession of the entire $50,000 ransom and had lost it in his ventures on the stock market. But Reilly said this was far from the truth: "They write the scenario and they say, 'Well, look at what Hauptmann did. He went into Wall Street. He spent money in Wall Street.' They add up a set of figures and they show you that from the 2nd of April, 1932, down to the time of his arrest, he spent $50,000, or $35,000, just enough to make, with the $15,000 found in the garage, the $50,000 of the Lindbergh money.

"And when we look at the accounts with Hauptmann and their inspector for the United States Government was sitting here---I think his name was Ward or something like that, the man that was sitting here checking with them,---we ask, 'Did you buy this?'

"'Yes.'

"The sales offset the buying. He showed it clearly. Nobody went back on the stand and contradicted him. He lost $5,000. They would have you think that he was spending Lindbergh money down to the day of his arrest, and yet when you look at the accounts, as you will, you will see that in July, 1933, when Isidor Fisch gave him the last $4,500 to balance the account, from July 2nd , I think it was, 1933, down to the day of his arrest, this defendant didn't put one dollar into his Wall Street account excepting one or two small dividend checks that came in that were credited to his account.

"Now why try to fool you? Why try to drag this poor defendant in here and have you people fooled, send a man to the electric chair, send him away for life, in order to close this unfortunate chapter in American home life?

"It isn't right and it isn't decent. Not a dollar of that money, of that ransom money, ever went through Wall Street or ever went through a bank. One bank might slip up. But there was a bank in Mount Vernon. There was a Central Savings Bank. That was the bank that the brokers did business with. Then there was another brokerage account. I think there were three brokerage accounts. There were three or more banks. And not a brokerage account, not a bank account from anybody in the world found a dollar of this money.

"Now, how can you say or anybody else say that Hauptmann used ransom money just because a set of figures added up on one side, but they forgot to correspond with the sales on the other side. And I think we have demonstrated that this defendant who was in the market long before the baby was kidnapped, who had money before the baby was kidnapped, who saved his money, went into the market, played, as the man said on the witness stand, that you could go into the market with three or four thousand dollars and you could shoestring it up to a million as many-a-man has done if he was fortunate in his tips.

"Then Hauptmann up in the Bronx, in August, finds a box.; Now what is unusual about that? He says Fisch gave it to him. Was there such a man as Fisch? Yes. Was he in the fur business? Yes. Was he in the fur business with Hauptmann? Yes. Was he down in Wall Street with Hauptmann? Yes. Who says so? Their witness from Wall Street, who testified concerning the account, says, 'I saw Isidor Fisch in that room, in that market room, time and time again, with Hauptmann.

"They didn't expect that to come out, but he told the truth. Fisch was down there."

And then Reilly proceeded to rip into the New

Jersey State Police for barring the defense attorneys from entering the Hauptmann home. "But of all the crookedness in this case, of all the plants that were ever put into a case, this board on the inside of a closet is the worst example of police crookedness that I have seen in a great many years.

"And who found it? Did the ordinary patrolman find it? No. Did a detective find it? No. Did a lieutenant find it? No. Did a captain find it? No. And you go all the way up the grades, with all of these fellows, these blood hounds all over the house, a little voice led big husky Inspector Bruckmann into the closet and he turns around in the dark closet and says, 'Aha! I have found it.' The Chief Inspector of the Bronx. That puts him in the case. Condon's telephone number and Condon's address from a man they claim was writing to Condon on and after March 8th, 1932.

"Why, if Hauptmann, as dumb as they want you to believe in one minute, or as smart as they want you to believe in the next minute, ever wrote to Dr. Condon, you can bet he would never write down anything on wood in a closet that you have got to back into to find it.

"Well, they haven't a very good case in the Bronx against Hauptmann up to now, but now they have got the telephone and they rip out the board---telephone number---and they rip out the board. Well that won't do, there has got to be something else. Go out and get something else on this fellow now. We will rent the apartment to the New Jersey State Police at sixty or seventy-five dollars a month, and we won't let anybody in to look at it, and when we are getting ready for trial, and during the trial, when we ask permission to go into the attic and into the Hauptmann apartment it is denied. What are they hiding? What are they hiding from us that they don't want us to see where this board was ripped out, if it ever was ripped out? What is the State of New Jersey, if it is on the level in this case, hiding from the defense? Even after the trial starts we can't get in the house. We go over and Mrs. Rauch says, 'No, the State Police have got it, you can't go in.' Go to the State Police and they say, well, we can't get in. What are they hiding? Your great State and its prosecuting officers are supposed to be absolutely free from anything in the line of hiding, and I think the prosecuting officers are free, but I put all of the bungling and all of the monkey business in this case on the State Police here and the City of New York Police; and no doubt tomorrow the General will say every lawyer that ever stood before the Bar when he has a weak case damns the police. I am not damning them because I have a weak case. I say that a house that is inspected day after day by detectives who are supposed to be bright and know their business, and go over every inch, it is a mighty peculiar thing that they cannot find anything. But the big inspector backing into the closet, he can find a number that nobody else could find."

The defense attorney lauded the honest testimony of other defense witnesses: "Now Dr. Hudson says, 'I examined this ladder at the request of the State Police. I went all over it. A microscopic camera went over every inch of this ladder. Over five hundred photographs of fingerprints were taken.'

"Now I would like to see, and so would you, the microscopic camera prints, the little prints that show the four holes in this side of the ladder that they say were there March the 8th, 10th, 9th, 11th, or whenever Dr. Hudson was down there, 12th, 13th or 14th, 1932. You didn't see it and I didn't see it.

"Let me have those photographs, please, the big photographs with the four holes.

"Dr. Hudson, I don't believe, would commit perjury for President Roosevelt. I don't think he would commit perjury for anybody, much less for Hauptmann. Dr. Hudson stakes his professional integrity and honor on that witness stand. He says there was one hole: 'Oh, we will get around that; we will bring in the photograph taken when Koehler saw it in 1932,' and they bring in a great big photograph that was so fresh, so nice, and so clean you could almost see that it had been printed within 48 hours. His photographs that were taken 'way back last September or October; see the way they have been handled and torn.

"Now watch these when they come in---if they find them---brand new, lovely, clean, big photographs."

Here is his estimation of the Koehler testimony. He began by attacking his testimony from start to finish. Reilly berated the State and its witness by attacking the preposterous testimony of the so-called "wood expert", a man he identified as being nothing more than a "lumber cruiser", one who goes around the country spotting groves of trees to see what they are good for, and then reports his findings down to Washington.

"Reilly said Koehler's ludicrous affirmation, claiming that he was certain the "now famous" rail 16 of the kidnap ladder and the floor board in Hauptmann's attic had at sometime (before March 1st, 1932) been one piece of lumber, should appear to any sane thinking person as being nothing more than poppy-cock.

"Now he'd have you believe by his testimony---and I don't see how he can sleep at night after giving that testimony where a man's life is at stake---that this carpenter, this defendant Hauptmann, who could buy any kind of wood in a lumber yard up in the Bronx, went out and got two or three different kinds of wood to make this ladder: North Carolina pine, some other kind of pine, some fir in it, too. And he says to himself, 'My goodness, I am short a piece of lumber! What am I going to do?'

"There is a lumber yard around the corner. There is wood in the cellar, belonging to Rausch, so he crawls up into his attic and tears up a board. So he crawls up into his attic and tears up a board and takes it downstairs some place and saws it lengthwise and crosswise and every other wise to make the side of a ladder, the upper joint of which he never used or never needed."

The attorney continued on as he lauded the claims presented by Charles De Bisschop: "We brought down here a man from Massachusetts, and I will stake his common, good old garden variety type of horse sense against any Koehler. Here is a fellow who has been up in Massachusetts for years, yes, he is a builder, a contractor, and an excavator. He has thirty thousand or more trees on his different estates. He plants them and he grows them and he watches them grow. He knows North Carolina pine because he grows it. Not Koehler, from the books. This fellow grows it, lives with it, brings it down here, shows it to you. He says, 'You see this mark here? That is a bruise, that is a bruise, that tree got a bruise early in life.' Koehler says, 'I don't know, it might be some of the chemical left over from washing the board.'

"Now, whose word are you going to take? I am not going to go all over Koehler's evidence. You got it and you got De Bisschop's evidence and you have got old Mielk, an old gentleman who has his own mill.

"Now, the standard, as I understand, in these mills is the same all over. A two-foot measurement of gauge in a mill in North Carolina is the same two feet in Alaska. The difference doesn't change the two-foot rule. And the bevel is the same. The log goes into the mill and it is cut, I believe, into one or two inch boards; then it is taken out and it is planed down. You men on the jury have handled boards. Here we have down in North Carolina, South Carolina, billions and billions of board feet a year; and then Koehler has the nerve to come in here and tell us, I suppose they are like fingerprints,---there never were two boards in all the billion feet alike; and he says, 'This board here was once a part of this board here.'

"De Bisschop says, 'Nothing of the kind. The grain isn't alike; the knots are not alike. The general appearance and the general characteristics of this board are nothing like this board.

"'How do you know?' says the Attorney General.

"'Well, here are two boards,' he says; 'they perfectly match.'

"He shows it to you. One, he says, forty-seven years old; the other, five years old. Both the same age when their individual and respective trees were cut, and they match perfectly, the grain, the age.

"Mr. Pope's examination developed, as you will remember, perfect markings in these two.

"Koehler goes on the stand; his reputation is at stake; he is a great man from Washington. He looks at it and he says, 'Ridiculous! because he can't go back to Washington and face the other fellows in the different departments and get laughed at.

"We started this case with practically nothing, but we sent an appeal out through the radio and through the news and in the theaters: 'If there is any soul on God's earth that knows anything about this case, please come forward and tell us.'

"And this man, De Bisschop, up in Massachusetts, who doesn't know a soul in this courtroom, reading the Koehler testimony, says, 'That fellow is wrong, and I am going down there and I am going to show he is wrong.'

"Now would he come down here and commit perjury, come down here and make a fool of himself, go to all this trouble? And his stuff rings true. He points out to you that it is true and he says that board and that board were never the same. We can't get in the attic and see where the board came from.

"I don't know who cooked up this idea of trying to make this ladder and this board agree but I don't think this jury is going to stand for that kind of evidence.

"Koehler was wrong many times. He was wrong on his measurements. They look alike; they are alike; they are absolutely the same. Mr. Pope took them over with a measuring instrument and found, I think it was 1-16th or 1-12th of an inch out of the way, planed differently, different saw marks.

"Now, what are you going to do with that kind of testimony?

"The case is too perfect from the prosecution's viewpoint; and what they produced here. There isn't a man in the world with brains enough to plan this kidnapping alone and not with a gang,---that master mind wouldn't be a carpenter---and then sit down and make the foolish mistake of ripping a board out of his attic and leaving the other half of it there to make the side of a ladder, a portion of which he never used.

"Now what does Hauptmann say? Hauptmann says. 'I was not there. I don't know anything about Hopewell. I wasn't there. I never visited the Lindbergh estate. I was up in Fredericksen's calling for my wife.' Mr. and Mrs. Fredericksen come down here. Mrs. Fredericksen says 'I was out. That is my regular Tuesday night.' Fredericksen says, 'I was there. I didn't see him, but Anna was waiting on the place.' And I can imagine in a restaurant, a bakery like that, people coming in and going out, and eating, Hauptmann calling every Tuesday and Friday night for his wife, wouldn't be asking these customers who they were, wouldn't be bothering about them at all, never anticipating a kidnapping trial, minding his own business.

"So the appeal goes out and the response comes back. Young Christenson says, 'I was there,' and comes down here as clean an individual as took the stand in this case. 'I was there. I went up to see a girl. It was too late and I didn't see her. I liked her.' He wouldn't be the first boy that liked a girl that the girl didn't like. He was only just a poor, little laborer. 'And I went in and ate. Hauptmann was there.'

"Maybe you didn't pay particular attention, I was hoping you would, at the cross-examination of Christenson. The General just sat here and he stalled along and he asked him about his grandmother, his grandfather, while the messengers dashed for that room back and forth, wires opened to New York, back and forth, wires opened to New York. The little boy said, 'I told Mrs. Strauss in her kitchen down in Lindbrook, I think it was, 'Long Island, when I read this in the paper. I said 'Mrs. Strauss, I know that man, I was there that night.'

"Well, Mrs. Strauss didn't come over here and tell you that he didn't tell her, did she?'

"Manley leaves his sick bed. 'I saw that man and even though I am sick, get out of bed, I have got to go down there and tell them that man was in Fredericksen's restaurant March the 1st when I was there.'

"Not a dime from us, no bought and paid testimony like these experts for the State. He was there, he said. Well, if he was there, he wasn't in Hopewell.

"Mrs. Bonesteel, 'I saw Violet Sharpe.' Sommer's: 'I saw Violet Sharpe.' 'But, you were a witness in the Hall-Mills case, weren't you?'

"'Yes.' Well, we can't go out and pick these people out of colleges. Anybody could be on a trolley car or a ferryboat, whether they had been Hall-Mills witnesses or whether they had testified in a civil case, or no matter how they testified, they were there.

"Sommer says---and here is the sincerity of his story: 'I reported the next morning to a detective in the Ralph Avenue Station House.'

"Now, I don't care whether Sommer had been in Sing Sing 25 times, if he saw Violet Sharpe with a baby and a man, and a blanket, and he went to the station house the next day and said to a detective, 'I saw this, here is my name and address,' and if he didn't, why don't they bring the detective down here? And you know they checked him, and of course the reason why he is not here is because Sommer did report it, and so it goes all the way down the line with our witnesses."

And the list went on and on as Reilly mentioned Lou Harding who had testified as having seen two men in a car which contained a ladder. The date had been Tuesday, March 1st and Harding had said neither of the men was Hauptmann. " He had been a good enough witness to be brought to Colonel Lindbergh's home; March the 2nd, 1932, and asked, 'What did you see?' 'I saw a car and I saw a ladder in it.' And if they didn't bring him before Hauptmann after Hauptmann's arrest and ask him 'Is this the man that was in the car?' That's more bungling. So he answered our appeal."

Ben Lupica, the Princeton preparatory student, who should have been recognized as an important witness for the defense. It was he who willingly gave the police information that he had seen a man in a car with a ladder near the entrance to Lindbergh Lane early in the evening of Tuesday, March 1st, 1932. Had his testimony been favorable for the prosecution's use, he could have then and there "nailed Hauptmann" to the chair; but unfortunately for Wilentz's case, Lupica's testimony could not be used. Instead his testimony should have been regarded as a strong witness for the defense since he testified that, although he resembled Hauptmann, he definitely was not the man he had seen in the car.

"And all of a sudden the trial is suspended to bring in this girl (Hildegard Olga Alexander) from the Bronx. Dr. Condon never, in all his testimony said he ever was in the Pelham station sending a telegram or having an argument with anybody. But they bring this dizzy young lady from the Bronx who is looking for a movie contract or something and she tells the impossible story,---plant number 999.

"Now why put people like that into the case if your case is on the level? In the Pelham railroad station that she couldn't pick out on the map after coming home on the subway she walks downstairs, across the street into this railroad station where she passed telephone booths galore in the subway station and Dr. Condon is having an argument at the counter with the telegraph operator and Mr. Hauptmann standing over behind him with his arms crossed like Hawkshaw the detective, and she looks.

"But why didn't they call back Condon and have Condon tell us that he never was in that station or ever talked to that man? Of course not. She was a liar and they realized it as soon as she left the stand. Now, why plant people in this case?

"Then they are going to have him pass money. 'Oh, yes, we will have him passing money; long before he met Fisch we will have him passing money.'

"And who do they bring in? Cecile Barr, from the moving picture theater, November the 26th, which just happened to be Hauptmann's birthday, Sunday night, about 15 or 20 miles away from Hauptmann's house, down in Greenwich Village, at the New York entrance of the Holland Tunnel, and he lives almost to the Yonkers line, this man would walk in with a folded five-dollar bill, folded, I think, in eight pieces, and give it to her; and after all these years she can come down and say, 'Yes, that's Hauptmann.'

"A notoriety hunting young woman, trying to get her picture in the paper, and got it there. Very likely she thought she was advertising her theater, that everybody in New York would flock to her theater and buy tickets from her to look at her.

"Well, do you believe the people that were at his birthday party: good, honest, decent people? Yes, they are friends of his; but you saw the kind of people they were: hardworking, industrious people; no crooks, no convicts.

"April the 2nd, he is supposed to be in St. Raymond's, behind a fence, getting $50,000, Kloppenburg said, 'I was in his house.'

"Yes, Kloppenburg is a friend of his, but he is telling the truth.

"And so it goes down the list and down the line and witness after witness comes here and testifies for this defendant. The man in the brokerage house says, 'Yes, Fisch was there.'"

Reilly continued with a perfectly reasonable explanation as to why Anna Hauptmann failed to see the package Richard had placed on the top shelf of the broom closet: "And Isidor Fisch gives him the bundle and he puts it up in the closet, shoves it in the back, he doesn't know what is in it, and because Mrs. Hauptmann doesn't climb up and clean the top shelf of a broom closet, she isn't telling the truth.

"Well, I wonder how many women of her size, who are going to have a baby are going to reach and climb up into a broom closet. The baby, I think, was born about sixteen or seventeen days before that birthday party, and after that, in 1934, she is nursing the baby and she is not climbing up---the poor little woman is not climbing up into a broom closet to look at a top shelf.

"And the water comes down and the closet is wet, and the plumber comes here and he says, 'I looked at it and I went up in the attic and the board was not missing.'

"Now what is he lying for? He doesn't know Hauptmann except that he lived there. He was Rauch's plumber. Everybody connected with the defense, because for the sake of humanity and justice they came here to help this man who is unjustly charged with crime, must be a perjurer.

"But the girl who saw Condon, she is no perjurer; Cecile Barr, she is no perjurer, she can remember every five-dollar bill she ever saw when she was at that place---she is no perjurer, they must be treated with kid gloves, they are the prosecution witnesses, but everybody who comes here because the inherent drive of their soul and conscience sent them here, they are the crooks."

Many times Reilly had resorted to a flair of the dramatic during his summation. He often used his "closed fist" technique; coupled with a deep voice approach to emphasize a point; or a desk pounding routine, making it clear by using a resonant voice; and then his hushed, subdued, almost a whisper, utterance, as he struggled to take advantage of a crucial issue. The pompous attorney, red faced from the effects of regular indulgences at "Nelly's Taproom" in the Union Hotel and the strenuous task of presenting a rather redeeming summation, Reilly ended his impassioned plea for his client's acquittal by turning to face Colonel Lindbergh, saying: "May I say to him, in passing, that he has my profound respect and I feel sorry for him in his deep grief, and I am quite sure that all of you agree with me, his lovely son is now within the gates of heaven."

After making a slight bow to the jury and spectators, he returned to his chair at the defense table where he joined his associates.

At 4:37 P. M. court was adjourned until ten o'clock the next morning, Tuesday, February 12th, 1935.

But, with the conclusion of that day's court session, regardless of the multitude of arguments yet to be put forth by the prosecution in their efforts to prove Hauptmann's guilt and the persuading factors already presented by the defense to prove his innocence, one great "unanswerable" question remained: "How was it possible for Hauptmann to have committed this crime by himself?"

In the first place, he would have had to know that the Lindberghs were going to be in Hopewell on that Tuesday night since it had always been their practice to return to Englewood on Monday mornings. In addition to this he would have had to know what room the child was in; he would have had to know whether the Lindberghs were at home or not; he would have had to know when little Charles would be put in his crib; he would have to know that none of the occupants of that home were in the nursery at the time he opened the shutters and raised the nursery window. As Reilly clearly stated: "A man can't come up to a strange house with a ladder and stick it against the wall and run up the ladder, push open a shutter and walk into a room that he has never been in before. That is what they would have you believe."

CHAPTER FIFTY THREE

The Dependable Wilentz And An Accommodating Judge!

Of all the disgusting and repulsive summation addresses ever offered to any jury by a prosecuting attorney, the one given by Attorney General David T. Wilentz at the trial of Bruno Richard Hauptmann on Tuesday, February 12th, 1935 in Flemington will always remain at the top of the list.

It was evident from the start of his summation that he had adopted a plan to not only present his strongest possible case, but one, of course, loaded with the "manufactured evidence" he had assembled against the unfortunate Bronx carpenter. In addition to this, he had decided that by means of some clever courtroom theatrics, he could effectively display his personal resentment toward the Germans who had already started to persecute the Jews in Hauptmann's homeland. Wilentz had made it quite clear that Hauptmann had been a machine gunner in the German army during World War 1; and now, by prosecuting Hauptmann, the brash attorney was being afforded the opportunity of being a front-running standard-bearer for the growing number of outspoken persons in America who had already been voicing their opposition to the Nazi brutality being committed against the Jews. To put it bluntly --- Wilentz was not about to miss a trick in his devious attempt to put Hauptmann in the chair.

"I have been governed with the thought that has always been with me that I am here as the Attorney General of the State of New Jersey and I am not only here for the State of New Jersey, men and women, but I am here representing the people of this country.", he began his long summation which was to continue throughout the day.

"My delightful adversary says that you are not to be governed by the clamor of the mob that wants the life of this man. Let me say to you that if there is such a clamor, if there is such a demand for the life or for the sentence of this man, it is not because of anything that you have done or that I have done. It must be because of the evidence that has come from the lips of credible witnesses sitting here under oath.

"'Judge not, lest ye be judged,' my adversary says, but forgets the other biblical admonition, 'And he that killeth any man shall surely be killed,' 'Shall surely be put to death.'" He then walked to the exhibit table and gently placed the Bible there where it remained in view as a constant admonition.

"For all these months since October, 1934, not during one moment has there been anything that has come to the surface or light that has indicated anything but the guilt of this defendant, Bruno Richard Hauptmann, and no one else.

"Every avenue of evidence, every little thoroughfare that we traveled along, every one leads to the same door: Bruno Richard Hauptmann."

Before commencing with his diatribe against Hauptmann, he told the jury that "the very thought of prosecuting a man for a crime goes against the very soul and the very grain of my system." And then he said: "I want to return to my family, and get away from this business of running up every morning with these maddening crowds and publicity seekers. I want to get away from it all. I am naturally a homeloving person. I want to get back evenings to my children.", and having said that, he lashed out like a caged lion ready to be set loose for the kill.

"There may be some questions you can't answer, but there sits the man that can answer them. He will be thawed out, he is cold; yes, he will be thawed out when he hears that switch; that's the time he will talk."

Wilentz extolled the character of Colonel Lindbergh, mentioning the instant fame he received when he made his solo flight over the Atlantic Ocean to Paris in 1927. And then asked: "Who would be the type of person that would take a child like that and murder it? Who could there be?

"Why men and women, if that little baby, if that little curly-haired youngster were out in the grass in the jungle, breathing, just so long as it was breathing, any tiger, any lion, the most venomous snake would have passed that child without hurting a hair on its head.

"Now, what type of man, what type of man would kill the child of Colonel Lindbergh and Anne Morrow?

"He wouldn't be an American. No American gangster and no American racketeer ever sank to the level of killing babies. Ah, no! An American gangster that did want to participate in a kidnapping wouldn't pick out Colonel Lindbergh. There are many wealthy people right in the City of New York, much more wealthy than Colonel Lindbergh. I don't know that the Colonel is wealthy at all. As a matter of fact, I think he had a tough job scraping up the few dollars here, there and everywhere to make up the ransom money.

"There are many wealthy people in New York.

"Oh, no, it had to be a fellow that had ice water in his veins, not blood.

"It had to be a fellow who had a peculiar mental make-up---who thought he was bigger than Lindy, that when the news of this crime came out he could look at the headlines screaming across the page, just as the headlines screamed across the pages when Lindy made that famous flight.

"It would have to be the type of man that wouldn't think anything of forsaking his own country and disgracing his own nation; it would have to be the sort of a fellow that would leave everything behind and flee and go to another country and another land, a strange land; it would have to be the type of man who would forsake his own mother, sixty-five years of age and run away. Yes, it would have to be the type of man who would hold up women at the point of a gun, women wheeling baby carriages. And let me tell you, men and women, the State of New Jersey and the State of New York and the Federal authorities have found that animal, an animal lower than the lowest form in the animal kingdom, public enemy Number 1 of this world, Bruno Richard Hauptmann; we have found him and he is here for your judgment.

"Why, men and women, this case is a perfect case. Why, I sleep it, I eat it, I dream it, I live it, and every moment it is Hauptmann, Hauptmann, Hauptmann, all the time!"

The attorney general next extolled the virtues of the great number of police officials whose diligent work had resulted in the successful arrest of Hauptmann; the many "experts" who had come to testify from all sections of the country and whose testimony they dare not question because each one had "proven" Hauptmann's guilt.

And then came his complaints that the defense had no right to question the honesty of any of their witnesses; at the same time challenging the statements of Dr. Hudson as being dishonest, because he had testified that in March, 1932, the time he had seen

"Rail 16", it clearly had only one nail hole in it.

"Every place every one---Hauptmann.", he continued, "But they are just so much a day.

"What do you think of that? They have to be assassinated for Hauptmann---Hauptmann the convict, Hauptmann the burglar, Hauptmann the murderer. They have to kill everybody in his path---just to clear the way for Hauptmann."

Wilentz, who knew the great expenditure the State had made to bring in its witnesses and prepare the evidence for court, had the audacity to seriously question the lack of funds the defense had in presenting their case to defend Hauptmann. While the State had its wealth to draw on, the defense were virtually paupers. Wilentz ranted on: "They talk about the defense not having any money, handicapped for money. There is not a scintilla of evidence, there is not one word of evidence, there is not the slightest bit of proof that they haven't money.

"I think they have got lots of money. That is my notion against their notion that they haven't got money; money coming from cranks and idiots and fools, un-Americans all over the country, pouring in enough money to hire what they consider the four best lawyers available, to get the best criminal lawyer in the East.

"There wasn't a lawyer in the State of New Jersey that they thought could do the job as well, a man with a reputation of thousands of cases, a man who has represented more criminals in the big Metropolis than any other man, according to reputation.

"So there must be something about this case, there must be some money somewhere; certainly they wouldn't represent a murderer just to represent him.

"What is there that would attract high-priced lawyers and famous lawyers to a man charged with the murder of the Lindbergh child?

"Certainly they don't want to glory in the blood of the Lindbergh baby. It must be because of their oath to their professional duty. It must be because of that and because they are paid to do the work.

"No money? Who said no money?

"Enough money to bring the handwriting expert from East St. Louis and a lumber man from Massachusetts or Connecticut, and another man from the other place, and the witness who testified to nothing from Warsaw, New York; enough money for radios and everything else.

"No money?

"Just an effort to prejudice this jury; just an

effort to appeal to the jury.

"Why, I think they have probably spent more money than the State has."

Oh, what a pack of foolish statements from a man who certainly knew better. He knew very well that Reilly had been hired by William Randolph Hearst, the newspaper giant, to defend Hauptmann. Reilly had received his recompense in order that the Hearst newspaper chain be given "exclusive" stories from Mrs. Hauptmann and those close to her. As for the defense witnesses, most came to Flemington without any monetary remuneration other than having their expenses paid from out of the small defense fund. The Wilentz charge that the defense had more money than the State was purely ludicrous and certainly out of order. However, this was not the only perversion of truth, stated as factual by the attorney general, that had been allowed to stand without censure by the presiding justice.

"Why", Wilentz went on, "if this wasn't a case concerning Colonel Lindbergh's child---you talk about the prestige of Colonel Lindbergh and the position of the Morrows---if it were the child of an ordinary citizen this case would have been over in one week, and that man would have paid the penalty by this time. But the fame and the glory of the name of Lindbergh has attracted lawyers. It has attracted newspaper men. It has attracted photographers. It has attracted curiosity seekers. It has attracted convicts. It has attracted idiots, lunatics. The whole world wants to get in under the glory of the Lindbergh and crush him more and more, just to get a little notoriety.

"It would have been over in a few days if it was anybody but Colonel Lindbergh.

"You and I know, of course, that there can't be any more serious crime than the crime of murder. There can't be, because it involves the taking of a life. And with all our civilization and with all our mad desire and rush for money and for everything else, with all the jealousies and everything that there is in the world, with all the ambition, the taking of a life has always been considered the most serious crime.

"Let me tell you, men and women, that even that, the crime of murder, which shrink into absolute insignificance, this murder even of the Lindbergh child would shrink into absolute insignificance in comparison to the crime that would be committed if this man were freed. That would be the crime of the century.

"To let him roam the streets of this country and

make every woman in her home shudder again; that would be a real tragedy, an American tragedy!

"That is why I told you men and women, that is why I told you I am so consumed, every inch of me, every ounce of me cries out to you, 'Please do your duty!'

"And if you ever freed this man---it couldn't be, it wouldn't be possible---but if any such thing were to happen, the murder of the Lindbergh child, as I say, that murder even would shrink into insignificance compared with the crime of which you would be guilty in letting this man roam the streets."

The attorney general had reached such an emotional high in his "plea for justice" against this "beast of a man" that he apparently had forgotten what he had said to the jury in his opening remarks to them on the opening day of the trial. At that time he had clearly stated: "Then as he went out that window and down that ladder of his, the ladder broke. He had more weight going down than he had when he was coming up. And down he went with this child. In the commission of that burglary, that child was instantaneously killed when it received that first blow. It received a horrible fracture, the dimensions of which when you hear about it will convince you that death was instantaneous."

But, lo and behold, the eminent attorney general suffered a memory lapse. In his summation he went on to present an entirely different cause of death---and then apparently expect the jury to believe it, which it apparently did, because forty-two days later he said: "But let me tell you this: this fellow took no chance on the child awakening. He crushed that child right in that room into insensibility. He smothered and choked that child right in that room. That child never cried, never gave any outcry. Certainly not. The little voice was stilled right in that room. That's a fair inference that comes from its failure to cry; either there in the room or outside." And then, as though he had another memory lapse, he offered another way that could have caused little Charles' death: "Did he use the chisel to crush the skull...? Is that a fair inference? What else was the chisel there for?" Wilentz was either in a quandary or a dilemma. And then he implored the jurors to believe him, which they did.

"He wasn't interested in the child. Life meant nothing to him. That's the type of man I told you about before that we are dealing with.

"Public Enemy Number One of the World! That's what we are dealing with.

"You are not dealing with a fellow who doesn't know what he is doing. Take a look at him as he sits there. Look at him as he walks out into this room, panther-like, gloating, feeling good.

"Cruelty. Why he would cut your heart honestly with a razor and think nothing of it and go upstairs and eat. That's how cold-blooded this murderer is.

"The only trouble I find is that we have treated this fellow entirely too well.

"I never even walked in to ask him a word. I never went in to annoy him for a second. I wouldn't get close enough to him. If I had my choice I wouldn't get in the same room, I wouldn't become contaminated, I wouldn't want to breathe the same air.

"I think too much of my friends and my wife and my kids to be around him at all--- I feel itchy, I feel oozy, I just couldn't stand being anywhere near him. I never walked into that jail even to get a confession from him.

"All right, we are still working, we are still working, and we get up into his attic.

"Oh, they say we wouldn't let them get up into the attic. The poor boys, we wouldn't let them--- terrible thing, we wouldn't let the defense do this and we wouldn't let them do that.

"The only trouble I find is that we have treated this fellow entirely too well. We have treated him too well, and they say we won't let them get up into the attic. Why do they have to get up into the attic? What is there about the attic that he doesn't know? He has lived there. What is there about the attic that Mrs. Hauptmann doesn't know? Why can't they get all the information?"

Wilentz "pulled out all the stops" by grouping together the decision of the State's handwriting "experts" by quoting the opinion of J. Clark Sellers, whom he identified as "one of the most famous men and one of the most delightful citizens of this world, from Los Angeles, a man that was appointed by the Court in the Rudolph Valentino case, in the case of Jean Harlow's husband, the man who was called upon to determine the handwriting in the Hickman murder case--- that was another kidnapping and murder case--- and the man whose record on this stand never indicated one reversal.

"And that sums up the opinion of every one of these men: Osborn, Stein, Tyrrell, Walter Cassidy, Souder.

"'I am convinced absolutely that Mr. Hauptmann

wrote the ransom notes and addressed the envelopes in which they were sent, and addressed the wrapper in which the sleeping suit was returned. I am not only saying that Hauptmann wrote the ransom documents, but I am saying no one else did. So convincing to my mind is the proof that Mr. Hauptmann wrote each and every one of these ransom notes that he might just as well have signed each and every one of them.'"

I am certain the name-dropping used as he introduced the statement of Sellers gave Wilentz more points to add toward the conviction of the helpless Hauptmann that he, thus far, had so "honorably" gained.

It is difficult to wonder whether Wilentz was entirely rational when his "staged humbleness" was marred by his consistent use of the pronoun "I", as he exuberantly explained certain aspects of the case. One point in particular was the enthusiastic fervor he exhibited in explaining the peculiar signature at the bottom of the ransom notes: "But this fellow, this fellow was no fool; he wasn't going to let anybody get that fifty thousand. So he put down at the bottom of each note: 'Our singnature.' And he put his signature on there. There was no mistake about that. There it is. You couldn't reproduce it. There it is; the blue circle, the red center and the holes; "B" in blue, for Bruno; "R" in red for Richard; holes, "H" for Hauptmann. 'Our singnature.' Nobody could reproduce that except Bruno Richard Hauptmann; and to make sure they were right he made all those papers of the same kind."

The enthusiastic pride Wilentz displayed as he explained this "proof of Hauptmann's guilt", which he felt should be accepted, without any question, as proof positive, could not help but cause some wonder throughout the courtroom as to the saneness of the prosecutor. Although Wilentz was enthused over this, it creates the question as to why any person involved in such a horrible crime would be stupid enough to "sign his own death warrant" by using a code that would be a dead giveaway. Although the coincidence exists, and the jury possibly accepted it as fact, it proves absolutely nothing.

And then we have the unfair allegation that Mrs. Hauptmann had enjoyed her trip to Germany by spending ransom money while she was there. Wilentz claimed: "He sends his wife to Germany when he isn't working. He dresses her. He gives her a trip to Germany. She bought a chest of silverware there. God! I don't care if she buys five thousand sets of silverware. There isn't anything I wish---people, if they want to go to Germany, it is all right with me. I am not a bit envious of anybody. But all I want them to do is not to take this money as the result of a murder. That is all.

"She bought her silverware in Germany with money and the fruits of this ransom money which he got because he had the baby's sleeping suit."

Wilentz went on and on in his dramatic fashion: "Hauptmann made us the victims; he picked Hunterdon County, he picked the State of New Jersey, as the scene of his crime and we, as victims, have got to suffer for it.

"Now my adversary took the liberty of addressing Colonel Lindbergh in his closing, and I am going to do the same thing.

"I want you to know, Colonel, that we cannot return your baby. No king, no nation, no country can. There is no question about that. We could try this case forever, we could go on for days and days---we couldn't do anything for Colonel Lindbergh. But we could do one thing in this case, let me tell you---this jury can, by its verdict, do one thing for the Colonel, for Anne, for the country---we can make the country a little bit more secure, we can make the children a little safer, we can make women a little happier.

"This fellow has been the inspiration for the greatest series of the meanest crimes in the history of the world.

"Why, the American gangster never knew what it was to murder a child or murder anybody kidnapped. He would take the person and he would return him for the money. There was some honor amongst thieves. There was some honor in those gangs. When they took a man and they said, 'Pay the ransom,' they gave the man back. They wouldn't take a child and murder him. He taught them a new system.

"He said, 'Take the fellow you are going to kidnap, murder him, and they can't catch you. How can they catch you, because you haven't got him? How are they going to get you?'

"He taught them that and since that time this country has been cursed with the meanest and worst series of crimes it has ever experienced. He hastened the death of Violet Sharpe. He disgraced Betty Gow. He has brought shame down upon Condon, unfair shame, in this court room, vilification and abuse.

"Why, he has left in the train of his activities not only the meanest series of crimes and been the inspiration for them, but he has caused more sorrow in millions of homes in this country than anybody could calculate.

"Why, for months, for years, as soon as a mother came into a house and found a child was missing, the first thought was, 'The child is kidnapped.' Panic in every home, sorrow in every home.

"And I want to tell you, men and women, yes, we can't restore this child. We can't do it. I have no doubt that people in this country would lay down their lives for him, but we can't do it and they can't do it in any other country.

"But if this jury will do its duty, we can translate Colonel Lindbergh's loss and worry into some gain for civilization, to show that whether we catch a man walking into the room or not, we can crush them, we can crush these snakes, we can crush these criminals, that society isn't so weak that we can't deal with them. That's the job that you can do. You can serve society so society will gain, even at Colonel Lindbergh's loss; and I know that if civilization will have some little gain out of it, as difficult as it is, Colonel Lindbergh will feel that the effort in this case has been worth while, notwithstanding his great loss."

After extolling the virtues of each of the lawyers for the State who had worked strenuously, putting in endless hours to bring a conviction against Hauptmann, Wilentz proudly stated: "We want nothing but a square deal for the people. There is no gain in it for this table---Tony Hauck, who doesn't get an extra dollar for every one of these days---men who have spent their lives, day and night, working. Why? Men who never wronged anybody, never an evil thought has crossed the mind of a fellow like Tony Hauck. He couldn't sit at that table if he didn't think and wasn't convinced this fellow was guilty. The same thing with Judge Large, Bob Peacock, Joe Lanigan, Stockton and the rest of the boys.

"Let me tell you, all we want is a square deal. We want no disgrace on the State of New Jersey.

"Gosh! how we have worked for that, to present this case and this proof with fairness, with decency, so that the United States of America and the world would feel, 'Yes, we will convict him, but we convict him fairly.'

"Mr. Reilly says the case is too perfect. No case can be too perfect. But it is perfect; and it is only perfect because of his conduct. Every piece of evidence that we have he has presented to us.

"Now, men and women, as I told you before, there are some cases, there are some cases in which a recommendation of mercy might do. But not this one, not this one. Either this man is the filthiest and vilest snake that ever crept through the grass. or he is entitled to an acquittal. And if you believe, as we do,you have got to convict him.

"Did you ever see that scale, the American scale of justice? Here is how it hangs now (indicating), way up there is the testimony of the State of New Jersey, way down in its lowest ebb is Hauptmann, Hauptmann, dangling on there, dangling on the hope and on the straw, right at the bottom of that scale, hoping that one juror, one juror may do it, may do it for Fisher, may do it for Reilly, may do it for somebody else, hoping that he will get life imprisonment instead of death.

"What does life imprisonment mean? Nothing. Maybe in fifteen years he will walk the streets again. The scales are up there with Hauptmann dangling down there, only because of the testimony.

"We have proven it overwhelmingly, conclusively, positively. Now, jurors, there is no excuse, you would never forgive yourself if you didn't do it, you wouldn't be happy, you wouldn't feel right, honestly you wouldn't.

"You convict this man of murder in the first degree. The Grand Jury of the County of Hunterdon had the courage to do it. The State of New Jersey has the courage. They stand here unafraid and ask for the penalty. Why? Because they know they are right.

"Now, jurors, it is up to you, we leave the burden with you. I assure you, when I sit down, that is the end of this case with me.

"It is your responsibility and grave as it is, important as it is, it is still your responsibility and don't shirk it. You have got a chance to do something for society that nobody else in the entire county of Hunterdon will ever have an equal chance and you have got to do that, you have got to do it. If you bring in a recommendation of mercy, a wishy-washy decision---yes, it is your province, I will not say a word about it, I will not say another word, once I sit down here in this case so far as the jury and its verdict is concerned. But it seems to me that you have and you will have the courage if you are convinced, as all of us are, the Federal authorities, the Bronx people who were there, the New Jersey State Police who were here, the lawyers who were here, Colonel Lindbergh who was here, everybody that has testified, if you believe with us, you have got to find him guilty of murder in the first degree."

With those words Wilentz closed his arduous summation, but as he did so, a voice pierced the silence of the courtroom. "If your honor please, I have a confession that was made to me by the man who committed this crime---". Several guards, acting immediately, rushed to the man and muffled the remaining words of his statement, as one of them clamped a hand over his mouth. Fortunately, only the guards and those nearby heard him say: 'I have a confession, etc.'. The shout had come from a man dressed in clerical attire who, rising to his feet, had attempted to make his startling announcement. However, he was quickly silenced and forcefully removed from the courtroom.

The immediate thoughts of the lawyers on both sides were, due to the interruption, the case could be called a possible mistrial. However, Justice Trenchard ruled that since neither he nor the jury had heard anything more of the outburst than the words "your Honor", there was no need for a retrial.

The man was later identified as the Reverend Vincent Burns, pastor of an interdenominational church in Palisades, New Jersey. He was a brother of Robert Elliot Burns who had received national notoriety for his escape from a Georgia chain gang several years earlier. Reilly said he met the Reverend Burns when he came to his office and told him that on Palm Sunday 1932 a man had come to his church and confessed to him that he was the kidnapper and murderer of the Lindbergh baby. Although Burns was convinced that his confessor had told the truth, Reilly said he had not been at all impressed and had the troopers throw him out. He said he found him to be an eccentric person who, based on his latest tirade, should have been committed to an insane asylum.

Nevertheless, with the commotion now subdued by the removal of Burns from the courtroom, and David T. Wilentz having finished his "masterful" summation, Judge Trenchard, at 4:10 P.M., due to the lateness of the hour, adjourned court until the next morning, Wednesday, February 13th, at ten o'clock at which time he announced he would deliver his charge to the jury.

The damage inflicted by Wilentz's very unfair summation was about to take its toll.

CHAPTER FIFTY FOUR

Trenchard's Charge!

On Wednesday, February 13th, 1935, the thirty-second day of the trial, the time being exactly 10:04 A.M., Justice Trenchard turned to face the jury members in the box at his left and began his charge of instructions for them. These instructions were being given for their use as guidelines as they considered and ruled on each point of evidence that had been presented during the trial. The hours of their time of deliberation were fast approaching.

"In this, as in every criminal case, the defendant is presumed to be innocent, which presumption continues until he is proved to be guilty," Justice Trenchard explained.

Now this was a difficult thing for them to do since their minds were still "swimming" with the ranting and raving of the attorney general and his diatribes of fierce accusations leveled at the innocent Hauptmann, who, because of Wilentz and his unethical summation, was already down and ready for the count.

Or, as Anthony Scaduto phrased it so well: "And then, assuming the arm of God, Judge Trenchard reached out and condemned Hauptmann to death."

Judges in criminal court deliver their customary charge to a jury knowing very well, as do attorneys, that the inflection of their voice, used at the proper time and in the proper way, can go far toward influencing members of a jury. Therefore, a statement or question, heard audibly in court, could be deemed prejudicial because of the intonation given the words. When that same statement or question is read at a later date from a printed journal there can be a great difference in one's ability to completely understand its full intent. The statement has lost its emphasis from the spoken to the printed word.

Quite often this was the case with Justice Trenchard's charge to the Hauptmann jury as he chose to emphasize his personal preference to statements and questions. If at this point in the case, there were a few jurors who were still uncertain of Hauptmann's guilt, there can be little doubt that Judge Trenchard's "unfair" charge won them over --- because it seemed quite apparent that he, acting as juror 13, believed Hauptmann to be guilty. And this was shown by a clever voice inflection when he frequently asked, "Do you believe that?" which could not fail to "telegraph" his personal belief of Hauptmann's guilt directly into the minds of the jury.

And so, after first briefly instructing the jurists:---"In this, as in every criminal case, the defendant is presumed innocent, which presumption continues until he is proved to be guilty." Justice Trenchard then went on to state: "If there is a reasonable doubt whether the defendant be guilty, he is to be declared not guilty."

It is difficult to consider even a remote possibility that at least a few of these honest jurists didn't have some reasonable doubt. However, understanding the true facts, as we know them, this thought would not be possible. Why? Because we must take into consideration that the twelve persons, in whose hands rested the ultimate fate of Hauptmann, had just had their minds cluttered by the outright lies, manufactured evidence, innuendos, and other false evidence, that it would have been difficult for them to entertain any thoughts that could be judged as even slightly controversial due, of course, to the devastating evidence which had been brought into court. Realizing this, they were allowed no alternative. Of necessity they had to go along with what they had heard within the confines of the courtroom. Had they not done this the reaction of the public would have been unspeakable and indescribable. Hadn't Wilentz already labeled Hauptmann as Public Enemy of the World? Of course he had, and any verdict other than guilty of murder in the first degree would have been highly unacceptable to the multitudes who had already "tried him out of court" and found him guilty by their own standards of how a "kangaroo court" should be run.

Trenchard began with a review of the case beginning with what had taken place in the Hopewell home on the night of the kidnapping. He covered each of the events as they took place during the investigation, the ramifications of each, and the consequences which led to the arrest of Hauptmann. He then discussed the testimony of both State and defense witnesses, often subtly "telegraphing" his doubts about that of Hauptmann and the defense witnesses. By ending many statements with his voice inflected question: "Can you believe that?", he left little to the imagination that his own answer would be: "Well, I don't, and I don't think you should either."

This fact was apparent to more than a few of the court's spectators. Later, as he was reading the court transcript, Colonel Lindbergh himself was made aware that Trenchard's charge read with less impartiality than it had sounded when he gave it in court. Harold Nicholson, who was writing a biography of Lindbergh's father-in-law, the late Senator Dwight Morrow, was told by the colonel: 'For instance he (Trenchard) kept on saying to the jury, in going over some of Hauptmann's evidence, "Do you believe that?" Now that sounds all right in print. But what he actually said was, "Do **you** believe **that**?"'

"It is argued," he continued, "that Dr. Condon's testimony is inherently improbable and should be in part rejected by you, but you will observe that his testimony is corroborated in large part by several witnesses whose credibility has not been impeached in any manner whatsoever.

"Of course, if there is in the minds of the jury a reasonable doubt as to the truth of any testimony, such testimony should be rejected but, upon the whole, is there any doubt in your mind as to the reliability of Dr. Condon's testimony?

"If you find that the defendant was the man to whom the ransom money was delivered, the question is pertinent: Was the defendant the man who left the ransom note on the window sill of the nursery, and who took the child from its crib, after opening the closed window?

"It is argued by defendants counsel that the kidnapping and murder was done by a gang, and not by the defendant, and that the defendant was in nowise concerned therein. The argument was to the effect that it was done by a gang, with the help or connivance of some one or more servants of the Lindbergh or Morrow households.

"Now do **you** believe **that** ? Is there any evidence in this case whatsoever to support any such conclusion?"

Another prime example: "The defendant says that these ransom bills, moneys, were left with him by one Fisch, a man now dead. Do **you** believe **that?**"

There were times during his discourse when Trenchard stated the facts in proper fashion; however, for the most part his discourse pointedly favored the evidence the State had presented. The following portions are pointed examples: "The defendant says that he found the ransom bills in a shoe box which had been reposing on the top shelf of his closet several months after the box had been left with him, and that he then, without telling anybody, secretly hid most of the bills in the garage where they were found by the police. Do you believe his testimony that the money was left with him in a shoe box, and that it rested on the top shelf of the closet for several months? His wife, as I recall it, said that she never saw the box, and I do not recall that any witness excepting the defendant testified that they ever saw the shoe box there."

And then there was this: "There is evidence from which you may conclude, if you see fit, that the defendant built the ladder, although he denies it. Does not the evidence satisfy you that at least a part of the wood from which the ladder was built came out of the flooring of the attic of the defendant?"

Pertaining to Hauptmann's denial of having been on the Lindbergh estate, Trenchard said: "The defendant denies that he was ever on the Lindbergh premises, denies that he was present at the time that the child was seized and carried away. He testifies that he was in New York at the time. He denies that he received the ransom money in the cemetery and says that he was at his home at that time on the evening of April 2, 1932."

And then he interjected: "This mode of meeting a charge of crime is commonly called setting up an alibi." He went on to explain that this was not looked upon with any disfavor in the law, for,: "whatever evidence tends to prove that the defendant was elsewhere at the time the crime was committed, at the same time tends to contradict the fact that the crime was committed by the defendant, where as here, the presence of the defendant is essential to guilt, and if a reasonable doubt of guilt is raised, even by inconclusive evidence of an alibi, the defendant is entitled to the benefit of that doubt."

However, in his next statement, he said: "As bearing upon the question of whether or not the defendant was present at the Lindbergh home on March 1st, 1932, you, of course, should consider the testimony of Mr. Hochmuth, along with that of other witnesses. Mr. Hochmuth lives at or about the entrance of the lane that goes up to the Lindbergh house." And then he went on to amplify Hochmuth's statement by telling the jury:

"He testified that on the forenoon of that day, March 1st, 1932, he saw the defendant at that point, driving rapidly from the direction of Hopewell; that he got in the ditch or dangerously near the ditch, and that he had a ladder in the car, which car was a dirty green.

"Do you think that there is any reason, upon the whole, to doubt the truth of the old man's testimony?"

On and on Justice Trenchard, with his biased presentation of the facts, "guided" the jurors as to the verdict he wanted them to render. "One by one by ghastly one, each point condemned Hauptmann to die.", wrote Scaduto in *Scapegoat*. "He just strapped Bruno to the chair," Damon Runyon said at the conclusion of the charge to the jury. Even Lindbergh, later that evening during dinner, told a guest that Trenchard's summation was biased. The judge's repeated phrase, whenever he discussed Hauptmann's defense, "Do you believe that?", did not appear as horrible in print in the evening paper, Lindbergh said, as it did in the courtroom. For what the judge actually said, what Lindbergh and everyone in court had heard, were icy intonations calling Hauptmann a liar---"Do you believe THAT?"

"Do you believe that?" "Is there any reason to doubt that prosecution witness?" "Is there any reason to believe the defendant?" These are all questions Justice Trenchard must have rehearsed before he entered the courtroom that day.

To put it mildly, shouldn't we be incensed about Hauptmann's "bum rap"? Indeed we should! Must we remain passive about the treatment we know he received? Never! That is why this book had to be published.

It is possible that you entertain thoughts that I have been unfair in presenting my evaluation of Judge Trenchard's charge and the conduct of the entire trial. In this event, in order that you understand I am not alone with my feelings which you might call prejudiced toward Richard Hauptmann, I quote a few of the comments of others of that day.

The following is a quote taken from *Editor and Publisher*, the recognized "mouthpiece" of the newspaper field:

"No trial in this country has so degenerated and degraded the administration of justice....If the life of one man and the unhappiness of hundreds are to be commercialized for the benefit of entertainment, of radio broadcasters, newspaper publishers, newsreel producers; if a public trial means protection from star-chambered tyranny, but not from the indignities of the mob, then the ancient institution of trial by a jury of peers is without meaning."

And a report from the American Bar Association's Committee on Criminal Procedure in Boston, 1936, we quote this paragraph:

"Both Mooney and Hauptmann based their appeals on the ground that they were tried and condemned by the press and that their court trials and convictions were therefore unfair and not according to law. No responsible American lawyer or newspaperman would feel that such appeals are completely answered by a retort that both defendants were guilty and got what they deserved. The better answer must always be that the defendants in any criminal case have received a trial which was essentially fair, dignified, and according to law."

In the popular magazine *Forum*, a distinguished New York attorney, Richard A. Knight, commented:

"Hauptmann was tried and found guilty, allegedly on circumstantial evidence, not of kidnapping nor of extortion, but of murder....And in the record compiled at that trial there is no more evidence that the man is guilty of murder than there is that you are or I am....No reasonable man can believe that an adult and a baby can fall off a ladder into soft mud without making an impression in the mud. No reasonable man can believe that the baby, in falling...can have its skull crushed in three places by the wall of a house or the rungs of the ladder....In the alternative no reasonable man can believe that a baby can be done to death in its cradle with a chisel without either the bedclothes or the chisel retaining any evidence of the deed....A child's murder can set no legal precedent, but a judicial lynching can."

A few comments taken from some of the newspapers during the course of the trial are well worth noting:

"Men and women sat on windowsills and jammed the small space between the bench and the walls." --- "The fourth broken courtroom window was registered today." --- Among questions discussed was the practice by attorneys from both sides of issuing subpoenas ostensibly to "witness," but in reality to friends seeking a seat in the courtroom." --- "Half-hysterical crowds...paw and claw and shove and jostle their way...circus spirit...thronging as they would at a bullfight....It's a side show---a jamboree....Thousands laughingly gathered to see a man fight desperately for his life."

It was a three-ring circus, a debacle, resembling a Roman carnival minus the gladiators and lions. All set for the kill of one innocent man.

Samuel Liebowitz, one of the most noted criminal lawyers of that day was a great stickler for the law being carried out to its full extent and in the proper manner. Commenting on the case he said: "Kidnapping was a continuous crime and so long as the baby was in the possession of the kidnapper he was guilty all the time. However, the charge was not kidnapping, which in 1932 in New Jersey didn't carry the death penalty, but murder in the course of burglary, which did. Yet burglary was not a continuous crime and to make the death penalty stick, the death of the child had to take place while the burglary was being committed. Where was the evidence that the child was killed during the perpetration of the burglary? What is there...which does not show it is just as likely that the baby was killed a hundred yards from the Lindbergh home, a mile or three miles away, hours after the burglary, or minutes or days?"

Regarding the conduct of the trial itself, Liebowitz had this to say after sitting in the courtroom and hearing the proceedings: "I was appalled. No matter how much a prosecutor feels he must obtain a conviction, he must be fair in his analysis of the evidence. No prosecutor has the right to say to a jury, 'I know that this defendant is guilty.' No prosecutor has the right to use inflammatory, incendiary arguments calculated to arouse the passions of the jury instead of cold arguments based on reason and logic."

And in violation of this, Wilentz stands guilty of all!

Again, I say, the innocent Hauptmann didn't stand a chance against such odds!

C H A P T E R   F I F T Y   F I V E

The Sentence!

As Judge Trenchard completed his instructions to the jury, he directed Clerk of Court Fell to swear in six constables, three men and three women, "to safely keep the jury until they have agreed upon their verdict.", and at 11:14 a.m. the constables were duly sworn. Sheriff Curtiss stated that the jury room was ready, that it had been searched for any hidden microphones. And then, at 11:23 a.m. the presiding justice announced, "The jury may retire." Led by Chief Constable Oden Baggstrom, the jury moved from the courtroom passing in front of Hauptmann. However, not one of them was seen to glance his way. Soon, a guard carrying the 366 exhibits followed them to the jury room, where the physical evidence would be placed in orderly fashion to be used as an aid to the jurists for their personal inspection during their deliberations.

At side Bar Justice Trenchard next heard the lawyers enter their exceptions to his charge. These were granted, to be used at a later date should an appeal become necessary. The courtroom was then ordered to be emptied until such time as the jury returned with its verdict. At 12:09 p.m. Bruno Richard Hauptmann was remanded to the custody of the sheriff and taken to his cell shackled between Deputy Sheriff Hovey Low and Trooper Stockburger.

Hauptmann's cell was located directly under the jury room and as he entered, the door was immediately closed and locked. The weary prisoner sat down on the cot where he had spent many hours pondering over the events of the past 32 days. He wondered if the jurors believed him. As he neared his cell he had asked Hovey Low, one of his regular guards, what he thought the jury's verdict would be. Low, who had grown fond of his prisoner, said: "Richard, that's in the lap of the gods.", to which Hauptmann had responded: "I am innocent!" With a slight smile, Low uttered all he could muster by whispering: "Don't worry."

With the cessation of testimony and the jury

retired, time seemed to have suddenly stopped. Throughout the afternoon Hauptmann spent the time pacing nervously about his small cell, sitting on his cot, lying down without sleeping, his eyes ever open. The hours seemed to drag on endlessly. The silence was torturous as Hauptmann and his guards followed Sheriff Curtiss' order forbidding them to converse.

Upstairs the jurors continued to deliberate. At 3:00 p.m. they inquired of Constable Baggstrom if he could obtain a magnifying glass for their use in studying some of the exhibits. The jurors from the time of their entrance into the jury room had decided that Hauptmann was guilty; however, several had argued for a recommendation of mercy instead of the death penalty which delayed their united decision for death.

Outside the court house a crowd estimated at ten thousand men, women and children had gathered, creating a carnival atmosphere minus the music. As time moved on, their hooting and howling grew louder, turning into chants, as the impatience of the mob became greater due to the cold chill of the February night air which seemed to penetrate their very bones.

At 9.24 p.m. a crash and the sound of breaking glass was heard as the lights in the courtroom went out. A rock, thrown by an angry man, had been hurled through the fan-shaped glass window over the portico of the impressive court house. Instantaneously the lights went out inside the courtroom. The wildly thrown rock had not been the offender. A guard, after a six minute search in the darkness, found a blown fuse to have been the cause. The lights in the jury room and Hauptmann's cell had not been affected and they remained unaware of the disturbance.

However, the chanting was clearly heard and understood by Hauptmann in his cell as well as by those in the jury room upstairs. Hundreds of persons, chanting in unison, "Kill Hauptmann! Kill Hauptmann! Kill Hauptmann!" exercising their lungs; voicing their hatred and crying for the blood of the innocent Bronx carpenter. All this within earshot of the twelve people who were deciding his very fate. Innocent? Guilty? Life? Death? "Kill Hauptmann! Kill Hauptmann! Kill Hauptmann!" Innocent? Never! Innocent didn't stand a chance of winning since it was inevitable that Guilty and Death must win.

The jury members had finished their second meal of the day, and continued on with their deliberations into the night hours. In addition to supplying the meals, the employees at the Union Hotel had been kept busy "hustling" coffee and sandwiches to the twelve who had been informed by Constable Baggstrom that they would not be permitted to leave the jury room until they had reached a verdict. This order provided a new concern, one which clearly spelled out the possibility that they might have to remain in the room all night, or at least throughout the evening and into the early hours of Thursday if they could not agree on a verdict.

All the while groups of reporters sat languishing in chairs and on tables around the courtroom with nothing more to do than await the jury's return. Joking together, many swapping stories of other trials they had covered, while others resorted to games of checkers as they wiled away the idle time they shared together.

The trial had ended; and now the climax of the "circus" was nearly at hand. Millions of words had been written and spoken about the events of the past thirty-two days. Stories had been put together hurriedly by many of the nation's best writers who had personally covered every day of the trial. Well known writers had been assigned to cover the case since it began. And now, in the Flemington Courtroom, famous writers including Damon Runyon, Ford Madox Ford, Edna Ferber, Arthur Brisbane, Alexander Woollcott, Fannie Hurst, John O'Hara, Jim Kilgallen and his daughter, Dorothy, Sheilah Graham, and Adela Rogers St. Johns had written reams of copy to supply the public, hungry for each days news, with the dramatic story of the trial.

St. Johns, with her flare for the dramatic, reported daily for her paper, the *New York Journal* owned by William Randolph Hearst who had hired Reilly to represent Hauptmann, thus guaranteeing his papers, which competed among themselves, exclusive stories of the day's events at the trial. Some portions of her coverage read as follows:

> ADELA ROGERS ST. JOHNS SAYS: Somebody kidnapped that baby, somebody killed him and left Lindy and Anne to those nights and days of hell and crucifixion. Who was it? Today we begin the trial of Bruno Hauptmann for that crime.
>
> ADELA ROGERS ST. JOHNS SAYS: In this small, drab old courthouse packed with humanity, we are again living every horror, every anguish, every suspense, every dastardly step of the murder of our Little Eagle.

ADELA ROGERS ST. JOHNS SAYS: Not one person in that courtroom would have been surprised if suddenly Lindy had risen from his seat and grasped Hauptmann by the throat...we were waiting for it.

ADELA ROGERS ST. JOHNS SAYS:

KEEP YOUR HANDS OFF OUR CHILDREN

And while they waited expectantly for the imminent return of the jury, Miss St. Johns pounded out on her typewriter her own evaluation of the trial by using her individual sensational style. She wrote: "Trenchard: 'true as steel, wise as Solomon, undismayed by uproar and undisturbed by excitement'; Wilentz: 'beating himself to pieces with his own desperate conviction of Hauptmann's guilt'; Reilly: 'big and bland, able and quiet, persuasive as only an Irishman can be.' These weeks have been horrible, haunting, desperate, even when for a few brief hours they touched laughter, laughter which was a little hysterical with sheer relief...a trial none of us will ever forget.'

The prejudices of the writers could not be ignored. Public sentiment had been swayed by the hatred the journalists exhibited toward the unfortunate Hauptmann. But, as one sided as the sentiments of most of the press seemed to be, there were some who voiced their opinions of Hauptmann's possible innocence. One of these was Ford Madox Ford who said: "I have no hesitation about the matter. I should vote for acquittal and I would stand for acquittal till the skies fell...I cannot think the fox was given enough grace. The prosecution was too keen. It is in my blood to think that prosecutions should have some of the impartiality of Justice herself...There must remain, over the vast expanses that the record of this affair will reach, some reasonable doubt."

Dorothy Kilgallen was another reporter who had not been won over because of the enormous amount of evidence that had been produced against the poor Hauptmann. She had watched him and observed his reactions, as best she could, during the course of the trial. On the day the ladder was produced in court by the State, she happened to be seated directly behind him. Dorothy leaned over, tapped him on the shoulder, and asked: "Well, Richard, what do you think of that?" His short reply had been: "The man who made that ladder vas a bum carpenter!" Dorothy Kilgallen definitely could be numbered among the accused man's few sympathizers.

It is possible that you might feel that I have

been much too harsh, and possibly unfair, in my evaluation of Judge Trenchard's prejudicial charge to the jury as he swayed his remarks heavily toward his very apparent personal belief of Hauptmann's guilt. I am firmly convinced that some judges often form their own opinion, at times even prior to a trial, as to the guilt or innocence of the accused person. A good example of this follows.

My claim of this must be accepted as a reasonable one when we read in Lee Isael's book titled *Kilgallen*, a biography of Dorothy Kilgallen, (Delacorte Press, New York 1979) of an interview Dorothy had with Judge Edward Blythin, a former mayor of Cleveland, who had been judge of the Common Pleas since the year 1948. Blythin, had been assigned to conduct the trial of Doctor Sam Sheppard, an osteopathic physician, who in 1954 had been accused of murdering his wife Marilyn in their Bay Village, Ohio home. The judge had requested to see Dorothy in his chambers before the trial began. Israel relates it this way: "Miss Kilgallen," a bailiff said to Dorothy, as she prepared to take her seat in the press section of the tiny Common Pleas Court in Cleveland, "the judge would like to say hello to you."

"When she entered his chambers, Judge Edward Blythin, angular, seventy, and bespectacled, was donning his robe. He extended his hand to Dorothy.

"I'm very glad to see you Miss Kilgallen. I watch you on television very frequently and enjoy the program. What brings you to Cleveland? Why come all the way from New York to cover this trial?"

"It has all the ingredients of what in the newspaper business we call a 'good murder,'" she replied. "It has an attractive victim, who was pregnant. And the accused is an important member of the community---a respectable and attractive man. Then, added to that, you have the fact that it is a mystery as to who did it."

"Mystery?" Blythin said. "It's an open-and-shut case."

"What do you mean, Judge Blythin?" she asked.

"He's guilty as hell," the judge replied. "There's no question about it."

This statement of Judge Blythin to Dorothy Kilgallen was also reported in the classic *Dr. Sam An American Tragedy* by Jack Harrison Pollack (Avon Books, New York 1972). Pollack in his definitive book on the famous Sheppard murder case quoted a portion of Miss Kilgallen's syndicated column written by her at the time of the trial. Pollack wrote: "One newspaper woman was enraged by the verdict. Dorothy Kilgallen, who represented the *New York Journal American* and *King Features Syndicate*, a crime reporter for 30 years before achieving nationwide prominence as a Broadway columnist and television panelist, wrote, 'The prosecutors for the State of Ohio did not prove he [Sam Sheppard] was guilty any more than they proved there are pin-headed men on Mars. Astounding is the word for the verdict! I heard the same evidence the jury heard...I could not have convicted him of anything except possibly negligence in not locking his front door....It is the first time I have ever been scared by the jury system...and I mean scared....' Her syndicated column was dropped from the Cleveland newspaper the next day."

These statements in themselves could be taken as "just a matter of whatever". But, we must realize that, although Dr. Sheppard was found guilty of second degree murder and sentenced to spend the rest of his natural life in jail, the irony of the entire travesty of the case shouts out to us the fact that after he had served ten years, he was released, and re-tried with the brilliant criminal lawyer, F. Lee Bailey, defending him. He was judged not guilty --- a verdict which should have been handed down ten years earlier.

Doctor Samuel Sheppard had been the unfortunate victim of a prejudicial press, a prejudicial public, and a prejudicial court system. So also was Richard Hauptmann. However, in the Hauptmann trial, the accused man had the additional task of explaining his innocence as he faced the lurid false accusations "belching forth" from the mouths of many liars and perjurers plus trying to untangle himself from the unexpected manufactured evidence that was brought in and "aimed" directly at him.

Returning to the affairs of the Hauptmann trial, the time had reached the mid-evening mark. The jury was still in session. Shortly after ten o'clock, Judge Trenchard informed Sheriff Curtiss that if a decision was not reached within another hour he planned to leave for his home. He told Curtiss the jury should continue deliberating, but if they should reach a verdict after he had gone, they should put it in a sealed envelope to be given to him the next morning, at which time he would read it when court reconvened at ten.

Nevertheless, the atmosphere in the courtroom was taking a decided change. Reilly and Judge Large had returned from the Union Hotel across the street; anxious stirrings among members of the press drew the attention of the spectators who had decided the time had arrived for them to re-enter the room; anticipation of the imminent return of the jury caused many to search for some choice seats still remaining empty; people moving about the previously abandoned courtroom were creating an ambience of growing activity. The sensation that something important was about to happen seemed to permeate the room. Each person present appeared to be experiencing a feeling of "electrifying excitement" as they anxiously awaited the approaching verdict of the jury that had been deliberating for almost eleven hours.

The anticipation of those in the courtroom was short lived. Things began to happen with greater rapidity. Action among the principals was noted as Sheriff Curtiss hurried to see Constable Baggstrom, after which he made a hasty visit to Judge Trenchard's chambers. At his heels was Attorney General Wilentz who also entered and came out within minutes. The attorney general nodded to Colonel Schwarzkopf; the long dark green window shades were pulled down to their full length by state troopers; and at the hour of twenty minutes past ten the bell in the courthouse steeple started its dismal toll announcing that the jury had reached a verdict.

Richard Hauptmann clearly heard the sound of the bell as did all the residents living within miles of the courthouse. He soon became aware of the footsteps of two men approaching his cell. One was a state trooper, the other in civilian clothes, each holding a pair of handcuffs. Richard inquired: "Why handcuffs? They never put on handcuffs before?". As his right wrist was manacled to Trooper Stockburger's left, and his left wrist to Deputy Sheriff Low's right, Stockburger answered curtly: "Doesn't mean anything special, just regulations."

With Sheriff Curtiss leading the way, followed by five State Troopers, Hauptmann was led into the courtroom restrained by the handcuffs which held him coupled between his two guardians. His customary neat appearance was marred somewhat by a weary look that permeated his usual pleasant expression; the man was literally tired, not able to sleep during the long ordeal of waiting for his expected verdict. The occasional smile he gave to Anna was not seen as she attempted to converse with him. Although they both knew of his innocence, they were not able to conceive that a court could find him guilty of something he did not do.

They were certain, from the time of his arrest and continuing all during the trial, that they would return home together and their long time of tribulation would be over.

But there was something neither had counted on. There were those people who had lied about him. There were those who had perjured themselves. There was all the manufactured evidence they had fabricated and used against him. He remembered all those people who had said such untrue things about him. He could not help but think, "What if the jury believed them instead of me? What will I do then?" He had been called such terrible names.

Richard had never wanted Anna to know he was worried. Never had he, in the slightest way, let on to her that he was. After all, he conceded, I am innocent and in a court of law, at the bar of justice, I will prove it. And yet now, as he was being led back into the courtroom, he could not help extinguish the feeling of shame that suddenly crept over him.

Quite frankly, Bruno Richard Hauptmann was frightened and worried. The stark reality of the moment suddenly overcame him. The hour of decision was now approaching. And so, feeling nothing which could be interpreted as a carefree mood, we can readily understand why, as Anna was taking her seat near him and was sending him her usual loving smile, he could not command enough facial muscles to return it.

The time of the clock on the courtroom wall read 10:37 p.m. as the jurists came filing back to reclaim their seats in the jury box. Eleven hours and fourteen minutes had passed since they had adjourned to begin their deliberations. A fleeting glance at each face revealed only that all were weary. Not a sign was given by any of them that could be construed as a hint or a clue as to their verdict.

Hauptmann attempted to find some hope hidden in the faces of the jurors as he searched for even a vague smile from one of them. Finding none, he turned away, face down. The arm of Lloyd Fisher rested lightly around his shoulder. With an attempt to appear cheerful, the attorney spoke quietly to his client, "This is only the beginning Richard. Don't show a sign." Turning to face Anna, he placed his arm around her shoulder. Lloyd Fisher was emotionally involved --- he firmly believed in Richard's innocence.

Sheriff Curtiss, following a brief conference with the attorneys, was seen entering the door to the judge's chambers. The tense moments as they were experienced by those in the courtroom that evening are dramatically related by George Waller in his great book *KIDNAP* [Dial Press, New York, 1961]. Because his account is so graphic, and cannot be improved, I have taken the liberty of relating it exactly as he told it to his readers:

"Charles Lindbergh's usual seat was empty. A trooper told a newspaper friend he understood the Colonel had returned to the Morrow place in Englewood to be with Anne when the verdict was announced; they'd hear it soon enough. Henry Breckinridge sat beside the empty chair.

The mob's roar had dwindled, died to nothing; aside from an occasional tinkly pop as boys shattered old flash bulbs, the street was as quiet as the courtroom.

Richard and Anna Hauptmann watched the judge's door. He did not appear.

Sheriff Curtiss came out and Wilentz, Reilly and Fisher got up and walked over to talk with him. He nodded and turned back through the door.

Why so long? Hadn't everyone waited long enough?

'He hasn't gone home, has he?' the newspaperman whispered to his friend the trooper.

'He's here, all right.'

'It's ten forty-three. Almost ten minutes since the jury came back.'

'Here he is.'

Judge Trenchard walked to the bench, rapped twice with his gavel and sat down. The jury was polled; answering 'Here,' their voices' tone told nothing else. The judge nodded to the court clerk.

'The jury will rise!'

Then the judge spoke.

'Let the defendant stand.'

Hauptmann got up so quickly the men locked to him were caught off guard. The bands yanked at their wrists. Their prisoner looked earnestly at the judge.

The court clerk said:

'Members of the jury, have you agreed upon your verdict?'

'We have.'

'Who will speak for you?'

'The foreman.'

'Mr. Foreman, what say you: Do you find the defendant guilty or not guilty?'

The defendant's eyes did not move from the judge.

Foreman Charles Walton said:

'Guilty.'

It was a whisper. The court clerk hastened to prompt him: he must announce the verdict formally. Charles Walton's hand fumbled at a pocket; the fingers shook. He drew out a folded paper and looked at it as if surprised to find it there. He had difficulty unfolding the paper.

'Read in a louder voice,' the clerk said confidentially.

The foreman's voice sounded oddly cracked, now deep, now high, as if he were a boy, very nervous, whose voice was changing.

'We, the jury, find the defendant, Bruno Richard Hauptmann, guilty of murder in the first degree.'

No recommendation for life imprisonment. **If you should return a verdict of murder in the first degree and nothing else,** the judge had charged, **the punishment which would be inflicted on that verdict would be death.**

Anna's eyes blinked. Hauptmann stared at the judge.

'Members of the jury,' the clerk said briskly, 'you have heard the verdict, that you find the defendant, Bruno Richard Hauptmann, guilty of murder in the first degree, and so say you all?'

'We do.'

The AP man with the brief case flashed a second signal and the AP man in the garret realized that someone had blundered; how many verdicts could any one jury declare? He informed his organization's members over the wires that the first bulletin was in error. The correct news was HAUPTMANN GUILTY GETS DEATH.

Ed Reilly asked, 'May we have a poll?' Judge Trenchard nodded; the clerk repeated his question and each juror in turn repeated the words Walton had read. Lloyd Fisher said to no one, 'This is a cry for blood.'

Hauptmann's guards sat down. The steel links tugged at his wrists and he sat down too. Anna's face was carefully stiff; they didn't look at each other. David Wilentz, the victor, did not seem to know what to do with his victory. The judge reminded him of the necessary next step.

'Do you wish to make a motion for sentence, Mr. Attorney General?'

Wilentz gave a little start. 'The State moves for immediate sentence,' he said.

An eager messenger had got out of the courtroom and raced to a second-floor window. He threw it open and shouted, 'Guilty---death!' The mob screamed. Hearing it, Fisher murmured again, 'A cry for blood.'

Judge Trenchard said, 'The defendant may stand.'

Hauptmann stood up. The guards were alert this time and rose with him.

'Bruno Richard Hauptmann, you have been convicted of murder in the first degree. The sentence of the Court is that you suffer death at the time and place and in the manner provided by law.'

The mob was still screaming. Judge Trenchard set the execution for the week beginning Monday, March 18, 1935. Then he said:

'You are now remanded to the custody of the sheriff.'

Hauptmann's guards started him toward the door. Fisher hurried over and whispered, 'Remember, it's only the beginning!' The prisoner half nodded. His wife watched him go. The instant he was through the door her heavy face creased and sagged, and she wept.

Time: ten minutes to eleven.

They marched the prisoner to his cell and unlocked the handcuffs. Breaking the steel bands seemed to break a steel rod in his body; he doubled over and fell. His face hit the floor. They lifted him to the cot. He put his hands over his bruised face, and the guards heard Richard Hauptmann sobbing. They had not thought that he would ever cry. It embarrassed them."

It did not take long for the courtroom to empty. The show was over, the "circus" had ended, the "carnival tents" were being lowered. And Anna, as she watched Richard pass from her sight, could not rise from her seat. She remained seated staring at the floor. This brave woman, who had won the admiration of so many for the faithfulness and belief she had shown in her husband, had now reached the breaking-point. Anna Hauptmann could not hold back the tears any longer. Her small shoulders were shaking as she wept silently, dabbing her eyes with a small blue handkerchief she had removed from her pocketbook. This brave Anna Hauptmann was at last inwardly experiencing the pathos that had been building within her during the past twenty-two months.

John Walters, Flemington's Chief of Police, noticing her despair, stepped to her side and encouraged her to allow him to take her to the home of Mr. and Mrs. William Opdyke where she had conveniently rented a room just a block away from the courthouse. It was near dawn before Anna was able to find only fitful sleep.

As for Hauptmann, the guards outside his cell said the prisoner wept at various times throughout the night. They also reported hearing him whisper: "Little men, little pieces of wood, little scraps of paper" claiming that Hauptmann seemed to be completely broken in spirit. Is there any possible reason why we should wonder why?

Although the big trial had been a sensational one for those who had followed it by radio and newspapers around the world, it had been an agonizing one for almost everyone who attended. Many people were inconvenienced with the necessity to share housing accommodations with others because of the lack of space; inclement weather conditions became a factor for travel, being far from pleasant for those making the trip back and forth each day between New York, Philadelphia, and other distant points. Some of the most miserable days were Tuesday and Wednesday, January 8th and 9th that proved to be exceedingly dangerous for travel due to a heavy fog that was mixed with a steady drizzle that preceded a heavy rainfall. However, the most trying of all the days during the trial was the extreme cold weather the participants and visitors were forced to endure happened to be Wednesday, January 23rd, which started with an extreme wind and gusts of snow that continued for most of the day. While the crowd stomped their feet to keep warm and waited to gain entrance to the courthouse after the noon recess, a heavy snow had already covered the countryside and sleigh bells could be clearly heard in the distance. Nevertheless, everyone stayed with the crowd, not willing to retreat to any warmth other than what the court house offered, lest they should miss an opportunity to see one or more of the major participants of the trial that day. All of these inconveniences had now ended; life for most of the people who had attended the trial each day would now return to normal.

The big show was over. The "carnival tents" were being lowered. Only a few remained to clean up the debris. The "play" had ended, the final bows of each of the "good guys" had been given, and now the lights would soon be extinguished inside the courthouse and the scene of all the action would soon dissipate into total darkness.

It's lamentable to say, but nevertheless true --- darkness for this trial was nothing new. There was a constant darkness which had hovered low over the trial proceedings even during the brightness of each daylight hour. It was a terribly "sad" trial --- especially for Richard and Anna Hauptmann.

Harold Nicholson, the famed English writer, had arrived at the Morrow home, "Next Day Hill", in Englewood the day before the jury's verdict. He had been extremely busy writing a biography of the life of Anne's father, the late Senator Dwight Morrow, a book that was nearing completion. Nicholson vividly describes the atmosphere in the home the next evening as the Lindberghs and their guests waited for news of the verdict:

"They knew that the first news would come over the wireless, so that there were two wirelesses turned on - one in the pantry next to the dining room and one in the drawing room. Thus there were jazz and jokes while we had dinner, and one ear was straining the whole time for the announcer from the courthouse. Lindbergh had a terrible cold which made it worse. Then after dinner we went into the library, and the wireless was on in the drawing room next door. They were all rather jumpy. Mrs. Morrow, with her unfailing tact, brought out a lot of photographs and we had a family council as to what illustrations to choose for the book. This was just interesting enough to divert, but not rivet, attention. Suddenly Betty (Gow) put her head round the huge Coromandel screen. She looked very white. 'Hauptmann,' she said, 'has been condemned to death without mercy.' We went into the drawing room. The wireless had been turned on to the scene outside the courthouse. One could hear the almost diabolic yelling of the crowd. They were all sitting round - Miss Morgan with embroidery, Anne looking very white and still. 'You have now heard,' broke in the voice of the announcer, 'the verdict in the most famous trial in all history. Bruno Hauptmann now stands guilty of foulest ...' 'Turn that off, Charles, turn that off.' Then we went into the pantry and had ginger beer. Charles sat there on the kitchen dresser looking very pink about the nose. 'I don't know,' he said to me, 'whether you have followed this case very carefully. There is no doubt at all that Hauptmann did the thing. My one dread all these years has been that they would get hold of someone as a victim about whom I wasn't sure. I am about this --- **quite** sure. It is this way ..."

What made you **quite** sure Charles A. Lindbergh? Was it the coercion of the police? Your belief in the manufactured evidence? Your willingness to readily accept the testimony of known liars? Your own agreement to bend the truth and lie? Or was it a combination of all these things? What made you **quite** sure that Hauptmann, the man whom you described as having "little eyes, like the eyes of a wild boar, that were mean, shifty, small and cruel" was guilty? What made you **quite** sure "Lindy"?

There should be no misunderstanding as to why Richard cried and spent a sleepless, restless night?

Nor can we find any reason to doubt the opinion of the famous author and writer, H.L. Mencken, known as "the Sage of Baltimore", who said, "It was the greatest story since the Resurrection, with something in it for young and old alike."

END OF BOOK TWO

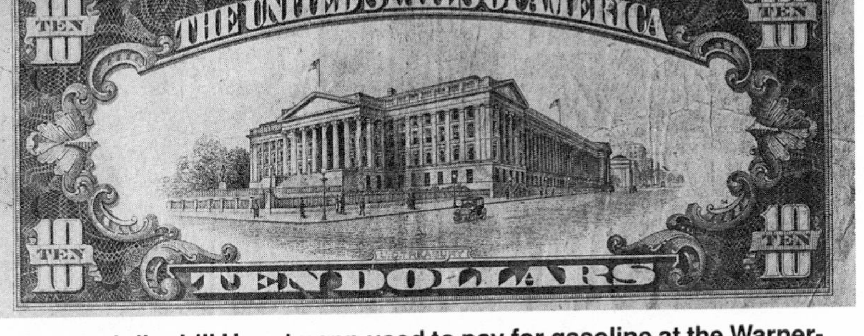

The ten dollar bill Hauptmann used to pay for gasoline at the Warner-Quinlan Station. (Author's collection, New Jersey State Police)

The Hauptmann home at 1279 E. 222nd Street, Bronx, New York, on the day of his arrest. (UPI/Corbis-Bettmann)

The demolition of the Hauptmann garage on September 20, 1934. (UPI/Corbis-Bettmann)

Anna Hauptmann (right) with her friend Johanna Tolksdorf, in 1929.

Richard and Anna Hauptmann, shortly after their marriage. (Author's collection)

Isidor Fisch, who brought shoebox filled with ransom money. (AP/Wide World Photos)

Hauptmann with the Fredericksens' dog, "Whoppie," on one of the frequent nights he waited for Anna to finish her work in the bakery. Picture taken sometime during the winter of 1932. (Author's collection)

The following pictures were all taken on the spot coverage of events in and around Flemington, New Jersey, during the Hauptmann trial in 1935. The picture captions appear as they were originally typed in haste, hence some of the misspelled words. The original prints are property of Mrs. Thelma Miller, Three Bridges, New Jersey, whose father, David Kline, was one of the officials who guarded Hauptmann during the trial.

View in front of the courthouse showing the usual crowd, kept back in this instance, and the cameras on top of the cars by the reporters. This also shows the great number of extra wires which were run into the courthouse for the use of the reporters.

Looking south on Main Street in Flemington, showing the crowded condition with the courthouse and Hall of Records on the right.

1. David T. Wilentz-Att'y General - State of N.J.
2. Edward J. Reilly - Chief of Defense Counsel

Hovey Low, Deputy Sheriff; Corp. Alan Smith,Hauptman guard and and Mrs. Hauptman talking to Bruno Hauptman

Defense counselors Egbert Rosecrans, Edward J. Reilly (back to camera) C. Lloyd Fisher, Bruno Richard Hauptman and Deputy Sheriff Hovey Low, January 21st as the fourth week of the trial got under way.

With automotive travel impossible following a near blizzard, the town-folk in Flemington got out their old sleighs. Here is one passing in front of the Hunterdon County Courthouse, January 24th.

The Flemington Union Hotel with members of the jury exercising on the upper porch.

Crowded lobby in the Union Hotel, Flemington, directly across from the Hunterdon County Courthouse. Walt Boyd, manager is in the foreground.

Walter Winchell, popular Broadway columnist, and Fannie Hurst, well known novelist as they attended the trial. January 30th.

Deputy David Kline, Charles Lindbergh and Col. Schwartzhoff going down the back steps to the jail going into the court room

:rs. Bruno Richard Hauptman, wife of the alleged Lindbergh kidnaper who
/ill take the witness stand in his behalf, January 29th.

Ladder Used in the Kidnapping

Edward J. Reilly, defense attorney questioning Bruno Richard Hauptman.

Corp. C.A. O'Donnell, Hauptmann guard; Bruno Hauptmann, Hovey Low, Deputy Sheriff:
Allen Smith, Hauptmann guard.

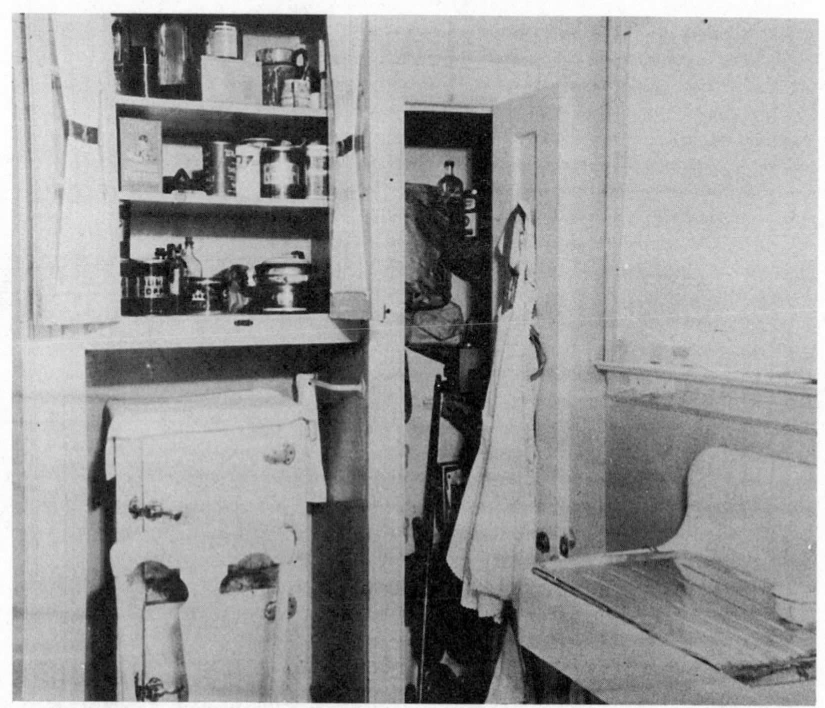

Above is a copy showing the broom closet in the home of Hauptman in which he claims he placed a box containing Lindergh ransom notes given to him by the late Isidor Fisch. It was introduced by the State in its cross examination of the defendant.

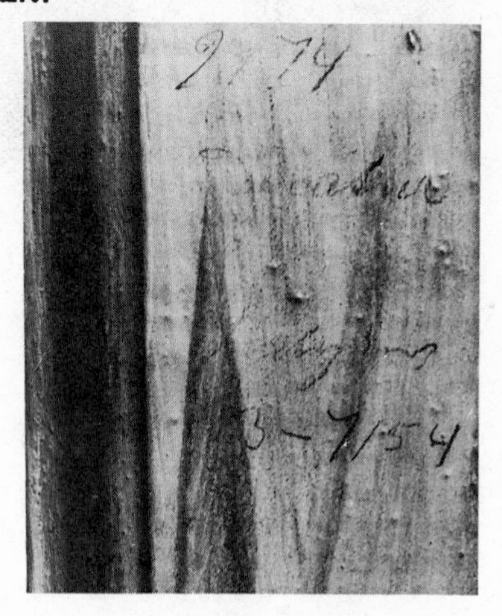

"The Bruckman-Cassidy closet"

Judge Trenchard

1. Elmer Smith; 2. Ethel Stockton; 3. Charles F. Snyder; 4. Verna Snyder; 5. Rosie Pill; 6. Chas. Walton, Sr.—Foreman; 7. Robert Cravatt; 8. Philip Hockenbury; 9. George Voorhees; 10. May P. Brelsford; 11. Liscom C. Case; 12. Howard V. Biggs; Constables: John H. Reed; Harry Fields; Oden Baggstrom.

Bruno Richard Hauptman's car

When jury has agreed upon its verdict this bell in the courthouse will be rung in accordance with the custom of years, by William Saunders

1. Arthur Koehler, wood expert—U.S. Forest Service; 2. Lewis J. Bornman; 3. Beauke Carter—News Commentator; 4. Walter Winchell—News Commentator; 5. C. Lloyd Fell—County Clerk; 6. Annie Hauptmann—wife of defendant.

A copy of a photograph, introduced by the prosecution which shows the attic of Hauptman's home in the Bronx. It is the State's contention that the board missing from the part of the floor covered was used in the ladder which enabled the kidnaper to enter the baby's room.

THE TRIAL OF THE CENTURY

A copy of the Hauptmann Trial stationery bearing the signatures of the chief participants, members of the press, and famous guests who attended the sessions

B O O K T H R E E

THE AFTERMATH

C H A P T E R F I F T Y S I X

Rumblings!

"I want to tell the people of America that I am absolute innocent of the crime of the murder. My conviction was a great surprise. I never saw the Lindenberg (sic) baby and I never received any money. I want to appeal to all people everywhere to aid me at this time. A defense must be raised to carry my appeal to a higher court. Before God, I am absolute innocent. I have told all I know about the crime."

Standing in his cell while newsreel cameras cranked away, Bruno Richard Hauptmann, having regained control of his emotions from the shock of the verdict the night before, recorded on film for posterity that statement which was never more true than it is today.

Hauptmann had been granted permission to wear a shirt and tie while the film was made, but as soon as it was completed he was ordered to don his prison attire. After making the change he was questioned by two reporters. They asked if he had been offered a large sum of money in payment for his confession. His immediate answer was, "If I had anything to confess, I would have done so months ago, so as to spare my wife and mother all they have gone through. If they came to the door and opened it and said, you can go free if you tell the whole truth, I couldn't tell them anything because I have already told the whole truth." When they inquired of his reaction to Koehler's testimony that Rail 16 of the ladder had been taken from his attic flooring, he smiled slightly and said, "That was the most ridiculous thing. I got so many boards in my garage, why should I want to go to the attic?"

"I was sentenced to death for murdering a little child I never saw in my life.", Hauptmann concluded.

Before another twenty-four hours had passed, newspapers and radio stations were repeating comments made about the trial by persons from all walks of life, some quite famous. Mrs. Franklin Delano Roosevelt, wife of the President, said, "The entire trial has left me with a question in my mind."; Clarence Darrow, America's famous criminal lawyer, stated, "No man should be executed on such flimsy evidence." Nor was *The New York Times* any more positive of Hauptmann's guilt, stating: "The long trial at Flemington, the charge of the judge and the verdict of the jury established a crime but did not clear away a mystery. We do not yet know exactly what happened on that tragic night at Hopewell. This is a leftover disappointment of the case. One motive which millions of people had in reading every scrap of the testimony was the hope that either the evidence of the police or the admissions of Hauptmann would show precisely who the kidnapper was and what were his preparations and methods of operation. As it is, they remain an unsolved mystery....This is as far as the trial took us. Nothing but a confession or the turning up of new evidence can now be expected to throw further light upon a mystery which has all along been one of the most puzzling in criminal annals."

On Friday morning Hauptmann signed a petition declaring himself a pauper. This had been necessary in order to clear the way for his attorneys to apply to the State of New Jersey for money they would need to pay for their client's appeal before the Court of Errors and Appeals.

For a brief time on Saturday, February 16th, Hauptmann found himself able to draw into his lungs some fresh clean air, to view life outside the confines of the prison, to look up to the sky. Things he had been deprived of since the day of his incarceration in the Hunterdon County jail four months earlier. Shortly before dawn he was escorted from his cell to begin the preliminary arrangements necessary for his transferral to his place of permanent confinement, the death house in New Jersey's State Prison at Trenton.

Taking advantage of every opportunity, the authorities continued to play their parts well as they made "a big show" of Hauptmann's move to the death house by obtaining more "sensational" publicity relating their further involvement in the "crime of the century". To begin with, they made a mockery of the mild mannered Hauptmann, their dangerous unarmed criminal, by inferring that he might have entertained thoughts of trying to escape. No less than fourteen armed State Troopers, riding in three sedans, had been chosen as the official convoy to transport this unfortunate convicted man to the place where his life would deliberately be taken from him for a crime of which he knew nothing. The gendarmes, however, formed only the official convoy;

more cars filled with reporters and photographers followed as they pulled away, passing slowly by the courthouse.

And so, as the clock neared the hour of 9:40 a.m., with the car's sirens screaming and their lights flashing, the "parade" turned south, heading in the direction of Trenton. By doing this, the convoy had ceremoniously announced the start of its forty minute journey to the State Capitol.

Bruno Richard Hauptmann, sitting rigidly, handcuffed between two officers, was now experiencing his last opportunity of seeing, and possibly enjoying, the vast beauty of life outside prison walls. However, with nothing but depressing thoughts of what faced him at the end of the journey, it is difficult to imagine that he appreciated any part of the gorgeous countryside they passed through along the short twenty-three mile drive.

It was about 10:30 as the cars in the entourage eased their way to the curb near the main gate of the prison, the entranceway which, in many ways, looked like that of the Tombs, New York City's famed penitentiary. The stone edifice resembled that of a fortress embellished with its carved figures in myriads of collages made up of kneeling persons, mythological creatures, serpents, eagles, and rams, all effigies which garnished the wall on which had been erected an attractive white cupola resembling the ones traditional to New England.

Stepping from the car, still securely manacled to his two guards, the prisoner received encouraging remarks from the gathering crowd of on-lookers. The voice of one man was clearly heard to shout' "We all know you're innocent, kid.", which certainly proves that, as early as the week of his conviction, people were indeed finding great difficulty with the verdict.

As he mounted the steps to enter the prison's door, he paused momentarily for the photographers to snap his picture. Neatly dressed in a double-breasted suit, necktie and hat, he briefly smiled, a possible indication of his appreciation of the encouragement he was receiving from the crowd surrounding him.

Following a physical examination, being fingerprinted and having his official prison photograph taken, the prison barber cut his hair. After putting on the regulation prison garb consisting of blue shirt, blue trousers and heavy shoes, he now became Prisoner Number 17,400. As he was led to his cell, Hauptmann passed in view of the prison's six hundred inmates who had gathered in the mess hall for their noon meal. Seeing him prompted a great volume of hisses, oaths, jeers and cat-calls to burst forth spontaneously from the mouths of most of these prisoners. Prisoners, whose crimes were of every possible description, but nevertheless all of one accord, hating with a passion a killer of little children. Especially Bruno Richard Hauptmann who had killed the infant son of the world's most famous hero Charles A. Lindbergh.

As Hauptmann and his guards arrived at the death row cell block located at the other side of the prison, he was led to Cell Number 9 located on the lower tier. In the upper tier were six other convicts who also faced death by electrocution. However, Hauptmann was alone on the first floor, his cell only a few steps away from the door of the death chamber where the electric chair stood in mute silence awaiting his turn to sit in it.

The section of the prison where the death house was located had been built in the year 1907, when hanging was replaced by electrocution as the form of enacting the death penalty. It consisted of eighteen cells, nine on each tier, and at times in the past every cell had been filled with condemned prisoners, with an overflow waiting to be moved in from the main section of the prison.

Hauptmann entered his small 10 by 9 foot cell where he was destined to spend the next thirteen months. Its contents consisted of a combined lavatory and wash-basin, a folding bed and a desk and chair. He sat down, no doubt pondering his fate. The cell door slammed shut. As his guards turned to leave Hauptmann raised his head and called after them, "May I please have a Bible?"

Lloyd Fisher, realized the importance that Hauptmann's defense lawyers must obtain a transcript of the trial testimony as soon as possible, something that could cost as much as twelve thousand dollars. This coupled with Richard and Anna declaring themselves penniless, the need for money was great in order that they appeal for a reversal of the trial verdict so that a writ of error be obtained, which in turn would automatically cause a postponement of the execution date allowing for a review of the trial by the Court of Errors and Appeals.

Reilly, however, saw no need for any great hurry, and so a dispute broke out between him and Fisher. It was "Big Ed's" contention that since David Wilentz was vacationing in Florida, "the gentlemanly practice of law" must be observed, and that a short wait until his return would not harm Hauptmann's intentions of appealing. But Fisher grew antagonistic toward Reilly as he attempted to explain that each day their client languished in the death house with nothing accomplished was a valuable day lost to their cause of properly defending Richard. Reilly remained adamant in his stand and would not bend.

With this Fisher exploded, "Mr. Reilly has not conferred with any of us, and I think it is an outrage. When our man is scheduled to die the week of March 18th, we should not be wasting time waiting for Mr. Wilentz to return from Florida. It will be a job to get that record printed in time now, and if we were to follow Reilly's suggestion, he would be dead and buried before we can get it." By getting that out of his system, Fisher went on to castigate Reilly for the manner in which he had conducted the entire case, being critical of some of the witnesses he had called. This charge naturally prompted Reilly to retaliate with his own boastful accusation, "I am sick and tired of all this fooling around, and Fisher's double-crossing."

Taking it upon himself, Fisher visited Hauptmann and explained the predicament he faced. He obtained Richard's signature granting him the authority to act immediately; and on Thursday, February 21st, he received a writ of error requiring that on March 12th a request for a copy of the trial transcript be filed. With this action taken an indefinite postponement of the execution was obtained. Fisher was appointed trustee of the fund.

Realizing the need for additional money in order that the necessary appeal be made, several public meetings were held the following week in the Yorkville Casino, the center of New York's German-American section, located in the Bronx. Here, Anna Hauptmann, standing on a stage at the front of the large hall, made a heart-rending appeal for help before a crowd of twenty-five hundred people, with an estimated three thousand more outside attempting to enter. Her appeal brought a deafening ovation from the large audience who sympathized with her need. Forty ushers wearing a green armband bearing the inscription HAUPTMANN DEFENSE FUND passed baskets throughout the audience. The collection netted slightly over $700 which was added to the $625 already tallied from the twenty-five-cent cost of admission.

Several other successful meetings were held in

quick order. On Sunday, March 3rd, at Passaic, New Jersey, she pleaded in her native language to: "Help me get a new trial for my husband. Whatever you give will help me and our baby." The result was $1200. Throughout the month of March, Anna continued to speak largely to German-American audiences, telling them, with her eyes brimming with tears: "I know my husband, and I know he is not capable of a crime like that." The results of these meetings proved to be very favorable for the defense of Hauptmann. At each rally reporters, assigned to cover the meetings, were given every assurance that none of the meetings bore any political, pro-Nazi, or anti-Semitic overtones, (emphasizing that their plea has absolutely nothing to do with a message published in some pamphlets being sold outside) which could be misconstrued in any way with the Hauptmann Defense Fund.

When it became common knowledge that money was being raised for Richard's appeal, donations began arriving for him at the prison. These were largely checks made out for the sum of one dollar, which of course, required his endorsement. Most of the contributors apparently were willing to send this small stipend in order to obtain Hauptmann's signature.

The public appearances of Anna Hauptmann continued with the fund steadily growing with financial aid contributed from the host of people who were among her husband's sympathizers. However, on Wednesday, April 3rd, she received some shocking news. Edward Jay Reilly submitted his personal bill to her for $25,000 for services already rendered.

Reilly's greed for a portion of the money being raised through Anna's meetings had become quite evident. A week earlier, because of his insistence, she had paid him $5,000 from the fund over the objections of Fisher, Pope and Rosecrans. And now his demand for $25,000 led to an open confrontation between Reilly and the other defense attorneys.

Reluctantly she brought the news to her husband who insisted that Reilly be discharged of any further responsibility of defending him. They agreed that Lloyd Fisher should now be in charge of any future defense actions necessary.

A registered letter was sent informing the flamboyant Reilly of their decision to release him, which goaded him to issue this hasty response, "If I'd tried this case in New York my fee would have been one hundred thousand dollars.", and going on to make the ridiculous charge that both of the Hauptmanns had agreed to pay him the twenty-five thousand dollars. Anna's honest response to this unfair accusation was made publicly to the press by her straightforward answer: "Mr. Reilly should know, if anybody should, that the defense fund has not any such sum as he demanded for his fee. We are struggling very hard to get our defense fund to meet the appeal's expense." This public statement of Anna's ignited the fire between them even more, causing an infuriated Reilly, while addressing a Masonic Luncheon Club in Brooklyn, to make the following threat: "Lawyers must be paid. Whether Anna likes it or not, she is going to pay, and pay through the nose."

Reading these statements, the public believed "open warfare" had sprung up in the Hauptmann camp.

But such was far from the truth. Hauptmann's three other lawyers agreed to work diligently without charging a fee for their efforts to prove their client's innocence. All agreed they were in it "for the love of the cause" each passionately pleading for someone to understand the injustice the State of New Jersey had bestowed on their client; while Reilly merely stated, "The man who did this crime deserves to be drawn and quartered, but that man was not Bruno Richard Hauptmann." Although Reilly still said he believed Richard was innocent, he said he looked toward a date somewhere in the future, when someone, possibly on their deathbed, would admit their guilt in the crime.

Nevertheless, Fisher, Rosecrans, and Pope remained firm in their belief that Hauptmann was not only innocent but that he had not been given a fair trial. On Thursday, May 2nd, they took their case before the Court of Errors and Appeals in their room in the State House annex at Trenton. The hearing was held before Chancellor Luther A. Campbell, the highest judicial officer in the State of New Jersey, Chief Justice Thomas J. Brogan, and, since Justice Trenchard had disbarred himself, the balance of the trial panel consisted of the remaining seven Supreme Court Justices and four lay members. Before these men the defense cited each of the exceptions they had made during the trial, including the circuslike atmosphere of the courtroom, and the fact that the jury had not been properly sequestered, and that the press and radio reports were flagrantly prejudicial. However, the only point granted which could possibly favor the defense, had to do with their claim that the Attorney General's summation had been inflammatory, far beyond the evidence, and had possibly unduly influenced the jury against the defendant.

The hearing of the main appeal, during which Hauptmann's three attorneys asked the high court to reverse the verdict of their client's guilt, was held on Thursday, June 20th, in the same room of the State House annex. Strong security measures barred the public from attending, with only reporters permitted inside. Neither Hauptmann nor his wife were allowed to attend. And no one could enter or leave while the court was in session. The six hour hearing held none of the inconveniences as those of the overcrowded, unventilated Flemington courtroom. Instead, the judges at the front of the spacious room sat in two rows of high-backed leather-cushioned mahogany chairs facing the thick deep purple carpeting that muffled the sound of footsteps in the large room. Looking out its giant windows, one could observe ships passing by on the famous Delaware River. It gave one the appearance of a room in a palace awaiting the entrance of nobility.

But, regardless of how stately the hearing room appeared, the final ruling came with the judge's decision that, although the charge by Wilentz might have been objectional to them, the defense lawyers should have objected at the time by calling it to the attention of the trial judge.

An angry Wilentz lost no time in defending himself for anything he had said in his charge to the jury. He argued he had every right to call Hauptmann the "Public Enemy Number One" and "an animal" because that was exactly what he was.

Pointing out that it was the duty, as well as the negligence, of Reilly, chief defense attorney, to have objected, Egbert Rosecrans in answer to this preposterous charge, went on to say, "We may have been neglectful and we may have been ignorant, but that doesn't make any difference. The trial judge should not have allowed these things to go on. Because counsel did not object is no excuse." Again Reilly had proven himself incompetent.

As court adjourned at four o'clock, it was a rather confident group of lawyers that left the State House with elation, feeling they had presented their objections of irregularities at the Flemington trial favorably enough to win a decision in Hauptmann's favor. They knew it would take the better part of the summer before the fourteen judges would reach an agreement. A tie would sustain the conviction, while a simple majority vote would reverse it. Regardless, the date set for his execution was canceled until the Court decided whether he must serve a life term in prison or be executed as the jury agreed the penalty should be.

During the summer months Fisher, Rosecrans and Pope spent endless hours running down leads they hoped might be beneficial toward helping Richard gain new and vital evidence that would conclusively prove his innocence. Anna's appeals had run into a dead end and no new dates were arranged. A proposed meeting in Chicago was dropped because of the indifferent attitude of people throughout the mid-west who were expressing themselves as being unwilling to do anything that would help Hauptmann. Only one glimmer of light appeared on the horizon, that being the refusal of the Brooklyn Supreme Court to honor Reilly's request that Anna Hauptmann be ordered to pay the $25,000 he claimed she owed him for services rendered.

Sixteen weeks passed before The Court of Errors and Appeals handed down its judgement on Hauptmann's appeals. It was Wednesday, October 9th, when Justice Charles W. Parker read the more than twelve thousand words in his answer to the lengthy seventeen major contentions that had been presented by Rosecrans. After listening to the explanation and consideration the judges had given to each major exception the defense had asked for, Justice Parker concluded, "The decision of the Court of Errors and Appeals is unanimous. The appeal for the verdict's reversal is denied."

As Richard sat alone in his cell pondering over the thoughts that the following day would be the tenth anniversary of his marriage to his beloved Anny, and the happiness they had shared together during the intervening years, he was suddenly alerted that someone was approaching. It was Lloyd Fisher, his friend and now his chief attorney, who honestly sincerely believed in his innocence. Fisher had taken it upon himself to be the informant of the bad news that the court had ruled against them. However, he told Richard, much hope still remained and their team had just begun its fight to have his innocence declared and him set free. Regardless of this, Richard could not help but realize the news of the court's rejection was far from the nice gift he had hoped to give his dear wife on their wedding anniversary.

On Tuesday, October 15th, Hauptmann's defense counsel was granted a second stay of execution. This stay was necessary to allow time for an appeal to be made before the United States Supreme Court. Therefore, on Tuesday, November 12th, the Supreme Court was petitioned by Egbert Rosecrans, who again cited in detail his reasons that they review the denial handed down by the New Jersey Court of Errors and Appeals on October 9th.

Meanwhile, New Jersey's governor, Harold Giles Hoffman, had been receiving all manner of complaints relative to the unfair treatment Hauptmann had received --- and was still receiving at the hands of the Jersey authorities. Hoffman was easily persuaded by the inquiries coming in because he also had more than a few doubts that Hauptmann had been adequately represented in a trial that ended with so many unanswered questions, so many loose ends still "swinging in the wind."

Dissatisfaction expressing the way the Hauptmann case had turned was being brought to the governor's attention from people throughout all parts of America and the world. Hoffman, too, agreed that the convicted murderer had been tried in an atmosphere which was prejudiced. Hate and bias, he claimed, had played a large part among the members of the jury which had unfairly influenced them in their guilty verdict with death as the penalty.

Harold Hoffman, armed and fortified with all the complaints he had in his possession, decided he must do something about it. Hoffman, a friendly chap, with a winning smile that covered his round face, was probably the most popular person in the state. He was a joiner, with membership in the Masonic Lodge, the Rotary Club, the Shriners, the Odd Fellows, the Eagles and the Elks Clubs. He thoroughly enjoyed the practical jokes and horseplay as a member of the Order of Circus Saints and Sinners, a group that raised money by hosting dinners, luncheons and entertainments for needy causes.

He was born in South Amboy, New Jersey, near the banks of the Raritan River. He served in the infantry during World War 1, entering as a private and coming home a captain, a rank earned because of his military bravery. In 1925, at the age of twenty-nine he was elected mayor of South Amboy to become the youngest mayor in the state; 1927 saw him win a great victory, a term in Congress, an accomplishment he repeated during the next election as he was returned to Congress to serve a second term.

Harold Hoffman was regarded, by those who knew him personally, as a family man. He lived with his wife, Lillie, and their three daughters, fourteen year old Ada, nine year old Lillie, and little four year old

Hope. In 1935 Harold Hoffman was a happy man. He was thirty-nine years old. He was a member of the South Amboy Methodist Church; he was a very popular Republican, one who had never been defeated in an election, who was now seriously considered being placed on the ballot for the Vice Presidency, or possibly even their candidate for President. Harold Hoffman had many, many friends; even Democrats liked him and many would have voted for him. He was a very popular man.

However, as popular as Harold Hoffman was, little did he realize in the fall of 1935, that his intervention, only to make certain that Hauptmann received nothing more than the fairness he deserved, was to ultimately bring about his fall from the high esteem where most of his friends had extolled him during his adult lifetime.

But, with Hoffman realizing the chance he was taking by questioning the decision the jury had made, and now choosing to "take sides", as the majority accused him of doing, in an effort to help the unpopular Hauptmann, was in the eyes of the public, a crime on the part of their governor that must not and could not be forgiven. Helping Hauptmann in any way was to damn and doom forever Hoffman's future political career. At this point it is pertinent that you read excerpts from his own account of the story as he told it in his series of articles which appeared in *Liberty* magazine in 1938:

"Early in October, 1935, my desk in the executive office at Trenton was piled high with disorderly evidence of tax troubles, political troubles, and every other kind of 'headache.' Into this scene walked Colonel Mark O. Kimberling, principal keeper of the New Jersey State Prison, and in his calm, soft voice, which belies the power and the firmness of the man who practically organized the New Jersey State Police, he said:

"'Governor, Hauptmann has asked to see you.'

"I lifted weary eyes from the pile of letters waiting signatures. '<u>Me</u> see Hauptmann, Mark?' I said. 'What for?'

"'I don't know exactly, Governor, he replied. 'But he keeps asking for you.'

"The Colonel left, and, giving but little thought to the unusual request, I plunged back into my job.

"Several days passed, with new burdens of work piling up on me. But there were frequent mental flashbacks to that unusual request, 'Hauptmann wants to see you.'

"Extra! Hauptmann guilty!

"Guilty? Sure. Hope? None.

"Of course I had heard rumblings of doubt; but then, I had been too busy to follow the case and the trial very closely. In the press and upon the radio Hauptmann had been convicted before Flemington.

"Then one morning there came a telephone call from Washington. It was from Charles Curtis, former Vice-President of the United States. I had, of course, known Charlie Curtis, for as Vice-President he had been the presiding officer of the United States Senate when I served as a member of the House of Representatives. My acquaintance with him, however, was limited to a few rather casual official and social contacts.

"'Governor,' he said, 'are you looking into this Hauptmann case?' I told him that I hadn't been especially interested. I mentioned, I think, that Hauptmann had been convicted in the Hunterdon County Court of Oyer and Terminer, and that the conviction had been sustained by our Court of Errors and Appeals, but that the matter would shortly be before the court of Pardons of which I was a member.

"'I think,' said Mr. Curtis, 'that there are a lot of funny things about that case.' He went on to tell me some of the doubts he had entertained and he expressed the opinion that, as governor, I should go carefully into the matter before Hauptmann's final appeal for life was made. 'I've read a lot of testimony,' he added, 'and it doesn't seem to me that he was adequately represented--or that he got a very fair deal.'

"I started to think more seriously about seeing Hauptmann. My mail, increasing each day, brought protests against the electrocution of Hauptmann upon evidence that was so largely circumstantial. Even the prosecution had admitted that there were a lot of things in the case that had not been explained. It would be important, I convinced myself, to learn how one man could conceive such an atrocious crime, executed successfully by himself, and baffle the police of the world searching for him for over two years. Yes, it would be a great and a necessary contribution to the science of crime detection and prosecution to learn by what process such a ghastly feat could have been accomplished.

"In my mind, ever recurring, were those words of Colonel Kimberling: 'Governor, Hauptmann has asked to see you.'

"I decided to visit the death house. If Hauptmann

was guilty, the chair was too good for him. If he was innocent, and could prove it, under no circumstances should his life be taken while I was governor of New Jersey. As to the propriety of my going, one of the highest judicial officers in the state assured me that such a visit would not conflict with any existing statute. Not only that; governors before me had visited the death house.

"It was not until the night of October 16 that I found the opportunity. My recollection is that there had been a last-minute cancellation of an evening engagement. I know that it was not until after dinner on that evening that I thought of visiting Hauptmann that night.

"From my suite in the Hotel Hildebrecht I called Colonel Kimberling. 'Mark,' I said, 'I'm coming down to see that fellow. Will tonight be O.K.?' Getting an affirmative answer, I told him I would phone him again and give him the approximate time of my arrival.

"And now another thought occurred to me. It concerned the woman in the evening gown--about whom so much conjecture had been spun. I made a long-distance phone call and finally succeeded in reaching her. She was at a social gathering, but promised to break away at once and meet me within the hour at the residence of Colonel Kimberling, adjoining the State Prison.

"I arrived there before she did. When I told her that I wanted her to accompany the Colonel and myself to the death house, she blushed, looked at her formal attire, and protested, 'But Governor, I simply can't go in there dressed like this.'

"Colonel Kimberling and I agreed with her, and he got her one of his overcoats. She put it on and it reached down to the tops of her satin slippers. Then the three of us got in her car and drove around to the Third Street gate of the prison. Standing near the gate, where he had been stationed at Colonel Kimberling's direction, was Lieutenant Colonel George Selby, the deputy warden, who had served with me overseas as an officer in my regiment, the 114th Infantry. I made no particular note of the time. I believe it was a little after ten.

"Once inside the prison gate, we turned to the right and entered, through a little door, New Jersey's death chamber. As the door opened, the beam from a prison guard's flashlight fell directly on the chair in which Hauptmann was later to die. Death Row is separated from the death chamber by an iron door.

"I turned to the woman in the evening dress and Colonel Kimberling's overcoat. I told her to take a seat on a little bench near the electric chair and that I would call her when and if I needed her. She seated herself and waited. I shall now disclose her identity.

"She was Mrs. Anna Bading, for years secretary to Ellis H. Parker, I had been given to understand that Hauptmann could not express himself very well in English, and had thought I might need an interpreter. And, of course, I had figured I might need a stenographer, particularly if he wanted to make a confession. My first thought, therefore, had been of Mrs. Bading. She was an expert stenographer, spoke German fluently, and could be depended upon to maintain the confidence that I thought essential to my plan.

"That night Mrs. Bading had been attending an affair being held by the Eastern star, which had honored her by selection as Worthy Matron of the chapter. Getting my phone call, she had raced in from Mount Holly, some fifteen miles distant, with no chance to change her clothes, stopping only long enough to pick up a stenographer's notebook and several sharp pencils.

"Colonel Kimberling gave an order. The door opened. A quick turn to the right, and he stood before the bars of cell 9 saying softly to the man behind them: 'Richard, the Governor to see you.'

"A guard turned another key and the grated cell door was opened to admit me. The key turned again and the guard left. I was locked inside with Hauptmann. Colonel Kimberling, saying, 'Call me, Governor, if you want me,' walked away to join the guard at the other end of the death-house corridor.

"I motioned to Hauptmann to sit down on his cot, and I sat down beside him, making at the same time a hasty survey of the cell. I can now remember only the convicted man, attired in a blue-gray shirt, open at the neck, and dark prison trousers; a stand with a pitcher and a basin; and a table covered with papers and books--a Bible, several works of philosophy and astronomy, and the paper-covered volumes containing the testimony taken at the Flemington trial. There were pictures of his 'poor Annie' and his 'Bubi.'

'I said something--just what I do not recall--designed to put him at his ease; but I did not then, or at any time during my visit, promise him aid or make any expression of sympathy or belief in his statements to me.

"Hauptmann looked me in the eye and asked:

'Governor, vy does your state do to me all this? Vy do they vant my life for something somebody else have done?'

"Well, you have been found guilty. The courts--"

But, since the courts had already spoken, having "had their day in court", so to speak, we can readily understand why Hauptmann had asked to see the governor. All he could hope to gain was Hoffman's intent and considerate understanding as he sat listening to the impassioned and straightforward questions presented by a man who had been condemned to die for a crime he did not commit.

CHAPTER FIFTY SEVEN

Hauptmann's Questions

"'Lies! Lies!' He pointed to the record of the trial." All lies! Vould I kill a baby? I am a man. Vould I build that ladder? I am a carpenter.'

"I soon realized that I was to hear no confession, that I was to listen to no terms of a proposed bargain. Not once in the hour that I spent in death-house cell 9 did Hauptmann beg me to save his life. He did ask for more investigation. His most earnest plea was for the use of a 'lie detector.' 'Vy won't they use on me that,' he asked, 'and on Doctor Condon also use it? They haf too some kind of drug, I haf heard. Vy don't they use on me that drug? And on Doctor Condon use it too?'

"I hold no brief for Hauptmann. But this thing I am bound to say: that his story and his unanswered questions put new doubts in my mind and aided in fashioning a firm resolution to search out, within the limits of my resources and my ability, the truth--and the whole truth--in this mysterious case.

"Here was no cringing criminal pitifully begging for mercy, but a man making a vehement claim of innocence, bitter in his denunciation of the police and the prosecution and their methods. And bitter, too, in his excoriation of his former chief counsel, Reilly.

"'Could a man do for dollar,' he asked, 'vat Reilly haf done to me? Only once, for about five minutes, did I haf a chance to explain my case to him, really. Sometimes he came to see me, not often, for a few minutes. How could I then talk to him?'

"I looked through the bars to the heavy steel door that led to the death chamber. Cell 9 was right next to that lethal room. The electric chair, through the steel door, was only about fifteen feet from where I was sitting beside a man who was destined to sit in it. When the door opened, that chair, covered with a piece of white muslin and resembling a seated ghost, could be seen by the occupant of Hauptmann's cell. At least six men, at night, had shuffled past the German carpenter, some of them silent, some sobbing, some shrieking, to be strapped in that chair.

"I wondered if they--

"But Hauptmann kept on talking: 'Vy did they take from me all my shoes? When I was arrested they took, among many things, all my shoes. Vot for I could not imagine, but now I haf found out. Because they haf a footprint.' He went on to say that there had been a footprint of a woman in the mud outside the nursery window at Hopewell, according to the testimony. It has been sworn that that print was made by Mrs. Lindbergh.

"'But,' he said, 'there was, too, a footprint of a man, who, according to the prosecutor, climbed the ladder to get the unfortunate child. It is to me a riddle, for, said the prosecutor, it was many feet and all soft earth from this window to where the ladder was found--how could it haf been but one footprint? Vy did they not produce at the trial the impression of which they cast a model? Vy? They cannot say that my foot has become larger or smaller. So too the footprint which was found in the graveyard from where Doctor Condon swore that he gave to John fifty thousand dollars. Also here my shoe certainly did not fit. Vy did they not produce here the plaster model that was made?'

"He spoke about the phonograph record that was made after Condon met 'John' and upon which the aged negotiator is supposed to have recorded his conversation;. 'Doest any one think,' he queried, 'that those footprints and this record haf been held back out of pity for me? Oh, no. For me, no pity!

"'Is it not true that in every case when a person is arrested they take his fingerprints? So they did vith me. A few days after, two New Jersey state police came to me in Bronx Prison and vanted further prints. I told them these had already been taken. These men replied the ones they took haf not been clear enough, so they take very firmly about six sets. Then one or two days later they came again with the statement that still there are several spots not plain enough. So they took more--and also the sides of my hands, which they did not take before, and then especially the joints of the fingers and the hollow parts of my hand.

"'Then at the trial, when my counsel asks about fingerprints the prosecutor say simply, 'There are no fingerprints.' If that is so, no fingerprints on the ladder, on the letters, on the window sill, in the room, vy would they vant so many times my fingerprints?

"'I can only think they haf fingerprints, but they are not like mine, so they say they haf none. But they invent another story. They say I haf worked vith gloves. Is this not a worthless lie? Because since in that room they found no other fingerprints--not of the parents, or the child's nurse or the other servants--can this statement be possible? It is even said that Mrs. Lindbergh and the nurse Betty together pulled down the window which was stuck but there are no fingerprints found on the window frame. Do the parents, then, ven they go to the room to take joy in their child, and all the servants, also wear gloves?'

"The prisoner spoke about an expert from New York (Dr. Hudson) who took many fingerprints from the ladder. 'But,' he said, 'there were nowhere any of mine. The jury would not believe this expert because he would not say anything to convict me.'

"(I was later to learn that these fingerprints were processed by Dr. Hudson but photographs were taken and the negatives were held in the possession of the State Police. J. Edgar Hoover, Director of the Federal Bureau of Investigation, has since stated to me that these photographs were never sent to Washington for a check against the prints of thousands of known criminals in the United States.)

"I am quoting Hauptmann faithfully, telling just what he said to me. He went on:

"'Among my carpenters' tools they found a chisel which looks in part like the one found at the Lindbergh place near the ladder. That my chisel is ground differently, is a different size, and has quite a different handle, made no difference. They simply said 'No, this is Hauptmann's chisel,' and the jury believed them. They do not believe me when I say that my chisel set is an entirely different one from the one they found. For my set was a Stanley set, one fourth inch to one and one half inch. They must haf taken out some sizes and put among them others like the one they found, except the three-quarter-inch chisel. For the one they found is a Bucks Brothers chisel.'

"(The chisel found on the Lindbergh estate was made, it was estimated at the factory, about thirty years ago, long before Hauptmann entered the United States.)

"'At the trial,' he continued, 'much weight was given to my letters to Pincus Fisch, the brother of Isidor Fisch. Ven I write letters to Germany I write them first in pencil and then copy them in ink--not just the same but much similar. I always saved these pencil letters, and I saved carefully the letters Pincus Fisch sent to me.'

"'In my first letter I had written everything to Pincus Fisch as Isidor had told me, and did not then know he was lying to me, for I always believed him. When I received my first letter from Pincus it made me think something was queer, and for this reason, and also because it was a case of death, I decided to carefully preserve all our exchange of letters, for, I thought, Pincus Fisch will hold me responsible for the things Isidor said were his in the country.'

"'So all of these letters--I think six or seven--I haf saved and put in a large envelope in my desk from which the police took them.' Hauptmann rose from the cot and picked out a volume of the Flemington testimony. 'But when we ask for these letters at the trial I received the answer, 'Ve haf none.' God in heavens! All the letters were together. One of the letters I never could get clear, for it said that shortly before Isidor died he called for me and seemed to vant to say something about me. But he was too weak or did not vant to. So he took to his grave that vhich would be of great help to me now.

"'Also Pincus wrote me to keep Isidor's death secret if it were necessary, but I did not then know vy that should be necessary, and I did not do so. No, vy did Vilentz say that he did not haf these letters, when my letters answering them were there? No, these letters did not fit into the state viewpoint, so they had to disappear. But they took precautions and had the Fisch family and the nurse come to America. They surely expected that I would insist more on these letters and say what vas in them. But ven I could recall only in parts the contents and the jury would not haf believed me, I was obliged to say nothing. For if I told vat I had remembered, vould not the Fisch family, who vere paid for coming here, haf said the opposite upon the suggestion of the prosecutor?

"'For vat else was the family brought here? So Pincus Fisch vas not called to the stand, and so, too, the nurse vas not called. Thus all direct evidence vich might haf freed me disappeared.'

"(There are now in my possession copies of the letters referred to by Hauptmann, supporting his claim, certified by German police officials of Leipzig. The copy of the pencil draft of Pincus Fisch's letter verifying the fact that Isidor, in his last moments, kept calling for Hauptmann and 'wanting to tell us something about you,' together with other important material was secured from Germany.)

"The 'most hated man in the world,' prison pallor in his cheeks, looked me directly in the eye as he answered my questions. Often he prefaced his answers with 'I am glad you haf asked me that.' It may be said that I did not ask him the right questions--but I think I did. He did not hedge an answer. Most of the replies were simple and direct; some were not altogether satisfying, but they formed the basis for subsequent investigation.

"''Vould I, a carpenter, make for a crime like dot a ladder dot vould not bear my own veight vidout breaking?'

"Hauptmann arose from his cot and stood before me as if he wanted me to appraise his height and weight. A dim light burning in the corridor outside cell 9, cast the shadows of prison bars in vertical stripes down his gray woolen shirt, open at the neck. His attitude, as at the Flemington trial, seemed to reflect pride in his craftsmanship. There he had answered the question of his chief counsel, Reilly, 'Did you build the ladder?' with the statement, 'I am a carpenter!'

"The prisoner turned abruptly and went to the table bearing his books. He picked out one of the volumes of the trial testimony, Henry E. Bruckman of the Detective Division of the Bronx. He pointed to the damaging evidence of Bruckman, who had testified that he had found inside a closet at the Hauptmann home the piece of board bearing the penciled notation of Dr. Condon's address and telephone number.

"I wanted to ask you about that," I said. "You did admit that it was your writing, didn't you? And that it was the Doctor's telephone number? How do you account --"

"'Dot is von of the things def haf done to me,' answered Hauptmann. 'A few days after my arrest my Annie and the child could stand it no longer in the house because the baby could no longer sleep because of all the police and people who vere there; so dey vent to relatives. Now I can see it vas the wrong thing to haf done, for the police could manage to do as dey vished.

"'Some days after I am arrested, vhen everything seems so mixed up, the police appear with a board on vhich is some writing. Dey say the board is from the closet in my home, and vhen I look through a glass at the writing it looks like mine and I say it must be mine because often it is my custom to write down things like many carpenters, on pieces of vood. But den dey tell me it is Doctor Condon's telephone number and the number of his house. Dear God! If I dot number had written and knew vhat it vas, vould I so haf told the police? No! Vith my dying breath I vould haf said I haf never seen it before.'

"'Besides, if I had commit this crime, vould I haf marked down in my own house this number? Because in my Bronx house I haf no telephone and must go some distance to telephone. Vaht good vould be to me a number written inside my closet vhich is the broom closet and very small and vhich I vould haf to get inside to see the number? And too, the closet is dark.'

"Hauptmann went on to explain that any telephoning done by him had to be from a pay station and that there were always telephone books containing Doctor Condon's phone number. 'They haf tried to make people think,' he said, 'dot this vas a secret number, but is shown dot it is not so and the number vas in all the books.'

"(Later, in *Liberty*, even Doctor Condon was to admit the improbability of Hauptmann's having written his phone number on the inside of the closet. Telling of long-distance calls from distant cranks who reversed charges, running his telephone bill up to nearly fifty dollars a month, he writes in *Jafsie Tells All*: 'Angry, I arranged for a private listing. Later, much was to be made of the fact that I had a private listing and that, despite this, my telephone number was found written in a closet in the kidnapper's home.... The number so found was Sedgwick 3-7154, the old number by which I was listed in the Bronx telephone directory; at the time of the kidnapping and <u>before</u> I obtained a private listing.... To this day I cannot bring myself to accept the written telephone number and address in the kidnapper's closet.')

"Hauptmann said to me, 'I am now certain that the numbers on the closet wainscoting haf been made either by police or by reporters who tried to write like me.'

"Frequently Hauptmann reverted to the ladder, which Attorney General Wilentz, before the trial, is reported to have said that the state would "hang around the neck" of the accused man.

"'Is it not unbelievable,'he asked, 'dot to make von support for the ladder, out of six, I vould haf from the floor in my own house tear up von of the boards? This is the von dey call 'rail 16.' In the first place, it had in it some large knots vhich alone vould prevent a carpenter from making a ladder of it. Anyvay, it is not altogether a ladder--it is only a wooden rack. Its construction shows dot it did not come from the hand of a carpenter, not even a poor von. The prosecutor tried to say dot I vas not a good carpenter, but I say I haf often worked for myself and as a foreman. Every master could depend on me. I haf often figured out whole requirements for vood for new construction and order material, and often I vas responsible for the whole job.

"'But the ladder rail. It vas said to the jury, and by experts, dot it came from my house. Vhether it really came from the house I do not know, but if it did, den I make responsible the persons who vere dere after my Annie left the house.'

"Again Hauptmann rose from the prison cot and stood before me. 'Listen,' he said, 'Vilentz says I am smart criminal. He says on dese hands I must haf vorn gloves, because dere are not fingerprints. He says on dese feet I must haf vorn bags, because dere are no footprints. If I vas a smart criminal, if I vould do all dose things, vy vould I go in my own house and take up half of one board to use for one piece of the ladder--something dot always vould be evidence against me?

"'If I vanted to make a ladder, could I not get around my yard and around my garage all the vood like this dot I vould need? I haf lots of boards like dot. Besides only about von block from my house is a lumber yard vhere for a few cents I could buy such a board.'

"Hauptmann went on to point out that there was no stairway leading to his attic, only a trap door that could be reached awkwardly by climbing up on closet shelves. The entrance to the attic would then be completed by lifting oneself up by the use of hands and arms. It seemed inconceivable to him that any one could believe that, for the sake of saving a few pennies, a board from the floor would be pried up. He said that, according to the testimony, the flooring was of the tongue-and-groove type and held to the floor by square five-penny nails. It would take a man of unusual strength with his hands alone to pry up such a board. 'Besides,' he added, 'since on the ladder rail there vas no tongue and no groove, in addition to all the other trouble it vould be necessary to ripsaw or plane such a board down both edges to make it the size of the ladder rail.'

"Hauptmann, doomed to die, was particularly bitter in his denunciation of Arthur Koehler, the government wood expert. The prisoner pointed out that, in order to show that rail 16 and the lumber said to remain in Hauptmann's attic had at one time been part of the same board, Koehler had to assume in his testimony that there was a piece of lumber two or three inches in width missing between the end of the ladder rail and the beginning of the piece left in the attic. By the use of one's assumptions, he said, anything might be conceived.

"He did not seem to think that there was anything particularly brilliant or impressive in Koehler's tracing a shipment of lumber, cut in a certain way, to a retail lumber yard in the Bronx. Many hundreds of thousands of feet of lumber cut with the same saws or knives would be produced by the same mill, he argues. Koehler himself had traced many shipments of the lumber to different cities in the country. Hauptmann claimed that if a suspect had been held in any one of those cities, say Buffalo, Easton, Richmond, it could have been said that the lumber which was milled and planed in the same South Carolina mills had been traced to a retail lumber yard in the suspect's neighborhood.

"'Vy vould the jury believe Koehler?' he asked, 'vhen he testified dot two pieces of lumber vhich were given him in the courtroom vere from the same board? Then ve show with Mr. DeBisschop, a fine witness, dot dey come from different places; von almost new--five or six years old--and the other from an old building nearly forty-seven years standing before it vas torn down. But vhen Koehler say dot two other pieces of board, von on the ladder and von vot they lie vas part of my attic floor are from the same board, he is believed. Vy?

"'I know vy!' Hauptmann had a far-away look in his eyes, although his thoughts were probably only a few feet away, upon the cloth-covered chair that was being watched, unknown to him, by Anna Bading, in the course of her lonely vigil in the death chamber. 'It is because, even though a piece is missing dot must be supplied by the mind, dey vant to believe this von thing vhich vill help take my life. Because vhen my life may depend upon a mistake of Koehler's, dot is not important.

"'Oh, no!' he concluded bitterly. 'The poor child haf been kidnapped and murdered, so somebody must die for it. For is the parent not the great flyer? And if somebody does not die for the death of the child, den alvays the police vill be monkeys. So I am the one who is picked out to die.'

"Hauptmann, I believe, could have gone on for hours talking about the wood--the ladder rails, the dowel pins, the crosspieces, the attic flooring, the nails; about discrepancies in the testimony of Koehler. He expressed himself as believing that the testimony concerning the plane marks on the ladder rails and the attempt to show that these marks were made by his plane was such obviously doubtful evidence that the jury should have disregarded the rest of Koehler's testimony. 'Can any von honestly believe,' he asked, 'dot I, vorking many times as a carpenter, vould for two haf a plane dot vould not be sharpened and vhich vould haf today the same nicks as it would haf two years ago?

"'Besides, even the same blade of the plane vould make different marks vhen used by different people. But Koehler, he proves dot dis plane today, by different people, makes exactly the same marks dot it made vhen supposed to haf been used by me two years ago. The ladder has been taken apart many times and handled by many people. It must be shown dot I vas not alvays in the Bronx, but at Hopewell--so some von, maybe the police, might run my plane on the ladder rails.'

"Sadly he added, 'Dot I cannot prove. If, like the state, I haf many hundreds of thousands of dollars to spend, maybe I too could haf many "experts."'

"I was anxious to get on to other phases of the case, and the testimony that had condemned Hauptmann. His mention of the wood "experts" gave me a chance to veer from the woodwork angle and question him about the handwriting on the ransom notes.

"'Right after my arrest I had to write,' said Hauptmann. 'I did not know at the time vy dey vanted specimens of my writing. If I had any idea, den I vould not haf let dem dictate to me so to write down mistakes. Of course I make mistakes in writing. Still, not such blunders as vere dictated to me. Den dey took out of all my writings dose things vhich looked like the ransom notes. In the note dot was found in the baby's room dey found only von little word 'is', dot dey say looked like mine.

"'It vas after twelve o'clock at night vhen dey come back and forced me to write more. I did not vant to write more den, because I had been on the boat the night before to say good-by to a relative, and I had almost no sleep. But dey dictate to me vhat I should write, so I did it. I could hardly keep my eyes open; still, I remember some of the things dey told me to write. I recall very clearly some things, for vhen I write the vord 'not' dey told me to add 'e' to it. Dot seemed very strange, but now dey say dot is not in my writings. So some of the sheets vhich I wrote haf been torn or are missing.

"'Many times dese handwriting 'experts' haf been wrong. One of dem testifying against me admitted dot as a result of a mistake he made an innocent man serve three or four years in a prison out Vest.'

"(Hauptmann was incorrect in the statement that the trial testimony had shown that the 'innocent man' had served time in jail; but it is a fact that, after making an unsuccessful effort to evade the question of defense counsel, John F. Tyrrell, one of the state's 'experts' admitted that he gave handwriting evidence upon which one Gordon Morgan, in a Milwaukee court, had been convicted of forgery and sentenced to prison. The day after the conviction, Tyrrell reluctantly stated at Flemington, a man by the name of Herman Eckert confessed that he had written the checks in question. The case was reopened and Morgan was discharged.)

"The doomed Hauptmann continued earnestly: 'Dey admitted dot many times dey had been wrong in important cases. Sometimes dey are hired by one side and again by another in a case. Sometimes dese big 'experts' oppose each other; von says the handwriting is right, the other says it is wrong for the person accused.

"'In my case,' he went on, 'Lloyd Fisher haf told me dot the state haf spent more money for handwriting experts alone dan ve haf for our whole defense. So, vhen it is a question of sending me to the electric chair, right avay the state, vith many thousands of dollars, get all the experts who are vell known in the country and haf dem on their side against me.'

"Rising quickly, the prisoner brought two volumes of the trial testimony almost completely filled with the handwriting examination. He ran through the pages, looked at me, and said, 'Governor, If you haf been a man who vas picked up vith some of the Lindbergh money--even though dot money might haf passed through ten hands before it came to you--I think dot easy some of dese man vould prove, from all your writings, dot you vere the von who haf written the ransom letters.

"'Nearly $40,000, I am told, the state paid dese men who testified dot here and dere is a letter I haf written, or a vord, dot the jury vould believe is like some of dose in the Lindbergh letters.'

"I asked Hauptmann many questions about his relationship with Isidor Fisch, the man from whom he claimed to have received the $15,000 proved after the arrest to be part of the Lindbergh ransom money. It had always seemed to me that the Fisch story represented the weakest part of Hauptmann's defense; it seemed unbelievable that Fisch, leaving for Germany, would have left the ransom bills in Hauptmann's custody, and that he would not have ascertained until after Fisch's death in Leipzig that the package contained currency.

"As I sat beside him on his cell cot, Hauptmann related this story; That he met Fisch, for the first time, in March or April of 1932 at Hunter's Island, and that he later drove Fisch and another friend, whose name he could not remember, to the subway station. It was about three weeks later when he again met Fisch at Hunter's Island, and after that they met two or three times a week. Fisch told him that he was interested in the stock market and Hauptmann asked him to accompany him to Steiner and Rouse's on Eighty-sixth Street. Although Hauptmann at that time still carried his account with Mott, he watched the reports at Steiner and Rouse's, and later he transferred his account to that firm.

"Fisch told Hauptmann that he was in the fur business, and added, according to Hauptmann, that there 'vas good money in it.' He finally interested Hauptmann in it and was given $500 to invest in furs. Hauptmann at the same time was to buy some stocks for Fisch, and each was to pay the other their respective profits or losses. They carried on these transactions for some time, with Hauptmann buying and selling stock for Fisch--including one $9,000 purchase of Alaska Juneau--and reinvesting in furs the profits which Fisch represented were being made on his original $500 investment, until he had $6,000 or $7,000 in furs.

"Fisch, who was sickly, one day announced that he was going to Germany to visit his parents, and, about four weeks before leaving, told Hauptmann that he had purchased 2,000 Hudson sealskins. He said he had sold 1,600 of them but wanted Hauptmann to keep the remaining 400. 'At first,' said Hauptmann, 'he said he vanted me to come down vith him to the fur district, but den he changed his mind and said I should come to his home on 127th Street. So I vent to his house and ve took the skins and vent to my home. About von veek later he brought to my house a moth box and he showed me how to vet and stretch the skins.

"'Later on he asks me vhen he goes to Germany if he can leave with me some of his belongings, and I vent to his home again, for the second time, and took to my house two satchels, a big von and a small von. He says,

'Dere is not much in dere, only old stuff--you may put it in the garage.' He showed me some books in the little von and told me I could read them, and I did during the vinter. I kept dot satchel in my big closet in the living room.

"'Den, the Saturday before Isidor left for Germany, my vife and I gave for him a farewell party. He brought along in his arm a cardboard box, wrapped up--I think about nine o'clock--and he asks me to put it in a closet for him and keep it until he comes back from Germany. I thought maybe in the box vere some things he forgot to put in the satchel, maybe papers and letters. Vhen he came in ve vere in the kitchen, so I put the package for him on the upper shelf of the broom closet. After a vhile dere vere rags and things on the shelf covering up the box and I forgot all about it. He told me he vould be back again in two months, maybe earlier.'

"Hauptmann continued: 'Isidor wrote me a few times from Germany, and den, in March or April, from his brother Pincus I get a letter saying he, Isidor, haf died. He asked me, in his letter, as he knew I vas a friend of Isidor's to look after his financial business in dis country. So I wrote and told Pincus how ve stood in the stock and fur business.

"'Fisch had told me vonce that he had bank accounts and a safe-deposit box and dot he also got $10,000 in some company dot bakes pies; also lots of furs; and dot a friend, Mr. Falek, owed him $2,000. But vhen I haf news dot Isidor haf died and I start to look around, I find dot the pie company is a fake and vorth nothing, also dot Fisch haf owed Falek $800 and to Mrs. Heil, Mr. Henkel's mother-in-law, he owed $4,000. Henry Uhlig, who knows the fur business and who had gone to Germany vith Isidor , vent looking around vith me, and we find Isidor haf no furs except the 400 skins at my house, vhich are not vorth vot he haf told me. So I am all mixed up.

"'I vent with Uhlig to a lawyer named Plitzer (I later found the name to be Louis Blitzer) to see how I could protect myself with my losses from Fisch, for I thought surely somevhere he must haf money or furs or property. Plitzer, I think, belonged to the same lodge as Isidor, and he said that in 1930 he was settling for Isidor a case about the pie company and also something about paying taxes in Albany.

"'I asked him if dere vas any chance of getting to open the safe-deposit box, and he said no, not unless Fisch's relatives should issue orders. But Mr. Falek,

I think, had some kind of a paper and he opened the box. Uhlig told me dot dere is nothing in it, just some little notes.

"'Even up to that time I haf not thought of the little box, but three or four veeks before I got arrested it has been raining and the water comes in the broom closet and I run across the box soaking vet. Vhen I look I find it is full of money. Oho! I say to myself; dot is vhere Isidor's money haf gone. Vot he has saved he has put in gold certificates to be safe. I put it in a pail and took it to my garage, vhere I dried it and hid it like the police found it, except for the few bills I haf spent. I did not put it in the bank because vith gold certificates I think I should haf trouble.

"'Before dot I haf written to Pincus he should come to the United States to settle up Isidor's business. Now I felt, since Fisch haf owed me so much money and haf tried to cheat me, dot the money largely is mine.

"'Could I haf known dot the money vas the Lindbergh baby money? No! How could any sensible person think dot?' Hauptmann then touched upon a point that had always puzzled me, even in the days when from a casual reading of the newspaper accounts I had been thoroughly convinced of his guilt. 'For vas it not testified at the trial, and truly so, dot to the gasoline station man I haf said, vhen I gave him the bill, 'I haf a hundred more like dot'? Vould I say dot if I knew dot dese bills maybe could take my life some day?'

"(It was true that at Flemington Walter Lyle had testified to that effect. His exact testimony was that, when Hauptmann had handed him the ten-dollar gold certificate, he looked at it, turned it over, and said, 'You don't see many more of these,' and he (Hauptmann) said, 'No, I only have about a hundred left.'

"Hauptmann talked on rapidly, without excitement, of the circumstances surrounding his arrest; how he first believed he had been picked up for speeding, but knew it was more serious when the police clapped handcuffs on him. He frankly admitted that he had lied about the amount of money in his garage because he 'vould get in so much trouble if they knew I had so much gold money, and besides, near the money I haf hidden also a pistol vhich I know I am not supposed to haf.'

"He told of an alleged beating to which he was subjected in a police station in New York. 'I vas handcuffed in the chair and the police give me such a terrible licking dot I fall downvard to the floor. Dey showed me a hammer and den dey put out the lights and started to beat me on the shoulders, the back of the head, and the arm. Den, too, dey kicked my legs vith their feet and kept yelling, 'Vhere is the money?' 'Vhere is the baby?' 'Ve'll knock your brains out!'"

"I was later to obtain a copy of the oral and physical examination of Hauptmann by Thurston H. Dexter, M.D., F.A.C.P., made in the presence of James M. Fawcett, then attorney for the accused man, and Louis L. Lefkowitz, assistant medical examiner; dated September 25, several days after the alleged 'third degree.'

"That report is before me as I write this record of the much talked about prison interview with the man who has long since gone to his death, legally at the hands of my state. It reads in part: 'Scab and abrasion between left eye and molar region, and under the lid a faint yellow discoloration ... on right shoulder tender lump, an inch and a half, and a lump on the spine of the right scapula and above it ... all of lower shoulder blade shows a swollen welt with discoloration and abrasions ... a large mark and discoloration, yellow and blue, extending into the axillary region ... in the left lower quadrant of the abdomen, close to the groin, an area of three by five inches of faint greenish-yellow discoloration ... in the upper chest region, involving principally the sternum, a large irregular region discolored yellow and faint blue, superficially abraded ... right thigh much swollen, very tender, and markedly discolored.'

"Dr. Dexter closes his report with: ' I conclude from this examination that he had been subjected recently to a severe beating, all or mostly with blunt instruments. The injuries resulting from this are general and include the head, back, chest, abdomen and thighs.'

"Hauptmann told me, as he had told Dr. Dexter, that he had been treated kindly while in the jail in the Bronx.

"Time and time again he referred to the intermediary, Dr. Condon. He used, in that interview, the same phrase used in a later statement given out by his counsel: 'Doctor Condon holds the key to my cell. If he vill tell the truth I must be a free man.'

"'The prosecutor does to me funny things,' he said. 'Dey place on the vitness stand a voman who testifies she sees me, after the crime, limping around vith a cane. Dot is to show dot it must be I who vas hurt vhen the ladder broke. But den comes Doctor Condon, who says dot, a few days later, I jump a high vall at the cemetery and run avay like an athlete.'

"The primary point in Hauptmann's mind concerning Condon seemed to be this: That the kidnapping took place in March, 1932. During all the following summer and the summers of 1933 and 1934 Hauptmann was at City Island three, four, and five times a week. He was there practically every week-end. He went swimming there, played soccer, and had picnics there with friends. For a long period of time he kept his canoe at Dixon's Boat House. During that same period Condon had a real-estate office on City Island, and to get there, according to Hauptmann, had to go past the Dixon boathouse. The Doctor admitted that he frequented City Island, went there week-ends, and was supposed to have even used the same boathouse.

"Hauptmann could not conceive that three full seasons could have passed, with both Condon and himself frequenting this place so continuously, without an identification. 'How could anybody believe dot,' he asked, 'vhen Doctor Condon vas looking as he says all over the country for 'John,' who he now says is me, vidout coming face to face vith me? Condon says dot he could identify 'John' vhen 'John' vas valking along a street and he vas on the top of a bus, yet on City Island nearly every day he vould not see me and pick me out as 'John.'

"'If I vas the kidnapper and I got the money from Condon, vould not I know, too, dot the Doctor vas in City Island many, many times? And vould not I haf stayed avay from City Island because I vould haf been afraid of being identified by Condon? Even after the Doctor haf seen me in vhat dey call the police 'line-up' in New York, vy vould he keep going around all over trying to find 'John' to whom he paid the Colonel's money?'

"It was evident that Hauptmann was quite confused about the aged negotiator's activities. He queried, 'Vould any man be fool enough to come to get the ransom money, and den, vhen he found Condon vas dere at the cemetery, to say, 'Vait a vhile so I can go get instructions,' and den disappear for fifteen minutes before returning? Vy, vhen he came back there vould be a thousand policemen to catch him. Anyvay, dey should haf done dot. Den I vould not be here. Dey knew dey vere going to pay the money, so vy did not the police surround the cemetery and catch dose who commit the crime?

"'The man who vas talking vith Doctor Condon at Voodlawn Cemetery vas said by him to veigh between 155 and 160 pounds; for did not the Doctor say he could tell, and he felt the arms of 'John'? But my veight at about that time vas 175 pounds--it shows so on my automobile license.'

"Hauptmann told about Doctor Condon's visit to him in the cell at the Hunterdon County Jail. 'Dere vas no guard inside the cell,' he said, 'but outside in the vindow of the jail hallvay (corridor) in front of the cell there vas a guard, vith some man--I think the prosecutor. Doctor Condon vas vith me on a bench in the cell, and he vas asking me if I haf any athletic training. I said 'yes'. Den he asked me if I haf von any prizes, and I told him sixteen or seventeen in Germany for running and jumping. Den it looked like he vas going to cry. He took a piece of paper and marked it in four parts and said he divided the case in four parts. Von part he said vas the baby, and in another part he made a little house vith a bench. He called me 'John' many times. He pointed to the first square and said 'Dot is the baby--dot comes first.' Den he pointed to the second space and said, 'Dot is the man I spoke vith--the go-between.'

"'I asked him vhat vas a go-between, and he explained to me dot he vas a go-between for Colonel Lindbergh, and the fellow who sat vith him in the cemetery vas the go-between for the kidnappers. He said this fellow said there vas five or seven men in the gang, and he told Doctor Condon how to fix the $50,000 in bundles.

"'He said if I know anything I should confess, because there vas no connection between the money and the kidnaping and I vould clear myself and himself. He said the police vere treating him roughly. But he never said I am the fellow--and vhen he left he asked could he come see me again, and I said 'yes.'

"'Vhen Doctor Condon did not identify me as 'John' in New York and again in Flemington, vhat should so suddenly make him change his opinion and say qvickly dot I am the man to whom he has given the money? Can it be like the man Curtis, who has been condemned for having contact vith kidnappers, dot the police, too, have made the Doctor say I am the man or they vill also prosecute him? For surely he, to, must haf had contact vith the kidnappers, since he paid to dem the money.

"'Den, too,' Hauptmann asked, 'can the woman Barr--dot cashier in the theater--be believed in the story she haf told? Can any one believe dot on the night of my birthday--dot vas November 26, 1933--I vould go from my home in 222nd Street vay downtown to Greenwich Village to see a moving picture? Can dey believe on dot night a man who is supposed to haf $50,000 to spend vould be vithout overcoat? Or dot for over a year a cashier who must vait on thousands of people vould remember one man who bought from her a ticket?

"'Dere vas no one else to say dot she vas telling the truth, but for me dere vere plenty of vitnesses who strongly cover this night and prove dot I am at home vith a little birthday party.

"'Den dere is the old man, Hochmuth, eighty years old and more, who says he sees me go by his house at Hopewell in a green car vith very red face and eyes like a ghost looking out of the automobile vindow. Dis man can hardly see. He admits on the vitness stand dot the police haf him in the jail at Flemington looking at me in the cell for over half an hour, but he says he could not see me--only a figure. But he, like all the state vitnesses, seems to be believed, although it is shown dot he cannot see, and further dot he untruthfully said he lived in New York vhen he really lived in New Jersey so he could get money for relief.

"'Yet my vitnesses are not believed--the five people who saw me in New York in the bakery with Annie at the time dot the crime was committed. One of these, Manley, an old gentleman, arose from a sickbed and he swore dot on the night of March 1, 1932, he saw me at nine o'clock in the bakery.'

"I asked Hauptmann about his prior record in Germany. He briefly recounted his experiences during the war, his home life, and said that after the war he returned to his native village improperly clad and hungry. 'So, too,' he added, 'were my mother and my brothers and sisters. I did steal an overcoat and I stole food. I vas almost a boy. Dese things are wrong, yes, but many times dey vere done in my country after that var. Maybe here, too, dere vere many cases like dot. But never once have I injured a human being.'

"In the shadow of the electric chair that within six months would whisk him into eternity, Hauptmann continued to ask questions that I could not answer. Thinking of Anna Bading, sitting outside in the gruesome atmosphere of the death chamber, I was anxious to bring my interview to a close.

"But the prisoner seemed reluctant to let me go without answers to his questions, fired at me with machine-gun rapidity:

"'Vy don't the police keep on looking for the man Faulkner who deposit nearly $3,000 of the Colonel's money?

"'Vy is it just von--me--dey vant to get for the death of the poor child?

"'Vy don't dey find whose vere the fingerprints, not mine on the ladder?

"'Vy do dey believe fairy story about the support from the child's sleeping garment (thumb guard) found by the nurse Betty Gow and the housekeeper a month after the crime, right vhere it vould haf been seen so many times by hundreds of people on dot road?

"'Vy do dey try to prove I haf had and spent $50,000 when only maybe $15,000 has been found?'

"I could not answer many of Hauptmann's questions. I, too, was to start out on a trail rough with bitterness and censure, searching for answers to some of the same questions--and some others that were beginning to form in my mind.

"I, too, was to feel some of the futility of the search, to sense that indefinable, mysterious force threatening to destroy any one who dared to question that the Lindbergh crime had been solved and that full and complete justice had been meted out to all participants.

"I called to Colonel Kimberling, who came down the corridor with a guard, to turn a key in the cell lock so that I might emerge. The prisoner looked at me hopelessly. 'Vot harm could I do anybody behind dese bars? Vhen dey kill me dey kill an innocent man. But I know--dey think vhen I die, the case vill die. Dey think it vill be like a book I close.'

"Stepping into the corridor, I heard the cage key click in the lock of cell 9. I stepped to the steel door of the death chamber, took one look back at the pale face--the last time I was to see it--behind the bars.

"'Good night, Governor--and thank you for coming.'

"I said good night, stepped through the doorway, and said to Mrs. Bading, 'Come along, Anna--it's over.'"

CHAPTER FIFTY EIGHT

A New Investigation

Governor Harold Hoffman, because of his investigation into the proprieties of the Lindbergh kidnapping case and the subsequent trial of Bruno Richard Hauptmann became a victim, being charged as "a seeker for publicity." Editorials appeared in major newspapers stating that "the courts had spoken"; that the case was closed and the Governor of New Jersey had no right to investigate any further. The American Bar Association, at its annual convention held in Los Angeles in 1935, appointed a special committee to investigate the conduct of the Hauptmann trial. Governor Hoffman was fortunate in having the privilege of receiving, and the opportunity of reading, a copy of the report of that committee in its original, untouched, form, "before it was altered to meet the desires of some New Jersey gentlemen", the governor angrily charged.

Governor Hoffman in his writings states: "The alteration includes the insertion of several pages which condemned my 'interference' with the course of justice and 'deplored' my 'search for publicity.'" Continuing Hoffman said:

"In making this late alteration the special gentlemen of the Bar Association did themselves what they always protest against when it is done by any one else; they undertook to look into my mind and read what they thought they found there.

"Aside from this interpolation, the report of the Bar Association was almost a textbook for the conduct of my investigation. That report condemned the trial and the conduct of the trial. It described the Flemington proceedings as a madhouse of publicity. It told of the shouting of reporters and the telegraph messengers which drowned the voices of the witnesses. It told of the peddling of subpoenas among stars of the stage and screen and society--subpoenas issued only for the purpose of securing for the recipients front-row seats in the courtroom. The report told how the judge and the sheriff repeatedly protested against the issuance of these subpoenas, without effect.

"The committee stated as their conclusion the belief that a fair trial under such conditions was impossible."

Governor Hoffman continued, relating the findings of a later meeting of the American Bar Association where another special report was submitted that contained this statement: "Your committee has considered with great care recommendations which close the so-called 'Hallam Report.' They deal in great detail with the particular problems suggested by the trial of Bruno Richard Hauptmann, which exhibited, perhaps, the most spectacular and depressing example of improper publicity and professional misconduct ever presented to the people of the United States in a criminal trial.

"The committee recognized the inadvisability of a harsh use of the power to punish for contempt by courts, but at the same time appreciates that power, inherent in every court, must be used as far as is necessary to protect the fairness of the proceedings, and that it may also be used sympathetically to protect the part of the Press which respects the real object of judicial proceedings, against the unfair competition of agencies or publicity which recklessly disregard that object and seek to capture customers of their competitors by publications of a sensational, scandalous, and inflammatory kind."

With statements such as these, together with the unanswered questions asked him by Richard Hauptmann, we can understand why Harold Hoffman, governor of the State of New Jersey, was motivated to look further into the case in search of some honest answers. And so, a new investigation was opened, undoubtedly without the sanction of the prosecuting authorities.

From the time of the first news broadcasts telling of the abduction of the Lindbergh baby became public knowledge, Ellis H. Parker, the famous Mount Holly detective, was motivated by a compelling desire to put his phenomenal ability in crime detection to work on the case.

The Burlington County New Jersey detective did not have to wait long. Within a few days of the crime, he was asked by Governor A. Harry Moore, in office at the time of the kidnapping, to officially look into the case. However, State Police Superintendent H. Norman Schwarzkopf resented the intrusion of any outsiders in the investigation. And that included Parker. The superintendent evidently believed the crime could, and would, be solved by none other than his State Police constabulary. Hence, Parker was barred from any official capacity in the investigation.

The "Old Fox of Mount Holly", a name by which he had become known all over the world due to his uncanny success in solving more than three-hundred major criminal cases, nevertheless took it upon himself, and lost no time by "unofficially" fulfilling the request of Governor Moore, by looking into the few known facts of the case.

Parker was certainly no novice when it came to his knowledge of crime detection. The famous "homespun" detective, for over 40 of his 59 years, had successfully solved tough criminal cases by ferreting out the answers from his office, a tiny cubicle located on the second floor of the Mount Holly Court House. He was known by almost every one of Mount Holly's residents. He also knew them, and was held in high regard for the uncanny ability he possessed in "cracking the toughest of criminal cases."

During the initial months of his investigation Parker had gathered information, passed on to him by a number of sources about the suspicious activities, at the time of the kidnapping, that had been made by an individual, living in the area, and well known for his past criminal activity. Parker, "old fox" that he was, had earned his nick-name by using clever, (sly) methods to great advantage in solving crimes. Shortly after the kidnapping he put to use another ploy. Taking the information he had already received of the nefarious activities of their suspect prior to the kidnapping, and adding to this the result of his own investigation into the man's movements, Parker decided to use the news media as an aid in his investigation. In a statement to the press, he made an offer to the boss of the kidnappers saying that if he, their leader, would come forward and talk to the detective, he, Parker, in turn would do everything in his power to see that the kidnappers would not be punished. At that time Parker's primary interest was to obtain the safe return of little Charles Lindbergh and by doing this it was his impassioned desire to draw out the kidnappers.

And, as usual, Parker's plan, did not go without results. As expected he received many calls and letters from across the country from persons willing to confess to something they didn't do in order to receive recognition and notoriety --- courtesy of the cooperating reporters. Writer Alan Hynd would describe them best as "Nut cases".

But, from among the many "weirdos", there came a telephone call from none other than the detective's prime suspect. Although the caller attempted to disguise his voice, both Parker and his secretary, Anna Bading, who was listening on another line, recognized the voice as that of Paul H. Wendel, a man both had known since he was a child.

Regardless of the fact that Wendel was the son of a minister, the caller's life had been a checkered one, much to the embarrassment of his family. As a young man he had studied for the ministry but never entered it. Instead he worked for a short time as a pharmacist, during a period when he "faked" a holdup against his store in an effort to collect insurance. Escaping this charge with a mere reprimand, he changed his mind again, deciding now to be on the side of law and order, to eventually become a practicing lawyer. Nevertheless, he became a disgrace to himself and his latest chosen profession, being convicted for embezzling funds from his clients, a crime which brought him a term in jail. Incidentally, it was Ellis Parker who aided Wendel in obtaining a parole from prison for this crime. After his release the Mount Holly detective made an attempt to have him reinstated with the Bar Association, but his effort fell on deaf ears.

Parker, who knew Paul Wendel better than anyone other than his family, claimed that the man was, without doubt, one of the smartest men he had ever encountered in all of his forty years of crime detection. Parker said the man had a brilliant mind, that he could absorb anything he studied, but had great difficulty sticking with anything for any length of time. However, young Wendel was also not able to stay out of trouble.

Soon after his release from jail numerous warrants were issued calling for his arrest because of worthless checks he had written. He had fast become a disgrace to his chosen profession. But, in spite of his being a fugitive from the law, he did not cease to keep in touch with Parker. He considered the detective to be his friend and often phoned him, informing him of his status with the police from whom he was usually fleeing, and at the same time asking for advice.

On occasion Wendel would call Parker when he was in a desperate strait, feeling the police were closing in on him. He would then be advised to "go away someplace" until the pressure is off and things can be straightened out. At times like these he would leave his wife and two children in Trenton and flee to an unknown location where sometimes he would have to hide out for a considerable length of time. At the time of the kidnapping Wendel was a fugitive from justice with several warrants being issued for him because of his passing worthless checks.

It was during one of these absences while "away from home" that Wendel called Parker, this time in response to his plea that the kidnappers contact the detective, with the hope of arranging details for the possible safe return of the baby.

Wendel's call to Parker was first received by Anna Bading. Although he spoke in a disguised voice, she recognized it as being that of Wendel's. He told Anna he had some vital information for the man who put the ad in the paper. He said friends of his had the Lindbergh baby and he wanted to come and give Parker the information. Mrs. Bading asked if he could call him back, but Wendel was determined to talk to Parker personally and find out what he meant by that which had been printed in the paper about the baby.

Signaling to her boss, Parker picked up his telephone extension, motioning to his secretary that he also recognized the voice as that of Paul Wendel. As Parker identified himself, the caller wasted no time delivering his message, insisting that he, not only knew, but had contact with the actual kidnappers, and would like to make further contact with Parker. In spite of the effort to hide his identity by using a masqueraded voice, which resulted in nothing more than a partially deceptive one, Parker was absolutely certain the voice was that of Wendel. This also was confirmed by Anna Bading.

Wendel called Parker on two other occasions, both of which the detective had the calls traced to Wendel's temporary living quarters, a room in the Hotel Stanford in New York City. Parker, who already suspicioned the dis-barred lawyer as being personally involved in the kidnapping, had checked his criminal record and found there were presently seven outstanding indictments which had been issued in Mercer County against him for charges of embezzlement, false pretenses, the utterance of worthless checks, and fraud as an executor, and that he had also jumped bail and was a fugitive from justice. During his next telephone communication, Parker promised him immunity if he would come to Mount Holly and tell his story personally.

And Wendel did just that, after being assured by

Parker that he would not turn him over to the neighboring Mercer County authorities. Parker, a law enforcement agent in Burlington County, had no jurisdiction in another county. Neither could he have informed them of Wendel's presence there, since he had no advance knowledge of when his suspect would appear. Furthermore, Parker reasoned correctly. Since his primary concern was the safe return of the baby, and because of the trust Wendel, the son of an old and valued friend of his, had placed in him, he believed he was acting correctly in learning first of all where they were holding the baby.

When Wendel arrived at Parker's office he implored the detective to "take him on" by letting him work on the case, stating that, "I have contact with people who have the baby and I'd like to work on this." But, in no way was Parker convinced that the kidnappers, who Wendel insisted were friends of his, could only be apprehended and the baby returned if Parker allowed him to work on the case.

However, Parker decided to play along with Wendel, and told him to go ahead and see what he could find out. During the early days of the investigation Wendel told the detective several things that he could only have learned through a personal contact with the kidnappers. Because of this Parker's suspicions of Wendel as the possible brains of the kidnapping became acute. He insisted, even after the corpse was found, that the baby was still alive; he also claimed the kidnapper had not descended the ladder with the child, but had used the front steps of the home and gone out the front door. He was confident the chisel found by the police had not been used to pry open the window, but instead, a screwdriver had been applied to raise it.

As time went on Parker's suspicions of Wendel became greater as he evaluated the things he remembered of the man's past. He thought of things Wendel had told him many months before the kidnapping when he had expressed his opinion about life, about the world and its people. At many times he had complained to Parker that "nothing good ever happens to me because everybody is against me", expressing his feelings to an even greater extent, "The world has always mistreated me, Ellis, but one day I'll do something that will make the world sit up and take notice. I'd like to get my hands on fifty thousand dollars. I'd show them I'm a smart man", he said with bitterness and hate evidenced in his manner.

It was because of these wild ramblings of Wendel and his unsavory past that caused Ellis Parker to label him as "a psychotic, a very brilliant man with a criminal twist to his mind." A man who needed to be watched very closely.

During the period of excitement generated by the news announcing the kidnapping of Lindbergh's child, Parker was motivated by a strong desire to test his personal ability at solving crimes, to first of all, make arrangements to see that the baby was returned home in safety. It was for this reason that Parker had expressed his belief that the police should have been withdrawn from the Lindbergh home in order to make it possible for the kidnappers to make a personal contact with the parents. However, although this suggestion was a good one which met with the approval of Colonel Lindbergh, it had not been carried out. It was at this time that Parker decided to issue his statement to the press, hoping it might lead to a contact, which it did almost immediately with the telephone contact made by Paul Wendel.

However, because of the "powers" already at work on the case, and in spite of the fact that the governor had asked Parker to join the investigation, he was blocked at every turn in any "official" move he might have made to help them. Hence, Ellis Parker realized that, regardless of his past successful record in crime detection, he was being forced to act "unofficially", thus allowing the "big boys" a clear and free run in their "botched" attempt to solve the case in their own time and solely without any help whatsoever.

Being thwarted in every attempt to help the authorities, Parker's keen mind went to work, as it had in hundreds of earlier cases when he had successfully ferreted out the criminals. His thoughts turned to Wendel, who had recently reached him and said, "I have contact with people who have the baby and I'd like to go to work on this." The shrewd detective deliberated about things he already knew of Wendel, wondering if his "sick mind" had motivated him to actually kidnap the Lindbergh child to "get even with the world that was always against me"? Is it possible that because Lindbergh was an international hero, Wendel could rationalize that "if I can successfully kidnap his baby, then I would actually be more famous than Lindbergh, because no one would know that I did it." Parker's thoughts continued to seek further justification for Wendel's distorted criminal mind to lead him to actively take part in a crime as violent as kidnapping and murder. But then, Wendel had told him, "Ellis, I know the baby is not dead", a fact which the detective already knew. Parker was left with many thoughts. Troublesome thoughts, thoughts that bothered him, thoughts which would lead him into a continued and concentrated investigation of the mysterious activities of Paul H. Wendel.

Meanwhile Governor Hoffman, in addition to making a detailed study of the case, was soon asked by the press to explain why he had visited Hauptmann in his death cell at Trenton. Although his personal interview with the condemned man had taken place on October 16th, it had not been known, except for a few close friends of the governor, by anyone until December 5th.

On this date Governor Hoffman, addressed the members of the New York Ad Club. Following the noon meeting, the governor was approached by Pat McGrady of the *Associated Press*, who was accompanied by ten or more other reporters representing New York newspapers and press services. McGrady asked Hoffman: "Governor, have you ever seen Hauptmann?" His affirmative answer, "Yes, once," naturally opened the door for the next inquiry, "Where?", to be followed by the governor's prompt reply, "In the State Prison", which suddenly generated a wild scramble, as the reporters dashed away to find telephones in order to reach their newspaper editors with the latest scoop they had obtained in the bizarre Lindbergh-Hauptmann case.

Governor Hoffman relates it best as he tells what happened, for after all, he lived it: "In spite of my newspaper training, I did not realize that the simple question and its direct answer would create such a furor. My newspaper apprenticeship had been served in the city room of the *Perth Amboy Evening News*, where placards had been posted over the desk of every reporter, bearing in three-inch type the word ACCURACY as a reminder of a quality of news reporting that was then essential. I had never covered a Lindbergh case. I did not understand that my visit to the prison, with its wealth of opportunity for misrepresentation, would give to such newspapers as desired it a long-sought chance to keep the story--and circulation--alive until Hauptmann was dead.

"Before I returned to New Jersey the papers were carrying garbled accounts of the happening and the fantastic stories of the intensive 'investigation' I had ordered for the purpose of saving Hauptmann.

"Reporters from all parts of the country hastened to Trenton. The New Jersey State House correspondents, many of whom made no attempt to conceal the fact that they were incensed over the action of the Governor in 'going to New York to give out' a choice bit of news, and were covering up their chagrin at their own failure to ask the question--which would have received the same honest answer--started in upon a campaign of hounding, heckling, and misrepresentation. There were, of course, exceptions, but the abuse was quite universal.

"My old paper, the *Perth Amboy Evening News*, in an editorial outburst of shocked sensibilities, pointed to the 'impropriety of Governor Hoffman going to the New York Advertising Club to make a speech about the Hauptmann case.' (The 'accuracy' signs must have been taken down.) Generally the press accused me of seeking 'publicity.'

"When it was pointed out that I had visited the prison on October 16 and it had not become publicly known until December 5--something that would hardly be expected of a seeker for publicity--the press suddenly veered to the designation of my visit as 'secret,' 'stealthy,' and 'clandestine.' The same editors who had raised the cry of 'publicity' now seemingly took me to task for failure to take reporters, cameras, and newsreel men along when I went to the prison.

"Standing out in my memory of these mad days following December 5 is an editorial from the *Newark Sunday Call*, sounding a lone and undeniable expression of truth and sanity: 'Governor Hoffman's visit to the convicted murderer of the Lindbergh baby in the State Prison death house was an action entirely within the authority of the Chief Executive, and for which he is required to answer to no one.... Governors times out of mind have exercised this prerogative as a duty ....It is a dreadful responsibility to determine whether a man should live or die. Anticipating the necessity of undertaking this responsibility, the Governor's duty to seek every possible bit of information is obvious, and the presumption is that he is doing so with a proper sense of his heavy obligation to the cause of Justice.'

"On December 7, pressed to make a statement as to my position, I said, in part:

"'The case of Bruno Richard Hauptmann is one with which the dimensions of American justice will be measured by all Americans and by the world. Because of the unprecedented prominence given to the trial of this man there have been thousands of rumors in circulation.

Some of these rumors allege the existence of evidence not presented at the trial. Some of them allege other conditions disadvantageous to either the prosecution or the defense....The offense charged was a dastardly crime, threatening our whole system of living in mutual confidence. No person participating in this crime can be allowed to escape the full penalty....If the defendant in this case is guilty beyond a reasonable doubt, he must pay the penalty demanded by law. That is required for the protection of society against the criminal. If he is not guilty, he should not be punished. That is required for the protection of society against itself.'

"In spite of this statement of my position, which I challenge any one to disprove as to soundness, and which I reiterate today with all the force at my command, the newspapers and some sections of the public were insistent upon their own interpretations of the things that were in my heart and mind. I was 'intruding,' they said, and 'interfering with the orderly processes of law,' challenging 'Jersey Justice,' and 'trying to save a murderer.'"

It is noteworthy to mention at this time that, regardless of the opposition Harold Hoffman received for his "interference" during, what he called the "hysterical weeks", there appeared to be one encouraging factor. From among the nearly 800,000 letters and telegrams he had received, the greater number expressed strong feelings that, in spite of the biased newspaper editorial writers who almost unanimously opposed the governor's "interference", they had been intelligent enough to have "read between the lines" and were now expressing strong approval of what Hoffman was attempting to do.

The wheels of the law continued to grind on. It had been no surprise to learn on Monday, December 9th, that the United States Supreme Court refused to hear the case. The date of Hauptmann's execution was drawing nearer when, on Friday, December 13th, Justice Trenchard set the new date as sometime during the week of January, 13, 1936.

Trenchard's announcement evidently prompted Hauptmann to write to the governor, once again expressing his innocence. Three days later Hoffman received a letter, which read in part: "With clear conscience I have fought my case. In my heart I can not believe that this state will break the life of an innocent man....I would be very thankful for permitting any able person, whom are free of any opinion in this case, to take a test with so-called lie detector, serum, or whatever science may offer. I hope for myself and in the course of justice that this, my wish, may inspire Dr. Condon to do the same. I have a deep interest in what kind of force made him change his saying. Because when he was visiting me in my Flemington cell, he said all excited, to the prosecutor 'I can not testify against this man.'....

During Hoffman's investigation, while attending to state business in Washington, he grasped the opportunity to visit Mrs. Evalyn Walsh McLean at her beautiful historic home "Friendship", where Colonel Lindbergh had been a guest during the trial of Gaston B. Means in 1932. In confidence Mrs. McLean told Hoffman many things she had personally learned about the case and that she was absolutely certain Hauptmann was an unfortunate victim. She informed the governor that it was during a gathering in her home, attended by former Vice-President Charles Curtis and several United States senators, they had unanimously agreed that the trial had been unfair and the solution not complete. It was then that Mrs. McLean had told them it was her intention to contact the governor, tell him of the information she had, and ask if he would investigate. However, Mrs. McLean's intent was met with just mild approval.

"They told me that Governor Hoffman wouldn't dare to go into the matter--that the forces at work in this case would ruin you. I told them if Governor Hoffman won't, I'm going to the President. You will recall, Governor, that I called you and warned you that my friends had said the case should be investigated, but that any one who had nerve enough to do it would ruin his political career.", she emphasized to Hoffman.

It was due to the topic of conversation, chiefly pertaining to the Hauptmann injustice, at the party that evening in the McLean home that prompted Charles Curtis to place his call to Hoffman when he inquired, "Governor, are you looking into this Hauptmann case? I think that there are a lot of funny things about that case." Before hanging up the phone, the former Vice-President had made the request that Harold Hoffman visit Mrs. McLean. This he had accomplished, only to take his leave with a mind now filled with additional unanswered questions.

On December 23rd Hauptmann filed an application with the New Jersey Court of Pardons in a plea for clemency, stating "I am not guilty of the crime charged", and on New Year's Day he issued a statement repeating his innocence.

It had been decided that Friday, January 17th, was to be the day when Hauptmann would be executed; and on January 7th, Warden Mark O. Kimberling issued eighteen invitations to the witnesses who were to be present that night in the death chamber to view the execution.

By this time the United States Circuit Court of Appeals had already handed down its denial for Hauptmann's appeal for a writ ordering a stay of his execution; and on Saturday, January 11th, it was learned that the New Jersey Court of Pardons, of which the governor was a member, had refused to commute his sentence to a life sentence in prison. Hoffman, one of this court's eight members, was the only person who had voted to grant Hauptmann a lifetime behind bars. This was the condemned man's last vestige of hope.

However, on Wednesday, January 15th, Governor Hoffman on a business trip to New York City, while staying at the Hotel New Yorker, learned that David Wilentz was in the Terrace Room downstairs. Without any prearrangement for a meeting, their paths crossed and the two men spent several hours seriously discussing the merits, the pros and cons, and the possible innocence of Bruno Richard Hauptmann as Hoffman contended. Wilentz was unyielding in his determination to see that Hauptmann was executed.

Regardless of the heated arguments put forth by the two men, neither of whom "pulled any punches" as Hoffman described the tempo of the meeting, one thing was resolved. The governor had agreed to comply with the attorney general's request that he see Anna Hauptmann and inform her there was nothing more he could do to help her husband unless he told the truth.

Before returning to Trenton with this burdensome and foreboding task facing him, Hoffman visited another room in the hotel where, coincidentally, J. Edgar Hoover, Chief of the Federal Bureau of Investigation, was staying. After a talk with Hoover, which lasted long after the midnight hour, the governor, after only three hours sleep, left on the seven o'clock train for Trenton. His head was now filled with more unanswered questions which had been asked by the FBI chief.

Arriving in Trenton, the governor at once made arrangements with George Crocker, the manager of the Stacy Trent Hotel where Mrs. Hauptmann was staying, to meet with her privately in his personal suite. It had been agreed that Hoffman would enter the hotel through a rear entrance in order to avoid the host of news reporters, photographers and newsreel people who had been milling about the lobby awaiting some sign of Mrs. Hauptmann. However, an over zealous hotel employee had tipped off the news media of the governor's visit, which caused Hoffman's planned "secret" entrance through a rear door and the use of a freight elevator, to still be made amid a swarm of reporters, many inquiring with hostility the reason for his visit.

Following a brief exchange of greetings, Governor Hoffman proceeded to get right to the issue at hand. It is best here, that we have him tell it exactly as it happened: "Mrs. Hauptmann," I said, with an assumed air of finality, "tomorrow is the day when, under the law, your husband is to die. I wanted to help him, but he has not been telling me--or any one else--the truth."

"No! No! No!" Anna Hauptmann screamed. "Dot isn't so. Richard did tell the truth! He is telling the truth!"

Her face, which had gone almost chalky white, suddenly flushed with anger. She clenched her fists and started to beat them against my chest. "Listen to me, Gofe'nor, listen to me!"

"Things look bad for your husband, Mrs. Hauptmann. Every one seems to believe that he is guilty. There is only one way in which he can save his life."

"Eagerly the frantic woman shot at me the question, "Vot vay is dot?"

"Well, Mrs. Hauptmann," I replied, "last night I met with Attorney General Wilentz, over in New York.

"A bitter look came into Anna Hauptmann's eyes as I went on: "He thinks it is important--I do too--to get the whole true story of how this thing happened. If your husband committed this crime--"

"He didn't! He didn't! He didn't! He didn't do it, I tell you--he couldn't do it!" Once more she closed her hands into tiny fists. I motioned to a chair and she sat down.

"Listen, Mrs. Hauptmann," I said, "until I finish. Your husband had some of the money. No one believes his story as to how he got it. He has been convicted; he has been sentenced to die tomorrow. But you can save him. The Attorney General says that if Richard will agree to tell the whole story, he will go--or one of his assistants--to the prison with me, and if he is convinced that the story is true, even if it shows that your husband was the only one who committed the crime, he will go with me before the Court of Pardons and ask to have his sentence changed to life imprisonment. There is no doubt that the court, with both the Governor and the Attorney General making this request, will commute your husband's sentence."

"The woman's face reflected at once defiance and disappointment--defiance at the implied accusation of her husband's guilt; disappointment that this charge, hurled so often and so vehemently in the courtroom, in the press, on the air, was coming from a man who, she had been given to understand through the sources of news, was 'on her husband's side.'

"My next words brought her, shrieking, from her chair:

"You must go to the prison this morning. You must see your husband. You must tell him that he can save his life. You must tell him that you want him to tell the truth."

"No! No! No!" she screamed. "I couldn't do dot! He vould turn his back to me. He would think dot the last von in the vorld to know that he is innozent should think, too, dot he haf commit this crime!"

"Drab, colorless Anna Hauptmann rose to the peak of human emotion. It was the first time I had ever seen this woman. She had been pictured as a typical German housewife. In spite of the tenseness of the situation, I had so appraised her in the first few moments of our meeting. Yet I was now face to face with a fatigued woman, red-eyed from constant crying, who was either telling truth that burned deeply into her heart or was staging a scene that, in my opinion, would dwarf the emotional appeal of any of the great dramatic actresses who had ever appeared upon the American stage. And it is hard to think of Anna Hauptmann as an actress.

"My husband haf only a few hours to live! Could I do dot to him--make him think I, like dot judge--like dot jury--believe too dot he vould kill a baby? Vould I make Richard think I too haf believed dose lying vitnesses who for money vould send a good man to die?"

"No! No! Never vould I do dot! Not even to save my Richard's life vould I do dot!"

"Mrs. Hauptmann walked away as if to look out of a window. She raised a handkerchief to her eyes, and then turned suddenly around to face me. "How could he do a thing like dot vidout me--his wife--knowing he vas doing it? How could he cut from the attic floor a board and take it out to make such a ladder? No! Vidout me he couldn't commit dis!

"Vy don't your state take too my life? If Richard is guilty I must also be guilty. I too should go to the electric chair.

"Vidout him I do not vish to live! My little boy--"

"She dropped, now sobbing, into a chair. "He is not guilty, my Richard--I swear it! Like almost every night, dot night he comes to the bakery. People saw him dere--vy vould dey not believe these good people who tell the truth? Yet liars they vant to believe!

"No;! No!" she continued, between convulsive sobs. "Dot night Richard he go home vid me together. I remember the next day a neighbor came to me like dis." She stretched out her arms in the motion of holding up a newspaper. "'Look vot happened!' And I too, like all vimmen, felt terrible for the little child who haf been took from his home. Vy? Vy? vould they tell such things to take my husband from me?"

"I tried to reason with her; to make her see that I was opening a door that would lead to the saving of her husband's life; but every time I repeated that phrase, 'Get him to tell the truth,' she would flare up.

"The truth he has told!" she cried. "Vot more can he say? Yes, maybe he could make up lies to say he did it and save his life. But soon it vould be found dey were not the truth. No! Alvays I--and some day our Bubi--vould be sorry dot he vould say he haf done such a thing even to save his life!"

Mrs. Hauptmann referred to the rumor, then so current, that her husband would have confessed, involving others, but for the fears he entertained for the safety of his wife and his little boy. "Dot, too, is a lie," she said. "Alvays ve vould be safe vith the law until dose people could too be put in jail. Besides, vy should ve vant to lif? My Manfred must some day have eferybody point at him deir fingers and say dot his father haf been a kidnapper and a murderer. So too dey vill alvays say of me, 'She is the vife of Hauptmann, who haf killed a baby.'"

"For a while I veered from the plan upon which the Attorney General and I had agreed, and talked about other phases of the case. When I felt that she had calmed down sufficiently, I broached a secondary proposal: "Will you do this, Mrs. Hauptmann? Go down to see your husband and ask him if he will talk to the Attorney General and to me and answer any questions? Perhaps the Attorney General will not go, but he will send one of his best men. Maybe Richard will say something to help. He might even say something that will save his life."

"'Dot I vill do," was the reply, "For Richard he haf always said dot gladly he vill answer questions dot anybody vant to ask him.

"But," she added, "I vill not say to him--his vife--dot at last he should tell the truth, ven alvays I know dot he has told the truth dot he did not do dis terrible thing."

"I gave Mrs. Hauptmann my telephone number at the Hotel Hildebrecht and told her to call me after she had visited the prison.

"In about an hour there was a call from Colonel Kimberling. He put Mrs. Hauptmann on his office telephone: "Richard says he vill be glad to see you and Vilentz--he vill be glad to see anybody. But, Gofe'nor, the story is just the same; he haf told eferything he knows--nothing more he can tell."

"I immediately called the Attorney General, told him of my experience with Mrs. Hauptmann at the Stacy Trent, her refusal to ask her husband 'to tell the truth,' and of his message that he would be glad to see us but that his story was 'just the same.'

'The hell with it, Harold,' was Wilentz' curt decision. 'If that's still his attitude, I'm damned if I'm going to do anything to help him.'

"Hauptmann was not interviewed."

When the governor returned to the State House he learned of some new evidence which had been unearthed in the renewed investigation. This, together with some fresh doubts of his own of the possibility that Richard Hauptmann might, after all, be innocent of the crime, Governor Hoffman, on Thursday, January 16th, announced that he was granting him a thirty-day reprieve.

This, however, was done to the chagrin of many persons who were already calling for his impeachment. When pressed for a reason why he had granted the reprieve, he stated in the face of his antagonists: "I entertain doubts, shared by many thousands of people, that complete justice has been done. There should be further time provided for what I hope might be an orderly investigation." The reprieve established the new date for the condemned man's death as February 15th, 1936.

During this extended period, an influx of amateur "detectives" came upon the scene, most of them with a sincere desire to add whatever skills they possessed in helping the man, most of them believed had been framed, prove his innocence.

However, from among these emerged bonafide investigators who, through the years, had proven themselves to be "champions" in their field. They were Lieutenant Robert W. Hicks of Washington who had moved to Trenton, a location which proved to be more convenient for his work, not only in New Jersey but in New York City as well. Hicks was a shrewd man who had many "theories" about the case that he backed up with, what he termed to be, "a carload of evidence." Harold Keyes, who at one time had worked in the government service, was presently an investigator for Mrs. Hauptmann, a person who was quite qualified to work on the investigation; as was William Pelletreau of Jersey City, a private investigator, who had put together various handwriting exhibits which proved to be valuable as evidence that Hauptmann could not possibly have written the ransom notes, thus providing additional evidence which supported the testimony already given in court by Arch Loney and Roy Knabenshue. In addition to those giving support in the new probe for truth was detective George Foster, who had worked as an investigator for James Fawcett, Hauptmann's lawyer shortly after his arrest.

At the start of Governor Hoffman's quest for evidence that would be contradictory to that which had already become the official court evidence against Hauptmann, none was more evident than what he learned during the conferences he held with Samuel Small, a professional penman who was a graduate from the Palmer-Zaner College of Penmanship. Again we call on the governor to tell of his own story: "Small, who had for years studied types and styles of handwriting, convincingly argued that Hauptmann could not possibly have been the writer of the ransom notes. A Jew, submerging all racial prejudice against the German prisoner, so apparent in those wild unbelievable days, Small held that Osborn had testified in contradiction to his own writings, his own beliefs. 'In a lifetime of painstaking effort,' declared Small, 'a man cannot change the way in which he was taught to write. Look at these!'

"Before me Small spread out, magnified perhaps a hundred times, photostatic reproductions of Hauptmann's admitted writings, before and after his arrest, and the blown-up sections of the writing upon the ransom notes. 'Look,' he said. 'The shadings are different--the down-strokes and the upstrokes. Every letter has different characteristics--they are started in different places. The smartest criminal in the world, with all the writing in the ransom notes, couldn't do that.' He explained the differences in the methods of the Spencerian and vertical round-hand systems, used long before the Palmer system--and Hauptmann--came into being.'

"The night before the final session of the Court of Pardons, Small in my hotel room begged permission to go before the court, and was told that, under the rules, it would be impossible. 'But,' he said, as he actually broke down and cried, 'do you mean to say that your state will send to the chair a man who couldn't possibly have written those notes? I could show them, Governor. Even a child could tell from these'---he pointed to his enlarged exhibits--' that Hauptmann couldn't have written the nursery note or any of the other ransom letters.

"'Listen!' Small cried. 'It isn't a question if Hauptmann wrote those letters. It is a question whether he could write them. I tell you, Governor, that if you went to the prison and said to Hauptmann, 'I will let you free if you can write a single sentence the way it is written in the ransom letter,' Hauptmann would have to stay in prison the rest of his life. Any expert who has studied types and methods of handwriting will tell you that.' Small insisted, and pointed as proof to sections from Osborn's book and from the statements of other known authorities on writing, that a person cannot disguise his handwriting from one known system to another without conflicting them."

With information they had already gathered pointing to other discrepancies and contradictions of the evidence that had been presented against Hauptmann at the trial, Governor Harold G. Hoffman, on Thursday, January 30th, ordered Colonel Schwarzkopf to reopen the investigation. By this time, the chief executive had sincere doubts as to the guilt of Hauptmann, and so, the main objective of the new investigation was to conduct a concentrated search for the persons who had actually orchestrated the crime.

In a letter to Schwarzkopf, Hoffman pointed out that "either the state's principal witnesses had not told the truth, in which their whole testimony might be questioned, or that there were other participants in the kidnap, the murder, or the extortion."

The answer to Hoffman's directive brought the following results, and he tells of it here:

"I then received a series of weekly 'reports' from

Colonel Schwarzkopf. He had advised Director Hoover of the F.B.I. and Police Commissioner Valentine of the contents of my letter. There had been a weekly 'conference' of officers. I can imagine the proceedings at those conferences. There was no indication of police desire or interest in finding any one else connected with the crime. Hauptmann had been convicted and was being hurried to the chair. Any one else found in possession of ransom money might have given information that would upset the lone-wolf theory of the police and the prosecution. Such a thing would, of course, 'reflect' upon the courts. It was forgotten that in the Curtis case the prosecution had 'proved' that there was a gang of kidnappers and that Curtis knew them.

"Banks were notified that it was no longer necessary to look for the ransom money. Notified on March 28 by John Edgar Hoover that the Philadelphia Reserve Bank had advised that it had 'accumulated forty-nine thousand A and B series five-dollar Federal Reserve notes which are available for examination,' Schwarzkopf wired the director as follows:

THIS DEPARTMENT CONTEMPLATES NO EXAMINATION OF NOTES REFERRED TO IN YOUR TELEGRAM THIS DATE STOP SUGGEST THAT ANY IDENTIFIED NOTES BE TAKEN OUT FOR DESTRUCTION.

"When I asked for a copy of a State Police report for use in checking I was generally handed--reluctantly, it seemed-- the material I requested; but several times I was advised that a certain letter--or a certain report--was 'in the hands of the Attorney General and not available.' This in spite of the fact that ordinary police procedure would demand the retention in the files of at least a copy of any important communication or report.

"On February 28, "fed up" with the weekly routine reports by Schwarzkopf concerning "conferences" and "progress" when there was no progress, I wrote the then Superintendent of Police that I was not interested in receiving further weekly reports simply indicating that the usual conferences were being held. "If you feel that the Lindbergh case has been completely solved and that no persons other than Hauptmann were involved, it is your duty to advise me and to give me your answers to the questions I have submitted. My opinion, which is shared by thousands of our people, is that the kidnapping, murder, and extortion was not "a one-man job." Had sound and ordinary police methods been used following the commission of the crime, many doubts entertained today might have been eliminated and two and one half years might not have elapsed before the arrest of a person who, through the efforts of a gasoline-station manager and a bank teller, could be charged with the crime."

When I referred in the Schwarzkopf letter to the Lindbergh investigation as representing "the utmost bungled case in police history" I was stating an opinion by outstanding criminologists.

This general opinion of police officials and scientists in crime detection, referred to by Hoffman in his letter to Schwarzkopf is summed up best by Henry Morton Robinson in his book *Science Verses Crime*. Quoting from his book, Robinson said: "To summon up a ghastly remembrance of police tipstavery, bend your glance backward to the opening chapter of the Lindbergh case. Do you remember--could any one ever forget--the foaming and senseless cataract of gorgeously uniformed state troopers that descended on the Lindbergh home in motorcycles, roared up and down the road trampling every available clue into the March mud, systematically covering with impenetrable layers of stupidity every fingerprint, footprint, dust-trace on the estate? Hauptmann has been convicted and doubtless deserves the punishment that will be meted out to him, yet there are many impartial and legally trained minds which dispute the value of the evidence that placed him in the Lindbergh nursery on the night of the kidnapping.

"What wouldn't Prosecutor Wilentz have given for a lone conclusive fingerprint on the crib, windowsill, or ladder? How effectively he could have introduced a moulage reproduction of that footprint underneath the nursery window! Or a handful of dust intelligently swept up and later analyzed for evidence. A European prosecutor would have had all these aids as a matter of routine; the first investigator who reached the scene would have protected with his life (and reputation) that footprint in the mud."

With such critics as these, plus the host of persons who believed in Hauptmann's innocence, there can be no question whatsoever as to why Harold Hoffman was moved, in spite of the mad cries of the "hateful prejudiced" who were demanding that Hauptmann be "thrown to the wolves" in order that the case be termed "successfully closed" regardless of the evidence which could and would prove his innocence.

But the drum beat of "guilty" banged the loudest. The United States Supreme Court turned down a writ of habeas corpus, disallowing any stay of execution. Hauptmann's reprieve had ended, and Justice Trenchard called for his execution to take place the week of March 30. Colonel Kimberling then set the night of Tuesday, March 31st as the time Hauptmann would take his short walk to the electric chair. His time on earth was growing shorter. His friends must quicken their pace in order to help the oppressed, unfortunate and guiltless Hauptmann.

The odds of this happening, however, had already been set against him, arranged by the malfeasance of one, or possibly more, of the prosecution staff; the willingness of a few police officers who were not fit to wear or carry a badge; the inferior defense lawyer who had been hired to defend him; the persons who manufactured the evidence used against him; and the weak members of humanity who were willing to perjure themselves either for the prominence of "short lived fame" or a share of the spoils - or both. What a deplorable shame!

C H A P T E R   F I F T Y   N I N E

The Great Defender!

About the middle of February, Governor Hoffman was informed that Samuel Liebowitz, the famous criminal lawyer, had recently become associated with the Hauptmann defense counsel. This news had been surprising, as well as puzzling to Hoffman, since soon after Hauptmann's arrest, Liebowitz had made it known in his newspaper interviews and radio comments that he frankly held a firm belief of Hauptmann's guilt.

Liebowitz visited Hoffman at his home in South Amboy, New Jersey, and informed the governor that he had gone to the prison and had had a long interview with Hauptmann. The purpose of his visit with Hoffman, who was spending his first day at home after a short stay in the hospital for minor surgery, was to give him one precise message: "Governor, I can make this fellow tell the truth. I am certain of it. But I need your help!"

Because of the vital and integral part Samuel Liebowitz played in our study of the last minute activities which took place immediately before the execution of Richard Hauptmann, it is necessary that, once again, we use the first hand story as it was told by Governor Hoffman.

"'Well, Mr. Liebowitz,' was my reply to the man who had been known as the Great Defender, 'if you have a plan to get the truth, I'm one hundred per cent for it. That's the thing I've been searching for, but I'm still a long way from it--and so is everybody else!'

"Then the noted Brooklyn lawyer unfolded his plan.

"My amazement deepened.

"Long before the verdict in the Flemington trial--even before the defendant had taken the witness chair--Liebowitz had declared writing for the *New York Evening Journal*, that Bruno Richard Hauptmann was guilty. He had reiterated it, I understood, in his radio broadcasts. And yet this man, standing before me in my home--now, God save the mark! a member of the 'defense counsel'--was once more expressing his opinion that Hauptmann was guilty and requesting my co-operation in a plan to get his confession.

"Subsequently Sidney B. Whipple, in one of the great number of books dumped upon the market to convince the public of Hauptmann's guilt and the fairness of the trial, was to say: 'The Governor succeeded in interesting a noted New York criminal attorney, Samuel Liebowitz, in the case.' This was not the most glaring in a series of inaccuracies in Mr. Whipple's book, for this prolific writer on crime, whenever the necessity appeared for furnishing a missing link in the chain of literary evidence against a German carpenter, apparently drew heavily upon his imagination. But at this point, for the information of the public, it seems to be necessary to supplant fiction with facts.

"I had no part in getting Mr. Liebowitz interested in this case. I was, as previously stated, in Mercer Hospital, Trenton, convalescing after an operation, when I first learned of Mr. Liebowitz' entrance in the matter. I never saw nor had I communicated with the attorney until after he had visited Hauptmann in the State Prison.

"To Mrs. Hauptmann, the distracted wife of the man who was shortly to walk to his death, it had been represented that Liebowitz could and would save her husband from the electric chair. Preyed upon by nearly every one with a theory or a plan, the frantic woman had visited the prison and prevailed upon her husband to name the Brooklyn man as a member of the defense counsel--for only in that way, under the New Jersey law, could Liebowitz have obtained access to the prison and to cell 9, which held the doomed prisoner.

"On February 11 Hauptmann wrote to Colonel Mark Kimberling, 'I do not care to see Lloyd Fisher or any of my other attorneys until I notify you personally in writing at a near future date. I wish to thank you in advance for your co-operation in this matter and further trust it meets with your approval. For your information I am very desirous of seeing Mr. Samuel Liebowitz (this name had been inserted in handwriting other than Hauptmann's). It is my definite understanding that all arrangements have been made by my wife for such a interview.' The newspapers carried the information that Hicks had prevailed upon Mrs. Hauptmann to use Liebowitz as a member of the defense counsel.

"Before seeing me Liebowitz had twice seen the prisoner; once with Mrs. Hauptmann and again with Pastor Matthiesen. He had gotten nowhere. He admitted that to me, although to the press he continued to express his belief that Hauptmann was guilty. Never once in these conversations--and this was verified by prison guards who had been in attendance at the interviews--had Hauptmann made the slightest admission, nor had he been trapped during the grueling cross fire of the lawyer's questions. Liebowitz' visit to me, his plea for my help, was further proof that he had not accomplished what was apparently his mission.

"I listened attentively to his plan.

"'Governor', said Liebowitz,' this fellow is guilty--guilty as hell-but he won't admit it.'

"'But, Mr. Liebowitz,' I said, 'you have been saying for many weeks that he was guilty. You said long ago (*New York Evening Journal*, January 29, 1935: Bruno, Seeing Chair, Will Name Accomplices) that Hauptmann was guilty and that when he was convicted and sentenced he would name his accomplices or the principals to whom he was an accomplice.'

"'Yes,' said the lawyer; 'and he will still do it, when I get at him.'

"'But you have been at him,' I replied, 'and yet he hasn't named any one.'

"'The reason for that,' was Liebowitz retort, 'is that Lloyd Fisher keeps continually telling him that he is innocent, and that he will save him--that you will save him. Now, what I want you to do is ask Fisher to go with me to the prison and tell Hauptmann in my presence that he believes he is guilty--that you will no longer help him. There isn't a guilty man in the world that I can't break down--I'll have him crying for help if you'll get Fisher to do that.'

"I said I would talk with Fisher, and I did. Fisher at first wanted nothing to do with Liebowitz. 'He came into the case without my knowledge,' he said. 'He and Hicks worked on poor Mrs. Hauptmann and she convinced Richard that Liebowitz was going to save his life. They pushed me out of the case.'

"I finally obtained Fisher's consent to see the Brooklyn lawyer, but he insisted that I accompany him. Once more I became a party to a plan suggested as a "sure-thing" way to obtain Hauptmann's confession. But if it would aid in getting the truth it was a worth-while venture. Here was a man with a reputation as one of the greatest criminal lawyers in the nation bubbling over with confidence in his own ability to make Hauptmann "crack." That "cracking" of the convicted man might remove the doubt, might supply the missing information demanded by the thousands upon thousands of people who insisted that the doubt be removed before a human life was taken by my state.

"After Liebowitz' second visit to the prison he had issued press statements indicating that he still believed Hauptmann guilty. The distraught wife and her adviser, Lieutenant Hicks, realizing their mistake, implored Fisher to come back into the case. Hicks called Fisher at Flemington at three o'clock the following morning, stating that he was on the way to the Clinton House, at Clinton, and wanted Fisher to join them to discuss the Liebowitz situation. Fisher replied that they had created the situation; that he would not go to Clinton at that time in the morning; that there was nothing to do but allow Liebowitz to continue his visits.

"The young defense lawyer, however, did go to Clinton later in the morning, and found a bitter woman and a contrite 'criminologist' imploring his aid. They urged him to go to the prison to have Richard sign a letter removing Liebowitz from the case and advising the warden to deny him access to the prison. Fisher refused, saying that the barring of the lawyer-journalist would be accepted as indicating that Hauptmann was afraid of being questioned. He knew that the prisoner then, as always, had invited questioning. 'Let Liebowitz play out his string,' was his advice.

"But Liebowitz, not discouraged by his two futile attempts to make Hauptmann break down, called me to arrange a visit with Fisher. He called Fisher directly. Fisher and I agreed to meet Liebowitz at the Hotel Towers in Brooklyn, that night. We met at the Hotel New Yorker and went to the Brooklyn hotel by cab. Although Liebowitz had assured us of the utmost secrecy, reporters quickly made their appearance in the hotel lobby and followed us to the rooms the lawyer had engaged. Photographers were there, too, and we insisted upon privacy for our talk. The manager of the hotel placed his suite, on an upper floor, at our disposal, and there Liebowitz, Fisher, and I had our conference. John Terry, Liebowitz' assistant, came in during part of the session.

"The fiery Fisher let Liebowitz know in no unmistakable terms that he resented his intrusion into the case under the representation that he was a member of the defense counsel; that he considered it unethical to gain admission to Hauptmann's cell and, after a lengthy questioning that produced no results to warrant such a declaration, to state publicly later that his client was guilty.

"'But,' said Liebowitz, 'the important thing is to get the truth.' I assented to that; restated my burning desire to get the truth, whether that truth indicated that Hauptmann was the lone criminal, whether he was innocent, or whether there were others involved.

"To Fisher Liebowitz said: 'This fellow would have confessed long ago but for you. You are his 'prop'--his 'crutch.' He is leaning on you to save his life. Instead of telling him that he is guilty you are bolstering up his courage by your belief that he is innocent.'

"'He is innocent,' angrily retorted Fisher, 'and you know it, too. But you have said and written that he is guilty and that he will name his accomplices. And you don't want the world to know that the great Liebowitz could made a mistake!'

"I succeeded in getting Fisher calmed down. 'How, Mr. Liebowitz, do you think you can get a confession?'

"'By Lloyd going with me to the prison tomorrow and, in my presence, telling Hauptmann; not that he is innocent but that he is guilty. I want him to tell Bruno that the jig is up; that you do not have the power--and you haven't--to save his life. If Fisher will do that, Hauptmann is sure to break. We'll get the truth!'

"Suppose you don't,' interposed Fisher. 'Will you then tell the world that he is innocent?'

"'Yes,' agreed Liebowitz. 'But don't worry about that.' He smiled complacently. 'When I get through with him you'll find out that he is guilty. He'll be crying for mercy.'

"Fisher went through with his bargain. In the interim he did not see Hauptmann. The day following the Hotel Towers interview he went with Liebowitz to the prison--the longest, and one of the strangest, prison interviews on record. But Liebowitz forgot his part of the bargain. Emerging from the prison disheveled and tired, he said, 'My opinion as to Hauptmann's guilt, which I had after close study of the evidence in the case, has not been changed one bit by the three intensive and exhaustive conferences at the death house.'

"The Great Defender forgot that part of that early 'opinion' was that the convicted Bruno had several accomplices; that he would name them when he was within sight of the electric chair. Announcing that he was 'withdrawing' from the case, Liebowitz, baffled in his efforts to secure a confession, admitted that Fisher had helped in every way possible. 'Lloyd Fisher today has been more than co-operative.' he said.

"But let Lloyd Fisher tell the story of that prison visit:

"'Without any word of warning to Hauptmann, we went to the death house for what turned out to be the weirdest death-cell interview ever held. We were there for four hours and twenty minutes--from two o'clock until six twenty. Liebowitz, in the most brutal language possible, pointed out to Hauptmann that the chair was inevitable; that there wasn't a chance in the world to escape. He drew mental pictures of the chair; talked about the smell of burning flesh. He pointed to the death chamber just a few feet away.

"'He went into lengthy theories, asking Hauptmann, too, his opinion as to how the crime had been committed--and what not. He started playing with figures in connection with the handwriting, and finally had it worked out to a point where it was 670 to 1 that Hauptmann didn't write the ransom notes. As Liebowitz would make what he considered to be a telling point he would look at me and ask, 'Isn't that so, Lloyd?' and in line with the arrangement, whether or not the statement was true, I would agree with him. After four hours Liebowitz reached a point where he could stand little more. He was perspiring and bedraggled and he had broken a small vein in his eye. Every argument he had advanced had been met, freely and frankly, by Hauptmann. Finally Liebowitz announced that he was ready to leave.'

"A grim sense of humor was shown by the prisoner at that time. 'As we took our departure,' said Fisher, 'Hauptmann, through the bars, said, 'Come back, Mr. Liebervitcz, if you haf any more questions to ask.' Then he added: 'You know, I haf lots of time.'"

"Liebowitz' association, in the public mind, with the defense counsel and the reaffirmance of his belief in Hauptmann's guilt after three long prison interviews was accepted widely as further proof that Bruno was the sole perpetrator of the Lindbergh kidnap. Yet, according to those who accompanied the lawyer to the cell and who heard the merciless grilling, there had not been the slightest break from Hauptmann's oft-repeated protestations of innocence nor a perceptible swerve from the story he had told at Flemington."

While Governor Hoffman's primary interest at this time, had been the attempt of Liebowitz to obtain a confession from Hauptmann, Ellis Parker had been intensely forging ahead establishing proof that Paul H. Wendel had actually been the "brains" of the kidnapping gang, in the performance of a crime which could not have been committed by one person working alone. This had been the only sensible and logical conclusion, agreed upon by all the police authorities, at the time the crime was committed. This belief included Parker who, at the time of Hauptmann's arrest as the lone perpetrator, had informed the governor: "Harold, they've got the wrong man!"

So relentless had been Parker's quest for the truth, due largely to the approaching date of Hauptmann's execution, that he dug deeper into the facts he already knew of Wendel's involvement, making what turned out to be, a desperate effort to help save an innocent man's life, as he so stated: "A man is sitting in the death house about to be executed for a crime he's completely innocent of."

Now Wendel, who had visited Parker on numerous occasions, continued to feed the detective with segments of his knowledge as to how the kidnapping had been performed, insisting that he was absolutely certain that the kidnapper never came down the ladder with the baby but, contrary to popular belief, had taken him out of the front door of the house. In his earlier contacts with Parker he had claimed he was in a position where he would be able to return the child to his parents. Furthermore, during his later contacts, Wendel had been insistent that Bruno Richard Hauptmann was innocent, having had no part in the crime.

In addition to other factors which had contributed to his "ever tightening" case against Wendel was a name that had been mentioned invariably by Hauptmann at his trial in Flemington. The name happened to be that of Isidor Fisch, Hauptmann's partner in the fur business. Although Parker had also run across a mention of this name in his investigation, he found it necessary to review his notes to find a connection. A short search revealed that Paul H. Wendel, as a practicing lawyer, had represented Isidor Fisch in a court case in Trenton, thus proving by a case of record that the two knew each other and were friends.

However, this fact alone proved very little towards helping Parker, since the authorities had "laughed" at Hauptmann's referral to Fisch, calling it his famous "Fisch story", his only alibi, and a weak one at that, since, after all, the "little man" Fisch was dead.

But, at this point Parker lacked anything conclusive which could link Wendel with Fisch in any criminal activity. Although his investigative mind led him to believe the possibility of an illegal connection between the two, and in spite of the insistence by Wendel that he believed Hauptmann had innocently received the money from Fisch, the suspicious detective could find nothing factual in the way of evidence cementing the two names together other than the court case in Trenton where Fisch had been represented by Wendel at some time in the past.

That was the way things stood until Detective Parker was introduced to two men from Pennsylvania who visited his office in Mount Holly, New Jersey in early 1936, prior to Hauptmann's death. This visit was to <u>prove the involvement of Isidor Fisch and give truth to Hauptmann's only alibi as to where he got the money.</u>

From the information offered him by his two visitors Parker learned some new facts concerning the involvement of Isidor Fisch in the Lindbergh case, something not previously known, but which proved to be more incriminating in support of Hauptmann's insistence that he had innocently obtained the $14,600 of Lindbergh ransom money from Fisch.

Armed with this "fresh ammunition", which added support to Parker's belief that Fisch had obtained possession of some of the ransom money from Wendel, something Wendel had inferred in previous statements to the detective, Parker decided to act since the time of Hauptmann's execution was near at hand.

On Monday, March 30th, the Court of Pardons once again refused Hauptmann's plea for a commutation of sentence; to be followed by an announcement issued by Colonel Kimberling that he had set the next evening, Tuesday, March 31st, as the night of Hauptmann's electrocution.

Parker, realizing the shortness of time, acted with speed as he added to the confusion of the hour by hauling Wendel into jail complete with his complete "confession". Governor Hoffman tells of the events as they happened: "*The Labor News*, a Trenton weekly newspaper, carried the story that Paul H. Wendel, whom I had known as Parker's suspect, had confessed to the commission of the Lindbergh crime. It became known that Wendel was somewhere in Parker's custody. Excitedly Attorney General Wilentz directed Colonel Schwarzkopf to demand the production of Wendel. Schwarzkopf wired Parker to produce Wendel, and the Burlington County detective delivered him up to James Kirkham, a detective serving under the staff of Prosecutor Irwin Marshall of Mercer County. Kirkham promptly lodged Wendel in the Mercer County Jail and charged him (Kirkham subsequently told me that this was done upon orders of the prosecutor) with murder.

"The night Wendel was lodged in the jail the Attorney General and several members of the State Police force were at the Stacy Trent Hotel, and upon being informed that this man was incarcerated, Wilentz, Schwarzkopf, and others visited Wendel in his cell, and emerged after their conference with the statement that the "confession" was false and that it had been obtained under physical duress. It was announced nevertheless, that the Mercer County Grand Jury would conduct a hearing.

"The Court of Pardons met on March 30, and the Wendel "confession" added to the confusion before that body considered, and refused, Hauptmann's application for commutation to life in prison. In his application, which was presented by Lloyd Fisher and Fred Pope (his request to appear in person had been denied), Hauptmann attacked the testimony of the identification witnesses Whited, Hochmuth, Alexander, Rossiter, Condon, Barr, and Perrone, and cited reasons for disbelief in their evidence. The petition requested the Court of Pardons 'to pass on these facts and matters with cool and calm deliberation--with deliberation that is not incited by the cry of the mob, nor by an overwhelming desire on the part of police officials to clear from their records a matter which has been baffling and embarrassing.'

"But Hauptmann once more maintained that he was completely innocent of the crime. Even though he had been given assurance that such a statement might entitle him to leniency at the hands of this court of mercy, he steadfastly refused to say that he had had a hand in the kidnap and murder of the infant Lindbergh.

"It was at the Court of Pardons that I saw <u>for the first time</u>, Messrs. Whipple and associates to the contrary notwithstanding, the purported Wendel confession. Parker had given copies of the confession to Judge Harold Wells of this court. Judge Wells had turned these copies over to the Chancellor, who, in turn, gave them to the Attorney General. Chancellor Campbell gave me one of the copies.

"The Court of Pardons gave deaf ear to Hauptmann's plea. Mrs. Hauptmann, seizing what appeared to be the last straw to save her husband's life, made a charge of murder against Wendel in Hunterdon County. The Mercer County Grand Jury proceeded with its investigation. Parker, members of the Wendel family, Attorney General Wilentz, and many others were summoned before it.

"There was a feeling of intense bitterness and a myriad of flying rumors as the hour set for Hauptmann's death approached. On the evening of March 31, as the witnesses were gathering in the death house, I was sitting in my hotel suite at the Hildebrecht, with three or four of my associates, when a telephone call came from Colonel Kimberling, the warden, announcing that he had postponed the execution upon the request of the Mercer County Grand Jury, transmitted through the foreman, Major Allyn Freeman.

"I was once more charged with giving the prisoner a fresh lease upon life, although as a matter of fact I had no intimation, prior to the Kimberling call, that there was to be a postponement. Justice Trenchard had ordered the warden to execute Hauptmann during the week of March 30. Colonel Kimberling was with complete authority to postpone the death until, and including, Saturday night of that week, and he exercised it.

"On the following day, upon the foreman's request, I appeared before the Grand Jury and told what I knew about the Wendel affair. The courthouse was jammed. There were more flying rumors. Assistant Attorney General Richard Stockton and Sergeant Ritchie, Colonel Schwarzkopf's chauffeur, occupied a room adjacent to the Grand Jury room, apparently interested in Wendel's defense.

"Many witnesses were called. Doctor Condon was requested to appear, and declined. It was a mad, exciting period."

Now, in fairness, we should consider the contents of this confession given by Wendel as we look back to the events preceding the hour that Parker turned him over to Detective James Kirkham in the Mercer County Jail.

As Parker's investigation of Wendel progressed he succeeded in recruiting the help of several men; namely Murray Bleefeld, Harry Weiss, Martin Schlossman, (brother-in-law of Bleefeld) Harry Bleefeld, (Murray's father) and his own son, Ellis, Jr. Each one was properly deputized by Parker in his Mount Holly office and instructed as to what he expected them to do.

Time being a factor, Ellis advised them to pick up Wendel in New York City at the Hotel Stanford on West Thirty-second Street where the detective knew he was staying. Three of the deputies, Bleefeld, Schlossman and Weiss, decided it would be more favorable for them to approach him when he left the hotel. In order to do this they rented a room in the Hotel Martinique, which permitted them to observe Wendel's departure through windows which faced Wendel's room in the Stanford. Only a courtyard separated the two hotels, and with the aid of binoculars they had no trouble watching any activity within his room. At various times Ellis, Jr. joined them in their watch.

At some time about the middle of February as Wendel stepped to the street in front of the Hotel Stanford, Bleefeld and Weiss approached him, and identifying themselves as detectives, told him that Jim De Louie, a New Jersey detective, wanted to see him. Wendel, recognizing the name and believing he had finally been apprehended, went along without opposition, expecting to be taken over to Jersey. Instead he was placed in the back seat of Schlossman's car, between Weiss and Bleefeld, and taken across the Manhattan Bridge. As they proceeded down Flatbush Avenue and Ocean Parkway, Wendel had been placed on the floor in order that the "kidnapped" man would not recognize exactly where he was.

As they arrived at the home of Harry Bleefeld, the three men took him to a furnished room in the basement. Here a blindfold was put on him and a regular guard set up outside the door. Regardless of what Wendel was to testify to and have published at a later date about the terrible treatment he received there, he had not been treated maliciously. Instead, he had bathing privileges provided, he ate well, he had bathroom facilities, he slept on a cot and had a radio to hear music and the news.

Parker had instructed his deputies to tell Wendel that they were mobsters who knew that Wendel had kidnapped the Lindbergh baby. Schlossman was called Hank, Weiss was known as Spidella, and Bleefeld took the name Tony. With names such as these, coupled with their rough demeanor, Wendel naturally believed them to be members of a notorious mob of gangsters.

During the time of his incarceration, Wendel was subjected to intense questioning by his captors. The questions were centered and, with many of them taking the form of accusations, based on "information they told him they knew about, he planned and effected the kidnapping of the Lindbergh baby." While this was taking place, Bleefeld was reporting very little progress being made on his regular trips to his boss in Mount Holly.

It was on one of these visits that Parker said, "Don't worry. One day, Murray, when you least expect it, this man will break down and tell you the whole story. This man is dying to tell the story to somebody. He wanted to tell it to me, Murray, but he was afraid. I know he'll tell it to you because he thinks you're criminals and he'll want you to know that he's the master criminal who did this thing. I know how his mind works, I've known this man for a long time. Just keep telling him how tough he's making it for the boys to make a living because the police are putting the heat on them and he'll eventually break down and tell you the whole story."

Parker's speculation had been correct. They did not have long to wait since the constant coercion Wendel had been subjected to finally convinced him to tell the facts he had thus far been withholding from them. Murray Bleefeld gave author Anthony Scaduto the story of what it was like when Wendel confessed, and Tony told of it in his book *Scapegoat*: "Now, on the fifth or sixth day Wendel breaks down hysterically, he cries and cries and he tells a story from beginning to end, how he kidnapped the Lindbergh baby. Of course, this man was in a basement. There were electric lights but there was no sun, no outside environment. Whether the man realized he was going to be held there until he told us what he did, or whatever reason, just the way Parker described it was the way it happened. He just broke down and started telling us all about it. Nobody hit him with a baseball bat. Nobody mistreated him, nobody... We didn't beat anybody. Ellis didn't do things that way, he used psychology."

Scaduto suggested the possibility of Wendel's confession being brought about because he was being held with no outside environment provided, that possibly he might have thought he would be held there forever. To this suggestion Scaduto wrote that Bleefeld answered "with a large dose of fervor: "No way! I was there, I heard him, I saw him. I believed every word that man said, I know every word was the truth. I can't explain any better than that---just that I <u>knew</u> he was telling the truth."

"Okay. What did he say?", inquired Scaduto, as Bleefeld continued: "Crying hysterically as though he were talking to a thousand people, as though no one were there, oblivious to everything and everybody: he was going to do something that the world would take notice of. He decided that Lindbergh was an international hero and he waited and waited, until that baby was born, until such time that he felt he would have an opportunity to kidnap that baby. And doing this he was going to get even with the world. The world! He was going to kidnap Lindbergh's baby and get money to boot, so he would get everything that he felt the world owed him."

And when asked by Scaduto as to what Wendel said about the actual kidnapping, Bleefeld said: "He talked about watching the house with binoculars for months on end, while the house was being built, when the Lindberghs go, when they come back. And he watched them, he watched them coming back to the house with that baby. He said 'The world believes that somebody went up the ladder and came down the ladder. I went up the ladder. I made those ladders. They were make-shift ladders but they were enough for me to go up to the bedroom. And they were a little too short because I made pieces, three pieces to fit into one another. And they were short but I was tall enough to get over the windowsill and get inside.'"

There is no point to be gained by disclosing any more of Wendel's confession. The events described and related by him cannot be denied, principally because they dove-tailed with occurrences already known in the chronology of the case. However, that is true with but one exception. The fact that the name Hauptmann had already been "forced into" those empty spaces created a major problem for them. With the name of Wendel now provided and made available for their just and honest consideration, based on facts learned by Ellis Parker, the authorities recognized they had a quick decision to make. As expected, their answer was that under no circumstances would they even consider removing the name of Hauptmann and replacing it with the name of Wendel in those empty spaces. It goes without saying the fit would have been much, much better. The police frame-up would not have been needed.

However, returning briefly to the Wendel confession, it is important to note here that in his references to Isidor Fisch, and the connection the two men had together in the kidnapping, he alluded to him as "the man who done me in". According to Wendel, as he was giving Fisch his share of the money he had earned, he told him they were counterfeit bills. Nevertheless, Fisch knowing it was ransom money, grabbed a larger part of it and walked away telling Wendel to "Get lost, you bum."

Having obtained Wendel's written confession, his captors asked him whom he would like to have intercede for him when the news of it became public. They suggested the governor, Colonel Schwarzkopf or Wilentz as those who might possibly be able to obtain a sentence other than death for him. But Wendel insisted there was no one but Ellis Parker, "My friend who helped me when I was disbarred." that he would trust.

Wendel signed his handwritten confession, addressed the envelope, and asked that it be mailed to Parker. Instead Ellis, Jr. called his father and told him of their success and was asked to bring it to him at Mount Holly. Bleefeld and Ellis, Jr. delivered it personally, Parker instructing them to wait several days since Wendel believed the letter was in the mail. Three days later, Schlossman, Bleefeld and Weiss drove Wendel to Parker's Mount Holly home, arriving there about 8:00 p.m.

The following evening Parker told Bleefeld that he had taken Wendel to the New Lisbon Colony, a state mental home. Here he was provided the comfort of a two-room apartment, a living room and bedroom. He was kept there under guard for several weeks, all that time being questioned by Parker, Ellis, Jr. and Mrs. Anna Bading, Parker's secretary, as they learned more of the details from him.

Because of the short time existing until Hauptmann's scheduled execution, Bleefeld told Scaduto that Parker made what he termed a serious mistake, by sending copies of Wendel's confession anonymously to every member of the board of pardons, instead of calling a press conference.

At the time this was taking place an editorial was published in the *Labor News* at Trenton arousing rumors in the form of questions as to: "Who is the person that Ellis Parker has been holding who has confessed to the actual kidnapping of the Lindbergh baby?" Wilentz promptly sent Parker a telegram demanding that he turn his prisoner over to the proper authorities.

There can be little doubt that when Ellis received the order he realized his grave mistake. He told Bleefeld: "Murray, I'm still going to do everything in my power to see that the truth comes out. Even though Wilentz now holds all the cards and will try to make Wendel appear a hero, I'm going to fight this until my dying day. An innocent man's life is at stake." When

Kirkham gets Wendel he has to tell Wilentz about this prisoner he's holding for the Lindbergh crime. Wilentz, in his not so innocent way, and Schwarzkopf in his not so innocent way, let everybody know that there was a man lodged in the Mercer County jail and he was going over to see him.

"So by the time he goes to see him there are cameras, lights, a Hollywood setting. Now he comes to the jail. The entrance is lit up like daylight. Mobs of people surrounding this jail. The public believes they finally got the kidnapper. Now Wilentz comes to the jail. Imagine you're in that jail house, you're Wendel, the guy that was disbarred because you were convicted for embezzlement of a client's funds. You're the guy that Mercer County has warrants out for your arrest for issuing worthless checks. You're a criminal. You're in the jail but you're not in a cell, they got you in a reception room. You're waiting for the attorney general of the state to come in and greet you. And greet him he does. When they walked into the jail they walked up to Wendel, Wilentz, Schwarzkopf, and others. And Wilentz says, 'Hello Paul.' And Paul sticks out his hand and Wilentz takes the criminal's hand and shakes it. And Wendel now becomes instead of a criminal a hero, overnight. Wendel said to him, 'Am I glad to see you.' And Wilentz says, 'Don't worry, Paul, nothing is going to happen to you.' Sure as shooting it's not gonna happen. Not with the attorney general having tried and convicted a man who is in the death house. He isn't going to turn around and tell the world he made a mistake. Not after having fought on the record to tell the world he was convicting the kidnapper of the Lindbergh baby. He isn't apt to tell them that he made a mistake and now he has the real kidnapper. Because if he admits this he makes a complete fool of himself, he'll never be governor, he's liable to be an office boy. Now the camp represented by Wilentz, Schwarzkopf, and all, they go to work to disprove everything that Parker and Hoffman and everybody else did.

"Right away Wendel began to deny his confession. He said, 'I'm glad you're here now, this is what was done to me, this is what I've got, a broken leg and a broken head and a broken mind.' And Wilentz is going to accept it all because he's not about to tell the world that this is the man even if it is the man. And it was the man. And Parker was right and went to his death believing it, and Hoffman died believing it, and my father died believing it. And I'll die believing it. Because it was the truth. Wilentz says to Paul, not Wendel, Paul, sit down Paul, in the Mercer County jail--Parker told me, Hoffman told me, I was talking to these people all the time, I was the active deputy--Wilentz told him to sit down and write everything out, repudiating his confession. He shot it full of holes. The whole thing. He's talking to a criminal to sit down and write it. Imagine telling you or me to do something like this. Then Wendel became a hero. They allowed Wendel to be taken from Mercer County after they got through and Hauptmann was electrocuted . . ."

Scaduto forced a momentary break in Bleefeld's highly spirited explanation with a question: 'Wait. They have a repudiation and a confession. Doesn't it go before a grand jury?'

"Hoffman is still trying to save the pieces. He gives Hauptmann a reprieve for seventy-two hours and he goes before the pardons board begging them to commute the sentence since there is so much evidence of Hauptmann's innocence and so much evidence of Wendel's guilt. All he can get for Hauptmann by law is those three days, he can't give the man more time, during which time a new grand jury will hear the evidence against Wendel and decide whether to indict. If they indict, then the pardons board can't let Hauptmann die.

"But they don't indict. Because Wilentz---the man who would be made a complete fool of should Hauptmann be proved innocent, the man who might even be in a lot of trouble himself if it could be shown that he had a hand in framing Hauptmann---Wilentz is the guy to present the evidence to that grand jury. And what does he do? He makes sure that the official sheet of paper charging Wendel with the murder of the Lindbergh baby, the paper filled out by Mercer County chief of detectives Jim Kirkham, never gets to the grand jury. Since there is no official charge, the grand jury has nothing to investigate."

"Did you hear anything about how Wilentz handled that grand jury? Scaduto asked. "You know as well as I that grand juries are guided and controlled by the prosecutor who's presenting evidence. Did Wilentz control that grand jury?"

"Parker later told me, he knew because the foreman of the grand jury was his close friend, he said Wilentz handled it like he handled the Hauptmann trial. He told them the confession was a lot of poppycock. The man was beaten and tortured, there was no confession, this isn't the man. So they didn't vote an indictment. The case against Wendel is dead.

"And so is Hauptmann. He was executed a couple of nights later. The poor fellow never had a chance. Not with Mr. Wilentz and the honorable Colonel Schwarzkopf, that frame-up artist, and all the power of the mighty state of New Jersey doing their damnedest to spill the blood of the first fall guy who comes along and can be pinned with the kidnapping."

These are the events which had taken place before the execution of Hauptmann, which resulted in a confession made by a man who had voluntarily, with his own free will, answered Parker's request that someone who had knowledge of the stolen child's location get in touch with him. And this resulted with an immediate telephone call, with other calls following, which were all traced to Paul Wendel. Wendel, a former Trenton attorney, once disbarred and then reinstated. Wendel, who was under fire again for unethical transactions. Wendel, who had resigned from the bar. Wendel, who had been a druggist with a knowledge of chemistry that was to fit into a theory that Parker was later to entertain in connection with the finding of the baby's body. Wendel, who had seven indictments then standing against him in Mercer County with charges of embezzlement, false pretenses, uttering worthless checks, and fraud as an executor. Wendel, who had jumped bail and was at the time a fugitive from justice. Wendel, who under the pretext of a charade which caused him to fear he had been kidnapped by gangsters had willingly admitted that he was the kidnapper of the child. Wendel, who after signing his confession, had sought out the help of Ellis H. Parker, the only man he believed he could trust. Deception, yes! Deception used by the world's greatest detective in his effort to solve the world's "Crime of the Century."

But with the aid of his greatest ally, the "honorable" David T. Wilentz, who, the moment he learned of Wendel's confession, sprang into action, by disallowing and disregarding every word of it. Every last word of it and for one reason only --- he the great Wilentz had "proved" otherwise in a Flemington courtroom a year earlier that no one other than Bruno Richard Hauptmann had been the lone kidnapper and killer of Lindbergh's little son.

And so, Wilentz had Wendel quickly write a retraction, a repudiation, of the entire confession. In it Wendel charged Parker and his associates by accusing them of "torturing" him into making a false confession.

In a series of articles Wendel later wrote for *Liberty* magazine, he stated: "Here was I, a simple law-abiding citizen, snatched from the peaceful routine of my daily life." To this Governor Hoffman responded: "It is my opinion that Wendel deserves no sympathy. Undeniably he communicated with Parker, representing that he was in a position to return the child. Those representations exist in his own handwriting; for there followed a long series of communications, some of them written in code, from all parts of the country, to Parker and Anna Bading.

"Parker had devoted his life to the cause of law and order. Books and magazine articles had been written about his successful exploits in crime detection. His name as a detective was legendary in New Jersey; he had solved over three hundred crimes of violence there and in other states."

The hour of Hauptmann's execution had arrived. All hope of another reprieve had passed. Governor Hoffman, once again, brings our memories into sharp focus as he describes the activities that took place both outside and inside the walls of Trenton's State Prison that night of Friday, April 3rd, 1936.

"Radio microphones were being installed; the police were already on duty to keep back the morbidly curious near the State Prison; there was a head being shaved, a trouser leg being slit. Elliott, the gaunt executioner, was testing the current. It was getting dark.

"I sat alone for a few minutes in my office. Then I opened the door and walked out into the reception room, where the reporters had gathered. Curiously enough, it was not sympathy that moved me as I swallowed hard and said:

"'There will be no further reprieve--Hauptmann will die tonight.'

"I was thinking of a figure, blindfolded, holding a sword in one hand and in the other a set of scales--scales supposed to be evenly balanced."

CHAPTER SIXTY

Look, I See A Star!

"Ich bin absolut unschuldig an dem Verbrechen das man mir zur Last legt."

"What did he say?" The Rev. John Gourley, the prison chaplain, turned his eyes from the pasty, greenish-white face of Hauptmann to gaze eagerly at the lips of John Matthiessen, standing by the side of the prisoner.

"He says," replied the German pastor, "that he is absolutely innocent of the crime that has been laid at his door."

The dialogue above was taken from the account of Hauptmann's final moments exactly as Governor Hoffman wrote it for his series of articles which appeared in *Liberty* magazine in 1938.

I have used this because I believe, if possible, it is appropriate that you sense an inkling of the trauma that permeated the inner walls of the Trenton State Prison as Hauptmann awaited his death.

I trust that you have been convinced of Richard Hauptmann's complete innocence. If so, then you should be able to wholly relate to this, and I would ask you to come along with me to the Trenton State Prison and picture yourself as suddenly being accused of committing a very tragic and brutal crime of which you know absolutely nothing, nothing more than Hauptmann did, and with nothing more to answer your accusers than your truthful plea of innocence, but sadly enough, one that the greater majority of the nation's people refused to believe.

There is great pathos, great sadness, in the words that follow. Therefore, it becomes necessary that you envision, as best you can, what took place on the night of Friday, April 3rd, 1936 as the innocent Richard Hauptmann was being prepared for that moment when he would shortly draw his last breath, when his life would be taken for a villainous crime in which he had been diabolically and maliciously "blamed", as the lone criminal, a scapegoat, held and "proven" guilty as charged, for something he knew absolutely nothing about. And as you read, try to empathize with Anna Hauptmann who was never to see her husband alive again. The man she deeply loved was to be taken from her - and he would never return to his dear Anny. The scene is a sorrowful one.

Governor Hoffman's vivid, heart-rending account follows:

"In a few minutes five men - two men of God, two blue uniformed prison guards, and a man accused and convicted as the murderer of a blond curly-haired child loved by the whole world--started in a hideous procession through a steel-flanked doorway that led to a sinister object in the center of New Jersey's death chamber. The five men walked about seven paces. Only four of them walked back.

"The man who did not walk back had spent over sixteen months behind prison bars -long months that led up to what must have been three last days of almost unbearable mental agony and physical distress. And those last days seemed to reach a climax - a peak of human futility and suffering - at just about quarter after eight on the night of April 3. From that moment on it seemed that bitterness left Bruno Richard Hauptmann and a peaceful calm descended upon him.

"I am writing this account of the manner in which Hauptmann met his death meted out to him by the law in the very room where, nearly two years ago, Lloyd Fisher cried as he told me of his last moments with his doomed client. It is the same room from which I departed on the evening of October 16, 1935, to visit Hauptmann; the same room to which I returned to jot down the record of my strange prison interview with the strange man who had been the lone hated figure in a strange case.

"Across my desk in this room, but a few minutes ago, I looked into the faces of two men who had been with the fiercely condemned German carpenter many hours during those last days. One of them, Fisher, had squeezed Hauptmann's arm through his cell bars and had said good-by to his client an hour before he was strapped in the lethal chair. A soldier who had often seen death claim other men in France, this fighting young lawyer could not bear to see a man die - a man who he believed, deeply, intensely, to be innocent of the crime for which he was to pay the penalty.

"The other, the Rev. John Matthiesen, the German Lutheran minister who had been the spiritual adviser of

Hauptmann, had been at the left side of the convict, reading the Scriptures in his native language, as 2,000 volts of electric current burned out the life of him.

"They told me - they can never forget them - their last experiences with Hauptmann.

"'When I went to see Hauptmann on March 31, the day first set for the execution by Kimberling,' said Fisher, 'my client seemed terribly broken up. He had been moved out of cell 9, in which he had pictures of his wife and baby and some fairly comfortable furnishings, into an adjacent cell. Hauptmann wanted to know why this was done. 'I haf been a good prisoner,' he said. 'I haf nefer made anybody any trouble. I nefer haf broken a rule. Vy should dey do dis to me?' He mentioned that Charles Zeid, who was scheduled to die the same night, had not been moved from the cell he had occupied. Pointing to a chair, the lone article of furnishing in his cell, he said, 'Vy should I be pushed around ven dis is my last day to live?' I explained to him that it was one of the prison rules to move a prisoner on the last day, but Hauptmann still seemed to be terribly excited over the occurrence at the time I left.'

"Fisher continued: 'I went back at about three thirty that afternoon, and told him that the Wendel matter was being considered by the Grand Jury and that I would return if there was any news. That night at eight twenty I went and told him that a forty-eight-hour stay had been granted by Kimberling. He had in some way sensed it - or had been told already by one of the prison officers - for he did not seem surprised.

"'When I went back to see him on the 3rd I had a long earnest talk with Richard. He reiterated his innocence; said he had told everything he knew. 'You don't know, Lloyd,' he said, 'vhat I vent through vith three days ago. Efen now I don't know vat to do. If I cry like often I vant to do vhen I think of Annie and Bubi, everybody dey vill say I am guilty. If I fight vith my heart and soul dey vill say I am cold-blooded fellow like von who vould commit such a crime.'

"Lloyd went on: 'Each time I left, Richard asked me if I would go to see his wife and tell her he was all right. He asked me especially not to tell her about moving him from one cell to another. I went to the prison at about seven thirty on that last night. They held up a parade of official witnesses to let me pass through the prison yard. When I got to the cell Dr. Gourley, the prison chaplain, and Pastors Werner and

Matthiesen were not there.

"'The pastors stepped away from the cell. The usual screen was down and I talked with Hauptmann through the bars. 'I can see by your face, Lloyd, dot it is bad news. Have you seen the Gofe'nor?' 'Yes, Richard,' I said, 'and his hands are tied. He can't do anything. My God! Isn't there anything you can tell me - anything at all you know? If you can say something maybe I can still stop this thing.' He looked at me as if pained at my implying that he might know something further. 'You know, Lloyd, dere isn't anything I can say. You know me as better as any von down here, Lloyd, and you know I know not'ing about dot crime.'

'Yes, I believe that, Richard,' I said, shaking his hand through the bars. I'm going to the warden's office, and I'll wait there.'

"'I had walked two or three paces away when he called 'Lloyd' in such a low voice that one of the guards was obliged to call my attention. I walked back and Hauptmann said, 'I vant to say good-by to you again, Lloyd; you haf been very kind to me.' At that time there was certainly no sign of physical or mental breakdown. He talked to me as clearly and as concisely and as intelligently as he had all through the case. For that reason I can't subscribe to the theory of Courtney Ryley Cooper, who says that Hauptmann died in the dressing room or that he was mentally dead when he entered the death chamber. His voice and his actions were as firm as they usually were.'

"Pastor Matthiesen, too, bore out Fisher's testimony to Hauptmann's courage in the last moments - you can hardly call it bravado in the light of the clergyman's story:

"'I arrived at Hauptmann's cell at seven thirty. His head had been shaved. Dr. Gourley and Mr. Werner were there. We took turns reading the Scriptures. I read the Fourteenth Chapter of John. Suddenly Hauptmann turned away from us. He went to the opposite side of his cell, dropped on one knee, and bowed his head. Later some one - I think it was one of the guards - told a story that he cried and fell down to the floor. That is not so. Hauptmann was praying.

"'After five or six minutes he got up and came over to us. He was smiling. 'I am happy now,' he said. 'I am at peace with my God and I am not sorry to leave a world that does not understand me.' He spoke to me in German and exacted from me several promises - to assist his wife, to do everything possible to clear his name, and to fight against the taking of life by the law on circumstantial evidence. Then he said, 'You may now open the door.'"

"Outside the cell Hauptmann stood up straight like a soldier. He thanked the guards, and turned and faced the door to the death chamber. As we started to walk he looked up at the skylight in the roof of the death house. 'Look,' he said: 'I see a star.'

"'Then he turned to the right as we passed cell 9 where he had spent nearly thirteen months. 'Please,' he said, 'let me look once more at Bubi's picture.' We stopped a moment as he looked at the photograph on the wall of his old cell and then moved on through the door to the death chamber, where all the reporters and witnesses were waiting. Hauptmann was walking between two guards, but they did not touch him. They did not need to. He walked straight to the chair and sat down. He did not tremble; he did not shake. That man was not afraid.'

"There was a strange glare in the death-chamber lights. Warden Kimberling had ordered the witnesses 'frisked' for cameras and had installed special bulbs that would defy photography. There was to be no repetition of the shoetop-camera episode that had shocked public sensibilities in connection with the Ruth Snyder execution. A screen of cloth, waist-high, had been stretched between the witnesses and the electric chair.

"But there were no photographs as the prison officers, directed by Elliott, tightened the straps around Hauptmann's arms and legs, or as they fastened the mask to hide the distortions of the eyes and mouth.

"The guards stepped back. Pastor Matthiesen, in a clear voice, read now from the Ninetieth Psalm: 'And let the beauty of the Lord our God be upon us: and establish thou the work of our hands -'

"The executioner turned a wheel. There was a sudden creaking of straps. A tiny wisp of smoke. And another.

"A doctor stepped forward with his stethoscope. A chest was bared. A few words were mumbled. Guards with busy shaking fingers loosened some straps and carried a limp something into a barren little back room.

"With an oath, a newsman shouted, 'it's terrible!'

"The little door in the other end of the death chamber was opened. There was a mad rush for telephones, telegraph instruments - and fresh air. The public was waiting. The radio was the first to carry the news:

"BRUNO RICHARD HAUPTMANN IS DEAD!"

"Sitting in my office in the State House. Governor of the State of New Jersey, I heard that statement - and wondered. I wondered, among many things, just how many people, in any corner of the world, would hear that news and give a sigh of relief - a sigh that would be an indication of more than mere satisfaction that vengeful society had taken its exacting toll for the murder of Charles Augustus Lindbergh, Jr.

"At the Stacy Trent Hotel, less than a half mile from the prison, a sobbing woman waited until a knock was heard at the door. Miss Adams, companion-newspaper writer, opened it to admit Fisher's secretary, Laura Apgar, bearing the grim news: 'Sorry -it's all over!'

"Crying hysterically, Mrs. Hauptmann rushed into the bathroom and locked the door. There had been talk of intended suicide. Excited hands were hammering upon the door when Fisher arrived, accompanied by the German clergymen. One of them, in German, entreated the frantic woman to come out. Finally she emerged, to rush in another room and throw herself on the bed. Now and then she would beat her hands on the wall. Words of comfort had no perceptible effect on the grief-stricken widow of Hauptmann and the mother of "Bubi".

"A New York reporter, "Mike" Something-or-Other, a cameraman, and two other reporters who had forced their way into the room tried to get her to talk and to pose for pictures. 'Our editors - ' they started.

"'Get out!' yelled Fisher. 'Let this poor woman alone!' Then the young lawyer put his hand on Annie Hauptmann's shoulder, started to talk, and stopped. He turned, took a handkerchief out of his pocket, and softly walked out of the room himself.

"Fisher came straight to my rooms at the Hildebrecht. After a brisk talk, already related, he left. I went to bed, but didn't sleep.

"Sergeant Steve Barnocky, my chauffeur, came in early in the morning with six or seven newspapers. I sat up in bed and glanced at the front page of the *New York American*. There was a story with Damon Runyon's by-line and the heading:

BRUNO DIES IN CHAIR

"All the papers had a lot of information about Hauptmann. Claiming steadfastly that he was 'innocent' and, after his last moments in prayer, urging his spiritual advisers to fight against the further taking of human life on circumstantial evidence, he had paid the ultimate penalty demanded by justice.

"I read some of the accounts of the execution:

"... mentally dead when he entered the death chamber."

"... held up by two prison guards."

"... didn't talk; perhaps he was too weak to talk."

"My mind went back to a prison cell on an October night. A white-faced man was sitting beside me on a gray-blanketed cot. 'Lies! Lies! All lies!' he was saying.

"Whether or not conscienceless untruth or proven fact had been responsible, the seared body of this man Hauptmann, on that bright morning of April 4, was lying upon a cold slab in the whitewashed room that is a necessary auxiliary of New Jersey's death chamber.

"Accompanied by Henry Stolzenberger, an undertaker of the Bronx, a bitter woman, still sobbing, went to claim her dead. To the man Colonel Kimberling handed a letter reading, 'Under Chapter 79, Laws of 1906, no religious or other services shall be held over the remains after such execution -'

"On the day he entered the prison Hauptmann had told Fisher, 'Lloyd, I come in here today a man; maybe some day soon I got out just a piece of clay.'

"The 'piece of clay' was taken to a crematory and was reduced to ashes. Anna Hauptmann, a few days later, went to the Trenton Prison and signed a receipt for a toothbrush, some books, some letters, and some pictures, 'the property of inmate No. 17400.'

"Cell 9 was cleaned and tidied up, awaiting the occupancy of the next man to be thrown into the electric maw of death. No trace was left in that cell of the man who, in the summation of the state before the Flemington jury, was called an 'animal lower than the lowest form in the animal kingdom ... public enemy number one of the world ... pantherlike ... coldhearted ... a fellow with ice water in his veins, not blood ... vilest snake that ever crept through the grass ...'

"It was in cell 9 that Hauptmann had bitterly protested to me, 'Nefer once haf I injured a human being.'

"It was in front of that cell that Hauptmann,

walking to the chair, had turned for a last look at the photograph of his baby boy Manfred. In front of that cell, too, he had turned his eyes upward to the death-house skylight, saying, 'I see a star.'

"Lloyd Fisher told me an interesting story about that skylight, Hauptmann, and a bird. 'The skylight,' said Fisher, 'was in the ceiling of the corridor directly in front of Hauptmann's cell. It is built of heavy glass, in metal frames, forming a sort of compartment that extends above the death-house through the skylight; in a grating of iron bars, covered with meshed wire.

"'One afternoon when I went to see Hauptmann he was visibly agitated. 'Look', he said, pointing through the bars to the skylight. A sparrow had flown through an opening where the frames were parted to admit a little fresh air. It was fluttering about aimlessly and hopelessly, beating its little wings against the wire and the bars. 'Do somet'ing, Lloyd,' asked Richard; 'a free t'ing like dot should nefer be in dere.' I called one of the guards - I think it was Lou Happ. He got a long pole and we tried to release the bird, without success. During all my talk with Hauptmann the rest of the afternoon his mind and his eyes seemed to be continually upon the imprisoned bird. I never thought of it again until just now, when you mentioned Matthiesen and the incident about the skylight. I wonder if the sparrow got out - or if Hauptmann saw it die.'

"Fifty-five people - more than twice the number that had ever witnessed an execution in New Jersey - saw Hauptmann die. They jammed the little death chamber, some morbidly curious, some vengeful, some inwardly rebelling - just as others had jammed the little courtroom at Flemington to watch Hauptmann, trapped, beating hopelessly against the legal net that had been woven to hold him.

"He had become, as he predicted, 'another dead to the Lindbergh case.' The list was and is growing: the cruelly murdered baby, Ollie Whateley, Elsie Whateley, Violet Sharpe, Isidor Fisch, Hauptmann, two jurors - and who can tell how many others? Others who may have taken to the grave - or to the crematory - secrets that, told, might have solved the riddle of the case that still challenges the world.

"I use that phrase 'challenges the world' advisedly.

"The police appear to have abandoned the Lindbergh

case, a foundling on the doorstep of Time. But that foundling, nurtured at the breast of suspicion and reared in an environment of doubt, is alive, very much alive, today. The electric chair did not become the dead end in the Lindbergh trail. That trail is still being trodden by hundreds - perhaps thousands - of searchers for the complete truth. They are searchers who will never be satisfied with the net of evidence that was strong enough to bring the death penalty to a lone suspect and yet so weak that it could not kill the doubts of the American people.

"It is a queer trail, the trail of the Lindbergh case, with many mysterious twists and turns. At times the searchers proceed upon firm ground, in the open light, only to be enveloped shortly in the ominous shadows of the forest of incredulity. There are places along that trail where tiny paths, marked by mysterious footprints, branch off boldly, only to vanish.

"There are some who claim that this trail winds way back into the bustling Bronx. There are others who profess to find its origin in exclusive Englewood, perched near the crest of the beautiful Palisades. Wherever the origin of the trail, there is general agreement that the first discernible landmark is to be found in staid old Hunterdon County, New Jersey, where an imposing home of whitewashed fieldstone, of the French-manor type, had been reared, secluded and almost inaccessible, close to the crest of the Sourland Mountains."

True, it was here the Lindbergh case began! However, before we reveal the maze of heretofore unknown truths, the labyrinth of facts, which, not only, conclusively prove the innocence of Bruno Richard Hauptmann, has made his final words remain alive over the past fifty-nine years. Never were truer words spoken.

"They think when I die, the case will die. They think it will be like a book I close -- but the book it will never close."

Bruno Richard Hauptmann

At Kent, England, as all the British newspapers were publishing full accounts of Hauptmann's death during the days following the execution, the Lindbergh's remained in seclusion at their home "Long Barn" for the next few days.

For them, they believed the book had finally been closed --- forever.

CHAPTER SIXTY ONE

Richard's Faith!

Warden Kimberling's answer, when asked if Hauptmann had made any statement before he went to the chair, had apparently been a disappointment to the press since more than a few in the news media had expected him to make a complete confession. They found it hard to believe that they had already heard everything Hauptmann had to tell. As he had previously stated on every occasion: "I have told all I know about the crime.", they had simply refused to accept this as factual. But it was nevertheless true since Hauptmann, very plainly, had absolutely no confession he could have found possible to make.

However, true as the warden stated: "He said nothing!", his reference was to the minutes remaining immediately preceding Hauptmann's execution. Certainly everyone had been made aware that prior to his final day of life Hauptmann had said much as he fervently proclaimed his innocence.

It is noteworthy that we repeat the many statements he made during his incarceration. It is only fair that we review exactly what he did tell the authorities when, for the very first time, he came to the realization that the $14,600 found in his possession was undoubtedly and undeniably Lindbergh ransom money.

Finding the ransom money in Hauptmann's possession was certainly very incriminating evidence to say the very least. However, we must bear in mind that as incriminating as any evidence is which favors the guilt of any person accused of any crime, this fact alone does not and should not be enough to reach a conviction of guilt. This would be especially so if that person presents undeniable factual evidence which would go far to support that person's claim of his or her innocence. This should also be the case if the accused person presents a logical explanation, and a possibly believable one, that would have accounted for his or her actions.

Hauptmann's reasonable explanation as to how he

came into possession of the ransom money has been dealt with earlier in the text of my story. But now, we must look at the statements he made following his arrest, those made at his hearings and subsequent trial, and even more importantly, those made as he awaited his execution. All I urge you to do is use your God given power of fair reasoning as you study and absorb his statements. However, we must keep in mind that these were expressed by an innocent man, one who was fighting for his very life. Now let's look at what Hauptmann did say!

Speaking to the press from his cell in Flemington, New Jersey, the day following his sentencing: "I want to tell the people of America that I am absolute innocent of the crime of murder. My conviction was a great surprise. I never saw the Lindenbergh (sic) baby and never received any money. I want to appeal to all people everywhere to aid me at this time. A defense must be raised to carry my appeal to a higher court. Before God, I am absolute innocent. I have told all I know about the crime."

Other reporters, after being told that he was attempting to raise some money from the public, inquired as to whether it was true that he had been offered a large sum of money if he would confess his involvement in the kidnapping. Hauptmann explained: "If I had anything to confess I would have done it months ago, so as to spare my wife and mother all they have gone through. If they came to the door and opened it and said, you can go free if you tell the whole truth, I couldn't tell them anything because I have already told the whole truth."

When he was asked if he was afraid of dying in the electric chair, he replied: "You can imagine how I feel when I think of my wife and child. It is them that I fear for. For myself I fear nothing, because I am innocent."

Many journalists had written stories that presented Hauptmann as not being a religious man, and when asked if this were true, he replied: "I am probably more religious than most people who go to church. I am a friend of nature. I have always been a Lutheran. I pray in my heart and not only since I was here. If there is anybody in the United States to whom I did any wrong and from whom I took a penny in any dishonest way, I'd like that man or woman to step forward and say so ... I make an appeal to the whole American public to help me ... so I will not have to die in the electric chair."

At this time Hauptmann had less than six months to live. His visitors were mainly his loyal wife Anna, his attorney, Lloyd Fisher, and his two spiritual advisors, the Reverend John Matthiesen, a German Lutheran minister, and the Reverend D.G. Werner of the First Adventist Church.

The Bible and the trial testimony were his principle items of reading material. His constant faith that God would open the prison doors for him remained strong. He firmly believed in miracles which only God alone could do. He studied the many promises and prophecies of Christ and his second coming to this earth, and claimed the hope in the stirring opening verse of Psalm 121 which reads: "I will lift up my eyes unto the hills, from whence cometh my help."

Christ had become so real in the life of Richard Hauptmann that as three of the seven prisoners on the top tier of the death house cells, while passing his cell on their way to the execution chamber, all paused to shake his hand as they bid him a final farewell. As they spoke their final words to one another, he urged each one to pray and receive Christ as their saviour.

During Hauptmann's incarceration, many ugly and unfair rumors were fostered on the public, primarily by those who wanted to paint a picture of the man as some sort of fiend who lacked any morals whatsoever. But, contrary to the host of false charges, innuendos, and untruths that were leveled at him, especially regarding a so-called unfaithfulness to his wife Anna, nothing could have been further from the truth. From the time of their first meeting, which eventually led to their marriage, he had remained faithful to her in every sense of the word. And she to him. His beloved "Anny" was the object of his every affection. This love was shared only after the birth of his little son, Manfred, in 1933. He was known among his friends as a family man.

Hauptmann's devotion to his wife can be clearly seen in this letter he wrote to her from his cell during the summer of 1935.
It reads:

My dear Anny,

It is nearly two weeks since I saw you last time, so therefore I will write to you; if it would permit it to write in my mother tongue, you certainly would get one letter after another. But you know, dear Anny, I can not express myself as I would like to and as I feel in my heart.

The last time you was visiting me you said you would like to bring our baby to me. O dear Anny, you know how I would like to see my baby, all my thoughts are by him and you. But I can not allow you to bring our child, our sunshine, behind these walls. Even when he don't know where he is when he see me, this would not give me any justification. As long as I can prevent it, our child shall never come behind these walls. So, therefore, I have to wait till I come home again.

Furthermore, dear Anny, can you imagine how I would feel when I see you and the baby, my heaven on earth, going from me and I have to stay in this terrible place. It would be a struggle against madness. I have stand a great deal of suffering already, but that would be the end. You said, people said I was never asking to see my baby. Of course they will say I must be a madman. Did people ever understand me or was trying to understand me? They probably will better when they have read my life story.

Dear Anny, I know positive that I will be home again and then our happy family life will continue. Just now, I have to be satisfied to have only the picture from you and the baby in here. Every night between seven and eight, I kiss the baby and you, like before as we did together. Brahm's beautiful lullaby, I know it is the time to put the baby to bed. To be in thought of my family is one thing nobody can take away from me; it is all what remains left and there is no possibility for stealing it.

My love for you and the baby and my belief in God, no one can lay his hand on it. These are two supremes that cannot be stolen through circumstantial evidence.

Dear Anny, when I say I am positive sure, that I have to come home free, and is based only belief in God. I know He never permit that some persons commit a murder on me. Just now, I am like a ball in a child's hands and they like to play with it. But the dishonor will not rest on my shoulder, but it will rest on the shoulder of the State. Because the State must be responsible on the group of men who was working only in their own interest and not in the course of justice, this was only a matter of secondary consideration, but to win this case and so to climb higher on the political ladder was more important as justice. Therefore this false sentence never will stand, not before God and not before the American nation.

Dear Anny, you are wondering always when you come visiting me that I am so happy. It is not only the happiness in seeing you, it is also a quiet happiness that I have in my heart that I know the time will come when the truth comes out and then the people will say I am innocent. For this time, my dear Anny, let us pray together and fold the hands of our child to pray to God; God is with us, then we will soon be together in happiness and love.

Your Richard

Kiss the baby from me and when possible bring some pictures to me.

Paulina Hauptmann, Richard's mother, in a letter she wrote to Governor Hoffman from her home in Germany, confirmed her faith in her son's innocence:

As the mother of the condemned man, who bore and raised him in a God-fearing family, I may be forgiven if, nevertheless, I cannot believe in Bruno's guilt. Although certain outward appearances may be irrefutably against him, I feel distinctly that Bruno, who was always a model son to me, and is himself the loving father of a little boy, could not be and is not the real perpetrator of this dastardly crime.

Up to the very last of the many letters which Bruno has written me from his prison cell, he has again and again firmly stated his innocence. Moreover thousands of people, personally unknown to me, who followed all the details of the trial, have spontaneously written me that the prosecution merely insisted on having him pay the penalty of death because, otherwise, the blame for not having cleared up the mystery of the murder would permanently rest upon them.

Almighty God in His infinite wisdom has invested Your Excellency with the supreme prerogative of pardon and clemency. I beseech you to exercise them for the benefit of Bruno Hauptmann, my beloved son, whose ignominious death on the electric chair would break my heart. I implore you, Mr. Governor, to use the dignity of your high office in not permitting that a man undergo the one penalty that is irreparable on merely circumstantial evidence.

Reverend John Matthiesen, pastor of Trinity Lutheran Church, also convinced of Hauptmann's innocence, expressed this belief in a letter to the New Jersey Court of Pardons. However, because of the stand he took in Hauptmann's behalf, he was rebuked by his parish council. His letter, in part, reads:

I have had fifteen very intimate and soul searching interviews with Bruno Richard Hauptmann, and am convinced that he tells the truth. If Hauptmann had had a reliable defense lawyer at the outstart, and if he had asked for an interpreter during the trial, the very evidence used against him would have spoken in his favor. Hauptmann felt no need for them until it was too late. After careful study of that case I have come to that conclusion.

First, know Hauptmann as he really is, and his wife Anna, and then study the evidence; and you will arrive at the same conclusion. Hauptmann does not fit into the frame of circumstantial evidence. I bring these findings to your honorable members of the Court of Pardons not because of sympathy for Hauptmann, although I claim to know him better than anyone with the exception of his wife, but I want to see justice prevail.

I would ask for the supreme penalty if Hauptmann were guilty. My creed has no objections to that. There is nothing else in my mind than this: that I may serve the state of New Jersey with my findings. I feel it is a sacred duty I have to discharge.

Lloyd Fisher, Hauptmann's attorney, following the Court of Pardons refusal to commit his client's sentence to life in prison, once again told the press: "I believe that Hauptmann is innocent and nothing has happened in any shape, form or manner to change that. He is as guiltless as any of you."

For the most part the news media of that day did their usually excellent job of portraying Hauptmann as a heartless, arrogant man, one who had no feeling of love and compassion toward the world around him. But, once again, nothing could be further from the truth. On the contrary, Richard Hauptmann was a gentle and mild-mannered man. When he finally realized the depth and seriousness of the charges which had been brought against him, and knowing within himself that the charges were false, he did not strike out savagely at his accusers, but instead honestly attempted to rationalize how it could be possible that his fellowmen could, by such deception and trickery, lay such unfair and untrue charges at his feet.

The claim that Richard was incapable of expressing any tender feelings was equally untrue and definitely unfair. During the time of his imprisonment he shed many a tear. There were many times when he broke down completely. Following his sentencing, his eyes brimming with tears, he spoke lovingly and emotionally of his wife "Anny" and his little "Bubi", the affectionate name they called their young son Manfred. But, in spite of these facts it served his accusers far better to portray him in another light - that of a beast. During the early morning hours of March 31st, 1936 the condemned man sat in his cell and penned the following letter to Governor Hoffman. At the time of its delivery at the executive mansion, 11:30 a.m., Hauptmann fully expected to die that evening. However, a last minute reprieve delayed the execution until three days later. Here is the letter:

Trenton, March 31, 1936

Your Excellent Governor,
Harold G. Hoffman,
Your Excellence:

My writing is not for fear of losing my life, this is in the hands of God, it is His will. I will go gladly, it means the end of my tremendous suffering. Only in thinking of my dear wife and my little boy, that is breaking my heart. I know until this terrible crime is solvet, they will have to suffer unter the weight of my unfair conviction.

In passing away, I assure your Excellence that I am not guilty of this crime. Over and over again I was trying to convince the prosecution that they murder an innocent man. I offert myself to any test what science may offer --- but I was begging in vain. I did this, not to force the prosecution to put me free, but only to convince the world that I am innocent.

In living my last hours of my life, I wish I could bring some light in this case, but all what I can do, is to give a description of the friend of Mr. Fisch, whom I sah the first time when I meet Mr. Fisch. (Description I have given already, also all the circumstances.)

Were I connected in any part of this terrible crime, I never would have trouble your Excellence in any way. This same I never would have ask the Court of Errors and Appeals, also the Court of Pardons to take my cause in consideration. I know in my one sense of justice that a person guilty of such a crime, can't deserve any consideration. But I was fighting with clear conscience I did have a right to do so before God and the world.

May I ask fair thinking people --- would I have

been convicted of this crime without the circumstantial evidence, and them false witnesses --- No! Never and Never. Why did people say on the witness stand they saw me near Hopewell. The motive can be only money and to play an important part in the Lindbergh case. Up to the present day I have no idea where the Lindbergh house in Hopewell is located.

Why did, and does Dr. Condon hide so many things he knows? It is not for the course of justice that this man says everything. Why did Dr. Condon say in my cell he cannot testify against me? My God, Dr. Condon and your witnesses, did you ever realize what you did? In a short time I will stand before a higher Judge and you will live a little longer, but you and you never can leave this world with a happier inner feeling as I do.

Gentlemen from the prosecution where are all the direct evidence? Fingerprints, footprints, you all know there are some in existence. Oh yes! For what did the police take right by my arrest all my shoes? Why all them special fingerprints from part of the hand from where the usual never take?

Why was it said to the jury I had $49,984 Dollars of Lindbergh money? You know it was not true, or half hour after my conviction your self send an officer to me that I should say where are the other $30,000 Dollars. Why did you say to the jury that people saw gold bills in our house but never brought this people on the witness stand? For what did you through all this same in the eyes of the jury, them two persons whom are judging offer my life?

Who is responsible for building up all the circumstantial evidence? Is there really a man who can believe that I, a carpenter, should have built such a ladder?

I stated that I found the money middle of August, 1934, and that I past the money without knowing it was Lindbergh money. Is there any person who can say that I past one single bill before that date?

Why did my Chief Lawyer send important witnesses home without even bringing them on the stand. My God, my God, I hardly can't believe on all that what happened by my trial. But it was necessary to convict me and so close the books on the case.

Mr. Wilentz with my dying breath, I swear by God that you convicted an innocent man. Once you will stand before the same judge to whom I go in a few hours. You know you have done wrong on me, you will not only take my life but also all the happiness of my family. God will be judge between me and you.

I beg you, Attorney General, believe at least a dying man. Please investigate, because this case is not solvet, it only adds another dead to the Lindbergh case.

Your Excellence, I see this as my duty, before this State takes my life, to thank you for what you have done for me. I write this with tears in my eyes. If ever prayer will reach you, they will come from me, from my dear wife and my little boy.

In all your effort to save my life and see that justice is done, I assure your Excellence, that your effort was spent to an innocent man.

I thank you Excellence, from the bottom of my heart and may God bless you,

Respectfully,

Bruno Richard Hauptmann

Why was not any consideration given to my four witnesses whom saw me in the same hour between 8 - 9 in the Bakery in New York? On the 1st of March 1932? There were no friends of mine. There are all strangers to me. Even one of them came in very bad condition from the sick bed. No witness from the State came up at all to cover this particular period, to place me in New Jersey.

The words of that letter were those of an innocent man who had expressed his feelings from the very depth of his heart. A man who had attempted to explain his innocence to a society outside the prison walls, who largely did not believe him, did not want to, and did not intend to. And because Governor Harold G.Hoffman put forth some effort to help the condemned man, he was publicly criticized by the news media of that day.

Hauptmann's remaining time on earth was spent largely in hours of prayer and in reading the Bible. The visits of pastors Werner and Matthiesen proved to be of great spiritual help to him as they knelt in prayer together in the small cell. It was during this time that Hauptmann wrote an article which he requested to be printed after his death. I believe the final paragraph exemplifies his sincere plea that someone, somewhere believes in him. It reads:

> "And so I sit, ten feet removed from the electric chair, and unless something can be done to aid me, unless something

> can be done to make some one tell the truth, or unless some one does tell it, I shall at eight o'clock Friday evening, in response to the call from my keepers, raise myself from my cot for the last time and shall walk that "last mile." I suppose there will be in that chamber some of those who have had part in the preparation of my case for the prosecution. It is my belief that their suffering, their agony, will be greater than mine. Mine will be over in a moment. Theirs will last as long as life itself lasts.

The final statement made by Hauptmann was one written in German and later translated into English. It had been composed on a single sheet of paper and handed to Lloyd Fisher by the reverend Matthiesen. It read:

> "I am glad that my life in a world which has not understood me has ended. Soon I will be at home with my Lord. And as I love my Lord, so I am dying an innocent man.
>
> Should however my death serve for the purpose of abolishing capital punishment ... I feel that my death has not been in vain.
>
> I am at peace with God. I repeat, I protest my innocence of the crime for which I was convicted. However, I die with no malice or hatred in my heart. The love of Christ has filled my soul, and I am happy in Him."

A reporter was assigned to call on Paulina Hauptmann at her home in Kamenz, Germany the morning after Richard's electrocution to inform her of her son's death the night before. Her faith that God would prevent this from happening had been so great that the news was a severe shock to her. Muttering, "It can't be, it can't be, it's impossible.", in shock, she broke down completely, trembling and crying, "Oh my dear son, my only hope, what have they done to you? Oh, God, how could it happen? Richard was innocent." Paulina Hauptmann loved her son dearly and had expected to receive a letter from him. However, she was prevented from experiencing the joy of reading his final expressions of love for her --- simply because Warden Mark O. Kimberling "forgot" to mail it to her. Richard's last letter to his mother was found among the warden's possessions at the time of his death.

I am sure you can now better understand why Lloyd Fisher said, "This (the Lindbergh case) is the greatest tragedy in the history of New Jersey. Time will never wash it out."

CHAPTER SIXTY TWO

Anna's Faith!

It had been expected with the arrival of the year 1936 and the ensuing execution of Bruno Richard Hauptmann that the annals of the Lindbergh kidnapping would now be deemed "satisfactorily" closed forever. Aside from the diversion the case had provided the country's citizens during the preceding four years, the crime would now pass, and rest comfortably, in the back of our minds to receive mere fleeting thoughts --- possibly every ten years --- as merely another historical event from out of our past. But, such was not to be with the "Crime of the Century" and the "Trial of the Century". As Hauptmann had said, "the case will never close."

Governor Hoffman, for months after the execution, kept Hauptmann's statement alive as he continued his search for additional facts which he sincerely believed could add more credibility to the story Hauptmann had told. He had strong faith in his ability, which many people ridiculed as a remote chance, to uncover key information that would eventually lead to proving the man's absolute innocence. Hoffman's intense conviction of this had been far from wrong.

As time passed, there were important truths which had been "hidden, shrouded and buried" by the "great" prosecution staff, that were "dug up and uncovered" by future investigators, who through the intervening years, were now able to put all the facts together as they should have been to finally declare that Richard Hauptmann was undeniably and unequivocally innocent. Unfortunately, Governor Hoffman did not live to see the glorious results of the faithful efforts he put forth to help the condemned man. Faithful efforts for which he received only the "stinging, mocking, hatred" voiced by those who desired to see "Hauptmann fry" regardless of the evidence. Not with factual evidence, but with evidence which had been built upon nothing more than occurrences and happenings put together with "weak", circumstantial evidence, embraced with "hundreds of doubts", that, after the first seventy-two hours of his arrest, should have clearly exposed him to the police as an innocent man. These doubts were strong enough to have cleared him. These were doubts, which at the very least, should have kept the man alive. But no --- New Jersey hammered on demanding its "pound of flesh."

Harold Hoffman's continuance of his investigation into the Hauptmann irregularities proved that many things Richard had insisted to be true, were that indeed. These were important issues the police continually made light of, by simply calling them blatant lies spawned by the criminal mind of their prisoner.

With Hauptmann no longer living, a feeling much greater than mere frustration engulfed the souls of those who were endeavoring to prove his innocence. As additional facts were learned it became agonizing to realize that this innocent man had been nothing more than a martyr's pawn in the "game of life". A martyr "fabricated with lies" in order to satisfy the "wishes of the politicians" who were "cheering", not only in the main arena, but on the side-lines as well, with all of their fat thumbs pointing downward.

It was indeed "gut-wrenching" to face the fact that a man had paid with his life for a crime he did not commit. But even more so, --- for a crime he knew absolutely nothing about as a participant.

Governor Hoffman's continued investigation uncovered many more truths which had been "buried." But, unfortunately they could no longer be of help to the dead Richard Hauptmann. Had they been seen in "the clear light of day" during his trial, and had been used to verify his statements, his life would "possibly" have been spared by an acquittal.

The compelling facts of the governor's "findings" had to do with things Hauptmann had said, (naturally "pooh-poohed" by the state) but were found to have been absolutely factual, and would have favored him in court.

It should be remembered that both of the Hauptmanns had said that Fisch had brought some of his personal belongings to their home, for safe keeping, before he departed for Germany. These included, as Anna described them, "boxes, like cardboard boxes ... with furs, and he had a valise with books, he said ... filled with books in it." Hauptmann had also informed Governor Hoffman during his prison interview that Fisch had brought a suitcase containing books, and that Isidor had given him permission to read them during the winter evenings, and that he had taken advantage of his offer.

In his summation for the prosecution, David Wilentz obviously convinced the jury that the entire Fisch story had been a mass of fabricated lies as he stated: "Fisch left his books with Hauptmann. Do you remember Mrs. Hauptmann's story? He left those satchels. There were some papers and books of Fisch's when he went to Europe." The attorney general sneeringly attacked Hauptmann's truthful claim, "Of course he destroyed those--very likely? They weren't there when we got there...."

But Harold Hoffman's investigation, after the departure of H. Norman Schwarzkopf, the "big shot boss" of the State Police, allowed him to look over the records of what had been found in the Hauptmann home. The governor described his findings: "My eye alighted on this sentence in a report made by Detective Sergeant John Wallace, who searched the Hauptmann home on September 22, 1934: 'The undersigned searched the chiffonniers located in the Hauptmann bedroom and found several books with Isidor Fisch's name in same.'

"Unimportant?", said the governor, "Perhaps; yet it would seem to substantiate Hauptmann's claim that the seizure of his home and his belongings, and the refusal to produce articles of defense evidence, placed him under an unfair handicap."

The evidence exists showing that the defense was continuously denied the right to visit both the Hauptmann home and the Lindbergh home. Hoffman discovered that the state police who had rented the Hauptmann home, had refused any of the defense counsel admittance to the home at 222nd Street in the Bronx under the express orders of the "honorable" David T. Wilentz. Furthermore, admission was to be granted only when the now famous "wood expert" Koehler could be present.

On a day arranged for an examination of the premises by the defense team, it was found to be inconvenient for Mr. Koehler. Hence another date, which would have been agreeable to all, was never found to meet with Koehler's availability. In addition to this, the counsel for the defense insisted they had been barred from entering the Lindbergh home as well.

If you think that I am unfair in my statements by which I show my disdain toward the New Jersey State Police, I want it to be clearly understood that my feelings are not all inclusive. There were then, as there are now, a great majority of the "men in blue" who are excellent officers serving well the people of their state. However, I make no apology whatsoever for my judgement of those who were willing to lend themselves to bend and pervert the truth in order to frame Richard Hauptmann, or for that matter, any person ever brought into the law courts of our communities. These reprobates are a disgrace to the badge they wear and should be stripped of their right to wear the uniform that distinguishes them as law enforcement officers.

Such a one we find in the person of 37 year old H. Norman Schwarzkopf, who had graduated from the United States Military Academy at West Point, served a hitch in the military during World War One, earning the rank of Colonel, and finding employment as a floor-walker in Bamberger's Department Store at Newark, and finally taking the position of chief-of-staff of the New Jersey State Police. Schwarzkopf, the handsome young colonel with his crew cut hair and waxed blond moustache, who had never before patrolled a beat or arrested a criminal, now found himself in charge of an investigation whose chief aim was to solve the "Crime of the Century", the abduction of the Lindbergh baby as soon as humanly possible.

Here we have a man who was totally unqualified for the job he was called to perform. The state was "saddled" with a man who, not only was inept for the work his title called for, but one who was determined from the very beginning that his troopers would solve the case without the help of any outside police agency, the FBI included.

Amid the official records of the investigation of the case it is very evident that there were police "bungles" made, many of them due to the "wrong turns" which were given at the direction of Colonel Schwarzkopf. There were times when the man seemed to be uncertain as to what moves to make. In addition to this, he proved himself to be a very poor witness in the Flemington court room. One prime example is shown by the following excerpt from the trial testimony:

Q. Colonel, did you issue a statement saying that the suicide of Violet Sharpe virtually solved the kidnapping? A. Such-- I don't recall any such statement.

Q. To the press. Do you say that you didn't issue such a statement? A. I am quite sure that I didn't.

Q. Will you say positively whether you did or you did not, to the best of your knowledge? A. I cannot tell you that, Mr. Fisher. I say I am quite sure that I didn't.

Q. Well, did you feel that it did solve the kidnapping--the death of Violet Sharpe went a long way towards solving the kidnapping? A. No, sir.

Q. Then you know that you never issued such a statement? A. Yes. I am quite sure that I didn't.

Q. If you had no such idea, Colonel, there is no question in your mind about it, is there? A. No.

But it so happened that Colonel Schwarzkopf did issue a statement of this kind and it is found in the files of the Lindbergh case releases from the State Police. Yet, while Richard Hauptmann was being tried for his life in Flemington, Schwarzkopf very conveniently, while under oath, "could not recall" that he had ever issued such a statement, maintaining that he never felt that Violet Sharpe's death went a long way toward solving the crime.

Can we put any confidence in anything Schwarzkopf said? No, of course not. The chief of the New Jersey State Police was known to encourage perjured testimony as long as it was used to convict someone he already believed to be guilty. The great Superintendent of the State Police, shortly before the trial started, had told reporters he considered Lindbergh one of his dearest friends and said he "would do anything for that man". Convict Hauptmann at all costs, had been his battle cry. And then, following the trial, in a newspaper article published in the February 15, 1935 issue of the *New York Journal*, he was quoted as saying: "I have made a friend. There is nothing I would not do for Colonel Lindbergh. There is no oath I would not break if it would materially help his well-being. There is not a single man in my outfit who would not lay down his life for Colonel Lindbergh." Schwarzkopf reverenced Lindbergh, he worshipped him, he idolized him.

Knowing these facts, is there any wonder that Anna Hauptmann demonstrated her anger at the irregularities her husband was forced to endure at Flemington. "See what we had to face," she shouted with great emotion. "This man admits he would break an oath, he would lie, for Colonel Lindbergh. That's why Richard was convicted, why they faked the evidence against him once they found he had Lindbergh money. Lindbergh was a prominent man, a hero to everybody. Richard was an alien, a workingman. His character was as good as Lindbergh's--Richard was not a liar--but his social standing was nothing. And the jury was taken in because the man who accused my husband had a high social standing, rich and powerful and a hero, like a god. I remember reading after, what the jurors said in stories they wrote, that Lindbergh convinced them. But Lindbergh lied. The way Schwarzkopf said he would lie for Lindbergh, the way Schwarzkopf did lie for him and got his police to lie and to fake evidence."

Anna Hauptmann spoke only truths in her diatribe which was long overdue. Richard's faithful wife had held off as long as she could before exercising her privilege to be heard. Both she and Richard held the firm belief that he would be acquitted for one reason---his innocence. However, as the trial progressed she began to realize what they were facing -- the lying, cheating, perjurers, and the rotten court system. Tony Scaduto, while preparing data for his book *Scapegoat*, asked her when she first began to realize that the prosecution was distorting evidence and calling on perjurers to convict Richard. He received this answer:

"I think I began to be afraid in the Bronx court. We always thought that whatever happens we are not afraid because we didn't do anything. I didn't realize it would be so bad to take Richard over to New Jersey for the trial. But in the Bronx, with the witness Whited lying that he saw Richard, and that Osborn, the handwriting man, I began to worry.

"But my feeling all along I think was still, he will be acquitted in the New Jersey trial. Until I saw everyone lying. 'My God,' I said, 'what can we do if they lie?' But despite the lies, inside I felt Richard would come out all right because he didn't do anything wrong.

"Even the people who did not lie, they just stood by and let all the others lie. Like Mr. Foley, the Bronx district attorney, and his assistant, that Mr. Breslin. They were at the trial in Flemington almost every day, maybe every day. I don't remember for sure now. But they were there. Foley and Breslin knew about the letters from Fisch's brother, that Wilentz said didn't exist. They knew about Richard's ledger book. They knew Condon was a liar. They knew all these things, and more, and they never said anything. I always wondered why men like Foley and Breslin, when they heard these lies and read about them, didn't come forward and tell the truth."

Many FBI agents, as well as its director, J. Edgar Hoover, held serious suspicions of improprieties being used against Hauptmann in the New Jersey court house. It had become apparent that, for the sake of keeping such suspicions from becoming public knowledge, although the agents who were more familiar with the case, "shook their heads in unbelief", they kept their mouths closed since it was not their case to prosecute. They were not involved, and if the authorities up in New Jersey chose to take a chance by using manufactured evidence, well then, it simply was not their problem --- neither that of the FBI or the Bronx officials. They just closed their eyes to it all and hoped this would serve as a balm to their consciences.

"And how do they sleep at night? How do they face their God when they die? This I want to know.

"I just couldn't believe the lies at the trial. But even so, I thought our witnesses showed that Richard was in the bakery with me that night of the kidnapping, I thought we had won. That afternoon, when the jury was given the case, I did all the washing that had piled up, mine and Manfred's. I was so certain Richard would be with us that evening as soon as the jury found him not guilty, that I was least nervous of those around me. A reporter asked me if I was nervous and I said, 'Certainly not, I know Richard will be free and Richard knows it, too. That's why I'm washing my clothes and the baby's clothes, so they'll be nice-looking when the three of us we get home together.' Never for a moment did I think Richard would be found guilty.

"The police came for me when the jury was ready to report and drove me to the courthouse where I knew I would hear a verdict of acquittal. But as I got out of the car I think I had a little premonition. There was a terrific mob there, thousands of people with the bright lights turned on them for the newsreel cameras. People in the crowd wished me good luck, said nice things, but I was almost overcome by the amount of people. I thought, 'It is like the crucifixion. Like the sacrifice of human life.' And when I got inside and saw Richard handcuffed between two guards, I thought, 'Well, it must be the worst or they would not take such precautions.'"

Asked if she was shocked at the verdict: "Oh, yes, I was shocked. I don't have words to tell how I felt. What I remember most, it is so clear I can still see it---the jury would not look at me. I stared at them, at everyone of them, trying to get them to look in my eyes while we were waiting for the judge to come in and hear the verdict. But not one of them dared to look at me or at Richard. Even when they answered, when they said guilty, they stared down at the floor. I think they knew they were doing something dreadful, many of them knew they were killing my Richard because of the lies of witnesses.

"I know that when I heard the verdict I wanted to cry out, but I couldn't. I don't remember too much after that because I was like in a dream, with shock. One thing I remember is when I returned to Manfred, I threw myself on the bed beside him and cried, 'My baby, what have they done to your father?'

"All of my life I have prayed that the truth will come out. I feel when the truth is finally written I can die and be with Richard."

It was her strong faith that had given Anna Hauptmann the assurance that God would permit her to remain alive so that she would see her prayers answered.

Mrs. Hauptmann explains it this way: "Can you imagine? I'm not talking for myself, I mean any person who would go through what I went through, sitting in a courtroom day after day and hearing people telling lies, looking at Richard and telling lies. And I knew it, that he was innocent and he was killed by lies, I knew it day after day and year after year. Sometimes I wonder how I lived through it. Sometimes I thought I could almost go insane. Thinking, saying, 'God, you let it happen. You know the truth. Why did You let it happen?'

"I talked to my pastor. I told him, 'God knows Richard is innocent, He above all knows it. Why did He let Richard die?' And he said, 'Mrs. Hauptmann, we must not ask questions about what God does. He must do it for some reason. I sometimes ask why He let me get sick, so that I can't complete the work I want to do, and then I understand He does it for some reason.'

"That helped me. But still, I always wanted the truth to come out. I did not want to leave it that just God knew the truth. Maybe in a certain time the truth will come out and people will say, 'Oh, how wrong we were in our judgment. We must never do this again.' And I used to think, 'What will all those people say then, the jury, the prosecutor Wilentz, all those witnesses who lied. What will their excuses be when the truth comes out?'

"'I wonder what Wilentz will say?', she was asked. 'He'll never admit he had a knowledge of it.'

"'I believe in his heart he knows Richard was innocent,' Mrs. Hauptmann said.

"'He knew some of it, he had to,' Scaduto said. 'He must have seen the evidence ...'

"'I am not a religious fanatic,' Mrs. Hauptmann continued. 'But I believe God was with me through the trial. Wouldn't those people who lied think that some day there will be a higher Judge they must face? Those people who perjure themselves, some of them must believe in God.'

"'I believe in a God in heaven.' Mrs. Hauptmann continued. 'I find out so many times, I get strength from that belief. If I didn't have this, I have nothing. It helped me survive. You know, there's a thing about right and wrong, lies and conscience, it means to me more than all the riches in the world, to tell the truth. I don't complain. God has been with me all the time, all these years, that's all I need. To the last breath I have I know Richard was innocent and I'm not afraid to die, I'm not afraid of anything.

"'I wouldn't want to change with Wilentz or any of them. You know, I had the strength of my faith, I could take it. But I feel so bad about Richard's mother and my parents. Just think what those people went through. Richard wrote to them many times and told them the truth of what happened, what was done to him. But they didn't know he was innocent, the way I knew, and they must have suffered terribly.

"'You see, I never doubted that Richard was telling the truth. He was with me that night, when the baby was taken. Maybe if he hadn't been with me, I might have doubted him and wondered if he could have done it. But I was certain with the certainty that only a wife has---he was with me all night and we went to sleep together.'"

Anthony Scaduto, during one of his visits with Anna Hauptmann in her home in Yeadon, Pennsylvania, was the recipient of her courtesy as she granted him the privilege of reading the last letter Richard had written to his loyal wife.

Once again, I wish to express my sincere appreciation to Mr. Scaduto for allowing me to share with you so many passages from his book, *Scapegoat*. We continue as we read Richard's final, intimate, letter to his wife Anna, together with her comments.

"'This is his last letter to me. He couldn't finish it, he couldn't even sign it. I would like to know what they did to him in those last days to make him write like this. Could they have beaten him to make him confess to something he didn't do or to make him tell them where the money was that Wilentz proved he spent every penny of? Here, look at it, look what they did to him.'

"The letter was written in German and I did not understand it. But it was plain that something had happened to Richard in the days just before he was electrocuted. The script is small and tight and written in a palsied hand, unlike all the other letters I've seen written by Hauptmann. It was the writing of an elderly man, a man who had deteriorated overnight.

"'I want the world to see that,' Anna Hauptmann said. To see what they did to Richard.'

"We had the letter translated. Dated April second, the day before his death, it says:

My dear Anny,

I received your letter just at the moment when I started to doubt God. Forgive me, my dear Anny, but my inner life has collapsed. This was a result of the treatment I was given during the past ten hours. Oh, how little faith I had, why do I let myself be misled by the people of this world. I should know better from my past life. They only want my death in order to solve a case in the wrong manner; however, dear Anny, again and again I still expected that they would come to their senses and shy back from committing a murder. I myself can hardly understand that they could make me doubt my own faith. How weak we are, we human beings; God has shamed me in my weakness. However, He had put it into my heart that I should live and that I should see you and Manfred again. God forgive me and help me in my lack of faith. From now on I shall leave everything in His hands because He will do the right thing: He will stay with me whatever may come. I am praying, dear Anny, that He may also be with you and our baby and with mother and with the whole world.

"'Please publish that for the world to see,' Mrs. Hauptmann asked again."

Anthony Scaduto answered her request on Pages 472-473 of his *Scapegoat*. I also have answered her request on this page.

C H A P T E R   S I X T Y   T H R E E

The Truth Slowly Surfaces!

When Harold Hoffman became aware that since the time of Hauptmann's arrest, not one of the defense counsel had been permitted entrance into the accused man's home in the Bronx, and knowing that such a denial was a highly irregular procedure on the part of the prosecution and the state police officers, the governor decided it was high time the defense lawyers were granted this request. However, it was not until Tuesday, March 24th, 1936, only eleven days before Hauptmann's execution, that this visit was consummated.

Entering the front door at East 222nd Street in the Bronx on that date were Governor Hoffman, defense attorney Lloyd Fisher, Attorney General Wilentz, Arthur Koehler, the "now famous expert on wood" and several other officials. This visit proved to be very revealing especially to Hoffman, and although we have covered the Hauptmann attic and "rail 16" in other sections of this book, we dare not eliminate the findings made on this date since they are necessarily important to show you more evidence toward proving the innocence of defenseless Richard Hauptmann.

In order to do this, we again turn to the report made by Governor Hoffman: "It must be understood that the attic flooring had never been completed. Flooring laid across the beams covered about two thirds of the attic, but did not extend back to where the sloping roof met the beams upon which the remainder of the floor had been laid. On March 24 the floor, minus the disputed board presented as evidence at Flemington, was entirely symmetrical, a good carpenter job. From the dead center of the floor, as determined by a plumb line dropped from the apex of the roof, there were thirteen boards on each side--a total of twenty-six pieces of flooring. If the disputed board had actually been a part of the flooring there would have been thirteen boards on one side and fourteen on the other.

"The flooring is laid with what is known as

toenailing--that is, the nails are driven through the tongue of the boards at an angle of about forty-five degrees. In all twenty-six boards in the attic flooring there appeared to be only <u>seven perpendicular nails</u>, while in the beams or joists where board S-226 and rail 16 are alleged to have been laid there were holes indicating that <u>twenty-five perpendicular nails</u> must have been driven in that one board. Mr. Koehler, in his report, explains that 'this board undoubtedly was the first one laid, and it had to be fastened securely so that the others could be driven against it.' Carpenters have advised me that it would not take anywhere near twenty-five nails to anchor the first board, and they have also pointed out that approximately the same number of nails required to anchor the first board would have been required to anchor the last board laid.

"In the course of the examination it was found that the disputed nail holes in the joists were not deep enough to accommodate the eightpenny cut nails that Detective Bornmann said came from the attic floor. Wires, match sticks, and other probing materials were used, and it was found that none of the holes had the required depth of 1-3/4 inches. This seemed significant, and it was suggested that pieces of the joists containing the nail holes should be split open to see whether or not the nails had been driven to their full length. The blocks were cut out and taken to the Physics Department of Columbia University, and when the samples were split open, through the nail holes, all but one of the nail holes were deep enough to have accommodated the nails to their full length. The reason why the wires and sticks had not probed the nail holes to the full depth was that the holes had been partially filled with what appeared to the naked eye to be sawdust. Koehler's report shows that he examined this material under a microscope and found it 'to be made of fragments of wood fibers mixed with a very small amount of gritty material, apparently dust from the attic.'

"I have in my possession several of these blocks from the joists, split through the nail holes. Every person to whom I have shown them--and this includes carpenters, crime analysts, and other citizens--has been convinced that these <u>nail holes are comparatively fresh</u>. The wood fibers surrounding the nail holes have not died, there are no signs of rust from the nails, and it is apparent to any one with an open mind that eightpenny cut nails had never remained in those holes for the nine or ten years that the flooring had been laid. Other nail holes in the beams, undisputed, present a far different appearance. They are lined with rust and there are no projecting fibers.

"It seems to me that the evidence is clear that the disputed nail holes were made by nails driven in the joists and pulled out almost immediately. When a nail is driven in most wood, I am advised, and immediately extracted, some of the displaced fibers spring back into place. I am convinced that this is what was done in making the nail holes that 'fit' with the alleged nail holes in the kidnap ladder, and that subsequently these pieces of fiber, breaking off because of repeated probes into the nail holes, supplied the material that partially filled the nail holes.

"It was a startling 'discovery' that the wood in rail 16 of the ladder matched with the remaining piece of flooring in the Hauptmann attic that supplied the connecting link between the Bronx and Hopewell, and placed Hauptmann at the scene of the crime. The 'discovery,' however, seems to me to have been a little too perfect. Let's look into it.

"From September 19, 1934, when Hauptmann was arrested, until September 26, when the 'discovery' was made, there had been repeated searches of the Hauptmann apartment, including the attic. I have been unable to examine any of the reports of New York City Police and Department of Justice investigators, since they were not made available to me, but I do have several reports of State Police officers, and not one of them shows that a search of the attic prior to September 26 disclosed that part of one floor board had been saved out of the attic.

"This important evidence is something that should have struck any experienced investigator 'smack in the eye'; yet, if it was there, New York City Police, F.B.I. investigators, and the New Jersey sleuths passed it by until Bornmann arrived on the scene, September 26, and, accompanied by two carpenters from the New York City Police Department, discovered the important evidence that had been waiting, for a week, for him to find.

"Corporal William Horn, in a report of his activities for September 19, says that he searched the Hauptmann residence with representatives of the New York City Police Department and the U.S. Department of Justice, under the supervision of Lieutenant Keaten of the New Jersey State Police and Inspector John Lyons of the New York City Department. The partially missing floor board is not mentioned in this report.

"On September 20 Corporal Samuel Leon reported

that, with Lieutenant Frank McCarthy of the New York City Police and Agent Wright of the Department of Justice, he searched the Hauptmann garage, and he adds: 'We then searched the kitchen, bedroom, nursery, parlor, attic, and cellar, but were unable to find anything connected with the Lindbergh case.'

"On September 22, in compliance with the orders of Lieutenant Keaten, Sergeant A. Zapolsky of the New Jersey State Police went to the Hauptmann home, accompanied by Sergeant P. Kelly and Sergeant Wallace of his department, and four New York City detectives. 'We were assigned,' writes Zapolsky, 'to search the attic.' He adds: 'In the attic we picked up a mason's bag containing two trowels, two pieces of pipe, one ruler, one plane blade, and one empty fiber suitcase.' There is no mention of the partially missing floor board.

"Can it be possible that all these sharp-eyed Sherlocks--several Department of Justice investigators, a half dozen or more New York City detectives and policemen, and eight New Jersey State Police officers--had gone repeatedly to the Hauptmann attic to search it, and had passed over what subsequently turned out to be the most important piece of evidence in sending Hauptmann to the electric chair?

"But read this report signed by Detective Bornmann, and setting out his activity of September 26, the day the evidence is supposed to have been found: 'This date detailed by Captain Lamb to continue search on the above-captioned home. Meeting Detective Tobin, two police carpenters, and Superintendent Wilson on the premises at 9 A.M., we immediately proceeded to make a thorough search of the attic. Nothing of value was found, with the exception of several small pieces of wood and shavings and several cut nails that may possibly have a bearing on the case.'

"It is true that there are several supplemental reports citing the 'great find,' but I am at a loss to understand why Bornmann, in what apparently was his first written report of that day's activities, maintained that 'nothing of value was found.'

"Bornmann, you will recall, is the State Police officer who, according to his testimony, pulled up the remaining half of the floor board, filled with nails, and with a tongue inserted in the groove of the adjacent floor board, with his bare hands. He certainly played an important part in sending Hauptmann to his doom. Bornmann didn't apply for any of the New Jersey reward money.

"The wood angle represents another phase of the case upon which whole volumes might be written.

"Hundreds of pages of testimony were devoted to the wood angle, undoubtedly confusing the jury. Some of the claims made were absurd, but they were undoubtedly swallowed by the expert-awed jurors.

"I have in my possession a photograph of the ladder made the day after the commission of the crime. It is a clear photograph, in which the knots and grains are distinctly shown and rail 16 can be easily identified; but in neither the original nor in a copy magnified ten times can the alleged nail holes be found."

It is my sincere belief that we are justified in our appraisal of the attic wood testimony as being nothing more than a "batch of ridiculous lies and manufactured evidence" that were brought into that courtroom and unfairly used against Hauptmann. Unfortunately these lies were accepted by the jury as truths which were not to be contested.

When we use our God-given good common sense we are certain to arrive at only one conclusion. Are we expected to believe that Hauptmann would be dumb enough, while planning to kidnap the world's most famous baby, to go up into his own attic, into which he had to gain entrance by first removing the shelves from a linen closet, (since there were no stairs) then climb up on the cleats which had held the shelves, remove a small wooden trap-door, and then pull or hoist himself through a small opening into the attic? Are we then expected to believe that he went to work sawing a ten foot section of one floor board, creating evidence that could later be used against him, and then going through the difficult task of taking the board down through the closet? And all this without Anna taking notice of it? Of course we don't believe these "foolish" allegations which were used as "proof positive" of his guilt. Hauptmann, an expert carpenter, if he needed an extra piece of lumber, would have no doubt used any of the odd pieces in his garage or cellar to complete the ladder. Or, for that matter, he could have purchased the odd piece he needed from the National Lumber and Millwork Company just several blocks away without arousing suspicion. But, this would not follow the script the prosecution had written. They said we found the "incriminating lumber". It was taken from Hauptmann's own attic --- and nobody had better doubt it. Well, we certainly do! The whole seance was conceived by the "sick minds" of persons who had no desire whatsoever to trust in unadulterated truths in their attempt to convict an innocent man.

Furthermore, before we turn to other aspects of the case, we must make one closing comment on the wood testimony. It is inconceivable that more emphasis was not placed on the improbability of Koehler's claim that he could successfully trace the grain of one piece of lumber into another piece, with nearly two inches of board missing between the two, by using nothing more than his imagination to "draw in" the missing grain. However, he did it, much to the satisfaction of the prosecution staff, the judge, and jury. Attorney Reilly missed every opportunity to press Koehler on this "false fact", while Governor Hoffman also questioned the ridiculous claim: "The flooring was of the tongue-and-groove type, which means that Hauptmann, in addition to being dumb enough to use one of his own floor boards, would have had to use a ripsaw and plane; for the famous rail 16 of the ladder bore no evidence of either a tongue or a groove, and, in addition, both ends of the board had been cut. It was only by 'imagination' that the eye could trace the missing piece of board which, it was claimed, had once joined the piece of flooring known as S-226 to the board from which rail 16 was cut.

"Koehler let his eye trace identical grains from one piece of the board to another; persons less imaginative could not concede a matching of the grains."

During the Hoffman investigation several other revealing pieces of information surfaced which made crystal clear some other improprieties that had been used against Hauptmann. Take the case of Amandus Hochmuth, the 87 year old witness who claimed he had seen Hauptmann for a few fleeting seconds on the day of the kidnapping.

To allow this man to testify was a crime in itself since the prosecution staff, at least some of them, had to know he was a liar in every sense of the word. It is a clear fact that back in 1932 Hochmuth did not and could not identify Hauptmann as a man he later said he had seen near the Lindbergh home simply because he had seen no one. And yet, after Hauptmann's arrest, and his picture had been published in many newspapers, Hochmuth, who had given his addresses as 595 East 134th Street, and 370 Willis Avenue, the Bronx, but who claimed he was living in Hopewell, New Jersey near the Lindbergh home, all the while collecting aid as a resident of New York City, was taken to the Flemington jail to say he now identified Hauptmann as a man he had seen with a ladder on March 1st, 1932, to then be "hauled" into the Flemington court room to testify under oath that Hauptmann was the "imaginary" man he said he had seen is nothing more than a blatant travesty of justice at its highest degree. It is pure unadulterated hogwash. This entire "scenario" should never have escaped the "lurid minds" of the prosecutors, but was, nevertheless, permitted to run rampant as "manufactured fact" providing more "evidence" that pointed an innocent man nearer to his grave.

This testimony used against Hauptmann was in itself, as stated before, a horrible crime. It should be remembered that on Wednesday, June 29th, 1932, this man Hochmuth when appearing before Investigator Edward Carey of the Division of Old Age Security, was found to be in very poor health. His record #14106 reads: "Health very poor, applicant partly blind, suffering from a complication of diseases." And then on Thursday, August 4th of that same year, before Inspector Joseph A. McGovern, the record stated: "Frail...failing eyesight due to cataracts."

We now see Hochmuth performing in a "starring role" at the Hauptmann trial in 1935, giving a stellar performance, one worthy enough to receive a portion of the reward money. In the performance of his "final act" in the Hauptmann drama, he appeared on Wednesday, December 15th, 1937 in the office of Governor Hoffman to receive that reward. Here he was called upon to give two "outstanding" demonstrations. The first was to establish his "excellent eyesight", the other his "profound memory" together with his "vivid imagination" and ability to concoct an utterly "unbelievable story".

Governor Hoffman relates this incident:

"Hochmuth, in my office on December 15, 1937, could not identify an eighteen-inch silver loving cup, filled with flowers, on top of a cabinet located within ten feet of the chair in which he sat. On that day, when I examined Hochmuth in connection with the reward, in the presence of Leon Hoage, a crime analyst, the old man gave the following fantastic story, never told before, in an effort to convince me that he had really seen Hauptmann and was entitled to a share of the reward; I am quoting from the stenographic record:

"'Well, when the baby was killed, that was on March 1, I saw Hauptmann, and before that I saw a fellow hanging on the bridge there---this is the first time I have mentioned it. He was hanging on the bridge, and we have a good many Germans coming to the neighborhood, and I said, 'Are you looking for a job?' and I didn't get a satisfactory answer, but I saw he was a German and I spoke German to him and we had quite a talk. I said, 'I am from Hamburg,' and he said he came from Saxony. I said, 'What is your name?' and he said, 'Hauptmann.'"

"Get the picture, readers, of Hauptmann, planning a crime that would shock the world, prowling around Hopewell telling people his name and origin! Hochmuth repeated this fabulous story in the presence of over twenty newspaper reporters on the day that the reward announcement was made; but little was said about it in the public press. Nothing must be done to discredit a witness in the Hauptmann case!

"And Justice Trenchard, in his charge to the jury, referring to Hochmuth, asked, among other things, 'Do you think there is any reason, upon the whole, to doubt the truth of the old man's testimony?'

"The jury evidently believed him. Remembering that he was one of the important witnesses who placed Hauptmann at the scene of the crime; that he was drawing relief in New York City while a resident of New Jersey; that there were wide discrepancies in his statements and the testimony he gave on the stand; that for over two years after the crime he kept a 'secret' that he had seen a man in the car with the kidnap ladder, do you believe him?"

But Hochmuth wasn't the only witness whose testimony was "swallowed hook, line and sinker". We also have Millard "the amazing liar" Whited, who was known by everyone, including his brothers, as one who "never tells the truth", and Charles B. Rossiter, "who came from out of the shadows" on Saturday, September 22nd, 1934, to tell Sergeant V.G. Varrelman of the Mount Ephraim barracks of the New Jersey State Police that on the Saturday evening before the kidnapping he had seen Hauptmann on a road between Princeton and Bellemead. The serious problem we have believing him is due to the discrepancies in his testimony. Rossiter had described the car "Hauptmann" was driving, which he said appeared to have been driven into a ditch, as green, (the Hauptmann car was blue), and he also described the car as having a "spare tire mounted on the rear on a three-prong tire carrier", (the Hauptmann car had a trunk on the rear, the tire was carried in a well on the front left fender). As for the man he identified, (whom the jury very obligingly accepted as being Hauptmann), he merely said that the man "looks very much like him".

Good grief! Is this the "brand" of testimony the Flemington jury placed its faith in? Yes, indeed it did! But then, why didn't anyone have the gumption to raise the question as to why Rossiter had waited two-and-one-half years to report this "imaginary car and its phantom driver"? What a travesty of justice!

The reports Governor Hoffman received during his inquiry into Rossiter's reputation proved his integrity to be next to worthless. It was discovered that Colonel Schwarzkopf, in the investigation his own troopers had made of the man's veracity, had also been aware of this same information, yet the state police chief had deemed it valuable enough, despite his questionable character, to allow Wilentz to use Rossiter as an "important" eye-witness, all done to put Hauptmann in the electric chair.

Facts which were cleverly hidden by Rossiter's blatant testimony were revealed in various police reports found by Governor Hoffman. Detective Nuncio De Gaetano reported in one of his reports of Rossiter's character: 'Visible signs of financial distress ... fired for some unknown reason ... failed to turn in collections ... said some one had entered his house when he and his wife were away and stole the $400 collections ... a trial was given him but after two months he returned to his old practices, which again caused his dismissal ... Mr.-----(an employer) says: brands him as being a good composer and a wonderful liar ... Mr. --- (another employer) says: ... This company received a telegram from New Rochelle, New York, signed by Charles B. Rossiter, stating that he was held up and robbed and requested more money ... received $60 worth of merchandise he has failed to account for."

Governor Hoffman sums up his findings of Whited, Hochmuth, and Rossiter in this fashion: "Voluntarily, a number of other employers of Rossiter have written to me stating that Rossiter had been dismissed for irregularity in financial transactions. When he was used as a witness, in the face of knowledge that he had an unenviable reputation, he told a story, under oath, differing widely from the initial statements he had given the State Police. But such witnesses as Whited, Hochmuth, and Rossiter, none of whom had been heard from prior to Hauptmann's arrest, evidently convinced the jury that Hauptmann, in different cars, answering different descriptions, had been seen in the vicinity of the Lindbergh home. The jurors might have been impressed by the consistency with which the defendant had followed his habit of running cars into ditches."

And then, we dare not eliminate the "trustworthy" Mrs. Cecile Barr, the cashier at the Loew's Sheridan Square Theater down in Greenwich Village. The Mrs. Barr whose testimony should have, at its very best, been considered very, very questionable. Here we have a woman who said she sold Hauptmann a theater ticket on Sunday, November 26th, 1933. Although records show that Mrs. Barr sold tickets to approximately 1,500 people on that date, she possessed the amazing ability to pick out Hauptmann as the man who had paid his admission to the theater with a folded five-dollar ransom bill.

Now, this fact in itself would appear, on the surface, to be entirely plausible. However, we seriously dispute it with a series of incidents which leave the entire drama Mrs. Barr pictured as being "highly suspect." In the first place, the date was Richard Hauptmann's thirty-fourth birthday. Because of this, there was a party in progress at the Hauptmann home at the very hour Mrs. Barr claimed Hauptmann had tossed her the folded bill. Present at this party were many witnesses who corroborated Hauptmann's alibi that he had been present there the entire time. This prompts us to ask this question, "Why would Hauptmann choose the date of his birthday to travel 14 miles away from his home, on an exceptionally cold night, without wearing an overcoat, to see a movie alone? Furthermore, Mrs. Barr claimed the man did not have an accent and was "apparently an American."

Sidney B. Whipple, author of the book *The Lindbergh Crime*, also had trouble digesting the story told by Cecile Barr. He wrote: "Of the evidence linking Bruno Richard Hauptmann to specific appearances before and after the crime, that relating to his supposed visit on the evening of November 26 to the Sheridan Square Theater has always seemed to many persons, including the writer, the most tenuous and susceptible to attack. ...There was considerable evidence to place Hauptmann in his own home that evening as against the uncorroborated evidence of the cashier. Of the fact that the defendant's birthday fell on that date there is no doubt. ... That there was a little birthday celebration at the Hauptmann apartment there was considerable evidence." Whipple continued on to explain that there is a possibility "that the bill had been in circulation for several days and that it reached the hands of the cashier through some innocent person, wrongly identified as Hauptmann."

Again we say --- what a travesty of Jersey justice! And for this Cecile Barr received a generous portion of the reward money! What a mockery the trial proved to be.

Governor Hoffman made it very clear that the information he learned about the state's witnesses had all been gained by searching through the police records, and that nothing he found was based on hearsay. And today, these same records continue to exist as a small, but silent, voice as the years continue on ---. However, soon the investigation of Hauptmann's innocence will blaze forth in a crescendo of truths that will literally amaze you as we uncover the facts of the Lindbergh case that prove to you how innocent the state's "scapegoat" really was.

C H A P T E R   S I X T Y   F O U R

A Man Named Stover!

In 1936, following the electrocution of Hauptmann, the Lindbergh kidnapping was being reviewed in retrospect by a large number of people as a tragic crime which could be likened to that of a huge cryptic jig-saw puzzle which would linger on as one far from completion. They argued that more than a few of the extremely important "pieces" were still missing, at the same time insisting that it was impossible for them to accept any "abridged facsimile" until a complete picture, showing all the true facts, could be conclusively seen without distortion.

However, the reflective judgmental opinions of the majority of our nation's citizens seemed to be one of satisfaction with the outcome of the case. They were willing to "settle" for exactly the way the authorities "said it was" and then move along to other things. In other words, and to put it briefly, they absolutely believed Hauptmann to be the "beast" he was painted as being, hence he was guilty and had rightly paid for the ghastly crime he had committed. To put it another way, they were willing to believe everything they read and heard, regardless of any contradictory facts, no matter how convincing they might be.

Many of these people still remain with us to this day. However, through the passing of time, a great multitude of those who once sincerely believed in the guilt of Richard Hauptmann have today entered the "camp" of those who whole-heartedly know he was completely innocent. Their new belief has been fostered because of the many, many truths which have been unearthed since the very hour of his death.

As for my personal belief at the time of Hauptmann's execution, I would have to say my opinion as to his guilt, was one of confusion. I was confused, largely because of the conglomeration of news reports carrying conflicting stories. I had followed the case, reading every news item I could get my hands on, since Lindbergh's baby had been stolen. Now I was experiencing a strong feeling of remorse because of his death. I could not dismiss the uneasy sensitivity I held which prompted me to honestly doubt that the case had been far from successfully solved with the death of Hauptmann. But, regardless of this, I succeeded in rejecting any uneasiness I held, with thoughts of "Who am I to question what the authorities have proven to be factual? Why should I, a young man of 22 living over in Pennsylvania, even though I have an avid interest in crime detection, even dare to wonder if they were right?" And so, as best I could, I "accepted" the fact --- Hauptmann was guilty! But yet, I always had a "sincere doubt" hiding deep within me, one which kept resurfacing to the forefront all too often.

I do believe, however, that my interest in the Lindbergh case was generated by a natural attraction instilled in me when I was just a youngster. During my early childhood I became intrigued as I listened to my parents and their friends discuss infamous criminal cases which happened during the 20's. Among these were the Leopold-Loeb case, the Hall-Mills murder, and the Snyder-Gray case. The famous unsolved murders in Fall River, Massachusetts, in 1892, which made the name of Lizzie Borden a legend; and the kidnapping of little four-year old Charlie Ross from his home in the Germantown section of Philadelphia on July 1, 1874, both held my special interest. Whenever I would hear discussions of these cases, plus many others, I found them to be extremely fascinating. So, with this background, I was certainly "primed" for the "Crime of the Century" when it occurred in 1932.

Now, March 1, 1932 happened to be my sixteenth birthday. On that same date in 1916, at approximately 7:45 p.m., I was being ushered into this world at the home of my parents in West Philadelphia; while sixteen years later, at approximately that identical hour, little Charles Augustus Lindbergh, Jr. was being tucked into his crib for a night of rest. I do not attribute this as being even remotely responsible for generating my interest in the case. I have made mere mention of it for whatever rarity it might prove to be.

I needed nothing more than the first announcement of the abduction, made shortly after 11:00 p.m., to arouse my interest in the case. I became stimulated more and more as each terse news bulletin relating the latest developments came through the speaker of our radio. After all, this was a case with mammoth proportions --- Colonel Lindbergh's little son had been kidnapped! The entire world was being alerted and its people were genuinely concerned. His baby must be found and returned immediately. Our world hero had been injured and was grieving.

The writers of history have briefly recorded for us the progress made by the investigators. A man was eventually arrested for stealing the baby and killing him. The man was tried, convicted, and executed for the felony of murder. But what most historians failed to chronicle was the vast uncertainty among the world's citizens pertaining to the man's actual guilt. Agreement on this was far flung, and rightly so. Since there was so much doubt, it prevalently displayed the failure of the authorities to successfully prove their case against the man. There remained nothing more, nor less, than bitter controversy, which at times became quite heated, particularly by those who vehemently argued that he was guilty simply because the great authorities in New Jersey "had proved" he was.

As for me, I refused to debate any thought I might have of his possible innocence. I remained merely skeptical since I did have some honest feelings about this conceivable possibility. However, I, as best I could, decided to put the case against Hauptmann to rest. This, I reasoned, I would be able to do, largely because the prosecutors had been successful in having a guilty verdict rendered against him. At this point I had no reason to suspect that anything illegal had been used to obtain that verdict.

During the months following the "official" closing of the case, only occasional articles were appearing in the newspapers pertaining largely to the distribution of the reward money and other insignificant details and comments made by some of the principals in the case. Aside from conversations one would hear concerning the proprieties of the Lindbergh-Hauptmann trial, the case was now considered to be a dead issue.

But that appraisement was far from the truth. The remainder of this book reveals all the new and shocking developments which were previously unknown. Had the authorities been aware of these facts, and the astonishing information surrounding them, they certainly did an excellent job of keeping the truth "under cover". Instead, however, I firmly believe they were kept much too busy "manufacturing evidence" to be used against Hauptmann to have allowed themselves to become "distracted" by any semblance of evidence which might have inspired them to look in "another direction."

Evidence of this is clearly seen when Colonel Schwarzkopf ordered the search for additional Lindbergh ransom bills to be discontinued. Apparently, he considered it needless to continue the search, therefore dismissing the hope he should have held, of apprehending any accomplices, or, for that matter, even the possibility of obtaining additional evidence against Hauptmann.

This was clearly demonstrated when we learned that Colonel Schwarzkopf, after the arrest of Hauptmann, was advised by J. Edgar Hoover, Director of the FBI, that large numbers of five-dollar Federal Reserve bills of the kidnap series were available for his inspection at Philadelphia. Schwarzkopf's response to this was a return wire, which stated that the New Jersey State Police were not interested and suggesting that "any identified notes be taken out for destruction."

Saturday, April 4th, 1936 was a day of mixed emotions for me. First of all, I found it virtually impossible to turn my thoughts away from Gabriel Heatter's, lengthy and very graphic, discourse of the Lindbergh case as he had broadcast it the night before. I had spent hours by the side of our radio awaiting his terse announcement: "Bruno Richard Hauptmann is dead!" There it was! The end had come! And, now it was over --- and I was left alone with my thoughts --- the authorities had said he was guilty --- and that should settle it!

But was he, really? My thoughts seemed to be occupied with many discomforts. Too many doubts. However, I reasoned --- they, who had been closest to the case, said he was guilty --- so, he was guilty. I tried to reason it this way, and then I would go about trying to justify my reasoning. Is it possible the wrong man died? Yes, it wouldn't be the first time an innocent man had paid with his life for a crime he did not commit. Well, anyway, I said to myself, I am going to forget all about it and turn to other things. However little did I realize then that the Crime of the Century would soon be absorbing a great share of my attention during the remaining years of my life. Well, it did, and of this I have no regrets.

Due to the extent of new information that has been gathered during the past 57 years, I wish to emphatically state that it has not been luck that has brought us to where we stand today. Now we are able to state undeniably that Bruno Richard Hauptmann was not guilty of the kidnap-murder of Charles A. Lindbergh, Jr.

This statement is made in obedience to God as His answer to Anna Hauptmann's heartfelt prayer to Him on the night of her husband's death in 1936.

I want it to be known that "luck" played no part in it. I sincerely believe with all my heart that each of us, the late Harold G. Hoffman, former governor of New Jersey, Anthony Scaduto, Ludovic Kennedy, and I, as well as many others, have been used by God in His move to answer Anna Hauptmann's prayers. Truly, our quest for the truth has been exciting, but also a very humbling experience.

Here now, is the way it all happened.

It was during the late fall of 1936 that Harry P. Young came to see me. I hadn't seen my friend for quite some time, not being a close friend of his, although I had known him for quite a few years. My visitor was a friendly dark complexioned man with rugged features and coal black hair. He was the owner of a radio shop on Main Street hill where he not only sold radios, but repaired them as well. We both lived in Phoenixville, a small Pennsylvania iron town of nearly 13,000 residents, located 4 miles west of historic Valley Forge and about 25 miles northwest of Philadelphia's center city.

My reason for enjoying Mr. Young's visit was largely due to the sudden turn our conversation had taken. No sooner had we exchanged pleasantries than he jumped into a discourse of the Lindbergh kidnapping as he excitedly divulged some additional information he claimed he personally knew about it and wanted to share with me. Although, I must admit, I found his story quite interesting, I mentally dismissed it as totally unbelievable. Aside from his claim that Hauptmann was innocent, to which I nodded my agreement, the rest of his tale seemed preposterous. As a matter of fact, I accepted his information much too lightly. To me it had a somewhat humorous vein, and failing to hide a slight smile, he mildly rebuked me for my apparent disbelief. "Don't laugh, Wayne", he almost shouted, "I'm telling you the truth. Governor Hoffman and Parker know all about it. They know the truth. That wood for that ladder was bought right here in Phoenixville, down at Andrews."

So incensed was Harry during his attempt to relate his story, that his dissertation of it was broken and fragmentary and hard for me to follow. However, before he left nearly two hours later, I finally came to grasp most of his story, which went like this:

About the middle of February, 1932, he said he had received a telephone call from his brother-in-law, Per Stover, who operated a shoe store at 224 Bridge Street in Phoenixville. Stover and his wife, Hannah, who was Harry's sister, lived above the store, just a short distance from Young's radio shop. Stover informed him that his brother Martin had just arrived from South America and was paying them an unexpected visit and wanted him to come down and meet his brother.

Young told me his meeting with Martin Stover was a fascinating one. He said they sat for hours listening to Martin relate the exciting life he lived in the Andes mountains where his home was located. Martin said he was a dealer in furs, who raised various animals for their pelts, and would then personally transport the valuable skins to fur dealers in the United States. After bringing them in, usually without paying an import tax, they would be sold to furriers and tailors who would transform the raw skins and hides into beautiful coats for the ladies. At this point, Mr. Young amplified to me that Stover said it was a dangerous "game" he was involved in because he was actually smuggling the furs into the country without paying a duty on them.

At last Harry came to the crux of his "astounding" story as he related it to me. On his visit with Per and Hannah Stover, Martin had brought with him four wooden crates in which were eight live chinchillas, two in each crate. Chinchillas are small rodents largely found in the Andes mountains of South America. They have long, soft pale or silver-gray fur, and are often described as resembling a small domestic cat with short ears. They generally measure about 15 inches in length including their tail. As for their commercial value they have always been classed as very expensive animals.

Aside from the curiosity they generated, the cute furry little "critters" also posed a problem for Martin. "Do you know where I can board them for a few days?", he asked. And Harry told me he immediately said that he did, and that he would drive him out there. "So," he said, "I took him and his chinchillas out to the Ott fur farm in Charlestown Township." It was here that they met Mr. Harry Ott who granted Stover permission to leave his chinchillas there. While there, they met Stinson Markley, the Chester County game warden, who sold Stover some grain to feed the little rodents.

During Martin Stover's stay in Phoenixville, Harry told me he spent many hours with him; saying he was good companionship because of the interesting stories he told of his life in South America. On one of their jaunts together, Harry said Martin asked him where he could purchase some lumber. "I wondered what he wanted the wood for and so I asked him. Without any hesitation he said he needed it to build a pair of steps", my visitor told me. Then he went on to say that he took him down to the Frank C. Andrews Lumber Company on Bridge Street, where Stover made a small purchase. "I was with him when he bought the lumber.", Young made it clear that I understood.

As Harry unraveled his story he became more insistent that I fully understand the implications he was making, but at this point I must admit my interest was waning. But, he continued telling me what else had taken place shortly before Martin left Phoenixville for New York City. "I was in the kitchen of Per's home with Martin and my sister Hannah, and he was telling us he had to leave for New York soon and would not be coming back this way. Hannah asked him how long he would be in New York and he said 'Several days and then I will leave for home. I have to take a kid back with me.'"

Hannah's reaction to his answer, Harry explained was nothing short of amazement, as she quickly retorted with another question: 'Why do you have to do that, you haven't got any kid?' But Martin went on to explain to them that although he didn't especially like the idea of a grown man taking a young boy that distance, he had to do it, adding that, 'when you don't have money you must do lots of things you wouldn't do if you had money.' "He also told us", Harry related to me, "that he wasn't going to take the boy up into the mountains, but was 'going to deliver him to some one or some society, whoever they tell me to.'"

Harry Young was normally not an excitable person, but nevertheless, he had related this information to me in a very stimulated, animated fashion, which I must say, I found hard to follow. He concluded his story by explaining that Martin Stover was a carpenter, and when he bought the lumber at Andrews, "I asked him if he was working at his trade, and he said: 'Oh, no. I'm just going to build a ladder and a pair of steps.'" Young also had informed me that one of Stover's valuable chinchillas had died while it was at the Ott fur farm.

His discourse was evidently concluded, and I told him it was quite a story, at the same time inquiring as to why he had come to me with it. "Because", he said, "of your interest in police work, and I thought you could be of some help."

"Yes, Harry. I am very interested in anything pertaining to the Lindbergh case. I also believe Hauptmann was not guilty, but what is your point? I see no connection. Surely you don't base your suspicions of Martin Stover's involvement on his purchase of wood and his statement that he was taking a child back to South America."

Either I had missed a point in Harry's story or he had overlooked telling me the one important factor. As I explained my lack of comprehension, he began reviewing the points as he had related them, but this time he accentuated the key element of his narrative. "Don't you see," he explained, "the names on the crates of chinchillas was Isidor Fisch. Martin was delivering those chinchillas to Hauptmann's partner, Isidor Fisch." He went on to explain that it was during Hauptmann's trial he read the name Isidor Fisch as the man from whom Hauptmann had said he obtained the box containing the ransom money. "And when I read it, I said to myself, where did I run across that name before? And then I realized it was the same name that was on those crates, same address too, 126th Street, in the Bronx." Harry seemed pleased that I now understood the connection.

I must admit again that Young's story now made slightly more sense to me. He explained that reading the name of Fisch had triggered his memory to reflect back on things that had occurred in February of 1932 when he and Martin Stover had spent so much time together. He reasoned that if Stover delivered those crates to Fisch, then he must have known him. And it would be quite natural, he thought, since they were both in the fur business. Harry's mind by this time was running away with his thoughts.

Young said he told his wife Leanore about his idea that his friend Martin Stover was also a friend of Hauptmann's partner, Isidor Fisch, but her reaction had been unemotional. She merely "wrote it off" as a possible coincidence, and much to Harry's disappointment, was her unbelief, all which added to his frustration.

But his overly active mind continued to assemble the various incidents in a structure of guilt that pointed to Stover, as he thought back to his purchase of lumber. Could he have possibly built that three-sectioned ladder with the wood from Andrews? After all, he reasoned, some of the same lumber that had been used in the actual kidnap ladder had already been traced into

Phoenixville. "You remember this, Wayne," he reminded me, "it was in the paper when the two FBI men came to the Andrews lumber company and told Doll Lessig that the wood they sold there was the same?"

Yes, I had to admit, Harry had made his point. I did remember that in late 1933 or early 1934 it was common knowledge in Phoenixville that two investigators (my guess would be that the two were Bornmann and Koehler since they were the men working on the wood angle) had come to the office of the Andrews Lumber Company and talked to L. Darlington Lessig and George M. Andrews, informing them that a portion of lumber still remaining in their yard was identical to that in the famous kidnap ladder used in the Lindbergh kidnapping. As Harry Young had said, this fact had been printed as a news item in *The Daily Republican*, Phoenixville's newspaper.

Now, Harry drove home his main point. "Didn't I tell you that Martin told my sister Hannah and me that he had to take a kid back to South America with him. Whose kid do you think it was? Lindbergh's kid that's whose it was! Don't you see the complete tie-in? The chinchillas were being taken to Fisch, Hauptmann's partner, Martin bought the lumber here and used it in making the ladder to take Lindy's kid out of the house, and then Martin took the kid to South America. There's no doubt about it. It's the truth Wayne, I swear to God, it's the truth!", Harry was quite incensed as he rambled on about his knowledge of the truth of the Lindbergh case, and Hauptmann's innocence.

"Even my wife won't believe me, but that doesn't make any difference. I know I'm right. She's afraid, she says I'll get myself killed, but I don't care. I know it's the truth. My name is good. I wouldn't make up such a story. These things really happened, and I can prove it. My sister knows the truth, too", Mr. Young continued on, apparently sensing my disbelief in all he had told me.

There was one thing Harry had said which could not be disputed. Harry Pennypacker Young had a good reputation for his integrity. He was a person who always shied away from the lime-light. However, he was never hesitant to tell anyone about his good marriage to Leanore Hartzell and their two children, little Harry and Leanore. He was proud of his family, and rightly so. He also took great pride in having it known that he was a relative of Pennsylvania's former governor, Samuel Whitaker Pennypacker, for whom Harry had been given his middle name.

Although Harry was known for his integrity, I just could not find myself able to grasp his story. I would certainly need more facts, more proof, I told him. He left me as I mulled over what he had told me. The whole thing was preposterous, unbelievable. Who could ever believe that Phoenixville, Pennsylvania had played a part in the kidnapping of Lindbergh's baby? Well, I certainly knew of one now --- Harry Pennypacker Young. As he left me I certainly had much more to think about. This thing could not possibly be true, I reasoned almost audibly. Or could it? I would think about it. And I did, more than I really intended to.

After Harry's initial visit, many others followed. By this time I had taken a position as manager of a stationery store on Main Street hill, directly across from the Young Radio Shop, the location of which made it very convenient for Harry to come across the street, buy his morning paper, and then spend considerable time "visiting" in order to discuss the merits of what he considered to be, his very reasonable claims.

It wasn't long before he came accompanied by a nice looking man I had never seen before. He introduced him as Mr. Stinson Markley, the game warden of Chester County, who lived in Charlestown Township adjacent to Phoenixville. He asked his friend, the pleasant, soft-spoken Mr. Markley to tell me what he knew about Martin Stover and the association he had with him a few years before. He reiterated the account Harry Young had told me, but he went a bit further, telling me that Stover had asked him if he would like to go back to Argentina and work for him. He had shown Markley some pictures of his home in the Andes mountains and said the work would be rather dangerous. Mr. Markley said he immediately declined his offer. I asked the game warden if he believed Mr. Young's perception as to Stover's probable connection with the Lindbergh case, and he assured me that he "certainly thought it was possible". He also supported Young's claim that the name on the tags attached to each crate of chinchillas had been that of Isidor Fisch, the Bronx, New York.

I am sure Harry Young found me to be a disappointment in his search for sincere believers in his story. He seemed to think that due to my interest in crime detection, I would have virtually jumped in and run with the information he had given me by getting involved and helping him clear the name of Hauptmann. But, even if I had, who was I to even as much as think that anyone would believe us. They would more than likely have had us committed as a pair of "loonies".

"But", Harry insisted," "Ellis Parker believed me. He said he knew all about Stover's connection with Fisch and a guy named Wendel. He said Hauptmann was innocent and that he was about to make an arrest. He said Hauptmann was not going to die. But he did, and then they arrested Parker. He knew all about Stover, he told us, Detective Campbell and me." Young's faith in his story did bother me. I could not seem to lay it aside in my thoughts.

Through the ensuing months I continued reading various documents and books on the case. I had acquired copies of the abridged version of *The Trial Of Bruno Richard Hauptmann* by Sidney B. Whipple, and *The Lindbergh Case* by the same author. As I read and studied these books night and day, and poured over the condensed version of the trial transcript, before very long I could clearly see some other glaring inaccuracies in the Hauptmann trial.

In addition to this, I was at a loss to understand how the findings of Ellis Parker and his associates could have been taken so lightly. It was after Hauptmann's execution, in late April of 1936, that Ellis Parker, Jr., of Mount Holly, New Jersey; Murray Bleefeld of Trenton, New Jersey; Harry Weiss and Martin Schlossman of Brooklyn, New York, were arrested for the kidnapping of Paul H. Wendel and incarcerating him in the home of Harry Bleefeld, at 3041 Voorhies Avenue in the Sheepshead Section of Brooklyn. Harry Bleefeld had also been arrested.

These arrests had been made at the command of William F.X. Geoghan, the Kings County District Attorney, who, after confirming Wendel's repudiation as acceptable, added that he looked at Wendel's confession as false and that Ellis Parker, Sr. had framed and tortured the lawyer into making an unbelievable "confession". An indictment against Ellis, Sr. was issued, and on Wednesday, June 3rd, none other than Lieutenant Lewis Bornmann of the New Jersey State Police, who must have experienced extreme pleasure, walked up to the "Old Fox of Mount Holly" and snapped the handcuffs on his wrists as he left the Elks Club in his home town.

However, Governor Hoffman refused to extradite the two Parkers to Brooklyn for trial. His main reason was because of his lack of trust in Geoghan's motive in issuing the warrants; Hoffman considered the matter to be entirely a political one. Wendel was then advised to take the matter into his own hands. He informed the United States Attorney General of his problem, asking him if the indictments should not be the concern of New Jersey's federal grand jury. In this the attorney general was in complete agreement, and in October, 1936, after listening to Wendel's "pathetic story" of the beatings to which he had been subjected, the grand jury handed down an indictment charging the Parkers with conspiracy under the Lindbergh law.

My personal feelings regarding the Wendel confession, prompted by a belief I held at the time, provoked me to reason that any action as to the validity of the confession should have been taken into court before Hauptmann was executed. Why, I had questioned, was there such a big rush to get rid of Hauptmann? I had real trouble understanding this - and still do.

But, the wheels of justice ground ever onward. For their part in the "abduction" of Wendel, Murray Bleefeld, Harry Weiss, and Martin Schlossman were tried in Brooklyn in February, 1937. They were convicted of violating New York State's kidnap law and were sentenced to serve twenty years in Sing Sing Prison at Ossining, New York. The trial for the two Parkers was held in federal court in Newark, New Jersey and lasted seven weeks. Both were convicted under the Lindbergh law. The so-called "justice" that had been demonstrated by the prosecutors in the sentencing of Hauptmann, now was being openly exhibited as Judge William Clark directed his remarks to Ellis, Sr.: "I have the impression that your life as a law-enforcement officer and your position in the community have given you the feeling that you are above the law, and that is the cause of your making a mockery of the processes of justice in New Jersey." Although the jury felt compunction enough to have recommended that leniency be granted the elderly detective, Judge Clark saw fit to sentence him to six years in the Federal Penitentiary at Lewisburg, Pennsylvania. This was the "thank you" he received, with no mention of his faithfulness to his state in a career that spanned over four decades, during which time he solved thousands of crimes. Known in those years as the world's greatest detective, his record of successful cases included his solving 226 murders, out of the 236 he investigated. He was a man who ascended to a brilliance of exhibiting great intellect whenever it came to solving mysterious crimes. He was a man who combined whatever scientific detection methods were available and then use a combination of brilliant deductive reasoning plus just his own plain common sense.

And so, for all of this he had now been thanked with a harsh six year prison sentence. Another example of Jersey "justice", mixed with a generous portion of, what seemed to be, Jersey politics. Ellis, Jr's sentence --- for helping his dad --- three years in a federal pen. Their subsequent appeals were, quite naturally, denied.

Without enjoying another day of freedom, on Sunday, February 4, 1940 the famous detective, Ellis Parker, the "Old Fox of Mount Holly", died of a brain tumor in the prison hospital at Lewisburg, Pennsylvania. Ellis, Jr. was released late in October the following year. As far as the authorities in New Jersey were concerned, justice had at last been served. Now, they agreed with one another, we will move ahead to other things.

Publicity about the case had dwindled to almost nothing. With the exception of an occasional article, telling of the death of a principal subject or an interesting tid-bit about someone who had played a part in the case, articles pertaining to the Lindbergh kidnapping were no longer considered front page news.

However, it had already become a practice of mine to clip every item I found on the case for any future reference I might want to make. But these became nothing more than collector's items which would possibly be pasted in a scrapbook at some time in the future.

Aside from the visits, made almost daily by Harry Young, and listening to his intense arguments as he attempted to "sell me" on his South America story, I rarely discussed the case with anyone else. To be truthful about it, Harry's story had started to wear rather thin with me. I couldn't help but feel that he was suffering from possibly a mental delusion of some kind. But then, I remembered, Stinson Markley had supported his story, as had Harry Ott and Mrs. Young, Harry's wife.

It was on a Saturday evening, during the fall months of 1937 that Harry came hurrying to see me. I had no problem noticing that he was visibly excited about something. Pushing a newspaper into my hand, he shouted, "Now maybe you'll believe me! I told you the kid was in South America. Here, read this!" I took the folded paper from him. It was a copy of a New York City paper, an early Sunday morning edition. I scanned the article he had pointed to, and as I read, my interest was aroused. My attention had been immediately drawn to a simulated picture of a child pointing to a photograph of Colonel Lindbergh which was hanging on the wall of a home somewhere in South America. The accompanying article unfolded a story which went far to confirm Harry Young's contention that the Lindbergh baby had been taken to South America. Experiencing amazement as I read through the story, I must admit it was also somewhat exciting.

The essence of the article related the following: In early March of 1932 two men had brought a child into a Colombian city in South America and deposited the male youngster in the home of a woman who had promised to take care of him. While the child was there he noticed a picture on a wall in one of the rooms, which prompted his incessant pointing to the picture while repeating the word "Daddy". The picture was that of Charles A. Lindbergh, Sr.

The fascination shown by the child toward the picture had aroused the curiosity of the woman who was caring for him. Naturally she had wondered who the child was and from where he had come. The only thing she did know about him was this. Two men, both strangers, had come to her door a few days earlier, and asked if she would keep him for them for a short time. She had consented and they paid her well for her trouble. But now she found herself faced with a slight problem. She could not understand what caused the youngster to become excited whenever he saw Lindbergh's picture, as well as what he was saying when he pointed to it? She attempted to fathom the mystery herself, but without success.

As she went about the community asking her questions she was told that the youngster was speaking the English word "daddy". Her alert mind immediately reasoned that the present date on the calendar coincided within days of the kidnapping of Lindbergh's child, and since he had not yet been found and returned to his home, she concluded that the child she had in her home was the stolen Lindbergh baby.

Her anxiety over this "strange possibility" naturally inspired her to tell others. She lost no time going about the neighborhood spreading her exciting news. The Colombian authorities were notified, and although they had serious doubts, they promptly informed the New Jersey investigators. They also forwarded the information on to Colonel Lindbergh himself. But regardless of this, there had been no response whatsoever to any of the telegrams they sent. No one seemed to be the least bit interested - and yet, in spite of this "valued information" offered to them by the Colombian officials, a mammoth search was being conducted at the same time up in the States without any success.

Regardless of the very apparent lack of interest in the "reported unknown child" located down in Colombia, there was, however, great concern expressed by the South American citizens who were now reading about it in their local newspaper. The interest down there was especially demonstrated by two men. One, a Colombian priest, and the other a friend of his, a private detective. To say the very least, these two were certainly sympathetic to the cause, as they went about conducting a private investigation of their own. Their findings prompted them to arrive at the conclusion that the child very definitely could be the lost son of Colonel and Mrs. Charles Lindbergh.

By this time the youngster had been reclaimed by the two men and taken further south to the little town of Popayan. Because of their desire to hopefully solve the case of the missing Lindbergh baby, the priest and detective followed the path of the two "abductors" into Popayan, where in front of the Hotel El Paso, they were brutally assassinated by gunfire from an unknown origin. And, with that, the story concluded.

Well, what did I think of it all? The article was awe inspiring, but it failed to prove anything absolute. It was just a story. It could have been fictional. And, of course, there was always the possibility that it could have been factual.

I found it difficult to think clearly. Harry Young was very, very excited about every detail of it, as he continued to "dance and prance" around me to a point that it all bordered on being amusing. "Can't you see it? I told you Martin Stover took Lindbergh's kid to South America, didn't I? He was one of the guys that took the kid to the woman to keep.", Harry shouted and stammered, occasionally pounding his fist on the counter to emphasize a point. He was beside himself with exuberance as he made it clear he was proving himself correct about Stover's taking a child to South America.

I had to admit there now existed a strong possibility that Harry had known something completely different about the case. That is something other than what we had been led to believe from reading and hearing the commonly accepted stories throughout the years which had been printed and dispatched by the news media. At least this article did add more credibility to his story.

From this time on the realization enveloped me that I had already taken a new outlook on the case. I could not toss off the intensity of the feeling that overwhelmed me. Could there actually be any truth to Harry Young's story? It seemed absurd, incredible. And yet, there were a number of people who had met Martin Stover, had seen his chinchillas, had heard his stories. In addition to Harry, there were his wife, Per Stover and his wife Hannah, Stinson Markley, Harry Ott, two of Per's sons, Percy Stover, and Alan Stover who operated an electrical appliance store on East Bridge Street in Phoenixville, his repairman, Joseph Fulmer, and his salesman, Sydney Slemmer. In addition to these, there was attorney Fred W. Deininger. But then there were the things I had been told personally by George B. Campbell, the detective whom Harry had initially consulted when he first had become aware of Stover's involvement.

I was working on a criminal case with detective Campbell, and I remember the incident well. It was a Saturday morning as we were riding together through nearby Oaks, Pennsylvania. George, who was driving, suddenly changed the subject from that of the case we were investigating to that of the Lindbergh case. Suddenly, without any preliminary remarks, he stopped the car and said: "Wayne, do you know that Hauptmann was innocent of kidnapping and killing the Lindbergh baby?" I assured him that I also believed this. He then went on to tell me of his belief that Martin Stover had been deeply involved with Isidor Fisch. He told me of his trip with Harry Young to see Ellis Parker in Mount Holly, New Jersey, and that Parker had told them that Hauptmann was not going to die. "He told us he knew all about Martin Stover, that he was working with a man named Wendel, the brains of the whole thing, and that soon he would be making an arrest", is what Campbell told me. I informed him that Mr. Young had been confiding with me and had brought me up to date with the latest developments. "But," said the detective, "things didn't work out right, Hauptmann did die and Parker went to prison for trying to do the right thing. Parker was on the right track, you know." I could not do any more than agree whole-heartedly. And, at this point, I will add that George B. Campbell had an excellent reputation locally as a detective similar to Ellis Parker, because his record as a criminal investigator could be compared, in a much smaller way, to that of the world renowned detective. He too, was a homespun man with the gifted intellect to solve many of the most difficult crimes.

From the time I had acquired this first hand additional information from Detective Campbell, I felt compelled to visit a few of the locations in New Jersey where the crime had taken place. I was anxious to talk to some of those involved, those who might have personal knowledge of what had actually taken place at the time of the crime. I wanted to get some of their viewpoints, to study their reactions to some questions I would like to ask. No, I had no desire to play detective. It was just a compelling interest I had, nothing more, nothing less. I guess it was just a morbid curiosity to possibly learn a few more things which might be just "contrary" to those we had already learned from the press. Nothing as great as Harry Young's South America story, but, just maybe, something to fill in a chink or two.

I decided a good place to start was at the Hopewell home of the Lindberghs, visit the Flemington court house, or possibly obtain some information from a State Trooper who had worked on the case. I decided the latter would possibly be the best avenue to take. Doing this, I found I could not have chosen a better course.

Elwood Hochstetter, a close friend of mine who was aware of my interest in the Lindbergh case, at one time had told me that a relative of his, a New Jersey state trooper, had actively worked on the case from the time the child was abducted. He had offered to take me to meet the trooper, if I so desired, since he thought I would enjoy talking with him. I decided that time had arrived, so I called Elwood and made arrangements to go with him on the following Sunday. The year was 1940, a few years after I had read Harry's newspaper article.

My trip with Elwood proved to be a fruitful one. I not only met New Jersey State Trooper John Opdyke, and found him to be a very congenial person, I had the pleasure of meeting his family in their home. Trooper Opdyke was more than willing to drive us around "Lindbergh Land", as it had now become known. We saw the various points of interest, a view of the Sourland Mountains with the white washed stone walls of the Lindbergh mansion silhouetted against them. We visited the jail where Hauptmann had been confined during his trial, we sat in the witness chair from where all of the Lindbergh-Hauptmann "notables" had testified.

All this had been quite entertaining. I thoroughly enjoyed the time spent with Trooper Opdyke. However, my trip had not produced one shred of evidence that I could put together with anything I already had which could be used toward helping Richard Hauptmann, even if I had wanted to. Until ------.

As we were about to say good-bye, I was standing by the side of Trooper Opdyke at a location approximately halfway toward the back of the court room in the spectator's section. As we stood there a strange thought crossed my mind. I wondered if I were bold enough to ask the trooper a question, one which might elicit a direct yes or no answer. Not wanting to forever lose such an opportunity, I went ahead and rather sheepishly inquired: "John, do you believe Hauptmann was guilty?" There was only a pause of a second or two, and then I watched as he closed his eyes and raised his head to face the ceiling, as he answered very deliberately: "Well, the big boys said he was!"

Trooper John Opdyke had given me his answer.

I needed no additional motivation. At that moment I determined with all my heart to do all in my power to prove Hauptmann's innocence.

CHAPTER SIXTY FIVE

In Search of Truth!

Progress made by police departments toward obtaining successful solutions of major criminal cases is usually a lengthy procedure. Generally, their investigation is not only tedious and tiring, it sometimes turns out to be very despairing work. This was without doubt true of the investigation into the kidnapping of the Lindbergh baby. But, it was true even to a greater extent, not solely due to the magnitude of the crime against America's number one hero, but because, after two-and-one-half years, the skills of three major criminal units had been unable to solve a crime, with so many clues having been left behind. And then, when they finally "stumbled upon the man they believed was involved", they were unable to prosecute him without the aid of manufactured evidence and perjured testimony, thus leaving a great number of people with honest doubts about his guilt.

I was one person who had been left with many honest doubts. But, I had more than just honest doubts. I had the facts Harry Young had told me, and the confirmation of this by others, plus the article in the New York newspaper supporting Harry's story. I was in a dilemma. I wanted to do something about it all, but I didn't know where or how to start.

With the words of Trooper Opdyke of the New Jersey State Police still fresh in my mind, I now found myself, one alone, with a burning desire to lend some aid toward discovering the real truth, and possibly what lay behind it. But surely, I could not do this without help, or could I? I decided to try.

Going about the town where you are known, telling friends that you know the real truth about the Lindbergh kidnapping, that Hauptmann was innocent, and that you know the names of some of the kidnappers, is not the greatest way to win friends. Instead, I found more and more persons willing to commit me to the "loony bin", claiming I had gone off my rocker. However, regardless of this, whenever I found some interested listeners I would tell them Harry Young's story, assuring them that I too believed it all. For this I was labeled a "fourteen-carat nut" who was capable of believing anything. Mockery, oh, what mockery.

Finally after arriving at the conclusion that I was getting absolutely nowhere with this approach, I decided to continue making visits to Hopewell and Flemington, New Jersey. After discussions I had with many residents in both towns about the case, I was encouraged with the responses I received, namely as to their reluctance to believe in Hauptmann's guilt. I was surprised to learn that so many of them also nurtured the belief that Hauptmann was innocent, some even insisting that he was framed. Their answers had been an exact reversal of what I had expected.

In addition to the one-on-one confrontations with friends, I was now being asked to address small groups of people, who by this time, had heard about my defense of Hauptmann and were anxious to hear me explain it to them first hand by telling them my version of the crime. The initial one of these speaking engagements was an appearance before an interested group of Boy Scouts. It was one I remember well, since their troop leader, who was an ardent student of the Lindbergh case, voiced his personal opinion about the verdict in no uncertain terms. I was pleased indeed, to hear him say his beliefs were the same as mine - Hauptmann was completely innocent.

Soon I was speaking frequently at public gatherings, and I must say rather boldly, as I told them of my earnest belief that Hauptmann had been framed, emphasizing the strong feeling I held that Harry Young's story should be looked into further as to the veracity of Martin Stover's involvement. However, the only feed-back I acquired was either from the scoffers, those who openly opposed my stand, or those who merely walked away, plainly indifferent toward seeing justice done. Strangely enough, the biggest obstacle I had to surmount was their skepticism. "Oh, yeah," they would point out, "don't expect me to believe that Phoenixville had anything to do with that kidnapping." Or, they would retort, "Don't try to tell me that the ladder wood came from here." And in my attempts to give them my reasonable answer, they didn't want to hear it.

If I had expected any thanks for my faith in Hauptmann's "Fisch Story", I would have been sorely disappointed. Instead I was on the losing end from the very start. I was chastised, ridiculed, and mocked, which sometimes extended to even pity and sympathy from friends who thought I was experiencing some sort of mental problem, bordering on lunacy. However, regardless of this, there remained within me the constant and deep rooted desire that kept me faithful to the possibility that at some time in the distant future the complete truth might be learned.

Was it too much to hope that it would be revealed, to the satisfaction of all, what actually did take place on the evening of Tuesday, March 1st, 1932 and the succeeding days which lead to the diabolical travesty of justice in the execution death of Bruno Richard Hauptmann on Friday evening, April 3rd, 1936? Not at all, I had reasoned with myself.

And yet, I must admit, I had nothing more than a "shaky hope" that the truth would some day be disclosed. As to when, or how, I naturally had no foreknowledge - I merely held a "shaky hope." However, as small as this hope was, I could not abandon it. And so, I continued to carry my "shaky hope" down through the years, primarily because I had embraced, and refused to deny, the truth of the amazing story Harry Young had told me.

During the ensuing years, it had never actually dawned on me that there could possibly be anyone else seeking the truth of the Lindbergh case. Other than Ellis Parker who had been committed to a prison where he eventually died for his belief that Paul Wendel had been involved, it never had occurred to me that there could be anyone else interested enough to have seriously attempted to "dig into" the inequities of the case that had been used to convict Hauptmann. Although Mrs. Hauptmann had hired a private detective to look into the case, with the hope of having him unearth something which could be considered of major importance to prove her husband's innocence, the results of his efforts were recognized as inconsequential.

As time moved on I came to realize that there were more than a few "private investigators" who had not been satisfied with the outcome of case, and were now, by means of their own initiative, trying to solve the mystery of the great Lindbergh kidnapping. Every so often an article would appear in the newspapers giving an account of their "beliefs" usually based on nothing more than rumors backed up with nothing but some person's supposition.

Stories such as these added nothing to help me along in my so-called private "investigation" which had already literally come to a stand-still. I had done very little, simply because I did not know what I could do. Per Stover had died and his obituary had mentioned that he had a brother living in South America --- Something I already knew, but the printed article did confirm his existence down there. Harry Young passed away in 1960. Martin Stover, who had not returned to the United States died during the 1960's and had been buried at his home in Argentina. Truthfully, I considered my investigation to have come to a stand-still. After all, I counseled myself, I am one-alone. What can I ever expect of myself. I have no resources. I don't have the "know-how" to put it all together anyway. Possibly I should forget it all and save the "wear-and-tear" on my brain, was a familiar thought.

However, unknown to me, someone over in New York City was already doing some intensified investigating which would eventually openly expose, for the public to clearly see, the "batch of lies" that had been unethically used to convict Hauptmann. The work done by this one man was to lead to the clearing of his name.

I wish to make it very clear that without the diligent and relentless investigation conducted by Anthony Scaduto, my work on the case would have fallen far short of allowing me to give you the complete story of the Lindbergh kidnapping. We needed to join forces. We did, and here is how it eventually happened.

In the year 1973, Tony Scaduto, a prize-winning reporter on the staff of the *New York Post*, was approached by means of a letter mailed to him by Murray Bleefeld, one of the men who had assisted Ellis Parker in the Wendel fiasco of 1936. The letter read: "I have the true 'Lindbergh Story.' This will be a story the world has never heard. I was there. I worked on the case. I can prove Bruno Richard Hauptmann was innocent. Perhaps you can help me write my book. Please contact me by calling Assistant U.S. Attorney...." The receipt of this letter started Tony on a three-year search for the answers, which he eventually obtained, proving to him that "the trial and execution of Bruno Richard Hauptmann may be the most terrifying example in American history of the defects in our system of criminal justice and of the arrogance of police power."

A short time later, Scaduto received a telephone call from Bleefeld who identified himself as one of Ellis Parker's assistants who had served a prison sentence for helping the old detective. Tony pressed him for more information, only to have his caller tell him the information he had was much too complicated to explain over the phone. But, regardless of this, Bleefeld went on to say that he knew that Hauptmann had nothing to do with the case, saying that it was Paul Wendel who had planned it all.

Scaduto probed further, inquiring as to why he was so certain Wendel had done it. "Because he confessed.", Bleefeld quickly answered.

"But Hauptmann was executed," Tony retorted, which induced Murray to give him the following explanation: "Because of David Wilentz, the prosecutor. He got to Wendel and before anybody knew what was happening Wendel twisted around everything in his confession---I tell you the man had a brilliant mind---and he made it look like we beat the confession out of him. It was politics. David Wilentz wasn't going to permit the governor and Ellis Parker to cast doubt on his solution of the crime of the century---that's what they called it and that's what it was, the most incredible crime in history. David Wilentz was the man sending Hauptmann to the chair and he wasn't going to admit he made a mistake because he had a big political future to worry about. So Hauptmann did go to the chair and I went to prison for trying to get the truth---me and Parker and his son, everybody connected with the Wendel case. We all went to prison and the real killer became a hero, wrote a book and magazine articles and all that. Ellis Parker died in prison, he died of a broken heart---forty years a detective and he was sent to prison to die because of politics."

Bleefeld had certainly given Tony Scaduto much to think about. After telling his informer that he would read some material he had on the Lindbergh case to refresh his memory, he suggested that they meet, at which time he could tape the interview.

While waiting for his meeting with Bleefeld, Tony devoted a lot of time reading and re-reading the books he owned that had been written about the famous case. He also made note of some variances which caused his concern; why certain omissions had not been checked out; why apparent discrepancies had been allowed to stand without questioning.

One of the points which had been stressed during the early days following the kidnapping, and one that bothered Scaduto, was the claim made by a young New York psychiatrist, Dr. Dudley D. Shoenfeld, who said that when "Cemetery John", the lone kidnapper of the child was arrested, the police would find "in John's pocket at least one ransom bill, which he would carry as a reminder of his omnipotence, and that bill would be folded; tightly folding the bill was a subconscious manifestation of John's personality---methodical, extremely cautious, inner-directed, and probably struggling to hold back his homosexual tendencies(!)"

It is no wonder that the statement of this "intelligent" Shoenfeld, who had spoken out with all the authority he could muster, had caused a bit of wonder in Tony Scaduto's mind. Why, he reasoned, when Hauptmann was arrested, the bill in his wallet was not folded, but was laid out flat in the bill pocket. And none of the other five bills attributed to being spent by Hauptmann had been folded. Why then, when all the ransom bills passed in 1933 and early 1934 were found to be folded, were those the authorities had traced to having been definitely spent by Hauptmann not been folded, as had been so confidently predicted by the "expert" psychiatrist? Shoenfeld's "prophecy" had fallen flat on its face.

One other interesting question was raised by Tony Scaduto. It is a point we dare not overlook when it comes to proving Hauptmann's innocence. He makes the issue very clear in his book *Scapegoat*: "While following this tangential lead, this search for information about the compulsively folded bills (as the psychiatrist had called them), I was driven off on an even further side trip by a paragraph in George Waller's *KIDNAP*. What Waller had written was farther down the road than I'd reached in my chronology, but I made notes anyway and thought about it for hours."

"By now, in Waller's chronicle, Hauptmann had finally been told he was under arrest as a suspect in the Lindbergh crime and he had attempted to explain how he'd come into possession of Lindbergh ransom money: a shoe box full of it had been given Hauptmann for safekeeping in December 1933 by a friend who had gone back to Germany to visit his family; the friend had died there and when Hauptmann discovered the box contained money he'd begun to spend it for household expenses because the friend owed him several thousand dollars. What lured me into this tangent forking off another tangent were two sentences in Waller's text. They came at the end of a long recitation about the witnesses who would be asked by police to attend a lineup and to identify Hauptmann. The witnesses were vital, Waller wrote, for possession of ransom money was not nearly enough to convict Hauptmann of kidnapping and extortion, or both; witnesses must place Hauptmann in the vicinity of Lindbergh's home on the day of the kidnapping or in the cemeteries during the negotiations, to construct an unassailable case against him. After listing the possible witnesses, Waller had written:

'Of equal importance now was an East Side storekeeper who had been given one of the ten-dollar gold certificates as far back as March 1, 1933; he might prove that Hauptmann was lying when he said that the ... gold notes had been turned over to him ... in DECEMBER of '33. The storekeeper had told detectives that he'd remember his customer if he saw him again.'

"Waller did not name the East Side storekeeper, nor did he give any details of the transaction in which the ransom bill was passed. Checking through several books which provided a complete list of witnesses at Hauptmann's trial and a brief summary of their testimony, I realized that that "East Side storekeeper" had not testified. "He could not identify Hauptmann, I thought. I was certain of that. If he had been able to identify Hauptmann, the prosecutor would certainly have put him on the witness stand to destroy Hauptmann's main defense, that he did not begin passing the ransom bills until the summer of 1934, following the death of the friend who'd given him the box of gold notes. The only possible reason that witness was not called is because he had been unable to positively identify Hauptmann or, perhaps, had even said that Hauptmann was most definitely not the man who had passed him the Lindbergh gold note."

Another obstacle that Hauptmann had to overcome was that of the trial itself. It proved to be an antagonistic barrier from beginning to end for the defense counsel to hurdle. Tony Scaduto found this to be true as he perused the accounts published prior to the trial, as well as those who gave reports of the daily happenings, not only within the confines of the Flemington court room, but on the outside as well. Reporting during the time of the Hauptmann trial had established a new low in journalism.

After reading the various reports, Scaduto told of them in his book, together with his personal feelings. As we read we can clearly see the irregularities which were used by the press in this most dastardly phase of unfair treatment aimed at Hauptmann from the time his arrest was made public. Scaduto writes: "The country was treated to a spectacular circus that angered even

EDITOR AND PUBLISHER, the normally uncritical organ of the journalistic profession. The magazine complained, after Hauptmann was convicted:

'No trial in this century has so degraded the administration of justice. If the life of one man and the unhappiness of hundreds are to be commercialized for the benefit of entertainment, of radio broadcasters, newspaper publishers, newsreel producers; if a public trial means protection from star-chamber tyranny but not from the indignities of the mob, then the ancient institution of trial by a jury of peers is without meaning.'

"Most certainly it was spectacle more than trial; low camp theater masquerading as justice. For about a month before the trial opened, technicians were busily decorating Flemington with telephone and telegraph cables in order to transmit to the world what every journalist called the story of the century. Several American newspapers established branch offices in the little town, enriching the citizens who threw open their spare bedrooms to reporters at five dollars a night. The more affluent papers announced with pride that they had acquired the services of Edna Ferber, Fannie Hurst, Damon Runyon, Adela Rogers St. Johns, Alexander Woollcot, Walter Winchell, Kathleen Norris, and a dozen other journalists of equal rank and popularity to write "special reports" in their own inimitable styles. The *DAILY MAIL* and *DAILY EXPRESS* of London were sending special correspondents. So were *PARIS-SOIR* and a score of equally important European publications. The goal of all was commerce, the boosting of circulation. Before the trial, the papers and radio stations conducted advertising campaigns to boast about the enormous effort and expense the publication or broadcaster was going through for the benefit of the public, trying to convince that public to buy this paper or listen to that station. An example from one of the Hearst papers:

NATION ITSELF ACTS AS JURY TO TRY HAUPTMANN

Adela Rogers St. Johns is at Flemington to write a special article on the trial of Bruno Richard Hauptmann for the kidnap-murder of the Lindbergh baby. Read her story everyday in the *NEW YORK JOURNAL*.

"In these circumstances, justice and the

determination of truth were incidental to the entertainment of the masses. There were, as Alan Hynd wrote, several Hauptmann trials occurring simultaneously but separate and distinct from one another. There was the relatively minor trial in the courtroom, a drama whose climax was known to all, since every citizen had been told for months that Hauptmann was beyond doubt the baby-killer. There was the trial in the newspapers in which experts, especially psychiatrists, most of whom had never seen nor spoken with Hauptmann, explained the compulsion that had led him to kill the son of the nation's hero. There was the trial over the radio in which the 'hacks of the airwaves' distorted the evidence with their vocal nuances; one of the most popular of these commentators was the noted defense attorney Samuel Leibowitz, later a New York State supreme court justice, who repeatedly told his radio audience that the evidence made it increasingly clear Hauptmann was guilty.

"'All four trials had one thing in common---an arresting switch applied to the tenet of American jurisprudence that holds that a man is innocent until proven guilty,' Hynd wrote. 'Hauptmann was presumed guilty unless proved innocent. The only question was: how guilty was he? The suspense over the outcome of the four trials was confined to speculation as to whether Hauptmann would get the chair or life imprisonment.'

"The spectacle most definitely affected the jury. Under New Jersey law, a jury in a capital case must be sequestered. The Hauptmann jury was housed on the third floor of the little Union Hotel, across the street from the courthouse. The hotel was the nerve center of newspaper and radio journalists. During its meals the jury was seated in the public dining room, separated from other diners by only a flimsy cloth screen. At each meal they heard the boisterous newspapermen and women commenting on the events in court; most reporters, with the exception of Damon Runyon, were vocal in their condemnation of 'Hauptmann the baby-killer.' To Eddie Mahar, the Hearst chain's bureau chief at Flemington, Hauptmann was a Nazi monster, and most other writers agreed.

"'Bruno Richard Hauptmann looks like this new guy they have got over in Germany,' Mahar told St. Johns and other Hearst writers as the trial was about to begin. 'The one they call Der Fueher, that Hitler. You got to remember Hitler and Hauptmann had exactly the same experience in the war, they were both corporals in the German army. They must have learned the same kind of brutality. Same type, you look and you'll see it.'

"Loud enough to be head by everyone, Runyon said, 'That doesn't make him guilty. I think we'd better keep open minds.'

"A strange silence fell, St. Johns later recalled.

"Four times daily, on its trips between the hotel and courthouse, the jury was required to pass through a carnival of reporters standing on the courthouse steps making bets on how long it would take the jury to convict Hauptmann; citizens participating in the curbstone trial, rendering the popular verdict by shouting at the jurors, 'Burn Hauptmann'; newsboys shouting headlines about Hauptmann's impending doom; souvenir sellers hawking reproductions of the kidnap ladder. And at night the jurors could hear from the broadcasters' room, directly over their own, radio commentators like Leibowitz and Gabriel Heatter informing their audiences that Hauptmann had come one day closer to the electric chair.

"Through it all, the fiction was maintained that the jury was intelligent and sophisticated enough to ignore the mob and reach an impartial verdict. When a change of venue was demanded by Hauptmann's attorneys, it was denied by the trial judge, Thomas W. Trenchard, who obviously felt, as Waller rather naively expressed it in *KIDNAP*, that the jury, 'well-balanced, soberly respectable, seemed qualified' to order their minds unaffected by the circus atmosphere outside. In truth, however, twelve Solomons could not have withstood the demands of public opinion."

Anthony Scaduto was learning fast. The more he read about the case and its irregularities, the more incensed he became as he learned of the treatment Hauptmann had received at the hands of dishonest people. This, coupled with a strong desire to prove to the public that Hauptmann had suffered an unnecessary death for a crime he did not commit, motivated the police reporter to seek out the real truth.

Just the rantings of Murray Bleefeld, claiming that Parker and the rest of them had been "set-up", something very apparent and important in his final "proof-positive" verdict, would not be sufficient. He needed more than the irregularities he had read about in various publications. He needed much more. He needed to acquire bonafide proof of the Hauptmann frame-up which he could then use to support the dead victim's claim that he was innocent. Just as I, Tony Scaduto wondered where he should go to find persons, so many years after the kidnapping, who would be willing to give him accurate, and more importantly, truthful answers. However, fortunately for him he had one great advantage, he worked in New York City and had friends who might help. Or, at the very least, friends who would be willing to intercede with those who might possibly aid him in his venture.

More disturbing to Scaduto than many other discrepancies were the apparent untruths told by Condon and the way they were "believed" by the authorities without any question. There could be no denial that "Jafsie" had been judged by many of the police as a possible accomplice. He told so many lies, and avoided so many direct questions put to him, that it was difficult for them to distinguish truth from fiction. If the authorities expected us to believe that Hauptmann was the only person involved in the crime, then where were the others that Condon said he had both seen and heard? How had they mysteriously and conveniently disappeared? This was one of the many inconsistencies that more than bothered Tony. They plainly disturbed him.

Scaduto picks up the story here with his own questions:

"For example, in recreating the trip Condon made with Al Reich to Woodlawn Cemetery, where he met John for the first time, Condon testified: 'I got out of the car with the letter that I had picked up at the frankfurter stand and went over to the middle of that space, like a little piazza or area in front of the gates. I took the letter out. One man walked down from 233rd Street in the direction of the automobile, between me and the automobile. Mr. Reich was in the automobile and I saw this man come down there, but I didn't pay any attention or any account to him.'

"Almost immediately, he said, he saw a handkerchief being waved inside the gate. The man waving it turned out to be John.

"*But who was the first man*? I wondered. Condon was convinced he was dealing with a gang, including the Italian who had said '*statto citti*' and the Italian woman who asked him to meet her at the Tuckahoe station. I thought: *If he was so convinced a gang was involved, wouldn't he have believed this man he first saw at the cemetery was a lookout*? *Wouldn't he be very curious about this man*? *He most certainly would have been. Then why did he skim over it so lightly in his testimony and in his book*?

"Again I wondered once more why there was no mention of the Italian man Condon had heard over the telephone and the Italian woman who had approached him at the charity bazaar. But now my suspicions went even further. Obviously, the defense didn't know about these two incidents which established that more than one man had been involved in the extortion plot. Just as obvious, the prosecution had suppressed this evidence because it would have made a mockery of the claim that Hauptmann had acted alone. And if that evidence was kept from defense and public, how much other evidence helpful to Hauptmann had been similarly concealed?

"Another question: During Condon's long recital of his experiences with John, he again slid quickly past an incident which could be vitally important. After the ransom had been paid, Condon told federal agents, John had climbed a low railing in the cemetery and leaped to the other side, landing on a freshly dug grave. Perhaps he had left his footprint, Condon suggested. Condon returned to the cemetery accompanied by his son-in-law, Ralph Hacker, and federal agent Thomas Sisk. They found a print where Condon said it might be. A plaster of paris cast of the footprint was made. But it was never introduced into evidence. Had it matched Hauptmann's shoe, I was certain, the prosecutor would have put it into evidence because he held back no evidence in his files that could have convicted Hauptmann. His failure to use the plaster cast against the prisoner must have meant that it didn't match Hauptmann's shoes. Was this also deliberately suppressed?"

During the course of my own investigation, as I read the testimony of Condon at the Flemington trial, it became very apparent to me that he never referred to Hauptmann by any other name than "John", the name used by the emissary of the kidnappers with whom he had sat on a bench in Van Cortlandt Park on the night of Saturday, March 12th, 1932, and then three weeks later, on Saturday, April 2nd, had paid this same man "John" $50,000 of Lindbergh's money for the return of the child he failed to deliver.

As much as I tried, I could not rationalize why the pompous Condon avoided calling the prisoner by his proper name, a name he now knew and had identified earlier by that name, as the man who had "positively bilked" Colonel Lindbergh of $50,000. His failure to do this bothered me. However, I soon wrote it off as just another queer incident in the record of the Lindbergh case, one that I allowed to pass by without an answer.

It was a small issue. Why should I worry about trivia, when there was so much more of major concern to deal with, was my reasoning. But, how foolish I had been to dismiss it so readily. Years later, it took the more alert mind of Anthony Scaduto to render his forthright reasoning into the question as to why Condon constantly referred to Hauptmann only as "John".

Here is Tony's reasonable explanation for Condon's "intentional omission" of the name Hauptmann in the Flemington court room:

"Another thing that further aroused my curiosity about Condon's honesty was his strange inability to speak Hauptmann's name. Early on, Condon had identified Hauptmann as John. Yet during all his long recitation about his meetings and discussions with the extortionist, Condon never called him 'Hauptmann' from the witness chair but always referred to him as 'John.' Perhaps I was over-reacting, searching for flaws in his testimony. Perhaps I was too anxious to destroy Condon's story. Fearing so, I reread his testimony for perhaps the sixth time. And I knew I was absolutely correct: on page after page the question is asked of Condon, 'Who said that?' and Condon replies, 'John.' In one instance Wilentz attempts to give him an opening by asking, 'Who asked who was up there, the defendant?' And with the defendant, Hauptmann, sitting only a few feet away, Condon replies, 'John asked me who was up there.'

"Wilentz finally found it necessary to ask Condon, 'And John is who?' in order to get the desired response, 'Hauptmann'. And to remind the jury that Hauptmann had really been identified by this witness who was so reluctant to utter that name.

"Several times Condon insisted that he was 'an honest man,' and I suspected that he was finding it difficult to truly associate Richard Hauptmann with John, that deep in his psyche he had the gravest doubts. There seemed to be a conflict between his memory and the public ritual he was being required to perform at Flemington. My intuition told me Condon was lying. When he identified Hauptmann as John, his very being must have been affected, because he valued so highly his reputation for morality and honesty. He could not continue to lie and so he called the extortionist 'John' even after saying it was Hauptmann.

"Finally, one thing more made me suspect Condon of lying. Made me believe, in fact, that his testimony had been rehearsed. I returned again to Reilly's question,

'Did you tell reporters at that time that Hauptmann was not John?' And Condon's reply: 'Oh, I never did. I never told or mentioned his name to them in public, never---note the words---of affirmation or denial. I make a distinction between identification and declaration of identification.'

"Immediately after denying he had made such a statement to reporters, Condon leaped into his explanation of his distinction between mentally identifying someone and verbally declaring that identification. It all came too fast, I felt. Condon had not been asked why he had failed to identify Hauptmann at the police lineup. He volunteered his explanation. It was as if he had struck upon the perfect explanation, or rationalization, only very recently and couldn't wait to relay it to the world that was so anxiously awaiting his testimony.

"And so I constructed in my mind a scenario that might have been acted out in the prosecutor's office. It is several weeks before the trial. Condon is sitting in the office of Attorney General Wilentz (a meeting that actually occurred). Several police officials and assistant prosecutors are with them. Condon is being asked the details of the story he will tell from the witness chair, for it is accepted practice to determine in advance what your witness will testify to. And someone at the conference asks: 'Reilly will want to know why you didn't identify Hauptmann at police headquarters. What will you tell him?'

"Condon: 'I wasn't too certain at that time.'

"Voice: 'Was it because of uncertainty or because you wanted to be absolutely fair?'

"Condon: 'Oh, I want to be fair when a man's life is at stake.'

"Voice: 'Then you decided to withhold your verbal identification for a while?'

"Condon: 'Yes, that is correct. I knew it was Hauptmann the moment I saw him. I just did not want to say it until everyone calmed down.'

"Voice: 'Then you simply refused to declare your identification because ...'

"Condon: 'That's absolutely correct. There is a distinction between the identification I make in my mind, and the declaration of identification I make to the world ...'

"Was I so anxious to prove Hauptmann's innocence that I was reading too much into words a man had spoken under stress? Perhaps so. Yet the weight of my own certainty was too heavy to ignore: Condon had been lying; the police and possibly the prosecutor had known he was lying. I hoped I could eventually prove it, but I was afraid that the old man may have had, as Thomas Carlyle once put it, 'the talent of lying in a way that cannot be laid hold of.'"

Day by day Tony was beginning to perceive the maddening inaccuracies that were brought into existence by the connivery of "monsters on the side of the law" to be used against an innocent victim. I am certain he must have experienced the same "gut wrenching" feeling I had when I came to the realization that Richard Hauptmann had been undeniably innocent, and that without a doubt there existed evidence which proved, in addition to this, that he had also been maliciously framed.

Murray Bleefeld's contact with Scaduto had produced many sleepless nights for the police reporter as he found himself delving deeper and deeper into the case. Troubled at every turn, Tony was disturbed at the way Hauptmann had been forced to write hour upon hour on the night of his arrest until the police believed they had found something suitable for a close comparison to the writing of the ransom notes. He was deeply critical of Reilly's admission, without a question, that the corpse found on May 12th, 1932 was that of Lindbergh's son. He wondered why the defense counsel had accepted the records of the Catholic orphanage which showed no children missing, while in actuality a report existed that a body of a child resembling the Lindbergh baby had been stolen from the orphanage, shortly after its death, around the time of the kidnapping.

Scaduto pin-pointed every breach of proper court procedure, every violation of legal jurisprudence --- and there were many. Some of the same irregularities I have already mentioned in earlier chapters were being observed, noted, studied, and alarming the alert Tony. Hauptmann's irate reaction to the lies told on the stand by agent Thomas Sisk of the Justice Department, when he claimed the defendant had admitted to him that he had buried some of the ransom bills in a metal can a foot below the earthen floor of the garage. Sisk had said this because the can they discovered had nothing in it but water. It is quite evident that his statement was made to refute Hauptmann's claim that the bills were wet due to water dripping on the shoe box from a broken water pipe in his closet. And when Hauptmann refused to remain silent and listen to such lies, and had jumped to his feet shouting: "Mister! Mister! Mister, you stop lying. You are telling a story!", he was severely reprimanded by Judge Trenchard.

In graphic fashion, Scaduto explains Hauptmann's reaction: "Hauptmann's head fell to his chest. He understood what was being done to him. Reilly had thrown away a major part of his defense in a single brisk sentence. Now Sisk was destroying in advance another piece of his defense. During the days of questioning after his arrest, Hauptmann had told police he remembered Fisch's shoe box with "important papers" only after rain had dripped into the closet and soaked that box. He had accidentally found the money, soaking wet. Now Sisk, in a swift thrust like an infantryman slashing his bayonet to the enemy, sliced and punctured Hauptmann's defense: the gold notes had been soaked because Hauptmann had placed them in a jug that later became partially filled with water.

"Yes, Hauptmann understood this personal disaster: 'Mister ... you stop lying.... You are telling a story'---words of a man who suddenly realizes the bars keeping the lions from him are built of twine.

"And now flowing over me was an aching need to know, a hunger of the mind. Was Condon lying? Was Lindbergh, even Lindy, the hero, was he lying? Was Sisk lying? Would Hauptmann have been so grievously provoked had Sisk been telling the truth? Were they all lying?

"But why? Anti-German feeling because of Hitler? It had to be more than that. Perhaps ... let us suppose that each of them, each man and woman of them, knew with absolute certainty that Hauptmann was guilty. The police said so; there was the money in his garage; the 'Fisch story,' as they so cavalierly dismissed Hauptmann's explanation of how he came by the ransom money; his profession, carpenter, his resignation from his job the day the ransom was paid; his weak alibi. Each of these witnesses knew Hauptmann's alibi had collapsed, for police and press had told them so. And so, for the glory of being part of a well-publicized justice, of official retribution, of carnival and theater, a chance to step onto center stage for a brief moment of media fame, perhaps, for those with a longer view, to become a footnote in history, a need for immortality of sorts, or even possibly to share in the $25,000 reward---each of them believed that a little embroidery in the official fabric couldn't hurt. Hauptmann was so guilty that a little piece of distorted evidence, a small lie, would not be very dreadful. The other witnesses are convicting this man, not me, each of them might have thought, the burden of his doom falls on everyone else ... me, I'm just adding a drop to an ocean, I'm just a minnow among larger fish ... what's the harm?

"Yes, Hauptmann was the man who ..."

Jack B. Weinstein, former professor of law at Columbia University, very clearly interpreted the purpose for the establishment of courts of law in these great United States of America. He said: "No person or entity, including the government, is powerful enough to trample on the rights of the weakest of our citizens while he has access to the courts and an advocate to press his case." His explanation had been correct. However, in spite of this, Hauptmann's experience at Flemington was a mockery to every intent of Professor Weinstein's well defined statement.

Richard Hauptmann could be classified as one of our weak citizens. Although he had access to our court system, having been arrested for a crime of which he pleaded innocent, Reilly, his chief advocate hired by William Randolph Hearst, did more to convict his client than defend him. And then, in this great "court of law", where fairness was believed to prevail, his rights were not just trampled ... his rights, hopes, and prayers were "smashed to smithereens" by a corrupt system made so by a few dishonest and unscrupulous persons who sold themselves to Satan in order to complete their diabolical travesty.

In order to prove our point we don't have to look beyond the integrity of the "big champion", the honorable H. Norman Schwarzkopf, Superintendent of the New Jersey State Police, whose "moral turpitude", as head of this great body of police officers, was known to have stated for publication to a group of reporters shortly before the start of the trial that Colonel Lindbergh was one of his dearest friends, and that he 'would do anything for that man', even willingly 'break an oath', because he considered him a hero who could do no wrong.

When we realize the tremendous adoration Schwarzkopf held for Lindbergh, the man to whom he would virtually "bow down and kiss his boot-straps", we should not be surprised to learn the details of an incident that took place as the trial in Flemington was in session.

John Hughes Curtis, the shipbuilder, who had been sentenced to pay a $1,000 fine and a suspended term in jail for leading Lindbergh on a "wild goose chase" in a search for his son, had been anxious to regain the esteem he once held in his home town of Norfolk, Virginia. So, Curtis fabricated a possible workable plan that would regain for him, not only his credibility in the community in which he lived, but would also see his $1,000 fine returned to him. He contacted Schwarzkopf and offered to come to Flemington and testify to the effect that Bruno Richard Hauptmann was, without a doubt, one of the men he had been dealing with in Cape May, New Jersey.

Scaduto's comments on this incident are excellent: "Curtis telephoned Colonel Schwarzkopf, head of the state police, and offered his testimony against Hauptmann. If he could be exonerated by the state, if Lindbergh would pose with him, shaking hands, to restore his reputation, he would testify against Hauptmann.

"And Schwarzkopf, that honorable man, that upholder of the law and the dignity of justice, said it sounded like a brilliant idea and he would put the proposition to Lindbergh. But Lindbergh said no and that was the end of it.

"Unbelievable! Schwarzkopf was willing to go along with an absolute lie in order to further condemn Hauptmann. The head of the police, the man whose morality or lack thereof sets the tone for every member of his force, would have helped put a perjurer in the witness chair. And I remembered something else I'd read about Schwarzkopf. Shortly before the trial began he had told reporters he considered Lindbergh one of his dearest friends and said he 'would do anything for that man.' Including, obviously, accepting a concocted story from an admitted swindler. Schwarzkopf's attitude most certainly must have been communicated to every one of his investigators: convict Hauptmann at all costs. Is that why the closet board had turned up? Could I be far wrong, then, in suspecting Wilentz's witnesses were lying? No ... my suspicions only touched the surface, of that much I was certain. And the lies probably went beyond an individual here swearing he saw Hauptmann in the cemetery, an individual there swearing he saw the man near Lindbergh's home. The few discrepancies I had uncovered so far gave promise of a total fraud, a broad conspiracy by dozens of men and women acting out of varying motives, all intent on convicting Hauptmann. Conspiracy? I'd always shuddered at that word, so much a part of the paranoia of the sixties that became a reality in the seventies, but now it sounded right."

Schwarzkopf's agreement to permit John Hughes

Curtis to come to Flemington to testify "falsely" against Hauptmann, absolutely pales when we heard what Tony Scaduto related publicly on television. Scaduto tells us that in the Lindbergh files at New Jersey's State Police Barracks he saw a document relating to the Lindbergh child being seen in South America. In it Schwarzkopf told Albert Osborn the "handwriting expert" to "keep it quiet and don't tell anyone here in America. Tell your friends to keep it quiet." But then, we must not forget that Colonel Schwarzkopf said he would do anything for Colonel Lindbergh, even to breaking an oath. Oh well, what's new?

The law of justice states: "No person or entity, including the government, is powerful enough to trample on the rights of the weakest ..."

Disturbed by all we had learned is putting it mildly. Angered is a far better word to describe our emotions. Anthony Scaduto, in New York City, pledged to himself to "dig even deeper and more intently" for the truth; while I, at the same time, over in Phoenixville, Pennsylvania, after learning she was somewhere in the Philadelphia area, had been doing my level best to locate Anna Hauptmann.

CHAPTER SIXTY SIX

Scaduto's Investigation!

It was very evident that Tony Scaduto was a man of strong will. In spite of the odds that were stacked against him, he apparently was not one to accept defeat without a fight. And this seemed to be especially true of his "unofficial" investigation into the multitude of injustices committed by the prosecutors in the Hauptmann case. Alarmed at the many things he had already uncovered which had been used to convict the alleged kidnapper (alleged was never true, declared is the correct description) Scaduto was spurred on to complete the job still facing him, the challenge of forever clearing Hauptmann's besmirched name.

The Bornmann frameup of the attic wood! What a ridiculous farce that proved to be. But the jury had swallowed it hook, line and sinker. The testimony of the detective was "sickening" and certainly should have been challenged by the defense. Scaduto reviewed it in this fashion in *Scapegoat*:

"Wilentz asked: And did you again search that apartment?

"Yes, I did, Bornmann said. It was on September 26 (seven days after Hauptmann's arrest) that I conducted another search of said premises with other police officers. Said search took us to the attic. We gained access to the attic by entering a small linen closet, pushing up a trap door in the ceiling, climbing up the closet shelves, and pulling ourselves through.

"When you got into the attic what did you find?

"Well, first we searched for money and during the search I noticed that a length of one of the attic floorboards had been removed. About eight feet of it had been sawed off one end of this long floorboard. I knew it had been cut off because there were holes still in the beams and between the seventh and eighth beam there was a small pile of sawdust lying there. Also, on the floorboard adjoining the end of the piece that had been sawed away, you could see a small saw cut where the saw bit into the adjoining board.

"So, he continued, I called Arthur Koehler, a wood expert for the U.S. Forest Service. Koehler had been helping us trace wood in the kidnap ladder for two years. And he came as soon as he could get away and on October 9 we returned to the attic and said premises.

"What did you do when you arrived there?

"Well, we brought with us one of the side rails in the ladder, one of the uprights. It's marked Rail 16, that's what we marked it when we tagged each piece of it for lab analysis. Rail 16. There are four nail holes in Rail 16. Up in the attic, we put Rail 16 down on the beam that also had four nail holes. Then we pushed nails into the holes in Rail 16 and they went right in with just a little finger pressure and they went right in and right down into the holes in the attic beam. They fit perfectly, no doubt about it.

"The prosecutor paused, turned to the jury with a smile, let it sink in. An earlier witness, the owner of the house, had testified that when the Hauptmanns moved into the apartment in October 1931, the attic floor had been intact. A couple of the jury members nodded. It was plain now. Hauptmann had run short of wood and had removed a length from his attic to finish the kidnap ladder.

"Now, Detective Bornmann, I show you a board. Did you take this board from Hauptmann's attic?

"Yes, sir, I did. That's the board that had a piece cut from it.

"Who removed that from the attic floor?

"I did.

"Was it the same color as it is now?

"Oh, yes sir, it is.

"And what was the color of Rail 16?

"The same color as the attic board.

"Your witness, the prosecutor said. He sat down, quite pleased. The kidnap ladder had now been rammed home---right into Hauptmann's attic.

"Frederick Pope, a local lawyer, one of the assistants to Reilly and Fisher, rose to challenge for the defense.

"He asked: Before you put Rail 16 into place there was nothing between the attic board and the end of the building, was there?

"No, sir. Bornmann replied. There was about eight feet missing from the floor, the board that was cut out was about eight feet long.

"Now, even after you put Rail 16 into place it didn't reach from the end of the floorboard to the end of the building, did it?

"No sir, there was a space about an inch and a quarter between the board on the floor and the beginning of the ladder rail. When we put the ladder rail into place with the nails, there was this gap of more than an inch.

"Yes, the defense attorney said, but I'm talking about the other end also. The missing length even after laying Rail 16 down is about thirty-six inches, isn't it?

"Well, Bornmann said, about eight foot of it had been taken out and Rail 16 is about six foot, eight and a half inches.

"The implication was clear to the spectators and the jury. Hauptmann, a skilled union carpenter, had removed a board from his attic that was between fifteen and thirty-six inches too long and had cut a foot or more from it. Or, perhaps---another inference that could be drawn---was it that Bornmann had been so sloppy in manufacturing his evidence he cut off and threw away a length of attic floor a couple of feet longer than the board he was going to claim had come from Hauptmann's attic?

"But it wasn't made sufficiently clear to the jury. The cross-examination had been too brief. Nowhere in it does the lawyer shout: 'Do you expect this jury to believe this ladder upright, Rail 16, came from that attic? Let us see what you expect this jury to believe. Wasn't there a lumberyard two blocks from the defendant's home? Didn't you find enough wood in his garage and in the basement to make this upright? Is it your expert police opinion that Hauptmann climbed into his attic in search of a length of wood to complete his ladder? He knows he needs precisely six feet, eight and a half inches. He is a carpenter, he measures his work, he knows the length he needs. In his attic, he begins to saw. Without measuring. Is it your expert opinion he sawed off a piece about eighteen inches too long? That he took it down through the trap door into his house and then down into his garage and sawed off the eighteen inches? And then, finding it was still too long, he cut off another inch and a half from the opposite end? Is that the expert police opinion you expect this jury to believe? Or is it more logical to believe there was an inch-and-a-half gap between the ends of those two boards in the attic because that was the only way to get the nail holes to match up? Did you, Detective Bornmann, drive nail holes in the beam so they'd match the holes in the rail?'

"But the questions were not asked. The information received by the jury was that the board had come from the attic. More than a foot off one end, an inch and a fraction off the other. Nuances never highlighted by questions to force the jurors to think. Nuances suggesting manufactured evidence.

"Coils of suspicion uncoiled in my mind. Eyewitnesses, suspect. Handwriting analysts, suspect. A board from the attic, suspect. A commander of police willing to suborn perjury, suspect ... suspect. Was it all like this? Layer upon layer of perjury, a meandering river of lies that swallowed Hauptmann and carried him over the abyss?"

These were but a few of the troublesome questions Scaduto had run into. Why had things been done in this fashion? Why had not this been done? Why were not more pointed questions asked in order that the jury be properly informed? Why did Reilly fail to do this ... or that? So many questions not asked, so many points not made? Why, why, why? Plain logic supplied him with the answers. However, logic would not be enough. Somewhere buried among the archives were to be found the true answers to many of these veiled questions which had been laying dormant during nearly sixty agonizing years of Anna Hauptmann's life.

As Scaduto continued reading the court transcript it became very evident to him that Attorney General Wilentz had been quite unfair in his "badgering" of Hauptmann during his cross-examination. One example of this was his deliberate failure to allow the prisoner ample time, taking unfair advantage of Hauptmann, as he searched for the correct English words to render his honest answer. This was clearly illustrated throughout the trial as Hauptmann seemed hesitant to answer. But at one point he explained his reason. Tony Scaduto emphasized this point in his book: "During cross-examination about the closet trim board with Condon's address and phone number on it, Hauptmann made a statement which brought into focus the reason he'd been such a poor witness. The prosecutor insisted that Hauptmann tell the jury whether he'd been speaking the truth when he said the writing on the board was his. Hauptmann appeared to be thinking the question over and when Wilentz thundered at him, 'Why do you hesitate?' 'Why don't you answer?' Can't you say yes or no?'

"'You will have to give me a chance,' Hauptmann said.

"'I will give you all day but you ought to know whether you told the truth.'

"And Hauptmann said: 'No,I have to trans---I am thinking in German and I have to translate it in American language, and it needs quite a bit of time, so excuse me.'"

Hauptmann had been placed at a decided disadvantage in giving an immediate answer to many of the questions hurled at him in machine-gun like fashion by Wilentz. During one of these diatribes by Wilentz, attorney Fisher rose to his feet objecting that the Attorney General was not permitting Hauptmann to answer. Faithful and fair Justice Trenchard happened to agree stating that Hauptmann "should be permitted to make his explanation now, if he has any". And, as Tony Scaduto emphasized, Trenchard's insinuation of his own possible doubt had been used to advantage by the inflection of his voice which targeted his own feelings and had, most certainly, not been lost by those listeners of his remarks who really counted --- the members of the jury and the press.

In the many meetings he had with Murray Bleefeld, Scaduto learned of the detailed conversations he had with Paul Wendel. The things Wendel had voluntarily revealed to him about his part in the kidnapping; how he actually seemed anxious to "surrender" to Parker "so that he could get it off his chest". Among other things, Bleefeld told Tony of an occurrence which had taken place in the Parker living room shortly after the apprehension of Wendel. Ellis, Sr. had sent his son to Trenton to bring in Wendel's nineteen-year-old son, Paul, Jr. As they pulled up in front of Parker's Mount Holly home, old Ellis said to Bleefeld. "Murray, I want you to listen to this." And he tells me to go into the dining room, stay just behind those big old-fashioned sliding wood doors and listen. Which I did.

"Paul Wendel, Jr. is brought into the sitting room. Parker says to him, 'Paul, sit down.' The kid sat. 'Paul, I brought you here to tell you that I'm holding your father. He's sound. He's safe. He's in good health. I'm holding him because he confessed to the kidnapping of the Lindbergh baby.'

"This is the son, now. Just like Hauptmann told the truth when he said, 'I know nothing, I'm innocent,' so Paul Wendel, Jr. was telling the truth when he answered; **'I always knew they'd get my father for this.'** I heard it myself. This man's own son said he knew his father would get caught for kidnapping the Lindbergh baby. If I couldn't believe anything else about this case I could believe that, the son admitting his father was involved."

Scaduto's search for Parker's records lead him to a dead end. Everything of value had been destroyed. Only the memories of associates and friends of Ellis substantiated much of what Bleefeld had told him. However, an affidavit was found which was sworn to by Parker's lawyer, Harry Green, stating that on the first or second Sunday after the kidnapping, Paul Wendel visited a Frank Cristano of Leonia, New Jersey, and offered him the following proposition. Wendel, knowing that Cristano had contacts with underworld figures, told him that he knew where the Lindbergh baby was being kept, that he could produce the baby and by his doing this they both could make a lot of money by sharing in the $50,000 ransom. Wendel asked Cristano if he would get in touch with his friend Al Capone and arrange for the baby to be turned over to the Chicago gangster. By doing this Capone could receive the plaudits for the child's safe return, thus making him a hero, and permitting him to propose a bargaining agreement with the government in order to "get out of his income tax troubles." But, Cristano absolutely refused to get involved in Wendel's dire scheme "because he regarded Wendel as a faker and a swindler by reason of a transaction several years before, in which Wendel had embarrassed Cristano seriously with Capone."

Although the success Scaduto was experiencing was largely based on "scuttlebutt", hearsay evidence that was undoubtedly true, it nevertheless remained unproven as being factual. Tony was disturbed at the claims Hauptmann made of things he was positive had taken place, only to have the prosecutors make light of his explanations by "pooh-poohing" them as nothing more than "poor excuses" of things they knew "very well" to be untrue. Among these "things" was Hauptmann's original statement that he had worked at the Majestic Apartments on Tuesday, March 1st, 1932. This mystified Scaduto. How could Richard Hauptmann have been so certain he had worked all that day, and later believe the "proof" of the attorney general, that he had not worked on that date? And, Hauptmann's original statement had been strengthened by affidavits of his employers. Was it March 1st, or had it been March 15th, as "proven" in court, or possibly March 21st as his employment card "appeared to prove"?

Tony reasoned that if the original work records of

Hauptmann's employment at the Majestic Apartments still existed they would be found in the files of either the Bronx district attorney's office or the New York City police department. He decided to seek the answers by first searching the files in the district attorney's office. After informing the officials there that he was doing a book on the Lindbergh case, he was granted permission to examine anything he found pertaining to the crime and to make copies of whatever he needed.

He had searched only a short time when he discovered a revealing piece of evidence. In his hands he held something which convincingly proved that Hauptmann had worked, as he said, on the first day of March, 1932, and that the prosecutors deliberately had kept this fact concealed from Hauptmann's lawyers.

Scaduto held little hope that he would find much that would support Hauptmann's statements. His feelings were largely based on his belief that it was inconceivable for a prosecutor to retain something in his files that he had denied ever existed. Unless, Tony reasoned, "he was so arrogant he felt certain his files would never be examined by an outsider." Or plainly "stupid".

A small sheet of yellow legal paper almost escaped his attention. But, by the grace of God, Tony picked it up and saw that it was a hand-written receipt which read:

> Received from Asst. D. A. Breslin, the following records:
> Employment card record of Richard Hauptmann,
> Carbon copy of payroll Feb. 29, 1932,
> Carbon copy of payroll March 15, 1932 . . .

Here in his hands was the proof he needed. A receipt for the semimonthly records covering the dates surrounding the kidnapping. The payroll records did exist after all, proving beyond a doubt that Richard **had** worked on Tuesday, March 1, 1932. Realizing that the officials had known this and had deliberately suppressed it and lied about it put Scaduto in a state of rage. The more he thought about the collaboration between Foley and Wilentz and Knapp and everybody else involved in the lurid conspiracy made him "sick". All had known of the existence of the very records that could have helped Hauptmann, and yet had allowed themselves to doom him by suppressing them.

What a crime that those involved had escaped the very law they had sworn to defend while Richard

Hauptmann had to pay with his life for a crime he did not commit. What a crime that the Ellis Parkers, and others were defined as the "bad guys" and had to pay with imprisonment, and defamation of character because of their honest attempts to apprehend the actual kidnappers.

You have been informed of the four men in the employment and payroll departments at the Majestic Apartments in Manhattan where Hauptmann was working at the time of the kidnapping and how he insisted he had spent the entire day of March 1st at his job. Hauptmann's lawyer shortly after his arrest was James M. Fawcett who obtained statements from the four men authenticating his claim of being at work all that day. However, by the time of Hauptmann's hearing in the Bronx, these men denied their "certainty" of the fact and were conspicuous by their absence. The "wheels of justice" had reached them and persuaded them into saying they were "not quite sure any longer" of what they had originally testified to as factual. In other words, the bums had them change their original statements for "convenience sake". The convenience of "nudging" Hauptmann just a little closer to the electric chair.

Yes, Tony Scaduto had found an incriminating bit of evidence that was to lead to the bonafide fact that Joseph M. Furcht, Edward Morton, E.V.C. Pescia, and Howard Knapp had been coerced into repudiating their original statements which they claimed to have been honest and forthright. Investigative reporter, Anthony Scaduto, was stripping off the "blanket of deception" the authorities had thrown over the annals of the Lindbergh kidnapping -the Crime of the Century, and was fast turning it into the "Shame of the Universe!

C H A P T E R S I X T Y S E V E N

Where Have You Been?

The aid of a New York City police officer, one whom Scaduto had befriended years earlier and who was willing to search the city files of the Lindbergh case for him, reaped even greater rewards. With his friends help he came up with proof positive that Joseph Perrone, the cab driver, had been running around everywhere "identifying dozens of guys who didn't resemble the extortionist in any way." At one point Perrone told the police the man who had given him the note to deliver to Condon, "had a full face and had heavy eyebrows about the same color as his hair" which he informed them was dark-brown. He said all this about a man whom he identified after having seen him for just a few seconds. The man he testified was wearing a hat. Perrone said he had taken a good look at the man because their conversation had taken place under a streetlight. However, we must remember that the light had been twenty feet above the street and would have cast shadows on the face of the man, making it almost impossible to obtain a good look at him in order to give any kind of positive identification.

As for Condon, Tony's informant said, he had not only given different descriptions of Cemetery John, but that "the police had believed he was tied in with a few guys who could have been the real kidnappers." However, when they "bagged Hauptmann" for the crime, they dropped their investigation of Condon like a hot potato. They now had the "one and only real kidnapper" --- so they thought. Now all they had to do was prove it --- and "prove it they did by hook and crook."

In addition to the incriminating evidence which proved that both Condon and Perrone had definitely perjured themselves, more evidence of value was found by the friendly police officer who was assisting Tony. "I found a carbon of that receipt for the employment records. It shows that the records for February and March did exist, so they were lying about it like you guessed.", he told Scaduto, who inquired: "Did you find the records themselves?" "No.", he was informed: "From the looks of the receipt, they went over to New Jersey, 'cause the receipt is signed by an Inspector Walsh of some Jersey police department, I think Jersey City."

The police officer also informed him that although he had not found Hauptmann's ledger book, believing that it had also been sent over to New Jersey, he had located a Justice Department summary of the book which contained an analysis of the records in the book. Its pages revealed the fact that Hauptmann and Fisch had been partners, giving dates when stocks were bought and sold, and dates when they had purchased and sold furs. Tony's informer said it told "the whole works".

Had it not been for the investigative reporting of Anthony Scaduto, much of the material, the undisputed evidence he uncovered, would in all probability, never have been found. Scaduto did a yeoman's job in obtaining the necessary evidence which reaches into the very core of the case to prove to you the innocence of Bruno Richard Hauptmann. For this he should have received, from our nation's officials, its citizens and the news media, a recognition he so richly deserved. Just their heartfelt thanks for finally "setting the record straight", by erasing a horrible "mistake", a wilful error, which had eroded, for forty years, the annals of our criminal "justice" records. However, this was not to be, largely because of the skepticism of some, or possibly the failure of many to read his book *Scapegoat*, but also because of the put-down his great volume received as being nothing but "pure unbelievable rot" by those who wanted the eye's of the public to remain blind to the very truth his writing held. Well, regardless of this, I again thank Anthony Scaduto for the great work he did by helping me prove Hauptmann's innocence.

Another important discovery made by Tony in his search of the police records. You should remember that Richard Hauptmann told the authorities he found the money left with him by his friend Isidor Fisch on a rainy Sunday afternoon in August, 1934. Again Scaduto tells of his finding:

"I learned from the documents copied for me, that Hauptmann had been telling the truth when he described how he had found the money in the shoe box because of a leaking rain on a Sunday in August and, more important, that he'd been telling the truth when he said he did not begin passing ransom notes until after that rainy day one month before his arrest.

"That evidence is contained in reports by Lieutenant Finn and other New York City police officers. From the very first ransom bill recovered from banks and merchants, and up to June 1934, all Lindbergh ransom money that came into Finn's office was sent to the police laboratory for analysis.

"The lab report on four of the bills which were submitted for analysis in June 1934---two months before Hauptmann says he found his particular cache of money in the shoe box---is similar to most of the previous reports. In it, the police chemist reports the frequent presence of lipstick and mascara on the bills, and police noted that earlier bills sent for analysis had also revealed the presence of blond, brunette, and red hair. Taken together with the fact that several bills had been passed at burlesque houses and restaurants, this finding indicated the man who was spending ransom money was living a somewhat flashy existence. These details, of course, did not fit the very conservative Hauptmann. Microscopic examination also disclosed that these four bills, like many tested earlier, were found to have stuck to them "a number of gold or brass dust particles" and a "fatty substance, apparently oil or grease." Police surmised, according to Lieutenant Finn, that the bill-passer was a mechanic of some kind, probably a machinist who had a lathe or drill press and who worked with metal; oil applied to the work probably flew off the machine with the metal particles and both were transferred to the bills, perhaps by the man's hands.

"This report concludes: 'All of the four bills apparently fold straight through the center lengthwise and then through the center crosswise and once again crosswise, making a double fold crosswise, resulting in a compact arrangement---apparently to fold them in such a size as to be carried in a vest pocket or a watch pocket.'

"Once more, we can see that these bills passed up to June 1934 had been placed in circulation by the man Cecile Barr, the theater cashier, had seen, the man who folded his money and kept it in his watch pocket. The bill recovered from Hauptmann on the day of his arrest, we've already noted, was found in his wallet and was lying flat. During one of the interrogation sessions at the Greenwich Street station, when Inspector Lyons pressed Hauptmann on the point, asking: 'Where do you keep the bills you carry around with you?' Hauptmann replied, 'Here, in my wallet,' and it appears from the transcript that Hauptmann pulled out his wallet to demonstrate. Lyons does not call him a liar, does not press the point. He seems to be satisfied Hauptmann is telling the truth.

"The bills discovered in Hauptmann's garage were also submitted for laboratory analysis. Those bills showed entirely different characteristics than the bills passed earlier.

"The garage bills, the lab report stated, were 'in a rather damp condition . . . watersoaked . . . .' Lieutenant Finn said in one of his summaries that 'there was a strong musty odor' on these Hauptmann bills, 'as if the bills had been buried in the ground or in a damp receptacle.' Since none of the earlier bills recovered had been wet or possessed a musty odor, it is possible Hauptmann did not come into possession of that money until shortly before the first one he is known to have passed, in early September.

"And what is just possible, at first examination of the documents, approaches likelihood as the search continues. For one of the lab reports on Hauptmann's bills says that they had been wrapped in newspapers dated June 25, 1934, and September 6, 1934---Hauptmann had said that after he dried out the bills in his garage at the end of August and beginning of September he wrapped them in newspapers lying around the house. Most telling of all, in these reports, are other different characteristics of the bills discovered by the lab technicians. The early bills had traces of lipstick, mascara, and several shades of hair, indicating they'd been in the presence of women. Hauptmann's bills lack these substances. The early bills had on them gold or brass particles, suspended in what appeared to be machine oil. Hauptmann's bills had on them a fatty substance that was probably machine oil, but clinging to it were traces of emery dust. In Hauptmann's garage was an emery wheel which he used for sharpening his tools. There was no lathe or drill press or any equipment on which brass or gold could have been worked, nor was there any trace of brass or gold dust. Seemingly, the earlier bill-passer was a different sort of mechanic than Hauptmann was and caused different kinds of particles to become affixed to his collection of ransom money.

"There is further circumstantial evidence indicating Hauptmann did not begin to pass the ransom money until late August or early September, 1934. An examination of the testimony of federal agents, bank employees, and brokerage house customer's men at the trial and a study of documents relating to Hauptmann's bank accounts and stock market transactions show that of dozens of people to whom Hauptmann passed money, and who were later questioned, not one of them---without exception---could say they had ever received a Lindbergh ransom bill from Hauptmann. Most of them, in fact, stated that they had never been notified by the banks in which their firms made deposits that Lindbergh ransom money had been turned in. In a number of cases, the banks specifically said that no ransom money had ever been found in the deposits by Hauptmann's brokerage firms.

"To cite but one example, found in an FBI report on the tracing of money which Hauptmann deposited in either banks or brokerage accounts. The report, Bureau of Investigation File Number 62-3057, made by agent J.A. Genau on October 18, 1934, says of currency Hauptmann deposited to his brokerage account:

In regard to the $1,000 deposit of currency appearing in the account on January 26, 1934, Mr. Allan Wilcox, clerk in the cashier's cage of E.A. Pierce and Company, who accepted and counted this deposit, stated that he cannot remember the denominations of this currency; that he cannot remember if any gold certificates were contained therein; that no record was kept of gold certificates.

This $1,000 was deposited in the main office of the Bank of Manhattan Company, 40 Wall St. Mr. M.W. Williams, cashier of the bank, stated that the deposit was not made up of gold notes; that the bank kept a record of all gold notes in deposits in excess of $100.

"Throughout this and other documents relating to an FBI search for evidence that Hauptmann had used gold certificates in his stock market trading, investigators state that no such evidence was ever developed. The reverse, in fact, seems to have been true---when Hauptmann needed money to purchase stocks or respond to a margin call for more cash, he invariably took those funds out of one of his bank accounts. On January 18, the week before the $1,000 transaction quoted above, Hauptmann opened his margin account with E.A. Pierce by withdrawing $2,500 from a savings account.

"Hauptmann, of course, had he been the extortionist who received all or part of the Lindbergh ransom money in April 1932, might have been acting very cautiously by getting rid of the gold certificates elsewhere and depositing "clean" money in his accounts. But then, how does one explain his absolutely stupid behavior in passing notes in 1934 in stores where he was known? Such illogical behavior is inconsistent with what we know of Hauptmann.

"The FBI also considered the possibility that Hauptmann deposited ransom money in a bank account and then withdrew untainted money to deposit in his brokerage account. But the banks reported that no ransom bills had ever been deposited by Hauptmann.

"There is further evidence, in this FBI report by agent Genau, that Hauptmann was telling the truth when he maintained he did not find the money until August 1934, at which time he began spending small sums for living expenses.

"On March 27, 1933, Hauptmann opened an account with the brokerage firm of Steiner, Rouse and Company, in his wife's maiden name, Anna Schoeffler, although he had full control over the account: (Hauptmann told police he put the account in Anna's name because he had had an auto accident in which he broke a man's leg, and an attorney had advised him to transfer his assets in the event the man sued. The accident victim settled for a few hundred dollars, but Hauptmann didn't bother changing the name on the account. His story was verified by police.) Hauptmann was doing a lot of short-term trading in this account; it is the account which permitted a federal agent to testify that Hauptmann had $250,000 in the stock market when, in actuality, the "largest credit balance appeared on June 6, 1933, in the amount of $8,431.39," to quote this FBI report. But the distorted testimony is unimportant, for the moment. The main point is that, because it was a margin account and because Hauptmann frequently had a large credit balance, he was in the habit of periodically withdrawing sums of money from this account. Most of those withdrawals were of small sums ranging from $30 to $150, which Hauptmann said was for living expenses since he did not have a steady job.

"The last two withdrawals, totaling $175, were made in the final week of July 1934.

"In the following month, Hauptmann claimed, he discovered the gold certificates in Fisch's shoe box. The FBI accounting document makes it seem likely he was telling the truth, for he stopped taking money from his brokerage account at the end of July even though at the time of his arrest that account had a credit balance of

$1,242.61 and also held shares of stock with a market value of close to $4,000.

"Further, Hauptmann went on a hunting trip to Maine in the summer of 1933. No ransom bills ever turned up in Maine. He took a vacation with Anna in Florida; no ransom money was recovered in Florida. He went to Canada some time later, according to Lieutenant Finn, 'but he spent nothing but good money across the boundary.' If anything, Hauptmann would have been unloading Lindbergh money where he was unknown, rather than spending it, as he did, near his home in stores where he customarily shopped.

"One piece of negative evidence supports the conclusion that Hauptmann was not the man, or one of the men, who had been passing the ransom money in the first couple of years after the kidnapping, that he did not begin passing the money until he says he did, in September 1934. That evidence is found in a laboratory analysis of all the bills then in possession of authorities, almost $5,000 worth. The analysis by the Justice Department, dated August 7, 1934, goes into exhaustive detail about the gold particles, lipstick, mascara, and other substances found on the bills. And two paragraphs leap out:

> "Three hundred and ten of the individual bills were chemically treated in an effort to develop latent fingerprints invisible to the naked eye.
>
> "In all, five fragmentary latent prints were developed and on such prints appeared sufficient characteristic ridge detail to permit identification upon direct comparison with fingerprints or palm prints of the person who left them [emphasis supplied]. There was not, however, sufficient characteristic ridge detail to permit a classification of these prints for the purpose of a search.

"When Hauptmann was arrested less than two months after this report was made, his fingerprints were compared with those found on the bills. They did not match.

"There is still another laboratory report of interest. After Hauptmann was arrested, Lieutenant Finn personally supervised an examination of Hauptmann's car. Police assumed it transported Lindbergh's gravely injured child from Hopewell to the point four miles away where the boy was dumped into the woods. Finn ordered the lab technicians to test "every inch of Hauptmann's car" for bloodstains, for the autopsy report indicated the child had probably been bleeding as a result of his skull fracture. No trace of blood was found.

"At this point in my review of but a small part of the foot-high pile of documents on my desk I suddenly recalled something Sidney Whipple had written in his introduction to the Hauptmann trial transcript that he edited and published. In attempting to answer the charges Governor Hoffman had made after his own investigation into the case, Whipple ignored the evidence Hoffman had made public and dismissed it in its entirety with this statement:

'The governor, while not shouting "frame-up" as loudly as defense counsel had shouted it, nevertheless indicated that he was seriously considering that possibility. Again he ignored the obvious argument that such a frame-up, assuredly unparalleled in American jurisprudence, would have entailed collusion between: all the prosecuting authorities of the State of New Jersey; the investigating authorities of the United States Department of Justice [here Whipple went on, naming six or eight agencies] and all the minor officials engaged on the case from 1932 to 1934. Such a conspiracy would have necessitated collusion among some six hundred individuals. In the words of Mr. Justice Trenchard, now do you believe that?'

"A terrible choice of words, that last sentence, considering Judge Trenchard's obvious bias. But those were simpler times, those days when most reporters had absolute faith in all institutions of government. . . . Whipple was wrong. It did not require 'collusion among some six hundred individuals' to construct the script which sent Hauptmann to his death. It did not require a 'conspiracy' in which Lindbergh, Schwarzkopf, Sisk, Condon, and all the rest came together to plot against Hauptmann. All that was required was for some dozen or so prosecution witnesses to lie, individually and for their own peculiar motives. And no single man or woman among them had to know all the others were lying or had to be in collusion with any others. . . . That there were lies, distortions, suppression of evidence was clear from the documents that I had so far examined."

Tony was convinced the police had suppressed their

lab reports: "I found that those reports showed quite clearly that the ransom bills definitely known to have been passed by Hauptmann differed, under microscopic examination, from ransom bills passed earlier. Only the bills spent by Hauptmann or found in his possession had once been watersoaked; the unique condition of Hauptmann's bills created a strong inference that he'd been telling the truth about discovering the box of money after it had been soaked by a leaking roof.

"Thus far I had found evidence that about a dozen men and women, among them police officers, had lied, and that police and prosecution hid from the defense evidence that would have supported Hauptmann. And now I turned to what was perhaps the most crucial of the suppressed evidence --- the 'Fisch story.'"

Hauptmann's only alibi, pertaining to his possession of the $14,600 of Lindbergh ransom money, was his honest explanation that he had been given the shoe box, containing the money, but without any knowledge that it was money, by his friend and partner Isidor Fisch. But the authorities did not believe him, simply because they did not want to believe him. Although they knew his explanation could have possibly been very logical, they refused to accept it because to do so would have been tragic for them. Had they believed him they would have destroyed their entire case. At last they had the "lone" culprit, the one they had been searching for unsuccessfully for two-and one-half years. And now, at last they could, and would, nail him despite Hauptmann's "unbelievable" Fisch story. And this they decided to do with all kinds of "trumped-up evidence" in order to erase the humiliation they had suffered through their failure to solve the "crime of the century."

Because he had no alternative, Attorney General Wilentz was so very gracious as he acknowledged the existence of Fisch, by saying at the trial: "Of course there was a man named Fisch, we concede that, Mr. Hauptmann didn't simply pull his name out of the air." Utter rubbish!

Since the object of Mr. Scaduto's book, and the one you are now reading, is to prove, beyond the doubts of every person, that Hauptmann's "Isidor Fisch story", the one and only explanation he ever gave for his possession of the ransom money, was absolutely true in every detail, it is imperative that you believe it.

"Isidor Fisch, it appears from the documents available, was most certainly dishonest. He also seemed to have been persuasive enough to make one group of friends believe he was starving, so that he could cadge money from them and from an immigrant society to which he belonged, at the same time he was getting another group of friends (Hauptmann and his acquaintances) to believe he was a wealthy fur speculator and investor in small expanding businesses so that he could borrow money from them by claiming he was temporarily short of liquid capital but didn't want to miss out on a sure winner. None of the money Fisch borrowed was ever repaid."

I assume that you closely followed the detailed explanation of Hauptmann's finances. Possibly you might have found it rather boring, as did the Flemington jury when William Frank, the federal accountant, who went to great lengths to "prove", by bending the truth and cleverly exaggerating and distorting non-existent figures, that Hauptmann had been responsible for spending "to within a few dollars" every cent of the Lindbergh ransom money. However, it is extremely important that you clearly see and understand the deception the authorities had taken to keep Hauptmann's ledger and record book from the eyes of the defense attorneys. Because we are proving to you Hauptmann's innocence, it is vital that we present you with every true facet of the case. Although the authorities were quite willing in 1935 to use "criminal tactics" to railroad an innocent man to a seat in electric chair, we have chosen to expose it all by telling the unadulterated truth.

It should certainly not be hard for you to have already perceived the despicable practices fostered on Hauptmann. The deceptive methods they used were even suspect to the FBI. The federal arm of crime investigation withdrew from the case on Wednesday, October 10th, three weeks after Hauptmann was arrested. Director J. Edgar Hoover had his doubts as to the validity of the charges and the way the New Jersey police authorities and the prosecution attorneys were handling things in the preparation of the trial. Hoover was extremely disappointed with the help he had received from Colonel Schwarzkopf's staff, having been refused the privilege of allowing his agents to examine the fingerprints found on the kidnap ladder. It was clearly shown that Hoover wanted his department separated from any part of the case because of his dislike of the way it was being handled.

As one person so plainly stated: "The FBI knew, J. Edgar Hoover knew. It wasn't their case. They weren't involved. If New Jersey wanted to take a chance on manufactured evidence, it wasn't the problem of the FBI or the Bronx prosecutor. They just closed their eyes."

God bless Anthony Scaduto! Without his determination to get to the bottom of this case, largely through the insistence of Murray Bleefeld, this book would in all probability never have been written. At least it would not have contained the many vital segments of information you have read, since it was only because of Tony's diligence that he was able to gather all of the new, true, and detailed knowledge you have learned.

In 1976 Tony Scaduto had his 512 page book *Scapegoat* published. It proved to be dynamite to those of us who truly believed in Hauptmann's innocence, but, nevertheless, had almost given up with our intent and hope to prove it. The book was loaded with some of the most astounding facts ever published about the Lindbergh kidnapping and the subsequent irregularities of the trial. Proven truths were learned, truths that I never could have guessed would ever be obtainable for the public's knowledge. It gave new hope to all of us who had never been satisfied with the conviction of Hauptmann as the lone kidnapper.

I had learned of Scaduto's forthcoming book approximately six months before it made its appearance in the book stores. Quite frankly I could not wait to get it in my hands since it was the first major publication on the case since Waller's *Kidnap* in 1961, a book that had proven to be a disappointment to me since he believed "conclusively" in Hauptmann's guilt. So, you can readily understand why I was so anxious to read and study *Scapegoat* because I had read that Scaduto believed in Hauptmann's innocence. He was evidently on my side --- or I on his. I was now more than anxious to read what he had to say. Was I possibly about to learn of any more facts that I could add to my limited evidence?

I had not long to wait. It was November, 1976, shortly before Thanksgiving Day that I journeyed to the nearby King of Prussia Plaza and purchased my copy of *Scapegoat*. It took me only two days to read it and absorb its valuable contents. I was amazed at the revelations it contained; many, many things I could never have hoped to obtain. They all clearly spelled out Hauptmann's innocence. I was enthralled.

As fine as the volume was, I found that it lacked one thing. It was proof of a definite tie-in of Isidor Fisch with the actual kidnapping. This was the one thing Tony needed --- and I sat here in Phoenixville, Pennsylvania with this missing link.

I decided to reach Scaduto immediately and commend him on his wonderful book. I was fortunate in making contact with him by telephone at his Ridgefield, Connecticut home several days later. "Hello, Mr. Scaduto," I asked? A voice informed me that I was speaking with him. I then proceeded to tell him how much I enjoyed reading his recently published book and that I too had been exploring the innocence of Hauptmann for the past forty years, telling him that I had evidence which proves, beyond a doubt, that Isidor Fisch was directly connected with the actual kidnapping of the Lindbergh baby.

And as I finished giving him that bit of information, his next words have been indelibly planted in my mind. I shall never forget, as long as I live, the forceful question he asked me---"WHERE HAVE YOU BEEN?"

CHAPTER SIXTY EIGHT

Doubts of the FBI!

"Where have YOU been?". My answer had been spontaneous since I had had no previous knowledge of Anthony Scaduto or the book he had been writing on the case.

During our conversation I related all I knew about the crime and how I had pursued the information I had learned from Harry Young relative to Isidor Fisch and his connection with Martin Stover, who had taken Lindbergh's child to South America. I told him I believed Young's story because I read an article published in a New York City newspaper about the child being seen in South America in March of 1932.

Scaduto was amazed with what I told him. He was very friendly, quite interested, and wished me much success in my endeavor to dig up more information about the mysterious Isidor Fisch who had been Hauptmann's only alibi.

As I was about to end our conversation, I entreated Tony to use the facts I had given him in his next book on the Lindbergh case. My remark brought his immediate reply, "Oh, no! I'm not going to do another book on the case. Now, it's your turn. You can tell your story in your own book. It's your story." After again thanking me for my words of praise for *Scapegoat*, the knowledge I had given him, and my desire to have Hauptmann's name cleared, my initial contact with Mr. Scaduto was completed.

With thoughts of his remarks, "Now it's your turn. You can tell your story in your own book. It's your story", still fresh in my mind, I briefly mulled over the idea he had given me, but immediately "chased it away" as being rather foolish. After all, I reasoned, I really didn't have that much to tell. Tony had already dug up the real facts on how Hauptmann had been framed, and what was more, I never considered myself to be much of a writer. How could I ever venture having a book published?

However, as ridiculous as Tony's suggestion had

originally seemed, time moved on and I did obtain much more conclusive evidence proving that Harry Young, back in 1935, held the key that was to unlock the door to the true story of the Lindbergh kidnapping.

And, with the passing of time, since I seem to be the only person who can relate all of the many new facets of the case, it seemed necessary for me to follow the suggestion of Scaduto and write a detailed account of the true story of the Lindbergh kidnapping as we now know it.

In 1980 I was interviewed in my home by a reporter from the *Philadelphia Inquirer*. After spending a total of six-and-one-half hours with me, and then making a trip to Washington, D.C. to check the authenticity of my story in the archives there, he returned to my home exclaiming: "My God, you have an earth-shaking story. Everything you said is true, I saw the telegrams myself!". The newsman went back to his paper, quite excited with his "scoop". However, after quite a few delays, stalls, and postponements, it became very evident the *Inquirer* was not going to print the story. I can only foster a guess as to why. The "big boys" were either protecting the "super sleuths" over in Jersey, or they didn't have the guts to print it! You can take your own guess.

At any rate, had the newspaper published the news I gave them in 1980, there would probably have been no reason for this book to have been written thirteen years later.

As stated earlier, I had started to publicly tell of my belief in Hauptmann's innocence by speaking largely in the vicinity of Phoenixville to civic groups such as Lions, Rotary, and Kiwanis Clubs. My claim, of course, was based primarily on Harry Young's story, and for the most part, I felt that I was not reaching my audience with anything more than a fantasy or theory. In other words, I was falling far short of convincing the listeners of anything more than providing them with a program of entertainment they could very well have missed. A few of them, however, would occasionally acknowledge my talk with their smiles and unbelieving snickers. To say the least, it was quite disappointing to me, since I was so desperately anxious to find believers among them. Many times I felt very much like someone crying in a wilderness of unbelief. At times I probably doubted my own sanity. But then, I would rationalize, I had been made aware of the true facts of the case, and the day was bound to come when I would find someone who would not only listen, but believe as well. Or, was I hoping for too much?

My "investigation", if it can be called such, during the 1940s amounted to nothing more than trips into the New Jersey area, namely Hopewell and Flemington, where the events of the crime had been centered. Although I talked to many residents, getting their reactions and opinions of the case, some of them basking in its notoriety, I actually obtained nothing more than a nostalgic and emotional awareness of the very countryside through which I was driving and walking, and the part each section played in the crime of the century. If I obtained any encouragement through my trips there, it would have to be based on the majority of the answers I received when I inquired of various people if they believed that Hauptmann was guilty. Most had answered that they had their doubts, and that if he was guilty, he had his helpers. None said they believed he was the lone kidnapper, in spite of the fact that the prosecutors established that he had acted alone.

But, on the other hand, with the help of God and the use of pure common sense, I should be able to prove that the prosecutors were tragically wrong. And here I was, feeling alone, thinking I might be able to solve the crime of the century. There can be no wonder that at times I felt "wacky".

Shortly after Harry Young's death in 1960, I went to see his wife, Leanore, who was then living in Spring City, Pennsylvania. The purpose of my visit was to possibly procure any physical evidence Harry might have acquired during the years of his personal research into the case. My hope of this was sadly blown away. To say the very least, I was disappointed beyond words. I was certain she would be glad to hand it over to me, but instead she informed me she had destroyed every bit of his collection. "Wayne", she said: "I couldn't wait to get rid of it. It scared me to have it around. I was always afraid of Harry being mixed up in it. No, I don't have anything around. I know he thought he knew everything about it, but it scared me to even hear him talk about it. That's all he ever wanted to talk about, he told everybody he saw about it, and I was scared for both him and me."

Although I could understand her fear, my hopes were bashed. Harry had told me on several occasions that he had it all written down for his two little children, as they grew older, to read about his knowledge of the case. I, of course, had high hopes of reading it and making a copy of all its details. And now that opportunity was lost. Gone forever were Harry's handwritten account, tossed asunder, or possibly burned. It didn't matter how they had been destroyed ---whatever help they might have been to me, they were gone forever.

Although I had never considered myself to be much of a religious man, it was during this time that I started to pray to God, asking Him for help. I don't know whether I held any faith that He might do it, but I did pray. After all, it could do no harm to try. I even was bold enough to ask my wife to try it, only to have her tell me she had already been doing that.

Shortly after this, C. Raymond Davis, a friend of mine, a building contractor in nearby Kimberton, met me in downtown Phoenixville, and without any knowledge of my financial trouble began telling me that I should consider receiving Christ into my life. I had been acquainted with Mr. Davis for many years and always knew him as a rough, tough individual known for his loud profane vocabulary. And now he was telling me Christ could change my life as He had his. Well, certainly something had changed him into becoming a mild soft-spoken person. Because I had always respected Mr. Davis as a fair and honest man, I took note of what he told me and pondered over his words. For days on end I read the literature he had given me, and in addition to this my wife Anna Mae and I had been faithfully watching the Reverend Billy Graham on television.

At this point it is very important that I tell you of a commitment I made that changed my life and the events which followed. On Friday night, July 19, 1957, after going through a day of depression, wondering where I could go for the help I needed, I cried out to God and received Christ as my saviour. Two weeks later my wife Anna Mae was saved.

It was shortly after this that I realized that things I had once dismissed from my mind were again being restored. One of the major changes had been the revival of my interest in the Lindbergh case. The names of Martin Stover and Isidor Fisch were again brought into the sharp focus of my thoughts. My desire to see Hauptmann's name cleared seemed preeminent. The case that had absorbed my attention for so many years, now seemed more important than ever to me. With renewed interest, and an intense awareness that I would be pleasing God, without any hesitation I again began to tell everyone who would listen the truth about the Lindbergh case.

As I obtained additional speaking engagements I made it a point to stress with increased intensity the terrible miscarriage of justice that had been thrust upon a man who paid with his life for a crime he did not commit. I also made a point of showing the extended suffering, through the intervening years, brought to bear on his loyal wife Anna. Although there was a possibility that it might have been nothing more than imagination, it seemed to me that more of my listeners were coming to me after my talks expressing their own firm belief in Hauptmann's innocence. Was it possible I was making some inroads? Was I at last gaining some ground? I believed I was.

Each day, as time allowed, I continued with my probe to find additional facts which would aid me in turning more people who had "possible doubts of Hauptmann's guilt" into "solid believers" of his innocence. Truly, I was gaining ground.

One convincing factor which proved that Hauptmann spoke the truth in the Flemington courtroom was the discovery of the motion picture sound track that had recorded the proceedings as the defendant was being mercilessly grilled by Attorney General David T. Wilentz. The film's sound track was played back in order to test the honesty of Hauptmann's answers by use of the truth-detecting device known as the Psychological Stress Evaluator (PSE). The recordings of Hauptmann's voice were from films made during his trial and statements made during the filming of him shortly before his death.

The result of the testing of Hauptmann's voice was overwhelming. Its playback proved that Richard Hauptmann had told the truth in both instances. Charles R. McQuiston, a co-developer of the voice stress evaluator, stated after obtaining the results: "I have no doubt in my mind that Hauptmann died an innocent man. We executed the wrong man, and the real kidnapper got away with the crime."

A few portions of the Psychological Stress Evaluator's verdict of the cross-examination of Hauptmann by Wilentz as it was filmed in court went as follows, with Mr.McQuiston's evaluations:

Wilentz: "Did you take the Lindbergh baby?"
Hauptmann: "No. I did not."
McQuiston: "This response shows a complete lack of stress. I have to believe him."

Wilentz: "Did you not lie under oath?"
Hauptmann: "No."
Wilentz: "You lied under oath."
Hauptmann: "I did not."
McQuiston: "Hauptmann's statement is made with great emphasis, but without stress. He is telling the truth."

The readout of the PSE clearly shows, without any stretch of the imagination, that Hauptmann was definitely telling the truth, when in answer to Wilentz's accusing assertion, "You lied under oath," Hauptmann replied in a straightforward manner, "I did not."

The impassioned plea for help that Hauptmann made from his jail cell shortly before his execution had also been filmed. In essence you will remember this is what he said: "I want to tell the people of America that I am innocent of the crime of murder. I never saw the Lindbergh baby and I never was in Hopewell or near Hopewell and I never received any money from Dr. Condon."

As McQuiston proceeded to break down Hauptmann's message line by line and word by word, and after running it through the PSE, he concluded there was absolutely no stress to be found in Hauptmann's voice, hence the convicted man was telling the truth without any question.

Arthur Koehler, the "wood expert" whose damaging testimony of the attic wood, "rail 16", as having been taken from the Hauptmann attic, in order to doom Hauptmann, because he "traced the graining" across an open space of a one-and-one-quarter-inch, span, thus "proving that it was once one piece of lumber", was also subjected to the scrutiny of the PSE. The following answer of Koehler allows us to summarize his entire testimony:

"I noted that the grain of the two matches up perfectly." To which McQuiston rendered these findings:

"This man is saying he's very sure, but there is strong stress on the words 'that' and 'matches.' This leads me to believe Koehler was either lying, or not as certain about his findings as he testified in court. If Hauptmann were tried today, he would walk away a free men. I am thoroughly convinced of that."

It is possible that the thought might have crossed your mind as to the reliability of the Psychological

Stress Evaluator. If so, let me assure you that at that time it had been proven to be credible as court evidence in five states, as well as its having been used by over 100 government investigative agencies to combat crime.

The attitude taken by agents of the Federal Bureau of Investigation during the investigation of the case, as well as that of their boss, Director J. Edgar Hoover, is indeed interesting. Three days after Hauptmann's arrest Hoover stated: "It is entirely possible that two men were involved and that possibly Fisch was involved with Hauptmann in the outside work." And then on October 10, 1934, three weeks later, Hoover called his men off the case by withdrawing them from any further work in the preparation of Hauptmann for trial. The reason for this was expressed by Agent Hugh H. Clegg who summarized the feelings of the other agents when he stated: "There are logical reasons which would point to the presence of someone else but there are an equal number of logical reasons why there is only one person."

There is additional evidence which clearly points out the bitter FBI hostility of the other agencies that had been investigating the "weird" case. On October 11, 1934, the day following Hoover's withdrawal of his "troops", Mr. Hoover wrote that "the real work was done by agents" of the bureau, and predicted that New Jersey police and prosecutors "will probably find a situation which they cannot handle", while another FBI memorandum, dated September 21, 1934, also made after Hauptmann's arrest, stated that: "Mr. Hoover said that at New York everything was against the division [FBI] 100 percent," and if he had not gone to New York the division would not even have been mentioned."

Along with this we have evidence that on March 28, 1936, Governor Harold Hoffman received a memorandum from Director Hoover in which he informed the governor the New Jersey State Police had ordered his agents away from the Hauptmann attic while state troopers were working there with a Federal Forestry Service expert. The "expert" had been Arthur Koehler, who in a later FBI memo dated May 26, 1936, was criticized for a talk he had given in which "Mr. Koehler's speech was not consistent with the evidence."

The most damning of the FBI memorandums had to do with the ridiculous claims of Koehler. The memo said that identification of the ladder wood as "identical" with Hauptmann attic wood came after the FBI withdrew from the investigation "and occurred after the New Jersey state police had rented the Hauptmann residence."

It went on to say "the Hauptmann defense lawyers were expected during the 1935 trial to subpoena FBI records to prove this identification was 'fabricated' by the joint efforts of the New Jersey State Police and the New Jersey prosecutor's office in cooperation with Arthur Koehler"; however, "this request was not received by the bureau from the defense attorneys."

As we weigh this FBI statement with Hauptmann's claim that there were times when he thought his attorney Reilly was working along with the prosecution, it certainly validates his charge. Because the Federal Bureau of Investigation, after having said they did not "swallow" the state's claim about the attic wood, had chosen not to testify of their belief simply because "they had not been subpoenaed" is certainly one of the greatest of "injustices" committed throughout the entire case against Hauptmann.

Chief Agent Thomas H. Sisk, working directly under Hoover, offered much evidence stating that, "if Hauptmann was guilty at all" he had to have had help. Sisk said: "there are others connected with this case." And this he based primarily on his belief of Hauptmann's inability, due to his size and weight, to have entered the nursery window alone. Furthermore he had contended that if Hauptmann was involved as they said he was, "he must have had a lot of help in the passing of the money, and what is more there is also some indication that someone in the vicinity of Hopewell may have been involved with him."

Another FBI agent, Leon G. Turrou, reported that on September 21, 1934, Dr. Condon had told him, after first looking at Mr. Hauptmann in police custody, that "the real John" was Mr. Hauptmann's "brother", going on to say that Condon, "asserted that the real John was killed long ago and that the money was taken away from him by his confederates. He intimated that the real men who are responsible for the kidnapping and murder of the Lindbergh child are now somewhere in Long Island around Bay Shore."

Just another example of "embellished fantasy" from the "lying lips" of "Jafsie" Condon. At every turn Hauptmann had been trapped in a maze of lies ---with no one to help him.

Another example of the prosecution's blatant disregard to accept any segment of evidence which might have proven helpful to Hauptmann can be clearly seen in this report of Federal Agent Turrou, who stated that in a memorandum dated October 5, 1934, Doctor Condon complained that the police had attacked "his character, and particularly so since the time he failed to positively identify Hauptmann when confronted with him at the time of his arrest." The memo contained this additional information: "Doctor Condon," further advised the writer that he "studied the photograph of Isidor Fisch which appeared in the newspapers and that it is his belief now that when on March 12, 1932, he went to meet 'John' at the Woodlawn Cemetery he saw a party strongly resembling the features and description of Isidor Fisch pass the car in which he and Al Reich were sitting." The very knowledge of such things having taken place within the criminal justice system of our great nation is nauseating.

Other FBI memos mentioned "the questionable tactics that extended to virtually every aspect of the state's case, including virtually every piece of evidence." Another memo in particular, dated October 1934, made mention that the New Jersey state police "did not have one single reliable witness who could place Hauptmann in the vicinity of Hopewell prior to or on the date of the crime." But regardless of what the memo stated, witness after witness, of questionable character, testified they had seen him near the Lindbergh home.

But, there were more amazing facts discovered during the intervening years following the closing chapter of Tony Scaduto's great book.

One of the most unfair things done to hurt Hauptmann was perpetrated as he was awaiting his execution. For no good reason, the authorities took it upon themselves to thwart his wish to communicate by letter with his mother Paulina in Kamenz, Germany. This fact was kept a tight secret until forty-one years later when the news of this was revealed by the *Associated Press* and the *New York Daily News* during the month of March, 1977.

The following is a humble request Richard Hauptmann made to the warden of the New Jersey State Prison at Trenton ---

Col. Kimberling.

Dear Sir:
Your translation of this letter
I really would be very thankful.
What I have written is only the truth.
The same I would be glad if the

Governor would read this letter over.

I know dear Sir it is quite some trouble for you, but I really don't know to whom I shall go in my present affair.

Thanks for your kindness.

Very respectfully

R. Hauptmann

And here is how it was treated by Colonel Mark O. Kimberling.

On the night of Friday, December 27, 1935, Hauptmann started to write a letter to his mother whom he had not seen since he left his home in Germany in 1923. In this letter he poured out his heart to her as he bitterly declared his innocence of the crime. However, after completing the letter and handing it to Colonel Kimberling, who personally read the contents, since it was his duty to censor the inmate's mail, decided it was necessary that the letter not be mailed.

Hauptmann, having written the letter in his tight, neat German script with blue water ink on white stationery, had requested that Kimberling first have it translated into English and a copy of it then sent to Governor Hoffman. The warden had two members of the prison staff translate the letter, and on Friday, January 3rd, 1936, exactly three months before Hauptmann's electrocution, Hoffman was mailed a copy. Enclosed with the letter was a personal note from Kimberling to the governor in which he said: "I am of the opinion that it might receive some press comment over in Germany, which might result in some unfavorable reaction, or, at least in placing us in an embarrassing position for having released it from state prison."

Because Governor Hoffman never answered or acknowledged in any way his receipt of the letter, it seems quite reasonable to wonder if possibly he also had not seen it. Regardless, it was Kimberlings duty to follow Hauptmann's request and mail the letter to his mother. But, the letter was never mailed and Hauptmann went to his death on April 3rd, 1936 believing his mother had received it. And Paulina Hauptmann went to her death without the knowledge that her son had written to her. Just more evidence of criminal injustice in the Lindbergh-Hauptmann case.

Although Kimberling died in 1964, his private

papers and news clippings relating to Hauptmann and the fourteen months he spent on New Jersey's death row were not found until the time of Mrs. Kimberling's death. Among other things in the warden's personal file were routine communications between him, Hoffman, and others pertaining to the news coverage of the execution, and offers by various members of the clergy who wished to be of aid to Hauptmann. Another thing found was an eyewitness account of the electrocution written by Dr. Charles H. Mitchell, the Mercer County medical examiner who signed Hauptmann's death certificate.

During 1935, as he sat alone in his cell, Hauptmann spent the bulk of his time writing his memoirs. There has been much controversy as to what became of it. It is my personal belief that a condensed version of it was published posthumously in the *New York Mirror*. Anna Hauptmann remembers that she, at one time, had Richard's complete hand written manuscript, but foolishly had loaned it to a woman who claimed to be a writer who promised to have it published. Unfortunately, the "writer" claimed it was stolen from her automobile and it has never been seen since. Nevertheless, among Kimberling's collection were some of the pages from Hauptmann's memoirs with additions and corrections. The first 87 pages, according to an evaluation of Kimberling, "refers to the boyhood home and army experiences and there seems to be nothing outstanding to anything but a normal life." One of the pages numbered 193-A told of an early summer experience in New York, shortly after his arrival from Germany, when his fiance Anna almost drowned and he had dramatically saved her life. On another page, 285-A, he expressed the bitterness he felt toward his attorney, Edward J. Reilly, for not properly defending him. Hauptmann's complete memoirs were believed to have totaled nearly 300 pages, and although they are lost today, it is my belief that the day will come when they will be found.

The failure of Kimberling to mail the letter to Hauptmann's mother is unforgivable. Regardless of any reason he gave for his neglect in carrying out Hauptmann's only possible means of reaching his mother is a sacrilege that demonstrated the complete disrespect he held for his hapless prisoner. Especially so, when we read the contents which expressed his feelings as he wrote his message from the depths of his innermost being, with a broken heart that was soon to be stilled:

"Dear mother, this letter will be somewhat long, for I want to go into some points regarding my trial. I will always and must always, suitable to my situation, go according to the records. Also, a lie cannot help me but would rather hurt me.

"Where I was arrested, they almost crippled me by beating in order to apprehend something which is not in me. There are, indeed, societies for the prevention of cruelty to animals, but, unfortunately, not for men.

"If I were guilty, I would submit to my verdict, for I would only receive what my deeds were worth. I cannot be silent and must defend myself and this I do with a clear conscience.

"I only wish that the world will recognize me as I am and not as they have painted me. If there is any shame in this case then it lies on the shoulders of the prosecutor, for I have carried on in this case with a clear conscience."

Writing of his attorney Reilly, he made great emphasis of his belief in the man's disloyalty: "I suffered more from the actions of this man than from any other man. I am 100 percent certain when I say that he worked together with the prosecutor I had an opportunity to explain my case to him only five minutes. He simply did not come to me, or if he came for three or five minutes, he was often drunk."

Hauptmann's letter explained his feelings about the ladder used in the kidnapping: "It is only a wooden rack, and I do not believe even now that this rack was ever used as a ladder. Its construction shows too plainly that it never came from the hand of a carpenter, not even a poor one. Whether it really came from the house, I do not know but if it did, then I make responsible the persons who were there after Anny left the house.

"Dear mother, you can hardly conceive how I feel when I think about the whole built-up affair. I cannot see my child in whom my whole heart is placed, in this place. My God, My God, where is justice in this world? I simply cannot believe that this state in order to cancel a case, will break the life of an innocent man in such a way. This would be not only more than ordinary murder but also **MURDER OF JUSTICE**."

Richard's letter of 5,000 words, was a lengthy one. When it was discovered that it had never been mailed to his mother, the authorities voiced a weak excuse that if she had received it and divulged its contents to the press over there, they believed the authorities of that day held an honest "fear" it would produce anti-American sentiment in Nazi Germany.

With the announcement of the discovery of the unmailed Hauptmann letter, plus the clamor caused by those who had read Scaduto's *Scapegoat*, and reports of other new evidence turning up, the New Jersey State Police reported that they were "taking another look" with the assignment of an officer to work full time at reconstructing the case in an attempt to learn how well the evidence by which Hauptmann was tried would "hold up" by the standards of the 1970s. Anna Hauptmann, who had officially requested that a review of the case be made, suffered another disappointing blow as Colonel Clinton A. Pagano, superintendent of the New Jersey State Police, after more than a year of "re-studying" the evidence, announced: "I have seen nothing anywhere that would indicate anything other than the original findings."

Of course he didn't. Why should he look for anything that would tear down and destroy the case that had been so expertly "built-up" by the "big boys", as Trooper Opdyke had politely called "the destroyers" that day in Flemington's empty courtroom.

CHAPTER SIXTY NINE

Martin Stover, Hauptmann's Best Witness!

It was during the decade of the 60s that I had many serious thoughts of forgetting, if it were possible, everything I ever knew about the case. Invitations to speak had fallen off considerably, and as I reassessed every element of the crime, I must admit I thoughtfully considered giving up any hope of ever getting enough evidence to prove that Richard Hauptmann was innocent of the kidnapping. Although my interest had dwindled, I became aware for the first time that it would take someone with far more logic than I to accomplish this goal. After all, how would I who knew the truth, here in Phoenixville, Pennsylvania, with no clout whatsoever be able to generate the interest needed to prove that Hauptmann had nothing to do with the crime of the century. As stated before, my voice was as one crying out into a wilderness of unbelievers.

I constantly questioned my sanity as to my involvement in the case. The whole thing seemed preposterous, absurd, asinine. Or was it? No, I rationalized, I think I'm as normal as most people. Then I should forget this foolishness and prove that I am. Not to do it had become my consistent line of poor reasoning. But since I happened to know more about the crime than the average person --- why then should I drop it? I found myself in a chaos of confusion.

Had my decision been to forget the case, I seriously doubt that I could have done it. This I base on something strange that had been occurring. As I went about carrying on my daily tasks, predominate among my normal thoughts, the name of Martin Stover would invariably come to my mind. This had been happening night after night and day upon day for quite some time. When my thoughts were completely centered on some activity I was engaged in, probably sports, my work, a meeting I was attending, again and again his name would crowd out the matter at hand and my thoughts would be diverted to Martin Stover, MARTIN STOVER, MARTIN STOVER, **MARTIN STOVER!** And with it came thoughts of my knowledge of the Lindbergh kidnapping and the innocence of Richard Hauptmann. I could not escape the driving and intense desire to continue on with my work on the famous crime. The name of Martin Stover was "bugging me" into a near frenzy. Why, I rationalized, I couldn't drop this case if I wanted to, because something greater than I was driving me on.

Following, what must have been weeks of this "torment" I decided there was nothing else I could do but search the "hinterlands" for more evidence. But I didn't know where to go or where to look, so I decided to wait and see. Now, if you think at this point I was bordering on the verge of insanity, that is your privilege, since possibly I thought the same. However, developments which were soon to unfold proved that I was without any doubt on the right wavelength.

Once again, I set forth on a new course of action. I had already decided it was high time I put on a more intensified search for Mrs. Hauptmann, since I realized it was important to talk with her, inform her of my knowledge of the case, and find out directly from her some things that were still unclear to me as well as those things I did not understand. Various news articles published throughout the years had reported that she had remarried, was living under a fictitious name, or had left the country and was now living in her homeland Germany. However, the majority of these reports stated that she was residing in the Philadelphia area, had not remarried, and had never attempted to hide her identity regardless of the turmoil and notoriety the arrest, trial, and execution of her innocent husband had unjustly thrust upon her and little Manfred.

I decided to intensify my search for her, but without any plans as to how I was going to do this, I naturally failed in every attempt I made. However, I was not at all disappointed because I had a belief, a strong feeling, that convinced me I was soon going to find Anna Hauptmann. My faith never wavered.

My first lead came when I learned through a published story in the *Philadelphia Evening Bulletin* that she was working in a bakery in Philadelphia. I quickly found the shop, identified as the D'Ambrosio Bakery, at 1713 South 22nd Street in Philadelphia. Accompanied by my friend Herb Coale, my chauffeur for the day, we entered the store. Inquiring if this was the place where Mrs. Anna Hauptmann was employed, a pleasant young lady named Edith informed us that she had worked there until recently, but was now retired. Although we implored her to tell us where we could find her, Edith was faithful to a promise she had made to inform no one of Mrs. Hauptmann's home address. But our pleading was not entirely in vain since she did try to be of aid when we told her we had information that would clear Richard Hauptmann's name. She could not hide her desire to help us, going so far as to telephone her boss, Vincent D'Ambrosio, and asking for him to grant her his permission to tell us where Anna lived. But she failed in this, since he too, in loyalty to Anna refused to give her the information we needed. However, after another visit to the bakery, I learned that Mrs. Hauptmann resided somewhere in Yeadon, Delaware County, a suburb near Philadelphia.

Armed with this information, I could now direct my search to one definite community. But, when I visited Yeadon I was again faced with the same obstacle that had been presented to me by Mrs. Hauptmann's friends at D'Ambrosio's Bakery. Most people said they knew she "lived here someplace", while others who told me they knew her address, refused to cooperate. The police and mailmen who were aware of the location of her residence were also committed to their pledge not to reveal to "anyone" where Anna Hauptmann could be located. And, although no one agreed to make it any easier for me, I must say that I certainly admired them for their silence, however, I must admit that every refusal to help made it more frustrating.

Anna Hauptmann was, along with her husband, an unfortunate victim of the crime of the century and should never have been "hauled around the country" to be placed on exhibition for the gawkers to stare at as some oddity. And so, I say God bless all of you who have known her and have seen to it that her right to privacy was never violated. Mrs. Richard Hauptmann has suffered these many long years as no other person can ever understand. On September 19th, 1934 her husband had been unjustly stripped of the privilege of returning in freedom to his home and to the wife he loved so dearly. A home to which he never returned, thus robbing Anna Hauptmann of the security, comfort, and love she should have been enjoying these past 64 years, and denying her son, Manfred, the joy of knowing his father's love. Mrs. Richard Hauptmann deserved much more than the taunts of a public who still refuse to understand and believe the truth of the kidnapping. But, on the other hand, I say God bless all of you who have befriended her through the years and have shown her the compassion and understanding she so rightly deserved.

As frustrating as my search for Mrs. Hauptmann proved to be, I had one proverbial "ace in the hole" from which to draw, especially so, since I was now certain that she lived in Yeadon. I called my friend Joe from a street telephone and explained my plight to him. After promising not to reveal his name, he told me it would take him a few minutes to get it for me and that he would then return my call. Suddenly it dawned on me that I had failed to inform him that I had called from a pay phone, therefore, he would believe I had called him from either my home or office. However, after waiting a reasonable length of time, during which I suffered the pangs of possibly an additional disappointment, I called him again and found him waiting to give me the address I needed. Hallelujah, I felt like shouting. The feeling of victory overwhelmed me. Giving my driver, Bill Stow, the address, he drove slowly as we searched for the street and house number. The date was Thursday, June 23, 1977 and soon I would meet Mrs. Hauptmann.

Before too long we were driving by her house. I asked Bill to continue on down the street and park a distance away. Her home was in a quiet residential area of Yeadon, the street on which she lived was amply shaded by old trees. On foot I approached the small neat looking frame duplex home, and as I walked nearer I could see that an upstairs window was open. Stepping onto the porch, I noticed that beyond a closed screen door, the front door was standing partially ajar, causing me to feel reasonably sure I would find her at home.

With slight trepidation I knocked gently on the screen door and waited. Within seconds an elderly lady of small stature appeared. "Yes?", she asked. Her pleasant response to my summons did not hide her apprehension at being approached by a total stranger. At once, I recognized her as the person I had been searching for. "Mrs. Hauptmann", I said, "I am a friend. I have evidence which can prove your husband was innocent and that he was framed." And then I followed with, "I believe God sent me to help you."

Now, please don't misunderstand me. I fully realize that there were, and still are, thousands upon thousands of persons who are still "prancing" around the country hooting, howling, and dancing to a "piper's tune" quite similar to what I said to Mrs. Hauptmann when I first met her.

From the time the first news of the kidnapping was broadcast, the police investigators had been deluged with messages from "kooks" of all kinds. Some of them were very sincere, claiming they had a special message sent to them from God, who had told them where the baby would be found, as well as other claims they had received from soothsayers and mediums of all kinds. Without exception, all of the stories they had volunteered to tell proved to be fruitless for use by the police. As sincere as many of them were, the police wrote most of them off as being nothing more than "crackpots", "weirdos", "loons", "fruitcakes" or one of the horde of "nut people", Alan Hynd called them.

Although I had mentioned to Mrs. Hauptmann that I believed God had sent me to help her, I trust that you will not hastily classify me as being in the same category as those I enumerated above. Ever since that night in July of 1957 when I was converted to Christ, I had been experiencing help in my investigation of the Lindbergh kidnapping that I never had before, help that seemed to come from a compelling force that prompted me to search where I would soon find the correct answers. My attention was now being directed to people who gave me help in my quest for pertinent information. Because of this I had come to realize that my chief concern should be to do things pleasing to God. By no means had I ever considered myself as being a religious fanatic. However, I must admit that the help I received bordered on something I now recognized as coming to me by God's direction. And so, I found new strength by admitting that any success I experienced was coming from spiritual help, and because of this I felt no shame by saying that God was on my side helping me. That is why I greeted Mrs. Hauptmann as I did.

"Come in," she invited, opening the door for me to enter. "What have you to tell me?" she asked with enthusiasm. "Mrs. Hauptmann," I said, "I have been working on the case for over forty years and can prove without a doubt that Isidor Fisch was involved in the kidnapping. I have the evidence needed to prove that Richard did get the money from Fisch as he said he did, and that Fisch was deeply involved in the kidnapping."

Anna Hauptmann was overjoyed as I told her I had living witnesses who had verified that Fisch, through his fur dealings, had been associated with a man named Stover who had taken a baby, believed to be the

Lindbergh child into South America in 1932. I asked her if she had known Stover, and after thinking a moment, she assured me that she had never heard of him. She also stated that she was reasonably sure Richard had never met him. She was quite happy, in fact overjoyed and appreciative that I had brought her more conclusive evidence of Isidor Fisch's involvement, explaining that she had another very important link which connected Fisch with the kidnapping. Mrs. Hauptmann appeared excited and fairly shouted with emotion: "Why this proves that Fisch had the money. That's what Richard tried to tell them, but they wouldn't believe him. They wouldn't listen. Isidor was a crook, but we didn't know it until after he died. We trusted him and he cheated us. He owed Richard $7,500. That's why when Richard found the money in the closet he dried some of it out and started to spend it. He had no intention to keep it all." Mrs. Hauptmann's excitement of my news to her thrilled me. She had realized immediately this proved that Richard's story was true. To say the least, she was ecstatic.

During my visit with Mrs. Hauptmann I could not help but notice the tidiness of her small home as she went hurrying about gathering together some items she wanted me to see. It was immaculate. As I waited for her return, I could not help but delight in the satisfaction that I had finally found the person for whom I had searched these many years.

Contrary to any belief you might possibly consider, that I was experiencing a sense of awe as I talked with Mrs.Hauptmann, let me assure you that as I sat in her home, in the very presence of the lady the whole world recognized as the wife of the man who had been accused of kidnapping and murdering the Lindbergh baby, my only thoughts were to "match notes" with her and be of some help to her in clearing her husband's name. However, I must admit that I was overwhelmed at my success in finding her and the first hand information I gained from this initial meeting with her.

As we sat together on the maple couch in her living room, she had me repeat again the evidence I had hurried to tell her as I first entered her home. "Oh, this is so good, it will prove that Richard spoke the truth about Fisch and the money." Anna Hauptmann had tears as she seemed to grasp with each passing moment the importance of the connection of Fisch and the man from South America.

As we discussed the case, she seemed to dwell on

Isidor Fisch, how they had trusted him, how they had received cards from him after he had gone back to Germany in 1933 in which he related the good times he was having going to burlesque shows and other entertainment. "But, this was not true at all," Mrs. Hauptmann told me, "Isidor was a sick man when he arrived in Germany. He was so sick Henry Uhlig had to help him off the boat, he was taken to a hospital and he never regained his health. He died in the Leipzig hospital the following March." She also questioned why he wrote to them of the good times he was having when it was not true. "Isidor was not only a crook he was also a liar.", she told me, emphasizing that after he died they were informed by Louise Helfert, who lived a floor above Fisch in the rooming house, that he had her type fake bills for purchases of furs he never owned. She said she also had typed bills at his insistence for his fake Knickerbocker Pie Company.

She brought out pictures that had been taken during the years she and Richard had shared as husband and wife. She talked at length about the happy days they had enjoyed together, the walks they had taken as they walked side by side in Bronx Park and along the bank of the river. With pride she showed me a handsome chest that Richard had made for her, one he had designed and constructed by inlaying wood of different hues and tones. Only a master carpenter could have fashioned such a chest by using selected varieties of wood. "Let me show you something else", Mrs. Hauptmann said as she hurried off to open a drawer of a cabinet in her dining room. As she returned she held out a large colored picture of her husband. I commented on the handsome appearance of Richard. "That's just it," she stated, "When I was in Germany visiting my mother in 1932, Richard sent this picture to me together with a letter in which he expressed his love for me and explained that he had sent the picture "so that I can be with you over there." Mrs. Hauptmann went on to tell me that the picture had been taken after she had embarked for Germany, at a photographer's studio located on East Eighty-sixth Street. She said the photographer had placed it in a window in his shop where everybody could see it and that he passed that shop every day when he went to the stock market office. "Why would he do this? Why would he allow his picture to be put so prominently in a window if he had been the man Condon said he met in the cemeteries? Would a kidnapper who got all that money from Lindbergh allow his picture to be seen on one of New York's busiest streets? Richard had nothing to hide or be ashamed of... No, they would never print this picture of Richard. He looked too kind, too human, too handsome for the newspapers. They only used pictures taken of him when he was tired from having no sleep. They wanted to make him look evil, not handsome as he is in this picture.", she reiterated as she fondly embraced the picture of her husband.

Mrs. Hauptmann and I talked at length about the number of discrepancies in the state's case, dwelling on Reilly's failure to allow witnesses to testify who could have helped her husband. She was very incensed at the deception of certain reporters, who at the time of the trial, were aware of some vital truths about the case. These reporters, instead of helping her as they had promised to do by printing the facts, had failed her by remaining silent about things which could have been helpful to Richard.

She mentioned several instances where she felt she had been deliberately deceived by reporters. One particular time had to do with a reporter who worked for the *New York Journal*. Mrs. Hauptmann then went on to tell me of that instance. "Shortly after Richard was arrested I received a letter from a lady who lived in Jackson Heights, New York. She told me she had seen Richard in Fredericksen's Bakery on March 1st, 1932, but that she was afraid to go to the police with her information because she knew what the police do to witnesses. Well, anyway, this reporter said he wanted to help me locate the letter writer and encourage her to go to the police with the information. I willingly gave him the letter but that's the last I ever heard of him. He deceived me like so many of the others did. Here is what she told me in her letter: 'Mrs.Hauptmann I would like to help you, but I am afraid because I know what the police do to witnesses. But I must tell you that I was in Fredericksen's Bakery that night and from seeing your husband's pictures in the papers I am positive he was in the bakery talking to you at the counter. I was sitting at the counter having a cup of coffee and your husband came in and talked to you a little while and then he walked the dog.'

"Don't you see it, Wayne?", she went on, "She told me this before it was made public during the trial. She would not have known this unless she had been in Fredericksen's. She was telling the truth and wanted to help me. She was there and saw us, but what good did it do? It didn't help my Richard. That reporter, whoever he was, hurt us badly. But then, what did it matter? They probably wouldn't have believed her anyway, since they didn't believe any of Richard's other witnesses." At this point my empathy for Mrs. Hauptmann hit a new high.

Anna Hauptmann had absolutely nothing good to say for her husband's chief defense lawyer, Edward J. Reilly. She showed nothing but contempt for him, and rightly so, because it is very possible Reilly did the "poorest" job of representing a client in the history of all the major cases ever conducted in the history of the American criminal jurisprudence system. The man was a total mess.

Tony Scaduto in his interview with Mrs. Hauptmann asked her why Reilly had not presented certain evidence in Richard's behalf, and received her caustic answer, "Who knows why Reilly did what he did? Who knows what that man was doing." And then she went on to say: "Reilly wanted me to lie about the shoe box. I told him I never saw it there and that was the truth, but he wanted me to swear I did see it. I couldn't lie, I'd be red in the face and shaking." Her hand reached for the Bible on the table next to her, as if she were recreating the oath she swore when she took the witness chair. "As much as I loved Richard," she said, "to lie would be wrong. You could put all the money in the world in front of me and I couldn't lie for it. Nothing is as strong as the truth."

The time I spent with Anna Hauptmann proved to be very profitable. I grasped from the intensity of her demeanor, the sincerity of her voice, that she was telling the truth as we discussed each point of the case. But above all, she told me that at the time of her husband's death in 1936, she had asked God to clear Richard's name by having the real truth known, thus proving his innocence, before the time she too would be called home to heaven where she knew Richard would be waiting.

When I first entered her home I immediately sensed that Mrs. Hauptmann was a devout Christian. I noticed her well-read Bible laying on the top of an end table in her living room, and with it a copy of *The Daily Bread*, a daily devotional booklet published by The Radio Bible Class of Grand Rapids, Michigan, one of which I also was familiar. When she learned of my faith in Christ, our conversation naturally turned to God's goodness of having me locate her to offer whatever help and strength I could. She seemed overjoyed to learn that I was a firm believer in the divine guidance of God as I went along assuring her that I knew He was going to produce more evidence that would be helpful in proving Richard innocent. Although I truly believed this, I had no idea how He was going to perform this, what seemed to be an insurmountable, task still facing us.

But regardless of this, we both had the faith to believe that God would answer Anna Hauptmann's prayers. And so, before I made my departure, we joined hands and had a word of prayer together, asking Him to guide us and help us to, at last, prove the innocence of Richard Hauptmann, an innocence that would meet with the satisfaction of all.

My initial meeting with Mrs. Hauptmann, as well as additional visits in our respective homes, all proved to be informative sessions, resulting in heart-warming discussions during which she related hundreds of stories about her life with Richard. But the pathos brought on by the diabolical tragedy of having been caught up in such a "fatal snare", manufactured by devilish authorities, it is important that you learn, as only Anna Hauptmann can tell it, the full impact of the case as she lived it personally during her married life with Richard and the ensuing years that followed.

Because of the significance and gravity of this traumatic period, and since Anthony Scaduto relates his first meeting with Anna Hauptmann in such a warm and engrossing style, it is with his permission that I have again borrowed excerpts from his excellent book *Scapegoat*.

"She began to ask questions about what I had found, and where I had found it, and I told her about the missing letters from Pinkus Fisch, the evidence that the employment time sheets for March first had existed, the summary of Richard's ledger book---rattling off everything I could remember about all the distortions and lies that had been told by police and prosecutor. And I realized she was not getting excited, as I expected her to, and she didn't seem to be very interested in my recital, in fact. I wondered whether she had indeed decided to forget about fighting to prove her husband's innocence, as I'd been told. But I was wrong.

"'I think about this often,' she said. 'Sometimes, when I think about it, I can't sleep. Two years ago, I woke up in the middle of the night and suddenly remembered something important. Richard made a cabinet for Fredericksen's bakery, very primitive, just two shelves to hold bakery boxes. He made it with the wood he bought in the lumberyard that they said he made the ladder with. I woke up and thought, 'Why didn't I remember that during the trial? Maybe that could have saved Richard.' And I wondered whether there were other things Richard made with that wood that would have proved he didn't make the ladder."

"We sat with Mrs. Hauptmann for about three hours that first day and she talked openly about Richard, their relationship, the trial, and Isidor Fisch.... 'It is so good to be able to talk to someone about this,' she said. 'I can't talk to anyone. It is so good that you came.'

"But now, at our first meeting, she was still wary. 'I have been made promises by reporters so many times,' she said. 'Years ago, they come to interview me and promise to print our side of it but they never do, they write how I'm living, how the wife of a famous murderer gets along. Never anything about Richard's innocence. So I don't trust writers anymore.'

"We asked her about Fisch, the man initially responsible for sending Richard to his death. Her eyes clouded for a moment, but then she straightened her shoulders and leaned forward in her easy chair.

"'When Richard found Fisch's money, that Sunday in the summer,' she said, 'he was moving a snake plant for me, out of a small pot into a larger one, because the roots were coming through. Richard was working at the kitchen sink, transplanting, and he spilled a little dirt. He went to the closet to get the broom and dustpan from the nail on the wall and when he was taking down the broom the handle hit something on the top shelf. He told me, 'It was like electricity and I thought, Isidor's box.'"

"When did Richard say this?"

"'In the Bronx jail, two days after his arrest, when I asked him about the money they found. He told me the box was falling to pieces from the water that leaked in, and when he saw that it was money he took it out to the garage to dry it. He told me, 'Annie, Isidor cheated me out of seven thousand dollars. I was drying out the money to take my share, what he owed me, and I was saving the rest for Fisch's brother, for when he came to America.'

"'Maybe, if I had been different, Richard would still be here,' she went on. 'A few days after he found the money I almost learned about his secret, but I didn't want to pry. I'm sorry I didn't. You see,

Richard would take a few pieces of money out and hang them up to dry, and when they were dry he would put them away and hang up a new set. Every day before he went to the office, to the stock market, he would work in the garage with the money. One morning I went outside and Richard saw me from the garage. He shut the garage door very quick. I wondered, 'What's going on in there, he's so secretive?' I thought I would go and check later, I was so curious. You know what we women are,' she said with a girlish smile. "But I thought, 'What if it's a surprise like the wardrobe closet he built for the baby?' And then I felt so cheap wanting to look. I didn't look because I thought he was building something and I didn't want to spoil the surprise.

"'This was after Fisch died, after we learned Fisch was a liar and a crook. He told us he loaned a friend two thousand dollars to open a delicatessen and I told Richard, 'How nice, Fisch lends that man his money like that.' I always liked Isidor, he was so smart and so nice. But after he died the man sent a note to Richard and asked him to come and see him, something about Isidor. Richard went to see him and the man told him that Fisch owed him two thousand dollars. Richard said, 'I thought Isidor lent **you** the money.' But the man had a receipt to prove that Fisch lied, that he borrowed the money, he didn't lend it to the man. The man wanted Richard to help him get the money back, but Richard said he didn't know where Fisch kept his money or the furs he was supposed to have. Later, the man was there when they opened the safe deposit box, but it was empty.'

"'I liked Isidor, but some things about him were very funny, very strange,' she said as an introduction to a long anecdote. Shortly after Manfred was born she received a letter addressed to him. 'I thought it was a card for him, something like that, and I opened it. It was a letter. I read it and I was very upset. It said such terrible things, 'I hope you live an awful life and die young,' things like that. It was typed, but I showed it to people and tried to find out who would do such an awful thing. I showed it to Isidor because he was always interested in writing and he said, 'Let me have it, I'll try to find out who did it.'

"'He came back a few days later and he said, 'This is a joke for Richard, not for Manfred. See, up in the corner, in pencil, is November twenty-six. That's Richard's birthday.' I looked and there in the corner was the date. I didn't see it before Isidor saw it.

Then Isidor told me he was certain Gerta Henkel and her sister, Erica, wrote the letter. I couldn't believe that, but Isidor said he was certain. I went to Gerta and showed it to her and told her what Isidor said. She denied it, she couldn't understand why Isidor said that. Why was Isidor stirring up trouble like that!

"'I feel certain Isidor had something to do with the ransom notes. I don't ever want to accuse anybody without proof because I know what they did to Richard without proof. But Isidor was always interested in handwriting and somebody disguised the ransom notes to look like Richard's writing. In the Bronx jail, when I talked to Richard, he told me, 'Annie, if I didn't write those notes, I would say they were my handwriting.'"

"But Richard and Isidor didn't meet until after the kidnapping," I said. "He couldn't have copied Richard's writing."

"'I know,' Anna Hauptmann replied. 'Isidor wrote in perfect English, he studied at school. Maybe he disguised the writing to look like German and just happened to ... I don't know, that's one thing I have never been able to understand, how it should look so much like Richard's writing.

"'Isidor, we thought he was our friend. Still, Richard and I always thought there was something strange about Isidor's going-away party. Isidor never wanted to go to parties, never wanted to meet too many people. But he asked Richard to give him a going-away party, for leaving to Germany. After Richard was arrested we began to think that Isidor asked for the party as a plan to give Richard the money, in the shoe box.

"'There were many things a little strange about Isidor. When he was going down to the boat, to go to Germany, Gerta and Erica decided they would go down and say goodbye, to surprise him. They went aboard and they saw Isidor standing with four or five men. When Isidor saw them he left his friends and came over to Gerta and said, 'What are you doing here?' He was angry. Gerta said, 'We wanted to surprise you, to say goodbye and make you surprised.' Isidor showed them to his cabin, then told them he was busy and made them leave right away. Gerta and Erica told me this, after Isidor died and things began to come out about him. We didn't know it until later, but Isidor kept one group of friends apart from another and he even kept people in the same group away from other people in the group.

"'That's why he didn't want Gerta to meet those men. He was telling you and your friends how rich he was, what a great businessman he was,' I said, 'and he was telling his other friends that he was poor and starving so he could borrow money from them. He was deceiving everyone."

"'That's what Hans always said, that Isidor tries to keep everybody apart,' Mrs. Hauptmann stated. 'He didn't want anybody to know what he was telling anybody else. Like when we play cards, just for pennies, you know, we had so much fun where he had that furnished room. And that lady who made the bills for him, Marie Helfert and the Henkels, we played cards there. And Mrs. Hile, she was a cook in rich people's house, she would come sometimes. And Isidor would go to the subway station, he was the one who took her to the station. He wouldn't let Karl Henkel do it. 'No, no, no, I'll take her,' he always said. See, nobody should know anything, she had no chance to say anything to anybody. And Hans always said that Isidor always had a split in between everybody, don't let them get together and find out. Because he was lying to everybody.'

"You must have felt so terrible when they told you why Richard was arrested," I asked. "It would be such a shock to any woman."

"'Oh, yes,' Mrs. Hauptmann said. 'They didn't tell me anything for a long time and I couldn't see Richard right away. The second day, before I really knew what it was all about, reporters were in my living room and I heard one reporter keep saying, 'He's going to burn for this, he's going to burn for this.' Burn? What were they talking about? I didn't know.

"'I was so dumb,' she continued. 'I trusted everybody, even the police. I believed they would get at the truth, that Richard was innocent and the police only wanted to learn the truth. When Richard was first arrested, Gerta said to me, get a lawyer, and I said, no, no, Richard will be home tomorrow. If I only knew what they were doing to him, how they planned to murder him, I would get a lawyer and I would never move out so they could fake the evidence in the attic. But I was too trusting, and Richard died.'"

Yes, it was true, Mrs. Hauptmann had been too trusting. And so had Richard. But you must understand that they both had a perfectly good reason for that trust. Being innocent, and knowing all too well there was no possible way for the authorities, the honest police officers, to prove any guilt whatsoever, certainly prompted good reason for complete trust. Especially so, when one's trust is placed in the ramifications of a system which should never fail to prove a person's innocence. Both Anna and Richard believed that "a person is innocent until proven guilty", and they were right in this belief. Knowing that Richard was innocent they felt very comfortable as the trial began. However, the Hauptmanns had no idea, especially before the start of the trial, that they were dealing with members of the human race, who had put together a "stacked deck" of persons who, regardless of the facts, were ready to turn Richard's innocence into "uncontested proven guilt" by shuffling "cards from under the table" by whatever means they could devise. And because of this Richard Hauptmann was never presumed to be anything but guilty. From the time of his arrest, throughout his trial, until he went to his death in the electric chair, there was never a fraction of time when he was presumed to be innocent, as the law clearly states he should have been. He was proclaimed guilty (and there had better be no ifs, ands, or buts about it) by most of the authorities who prosecuted him. And this proclamation was "sold" by a corrupt system on to the news media who passed it along to a hungry public who insisted on the facts, no matter how distorted they were, thus allowing them "freedom's right" to shout "kill the kraut".

Understanding this, we cannot fault Hauptmann for constantly telling his wife he soon would be at home with her. Nor can we question Anna's faith for believing him. Because of his innocence, they firmly believed the system would soon set him free. But, as the trial progressed and they heard the assortment of "beastly lies and distortions" that were being thrust their way, their faith began to waver as the butt of a candle which was soon to be snuffed out.

During the years since we first came to know Anna Hauptmann, each member of my family has had many lengthy conversations with her. And, due to this we have been especially blessed to learn personally from her the amazing details of experiences she has encountered. Her disappointments, her sadness, her happiness, as well as some triumphs, could fill the pages of another book. A host of these had to do with her married life with Richard, while many others pertained to the treachery they both suffered at the hands of certain police and prosecuting officials. Her stories, as she relates them, are filled with pathos and remorse. As we would listen to her tell of these times, it was difficult to remain dry eyed as she spoke. We empathized with her emotionally as she recounted the events during her life of extreme tragedy, a life which to this day remains unequalled in suffering by any other woman.

It is difficult to name any one outstanding characteristic that I can apply as exemplifying Mrs. Richard Hauptmann. She was kind, loving, honest and loyal, and reluctant to be critical until she becomes aware of the treachery of an adversary. But what is more, she was gifted with a brilliant memory, especially of facts relating to names, places, dates, and incidents of the Lindbergh case in which her husband became involved and entrapped through the skulduggery of the police and prosecutors. In this she was truly exceptional. And without hesitation, we attribute this to her absolute faith in God who bestowed her with such an unfailing memory as she relentlessly plodded along, usually by herself, during the years that followed in her quest to clear her dear husband's name.

The betrayals she suffered remain primary in her memory. The disappointments she was forced to face when witnesses they had been counting on to verify specific truths in Richard's favor had been coerced to perjure themselves and change their promised valuable testimony with damaging untruths, each helping to place her husband on a whirlwind toboggan slide to the electric chair.

One of Mrs. Hauptmann's greatest disappointments was the reversal of Doctor Condon's original statement in which he said on several occasions that he could not testify against Richard. She clearly remembered the joy her husband exhibited when she visited him at the Flemington jail immediately after Condon had left. "I don't understand how he could do it. He was standing outside Richard's cell talking to him and all at once he became very excited and started to pace up and down the corridor outside waving his arms and shouting 'I can't testify against this man. I can't testify against this man.' Richard was so glad to hear him say this because he knew he wasn't the man. And then while Condon was shouting this, a guard told him to shut up." Mrs. Hauptmann went on to tell us more about Condon's refusal to identify her husband in the Greenwich Village police station in New York. "He knew Richard was not the man he met in the cemeteries, but the police made him say he was when he testified in Flemington. How could he have done this to us? Didn't the man have a conscience? He wanted to look so righteous. My God, how could he do this?"

At the mention of Lindbergh she asked my opinion as to whether I thought he lied when he identified her husband as the man who had called out to Condon from inside the gates of St. Raymond's Cemetery in the Bronx. I assured her that I believed he had, after having been urged by the police to say that it was Richard. I mentioned that originally Lindbergh, as had Condon, told them in District Attorney Sam Foley's office in New York, that he was, at that time, not certain at all that the man who had called out the words "Hey, Doctor," on Saturday, April 2nd, 1932 had been her husband. Mrs. Hauptmann had been aware of this and agreed with me that it was just another reversal brought on by the use of corrupt police persuasion. However, she did admit that she didn't know too much about it, since she could not remember Richard ever saying anything pertaining to it.

Nevertheless, she did relate something she had learned from a member of the Bronx Grand Jury which had to do with Lindbergh's testimony before them. "A man wrote me a letter and told me, 'Mrs. Hauptmann, I am breaking an oath as a grand juror by telling you this, but I can't help it. I have to tell you. When Lindbergh testified before us, he couldn't identify the voice.' That's what the man told me in the letter. But I don't have the letter because a reporter took it away from me. He said he would use it to help me, but that's the last I saw of it. He betrayed me too, like some other reporters did."

Tony Scaduto in one of his interviews with Anna Hauptmann had asked her if she had ever had an occasion to talk to Lindbergh during the trial at Flemington. He tells of an unfortunate happening brought on by her desire to confront the famous flier, she told him she wanted "to look him in the eye" to see how he'd react, whether he'd say anything to her. "Also, I wanted to show him what I was like, that we're not the kind of people to do this, to say to him, 'How could you believe we could do something like this, that Richard could have done this thing?'" At the end of one trial session she hurried out of the courtroom and went down a private stairway that Lindbergh used in order to get in and out of the courtroom and avoid the crowds.

"'I was waiting down there, near the sheriff's office, when Lindbergh came down. He saw me and he turned his face to the side and looked down when he walked past me. Like he was embarrassed and afraid to look at me. I followed him, I walked alongside him, but I never said a word. I just wanted him to look at me.

He wouldn't. And the next day the door was locked and court people told me, 'Don't go there anymore.'

"'They used tactics to try to trick me. Once, they asked me if I'd ever been to Hopewell and I said, 'No, of course not, I don't even know where it is.' They asked me if I'd like to see it. I knew that if I said no they would think I was afraid to go there, I was hiding something. I didn't have anything to hide---I always believed that telling the truth would make everything come out right.

"'We went in a limousine, three or four detectives and me. We drove past the little house---what do you call it? the gate house---and drove up to the big house. I said, 'Yes, it's a big house.' Very calm and plain. 'Have you ever seen this house or been at this house?' they asked. I said no. We got back in the car and drove along the road a few miles and stopped. They asked me to get out of the car and we walked into the woods a little ways. A detective pointed to a spot on the ground and said, 'This is where the baby's body was found.'

"'I said, Oh, so far away? I thought it was near the house.'

"'I knew they took me out there because they hoped I would break down and cry and confess that Richard did it, maybe that I helped him. I knew that's why they wanted me to go out there. I went with them because I didn't want them to even think I was trying to hide anything..'"

One of the times Anna was happiest was when she told of the love Richard had for children. "He loved them all" she told us. "And you know, the children all loved him. Little Viola, the daughter of our neighbors downstairs, the Schusslers, always waited for Richard to come home in his car. When she saw him coming, she would excitedly run out to the car to meet him at the curb, and he would let her, and sometimes a few of the other neighborhood children, get in and he would take them just a short distance to the garage at the back of the house. He loved this and looked forward to it, and when they got out of the car they would romp with him and climb all over him. That was my Richard, he loved children and was so happy when our Manfred was born. But all this happiness ended when he was taken away from me by the police. It all happened so fast."

And Richard Hauptmann had a deep love for animals, too. Anna often related stories exemplifying the compassion her husband had for an unfortunate dog or cat. She told Tony Scaduto of an incident that happened when she and Richard were returning in their car from a shopping trip. "Viola Schussler, the little girl downstairs, was with us in the back seat with all the bags of groceries next to her. I didn't see anything, but suddenly Richard stopped short. Viola and the bag of groceries fell off the back seat and I could smell that a bottle of ammonia broke. I rushed to get Viola out and after we got everything straightened up I asked Richard why he stopped so suddenly. He said, 'A little dog ran in front of the car, Annie, I couldn't run it over.' That's the kind of man Richard was. A good man who loved children and pets. Could he have done such a thing?"

"'I know my Richard couldn't do such a thing. And I know something else. You see, there were only two things that gave me the strength to continue through all this. One was the knowledge in my heart that Richard was innocent, because he was with me that night and nothing anybody said could change that. He was with me. The other thing that gave me strength was to protect my baby.'"

As a child growing up little Manfred soon became an innocent victim of a "hate filled" society that continued to castigate his guiltless father. Terms used by Wilentz as he referred to Hauptmann in the Flemington courtroom, were mentioned during family conversations in the domesticity of homes, and were "picked up" by children and carried on to schools and playgrounds all over America. The chides that were uttered, and the pointed fingers of accusing classmates, when they were told "that boy over there is the son of the man who murdered a baby," were far greater than mere words can ever express. And little Manfred was stung by these unfair, never to be forgotten, accusations. The children who said these things can easily be excused. They knew no better. But, as for the adults, they also were ignorant, an ignorance which can be blamed on their own lack of enlightenment of the real truths and were more than willing to "swallow" the "garbage" the press put out.

"'Yes, yes, more than anything I blame the reporters for permitting Wilentz and the police to murder Richard', Anna told Tony Scaduto. 'Many of them knew what Wilentz was doing to Richard, with the fake evidence and the lies of the witnesses. I remember one of them so well, Pat McGrady, I think he worked for the *Associated Press*. He was one of them who believed

Richard was being murdered by the police. I asked him why the newspapers wouldn't do anything to help us and he said, 'Mrs. Hauptmann, the newspapers are afraid to print the truth. They said so many things about your husband that if they printed the truth now and Richard went free, he could sue every one of them for libel. So they won't ever print the truth.'

"'They were also afraid of Wilentz,' she went on. 'Nobody would publish Richard's story when he was alive. He wrote his own story after the trial, in German. I later dictated it to Mrs. Bading because she knew German, and she put it into English. The papers were going to print it, but Wilentz told them not to. They didn't print it until after Richard was dead, in the *Mirror*.'

"'When the police asked me if Richard was with me that night the Lindbergh baby was kidnapped, I said I didn't know because I didn't remember it was a Tuesday night. Then when they told me it was a Tuesday, I said he **usually** was with me on Tuesday nights. I thought 'usually' meant 'always' because my English wasn't too good back then; I meant he was **always** there on Tuesday nights because he **was**.

"'But when I tried to explain it in court, that Wilentz made me say that I told the police 'usually' and he wouldn't let me explain, the judge wouldn't let me explain. They wouldn't let me explain why I said I didn't know if he was with me that night because I didn't remember it was a Tuesday, they wouldn't let me explain anything. That wasn't right. Why is the law like that? You can only say yes or no, you can't explain. They murdered Richard in the electric chair because we couldn't explain.'

"I can understand the law doing that," Tony broke in, "because the law is made for lawyers and not for people. But what I can't understand is why the reporters ignored all the contradictions. The whole question of whether Richard was working on the day of the kidnapping---Wilentz and Foley said in the Bronx that he was working a half day, something like that, and then in Flemington, Wilentz proved he didn't start working until much later in March and he claimed the employment records didn't exist for the first week in March. I can't understand why the reporters didn't jump on that---it was obviously a lie."

"'Because all they cared for was sensationalism,' Mrs. Hauptmann said. 'That's what Jack Clements told me, the *Hearst* reporter who made me sign a contract so we could get a lawyer without charge. I remember one time I visited Richard, I think it was in Flemington just before the trial started. And Clements wrote in his story that I was crying when I came out. I never cried. I wanted to, many times, but I wouldn't show that to the reporters because Richard would read about it and it would upset him.

"'I read the story the next day and I got very angry with Clements. 'This is a lie,' I told him. 'I didn't cry' and Clements said, 'What difference does it make? The public wants sensationalism and it won't hurt you to give them a little sensationalism.'

"'I knew Clements and the *Hearst* people were taking advantage of me. But what could I do? We had no money. The police took everything. We had two mortgages, and they took them, they took our bank book, my citizenship papers, they even took a silver spoon from the baby that was a christening present from my sister. So when Jack Clements came to me and said the *Hearst* papers would pay my expense in Flemington, my room in a private house and give me a few dollars to live on, and pay the best lawyer around---this Mr. Reilly---I accepted because ... well, what was I to do? I had no place to turn.'

"During the trial, Anna Hauptmann said, a woman reporter from a Boston paper slipped past the *Hearst* men guarding the rooming house she was living in and knocked on her door. Anna opened it.

"'She was very nervous, very frightened. She said she had just sneaked up the stairs and she wanted to talk to me. I told her to come in. She said she wanted to write a story about my life with Richard, what Richard was really like, a story in Richard's favor that no paper ever wrote before. I gave the interview because it would help Richard's case, I thought.

"'Jack Clements was furious with me when he read the story the next day. He waved the paper at me and he said, 'Did you say these things?' I told him I did. He said, 'You can't do that, you can't talk to other newspapers. You have a contract with *Hearst*.' I told him, 'Why didn't you ever print this story? I told you all of this, but you never wrote a story like this.' He couldn't answer. All they cared about was the sensationalism, selling newspapers. They didn't care about the truth. Richard was killed because nobody cared about the truth. The newspapers were getting rich, Wilentz was getting famous, Lindbergh was getting ... I don't know what he was getting, but he also didn't care about the truth.'"

Again I would like to express my sincere thanks to Anthony Scaduto for the realm of information he has allowed me to use from the pages of his book *Scapegoat*. His work as an investigative reporter in "rooting out" the truthful accuracies, and at the same time, revealing the horrible inaccuracies of the Lindbergh case that for too many years had been allowed to remain stagnant, has been super. At every opportunity I am extended the privilege to speak on the innocence of Richard Hauptmann, I never fail to mention Tony's great book. Although *Scapegoat* is now to be found only in libraries and used book stores, I heartily recommend that you search for it. It is excellent reading.

During the many pleasant hours my wife Anna Mae and I, as well as other members of my family, had spent with Mrs. Hauptmann, the topic of conversation usually turned, at some time or other, to the mutual faith we all had in God and His direction for our lives. On occasion she would remind me of what I had said at our first meeting, as she stood on the other side of her screen door in answer to my knock. "You said you believed God sent you to help me. That is the only reason I agreed to let you in. I had a strong feeling I should talk to you because you said God sent you to see me." Essentially that is what I had told her. However, I must assure you that my greeting was not a ploy I used to gain her confidence. I had not rehearsed, or for that matter given any forethought, what I might say to her. My mention of God had been used very naturally. Nevertheless, I am certain my first words to her were chosen at God's direction.

Anna Hauptmann told us many times of Richard's personal faith. "He loved God." she said. "Up until the time of his execution he spoke boldly of his faith and tried to tell some of the other prisoners who were also awaiting their execution that they should trust in Christ. But, you know, there was a time when his faith was almost broken as a result of the treatment he received in prison. He told me about this in a letter he wrote to me the day before he died. But he never finished it and it was not signed and never mailed. He was in such agony, even his handwriting was not in his usual style. I didn't know anything about the letter until I found it among his things when I went to the prison to collect them after Richard died. It was very depressing, they almost caused him to turn his back on God. "Anny,", he had written, 'I almost lost my faith in

God. You can never know how terrible the last twenty-four hours have been.' "I can understand why he wrote this, Wayne. "You see they moved him out of his cell he had been in for months, they had shaved his head, took all the pictures of me and the baby away from him. They did everything to him, even making him sleep on the cold cement floor. My dear God, how could they do this?"

Although it is difficult to comprehend why such treatment had been measured out to their prisoner during the final hours of his life, it is possible to conceive that those who did this were merely following the orders being issued by someone "higher up". The "big boys" as Trooper John Opdyke called them in that Flemington Courtroom in 1940. Persons who were hoping that by using this treatment they would bring about, at the 11th hour, a possible confession from the lips of a man who knew absolutely nothing about the crime, and who, to the very moment of his death, could not possibly have understood all that had happened to him.

To the very day of her death, Anna Hauptmann along with her son Manfred have lived under an unfair stigma of guilt thrust on them, with malice aforethought, by an orchestration of authorities within the states of New Jersey and New York in order that they be able to, not only falsely accuse, but fraudulently convict and maliciously kill an innocent husband and father --- Richard Hauptmann.

During these many years Anna Hauptmann had suffered many disappointments. She had agonized in prayer for the vindication of her husband, and at times there seemed to be a ray of hope. Along came Anthony Scaduto and his revealing work. Next appeared Ludovic Kennedy and his helpful discourse on the case. But, she always looked for the sun to rise above the horizon.

One of the most heart wrenching experiences Anna Hauptmann was forced to endure was that of Richard's absolute refusal to allow her to bring their little son Manfred to see him during his imprisonment. "At the time of Richard's arrest Manfred was less than a year old and I took the baby to see him before he was moved to Flemington, while he was still in the Bronx prison. But that was the last time Richard saw Manfred because he didn't want me to bring the baby to see him behind bars. He told me, Anny, I don't belong here," he said to me. "My baby will never come here, my baby will never see me in jail. I am innocent and I will be coming home to you and Manfred, and I don't ever want him to see me behind these bars. I honored his wish, and during that period of over eighteen months he never saw his baby again."

"This all took so much out of me, seeing what that Wilentz did to him, taking from Richard his baby, making it impossible for Richard to see his baby for a year and a half, until they murdered Richard. That's what they did to us."

Mrs. Hauptmann clearly stated that if she had been alone at the time of Richard's execution, she would have fought desperately to prove his innocence. But she had her little Manfred to care for, to protect, to see that he was raised as normally as possible in a world cluttered with citizens who had despised her husband, and had little room for her.

And so, Anna Hauptmann purposely disappeared from the eyes of the public. With the exception of her dear friend Toni Rafferty in Yeadon and a small minority, those few who found her, came to know her, respect her, love her, and protect her identity, she virtually, along with her small son, became lost to the host of busybodies and curiosity seekers of that day.

Manfred Hauptmann, having grown to manhood, a handsome man who strongly resembles his father, would on occasion learn of his mother's disappointment over another failure in her latest effort to prove his father's innocence. At such times as these he would lovingly admonish her with words such as these, "Mother, you must forget it. We are poor people. We cannot fight it. What can we do? Who will listen to us?"

This advice was given by a son who loved his mother dearly. A son who knows, together with his wife Erica of their dad's innocence, both of whom lived near their mother, seeing to it that her every need was met. A son, who more than we can ever dare to realize, understood the suffering his mother was forced to bear by those who murdered justice.

However, as we come to understand that Manfred's wisdom was the very best he could give to help his aging mother --- the wisdom of God is always far greater. His plan from the very beginning was to answer the prayer of a bereaved wife and mother who asked Him to clear her husbands's tainted name back on April 3rd, 1936.

The 1980s had arrived. It was His appointed time. Success at last. The exciting conclusion is unearthed. The facts of the Lindbergh kidnapping case must now be re-written. The truth is at hand!

CHAPTER SEVENTY

Unexpected Evidence!

I considered locating Anna Hauptmann to have been a major accomplishment. For many years she had been lost to me somewhere in our great sea of humanity, and because of this, I had no idea where she was living. However, now that I had found her and heard her personally tell of the atrocious things that were done to her husband, and of her absolute faith in him because she knew they had been together on the night of March 1st, 1932, I must admit that I believed I had reached the end of my trail, thus convincing myself that there could only be a slight possibility remaining for me to personally develop anything more that would help me prove my cause that --- I knew for a certainty that Bruno Richard Hauptmann was innocent.

As I basked in my achievement, I continued to accept new speaking engagements, now augmented with some experiences Anna Hauptmann had personally related to me. More and more I found the customary "Hauptmann condemnations" to have almost vanished; the "anti-Bruno" accusations had practically made a complete reversal, to be replaced and voiced by ones coming from a very positive "pro-Richard" attitude. I attribute this turn-about largely as coming from those who read, and passed on to others, the new evidence revealed in the book *Scapegoat*. By this time the public, due to Anthony Scaduto's relentless investigative reporting, had finally learned of the many major portions of heretofore unknown and distorted truths. And the clamor was still being heard for more. Within me, I could only hope that it would be possible for me to tell them -- "the more".

Although Tony Scaduto encouraged me to do so, neither of us in our wildest dreams could have guessed that with the passing of the government's Freedom of Information Act, plus some amazing new and astounding developments, lay the unequivocal truth which would make it impossible for anyone to ever seriously question, dispute, or deny Richard Hauptmann's complete innocence of the crime which was unfairly laid at his feet.

Harold G. Hoffman, Governor of New Jersey, who insisted on the continuing investigation that could probably prove Hauptmann's innocence. (UPI/Corbis-Bettmann)

Ellis H. Parker—Burlington County, New Jersey, detective known as "the old fox of Mount Holly," with his son Ellis, Jr. (UPI/Corbis-Bettmann)

Paul H. Wendel—disbarred New Jersey lawyer who confessed to committing the crime. (AP/Wide World Photos)

Harry P. Young—friend of the author who told author facts about the case that, at first, seemed unbelievable. (Author's collection)

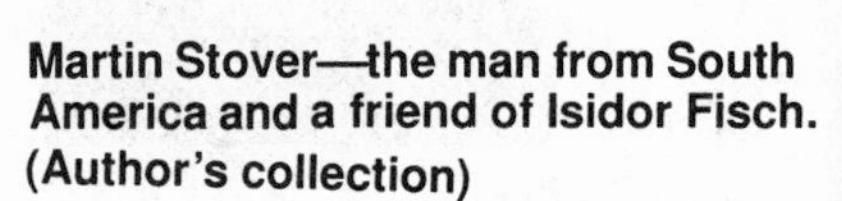

Martin Stover—the man from South America and a friend of Isidor Fisch. (Author's collection)

George B. Campbell—Chester County, Pennsylvania, detective who vouched for the truth of Harry Young's story. (Author's collection)

Anthony Scaduto—whose brilliant and investigative reporting uncovered evidence of a frame-up used against Hauptmann. (Author's collection)

Author standing at the door of the Frank C. Andrews Lumber Yard in Phoenixville, Pennsylvania, where some of the wood used for the kidnap ladder was traced. (Photo by David Barberri—Author's collection)

Author with the original kidnap ladder—taken at the West Trenton, New Jersey, State Police Barracks. (Author's collection)

SOURCE OF RUMOR TRACED.

$5,000 Was Offered to Colombian Woman to Care for a Baby.

CALI, Colombia, March 29 (AP).—Major Samper, District Chief of the National Police, revealed today the source of a rumor last week that led authorities to suspect that the kidnapped Lindbergh baby might be near the Colombian city of Buenaventura.

He discovered that an unidentified baby had been offered to a woman at Buga, midway between Buenaventura and Cali, for keeping on March 17.

Buga is an old Colonial city of 30,000 inhabitants. Two strangers, one a Colombian, the other a foreigner, arrived at the home of Señora Soledad Fernandez de Panesa, a respectable middle-aged woman of moderate circumstances, and offered her $5,000 to care for a boy about 19 months old.

Señora Fernandez said she would have to ask her husband and the strangers left. The señora told her friends and gossip spread ten days before it reached the authorities.

Front page article which appeared in the *New York Times* edition dated March 30, 1932.

Anna Hauptmann in the home of the author and his wife—taken March 25, 1991 during her last visit to Phoenixville, Pennsylvania. (Author's collection)

Mrs. Thelma Miller—who graciously contributed her pictures of the Flemington trial. (Author's collection)

Dick Cass, "film producer," who firmly believed in Hauptmann's innocence and was a great help to the author. (Author's collection)

Author's daughter, Barbara Vickus, reading a copy of Harry Young's account of Martin Stover's visit to Phoenixville in 1932. (Author's collection)

As the dates on our calendars told us we had entered the 1980s, events took an upward turn for those of us who were certain of Hauptmann's innocence. More and more people were by now signifying their partial belief, nevertheless, were saying that our "proof" was not enough. They wanted undeniable proof, not just a "theory", as they termed my story. I fully realized what they were demanding of me was that I prove it without any question. However, my common sense told me what I first needed was a big break. Something "with teeth in it", something of importance had to happen, and that something must be undeniable. Unbeknown to me that big break was soon to come.

With the passing of the Freedom of Information Act in 1978, it now became lawful for persons to be granted entrance to federal offices and institutions and permit them to search the association's confidential files. Files that held valuable and important documents, letters, papers, and pictures, had now been literally "thrown open" for the perusal of the general public. Historical chronology which had heretofore been safely retained under lock and key was now available to anyone who held interest enough to go and search through the many musty and yellowed records the files contained. Because of the enactment of the Freedom of Information law, the files of the Lindbergh kidnapping case, at both state and national levels, became a bonanza of renewed interest to people from all walks of life who wanted to gain more information about the famous crime. This was seen to be particularly true of the many amateur sleuths (among these I include myself) as well as a few authorized investigators who journeyed to search the files not only in New Jersey, but in New York City and Washington D.C. as well.

As mentioned earlier, I was hoping, but not actually looking, for the big break I needed. And when it finally came, I must admit it was so unanticipated, it jarred me with the magnitude of an unexpected electrical shock. It came as a bolt out of the blue, because the facts I was about to learn were much more than I could have ever hoped for.

The date was Thursday, June 12, 1980, and I had a speaking engagement scheduled for twelve noon at the Union League in Philadelphia. Since we had arrived in Philadelphia with about an hour to kill, Ray Trego, my chauffeur that day, came with me on a short walk to the open air art show in nearby Rittenhouse Square. Here we had the pleasure of meeting my friend, Sandra

Giangiulio, whose remarkable watercolor creations are recognized and enjoyed internationally. After admiring her work, and spending a short time renewing our friendship, we returned to the Union League where I was scheduled to present my talk. Never could I have guessed that this day was destined to become such a memorable one. Especially so, because it gave me the most outstanding phenomenal experience I ever encountered in my quest for facts to prove Richard Hauptmann's innocence.

Aside from my realization that I was speaking to a group of professional men in the original club house, the esteemed bastion of Republicanism at Broad and Sansom Streets, that had been founded 124 years earlier during the lifetime of Abraham Lincoln, my talk was the same as those I had given many times before. The shocker came at the close when I asked, as I always did, if anyone in the audience had any questions. To my great surprise a man arose and stated: "Fellows, I want you to know that what Mr. Jones has told us here today is the truth, especially the part about South America. You see, I knew Martin Stover and Isidor Fisch when I was stationed there in Colombia as a member of the United States Army Air Corps Intelligence Service."

Truthfully, I had a hard time believing what I had just heard. Had I at last found a man who was living in South America in 1932 and would now back up my story that Martin Stover had taken the child into South America? Of course I had, my ears had not deceived me. After promptly informing the gentleman that I must talk with him, the meeting ended and the room finally was cleared of the other members.

The man's name was William H. Wright, a resident of Philadelphia. I found Mr. Wright to be a pleasant, engaging man in his seventies, who was more than willing to answer all my questions. He did not hesitate with any of his responses. His alert mind was trigger-like as he furnished me with names and places I needed. The information he gave me was overwhelming.

Realizing that I must arrange a time and place where I could sit and talk at length with Mr. Wright, he suggested that I come to his home and record the evidence he would pass on to me. This I agreed to do, and on Wednesday, July 9th, Ray Trego and I again journeyed to Philadelphia, this time to meet in the home of Mr. Wright.

Because the facts I have learned from my various interviews with Bill Wright, including those from personal contacts, telephone exchanges, television, and radio programs on which we have both appeared, all play such a significant part in helping me prove Richard Hauptmann's innocence, I have assembled them together in one statement. This statement was authorized as being "factual and true in every sense of the word" for my use by Mr. Wright on Wednesday, December 5, 1984.

In fairness to Richard Hauptmann, I trust that as you read this statement, you will bear in mind that the only explanation Richard had for his possession of ransom money was that he had received it from Isidor Fisch with no knowledge whatsoever that the wrapped box contained money. Although the police laughed at Hauptmann's "alibi", calling it his famous "Fish Story", I am certain that after you have read Mr. Wright's statement, you will agree that Isidor Fisch was not "the innocent dead man" the police made him out to be.

The following is William Wrights's astounding official statement:

"I, William H. Wright of Philadelphia, Pennsylvania, do hereby swear that the following statement is true and correct in every detail:

"During the years of the 1930s and 1940s I was stationed in Colombia, South America as a member of the United States Army Air Corps Intelligence Service. While there I became acquainted with many people. Among them was a rather small, slightly built man, named Isidor Fisch. Mr. Fisch was well known in Colombia as a handler of illicit skins and furs. He would sell them to dealers down in Argentina, who in turn, would ship them up to Bogota, Colombia, from where they would be sent north into the United States and Europe. Fisch had connections with the indians who lived in the southern part of Colombia, and he seemed to have access, knowledge and contacts with those involved in the transfers or movements of furs from Popayan down the entire west coast. He spent much of his time in and out of the United States, making frequent trips to Germany. During the time he spent in South America he was always known as a man who carried lots of money.

"Many Germans lived in Colombia during those years and certain numbers of them were associated with Fisch and two of his closest friends, Martin Stover and a man by the name of Weismann, a powerful Nazi who had great wealth and seemed capable of financing almost anything, including many of those in which Isidor Fisch was involved.

"It was shortly after the kidnapping of Colonel Lindbergh's baby in 1932 that word spread throughout the areas in and around Popayan and Cali that a baby believed to be the kidnapped child had been brought there. The newspapers got hold of the story and played it up to such an extent that, according to its prominence, you would have thought the actual kidnapping had occurred down there.

"During this period of time rumors persisted about the child and it was soon learned by the local authorities there that a Missionary priest had brought in a private investigator from up in the states to ferret out the truth of this story. The detective journeyed to Colombia where he met his friend, the priest, and the two men quickly began a concentrated effort to inform the authorities in New Jersey of the validity of the rumor since they, the two investigators now firmly believed that Lindbergh's baby had been brought down there. But it all went to no avail. The authorities up north turned a deaf ear to their pleas.

"I know for a fact that the United States Embassys in Colombia and Peru never bothered to investigate. We learned from authoritative sources that they were, as they stated, "called off from above." As a matter of fact they continued to refuse the help of other investigators who, as late as 1934-1936, attempted to follow up the story of the appearance of the Lindbergh baby in South America. Absolutely no pressure was applied by the American Embassy. In spite of the many newspapers carrying their headlines and stories about Isidor Fisch, the embassy consuls clamped up tight, refusing to make any comment. The Embassy absolutely made no move to investigate. The same thing occurred in Ecuador. This simply amazed us since our own investigation of the story proved to us that there was much credence to it.

"At any rate, a shocking surprise came when both the priest and detective were killed. It was an overwhelming belief among us that they had been assassinated because their deaths would put an end to their investigation of the mysterious baby. The two men had been intent on solving the South American mystery of having the child identified by the northern authorities and making an arrest of the actual kidnappers, Fisch, Stover, and the unidentified woman. You must understand that by this time the investigation had proven beyond a shadow of a doubt, at least to the priest and investigator, that it was definitely the Lindbergh baby who had been brought from the states into Popayan.

"The priest was stabbed and shot while he was walking on the street in front of the Hotel el Pazo in Popayan. He died on the floor of the dining room where he had been dragged indoors. For years his blood was not washed away and many persons claim traces of it can still be viewed there today. Although I believe the private investigator was also killed there, I must admit I am not too certain of that, since it may have been that he was slain in either Ecuador or Peru. But, regardless of where he was killed, we know he was definitely on his way to meet the priest in Popayan since he had some valuable information to turn over to the priest, information that was vital to the success of their investigation.

"I think it is worth mentioning that the name of the Hotel el Pazo was later changed to the Lindbergh Hotel, not as an honor to Lindbergh the famous aviator, but because of the death of the Colombian priest who had been slain there because of his certainty that the Lindbergh baby was in Popayan. The hotel management explained the reason for their decision to change the name was prompted by an effort to attract the interest of the many tourists passing through the area.

"One of the informants from whom we learned many facts was a man by the name of Ernie Benkert, another Nazi, who had the habit of drinking too much, and when under the influence of alcohol, would tell those of us in the intelligence service much of what he knew of the activities that were taking place in Colombia. He told me that whenever Fisch would show up with so much money he would inquire of him where he had obtained it all. He claimed Fisch blatantly declared he had received it from friends of his in high places up in the United States. He told us one thing further that proved to be self-incriminating, that being that Fisch claimed some of the money was given him to take care of a very famous baby that had to be kept out of the United States. This claim of his ran rampant and, of course, left little doubt with almost everyone that the baby he referred to was the child of Colonel Lindbergh.

"A friend of mine, a Colombian, a man I imagine is dead today, also knew Ernie Benkert quite well, and he insisted that he knew for a fact that the information the private detective had obtained would have convinced the authorities beyond any doubt that the Lindbergh baby had been brought to South America. He said he also knew it was for this reason the two men were murdered.

"Peter Von Bauer, an Austrian German, was a pilot for the Scadta Airplane Lines in those days. The line was German oriented and was located in Colombia. It was regarded as the first commercial airline in the New World. Its headquarters was in Medellin, with its jump-off place at Popayan to points along the west coast of South America, below the Republic of Colombia, into Ecuador and Chile.

"Quite naturally, we of the intelligence service, were very anxious to investigate the authenticity of these rumors that were being so widely circulated as factual. We certainly did this, and this is what we discovered.

"It was true that a baby had been brought into South America by the man we knew to be Martin Stover. I believe he was a German, but of that I am not certain. He had been accompanied by a woman who was either a Latin American or mixed indian. In early March of 1932 they had been flown in from Panama, landing at Medellin where they made a short stop-over. They then continued their flight on to Cali where they made contact with Isidor Fisch who had arrived earlier and was waiting for them. Stover and the woman then took the child by train to Popayan where they stayed at the Hotel el Pazo. It was here they were joined by Weismann.

"Some time later Fisch met them at the el Pazo, once again loaded with money and bragging that it came into his possession from friends of his in high places in the United States. It was not only known, but was a well established fact, that these persons were all at the hotel when the assassinations took place.

"Peter Von Bauer, a Scadta pilot, who lived at the Hotel Europa in Medellin, spoke quite openly as he bragged to us that it had been he who flew Martin Stover, the baby, a woman, and Weismann into Cali where a man he knew to be Isidor Fisch met them. Somehow he seemed to know that the money Fisch received on a regular basis was picked up by him in one of the older banks in Bogota. Quite often he would talk about Fisch and his unscrupulous business tactics. All of the men in our group agreed that Isidor Fisch was certainly a man of mystery.

"In early 1941, when the Scadta airplane lines were closed down prior to the war, we searched through the records of the defunct airline, and there, sure enough, just as Von Bauer had claimed, were the names of Stover and a child on the passenger list. We never did learn the woman's name and could not identify her from among the other passengers. If Weismann made the trip with them, as Von Bauer claimed, there was no record of his name on the list. Further airline records were non-existent since only small planes made the trip south of Cali. However, it should be noted that their journey into Popayan was made by train over a rather good railway system. Incidentally, the Scadta airline was taken over by Pan-American Air Lines until it finally became known as Avianca.

"As early as 1931 Martin Stover had been bringing furs into Colombia. He was a fur buyer. As far as I know, Stover did not smuggle furs into the country, but on the other hand, he made a practice of not paying full duty on them. He supplied live furry animals and exported them from Putumayo in southern Colombia after bringing them to the trading post and furriers located along the Putumayo River. Quite often I would see him with Fisch after he had brought his animals up to the post after an exciting trip through the Andes Mountains. He had any number of contacts and was usually loaded with furs. He spoke with an Argentinean accent and was very well known by the fur dealers in South America, especially in those places where he and Fisch holed in quite often, usually in Santiago, Chile, the La Paz in Bolivia, a place run by an Argentinean Jew, and the Cali Real in Bogota. It was here that I had many conversations with Fisch.

"Stover, who was known as a German National, was a traveler, not staying in one place for any great length of time. He resided at the Hotel Botami when he was in Bogota. He spent a great deal of time at the Hotel Europa in Medellin, and when he went to Lima, Peru he lived in the Hotel Royale. His permanent home, if you can call it such, was at Chuchumanga in Ecuador. It was a ranch-like place that served as a meeting place for Germans whom we believed were deeply politically involved in Argentina. From his residence it was quite easy to get to Quito, Ecuador and not at all difficult to get out of Quito into the many key points where clandestine meetings were held by them on many occasions. Chuchumanga was in an isolated section of the country where at one time much agricultural work was conducted, chiefly by the German people, with the help of Austrians, Hungarians, and Czechoslovakians. I am not at all certain if Martin Stover ever held a full residence visa. He probably had been issued a semi-permanent one due to his owning property.

"The fact nevertheless remains that the chief topic of conversation during these days was the kidnapping. No one had to be convinced in and around Cali and Popayan that the mysterious baby was not the Lindbergh baby. Everyone was certain that he was the stolen baby and that Martin Stover had brought him down from the states. Talk among the guests in the Hotel Alfredez Royale ran rampant on the subject, but despite this, the local authorities could do nothing about it because of the lack of cooperation up north. It did seem strange, however, that following the assassinations of the priest and private investigator, and the news of their deaths spread into Ecuador, Peru, Bolivia, and Chile, the anxiety of the German community relaxed considerably.

"Ernie Benkert was involved with several German groups in Colombia that were located along the west coast of South America. He was an engineer by profession and was also known to be quite wealthy. He was in Colombia at the time of the kidnapping and was a close friend of both Fisch and Weismann. Another friend of theirs was Ernest DuPerlee, a close associate of Benkert. Peter Von Bauer, a financier who backed the Scadta Airplane Lines, had finances that were known to come strictly from an industrial movement in Germany. Another friend of mine, Hector Vargas, an elderly Colombian, was a chauffeur for the owners of the Scadta Airlines, and was also well aware of these sinister activities which centered on the Lindbergh kidnapping of 1932.

"The woman involved with the removal of the baby can best be described as being rather short and strictly Colombian. She served as a nursemaid for the child. Both Stover and Fisch were men of small stature. Incidentally, I was well acquainted with a family living in Buga, Colombia, during those years, and some time during the middle of March, 1932, one of its members, Senora Soledad Fernandez dePenesa, was approached by two strangers who asked her to take care of a small child for which she in turn would receive a payment in pesos, not in United States currency. I learned that she did take care of the youngster for a short time and that it was later taken to Popayan and points south. Buga is a small city of about 30,000 people located inland from Buenaventura almost midway between Pereira and Cali. I am not absolutely certain that it was here that the baby saw a picture of Lindbergh and called him "daddy" or not, but I do know the incident took place somewhere in

Colombia and that it was because of this that the story spread like wild-fire throughout the area and caused the investigation to spring into action.

"Summing everything up concisely, it is a definite fact that Martin Stover and a woman, never identified, brought a baby down to South America from the United States. Isidor Fisch and Martin Stover were closely connected and involved in many unscrupulous deeds. When the child was brought to Popayan and believed to be Lindbergh's baby, and consequent attempts were made to reach the authorities in New Jersey with the news, nothing developed because the police authorities there appeared as though they were not at all interested in ferreting out the truth of the South American report. They apparently wrote it off as being nothing more than a wild rumor or that someone's imagination had run wild.

"As for a possible question as to where the baby was finally taken, I can only report that when things in Popayan became too hot for those who were holding the child, Fisch and Stover at once took the baby into Buga from where they travelled by bus or car down into Ecuador. The baby was never seen down there again, however both Fisch and Stover reappeared and continued on with their other activities.

"Regarding my personal feelings about the "so called" solution of the case, I have one major thought about the matter, based largely on my knowledge of the things that tookplace in South America and my ultimate investigation of them. From the time I first learned from the newspapers in their reports of the Hauptmann trial that the defendant claimed he obtained the money they found in his possession from a friend of his named Isidor Fisch, I was more than satisfied that the baby we had seen down in Popayan had definitely been the stolen Lindbergh baby. You see, I had already been convinced of the involvement of Fisch in the crime years before Hauptmann named him as his alibi, one the police laughed at. Knowing Fisch as I did, I was certain he was guilty because I knew him as a man who could, without his conscience bothering him, involve an innocent person in the crime and then go on to lie his way out of his own involvement in it. Fisch was known to all of us as one mean man, if I can call him that, who had the ability to con people into almost anything.

"As for my personal feelings about the guilt of Bruno Richard Hauptmann, I am certain that his explanation about Isidor Fisch should have been followed up with a thorough and intense investigation being conducted on the reported events, proven to be true, down in Colombia, South America. I firmly believe that Hauptmann was innocent, entirely innocent, of any part of this terrible crime that shocked the world."

After reading the above statement and absorbing the facts expounded by Mr. Wright (the involvement of Isidor Fisch, Martin Stover and a baby he had brought to South America) we must then remember the story told to me years earlier by Harry Young, Stinson Markley, and George Campbell: The chinchillas that were delivered to Isidor Fisch by Martin Stover; the purchase of lumber by Stover in Phoenixville from a shipment, the same as that used in the kidnap ladder; and finally, Stover's admission that he was taking a child to South America. We must then remember Richard Hauptmann's truthful response, when he was asked how he had come into possession of the money. He said, very simply and honestly, that he had obtained it, with no knowledge that the box contained money, from his friend and partner Isidor Fisch. Unfortunately the police refused to believe his "alibi" because of their failure that had extended through a humiliating two-and-one-half year time span, to solve the case. With the arrest of Hauptmann, they realized they "had in their clutches a suitable scapegoat" who would conveniently help them "solve the case," and so they pinned it on him.

However, the statement of William Wright certainly puts a volume of credibility to Hauptmann's story; not to any alibi he might have concocted, but to the solid veracity of his very logical explanation. Bruno Richard Hauptmann had told them the truth.

After I had properly put together all the information Bill Wright had related to me about the activities in South America, I began using a good portion of it when I spoke publicly on the case. During most of these talks I noticed the increased attention I was receiving as I addressed the audiences. In many cases one could have heard a pin drop; they sat as though transfixed with none leaving the room. Another noticeable sign was the increased number of listeners who would generally meet me at the meeting's end with their personal questions. It thrilled me to hear so many agree that they also believed that Hauptmann was innocent. Because of this escalated and intensified interest with so many persons telling me "the whole world should know this", I decided to do something about it. Without any hesitation I contacted, *The*

Philadelphia Inquirer informing them that I had some new developments relative to the Lindbergh kidnapping. They informed me a reporter would be up to see me.

Whoever took my phone call evidently perceived some urgency in my message and passed it along to one of the paper's suburban reporters who appeared at my door within a day or two. His name was Steffin Salisbury, a very friendly, nice looking young man. After showing rapt and undivided attention as he listened to the basics of my story as my wife and I related it to him, he exclaimed, "My God, you have an earth shaking story!", and without any hesitation, I quickly responded, "I know I have. That's what I've been trying to tell everyone all these years."

He whole-heartedly agreed with me that it <u>must</u> be told. After three-and-one-half hours had passed, Steffin put in order the many notes he had made and announced that it was time for him to leave. His enthusiasm had reached a new high as he promised that he would get back to me very soon.

Within a very short time I received his phone call informing me that he wanted to see me that day. A few hours later Steffin was in our home, again this time expounding to us the news that since his first visit with us he had traveled to Washington D.C., where he spent hours searching the files in the Smithsonian Institution. As he related to us the result of his discoveries there, he could not camouflage the merging of his combined excitement and enthusiasm. Steffin Salisbury was overjoyed with his findings. "Why everything you said is true. I found the telegrams that were sent from South America to the authorities up in the United States. Why didn't they act on this information?"

Steffin, with renewed fervor, said he was now equipped with all the information he needed to write the story that had caused him to exclaim when he first heard it: "Why you have an earth shaking story!" After spending another three hours with us that day, and with one of my copies of Tony Scaduto's *Scapegoat* in his hand, Steffin made a hurried departure, promising that he was going to start working on this terrific news story immediately and that soon the whole world would know about it after reading it in his newspaper, *The Philadelphia Inquirer*.

However, as time moved on, and after waiting a reasonable number of days and not having received any word from Steffin on the progress he was making, I phoned him and he explained that, apparently "his boss or bosses" had decided to hold the story and publish it after Labor Day when additional readers would by this date have returned from their vacations. I explained to Steffin that Mrs. Hauptmann was getting along in years and that we were anxious for the citizens of the world to know about her husband's innocence. It was during this conversation with him that he emphatically told me that he had finished reading *Scapegoat* and was thoroughly convinced of Richard Hauptmann's innocence, and that he had no doubt about it. I was encouraged to have him tell me this, however, I was extremely disappointed that Steffin's story was being delayed. He told me it was best that we wait --- and I believed him. After all, there was nothing I could do about it.

Time continued on and I put through another call to Steffin. Labor Day had come and gone. This time the date "they" had decided to use the story was "sometime after the election was over", since prior to the election everybody would be reading the political news, and my "earth shaking story" must wait. More days passed and more excuses were handed me, with the explanation that the new date of "Thanksgiving Day" was "chosen or selected by them" as the best possible time to inform their readers of the great Lindbergh injustice. You will just have to wait until the proper time, I was told, whenever that would be I thought.

Finally Steffin admitted to me that he could not tell me when the proper time would be. That "they" hadn't decided how to use it. I had already guessed that I was being given the old run-around --- and now I knew it! *The Philadelphia Inquirer* had no intention of publishing my "earth shaking story" that Steffin Salisbury, their own reporter, confirmed was true.

Naturally I was extremely discouraged as I learned of their decision. The greatest discouragement my wife and I experienced was our failure to be of aid to our dear friend Anna Hauptmann, whom we were certain would rejoice when the Salisbury story appeared and clear her Richard's name. And now we had failed her. We suffered emotions of anger at the betrayal of *The Inquirer*, and sincere grief in the disappointment to Anna.

Many of my friends had tried to tell me that the *Inquirer* would refuse to print the facts I had. Nevertheless, my hopes were high. They told me of a giant cover-up that had been put in motion years before in order to protect the guilty persons involved in the frame-up of Hauptmann; who, if the truth were to become known, would be subject to arrest and prosecution --- and, above all, suffer the shame and humiliation of their guilt.

What a mockery, what a travesty, to place the feelings of these people, the guilty, as being of greater importance than the lifetime of disappointment, grief, and despair suffered by Anna Schoeffler Hauptmann and her son Manfred.

It is a horrible disgrace! This murder of justice lowers itself into the very ultimate depths of degradation to clearly and plainly exhibit for all to see --- "MAN'S INHUMANITY TO MAN!"

CHAPTER SEVENTY ONE

A Book Is Found!

With the advent of the 1980s it had become quite evident that progress was being made as we gathered more evidence which pointed to the frame-up of Hauptmann. The close friendship my family developed with Mrs. Hauptmann enabled us to learn personally from her the many undeniable injustices the authorities had thrust against her and her husband. In addition to this, I had the opportunity, thanks to the passage of the Freedom of Information Act, of making some new discoveries from the files in the State Police Barracks at West Trenton, New Jersey.

In 1977 I had been contacted by a man named William Simons who told me he was certain he was the kidnapped son of Charles and Anne Lindbergh. Although I was skeptical, I visited his home in nearby Eagle, Pennsylvania, where he showed me much evidence which certainly would make him a very probable contender for the title which some two dozen other men were attempting to claim. Due to our friendship, Bill and I made several visits together to the State Police Barracks in New Jersey.

In the meantime I was fulfilling requests to speak to groups in Universities and Colleges, as well as to students in high schools. I was amazed at the intense interest shown by teen-age students in various schools, most of them expressing their opinion that Hauptmann was innocent. In 1983, one particular group of students searching for information on the case were those of Sharon High School, Sharon, Massachusetts. Their class, titled Historical Research Seminar, was formed to study controversial cases in the history of the criminal court system. Miss Dana A. Kamya, the corresponding secretary, exhibited her interest by contacting me several times asking my personal opinion regarding several points in the historic case. Miss Kamya and her classmates also received letters from Anthony Scaduto, Harold R. Olson, (another person claiming to be the kidnapped child), and the New Jersey State Police, each expressing their beliefs. The Lindbergh kidnapping has never ceased to hold a special fascination to the youth of our nation.

With the increased newspaper publicity I was acquiring because of the outcry I was making as I proclaimed Hauptmann's innocence, I began receiving invitations to appear as a guest on some of Philadelphia's radio and television talk and variety shows. Bill Simons and I were seen as we appeared live together on the Maury Povitch "People Are Talking" show on two different occasions; one during which Bill Wright telephoned and confirmed his first-hand knowledge of the Fisch-Stover South American connection.

But it was the day following my second guest appearance on Bernie Herman's four hour evening radio talk show that I received a tremendous surprise. As I left the radio studio that evening I was quite pleased with the way the program had gone, especially so since the response of the callers had largely been in agreement with me, stating their belief that Hauptmann had been framed. To my amazement I found that even Bernie Herman could see Hauptmann's innocence shining through, a great accomplishment for me, since at the time of my first visit on his popular show, he had briefed himself on the case by reading George Waller's *Kidnap*, but in so doing, had not been convinced of the man's innocence. But now, after reading Tony Scaduto's *Scapegoat*, he required no more proof. He was sold on Richard's innocence.

My big surprise came the day after this radio interview. During the early evening I received a telephone call from a man who refused to identify himself. His voice, however, had the resonance of a young person. He stated that he had heard me on the Herman show and that he called to inform me that I knew what I was talking about when I said the 'kid' was taken to South America. And then he proceeded to tell me he knew all about it because he owns "a book that tells all about it." "You what?", I almost shouted into the phone. He went on to explain that what he had was not in the form of a published printed book, but rather a hand written notebook, the contents of which included Martin Stover's visit to Phoenixville in 1932. I was perplexed with what I was hearing, but at the same time, could not help but be thrilled at the almost remote possibility that what my caller possessed might be something Harry Young had put together in the '30s relating to the existing facts as he knew them at that time.

The more he talked, attempting to explain the contents and condition of the "book", I was certain he was possibly a relative of my old friend Harry Young. I appealed to him to tell me his name, but he was determined to remain nameless. He wanted to know just how much the "book" would be worth for me to own. I assured him it was worth nothing at all to me until I could look it over, but that since I already knew everything to be known about the South American story, I doubted if it would be worth much. Refusing to give me the phone number where he could be reached, he asked me to put a figure on what I would be willing to pay for it, and after saying he would get back to me within a few days, he hung up.

Of course my mind ran its course of bewilderment. I could not quell the excitement I was experiencing, in fact I didn't want to stifle it. Was it possible that more evidence telling about Lindbergh's child being transported to South America had been unearthed? Just what was this book, I asked myself? As soon as I could collect my thoughts into some sense of normal reasoning, my wife and I discussed the possibilities as to whom it might have been that had called me. Between us we concluded that my caller had possibly been one of Harry Young's relatives, probably a grandson, which seemed to us entirely reasonable. However, we could only speculate on this since my informant had promised to call again within several days, leaving me with nothing to do but wait.

Days passed and I heard nothing. After waiting a reasonable length of time I decided to pursue the matter by visiting Mrs. Young at her home in Spring City. Without telling her the actual purpose of my call, I spent a pleasant time with her during which she again described the great fear she lived under back in 1935 when her husband originally became obsessed with the involvement of Martin Stover in the Lindbergh kidnapping. As I rose to leave I inquired about her two children, how many grandchildren she had, and at the same time learned that her eldest grandson lived in Phoenixville. When I asked for it, she willingly gave me his name. Obtaining this had been the sole purpose of my visit, and now I was ready to play my hunch.

Arriving back in Phoenixville, I perused my telephone directory and lost no time dialing the number I found behind the name I had been given. Soon, a male voice answered and I went right to the point of my call, by inquiring if it were he who had called me two weeks earlier about a book he owned that told about the South American connection with the Lindbergh kidnapping? My question brought his somewhat delayed answer, "How did you find me?" He seemed astounded to hear my voice, and more pointedly, my question. "Don't worry about how I found you", I retorted. After admitting that he was the person, he asked if I had come up with a price that I would be willing to pay for it. I assured him that I definitely had not done so, nor did I intend to, informing him that if he had such a book he should get it back into the hands of its rightful owner since it contained vital facts about the kidnapping. It was evident that my advice had been well taken. He explained that he had "borrowed" the book from his mother "without her knowledge", and then asked me to grant him a few days time, during which he would return it to her "without her knowledge", and then he assured me I would have his absolute "uncontested permission" to approach his mother about "the book." My mystery man's offer sounded like a reasonable one to me, and with success so close, I had nothing to lose by waiting a few more days. Surely, within a short space of time, I would have "the book" in my hands.

When I finally contacted Harry Young's daughter, Leanore, she told me she did have her dad's book, and although she had not seen it in quite some time she promised to search for it and call me as soon as she found it. Leanore's verification of this now put to rest any doubts I had. I now had assurance that Mrs. Young had not destroyed, as she had claimed, all the notes her husband had made relating to his connection with the case. At least something existed and I would soon see it.

But, as it turned out, it was not to be all that simple a task. When I next contacted Leanore, she informed me that she had placed the book in the hands of her attorney, Ronald F. Brien of Spring City, and that if I wanted to see the book I must contact him. When I phoned Mr. Brien I was told that I would have to come to his office. After a convenient arrangement was made, my son David agreed to drive me there, and I must say I experienced increased anticipation each mile of the way, wondering what "the book" contained that I would soon hold in my hands to personally examine. As we waited for the attorney to come out of his private office I sensed a high degree of tension and excitement. Was it possible that at last I would have some physical evidence with which to prove that Harry Young's story, as he told it to me back in 1936, coupled with William Wright's confirmation of it in 1980, was now solidly grounded by a firm foundation. Was I now on the brink of something far greater than what had originally been classed as being merely a theory, or a fantasy, as some folks called it? One, they claimed, that had been developed out of "thin air" by people with distorted minds.

As I pondered these thoughts I suddenly became conscious of things about me. Mr. Brien had come out of his office. My eyes were fixed on the object he was holding --- it was <u>the book</u> I never expected to see. It had at last become a reality. The front cover revealed that it was nothing more than an inexpensive composition book, one that could be purchased by any school child of the 1930s for as little as ten cents. A hasty examination of its 53 pages, all written with ink in long-hand, contained what I had expected, much information verifying Martin Stover's visit in Phoenixville in February, 1932 and his subsequent trip to South America with a child. I also noticed that he mentioned Isidor Fisch. Across the top of the front cover Mr. Young had written this salutation: <u>Dear Children from Daddy</u>:, making it clear that he had written the book for his children, hoping that in the years to come they would read, and believe, his personal hand-written account of the private knowledge he had regarding the Lindbergh kidnapping.

I had hoped to take the book with me and read it slowly and thoroughly in my home, but was told that this was impossible, that the book must remain there under lock and key where it would be safe. Although I assured Mr. Brien that it would be kept "really safe" with me, he refused my request. I did, however, get his permission to come to his office at another time and record the contents as I read it audibly. This was done, and although Harry Young's handwriting was reasonably discernable, my transcribing it as I read through it audibly for the first time proved to be poor and highly unsatisfactory for study purposes.

At some time in the months that followed, during one of my conversations with Leanore, I learned that her father's book was back in her possession. I implored, I practically begged, her to allow me to borrow it which would allow me the opportunity to have copies made. At the same time I was trying to impress upon her the great value the book held, that its contents were a credit to her father and that it was important that the people of the entire world must be told about it. She seemed to understand the point I was attempting to make and promised to contact Mr. Brien and ask him to grant me his permission to do this. I called her a week later and she told me that I could pick up the book at her home in Royersford at any time. Believe me, I lost no time getting there.

The book turned out to be everything I had hoped it would be. In it Harry Young had written a detailed account to his two children, telling them of the events which had taken place in their hometown of Phoenixville, Pennsylvania, prior to the kidnapping of the Lindbergh baby, as well as accounts leading up to the trial and execution of Bruno Richard Hauptmann for the child's murder. The book held many significant facts, more than I had expected to find. I found it rather difficult to interpret some of Mr. Young's handwriting since some of it was poor, probably due to writing it in haste. Much of his story had to do with personal things he wanted to share with his children, however the main thrust of the book held the information I needed. Information that Mrs. Young had told me years earlier she had disposed of, and now, thanks to God, I held in my hands the conclusive evidence I needed to prove that Isidor Fisch was very deeply involved in the kidnapping.

As evidence of this, we have the testimony of Harry Young, William Wright, and Richard Hauptmann. Hauptmann, a man who had never heard of either Young or Wright, claimed he had obtained the money found in his closet from Isidor Fisch. Fisch, a friend of Hauptmann, whom Hauptmann found difficulty believing was involved in the kidnapping. But, in spite of this, we have both Young and Wright telling us he was --- because both of them knew he was. And although the authorities of that day refused to, or didn't want to believe Hauptmann's "fish story" as they called it, does not make it any the less true. Hauptmann was innocent because there were at least two men, plus others, who could have produced the evidence needed to back-up Hauptmann's story --- but they didn't want any evidence of that kind. They wanted to murder their innocent scapegoat in order to close the case forever. But, in this they were unsuccessful. Proof of this is contained in the following excerpts, all the important portions, pertaining to the South American story as taken from a letter, (spelling and punctuation) <u>exactly as it was written</u> in 1935 by Harry Young to his children

Dear Children from Daddy:< This appears on cover.

Harry H. Young and little Leanore Estelle Young this is just a little true story Daddy thought you can read when you grow older about your Uncle Per N. Stover's Brother

Martin Stover
South America

Harry this is a little story about your uncle Martin Stover. Several years ago probably 30 or more years he was a young man then and he had just finished his trade as a carpenter in Sweden and he was very anxious to make good in the world and of course there were greater opportunities here in America and so he decided to come here and make good. So one day he decided he would come, so from Sweden he came down to England, and of course funds being not very plentiful decided he would work his way over on a boat. Well he couldn't speak English and it was hard for him to make himself understood but after a great deal of explaining he was permitted to go on board and work his way to America. So after being on board several days he learned he was headed for South America. Well going across the equator he contracted a fever and when the old boat finally dock [sic] he was sent to quarentine [sic] to get well, well he was very sick and he laid in bed for weeks and weeks he thought he would never get well and eats were very poor and not enough to get well on according to your aunt Hannah Stover's story he was lying on his bed in the hospital one day and a small boy was painting the stone walls and the paint would run and he was not making a very good job of it and two sisters came in and were not so pleased and they criticized his work very much and Harry your uncle Martin took pity on the poor little fellow and he made motion to the boy to bring his can and paint and turpentine over along side of his bed and he mixed the paint for him and then the little boy went back and started to paint again and this time the paint stayed on the walls and he was making out fine when again in came the sisters and of course they were surprised to see such a nice job being done they asked him what he done and of course he pointed to your uncle Martin. Well Harry according to your aunt Hannah's story Martin said they brought him lots of meat and potatoes and it wasn't long before they had him out of bed and then of course they had him do all the little jobs around the place and when they were all done he wanted to go across the bay to the main land. Well he couldn't speak English and by their motions or gestures they wanted him to go back to bed. Well while he was up and around he found out where his clothes were and he got acquainted with someone who volunteered to row him across the bay so one night he made his escape from quarentine [sic] onto the mainland. Well Harry he was handicapped because he couldn't speak neither Spanish which everyone speaks down there or English but according to her story he hadn't very much money only a few dollars but the weather was nice and one day while he was sitting on a bench in one of the parks down there in Argitena [sic] he met a man who seemed to take a little interest in him and they talked lots together and the man finally managed to get work for him digging a sewer ditch well he soon learned a little Spanish and he got along fine. Well Harry your uncle Martin was very thrifty and he saved a little money and bought himself a boat and on Saturday afternoons he would get in his boat with his dog and up the rivers he would go. He soon became acquainted with some Indian traders and so he bought a lot of furs and sometimes took up coffee and sugar and shoes and bullets to the natives and allways [sic] brought down hides and he had quite a collection of Beaver, Irish American lion and bob cat [sic] and other hides and then came the world war so he sold his pelts to the English Government for aviation caps and coats and he made himself some money so one day he headed for home he went to Sweden to see his folks he came here to Phoenixville to see his Brother and family and we all met him and were very proud of him but his work was down there and of course he had to go back well Harry it seems he made money and lost money in the fur business so finally he was going to try a new line of fur business so he and a trusty indian went off into the mountains in search of Chinchilla the fur of which is very valuable well they had to wait about three months and finally got one and in six or eight months he had another which was a pair a pair of live chinchillas is worth about $3,500 in American money so he decided to breed chinchilla and after several years he now has a very large farm and silver foxes and deer and other animals. Well Harry on one occasion in ninteen [sic] thirty two your uncle Martin came up here with four pairs of those chinchillas in especially constructed wire and wooden boxes easy to carry and at the same time the animals could get air and sunshine and then they could get inside if they wanted to out of the weather. Now then Harry it was in early spring the last of February or the first of March when my sister your aunt Hannah Stover called on the phone telling me Martin Stover from South America was here and had some chinchillas with him and asked me to come over to see them so of course I went over right away, and as I had never seen a live chinchilla before they were very interesting and of course Martin had a terrible time getting them into U.S. he said coming across the equator they almost died from the heat he laid on the deck of the freighter boat and poured water on them to keep them alive and then I asked him how he got them into New York he said the custom house officers asked him what he had in the boxes and he said rats and all they charged him was six or eight dollars which I thought was very little well Harry Martin wanted to know what kind of vegitation [sic] we had around here to feed them and so Daddy took him out in the country to a farm where they had a hay mow full of alfaffa [sic] which he said was just right for them of course it was dry and there was no green clover well then Martin wanted to know where he could get some light sand for them they would lay on their backs and shower themselves like good fellows Allen Stover got some sand down at the Iron Co. Steel plant and then they were fixed up pretty good Harry they were beautiful with little ears like a mouse and a tail like a squirrel's which raised up over their little backs Harry uncle your uncle Per Stover's brother was here in Phoenixville for several weeks and while he was here your daddy took him most every where hereabouts and daddy enjoyed hearing him tell all about his animal farm down there in South America he had silver foxes and deer and goats and these chinchillas and he had a trusty old indian take charge of the place and Martin would go here and there selling his furs he also said he had a salesman selling his furs in Europe I guess he does pretty good but it was hard for him until he got established Martin said the reason he was in Phoenixville at this time in nineteen thirty two early spring with these chinchillas was his salesman in Europe wrote him a letter telling him to come to New York and meet him there as a man by the name of Fisch was coming over here from Germany to see them and if he liked them he would buy them well he waited and waited and mr [sic]

Fisch did not come and of course in need of money his expenses were going on all the time so he left word there and they were to drop him a card he came here to Phoenixville with his animals he was afraid fellow Fisch would not come over from Germany so he tried to sell them to someone else Allen Stover his nephew tried to sell them to a very rich game man by the name of Frank B. Foster out here in Charlestown but Mr Foster said he was not interested in animals he wanted birds but Mr Foster was a big game hunter of some importance later Harry your uncle Per Stover's brother Martin was here quite some time around the later part of February and March and then one day I think it was on a Tuesday I just forget the date Daddies [sic] sister Mrs Per Stover called on the telephone and said Martin was going back to South America and if I wanted to see him I better come over of course I went right over and he said a man was here he liked the chinchillas very much and agreed to take them I just forget the full price but they paid I think he said three Thousand dollars down and Allen Stover was to keep the chinchillas until the full amount was paid and when each payment was paid Allen was to airmail Martin every thing but tenpercent which he was to keep for his trouble which I guess he did and when it was paid Joe Fullmer Allen Stover's appliance salesman and Percy Stover Allen's brother delivered the chinchillas to New York to whom I do not know but I do know that the day my sister Mrs. Stover called me oversomething strange happened Harry your daddy said to Martin how are you going back? By way of Phila. or New York and Martin said By way of New York and I said isnt [sic] that longer and he said yes but he guessed the boys down in New York were going to have a party for him he said my they certainly have nice girls down there and he might have to take a kid back home back home with him and Harry your aunt Hannah Stover's eyes got as big as moons she stared him in the eyes and said why you dont have any kid and Martin said no I know but I guess I'll have to take one with me and daddy said well Martin you dont have to take a kid with you if you dont want to do you and he said well Harry you know when you dont have money you got to do lots of things you wouldn't do if you had money he said I dont like the idea it dont look god a big man like me taking a little boy by the hand and especially on a boat taking a long voyage it dont look good and I again said well you're not going to take him away up there in the mountains the mountains two hundred miles away from the nearest house are you and he said no and I again said well what are you going to do with him then and he said deliver him to some one or some society whoever they tell me to Harry I don't know who he means but it sure sounds funny to daddy and daddy also asked him how he spent his time over in New York while he was waiting for Mr Fisch to come from Germany and he told daddy working. knowing he had learned the carpenter trade when he was a young man I asked him if he was working at his trade and he said Oh! No! built a ladder and a pair of steps. Well Harry Daddy doesn't know if he did build a ladder and a pair of steps or not and daddy doesn't know if he did take a little boy to South America or not but it certainly did not look good to daddy and of course it was Just at the same time Mr. Charles Lindberg [sic] lost his boy and hope he isnt mixed up in a case like that was you can never Mr. Fisch and Mr. Hauptman [sic] were in the fur business and he was selling Mr Fisch his chinchillas to go to Germany and Martin said he was going home through Cuba and the Panama canal he said he expected to meet some one of authority on the boat and he wanted to see this party so he could make arraingments [sic] to get his animals out of Argentina over the Andes Mountains through Chili without paying any duty. and he expected to leave this boy in Chili he didnt seem to like the trip through Chili up over the mountains to his farm he said bandits lay up in the Mountains and just shoot you down without any warning and then take your belongings and think nothing of it. Harry it was quite a long time after he went Back to South America before any one heard from him daddy has not heard from him at all as Daddy and Your aunt Hannah Stover have never talked a conversation since and Harry Daddy knowing all these things I was very much troubled and daddy just couldn't understand with the State Police and Ellis Parker one of the countries [sic] best detectives and all the police at hand how they could make any mistakes but I still think they took the wrong road. Well Harry finally came the Hauptman [sic] Trial and It Just seemed to [sic] bad they kept that poor fellow in Jail and worried the life out of him and then came the first reprieve well Harry daddy was so worried before this reprieve cause Daddy was very dumb about courts and lawyers and police depts and governments he didn't know what to do so every night I would pray and one night daddy prayed as hard as he knew how and asked for guidance and well daddy's prayers were sure answered about one thirty in the morning daddy got such an awakening well if any one ever gets an awakening they will never forget it. it sure came from God himself or the power from Heaven and I was I would have to put my confidence in someone of authority and I tried to think who and then it came to me I must go see George Cambell [sic] right away well I thought I would wait till morning. and I did. and when I went to see him this day I was to do as he told me, and I did. He said keep your mouth shut dont tell no one only my closest friends and he said we would make affidavits and we did in Jim Foxalls office West Chester and then we came home and he wrote Governor Harold G. Hoffmans office I have a copy of the original letter and Daddy offered to go down there if they wanted me but We received a letter from Governor Hoffmans office and they told us Governor Hoffman had gone to Florida and had turned the whole thing over to Mr. Ellis Parker his detective and we should get in touch with him but they wanted to know who the author of the affidavit was. he said he was under bond and if they wanted us they had his address on his stationery but they didnt send for us and then he wrote to Ellis Parker and we received a couple of letters from him but he said Hauptman [sic] would not go to the electric chair and of course we thought he should know but we were sorry we didn't go down but he said we would get killed and Harry daddy had you and mother to think of and he said I done my duty couldnt do any more but when the time came to the fatal night and they pulled that switch and killed Bruno Richard Hauptman [sic] it was no good then and daddy feels bad ever since and Harry I guess we must have done the right thing and I believe God was pleased because quite sometime later I know it was after Col Lindberg [sic] came back from England Daddy rec'd another message and this time Daddy was told Col Lindberg,[sic] Mrs. Morrow and Ann have just been informed their son Charles is alive and well and I could see Mrs Morrow and Mr Lindberg [sic] and Ann it just seemed we just stood there and stared at one another and I certainly could not sleep any more that night and Harry then another time daddy was told Mr. Cambell [sic] had given his affidavit away but I do not know who got it so I went out to Detective George Cambells house on Washington Ave to see if he really did give it away and when I asked him if he had it he said I dont know where it is and I never seen it since I dont know if he gave it to Mr. J. Edgar Hoover or where it ever got to and I dont know what became of the letters from Mr Hoffmans office I sometimes think he gave them to Dr. Anthony he always spoke so highly of Him and then again Daddy had a terrible well not so terrible dream one night daddy was dreaming he was going through a field and I never saw so many snakes in my life before and it seems someone was leading me by the arm and I said to this party who it was leading me look at those snakes and they would run right up to me and look me in the eyes and not a one of them even touched me and he said come on they wont hurt me and they didnt and then we went into the next field and then he said you are alright now. now when you get big mebby [sic] you can figure it out I dont know what all these things mean I sure am lost but daddy has lived a guided life. all my life is like miracles. Harry it just seems so strange Daddies Parents were German and then again daddy was lost on the railroad tracks and picked up and fathered by a German and then was guided to stay away from there and then again a young man worked in daddys radio Store helped to build airplane Mr Lindberg [sic] flew to China in and then John's wifes cousin was a student Dr in John Hopkins university and said young Charles Lindberg [sic] was down there for six months and he said the poor boy couldnt talk right and they couldnt do anything for him so they shipped him home to Flemington and it was soon after that when he dissapeared [sic] it just seems my whole life is for this case and yet they never called me. ....

At this point Mr. Young deviated from his account of Martin Stover and references to the Lindbergh kidnapping. Instead he related some personal experiences he encountered during the lean times of his life, alluding to several Phoenixville residents who had helped him when he most needed it during those years. In several places he told his children of the confidence he had in God helping him, stating that "I guess God knows and it Just looks as if God directs every thing daddy does and gets." He further instructed his children by writing: "Harry please go to your church. and be a good boy and God will always take care of you and sister too."

Harry Young's final reference to the Lindbergh

case was made in his closing statements when he wrote this: "Harry Daddy almost forgot on another occasion daddy was told it would be from six to eight years after the trial of Bruno Hauptman [sic] before any thing would happen I sure have faith there will be and if they do what a story they will have to listen to Hey wot?

This final statement sent my thoughts soaring back to Steffin Salisbury of the *Philadelphia Inquirer*, when, sitting in my home in the year 1980, he excitedly said to me: "Wayne, you have an earth shaking story."

The handwritten composition book closes with this expression of a father's love for his children: "Just a little story to let you know how God watches you every minute ... and if we behave and do every thing that is good he watches day and night never fails so many times he has watched over me.

These little stories are true.

Yours very Lovingly
Daddy Harry P. Young
X X X

It was for a very noteworthy purpose that I had you read such a large portion of Harry Young's composition book. Since I had known Mr. Young for a number of years, I believe I qualify to speak for the man's honesty. His reputation in the community was spotless. Although I had not known him to be an extremely religious person, I did know him to be a kind man, and very fair and thorough in his retail business of selling and repairing radios. As a matter of fact, my family dealt with him and that is how we became acquainted. Because I can vouch for his integrity, I wish to impress you with the man's sincerity, and at the same time attempt to persuade you to realize that Harry Young actually had nothing to gain by relating his story of Martin Stover to a largely mocking "unbelieving" audience. Even I, knowing his reputation for honesty, at first refused to believe any part of it, and on occasion I thought the man "had gone off his rocker" and was suffering from delusions. But, Harry continued to tell it until his final moments on earth.

The reason for this is easily understood --- Harry Young knew it was the truth, every portion of it! And because Harry Young trusted in God, his desire was that the world should know the truth. As you read through his message to his children, the very truth of his story shouts out to us. And since we now know of the involvement of Isidor Fisch, as testified to by Harry Young, and years later by William Wright, we now find the defendant Bruno Richard Hauptmann was innocent as he claimed and nothing more than a "manufactured and manipulated" scapegoat.

And when Harry Young finally proved to me that his story was true and I soon became conscious that God Himself was guiding me by leading me to Bill Wright at the Union League in Philadelphia, and by protecting Harry Young's written message to his children, and later allowing me to procure it, plus the finding of many other vital and important pieces of evidence, we should never deny in any way the greatness of God in the moves He has made to answer the prayer of Anna Hauptmann.

Because the story Harry Young had told me back in 1936 had been validated firmly in my mind and was now supported with physical evidence, I reasoned that I should acquire some additional affidavits from a few other witnesses, people who could personally substantiate the facts. L. Darlington Lessig was one of these.

Mr. Lessig verified that he had been informed by the Lindbergh investigators, when they personally visited him at his place of employment in 1933, that "the wood used in the kidnap ladder had been cut and planed by the Dorn Company in South Carolina, and the lumber which came to our company in Phoenixville (The Frank C. Andrews Lumber Co.) had evidently been included in the same shipment.)"; I also hold an affidavit signed by D. Sidney Slemmer, in which he states that he was working in an electrical appliance store in Phoenixville that was owned by Alan Stover, a son of Per Stover. Mr. Slemmer verifies that he very clearly recollects Martin Stover's visit to Phoenixville in 1932. He stated further that he saw the live chinchillas not only in Alan's store, but also in the home of Per Stover, adding that he remembers reading about the ladder wood being traced to Phoenixville shortly after the kidnapping. Another affidavit I was able to obtain was one given by the late John Jacob who relates a personal experience he had with Lindbergh on a summer afternoon in the year 1930 when the aviator and his wife Anne were living in the farmhouse near Princeton. His affidavit lends another interesting fact relating to Lindbergh's many idiosyncrasies.

Armed with these affidavits and depositions from

the others I have already mentioned, I now felt I was fortified with all the added proof I might need.

It was in 1981 that I first met Thomas Kelly and his nephew James Kelly. Both, I learned, were from the nearby Philadelphia area, and although we had all been studying the Lindbergh case for many years, our paths had never crossed. The two men were firmly convinced of Hauptmann's innocence. They had personally talked to many of the principals of the case and had gained a realm of information which leaned heavily toward the frame-up of Richard. They supplied me with an audio tape they had obtained from recordings of Hauptmann's voice which had been submitted to voiceprint testings. The result supported their view that Hauptmann's plea of innocence was an honest one. The test made of John F. Condon's voice proved to be otherwise.

The Kelly's and I visited Hans Kloppenburg at his home in Jackson, New Jersey and taped a lengthy interview with him, in which he reiterated his belief in his friend Richard's innocence. He told us personally about his "not so gentle persuasion" on the part of the police and Wilentz as they told him just how he should testify, with their threat of arrest to himself if he did not follow their orders. He said Wilentz had ordered him not to say the package he saw Isidor Fisch hand Hauptmann was "the size of a shoe box."

Jim Kelly asked me one of the most perplexing questions ever asked in the annals of the Lindbergh case. This is true because his question is a very logical one. Yet, it is a question the police most certainly had first asked among themselves, and then most definitely had asked Hauptmann. Jim and I, (his uncle Tom had since passed away), agreed that when they asked the question of Hauptmann, he had given them an answer which, because of supporting evidence, could not be broken. And then, we believe the police deliberately "backed off" and away from the question, hoping it would never be asked in any court room, or for that matter, by some of the more friendly press.

Here is the question as Jim put it to me. "Wayne, have you ever read or heard of Hauptmann's explanation as to where he was on Saturday night, March 12th, the night the kidnapper met with Condon at Woodlawn Cemetery and sat with him for all that time in Van Cortlandt Park? What alibi did Hauptmann give them?" I assured Jim, I simply did not know, I had never read what he told them. Jim responded immediately: "Sure, of course you haven't. Don't you think that's funny?" I assured him that I did, which was followed by Jim's reaction: "That's just it. The police were so intent on framing Hauptmann about his presence in Hopewell on Tuesday, March 1st, after he gave them his legitimate alibi; and then on Saturday, April 1st, when he gave them his honest answer as to where he was, they said he was lying; and then on Sunday, November 26, 1933, when he had witnesses testify that he was at a birthday party given for him in his home, they said he was lying, that he was seen at a movie theater in Greenwich Village, don't you think it strange that they didn't press him as to where he was on Saturday, March 12th, the night Condon said he talked to Hauptmann for an hour and a quarter on a park bench?" I instantly agreed with Jim that the only explanation as to the reluctance of the police to press their prisoner any further as to where he was on that date can only be answered with a very positive statement: HAUPTMANN MUST HAVE HAD AN IRONCLAD ALIBI AS TO HIS WHEREABOUTS ON THE EVENING OF SATURDAY, MARCH 12th, 1932. That's the only line of reasoning we can give, otherwise they would have ripped it to shreds as they had "successfully" done with his others. Had they been able to "nail him" with anything more in the way of even "shaky evidence" that would have suited their purpose of framing him further as to his whereabouts that evening, with accusations that "he was not where he said he was", they would have done so.

As we know, so much was said about the overwhelming and "very conclusive" handwriting evidence that was used against Hauptmann. Why then, I must ask, was his "demand" writing used, that taken from him on September 19, 1932, the day of his arrest, to be compared with that of the ransom letters, which they argued was definitely a disguised writing? Why did they not compare the ransom letters with his natural writing taken from legal documents he had written, when not under duress or compulsion? Good examples they could have used, had they suited their need, would be his signature from legal documents, his automobile license, mortgages, etc.? None of these matched, in any stretch of the imagination, any of the ransom writings.

Proof of this is evident in a short letter Hauptmann had written on December 9, 1933 to the wife of a Mr. Alexander Begg, who as a pedestrian had crossed the street in front of him as he was driving his Dodge. Richard, not being able to stop in time, had struck Mr. Begg, knocking him to the street, resulting in Mr. Begg suffering a broken leg. Although Richard believed the injured man had stepped out against the traffic light, he acknowledged his guilt and readily agreed to reimburse the man for his medical expenses in the amount of $300. In the letter to Mrs. Begg, Richard wrote:

> Dear Madam:
>
> I received your letter and I am very sorry Mr. Begg is not well. If I had more, I would have send you the money long ago, but I try to send you ten or twenty Dollars before Christmas.
>
> My wife has a baby since five weeks and so the few Dollars I made I needed badly. As soon as I am able to I will send you the rest of the money.
>
> I wish Mr. Begg will get better soon.
>
> Yours Truly
>
> Richard Hauptmann

Here we have read a compassionate letter in which he expressed his good wishes to Mr. Begg, explaining his inability to send them more money at that time because of his lack of available cash.

As we use every means of good reasoning, isn't it perfectly logical that if Hauptmann had possession of the kidnap money in 1933, as the police said he did, he would most certainly have sent Mrs. Begg the small amount she asked for, the $300? Good common sense tells us he would have done this, however, it was impossible for him to do this simply because he did not have it.

Where, I must ask, was the wealthy Bruno Richard Hauptmann the police claimed he was in 1933? He, Anna, and little Manfred were an average family living on moderate means in those days of the depression.

Another point I make pertains to his signature at the close of the letter where he signed it merely Richard Hauptmann, the name he had used since he landed on the shores of America, the only name Anna had ever heard from his lips or read from his writings. It most certainly had not been used to serve him as an alias. Certainly no crime had been committed by a man who merely desired to make his name shorter in an effort to help him begin life anew in the new world.

All the hullabaloo raised over the arrest and conviction of Hauptmann, most all of it based on mere conjecture and wild guesses, aided by their evilly contrived evidence, finally vanishes into a disappearing mist as you read the revealing final chapters.

CHAPTER SEVENTY TWO

Convincing New Evidence And Letters Of Proof!

Many interesting things happened during the 1980s. Things that turned out to be very helpful in Anna Hauptmann's valiant fight to prove the innocence of her husband. It was in 1981, after the passage of the government's Freedom of Information Act, that a noted lawyer, Robert R. Bryan, of San Francisco, visited Mrs. Hauptmann at her home in Yeadon, Pennsylvania and informed her that he had obtained enough documents from the FBI files in Washington to clear her husband's name.

Mr. Bryan, a soft spoken pleasant man with nice features, enhanced by his sandy hair, had been actively involved in the kidnapping case when he was selected during the 1970s by Kenneth Kerwin to represent him in his legal battle as he attempted to prove that he was the kidnapped son of the Lindberghs. Bryan had offered his legal expertise to Anna Hauptmann, promising not to charge her a dime, because of the sincere belief he held of Richard's innocence.

True to his word, fortified by Anna's exuberance that he was sent to her by God, Robert Bryan fought a tough and difficult battle in the courts attempting to prove Richard's innocence. However, in spite of the facts he presented, it all went to no avail.

In October 1981, Bryan filed a $100 million wrongful-death suit against the State of New Jersey in Newark, contending that state officials had "maliciously" suppressed crucial evidence that could have proven Hauptmann's innocence, and that the 1935 trial was a fraud because information that would have cleared Hauptmann of the crime was concealed. In addition to the State of New Jersey, individual state police officers Lewis J. Bornmann, William F. Horn, John B. Wallace, Joseph A. Wolf, and Hugo Stockburger were named in the suit, as well as David T. Wilentz, who in his capacity as former Attorney General of New Jersey, had prosecuted Hauptmann. The arguments were heard by United States District Judge Frederick B.Lacey, and defended by Eugene Sullivan, assistant New Jersey Attorney General, who argued that a wrongful-death charge may only be brought within two years of the death in question. Bryan countered to this charge, asserting that Mrs. Hauptmann had not learned of the additional evidence and therefore, could not have proved her husband's innocence until 1981 when the State Police files and FBI files had been ordered open for the public's inspection under the Freedom of Information Act.

Bryan had based his case on findings which he claimed showed a pattern of perjured testimony, suppressed documents and contradictory testimony. However, Judge Lacey dismissed the suit without trial, stating that his ruling was based on a 1976 U.S. Supreme Court decision regarding public prosecutors who were granted "absolute immunity" from prosecution. And because of this Wilentz was "freed" from any possible lawsuits in the case. Attorney Sullivan went on to explain: "It is too many years after the fact to reconstruct the evidence." In addition to this Judge Lacey stated that the two-year statute of limitations had expired, and further ruled that Mrs. Hauptmann had failed to prove that New Jersey's authorities had withheld evidence and violated her husband's constitutional rights. Anna Hauptmann and her attorney lost all their appeals to this ruling without any opportunity to argue the merits of their case.

With the odds appearing to be decidedly against her as their appeals were being rejected, plus the refusal of the United States Supreme Court to even look at the case, Anna Hauptmann's faith never wavered. "Some miracle will happen. I don't know how. All I can do is pray and hope. Something must happen. It takes a long time, but Richard's name will be cleared. Why? Because my husband did not kidnap the Lindbergh baby. And there is a God in heaven, and He saw us drive home that night. They built the case on lies, and they knew it. They know it today. And they know they killed an innocent man. Murdered him. They are the murderers", she spoke boldly with a persistence that is admirable and at the same time obstinate.

During the time taken for the "enactment" of the Hauptmann case in civil lawsuits brought into the New Jersey courtrooms during the 1980s, the respect and sympathy toward Anna Hauptmann grew in immense proportions. The public with but few exceptions had shown great admiration for this lady who was soon to enter the 90th year of her lifetime. They sensed her honesty and sincerity as she told them, "I know he is innocent because we went home together that night." It had become a ritual with her because she knew nothing different. She had spoken the truth.

There were some, even among state officials, who outwardly expressed disappointment in Mrs. Hauptmann's failure to obtain her husband's vindication. However, the statement of Colonel Clinton L. Pagano, Superintendent of the New Jersey State Police at that time, reflected the attitude of the "officialdom" of the state when he said: "I feel empathy for the widow of a murderer, but I found not one ounce of evidence that's new or would ever dissuade me from believing that the jury found properly. Not one scintilla of evidence anywhere." So said Colonel Pagano. You see, the state was still marching to the beat of the same drummer as they did in 1935.

Robert Bryan, after poring over tens of thousands of documents pertaining to the Lindbergh case, at one point in his investigation made the claim that within a few months he hoped to reveal the true identity of the kidnapper, only to have Pagano smugly answer: "I'm waiting with bated breath." Yes, the officials of the state of New Jersey seemed to be very confident and content in their belief that nothing had been done improperly at the Flemington trial in 1935.

The arguments for Hauptmann's posthumous trial continued. Attorneys for the state believe they are protected from "whatever" by the statute of limitations which prevents them from agreeing to a possible trial by a jury. Their claim is based on the fact that Anna Hauptmann, having read the book *Scapegoat* in 1976, had learned of Scaduto's claims of Hauptmann's innocence with information which was made known to her by means of his book at that time. This fact, they argued, should then establish a new statute of limitations. The lawyers reasoned that since Richard Hauptmann's widow had been furnished with enough knowledge of "facts giving rise to a cause of action", this then, automatically re-set the clock for another two year period which they claimed had expired well before she filed her lawsuit in 1981.

But attorney Robert Bryan sees this another way. He has consistently stated that the case should be resolved by a jury, not by federal judges in New Jersey who have dismissed Anna Hauptmann's suits.

Every year, since the knowledge of her residence

became inadvertently known, Richard Hauptmann's widow had received hundreds of letters from writers in all parts of the world who poured out encouraging messages to her expressing their personal belief in her husband's innocence, at the same time urging her to press on with her efforts to prove it by means of her lawsuits.

These letters of support helped strengthen her. However, she would settle for nothing less than Richard's complete vindication granted officially by the state of New Jersey, either through the courts, the legislature, or the governor. It would be only then that Anna Hauptmann would rest from her efforts. She sought no financial gain from her lawsuits. "Only a letter of heartfelt apology for the terrible wrong they have done to us, is all I ask", she said glancing up with eyes brimming with tears as she fingered her wedding band she still wears.

"I am a Christian, you know, and although there were times in the past when I wondered if God really cared enough about me, I could not let go of my faith that a day would come when He would see that the truth of Richard's innocence is proven. I pray for those who are still living that were responsible for Richard's death. I know they can't be happy, but the Bible says we should pray for those who do wrong to us, and that we should forgive them, and I do, but I do pray that someone comes forward and tells the truth and admit that Richard was innocent. I pray for this every day", Anna continued as she again expressed her great faith in God.

Time, however, was now becoming quite an important factor. Attorney Bryan found himself confronted by several courtroom setbacks as his petitions on Anna's behalf for a new trial, always based on legitimate claims in his charge of wrongful death, were disallowed, in each instance, by federal court justices. Had one of these appeals been granted, a new trial would have been ordered, the case reopened, and Hauptmann tried again posthumously.

Undaunted, Bryan, the determined attorney he was proving to be, however, next arranged to have the Hauptmann case verdict heard by San Francisco's Court of Historical Review and Appeals, a court whose primary duty is to review the evidence which had been presented in controversial criminal cases, and after weighing the facts, then render a decision. There were times when this court's findings would be in complete disagreement with the decision of a jury in a criminal court of law that had originally tried the case. In such instances this would be followed with the suggestion that a new trial be held.

The controversial conviction of Hauptmann as the only person guilty of kidnapping the Lindbergh baby in the 1935 trial certainly presented ample cause for its application requesting that it be heard by this historical court. Hence, it was agreed, that due to the overwhelming debate created by the Flemington conviction, and although the historical court held no legal authority, it did however, serve the best interest of the citizens to again study these questionable points in an effort to review the possible flaws of the case, the Court of Historical Review and Appeals should scrutinize the Hauptmann case and render its unbiased verdict.

The decision rendered by the San Francisco court in 1986 was very favorable to the Hauptmann cause when Judge George Choppelas announced after hearing the case that "there is a historical need to reopen the case." However, he explained that this decision rests in the hands of the authorities of the state where Hauptmann was convicted.

The San Francisco trial had been a perfectly legal one, held before a qualified judge and jury with all the components of an official, present day lawsuit, including attorneys, witnesses, a court stenographer, and a courtroom packed with more than 100 spectators. Anna Hauptmann, who made a tearful plea on behalf of her husband, was also present. Her attorney, Robert Bryan, maintained that he had new evidence which proves that the kidnapping was "an inside job". "I know who did it and how many people were involved", he spoke with great conviction.

But, as expected, the New Jersey authorities refused to act on the advice of Judge Choppelas' recommendation to reopen the case. And so, once again the public was denied their right to the acquisition of the well kept "secret and hidden" facts of the Lindbergh kidnapping.

Realizing the success Robert Bryan experienced as he presented Richard's case before a jury in San Francisco, leads us to believe that the Flemington jury in 1935, even with all the perjured testimony and manufactured evidence with which it had to deal, would have brought in a verdict for acquittal if Hauptmann had been properly defended. As we already know Edward J. Reilly proved to be of little help to the prisoner. The man was absolutely a detriment to the defendant, who wasn't aware that James Fawcett had been removed from his case and replaced by "Death House Reilly", also known among his peers as "The Bull of Brooklyn". In reference to his new attorney's employment, Hauptmann had this to say: "In just what way Mr. Reilly became my chief counsel, I don't know. I can not remember ever having signed any agreement to that affect. I suffered more from the action of this man than any other man. Many times I requested of him that he come see me, through my wife as well as through Mr. Fisher, to discuss the case. When he would come, he remained with me only from three to five minutes. Indeed, once when the trial was in progress he came to me under the influence of liquor so it was difficult to talk with him. All that he said was 'don't worry, there is no jury in the whole world who can convict you'. Then he departed again, singing."

With a chief attorney such as Reilly defending him, Richard would have done better to have represented himself had he possessed more than just his limited command and grasp of the English language. Because Lloyd Fisher, second in command of Hauptmann's lawyers, firmly believed in his client's innocence, it is my contention that he should have been in charge of the accused man's defense. And furthermore, Fisher being a Flemington attorney, probably would have found much favor among the local residents. But, the Hearst people had to steer it another way, and so Reilly was hired for the task of "putting the skids" beneath Hauptmann as they sent him on his way to the electric chair. What a "snow job" they gave Anna Hauptmann!

During the 1980's, invitations for me to speak publicly on the case increased. This was largely due to the greater number of requests from organizations whose chief interest was to hear me personally relate how I had assembled my collection of heretofore unknown facts on the case over the passing of fifty years.

Word had been spreading by means of newspapers, radio, and television that "I was a guy who knew the truth and was not afraid to tell it." And that happened to be close to the truth, but the scope was not great enough. My lack of finances was of great hindrance to me. I had no agent, I had no grants to support my cause, and what was more, I had very limited funds to get me copies of important things I needed, as well as take me to the places I had to reach. From the very start of my investigation I promised myself never to charge anyone who wanted to hear me speak. I never wanted to be conscious stricken for being found guilty of making money on the long lifetime of sorrow that Anna Hauptmann had been forced to endure. Although I have been accused of doing otherwise, I can honestly state that the only remuneration I ever received was in the form of small gratuities, that were always offered and never demanded, but which many times barely covered the cost of my transportation.

I must add, however, that through the years it became necessary for me to invest a few thousand dollars in order to obtain things I realized I must own in order to prove and solidify the facts I have put together in this book. These are largely the documents, pictures, affidavits and depositions that now rest safely in my files. Among these things are the 4791 pages which contain every word of the court testimony taken in the 1935 trial of the State Of New Jersey vs. Hauptmann. This testimony is contained in six large hard bound volumes that were once owned by the former governor of New Jersey, Harold G. Hoffman. Included in them is all of the photographic evidence presented at the trial; the Briefs and Opinion of the Court of Errors and Appeals Petition; the Briefs and Decisions of the U. S. Supreme Court; as well as hundreds of valuable newspaper clippings of those days, all collected by the governor.

My acquisition of many important documents came from various searches I made during many visits to the New Jersey State Police Barracks at West Trenton. We must thank Brendan T. Byrne, New Jersey's governor, who in 1981, under rights granted him by the passage of the Freedom of Information Act, ordered the Lindbergh case files to be opened, making their inspection possible by the general public. On a few of my visits to the New Jersey State Police barracks, I was accompanied by Bill Simons, a man who claims to be the kidnapped Lindbergh child. I have known Bill since 1976 and have never doubted his sincere desire to prove his true identity. After our first visit to the barracks he came away elated with some new facts he had found which he claimed supported his belief.

I might add here that of the more than 25 persons, each with their own reasons, who claim to be the Lindbergh's stolen son, I happen to know three of them personally. Although I can't speak for the remainder, I must certainly defend the purpose of those I have known for many years. The three are Kenneth Kerwin, Harold R. Olson, and William Simons. Each one of these, in his own right, sincerely believes he is the son of

Charles and Anne Lindbergh who was kidnapped from his Hopewell, New Jersey home on March 1st, 1932. I have stated this in order to make it perfectly clear that anyone who knows the merits (if there are any), and the many "demerits" of this case, and then considers the sincerity behind the efforts of each of these men, should agree with me that the statements of New Jersey's former attorney general, Irwin I. Kimmelman, and the former superintendent of the state police, Colonel Clinton L. Pagano, should be taken as a personal affront when they blatantly labeled all of the claimants as nothing more than impostors. Naturally, I can only defend the three I know by stating for the record, "Impostors they are not!"

I made no attempt to cover up the reason for my interest in searching through the Lindbergh files. From my initial visit I had made it quite clear that I was there with a two-fold purpose --- to gather additional information which would help me prove my claim of Hauptmann's innocence, with the end result being my rendering needed help to his wife Anna. In spite of any animosity my trips to the New Jersey State Police Barracks might have drawn because of my belief, which I might add, was diametrically opposed to the beliefs of those officers in charge of the more than two hundred thousand documents on the case, I can never say that I was treated with anything more than complete courtesy and friendship by New Jersey's uniformed troopers. I spent many enjoyable hours there, occasionally having the privilege of eating lunch with them, discussing varied subjects, getting to know them as friends, and never looking at them as adversaries. Those troopers I especially thank for their patient help to me when I visited the New Jersey State Police Barracks were Detective Sergeant Cornel D. Plebani, Pat Kendig, and Sergeant Bob Felicito.

My files are filled with important documents and papers I acquired from the state police Lindbergh files. All of these were obtained legally because of the passage of the Freedom of Information Act. Please believe me when I tell you they make very interesting reading. Many of them support the accusations made by Hauptmann's defense counsel in their charges of illegal procedure.

If I had revealed all of the volume of incriminating evidence in my possession, another 500 pages would have been added to this book. However, in order to make it clearly seen what they did and by what methods they used, I have chosen some of the most convincing points to back up my charge that Bruno Richard Hauptmann was rail-roaded to the electric chair by dishonest scoundrels who were no better than any of those vile names attorney general David T. Wilentz called the accused victim.

First of all, let's look once again at the two "honorable identification witnesses" who were called to testify that they had seen Hauptmann near the Lindbergh home at the time of the kidnapping. The two who said they had seen no one until after the "convenient arrest" of Hauptmann. Take into consideration the deposition of Emma Irene Cooper, a resident of Hopewell Township, New Jersey, in which she stated that Millard Whited was indebted to her in an amount which totaled $283.00. She said she had a number of conversations with Whited asking him to pay this account and on each occasion he had said to her that he "cannot pay her until after Hauptmann is electrocuted and he gets his one-third of the reward." She said he told her that "one time after another." In her deposition she also stated that she had conversations with him at times other than when she asked him to pay the bill, and that on those occasions he told her that he was to receive one-third of the Lindbergh reward and that would amount to about $7,000. She went on to state that she had asked Sgt. John Wallace of the state police about this and that Wallace "had admitted to her that Whited had been promised one-third of the reward by Mr. Wilentz."

Mrs. Cooper also said in her sworn statement that she had heard Whited tell other people that he was going to have plenty of money "just as soon as Hauptmann was executed, because he was going to get one-third of the reward." She also said Whited told her that the state police had "continuously followed him" or as he called it "hounded him", so that it was impossible for him to get a job or keep a job if he got it. He stated further that "even after the case was over the police kept right on following him and hounding him." The Cooper deposition states that a man named Charles Schuhardt, who resided at the "old Poor Farm on the Rocky Hill road", had told her that he also was working near the Lindbergh home in the woods at the time of the kidnapping. He said: "I could have had $50.00 too like Mr. Whited got, if I had wanted to lie about seeing a man."

The deponent stated that she had no interest in the Hauptmann case in any manner, shape, or form, and that she made her statement only because it is absolutely true and because she felt it was her duty to do so. Her statement was sworn and subscribed to on the 9th day of March 1936 --- four weeks before Hauptmann's execution.

The Whited testimony, among others, is one of the most loathsome and repulsive in the Hauptmann trial.

But then, we must also consider that of Amandus Hochmuth. Among the interesting tid-bits I extracted from the state police files of the case was this letter received by Governor Harold G. Hoffman. It read:

Dear Governor:

I am giving you the same story that I also reported to Ellis several weeks ago. Several days before the trial started of Bruno Richard Hauptmann, I had an occasion to go and interview the daughter of Amandus Hochmuth, who lives at the corner of the road that leads up to the estate of Col. Lindbergh.

Mrs. Plum, stated to me in the presence of several other newspapermen from my office that her father had nothing to do with this case, and why would they ask an old man like him to tell a story about something that he did not know anything about.

She also spoke about his eyesight at that time and said that he never saw Hauptmann pass their house at all.

Mrs. Plum told that her father told the police when they called at the house for him that he knew nothing about the case.

They held my father up at the state police headquarters for three days and would not let him come home at all. We were worried until one day he called us and said he would be home soon. The state police went so far as to place a guard over him, and this guard went every place that the old man went. He was moved to New York, where he stayed with his other daughter.

I will give you the names of the other men that were with me at that time, all members of the *Camden Courier* staff. Charles Humes, William Connor, Phil Buxton, and myself.

Very Truly Yours, Russell (Hop) Stoddard

Amandus Hochmuth, the man with "terribly poor eyesight", who after making no attempt to inform the police "of what he claims he had seen" in March of 1932, was finally "conveniently located" by the state police in 1934, and then "urged and persuaded" to go into court in 1935 and swear before God that he had "seen and identified Hauptmann" as being near the Lindbergh home in 1932, and finally explained that his failure to report "what he claims he had seen" in 1932 was, in his own words, "because he hated to become involved in the case...that he didn't want to be the man, or the means, of sending any man to the chair." This is the man who allowed himself to be maneuvered by the police to falsely identify Hauptmann, even having the "guts" to go so far as to place his hand on the shoulder of the man he accused.

I have in my possession no less than thirty-three additional statements of Amandus Hochmuth that are very, very controversial. Reading them makes one wonder if the "old man", as Justice Trenchard insisted on calling him, ever did know what he saw, if he saw it, when he saw it.

Hochmuth, the man who did not wish to become "involved" in the case but later made an attempt to get a seat for himself at the execution. This is the man Justice Trenchard, in his "biased" charge to the jury said, using to advantage his usual voice-inflection, "Isn't this old gentleman to be believed - Is there any reason why this old gentleman should not be believed - Do you think that there is any reason, upon the whole, to doubt the truth of the old man's testimony?"

Oh, justice - sweet justice as it was found and exhibited in Flemington, New Jersey in 1935.

Now I realize that it is possible for you to have read the preceding 71 chapters and are still unconvinced that Hauptmann was innocent. However, I trust that if this is the case, you will now allow me to prove to you what I mentioned in an earlier chapter, the complete lack of cooperation that existed between the major police departments investigating the kidnapping from the time of its beginning until its end. This one factor alone was largely responsible for much of the bungling done by the police during the early days following the kidnapping. There was absolutely no reason for the break-down of communications that existed between the investigating bodies. However, the Jersey troopers seemed to hold the position that it was their case and it would be their men that would solve the case without the help of any others from the outside. This created a sense of jealousy which "fathered the failure" of the New Jersey State Police, under the leadership of their chief, Colonel H. Norman Schwarzkopf, to comply with the urgent requests made by their compatriots of other police departments.

I present here a series of letters that would be quite amusing if the matter at hand was not of such grave importance. Director J. Edgar Hoover of the Federal Bureau of Investigation must have been very frustrated with the lack of cooperation he received from Colonel H. Norman Schwarzkopf, Superintendent of the New Jersey State Police. The letters speak for themselves.

April 6, 1934

Colonel H. Norman Schwarzkopf,
Superintendent,
New Jersey State Police,
Trenton, New Jersey.

Dear Colonel Schwarzkopf:

In order that this Division may be informed concerning all available evidence in connection with the case involving the kidnapping and murder of Charles A. Lindbergh, Jr., not only for the intelligent conduct of any inquiries which may have to be made by this Division but also for comparison purposes with other data which may be received from time, it is respectfully requested that this Division be furnished with a list of all physical evidence in your possession in this case and with photographic or photostatic copies of all such physical evidence.

I have recently been advised that there were latent fingerprints developed on some of the ransom notes received in this case. If this is a fact, I would be glad to have these prints compared with all the fingerprints in the Division's single fingerprint file, with the view in mind of making some identification, assuming, of course, that the prints have not as yet been identified. I would appreciate your advising me as to this matter.

If you are unable to have photographic or photostatic copies made of such evidence because of the lack of equipment, if you will forward the originals to me I will be glad to have such copies made here at the Division, where the equipment is available, and return the originals to you immediately after the copies have been made.

Very truly yours,

J. EDGAR HOOVER Director,

cc - Mr. T. H. Sisk, New York Office.

----And then we have Schwarzkopf's answer----

April 11, 1934

J. Edgar Hoover, Director,
Bureau of Investigation,
Washington, D. C.

My dear Mr. Hoover:

Permit me to acknowledge receipt of your esteemed communication of recent date and with reference thereto, would state, that throughout this investigation it has been the policy of this department to retain all evidence in this case in our immediate possession and to make comparisons for other departments at their request. As you well know, it is my responsibility to protect the evidence, and I must take this responsibility very seriously. Should your investigation develop any matters which need comparison with the original evidence, we will be very glad to make such comparisons and submit reports of the comparisons.

For your information and in reply to your specific inquiry, would state, that no latent finger prints were developed on any of the ransom notes and all finger prints of any kind that we have gotten have been compared with our files and also forwarded to Washington for comparison.

Thanking you for your kind offers of cooperation and assuring you of our appreciation, I continue to remain, with kind personal regards,

Very truly yours,

H.Norman Schwarzkopf
Colonel and
Superintendent,
New Jersey State Police.

cc - T. H. Sisk, New York Office.

----Another letter from Hoover follows----

April 23, 1934

Colonel H. Norman Schwarzkopf,
Superintendent,
New Jersey State Police,
Trenton, New Jersey.

Dear Colonel Schwarzkopf:

Your letter of April 11, 1934, in reply to mine of April 6, has been received. I note your statement concerning the original evidence in the Lindbergh case, and it would appear from your communication that my request in connection with this matter was not understood, as I did not request that you surrender the original evidence in this case. You were requested to furnish this Division "with a list of all physical evidence in your possession in this case and with photographic or photostatic copies of all such physical evidence." I did offer, in the event you did not possess facilities for making such photographic or photostatic copies of this evidence, to make the copies for you. This Division did not suggest that you surrender the original physical evidence in your possession with this case.

This Division, by reason of its exclusive jurisdiction in Federal kidnapping cases, has gathered and is receiving voluminous information concerning individuals and activities of underworld characters engaged in this particular type of violation of the law. Obviously, it would be of considerable assistance to this Division in its efforts to intelligently analyze the evidence so received to have available a complete list of physical evidence in all kidnapping cases, together with photographic or photostatic copies of the physical evidence obtained in the various kidnapping cases which have occurred. This would enable the Division experts to make intelligent comparisons and to properly analyze and evaluate information which is received from time to time. The Division has been successful in obtaining such lists and copies of the physical in these various kidnapping cases, with the exception of the Lindbergh case, and it was with this purpose in mind that I wrote to you, asking, as I have indicated, for a list of the physical evidence which was obtained in this case, together with either photostatic or photographic copies of the same. I am hopeful that you may see your way clear to comply with this request in order that the proper assistance and intelligent cooperation may be rendered by this Division in this matter.

Very truly yours,

J. Edgar Hoover,
Director

cc - T.H. Sisk, New York Office.

----Which was followed by this acknowledgement----

April 24, 1934

My dear Director Hoover:

Permit me to acknowledge receipt of your communication of recent date, addressed to Colonel H. Norman Schwarzkopf, the Superintendent, and to state that the Colonel is away from the Office for a few days, but immediately upon his return your communication will be brought to his attention.

Sincerely yours,

Chas. H. Schoeffel,
Major and Deputy Superintendent,
New Jersey State Police.

J. Edgar Hoover, Director,
Division of Investigation,
U.S. Department of Justice,
Washington, D.C.

----Schwarzkopf replies----

May 1, 1934

My dear Director Hoover:

From your letter it appears that you did not understand just my meaning. In amplification of the same, would state, that when the Lindbergh case is finished I will be very glad to give you copies of everything you wish and will do my utmost to help you complete your file.

With kind personal regards,

Very sincerely yours,

H. Norman Schwarzkopf,
Colonel and Superintendent,
New Jersey State Police.

J. Edgar Hoover, Director,
Bureau of Investigation,
Washington, D. C.

----Hoover's patience is growing thin----

May 3, 1934

Colonel H. Norman Schwarzkopf,
Superintendent,
New Jersey State Police,
Trenton, New Jersey.

My dear Colonel Schwarzkopf:

I am in receipt of your communication of May 1, 1934 in which you refer to previous correspondence which I have had with you concerning certain information desired by this office in connection with its investigation of the Lindbergh case. I note you state that when the Lindbergh case is finished you will be very glad to give to this office copies of everything which is desired, and will help to complete our file. Of course, when the case is completed, the information which I have requested will be of practically no value to this Division. As previously indicated to you, the information which I have requested is for the purpose of assisting the investigators of this Division in their present investigative activities into the Lindbergh case. Obviously, without a list of the physical evidence which was procured by your investigators in this case, and without photographic or photostatic copies of such physical evidence, our investigators cannot approach the situation as intelligently as they could if they had this information available.

However, if it is contrary to your policy to make such information available to our investigators at the present time in the form of a list of the items of physical evidence, with photographs of the same, the Special Agents of this Division will make such effort as is possible to carry on their investigation without the information which I have requested.

Very truly yours,

Director.

cc - Mr. T. H. Sisk - New York Office.

----Evidently Hoover chose not to sign this letter since no signature appears at the bottom----

---

----More letters showing Schwarzkopf's refusal of compliance----

May 16, 1934

PERSONAL AND CONFIDENTIAL

Director
Division of Investigation
U.S. Department of Justice
Washington, D.C.

Re: Unknown Subjects
Kidnapping and Murder
of Charles A.
Lindbergh, Jr.

Dear Sir:

Reference is made to Division letter dated May 11, 1934 indicating that the ransom money discovered in this case to date was being obtained by the Division for scientific laboratory examination.

With reference to this matter, Lieutenant James Finn of the New York Police, confidentially advised me yesterday that the New Jersey State Police had learned through the Federal Reserve Bank that we obtained the ransom money, and, according to Finn "they were plenty sore about it." Lieutenant Finn stated that the State Police just recently obtained a loan of $5000 from Col. Lindbergh to be deposited with the Federal Reserve Bank to cover the temporary withdrawal of the ransom money. Upon arriving at the Federal Reserve Bank they discovered the ransom money had been sent to Washington a few days before. Lieutenant Finn further advised me that Col. Schwarzkopf is taking the matter up with the Attorney General of the State of New Jersey and that a protest may be lodged with the Attorney General of the United States on the grounds that the ransom money is evidence in the Lindbergh case and that the Division has no right to even temporary possession of it. Another objection is that we took the money out of the State.

Today, evidently as a retaliatory measure, Lieutenant Arthur Keaten, issued an order to Corp. William Horn, who has been working daily with Lieutenant Finn and Agent Seery on the ransom money, that neither Agent Seery nor any other Department of Justice Agent shall be allowed to ride in the automobile assigned to Horn and owned by the State Police. Corp. Horn advised Agent Seery of this order and stated that Lieutenant Keaten was "burning up" because the Division had the ransom money. Horn quoted Keaten's exact words as follows: "Don't let any of those G--D-- Department of Justice Agents ride in that car." Keaten also instructed Horn not to let Lieutenant Finn out of his sight and to accompany him everywhere, if possible.

It looks like a possible attempt on the part of the State Police to "freeze" the Division out of the ransom money investigation; obviously, of course, it won't work. Lieutenant Finn's opinion about the matter, as expressed to me, is that the State Police are making themselves ridiculous. It is pointed out that if Corp. Horn's superiors would let him alone, everything would be all right on this money investigation as he is an easy person to get along with and has worked smoothly right along with Agent Seery and Lieutenant Finn.

As the Division is aware, an arrangement has been in effect for some time whereby Corp. Horn of the New Jersey State Police, Lieutenant Finn of the New York Police and a Division Special Agent jointly investigate ransom money discovered in this vicinity. The practice has been for Corp. Horn and the Division Special Agent, presently Agent W.F. Seery, to call each morning at New York Police Headquarters and there meet Lieutenant Finn for the purpose of planning the day's work. When a ransom bill turns up the three investigate it together and have been travelling in the Buick Sedan owned by the New Jersey State Police and operated by Horn.

I have instructed Agent Seery to take a Division car with him in the future on the money investigations and in this connection both Corp. Horn and Lieutenant Finn have expressed their willingness to ride with Seery in the Government car. However, this arrangement will very possibly be upset when Lieutenant Keaten hears about it. He will probably instruct Horn not to ride with Seery in any car. If Lieutenant Keaten or whoever is responsible for these instructions to Horn assumes this attitude, he will make himself even more ridiculous. I do not believe we should refuse to allow Horn to accompany Seery in a Government car as to do so would be to place ourselves on the same footing with Lieutenant Keaten and company.

I have explained the situation exactly as it is to date and will keep the Division advised as to further developments. We are trying to be as diplomatic as possible in our contacts with both the New Jersey State Police and the New York Police and every effort, of course, will be made to avoid any trouble. However, we are not backing down or limiting our field as far as the investigation itself is concerned.

Very truly yours,

T. H. Sisk
Special Agent.

----AND THEN CAME THIS----

May 22, 1934

MEMORANDUM FOR THE ATTORNEY GENERAL

In connection with the investigation being conducted by this Division of the kidnapping and murder of Charles A. Lindbergh, Jr., I am transmitting herewith a copy of a letter dated May 16, 1934 from Special Agent Thomas H. Sisk who is in charge of this investigation which portrays the attitude of the New Jersey State Police and indicates the obstacles with which the Division is confronted in conducting this investigation.

The letter, as it will be noted, refers to the obtaining by the Division of ransom bills paid by Lindbergh in this case from the Federal Reserve Bank at New York City. The money was obtained through the

Secretary of the Treasury for the purpose of being treated scientifically by the Division's Criminological Laboratory to determine whether it bare any distinctive marks of identification on which might prove helpful in tracing it to the kidnappers. The majority of these bills have been located for over one year and the New Jersey State Police, apparently, have taken no steps to carefully examine this money from a laboratory point of view which was the Division's purpose in obtaining it. The money, after being examined, will, of course, be returned to the Treasury Department which will in turn return it to the Federal Reserve Bank at New York City.

To further illustrate the attitude of the New Jersey State Police in connection with this investigation, I am transmitting herewith copies of the correspondence between Colonel H. Norman Schwarzkopf, Superintendent of the New Jersey State Police, and myself. As will be noted, on April 6, 1934 I directed a letter to Colonel Schwarzkopf requesting that the Division be furnished with a list of all physical evidence in the possession of the New Jersey State Police and with photographic or photostatic copies of all such physical evidence, and advised him that it had recently come to my attention that latent fingerprints had been developed on some of the ransom notes, and suggested that if such prints were developed, I would be glad to have these prints compared with all the fingerprints in the Division's Single Fingerprint File with a view of making some identification which resulted in the attached correspondence:

Letter to Colonel Schwarzkopf dated April 6, 1934
Letter from Colonel Schwarzkopf dated April 11, 1934
Director's reply dated April 23, 1934
Letter from Charles H. Schoeffel to Director dated April 24, 1934
Letter from Colonel Schwarzkopf dated May 1, 1934
Letter to Colonel Schwarzkopf dated May 3, 1934

It will be noted in Colonel Schwarzkopf's letter dated April 11, 1934 that he states no latent fingerprints were developed on any of the ransom notes. The photographic copies of these notes in the Division's possession disclose that latent fingerprints were developed. The value of such prints, of course, is not known in that they may have been identified as the prints of individuals who handled the notes subsequent to their receipt. It will be further noted that Colonel Schwarzkopf advises he will submit a list of the physical evidence in his possession after the case has been solved at which time, it will, of course, be of no particular value. The Division was desirous of having the advantage of all the basic information in the case in order that a more intelligent investigation might be conducted.

Respectfully,

Director.

Enclosure #551387

----It is again evident that Director Hoover did not choose to sign this memorandum to Attorney General Wilentz, since his signature does not appear----

These letters certainly prove my charge that there was absolutely no cooperation exhibited by the New Jersey State Police with the other investigating bodies. Had they been agreeable to work with the other authorities, information might have been passed along which could possibly have resulted in an early solution of this major case, the one that was to become known as the "Crime of the Century". But despite this, the New Jersey State Police, under the leadership of their great commander, Superintendent H. Norman Schwarzkopf, stubbornly refused to give their help during the early stages of the case, and continued to do so until the time of Hauptmann's arrest, as evidenced by the dates the letters and memorandums were written.

The following memorandum and letters go far to prove the point I make.

May 22, 1934

-<u>MEMORANDUM FOR ASSISTANT ATTORNEY GENERAL KEENAN</u>-

For your information, I am transmitting herewith a copy of a memorandum directed to the Attorney General, a copy of a letter dated at New York City on May 16, 1934 from Special Agent T.H. Sisk, and copies of correspondence between Colonel H. Norman Schwarzkopf, Superintendent of the New Jersey State Police, and myself in connection with the physical evidence in his possession in the case of the kidnapping and murder of

Charles A. Lindbergh, Jr., which reflect the attitude of the New Jersey State Police.

Very truly yours,

(Signature)
J. Edgar Hoover
Director.

Enclosure #551388

The next interesting, and convincing, piece of information I found in the New Jersey State Police files was a letter sent to FBI Director, J. Edgar Hoover, from Harold G. Hoffman, Governor of New Jersey, who inquired of Hoover's knowledge of the incident related to Detective Bornmann's finding the board missing from the Hauptmann attic. The governor's letter of inquiry, dated January 18, 1936, read as follows:

Re: Lindbergh Case

My dear Director:

Will you please advise me if any representative of your Department was present in the Bruno Richard Hauptmann home in Bronx, New York, on September 26th, when Detective Bornmann, of the New Jersey State Police, made the discovery that part of a board had been removed from the unfinished floor of the attic?

It has been reported to me that representatives of the Federal Bureau of Investigation were not permitted to be present in the Hauptmann home at that particular time. Will you kindly advise me if this report is correct.

Sincerely,
(Unsigned)
Governor, State of New Jersey

----Director Hoover answered the governor's inquiry in a letter written January 23, 1936. Since it is rather lengthy, and much of it does not pertain to the specific questions asked by the New Jersey governor,

I have selected only his answers having to do with his knowledge of Bornmann's "amazing find" and New Jersey's lack of cooperation with the Federal Bureau of Investigation.----

---

Honorable Harold G. Hoffman
Governor,
State of New Jersey,
Trenton, New Jersey.

Dear Governor Hoffman:

No representative of this Bureau was present in the attic of the Hauptmann residence, when, on September 26, the segments of the ladder used in the kidnapping were compared with the boards in the attic floor.

Relative to your inquiry as to whether the ladder believed to have been used by the kidnappers of the Lindbergh child was examined by representatives of this Bureau, you are advised that the ladder was never submitted to this Bureau for any form of examination.

The foregoing responds to all inquiries contained in your five letters of January 18, I am transmitting herewith a duplicate copy of this letter, for your use in the event you desire to transmit the information in this letter to Attorney General Wilentz.

Sincerely yours,

John Edgar Hoover,
Director.

Enclosure #831336

As we absorb the contents of the letters and memorandums that passed between the chiefs of the Federal Bureau of Investigation and the New Jersey State Police, it can be readily understood why Hoover protested in one of the conferences held with his Agents, by stating that: "New Jersey is one State from which our department received no co-operation from the police... It's hard to believe, but we still haven't received from them the fingerprints of Hauptmann for our files---we never had them".

From additional evidence I procured, was this

statement reportedly made by Director Hoover on February 14, 1938. Since I had been able to obtain copies of Hauptmann's fingerprints as were taken in 1934 by both the New Jersey State and New York City police, I also found them to be nonexistent in Washington, D.C. My not finding them there certainly corroborates Director Hoover's claim.

These, among many other facts which I found in the New Jersey State Police files (thanks to the Freedom of Information Act), when put together, plainly show the great extent to which the prosecuting authorities extended themselves to put an innocent man in the electric chair. They literally "bent themselves out of shape" once they "found" an acceptable scapegoat worthy of "proving guilty" enough to put their bungled case to rest.

It was during the 1980s that I met many people, who after learning of my determination to clear Richard Hauptmann and the important information I had obtained, came to my home in Phoenixville and told me other facts that, prior to their visit, I had not known. One of these was Sydney L. Smith of West Chester, Pennsylvania who told me he had originally come from Hopewell, New Jersey and that he had known Millard Whited very well. We became fast friends since we were both of one mind regarding Hauptmann's complete innocence. We made a trip to Hopewell together, visiting Millard's grave and the Lindbergh's Sourland Mountain home from where the terrible tragedy began. As we stood at the Whited grave, Sydney impressed me with his personal knowledge of this man who had accused Hauptmann. He claimed, as did many others at the trial, that Whited was nothing but a "no good liar".

Mr. Smith, although vague as to the date, said he was certain that he had read in a newspaper, sometime in the 1960s, of a man from Argentina, South America, who had reportedly confessed on his death bed, telling of his participation in the kidnapping of the Lindbergh baby. Circumstantial of course, hearsay certainly, but not so if Mr. Smith had remembered that the death bed confession had been made by a Martin Stover.

During one of our frequent telephone conversations with Mrs. Hauptmann, she informed my wife and I that the following day we would be visited by a young man and his sister who were anxious to talk with us relative to the information I had acquired which proved Richard's innocence. It was early afternoon of the next day, April 8, 1987, when they arrived from their home in New

Jersey. Greeting them at the door, I continued in conversation with the young man, as I overheard my wife, Anna Mae, question his sister, "You look familiar, haven't I seen you before?", which was followed by another quick query, "Haven't we seen you on television?". To this question her brother answered with pride, "If you watched 'Call To Glory' you did." As he said this Anna Mae immediately recognized her as the girl who portrayed the daughter of Craig T. Nelson and Cindy Pickett in their award winning weekly series which depicted the life of a United States Air Force Colonel and his family during the 1960s.

Our guests were Andrew and Elisabeth Shue, a young actress. Both were convinced of the innocence of Richard Hauptmann, having looked into the facts of the case when they were elementary students and were not at all satisfied with what they were told. Elisabeth was a student at Harvard University while Andrew was studying at Dartmouth.

In their quest for the truth they had located Anna Hauptmann, and while visiting her, she had told them to see me. We spent a delightful time together as we reviewed the case, compared our knowledge of the "truthful" facts, and viewed video tapes of documentaries, docudramas, and file footage of the crime.

We learned that our visitors were leaving for Germany in several weeks, and while there it was their intent to visit Richard's native village of Saxony, where they hoped to find his birth certificate and bring a copy of it back with them to Mrs. Hauptmann. Until the time of her husband's arrest, Anna had always known him as Richard Hauptmann. The reason for this is easily understood. When Richard arrived on American shores in 1924 his one desire was to start a new life for himself. And in order to do so, he decided to refrain from using his given name Bruno any longer. And this he did, rather successfully. There is no record of Richard Hauptmann ever signing his complete name, Bruno Richard Hauptmann, until the New York City police learned of it from the police authorities overseas on the date of his arrest, September 19, 1934.

Everything he signed, his insurance papers, driver's license, owner's card, mortgage papers, etc., including his marriage license, all bore the name Richard Hauptmann. When Anna's future husband decided to start his new life in America he "buried" the name Bruno, never expecting that he would ever have use for it again. However, with the events which were destined to happen in his life, it proved to be a big mistake. Because of his arrest, the police naturally "resurrected" it and it immediately became a source of great confusion and mystery to his dear wife.

For years Anna Hauptmann innocently denied that her husband's name had ever been Bruno. "Where did they get Bruno?", she would ask. "Bruno? He is no Bruno!", she insisted. And for years, we also believed that it was the police and news media who were responsible for "tagging it on" in an effort to serve their purpose by making his name sound more brutal. Although we had seen letters from Richard's mother in which she referred to him as Bruno, we could not doubt what we had been told by his wife who certainly should have been told and known the truth.

However, this minor mystery was solved when Elisabeth and Andrew Shue returned from Germany with a copy of the record of Richard's birth. It had been recorded that he was born and baptized Bruno Richard Hauptmann, and although the truth of his name had at last been learned --- to Anna Hauptmann he will always be known as her dear Richard.

We entertained many interesting guests during the 1980s. In addition to Robert Bryan, Mrs. Hauptmann's attorney, we had the excitement of having an unexpected visit by a man who was anxious to hear me relate to him the story of the Lindbergh kidnapping as I knew it. He explained that he had heard of my interest in the case and was inquisitive enough about it to come to Phoenixville and hear me tell him personally the true story of the Lindbergh case.

Our guest's name was Dick Cass, who said his profession was film making. The man was certainly no novice, explaining that he had worked for many years with Hollywood's great stars and had been a cameraman on quite a few of Alfred Hitchcock's classic films. We soon learned that the main purpose behind his visit was to obtain, and study, the details of my attempt to clear Richard Hauptmann's name, and after speculating its possibilities, he said he would then seriously consider producing a documentary film about my work.

Mr. Cass, who had been convinced from the time of Hauptmann's execution that he had been unjustly accused, listened intently as I explained and exhibited the materials I had. He intently watched selected video tapes that had been made during some of my interviews, various file films of the case I had obtained, asking questions now and then, having me play back certain portions of tapes I had collected, all relating to major portions of the Lindbergh kidnapping.

Suddenly calling a halt to his visit, Mr. Cass arose and stated exultantly: "I have seen and heard enough. I am sure there is enough information here for us to make a block-buster documentary." However, he went on to explain that the chief problem he faced, was to complete a few projects he was presently working on. By doing this it would then allow him the time he needed to go full-steam ahead with the proposed Lindbergh-Hauptmann documentary. This initial visit of Dick Cass was made on Wednesday, July 1, 1987. Telling us that he would get back to us soon, after making nothing definite in the way of a firm commitment, Anna Mae's hopes together with mine were riding high as we rejoiced together in the realization that possibly, at last, the populace of the world was soon to learn the truth about the Crime of the Century and Hauptmann's innocence in every phase of it.

Our wait was a short one. On Saturday, July 4th, Dick called us with the good news. He said he was going ahead with the documentary, explaining enthusiastically, "This film will be so great, I have decided to make it a docudrama with actors and actresses portraying the actual participants. We will possibly have to make it a two hour film." More good news --- more cause for rejoicing. He said he still had to finish a few projects he was working on, but did promise to get back to us as soon as possible. Again he proved to be as good as his word. Two days later he called with the news we were waiting for - he was ready to start.

The next year turned out to be an exciting one. The preparation of the experimental format; choosing the site where the film would be shot; viewing and selecting from the extensive footage of file film scenes to be used; the taping of interviews provided by witnesses; and soliciting for the financial help required for the rather low-cost production which Dick planned to make, estimated to be about $300,000. Of all the problems we faced, raising the money for the production proved to be our greatest stumbling block.

When Dick Cass decided to move ahead with plans for our docudrama, he turned away from every avenue of employment offered him by others who wanted him to do film work for them. To better explain this, let me say he plunged in "head first" in every sense of the word. Never have I ever seen anyone devote themselves to anything as whole-heartedly as Dick did in this intense desire of his to make a successful film which was destined to, upon completion, clear the name of Richard Hauptmann. Dick gave up all sources of income he could have received. He invested every cent he had in the purchase of needed equipment. He read the many books that had been published on the case, he studied the films in his production studio, watching them over and over into the wee small hours of almost every night. He interviewed prospective assistants and helpers. He became totally absorbed with our project. Lengthy telephone calls were made each day; trips from Philadelphia to Phoenixville were nearly a daily occurrence; flights to Los Angeles were not rare. Dick Cass had become wholly committed and engrossed in the "hoped for" production of his "Hauptmann Was Innocent" film.

There is no way I can say that every effort we put forth to produce this docudrama turned into failure. We were quite successful in locating a suitable site for the filming. We received complete cooperation from our witnesses who willingly signed affidavits and depositions, in addition to spending hours before the cameras relating the information they knew and remembered so well. Chauffeurs were hired to furnish transportation for people to be taken to the various locations, when and where they would be needed. Nevertheless, with all the success we made in these secondary things, each one important in its own right, our main problem was our failure to find enough people with enough money to invest in our project. We did, however, find some folks who were willing to have some money put in escrow, but this was a far cry from the amount we needed.

Dick and I, however, were so certain of its success that, had we been able, would have financed the entire production cost. However, this was impossible since Dick's bank account had been drained so badly by the expenditure of his own money on the film, there was simply nothing left. As for any possibility of me investing in our project, through the years I had spent every dollar I could spare to obtain the evidence I now held. Nevertheless, remaining undaunted, we continued on until the news of the "big dip" in the stock market diminished all hope of gaining any new investors, since those whose money we already had in escrow pulled out.

Because of our failure at securing investors, we were forced to "shelve" the plans we had for Dick's proposed docudrama. And so, with reluctance, we temporarily abandoned our project, earnestly hoping that we would be able to produce it at a later date. In the meantime, my work on this book, which had been put on a "back burner" due to my activity on the "fizzled out" film, was begun again with even renewed vigor. I was more determined than ever to inform the multitude of our world's uninformed citizens of Bruno Richard Hauptmann's innocence, the unjust treatment he received, and the horrible death he suffered --- all for a crime he did not commit.

However, an excellent pro-Hauptmann television documentary, in which I took part, was produced by Peter Goldsmith for Channel WWOR of Secaucus, New Jersey in 1988. Mr. Goldsmith had a personal interest in producing the film since he happens to be one of many persons who firmly believe in Hauptmann's innocence. The film had its initial showing on that station's "Evening Magazine" program in February of that year and was eventually shown periodically on many TV stations across the United States. The response I received from many of the persons who saw it gave me much encouragement and reassurance.

In my search for the truth, there were times when certain pieces of information I found seemed to "boggle my mind". A lone piece of paper would catch my eye, and after reading its contents, it would develop into "a disturbing mystery" to me. Among these were many I brought to my home. They make very interesting reading, but nevertheless, I must admit, they baffle me as well.

Isn't there good reason for us to wonder just how those who were guilty of framing Richard Hauptmann could live with themselves? Didn't their consciences bother them at all? Were they so caught up with their "success" in solving the famous case that they had no feeling of remorse? Were not the moral ethics as taught in schools of law, and practiced by the other prosecuting attorneys, Richard Stockton, Robert Peacock, Joseph Lannigan, George K. Large, and Anthony M. Hauck, seen being violated in a blatant breach of proper court procedure, in a public exhibition by Attorney General David T. Wilentz? Again, I ask, didn't anyone's conscience bother them with this open "carnage" of a man's life?

One of the "lone" pieces of paper I found tucked away within the files at the New Jersey State Police Barracks gave rise to a possible answer of the question I asked --- Didn't the prosecuting attorneys feel any compunction as to what was being practiced in that Flemington courthouse by the attorney general? As evidence of the possibility that there was, I offer this telegram sent to the governor three days before Hauptmann's execution.

THE HONORABLE HAROLD HOFFMAN=
THE GOVERNOR OF NEW JERSEY
CONFIDENTIAL STOP YOU ARE GOVERNOR OF NEW JERSEY STOP BE GOVERNOR STOP AS SUCH YOU HAVE MANY POWERS AND DUTIES COMMA INCLUDING POWER AS COMMANDER IN CHIEF OF THE NATIONAL GUARD COMMA WHICH IT IS YOUR DUTY TO USE WITH SUCH INTELLIGENCE AS GOD MAY HAVE GIVEN YOU STOP AM DELIBERATELY OMITTING REFERENCE TO POLITICAL FEATURES OF CASE STOP IT IS TRUE THAT FROM EVIDENCE MADE PUBLIC NO IMPARTIAL THINKER CAN BE SURE THAT HAUPTMANN IS NOT GUILTY BUT IT IS EQUALLY TRUE THAT CONVICTION WAS ON CIRCUMSTANTIAL EVIDENCE AND THAT THERE IS ALSO STRONG CIRCUMSTANTIAL EVIDENCE THAT FULL TRUTH HAS NOT BEEN DISCLOSED STOP UNDER SUCH CONDITIONS THERE IS NO REASON FOR IMMEDIATE EXECUTION ON THE CONTRARY IT IS UNWARRANTED STOP I HAPPEN TO BE ONE WHO HAS SEEN DEATH ON A WHOLESALE SCALE AND WHO CONSEQUENTLY DOES NOT OVERVALUE THE LIFE OF ANY INDIVIDUAL BUT I REALIZE THAT, WHILE HAUPTMANN IS ONLY A POOR ALIEN COMMA A CONDEMNED MAN HELD IN PRISON MAY BE EXECUTED AT A LATER DATE BUT A DEAD MAN CANNOT BE BROUGHT TO LIFE STOP COMPLETE AND INTELLIGENT JUSTICE IN NEW JERSEY IS FAR MORE IMPORTANT THAN HASTE FOR ONE MANS DEATH STOP REGARDLESS OF WHAT OR WHO MAY BE INVOLVED COMMA GET ALL FACTS BEFORE ANY IRREVOCABLE ACTION IS TAKEN=

RICHARD STOCKTON 6TH.

Is it possible that this was sent to the governor by the Assistant Attorney General? If so, his conscience must have been bothering him.

As sure as time continues, speculation as to all that went wrong with the original investigation of the Lindbergh kidnapping, and what actually happened permitting them to convict an entirely innocent man, is certain to continue. Time alone will offer opportunities that will only allow more rumors to creep into the sordid story. Nevertheless, as I have set down the accounts as they actually happened, I have no reservations. It is with a clear conscience that I say - I have told you the truth!

CHAPTER SEVENTY THREE

Devious Deception! How Deep Can It Go?

We should remember that there were witnesses other than Anna Hauptmann who knew that her husband was present in Fredericksen's Bakery on the night of Tuesday, March 1st, 1932. Although Anna testified she was certain that Richard came for her there and took her home that evening, the prosecution staff literally scoffed at her words, writing them off as merely those of a faithful wife who was protecting her "guilty husband". However, among the other witnesses who said Hauptmann was there, was a Louis Kiss who gave testimony that he knew Mr. Hauptmann was there because he had seen Hauptmann there. Not that he imagined it, or thought it, his insistence of what he said could not be shaken. But in spite of this, the judge, jury, and prosecution staff would not, and for the most part, did not intend to believe him --- simply because to believe him, regardless of what he said, would seriously damage the case they had built up against their "trapped" prisoner.

Following is the deposition, sworn and subscribed to by Mr. Kiss, regarding attempts made to have him change his testimony as he gave it at the Hauptmann trial in the Flemington Courtroom in 1935:

STATE OF NEW YORK)
) ss.
COUNTY OF NEW YORK)

Louis Kiss, of full age, being duly sworn according to law, upon his oath deposes and says:

I testified on behalf of the defense at the trial of the indictment against Bruno Richard Hauptmann for murder in Hunterdon County, New Jersey. I testified on the thirty-first day of January 1935 and my testimony was in the nature of an alibi for Hauptmann on the night of the Lindbergh kidnapping. I testified that I saw Hauptmann at Fredericksen's bakery on the night the

Lindbergh baby was kidnapped.

The day following my testimony at Flemington I went to the studio of one Mr. Resko, a friend of mine, who at that time was located at 80 West 40th Street, New York City, to call on Mr. Resko. As soon as I came to his place, Mr. Resko said to me "Why did you go to Flemington to testify in the Hauptmann case?" and I asked him why, and he said "Just wait a minute, I will get Mr. Berko on the phone, he wants to talk to you". I knew Mr. Berko who was a lawyer in New York City, and I asked Resko why he wanted to talk to me, and he said, "Just a minute, he will talk to you about this case in a minute himself". Mr. Resko called Mr. Berko, and in about five minutes Mr. Berko came to Mr. Resko's place. At that time there wasn't anybody in the studio of Mr. Resko except Resko, Berko and myself. When Berko came in he said to me, "Listen, Kiss, I am a friend of yours and I want to save you from going to jail." I said "What do you mean" and I started to laugh, and then he said "Why did you go over and testify in the Hauptmann case?" And then he said, "Don't you know anything about Jersey Justice?", and I said to him that they couldn't send me to jail for telling the truth. Mr. Berko then said to me, "I have an open wire to Wilentz and I can arrange that you go tomorrow back to Flemington and tell that you made a mistake by an hour, that you saw Hauptmann earlier than you said", and he said "Mr. Wilentz will arrange that you won't have any trouble."

While we were talking, there came to the office a man named Weidenger, who was a friend of Resko and mine, and also a friend of Berko. He heard the conversation between Berko and myself. I then told Berko that there was nothing to patch up, that I had given my testimony to satisfy my own soul because I knew that Hauptmann had been in the restaurant and about the time the kidnapping took place, and that if I had not gone and testified to the truth, my conscience would bother me the rest of my life. Then Berko said to me, "Why don't you let that Son-of-a-Bitch Hauptmann go to the chair," and Resko said, "Yes, why don't you let him go to the chair?", and I said to them, "Don't bother me any more about it, I have done my duty, I have told the truth and I don't want to hear any more about it." Then somebody rang a bell and another party came in, and they took him in another room. I didn't see who it was that came in and he didn't talk to me. Berko told me that it was a G-man and I asked Berko what he wanted. I never saw the man who was supposed to be a G-man and he never said a word to me. Berko said to me, "If you don't change your story about the time, we will get Singer (Singer was the man to whom I was delivering the package, when I saw Hauptmann) and Singer will go over to Jersey and testify that you were at his place an hour earlier" and I said "I can't help that, I told the truth" and Berko then said "Wait, we will get Singer down here", and I asked why we should call Singer. He went in another room and when he came back he said he had called Singer and that he, Singer, would be there in a few minutes.

In about ten or fifteen minutes Singer came in and he said to me, "Listen, Kiss, why did you get me in this trouble", and I said "Singer, I couldn't help it, I had to tell the truth about where I was that night." He said to me, "Listen, you were at my house before eight o'clock, and I said "Mr. Singer, you are mistaken, I wasn't at your house at eight o'clock, I was in Fredericksen's bakery at eight o'clock, and it was nine o'clock when I was at your house." Then everybody except Mr. Weidinger and myself went in another room, and about that time a Mr. Rousand came in to the office, who was also a friend of ours. He stayed with Mr. Weidinger and I. After the rest had gone in another room, Rousand called Resko out and he said, to him, "If Kiss says he saw Hauptmann at eight o'clock, why are you trying to get him to change his story?" Resko got mad at Rousand and cursed at him terribly and Rousand left.

After Resko, Berko and the man said to be the G-man had been in conference about thirty minutes, Berko said to me, "You said you saw a radio clock in Singer's house, and that isn't true, because it wasn't there then," and I said "I have been to Singer's house several times and know that on one visit I saw a radio clock." Berko tried to get me to say I was wrong about the clock, and I told him I was not wrong about the clock and I was not wrong about seeing Hauptmann. About that time, a telephone rang in another room and Berko went to the phone. When he came back, he said "Now you are in trouble. I have just had Wilentz on the telephone and they are going to pin all this on you, that you and Hauptmann built a restaurant at Long Beach and that you had Isidor Fisch out there, and they are going to pin all this on you." I laughed and said to them, "Gentlemen you are going crazy. I had a restaurant, but I never knew Hauptmann nor Isidor Fisch."

By about this time three hours had elapsed. Before Mr. Weidinger left, he said to me "you go tomorrow to Mr. Reilly's office and tell this entire story to him."

The next day I went to Mr. Reilly's office. Mr. Reilly wasn't there and I went back on Sunday, and I saw Mr. Reilly and Mr. Edelbaum and three news reporters and in the presence of all these people I told all the facts as I have told them in here and I signed a statement and it was sworn to before a Notary Public in Mr. Reilly's office.

On Monday of last week, Berko called the Superintendent of my apartment house and said he wanted to talk to me. I was suspicious of Berko and I took Mr. Weidinger with me, and when we got to Mr. Berko's office, which is at 551 Fifth Ave., New York City, he was surprised to see Mr. Weidinger, he said he wanted to talk to me alone, and I told him that he could talk in front of Weidinger, and Berko said "alright, you are a friend of Weidinger and I want to talk to you heart and heart." He then said to me, "Now that some time has passed, don't you think you could change your mind about your testimony. If you could change your testimony it would mean my entire future and it would be a little money for you." He then said to me, "I tried to get a job on the legal staff of Mr. Dewey the special prosecutor of New York, but they turned me down because I lacked criminal experience. Last week at a dinner given for Mr. Harry Herschfield at the Hotel Astor, I ran into Mr. Wilentz and I asked him if he could help me get on Mr. Dewey's staff, and he said "why don't you get your friend Kiss to change his story, and if you do, I will be glad to help you get on Mr. Dewey's staff!" Berko went on to say that he had been practicing thirteen years, that he had never gotten along and that if he could get on Mr. Dewey's staff, it would be a lot to him. He said "You have only got a PWA job and you could use the money." He said, "Now, what do you say, will you change your story? and I said to him "You have talked to me thirty minutes, will you listen to me about two? You tell Mr. Wilentz I am a very poor man, $5.00 is a lot of money to me, but if Mr. Wilentz would come here and put on that table five million dollars, I would take that five million dollars and throw it in his face, because I have told the truth and I wouldn't change it because my conscience wouldn't let me." He said, "Well I can't make a living practicing law any more. I will have to go to South America." I told him I was sorry I couldn't help him and I started to leave, and he said "Well we are still friends" and I said "Yes" and I walked out.

Mr. Weidinger heard the conversation in Resko's

office and the conversation last above set out.

Sworn and subscribed to) Louis Kiss
before me this sixth)
day of January 1936.

Laura Apgar
Notary Public of N.J.

Although more proof of this attempted deception is not needed, the following affidavit supports that given by Mr. Kiss:

STATE OF NEW YORK)
) ss.
COUNTY OF NEW YORK)

Desider Weidinger, of full age, being duly sworn according to law upon his oath deposes and says:

I reside in New York City, and I have read the affidavit of Louis Kiss in connection with the Hauptmann case, and I state that in each instance Kiss mentions my name, the conversation as related by Kiss is correct.

Deponent states that in Resko's office he heard Resko and Berko attempt to get Kiss to change his story. He says that he did advise Kiss to go to Reilly's office, and tell what happened, and he says that last week he was present at Mr. Berko's office and heard Berko attempt to get Kiss to change his story. He states that he heard Berko say that Wilentz, the Attorney General of New Jersey, had promised that he would get Berko on Dewey's legal staff if Berko would get Kiss to change his story.

Deponent states that he has no personal interest in the Hauptmann case whatever, and that each and every statement made by Louis Kiss in the attached affidavit, which has been read by this deponent, is true so far as it relates to things said to Kiss and heard by this deponent.

Deponent further states that he is willing to appear and give testimony on this point at any time his services are desired.

Sworn and subscribed to)
before me this sixth) Desider Weidinger
day of February 1936)

A. O. Weinberg
Notary Public, Kings County.

Disgusting is a rather weak word to describe the attempted actions of Attorney General Wilentz. However, in light of all the other things he "manufactured" in order to convict an innocent man, anything beyond normal reasoning should be accepted.

Among the multitude of other "foul acts" that occurred during the many phases of the case, one of the most disturbing of all was the failure of "Death House" Reilly, Hauptmann's chief attorney, to accept the testimony of Mrs. Frieda von Valta, one more person who would have testified that Hauptmann was in the Bronx on Tuesday, March 1st, 1932. Her testimony would have been very convincing and could have helped the efforts of Hauptmann's defense team. Because her deposition is very much to the point, and does not deviate from her personal knowledge of Hauptmann's whereabouts that evening, it leads us to wonder why Reilly, the bombastic "Bull of Brooklyn", refused to use her invaluable testimony. Here is her deposition as she gave it in January 1936.

STATE OF NEW JERSEY)
: SS.:
COUNTY OF HUDSON)

I, Frieda von Valta, residing at 263 - 11th Street, Hoboken N.J., of age, being duly sworn and says:-
That she makes this affidavit in support of Bruno Richard Hauptmann in his effort to establish that he is not guilty of the kidnapping and or murder of Charles A. Lindbergh, Jr. of which he has been convicted.
That on the first day of March 1932, deponent says that she went from Hoboken N.J. to Mt. Vernon N.Y. around five o'clock p.m. on an ad in the german Staats zeitung reading in translation as follows: Woman for all housework, good home, little family, wages 40$, Hughes 436 Nuber Ave. Mt. Vernon.
On her way around Times Square deponent asked for the direction of different people when one man in company of another man answered I will help you find the right way. They rode with me after changing at 149th Street and after a while they left the train in the Bronx around 220th Street and one of the two told me that I have to change again to a street car at end station of the subway. When leaving he gave me ten cents in case I should not get the desired position to be sure to have car fare home, mentioning that he has a mother in the

homeland and somebody might do her a favor if she should be in need.
The deponent when seeing the picture of Bruno Richard Hauptmann in the papers recollected his face immediately as the man that helped her in the subway as described above. It was between six and six thirty in the evening when we got to the Bronx.
That I was threatened by the Hoboken police in case I should go to Flemington to testify for Bruno Richard Hauptmann. In spite of these threats I went to Flemington to offer myself as a witness to the then chief counselor Reilly who refused me. There it was where I met Pastor D.G. Werner whom I told my experience as described in this affidavit.
Deponent further says that from all the circumstances and from the entire knowledge as related above that she is convinced in her own mind that Bruno Richard Hauptmann could not be the kidnapper of the Lindbergh child.

Mrs. Frieda von Valta

Sworn to before me this
tenth day of January 1936.

Emil LeFevre
Notary Public of N.J.

Mrs. von Valta was very certain the day was Tuesday, March 1st because she had traveled to Mt. Vernon to apply for the advertised position on that date. But, regardless of her insistence, the "great" attorney Reilly did not deem it important enough to use her testimony. Another big "blunder" by the defense.

There was another additional person who had given the police some information, which had they followed it up, could have proven to be helpful to them in the apprehension of the kidnappers. It came from a farmer named Harry Conover who lived at the time of the kidnapping on the Hopewell-Wertsville Road, about three-quarters of a mile south of the entrance to the Lindbergh estate. Mr. Conover reported that just after dark on the night of the kidnapping he had observed the cowl lights of a car on Featherbed Lane, a road which ran just below and to the immediate south near the Lindbergh home. He told the police he had watched the car, but because it was several hundred feet down the road, it soon disappeared from view. However, he said he believed "the car had come to a stop" and that the driver had turned the lights out. He stated further that the car's motor sounded like that of a Ford. Again the police were negligent in not following a good lead, one which could have been quite helpful to Hauptmann. But, as clearly seen in the case of Benjamin Lupica, whose truthful testimony had failed to penetrate the minds of those who were sitting in judgement, there was no one to be found from among either the prosecution staff and/or the defense attorneys who were even minutely desirous of helping Hauptmann. That is with the exception of Lloyd Fisher who firmly believed in Hauptmann's innocence.

Again, I wish to reiterate that from the moment the investigators were able to assemble and sort out the facts that were clear to them from the evidence they found at the scene of the crime, they all had been of one opinion --- the kidnapping had been structured by a group of people. Furthermore, they had agreed it could not have been the work of one person, but that it had been that of a conspiracy. Adding to this unanimous conclusion had been the voices of the Lindberghs, Mrs. Dwight Morrow (Anne Lindbergh's mother), Colonel Breckinridge, Colonel Schwarzkopf, and anyone else who was closely connected with the investigation. In addition to this, many believed that the crime could not have been perpetrated and enacted as successfully as it was without inside help. Aid from someone, either on the working staff of the Lindbergh home in Hopewell, the Morrow home in Englewood, or both had been the popular opinion of the investigating authorities. This correct belief persisted, <u>strangely</u> <u>enough</u>, until the arrest of Bruno Richard Hauptmann. And then, suddenly the crime became exploited as that from the workings of the devious mechanism of a degenerative and twisted mind of a one man "beast" who had devised and committed the vile crime "all by himself."

The populous of the entire world seemed to "jump on the bandwagon" in agreement with this "mad perception." How wrong, how distorted, how "unfair" the minds of these people were to become as they were filled with the "many concocted and misconstrued conceptions" of what had actually happened. They had unwittingly allowed their thoughts to easily become entrenched in agreement with something which was diametrically opposed to that which had originally been agreed upon had actually taken place. We were now being called upon, myself included, to submit to the "covered up falsehoods" being fed to us by the news media through the "courtesy" of the officials who now had Hauptmann in captivity. But then, how were we to know the deception behind their statements? How were we to suspicion anything but the "truth of their statements" fed to the press? In innocence, we could only believe what we were told by these "great deceivers" who continued to pile up "falsehood upon falsehood".

So that you can better understand the above statement, I deem it necessary that you read portions of a letter from Dan Cowie, an attorney with the law firm of Burch, Geiger, and Cowie of Wichita, Kansas. The letter was received by Harold G. Hoffman, then governor of New Jersey, and it reads in part:

> ....From your conversation, I judged that you would be particularly interested in Colonel Lindbergh's attitude toward Dr. Condon, and the possibility of two or more persons being involved.
>
> I was taken to Colonel Lindbergh by George Medalie, U.S. Attorney, New York City. I spent considerable time with the Colonel reviewing the information I had, and he was not in the least reluctant to disclose all that he knew of the case and his participation in it. We were particularly interested in knowing who could be trusted by the investigator to be assigned, and that lead to a discussion of Dr. Condon. The Colonel advised me that the night of the pay-off, he drove Dr. Condon and was followed by Colonel Irey of the Intelligence Unit and Colonel Breckinridge in another car. He said that Dr. Condon left the automobile, went down the street, over into the Cemetery and for a few moments was hidden from his sight.
>
> In the meantime, another party walked past the automobile in which Colonel Lindbergh sat, looking at him very closely but with his face carefully guarded by a handkerchief which he held in his hand. That he came back and re-passed the automobile in which Colonel Lindbergh sat,

went up the street across from the Cemetery, waved his handkerchief and then dropped it. Dr. Condon came out of the Cemetery following this party out of Lindbergh's sight. Lindbergh advised me that this party directed Condon back to the Cemetery by pointing. This information was imparted to Lindbergh by Dr. Condon.

The Colonel told me further, **that he had absolutely no confidence in Dr. Condon and that he had mislead him very much to his sorrow;** that if the party to whom the ransom money was paid was ever arrested, **Dr. Condon would never identify him.** He said without any equivocation, **that Dr. Condon had aided and abetted those collecting the ransom.**

I might add that the story that has been given me, I, in turn, disclosed to the Attorney General of the United States, George Medalie, Lt. Snook, of the Jersey State Police, and Frank Wilson, of the Intelligence Unit, as well as Colonel Lindbergh. The one inference to be drawn from my information, was that more than one had participated in this abduction. Colonel Lindbergh told me **that there was no other deduction to be made; that it could not have been done by one man and one man alone, and that he would even go so far as to say that until this crime was solved, he and every member of his family and household, was a legitimate suspect.**

I wish to take this opportunity to commend you for your courageous stand in this matter.

Yours very truly,

BURCH, GEIGER & COWIE

BY: Dan B. Cowie

(Emphasis Mine.)

The examination Dr. Spiegel made of his patient, Isidor Fisch, during his visit to his office as late as the end of July, 1931, resulted in his finding that Fisch was suffering from tuberculosis of the right lung, a disease which, without any doubt, would have made it necessary for him to cough. It must be remembered here that the man Condon met with in Van Cortlandt Park on the night of Saturday, March 12, 1932, according to what Condon testified to under oath at Flemington, "He had a cough, it was a cough, it was what they call a hollow cough, I said the inroads of pulmonary disease." It could very well have been Fisch who met with Condon on that cold night, especially so, since "Jafsie's" description seemed to differ every time he tried to identify the man.

Another malicious rumor that the police used to encourage the public to believe Hauptmann was guilty was a "fable" they fed to the press which told of Hauptmann's "apparent attempt" to take his life while he was a prisoner in the Bronx. The story proved to be nothing more than another lie. However, the newspapers carried the sensational story under the bold headline --- BRUNO TRIES SUICIDE!

As it was reported in Waller's book, had been taken by him from the various newspaper accounts which told of "Hauptmann's attempted suicide." The story, proven later to have never happened, was no more than a purely fictional one that had been concocted by the authorities. Nevertheless, it was one that had been tossed to the press as an attempt to show that the "prisoner's fear, because of his guilt", had resulted in his attempt to end it all by taking his life. They reasoned that his "guilty behavior", was an aberration of his, that would undoubtedly prove that "his alibi was a lie". Although, and quite unfortunately, many people did believe that Hauptmann had made an attempt to take his life --- but such an occurrence never took place. It was simply another "manufactured" story used to direct the public's mind against Hauptmann, a man, whom because of their unfair preconceived thinking, they had already decided was a "very wicked man".

As I read this in George Waller's book *Kidnap*, I thought of what had been told to me by my friends, Tom and Jim Kelly some years earlier. With the knowledge I already had, that Waller had obtained the information for his book chiefly from the accounts given him by the police departments that had been assigned to the case, plus the printed newspaper accounts he researched, I commented that Waller had done a masterful job in covering the case for his book. However, I stated: "It was a shame that he was prejudiced against Hauptmann, largely because of his failure to obtain the true facts!" "But", both Kellys responded, nearly in unison, "haven't you heard? Today Waller is convinced that Hauptmann was innocent!", claiming they had been told this by the author himself. Apparently, this change of mind was made after he read of Tony Scaduto's new information on the case in *Scapegoat*, all which favored Hauptmann, that had prompted him to admit his radical change of opinion.

As I have revealed the previously untold truths in the Lindbergh kidnapping case (more properly termed "the Lindbergh crime"), these new truths now make it crystal clear that Hauptmann was innocent. Because of this we can clearly see that the "great crime" was committed by the authorities who allowed an innocent man to pay for a crime he did not commit. Since they had "quite unexpectedly been furnished a scapegoat" they busied themselves by committing their "own crimes" in their efforts to "paint a picture of extreme guilt" toward and around Richard Hauptmann.

Enormous perpetrated irregularities were committed by the police in order to frame Richard Hauptmann. In this book you have been told of these. There are possibly other police inconsistencies that were used against the man who was "very unfairly" prosecuted in this case, some deviations of which we may never become aware. However, regardless of this, it must be remembered that most of the police involved were honest God-fearing officers whose efforts put forth during the countless hours they spent working on the case were given with but one purpose only --- to see that the kidnapped baby would be safely returned to his mother's arms, and that no one but the guilty parties would be apprehended and called on to pay for their part in the crime. These are the persons we honestly admire and sincerely thank.

Yes, these are the ones who, in spite of the "botched up" initial investigation, came through the investigation in spotless fashion. This they did in every interpretation of the words "Proper Police Investigation", which are "packed tight with the meaning" that persons are defined and proclaimed as innocent until they are otherwise proven guilty. And we might add, proven guilty beyond any doubt in a courtroom where -- FAIRNESS PREVAILS!

But what did Hauptmann have with which to contend? First of all we have the hero of the entire world sitting in the courtroom every day of the trial; we have this hero admit he believed Hauptmann was guilty; we have him stating on the witness stand that it was Hauptmann he had heard three years prior utter the two words "Hey Docktor". The honest rural folks were sitting in that courtroom in absolute admiration and awe of the great aviator; and, as for the jury, we must ask how could they render a verdict completely contrary to that which Colonel Lindbergh had already testified? They could not and did not! To have done so, they no doubt felt would have been, in their eyes, "a great miscarriage of justice". Hauptmann didn't have a chance!

And then we have the great Colonel H. Norman Schwarzkopf, the great Superintendent of the New Jersey State Police, who on many occasions, stated his absolute allegiance to his "new friend" Colonel Lindbergh. As evidence of this we quote his statement made to the *New York Journal*, which appeared in its issue of Friday, February 15, 1935. (Again we must quote what Colonel Schwarzkopf said:)

> I have made a friend. There is nothing I would not do for Colonel Lindbergh. There is no oath I would not break if it would materially help his well-being. There is not a single man in my outfit who would not lay down his life for Colonel Lindbergh.

Once again my mind goes back to what New Jersey State Trooper John Opdyke said to me in answer to my question, "Do you believe Hauptmann was guilty?" As we stood alone near the back of the Hunterdon County Courtroom in Flemington, he looked up to the ceiling and very calmly said: "Well the big boys said he was." His gesture and words related, directly to me, his heartfelt answer.

Trooper Opdyke was undoubtedly "one of the good guys" in the Crime of the Century.

CHAPTER SEVENTY FOUR

Important Bits and Pieces!

My story has been told, I have told you the truth, but for the life of me, I am not completely satisfied. There remain too many disturbing questions, which no doubt, will probably never be answered. Nevertheless, a few folks have given me some answers that must be placed in an "unsatisfactory category", inasmuch as, if we were to accept their conclusions, too many "eyebrows would be raised". However, this book was written with one purpose in mind --- to clear for all time, the name of Richard Hauptmann. I am certain my objective has been reached. But, in spite of this, as I began my narrative, I decided not to accept any "wild guesses", which in turn, could cast aspersions toward the innocent. Due to this, in order to be fair, I decided that it was necessary for me to tell you all I know about the case, and from these facts you can draw your own conclusions. So, I will now proceed to inform you of these additional items for your consideration, and we will - "let the chips fall where they may."

During the early months of the police investigation, a "rumor", under the assumption of being quite factual, especially by those who told it, was being passed around with great rapidity. It, as far as my investigation, remains merely an unfounded rumor. However, it is one that still persists in being repeated by many persons, who to this very day, insist that they know it to be otherwise. The rumor had to do with the questioned physical and/or mental health of the Lindbergh baby.

During my study of the case I came across claims made by persons who said they knew of certain abnormalities the child was said to have. I must admit that although I had read some articles which definitely stated that baby Lindbergh had some mental and/or physical defect, I found there was nothing to confirm these tales. That is, with the exception of a minor overlapping of several of his toes, something which many children have during their early years of life. But, since this can be easily corrected, it was certainly not anything that could be considered serious.

At my speaking engagements, the occasion would be a rare one when I was not asked the question: "Isn't it true that there was something wrong with the baby?", to which I would invariably answer: "The youngster was as normal as any other child at the age of 20 months." I further dispelled all the "factual claims" they had heard about the child "not being perfect" as nothing more than rumor. However, I ceased making this statement during the mid-1980s, when more effort and time was being put into certain elements of research with the aid of my friend and associate Richard Cass.

For years I had been told, without any foundation for it, that Charles A. Lindbergh, Jr. had spent some time in 1931 as a patient at the Johns Hopkins Hospital in Baltimore, Maryland. Although items had been printed relating to this "fact", it had never been confirmed.

During his own research of the case Mr. Cass had also come across a number of inferences about the child being confined at this famous hospital. But, as I, he too, had found nothing to substantiate it as being factual. He inquired if I knew anything at all about this. Assuring him that I had read something to that effect, but, since it could not be confirmed, I had written it off as being nothing more than rumor. Hearing me say this caused him to "pop off like a firecracker", as he excitedly said: "Where there's smoke there has got to be a fire, and I'm going to do something about it. I'm going to check this out personally down at Johns Hopkins and find out if it's true." Being a man of action, he did just that and this is what he found.

Approaching the information desk he was greeted by a young lady who very pleasantly asked if she could help him. Affirming that she could, he stated that he was there to gain information about several persons who had been patients in her hospital many years ago. Dick said she seemed quite happy to help him as she inquired as to the patients names he desired. Giving her several names in order that his quest for information on the kidnapped child would not be emphasized, he gave her five or six names, among them that of Charles A. Lindbergh, Jr. Evidently the prominence of the name Lindbergh meant little or nothing to her as she skirted off to obtain the required files on the patients without any hesitation.

She returned after a short time, informing him

that of the files of the persons he had requested, she had been able to find only one, that of Charles A. Lindbergh, Jr. In relating his experience there, Dick said he became very excited since he was in proximity close enough to easily read the name Charles A. Lindbergh, Jr. clearly printed on the file folder the receptionist was handing him. "You can imagine how I felt. I actually held my breath. Here I was about to learn the real truth about the baby. Why, I practically had it in my hands when some woman, evidently her boss, came from out of somewhere and in no uncertain terms shouted: 'What are you doing there?' My young helper informed her that I had requested the files on this person, while at the same time her matronly "boss" actually pulled the file from her hands. 'You can't do that! Don't you know this is classified information that is not available to just anyone?' With that announcement, said in her very best "drill sergeant's demeanor, she marched back to somewhere with the files I almost had in my own hands."

As Dick and I later discussed the value of his visit to the Johns Hopkins hospital, although the outcome gave us nothing pertaining to the vital information he was hoping to obtain, it did accomplish one thing --- we now are certain that Charles A. Lindbergh, Jr. had most certainly been a patient at that hospital at some time during his short life. However, for what reason we still do not know.

Through the vast number of years I spent researching the many aspects of the Lindbergh case, and most importantly the innocence of Hauptmann, I held a strong hope within me that if I was successful in proving his innocence, the day would come when I would be able to have my findings published. That day has arrived!

While I probed for facts, it became necessary that I read many of the large number of published histories of the Lindberghs as well as those of the Morrows, including biographies and autobiographies. However, I soon realized, and rightly so, that the thrust of my book should not be the presentation of another "life story of the Lindbergh family", but instead, should serve as the true story of Bruno Richard Hauptmann and how he was rail-roaded into the electric chair for a crime he did not commit.

Nevertheless, it must be said, that through my reading of many books, I came to realize that Charles Lindbergh was a very complex man. A man who was greatly admired due largely to the heroics he displayed by successfully completing his daring solo non-stop flight from New York to Paris in 1927. For this feat, at the age of 25, he received instant fame --- And deservedly so. Two years later he married Anne Spencer Morrow, the daughter of a multi-millionaire. His fame spread, and rightly so.

But, soon after their wedding, his growing dislike for the news media became very apparent. Although his marriage and the subsequent birth of his son, Charles, Jr., on Anne's birthday, June 22, 1930, were correctly considered newsworthy to a great degree, his utter disdain and abhorrence for members of the press was displayed openly on many occasions. There were times when he actually threatened them with clenched fists. Occasionally he would stubbornly and furiously refuse the requests of reporters with what he called "the evils of the press."

Charles Lindbergh had quickly displayed himself as a person of many moods. From the days of his youth, which extended into the days of his barnstorming and mail flights of the 1920s, he became known as a practical joker. His friends claimed they had to be alert to his tricks at all times because he was capable of "putting fish in your camera, a blunt blade in your razor, putting frogs and lizards in your bed, putting a dead skunk in your pillow, putting your bed up on the roof, switching the keys in your typewriter, or having your bedclothes stripped back while you were sound asleep and drenching you with a bucket of ice-cold water." A close friend, Bud Gurney, was a victim of one of Lindbergh's most sadistic "pranks" when he drank from a jug he assumed contained ice water. By doing this, Gurney suffered from a badly burned throat and stomach, and had to be rushed to a hospital because Lindbergh thought it would be a "good joke" to substitute the water with kerosene.

"Slim", the name by which he had become affectionately known among his flying companions, apparently never learned the secret of restraining himself when an opportunity presented itself to "pull a practical joke on someone" --- regardless of the cost. And these desires he carried with him into his adult life. His wife often found herself the brunt of his "foolishness". One of these incidents took place when the Lindberghs were guests in the home of their friend, Jack Maddux, in Hollywood. Amelia Earhart, the famous female flier, who was also present, related the noteworthy happening in this way: "Anne, who was wearing a sweet dress of pale blue silk, was standing directly in front of Charles as he munched on a tomato sandwich. Suddenly he had the impulse to let drops of water fall in a stream on his wife's shoulder from a glass in his hand." Since water spots silk he had ruined a perfectly good dress. Later that same evening, Miss Earhart stated, "Anne, with one comprehensive movement swung around and -- very simply -- threw the contents of her glass of buttermilk straight over the Colonel's blue serge suit, making it simply a marvelous mess."

Continuing in his role as a father, it was evident that Lindbergh had not abandoned a craving of his to play his "self appointed" role of "All American Joker" in his own home. We have evidence of this in an affidavit given by Miss Marie Cummings, who preceded Betty Gow as the baby's nurse, which states that while the baby was still an infant, his father had removed the child from his crib and hidden him in a closet, much to the consternation and chagrin of the nurse and family.

Although the rumor-mongers claim that this "sick trick" of the child's father occurred on at least one other occasion, the fact remains that it did happen once --- which quite naturally prompted Betty Gow, when she found the baby missing from his crib, to earnestly inquire "Colonel Lindbergh, do you have the baby?", to immediately follow with her statement: "PLEASE DON'T FOOL ME!" There can be no doubt that Betty's initial hope was that Colonel Lindbergh was playing another of his "masquerades of deception", that he was famous for in the past.

To further validate Betty Gow's original belief that possibly Colonel Lindbergh had again hidden the baby somewhere, I quote here part of a paragraph from Anne Lindbergh's letter to her mother-in-law, written the day after the kidnapping, Wednesday, March 2, 1932. She wrote: "At ten Betty went in to the baby, shut the window first, then lit the electric stove, then turned to the bed. It was empty and the sides still up. No blankets taken. <u>She thought Charles had taken him for a joke</u>. <u>I did, until I saw his face</u>. (The emphasis is mine.)

In spite of my study of the many "moods and temperaments" of Lindbergh, it is very difficult to understand the one he seemed to "enjoy" as he "playfully" threw water on his "shipmates" during the time he was at sea hoping to make contact with the kidnappers, a time we should believe he, a distraught father, was "intently searching" for his little lost son.

Yes, although he was known to be a rather mild mannered person, "Lindy" did have a temper. This is best exhibited when Daffin, the Morrow's small white terrier was killed on Sunday, March 5, 1931 at their Englewood home, Next Day Hill. On this date some sight-seers, hoping to catch a glimpse of the Lindberghs, swung their car suddenly through the open gateway, and driving down to the open forecourt, they struck the little dog as he ran out barking at the intruders. The car did not stop, hurrying away with its occupants showing no remorse for the condition of Daffin who was writhing in pain until a veterinarian was called to put him out of his misery with a shot of morphine. When the Lindberghs, then living near Princeton, were informed of the tragedy, Anne showed tearful sorrow and then her natural anger at the irresponsible people. Charles' outrage at the incident could not be controlled as he ranted and raved: "If I'd been there, I would have shot them, I really would have shot them!" And I am certain if he had done this it would not have been considered another one of his "stupid schoolboy jokes".

Leonard Mosley, in his book *Lindbergh* (Doubleday, 1976) said: "Even Anne considered that she had married her intellectual inferior. He hardly ever seemed to have read a book except ones on aviation. He had no feeling for words and seemed to prefer doggerel to poetry. His knowledge of music was elementary and his liking for it apathetic. He still could not resist playing those stupid schoolboy practical jokes. He seemed altogether lacking in the attributes of an educated young man of the kind she had been brought up to recognize."

In my study of Lindbergh's personality, I am at a complete loss to understand why he, a man known for possessing such great characteristics pertaining to his preciseness, punctuality, dependability, and reliability in everything he did, had totally forgotten his agreement to speak before a large group of the NYU alumni in New York City on the evening of Tuesday, March 1st, the night of the kidnapping, and had driven home instead. Was it fate that had led him back to his lonely Sourland mountain home?

But, if this were so, then it must take its proper place among the other unanswerable incidents that have played their part in the maze of "mysterious pieces" from among the other oddities which we find no way of fitting properly into that "giant puzzle" which was to become known through the years as the infamous Lindbergh case.

I came across another rather strange coincidence regarding the information I learned from Bill Wright, the man whom I met in 1980 when I spoke at Philadelphia's Union League. Mr. Wright, you will remember, told me that he knew Martin Stover and Isidor Fisch when he was serving in Colombia, South America as a member of the United States Air Corps Intelligence Service. In his deposition Wright stated that the pilot of the plane which brought Stover, a baby, a woman, and a man named Weisman into Cali, was a man named Peter Von Bauer. Furthermore, it becomes quite evident as we read Wright's deposition that Von Bauer must have understood the importance of his mission since he "bragged about it", claiming that his passengers were met by Isidor Fisch when his plane landed at Cali. Then doesn't it seem rather ironic that Colonel Lindbergh would mention Peter von Bauer of SCADTA, the German airline which operated out of Colombia, in his *Wartime Journals* (Harcourt Brace Jovanovich, New York published in 1970)? It seems that coincidences of this kind never cease.

It must be clearly understood that in public domain no concrete proof exists that there was ever anything diagnosed as being physically or mentally wrong with the kidnapped Lindbergh child. In spite of many rumors contrary to this, I have never found any concrete evidence that would prove otherwise. However, because I have promised to tell you everything I know about the case, even though on the surface the following might cause one's eyebrows to be raised, and therefore interpreted as something "worthy of questionable speculation" thus warranting further investigation, it does not necessarily put any "seal of proof" to it. It could very well fall into the category of being "just another vicious rumor". However, since it is associated with Phoenixville, I feel constrained to use it. The information provided here is taken, in part, from an affidavit I hold in my possession.

"My name is Robert Coine. I reside at 30 Nutt Road, Phoenixville, Pennsylvania. This affidavit essentially contains information passed on to me by an aunt of mine, Miss Helen Coine, who at the time, lived at 301 Morris Street, Phoenixville. The time frame of this information, divulged, not only to me but to other members of my family, was shortly after the kidnapping of the young son of Colonel and Mrs. Charles A. Lindbergh in 1932.

"Miss Coine, now deceased, was a registered nurse at that time and had become acquainted with Betty Gow, the lady who had been hired by the Lindberghs to care for their child. Aunt Helen was proud to know someone who worked in the Lindbergh household.

"Prior to the kidnapping and during one of the meetings of these two women, Miss Gow related to my aunt that the Lindberghs had detected something in the child's mannerisms and demeanor that caused them great concern.

"It was because of this that Colonel Lindbergh, according to Miss Gow, took his child to Johns Hopkins Hospital in Baltimore, Maryland where he was hospitalized. It was here he underwent tests for diagnosis and possible treatment. I personally can only estimate the time as being in late 1931.

"As a result of this stay in the hospital, Miss Gow went on to reveal to my aunt that the child was diagnosed as having a serious hearing deficiency brought on as the result of a flight with his father in an airplane taken sometime earlier. The ultimate result of this flight was the bursting of the child's ear drums. Miss Gow was quite outspoken about what had taken place, referring to baby Lindbergh as a deaf mute, and according to Aunt Helen, was quite upset about the tragedy.

"When the baby was kidnapped and among the many discussions in the Coine household about the terrible crime and the many subsequent things that followed it was quite a natural thing for us to discuss the known fact, as related by aunt Helen, that the child was not a normal person. For years after, many people learned of these facts.

"I sincerely affirm that the above information is completely true and I have recorded it exactly as it happened to the best of my recollection.

"Witness my hand and seal this 3 day of August, A.D. 1987"

Robert Coine
30 Nutt Road
Phoenixville, PA 19460

One other observation which presents a question for us has to do with why it was necessary for Anne and Charles to both emphasize "so many times" upon the arrival of their second child, Jon Morrow Lindbergh, at Englewood on Tuesday, August 16, 1932, by stating that their new little 7 pound, 14 ounce boy was such a "perfect" baby?

Once more we must study Anne's diary of this event and the days which followed. (The emphasis shown here were all those of the child's mother). Her entry for the day of his birth reads: "A little boy. I wanted to know over and over again if the baby was all right, perfectly all right.... Then later all day I was blissfully happy, relieved, saying and thinking over and over, the baby is all right, all right, he is here, he's all right. .... a perfect baby. It was a miracle."

And then in a letter, written on that same date to her mother-in-law, Anne said: "I must write you tonight just a scribble because I am so happy and relieved. The baby here---a fine big (7 lb. 14 oz.!) boy, strong and well and absolutely perfect physically. I cannot tell you what a miracle it seems.

"Oh, to have that baby here, and so strong and fine and fit---nothing wrong! If I stress that, it is because I have felt since this winter so unsure of everything and so afraid that something might go wrong.

Although Anne repeatedly wrote, and no doubt expressed to many others, of the perfect baby that had been born to her, she probably was placing her emphasis primarily on a referral to the intense trauma she had endured, after having her first child stolen away, to forever rob her of the joy of cradling him in her arms again. In all probability she meant that her new child was a "miracle" since it was born free of any defects which could possibly have been brought on by the "hours of lead" through which she had carried little Jon. Nevertheless, for what ever were her reasons, she certainly stressed the fact that Jon, her new son, was a perfect baby.

It would be unwarranted for anyone to suggest that Anne never believed the corpse that was found was none other than that of her son. When Colonel Lindbergh informed his wife that the body of their son had been discovered a few miles from their home on that gloomy afternoon of Thursday, May 12th, she had absolutely no reason to doubt it. After all, both Betty Gow and her husband had viewed the skeleton in the Trenton morgue and identified it as that of her little son. She accepted their identification as factual with no reason to doubt it. As we read through *Hours Of Gold, Hours Of Lead* - Anne's Diaries and Letters 1929-1932 (Harcourt Brace Jovanovich 1973) one becomes drawn emotionally with sincere sympathy as she tells of the days of deep grief she lived through. In this book she pours out from her innermost being, time after time, her feelings brought on by the sudden loss of their little "fat lamb".

And yet in spite of this, there remains the possibility that even a small doubt might have existed, a slight hope may have remained, when Anne in her entry in her diary dated May 18, 1932, holding the belief that the baby had been killed and tossed in the shallow grave on the same night he was found, asked herself this question: "What happened to the diapers?". To which I might add, "What happened to the 'rubber covering' that Betty testified to in court as having placed over the diapers?" These rubber pants also were not found.

It now becomes even more apparent that, after Betty Gow, the child's father, and the police had agreed among themselves that the badly decomposed corpse had at one time actually been the kidnapped baby, their identification was made chiefly by identifying the fragments of clothing found clinging to it. This material was nothing more than mere scraps of cloth that Betty looked at and matched with material from which she had cut and made a flannel shirt for the added protection of the baby from any chill that might occur in the nursery that somber night. The blue thread Betty used to stitch-up the garment was their dominant argument in their "determination of proof" that the thread found in the "garment on the corpse" was most definitely the same as that used in Betty's needlework. All well and good if we can accept such a "hypothetical, speculative, or far-flung argument." And I have sound reasoning behind me as I say this.

Accepting the fact that Betty Gow did put together a small flannel night shirt for the baby, we must also realize that in a very detailed statement relative to her activities on the night of March 1st, given by Miss Gow on March 10, 1932 at the residence of Colonel Charles A. Lindbergh, Hopewell, N.J. to Lieutenant John J. Sweeney and Detective Hugh J. Strong, both of the Newark, New Jersey Police Department, she fails to mention that it was "blue thread" she used in stitching the garment. Another item for consideration is the fact that there was no mention as to any certain color of the thread until the time the skeleton was found. But following this much ado was made over the color --- simply because it "was proven" to match a spool of thread in the Lindbergh home.

During my study of the case and all of its ramifications I conducted an experiment in order to satisfy my curiosity about the "blue thread" evidence. On one of my trips to the New Jersey State Police Barracks at West Trenton during the 1980s, I closely examined the little faded and stained flannel shirt that had been found on the badly decomposed corpse. As I turned it over in my hands, one thing disturbed me. I simply could not understand how the garment appeared so tanned and "weather worn", naturally brought about by its exposure to the elements of the weather and temperature, and yet allow the blue thread to be easily detected by the brightness and intensity of its color. Why, I asked myself, does this little shirt show a normal deterioration and yet the thread does not show the same degree of deterioration in its color? How could it possibly hold the same color as that on the night it was stitched into the flannel? Why had it not faded and deteriorated as had the rest of the garment? There it was, "in all its glory", still a bright blue. It just didn't make any sense to me --- and I decided to conduct my own test and see what would happen.

As I arrived home and put my thoughts to work I realized that, in order to conduct my experiment fairly, I must wait until a certain date arrived on the calendar. Although I knew that the weather conditions of Chester County, Pennsylvania, would not coincide exactly to those which prevailed when the baby was believed to have been placed in his shallow grave in Mercer County, New Jersey many years earlier, I nevertheless, decided that the proper way to begin my test would be to start it on that infamous date of March 1st, which commemorates the day of the month when the child was kidnapped.

I located a piece of flannel cloth and stitched it with a bright blue thread. My next task was to find a suitable place to conduct my experiment, one that would provide me a place which would closely resemble the terrain as that near the side of the Hopewell-Princeton road where the skeleton was found. Without the involvement of a long search, I found a suitable area, one where the ground in which I decided to place the cloth would be partially covered by the earth and leaves, and at the same time, would be sheltered from the elements of the weather by the trees and bushes nearby.

The evening of March 1st finally arrived. At approximately 10:30, I carefully placed my experimental piece of flannel in its "partially submerged grave". My sole intention had been not to disturb it until 72 days later when the date of May 12th came up on the calendar. In order to satisfy my intense curiosity, I succeeded in doing this.

At approximately 3:30 on the afternoon of May 12th I visited the "burial site" of my experimental flannel and retrieved it from the spot in which I had originally placed it. I must admit that I was not at all surprised to see that the cloth had very decidedly changed its color. What had originally been a grey-white piece of flannel had changed its appearance to a dirty brown or rust color. But what was more, the bright blue thread I had used had lost its hue and was now nothing more than a thread, the color of which was close to that of the brown rust-color of the flannel I had redeemed. This too, didn't amaze me. It was nothing more than I had expected. However, realizing that my test proved nothing in any legal way, it did give more rise to my suspicions and questions as to why the bright blue thread used by Betty Gow when she made the "garment" for the Lindbergh baby on that fateful night had retained its intensity of color, while under similar conditions for 72 days during my test, my thread had not? Probably, I reasoned, she had used a far better quality of thread.

Even though my little test proved of no official value, it can, nevertheless be added as one more "minor fact" to the already existing evidence that the unrecognizable corpse found on May 12th, 1932 was definitely not that of the Lindbergh baby. It should be, however, just as "convincing" as Attorney General Wilentz appeared to be when, in court while questioning Anne Lindbergh, inquired of her: "I notice a green---I think it is---thread possibly I am mistaken about the color---is that a green thread on the right side? (Handing Exhibit S-13 to the witness)? To which question Mrs. Lindbergh answered: "It is blue."

"Blue. Was there a blue thread---I think you said Miss Gow sewed that afternoon", Mr. Wilentz countered, as the child's mother responded: "I did not sew the garment and I did not get the thread."

Where, in 1935, was the intensity of the blue thread? Had it also deteriorated to such an extent that the attorney general could not distinguish it as being either blue or green? Strange, is it not, that when I saw "this same thread" in "this same garment" its color was decidedly a bright blue.

One more brief mention of the "blue thread" Betty Gow used in sewing her improvised garment for little Charles. As Inspector Harry Walsh returned to again view the corpse at the scene, he had in his possession some of the "blue thread" Betty had given him to compare with those fragments found on the skeleton. George Waller in his book *Kidnap*, published in 1961, adds another implication to the finding and the matching garment: He tells it this way: "The flannel petticoat and 'fragments' of clothing matched. So did the 'blue thread', when held against the few stitches that were visible." True, the emphasis is mine. And so is the emphasis I make about the result of my own unofficial test. The stitches in my "garment" were also "not visible" when it came to identifying the silk thread used as being anything near the color of blue. We should make note of the fact that in the Flemington court room both attorney Wilentz and Mrs. Lindbergh also had difficulty distinguishing the color of the thread used in the garment as being blue.

I must amplify again the fact that Mrs. Lindbergh was not mistaken when she wondered "what happened to the diapers?" The diapers she knew had been put on her child that evening. When in court she was asked this question by Wilentz: "What else did the child wear that evening as bedclothes?", her answer had been very precise: "He had diapers, fastened to the small shirt, to the second shirt, and on top of that he had a sleeping suit, a wool sleeping suit." Again I must ask, "I wonder what did happen to his diapers?"

Is it possible that Laura Vitray, a reporter for the New York *Evening Journal*, who had been assigned by her boss to cover the Lindbergh kidnapping ten minutes after the story broke, found the missing diapers?

During the early days of the search for the baby, Laura along with Joan Lowell, a reporter from a Boston newspaper, were taking an active role by personally looking for the baby in the Sourland Mountains not far from the Lindbergh home. The two women had as their guide an elderly lady, Antonia Chowlewsky, known as the "Amazon of the Hills" who was well acquainted with the terrain they were covering. Their guide happened to be the owner of several empty shacks and an empty bungalow which had been boarded up tight for the winter. Mrs.

Vitray, in a book she wrote on the case in 1932, *The Great Lindbergh Hullabaloo*, tells of the following event: "The hut Antonia pointed out to us had its window frame neatly pried out and replaced. Inside, on a mouldy mattress, in a bedroom that caused us to shudder, lay a hatchet, a hammer and a shovel ... Behind the door of that same room hung a baby's diaper, that looked quite new." Just a coincidence, you might say. Well, possibly. However, I wish to point out that the diaper seen by Laura Vitray and Joan Lowell was found in a shack off Zion Road, the route it had been originally believed the kidnappers had taken as a retreat following their fiendish act on that cold night of March 1, 1932.

At any rate, as usual, the police deemed this coincidence to be as unimportant as they did many other things during the early days of their investigation.

One more disturbing item in the mysterious Lindbergh case is the identification of the baby's sleeping suit. We know that Anne Lindbergh identified in court a sleeping suit, purportedly to have been the one found on the body of the corpse, as the one she and Betty Gow had put on him when they placed him in his crib on the night of the kidnapping. The one that had been received by Doctor Condon at his home had also been identified as the one taken from the baby and then being washed before it was mailed to him. However, this suit was not accepted conclusively as being the same garment. It had only been accepted as the same kind of suit, and since this was so, two questions come to mind. Why, when they could not positively identify it as being the suit, did Colonel Lindbergh pay $50,000 to a possible extortioner? That being so, how could Mrs. Lindbergh identify in court, under oath, that the one she was shown, a Dr. Denton's No. 2, marked State Exhibit No. 15, when asked by Attorney General Wilentz: "And it is the sleeping suit then that your son wore that night as he went to bed?", answer immediately: "It is." Someone was definitely confused. Anne in her diary, identified by her entry reading Hopewell, Thursday, May 12, 1932, states: "They took the sleeping garment off him to use to extort money." Very confusing to say the least.

With clock-like regularity the years that have gone before us have taken their respective places in what is known as the deep annals of history. And with their passing, historians have recorded multitudes upon multitudes of note-worthy events. Among these were those that recorded the arrest, trial, conviction, and execution of Bruno Richard Hauptmann. Book after book has been written that detailed his guilt in the crime of kidnapping and murdering the child of Charles and Anne Lindbergh in 1932. Now that we are in the decade of the 1990s, and these years take their positions as part of the immediate past, the complete exoneration of Richard Hauptmann still remains to be recognized by all. Those who are the present authorities in the State of New Jersey, although they were not the guilty ones, hold positions which give them the legal right to take action to set the records straight and clear, once and for all, the name of this innocent man. By doing this, their action will be a glorious answer to the prayers of both his faithful wife, Anna, and his son Manfred.

In 1977 David T. Wilentz issued the following statement:

"If you disbelieve Lindbergh, disbelieve the handwriting experts, the government expert on wood---if you believe District Attorney Foley suppressed evidence, and I suppressed evidence---then of course you have a different story."

YES, MR. WILENTZ, WE HAVE A DIFFERENT STORY!

I trust that from what I have told in the foregoing pages, you are finally convinced, and will from this time on, acknowledge the total vindication of Bruno Richard Hauptmann.

CHAPTER SEVENTY FIVE

The Elusive Fingerprints!

Fingerprints? No fingerprints! No fingerprints of the kidnapper! Possible fingerprints of the kidnapper? Well, maybe! No fingerprints of the kidnapped baby? Probable fingerprints of the kidnapped baby! No fingerprints of the kidnapped baby! Yes, there were fingerprints of the kidnapped baby! What should we believe? What do they expect us to believe? We must believe what we know to be the truth!

On March 1, 1932, after completing his initial investigation into the mysterious disappearance of the child, Trooper Frank Kelly went on record by stating that he had found no fingerprints from anywhere in the nursery --- of anyone. In addition to this we know that no fingerprints of the baby existed anywhere, due to the fact that neither fingerprints, nor toe prints, were taken at the time of his birth, primarily because he had been born at home and not in a hospital.

And because we know this, we can understand the reason that Doctor Hudson was called to the Lindbergh home in early March of 1932 with the hope that by him using his silver-nitrate method of developing latent fingerprints, he could possibly find some undetected, hidden prints of the child. Doctor Hudson went about the home applying his expertise and was successful in raising, from the toys, tables, and high chair (all from rooms other than the nursery) enough latent fingerprints, agreed upon by those present, to be a complete set consisting of the eight fingers and two thumbs that were left by the touch of Charles A. Lindbergh, Jr. upon those surfaces. It was also agreed that these could be used for proper comparison, with others, by a qualified fingerprint expert, or for later identification by a qualified expert in a court of law if the need should arise.

The cards bearing pictures of these prints were then properly marked and identified for future use (possibly in court) by Doctor Hudson, as any qualified identification officer would do, labeling them with; 1.

The name of the person, (or as in this case the name of the one they believed them to be - Charles A. Lindbergh, Jr.); 2. From where they had been raised (in this case the card would have read - The residence of Col. and Mrs. Charles A. Lindbergh, Hopewell, New Jersey); and then 3. The date they were raised and by whom, and possibly showing the name of the photographer. Each individual photo would have a reference identifying the surface from which the latent print was raised.

The mystery of these all important prints deepened for me when, thanks again to the liberty allowed us by the Freedom of Information Act, I first visited the New Jersey State Police Barracks at West Trenton during the 1980s. I had been aware that the Jersey State Police had at least one set of the Doctor Hudson prints. This I knew simply because the doctor had stated that he had given them the original set. In addition to this set he had also provided a set each to Governor Harold G. Hoffman and Mrs. Evalyn Walsh McLean. In all, three sets had been made. Quite possibly he had retained a set for himself.

Since my early years of educational study, I became involved in a detailed study in the identification of fingerprints, and I must admit I was overly anxious to examine the state's copy of the latent prints of the kidnapped child. On my initial visit to the West Trenton barracks, made in the company of Bill Simons, one of the men who believes he is the stolen Lindbergh baby, the first thing I asked to see were the baby's latent prints. To my dismay, Sergeant Cornel Plebani of the State Police, the officer in charge of the Lindbergh-Hauptmann files, informed me that "we don't have them". As a means of proving his statement, he brought me a box, which although it was identified as one containing the baby's prints, when it was opened, proved to be empty, except for what appeared to be a very small piece from the corner of a photographic negative.

As I expressed my disappointment and asked how this could be, Sergeant Plebani, who was trying his best to be helpful, explained that they had been given to the Governor and had never been returned. "But", I questioned immediately, "Why would he have them when he already had a set of his own?" To this claim of mine, Plebani had no answer. "You sure had them in 1977, the day after Easter, when I came here and you took my prints and said you would check mine against those you had!", Simons explained emphasizing his words. "Why would you have bothered to take my prints if you had nothing to compare them with?", Simons had lost his patience. However, since both of us were disappointed at not being able to see the "mysterious prints", we busied ourselves throughout the remainder of the day gathering other important data we needed.

In spite of our failure to locate the missing, elusive pictures of the latent fingerprints, more light was being shed on the possible deception of the police. Since I had read Anthony Scaduto's *Scapegoat*, and later was informed by him through a telephone hook-up with a television program on which I was appearing, that he had been to the West Trenton State Police Barracks during the early 1970s and while there had seen approximately a dozen fingerprints of the child, and about 100 others of adults. When the state police were informed that he was making this claim, Scaduto told us, "They said at first I was mistaken and later claimed I was lying." --- Regardless of what the police say, I believe Tony Scaduto saw the baby's prints, and I'll tell you why.

On October 8, 1985, it was announced in the press that 10 file drawers filled with documents and letters pertaining to the Lindbergh case had been found in a garage in South Amboy, New Jersey, adjacent to the home where Harold Hoffman, the former New Jersey governor, who died in 1954, had once lived with his family. I must say, I wasted very little time reaching the designated address on North Broadway. In answer to my knock at the door, I was informed by a very pleasant housekeeper, Mrs. Hazel Carlisle, that no one had lived there since the death of Mrs. Hoffman the previous December. I was pleased to find Mrs. Carlisle quite helpful, as she went on to explain that at the time of Mrs. Hoffman's death, her only surviving daughter, Mrs. Hope Cross of West Bend, Wisconsin, had come east for the purpose of closing up the home in South Amboy, to dispose of many of her mother's possessions, settle the estate, and ultimately arrange for the sale of the house.

Among the possessions were the recently discovered file drawers loaded with approximately 22,000 Lindbergh-Hauptmann papers which had been found in the two-car garage adjoining the homestead where her mother, Lillie Mae, had been born. Mrs. Carlisle explained that Mrs. Cross had made a donation of these valuable papers to the East Brunswick Museum Corp., and that I should get in touch with a Mr. John Runyon in East Brunswick, New Jersey, the president of the East Brunswick Historical

Museum, to whom Mrs. Cross had given them.

I sought Mr. Runyon at the address Mrs. Carlisle had given me, but found no one at home there. Hoping that I could get some helpful information from the area newspaper, I soon found myself in the news room of *The News Tribune* at Woodbridge, New Jersey, where I met another very cooperative person, Joan Galler, a *News Tribune* staff writer, a young lady who had written some feature stories on the discovery of the long-lost Lindbergh kidnapping documents and seemed to be quite knowledgeable of the case.

Miss Galler went far out of her way to aid me by attempting to reach Mr. Runyon by phone, but when this failed, she handed me the directions to both the museum and his home, including the respective telephone numbers I would need. But my desire to personally speak with Mr. Runyon while I remained in East Brunswick proved unsuccessful.

However, when I arrived back in Phoenixville, I immediately tried to reach him at his home, this time with success. I found Mr. Runyon to be a very agreeable person, who seemed more than willing to speak with me. He explained that he had taken possession of the Lindbergh files, but that the Jersey State Police had learned about Mrs. Cross' gift of them to the museum, with the result that since many of the recently discovered documents had originally been the property of the state police (before Governor Hoffman had borrowed them as an aid to his own investigation into the possible innocence of Hauptmann, and had never been returned), they should now be put in their rightful place, the New Jersey State Police files where the other Lindbergh-Hauptmann memorabilia was lodged. Mr. Runyon further stated that since this was true, he and the police had reached an affable agreement, one that would permit him to have everything carefully inventoried at the museum, copies then made, with the originals to be transported to the state police headquarters at West Trenton. He thanked me for my interest saying he would probably see me at the news conference scheduled to be held the following day at the police barracks. Thanking him for his courtesy, I realized I couldn't have hoped to find a more cooperative person than John Runyon.

However, the press conference planned by State Police Superintendent Clinton L. Pagano did not take place until two weeks later, Tuesday, October 22nd. I learned about the new date from the news releases issued by the AP and UPI to various newspapers. Because of the advance publicity given the news conference, more than a few reporters from area papers called me for any possible comments I might wish to make regarding the cache of Lindbergh-Hauptmann documents that had been recovered, inquiring as to what I expected them to find "Will the child's fingerprints be among these things?", they asked. I strongly affirmed my belief that they would, based on two things of which I was aware. First, I was certain that Governor Hoffman had a set of the prints that I knew were furnished him by Doctor Hudson; and secondly, I was confident he had them because I had a copy of the receipt the governor signed in exchange for them.

The press conference held in the log cabin building on the grounds of the State Police Barracks at West Trenton was the largest one of its kind I ever attended. Representatives from all the major news services were there, as were reporters and camera crews from many television stations; one crew coming from a station in Australia. An atmosphere of intense expectancy prevailed both inside and outside the building, with reporters asking the time worn questions: "What do you think they found?", "Do you think they will find enough to clear Hauptmann?" My answers to most questions put to me were honestly stated: "I really don't know. I doubt if they'll find much new." However, I did make it known that I knew Hauptmann was innocent and had been given a bad rap. "Do you think they found the fingerprints?", they asked. To which I responded, "Yes, I'm sure they now have them!"

But the conference was, as I expected, nothing great. The officials were all there telling us there was nothing new. The massive enlargements made of the nine pictures, supposed to be those of the Lindbergh baby, were used as a back-drop of the table where the "big boys" were seated. Instead of the "big boys" of '34, '35, and '36, I had to listen to statements being issued by the "big boys" of 1985 as they reiterated over and over again that "there is nothing new that shows there was any kind of a frame-up of Hauptmann", oh, yes,- "we did find some evidence that shows he was beaten by the police in New York." And on and on it went - with the members of the press asking their questions, many times superfluous to the very crux of the matter. It was difficult to listen to those persons who claim to be Lindbergh's kidnapped son referred to as nothing more than impostors. This is especially so, since the three I know personally are convinced they have the credentials and documents that will go far to help them prove their case.

Regardless of this, however, there always was and still remains only one certain way to prove that any of them hold the right to their claim. The answer is always the same ---fingerprints! Oh, yes, those enlarged pictures of the child's prints that they now say were found, (in their original size, of course), in the Hoffman garage. Well, what about them? They said, "well we checked them out with the three main challengers, and none of them match, so we are certain these are the correct prints of the Lindbergh baby." Well, I'm not so sure and I'll tell you why!

Immediately at the close of the press conference I walked to the front of the room to inquire of State Police Sergeant Cornel Plebani if I could obtain one of each of the 8 x 10 inch glossy prints of the nine mammoth blow-ups they had so prominently displayed. He assured me that I could have them just as soon as I sent him $5.00 for each, a total of $45.00. Promising him that I would, my friend Cornel was as good as his word. The next week I had the nine glossies in my hands.

From the moment I took the pictures of the prints from the envelope I must admit I had the strangest feeling about them. Sergeant Plebani's accompanying note did not designate in any way what the material was that he had mailed to me, nor did it necessarily have to. I make mention of this merely as a means to have you understand that the note only signified that the enclosed was "the material I requested".

However, the important point I wish to make is the lack of any identification whatsoever. On not one of the prints did it signify that the print was one believed to be a fingerprint of Charles A. Lindbergh, Jr. Age 20 months. Latent print raised from the high chair in the home of Colonel and Mrs. Charles A. Lindbergh, Hopewell, New Jersey, on the 13th day of March 1932. Developed by Erastus Meade Hudson. Every picture lacked the information needed if it had been necessary to present it in court. Doctor Hudson knew this and furnished these details --- but where were they? The bare pictures tell us nothing. They could have been those of "Joe Blow" for all we know.

Since the year 1936, Anna Hauptmann had attempted to prove to all mankind that her husband was innocent of that terrible crime. And for some reason, the authorities, from the likes of those who framed and prosecuted him in 1935 to this very day have been fighting her by blocking every move that dear lady made in her every effort to accomplish this. Robert Bryan, her attorney, is attempting and using every legal means possible in his valiant fight to aid her --- only to see his moves thwarted at every turn. Mr. Bryan has been insistent in his charges that the Flemington trial was loaded with unfair tactics and maneuvers, and so do we, and so do many of the legal experts who actually are saying by their shenanigans that they don't intend to have the system of Jersey justice of 1935 to be seen as anything but honest and fair, and not as slanted, tilted, and bent out of shape as we clearly see it today. Oh, no, they keep saying, we must cover it up in order to maintain the good name of the court system in our great Garden State.

You probably question my reason for making such a strong accusation. O.K. here is why I do it. Based on all the true facts I have presented in this book, plus Robert Bryan's attempts to have a posthumous trial granted for Richard by putting forth strong arguments for this, only to have judge after judge in court after court refuse his petitions by saying there is simply no new evidence is simply ludicrous. To have the present legislative body, plus the others who have served in that capacity throughout the 1980s, after reading the excellent books written by Anthony Scaduto and Ludovic Kennedy, and not make as much as a murmur of a comment as to their personal beliefs is hard to believe, but nonetheless true and very hard to understand. And then to top the whole thing we see the request of Mrs. Anna Hauptmann, a dear 95 year old widow and mother, who has suffered more years of anguish than any other woman, when she asked to be granted an audience of ten minutes with New Jersey's former governor, James Florio, was refused without one word of explanation simply because his attorney general said he should not do this is absolutely sickening to the highest degree. We know why things are conducted in this legal fashion in New Jersey! It is because no one who has any voice of power is willing to get their fingers dirty by delving into the Lindbergh "thing" as it is called this day. Why should we help Hauptmann they all cried in 1936? And they're saying the same thing today.

Now let's get back to the fingerprints. It took only a few minutes for me to think the whole thing through. Since the prints I received from New Jersey had not been properly identified as actually those of the Lindbergh baby, I realized that the authorities expected me to "merely assume" that they were, based on nothing more than "this is what they promised to send me". To have done so would have shown plain stupidity on my part. Instead I became quite skeptical, largely because of my knowledge of fingerprint identification.

Because I knew of the many previous statements that had been made by the authorities in their efforts to apparently confuse the issue of the child's fingerprints, I had become very suspicious about almost everything I was told. I simply did not put any veracity in statements that came out from the West Trenton Barracks. After all, I had the word of Tony Scaduto and Bill Simons. Neither one had hallucinated and were absolutely certain of what they had seen there, and what was more I knew what I had seen. If they never had the prints as they claimed, then why had I been permitted to see an empty box bearing an inscription identifying its contents as the fingerprints of Charles A. Lindbergh, Jr.?

In the past, all of us had received so many unsatisfactory answers. Why, since the police at one time had the Hudson prints, and they were so sure they were the child's prints, is there so much deception about these prints today? The answer is quite evident. Because many people were aware that the cremated remains of the corpse found on May 12th, 1932 were not those of the Lindbergh baby there is still the possibility that the real Lindbergh child will be found and proven to be alive today. And if and when that happens, and it could, their entire case against Richard Hauptmann will fall into a "heap of ashes", the same kind as those of the remains of that cremated corpse. That is why there is so much ceaseless deception about the Hudson fingerprints of the child to this very day.

With the discovery of the prints found in the Hoffman garage at South Amboy (which I certainly accept as being those of the Lindbergh baby based entirely on Doctor Hudson's statement), and the necessary copies made in the East Brunswick museum, it would, once and for all time settle the argument as to who the Lindbergh child is, should he be alive today. All of those claiming to be the stolen Lindbergh baby should have their fingerprints compared at once with those found in the garage and that will end any argument pronto. The claims of those who do not match will end immediately, unless a comparison of at least the ridges of one finger can be made. Once that is done, that person must then be declared the son of Charles and Anne Lindbergh.

But, I again asked myself, let us assume they don't want anyone to be identified as the lost baby? I reasoned that it would be a grave mistake, a terrible error, to have someone prove he is Lindbergh's son today, especially so since those "brilliant cops and lawyers" back in the '30s said Hauptmann killed him all by himself. If anyone should prove today that he is that kidnapped baby, then it stands to reason that there was no murder, that Hauptmann did not kill anybody, and without going one step further, it would prove unquestionably that they all conspired to take the life of an innocent man who had shed the blood of no one. The state had committed murder, a terrible indictment.

With my vast knowledge of the crime, I am not gullible enough to believe that there are none among the intelligentsia, which includes those of the law enforcement body of the state of New Jersey, who refuse to believe that Hauptmann was not only innocent, but framed as well. Instead, I believe there are many whose conscience tell them that he was innocent, and because of this, they would like to do something about it, but nevertheless fear to do so. Probably these honest folk have been waiting, and hoping, that someone would start something in an attempt to clear Hauptmann's name. I believe Brendon Byrne, former governor of New Jersey, is one of these fair-minded persons. I heard him state publicly on television that he still cannot understand how one person (Hauptmann) could have committed that crime alone.

But on the other side of the issue, we have those persons we must deal with today. The present officials I speak of are those who, had they been living during those days of the "Flemington Fiasco" of the '30s, would have, in all probability, treated Hauptmann in the same manner as those corrupt officials when they developed their own "criminal science" of wantonly "successfully maneuvering and manipulating" an innocent man into the electric chair. Today, there are certain New Jersey officials who continue to throw smoke screens in front of the known facts, making it clearly evident that their primary purpose regarding the Lindbergh kidnapping case is to cover it all up to protect and save the faces of those "very honorable men", those "great dishonorable cads of power" who were willing to sell their souls and blatantly lie again and again to bring nothing but shame and dishonor to the great state of New Jersey.

Should you choose to disagree with that statement, then I must ask you how one can explain away all the moves that have taken place as the authorities in New Jersey still refuse Anna Hauptmann her legal right to protest the illegal method the state used to take the life of her husband when so much evidence exists today that prove his innocence? The courts say that her attorney, Robert Bryan, has shown nothing in the way of new evidence, even stressing that there was nothing irregular in the way the trial was conducted in Flemington. If new evidence is needed and they cannot see it, then I again ask them to read the books written by Scaduto and Kennedy, and then this one. No new evidence! What more do they want? Every plea ever made to them by Anna Hauptmann herself has been rejected, including her last one to Governor Jim Florio. I claim that New Jersey is running scared --- running away from having to eventually face the truth about the Lindbergh case. And I have many good reasons for making that statement.

After I received the pictures of the fingerprints I was expected to believe were those of the latent prints as developed by Doctor Hudson. I made a study of them. I soon became deeply bothered with a thought I could not pass off. A thought that constantly troubled me. It kept troubling me to the extent that I could not concentrate on anything else; my suspicious, investigative mind would not let me alone. I was being plagued with thoughts that caused me deep concern --- and anger. Had there been a switch? Is it possible, I kept asking myself, that these prints were not those of the Lindbergh baby? Had the baby's prints been substituted with those of another person? If that were true, then the ones I received were actually the fingerprints of some unknown person whose prints could never be matched with those of any of the men who are claiming to be Lindbergh's kidnapped son.

My thoughts raced on. To successfully do this there must have been someone at the New Jersey police barracks who was willing to substitute other latent prints of a "Mr. Unknown", or possibly a "Mrs. Unknown", or even those of a child, and then make a switch in their files? And then from that time on and forever after, to be identified and cataloged as the latent prints Doctor Hudson had developed in the Lindbergh home in 1932 and cataloged as those of the kidnapped baby?

My mind continued to run away with such thoughts of evil deception that possibly had been perpetrated by some Jersey authorities. At this stage of my investigation, my suspicious mind reasoned that anything was possible. I rationalized that those who made the actual switch in the files would not necessarily have been the ones involved in the possible "deception". Without knowing that a change had been made, they could have placed the "substituted" prints in the official files - thus, with absolute unawareness, they had performed their duty well, becoming an innocent party in another despicable act of deception planned by one or more persons in the state of New Jersey who were still making every attempt to save the reputations of the very "deceivers" who killed poor Richard Hauptmann by very unlawful means.

With thoughts such as these running through my over-active mind, I suddenly realized that my suspicions could possibly be proven. I remembered that John Runyon had told me in my first conversation with him that he was presently busy making copies of all the material that had been found in the Hoffman garage, and following the completion of this, the State Police were going to transport the originals to their West Trenton Barracks for proper filing with the rest of the Lindbergh case material. This fact had also been published in the newspapers.

Now, since this had been done, I reasoned further, the copies of the original latent fingerprints would have remained in the East Brunswick museum, the originals would then be taken to the State Police files, and then, if as I suspicioned, the actual originals could be replaced with the prints of "someone else", each place would then have different pictures, both to be exhibited with claims as having been the "authentic find" from the garage. The museum would be housing copies of the original, while the police would have a set of "phonies" in their files which they could now feel safe in "pawning off" to the public as the "real" fingerprints of the baby. My distrust must be unfair.

However, I reasoned further that if I wanted proof that my suspicions had any validity, I realized I must visit the museum where it would be possible for me to compare those that had been sent to me by Sergeant Plebani with the copies John Runyon had made from the originals in order that he would have a set for him to display in the museum. Since I was aware that the transaction, as agreed upon between the museum and the State Police, had been completed, and providing there had been no "hanky-panky", then I would find that the two sets, the original and the copy, matched in every detail; and the set I held would also dovetail, proving that no switch had been made. If I found this to be the case, then I could put my suspicions to rest.

But on the other hand, if a switch had been made, it would be forever impossible for a successful comparison to be made with the prints of any of the persons claiming to be Lindbergh's son. Could it be, I wondered, that this was their intent and purpose? How could I think such things, I asked myself? If someone had the gall to do this, the message it triggered was a clear one ---the "big boys" of today are still fighting every move Anna Hauptmann made to clear her husband's name, and now, by this final act, they have fostered another attempt to protect the names of their counterparts who perpetrated such evil conspiracies in the 1930s.

I could not rest until I visited John Runyon and examine the "child's fingerprints" he had retained at the East Brunswick Museum. But I soon found I would have to wait. My first trip to East Brunswick brought no results. My visit to a closed museum (a sign informed me it was open only on Saturdays and Sundays), and my knocks on the front door at the Runyon home brought no response, had made my journey fruitless. Nevertheless, I left notes at both doors asking that John telephone me since I deemed it rather important that I speak with him.

Several days passed during which time I waited anxiously for a call from the president of the museum. But I received none. Another visit was made to East Brunswick without success. Again more notes were left behind asking him to place a collect call to me. Still no answers. Recorded messages I left for him on answering machines remained unanswered. To say the least, I was becoming quite exasperated. It irritated me that a professional man, holding such an important position, and involved as he was in the Lindbergh case, could ignore my request to return a harmless telephone call after I had made at least eight or ten attempts to reach him. I must admit that I could not control my growing suspicions. I continually wondered why he was deliberately ignoring me. After all, I concluded, his failure to get in touch with me was downright intentional. Was there a solid foundation for the suspicions I held from the very start of my "fingerprint chase"? I simply could not believe it, and yet, what were they hiding? What hidden truths might I discover if I were to put forth a more earnest attempt to find them? Would I be unsuccessful by not finding any? I surely didn't know, but I was determined to try to find the answer. Without making any advance plans, my opportunity to do this came along unexpectedly.

A few days had elapsed since my last attempt to talk to John Runyon, and I was telling my youngest son, Rick, of my failure to reach John, explaining that I believed he was deliberately avoiding me. Our son, who live in Lancaster, Pennsylvania, was spending the day with us, and after hearing me explain my dilemma, he fairly leaped out of his chair, exclaiming, "Come on! We're going to the museum now! He won't know we're coming and we can catch him there!" Since it was a Saturday afternoon and I knew the museum would be open, no coaxing on my part was necessary. Off we went, headed for East Brunswick, New Jersey.

Arriving there, we entered the museum, and were approached by a very pleasant woman. We introduced ourselves and informed her that I wished to see Mr. Runyon, but was disappointed to learn that he was at his home. Relating that I had hoped to see him personally to discuss the recent acquisition of the Lindbergh material he had obtained for the museum, she immediately volunteered to reach him by phone and tell him of my visit. After a few minutes away, while she made her call, she returned to inform us that Mr. Runyon would be with us shortly. While we waited, our friendly hostess allowed us to glance in the closet where the Lindbergh files had been stored.

Approximately one half hour later, John Runyon mounted the steps and entered the building. I met him with a warm handclasp and a very friendly manner, telling him that since Rick and I were in the area, we thought we would drop in to say hello and at the same time had hoped to look at some of the Lindbergh memorabilia. However, my friendly demeanor failed to put John Runyon at ease. He generated a feeling that he was not at all glad to see me. I watched him constantly, hoping he would look me straight in the face, but he not only appeared to be, but was very much ill at ease.

Finally I asked him why he had not returned my phone calls, only to be told that he had returned them. I explained that the only calls he returned had been those prior to the press conference in West Trenton on October 22nd. Although he denied this, I reasoned there would be no purpose to argue that point since here I was now requesting permission to see the Lindbergh material. "Well, anyway, John, may I see the things you acquired?", I asked in my friendliest manner. "Oh, no, you can't see it unless I get the permission from my board of directors!", the man informed me. "But, John, you are the president. The things were given to you by Hope Cross back in April. This is a museum where people come to see things. Why can't you let us see them? I have a great interest in the case and want to see them", I fairly pleaded with him.

"I'll tell you what I'll do", Runyon replied. "If I can get the permission of my board, if they okay it, then you can see them", he stated. This explanation seemed somewhat ridiculous since Runyon was the president, and the gift of the collection had been made personally to him by Mrs. Cross. Why, I thought to myself, did he need the consent of the entire board of directors? I reasoned at this point that I would have to consent to this if it was necessary. If there was to be even a remote possibility that I was to see the material he had locked so safely away from the eyes of the public as well as those persons who were vitally interested in the case. "Let me go make a phone call.", he said. And off he went to make a phone call --- something I had not received from him when I needed his help.

As we waited, from my vantage point I could watch John Runyon as he discussed my request with "whoever". His conversation continued for a "long time", nearly ten minutes, while we waited "patiently" for him to return. By this time our minds began to play tricks on us: "Rick.", I said, "I think he's calling the State Police for instructions as to what he should do." Rick agreed: "I believe it. What would be taking him so long?" As we continued to mumble to each other in low tones about the way we were being put off, John returned.

"Well, I got it all straightened out. But you'll have to wait until the next board meeting, Okay?", John was beaming by now, he had been taken off the hook. "When is the next meeting?", I inquired. "Next Thursday night", John announced. "Fine," I assured him, "We can wait until then. John, will you be kind enough to let me know their answer?", I asked. "I sure will", the worthy president of the East Brunswick Historical Museum promised me. "Will you let me know the answer whatever way the decision goes?", I most graciously asked. "I'll be glad to, either way" was his friendly answer. We took our leave --- never to hear from John Runyon again.

What was I to think? Had my suspicions been unfounded? Could I have possibly been wrong? Or does the equation fit the problem? The enigma stems from someone stealing an innocent little 20-month old baby boy, an act which was to become known as "The Crime of the Century". A crime which brought millions of people to their knees in prayer in churches all over the world; one which brought thousands to their feet in prayer as they attended a boxing match in Madison Square Garden; one which pushed the news of the Japanese-Chinese War off the front pages of our newspapers; one that spawned and "gave birth" to such a host of liars during the Hauptmann trial, who by their evil deeds committed an even greater crime, the evidence of which remains forever on "our stage of life".

Richard Hauptmann had said: "The book, it will never close." Although that may be true, I am certain that his name has finally been cleared. This I can say to the glory of God, and to the lasting joy and relief of Anna, Manfred and Erica Hauptmann.

THE END!

EPILOGUE!

One of the questions I have been called upon to answer, more than possibly any others, has been: "If that wasn't the body of the Lindbergh baby, could he still be alive today?" And my well-worn answer has always been: "Absolutely, unless he has either died a natural or an accidental death in the meantime." And then, their questions are usually followed by: "Of all those who claim to be Lindbergh's son, which one do you think is?" And that, my friends, is more than a $64,000 question. Unless at least one of the <u>indisputable</u> fingerprints of the child is found, that question, in all probability, will never be answered. However, it is a question which presents itself as suitable for any of us who wish to offer an honest guess.

As I mentioned earlier, of those who made their claims to the title many years ago, each one earnestly believing himself to be the kidnapped son of Charles and Anne Lindbergh, there are three major contenders. These three are distinguished from possibly fifty others who also are seeking recognition for their claims. Personally I am not aware of their names, however, I do know each of the three major claimants, and not one of them is an imposter.

Harold Roy Olson is a computer supply salesman from Westport, Connecticut, who has spent twenty-eight years of his life attempting to prove his identity as that of Charles Lindbergh, Jr. During that time his efforts have cost him at least $100,000.

Mr. Olson, according to his birth certificate, has him registered as being born on April 8, 1928, a difference that would have him to be slightly more than two years and two months older than the Lindbergh child. However, Olson has quite a few bonafide arguments which makes one "sit up and take notice". In addition to a remarkable resemblance to pictures of Anne Lindbergh, he had undergone surgery on his face as a young lad, has been forced to hide in a basement to keep him from being seen, has a birthmark similar to one the Lindbergh baby had, has the turned-in toes, and other very persuasive points, even to the possible connection of Al Capone, the notorious gangster, being involved in the crime. To say the very least, there has always been, and possibly always will be, an aura of mystery pertaining to the identity of Harold Olson and the very significant likelihood of his being the Lindbergh child. Because I have only had the privilege of talking with Mr. Olson and his lovely wife on two or three occasions, I can honestly say that I found him to be a very fine and serious man who is quite sincere relative to his convictions of being the lost Lindbergh child. Very definitely he has not, in any way ever, presented himself as being an imposter.

The next fellow, Kenneth Kerwin, has through the passing of time, become a rather good friend of mine. He also is represented by attorney Robert Bryan. There have been several occasions when Ken and I have appeared together publicly as we bring the "true story of the Lindbergh kidnapping" to interested audiences. Kenneth William Kerwin was born, according to existing records on February 27, 1932, in Portland, Maine; with another certificate giving a record to his birth as having taken place on that same date in North Yarmouth, Maine. Both birth certificates coincide as to the names of both his parents. The recorded date of his birth would establish his age as approximately two years younger than baby "Lindy". Be that as it may, however, Mr. Kerwin also has much going for him in his arguments to prove "who he really is", something he started to do fifty years ago.

First of all, many of Kerwin's photographs, those taken as a child and as an adult, show a remarkable resemblance of him to the kidnapped baby and Colonel Lindbergh. Among the documents Kenneth has to fortify his claim is a sworn affidavit given by a Mrs. Laura LaDue, who claims that at the time of the kidnapping a couple lost their child through death and that the one found and identified as the Lindbergh child was actually theirs. Mrs. LaDue stated that the body of the couple's baby was switched with the live Lindbergh child, who today is none other than Kenneth Kerwin. This affidavit is substantiated by the Reverend Robert D. Witham, Pastor of The United Church of Northfield, Vermont.

Kerwin has given me a rather interesting account of what took place when he came face to face with Colonel Lindbergh: "I told him I had something to show him as I met him at the door of his home in Darien, Connecticut. He froze when he saw me. He refused to listen and told me if I had anything, to take it to the police. As I started to leave, the police arrived and took me into their custody. When they had me in jail the police looked over my documents and appeared to be very interested. Some of the police promised to take them to Lindbergh, but later told me he refused to even look at them himself. The police pressed no charges against me, so I was set free but told not to come back to Connecticut again."

Kenneth Kerwin continues to make a determined effort to prove himself Charles Lindbergh, Jr. He has developed his investigation to include a possible tie-in between families of the Kerwins to those of Doctor John Francis Condon. In addition, Kenneth has a letter in his possession from a gentleman who practices the science of extrasensory perception. It reads in part: "I declare Kenneth W. Kerwin to be the son of Col. Charles A. Lindbergh, who was kidnapped and later reported to be dead and cremated." It was signed by Alexander Tanous, who had determined his finding by "astro-projection and bi-location". Whatever that is, it should be considered, at the very least, another factor pointing to the fact that the corpse found was not that of the kidnapped baby. Again, I must say that Kenneth William Kerwin is not just another imposter. He is a very honest and sincere gentleman, seeking the identity of the person he believes himself to be.

The final one of the three major claimants whose wish is to be recognized as the first born son of the Lindberghs is a man named William Simons, formerly of Eagle, Pennsylvania. Of the three men, he has been the least publicized, merely because he had not been aware of the possibility that he could be the son of the famous aviator and his wife until the year 1977. And he has a very good reason for this. The following is a condensation of what he told me on the night he summoned me to see him at his home in 1977.

When he was a youth, Bill Simons was told that he was an orphan. The man who raised him had very bluntly informed him that he and his wife were not his biological parents. And from that time on young Simons attempted to trace his roots in an effort to locate his natural parents. The earliest record he found of himself was at the Rockingham County Farm, in New Hampshire where he had been brought on Sunday, May 15, 1932 as a ward of the state. (It would be well to note here that the date happened to be just three days after the discovery of the decomposed corpse along the Hopewell-Princeton highway, possibly only a coincidence.)

Simons continued his search, but with no success. The birth certificate he carried was proven to be false when it was determined that the person whose name it listed as his mother, was not authentic since the date on the certificate would have placed Bill as being born in prison while she was incarcerated. She definitely had no children during that time. Furthermore, she had only four children legally born to her. Bill would have been her fifth, proving to him that he was not her child. The years continued on and Bill gave up concentrating on finding his true parentage, and was more or less content with what little he had already found.

During the late winter of 1977, Bill, while doing some carpentry work in an empty house not far from his own, opened a drawer of a cabinet and found an old newspaper from the year 1932. Its front page carried the story of the Lindbergh kidnapping. Bill, thinking it was of no value to anyone, took it with him as a good collector's item.

Several weeks later, a few days before Easter, he took note of the picture of the kidnapped Lindbergh baby. He studied it for only a moment or two, and then shouted, "My God! That's me!"

Since that time, Bill and I have appeared together on television on three occasions. We have been together as we presented "the Hauptmann cause" at various service club meetings. There can be no doubt about it that Bill Simons does resemble Charles Lindbergh; while his daughter bears a remarkable likeness to Anne Lindbergh, so much so that when Bill exhibited her picture on live television, the audience gave a very audible gasp.

Quite seriously he says: "All I want to do is see my mother. When she sees me, she will immediately know that I am her Charles. Something deep inside her will tell her that. I know that she is my mother." Hearing him say these things, it is very hard to doubt him. He is quite sincere about it all.

Valerie Morrison, the renowned psychic, unequivocally states that Bill Simons is the lost son of the Lindberghs. It is not for this reason that I believe he is. Members of my family who have seen Bill in our home tell me they believe he is. "Why, he even stands like Lindbergh," says my daughter Barbara. It is not for reasons such as these that I could possibly believe that he is. But, it is for this reason that I think he certainly could be.

Bill has told me things he remembers as a child.

He recollects a train ride with a man and a woman, crying to be taken to his mother, while the woman attempted to comfort him, saying "We are taking you to your mother." He remembers nightmares as a little boy; of watching other little boys and girls go into a door together (possibly Elisabeth Morrow's "Little School" at Next Day Hill); he recalls being whipped and put in a closet at a place called St. Charles' Orphanage, among other things such as sitting on a wharf and watching the ships.

However, there is one thing that does disturb me so much that when I first heard it from Bill the sensation I experienced seemed to run up my spine. It caused me to accept Bill's explanation as a perfectly logical answer to a question I asked him: "Bill what was it that prompted you to say 'My God! That's me!' when you saw the picture of the Lindbergh baby on the front page of the newspaper?" Bill's answer was short and reasonable. "When I saw that kid's picture there, I saw myself. It was me, the way I looked when I used to see myself in mirrors when I was that age. It was like I was seeing me, and it shook me and I knew I was looking at me when I was a kid." Bill went on to explain to me about the strange driving force he had experienced, one which motivated him to go to the West Trenton barracks two days later.

I don't think we have the right to even question Bill's explanation. We should, however, keep in mind that the Bible tells us that the Lord moves in mysterious ways His wonders to perform. However, at this point in time no one knows if any of these men are the son of Charles and Anne Lindbergh, just remember --- no one will until the fingerprints are found.

Finding them still remains a possibility if we keep in mind what Doctor Hudson said after he developed those little latent fingerprints in the Lindbergh home: "From the baby's books and toys, we were able to produce enough palm and fingerprints ... to identify or disqualify, without dispute, any living Lindbergh baby that might be presented in the future." These prints were developed by Doctor Hudson on Friday, March 13th, 1932 --- the big question is, where are they today? And why are they hiding them?

Regardless of the truthful facts I made in my statement above, I must dispute one made by Irwin I. Kimmelman, former Attorney General of New Jersey, in which he said the documents, which included fingerprints taken from the child's crib and toys, "do not cast any doubt whatsoever on the justice of the verdict, nor do they in any way change the outcome of the trial." In addition to this he claimed "the state police compared the fingerprints to those of members of the Lindbergh household and three men who claim they are Lindbergh's son." These statements, made by Mr. Kimmelman, were taken from an article which appeared in the Fostoria, Ohio *Review-Times*, dated October 23, 1985. I would like to remind the former attorney general that <u>no prints were ever found on the crib, and that at no time did Mr. Olson, Mr. Kerwin, or Mr. Simons ever have their prints compared with those that were lifted in the Lindbergh home by Doctor Hudson</u>.

Another very pertinent question that I am asked, has to do with my belief as to "who was guilty" of the crime. My belief is based on knowledge which I have already expounded to in this volume. However, I will answer it here in a short concise form. From the facts as we know them, I name Oliver Whateley as the inside man in the Lindbergh home; Violet Sharpe as the informant-helper in the Morrow home; Isidor Fisch as "Cemetery John" and possibly the person who went up the ladder into the nursery; Martin Stover who took the child out of the country; and Paul H. Wendel who planned the kidnapping and directed the operation. By naming these, we still have two unidentified persons, the woman who met Condon at the bazaar while he was selling violins, and the person, a male Italian voice Condon heard on the telephone. A total of seven people, if there were any more I have no evidence of them.

My study of this famous case has taken me to many places, all of them locations connected with the crime. Because I am a very nostalgic person, together with being a very curious one, I always leave the reality of this present life whenever I visit these historic spots. At the Hopewell home of the Lindberghs my thoughts take me back in time to all that took place in that famous yesteryear of 1932; my thoughts at the Hauptmann home in the Bronx affect me the same way as I lose myself in memories of what took place there in 1934; a trip to Flemington and the famous old court house causes a sensation all its own as the trial comes to life again. (It actually did come to life for me on Sunday, September 30, 1990 when my good friend Charles Gutkowski and I had the privilege of sitting on the jury to see and hear the excellent re-enactment of the famous trial, which was so well written by Mr. Harry Kazman and his wife Reva, who helped him produce and direct it. The cast was well selected and did a superb job.) My emotions whenever I visit Woodlawn and St. Raymond's Cemeteries, Van Cortlandt Park, and the homes of the Hauptmann's, the Lindberghs, the Morrow's, Condon's and others always have strong nostalgic affect on me.

But of all the places I have visited relating to the history of the famous case none of them have the affect on me as my walk down the entire length of "Lindbergh Lane". And while my mind dwells on things from the past, primarily that this is the point from where tragedy struck so many years ago, I cannot help but wonder how Betty Gow and Elsie Whateley felt when their eyes fell upon the shiny thumb guard near the entrance of "High Fields" a month after the childs abduction? Is it possible that this was another practical joke of Colonel Lindbergh?

W.D.J.

CHRONOLOGY OF MAJOR EVENTS
IN THE LINDBERGH KIDNAPPING CASE

Tuesday, March 1, 1932 - Charles A. Lindbergh, Jr. is kidnapped from his Hopewell, New Jersey home between 8 and 10 p.m.
Saturday, March 12, 1932 - John F. "Jafsie" Condon meets with "Cemetery John" in Woodlawn Cemetery and Van Cortlandt Park.
Saturday, April 2, 1932 - "Jafsie" Condon, pays $50,000 ransom to "Cemetery John" in St. Raymond's Cemetery. No baby is returned.
Thursday, May 12, 1932 - A corpse is found off the side of the Hopewell-Princeton highway and is identified as the stolen baby.
Friday, June 10, 1932 - Violet Sharpe, maid in the Morrow home in Englewood, New Jersey, commits suicide instead of facing police.
Wednesday, September 19, 1934 - Bruno Richard Hauptmann is arrested and charged with the kidnapping and murder of the baby.
Friday, October 19, 1934 - Hauptmann is taken to Flemington, New Jersey to await trial in Hunterdon County.
Wednesday, January 2, 1935 - Trial begins in the century-old court house in Flemington.
Wednesday, February 13, 1935 - Hauptmann is found guilty of first degree murder and is sentenced to death in the electric chair.
Friday, April 3, 1936 - Bruno Richard Hauptmann is executed for the crime at the State Prison in Trenton at 8:47 1/2 p.m.

COST OF LINDBERGH CASE TO STATE OF NEW JERSEY EXCEEDED $1,888,000

Length of Trial - 32 days ---
Total Witnesses Called 156.
Total Exhibits - 380.
Trial Transcript - More than 1,500,000 Words In Printed Forms.

PERSONS WHO SHARED IN THE REWARD OFFERED

Walter Lyle - $7,500
William Allen - $5,000
William Cody - $2,000
William Strong - $2,000
Cecile Barr - $1,000
Amandus Hochmuth - $1,000
John Lyons - $1,000
Joseph Perrone - $1,000
Millard Whited - $1,000
Charles Rossiter - $500

OTHER CHILDREN BORN TO CHARLES AND ANNE MORROW LINDBERGH

Jon Morrow, born August 16, 1932; Land Morrow, born May 20, 1937; Anne Spencer, born in 1940; Scott Morrow, born in 1942; Reeve Morrow, born in 1945.

Colonel Charles A. Lindbergh died on August 26, 1974 at Maui, Hawaii and is buried at Kipahulu.

SOURCES

SCAPEGOAT by Anthony Scaduto, G.P. Putnam's Sons, 1976.
THE AIRMAN AND THE CARPENTER, by Ludovic Kennedy, Viking, 1985.
KIDNAP, by George Waller, The Dial Press, 1961.
HYSTERIA LINDBERGH KIDNAP CASE, by Andrew Dutch, Dorrance and Co., 1975.
LINDBERGH A BIOGRAPHY, by Leonard Mosley, Doubleday & Company, Inc., 1976.
THE TRIAL OF BRUNO RICHARD HAUPTMANN, by Sidney B. Whipple, Doubleday, Doran & Company, Inc., 1937.
THE LINDBERGH CRIME, by Sidney B. Whipple, Blue Ribbon Books, 1935.
THE HAND OF HAUPTMANN, by J. Vreeland Haring, The Hamer Publishing Co., 1937.
THE CRIME AND THE CRIMINAL, by Dudley D. Shoenfeld, M.D., Covici.Friede, 1936.
THE LINDBERGHS, by P.J. O'Brien, International Press, 1935.
LINDBERGH, A BIOGRAPHY, by Leonard Mosley, Doubleday & Company, Inc., 1976.
LINDBERGH OF MINNESOTA, by Bruce L. Larson, Harcourt Brace Jovanovich, 1971.
JAFSIE TELLS ALL!, by John F. Condon, Jonathan Lee Publishing Corp, 1936.
THE LINDBERGH KIDNAPPING CASE, by Ovid Demaris, Monarch Books, Inc., 1961.
WHERE MY SHADOW FALLS, by Leon G. Turrou, Doubleday & Company, Inc., 1949.
TRUE STORY OF THE LINDBERGH KIDNAPPING, by John Brant and Edith Renaud, Kroy Wen Publishers, Inc., 1932.
THE GREAT LINDBERGH HULLABALOO, by Laura Vitray, William Faro, Inc., 1932.
NORTH TO THE ORIENT, by Anne Morrow Lindbergh, Harcourt Brace and Co., 1935.
BRING ME A UNICORN, DIARIES AND LETTERS OF ANNE MORROW LINDBERGH, 1922-1928, Harcourt Brace Jovanovich, 1971, 1972.
HOUR OF GOLD, HOUR OF LEAD, DIARIES AND LETTERS OF ANNE MORROW LINDBERGH, 1929-1932, Harcourt Brace Jovanovich, 1973.

LOCKED ROOMS AND OPEN DOORS, DIARIES AND LETTERS OF ANNE MORROW LINDBERGH, 1933-1935, Harcourt Brace Jovanovich, 1974.
THE FLOWER AND THE NETTLE, DIARIES AND LETTERS OF ANNE MORROW LINDBERGH, 1936-1939, Harcourt Brace Jovanovich, 1976.
WAR WITHIN AND WAR WITHOUT, DIARIES AND LETTERS OF ANNE MORROW LINDBERGH, 1939-1944, Harcourt Brace Jovanovich, 1980.
LISTEN, THE WIND, by Anne Morrow Lindbergh, Harcourt Brace, 1938.
THE LAST HERO: CHARLES A LINDBERGH, by Walter S. Ross, Manor Books, Inc., 1964.
IN SEARCH OF THE LINDBERGH BABY, by Theon Wright, Tower Books, 1981.
THE MINISTER AND THE CHOIR SINGER, by William M. Kunstler, A Dell Book, 1964.
THE WARTIME JOURNALS OF CHARLES A. LINDBERGH, by Charles A. Lindbergh, Harcourt Brace Jovanovich, Inc. 1970
CHARLES A. LINDBERGH AUTOBIOGRAPHY OF VALUES, by Charles A. Lindbergh, Harcourt Brace Jovanovich, 1976.
THE SPIRIT OF ST. LOUIS, by Charles A. Lindbergh, Charles Scribner's Sons, 1953.
WE, by Charles A. Lindbergh, G.P. Putnam's Sons, 1927.
LINDBERGH ALONE, by Brendan Gill, Harcourt Brace Jovanovich, 1977.
THE STORY OF LINDBERGH THE LONE EAGLE, by Richard J. Beamish, The International Press, 1927.
THE LINDBERGH CASE, by Jim Fisher, Rutgers University Press, 1987.
WORD PICTURES OF THE HAUPTMANN TRIAL, by Gabriel Heatter
THE LINDBERGH-HAUPTMANN KIDNAP-MURDER CASE, by Marcet Haldemun-Julius, Haldeman-Julius Publications,
THE CRIME-THE CASE-THE CHALLENGE, WHAT WAS WRONG WITH THE LINDBERGH CASE?, by Harold G. Hoffman, Former Governor of New Jersey, (Personal Bound Volume), 1938.
THINGS I FORGOT TO TELL, by Harold G. Hoffman, Liberty Magazine, July 2, 1938.
MORE THINGS I FORGOT TO TELL, by Harold G. Hoffman, Liberty Magazine, July 9, 1938.
EVERYBODY WANTED TO GET INTO THE ACT, by Alan Hynd, True Magazine, March 1949.
THE CASE NEW JERSEY WOULD LIKE TO FORGET, by C. Lloyd Fisher, Liberty Magazine, August 1, 8, 15, 22, 29, September 5, 12, 1936.
WHY DID YOU KILL ME?, by Bruno Richard Hauptmann, Liberty Magazine, May 2, 1936.
HOW I CAPTURED HAUPTMANN, by Lieutenant James J. Finn

and D. Thomas Curtin, Liberty Magazine, October 12, 19, 26, November 2, 9, 16, 23, 1935.
WAS THE LINDBERGH BABY EVER REALLY FOUND? by Alan Hynd, Confidential Magazine.
WILL LINDBERGH SAVE HAUPTMANN? by Edward J. Reilly, Liberty Magazine, October 5, 1935.
WHY I AM STILL INVESTIGATING THE LINDBERGH CASE, by Evalyn Walsh McLean, Liberty Magazine, 1938.
A SCIENTIFIC VERDICT ON THE LINDBERGH HAUPTMANN RIDDLE, by Dr. Erastus Mead Hudson, Liberty Magazine, 1937.
DID THEY REALLY SOLVE THE LINDBERGH CASE?, by Craig Thompson, The Saturday Evening Post, March 3, 1952.
BRUNO RICHARD HAUPTMANN: KILLER OR VICTIM? by Peter Yerkes, The Philadelphia Inquirer, April 9, 1978.
DID THE EVIDENCE FIT THE CRIME?, by Tom Zito, Life Magazine, March 1982.
LEGACY OF A KIDNAPPING, by Ben Yagoda, New Jersey Monthly, August 1981.
50 UNANSWERED QUESTIONS IN THE HAUPTMANN CASE, by Lou Wedemar, Liberty Magazine, January 4, 1936.
FINAL VERDICT, by Adela Rogers St.Johns, Doubleday and Co., 1962.
STATE OF NEW JERSEY VS. HAUPTMANN, Official Trial Record and State Exhibits, Pages 1 thru 4791 with Appeals, 1935.
AN AMERICAN SAGA, by Robert Daley, Random House, 1980.
KILGALLEN, by Lee Israel, Delacorte Press, 1979.
SPECIAL PEOPLE, by Julie Nixon Eisenhower, Ballantine Books, 1977.
DR. SAM, AN AMERICAN TRAGEDY, by Jack Harrison Pollack, Avon Books, 1972.

ACKNOWLEDGMENTS

This book could not have been written had it not been for the help of many persons. For this, I will ever remain deeply grateful for the various contributions each one has made.

I first want to thank my wife Anna Mae for the countless hours she spent, working tirelessly hour after hour, compiling the thousands of pages of notes, and the arranging and the filing of them, which was necessary before the words could take their respective places in the manuscript of this book.

I am deeply grateful to my two daughters, Patty and Barbara, who spent many, many hours editing the text. My sincere thanks to my sons, Rick and Dave, his wife Debbie, and my son-in-law, Helmut who constantly gave me their words of encouragement, and for the help they offered.

My special thanks are forever extended to my good friends, Jim Overstreet and Bill West, my brother, Art Faddis and his wife, Peg, who when finances were so urgently needed, came to my rescue because of their faith in my project. They will never realize the help and encouragement they gave me. And then, to Jose and Pam Rivera, who not only helped me financially, but offered to finance a two-week trip for me to travel down to Colombia, South America. However, it was only the fear of many for my safety down there that kept me from making this trip.

As for Pam Rivera, who had the monumental task of taking on the final and complete editing of every word and page of this book and then laser printing it in its final form, I can never thank her enough. The efforts and hours she put into this work were always without complaint.

Bob New certainly deserves my special thanks. His monumental gift of a computer, a word processor, enabled me to complete this large volume in one-tenth the time it would have taken had I used a typewriter. To Bob I will always be grateful for his extreme generosity. To those good friends who were always willing to drive me to my many speaking engagements, Bill Stow, Ray Trego, Art Faddis, Charles Gutkowski, Frank Davis, Bill Scherfel, Don Foulke, Sam Barkley, Rich Kirkner, Bob New, Herb Coale, and Rick Rhoads.

I sincerely thank Thelma Miller of Three Bridges,

New Jersey, for allowing me to have copies made of her valuable collection of Hauptmann trial photographs, and to my friends Dave Smith for taking me to New Jersey on several occasions and making the copies, and Barry Taglieber who made such excellent enlargements for me.

Dick Cass and I became fast friends during the time we attempted to raise the funds to produce the docudrama on the case. Dick gave everything he had, his time and his money in our unsuccessful venture, and I shall be forever indebted to him for, not only his desire to produce the film, but for his unwavering faith in Richard Hauptmann's innocence.

To Bernie Herman who had me as a guest on his radio talk show on two occasions. The first time he was a doubter, the second time he was a believer. To Richard Hayes who invited me to come on his talk show and gave me the liberty to exploit the proof I had of Hauptmann's innocence from coast to coast, because he, too, was a believer. And then to Joe Lombardo, the talk show host in Baltimore, who was so kind by having me tell my story to his listeners along the Atlantic seacoast. To Peter Goldsmith for arranging and producing a great documentary for television seen across ths States. I certainly owe each one of these fine gentlemen my utmost thanks.

It is hard to express in words my grateful appreciation to Bob Stevens, and Peggy Jalcs, our neighbors, for their patience exhibited as they instructed me how to properly operate a computer.

My extreme gratitude is also extended to Bob Stevens, David Callihan and Russ Huff for the long hours they spent in laser printing the original manuscript.

To Wayne Rutter for the friendship, enthusiasm, and encouragement he gave me, especially at times when I needed additional motivation during the final months of work on my book, I extend my heartfelt thanks.

There remain many more whom I must thank for their kindness to me during the many years I have worked on the Lindbergh case. Limited space, however, does not permit me to elaborate on the part each person played. Nevertheless, I am sure each one knows what they did to help me, sometimes it was simply their words of encouragement they offered. To all I am very, very appreciative and I shall never forget any of them for their help during my investigation over the past 57 years. I especially thank Karen Strunack, Beth Besley, Sydney Weiss, Dolores Raisch, Cornel Plebani, Pat Kendig, Bob Felicito, John Eisenhower, Mike Jalcs,

Elliott Goldberg, Cindy Jones, Ed Bonekemper, David Holwerda, Harold Berger, Manney Berger, Sydney Smith, Catherine Vargo, Henry & Pearl Glovatsky, Jean Jeffries, Lydia Garcia, Pete Martin, Mark Sheplock, Anthony Scaduto, Ludovic Kennedy, Rich Kirkner, Bill Wright, Bea Kershenblatt, Walter & Shirley Straub, John Bezanis, Charles & Anita Gutkowski, Grace McGrady, Darlington Lessig, Jim Charley, Evelyn Overstreet, Nick Alexander, Margaret Mason, Andrew Shue, Elisabeth Shue, Fred Huber, Joseph Mooney, Donna Stevens, Dave Monyer, Les Reichard, Laurie Callihan, Harry Young, Jr., Peter Goldsmith, Gus Kraft, Steve & Joyce Bumball, Pam Jackson, Joan Galler, Harry & Reva Kazman, "B" Wexler Isaacson, John Pinter, Jean West, Toni Rafferty, Joe Rudick, Tom Schalata, Joe Slobodian, Sid Slemmer, Jim Kelly, Tom Kelly, Andrew Dutch, Erica Novak, Martin Clompus, Frank Fitzpatrick, Hans Kloppenburg, Bill Simons, Sinclair Orcutt, Nick Smola, Scott Armstrong, David Joseph, Kenneth Kerwin, Ronald Brien, Robert Coine, Mr. & Mrs. Eugene "Duck" McCullough, Howard Busch, John Wiegand, Stinson Markley, Bill Quinn, Diane Sharshon, Bill Feroe, Joe Sharkey, Harold Olson, Diana Mora, Tom Rivera, Frank & Michele Ross, Tom VanSteenburg, Chris Davis, Joe Dougherty, Henry Uhlig, Ed Petrucci, Jim Reed, David Richards, Nancy Meanix, John Jacob, F. Gonzalez, Lucy Oritz, L. Figueroa, J. Nogueras, Don Coppedge, Maury Povich, Valerie Morrison, William Hartman, Carl Weimer, Dave & Ida May Brunner, Steve Stewart, Jonathan Wilson, Tom Feeney, Bill Talero, Mrs. C. Lloyd Fisher, Mrs. Hazel Carlisle, Peg Barrett, Theodore Flint, John Bezanis, William Degen, Narcisco Lugo, Pervis Riley, Joseph King, Bill Hartman, Lou Yager, Leanore Young Favinger, Mrs. Harry Young, Jerry Rutter, Harry Mazer, Connie Bretz, Ty Inman, Steve Falk, Jack Armstrong, Joseph Pierson, Margaret Powers, Rich Jones, Sylva Smith, Bob MacFarland, Charles & Aina Novitski, Nancy Rhoads, Rick & Gloria Kratz, Margaret Fitzcharles-Kimasz, Don Campbell, Chrissie Jones, V. Leroy Skillman, Frank Bolger, Tom & Polly Croft, Liz Andrews Willow, Dorothy Mandell, Leo Custer, Mike Pesta, Charles LaPella, Tim LaPella, Joe Lombardo, Gunther Mason, Marie Manney, Charles Nagy, Albert Axelrod, Lou Toboz, Dan Willoughby, Ed Mack, Dollie Smith, Jim Heasley, Barbara Lynch, Richard Hunsinger, Ray Hookway, Tom Muth, Ron Graff, Kurt Tolksdorf, Richard Webber, Camilo Rincon, John Papandon, Warren W. Wescott, Joe Kaminski, and Greg Olley.

To D-I-MB-J-TK-D-DJ FOR KEEPING MY SHIP FROM SINKING. W.D.J.

Index

Achenbach, Ella, 242, 390, (court testimony 621-625), 626, 627, 672
Adams, Jean, 293
Alexander, Hildegarde Olga, (court testimony 530-541), 672, 797
Allen, William J., 135, 136, 139, 443-445
Andrews, Frank C. Lumber Co., 952, 1068
Arac, Benjamin, (court testimony 646-649)

Bading, Anna, 846, 869, 870, 900, 904, 1035
Baggstrom, Oden, 819-821, 825
Bailey, F. Lee, 824
Banks, Septimus, 166, 171, 175, 619
Barr, Cecile M. 213, 270, 542, 543, 672, 674, 797, 798, 944
Biggs, Howard V., 309
Birrittella, Rev. Peter, 616-620
Bitz, Irving, 53, 101, 105, 159
Bleefeld, Harry, 896, 897, 956
Bleefeld, Murray, 896, 898-900, 902, 956, 957, 967, 968, 978, 987, 988, 1001
Bornmann, Lewis J., 11, 200, 202, 203, 215, 277, 459, 460, (court testimony 461-467), 479, 480, 483, 485, 486, 495, 496, 501, 505, 509, 510, 514, 559, 635, 661, 672, 742, 773, 954, 956, 983, 1072
Braunlich, Hilda Zaeglain, 439, 440-442
Breckinridge, Col. Henry C., 9, 62, 64-66, 93, 94, 105, 107, 143, 144, 163, 303, 616, 617, 784, 1110
Brelsford, Mary F., 309
Breslin, Edward D., 496, 512, 513, 518, 521, 930, 989
Bruckman, Henry D., 635, (court testimony 639-646), 661-663, 791
Bryan, Robert R., 1072, 1074-1076, 1097, 1137, 1140
Burrage, Guy Hamilton, 89, 163, 164, 188
Bush, Oscar, 36

Campbell, George B., 961, 962
Capone, "Scarface" Al, 49, 988, 1146
Carlstrom, Elvert, (court testimony 716-717), 757
Carter, Boake, 299
Case, Liscom C., 309
Cashman, James, 279, 280, 512, 635
Cass, Dick, 709, 1097-1099, 1117
Cassidy, Thomas, 514, 515, 657, 660-665, 706, 710
Cerrita, Mary, 616-618
Chowlewsky, Antonia, 1128, 1129
Chrzanower, Young Mens Assoc., 619, 620
Clements, Jack, 292, 1035, 1036
Coar, Robert, 35, 137, 140, 183, 281, 282, 315
Condon, Dr. John Francis, 57-82, 93-105, 107-120, 142, 143, 159, 160, 180, 183, 189, 194, 210, 211, 216, 217, 263, 264, (failure to identify Hauptmann 265-271), 367, (court testimony 368-372), (discrepancies of Condon statements 372-396, 398-407), 499, 503, 527, 541, 590, 599, 617, 618, 626, 630, 631, 654, 657-659, 662, 663, 672, 674, 710, 741, 784, 785, 798, 974-976, 979, 986, 991, 1008, 1010, 1011, 1031, 1032, 1113, 1129
Consolvos, Col. Charles H., 128
Cramer, Anselm, 635, 672
Cravatt, Robert, 309
Cronim, Chester, 222, 223, 635
Cross, Hope, 1133, 1134
Curtis, Charles, 844, 876
Curtis, John Hughes, 87, 120-134, 145, 159-163, 183-188, 295, 900, 981
Curtiss, Sheriff John H., 284, 304, 819, 824-826

Darrow, Clarence, 833, 834
Davis, C. Raymond, 1006
DeBisschop, Charles J., (court testimony 758-764), 793, 794
DeGaetano, Nuncio, 11, 560, 943
Dexter, Dr. Thurston H., 289, 290
Dobson-Peacock, Rev. Harold, 88-92, 163, 188
Dormer, Elmira, 455
Dorn, Joseph A., 199
Dorn, M.G. and J.J. Co., 459, 496, 501, 504
Duerr, Dennis, 222, 223, 225
Dunninger, Joe, 616, 618, 619
Dutch, Andrew K., 332

Earhart, Amelia, 1119, 1120
Enkler, Charles F.W., 635, 672

Faulkner, Jane, 208
Faulkner, J.J., 208, 612, 618
Fawcett, James Mark, 275, 278, 283, 286-289, 291-293, 511-513, 515, 516, 520, 615, 659, 882, 1077
Felicito, Robert, 1079
Fell, C. Lloyd, 304, 309, 819
Finn, James J., 55, 165, 190, 191, 194, 206-210, 213, 214, 220-223, 226, 227, 280, 364, 502, 542, 631, 653, 661
Fisch, Isidor, 243, 245, 260, 273, 274, 493, 503, 542, 562, 566, 577-599, 601-605, 607, 611, 613-616, 618-620, 630, 654, 687, 713, 714, 727, 733, 735-737, 739-742, 755, 756, 770, 772, 790, 829, 893, 894, 899, 927, 953-955, 961, 992, 999, 1000, 1003, 1006, 1020-1022, 1026-1028, 1059, 1077, 1122, 1151
Fisch, Pincus, 261, 566, 587-589, 591, 592, 596, 598, 773
Fisch, Henna, 273, 598, 773
Fisher, C. Lloyd, 183, 295, 296, 303, 304, 332, 444, 456-458, 508, 509, 557, 615, 630, 674, 675, 733, 780, 826, 836, 837, 839, 841, 895, 919, 924, 935, 987, 1110
Fitzpatrick, Frank, 154, 155, 664, 666
Flemington, New Jersey, 297-300
Foley, Samuel J., 270, 275-277, 484, 512, 515, 516, 520, 524, 657, 658, 662, 663, 677, 930, 1032, 1035
Ford, Ford Maddox, 822
Frank, William E., 563, 566, 1000
Fredericksen Bakery, 242, 245, 248, 510, 565, 756
Fredericksen, Christian, 242, 244, 252, 278, 620, 795
Fredericksen, Katy, 242, 244, 252, 278, 542, 584, 620, 714, 795
Furcht, Joseph M., 286, 287, 511, 514-517, 522, 523, 525, 528, 990

Gaglio, P. Milton, 61
Galler, Joan, 1134
Garlock, Dr. John H., 290
Gebhart, Paul, 34, 138
Geissler, Carl Osewin, 208, 209
Giangiulio, Sandra, 1041, 1042
Gibson, Jane, 482, 667
Gloeckner, Charles, 244
Gloeckner, Emma, 244
Goldsmith, Peter, 1100
Gow, Betty, 1, 105, 106, 137, 140, 141, 184, 192, 831, 1120, 1127, 1128, 1152
Graham, Rev. Billy, 1006
Guggenheim, Col. M. Robert, 83
Gurney, Bud, 1119

Hacker, Myra Condon, & Ralph, 59, 94, 104, 107, 119, 210, 211
Hall, Rev. Edward Wheeler, 482, 667
Hall, Frances Noel, 666, 668, 670
Hall, William & Henry, 666
Hammer, Justice Ernest E.L., 275, 283, 514-516
Hann, Elmer, 303
Harding, Lou, (court testimony 723-725), 796
Hauck, Anthony M. Jr., 161, 163, 184, 187, 296, 303, 304, 307, 331, 778, 780, 809, 1100
Hauptmann, Anna, 228, 229, 231, 232, 241-244, 246, (inquisition of 250, 251), 255-258, 275, 277, 288, 289, 291-293, 303, 431, 460, 510, 542, 562, 565, 583, 603, 605, 606, 613, 620, 621, 678, 714, 716, 741, 757, 780,

798, 825-827, 829, 831, 837-839, 841, 846, 878, 895, 906, 916, 930, 950, 1013, 1015, 1018-1020, 1022-1025, 1031-1034, 1036-1040, 1053, 1071, 1073-1076, 1095-1097, 1130, 1136, 1140, 1145
Hauptmann, Bruno Richard, 221, 222, 224-227, 229-243, 245, 246, (inquisition of 247-263), 275-278, 283, 284, 286-288, 290, 291, 293, 295, 303, 304, 310, 314, 315, 330, 361, 364, 411, 412, 438, 459, 484, 488, 491, 492, 495, 499, 503, 506, 508-511, 514-519, 521-529, 541, 542, 557-560, 562, 564-566, 576, 577, 579, 582-584, 586, 588-593, 595-597, 600-605, 611, 614, 620, 628, 629, 631, 632, 634, 635, 650, 652, 654-660, 664, 666, 671, 673, 675-677, (court testimony 678-713), 728, 732, 733, 736, 737, 741, 755, 778, 779, 781, 783, 790, 797, 801-803, 805, 807, 810, 815, 819, 820, 822, 825-841, 843, 844, 846, 867, 873, 874-877, 881, 894, 895, 903-905, 915, (letter to his wife 916-918), 919, (letter to Gov. Hoffman 920-922), (final statements 922-923), 939-946, 948, 949, 952, 957, 965, 969, 970, 972, 976, 979, 980, 986, 988, 990, 992, 993, 1003, 1007-1011, 1014-1016, 1026, 1030, 1033, 1038, 1053, 1059, 1070, 1071, 1096, 1100, 1116, 1118, 1129, 1130, 1137-1139, 1141, 1145
Hauptmann, Manfred, 228, 245, 246, 255, 277, 562, 732, 846, 1017, 1027, 1034, 1038, 1039, 1071, 1130, 1145
Hauptmann, Herman, 233, 234 (Richard's father)
Hauptmann, Paulina, 233, 234, 236, 923, 1011, 1012 (Richard's mother)
Hauptmann, Herman, Max and Fritz & Emma, 233, 234 (Richard's brothers and sister)
Haussling, E.A., 12, 315, 635
Hawks, Dr. Everett, 190
Hearst, William Randolph, 292, 455, 804
Heatter, Gabriel, 299, 973
Helfert, Louise, 605, 1029
Henkel, Erica, 597, 1028
Henkel, Gerta, 243, 582, 595, 597, 601, 620, 714, 755, 1028
Henkel, Karl, 243, 582, 595, 597, 599, 601, 603, 618-620, 755, 1029
Herman, Bernie, 1055
Hibben, Dr. John Grier, 45
Hicks, Robert W., 151, 152
Hile, Augusta, 582, 586, 592, 597, 599, 601, 603, 620, 1029
Hockmuth, Amandus, 312, 333, (court testimony 334-343), 344, 345, 348, 559, 561, 672, 815, 941, 942, 1081, 1082
Hochstetter, Elwood, 962
Hockenbury, Philip, 309
Hoffman, Gov. Harold G., 156, 296, 305, 331, 332, 344, 345, 468, 469, 480, 509, 559, 578, 606, 842, 843, 848, (interview with Hauptmann 848-865), 866, 867, 873-877, (interview with Anna Hauptmann 878-881), 882, (personal investigation 882-892), 904, 905, (account of Hauptmann execution 906-913), 925, 927, (additional evidence of Hauptmann's innocence 935-939), 941, 943, 945, 950, 956, 968, 1009, 1012, 1132, 1133
Hoover John Edgar, 165, 268, 467, 481, 497, 652-657, 877, 949, 1000, 1009, (series of letters exchanged with Schwarzkopf and others exhibiting states lack of cooperation 1083-1094), 1095
Hoover, President Herbert, 45, 164, 205
Hopstatter, Russell "Hoppy", 665
Horn, Cp. William F., 213, 220, 222, 315, 331, 631, 1072
Hudson, Dr. Erastus Meade, 191-193, 481, 483, 652, 666, 669, 733, 739, (court testimony 743-753), 769, 770, 792, 802, 1131, 1135, 1136, 1138, 1140, 1150
Hughes, Howard, 273, 414, 415, 442
Hurney, Rev. Francis J., 84

Hynd, Allan, 150, 153, 457, 868, 972

Irey, Elmer L., 96
Irving, Clifford, 273, 414, 415, 442

Johnson, Elmer, 776, 777
Johnson, Henry "Red", 2, 211
Jung, Henry & Erna, 770, 773

Kassens, Gustav, 511, 514, 516, 522, 523
Kazman, Harry & Reva, 1151
Keaten, Arthur T. (Buster), 35, 137, 174, 222, 223, 225-227, 230, 283, 315, 444, 517, 627, 652
Kelly, Sgt. W.P., 279, 280
Kelly, Frank A., 11, 35, 137, 191-193, 482, 651-653, 666, 733, 738, 740, 744, 1131
Kelly, Tom & James, 1069
Kempairien, Emily, 175
Kennedy, Ludovic, 409, 410, 509, 512, 661, 765, 766, 950
Kerwin, Kenneth, 1078, 1147, 1148
Kilgallen, Dorothy, 822-824
Kimberling, Col. Mark O., 843-846, 877, 886, 896, 914, 924, 1011-1013, 1079
Kimmelmann, Irwin I., 1150
Kirkham, James, 895, 896
Kirsten, Erica & Gerta, 598, 599
Kirsten, Mrs. Hermann, 597, 603
Kirsten, Hermann, 598, 599, 601
Kiss, Louis, (court testimony 717-719), 757, (deposition 1103-1107)
Kloppenburg, Hans, 243, 244, 250, 252, 254, 255, 411, 564, 595, 599, 601, 603, 618-620, 714, (court testimony 730-733), 735, 798, 1069
Knabenshue, Roy, 486, 487, 509, 882
Knapp, Howard, 513, 514, 520, 524, 990
Koehler, Arthur. 196-203, 215, 216, 459, 460, 461, 468, 479, 480, 485-492, 495, 496, 498, 500-505, 508-510, 514, 633, 655, 664, 672, 759, 765, 766, 773, (court testimony 773-775), 792-794, 927, 940, 954, 984, 1008-1010
Kohl, Selma, 595, 599, 601, 602
Krippendorf, Willie, 209, 210, 286
Kubler, Louis, 193, 739, 740

Lacey, Judge Frederick B., 1072, 1073
Lamb, John J. "Jack", 35, 137-139, 153, 159, 185, 186, 196, 279, 280, 283, 330, 482, 483, 496, 517, 633, 652, 653, 666-669
Lanigan Joseph P., 184, 187, 303, 809, 1100
Large, George K., 303, 809, 1100
Lehman, Gov. Herbert, 283, 484
Lemke, Henry, 243, 244
Leon, Samuel J., 12, 35, 140, 183, 281, 282, 315
Lessig, L. Darlington "Doll", 954, 1068
Levenson, Joseph O., (court testimony 770-772)
Liebowitz, Samuel, 818, 887-892, 972, 973
Lindbergh, Anne (Morrow), 1, 138, 303, 801, 831, 1054, 1079, 1110, 1119, 1127, 1129, 1136, 1149
Lindbergh, Col. Charles A., 5, 93, 94, 104, 105, 107-118, 120-128, 133, 134, 143-145, 163, 185, 188, 211, 275-277, 303, 315, (discrepancies of statements 397-398), 413, 563, 654, 656, 672, 781, 782, 801, 804, 809, 811, 814, 827, 831, 872, 876, 913, 929, 947, 949, 959, 960, 982, 1054, 1079, 1110, 1115, 1118-1121, 1124, 1125, 1129, 1132, 1136, 1149, 1152
Lindbergh, Evangeline, 84
Lindbergh, Jon Morrow, 190, 1124
Loney, Arch W., 486, 487, 509, 882
Low, Hovey, 303, 819, 825
Lowell, Joan, 1128, 1129
Lupica, Sebastian Benjamin, 38, 312, 729, 730, 796, 1110
Lyle, Walter, 218, 219, 221, 618
Lyons, John A., 218, 219, 221
Lyons, Inspector, 222, 226, 227, 230, 252, 253, 265, 364

Madden, Arthur P., 96
Majestic Apartments, 245, 248, 278, 286, 288, 491, 510, 511, 512, 514-517, 520, 522-525, 564, 988, 990
Mancke, Gustave & Sophie, 615
Manley, Walter, 756
Markley, Stinson, 955, 958, 961
Marshall, George, 777, 778
Matthiessen, Rev. John, 905, 916, 918, 919
McGovern, Joseph A., 941
McGrady, Grace, 605, 606, 611, 615
McGrady, Patrick, 605, 873
McLean, Evelyn Walsh, 83, 129, 151, 152, 183, 212, 876, 1132
Means, Gaston Bullock, 83, 129, 149, 182, 183, 212, 876
Mencken H.L., 832
Merola, Mario, 517, 519, 521
Mielk, Ewald, 765, 766, 767
Miller, Gustave, 480, 741
Minners, Catherine, 776, 777
Minturn, James F., 191
Mitchell, Dr. Charles H., 140-142, 148, 149, (court testimony 449-454), 786, 1013
Moore, Gov. A. Harry, 45, 140, 142, 153, 283-285, 310, 443, 656, 669, 867
Morrison, Angus, 527
Morrison, Valerie, 1149
Morrow, Senator & Mrs Dwight, 46, 152, 171, 179, 191, 303, 778, 788, 814, 831, 1110
Morrow, Dwight Jr., 176
Morrow, Elizabeth, 166, 778, 788, 1150
Mosley, Leonard, 1121
Morton, Edward F., 512, 513, 525, 527, 990
Mueller, Maria, 252, 255, 277, 286, 542, 714, 733
Mueller, Hans, 277, 583
Mulrooney, Edward, 151

National Lumber & Mill Work Co., 202, 496, 497, 502-504, 564
Nicholson, Harold, 831

O'Brien, James, 365, 366
Olson, Harold R., 1078, 1146, 1147
Opdyke, John, 962, 963, 1015, 1038, 1115
Osborn, Albert D., 271, 272, 408, 410, 413, 432, 726
Osborn, Albert S., 252-254, 271, 272, 278, 410, 412-414, 416, 432, 484, 513, 806
Ott, Harry, 951
Ozmec, Miran John, 219, 220

Pagano, Col. Clinton A., 1015, 1074, 1079, 1134
Parker, Ellis H., 153-155, 157, 669, 846, 867-873, 894, 895, 897, 898, 900, 903, 904, 950, 955-958, 961, 966-968, 987
Parker, Ellis H. Jr., 896, 897, 900, 956-958
Parker, Charles W., 841
Peacock, Robert, 303, 461, 809, 1100
Perrone, Joseph Anthony, 67, 290, (court testimony 349-360), 361-366, 672, 991
Pescia, E.V.C., 245, 286, 287, 511, 514-516, 522-524, 990
Petrosino, James, 256, 634, 635
Petzold, Fritz, 235
Pill, Rosie, 308
Plebani, Cornel D., 1079, 1132, 1136
Pope, Frederick A., 295, 303, 364, 478, 672, 737, 767, 768, 794, 839, 841, 895
Povich, Maury, 1055

Quinn, George, 493

Rauch, Pauline & Max, 229, 231, 244, 277, 479, (court testimony about Hauptmann attic 480), 742, 791, 793
Reich, Alfred J., 60, 67, 68, 94, 104, 107, 108
Reich, Gus, 221, 222
Reliance Property Management Co., 511, 513, 514, 516, 520, 526
Reilly, Edward J., 292-296, 303, 438, 439, 455-458, 508, 524, 655, 674, 675, 713, 736, 737, 740, 755, 769, 780, 781, 792, 798, 799, 810, 822, 828, 836-841, 980, 1013, 1014, 1076, 1077
Reilly, William F., 496

Richard, George, 142
Ritchie, Thomas, 253, 271, 410
Robbins, Adam O., 185-187
Robinson, Henry Morton, 885
Roosevelt, Governor Franklin D., 45, 206, 216, 676
Roosevelt, Mrs. Franklin D., 833
Rosecrans, Egbert, 295, 303, 673, 737, 839, 840, 841, 842
Rosenbaum, Rosetta, 240, 241
Rosenhain, Max, 60
Rosner, Morris "Mickey", 53, 88, 101, 105, 159, 616
Rossiter, Charles B., (court testimony 543-557), 558-561, 672, 942, 943
Ruggiero, F.J., 600
Runyon, John, 1133, 1134, 1141-1144

Salisbury, Steffin, 1051, 1053
Scaduto, Anthony, 333, (critical review of Osborns handwriting testimony 414-430), 442, 456, 461, (comments on Bornmann testimony 469-473), (comments on Koehler testimony 473-478), 481, (comments on Cpt. Jack Lamb 481), 485, 486, 494, 497, 507, 517, 518, 528, 566, (explanation of Hauptmann finances 567-576), 593, 606, 613, 619, 664, 665, 736, 816, 898, 902, (interview with Anna Hauptmann 930-934), 950, 967-969, 973-975, 978, 979, 981-991, (evidence of not possessing ransom money 992-999) 1001-1004, 1011, 1015, 1032, 1034, 1035, 1037, 1040, 1074, 1114, 1133, 1137
Schaefer, Erich, 596, 597, 603
Schleser, Charlie, 580-582, 585, 586, 620
Schlossman, Martin, 896, 897, 900, 956, 957
Schoeffel, Charles H., 12, 35
Schoeffler, Anna, 239, 240
Schoeffler, Ernest, 735
Schoeffler, Frederick & Katherine, 239, 244
Schneider, Henry E., 96
Schuhardt, Charles, 1080
Schussler, Louisa & Viola, 228, 583, 1034
Schussler, Victor, 491, 735
Schwarzkopf, Col. H. Norman, 12, 35, 92, 104, 138, 139, 142, 153, 159, 160, 163, 178, 191, 194, 196, 268, 272, 303, 330, 331, 362, 363, 412, 414, 443, 460, 497, 509, 560, 616, 618, 653, 655, 669, (court testimony 733-735), 825, 867, 900, 901, 927, 928, 929, 943, 949, 980-982, 1110, 1115
Seery, William F., 220, 222, 223, 229, 280
Selby, George, 845
Sellers, J. Clark, 432, 806, 807
Sharkey, Joseph, 438, 439, 665
Sharpe, Emily, 166, 171, 182
Sharpe, Violet, 2, 166-182, 615-619, 727, 778, 787, 796, 929, 1151
Shepherd, Edward H. Gerald, 179
Sheppard, Dr. Sam, 823, 824
Shoenfeld, Dr. Dudley D., 194, 543, 968
Shue, Andrew & Elisabeth, 1095-1097
Simons, J.H., 213
Simons, William, 1054, 1055, 1078, 1138, 1148
Sisk, Special Agent Thomas H., 207, 220, 222, 223, 226, 227, 230, 231, 363, 627-629, 652, 656, 661, 978, 1010
Slemmer, Sydney, 961, 1068
Small, Samuel, 726, 882
Smith, Allen C., 303
Smith, Elmer, 308
Smith, Sydney L., 333, 754, 1095
Snook, Russell A., 35, 193, 738, 739
Snyder, Charles F., 308
Snyder, Verna, 308
Sommer, Peter H., 726, 727, 796
Souder, William T., 432, 806
Spiegel, Dr. August, 1113
Spitale, Salvatore "Salvy", 53, 101, 105, 159
Spitz, Stephe, 620
Springer, Arthur, 174, 175
Stein, Elbridge W., 432, 806
Steiner, Rouse & Co., 243, 564, 654

Steinweg, George, (court testimony 607-611), 612-614, 736, 737
Stevens, Willie, 669
Stockburger, Hugo, 819, 825, 1072
Stockton, Ethel, 308
Stockton, Richard, 303, 809, 1100
Stoddard, Russell M., 665, 1081
St. John, Adella Rogers, 719, 821, 822, 971, 973
Stover, Hannah Young, 951, 952, 954, 961
Stover, Martin, 951-953, 955, 956, 960, 961, 967, 1003, 1006, 1016, 1017, 1058, 1122, 1151
Stover, Per, 951, 952, 961, 1068
Stover, Percy & Allen, 961, 1068
Strawl, Manning, 518, 519
Strong, Hugh J., 35, 1125
Strong, William R., 219
Sullivan, Eugene, 1073
Sweeney John J., 35, 1125
Swayze, Walter H., 139, 141, 448, 449
Szostrom, E. Paul, 738, 739

Tobin, Maurice W., 258, 635, (court testimony 636-639)
Tolksdorf, Frank, 242
Tomlinson, J. William, 212
Trego, Ray, 1041
Trenchard, Judge Thomas Whitaker, 278, 296, 303, 304, 309, 347, 649, 673, 675, 689, 741, 755, 758, 811-813, 816, 819, 822, 824, 825, 827, 829, 875, 896, 942, 973, 987, 1082
Trendley, John W., (court testimony 432-438), 442, 726
Trost, Arthur H., 606
Turrou, Leon G., 256, 268-271, 410, 412, 484, 634, 1010
Tyrrell, John F., 411, 432, 806

Uhlig, Henry, 273, 274, 587, 592, 595, 597, 598, 601-603, 620, 736, 755, 756, 824
Union Hotel, 299, 309, 666

Van Henke, August, (court testimony 719-722), 757
Van Ingen, Dr. Philip, 147, 443
Varrelman, A.G., 559, 942
Vetterle, Paul, 542, 620, 714, 733
Vitray, Laura, 1128, 1129
Von Bauer, Peter, 1122
Von Richthofen, Baron Manfred Albrecht, 284
Von Valta, Frieda, 1108, 1109
Vorhees, George, 309

Wallace, Sgt. John B., 222, 223, 225, 226, 256, 630, 631, 634, 635, 661, 927, 1072
Wallace, William, 222, 223, 225
Waller, George, 499, 969, 970, 1001, 1113, 1114, 1128
Walsh, Harry W., 35, 137, 172, 174, 178, 179, 181, 186, 194, 210, 303, (court testimony 444-448), 618, 1128
Walter, Herbert J., 432
Walters, John, 829
Walton, Charles Sr., 304, 307, 308
Weinstein, Jack B., 980
Weiss, Harry, 896, 897, 900, 956, 957
Wells, Judge Harold, 895
Wendel, Paul H., 869-873, 893-895, 897-904, 956, 957, 961, 966, 968, 987, 988, 1151
Werner, Rev. D.G., 916
Whateley, Oliver & Elsie, 2, 105, 106, 184, 203, 204, 615, 616, 619, 788, 1151, 1152
Whipple, Sidney, 502, 612, 736, 895, 944, 956
Whitaker, Norman T., 212
Whited, Millard, 279, 281-283, 312, 315, 331, 332, (court testimony 316-329), 330, 480, 484, 513, 559, 561, 656, 672, 754, 942, 1080, 1095
Whitney, Harry, 291, 292
Wilentz, David T., 275, 278, 296, 303, 309-312, 316, 438, 484, 512, 513, 515, 516, 520, 524, 530, 587, 594, 621, 627, 633, 673, 676-678, 719, 727, 742, 743, 755-759, 765, 767, 778, 786, 800, 801, 806, 807, 812, 818, 822, 825, 839, 840, 877-879, 895, 901-903, 927, 935, 968, 976, 977, 983, 987, 999, 1007, 1034, 1035, 1072, 1100, 1127, 1130

Williams, Trooper M.W., 160
Williamson, Charles E., 9, 136, 444
Wilson, Frank J., 96, 159, 191, 207
Wilson, Orville, 135, 136
Wilton, George G., 769, 770
Wolf, Joseph A., 10, 35, 156, 279, 315, 444, 1072
Wolfe, Harry H., 9
Wollenberg, Louise, 243, 583, 620, 735
Wollenberg, Otto, 243, 583, 735
Woodcock, J. Mortimer, 488-490
Wright, Theon, 616, 618, 619
Wright, William H., 1042 (Mr. Wright's deposition of So. America connection 1043-1050), 1059, 1068, 1122

Young, Harry P., 950, 952, 954-956, 958, 960, 961, 1003-1005, 1058, 1059, (contents of book pertaining to Martin Stover's role in Lindbergh kidnapping 1060-1067), 1067

Zapolski, Andrew, 12, 136, 411, 444

The indexed names listed between pages 1-232 are of persons involved from the time of the kidnapping to and including the apprehension of Richard Hauptmann.

The indexed names listed between pages 233-832 are of persons involved in Hauptmann's apprehension, his trail, conviction and sentencing.

The indexed names listed between pages 833 to the book's end contain those of persons involved in the execution and further successful investigation which proves Bruno Richard Hauptmann absolutely innocent of the crime.